ips 입시플라이

반 배치고사+3월·6월
전국연합 모의고사

예비 고1 영어

Contents

Ⅰ	신입생 학급 배치고사	
01회	고등학교 신입생 반배치 기출	001쪽
02회	고등학교 신입생 반배치 기출	009쪽
03회	고등학교 신입생 반배치 기출	017쪽

Ⅱ	[3월] 전국연합학력평가	
04회	2023학년도 3월 전국연합학력평가	025쪽
05회	2022학년도 3월 전국연합학력평가	037쪽
06회	2021학년도 3월 전국연합학력평가	049쪽
07회	2020학년도 3월 전국연합학력평가	061쪽
08회	2024학년도 3월 대비 실전 모의고사 [특별 부록]	073쪽

Ⅲ	[6월] 전국연합학력평가	
09회	2023학년도 6월 전국연합학력평가	085쪽
10회	2022학년도 6월 전국연합학력평가	097쪽
11회	2021학년도 6월 전국연합학력평가	109쪽

●	[정답과 해설]	• 책속의 책 •

● 모바일 영어 듣기 MP3 이용 안내

① 스마트폰으로 QR 코드 스캔하기
② 입시플라이 or www.ipsifly.com 입력
   모바일 홈페이지 [듣기 자료실] 이용

반 배치고사의 시험 범위는 대부분 중3 과정이며, **일부 지역 고등학교에서는 교과 외 내용이나 심화 과정**을 포함하고 있습니다. 이 경우 함께 수록된 [고1] 3월과 6월 학력평가 문제를 함께 풀어보면 많은 도움이 됩니다.

"강력한 해설로 새롭게 출시된 「2024 리얼 오리지널」"

혼자서도 학습이 충분하도록 친절한 입체적 해설로 [직독직해, 구문풀이]부터 문제 해결 꿀~팁까지 해설을 전면 보강했습니다.

01

신입생 [반 배치고사] 완벽 대비

고등학교 배정 후 시행되는 신입생 반 배치고사를 대비해 [3회분] 기출 모의고사를 수록했습니다.

❶ 최근 시행되고 있는 반 배치고사의 출제 형식에 맞춰 문항 수 및 유형까지 완벽하게 시험지 형식을 재현했습니다.

❷ 문제를 풀기 전 50분 타이머를 맞추어 놓고 실제 반 배치고사와 똑같은 조건으로 풀어보면 실전에서 큰 도움이 됩니다.

02

고1 첫 시험 [3월 학력평가] 대비

입학 후 첫 시험을 대비해 [고1] 3월 전국연합 학력평가 [4회분] 기출 모의고사를 수록했습니다.

❶ 고1 3월 전국연합 학력평가는 중3 과정이므로 총정리와 함께 실제 수능 모의고사 형태로 미리 풀어 볼 수 있습니다.

❷ 3월 전국연합 학력평가는 전국 단위 고1 첫 시험이므로 입학 후 자신의 실력과 위치를 파악하는 기준이 될 수 있습니다.

03

고1·1학기 [6월 학력평가] 대비

고1·1학기 학교시험 [중간·기말고사] 학습 진도에 해당하는 6월 전국연합 학력평가 [3회분] 문제를 수록했습니다.

❶ 고1 6월 학력평가는 고1·1학기 과정이므로 예비 고1 수험생이 남보다 한발 앞선 준비를 할 수 있습니다.

❷ 학교시험에 학력평가 문제를 변형하거나 그림, 도표를 활용해 문제를 출제하는 학교가 많아 내신까지 대비 할 수 있습니다.

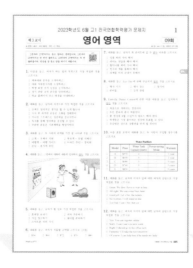

★ 모의고사를 실전과 똑같이 풀어보면
내 실력과 점수는 반드시 올라갈 수밖에 없습니다.

04

3월 대비 [실전 모의고사] 제공

고1 첫 시험! 3월 전국연합 학력평가를 대비해 3월 [실전 모의고사] 1회분을 부록으로 제공합니다.

❶ 3월 모의고사 점수가 내신에는 들어가지 않지만 "고1 첫 시험 점수가 고3 까지 간다"는 속설처럼 매우 중요한 시험입니다.

❷ 실제 시험과 동일한 조건으로 모의고사를 풀어보면 학력평가에서 좋은 점수와 모의고사에 대한 자신감까지 UP 됩니다.

05

영단어 VOCA LIST & 어휘 리뷰 테스트

회차별로 쉬운 단어부터 어려운 단어까지를 모두 정리한 [VOCA LIST]와 [어휘 리뷰 테스트]를 제공합니다.

❶ 3월과 6월 학력평가 회차별 문항 순서대로 수록했으며 문제편 뒤에 VOCA LIST와 어휘 리뷰 테스트가 매회 제공됩니다.

❷ 매회 VOCA LIST로 학습 후 본문에 있는 [어휘 리뷰 테스트]로 단어를 복습하면 어휘력과 독해력이 쑥쑥 올라갑니다.

06

실전과 동일한 OMR 체크카드

정답 마킹을 위한 OMR 체크카드는 실전력을 높여주며 부록 형태로 모의고사 문제편 뒷부분에 수록되었습니다.

❶ OMR 체크카드는 실전과 동일한 형태로 제공되며, 모의고사에서 마킹 연습은 또 하나의 실전 연습입니다.

❷ 답을 밀려 썼을 때 교체하는 연습도 중요하며, 추가로 OMR 체크 카드가 필요하면 홈페이지 자료실에서 다운로드 받을 수 있습니다.

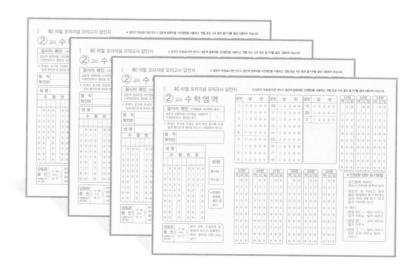

STUDY 플래너 & 등급 컷

① 문제를 풀기 전 먼저 〈학습 체크표〉에 학습 날짜와 시간을 기록하세요.
② 회분별 기출 문제는 영역별로 정해진 시간 안에 푸는 습관을 기르세요.
③ 정답 확인 후 점수와 등급을 적고 성적 변화를 체크하면서 학습 계획을 세우세요.
④ **리얼 오리지널**은 실제 수능 시험과 똑같이 학습하는 교재이므로 실전을 연습하는 것처럼 문제를 풀어 보세요.

● 영어(반 배치고사) | 시험 개요

문항 수	문항당 배점	문항별 점수 표기	원점수 만점	시험 시간	문항 형태
30문항	2점, 3점, 4점	• 각 문항 끝에 점수 표기	100점	50분	5지 선다형

● 영어영역 | 시험 개요

문항 수	문항당 배점	문항별 점수 표기	원점수 만점	시험 시간	문항 형태
45문항	2점, 3점	• 3점 문항에 점수 표시 • 점수 표시 없는 문항 모두 2점	100점	70분	5지 선다형

● 반 배치고사

회분	학습 날짜	학습 시간	채점 결과	틀린 문제	시간 부족 문제
01회 신입생 학급 배치고사	월 일	시 분~ 시 분			
02회 신입생 학급 배치고사	월 일	시 분~ 시 분			
03회 신입생 학급 배치고사	월 일	시 분~ 시 분			

● 영어영역 | 등급 컷 원점수

회분	학습 날짜	학습 시간	틀린 문제	채점 결과		등급 컷 원점수							
				점수	등급	1등급	2등급	3등급	4등급	5등급	6등급	7등급	8등급
04회 2023학년도 3월	월 일	시 분~ 시 분				90	80	70	60	50	40	30	20
05회 2022학년도 3월	월 일	시 분~ 시 분				90	80	70	60	50	40	30	20
06회 2021학년도 3월	월 일	시 분~ 시 분				90	80	70	60	50	40	30	20
07회 2020학년도 3월	월 일	시 분~ 시 분				90	80	70	60	50	40	30	20
09회 2023학년도 6월	월 일	시 분~ 시 분				90	80	70	60	50	40	30	20
10회 2022학년도 6월	월 일	시 분~ 시 분				90	80	70	60	50	40	30	20
11회 2021학년도 6월	월 일	시 분~ 시 분				90	80	70	60	50	40	30	20

※ 〈영어영역〉은 절대 평가에 의한 등급 구분 점수입니다.

● 실전 모의고사

회분	학습 날짜	학습 시간	채점 결과	틀린 문제	시간 부족 문제
08회 3월 대비 실전 모의고사	월 일	시 분~ 시 분			

출신중학교   성명   수험번호

○ 문제지에 성명과 수험 번호를 정확히 써 넣으시오.
○ 답안지에 성명과 수험 번호를 써 넣고, 또 수험 번호와 답을 정확히 표시하시오.
○ 문항에 따라 배점이 다르니, 각 물음의 끝에 표시된 배점을 참고하시오.

1. 밑줄 친 This[this]가 가리키는 것으로 가장 적절한 것은? [2점]

<u>This</u> is an ancient form of saying "Hello" when you meet someone. Long ago, men did <u>this</u> as a way of saying, "You can trust me." One man held out his hand to another to show that he wasn't ready to pull out his sword. Each saw that the other had no weapon in his hand, and knew that he could trust him. Today, people do <u>this</u> as a friendly gesture that means "Nice to meet you," or "Welcome." According to the Guinness Book of World Records(1977), Atlantic City Mayor Joseph Lazarow shook more than 11,000 hands in a single day.

* sword 검, 칼

① smiling   ② knocking   ③ handshaking
④ arm wrestling   ⑤ crossing fingers

2. 다음 글의 목적으로 가장 적절한 것은? [3점]

Dear citizens,

As you all know from seeing the pictures on television and in the newspaper, Central America has been hit hard by a series of hurricanes. Tens of thousands of people are homeless and without basic necessities like food and clothing. I feel that we need to do something to help. So, we are asking you to donate canned goods, warm clothes, blankets, and money. Please bring all donations to the community center between 10 a.m. and 4 p.m., Saturday, September 10. Thank you for helping your fellow human beings in their time of desperate need.

Sincerely,
George Anderson

① 자연재해의 위험성을 경고하려고
② 재난 사고 시 대처 요령을 안내하려고
③ 재난 피해자를 위한 기부를 요청하려고
④ 자원봉사 활동의 일정 변경을 공지하려고
⑤ 재난 피해자를 도운 것에 대해 감사하려고

3. 다음 글의 밑줄 친 부분 중, 어법상 <u>틀린</u> 것은? [4점]

The next time you face a difficult challenge, think to yourself, "In order for me ① <u>to resolve</u> this issue, I will have to fail nine times, but on the tenth attempt, I will be successful." This attitude lets you think creatively without fear of failure. It is because you understand ② <u>that</u> learning from failure is a forward step toward success. Take a risk and when you fail, no longer think, "Oh, no, ③ <u>what</u> a waste of time and effort!" Instead, learn from that misstep and correctly ④ <u>thinking</u>, "Great: one down, nine to go—I'm making forward progress!" And indeed you are. After your first failure, think, "Great, I'm 10% done!" Mistakes, loss and failure ⑤ <u>are</u> all flashing lights clearly pointing the way to deeper understanding and creative solutions.

4. (A), (B), (C)의 각 네모 안에서 문맥에 맞는 낱말로 가장 적절한 것은? [4점]

In most people, emotions are situational. Something in the here and now makes you mad. The emotion itself is (A) tied / unrelated to the situation in which it originates. As long as you remain in that emotional situation, you're likely to stay angry. If you *leave* the situation, the opposite is true. The emotion begins to (B) disappear / appear as soon as you move away from the situation. Moving away from the situation prevents it from taking hold of you. Counselors often advise clients to get some emotional distance from whatever is (C) bothering / pleasing them. One easy way to do that is to *geographically* separate yourself from the source of your anger.

	(A)	(B)	(C)
①	tied	disappear	bothering
②	tied	disappear	pleasing
③	tied	appear	bothering
④	unrelated	disappear	pleasing
⑤	unrelated	appear	pleasing

[5~8] 다음 빈칸에 들어갈 말로 가장 적절한 것을 고르시오.

5. When two people talk to each other, they normally speak toe to toe. If, however, one of the individuals turns his feet slightly away or repeatedly moves one foot in an outward direction (in an L formation with one foot toward you and one away from you), you can be sure he wants to take leave or wishes he were somewhere else. The person's body may remain facing you out of politeness, but the feet may more honestly reflect the brain's need or desire to _____.

[3점]

① talk   ② join   ③ argue
④ follow   ⑤ escape

6. Let me give you a piece of advice that might change your mind about _____. Suppose that your doctor said that you have six months to live and recommended that you do everything you ever wanted to do. What would you do? Have you always wanted to sky dive, or climb cliffs, or maybe live alone in the woods for a month but been afraid you might be harmed? What difference would it make if you now attempted it? You'd almost certainly live through it and it would enrich the time you had left. Wouldn't it be nice to go out saying you had faced all your fears? Why do you wait till you have a death sentence? If it's that important to you, do it now.

[4점]

* death sentence: 사형 선고

① being courageous
② helping others
③ making friends
④ recovering health
⑤ encouraging patients

7. An important part of learning to read for children is _____. A report by the National Literacy Trust highlighted that 40 percent of male parents believe their partner is more likely to read with the children than they are. What's more, up to 25 percent of children have never seen their dad read. But if fathers could find the time to read with their children, it would have a huge impact on the lives of their children. According to the Fatherhood Institute, reading results in a closer father-child relationship and can lead to improved child behaviour and higher achievement.

[3점]

① visual aids
② word memorization
③ competition with others
④ the input of both parents
⑤ the experience of writing

8. It is not always easy to eat well when you have a newborn baby. It can seem like you do not have time to prepare tasty nutritious meals or even to eat them. You will need to learn the following trick. Try not to wait until _____. When you have a newborn baby, preparing food will probably take longer than usual. If you start when you are already hungry, you will be absolutely starving before the food is ready. When you are starving and tired, eating healthy is difficult. You may want to eat fatty fast food, chocolates, cookies or chips. This type of food is okay sometimes, but not every day. [4점]

① your baby cries to be fed at night
② you find a new recipe for your meal
③ you are really hungry to think about eating
④ your kids finish all the food on their plates
⑤ you feel like taking a nap after a heavy meal

9. 다음 글의 밑줄 친 부분 중, 문맥상 낱말의 쓰임이 적절하지 <u>않은</u> 것은? [3점]

You have probably seen several ① <u>different</u> features of the land. Perhaps you have gone hiking to the top of a mountain. A mountain is a landform. A landform is a part of Earth's surface that has a certain shape and is formed naturally. Earth has several kinds of landforms. The most ② <u>visible</u> landform is a mountain. A mountain is a ③ <u>lowered</u> part of the land, usually with sharp sides, that rises above the area around it. Some mountains are high, rocky, and ④ <u>capped</u> with snow. Others are covered with trees. Another landform of Earth is a plain. It is a large land area that is mostly ⑤ <u>flat</u>. Plains often have rich soil and make good farmland.

10. (A), (B), (C)의 각 네모 안에서 문맥에 맞는 낱말로 가장 적절한 것은? [4점]

The laser pointer, which became popular in the 1990s, was at first typically thick to hold in the hand. Before long, such pointers came in slimmer pocket models and became easier to handle. Still, the laser pointer had its own (A) strengths / weaknesses . Batteries were required and had to be replaced, and the shaky hand movements of a nervous lecturer were (B) hidden / shown in the sudden motion of the glowing red dot. Moreover, the red dot could be difficult to see against certain backgrounds, thus making the laser pointer (C) inferior / superior even to a simple stick. To correct this problem, more advanced and thus more expensive green-beam laser pointers came to be introduced.

	(A)	(B)	(C)
①	strengths	shown	inferior
②	strengths	hidden	superior
③	weaknesses	shown	superior
④	weaknesses	hidden	superior
⑤	weaknesses	shown	inferior

11. 다음 도표의 내용과 일치하지 <u>않는</u> 것은? [3점]

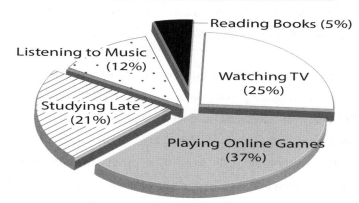

Reasons behind High School Students' Limited Sleep

Reading Books (5%)
Listening to Music (12%)
Watching TV (25%)
Studying Late (21%)
Playing Online Games (37%)

High school students in Korea slept five hours and 27 minutes per night on average last year. A survey was done to find the reasons. The above chart shows why most high school students couldn't sleep enough. ① Playing online games was the number one reason for the lack of sleep. ② A quarter of students replied that they couldn't sleep enough because they were watching TV. ③ Studying late had the third highest percentage in this survey. ④ Listening to music ranked higher than studying late. ⑤ Only 5 percent of students replied they didn't get enough sleep because they were reading books.

12. 다음 글의 분위기로 가장 적절한 것은? [2점]

It had stopped raining; the roads were clean, and the dust had been washed from the trees. The earth was refreshed. The frogs were loud in the pond; they were big, and their throats were swollen with pleasure. The grass was sparkling with tiny drops of water. Some boys were playing in the little stream that the rain had made by the roadside; it was good to see them and their bright eyes. They were having the time of their lives, and I could see they were very happy. They laughed with joy as one said something to them, though they didn't understand a word.

① sad and gloomy
② merry and lively
③ tense and urgent
④ funny and humorous
⑤ boring and monotonous

[13~14] 글의 흐름으로 보아, 주어진 문장이 들어가기에 가장 적절한 곳을 고르시오.

13.

> This genetic difference means that it is likely that the man's immune system possesses something hers does not.

Some scientists explain that our choice of a partner is a simple matter of following our noses. (①) Claus Wedekind of the University of Lausanne in Switzerland conducted an interesting experiment with sweaty T-shirts. (②) He asked 49 women to smell T-shirts previously worn by a variety of unidentified men. (③) He then asked the women to rate which T-shirts smelled the best and which the worst. (④) He found that women preferred the smell of a T-shirt worn by a man who was the most genetically different from her. (⑤) By choosing him as the father of her children, she increases the chance that her children will be healthy. [4점]

* genetic 유전적인 ** immune system 면역체계

14.

> However, shoppers should understand that getting any of these sources of information has costs.

Shoppers usually have a limited amount of money to spend and a limited amount of time to shop. (①) It is important to realize that shopping is really a search for information. (②) You may obtain information from an advertisement, a friend, a salesperson, a label, a magazine article, the Internet, or several other sources. (③) You may also gain information from actual use of the product, such as trying on a dress, test-driving a car, or taking advantage of a promotion at a fitness center. (④) These costs may include transportation costs and time. (⑤) Only you can decide whether to take the costs or not. [4점]

* promotion: 판촉 행사

[15~16] 다음 글에서 전체 흐름과 관계 없는 문장을 고르시오.

15. The water that is embedded in our food and manufactured products is called "virtual water." For example, about 265 gallons of water is needed to produce two pounds of wheat. ① So, the virtual water of these two pounds of wheat is 265 gallons. ② Virtual water is also present in dairy products, soups, beverages, and liquid medicines. ③ However, it is necessary to drink as much water as possible to stay healthy. ④ Every day, humans consume lots of virtual water and the content of virtual water varies according to products. ⑤ For instance, to produce two pounds of meat requires about 5 to 10 times as much water as to produce two pounds of vegetables. [4점]

* virtual water: 공산품·농축산물의 제조·재배에 드는 물

16. Early native Americans had to make everything they needed. ① The kinds of things each tribe used to make tools, clothing, toys, shelter, and food depended upon what they found around them. ② Also, the things they made fit their life style. ③ Most tribes spoke their own language, but could communicate with other tribes. ④ For example, the people of the Plains, who traveled a lot, didn't make clay pots. ⑤ Pots were too heavy and broke too easily when they were moved, so they made containers from animal skins. [3점]

17. 다음 글의 빈칸 (A), (B)에 들어갈 말로 가장 적절한 것은?

[3점]

While you're in bumper-to-bumper traffic that is moving at a painfully slow speed, you wonder "How can this traffic problem be fixed?" The answers are easy but not practical: increase the flow by widening the roads or constructing additional highways. ___(A)___, the reality is that unless you're the president or governor, you cannot make either solution happen. Thus your stress level rises along with your blood pressure. Your question was not a good one. ___(B)___, ask, "With an extra forty minutes in traffic, how can I use that time effectively?" Now you're asking a question that is productive. You might consider listening to music to entertain you or audio books to educate you.

	(A)		(B)
①	Therefore	......	Similarly
②	For example	......	Instead
③	However	......	Similarly
④	However	......	Instead
⑤	For example	......	By contrast

18. Farm Experience Days에 관한 다음 안내문의 내용과 일치하지 <u>않는</u> 것은? [2점]

Farm Experience Days

Come and enjoy our Farm Experience Days.

Here are some activities you can enjoy:
- Collect eggs from our hens
- Feed the cows, sheep, and pigs
- Walk around the farm to learn about the animals

- The activities of the day may change according to the weather.

- The fee is $50 per person. This includes a hearty, homemade lunch.

- Reservations are required.

- We're only open on weekdays.

For more information, please call us at 5252 - 7088.

① 소, 양, 돼지에게 먹이를 줄 수 있다.
② 날씨에 따라 당일 체험 활동이 달라질 수 있다.
③ 점심 비용이 참가비에 포함되어 있다.
④ 예약이 필요하다.
⑤ 주말에도 이용할 수 있다.

19. Maria Montessori에 관한 다음 글의 내용과 일치하는 것은?

[3점]

Maria Montessori was born on August 31, 1870, in Chiaravalle, Italy. When she was 14, her family moved to Rome. She finished her studies at the medical school of the University of Rome in 1896 and became the first female doctor in Italy. As a doctor, she mainly treated many poor and working-class children and began to research early childhood development and education. In 1907, she opened her first classroom called Children's House. By 1925, more than 1,000 Montessori schools had opened in the United States. Once World War II began, Montessori went to India, where she developed a program called Education for Peace. She died on May 6, 1952.

① 1870년 로마에서 태어났다.
② 이탈리아에서 최초의 여성 의사가 되었다.
③ 주로 상류층 아동을 치료했다.
④ 1925년 Children's House라 불리는 첫 교실을 열었다.
⑤ 2차 세계대전이 끝난 후 인도로 갔다.

20. 다음 글의 제목으로 가장 적절한 것은? [3점]

Give children options and allow them to make their own decisions — on how much they would like to eat, whether they want to eat or not, and what they would like to have. For example, include them in the decision-making process of what you are thinking of making for dinner — "Lisa, would you like to have pasta and meatballs, or chicken and a baked potato?" When discussing how much they should eat during dinner, serve them a reasonable amount; if they claim they are still "hungry" after they are through, ask them to wait five to ten minutes, and if they continue to feel hunger, then they can have a second plate of food. These are fantastic behaviors that, when taught properly, teach brilliant self-confidence and self-control.

① Be a Role Model to Your Children
② Hunger: The Best Sauce for Children
③ Table Manners: Are They Important?
④ Good Nutrition: Children's Brain Power
⑤ Teach Children Food Independence

21. 다음 글의 주제로 가장 적절한 것은? [4점]

Hydroelectric power is a clean and renewable power source. However, there are a few things about dams that are important to know. To build a hydroelectric dam, a large area must be flooded behind the dam. Whole communities sometimes have to be moved to another place. Entire forests can be drowned. The water released from the dam can be colder than usual and this can affect the ecosystems in the rivers downstream. It can also wash away riverbanks and destroy life on the river bottoms. The worst effect of dams has been observed on salmon that have to travel upstream to lay their eggs. If blocked by a dam, the salmon life cycle cannot be completed.

* hydroelectric: 수력 발전의 ** ecosystem: 생태계

① necessity of saving energy
② dark sides of hydroelectric dams
③ types of hydroelectric power plants
④ popularity of renewable power sources
⑤ importance of protecting the environment

22. 다음 글의 요지로 가장 적절한 것은? [4점]

It is important to recognize your pet's particular needs and respect them. If your pet is an athletic, high-energy dog, for example, he or she is going to be much more manageable indoors if you take him or her outside to chase a ball for an hour every day. If your cat is shy and timid, he or she won't want to be dressed up and displayed in cat shows. Similarly, you cannot expect macaws to be quiet and still all the time — they are, by nature, loud and emotional creatures, and it is not their fault that your apartment doesn't absorb sound as well as a rain forest.

* macaw: 마코 앵무새

① 애완동물에게는 적절한 운동이 필요하다.
② 애완동물도 다양한 감정을 느낄 수 있다.
③ 애완동물의 개별적 특성을 존중해야 한다.
④ 자신의 상황에 맞는 애완동물을 선택해야 한다.
⑤ 훈련을 통해 애완동물의 행동을 교정할 수 있다.

23. 주어진 글 다음에 이어질 글의 순서로 가장 적절한 것을 고르시오.

> I took a job on the night shift because the money was much better.

(A) I took a slightly longer break than usual and my boss wasn't too happy about that. So, we couldn't do it very often, but I loved it when they came.

(B) Unfortunately, working at night meant I could no longer have dinner with my wife and kids. A sandwich in the cafeteria isn't exactly the same thing as a hot meal at home.

(C) One night, my wife surprised me by packing up the kids and dinner and coming to see me at work. The five of us sat around the cafeteria table and it was the best meal I'd had in a long time.

[3점]

* night shift: 야간 근무

① (A) − (C) − (B)　　② (B) − (A) − (C)
③ (B) − (C) − (A)　　④ (C) − (A) − (B)
⑤ (C) − (B) − (A)

24. 다음 글에서 필자가 주장하는 바로 가장 적절한 것은? [3점]

Some people need money more than we do. For example, some people have lost their homes due to natural disasters or war, while others don't have enough food or clothing. So this year, for our birthdays, let's tell our friends and family to donate money to a charity instead of buying us presents. I know that some kids might not want to give up their birthday presents, and I understand. However, remember that we can live without new toys or games more easily than someone can live without food, clothing, or shelter. So, we should tell our friends and family that, for our birthdays this year, we want to give to others.

① 생일 파티를 간소하게 하자.
② 부모님께 감사하는 마음을 갖자.
③ 사용하지 않는 물건을 자선단체에 기부하자.
④ 값비싼 선물보다는 정성이 담긴 편지를 쓰자.
⑤ 생일 선물에 드는 비용으로 어려운 사람을 돕자.

25. 다음 글의 내용을 한 문장으로 요약하고자 한다. 빈칸 (A)와 (B)에 들어갈 말로 가장 적절한 것은? [4점]

> How does a fire change a forest? Small plants that some animals eat are destroyed. Thick bushes that provide shelter may disappear. But a change that is harmful to some organisms can be good for others. A fire can create new habitats. A habitat is a place where an organism lives. After a flood, people and animals may lose their homes. Plants die as muddy water covers them and blocks sunlight. But when the water dries up, rich soil is left behind. New plants can grow where they might not have grown before the flood.
>
> * habitat 서식지

↓

> Forest fires and floods first __(A)__ habitats but they can later create __(B)__ conditions that allow new plants and animals to live.

　　(A)　　　　　(B)
① support ······ beneficial
② harm ······ beneficial
③ protect ······ unsafe
④ harm ······ terrible
⑤ support ······ terrible

[26~27] 다음 글을 읽고, 물음에 답하시오.

I once watched Grandfather looking at a bush. He stood for half an hour, silent and still. As I got closer, I could see he was looking at a sort of bird, but I could not tell what kind of bird it was. Just as I was about to ask him, a common robin flew from the bush. I asked Grandfather what he was looking at. Smiling, he replied, "A robin." I said, "But Grandfather, it's just a common robin. What's so interesting about a robin?" He said, "Just a robin?" Then, he drew a picture of a bird on the ground with a stick and, handing me the stick, he said, "Show me where all the black marks on a robin are located." I said, "I don't know." "Then," he continued, "each bird is as _____ as you and I. No single bird is the same as another. We can always learn something new every time we observe a robin. That is also true of everything else in life, every experience, every situation, every bird, tree, rock, water, and leaf. We can never know enough about anything. Finally," he continued, "you do not even begin to know an animal until you touch it, and feel its spirit. Then and only then can you ever begin to know."

26. 위 글의 제목으로 가장 적절한 것은? [3점]

① Share Your Experiences with Other People
② Learn Something New from Everything
③ Touch Others with Kind Words
④ Be Happy Where You Are
⑤ Have a Positive Attitude

27. 위 글의 빈칸에 들어갈 말로 가장 적절한 것은? [4점]

① hardworking   ② different
③ friendly   ④ active
⑤ free

[28~30] 다음 글을 읽고, 물음에 답하시오.

(A)

Robby was a young boy who lived with his mother. His mother wanted to hear her son play the piano for her, so she sent her son to a piano teacher but there was one small problem. (a) He was not musically gifted and therefore was very slow at learning. However, his mother was eager to listen to him and every week she would send Robby to the teacher.

(B)

With a microphone in front of him, (b) he said, "I was not able to attend the weekly piano lessons as there was no one to send me because my mother was sick with cancer. She just passed away this morning and I wanted her to hear me play. You see, this is the first time she is able to hear me play because when she was alive she was deaf and now I know she is listening to me. I have to play my best for her!"

(C)

One day Robby stopped attending the piano lessons. The piano teacher thought that he had given up. Not long after, the teacher was given the task to organize a piano concert in town. Suddenly, the teacher received a call from Robby who offered to take part in the concert. The teacher told him that he was not good enough and that (c) he was no longer a student since he had stopped coming for lessons. Robby begged him for a chance and promised that he would not let him down.

(D)

Finally, (d) he agreed to let Robby play, but put him last, hoping that he would change his mind at the last minute. At last, it was Robby's turn to play and as (e) his name was announced, he walked in. As Robby started playing, the crowd was amazed at the skill of this little boy. In fact, he gave the best performance of the evening. At the end of his presentation the crowd and the piano teacher gave him a big hand. The crowd asked Robby how he managed to play so brilliantly.

28. 주어진 글 (A)에 이어질 내용을 순서에 맞게 배열한 것으로 가장 적절한 것은? [4점]

① (B) − (C) − (D)
② (C) − (B) − (D)
③ (C) − (D) − (B)
④ (D) − (B) − (C)
⑤ (D) − (C) − (B)

29. 위 글 (a)~(e) 중 가리키는 대상이 나머지 넷과 다른 것은? [3점]

① (a)   ② (b)   ③ (c)   ④ (d)   ⑤ (e)

30. 위 글에 관한 내용과 일치하지 않는 것은? [3점]

① Robby의 어머니는 아들의 피아노 연주를 듣고 싶었다.
② Robby의 어머니는 암으로 아팠다.
③ Robby는 피아노 선생님에게 기회를 달라고 간청했다.
④ Robby는 콘서트에서 첫 순서로 연주했다.
⑤ 청중들은 Robby에게 큰 박수를 보냈다.

---

* 확인 사항

○ 답안지의 해당란에 필요한 내용을 정확히 기입(표기)했는지 확인하시오.

출신중학교		성명		수험번호	

○ 문제지에 성명과 수험 번호를 정확히 써 넣으시오.
○ 답안지에 성명과 수험 번호를 써 넣고, 또 수험 번호와 답을 정확히 표시하시오.
○ 문항에 따라 배점이 다르니, 각 물음의 끝에 표시된 배점을 참고하시오.

---

1. 밑줄 친 This[this]가 가리키는 것으로 가장 적절한 것은? [2점]

This is essential to the drama and in forming the plot. It can be thought of as the problem the main characters have to work toward resolving. This is certainly not limited to characters arguing with each other, though that could be one aspect of the story. In a broader sense, this is an obstacle which the main character or characters must overcome before the end of the story.

① title　　　　② conflict　　　　③ theme
④ setting　　　⑤ motivation

2. 밑줄 친 He[his]가 가리키는 대상이 나머지 넷과 다른 것은? [3점]

Several years ago, one of my friends became ill. ① He became worse as time went on, and was finally taken to the hospital for an operation. The doctor warned me that there was little chance of my ever seeing him again, but ② he was wrong. Just before my friend was wheeled away, he whispered, "Do not be disturbed. I will be out of here in a few days." The attending nurse looked at me with pity. But, ③ he did come through safely. After it was all over, his physician said "Nothing but ④ his desire to live saved him. He would never have pulled through if ⑤ he had not refused to accept the possibility of his death."

3. 다음 글의 목적으로 가장 적절한 것은? [3점]

Breakfast eaters tend to have more energy and are less likely to be fat. So, skipping breakfast isn't such a great way to lose weight. If you are concerned about your diet, you might want to try some of these methods to grab a quick bite to eat before school. First, fill your fridge with breakfast-to-go choices, such as Greek yogurt, hard-boiled eggs, or fruit. Pack a breakfast to eat after your ride to school when you may feel hungrier. Plan the next day's breakfast the night before. Ask your parents to have it ready. Go to bed 30 minutes earlier, so you aren't as tired in the morning. Get up 10 minutes earlier, so your body has more time to wake up and get hungry.

① 건강에 좋은 요리법을 추천하려고
② 기상 시간과 성적 향상의 관계를 설명하려고
③ 식료품을 신선하게 보관하는 방법을 소개하려고
④ 아침형 인간과 저녁형 인간의 특성을 비교하려고
⑤ 아침 식사를 챙겨먹을 수 있는 요령을 알려주려고

4. 다음 글의 밑줄 친 부분 중, 어법상 틀린 것은? [4점]

It has become a thing of the past to rush to a farmhouse in the middle of the night to check all the crops. All farmers have to do now ① are to just stay in bed and touch the screen of their smartphones. This is all ② thanks to the new "smartfarm" technology. Such smartfarming apps run on the Internet of Things (IoT), a range of technologies ③ that can measure and analyze temperature, humidity and the amount of sunlight inside a greenhouse. All the data are transferred to a smartphone where farmers can check and control the conditions in ④ their greenhouses in real time. The new systems have improved productivity and the quality of crops, while ⑤ reducing manpower and the required energy inputs.

5. (A), (B), (C)의 각 네모 안에서 어법에 맞는 낱말로 가장 적절한 것은? [4점]

Feedback can be improved in many activities. Consider the simple task of painting a ceiling. This task is more difficult than it might seem because ceilings are nearly always painted white and it can be hard to see exactly (A) where / of which you have painted. Later, when the paint dries, the patches of old paint will be annoyingly visible. How should this problem be solved? Some clever person invented a type of ceiling paint that goes on pink when wet but (B) turns / turned white when dry. Unless the painter is so (C) colorblind / colorblindly that he cannot tell the difference between pink and white, this solves the problem.

	(A)	(B)	(C)
①	where	turns	colorblind
②	where	turns	colorblindly
③	where	turned	colorblind
④	of which	turned	colorblindly
⑤	of which	turned	colorblind

[6~9] 다음 빈칸에 들어갈 말로 가장 적절한 것을 고르시오.

6. Suppose that fifty thousand years ago you were traveling around the Serengeti with your hunter-gatherer friends, and suddenly they all started to run. Would you have stood motionless thinking whether what you were looking at was a lion or a harmless animal that could serve as meat? No, you would have rushed after your friends. We are the direct heirs of those who _____ others' behavior. This pattern is so deeply rooted in us that we still use it today, even when it offers no survival advantages. For example, if you find yourself hungry in a foreign city and don't know a good restaurant, it makes sense to pick the one that's full of locals. In other words, you imitate the local's behavior. [4점]　　*heir 후손

① copied　　　② blamed　　　③ ignored
④ corrected　　　⑤ controlled

7. Within every church, business, or nonprofit organization in need of change, there is a group of insiders who are aware of the changes that need to take place. They gather in the break room and complain to each other. But day after day they go about their work thinking nothing will change. So they keep their mouths shut. They do not lack insight into what needs to happen; they simply lack the courage to do anything about it. A leader is someone who has the courage to say publicly what everybody else is whispering privately. It is not his insight that sets the leader apart from the crowd. It is his courage to act on what he sees and _____ when everyone else is silent. [3점]

① to give up　　② to speak up　　③ to keep secrets
④ to praise others　　⑤ to refuse a favor

8. A group of marketing researchers has studied exactly what makes a bad gift and why people buy such presents. The researchers suggested that one reason for bad gifts is that the giver and the recipient focus on different things. The giver focuses on the moment of the exchange, wanting to surprise or impress the recipient, while the recipient focuses on the long-term usefulness of the gift. "What we found was that the giver wants to 'wow' the recipient and give a gift that can be enjoyed immediately, while the recipient is more interested in a gift that _____," said a study researcher Jeff Galak. [4점]　　*recipient 받는 사람

① shows the giver's taste
② provides value over time
③ is well-wrapped in ribbons
④ can impress his or her friends
⑤ remains in the giver's memory

9. Have you ever had pain caused by indigestion that made it feel like your chest was hurting? This sort of confusion happens because all the nerves that sense pain in the internal organs send signals through the same pathways in the spinal cord that carry information from the body surface. This leaves the brain uncertain about what is wrong. In fact, pain is felt in _____. For this reason, doctors learn that when patients complain about pain in their left arm, it may indicate a heart attack. Similarly, pain from a kidney stone may feel like a stomachache. [4점]

* spinal cord 척수 ** kidney stone 신장결석

① the lower back and upper legs
② the farthest part from the heart
③ a place other than its true source
④ the skin and muscles, not the bones
⑤ the mind made up by the imagination

10. 다음 도표의 내용과 일치하지 <u>않는</u> 것은? [3점]

The Cost of Water & Typical Daily Low Salary

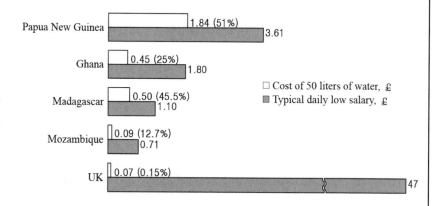

According to the report by *Water Aid*, some people pay more money for water compared to their typical daily low salary. ① In Papua New Guinea, 50 liters of water costs more than 50% of its worker's daily salary. ② The cost of 50 liters of water in Ghana takes up a quarter of its worker's daily income. ③ The cost of 50 liters of water in Madagascar takes up more percentage of its worker's daily salary than it does in Papua New Guinea. ④ The cost of 50 liters of water in Mozambique accounts for the smallest percentage in all countries except for the UK. ⑤ People in the UK pay less than 1% of their daily salaries for 50 liters of water.

11. 다음 글의 밑줄 친 부분 중, 문맥상 낱말의 쓰임이 적절하지 <u>않은</u> 것은? [3점]

In the movies, sharks are dangerous predators. They are ready to ① <u>attack</u> at the first sight of humans. But as many experienced shark divers will tell you, real-life sharks don't generally ② <u>fit</u> their movie image. Most sharks don't swim around the ocean looking for people to eat. While you can generalize about various species of shark, it is still true that sharks as individuals have very ③ <u>different</u> personalities. Some are relaxed and laid back. They don't become aggressive even when faced with human beings. Other sharks are extremely ④ <u>welcoming</u>, so they are quick to be very upset by an outsider entering their area. Yet, on the whole, most sharks are more ⑤ <u>afraid</u> of human beings than not.

12. 주어진 글 다음에 이어질 글의 순서로 가장 적절한 것은? [4점]

A new report says that by the year 2060, outdoor air pollution will cause as many as 9 million deaths per year around the world. This may not mean that pollution will hurt people directly. It can cause cancer and other illnesses like heart disease.

(A) However, the large dollar figures do not reflect the true cost of air pollution. Pain, suffering, and avoidable death from breathing in toxic air do not have a price. Neither does the experience of having you wear a mask just to play outside. These problems are more important than money.

(B) These threatening diseases will have a large effect on areas with a lot of people and high levels of poisonous dusts and gases. Many of these areas will be in cities in China and India. People will also see problems in Eastern Europe, parts of the Middle East, and other parts of Asia.

(C) The effect of air pollution is often discussed in dollar terms. By 2060, countries will lose a lot of money. These losses will be due to the health problems related to air pollution. Lower worker productivity, higher health spending, and lower crop harvest will all result in losses.

① (A)-(C)-(B) ② (B)-(A)-(C)
③ (B)-(C)-(A) ④ (C)-(A)-(B)
⑤ (C)-(B)-(A)

13. (A), (B), (C)의 각 네모 안에서 문맥에 맞는 낱말로 가장 적절한 것은? [4점]

Dogs learn in the context in which you teach them. If you teach your dog a behavior in the kitchen, he will think the behavior is (A) related / unrelated to the kitchen. If you always teach him a behavior in the living room and assume he will perform the behavior in the hallway when friends come over, he will probably (B) please / disappoint you. You didn't teach him the behavior in the hallway —you taught him in the living room! You have to teach a behavior in the environment in which you want it to occur. When training your dog, remember that when you (C) hold / change the environment, you may have to reteach him what you think he already knows.

	(A)	(B)	(C)
①	related	······ please	······ hold
②	related	······ disappoint	······ change
③	related	······ disappoint	······ hold
④	unrelated	······ disappoint	······ change
⑤	unrelated	······ please	······ hold

14. 다음 글에서 전체 흐름과 관계 <u>없는</u> 문장은? [2점]

Visitors to London who come from the United States have a problem being safe pedestrians. They have spent their entire lives expecting cars to come at them from the left. ① But in the United Kingdom automobiles drive on the left-hand side of the road, so the danger often comes from the right. ② Fewer automobiles on the road mean fewer traffic accidents. ③ As a result, many pedestrian accidents occur to American tourists. ④ So, the city of London came up with an idea to help them with good design. ⑤ On many corners, especially in neighborhoods frequently visited by tourists, there are signs on the sidewalk that say, "Look right!"
　　　　　　　　　　　　　　　　　　　　* pedestrian 보행자

[15~16] 글의 흐름으로 보아, 주어진 문장이 들어가기에 가장 적절한 곳을 고르시오.

15.

> In the past people didn't have a clue what caused the awesome aurorae.

If you're out and about during the long winter nights at the North Pole, and suddenly you see bright, flashing lights in the sky, don't panic. (①) This spectacular polar light show is called the aurorae. (②) It happens when electrical particles stream from the sun and bump into gases in the Earth's atmosphere. (③) So they made up stories to make sense of what was going on. (④) The Inuit people of Canada thought the sky was a dome stretched over the Earth and holes in the dome let light in and the spirits of dead people out. (⑤) They believed the aurorae were burning torches that guided the spirits to heaven. [4점]
　　　　　　　　　　　　　　　　　　　　* particle 미립자

16.

> However, early digital cameras failed on one crucial feedback.

Digital cameras generally provide better feedback to their users than film cameras. (①) After each shot, the photographer can see a small version of the image that was just captured. (②) This removes all kinds of errors that were common in the film era. (③) The errors ranged from failing to load the film properly to cutting off the head of the central figure of the picture. (④) When a picture was taken, there was no sound cue to indicate that the image had been captured. (⑤) Modern models now include a very satisfying but completely fake "shutter click" sound when a picture has been taken.

[3점]

17. 다음 Annual Teen Short Story Competition에 대한 내용과 일치하지 <u>않는</u> 것은? [2점]

Annual Teen Short Story Competition

Enter this year's teen short story contest NOW!

- Open to all teens aged thirteen to nineteen
- Stories should be 2,500 words or less written in your own words!

📖 **How to register :**

You can email your story and the application form, along with your contact details, to shortstory@tmail.com. You can also hand in your story in person to the nearest Baunt Books (along with a completed copy of the form). Please make sure they're typed, double-spaced and single-sided.

The contest is held until Sunday, January 8th, 2017. Results will be announced in April 2017, and winning stories will be published in May 2017.

---

① 13세에서 19세의 십대들을 대상으로 한다.
② 작품 분량은 2,500단어 이하여야 한다.
③ 지원서는 이메일로 접수 가능하다.
④ 작품은 가장 가까운 Baunt Books에 제출 가능하다.
⑤ 수상작은 결과 발표 후 그 다음 해에 출판된다.

18. blind snake에 관한 다음 글의 내용과 일치하는 것은? [3점]

Blind snakes are harmless snakes found mainly in Africa and Asia. They are not totally blind, but they can only tell light from dark. These snakes spend most of their life underground. It is very easy to mistake them for earthworms. Blind snakes could very well be the smallest snakes in the world. The adult snakes are very small and very thin. You cannot easily tell the head of the blind snake from its tail. It does not have a narrow neck. These snakes are unisexual and no males of the species have been discovered till now. The adult snakes have varied colors ranging from purple, charcoal gray to shining silver-gray.

① 시력을 잃어 명암을 구분할 수 없다.
② 주로 땅 위에서 생활한다.
③ 머리와 꼬리를 구분하기 쉽다.
④ 현재까지 수컷이 발견되지 않았다.
⑤ 완전히 자라면 모두 같은 색이 된다.

19. 다음 글의 제목으로 가장 적절한 것은? [3점]

In developed nations we tend to take water for granted because it flows easily out of the tap. But we are rapidly using up the global supply of fresh water, and this reality could potentially have serious effects. According to Water.org, less than 1 percent of the water on the earth is readily available for human use, that is, it is fresh—rather than salty—and reasonably clean. Salt can be removed from enough sea water through a special process, which is so expensive that it is rarely used as a practical solution for water shortage issues. Saving water is a straightforward, reasonable way to make the most of the fresh water.

① Recycling Water for a Low Price
② Various Factors of Water Pollution
③ Why We Should Not Waste Water
④ Water as the Future Energy Resource
⑤ Want Water? Sea Water Is the Answer!

20. 다음 글의 주제로 가장 적절한 것은? [3점]

The habit of reading is one of the greatest resources of mankind; and we enjoy reading books that belong to us much more than if they are borrowed. A borrowed book is like a guest in the house; it must be treated properly and formally. You must see that it does not get damaged. You cannot leave it carelessly, you cannot mark it, you cannot turn down the pages, you cannot use it familiarly. And then, some day, you really ought to return it. But your own books belong to you; you treat them with familiarity. You don't need to be afraid to mark up, or afraid to place on the table, wide open and face down.

① benefits of putting books in order
② ways we can read a book a week
③ things to consider when writing a book
④ the reason we should possess our own books
⑤ the importance of reading various kinds of books

21. 다음 글의 요지로 가장 적절한 것은? [4점]

Teens have something exciting planned with their peer group and do not want to go with the parents. The parents think of this as rejection or the lack of desire to be with the family. However, if the parents had recognized the teenager as a person (someone with independence and self-identity) and had consulted with the teenager at the planning stage, the teenager may have been very interested in joining the family. It is when we treat our teenagers as children and make plans for them that we get the impression that they don't wish to be with the family.

① 부모는 자녀의 또래 관계에 관심을 가져야 한다.
② 자녀와 함께 보내는 시간은 양보다 질이 중요하다.
③ 부모의 대화 방식이 자녀의 성격에 영향을 미친다.
④ 부모의 지나친 간섭은 자녀의 정체성 확립에 방해된다.
⑤ 가족 활동 계획 시 자녀를 독립된 인격체로 참여시켜야 한다.

22. 다음 글의 상황에 나타난 분위기로 가장 적절한 것은? [3점]

Bill took off his glasses and wiped them on his shirt. "Who knows we're here? Nobody knows where we are," said Bill. He was paler than before and breathless. "Perhaps they knew where we were going to, and perhaps not. But they don't know where we are because we never got there." Bill looked at the other boys. "That's what I was going to say," said Ralph. He looked at their serious faces and added, "Our plane was shot down in flames. Nobody knows where we are. We might be stuck here for a long time." The silence was so complete that they could hear each other breathing. Nobody said anything.

① hopeless   ② cheerful   ③ noisy
④ peaceful   ⑤ humorous

23. 다음 글에서 필자가 주장하는 바로 가장 적절한 것은? [4점]

A once-a-year day of volunteering is rarely enough for a child to adopt a charitable mindset. Look for ways to help your children experience the joy of giving on a regular basis: baking extra cookies for the lonely neighbor, singing at the nursing home to add a little joy. The goal of getting kids involved in charity is not about winning the Nobel Peace Prize, but giving them the opportunity to experience goodness. The truth is, kids don't learn how to be kind from reading about it in a textbook, but from doing a kind deed. The more children experience what it feels like to give in a regular manner, the more likely they will develop a charitable spirit.

① 봉사자는 수용적인 태도를 갖추어야 한다.
② 수혜자들에게 필요한 자원봉사가 이루어져야 한다.
③ 자원봉사 관련 프로그램을 다양하게 개발해야 한다.
④ 어릴 때부터 봉사와 관련된 책을 많이 읽어야 한다.
⑤ 아이들에게 정기적으로 봉사를 경험할 수 있게 해야 한다.

24. 다음 글의 빈칸 (A), (B)에 들어갈 말로 가장 적절한 것은? [4점]

Focusing on one's subject matter can be an important factor in gaining creative insights. Newton, ___(A)___, arrived at the law of gravitation by thinking over the problem all the time. Creative insights appear to be easiest to gain in fields where we have a lot of knowledge and experience. ___(B)___, there is a paradox here, for we tend not to think about what we think we know already. Existing ideas tend to make us unable to realize new possibilities. This means that creative ideas do not come to us unless we spend much effort in the activity you believe you know well.

	(A)	(B)
①	however	Besides
②	moreover	However
③	moreover	In addition
④	for example	However
⑤	for example	In addition

25. 다음 글의 내용을 한 문장으로 요약하고자 한다. 빈칸 (A)와 (B)에 들어갈 말로 가장 적절한 것은? [4점]

Potential customers were given two subscription offers—an "online only" for $56, and an "online + print" for $125. A large majority of customers chose the first option ($56). The publishers then introduced a third option that they knew nobody would prefer: "$125 for print only". As expected, no one chose the third option, but something magical happened! The majority now chose the second option ($125 for online+print)! The introduction of this third option made option 2 seem like a good bargain; you were getting an online version for free! What happened here? The first scenario with two options had nothing to compare either option to. But, with the introduction of the third option, options 2 and 3 were comparable and option 2 won. Option 1 had no comparison so it was left out.

* subscription 정기구독(표)

⇩

The introduction of a third option, which is less ___(A)___, can make a similar option (option 2) seem like ___(B)___ in comparison.

	(A)	(B)
①	creative	a better deal
②	creative	a bad decision
③	attractive	a better deal
④	attractive	a difficult choice
⑤	objective	a difficult choice

[26~27] 다음 글을 읽고, 물음에 답하시오.

Some people believe that having a lot of money will make them happy. For example, many people think that if they win the lottery, they will be happy. However, many lottery winners overspend and have many debts. Also, they have financial troubles because their friends and family want gifts, money or loans. These things make people unhappy. This example about lottery winners shows that, "money can't buy happiness." But, is that always true?

Michael Norton, a business school professor, has done experiments on how people behave with money. In one experiment, some university students spent money on themselves and some students spent money on other people. Afterwards, all the students were asked about their feelings. The students that spent money on themselves did not feel unhappy, but they did not feel happier, either. However, the research shows that students that spent money on others felt happier. Michael Norton did this type of money experiment all over the world, with people of all ages. Each time, the result was the same: Spending money on others _____ the happiness of the giver.

26. 윗글의 빈칸에 들어갈 말로 가장 적절한 것은? [4점]

① improved   ② blinded   ③ reduced

④ destroyed   ⑤ bothered

27. 윗글의 제목으로 가장 적절한 것은? [3점]

① A Wealthy Life is a Healthy Life
② The Key to Making Other People Feel Happy
③ Managing Your Finance after Winning the Lottery
④ Saving Money Will Save You from Your Troubles
⑤ Happiness Gained from Spending Money on Others

[28~30] 다음 글을 읽고, 물음에 답하시오.

(A)

Six years ago, my son, Nick, brought home a goldfish from the school festival. Finding a small container, I carelessly dumped it. Nick soon lost interest in that lone fish he named Fred. I took over as the caretaker. Beyond the bare necessities of food and fresh water, I did nothing to make (a) his home more interesting. Not an arch, plant, or rock.

(B)

So he took (b) him to our tiny neighborhood church, which had a beautiful pond. One other fish, a larger one, was there alone. When John put Fred in the water, he lay there, not knowing what to do, and John was worried that (c) he would drown. But suddenly the larger fish came over and tapped Fred gently, and slowly they went off together.

(C)

However, as time passed, I became closer to Fred. I'd worry when he didn't move around much; I thought he was dying, and I would tap loudly on his six-inch bowl to get (d) him moving. He would become lively and I was relieved. Mornings, I'd see him there and feel reassured.

(D)

Last summer, my husband and I went to Montana while Nick was at camp. We left our nineteen-year-old son, John, in charge of our house and Fred. Unknown to me he'd made the decision to set Fred free. (e) He could no longer bear to see him, day after day, trapped in such a small and lonely environment.

28. 주어진 글 (A)에 이어질 내용을 순서에 맞게 배열한 것으로 가장 적절한 것은? [3점]

① (B)-(D)-(C)   ② (C)-(B)-(D)   ③ (C)-(D)-(B)

④ (D)-(B)-(C)   ⑤ (D)-(C)-(B)

29. 밑줄 친 (a)~(e) 중 가리키는 대상이 나머지 넷과 다른 것은? [3점]

① (a)   ② (b)   ③ (c)   ④ (d)   ⑤ (e)

30. 윗글의 내용과 일치하는 것은? [3점]

① Nick은 시장에서 금붕어 한 마리를 사왔다.
② Nick의 가족은 Fred의 집에 식물과 돌을 넣어주었다.
③ 교회 연못에는 커다란 물고기 한 마리가 살고 있었다.
④ Nick은 아침마다 Fred가 움직이는지 확인했다.
⑤ John은 Fred를 놓아주겠다고 엄마에게 알렸다.

* 확인 사항

○ 답안지의 해당란에 필요한 내용을 정확히 기입(표기)했는지 확인하시오.

출신중학교 | 성명 | 수험번호

○ 문제지에 성명과 수험 번호를 정확히 써 넣으시오.
○ 답안지에 성명과 수험 번호를 써 넣고, 또 수험 번호와 답을 정확히 표시하시오.
○ 문항에 따라 배점이 다르니, 각 물음의 끝에 표시된 배점을 참고하시오.

1. 밑줄 친 He[him / his]가 가리키는 대상이 나머지 넷과 <u>다른</u> 것은? [2점]

On October 25, 1881, in Malaga in southern Spain, an art teacher and his wife had a baby boy. Years later that baby became known as the great artist, Pablo Picasso. Pablo's parents wanted ① <u>him</u> to be an artist. As a little boy, ② <u>he</u> often went to bullfights with his father. Pablo's first known painting was of a bullfight. ③ <u>He</u> was only about eight years old when he did it. Everyone thought he was gifted in art and they were right. When Pablo was thirteen, ④ <u>he</u> had his first art show. By then, his father saw that Pablo painted better than he did. So Pablo's father gave ⑤ <u>his</u> son all his brushes and paints and never painted again.

2. 다음 글의 목적으로 가장 적절한 것은? [3점]

We wish to express our worries about the bathroom facilities in the Grand Park on Main Street. Because of the park's convenient location, our neighborhood children spend many hours after school playing on the playground equipment. Some of us visited the facilities this morning and were horrified to see their condition. The water from the broken toilets flooded the floor. The children say that it has been that way for weeks. It is clearly a danger to the users. Please, repair them immediately. We ask that your office take action as soon as possible.

① 공원 화장실 이용 수칙을 안내하려고
② 학교 운동장 개방 시간을 공지하려고
③ 학생 안전교육의 필요성을 강조하려고
④ 손상된 공중화장실 시설 수리를 요청하려고
⑤ 체계적인 공중시설 관리 방안을 제시하려고

3. 다음 글의 밑줄 친 부분 중, 어법상 <u>틀린</u> 것은? [4점]

Your parents may be afraid that you will not spend your allowance wisely. You may make some foolish spending choices, but if you ① <u>do</u>, the decision to do so is your own and hopefully you will learn from your mistakes. Much of learning ② <u>occurs</u> through trial and error. Explain to your parents that money is something you will have to deal with for the rest of your life. It is better ③ <u>what</u> you make your mistakes early on rather than later in life. Explain that you will have a family someday and you need to know how ④ <u>to manage</u> your money. Not everything ⑤ <u>is taught</u> at school!

4. (A), (B), (C)의 각 네모 안에서 어법에 맞는 낱말로 가장 적절한 것은? [4점]

One of the best ways to know whether you've mastered something (A) [is / are] to try to teach it. Give students that opportunity. Give each student in a class a different aspect of the broader topic you're studying and then have them (B) [take / taken] turns teaching what they've learned to their classmates. And once they've got it down, give them a wider audience by inviting other classes, teachers or parents to learn what they have to teach. Also, at the start of a school term, ask students about their individual interests. Keep a list of your experts, and then (C) [call / calling] upon them as needed throughout the term. A classroom of teachers is a classroom of learners.

	(A)		(B)		(C)
①	is	……	take	……	call
②	is	……	taken	……	call
③	is	……	take	……	calling
④	are	……	taken	……	calling
⑤	are	……	take	……	call

[5~8] 다음 빈칸에 들어갈 말로 가장 적절한 것을 고르시오.

5. Recently on a flight to Asia, I met Debbie, who was warmly greeted by all of the flight attendants and was even welcomed aboard the plane by the pilot. Amazed at all the attention being paid to her, I asked if she worked with the airline. She did not, but she deserved the attention, for this flight marked the milestone of her flying over 4 million miles with this same airline. During the flight I learned that the airline's CEO personally called her to thank her for using their service for a long time and she received a catalogue of fine luxury gifts to choose from. Debbie was able to acquire this special treatment for one very important reason: she was a _____ customer to that one airline. [4점]

* milestone: 획기적인 사건

① courageous　　② loyal　　③ complaining
④ dangerous　　⑤ temporary

6. Today, 3-D printing technology is used only in companies and universities, but the prices are now getting lower and the quality better. We can imagine every home having a 3-D printer in the future. Note that 3-D printing technology doesn't require an original object to copy: any drawing will do, as long as it describes the piece precisely. Soon anyone can use a home sketching tool to produce the proper design, and then the home printer will be able to create the actual physical object. If you can _____ it, you can make it. For example, if you don't have enough dinner plates for your guests, you can "print out" some real plates from your sketch. [3점]

① mix　　② open　　③ draw
④ move　　⑤ taste

7. People eat significantly more when they are distracted at mealtimes and therefore are not paying attention to their food. In one experiment, the amount of attention that moviegoers paid to a film was related to how much popcorn they ate. Those who were more absorbed by the movie ate significantly larger amounts. In another experiment, people who listened to a fun story during their lunchtime ate 15 percent more food than those who sat in silence. Distractions while eating, such as watching television or reading a magazine _____. [4점]

* distract (주의를) 딴 데로 돌리다

① make us talk with others
② improve students' creativity
③ take some time to disappear
④ turn bad ideas into good ones
⑤ encourage people to consume more

8. Sarah Brosnan, the leader of a study, put female capuchin monkeys in pairs. The researcher trained the monkeys to exchange a small rock with the researcher. When a monkey exchanged a rock with the researcher within 60 seconds, she received a reward. Usually, the reward was a piece of cucumber. The partner of the capuchin who made an exchange also received a reward. Sometimes the partner got the same reward, but other times the partner received a better reward(a grape). Brosnan said the response to the unequal treatment was surprising. When a capuchin saw its partner get better treatment, it was unhappy. Some capuchins did not want to continue the test or eat the cucumbers they received. Some threw their food at the researcher. Brosnan realized _____. [4점]

* capuchin 눈목꼬리감기 원숭이 ** cucumber 오이

① the taste of a grape is sour
② female monkeys tend to be patient
③ they expect to receive fair treatment
④ writing letters is impossible for monkeys
⑤ the leader of the monkeys is treated better

9. 다음 글의 밑줄 친 부분 중, 문맥상 낱말의 쓰임이 적절하지 <u>않은</u> 것은? [4점]

   It's a small world, and business brings people from all cultures together. You may attend a meeting with a ① <u>foreign</u> visitor, or you may be sent off to a country with a language you don't understand. A language ② <u>gap</u> is a great opportunity for good manners to shine. The best course of action is a little ③ <u>preparation</u>. You can obtain a phrase book and learn a few ④ <u>basic</u> expressions - "Good morning," "Please," "Thank you," "I'm pleased to meet you," and "Goodbye." Making an effort to communicate in another person's language shows your ⑤ <u>disrespect</u> for that person.

       * phrase book: (여행객을 위한) 상용 회화집

10. (A), (B), (C)의 각 네모 안에서 문맥에 맞는 낱말로 가장 적절한 것은? [3점]

   Most of the world's energy comes from coal and oil. But burning them gives off dirty gases. This is the world's biggest cause of pollution. So scientists have been looking for (A) cheaper / cleaner ways to make energy. They've found some answers shining in sunlight. "Sun power is (B) useful / useless for the Earth," says Nancy Hazard, who works for a group that studies new kinds of energy. For example, the Tindo bus in Australia uses sun power for its lighting, heating, and air-conditioning. In addition, in Japan, people are building homes with special roof tiles that (C) catch / release sunlight. The energy kept by the tiles can make enough electricity for an entire family. About 70,000 of these homes will be built in the next few years.

(A)	(B)	(C)
① cleaner	useful	catch
② cleaner	useless	release
③ cleaner	useful	release
④ cheaper	useless	catch
⑤ cheaper	useful	release

11. 다음 도표의 내용과 일치하지 <u>않는</u> 것은? [3점]

World's Top International Tourism Spenders in 2014

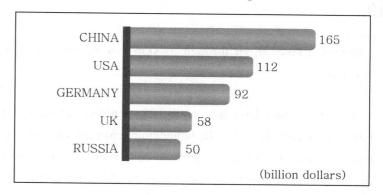

(billion dollars)

   The above graph shows the world's top international tourism spenders in 2014. ① China was at the top of the list with a total of 165 billion dollars. ② The United States of America (USA), the world's second largest spender, spent more than twice as much as Russia on international tourism. ③ Germany, which spent 20 billion dollars less than the USA, took third place. ④ The United Kingdom (UK) spent 58 billion dollars, which was less than half of the amount spent by the USA. ⑤ Of the five spenders, Russia spent the smallest amount of money on international tourism.

12. 다음 글의 상황에 나타난 분위기로 가장 적절한 것은? [2점]

   "Good night, sir," said the policeman, passing down the street, trying doors as he went. There was now a slight, cold rain falling, and the wind had become stronger, so now it blew steadily. The few people on the streets hurried sadly and silently along with their coat collars turned high and their hands in their pockets. And in the door of the hardware store, the man who had come a thousand miles to keep an appointment with his boyhood friends waited by himself.

① lively   ② lonely   ③ colorful

④ cheerful   ⑤ festive

[13~14] 글의 흐름으로 보아, 주어진 문장이 들어가기에 가장 적절한 곳을 고르시오.

13.

> Instead it takes in air through its skin and an opening under its tail.

A turtle doesn't have automatic body temperature control like birds and mammals. (①) Its temperature changes according to its environment. (②) When it gets too cold, it digs a hole deep into the mud at the bottom of a pond or into the dirt of the forest. (③) How can it breathe when it's buried? (④) The turtle stops breathing air through its nose and mouth. (⑤) And when spring comes and the ground warms up, the turtle digs itself out and starts breathing normally again. [3점]

* mammal: 포유류

14.

> But there will be times in your life when there is no one around to stand up and cheer you on.

It's great to have people in your life who believe in you and cheer you on. (①) They are truly interested in what you are trying to achieve and support you in all of your goals and efforts. (②) Each of us needs people in our lives who encourage us so that we can feel confident in our capabilities and move forward toward our goals. (③) When this happens, don't get depressed. (④) Instead, become your own cheerleader. (⑤) Give yourself a motivational pep talk because nobody knows your strengths and talents better than you and no one can motivate you better than you. [3점]

* pep talk: 격려의 말

[15~16] 다음 글에서 전체 흐름과 관계 <u>없는</u> 문장을 모두 고르시오.

15. As light shines through the glass crystal, you can look at the bands of color that appear. This shows that light is made up of all the colors of the rainbow. ① When light shines on a colored object, the surface of the object absorbs, or takes in, some of the light waves that strike it. ② The object absorbs some colors and reflects other colors. ③ You see the reflected colors but not the absorbed colors. ④ Light travels in waves and can pass through empty space. ⑤ Bananas look yellow because they reflect yellow light and absorb other colors. [3점]

16. Music study enriches all the learning — in reading, math, and other subjects — that children do at school. ① It also helps to develop language and communication skills. ② As children grow, musical training continues to help them develop the discipline and self-confidence needed to achieve in school. ③ Studying while listening to music causes students to have a difficult time learning the material. ④ The day-to-day practice in music, along with setting goals and reaching them, develops self-discipline, patience, and responsibility. ⑤ That discipline carries over to other areas, such as doing homework and other school projects on time and keeping materials organized. [4점]

* discipline: 자제력

17. 다음 글의 빈칸 (A), (B)에 들어갈 말로 가장 적절한 것은?

[3점]

Does parents' physical touch communicate their love to the teenager? The answer is yes and no. It all depends on when, where, and how. ___(A)___, a hug may be embarrassing if it's done when a teenager is with his friends. It may cause the teenager to push the parent away or say, "Stop it." ___(B)___, massaging the teenager's shoulders after he comes home from a game may deeply communicate love. A loving touch after a disappointing day at school will be welcomed as true parental love.

	(A)		(B)
①	In addition	······	However
②	In other words	······	In short
③	For instance	······	However
④	For instance	······	In short
⑤	In addition	······	Similarly

18. 다음 광고의 내용과 일치하지 <u>않는</u> 것은? [2점]

```
< Book Market >
    The Incheon Global Center is holding a special market for
used books to raise funds for a children's charity. Anyone who
wants to sell used books can join this event. Each person is
limited to selling 40 books. In addition, sellers are required to
give 10 percent of their earnings to the charity. To join this event,
you should submit your application form online by Feb. 25.


            When: Feb. 27, 10 a.m. to 5 p.m.
            Where: The Central Park
            Items for Sale: used books


    For more information, visit www.globalabc.com.
```

① 행사의 목적은 자선기금 모금이다.
② 개인당 최대 40권을 판매할 수 있다.
③ 판매자는 수익의 10%를 기부하도록 요구받는다.
④ 참가 신청서는 당일 행사 장소에서 제출해야 한다.
⑤ 행사는 2월 27일 오후 5시까지 열린다.

19. warthog에 관한 다음 글의 내용과 일치하지 <u>않는</u> 것은? [3점]

The warthog is a member of the pig family. This animal can be found only in Africa. Unlike most animals, warthogs can survive in dry areas without drinking water for several months. Warthogs can reach 4 to 6 feet in length and between 110 and 260 pounds in weight. Males are 20 to 50 pounds heavier than females. Warthogs keep their tails in the upright position when they are running. In that position, their tails look like flags in the wind. Warthogs have poor eyesight, but excellent senses of smell and hearing.

① 아프리카에서만 볼 수 있다.
② 물을 마시지 않고 몇 달 동안 버틸 수 있다.
③ 수컷이 암컷보다 무게가 더 많이 나간다.
④ 달릴 때 꼬리를 위로 세운다.
⑤ 시력은 좋지만 청력은 좋지 않다.

20. 다음 글의 제목으로 가장 적절한 것은? [4점]

Dr. John Ross was well-known for helping his patients. Many of his patients were poor farmers, and they could not always afford to pay Dr. Ross's small fee. The good doctor would accept vegetables, eggs, or even a simple "thank you" in payment. One winter afternoon, he went to a house to see a child with a fever. The girl's family had run out of the firewood they needed to keep their tiny house warm. Dr. Ross grabbed a spare blanket from his car and told the father to bathe his daughter's forehead with cool water. Then Dr. Ross left to take care of other patients. After setting a broken leg, delivering a baby, and cleaning an infected finger, he returned to the sick child's house with a load of firewood. He built a fire for the little girl and her family.

* deliver: 출산을 돕다

① A Warm-Hearted Doctor
② Folk Medicine Really Works
③ The Importance of Family Love
④ A Little Knowledge Is Dangerous
⑤ A Doctor Who Couldn't Cure Himself

21. 다음 글의 주제로 가장 적절한 것은? [3점]

Ask people whether they will be happier after spending money on themselves or others, and the vast majority will check the "me" box. The science shows that exactly the opposite is true. People become much happier after providing for others rather than themselves. The good news is that you really do not have to put aside a huge proportion of your income for friends and family. In fact, the smallest gifts can quickly result in surprisingly large and long-lasting changes in happiness. A few dollars spent on others may be one of the best investments that you ever make. And if you really can't afford to share your cash, remember that carrying out five nonfinancial acts of kindness on a single day also provides a significant increase to happiness.

① how to save money effectively
② disadvantages of wasting your money
③ giving more as a way to stay in happiness
④ suggestions for choosing appropriate presents
⑤ significance of spending money on your future

22. 다음 글의 요지로 가장 적절한 것은? [4점]

When your child begs for another toy car, it's easy to say no. But when he asks for a toy that helps with math, do you give in? In fact, all toys can be educational; the most educational ones are usually the simplest, like cars and dolls. It's not about how they're marketed—it's about how you play with them. Learning doesn't necessarily have to come from the expensive developmental toys. If your child is constantly playing with cars or trains, he can use them to practice reading and writing. With chalk, make roads in the shape of letters or words your child is struggling with and then make a game of it: call out the letter or words while passing through them. This game is a fun way to help your child recognize some important words.

① 장난감 구입 시 제품의 안전성을 고려해야 한다.
② 아이는 자주 가지고 노는 장난감에 애착을 가진다.
③ 모든 장난감은 활용 방법에 따라 교육적일 수 있다.
④ 아이의 발달단계를 고려한 장난감을 제공해야 한다.
⑤ 학습에 도움이 되는 장난감을 더 많이 개발해야 한다.

23. 주어진 글 다음에 이어질 글의 순서로 가장 적절한 것은? [4점]

> As industry developed, people's lives began to change. The factories created many new jobs, so many workers were needed.

(A) So they formed groups called labor unions. Many of the terrible conditions were corrected and the working conditions got better. Today there are about 16 million workers in the U.S. that belong to a labor union.

(B) People came from far away to work in the factories, because there were few jobs in the country. The new towns began to grow up around the factories.

(C) But living conditions were terrible in these towns. Some people had to work in dangerous conditions long hours. They were paid very little money. Many women and children also had to work. Workers felt the situation was unfair.

① (A) − (C) − (B)　　　② (B) − (A) − (C)
③ (B) − (C) − (A)　　　④ (C) − (A) − (B)
⑤ (C) − (B) − (A)

24. 다음 글에서 필자가 주장하는 바로 가장 적절한 것은? [3점]

Research has revealed that happy people move in a very different way than unhappy people do. Try walking in a more relaxed way, swinging your arms slightly more and putting a spring in your step. Also, try making more expressive hand gestures during conversations, wear more colorful clothing, use positively charged emotional words especially "love," "like," and "fond", have a larger variation in the pitch of your voice and speak slightly faster. Incorporating these behaviors into your everyday actions will increase your happiness.

① 지킬 수 있는 약속을 해라.
② 대화 중 지나친 몸짓을 피해라.
③ 친구의 애정 어린 충고에 귀 기울여라.
④ 건강을 지키기 위해 규칙적인 생활 습관을 가져라.
⑤ 행복하기 위해 행복한 사람이 행동하는 것처럼 행동해라.

25. 다음 글의 내용을 한 문장으로 요약하고자 한다. 빈칸 (A)와 (B)에 들어갈 말로 가장 적절한 것은? [4점]

> Natural boundaries between states or countries are found along rivers, lakes, deserts, and mountain ranges. Among them, river boundaries would seem to be ideal: they provide clear separation, and they are established and recognized physical features. In reality, however, river boundaries can change as rivers change course. Following flooding, a river's course may shift, altering the boundary between states or countries. For example, the Rio Grande, separating the United States and Mexico, has frequently shifted its course, causing problems in determining the exact location of the international boundary.
>
> * boundary: 경계

↓

> A river seems to be ideal in ___(A)___ boundaries, but in fact it isn't, because its course is ___(B)___.

(A)	(B)
① establishing	…… invisible
② establishing	…… changeable
③ removing	…… fixed
④ linking	…… fixed
⑤ linking	…… changeable

[26~27] 다음 글을 읽고, 물음에 답하시오.

The researchers of McGill University discovered an interesting result through an experiment involving 372 children. They left each child alone in a room for one minute with a toy behind them on a table, having told the child not to look at it during their absence. While they were out of the room, a hidden video camera recorded what went on.

The result showed that slightly more than 66% of the children looked at the toy. When those children were asked whether or not they had looked at it, again about 66% of them lied. More interestingly, children were less likely to tell the truth if they were afraid of being punished than if they were asked to tell the truth because it would please the adult. "The bottom line is that punishment does not promote truth-telling," says Victoria Talwar, the lead researcher on the study. "In fact, the threat of punishment can have the _____ effect by reducing the likelihood that children will tell the truth."

26. 위 글의 빈칸에 들어갈 말로 가장 적절한 것은? [4점]

① reverse   ② desirable   ③ productive
④ profitable   ⑤ educational

27. 위 글의 제목으로 가장 적절한 것은? [3점]

① Why Are Children Crazy for Toys?
② Can Telling a Lie Be a Good Excuse?
③ Does Punishing Children for Lying Work?
④ Curiosity: The Key to Improving Creativity
⑤ Truth: The Essential Value to Respect Parents

[28~30] 다음 글을 읽고, 물음에 답하시오.

(A)

Families don't grow strong unless parents invest precious time in them. In *New Man*, Gary Oliver writes about a difficult decision made by professional baseball player Tim Burke concerning his family. From the time Tim can first remember, his dream was to be a professional baseball player. Through years of hard work (a) he achieved that goal.

(B)

When Tim left the stadium for the last time, a reporter stopped him. And then (b) he asked why he was retiring. "Baseball is going to do just fine without me," he said to the reporter. "It's not going to miss a beat. But I'm the only father my children have and I'm the only husband my wife has. And they need me a lot more than baseball does."

(C)

While he was a successful pitcher for the Montreal Expos, (c) he and his wife wanted to start a family but discovered that they were unable to have children. After much thought, they decided to adopt four special-needs international children. This led to one of the most difficult decisions of Tim's life.

(D)

He discovered that his life on the road conflicted with his ability to be a quality husband and dad. Over time, it became clear that (d) he couldn't do a good job at both. After more thought, he made what many considered an unbelievable decision: (e) he decided to give up professional baseball.

28. 주어진 글 (A)에 이어질 내용을 순서에 맞게 배열한 것으로 가장 적절한 것은? [3점]

① (B) − (D) − (C)   ② (C) − (B) − (D)
③ (C) − (D) − (B)   ④ (D) − (B) − (C)
⑤ (D) − (C) − (B)

29. 밑줄 친 (a) ~ (e) 중에서 가리키는 대상이 나머지 넷과 다른 것은? [3점]

① (a)   ② (b)   ③ (c)   ④ (d)   ⑤ (e)

30. 윗글의 Tim Burke에 관한 내용과 일치하지 <u>않는</u> 것은? [4점]

① 열심히 노력하여 프로 야구 선수가 되었다.
② 마지막 경기 후에 기자로부터 질문을 받았다.
③ Montreal Expos 팀의 투수였다.
④ 네 명의 아이를 입양하기로 했다.
⑤ 가정을 위해 프로 야구를 계속하기로 했다.

＊ 확인 사항

◦ 답안지의 해당란에 필요한 내용을 정확히 기입(표기)했는지 확인하시오.

2023학년도 3월 고1 전국연합학력평가 문제지

영어 영역

제 3 교시

● 문항수 45개 | 배점 100점 | 제한 시간 70분

1

04회

● 점수 표시가 없는 문항은 모두 2점

04회

1번부터 17번까지는 듣고 답하는 문제입니다. 1번부터 15번까지는 한 번만 들려주고, 16번부터 17번까지는 두 번 들려줍니다. 방송을 잘 듣고 답을 하시기 바랍니다.

MP3

1. 다음을 듣고, 남자가 하는 말의 목적으로 가장 적절한 것을 고르시오.

① 아이스하키부의 우승을 알리려고
② 아이스하키부 훈련 일정을 공지하려고
③ 아이스하키부 신임 감독을 소개하려고
④ 아이스하키부 선수 모집을 안내하려고
⑤ 아이스하키부 경기의 관람을 독려하려고

2. 대화를 듣고, 여자의 의견으로 가장 적절한 것을 고르시오.

① 과다한 항생제 복용을 자제해야 한다.
② 오래된 약을 함부로 폐기해서는 안 된다.
③ 약을 복용할 때는 정해진 시간을 지켜야 한다.
④ 진료 전에 자신의 증상을 정확히 확인해야 한다.
⑤ 다른 사람에게 처방된 약을 복용해서는 안 된다.

3. 대화를 듣고, 두 사람의 관계를 가장 잘 나타낸 것을 고르시오.

① 관람객 – 박물관 관장
② 세입자 – 건물 관리인
③ 화가 – 미술관 직원
④ 고객 – 전기 기사
⑤ 의뢰인 – 건축사

4. 대화를 듣고, 그림에서 대화의 내용과 일치하지 않는 것을 고르시오.

5. 대화를 듣고, 남자가 할 일로 가장 적절한 것을 고르시오.

① 티켓 디자인하기   ② 포스터 게시하기
③ 블로그 개설하기   ④ 밴드부원 모집하기
⑤ 콘서트 장소 대여하기

6. 대화를 듣고, 여자가 지불할 금액을 고르시오. [3점]

① $70   ② $90   ③ $100   ④ $110   ⑤ $120

7. 대화를 듣고, 남자가 지갑을 구매하지 못한 이유를 고르시오.

① 해당 상품이 다 팔려서
② 브랜드명을 잊어버려서
③ 계산대의 줄이 길어서
④ 공항에 늦게 도착해서
⑤ 면세점이 문을 닫아서

8. 대화를 듣고, Youth Choir Audition에 관해 언급되지 않은 것을 고르시오.

① 지원 가능 연령   ② 날짜   ③ 심사 기준
④ 참가비   ⑤ 지원 방법

9. 2023 Career Week에 관한 다음 내용을 듣고, 일치하지 않는 것을 고르시오.

① 5일 동안 열릴 것이다.
② 미래 직업 탐색을 돕는 프로그램이 있을 것이다.
③ 프로그램 참가 인원에 제한이 있다.
④ 특별 강연이 마지막 날에 있을 것이다.
⑤ 등록은 5월 10일에 시작된다.

10. 다음 표를 보면서 대화를 듣고, 여자가 구입할 프라이팬을 고르시오.

Frying Pans

	Model	Price	Size (inches)	Material	Lid
①	A	$30	8	Aluminum	○
②	B	$32	9.5	Aluminum	○
③	C	$35	10	Stainless Steel	×
④	D	$40	11	Aluminum	×
⑤	E	$70	12.5	Stainless Steel	○

11. 대화를 듣고, 남자의 마지막 말에 대한 여자의 응답으로 가장 적절한 것을 고르시오.

① I don't think I can finish editing it by then.
② I learned it by myself through books.
③ This short movie is very interesting.
④ You should make another video clip.
⑤ I got an A$^+$ on the team project.

12. 대화를 듣고, 여자의 마지막 말에 대한 남자의 응답으로 가장 적절한 것을 고르시오.

① All right. I'll come pick you up now.
② I'm sorry. The library is closed today.
③ No problem. You can borrow my book.
④ Thank you so much. I'll drop you off now.
⑤ Right. I've changed the interior of my office.

13. 대화를 듣고, 남자의 마지막 말에 대한 여자의 응답으로 가장 적절한 것을 고르시오.

Woman: _____

① Try these tomatoes and cucumbers.
② I didn't know peppers are good for skin.
③ Just wear comfortable clothes and shoes.
④ You can pick tomatoes when they are red.
⑤ I'll help you grow vegetables on your farm.

14. 대화를 듣고, 여자의 마지막 말에 대한 남자의 응답으로 가장 적절한 것을 고르시오. [3점]

Man: _____

① You're right. I'll meet her and apologize.
② I agree with you. That's why I did it.
③ Thank you. I appreciate your apology.
④ Don't worry. I don't think it's your fault.
⑤ Too bad. I hope the two of you get along.

15. 다음 상황 설명을 듣고, John이 Ted에게 할 말로 가장 적절한 것을 고르시오. [3점]

John: _____

① How can we find the best sunrise spot?
② Why do you go mountain climbing so often?
③ What time should we get up tomorrow morning?
④ When should we come down from the mountain top?
⑤ Where do we have to stay in the mountain at night?

[16 ~ 17] 다음을 듣고, 물음에 답하시오.

16. 여자가 하는 말의 주제로 가장 적절한 것은?

① indoor sports good for the elderly
② importance of learning rules in sports
③ best sports for families to enjoy together
④ useful tips for winning a sports game
⑤ history of traditional family sports

17. 언급된 스포츠가 아닌 것은?

① badminton
② basketball
③ table tennis
④ soccer
⑤ bowling

이제 듣기 문제가 끝났습니다. 18번부터는 문제지의 지시에 따라 답을 하시기 바랍니다.

18. 다음 글의 목적으로 가장 적절한 것은?

> To whom it may concern,
>
> I am a resident of the Blue Sky Apartment. Recently I observed that the kid zone is in need of repairs. I want you to pay attention to the poor condition of the playground equipment in the zone. The swings are damaged, the paint is falling off, and some of the bolts on the slide are missing. The facilities have been in this terrible condition since we moved here. They are dangerous to the children playing there. Would you please have them repaired? I would appreciate your immediate attention to solve this matter.
>
> Yours sincerely,
> Nina Davis

① 아파트의 첨단 보안 설비를 홍보하려고
② 아파트 놀이터의 임시 폐쇄를 공지하려고
③ 아파트 놀이터 시설의 수리를 요청하려고
④ 아파트 놀이터 사고의 피해 보상을 촉구하려고
⑤ 아파트 공용 시설 사용 시 유의 사항을 안내하려고

19. 다음 글에 드러난 'I'의 심경 변화로 가장 적절한 것은?

On a two-week trip in the Rocky Mountains, I saw a grizzly bear in its native habitat. At first, I felt joy as I watched the bear walk across the land. He stopped every once in a while to turn his head about, sniffing deeply. He was following the scent of something, and slowly I began to realize that this giant animal was smelling me! I froze. This was no longer a wonderful experience; it was now an issue of survival. The bear's motivation was to find meat to eat, and I was clearly on his menu.

* scent: 냄새

① sad → angry
② delighted → scared
③ satisfied → jealous
④ worried → relieved
⑤ frustrated → excited

20. 다음 글에서 필자가 주장하는 바로 가장 적절한 것은?

It is difficult for any of us to maintain a constant level of attention throughout our working day. We all have body rhythms characterised by peaks and valleys of energy and alertness. You will achieve more, and feel confident as a benefit, if you schedule your most demanding tasks at times when you are best able to cope with them. If you haven't thought about energy peaks before, take a few days to observe yourself. Try to note the times when you are at your best. We are all different. For some, the peak will come first thing in the morning, but for others it may take a while to warm up.

* alertness: 기민함

① 부정적인 감정에 에너지를 낭비하지 말라.
② 자신의 신체 능력에 맞게 운동량을 조절하라.
③ 자기 성찰을 위한 아침 명상 시간을 확보하라.
④ 생산적인 하루를 보내려면 일을 균등하게 배분하라.
⑤ 자신의 에너지가 가장 높은 시간을 파악하여 활용하라.

21. 밑줄 친 The divorce of the hands from the head가 다음 글에서 의미하는 바로 가장 적절한 것은? [3점]

If we adopt technology, we need to pay its costs. Thousands of traditional livelihoods have been pushed aside by progress, and the lifestyles around those jobs removed. Hundreds of millions of humans today work at jobs they hate, producing things they have no love for. Sometimes these jobs cause physical pain, disability, or chronic disease. Technology creates many new jobs that are certainly dangerous. At the same time, mass education and media train humans to avoid low-tech physical work, to seek jobs working in the digital world. The divorce of the hands from the head puts a stress on the human mind. Indeed, the sedentary nature of the best-paying jobs is a health risk — for body and mind.

* chronic: 만성의　** sedentary: 주로 앉아서 하는

① ignorance of modern technology
② endless competition in the labor market
③ not getting along well with our coworkers
④ working without any realistic goals for our career
⑤ our increasing use of high technology in the workplace

22. 다음 글의 요지로 가장 적절한 것은?

When students are starting their college life, they may approach every course, test, or learning task the same way, using what we like to call "the rubber-stamp approach." Think about it this way: Would you wear a tuxedo to a baseball game? A colorful dress to a funeral? A bathing suit to religious services? Probably not. You know there's appropriate dress for different occasions and settings. Skillful learners know that "putting on the same clothes" won't work for every class. They are flexible learners. They have different strategies and know when to use them. They know that you study for multiple-choice tests differently than you study for essay tests. And they not only know what to do, but they also know how to do it.

① 숙련된 학습자는 상황에 맞는 학습 전략을 사용할 줄 안다.
② 선다형 시험과 논술 시험은 평가의 형태와 목적이 다르다.
③ 문화마다 특정 행사와 상황에 맞는 복장 규정이 있다.
④ 학습의 양보다는 학습의 질이 학업 성과를 좌우한다.
⑤ 학습 목표가 명확할수록 성취 수준이 높아진다.

23. 다음 글의 주제로 가장 적절한 것은?

As the social and economic situation of countries got better, wage levels and working conditions improved. Gradually people were given more time off. At the same time, forms of transport improved and it became faster and cheaper to get to places. England's industrial revolution led to many of these changes. Railways, in the nineteenth century, opened up now famous seaside resorts such as Blackpool and Brighton. With the railways came many large hotels. In Canada, for example, the new coast-to-coast railway system made possible the building of such famous hotels as Banff Springs and Chateau Lake Louise in the Rockies. Later, the arrival of air transport opened up more of the world and led to tourism growth.

① factors that caused tourism expansion
② discomfort at a popular tourist destination
③ importance of tourism in society and economy
④ negative impacts of tourism on the environment
⑤ various types of tourism and their characteristics

24. 다음 글의 제목으로 가장 적절한 것은?

Success can lead you off your intended path and into a comfortable rut. If you are good at something and are well rewarded for doing it, you may want to keep doing it even if you stop enjoying it. The danger is that one day you look around and realize you're so deep in this comfortable rut that you can no longer see the sun or breathe fresh air; the sides of the rut have become so slippery that it would take a superhuman effort to climb out; and, effectively, you're stuck. And it's a situation that many working people worry they're in now. The poor employment market has left them feeling locked in what may be a secure, or even well-paying — but ultimately unsatisfying — job.

* rut: 틀에 박힌 생활

① Don't Compete with Yourself
② A Trap of a Successful Career
③ Create More Jobs for Young People
④ What Difficult Jobs Have in Common
⑤ A Road Map for an Influential Employer

25. 다음 도표의 내용과 일치하지 <u>않는</u> 것은?

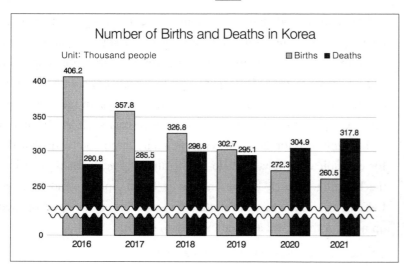

Number of Births and Deaths in Korea

Unit: Thousand people ☐ Births ■ Deaths

The above graph shows the number of births and deaths in Korea from 2016 to 2021. ① The number of births continued to decrease throughout the whole period. ② The gap between the number of births and deaths was the largest in 2016. ③ In 2019, the gap between the number of births and deaths was the smallest, with the number of births slightly larger than that of deaths. ④ The number of deaths increased steadily during the whole period, except the period from 2018 to 2019. ⑤ In 2021, the number of deaths was larger than that of births for the first time.

26. Lilian Bland에 관한 다음 글의 내용과 일치하지 <u>않는</u> 것은?

Lilian Bland was born in Kent, England in 1878. Unlike most other girls at the time she wore trousers and spent her time enjoying adventurous activities like horse riding and hunting. Lilian began her career as a sports and wildlife photographer for British newspapers. In 1910 she became the first woman to design, build, and fly her own airplane. In order to persuade her to try a slightly safer activity, Lilian's dad bought her a car. Soon Lilian was a master driver and ended up working as a car dealer. She never went back to flying but lived a long and exciting life nonetheless. She married, moved to Canada, and had a kid. Eventually, she moved back to England, and lived there for the rest of her life.

① 승마와 사냥 같은 모험적인 활동을 즐겼다.
② 스포츠와 야생 동물 사진작가로 경력을 시작했다.
③ 자신의 비행기를 설계하고 제작했다.
④ 자동차 판매원으로 일하기도 했다.
⑤ 캐나다에서 생의 마지막 기간을 보냈다.

27. Call for Articles에 관한 다음 안내문의 내용과 일치하지 <u>않는</u> 것은?

Call for Articles

Do you want to get your stories published? *New Dream Magazine* is looking for future writers! This event is open to anyone aged 13 to 18.

Articles
- Length of writing: 300－325 words
- Articles should also include high-quality color photos.

Rewards
- Five cents per word
- Five dollars per photo

Notes
- You should send us your phone number together with your writing.
- Please email your writing to us at article@ndmag.com.

① 13세에서 18세까지의 누구나 참여할 수 있다.
② 기사는 고화질 컬러 사진을 포함해야 한다.
③ 사진 한 장에 5센트씩 지급한다.
④ 전화번호를 원고와 함께 보내야 한다.
⑤ 원고를 이메일로 제출해야 한다.

28. Greenhill Roller Skating에 관한 다음 안내문의 내용과 일치하는 것은?

Greenhill Roller Skating

Join us for your chance to enjoy roller skating!

- Place: Greenhill Park, 351 Cypress Avenue
- Dates: Friday, April 7 － Sunday, April 9
- Time: 9 a.m. － 6 p.m.
- Fee: $8 per person for a 50-minute session

Details
- Admission will be on a first-come, first-served basis with no reservations.
- Children under the age of 10 must be accompanied by an adult.
- We will lend you our roller skates for free.

Contact the Community Center for more information at 013-234-6114.

① 오전 9시부터 오후 9시까지 운영한다.
② 이용료는 시간 제한 없이 1인당 8달러이다.
③ 입장하려면 예약이 필요하다.
④ 10세 미만 어린이는 어른과 동행해야 한다.
⑤ 추가 요금을 내면 롤러스케이트를 빌려준다.

29. 다음 글의 밑줄 친 부분 중, 어법상 틀린 것은? [3점]

The most noticeable human characteristic projected onto animals is ① that they can talk in human language. Physically, animal cartoon characters and toys ② made after animals are also most often deformed in such a way as to resemble humans. This is achieved by ③ showing them with humanlike facial features and deformed front legs to resemble human hands. In more recent animated movies the trend has been to show the animals in a more "natural" way. However, they still use their front legs ④ like human hands (for example, lions can pick up and lift small objects with one paw), and they still talk with an appropriate facial expression. A general strategy that is used to make the animal characters more emotionally appealing, both to children and adults, ⑤ are to give them enlarged and deformed childlike features.

* deform: 변형하다　** paw: (동물의) 발

30. 다음 글의 밑줄 친 부분 중, 문맥상 낱말의 쓰임이 적절하지 않은 것은? [3점]

The major philosophical shift in the idea of selling came when industrial societies became more affluent, more competitive, and more geographically spread out during the 1940s and 1950s. This forced business to develop ① closer relations with buyers and clients, which in turn made business realize that it was not enough to produce a quality product at a reasonable price. In fact, it was equally ② essential to deliver products that customers actually wanted. Henry Ford produced his best-selling T-model Ford in one color only (black) in 1908, but in modern societies this was no longer ③ possible. The modernization of society led to a marketing revolution that ④ strengthened the view that production would create its own demand. Customers, and the desire to ⑤ meet their diverse and often complex needs, became the focus of business.

* affluent: 부유한

[31 ~ 34] 다음 빈칸에 들어갈 말로 가장 적절한 것을 고르시오.

31. People differ in how quickly they can reset their biological clocks to overcome jet lag, and the speed of recovery depends on the _____ of travel. Generally, it's easier to fly westward and lengthen your day than it is to fly eastward and shorten it. This east-west difference in jet lag is sizable enough to have an impact on the performance of sports teams. Studies have found that teams flying westward perform significantly better than teams flying eastward in professional baseball and college football. A more recent study of more than 46,000 Major League Baseball games found additional evidence that eastward travel is tougher than westward travel.

* jet lag: 시차로 인한 피로감

① direction
② purpose
③ season
④ length
⑤ cost

32. If you want the confidence that comes from achieving what you set out to do each day, then it's important to understand _____. Over-optimism about what can be achieved within a certain time frame is a problem. So work on it. Make a practice of estimating the amount of time needed alongside items on your 'things to do' list, and learn by experience when tasks take a greater or lesser time than expected. Give attention also to fitting the task to the available time. There are some tasks that you can only set about if you have a significant amount of time available. There is no point in trying to gear up for such a task when you only have a short period available. So schedule the time you need for the longer tasks and put the short tasks into the spare moments in between.

* gear up: 준비를 갖추다, 대비하다

① what benefits you can get
② how practical your tasks are
③ how long things are going to take
④ why failures are meaningful in life
⑤ why your leisure time should come first

33. In Lewis Carroll's *Through the Looking-Glass*, the Red Queen takes Alice on a race through the countryside. They run and they run, but then Alice discovers that they're still under the same tree that they started from. The Red Queen explains to Alice: "here, you see, it takes all the running you can do, to keep in the same place." Biologists sometimes use this Red Queen Effect to explain an evolutionary principle. If foxes evolve to run faster so they can catch more rabbits, then only the fastest rabbits will live long enough to make a new generation of bunnies that run even faster — in which case, of course, only the fastest foxes will catch enough rabbits to thrive and pass on their genes. Even though they might run, the two species _____. [3점]

　　　　　　　　　　　　　　　　　* thrive: 번성하다

① just stay in place
② end up walking slowly
③ never run into each other
④ won't be able to adapt to changes
⑤ cannot run faster than their parents

34. Everything in the world around us was finished in the mind of its creator before it was started. The houses we live in, the cars we drive, and our clothing — all of these began with an idea. Each idea was then studied, refined and perfected before the first nail was driven or the first piece of cloth was cut. Long before the idea was turned into a physical reality, the mind had clearly pictured the finished product. The human being designs his or her own future through much the same process. We begin with an idea about how the future will be. Over a period of time we refine and perfect the vision. Before long, our every thought, decision and activity are all working in harmony to bring into existence what we _____. [3점]

　　　　　　　　　　　　　　　　　* refine: 다듬다

① didn't even have the potential to accomplish
② have mentally concluded about the future
③ haven't been able to picture in our mind
④ considered careless and irresponsible
⑤ have observed in some professionals

35. 다음 글에서 전체 흐름과 관계 <u>없는</u> 문장은?

Whose story it is affects *what* the story is. Change the main character, and the focus of the story must also change. If we look at the events through another character's eyes, we will interpret them differently. ① We'll place our sympathies with someone new. ② When the conflict arises that is the heart of the story, we will be praying for a different outcome. ③ Consider, for example, how the tale of Cinderella would shift if told from the viewpoint of an evil stepsister. ④ We know Cinderella's kingdom does not exist, but we willingly go there anyway. ⑤ *Gone with the Wind* is Scarlett O'Hara's story, but what if we were shown the same events from the viewpoint of Rhett Butler or Melanie Wilkes?

　　　　　　　　　　　　　　　　　* sympathy: 공감

[36~37] 주어진 글 다음에 이어질 글의 순서로 가장 적절한 것을 고르시오.

36.

> In the Old Stone Age, small bands of 20 to 60 people wandered from place to place in search of food. Once people began farming, they could settle down near their farms.

(A) While some workers grew crops, others built new houses and made tools. Village dwellers also learned to work together to do a task faster.

(B) For example, toolmakers could share the work of making stone axes and knives. By working together, they could make more tools in the same amount of time.

(C) As a result, towns and villages grew larger. Living in communities allowed people to organize themselves more efficiently. They could divide up the work of producing food and other things they needed.

　　　　　　　　　　　　　　　　　* dweller: 거주자

① (A) ― (C) ― (B)　　　② (B) ― (A) ― (C)
③ (B) ― (C) ― (A)　　　④ (C) ― (A) ― (B)
⑤ (C) ― (B) ― (A)

37.

Natural processes form minerals in many ways. For example, hot melted rock material, called magma, cools when it reaches the Earth's surface, or even if it's trapped below the surface. As magma cools, its atoms lose heat energy, move closer together, and begin to combine into compounds.

(A) Also, the size of the crystals that form depends partly on how rapidly the magma cools. When magma cools slowly, the crystals that form are generally large enough to see with the unaided eye.

(B) During this process, atoms of the different compounds arrange themselves into orderly, repeating patterns. The type and amount of elements present in a magma partly determine which minerals will form.

(C) This is because the atoms have enough time to move together and form into larger crystals. When magma cools rapidly, the crystals that form will be small. In such cases, you can't easily see individual mineral crystals. [3점]

* compound: 화합물

① (A) - (C) - (B) ② (B) - (A) - (C)
③ (B) - (C) - (A) ④ (C) - (A) - (B)
⑤ (C) - (B) - (A)

[38 ~ 39] 글의 흐름으로 보아, 주어진 문장이 들어가기에 가장 적절한 곳을 고르시오.

38.

Bad carbohydrates, on the other hand, are simple sugars.

All carbohydrates are basically sugars. (①) Complex carbohydrates are the good carbohydrates for your body. (②) These complex sugar compounds are very difficult to break down and can trap other nutrients like vitamins and minerals in their chains. (③) As they slowly break down, the other nutrients are also released into your body, and can provide you with fuel for a number of hours. (④) Because their structure is not complex, they are easy to break down and hold few nutrients for your body other than the sugars from which they are made. (⑤) Your body breaks down these carbohydrates rather quickly and what it cannot use is converted to fat and stored in the body.

* carbohydrate: 탄수화물 ** convert: 바꾸다

39.

It was also found that those students who expected the lecturer to be warm tended to interact with him more.

People commonly make the mistaken assumption that because a person has one type of characteristic, then they automatically have other characteristics which go with it. (①) In one study, university students were given descriptions of a guest lecturer before he spoke to the group. (②) Half the students received a description containing the word 'warm', the other half were told the speaker was 'cold'. (③) The guest lecturer then led a discussion, after which the students were asked to give their impressions of him. (④) As expected, there were large differences between the impressions formed by the students, depending upon their original information of the lecturer. (⑤) This shows that different expectations not only affect the impressions we form but also our behaviour and the relationship which is formed. [3점]

40. 다음 글의 내용을 한 문장으로 요약하고자 한다. 빈칸 (A), (B)에 들어갈 말로 가장 적절한 것은?

To help decide what's risky and what's safe, who's trustworthy and who's not, we look for *social evidence*. From an evolutionary view, following the group is almost always positive for our prospects of survival. "If everyone's doing it, it must be a sensible thing to do," explains famous psychologist and best selling writer of *Influence*, Robert Cialdini. While we can frequently see this today in product reviews, even subtler cues within the environment can signal trustworthiness. Consider this: when you visit a local restaurant, are they busy? Is there a line outside or is it easy to find a seat? It is a hassle to wait, but a line can be a powerful cue that the food's tasty, and these seats are in demand. More often than not, it's good to adopt the practices of those around you.

* subtle: 미묘한 ** hassle: 성가신 일

↓

We tend to feel safe and secure in ___(A)___ when we decide how to act, particularly when faced with ___(B)___ conditions.

	(A)		(B)
①	numbers	......	uncertain
②	numbers	......	unrealistic
③	experiences	......	unrealistic
④	rules	......	uncertain
⑤	rules	......	unpleasant

[41 ~ 42] 다음 글을 읽고, 물음에 답하시오.

Chess masters shown a chess board in the middle of a game for 5 seconds with 20 to 30 pieces still in play can immediately reproduce the position of the pieces from memory. Beginners, of course, are able to place only a few. Now take the same pieces and place them on the board randomly and the (a) difference is much reduced. The expert's advantage is only for familiar patterns — those previously stored in memory. Faced with unfamiliar patterns, even when it involves the same familiar domain, the expert's advantage (b) disappears.

The beneficial effects of familiar structure on memory have been observed for many types of expertise, including music. People with musical training can reproduce short sequences of musical notation more accurately than those with no musical training when notes follow (c) unusual sequences, but the advantage is much reduced when the notes are ordered randomly. Expertise also improves memory for sequences of (d) movements. Experienced ballet dancers are able to repeat longer sequences of steps than less experienced dancers, and they can repeat a sequence of steps making up a routine better than steps ordered randomly. In each case, memory range is (e) increased by the ability to recognize familiar sequences and patterns.

* expertise: 전문 지식   ** sequence: 연속, 순서
*** musical notation: 악보

41. 윗글의 제목으로 가장 적절한 것은?

① How Can We Build Good Routines?
② Familiar Structures Help Us Remember
③ Intelligence Does Not Guarantee Expertise
④ Does Playing Chess Improve Your Memory?
⑤ Creative Art Performance Starts from Practice

42. 밑줄 친 (a) ~ (e) 중에서 문맥상 낱말의 쓰임이 적절하지 않은 것은?

① (a)   ② (b)   ③ (c)   ④ (d)   ⑤ (e)

[43 ~ 45] 다음 글을 읽고, 물음에 답하시오.

(A)

Once upon a time, there was a king who lived in a beautiful palace. While the king was away, a monster approached the gates of the palace. The monster was so ugly and smelly that the guards froze in shock. He passed the guards and sat on the king's throne. The guards soon came to their senses, went in, and shouted at the monster, demanding that (a) he get off the throne.

* throne: 왕좌

(B)

Eventually the king returned. He was wise and kind and saw what was happening. He knew what to do. He smiled and said to the monster, "Welcome to my palace!" He asked the monster if (b) he wanted a cup of coffee. The monster began to grow smaller as he drank the coffee.

(C)

The king offered (c) him some take-out pizza and fries. The guards immediately called for pizza. The monster continued to get smaller with the king's kind gestures. (d) He then offered the monster a full body massage. As the guards helped with the relaxing massage, the monster became tiny. With another act of kindness to the monster, he just disappeared.

(D)

With each bad word the guards used, the monster grew more ugly and smelly. The guards got even angrier — they began to brandish their swords to scare the monster away from the palace. But (e) he just grew bigger and bigger, eventually taking up the whole room. He grew more ugly and smelly than ever.

* brandish: 휘두르다

43. 주어진 글 (A)에 이어질 내용을 순서에 맞게 배열한 것으로 가장 적절한 것은?

① (B) — (D) — (C)   ② (C) — (B) — (D)
③ (C) — (D) — (B)   ④ (D) — (B) — (C)
⑤ (D) — (C) — (B)

44. 밑줄 친 (a) ~ (e) 중에서 가리키는 대상이 나머지 넷과 다른 것은?

① (a)   ② (b)   ③ (c)   ④ (d)   ⑤ (e)

45. 윗글에 관한 내용으로 적절하지 않은 것은?

① 왕이 없는 동안 괴물이 궁전 문으로 접근했다.
② 왕은 미소를 지으며 괴물에게 환영한다고 말했다.
③ 왕의 친절한 행동에 괴물의 몸이 계속 더 작아졌다.
④ 경비병들은 괴물을 마사지해 주기를 거부했다.
⑤ 경비병들은 겁을 주어 괴물을 쫓아내려 했다.

* 확인 사항
○ 답안지의 해당란에 필요한 내용을 정확히 기입(표기) 했는지 확인하시오.

01
001 principal ⓝ 교장
002 big fan 열렬한 팬
003 excited ⓐ 기대하는, 신나는
004 cheer ⓥ 응원하다
005 put in effort 노력을 기울이다
006 incredible ⓐ 엄청난, 믿을 수 없는
007 amount ⓝ 양

02
008 catch a cold 감기에 걸리다
009 sore throat 인후통
010 see a doctor 병원에 가다
011 cabinet ⓝ 찬장, 캐비닛
012 prescribe ⓥ 처방하다
013 symptom ⓝ 증상
014 prescription ⓝ 처방(전)

03
015 preparation ⓝ 준비, 대비
016 I'm afraid that 죄송하지만 ~합니다
017 exhibition ⓝ 전시
018 painting ⓝ 그림
019 electrical ⓐ 전기의
020 exhibit ⓥ 전시하다

04
021 volunteer work 봉사활동
022 whale ⓝ 고래
023 How do you like ~? ~는 어때?
024 background ⓝ 배경
025 leaf(-leaves) ⓝ (식물, 나무의) 잎
026 butterfly ⓝ 나비

05
027 be busy ~ing ~하느라 바쁘다
028 rock band 록 밴드
029 reserve ⓥ 예약하다
030 actually ⓐ 사실, 실제로
031 upload ⓥ 업로드하다, 올리다
032 post ⓥ 게시하다

06
033 coffee pot 커피포트
034 originally ⓐ 원래
035 on sale 할인 중인
036 come in (사이즈나 색상이) 나오다
037 carry around 들고 다니다
038 credit card 신용 카드

07
039 in line 줄을 선, 줄 서서
040 by the way 그나저나
041 drop by ~에 들르다
042 duty free shop 면세점
043 wallet ⓝ 지갑
044 take a memo 메모하다
045 sold out 품절된

08
046 youth ⓝ 청소년, 청년
047 choir ⓝ 합창단

048 aged ⓐ 나이가 ~인
049 leave ⓥ 떠나다, 출발하다
050 entry fee 참가비
051 apply for ~에 신청하다, 지원하다
052 fill out (서류를) 작성하다
053 application form 신청서

09
054 announce ⓥ 안내하다
055 explore ⓥ 탐색하다
056 various ⓐ 다양한
057 note ⓥ 주목하다, 유념하다
058 be limited to ~로 제한되다
059 special lecture 특별 강연
060 registration ⓝ 등록, 신청

10
061 frying pan 프라이팬
062 pretty ⓐ 꽤, 상당히
063 spend ⓥ 소비하다
064 work for ~에 적합하다
065 material ⓝ 소재, 재료, 자재
066 lid ⓝ 뚜껑
067 keep A from B A가 B하지 못하게 막다
068 splash ⓥ (물 등을) 튀기다, 철벅거리다

11
069 edit ⓥ 편집하다
070 video clip (짧은) 영상
071 by then 그때까지
072 learn by oneself 독학하다

12
073 be about to ~할 참이다
074 drive home 운전하여 집에 가다
075 give a ride (~을) 태워주다
076 pick up ~을 (차에) 태우다
077 borrow ⓥ 빌리다
078 drop off ~을 (차에서) 내려주다
079 interior ⓝ 내부

13
080 harvest ⓥ 수확하다
081 cherry tomato 방울토마토
082 cucumber ⓝ 오이
083 pepper ⓝ 고추, 피망, 후추
084 look around 둘러보다
085 comfortable ⓐ 편안한

14
086 have an argument 싸우다
087 make a mistake 실수하다
088 have a long face 우울한 얼굴을 하다
089 get along with ~와 잘 지내다
090 apology ⓝ 사과
091 response ⓝ 응답
092 in person 직접
093 apologize ⓥ 사과하다
094 appreciate ⓥ 감사하다

15
095 reach ⓥ 도착하다, 이르다

096 mountain top 산 정상
097 all day 하루 종일
098 relaxing ⓐ 여유로운, 느긋한
099 drink coffee 커피를 마시다
100 sunrise ⓝ 일출, 해돋이

16~17
101 whole ⓐ 전체의
102 minimal ⓐ 최소의
103 equipment ⓝ 장비
104 easily ⓐ 쉽게
105 near ⓟⓡⓔⓟ ~의 가까이에
106 table tennis 탁구
107 indoors ⓐ 실내에서
108 how about ~ing ~하는 게 어떠세요?
109 the elderly 연세 드신 분들, 노인들
110 useful ⓐ 유용한
111 traditional ⓐ 전통적인

18
112 to whom it may concern 담당자 귀하, 관계자 귀하
113 resident ⓝ 주민
114 observe ⓥ (보고) 알다, 관찰하다
115 in need of ~이 필요한
116 repair ⓝ 보수, 수리
117 pay attention to ~에 주의를 기울이다
118 condition ⓝ 상태
119 playground ⓝ 놀이터
120 equipment ⓝ 장비
121 swing ⓝ 그네
122 damaged ⓐ 손상된
123 fall off 벗겨지다, 떨어져 나가다
124 slide ⓝ 미끄럼틀
125 missing ⓐ 없어진, 실종된
126 facility ⓝ 시설
127 terrible ⓐ 끔찍한
128 immediate ⓐ 즉각적인
129 solve ⓥ 해결하다
130 matter ⓝ 문제

19
131 trip ⓝ 여행
132 grizzly bear (북미·러시아 일부 지역에 사는) 회색곰
133 native ⓐ 토착의, 토종의
134 habitat ⓝ 서식지
135 at first 처음에
136 joy ⓝ 기쁨, 즐거움
137 walk across ~을 횡단하다
138 every once in a while 이따금
139 turn about 뒤돌아보다, 방향을 바꾸다
140 sniff ⓥ 킁킁거리다
141 deeply ⓐ 깊게
142 scent ⓝ 냄새
143 slowly ⓐ 천천히
144 giant ⓐ 거대한
145 smell ⓥ 냄새 맡다
146 freeze ⓥ 얼어붙다
147 no longer 더 이상 ~않다
148 issue ⓝ 문제, 이슈
149 survival ⓝ 생존

150 motivation ⓝ (행동의) 이유, 동기 (부여)
151 clearly ⓐ 분명히
152 jealous ⓐ 질투하는
153 frustrated ⓐ 좌절한

20
154 maintain ⓥ 유지하다
155 constant ⓐ 지속적인
156 attention ⓝ 주의, 집중
157 throughout ⓟⓡⓔⓟ ~ 내내
158 working day 근무 시간대
159 body rhythm 신체 리듬
160 characterise ⓥ ~을 특징으로 하다
161 peaks and valleys 정점과 저점, 부침, 성쇠
162 alertness ⓝ 기민함
163 achieve ⓥ 성취하다
164 confident ⓐ 자신감 있는
165 benefit ⓝ 이득
166 demanding ⓐ 까다로운, 힘든
167 cope with ~을 처리하다
168 warm up 준비가 되다, 몸을 풀다

21
169 adopt ⓥ 수용하다, 받아들이다
170 cost ⓝ 비용 ⓥ (~의 비용을) 치르게 하다
171 livelihood ⓝ 생계
172 push aside 밀어치우다
173 progress ⓝ 진보
174 remove ⓥ 제거하다
175 million ⓝ 100만
176 produce ⓥ 만들어내다
177 have love for ~에 애정을 갖다
178 physical ⓐ 신체적인
179 disability ⓝ 장애
180 chronic ⓐ 만성의
181 certainly ⓐ 분명히, 확실히
182 mass ⓝ (일반) 대중 ⓐ 대중의, 대량의
183 seek ⓥ 찾다, 추구하다
184 divorce A from B A와 B의 분리, A를 B로부터 분리시키다
185 put a stress on ~에 스트레스[부담]를 주다
186 sedentary ⓐ 주로 앉아서 하는
187 nature ⓝ 본성, 특성
188 health risk 건강상 위험
189 ignorance ⓝ 무지
190 endless ⓐ 끝없는
191 competition ⓝ 경쟁
192 labor market 노동 시장
193 get along (well) with ~와 잘 지내다
194 realistic ⓐ 현실적인

22
195 college life 대학 생활
196 approach ⓥ 접근하다, 다가오다 ⓝ 접근법
197 course ⓝ 수업, 강좌
198 rubber-stamp ⓝ 고무도장, 잘 살펴보지도 않고 무조건 허가하는 사람
199 colorful ⓐ 화려한, 색색의
200 funeral ⓝ 장례식
201 bathing suit 수영복

202 ☐ religious service 종교 의식	25	310 ☐ lift ⓥ 들어올리다	364 ☐ estimate ⓥ 추산하다
203 ☐ appropriate ⓐ 적절한	258 ☐ the number of ~의 수	311 ☐ paw ⓝ (동물의) 발	365 ☐ alongside prep ~와 함께
204 ☐ occasion ⓝ 상황, 경우	259 ☐ birth ⓝ 출생	312 ☐ facial expression 얼굴 표정	366 ☐ learn by experience 경험을 통해 배우다
205 ☐ setting ⓝ 환경, 배경	260 ☐ death ⓝ 사망	313 ☐ general ⓐ 일반적인	367 ☐ than expected 예상보다
206 ☐ skillful ⓐ 숙련된	261 ☐ decrease ⓥ 감소하다	314 ☐ emotionally ad 정서적으로	368 ☐ fit ⓥ ~에 맞추다
207 ☐ flexible ⓐ 융통성 있는	262 ☐ period ⓝ 기간	315 ☐ appealing ⓐ 매력적인	369 ☐ available ⓐ 이용 가능한
208 ☐ strategy ⓝ 전략	263 ☐ gap between A and B A와 B 사이의 격차	316 ☐ enlarge ⓥ 확대하다	370 ☐ set about ~을 시작하다
209 ☐ multiple-choice test 객관식 시험, 선다형 시험	264 ☐ slightly ad 약간	317 ☐ feature ⓝ 특징, 이목구비	371 ☐ there is no point in ~하는 것은 의미가 없다
	265 ☐ steadily ad 꾸준히		372 ☐ gear up 준비를 갖추다, 대비하다
23	266 ☐ except prep ~을 제외하고	30	373 ☐ spare ⓐ 여분의
210 ☐ social ⓐ 사회적인	267 ☐ for the first time 처음으로	318 ☐ major ⓐ 주요한, 큰	374 ☐ in between 사이에
211 ☐ economic ⓐ 경제적인		319 ☐ philosophical ⓐ 철학적인	375 ☐ practical ⓐ 현실성 있는, 타당한
212 ☐ get better 나아지다, 개선되다	26	320 ☐ shift ⓝ 변화, 전환 ⓥ 바뀌다	376 ☐ come first 가장 중요하다, 최우선 고려 사항이다
213 ☐ wage ⓝ 임금	268 ☐ unlike prep ~와 달리	321 ☐ industrial ⓐ 산업의	
214 ☐ working condition 근무 조건	269 ☐ at the time (과거) 당시에	322 ☐ affluent ⓐ 부유한	33
215 ☐ improve ⓥ 향상되다	270 ☐ trousers ⓝ 바지	323 ☐ competitive ⓐ 경쟁적인	377 ☐ countryside ⓝ 시골 지역
216 ☐ gradually ad 점차, 점점	271 ☐ spend time ~ing ~하면서 시간을 보내다	324 ☐ geographically ad 지리적으로	378 ☐ discover ⓥ 발견하다
217 ☐ time off 휴가	272 ☐ adventurous ⓐ 모험적인	325 ☐ spread ⓥ 퍼지다	379 ☐ explain ⓥ 설명하다
218 ☐ at the same time 동시에, 한편	273 ☐ horse riding 승마	326 ☐ force ⓥ (~이) 어쩔 수 없이 …하게 하다	380 ☐ biologist ⓝ 생물학자
219 ☐ transport ⓝ 운송, 이동	274 ☐ hunting ⓝ 사냥	327 ☐ in turn 결과적으로	381 ☐ evolutionary ⓐ 진화적인
220 ☐ industrial revolution 산업 혁명	275 ☐ wildlife ⓝ 야생 동물	328 ☐ reasonable ⓐ 합리적인, 적당한	382 ☐ principle ⓝ 원리
221 ☐ lead to ~을 초래하다	276 ☐ photographer ⓝ 사진 작가	329 ☐ equally ad 마찬가지로, 똑같이	383 ☐ evolve ⓥ 진화하다, 발전하다
222 ☐ railway ⓝ 철도	277 ☐ design ⓥ 설계하다	330 ☐ essential ⓐ 매우 중요한	384 ☐ generation ⓝ 세대
223 ☐ seaside ⓝ 해변	278 ☐ persuade ⓥ 설득하다	331 ☐ best-selling ⓐ 가장 많이 팔리는, 베스트셀러인	385 ☐ bunny ⓝ 토끼
224 ☐ arrival ⓝ 도래, 도착	279 ☐ safe ⓐ 안전한	332 ☐ modernization ⓝ 현대화	386 ☐ thrive ⓥ 번성하다
225 ☐ tourism ⓝ 관광(업)	280 ☐ end up ~ing 결국 ~하다	333 ☐ revolution ⓝ 혁명	387 ☐ pass on 물려주다
226 ☐ growth ⓝ 성장	281 ☐ work as ~로서 일하다	334 ☐ strengthen ⓥ 강화하다	388 ☐ gene ⓝ 유전자
227 ☐ factor ⓝ 요인	282 ☐ car dealer 자동차 판매상	335 ☐ demand ⓝ 수요	389 ☐ species ⓝ (생물) 종
228 ☐ expansion ⓝ 확장	283 ☐ go back to ~로 되돌아가다	336 ☐ complex ⓐ 복잡한	390 ☐ run into ~을 우연히 만나다
229 ☐ discomfort ⓝ 불편	284 ☐ nonetheless ad 그럼에도 불구하고	337 ☐ focus ⓝ 초점	391 ☐ adapt to ~에 적응하다
230 ☐ tourist destination 관광지	285 ☐ have a kid 자식을 낳다		
231 ☐ impact ⓝ 영향, 여파	286 ☐ the rest of ~의 나머지	31	34
232 ☐ various ⓐ 다양한		338 ☐ differ in ~에 관해 다르다	392 ☐ creator ⓝ 창조자
233 ☐ characteristic ⓝ 특징	27	339 ☐ reset ⓥ 재설정하다	393 ☐ clothing ⓝ 옷, 의복
	287 ☐ publish ⓥ 출간하다	340 ☐ biological clock 체내 시계	394 ☐ begin with ~로 시작되다
24	288 ☐ look for ~을 찾다	341 ☐ overcome ⓥ 극복하다	395 ☐ refine ⓥ 다듬다
234 ☐ intended ⓐ 의도된	289 ☐ be open to ~을 대상으로 하다	342 ☐ jet lag 시차로 인한 피로감	396 ☐ perfect ⓥ 완성하다, 완벽하게 하다
235 ☐ path ⓝ 길	290 ☐ article ⓝ 기사	343 ☐ recovery ⓝ 회복	397 ☐ nail ⓝ 못
236 ☐ rut ⓝ 틀에 박힌 생활	291 ☐ length ⓝ 길이	344 ☐ depend on ~에 좌우되다	398 ☐ turn A into B A를 B로 바꾸다
237 ☐ be good at ~을 잘하다	292 ☐ high-quality ⓐ 고품질의	345 ☐ westward ad 서쪽으로	399 ☐ picture ⓥ 상상하다, 그리다
238 ☐ be rewarded for ~에 대해 보상받다		346 ☐ lengthen ⓥ 연장하다	400 ☐ finished product 완제품
239 ☐ look around 둘러보다	28	347 ☐ eastward ad 동쪽으로	401 ☐ process ⓝ 과정
240 ☐ deep ⓐ 깊은	293 ☐ session ⓝ (특정한 활동을 위한) 시간	348 ☐ shorten ⓥ 단축하다	402 ☐ over a period of time 일정 기간에 걸쳐서
241 ☐ breathe ⓥ 호흡하다	294 ☐ admission ⓝ 입장	349 ☐ sizable ⓐ 꽤 큰, 상당한	403 ☐ before long 머지않아
242 ☐ slippery ⓐ 미끄러운	295 ☐ first-come, first-served 선착순	350 ☐ have an impact on ~에 영향을 주다	404 ☐ in harmony 조화롭게
243 ☐ take effort to ~하는 데 (…한) 노력이 들다	296 ☐ reservation ⓝ 예약	351 ☐ performance ⓝ (선수의) 경기력, 수행, 성과	405 ☐ bring into existence ~을 생겨나게 하다
244 ☐ superhuman ⓐ 초인적인	297 ☐ accompany ⓥ 동반하다	352 ☐ significantly ad 상당히, 현저히	406 ☐ mentally ad 머릿속에, 마음속으로
245 ☐ effectively ad 실질적으로, 사실상	298 ☐ for free 공짜로	353 ☐ additional ⓐ 추가적인	407 ☐ careless ⓐ 조심성 없는
246 ☐ be stuck 꼼짝 못하다		354 ☐ tough ⓐ 어려운, 힘든	408 ☐ irresponsible ⓐ 무책임한
247 ☐ employment ⓝ 고용	29	355 ☐ direction ⓝ 방향	409 ☐ professional ⓝ 전문가 ⓐ 전문적인
248 ☐ lock ⓥ 가두다, 잠그다, 고정시키다	299 ☐ noticeable ⓐ 눈에 띄는, 두드러지는	356 ☐ purpose ⓝ 목적	
249 ☐ secure ⓐ 안전한	300 ☐ characteristic ⓝ 특징		35
250 ☐ well-paying ⓐ 보수가 좋은	301 ☐ project onto ~에게 투영시키다	32	410 ☐ affect ⓥ 영향을 미치다
251 ☐ ultimately ad 궁극적으로	302 ☐ cartoon character 만화 캐릭터	357 ☐ confidence ⓝ 자신감	411 ☐ main character 주인공
252 ☐ unsatisfying ⓐ 불만족스러운	303 ☐ make after ~을 본떠 만들다	358 ☐ set out 착수하다	412 ☐ look through ~을 통해서 보다
253 ☐ compete with ~와 경쟁하다	304 ☐ deform ⓥ 변형하다	359 ☐ each day 매일	413 ☐ interpret ⓥ 해석하다, 이해하다
254 ☐ have ~ in common ~을 공통적으로 지니다	305 ☐ in such a way as to ~한 방식으로	360 ☐ over-optimism ⓝ 지나친 낙관주의	414 ☐ differently ad 다르게
255 ☐ road map 도로 지도, 로드 맵	306 ☐ resemble ⓥ ~와 닮다	361 ☐ time frame (어떤 일에 쓸 수 있는) 시간(대)	415 ☐ sympathy ⓝ 공감
256 ☐ influential ⓐ 영향력 있는	307 ☐ humanlike ⓐ 인간 같은	362 ☐ work on ~에 공을 들이다	416 ☐ conflict ⓝ 갈등
257 ☐ employer ⓝ 고용주, 회사	308 ☐ animated movie 만화 영화	363 ☐ make a practice of ~을 습관으로 하다	
	309 ☐ natural ⓐ 자연스러운		

417 ☐ arise ⓥ 발생하다
418 ☐ pray for ~을 위해 기도하다
419 ☐ outcome ⓝ 결과
420 ☐ tale ⓝ 이야기
421 ☐ shift ⓥ 바꾸다
422 ☐ viewpoint ⓝ 관점
423 ☐ evil ⓐ 사악한 ⓝ 악
424 ☐ stepsister ⓝ 의붓자매
425 ☐ kingdom ⓝ 왕국
426 ☐ exist ⓥ 존재하다
427 ☐ willingly ⓐ 기꺼이
428 ☐ what if ~라면 어떨까

36
429 ☐ Old Stone Age 구석기 시대
430 ☐ band ⓝ (소규모) 무리
431 ☐ wander ⓥ 돌아다니다, 배회하다
432 ☐ from place to place 여기저기
433 ☐ in search of ~을 찾아서
434 ☐ farming ⓝ 농사
435 ☐ settle down 정착하다
436 ☐ crop ⓝ 작물
437 ☐ dweller ⓝ 거주자
438 ☐ work together 함께 일하다, 협력하다
439 ☐ share ⓥ 나누다, 공유하다
440 ☐ axe ⓝ 도끼
441 ☐ as a result 그 결과
442 ☐ community ⓝ 공동체, 지역사회
443 ☐ organize ⓥ 조직하다, 정리하다
444 ☐ efficiently ⓐ 효율적으로
445 ☐ divide up ~을 나누다

37
446 ☐ form ⓥ 형성하다
447 ☐ mineral ⓝ 광물
448 ☐ in many ways 많은 방법으로
449 ☐ melt ⓥ 녹이다, 녹다
450 ☐ magma ⓝ 마그마
451 ☐ surface ⓝ 표면
452 ☐ trap ⓥ 가두다
453 ☐ below prep ~의 아래에
454 ☐ atom ⓝ 원자
455 ☐ combine into ~로 결합되다
456 ☐ compound ⓝ 화합물
457 ☐ crystal ⓝ 결정체, 수정
458 ☐ partly ⓐ 부분적으로
459 ☐ rapidly ⓐ 빠르게
460 ☐ with the unaided eye 육안으로
461 ☐ arrange ⓥ 배열하다
462 ☐ orderly ⓐ 질서 있는
463 ☐ element ⓝ 원소, 구성요소
464 ☐ in such cases 이런 경우에

38
465 ☐ carbohydrate ⓝ 탄수화물
466 ☐ simple sugar 단당류
467 ☐ basically ⓐ 기본적으로
468 ☐ break down 분해하다
469 ☐ nutrient ⓝ 영양소
470 ☐ chain ⓝ 사슬
471 ☐ release ⓥ 방출하다
472 ☐ provide A with B A에게 B를 공급하다

473 ☐ a number of 많은
474 ☐ structure ⓝ 구조
475 ☐ other than ~ 외에
476 ☐ be made from ~로 구성되다
477 ☐ rather ⓐ 다소, 상당히, 꽤
478 ☐ convert ⓥ 바꾸다
479 ☐ store ⓥ 저장하다, 보유하다

39
480 ☐ lecturer ⓝ 강사, 강연자
481 ☐ interact with ~와 상호작용하다
482 ☐ commonly ⓐ 흔히
483 ☐ mistaken ⓐ 잘못된, 틀린
484 ☐ assumption ⓝ 가정, 추정
485 ☐ characteristic ⓝ 특성
486 ☐ automatically ⓐ 자동으로, 저절로
487 ☐ go with ~와 어울리다
488 ☐ description ⓝ 설명
489 ☐ speak to ~에게 말하다, 이야기를 걸다
490 ☐ receive ⓥ 받다
491 ☐ contain ⓥ 포함하다, (~이) 들어 있다
492 ☐ be told ~을 듣다
493 ☐ discussion ⓝ 토론, 논의
494 ☐ impression ⓝ 인상
495 ☐ as expected 예상된 대로
496 ☐ original ⓐ 최초의, 원래의
497 ☐ expectation ⓝ 기대, 예상
498 ☐ relationship ⓝ 관계

40
499 ☐ risky ⓐ 위험한
500 ☐ trustworthy ⓐ 신뢰할 만한
501 ☐ evidence ⓝ 근거, 증거
502 ☐ almost ⓐ 거의
503 ☐ prospect ⓝ 예상, 가망성
504 ☐ sensible ⓐ 분별 있는, 현명한
505 ☐ frequently ⓐ 자주, 빈번히
506 ☐ product review 상품평
507 ☐ subtle ⓐ 미묘한
508 ☐ cue ⓝ 단서, 신호
509 ☐ signal ⓥ 알리다 ⓝ 신호
510 ☐ local ⓐ 지역의, 현지의
511 ☐ hassle ⓝ 성가신 일
512 ☐ tasty ⓐ 맛있는
513 ☐ in demand 수요가 많은
514 ☐ more often than not 대개
515 ☐ practice ⓝ 관례, 실행
516 ☐ particularly ⓐ 특히
517 ☐ faced with ~와 직면한
518 ☐ uncertain ⓐ 불확실한
519 ☐ unrealistic ⓐ 비현실적인
520 ☐ rule ⓝ 규칙 ⓥ 지배하다
521 ☐ unpleasant ⓐ 불쾌한

41~42
522 ☐ master ⓝ 달인, 고수
523 ☐ chess board 체스판
524 ☐ in the middle of ~의 한가운데에
525 ☐ in play 시합 중인
526 ☐ reproduce ⓥ 재현하다
527 ☐ position ⓝ 위치
528 ☐ from memory 외워서, 기억하여

529 ☐ beginner ⓝ 초심자
530 ☐ only a few 몇 안 되는 (것)
531 ☐ place ⓥ 놓다, 배치하다
532 ☐ randomly ⓐ 무작위로
533 ☐ reduce ⓥ 줄이다, 감소시키다
534 ☐ advantage ⓝ 유리함, 이점
535 ☐ familiar ⓐ 익숙한, 친숙한
536 ☐ previously ⓐ 이전에, 사전에
537 ☐ unfamiliar ⓐ 익숙지 않은, 낯선
538 ☐ domain ⓝ 영역, 분야
539 ☐ disappear ⓥ 사라지다
540 ☐ beneficial ⓐ 유익한, 이로운
541 ☐ expertise ⓝ 전문 지식
542 ☐ sequence ⓝ 연속, 순서
543 ☐ musical notation 악보
544 ☐ accurately ⓐ 정확하게
545 ☐ unusual ⓐ 특이한
546 ☐ movement ⓝ 동작, 움직임
547 ☐ experienced ⓐ 숙련된, 경험 많은
548 ☐ routine ⓝ 습관, (정해진) 춤 동작, 루틴
549 ☐ guarantee ⓥ 보장하다

43~45
550 ☐ once upon a time 옛날 옛적에
551 ☐ palace ⓝ 궁전
552 ☐ monster ⓝ 괴물
553 ☐ approach ⓥ 다가오다, 접근하다
554 ☐ gate ⓝ 문
555 ☐ ugly ⓐ 추한
556 ☐ smelly ⓐ 냄새 나는, 악취가 나는
557 ☐ in shock 충격을 받아
558 ☐ throne ⓝ 왕좌
559 ☐ come to one's senses 정신을 차리다
560 ☐ shout at ~을 향해 소리치다
561 ☐ get off ~을 떠나다
562 ☐ wise ⓐ 현명한
563 ☐ if conj ~인지 아닌지
564 ☐ take-out ⓐ 사서 가지고 가는
565 ☐ call for ~을 시키다, ~을 요구하다
566 ☐ gesture ⓝ 몸짓, (감정의) 표시, 표현
567 ☐ massage ⓝ 마사지
568 ☐ tiny ⓐ 아주 작은
569 ☐ brandish ⓥ 휘두르다
570 ☐ scare away ~을 겁주어 쫓아버리다
571 ☐ take up ~을 차지하다
572 ☐ than ever 그 어느 때보다

● 채점 : 맞은 개수 _____ / 80

TEST A-B 각 단어의 뜻을 [A] 영어는 우리말로, [B] 우리말은 영어로 쓰시오.

A	English	Korean
01	conflict	
02	mineral	
03	carbohydrate	
04	discussion	
05	unpleasant	
06	approach	
07	guarantee	
08	take up	
09	willingly	
10	release	
11	scent	
12	frustrated	
13	confident	
14	arise	
15	combine into	
16	cope with	
17	adopt	
18	adapt to	
19	maintain	
20	call for	

B	Korean	English
01	정착하다	
02	효율적으로	
03	포함하다	
04	~을 겁주어 쫓아버리다	
05	발견하다	
06	유전자	
07	무작위로	
08	지속적인	
09	(생물) 종	
10	조직하다, 정리하다	
11	질투하는	
12	이유, 동기부여	
13	추산하다	
14	돌아다니다, 배회하다	
15	원리	
16	인상	
17	공감	
18	서식지	
19	기대, 예상	
20	구조	

▶ A-D 정답 : 해설편 030쪽

TEST C-D 각 단어의 뜻을 골라 기호를 쓰시오.

C	English			Korean
01	picture	(	)	ⓐ 화합물
02	warm up	(	)	ⓑ 규칙, 지배하다
03	rule	(	)	ⓒ 상상하다, 그리다
04	expertise	(	)	ⓓ 영양소
05	refine	(	)	ⓔ 유익한, 이로운
06	compound	(	)	ⓕ 왕좌
07	faced with	(	)	ⓖ ~내내
08	alertness	(	)	ⓗ 준비가 되다, 몸을 풀다
09	run into	(	)	ⓘ 다듬다
10	thrive	(	)	ⓙ 우연히 만나다
11	bring into existence	(	)	ⓚ 결과
12	nutrient	(	)	ⓛ 미묘한
13	outcome	(	)	ⓜ 전문지식
14	dweller	(	)	ⓝ 이야기
15	beneficial	(	)	ⓞ 번성하다
16	throne	(	)	ⓟ 거주자
17	tale	(	)	ⓠ ~을 생겨나게 하다
18	assumption	(	)	ⓡ 기민함
19	throughout	(	)	ⓢ 가정
20	subtle	(	)	ⓣ ~와 직면한

D	Korean			English
01	질서 있는	(	)	ⓐ stepsister
02	영역, 분야	(	)	ⓑ no longer
03	원소, 구성요소	(	)	ⓒ careless
04	무책임한	(	)	ⓓ prospect
05	근거, 증거	(	)	ⓔ element
06	위험한	(	)	ⓕ interpret
07	현실성 있는, 타당한	(	)	ⓖ practice
08	해석하다, 이해하다	(	)	ⓗ orderly
09	수요가 많은	(	)	ⓘ familiar
10	더 이상~ 않다	(	)	ⓙ band
11	의붓자매	(	)	ⓚ in demand
12	조심성 없는	(	)	ⓛ from memory
13	예상, 가망성	(	)	ⓜ irresponsible
14	익숙한, 친숙한	(	)	ⓝ accurately
15	관례, 실행	(	)	ⓞ practical
16	(소규모) 무리	(	)	ⓟ sequence
17	외워서, 기억하여	(	)	ⓠ gesture
18	연속, 순서	(	)	ⓡ evidence
19	몸짓	(	)	ⓢ domain
20	정확하게	(	)	ⓣ risky

2022학년도 3월 고1 전국연합학력평가 문제지

1

제 3 교시

영어 영역

05회

● 문항수 45개 | 배점 100점 | 제한 시간 70분

● 점수 표시가 없는 문항은 모두 2점

05회

1번부터 17번까지는 듣고 답하는 문제입니다. 1번부터 15번까지는 한 번만 들려주고, 16번부터 17번까지는 두 번 들려줍니다. 방송을 잘 듣고 답을 하시기 바랍니다.

MP3

1. 다음을 듣고, 남자가 하는 말의 목적으로 가장 적절한 것을 고르시오.

① 농구 리그 참가 등록 방법의 변경을 알리려고
② 확정된 농구 리그 시합 일정을 발표하려고
③ 농구 리그의 심판을 추가 모집하려고
④ 농구 리그 경기 관람을 권장하려고
⑤ 농구 리그 우승 상품을 안내하려고

2. 대화를 듣고, 여자의 의견으로 가장 적절한 것을 고르시오.

① 평소에 피부 상태를 잘 관찰할 필요가 있다.
② 여드름을 치료하려면 피부과 병원에 가야 한다.
③ 얼굴을 손으로 만지는 것은 얼굴 피부에 해롭다.
④ 지성 피부를 가진 사람은 자주 세수를 해야 한다.
⑤ 손을 자주 씻는 것은 감염병 예방에 도움이 된다.

3. 대화를 듣고, 두 사람의 관계를 가장 잘 나타낸 것을 고르시오.

① 방송 작가 – 연출자
② 만화가 – 환경 운동가
③ 촬영 감독 – 동화 작가
④ 토크쇼 진행자 – 기후학자
⑤ 제품 디자이너 – 영업 사원

4. 대화를 듣고, 그림에서 대화의 내용과 일치하지 않는 것을 고르시오.

5. 대화를 듣고, 여자가 남자에게 부탁한 일로 가장 적절한 것을 고르시오.

① 장난감 사 오기   ② 풍선 달기
③ 케이크 가져오기   ④ 탁자 옮기기
⑤ 아이들 데려오기

6. 대화를 듣고, 남자가 지불할 금액을 고르시오. [3점]

① $14   ② $16   ③ $18   ④ $20   ⑤ $22

7. 대화를 듣고, 두 사람이 오늘 실험을 할 수 없는 이유를 고르시오.

① 실험용 키트가 배달되지 않아서
② 실험 주제를 변경해야 해서
③ 과학실을 예약하지 못해서
④ 보고서를 작성해야 해서
⑤ 남자가 감기에 걸려서

8. 대화를 듣고, Stanville Free-cycle에 관해 언급되지 않은 것을 고르시오.

① 참가 대상   ② 행사 장소   ③ 주차 가능 여부
④ 행사 시작일   ⑤ 금지 품목

9. River Valley Music Camp에 관한 다음 내용을 듣고, 일치하지 않는 것을 고르시오.

① 4월 11일부터 5일 동안 진행된다.
② 학교 오케스트라 단원이 아니어도 참가할 수 있다.
③ 자신의 악기를 가져오거나 학교에서 빌릴 수 있다.
④ 마지막 날에 공연을 촬영한다.
⑤ 참가 인원에는 제한이 없다.

10. 다음 표를 보면서 대화를 듣고, 여자가 주문할 소형 진공 청소기를 고르시오.

Handheld Vacuum Cleaners

	Model	Price	Working Time	Weight	Washable Filter
①	A	$50	8 minutes	2.5 kg	×
②	B	$80	12 minutes	2.0 kg	○
③	C	$100	15 minutes	1.8 kg	○
④	D	$120	20 minutes	1.8 kg	×
⑤	E	$150	25 minutes	1.6 kg	○

11. 대화를 듣고, 남자의 마지막 말에 대한 여자의 응답으로 가장 적절한 것을 고르시오.

① Why don't you rinse your eyes with clean water?
② Can you explain more about the air pollution?
③ I need to get myself a new pair of glasses.
④ I agree that fine dust is a serious problem.
⑤ We should go outside and take a walk.

12. 대화를 듣고, 여자의 마지막 말에 대한 남자의 응답으로 가장 적절한 것을 고르시오.

① That's not fair. I booked this seat first.
② Thank you. My friend will be glad to know it.
③ You're welcome. Feel free to ask me anything.
④ Not at all. I don't mind changing seats with you.
⑤ That's okay. I think the seat next to it is available.

13. 대화를 듣고, 남자의 마지막 말에 대한 여자의 응답으로 가장 적절한 것을 고르시오.

Woman: _____

① Smells good. Can I try the pizza?
② Great. I'll bring chips and popcorn.
③ No problem. I'll cancel the tickets.
④ Sorry. I don't like watching baseball.
⑤ Sure. Here's the hammer I borrowed.

14. 대화를 듣고, 여자의 마지막 말에 대한 남자의 응답으로 가장 적절한 것을 고르시오. [3점]

Man: _____

① Exactly. This is a best-selling novel.
② Sounds cool. I'll join a book club, too.
③ Not really. Books make good presents.
④ New year's resolutions are hard to keep.
⑤ Let's buy some books for your book club.

15. 다음 상황 설명을 듣고, Brian이 Sally에게 할 말로 가장 적절한 것을 고르시오. [3점]

Brian: _____

① You shouldn't touch a guide dog without permission.
② The dog would be happy if we give it some food.
③ I'm sure it's smart enough to be a guide dog.
④ I suggest that you walk your dog every day.
⑤ I'm afraid that dogs are not allowed in here.

[16 ~ 17] 다음을 듣고, 물음에 답하시오.

16. 여자가 하는 말의 주제로 가장 적절한 것은?

① activities that help build muscles
② ways to control stress in daily life
③ types of joint problems in elderly people
④ low-impact exercises for people with bad joints
⑤ importance of daily exercise for controlling weight

17. 언급된 운동이 <u>아닌</u> 것은?

① swimming
② cycling
③ horseback riding
④ bowling
⑤ walking

> 이제 듣기 문제가 끝났습니다. 18번부터는 문제지의 지시에 따라 답을 하시기 바랍니다.

18. 다음 글의 목적으로 가장 적절한 것은?

> Dear Ms. Robinson,
>   The Warblers Choir is happy to announce that we are invited to compete in the International Young Choir Competition. The competition takes place in London on May 20. Though we wish to participate in the event, we do not have the necessary funds to travel to London. So we are kindly asking you to support us by coming to our fundraising concert. It will be held on March 26. In this concert, we shall be able to show you how big our passion for music is. Thank you in advance for your kind support and help.
> Sincerely,
> Arnold Reynolds

① 합창 대회 결과를 공지하려고
② 모금 음악회 참석을 요청하려고
③ 음악회 개최 장소를 예약하려고
④ 합창곡 선정에 조언을 구하려고
⑤ 기부금 사용 내역을 보고하려고

19. 다음 글에 드러난 Zoe의 심경 변화로 가장 적절한 것은?

The principal stepped on stage. "Now, I present this year's top academic award to the student who has achieved the highest placing." He smiled at the row of seats where twelve finalists had gathered. Zoe wiped a sweaty hand on her handkerchief and glanced at the other finalists. They all looked as pale and uneasy as herself. Zoe and one of the other finalists had won first placing in four subjects so it came down to how teachers ranked their hard work and confidence. "The Trophy for General Excellence is awarded to Miss Zoe Perry," the principal declared. "Could Zoe step this way, please?" Zoe felt as if she were in heaven. She walked into the thunder of applause with a big smile.

① hopeful → disappointed   ② guilty → confident
③ nervous → delighted   ④ angry → calm
⑤ relaxed → proud

20. 다음 글에서 필자가 주장하는 바로 가장 적절한 것은?

When I was in the army, my instructors would show up in my barracks room, and the first thing they would inspect was our bed. It was a simple task, but every morning we were required to make our bed to perfection. It seemed a little ridiculous at the time, but the wisdom of this simple act has been proven to me many times over. If you make your bed every morning, you will have accomplished the first task of the day. It will give you a small sense of pride and it will encourage you to do another task and another. By the end of the day, that one task completed will have turned into many tasks completed. If you can't do little things right, you will never do the big things right.

* barracks room: (병영의) 생활관 ** accomplish: 성취하다

① 숙면을 위해서는 침대를 깔끔하게 관리해야 한다.
② 일의 효율성을 높이려면 협동심을 발휘해야 한다.
③ 올바른 습관을 기르려면 정해진 규칙을 따라야 한다.
④ 건강을 유지하기 위해서는 기상 시간이 일정해야 한다.
⑤ 큰일을 잘 이루려면 작은 일부터 제대로 수행해야 한다.

21. 밑줄 친 <u>Leave those activities to the rest of the sheep</u>이 다음 글에서 의미하는 바로 가장 적절한 것은? [3점]

　　A job search is not a passive task. When you are searching, you are not browsing, nor are you "just looking". Browsing is not an effective way to reach a goal you claim to want to reach. If you are acting with purpose, if you are serious about anything you chose to do, then you need to be direct, focused and whenever possible, clever. Everyone else searching for a job has the same goal, competing for the same jobs. You must do more than the rest of the herd. Regardless of how long it may take you to find and get the job you want, being proactive will logically get you results faster than if you rely only on browsing online job boards and emailing an occasional resume. <u>Leave those activities to the rest of the sheep.</u>

① Try to understand other job-seekers' feelings.
② Keep calm and stick to your present position.
③ Don't be scared of the job-seeking competition.
④ Send occasional emails to your future employers.
⑤ Be more active to stand out from other job-seekers.

22. 다음 글의 요지로 가장 적절한 것은?

　　Many people view sleep as merely a "down time" when their brain shuts off and their body rests. In a rush to meet work, school, family, or household responsibilities, people cut back on their sleep, thinking it won't be a problem, because all of these other activities seem much more important. But research reveals that a number of vital tasks carried out during sleep help to maintain good health and enable people to function at their best. While you sleep, your brain is hard at work forming the pathways necessary for learning and creating memories and new insights. Without enough sleep, you can't focus and pay attention or respond quickly. A lack of sleep may even cause mood problems. In addition, growing evidence shows that a continuous lack of sleep increases the risk for developing serious diseases.

* vital: 매우 중요한

① 수면은 건강 유지와 최상의 기능 발휘에 도움이 된다.
② 업무량이 증가하면 필요한 수면 시간도 증가한다.
③ 균형 잡힌 식단을 유지하면 뇌 기능이 향상된다.
④ 불면증은 주위 사람들에게 부정적인 영향을 미친다.
⑤ 꿈의 내용은 깨어 있는 시간 동안의 경험을 반영한다.

23. 다음 글의 주제로 가장 적절한 것은? [3점]

　　The whole of human society operates on knowing the future weather. For example, farmers in India know when the monsoon rains will come next year and so they know when to plant the crops. Farmers in Indonesia know there are two monsoon rains each year, so next year they can have two harvests. This is based on their knowledge of the past, as the monsoons have always come at about the same time each year in living memory. But the need to predict goes deeper than this; it influences every part of our lives. Our houses, roads, railways, airports, offices, and so on are all designed for the local climate. For example, in England all the houses have central heating, as the outside temperature is usually below 20°C, but no air-conditioning, as temperatures rarely go beyond 26°C, while in Australia the opposite is true: most houses have air-conditioning but rarely central heating.

① new technologies dealing with climate change
② difficulties in predicting the weather correctly
③ weather patterns influenced by rising temperatures
④ knowledge of the climate widely affecting our lives
⑤ traditional wisdom helping our survival in harsh climates

24. 다음 글의 제목으로 가장 적절한 것은?

　　Our ability to accurately recognize and label emotions is often referred to as *emotional granularity*. In the words of Harvard psychologist Susan David, "Learning to label emotions with a more nuanced vocabulary can be absolutely transformative." David explains that if we don't have a rich emotional vocabulary, it is difficult to communicate our needs and to get the support that we need from others. But those who are able to distinguish between a range of various emotions "do much, much better at managing the ups and downs of ordinary existence than those who see everything in black and white." In fact, research shows that the process of labeling emotional experience is related to greater emotion regulation and psychosocial well-being.

* nuanced: 미묘한 차이가 있는

① True Friendship Endures Emotional Arguments
② Detailed Labeling of Emotions Is Beneficial
③ Labeling Emotions: Easier Said Than Done
④ Categorize and Label Tasks for Efficiency
⑤ Be Brave and Communicate Your Needs

25. 다음 도표의 내용과 일치하지 <u>않는</u> 것은?

Percentage of UK People
Who Used Online Course and Online Learning Material
(in 2020, by age group)

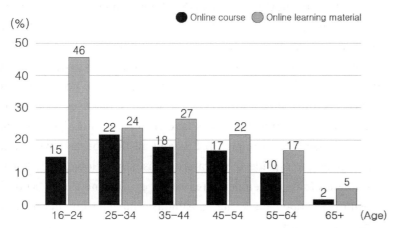

The above graph shows the percentage of people in the UK who used online courses and online learning materials, by age group in 2020. ① In each age group, the percentage of people who used online learning materials was higher than that of people who used online courses. ② The 25−34 age group had the highest percentage of people who used online courses in all the age groups. ③ Those aged 65 and older were the least likely to use online courses among the six age groups. ④ Among the six age groups, the gap between the percentage of people who used online courses and that of people who used online learning materials was the greatest in the 16−24 age group. ⑤ In each of the 35−44, 45−54, and 55−64 age groups, more than one in five people used online learning materials.

26. Antonie van Leeuwenhoek에 관한 다음 글의 내용과 일치하지 <u>않는</u> 것은?

Antonie van Leeuwenhoek was a scientist well known for his cell research. He was born in Delft, the Netherlands, on October 24, 1632. At the age of 16, he began to learn job skills in Amsterdam. At the age of 22, Leeuwenhoek returned to Delft. It wasn't easy for Leeuwenhoek to become a scientist. He knew only one language — Dutch — which was quite unusual for scientists of his time. But his curiosity was endless, and he worked hard. He had an important skill. He knew how to make things out of glass. This skill came in handy when he made lenses for his simple microscope. He saw tiny veins with blood flowing through them. He also saw living bacteria in pond water. He paid close attention to the things he saw and wrote down his observations. Since he couldn't draw well, he hired an artist to draw pictures of what he described.

* cell: 세포 ** vein: 혈관

① 세포 연구로 잘 알려진 과학자였다.
② 22살에 Delft로 돌아왔다.
③ 여러 개의 언어를 알았다.
④ 유리로 물건을 만드는 방법을 알고 있었다.
⑤ 화가를 고용하여 설명하는 것을 그리게 했다.

27. Rachel's Flower Class에 관한 다음 안내문의 내용과 일치하지 <u>않는</u> 것은?

Rachel's Flower Class

Make Your Life More Beautiful!

Class Schedule (Every Monday to Friday)

Flower Arrangement	11 a.m. − 12 p.m.
Flower Box Making	1 p.m. − 2 p.m.

Price
- $50 for each class
  (flowers and other materials included)
- Bring your own scissors and a bag.

Other Info.
- You can sign up for classes either online or by phone.
- No refund for cancellations on the day of your class

To contact, visit www.rfclass.com or call 03−221−2131.

① 플라워 박스 만들기 수업은 오후 1시에 시작된다.
② 수강료에 꽃값과 다른 재료비가 포함된다.
③ 수강생은 가위와 가방을 가져와야 한다.
④ 수업 등록은 전화로만 할 수 있다.
⑤ 수업 당일 취소 시 환불을 받을 수 없다.

28. Nighttime Palace Tour에 관한 다음 안내문의 내용과 일치하는 것은?

Nighttime Palace Tour

Date: Friday, April 29 − Sunday, May 15

Time

Friday	7 p.m. − 8:30 p.m.
Saturday & Sunday	6 p.m. − 7:30 p.m.
	8 p.m. − 9:30 p.m.

Tickets & Booking
- $15 per person (free for kids under 8)
- Bookings will be accepted up to 2 hours before the tour starts.

Program Activities
- Group tour with a tour guide (1 hour)
- Trying traditional foods and drinks (30 minutes)

※ You can try on traditional clothes with no extra charge.
※ For more information, please visit our website, www.palacenighttour.com.

① 금요일에는 하루에 두 번 투어가 운영된다.
② 8세 미만 어린이의 티켓은 5달러이다.
③ 예약은 투어 하루 전까지만 가능하다.
④ 투어 가이드의 안내 없이 궁궐을 둘러본다.
⑤ 추가 비용 없이 전통 의상을 입어 볼 수 있다.

29. 다음 글의 밑줄 친 부분 중, 어법상 <u>틀린</u> 것은?

We usually get along best with people who we think are like us. In fact, we seek them out. It's why places like Little Italy, Chinatown, and Koreatown ① <u>exist</u>. But I'm not just talking about race, skin color, or religion. I'm talking about people who share our values and look at the world the same way we ② <u>do</u>. As the saying goes, birds of a feather flock together. This is a very common human tendency ③ <u>what</u> is rooted in how our species developed. Imagine you are walking out in a forest. You would be conditioned to avoid something unfamiliar or foreign because there is a high likelihood that ④ <u>it</u> would be interested in killing you. Similarities make us ⑤ <u>relate</u> better to other people because we think they'll understand us on a deeper level than other people.

* species: 종(생물 분류의 기초 단위)

30. 다음 글의 밑줄 친 부분 중, 문맥상 낱말의 쓰임이 적절하지 <u>않은</u> 것은? [3점]

Rejection is an everyday part of our lives, yet most people can't handle it well. For many, it's so painful that they'd rather not ask for something at all than ask and ① <u>risk</u> rejection. Yet, as the old saying goes, if you don't ask, the answer is always no. Avoiding rejection ② <u>negatively</u> affects many aspects of your life. All of that happens only because you're not ③ <u>tough</u> enough to handle it. For this reason, consider rejection therapy. Come up with a ④ <u>request</u> or an activity that usually results in a rejection. Working in sales is one such example. Asking for discounts at the stores will also work. By deliberately getting yourself ⑤ <u>welcomed</u> you'll grow a thicker skin that will allow you to take on much more in life, thus making you more successful at dealing with unfavorable circumstances.

* deliberately: 의도적으로

[31 ~ 34] 다음 빈칸에 들어갈 말로 가장 적절한 것을 <u>고르시오</u>.

31. Generalization without specific examples that humanize writing is boring to the listener and to the reader. Who wants to read platitudes all day? Who wants to hear the words great, greater, best, smartest, finest, humanitarian, on and on and on without specific examples? Instead of using these 'nothing words,' leave them out completely and just describe the _____. There is nothing worse than reading a scene in a novel in which a main character is described up front as heroic or brave or tragic or funny, while thereafter, the writer quickly moves on to something else. That's no good, no good at all. You have to use less one word descriptions and more detailed, engaging descriptions if you want to make something real.

* platitude: 상투적인 말

① similarities
② particulars
③ fantasies
④ boredom
⑤ wisdom

32. Face-to-face interaction is a uniquely powerful — and sometimes the only — way to share many kinds of knowledge, from the simplest to the most complex. It is one of the best ways to stimulate new thinking and ideas, too. Most of us would have had difficulty learning how to tie a shoelace only from pictures, or how to do arithmetic from a book. Psychologist Mihàly Csikszentmihàlyi found, while studying high achievers, that a large number of Nobel Prize winners were the students of previous winners: they had access to the same literature as everyone else, but _____ made a crucial difference to their creativity. Within organisations this makes conversation both a crucial factor for high-level professional skills and the most important way of sharing everyday information.

* arithmetic: 계산 ** literature: (연구) 문헌

① natural talent
② regular practice
③ personal contact
④ complex knowledge
⑤ powerful motivation

33. Most times a foreign language is spoken in film, subtitles are used to translate the dialogue for the viewer. However, there are occasions when foreign dialogue is left unsubtitled (and thus incomprehensible to most of the target audience). This is often done if the movie is seen mainly from the viewpoint of a particular character who does not speak the language. Such absence of subtitles allows the audience to feel a similar sense of incomprehension and alienation that the character feels. An example of this is seen in *Not Without My Daughter*. The Persian language dialogue spoken by the Iranian characters is not subtitled because the main character Betty Mahmoody does not speak Persian and the audience is _____. [3점]

* subtitle: 자막(을 넣다) ** incomprehensible: 이해할 수 없는
*** alienation: 소외

① seeing the film from her viewpoint
② impressed by her language skills
③ attracted to her beautiful voice
④ participating in a heated debate
⑤ learning the language used in the film

34. One dynamic that can change dramatically in sport is the concept of the home-field advantage, in which perceived demands and resources seem to play a role. Under normal circumstances, the home ground would appear to provide greater perceived resources (fans, home field, and so on). However, researchers Roy Baumeister and Andrew Steinhilber were among the first to point out that these competitive factors can change; for example, the success percentage for home teams in the final games of a playoff or World Series seems to drop. Fans can become part of the perceived demands rather than resources under those circumstances. This change in perception can also explain why a team that's struggling at the start of the year will _____ to reduce perceived demands and pressures. [3점]

* perceive: 인식하다 ** playoff: 우승 결정전

① often welcome a road trip
② avoid international matches
③ focus on increasing ticket sales
④ want to have an eco-friendly stadium
⑤ try to advertise their upcoming games

35. 다음 글에서 전체 흐름과 관계 <u>없는</u> 문장은?

Who hasn't used a cup of coffee to help themselves stay awake while studying? Mild stimulants commonly found in tea, coffee, or sodas possibly make you more attentive and, thus, better able to remember. ① However, you should know that stimulants are as likely to have negative effects on memory as they are to be beneficial. ② Even if they could improve performance at some level, the ideal doses are currently unknown. ③ If you are wide awake and well-rested, mild stimulation from caffeine can do little to further improve your memory performance. ④ In contrast, many studies have shown that drinking tea is healthier than drinking coffee. ⑤ Indeed, if you have too much of a stimulant, you will become nervous, find it difficult to sleep, and your memory performance will suffer.

* stimulant: 자극제 ** dose: 복용량

[36 ~ 37] 주어진 글 다음에 이어질 글의 순서로 가장 적절한 것을 고르시오.

36.

Toward the end of the 19th century, a new architectural attitude emerged. Industrial architecture, the argument went, was ugly and inhuman; past styles had more to do with pretension than what people needed in their homes.

(A) But they supplied people's needs perfectly and, at their best, had a beauty that came from the craftsman's skill and the rootedness of the house in its locality.

(B) Instead of these approaches, why not look at the way ordinary country builders worked in the past? They developed their craft skills over generations, demonstrating mastery of both tools and materials.

(C) Those materials were local, and used with simplicity — houses built this way had plain wooden floors and whitewashed walls inside.

* pretension: 허세, 가식

① (A) − (C) − (B)　　　　② (B) − (A) − (C)
③ (B) − (C) − (A)　　　　④ (C) − (A) − (B)
⑤ (C) − (B) − (A)

37.

> Robert Schumann once said, "The laws of morals are those of art." What the great man is saying here is that there is good music and bad music.

(A) It's the same with performances: a bad performance isn't necessarily the result of incompetence. Some of the worst performances occur when the performers, no matter how accomplished, are thinking more of themselves than of the music they're playing.

(B) The greatest music, even if it's tragic in nature, takes us to a world higher than ours; somehow the beauty uplifts us. Bad music, on the other hand, degrades us.

(C) These doubtful characters aren't really listening to what the composer is saying—they're just showing off, hoping that they'll have a great 'success' with the public. The performer's basic task is to try to understand the meaning of the music, and then to communicate it honestly to others. [3점]

        * incompetence: 무능 ** degrade: 격하시키다

① (A) − (C) − (B)   ② (B) − (A) − (C)
③ (B) − (C) − (A)   ④ (C) − (A) − (B)
⑤ (C) − (B) − (A)

[38 ~ 39] 글의 흐름으로 보아, 주어진 문장이 들어가기에 가장 적절한 곳을 고르시오.

38.

> But, when there is biodiversity, the effects of a sudden change are not so dramatic.

When an ecosystem is biodiverse, wildlife have more opportunities to obtain food and shelter. Different species react and respond to changes in their environment differently. (①) For example, imagine a forest with only one type of plant in it, which is the only source of food and habitat for the entire forest food web. (②) Now, there is a sudden dry season and this plant dies. (③) Plant-eating animals completely lose their food source and die out, and so do the animals that prey upon them. (④) Different species of plants respond to the drought differently, and many can survive a dry season. (⑤) Many animals have a variety of food sources and don't just rely on one plant; now our forest ecosystem is no longer at the death! [3점]

        * biodiversity: (생물학적) 종 다양성 ** habitat: 서식지

39.

> Since the dawn of civilization, our ancestors created myths and told legendary stories about the night sky.

We are connected to the night sky in many ways. (①) It has always inspired people to wonder and to imagine. (②) Elements of those narratives became embedded in the social and cultural identities of many generations. (③) On a practical level, the night sky helped past generations to keep track of time and create calendars—essential to developing societies as aids to farming and seasonal gathering. (④) For many centuries, it also provided a useful navigation tool, vital for commerce and for exploring new worlds. (⑤) Even in modern times, many people in remote areas of the planet observe the night sky for such practical purposes.

        * embed: 깊이 새겨 두다 ** commerce: 무역

40. 다음 글의 내용을 한 문장으로 요약하고자 한다. 빈칸 (A), (B)에 들어갈 말로 가장 적절한 것은?

> The common blackberry (*Rubus allegheniensis*) has an amazing ability to move manganese from one layer of soil to another using its roots. This may seem like a funny talent for a plant to have, but it all becomes clear when you realize the effect it has on nearby plants. Manganese can be very harmful to plants, especially at high concentrations. Common blackberry is unaffected by damaging effects of this metal and has evolved two different ways of using manganese to its advantage. First, it redistributes manganese from deeper soil layers to shallow soil layers using its roots as a small pipe. Second, it absorbs manganese as it grows, concentrating the metal in its leaves. When the leaves drop and decay, their concentrated manganese deposits further poison the soil around the plant. For plants that are not immune to the toxic effects of manganese, this is very bad news. Essentially, the common blackberry eliminates competition by poisoning its neighbors with heavy metals.

        * manganese: 망가니즈(금속 원소) ** deposit: 축적물

↓

> The common blackberry has an ability to __(A)__ the amount of manganese in the surrounding upper soil, which makes the nearby soil quite __(B)__ for other plants.

	(A)	(B)
①	increase	deadly
②	increase	advantageous
③	indicate	nutritious
④	reduce	dry
⑤	reduce	warm

[41 ~ 42] 다음 글을 읽고, 물음에 답하시오.

The longest journey we will make is the eighteen inches between our head and heart. If we take this journey, it can shorten our (a) misery in the world. Impatience, judgment, frustration, and anger reside in our heads. When we live in that place too long, it makes us (b) unhappy. But when we take the journey from our heads to our hearts, something shifts (c) inside. What if we were able to love everything that gets in our way? What if we tried loving the shopper who unknowingly steps in front of us in line, the driver who cuts us off in traffic, the swimmer who splashes us with water during a belly dive, or the reader who pens a bad online review of our writing?

Every person who makes us miserable is (d) like us — a human being, most likely doing the best they can, deeply loved by their parents, a child, or a friend. And how many times have we unknowingly stepped in front of someone in line? Cut someone off in traffic? Splashed someone in a pool? Or made a negative statement about something we've read? It helps to (e) deny that a piece of us resides in every person we meet.

* reside: (어떤 장소에) 있다

41. 윗글의 제목으로 가장 적절한 것은?

① Why It Is So Difficult to Forgive Others
② Even Acts of Kindness Can Hurt Somebody
③ Time Is the Best Healer for a Broken Heart
④ Celebrate the Happy Moments in Your Everyday Life
⑤ Understand Others to Save Yourself from Unhappiness

42. 밑줄 친 (a)~(e) 중에서 문맥상 낱말의 쓰임이 적절하지 <u>않은</u> 것은?

① (a)   ② (b)   ③ (c)   ④ (d)   ⑤ (e)

[43 ~ 45] 다음 글을 읽고, 물음에 답하시오.

(A)

One day a young man was walking along a road on his journey from one village to another. As he walked he noticed a monk working in the fields. The young man turned to the monk and said, "Excuse me. Do you mind if I ask (a) you a question?" "Not at all," replied the monk.

* monk: 수도승

(B)

A while later a middle-aged man journeyed down the same road and came upon the monk. "I am going to the village in the valley," said the man. "Do you know what it is like?" "I do," replied the monk, "but first tell (b) me about the village where you came from." "I've come from the village in the mountains," said the man. "It was a wonderful experience. I felt as though I was a member of the family in the village."

(C)

"I am traveling from the village in the mountains to the village in the valley and I was wondering if (c) you knew what it is like in the village in the valley." "Tell me," said the monk, "what was your experience of the village in the mountains?" "Terrible," replied the young man. "I am glad to be away from there. I found the people most unwelcoming. So tell (d) me, what can I expect in the village in the valley?" "I am sorry to tell you," said the monk, "but I think your experience will be much the same there." The young man lowered his head helplessly and walked on.

(D)

"Why did you feel like that?" asked the monk. "The elders gave me much advice, and people were kind and generous. I am sad to have left there. And what is the village in the valley like?" he asked again. "(e) I think you will find it much the same," replied the monk. "I'm glad to hear that," the middle-aged man said smiling and journeyed on.

43. 주어진 글 (A)에 이어질 내용을 순서에 맞게 배열한 것으로 가장 적절한 것은?

① (B) − (D) − (C)
② (C) − (B) − (D)
③ (C) − (D) − (B)
④ (D) − (B) − (C)
⑤ (D) − (C) − (B)

44. 밑줄 친 (a) ~ (e) 중에서 가리키는 대상이 나머지 넷과 <u>다른</u> 것은?

① (a)   ② (b)   ③ (c)   ④ (d)   ⑤ (e)

45. 윗글에 관한 내용으로 적절하지 <u>않은</u> 것은?

① 한 수도승이 들판에서 일하고 있었다.
② 중년 남자는 골짜기에 있는 마을로 가는 중이었다.
③ 수도승은 골짜기에 있는 마을에 대해 질문받았다.
④ 수도승의 말을 듣고 젊은이는 고개를 숙였다.
⑤ 중년 남자는 산속에 있는 마을을 떠나서 기쁘다고 말했다.

* 확인 사항
○ 답안지의 해당란에 필요한 내용을 정확히 기입(표기)했는지 확인하시오.

VOCA LIST 05

01
- 001 ☐ **as you know** 아시다시피
- 002 ☐ **sign up sheet** 참가 신청서
- 003 ☐ **hand out** 배부하다, 나눠주다
- 004 ☐ **gym** ⓝ 체육관
- 005 ☐ **registration** ⓝ 등록
- 006 ☐ **method** ⓝ 방법
- 007 ☐ **register** ⓥ (공식 명부에 이름을) 등록[기재]하다
- 008 ☐ **fill** ⓥ 채우다

02
- 009 ☐ **in front** 앞쪽에
- 010 ☐ **pop a pimple** 여드름을 짜다
- 011 ☐ **annoying** ⓐ 거슬리는, 짜증나게 하는
- 012 ☐ **bacteria** ⓝ 박테리아
- 013 ☐ **spread** ⓥ 퍼뜨리다
- 014 ☐ **worsen** ⓥ 악화시키다

03
- 015 ☐ **climate change** 기후 변화
- 016 ☐ **inspiring** ⓐ 고무하는
- 017 ☐ **pollution** ⓝ 오염, 공해
- 018 ☐ **successful** ⓐ (어떤 일에) 성공한, 성공적인
- 019 ☐ **environmental activist** 환경 운동가
- 020 ☐ **make a suggestion** 제안하다
- 021 ☐ **perhaps** ⓐ 아마, 어쩌면
- 022 ☐ **comic book** 만화책
- 023 ☐ **discuss** ⓥ 상의하다
- 024 ☐ **business card** 명함

04
- 025 ☐ **decorate** ⓥ 장식하다, 꾸미다
- 026 ☐ **fish tank** 수조
- 027 ☐ **recognize** ⓥ (어떤 사람·사물을 보거나 듣고 누구·무엇인지) 알아보다
- 028 ☐ **starfish** 불가사리
- 029 ☐ **side by side** 나란히

05
- 030 ☐ **put up** 달다, 올리다, 게시하다
- 031 ☐ **doorway** 출입구
- 032 ☐ **take care of** ~을 책임지고 떠맡다, ~을 처리[수습]하다
- 033 ☐ **front yard** (집의) 앞뜰, 앞마당
- 034 ☐ **make a last minute change** 마지막 순간에 바꾸다
- 035 ☐ **garage** ⓝ 차고, 주차장
- 036 ☐ **grab** ⓥ 집다, 잡다

06
- 037 ☐ **eco-friendly** ⓐ 친환경적인
- 038 ☐ **bamboo** ⓝ 대나무
- 039 ☐ **plastic-free** ⓐ 플라스틱이 들어가지 않은

07
- 040 ☐ **check out** (책 등을) 대출하다
- 041 ☐ **head out** ~으로 향하다
- 042 ☐ **science lab** 과학실
- 043 ☐ **experiment** ⓝ (과학적인) 실험
- 044 ☐ **available** ⓐ 이용할 수 있는
- 045 ☐ **reservation** ⓝ 예약

- 046 ☐ **suffer** ⓥ 시달리다, 고통 받다
- 047 ☐ **hand in** 제출하다

08
- 048 ☐ **give away** 버리다, 거저 주다
- 049 ☐ **garbage** ⓝ 쓰레기
- 050 ☐ **treasure** ⓝ 보물
- 051 ☐ **cupboard** ⓝ 찬장
- 052 ☐ **breakable** ⓐ 깨지기 쉬운
- 053 ☐ **accept** ⓥ 접수하다, 수용하다

09
- 054 ☐ **instrument** ⓝ 악기
- 055 ☐ **borrow** ⓥ 빌리다
- 056 ☐ **performance** ⓝ 공연
- 057 ☐ **be limited to** ~로 제한되다
- 058 ☐ **on a first-come-first-served basis** 선착순으로

10
- 059 ☐ **handheld** ⓐ 손에 들고 쓰는
- 060 ☐ **vacuum cleaner** 진공청소기
- 061 ☐ **cross out** (선을 그어) 지우다
- 062 ☐ **narrow down to** ~로 좁히다
- 063 ☐ **washable** ⓐ 물에 빨아도[세탁해도] 되는

11
- 064 ☐ **sore** ⓐ 따가운, 아픈, 화끈거리는
- 065 ☐ **probable** ⓐ (어떤 일이) 있을 것 같은, 개연성 있는
- 066 ☐ **rinse** ⓥ 헹구다
- 067 ☐ **air pollution** 공기[대기] 오염

12
- 068 ☐ **Would you mind if ~?** ~해도 괜찮을까요?
- 069 ☐ **bother** ⓥ 귀찮게 하다, 성가시게 하다
- 070 ☐ **feel free to** 편하게 ~하다

13
- 071 ☐ **drop by** ~에 들르다
- 072 ☐ **give back** ~을 돌려주다
- 073 ☐ **by the way** (화제를 전환하며) 그나저나, 그런데

14
- 074 ☐ **resolution** ⓝ 다짐, 결심
- 075 ☐ **surely** ⓐ 확실히, 분명히
- 076 ☐ **benefit** ⓝ 이점
- 077 ☐ **experience** ⓝ 경험, 체험
- 078 ☐ **broaden** ⓥ 넓히다, 확장하다

15
- 079 ☐ **guide dog** 맹도견, 장님을 인도하는 개
- 080 ☐ **towards** prep (어떤 방향) 쪽으로, (어떤 방향을) 향하여
- 081 ☐ **reach out** (손을) 뻗다
- 082 ☐ **concentrate on** ~에 집중하다
- 083 ☐ **lose one's focus** 집중력을 잃다, 초점을 잃다
- 084 ☐ **permission** ⓝ 허락
- 085 ☐ **afraid** ⓐ 유감으로 생각하다

16~17
- 086 ☐ **joint** ⓝ 관절
- 087 ☐ **bone** ⓝ 뼈
- 088 ☐ **put stress on** ~에 무리를 주다
- 089 ☐ **relatively** ⓐ 상대적으로, 비교적
- 090 ☐ **impact** ⓝ 충격, 영향
- 091 ☐ **knee joint** 무릎 관절
- 092 ☐ **smoothly** ⓐ 부드럽게
- 093 ☐ **low-impact** ⓐ (인체에 미치는) 충격이 적은
- 094 ☐ **muscle** ⓝ 근육
- 095 ☐ **elderly** ⓐ 연세가 드신

18
- 096 ☐ **choir** ⓝ 합창단
- 097 ☐ **announce** ⓥ 발표하다, 알리다
- 098 ☐ **compete in** ~에서 경쟁하다
- 099 ☐ **competition** ⓝ 대회
- 100 ☐ **takes place** 열리다
- 101 ☐ **participate in** ~에 참가하다
- 102 ☐ **necessary** ⓐ 필요한
- 103 ☐ **support** ⓥ 후원하다
- 104 ☐ **fundraising** ⓝ 모금
- 105 ☐ **passion** ⓝ 열정
- 106 ☐ **in advance** 미리, 앞서

19
- 107 ☐ **principal** ⓝ 교장
- 108 ☐ **present** ⓥ 수여하다
- 109 ☐ **academic** ⓐ 학업의
- 110 ☐ **achieve** ⓥ 달성하다, 성취하다
- 111 ☐ **row** ⓝ 열, 횡렬
- 112 ☐ **finalist** ⓝ 최종 후보자, 결승 진출자
- 113 ☐ **gather** ⓥ 모이다
- 114 ☐ **wipe** ⓥ 닦다
- 115 ☐ **sweaty** ⓐ 땀에 젖은
- 116 ☐ **handkerchief** ⓝ 손수건
- 117 ☐ **glance at** ~을 흘긋 보다
- 118 ☐ **pale** ⓐ 창백한
- 119 ☐ **uneasy** ⓐ 불안한
- 120 ☐ **subject** ⓝ 과목
- 121 ☐ **rank** ⓥ 평가하다, 순위를 매기다
- 122 ☐ **confidence** ⓝ 자신감
- 123 ☐ **declare** ⓥ 선언[포고]하다, 공표하다
- 124 ☐ **this way** 이리로
- 125 ☐ **applause** ⓝ 박수갈채
- 126 ☐ **guilty** ⓐ 죄책감이 드는, 가책을 느끼는

20
- 127 ☐ **army** ⓝ 군대
- 128 ☐ **instructor** ⓝ 교사, 교관, 강사
- 129 ☐ **barrack** ⓝ 막사, 병영
- 130 ☐ **inspect** ⓥ 조사하다
- 131 ☐ **task** ⓝ 일, 과업, 과제
- 132 ☐ **require** ⓥ 필요[요구]하다
- 133 ☐ **make the bed** 잠자리를 정돈하다
- 134 ☐ **perfection** ⓝ 완벽, 완전
- 135 ☐ **ridiculous** ⓐ 우스꽝스러운
- 136 ☐ **wisdom** ⓝ 지혜
- 137 ☐ **prove** ⓥ 입증[증명]하다
- 138 ☐ **accomplish** ⓥ 완수하다, 성취하다
- 139 ☐ **pride** ⓝ 자존감
- 140 ☐ **encourage** ⓥ 용기를 북돋우다

- 141 ☐ **complete** ⓥ 완수하다
- 142 ☐ **turn into** ~로 바뀌다

21
- 143 ☐ **job search** 구직 활동
- 144 ☐ **passive** ⓐ 수동적인
- 145 ☐ **browse** ⓥ 훑어보다
- 146 ☐ **effective** ⓐ 효과적인
- 147 ☐ **reach** ⓥ ~에 이르다, ~에 도착[도달]하다
- 148 ☐ **goal** ⓝ 목표
- 149 ☐ **claim** ⓥ 주장하다
- 150 ☐ **purpose** ⓝ 목적
- 151 ☐ **serious** ⓐ 진지한
- 152 ☐ **direct** ⓐ 직접적인
- 153 ☐ **focused** ⓐ 집중하는
- 154 ☐ **possible** ⓐ 가능한, 실행할 수 있는
- 155 ☐ **clever** ⓐ 영리한
- 156 ☐ **else** ⓐ 다른
- 157 ☐ **rest** ⓝ (어떤 것의) 나머지
- 158 ☐ **herd** ⓝ 무리
- 159 ☐ **regardless of** ~와 상관없이
- 160 ☐ **proactive** ⓐ 상황을 앞서서 주도하는
- 161 ☐ **logically** ⓐ 논리적으로
- 162 ☐ **result** ⓝ 결과
- 163 ☐ **occasional** ⓐ 가끔씩의
- 164 ☐ **resume** ⓝ 이력서
- 165 ☐ **stand out from** ~에서 두드러지다
- 166 ☐ **sheep** ⓝ 양, 어리석은 사람

22
- 167 ☐ **view A as B** A를 B로 보다
- 168 ☐ **merely** ⓐ 그저, 단순히
- 169 ☐ **down time** 정지 시간, 휴식 시간
- 170 ☐ **shut off** 멈추다
- 171 ☐ **body** ⓝ 몸, 신체
- 172 ☐ **in a rush** 서둘러
- 173 ☐ **household** ⓝ (한 집에 사는 사람들을 일컫는) 가정
- 174 ☐ **responsibility** ⓝ 책임
- 175 ☐ **cut back on** ~을 줄이다
- 176 ☐ **problem** ⓝ 문제
- 177 ☐ **activity** ⓝ 활동
- 178 ☐ **important** ⓐ 중요한
- 179 ☐ **research** ⓝ 연구
- 180 ☐ **reveal** ⓥ 밝히다
- 181 ☐ **a number of** 많은
- 182 ☐ **vital** ⓐ 매우 중요한
- 183 ☐ **carry out** ~을 수행하다
- 184 ☐ **during** prep 동안
- 185 ☐ **maintain** ⓥ 유지하다
- 186 ☐ **enable** ⓥ ~을 할 수 있게 하다
- 187 ☐ **function** ⓥ 기능하다
- 188 ☐ **at one's best** 최상의 수준으로
- 189 ☐ **form** ⓥ 형성하다
- 190 ☐ **pathway** ⓝ 경로
- 191 ☐ **memory** ⓝ 기억
- 192 ☐ **insight** ⓝ 통찰력
- 193 ☐ **focus** ⓥ 정신을 집중하다
- 194 ☐ **pay attention** 주의를 기울이다
- 195 ☐ **respond** ⓥ 반응하다
- 196 ☐ **lack** ⓝ 부족
- 197 ☐ **cause** ⓥ 일으키다

VOCA LIST 05

¹⁹⁸ ☐ **mood** ⓝ 기분, 감정
¹⁹⁹ ☐ **in addition** 게다가
²⁰⁰ ☐ **grow** ⓥ 커지다, 증대하다
²⁰¹ ☐ **evidence** ⓝ 증거
²⁰² ☐ **risk** ⓝ 위험
²⁰³ ☐ **develop a disease** 병을 키우다

23
²⁰⁴ ☐ **whole** ⓐ 전체
²⁰⁵ ☐ **human society** 인간 사회
²⁰⁶ ☐ **operate** ⓥ 운영되다, 돌아가다
²⁰⁷ ☐ **future** ⓐ 미래의
²⁰⁸ ☐ **weather** ⓝ 날씨
²⁰⁹ ☐ **farmer** ⓝ 농부
²¹⁰ ☐ **monsoon** ⓝ (동남아 여름철의) 몬순, 우기, 장마
²¹¹ ☐ **plant** ⓥ 심다
²¹² ☐ **crop** ⓝ 작물
²¹³ ☐ **harvest** ⓝ 수확
²¹⁴ ☐ **knowledge** ⓝ 지식
²¹⁵ ☐ **past** ⓝ 과거
²¹⁶ ☐ **predict** ⓥ 예측하다
²¹⁷ ☐ **influence** ⓥ 영향을 미치다
²¹⁸ ☐ **railway** ⓝ 철도
²¹⁹ ☐ **design** ⓥ 설계하다
²²⁰ ☐ **climate** ⓝ 기후
²²¹ ☐ **central heating** 중앙난방
²²² ☐ **temperature** ⓝ 기온
²²³ ☐ **below** prep ～보다 아래에
²²⁴ ☐ **air-conditioning** ⓝ 냉방(기)
²²⁵ ☐ **rarely** ⓐⓓ 거의 없게
²²⁶ ☐ **beyond** prep 위로
²²⁷ ☐ **opposite** ⓝ 정반대
²²⁸ ☐ **technology** ⓝ 과학기술
²²⁹ ☐ **deal** ⓥ 처리하다, 다루다
²³⁰ ☐ **correctly** ⓐⓓ 정확하게
²³¹ ☐ **affect** ⓥ 영향을 미치다
²³² ☐ **harsh** ⓐ 혹독한

24
²³³ ☐ **ability** ⓝ 능력
²³⁴ ☐ **accurately** ⓐⓓ 정확하게
²³⁵ ☐ **label** ⓥ 이름을 붙이다
²³⁶ ☐ **emotion** ⓝ 감정
²³⁷ ☐ **refer to A as B** A를 B라고 부르다
²³⁸ ☐ **granularity** ⓝ 낱알 모양, 입상(粒狀)
²³⁹ ☐ **psychologist** ⓝ 심리학자
²⁴⁰ ☐ **vocabulary** ⓝ 어휘
²⁴¹ ☐ **absolutely** ⓐⓓ 절대적으로
²⁴² ☐ **transformative** ⓐ 변화시키는
²⁴³ ☐ **explain** ⓥ 설명하다
²⁴⁴ ☐ **difficult** ⓐ 어려운
²⁴⁵ ☐ **communicate** ⓥ 전달하다
²⁴⁶ ☐ **support** ⓝ 지지
²⁴⁷ ☐ **distinguish** ⓥ 구별하다
²⁴⁸ ☐ **a range of** 광범위한
²⁴⁹ ☐ **various** ⓐ 다양한
²⁵⁰ ☐ **manage** ⓥ 관리하다
²⁵¹ ☐ **ups and downs** 좋은 일과 궂은 일, 오르락내리락
²⁵² ☐ **ordinary** ⓐ 평범한
²⁵³ ☐ **existence** ⓝ 존재

²⁵⁴ ☐ **process** ⓝ 과정
²⁵⁵ ☐ **related to** ～에 관련된
²⁵⁶ ☐ **regulation** ⓝ 통제
²⁵⁷ ☐ **psychosocial** ⓐ 심리사회적인
²⁵⁸ ☐ **well-being** ⓝ 행복
²⁵⁹ ☐ **friendship** ⓝ 우정, 교우관계
²⁶⁰ ☐ **endure** ⓥ 견디다, 참다, 인내하다
²⁶¹ ☐ **argument** ⓝ 논쟁, 논의
²⁶² ☐ **beneficial** ⓐ 유익한, 이로운
²⁶³ ☐ **categorize** ⓥ 분류하다
²⁶⁴ ☐ **efficiency** ⓝ 효율, 능률

25
²⁶⁵ ☐ **course** ⓝ 강의
²⁶⁶ ☐ **learning material** 학습 자료
²⁶⁷ ☐ **age group** 연령 집단
²⁶⁸ ☐ **be the least likely to** ～할 가능성이 가장 낮다

26
²⁶⁹ ☐ **known for** ～으로 알려진
²⁷⁰ ☐ **job skill** 직무 기술
²⁷¹ ☐ **language** ⓝ 언어
²⁷² ☐ **Dutch** ⓝ 네덜란드어
²⁷³ ☐ **unusual** ⓐ 드문
²⁷⁴ ☐ **curiosity** ⓝ 호기심
²⁷⁵ ☐ **endless** ⓐ 끝없는
²⁷⁶ ☐ **make A out of B** B로 A를 만들다
²⁷⁷ ☐ **come in handy** 도움이 되다
²⁷⁸ ☐ **microscope** ⓝ 현미경
²⁷⁹ ☐ **tiny** ⓐ 아주 작은
²⁸⁰ ☐ **vein** ⓝ 정맥
²⁸¹ ☐ **blood** ⓝ 피
²⁸² ☐ **flow** ⓥ 흐르다
²⁸³ ☐ **pond** ⓝ 연못
²⁸⁴ ☐ **pay attention to** ～에 주의를 기울이다
²⁸⁵ ☐ **observation** ⓝ 관찰
²⁸⁶ ☐ **draw** ⓥ 그리다
²⁸⁷ ☐ **hire** ⓥ 고용하다
²⁸⁸ ☐ **describe** ⓥ 설명하다, 서술하다, 묘사하다

27
²⁸⁹ ☐ **flower arrangement** 꽃꽂이
²⁹⁰ ☐ **material** ⓝ 재료
²⁹¹ ☐ **scissor** ⓝ 가위
²⁹² ☐ **sign up for** ～에 등록하다
²⁹³ ☐ **refund** ⓝ 환불
²⁹⁴ ☐ **cancellation** ⓝ 취소
²⁹⁵ ☐ **contact** ⓥ 연락하다

28
²⁹⁶ ☐ **palace** ⓝ 궁전
²⁹⁷ ☐ **book** ⓥ 예약하다
²⁹⁸ ☐ **traditional** ⓐ 전통적인
²⁹⁹ ☐ **extra charge** 추가 비용, 할증요금
³⁰⁰ ☐ **visit** ⓝ 접촉 ⓥ 방문하다

29
³⁰¹ ☐ **usually** ⓐⓓ 보통, 대개
³⁰² ☐ **get along with** ～와 잘 지내다, 어울리다
³⁰³ ☐ **seek out** (오랫동안 공들여) 찾아다니다
³⁰⁴ ☐ **exist** ⓥ 존재하다

³⁰⁵ ☐ **race** ⓝ 인종
³⁰⁶ ☐ **skin** ⓝ 피부
³⁰⁷ ☐ **religion** ⓝ 종교
³⁰⁸ ☐ **value** ⓝ 가치관
³⁰⁹ ☐ **way** ⓝ 방식
³¹⁰ ☐ **as the saying goes** 속담에서 말하듯이, 옛말처럼
³¹¹ ☐ **feather** ⓝ 깃털
³¹² ☐ **flock** ⓥ 모이다, 무리 짓다
³¹³ ☐ **common** ⓐ 흔한
³¹⁴ ☐ **tendency** ⓝ 경향, 경향성
³¹⁵ ☐ **be rooted in** ～에 뿌리박고 있다, ～에 원인이 있다
³¹⁶ ☐ **species** ⓝ 종(생물 분류의 기초 단위)
³¹⁷ ☐ **imagine** ⓥ 상상하다
³¹⁸ ☐ **forest** ⓝ 숲
³¹⁹ ☐ **be conditioned to** ～에 조건화되어 있다
³²⁰ ☐ **avoid** ⓥ 피하다
³²¹ ☐ **unfamiliar** ⓐ 친숙하지 않은
³²² ☐ **likelihood** ⓝ 가능성
³²³ ☐ **similarity** ⓝ 유사점
³²⁴ ☐ **relate to** ～을 이해하다, ～에 공감하다
³²⁵ ☐ **level** ⓝ 수준

30
³²⁶ ☐ **rejection** ⓝ 거절
³²⁷ ☐ **handle** ⓥ 감당하다
³²⁸ ☐ **painful** ⓐ 고통스러운
³²⁹ ☐ **rather** ⓐⓓ 오히려, 차라리
³³⁰ ☐ **risk** ⓥ 위험을 감수하다
³³¹ ☐ **negative** ⓐ 부정적인
³³² ☐ **aspect** ⓝ 측면
³³³ ☐ **tough** ⓐ 강한
³³⁴ ☐ **reason** ⓝ 이유
³³⁵ ☐ **consider** ⓥ 고려하다
³³⁶ ☐ **therapy** ⓝ 요법
³³⁷ ☐ **come up with** ～을 생각해내다, 떠올리다
³³⁸ ☐ **request** ⓝ 요청
³³⁹ ☐ **deliberately** ⓐⓓ 고의로, 의도적으로
³⁴⁰ ☐ **discount** ⓝ 할인
³⁴¹ ☐ **grow a thick skin** 무덤덤해지다, 둔감해지다
³⁴² ☐ **thus** ⓐⓓ 따라서, 그러므로
³⁴³ ☐ **unfavorable** ⓐ 호의적이지 않은
³⁴⁴ ☐ **circumstance** ⓝ 상황, 환경

31
³⁴⁵ ☐ **generalization** ⓝ 일반화
³⁴⁶ ☐ **specific** ⓐ 구체적인, 명확한
³⁴⁷ ☐ **humanize** ⓥ 인간적으로 만들다
³⁴⁸ ☐ **boring** ⓐ 지루한
³⁴⁹ ☐ **platitude** ⓝ 진부한 말, 상투적인 문구
³⁵⁰ ☐ **finest** ⓐ 가장 훌륭한
³⁵¹ ☐ **humanitarian** ⓐ 인도주의적인
³⁵² ☐ **leave out** ～을 빼다
³⁵³ ☐ **completely** ⓐⓓ 완전히, 전적으로
³⁵⁴ ☐ **novel** ⓝ 소설
³⁵⁵ ☐ **main character** 주인공
³⁵⁶ ☐ **up front** 대놓고
³⁵⁷ ☐ **heroic** ⓐ 대담한, 영웅적인
³⁵⁸ ☐ **brave** ⓐ 용감한
³⁵⁹ ☐ **tragic** ⓐ 비극적인

³⁶⁰ ☐ **thereafter** ⓐⓓ 그 후에
³⁶¹ ☐ **description** ⓝ 묘사
³⁶² ☐ **at all** 전혀
³⁶³ ☐ **detailed** ⓐ 세밀한
³⁶⁴ ☐ **engaging** ⓐ 마음을 끄는, 몰입시키는
³⁶⁵ ☐ **fantasy** ⓝ 환상
³⁶⁶ ☐ **boredom** ⓝ 지루함

32
³⁶⁷ ☐ **face-to-face** ⓐ 대면의
³⁶⁸ ☐ **interaction** ⓝ 상호 작용
³⁶⁹ ☐ **uniquely** ⓐⓓ 유례없이
³⁷⁰ ☐ **powerful** ⓐ 영향력 있는, 강력한
³⁷¹ ☐ **simplest** ⓐ 가장 간단한
³⁷² ☐ **complex** ⓐ 복잡한
³⁷³ ☐ **stimulate** ⓥ 자극하다
³⁷⁴ ☐ **difficulty** ⓝ 어려움
³⁷⁵ ☐ **tie** ⓥ 묶다
³⁷⁶ ☐ **shoelace** ⓝ 신발 끈
³⁷⁷ ☐ **arithmetic** ⓝ 산수
³⁷⁸ ☐ **achiever** ⓝ 성취도를 보이는 사람
³⁷⁹ ☐ **previous** ⓐ 이전의
³⁸⁰ ☐ **access** ⓝ 접근
³⁸¹ ☐ **crucial** ⓐ 아주 중요한, 중대한, 경쟁적인
³⁸² ☐ **organization** ⓝ 조직, 단체
³⁸³ ☐ **conversation** ⓝ 대화
³⁸⁴ ☐ **factor** ⓝ 요소
³⁸⁵ ☐ **professional** ⓐ 전문적인
³⁸⁶ ☐ **regular** ⓐ 규칙적인
³⁸⁷ ☐ **practice** ⓝ 연습

33
³⁸⁸ ☐ **foreign** ⓐ 외국의, 낯선
³⁸⁹ ☐ **subtitle** ⓝ (영화·텔레비전 화면의) 자막
³⁹⁰ ☐ **translate** ⓥ 번역하다, 통역하다
³⁹¹ ☐ **dialogue** ⓝ 대화
³⁹² ☐ **viewer** ⓝ 관객
³⁹³ ☐ **occasion** ⓝ 경우, 때
³⁹⁴ ☐ **incomprehensible** ⓐ 이해할 수 없는
³⁹⁵ ☐ **target audience** 주요 대상 관객
³⁹⁶ ☐ **mainly** ⓐⓓ 주로
³⁹⁷ ☐ **viewpoint** ⓝ 관점, 시점
³⁹⁸ ☐ **particular** ⓐ 특정한
³⁹⁹ ☐ **absence** ⓝ 부재
⁴⁰⁰ ☐ **alienation** ⓝ 소외
⁴⁰¹ ☐ **impressed** ⓐ 감명[감동]을 받은
⁴⁰² ☐ **attract** ⓥ 끌어당기다
⁴⁰³ ☐ **participate** ⓥ 참여하다

34
⁴⁰⁴ ☐ **dynamic** ⓝ 역학
⁴⁰⁵ ☐ **dramatically** ⓐⓓ 극적으로
⁴⁰⁶ ☐ **concept** ⓝ 개념
⁴⁰⁷ ☐ **home-field advantage** 홈 이점
⁴⁰⁸ ☐ **perceive** ⓥ 인지하다
⁴⁰⁹ ☐ **demand** ⓝ 부담, 요구
⁴¹⁰ ☐ **play a role in** ～에 역할을 하다, 일조하다
⁴¹¹ ☐ **provide** ⓥ 제공하다
⁴¹² ☐ **resource** ⓝ 자원
⁴¹³ ☐ **researcher** ⓝ 연구원
⁴¹⁴ ☐ **point out** 지적하다
⁴¹⁵ ☐ **competitive** ⓐ 경쟁력 있는

416 ☐ **appear** ⓥ ~인 것같이 보이다
417 ☐ **perception** ⓝ 인식
418 ☐ **struggling** ⓐ 고전하는
419 ☐ **reduce** ⓥ 줄이다
420 ☐ **pressure** ⓝ 압박
421 ☐ **road trip** 장거리 자동차 여행
422 ☐ **increase** ⓥ 증가하다
423 ☐ **advertise** ⓥ (상품이나 서비스를) 광고하다
424 ☐ **upcoming** ⓐ 다가오는, 곧 있을

35
425 ☐ **mild** ⓐ 가벼운
426 ☐ **stimulant** ⓝ 자극제, 흥분제
427 ☐ **commonly** ⓐⓓ 흔히, 보통
428 ☐ **soda** ⓝ 탄산음료
429 ☐ **possibly** ⓐⓓ 아마
430 ☐ **attentive** ⓐ 주의 깊은
431 ☐ **likely** ⓐ ~ 할 것 같은
432 ☐ **have an effect on** ~에 영향을 미치다
433 ☐ **memory** ⓝ 기억력
434 ☐ **improve** ⓥ 향상하다, 개선되다, 나아지다
435 ☐ **performance** ⓝ 수행
436 ☐ **ideal** ⓐ 이상적인
437 ☐ **currently** ⓐⓓ 현재
438 ☐ **unknown** ⓐ 알려지지 않은
439 ☐ **wide awake** 아주 잠이 깨어
440 ☐ **well-rested** 잘 쉰
441 ☐ **further** ⓐⓓ 더욱
442 ☐ **in contrast** 반면에
443 ☐ **indeed** ⓐⓓ 실제로
444 ☐ **nervous** ⓐ 신경이 과민한
445 ☐ **suffer** ⓥ 악화되다

36
446 ☐ **century** ⓝ 세기
447 ☐ **architectural** ⓐ 건축의
448 ☐ **attitude** ⓝ 사고방식
449 ☐ **emerge** ⓥ 나타나다, 출현하다
450 ☐ **industrial** ⓐ 산업의
451 ☐ **argument** ⓝ 주장
452 ☐ **ugly** ⓐ 추한, 못생긴
453 ☐ **inhuman** ⓐ 비인간적인
454 ☐ **pretension** ⓝ 허세, 가식
455 ☐ **supply** ⓝ 공급하다
456 ☐ **perfectly** ⓐⓓ 완벽하게
457 ☐ **craftsman** ⓝ 장인
458 ☐ **rootedness** ⓝ 뿌리내림, 고착, 정착
459 ☐ **locality** ⓝ (~이 존재하는) 지역, 곳
460 ☐ **instead** ⓐⓓ 대신에
461 ☐ **approach** ⓝ 접근
462 ☐ **craft** ⓝ 공예
463 ☐ **generation** ⓝ 세대
464 ☐ **demonstrate** ⓥ 입증하다
465 ☐ **mastery** ⓝ 숙달한 기술
466 ☐ **simplicity** ⓝ 단순함
467 ☐ **plain** ⓐ 평범한, 단순한

37
468 ☐ **moral** ⓐ 도덕의
469 ☐ **necessarily** ⓐⓓ 반드시
470 ☐ **incompetence** ⓝ 무능
471 ☐ **occur** ⓥ 일어나다, 발생하다

472 ☐ **accomplished** ⓐ 숙달된, 기량이 뛰어난
473 ☐ **in nature** 사실상
474 ☐ **somehow** ⓐⓓ 어떻게든지
475 ☐ **uplift** 고양시키다, 들어올리다
476 ☐ **on the other hand** 반면에
477 ☐ **degrade** ⓥ 격하시키다
478 ☐ **doubtful** ⓐ 미심쩍은
479 ☐ **character** ⓝ 사람, 등장인물
480 ☐ **composer** ⓝ 작곡가
481 ☐ **show off** 과시하다, 뽐내다
482 ☐ **honestly** ⓐⓓ 정직하게

38
483 ☐ **biodiversity** ⓝ 생물의 다양성
484 ☐ **effect** ⓝ 영향
485 ☐ **sudden** ⓐ 갑작스러운
486 ☐ **dramatic** ⓐ 극적인
487 ☐ **ecosystem** ⓝ 생태계
488 ☐ **wildlife** ⓝ 야생 생물
489 ☐ **opportunity** ⓝ 기회
490 ☐ **obtain** ⓥ 얻다
491 ☐ **shelter** ⓝ 서식지
492 ☐ **react** ⓥ 작용하다
493 ☐ **environment** ⓝ 환경
494 ☐ **entire** ⓐ 전체의
495 ☐ **food web** 먹이 그물, 먹이 사슬 체계
496 ☐ **dry season** 건기(乾期)
497 ☐ **die out** 멸종되다, 자취를 감추다
498 ☐ **prey upon** ~을 잡아먹다, 괴롭히다
499 ☐ **drought** ⓝ 가뭄
500 ☐ **survive** ⓥ 살아남다
501 ☐ **rely** ⓥ 의지하다
502 ☐ **at the death** 종말에 처한

39
503 ☐ **dawn** ⓝ 시작, 새벽
504 ☐ **civilization** ⓝ 문명
505 ☐ **ancestor** ⓝ 선조
506 ☐ **myth** ⓝ 신화
507 ☐ **legendary** ⓐ 전설의
508 ☐ **connect** ⓥ 연결되다
509 ☐ **inspire** ⓥ 영감을 주다
510 ☐ **wonder** ⓥ 궁금하다
511 ☐ **element** ⓝ 요소
512 ☐ **narrative** ⓝ 이야기
513 ☐ **embed** ⓥ ~을 깊이 새겨 두다, 끼워 넣다
514 ☐ **identity** ⓝ 정체성
515 ☐ **practical** ⓐ 실용적인
516 ☐ **keep track of** ~을 기록하다
517 ☐ **calendar** ⓝ 달력
518 ☐ **essential** ⓐ 필수적인
519 ☐ **aid** ⓝ 보조 도구
520 ☐ **farming** ⓝ 농업
521 ☐ **seasonal** ⓐ 계절에 따른
522 ☐ **gathering** ⓝ 수집, 수확
523 ☐ **navigation** ⓝ 항해
524 ☐ **tool** ⓝ 도구, 연장
525 ☐ **commerce** ⓝ 무역, 상업
526 ☐ **explore** ⓥ 탐험하다
527 ☐ **remote** ⓐ 멀리 떨어진
528 ☐ **planet** ⓝ 지구
529 ☐ **observe** ⓥ 관찰하다

40
530 ☐ **layer** ⓝ 층
531 ☐ **soil** ⓝ 토양
532 ☐ **root** ⓝ 뿌리
533 ☐ **funny** ⓐ 기이한
534 ☐ **talent** ⓝ 재능
535 ☐ **nearby** ⓥ 근처
536 ☐ **manganese** ⓝ 망가니즈(금속 원소)
537 ☐ **harmful** ⓐ 해로운, 유해한
538 ☐ **concentration** ⓝ 농도, 농축
539 ☐ **unaffected** ⓝ 영향을 받지 않은
540 ☐ **damaging** ⓐ 해로운
541 ☐ **evolve** ⓥ 발달시키다
542 ☐ **redistribute** ⓥ 재분배하다
543 ☐ **shallow** ⓐ 얕은
544 ☐ **absorb** ⓥ 흡수하다
545 ☐ **concentrate** ⓥ 모으다, 농축시키다
546 ☐ **decay** ⓥ 썩다
547 ☐ **deposit** ⓝ 축적물, 퇴적물
548 ☐ **poison** ⓥ (독성 물질로) 오염시키다, 중독 시키다
549 ☐ **be immune to** ~에 면역이 있다
550 ☐ **toxic** ⓐ 유독한
551 ☐ **essentially** ⓐⓓ 본질적으로
552 ☐ **eliminate** ⓥ 제거하다
553 ☐ **competition** ⓝ 경쟁자
554 ☐ **poisoning** ⓝ 중독
555 ☐ **neighbor** ⓝ 이웃
556 ☐ **surrounding** ⓐ 주변의

41~42
557 ☐ **journey** ⓝ 여정, 여행 ⓥ 여행하다
558 ☐ **shorten** ⓥ 줄이다
559 ☐ **misery** ⓝ 불행, 비참함
560 ☐ **impatience** ⓝ 조급함
561 ☐ **judgment** ⓝ 비난
562 ☐ **frustration** ⓝ 좌절
563 ☐ **anger** ⓝ 분노
564 ☐ **reside** ⓥ 존재하다
565 ☐ **shift** ⓥ 바뀌다
566 ☐ **get in one's way** ~을 방해하다
567 ☐ **unknowingly** ⓐⓓ 무심코
568 ☐ **cut off** ~을 가로막다
569 ☐ **in traffic** 차량 흐름에서
570 ☐ **splash** ⓥ (물을) 튀기다, 끼얹다
571 ☐ **pen** ⓥ (글을) 쓰다
572 ☐ **review** ⓝ 후기
573 ☐ **miserable** ⓐ 비참한
574 ☐ **human being** 인간
575 ☐ **child** ⓝ 자녀
576 ☐ **pool** ⓝ 수영장
577 ☐ **statement** ⓝ 진술
578 ☐ **deny** ⓥ 부인하다
579 ☐ **forgive** ⓥ 용서하다

43~45
580 ☐ **village** ⓝ 마을
581 ☐ **monk** ⓝ 수도승
582 ☐ **field** ⓝ 들판
583 ☐ **reply** ⓥ 대답하다
584 ☐ **middle-aged** ⓐ 중년의
585 ☐ **come upon** ~을 우연히 만나다

586 ☐ **valley** ⓝ 골짜기
587 ☐ **unwelcoming** ⓐ 불친절한, 환영하지 않는
588 ☐ **expect** ⓥ 예상하다
589 ☐ **helplessly** ⓐ 힘없이, 무기력하게
590 ☐ **elder** ⓝ 원로들, 어른들
591 ☐ **generous** ⓐ 관대한

TEST A-B 각 단어의 뜻을 [A] 영어는 우리말로, [B] 우리말은 영어로 쓰시오.

A	English	Korean	B	Korean	English
01	announce		01	유지하다	
02	responsibility		02	전달하다	
03	passion		03	통제	
04	gather		04	흐르다	
05	task		05	낯선	
06	complete		06	마음을 끄는, 몰입시키는	
07	serious		07	경쟁력 있는	
08	insight		08	반드시	
09	temperature		09	재료	
10	recognize		10	영향을 미치다	
11	curiosity		11	전통적인	
12	handle		12	대담하다	
13	specific		13	실제로	
14	previous		14	관찰하다	
15	viewpoint		15	문명	
16	reduce		16	현재	
17	emerge		17	주장하다	
18	ecosystem		18	요소	
19	survive		19	평범한, 단순한	
20	eliminate		20	주로	

▶ A-D 정답 : 해설편 044쪽

TEST C-D 각 단어의 뜻을 골라 기호를 쓰시오.

C	English		Korean	D	Korean		English
01	harsh	( )	ⓐ 인종	01	거절	( )	ⓐ suffer
02	misery	( )	ⓑ 환불	02	입증하다	( )	ⓑ perception
03	ridiculous	( )	ⓒ 정반대	03	구성	( )	ⓒ accomplished
04	support	( )	ⓓ 좌절	04	이력서	( )	ⓓ element
05	craftsman	( )	ⓔ 기후	05	번역하다, 통역하다	( )	ⓔ occasional
06	confidence	( )	ⓕ 혹독한	06	수확	( )	ⓕ fundraising
07	distinguish	( )	ⓖ 고려하다	07	사고방식	( )	ⓖ stimulate
08	climate	( )	ⓗ 조급함	08	가끔씩의	( )	ⓗ resume
09	race	( )	ⓘ 얻다	09	고양시키다, 들어 올리다	( )	ⓘ construction
10	existence	( )	ⓙ 얕은	10	조사하다	( )	ⓙ demonstrate
11	shallow	( )	ⓚ 우스꽝스러운	11	용감한	( )	ⓚ instructor
12	obtain	( )	ⓛ 장인	12	모금	( )	ⓛ harvest
13	opposite	( )	ⓜ 자신감	13	악화되다	( )	ⓜ generalization
14	frustration	( )	ⓝ 존재	14	숙달된, 기량이 뛰어난	( )	ⓝ uplift
15	wisdom	( )	ⓞ 구별하다	15	교사, 교관, 강사	( )	ⓞ operate
16	consider	( )	ⓟ 불행, 비참함	16	요소	( )	ⓟ rejection
17	wipe	( )	ⓠ 농도, 농축	17	자극하다	( )	ⓠ inspect
18	refund	( )	ⓡ 후원하다	18	인식	( )	ⓡ translate
19	impatience	( )	ⓢ 닦다	19	운영되다, 돌아가다	( )	ⓢ brave
20	concentration	( )	ⓣ 지혜	20	일반화	( )	ⓣ attitude

2021학년도 3월 고1 전국연합학력평가 문제지

영어 영역

제 3 교시

06회

1

● 문항수 45개 | 배점 100점 | 제한 시간 70분

● 점수 표시가 없는 문항은 모두 2점

06회

1번부터 17번까지는 듣고 답하는 문제입니다. 1번부터 15번까지는 한 번만 들려주고, 16번부터 17번까지는 두 번 들려줍니다. 방송을 잘 듣고 답을 하시기 바랍니다.

1. 다음을 듣고, 남자가 하는 말의 목적으로 가장 적절한 것을 고르시오.
   ① 교내 청소 일정을 공지하려고
   ② 학교 시설 공사의 지연에 대해 사과하려고
   ③ 하교 시 교실 창문을 닫을 것을 요청하려고
   ④ 교내의 젖은 바닥을 걸을 때 조심하도록 당부하려고
   ⑤ 깨끗한 교실 환경 조성을 위한 아이디어를 공모하려고

2. 대화를 듣고, 여자의 의견으로 가장 적절한 것을 고르시오.
   ① 짧은 낮잠은 업무 효율을 높인다.
   ② 야식은 숙면에 방해가 될 수 있다.
   ③ 사람마다 최적의 수면 시간이 다르다.
   ④ 베개를 바꾸면 숙면에 도움이 될 수 있다.
   ⑤ 숙면을 위해 침실을 서늘하게 하는 것이 좋다.

3. 대화를 듣고, 두 사람의 관계를 가장 잘 나타낸 것을 고르시오.
   ① 파티 주최자 – 요리사
   ② 슈퍼마켓 점원 – 손님
   ③ 배달 기사 – 음식점 주인
   ④ 영양학자 – 식품 제조업자
   ⑤ 인테리어 디자이너 – 의뢰인

4. 대화를 듣고, 그림에서 대화의 내용과 일치하지 않는 것을 고르시오.

5. 대화를 듣고, 남자가 할 일로 가장 적절한 것을 고르시오.
   ① 영화 예매하기   ② 지갑 가져오기
   ③ 시간표 출력하기   ④ 학생증 재발급받기
   ⑤ 영화 감상문 제출하기

6. 대화를 듣고, 여자가 지불할 금액을 고르시오. [3점]
   ① $72   ② $80   ③ $90   ④ $100   ⑤ $110

7. 대화를 듣고, 남자가 보고서를 완성하지 못한 이유를 고르시오.
   ① 실험을 다시 해서
   ② 제출일을 착각해서
   ③ 주제가 변경되어서
   ④ 컴퓨터가 고장 나서
   ⑤ 심한 감기에 걸려서

8. 대화를 듣고, Spring Virtual Run에 관해 언급되지 않은 것을 고르시오.
   ① 달리는 거리   ② 참가 인원   ③ 달리는 장소
   ④ 참가비   ⑤ 기념품

9. Family Night at the Museum에 관한 다음 내용을 듣고, 일치하지 않는 것을 고르시오.
   ① 박물관 정규 운영 시간 종료 후에 열린다.
   ② 행성과 별 모형 아래에서 잠을 잔다.
   ③ 참가자들에게 침낭이 제공된다.
   ④ 6세부터 13세까지를 위한 프로그램이다.
   ⑤ 사전 등록 없이 현장에서 참가할 수 있다.

10. 다음 표를 보면서 대화를 듣고, 여자가 구매할 스마트 워치를 고르시오.

Smart Watches

	Model	Waterproof	Warranty	Price
①	A	×	2 years	$90
②	B	○	3 years	$110
③	C	○	1 year	$115
④	D	×	2 years	$120
⑤	E	○	4 years	$125

11. 대화를 듣고, 여자의 마지막 말에 대한 남자의 응답으로 가장 적절한 것을 고르시오.
    ① Oh, I should get it exchanged.
    ② Sure. I'll order a shirt for you.
    ③ Well, it's too expensive for me.
    ④ No. Please find me a smaller size.
    ⑤ Sorry, but this shirt is not on sale.

12. 대화를 듣고, 남자의 마지막 말에 대한 여자의 응답으로 가장 적절한 것을 고르시오.
    ① Good. Let's meet around six.
    ② That's okay. I don't like donuts.
    ③ I want to open my own donut shop.
    ④ Don't worry. I can do that by myself.
    ⑤ Thanks for sharing your donut recipe.

13. 대화를 듣고, 여자의 마지막 말에 대한 남자의 응답으로 가장 적절한 것을 고르시오. [3점]

Man: _____

① This coffee place is very popular.
② You can stop using plastic straws.
③ I'll order drinks when you're ready.
④ Your drink will be ready in a minute.
⑤ The cups come in various colors and shapes.

14. 대화를 듣고, 남자의 마지막 말에 대한 여자의 응답으로 가장 적절한 것을 고르시오. [3점]

Woman: _____

① Luckily, I didn't get hurt in the accident.
② I have enough money to get a new bike.
③ You really need one for your own safety.
④ You may feel sleepy after biking to school.
⑤ We can put our bikes in the school parking lot.

15. 다음 상황 설명을 듣고, Jasper가 Mary에게 할 말로 가장 적절한 것을 고르시오.

Jasper: _____

① Where is the audition being held?
② How about writing your own song?
③ Let's play a different song this time.
④ I think you should be our lead singer.
⑤ Don't you think we need more practice?

[16 ~ 17] 다음을 듣고, 물음에 답하시오.

16. 남자가 하는 말의 주제로 가장 적절한 것은?

① eco-friendly toys for pets
② roles of toys in pets' well-being
③ types of pets' unusual behaviors
④ foods that are dangerous to pets
⑤ difficulties in raising children with pets

17. 언급된 동물이 아닌 것은?

① cat   ② hamster   ③ dog
④ turtle   ⑤ parrot

이제 듣기 문제가 끝났습니다. 18번부터는 문제지의 지시에 따라 답을 하시기 바랍니다.

18. 다음 글의 목적으로 가장 적절한 것은?

Dear members of Eastwood Library,

Thanks to the Friends of Literature group, we've successfully raised enough money to remodel the library building. John Baker, our local builder, has volunteered to help us with the remodelling but he needs assistance. By grabbing a hammer or a paint brush and donating your time, you can help with the construction. Join Mr. Baker in his volunteering team and become a part of making Eastwood Library a better place! Please call 541-567-1234 for more information.

Sincerely,
Mark Anderson

① 도서관 임시 휴관의 이유를 설명하려고
② 도서관 자원봉사자 교육 일정을 안내하려고
③ 도서관 보수를 위한 모금 행사를 제안하려고
④ 도서관 공사에 참여할 자원봉사자를 모집하려고
⑤ 도서관에서 개최하는 글쓰기 대회를 홍보하려고

19. 다음 글에 드러난 Shirley의 심경으로 가장 적절한 것은?

On the way home, Shirley noticed a truck parked in front of the house across the street. New neighbors! Shirley was dying to know about them. "Do you know anything about the new neighbors?" she asked Pa at dinner. He said, "Yes, and there's one thing that may be interesting to you." Shirley had a billion more questions. Pa said joyfully, "They have a girl just your age. Maybe she wants to be your playmate." Shirley nearly dropped her fork on the floor. How many times had she prayed for a friend? Finally, her prayers were answered! She and the new girl could go to school together, play together, and become best friends.

① curious and excited   ② sorry and upset
③ jealous and annoyed   ④ calm and relaxed
⑤ disappointed and unhappy

20. 다음 글에서 필자가 주장하는 바로 가장 적절한 것은?

At a publishing house and at a newspaper you learn the following: *It's not a mistake if it doesn't end up in print*. It's the same for email. Nothing bad can happen if you haven't hit the Send key. What you've written can have misspellings, errors of fact, rude comments, obvious lies, but it doesn't matter. If you haven't sent it, you still have time to fix it. You can correct any mistake and nobody will ever know the difference. This is easier said than done, of course. Send is your computer's most attractive command. But before you hit the Send key, make sure that you read your document carefully one last time.

① 중요한 이메일은 출력하여 보관해야 한다.
② 글을 쓸 때에는 개요 작성부터 시작해야 한다.
③ 이메일을 전송하기 전에 반드시 검토해야 한다.
④ 업무와 관련된 컴퓨터 기능을 우선 익혀야 한다.
⑤ 업무상 중요한 내용은 이메일보다는 직접 전달해야 한다.

21. 밑줄 친 translate it from the past tense to the future tense가 다음 글에서 의미하는 바로 가장 적절한 것은? [3점]

Get past the 'I wish I hadn't done that!' reaction. If the disappointment you're feeling is linked to an exam you didn't pass because you didn't study for it, or a job you didn't get because you said silly things at the interview, or a person you didn't impress because you took entirely the wrong approach, accept that it's *happened* now. The only value of 'I wish I hadn't done that!' is that you'll know better what to do next time. The learning pay-off is useful and significant. This 'if only I ...' agenda is virtual. Once you have worked that out, it's time to translate it from the past tense to the future tense: 'Next time I'm in this situation, I'm going to try to ...'.

* agenda: 의제 ** tense: 시제

① look for a job linked to your interest
② get over regrets and plan for next time
③ surround yourself with supportive people
④ study grammar and write clear sentences
⑤ examine your way of speaking and apologize

22. 다음 글의 요지로 가장 적절한 것은?

If you care deeply about something, you may place greater value on your ability to succeed in that area of concern. The internal pressure you place on yourself to achieve or do well socially is normal and useful, but when you doubt your ability to succeed in areas that are important to you, your self-worth suffers. Situations are uniquely stressful for each of us based on whether or not they activate our doubt. It's not the pressure to perform that creates your stress. Rather, it's the self-doubt that bothers you. Doubt causes you to see positive, neutral, and even genuinely negative experiences more negatively and as a reflection of your own shortcomings. When you see situations and your strengths more objectively, you are less likely to have doubt as the source of your distress.

* distress: 괴로움

① 비판적인 시각은 객관적인 문제 분석에 도움이 된다.
② 성취 욕구는 스트레스를 이겨 낼 원동력이 될 수 있다.
③ 적절한 수준의 스트레스는 과제 수행의 효율을 높인다.
④ 실패의 경험은 자존감을 낮추고, 타인에 의존하게 한다.
⑤ 자기 의심은 스트레스를 유발하고, 객관적 판단을 흐린다.

23. 다음 글의 주제로 가장 적절한 것은?

When two people are involved in an honest and open conversation, there is a back and forth flow of information. It is a smooth exchange. Since each one is drawing on their past personal experiences, the pace of the exchange is as fast as memory. When one person lies, their responses will come more slowly because the brain needs more time to process the details of a new invention than to recall stored facts. As they say, "Timing is everything." You will notice the time lag when you are having a conversation with someone who is making things up as they go. Don't forget that the other person may be reading your body language as well, and if you seem to be disbelieving their story, they will have to pause to process that information, too.

* lag: 지연

① delayed responses as a sign of lying
② ways listeners encourage the speaker
③ difficulties in finding useful information
④ necessity of white lies in social settings
⑤ shared experiences as conversation topics

24. 다음 글의 제목으로 가장 적절한 것은?

Think, for a moment, about something you bought that you never ended up using. An item of clothing you never ended up wearing? A book you never read? Some piece of electronic equipment that never even made it out of the box? It is estimated that Australians alone spend on average $10.8 billion AUD (approximately $9.99 billion USD) every year on goods they do not use — more than the total government spending on universities and roads. That is an average of $1,250 AUD (approximately $1,156 USD) for each household. All the things we buy that then just sit there gathering dust are waste — a waste of money, a waste of time, and waste in the sense of pure rubbish. As the author Clive Hamilton observes, 'The difference between the stuff we buy and what we use is waste.'

① Spending Enables the Economy
② Money Management: Dos and Don'ts
③ Too Much Shopping: A Sign of Loneliness
④ 3R's of Waste: Reduce, Reuse, and Recycle
⑤ What You Buy Is Waste Unless You Use It

25. 다음 도표의 내용과 일치하지 <u>않는</u> 것은?

Devices Students Used to Access Digital Content

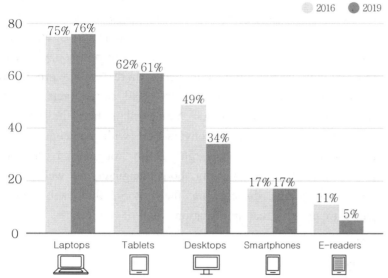

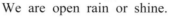

The above graph shows the percentage of students from kindergarten to 12th grade who used devices to access digital educational content in 2016 and in 2019. ① Laptops were the most used device for students to access digital content in both years. ② Both in 2016 and in 2019, more than 6 out of 10 students used tablets. ③ More than half the students used desktops to access digital content in 2016, and more than a third used desktops in 2019. ④ The percentage of smartphones in 2016 was the same as that in 2019. ⑤ E-readers ranked the lowest in both years, with 11 percent in 2016 and 5 percent in 2019.

26. Elizabeth Catlett에 관한 다음 글의 내용과 일치하지 <u>않는</u> 것은?

Elizabeth Catlett was born in Washington, D.C. in 1915. As a granddaughter of slaves, Catlett heard the stories of slaves from her grandmother. After being disallowed entrance from the Carnegie Institute of Technology because she was black, Catlett studied design and drawing at Howard University. She became one of the first three students to earn a master's degree in fine arts at the University of Iowa. Throughout her life, she created art representing the voices of people suffering from social injustice. She was recognized with many prizes and honors both in the United States and in Mexico. She spent over fifty years in Mexico, and she took Mexican citizenship in 1962. Catlett died in 2012 at her home in Mexico.

① 할머니로부터 노예 이야기를 들었다.
② Carnegie Institute of Technology로부터 입학을 거절당했다.
③ University of Iowa에서 석사 학위를 취득했다.
④ 미국과 멕시코에서 많은 상을 받았다.
⑤ 멕시코 시민권을 결국 받지 못했다.

27. Spring Farm Camp에 관한 다음 안내문의 내용과 일치하지 <u>않는</u> 것은?

Spring Farm Camp

Our one-day spring farm camp gives your kids true, hands-on farm experience.

When: Monday, April 19 − Friday, May 14
Time: 9 a.m. − 4 p.m.
Ages: 6 − 10
Participation Fee: $70 per person
      (lunch and snacks included)
Activities:
- making cheese from goat's milk
- picking strawberries
- making strawberry jam to take home

We are open rain or shine.
For more information, go to www.b_orchard.com.

---

① 6세 ~ 10세 어린이가 참가할 수 있다.
② 참가비에 점심과 간식이 포함되어 있다.
③ 염소젖으로 치즈를 만드는 활동을 한다.
④ 딸기잼을 만들어 집으로 가져갈 수 있다.
⑤ 비가 오면 운영하지 않는다.

28. Great Aquarium에 관한 다음 안내문의 내용과 일치하는 것은?

Great Aquarium

Opening Hours: 10 a.m. − 6 p.m., daily
      Last entry is at 5 p.m.

Events

Fish Feeding	10 a.m. − 11 a.m.
Penguin Feeding	1 p.m. − 2 p.m.

Ticket Prices

Age	Price
Kids (12 and under)	$25
Adults (20 − 59)	$33
Teens (13 − 19) Seniors (60 and above)	$30

* Ticket holders will receive a free drink coupon.

Booking Tickets
- ALL visitors are required to book online.
- Booking will be accepted up to 1 hour before entry.

---

① 마지막 입장 시간은 오후 6시이다.
② 물고기 먹이 주기는 오후 1시에 시작한다.
③ 60세 이상의 티켓 가격은 33달러이다.
④ 티켓 소지자는 무료 음료 쿠폰을 받는다.
⑤ 예약은 입장 30분 전까지 가능하다.

29. 다음 글의 밑줄 친 부분 중, 어법상 틀린 것은? [3점]

Although there is usually a correct way of holding and playing musical instruments, the most important instruction to begin with is ① that they are not toys and that they must be looked after. ② Allow children time to explore ways of handling and playing the instruments for themselves before showing them. Finding different ways to produce sounds ③ are an important stage of musical exploration. Correct playing comes from the desire ④ to find the most appropriate sound quality and find the most comfortable playing position so that one can play with control over time. As instruments and music become more complex, learning appropriate playing techniques becomes ⑤ increasingly relevant.

30. 다음 글의 밑줄 친 부분 중, 문맥상 낱말의 쓰임이 적절하지 <u>않은</u> 것은? [3점]

When the price of something fundamental drops greatly, the whole world can change. Consider light. Chances are you are reading this sentence under some kind of artificial light. Moreover, you probably never thought about whether using artificial light for reading was worth it. Light is so ① cheap that you use it without thinking. But in the early 1800s, it would have cost you four hundred times what you are paying now for the same amount of light. At that price, you would ② notice the cost and would think twice before using artificial light to read a book. The ③ increase in the price of light lit up the world. Not only did it turn night into day, but it allowed us to live and work in big buildings that ④ natural light could not enter. Nearly nothing we have today would be ⑤ possible if the cost of artificial light had not dropped to almost nothing.

* artificial: 인공의

[31 ~ 34] 다음 빈칸에 들어갈 말로 가장 적절한 것을 고르시오.

31. One of the most important aspects of providing good care is making sure that an animal's needs are being met consistently and predictably. Like humans, animals need a sense of control. So an animal who may get enough food but doesn't know when the food will appear and can see no consistent schedule may experience distress. We can provide a sense of control by ensuring that our animal's environment is _____: there is always water available and always in the same place. There is always food when we get up in the morning and after our evening walk. There will always be a time and place to eliminate, without having to hold things in to the point of discomfort. Human companions can display consistent emotional support, rather than providing love one moment and withholding love the next. When animals know what to expect, they can feel more confident and calm.

* eliminate: 배설하다

① silent
② natural
③ isolated
④ dynamic
⑤ predictable

32. When a child is upset, the easiest and quickest way to calm them down is to give them food. This acts as a distraction from the feelings they are having, gives them something to do with their hands and mouth and shifts their attention from whatever was upsetting them. If the food chosen is also seen as a treat such as sweets or a biscuit, then the child will feel 'treated' and happier. In the shorter term using food like this is effective. But in the longer term it can be harmful as we quickly learn that food is a good way to _____. Then as we go through life, whenever we feel annoyed, anxious or even just bored, we turn to food to make ourselves feel better.

① make friends
② learn etiquettes
③ improve memory
④ manage emotions
⑤ celebrate achievements

33. Scientists believe that the frogs' ancestors were water-dwelling, fishlike animals. The first frogs and their relatives gained the ability to come out on land and enjoy the opportunities for food and shelter there. But they _____. A frog's lungs do not work very well, and it gets part of its oxygen by breathing through its skin. But for this kind of "breathing" to work properly, the frog's skin must stay moist. And so the frog must remain near the water where it can take a dip every now and then to keep from drying out. Frogs must also lay their eggs in water, as their fishlike ancestors did. And eggs laid in the water must develop into water creatures, if they are to survive. For frogs, metamorphosis thus provides the bridge between the water-dwelling young forms and the land-dwelling adults. [3점]

　　　　　　　　　　　　　　　　* metamorphosis: 탈바꿈

① still kept many ties to the water
② had almost all the necessary organs
③ had to develop an appetite for new foods
④ often competed with land-dwelling species
⑤ suffered from rapid changes in temperature

34. It is important to distinguish between being legally allowed to do something, and actually being able to go and do it. A law could be passed allowing everyone, if they so wish, to run a mile in two minutes. That would not, however, increase their *effective* freedom, because, although allowed to do so, they are physically incapable of it. Having a minimum of restrictions and a maximum of possibilities is fine. But in the real world most people will never have the opportunity either to become all that they are allowed to become, or to need to be restrained from doing everything that is possible for them to do. Their effective freedom depends on actually _____. [3점]

　　　　　　* restriction: 제약　** restrain: 저지하다

① respecting others' rights to freedom
② protecting and providing for the needy
③ learning what socially acceptable behaviors are
④ determining how much they can expect from others
⑤ having the means and ability to do what they choose

35. 다음 글에서 전체 흐름과 관계 <u>없는</u> 문장은?

　Today's music business has allowed musicians to take matters into their own hands. ① Gone are the days of musicians waiting for a gatekeeper (someone who holds power and prevents you from being let in) at a label or TV show to say they are worthy of the spotlight. ② In today's music business, you don't need to ask for permission to build a fanbase and you no longer need to pay thousands of dollars to a company to do it. ③ There are rising concerns over the marketing of child musicians using TV auditions. ④ Every day, musicians are getting their music out to thousands of listeners without any outside help. ⑤ They simply deliver it to the fans directly, without asking for permission or outside help to receive exposure or connect with thousands of listeners.

[36~37] 주어진 글 다음에 이어질 글의 순서로 가장 적절한 것을 고르시오.

36.

　Almost all major sporting activities are played with a ball.

(A) A ball might have the correct size and weight but if it is made as a hollow ball of steel it will be too stiff and if it is made from light foam rubber with a heavy center it will be too soft.

(B) The rules of the game always include rules about the type of ball that is allowed, starting with the size and weight of the ball. The ball must also have a certain stiffness.

(C) Similarly, along with stiffness, a ball needs to bounce properly. A solid rubber ball would be too bouncy for most sports, and a solid ball made of clay would not bounce at all.

　　　　　　　　　　　　　　　　　* stiffness: 단단함

① (A) − (C) − (B)　　　　② (B) − (A) − (C)
③ (B) − (C) − (A)　　　　④ (C) − (A) − (B)
⑤ (C) − (B) − (A)

37.

If you had to write a math equation, you probably wouldn't write, "Twenty-eight plus fourteen equals forty-two." It would take too long to write and it would be hard to read quickly.

(A) For example, the chemical formula for water is H_2O. That tells us that a water molecule is made up of two hydrogen ("H" and "2") atoms and one oxygen ("O") atom.

(B) You would write, "28 + 14 = 42." Chemistry is the same way. Chemists have to write chemical equations all the time, and it would take too long to write and read if they had to spell everything out.

(C) So chemists use symbols, just like we do in math. A chemical formula lists all the elements that form each molecule and uses a small number to the bottom right of an element's symbol to stand for the number of atoms of that element. [3점]

* chemical formula: 화학식 ** molecule: 분자

① (A) − (C) − (B)   ② (B) − (A) − (C)
③ (B) − (C) − (A)   ④ (C) − (A) − (B)
⑤ (C) − (B) − (A)

[38 ~ 39] 글의 흐름으로 보아, 주어진 문장이 들어가기에 가장 적절한 곳을 고르시오.

38.

Meanwhile, improving by 1 percent isn't particularly notable, but it can be far more meaningful in the long run.

It is so easy to overestimate the importance of one defining moment and underestimate the value of making small improvements on a daily basis. Too often, we convince ourselves that massive success requires massive action. (①) Whether it is losing weight, winning a championship, or achieving any other goal, we put pressure on ourselves to make some earthshaking improvement that everyone will talk about. (②) The difference this tiny improvement can make over time is surprising. (③) Here's how the math works out: if you can get 1 percent better each day for one year, you'll end up thirty-seven times better by the time you're done. (④) Conversely, if you get 1 percent worse each day for one year, you'll decline nearly down to zero. (⑤) What starts as a small win or a minor failure adds up to something much more.

39.

Before a trip, research how the native inhabitants dress, work, and eat.

The continued survival of the human race can be explained by our ability to adapt to our environment. (①) While we may have lost some of our ancient ancestors' survival skills, we have learned new skills as they have become necessary. (②) Today, the gap between the skills we once had and the skills we now have grows ever wider as we rely more heavily on modern technology. (③) Therefore, when you head off into the wilderness, it is important to fully prepare for the environment. (④) How they have adapted to their way of life will help you to understand the environment and allow you to select the best gear and learn the correct skills. (⑤) This is crucial because most survival situations arise as a result of a series of events that could have been avoided. [3점]

* inhabitant: 주민

40. 다음 글의 내용을 한 문장으로 요약하고자 한다. 빈칸 (A), (B)에 들어갈 말로 가장 적절한 것은?

In one study, researchers asked pairs of strangers to sit down in a room and chat. In half of the rooms, a cell phone was placed on a nearby table; in the other half, no phone was present. After the conversations had ended, the researchers asked the participants what they thought of each other. Here's what they learned: when a cell phone was present in the room, the participants reported the quality of their relationship was worse than those who'd talked in a cell phone-free room. The pairs who talked in the rooms with cell phones thought their partners showed less empathy. Think of all the times you've sat down to have lunch with a friend and set your phone on the table. You might have felt good about yourself because you didn't pick it up to check your messages, but your unchecked messages were still hurting your connection with the person sitting across from you.

* empathy: 공감

↓

The presence of a cell phone   (A)   the connection between people involved in conversations, even when the phone is being   (B)   .

	(A)		(B)
①	weakens	…….	answered
②	weakens	…….	ignored
③	renews	…….	answered
④	maintains	…….	ignored
⑤	maintains	…….	updated

[41 ~ 42] 다음 글을 읽고, 물음에 답하시오.

As kids, we worked hard at learning to ride a bike; when we fell off, we got back on again, until it became second nature to us. But when we try something new in our adult lives we'll usually make just one attempt before judging whether it's (a) worked. If we don't succeed the first time, or if it feels a little awkward, we'll tell ourselves it wasn't a success rather than giving it (b) another shot.

That's a shame, because repetition is central to the process of rewiring our brains. Consider the idea that your brain has a network of neurons. They will (c) connect with each other whenever you remember to use a brain-friendly feedback technique. Those connections aren't very (d) reliable at first, which may make your first efforts a little hit-and-miss. You might remember one of the steps involved, and not the others. But scientists have a saying: "neurons that fire together, wire together." In other words, repetition of an action (e) blocks the connections between the neurons involved in that action. That means the more times you try using that new feedback technique, the more easily it will come to you when you need it.

41. 윗글의 제목으로 가장 적절한 것은?

① Repeat and You Will Succeed
② Be More Curious, Be Smarter
③ Play Is What Makes Us Human
④ Stop and Think Before You Act
⑤ Growth Is All About Keeping Balance

42. 밑줄 친 (a) ~ (e) 중에서 문맥상 낱말의 쓰임이 적절하지 않은 것은?

① (a)　　② (b)　　③ (c)　　④ (d)　　⑤ (e)

[43 ~ 45] 다음 글을 읽고, 물음에 답하시오.

(A)

Once upon a time, there lived a young king who had a great passion for hunting. His kingdom was located at the foot of the Himalayas. Once every year, he would go hunting in the nearby forests. (a) He would make all the necessary preparations, and then set out for his hunting trip.

(B)

Seasons changed. A year passed by. And it was time to go hunting once again. The king went to the same forest as the previous year. (b) He used his beautiful deerskin drum to round up animals. But none came. All the animals ran for safety, except one doe. She came closer and closer to the drummer. Suddenly, she started fearlessly licking the deerskin drum.

　　　　　* round up: ~을 몰다　** doe: 암사슴

(C)

Like all other years, the hunting season had arrived. Preparations began in the palace and the king got ready for (c) his hunting trip. Deep in the forest, he spotted a beautiful wild deer. It was a large stag. His aim was perfect. When he killed the deer with just one shot of his arrow, the king was filled with pride. (d) The proud hunter ordered a hunting drum to be made out of the skin of the deer.

　　　　　* stag: 수사슴

(D)

The king was surprised by this sight. An old servant had an answer to this strange behavior. "The deerskin used to make this drum belonged to her mate, the deer who we hunted last year. This doe is mourning the death of her mate," (e) the man said. Upon hearing this, the king had a change of heart. He had never realized that an animal, too, felt the pain of loss. He made a promise, from that day on, to never again hunt wild animals.

　　　　　* mourn: 애도하다

43. 주어진 글 (A)에 이어질 내용을 순서에 맞게 배열한 것으로 가장 적절한 것은?

① (B) − (D) − (C)　　　　② (C) − (B) − (D)
③ (C) − (D) − (B)　　　　④ (D) − (B) − (C)
⑤ (D) − (C) − (B)

44. 밑줄 친 (a) ~ (e) 중에서 가리키는 대상이 나머지 넷과 <u>다른</u> 것은?

① (a)　　② (b)　　③ (c)　　④ (d)　　⑤ (e)

45. 윗글에 관한 내용으로 적절하지 <u>않은</u> 것은?

① 왕은 매년 근처의 숲으로 사냥 여행을 갔다.
② 암사슴은 북 치는 사람으로부터 도망갔다.
③ 왕은 화살로 단번에 수사슴을 맞혔다.
④ 한 나이 든 신하가 암사슴의 행동의 이유를 알고 있었다.
⑤ 왕은 다시는 야생 동물을 사냥하지 않겠다고 약속했다.

★ 확인 사항
○ 답안지의 해당란에 필요한 내용을 정확히 기입(표기) 했는지 확인하시오.

VOCA LIST 06

01
- 001 □ administration office 행정실
- 002 □ rainstorm ⓝ 폭풍우
- 003 □ pouring ⓐ 쏟아지는
- 004 □ hallway ⓝ 복도
- 005 □ slippery ⓐ 미끄러운
- 006 □ stairway ⓝ 계단
- 007 □ especially ⓐⓓ 특히
- 008 □ careful ⓐ 조심하는
- 009 □ seriously ⓐⓓ 심각하게
- 010 □ hurt ⓐ 다친
- 011 □ slip ⓥ 미끄러지다
- 012 □ take care of ～을 처리하다

02
- 013 □ tired ⓐ 피곤한
- 014 □ having trouble ~ing ～하는 데 어려움을 겪다
- 015 □ fall asleep 잠들다
- 016 □ handle ⓥ 해결하다
- 017 □ pillow ⓝ 베개
- 018 □ tip ⓝ 조언, 팁
- 019 □ work ⓥ 효과가 있다

03
- 020 □ hold a party 파티를 하다
- 021 □ take charge of ～의 책임을 지다
- 022 □ depend on ～에 의존하다
- 023 □ chef ⓝ 요리사
- 024 □ No need. 그럴 것 없습니다.
- 025 □ fantastic ⓐ 환상적인

04
- 026 □ lecture ⓝ 강의
- 027 □ face ⓥ ～을 향하다
- 028 □ latest ⓐ 최신의
- 029 □ next to ～ 옆에
- 030 □ lighting ⓝ 조명
- 031 □ brighten ⓥ 밝히다
- 032 □ shoot ⓥ 촬영하다
- 033 □ microphone ⓝ 마이크
- 034 □ professional ⓐ 전문적인
- 035 □ go well with ～와 잘 어울리다

05
- 036 □ go to the movies 영화 보러 가다
- 037 □ discount ⓝ 할인
- 038 □ bring ⓥ 가져오다
- 039 □ office ⓝ 사무실
- 040 □ right away 즉시, 바로

06
- 041 □ recommend ⓥ 추천하다
- 042 □ bestselling ⓐ 가장 잘 팔리는
- 043 □ knife ⓝ 칼
- 044 □ convenient ⓐ 편리한
- 045 □ total ⓐ 전체의
- 046 □ purchase ⓝ 구입

07
- 047 □ borrow ⓥ 빌리다
- 048 □ report ⓝ 보고서

- 049 □ due ⓐ (제출) 기한인
- 050 □ experiment ⓝ 실험
- 051 □ experimental ⓐ 실험의

08
- 052 □ sign up for ～을 신청하다
- 053 □ race ⓝ 경주
- 054 □ upload ⓥ 업로드하다
- 055 □ record ⓝ 기록
- 056 □ location ⓝ 장소
- 057 □ registration fee 참가비
- 058 □ souvenir ⓝ 기념품
- 059 □ reasonable ⓐ 적당한

09
- 060 □ adventure ⓝ 모험
- 061 □ natural history 자연사
- 062 □ regular ⓐ 정규의
- 063 □ flashlight ⓝ 손전등
- 064 □ complete ⓐ 끝마친
- 065 □ planet ⓝ 행성
- 066 □ sleeping bag 침낭
- 067 □ register ⓥ 등록하다
- 068 □ in advance 미리
- 069 □ on-site ⓐ 현장의
- 070 □ registration ⓝ 등록
- 071 □ accept ⓥ 받아들이다

10
- 072 □ waterproof ⓐ 방수의
- 073 □ warranty ⓝ 보증 기간
- 074 □ option ⓝ 선택(할 수 있는 것), 선택권
- 075 □ go with ～을 선택하다

11
- 076 □ missing ⓐ 없어진, 빠진
- 077 □ button ⓝ 단추
- 078 □ exchange ⓥ 교환하다

12
- 079 □ delicious ⓐ 맛있는
- 080 □ meet ⓥ 만나다
- 081 □ around ⓐⓓ 약, ～쯤
- 082 □ by oneself 혼자서
- 083 □ share ⓥ 공유하다

13
- 084 □ reusable ⓐ 재사용할 수 있는
- 085 □ reduce ⓥ 줄이다
- 086 □ footprint ⓝ 발자국
- 087 □ amount ⓝ 양
- 088 □ throw away 버리다
- 089 □ huge ⓐ 큰
- 090 □ straw ⓝ 빨대

14
- 091 □ cool ⓐ 멋있는
- 092 □ refreshing ⓐ 상쾌하게 하는
- 093 □ together ⓐⓓ 같이
- 094 □ be good at ～을 잘하다
- 095 □ slowly ⓐⓓ 천천히
- 096 □ safety ⓝ 안전

15
- 097 □ form ⓥ 결성하다, 구성하다
- 098 □ competition ⓝ 경연 대회
- 099 □ audition ⓝ 오디션
- 100 □ completely ⓐⓓ 완전히
- 101 □ practice ⓝ 연습
- 102 □ amazed ⓐ 놀란
- 103 □ perfect ⓐ 완벽한
- 104 □ How about ~ing ～하는 게 어때?

16~17
- 105 □ companion ⓝ 동반자, 친구
- 106 □ pet ⓝ 반려동물
- 107 □ play a role in ～에 역할을 하다, 일조하다
- 108 □ scratcher ⓝ 긁는 장난감
- 109 □ tool ⓝ 도구
- 110 □ wheel toy 쳇바퀴 장난감
- 111 □ bond ⓝ 유대
- 112 □ joyful ⓐ 아주 기뻐하는, 행복한
- 113 □ entertain ⓥ 즐겁게 해 주다
- 114 □ parrot ⓝ 앵무새

18
- 115 □ successfully ⓐⓓ 성공적으로
- 116 □ raise ⓥ (돈을) 모으다
- 117 □ enough ⓐ 충분한
- 118 □ remodel ⓥ 개조하다, 리모델링하다
- 119 □ local ⓐ 지역의
- 120 □ builder ⓝ 건축업자
- 121 □ volunteer ⓥ 자원하다
- 122 □ assistance ⓝ 도움
- 123 □ grab ⓥ 쥐다
- 124 □ hammer ⓝ 망치
- 125 □ donate ⓥ 기부하다
- 126 □ construction ⓝ 공사, 건설
- 127 □ become ⓥ …(해)지다, …이 되다
- 128 □ place ⓝ 곳, 장소

19
- 129 □ notice ⓥ 알아차리다
- 130 □ park ⓥ 주차하다
- 131 □ across the street 길 건너에
- 132 □ neighbor ⓝ 이웃
- 133 □ be dying to 간절히 ～하고 싶어 하다
- 134 □ interesting ⓐ 흥미를 끄는
- 135 □ joyfully ⓐⓓ 즐겁게
- 136 □ playmate ⓝ 놀이 친구
- 137 □ drop ⓥ 떨어뜨리다
- 138 □ floor ⓝ 바닥
- 139 □ pray ⓥ 기도하다
- 140 □ curious ⓐ 호기심이 많은
- 141 □ upset ⓐ 속상한
- 142 □ jealous ⓐ 질투 나는
- 143 □ disappointed ⓐ 실망한

20
- 144 □ publishing house 출판사
- 145 □ following ⓝ 다음에[아래] 나오는[언급되는]
- 146 □ mistake ⓝ 실수
- 147 □ end up 결국 ～이 되다
- 148 □ in print 출간되는, 발표되는
- 149 □ happen ⓥ 일어나다

- 150 □ misspelling ⓝ 오탈자
- 151 □ fact ⓝ 사실
- 152 □ rude ⓐ 무례한
- 153 □ comment ⓝ 말
- 154 □ obvious ⓐ 명백한
- 155 □ matter ⓥ 문제가 되다
- 156 □ fix ⓥ 고치다
- 157 □ correct ⓥ 수정하다
- 158 □ easier said than done 행동보다 말이 쉽다
- 159 □ attractive ⓐ 매력적인
- 160 □ command ⓝ 명령(어) ⓥ 명령하다
- 161 □ make sure that 반드시 ～을 하다
- 162 □ document ⓝ 문서, 서류
- 163 □ carefully ⓐⓓ 주의 깊게

21
- 164 □ get past 지나가다, 추월하다
- 165 □ reaction ⓝ 반응
- 166 □ disappointment ⓝ 실망
- 167 □ be linked to ～과 연관되다
- 168 □ pass ⓥ 통과하다
- 169 □ silly ⓐ 바보 같은
- 170 □ interview ⓝ 면접, 인터뷰
- 171 □ impress ⓥ 인상을 주다
- 172 □ entirely ⓐⓓ 완전히, 전적으로
- 173 □ wrong ⓐ 잘못된
- 174 □ approach ⓝ 접근 방법
- 175 □ accept ⓥ 받아들이다
- 176 □ value ⓝ 가치
- 177 □ pay-off ⓝ 이득, 보상
- 178 □ useful ⓐ 유용한
- 179 □ significant ⓐ 의미가 있는, 중요한
- 180 □ virtual ⓐ 가상의
- 181 □ work ~ out ～을 파악하다
- 182 □ translate ⓥ 바꾸다, 번역하다
- 183 □ situation ⓝ 상황
- 184 □ get over ～을 극복하다
- 185 □ surround ⓥ 둘러싸다
- 186 □ supportive ⓐ 힘이 되는, 지지를 주는
- 187 □ grammar ⓝ 문법
- 188 □ sentence ⓝ 문장
- 189 □ examine ⓥ 검토하다, 조사하다
- 190 □ apologize ⓥ 사과하다

22
- 191 □ care about ～에 관심을 두다, ～을 걱정하다
- 192 □ place value on ～에 가치를 두다
- 193 □ ability ⓝ 능력
- 194 □ area ⓝ 영역, 분야
- 195 □ concern ⓝ 관심, 걱정
- 196 □ internal ⓐ 내적인
- 197 □ pressure ⓝ 압박, 압력
- 198 □ achieve ⓥ 성취하다
- 199 □ do well 성공하다
- 200 □ socially ⓐⓓ 사회적으로
- 201 □ normal ⓐ 정상적인, 일반적인
- 202 □ doubt ⓝ 의심 ⓥ 의심하다
- 203 □ self-worth ⓝ 자아 존중감, 자기 가치감
- 204 □ suffer ⓥ 상처를 입다, 괴로워하다
- 205 □ uniquely ⓐⓓ 특유의 방법으로, 독특하게

206 ☐ activate ⓥ 활성화하다	25	315 ☐ handle ⓥ 다루다	370 ☐ quick ⓐ 빠른
207 ☐ self-doubt ⓝ 자기 의심	263 ☐ device ⓝ 기기, 장치	316 ☐ produce ⓥ 만들어 내다, 생산하다	371 ☐ calm ~ down ~을 진정시키다
208 ☐ bother ⓥ 괴롭히다	264 ☐ access ⓥ 이용하다, 접근하다, 접속하다	317 ☐ stage ⓝ 단계	372 ☐ act as ~으로 작용하다
209 ☐ positive ⓐ 긍정적인	265 ☐ laptop ⓝ 노트북 (컴퓨터)	318 ☐ desire ⓝ 욕구, 욕망	373 ☐ distraction ⓝ 정신을 분산시키는 것,
210 ☐ neutral ⓐ 중립적인	266 ☐ e-reader ⓝ 전자책 단말기	319 ☐ appropriate ⓐ 적절한	주의를 돌리는 것
211 ☐ genuinely ⓐ 진정으로	267 ☐ kindergarten ⓝ 유치원	320 ☐ quality ⓝ 질, 품질	374 ☐ shift ⓥ 돌리다, 바꾸다
212 ☐ negative ⓐ 부정적인	268 ☐ educational ⓐ 교육의	321 ☐ comfortable ⓐ 편안한	375 ☐ upsetting ⓐ 속상하게 하는
213 ☐ reflection ⓝ 반영	269 ☐ a third 3분의 1	322 ☐ complex ⓐ 복잡한	376 ☐ attention ⓝ 주의
214 ☐ shortcoming ⓝ 단점	270 ☐ rank ⓥ 순위를 차지하다	323 ☐ increasingly ⓐ 점점 더	377 ☐ see A as B A를 B로 간주하다
215 ☐ strength ⓝ 강점	271 ☐ lowest ⓐ 최하의, 최저의	324 ☐ relevant ⓐ 유의미한, 적절한, 관련 있는	378 ☐ treat ⓝ 간식 ⓥ 대접하다
216 ☐ objectively ⓐ 객관적으로			379 ☐ sweet ⓝ 사탕, 단 것
217 ☐ source ⓝ 원천, 근원	26	30	380 ☐ effective ⓐ 효과적인
	272 ☐ born ⓥ 태어나다	325 ☐ price ⓝ 가격	381 ☐ harmful ⓐ 해로운
23	273 ☐ heard ⓥ 듣다	326 ☐ fundamental ⓐ 기본적인	382 ☐ quickly ⓐ 빨리, 곧
218 ☐ be involved in ~에 참여하다, ~과 관련	274 ☐ slave ⓝ 노예	327 ☐ drop ⓥ 하락하다, 떨어지다 ⓝ 하락	383 ☐ annoyed ⓐ 짜증 난
되다	275 ☐ disallow ⓥ (공식적으로) 거절하다,	328 ☐ consider ⓥ 생각하다	384 ☐ anxious ⓐ 불안한
219 ☐ honest ⓐ 솔직한	인정하지 않다	329 ☐ chances are 아마 ~일 것이다	385 ☐ bored ⓐ 지루한
220 ☐ conversation ⓝ 대화	276 ☐ entrance ⓝ 입학, 입장	330 ☐ artificial ⓐ 인공의	386 ☐ turn to ~에 의지하다
221 ☐ back and forth 왔다 갔다하는	277 ☐ drawing ⓝ 소묘, 데생	331 ☐ probably ⓐ 아마	387 ☐ etiquettes ⓝ 예의[에티켓]
222 ☐ information ⓝ 정보	278 ☐ earn ⓥ 얻다, 취득하다	332 ☐ worth ⓐ ~의 가치가 있는	388 ☐ improve ⓥ 개선하다, 향상시키다
223 ☐ personal ⓐ 개인적인	279 ☐ master's degree 석사 학위	333 ☐ cheap ⓐ 값이 싼	389 ☐ emotion ⓝ 감정, 정서
224 ☐ smooth ⓐ 순조로운, 원활히 진행되는	280 ☐ fine arts 순수 미술	334 ☐ cost ⓝ 비용 ⓥ (~에게 …의 비용을) 요하다,	390 ☐ celebrate ⓥ 축하하다
225 ☐ exchange ⓝ 대화, 주고받음, 교환	281 ☐ represent ⓥ 대표하다, 나타내다	치르게 하다	391 ☐ achievement ⓝ 성취
226 ☐ draw on ~에 의존하다, ~을 이용하다	282 ☐ voice ⓝ 목소리	335 ☐ pay ⓥ 지불하다	
227 ☐ pace ⓝ 속도	283 ☐ suffer from ~으로 고통받다	336 ☐ amount ⓝ 총액, 총계	33
228 ☐ lie ⓥ 거짓말하다	284 ☐ injustice ⓝ 불평등, 부당함	337 ☐ increase ⓝ 증가	392 ☐ ancestor ⓝ 조상
229 ☐ response ⓝ 반응	285 ☐ recognize ⓥ 인정하다	338 ☐ light up (불을) 밝히다	393 ☐ dwell ⓥ 거주하다, 살다
230 ☐ process ⓥ 처리하다	286 ☐ honor ⓝ 표창, 명예	339 ☐ turn ~ into ... ~을 …으로 바꾸다	394 ☐ water-dwelling ⓐ 물에 사는
231 ☐ detail ⓝ 세부 사항	287 ☐ citizenship ⓝ 시민권	340 ☐ nearly ⓐ 거의	395 ☐ fishlike ⓐ 물고기와 같은
232 ☐ invention ⓝ 꾸며 낸 이야기, 창작		341 ☐ possible ⓐ 가능한	396 ☐ relative ⓝ 친척
233 ☐ recall ⓥ 회상하다	27		397 ☐ gain ⓥ 얻다
234 ☐ stored ⓐ 저장된	288 ☐ hands-on ⓐ 직접 해 보는, 체험의	31	398 ☐ opportunity ⓝ 기회, 가능성
235 ☐ make up 만들어내다, 꾸며내다	289 ☐ experience ⓝ 경험	342 ☐ important ⓐ 중요한	399 ☐ shelter ⓝ 살 곳, 쉼터, 은신처
236 ☐ disbelieve ⓥ 불신하다, 믿지 않다	290 ☐ participation fee 참가비	343 ☐ aspect ⓝ 측면	400 ☐ lung ⓝ 폐
237 ☐ pause ⓥ 잠시 멈추다	291 ☐ include ⓥ 포함하다	344 ☐ provide ⓥ 제공하다, 주다	401 ☐ oxygen ⓝ 산소
238 ☐ delay ⓥ 지연하다	292 ☐ activity ⓝ 활동	345 ☐ care ⓝ 돌봄, 보살핌	402 ☐ breathe ⓥ 호흡하다
239 ☐ encourage ⓥ 격려하다	293 ☐ goat ⓝ 염소	346 ☐ need ⓝ 욕구	403 ☐ skin ⓝ 피부
240 ☐ necessity ⓝ 필요성	294 ☐ pick ⓥ 따다, 줍다	347 ☐ consistently ⓐ 일관적으로	404 ☐ properly ⓐ 적절히
	295 ☐ rain or shine 날씨에 상관없이	348 ☐ predictably ⓐ 예측 가능하게	405 ☐ moist ⓐ 촉촉한
24		349 ☐ sense of control 통제감	406 ☐ take a dip 잠깐 수영을 하다
241 ☐ an item of clothing 옷 한 벌	28	350 ☐ appear ⓥ 보이게 되다	407 ☐ every now and then 이따금
242 ☐ electronic ⓐ 전자의	296 ☐ aquarium ⓝ 수족관	351 ☐ schedule ⓝ 일정	408 ☐ dry out 건조하다, 바짝 마르다
243 ☐ equipment ⓝ 기기, 장비	297 ☐ daily ⓐ 매일 일어나는, 나날의	352 ☐ distress ⓝ 괴로움	409 ☐ lay ⓥ (알을) 낳다
244 ☐ estimate ⓥ 추산하다	298 ☐ entry ⓝ 입장	353 ☐ ensure ⓥ 반드시 ~하다, 보장하다	410 ☐ develop ⓥ 발달하다, 성장하다
245 ☐ spend ⓥ 쓰다, 소비하다	299 ☐ feeding ⓝ 먹이 주기	354 ☐ environment ⓝ 환경	411 ☐ creature ⓝ 생물
246 ☐ average ⓝ 평균	300 ☐ teen ⓝ 십대	355 ☐ get up 일어나다	412 ☐ bridge ⓝ 다리
247 ☐ billion ⓝ 십 억	301 ☐ senior ⓝ 노인	356 ☐ walk ⓝ 산책	413 ☐ land-dwelling ⓐ 육지에 사는
248 ☐ approximately ⓐ 대략	302 ☐ above prep …보다 많은, …을 넘는	357 ☐ hold ~ in ~을 참다	414 ☐ adult ⓝ 성체
249 ☐ goods ⓝ 물건, 제품, 상품	303 ☐ holder ⓝ 소지자	358 ☐ to the point of ~할 수 있을 정도로	415 ☐ tie ⓝ 관계, 연결
250 ☐ government ⓝ 정부	304 ☐ receive ⓥ 받다, 받아들이다	359 ☐ discomfort ⓝ 불편함	416 ☐ necessary ⓐ 필요한
251 ☐ university ⓝ 대학	305 ☐ booking ⓝ 예약	360 ☐ display ⓥ 보이다, 나타내다	417 ☐ organ ⓝ (신체) 기관
252 ☐ household ⓝ 가구, 세대	306 ☐ visitor ⓝ 방문객	361 ☐ emotional ⓐ 정서적인	418 ☐ appetite ⓝ 식욕
253 ☐ gather ⓥ 모으다	307 ☐ up to ~까지	362 ☐ support ⓝ 지지, 뒷받침	419 ☐ compete with ~와 경쟁하다
254 ☐ dust ⓝ 먼지		363 ☐ moment ⓝ 순간	420 ☐ rapid ⓐ 빠른
255 ☐ waste ⓝ 낭비, 쓰레기	29	364 ☐ withhold ⓥ 주지 않다	421 ☐ temperature ⓝ 온도, 기온, 체온
256 ☐ in the sense of ~이라는 의미에서	308 ☐ although conj (비록) …이긴 하지만	365 ☐ expect ⓥ 기대하다	
257 ☐ pure ⓐ 순전한, 순수한	309 ☐ usually ⓐ 보통, 대개	366 ☐ confident ⓐ 자신감 있는	34
258 ☐ rubbish ⓝ 쓰레기	310 ☐ correct ⓐ 맞는, 정확한	367 ☐ calm ⓐ 차분한, 온화한	422 ☐ distinguish ⓥ 구별하다
259 ☐ author ⓝ 작가, 저자	311 ☐ instrument ⓝ 악기, 도구	368 ☐ isolated ⓐ 고립된	423 ☐ legally ⓐ 법적으로
260 ☐ observe ⓥ 말하다, 관찰하다	312 ☐ instruction ⓝ 지침, 가르침		424 ☐ allowed ⓐ 허가받은, 허용된
261 ☐ difference ⓝ 뺀 것, (양의) 차이	313 ☐ look after ~을 관리하다, 돌보다	32	425 ☐ actually ⓐ 실제로, 사실
262 ☐ stuff ⓝ 물건	314 ☐ explore ⓥ 탐구하다	369 ☐ upset ⓝ 화남 ⓥ 화나게 하다	426 ☐ be able to ~을 할 수 있다

427 ☐ freedom ⓝ 자유
428 ☐ physically ⓐd 신체적으로, 물리적으로
429 ☐ be incapable of ~을 할 수 없다
430 ☐ minimum ⓐ 최소한
431 ☐ maximum ⓐ 최대한
432 ☐ possibility ⓝ 가능성
433 ☐ restrain ⓥ 저지[제지]하다
434 ☐ depend on ~에 좌우되다
435 ☐ needy ⓐ (경제적으로) 어려운, 궁핍한
436 ☐ acceptable ⓐ 허용 가능한, 수용 가능한
437 ☐ means ⓝ 수단

35
438 ☐ business ⓝ 사업
439 ☐ take matters into one's own hands
      스스로 일을 추진하다, 일을 독자적으로 하다
440 ☐ gone ⓐ (특정한 상황이) 끝난
441 ☐ gatekeeper ⓝ 문지기, 수위
442 ☐ prevent ⓥ 막다
443 ☐ let in ~을 들여 보내다
444 ☐ label ⓝ 음반사
445 ☐ be worthy of ~을 받을 만하다
446 ☐ spotlight ⓝ 주목
447 ☐ ask for ~을 요청하다
448 ☐ permission ⓝ 허락, 허가
449 ☐ fanbase ⓝ 팬층
450 ☐ rising ⓐ 증가하는
451 ☐ concern ⓝ 우려
452 ☐ outside ⓐ 바깥쪽의, 외부의
453 ☐ simply ⓐd 간단히, 단순히
454 ☐ deliver ⓥ 전달하다
455 ☐ directly ⓐd 직접, 곧장
456 ☐ exposure ⓝ 노출, 매스컴 출연
457 ☐ connect ⓥ 잇다, 연결하다

36
458 ☐ major ⓐ 주요한
459 ☐ hollow ⓐ (속이) 빈
460 ☐ steel ⓝ 강철
461 ☐ stiff ⓐ 단단한
462 ☐ light ⓐ 가벼운
463 ☐ foam rubber 발포 고무
464 ☐ center ⓝ 중심부, 중앙
465 ☐ type ⓝ 유형
466 ☐ weight ⓝ 무게
467 ☐ certain ⓐ 확실한, 틀림없는
468 ☐ bounce ⓥ 튀어오르다
469 ☐ solid ⓐ 순수한(다른 물질이 섞이지 않은)
470 ☐ rubber ⓝ 고무
471 ☐ clay ⓝ 점토

37
472 ☐ math ⓝ 수학
473 ☐ equation ⓝ 방정식, 등식
474 ☐ equal ⓥ 같다
475 ☐ be made up of ~으로 구성되다, 이루어
      지다
476 ☐ hydrogen ⓝ 수소
477 ☐ atom ⓝ 원자
478 ☐ chemistry ⓝ 화학
479 ☐ chemist ⓝ 화학자
480 ☐ all the time 항상

481 ☐ spell out 상세히 말하다
482 ☐ symbol ⓝ 기호
483 ☐ list ⓥ 나열하다, 열거하다
484 ☐ element ⓝ 원소, 요소
485 ☐ bottom ⓝ 아래
486 ☐ stand for ~을 나타내다[대표하다]

38
487 ☐ meanwhile ⓐd 한편
488 ☐ particularly ⓐd 특별히
489 ☐ notable ⓐ 눈에 띄는, 두드러지는
490 ☐ meaningful ⓐ 의미 있는
491 ☐ in the long run 장기적으로
492 ☐ overestimate ⓥ 과대평가하다
493 ☐ defining ⓐ 결정적인, 정의하는
494 ☐ underestimate ⓥ 과소평가하다
495 ☐ on a daily basis 매일
496 ☐ convince ⓥ 납득시키다, 설득하다
497 ☐ massive ⓐ 거대한
498 ☐ success ⓝ 성공
499 ☐ require ⓥ 필요로 하다
500 ☐ action ⓝ 행동, 조치
501 ☐ lose weight 체중을 줄이다
502 ☐ win a championship 결승전에서 이기다
503 ☐ put pressure on ~에 압박을 가하다
504 ☐ earthshaking ⓐ 극히 중대한,
      세상을 떠들썩하게 하는
505 ☐ tiny ⓐ 극히 작은
506 ☐ over time 시간이 지남에 따라
507 ☐ conversely ⓐd 역으로
508 ☐ decline ⓥ 떨어지다, 감소하다
509 ☐ minor ⓐ 사소한
510 ☐ failure ⓝ 패배

39
511 ☐ research ⓥ 조사하다, 연구하다
512 ☐ native ⓐ 토착의, 지방 고유의
513 ☐ survival ⓝ 생존
514 ☐ human race ⓝ 인류
515 ☐ adapt to ~에 적응하다
516 ☐ ancient ⓐ 고대의
517 ☐ skill ⓝ 기술
518 ☐ gap ⓝ 간극, 격차
519 ☐ rely on ~에 의존하다
520 ☐ heavily ⓐd 심하게, 많이
521 ☐ modern ⓐ 현대의
522 ☐ technology ⓝ 기술
523 ☐ head off ~로 향하다
524 ☐ wilderness ⓝ 황무지
525 ☐ prepare ⓥ 준비하다, 대비하다
526 ☐ gear ⓝ 장비
527 ☐ crucial ⓐ 매우 중요한
528 ☐ arise ⓥ 발생하다, 일어나다
529 ☐ as a result of ~의 결과로
530 ☐ event ⓝ 사건
531 ☐ avoid ⓥ 피하다

40
532 ☐ study ⓝ 공부[연구], 학습, 학문
533 ☐ researcher ⓝ 연구원, 조사원, 탐색자
534 ☐ pair ⓝ 짝
535 ☐ stranger ⓝ 모르는 사람, 낯선 사람

536 ☐ chat ⓥ 이야기하다
537 ☐ cell phone 휴대폰
538 ☐ place ⓥ 놓다, 두다
539 ☐ nearby ⓐ 근처의
540 ☐ present ⓐ 존재하는
541 ☐ participant ⓝ 참가자
542 ☐ report ⓥ 말하다, 전하다
543 ☐ relationship ⓝ 관계
544 ☐ partner ⓝ 상대
545 ☐ empathy ⓝ 감정이입, 공감
546 ☐ unchecked ⓐ 확인되지 않은
547 ☐ hurt ⓥ 손상시키다, 다치게 하다
548 ☐ connection ⓝ 관계, 연결
549 ☐ involved ⓐ 관여하는, 관련된, 연루된
550 ☐ weaken ⓥ 약화시키다
551 ☐ answer ⓥ 대답하다, 대응하다
552 ☐ ignore ⓥ 무시하다
553 ☐ renew ⓥ 새롭게 하다, 갱신하다, 재개하다
554 ☐ maintain ⓥ 유지하다

41~42
555 ☐ work hard at ~을 들이파다, 열심히 하다
556 ☐ fall off 넘어지다
557 ☐ nature ⓝ 본성, 천성
558 ☐ make an attempt 시도하다
559 ☐ judge ⓥ 판단하다, 판정하다
560 ☐ awkward ⓐ (기분이) 어색한, 불편한
561 ☐ ourselves ⓟron 우리 자신[스스로/직접]
562 ☐ rather than ~하기보다는
563 ☐ give it a shot 시도하다
564 ☐ shame ⓝ 애석한 일, 딱한 일
565 ☐ repetition ⓝ 반복
566 ☐ central ⓐ 핵심적인
567 ☐ process ⓝ 과정
568 ☐ rewire ⓥ 재연결하다, 전선을 다시 배치하다
569 ☐ network ⓝ 연결망, 네트워크
570 ☐ neuron ⓝ 뉴런, 신경 세포
571 ☐ technique ⓝ 기술
572 ☐ reliable ⓐ 신뢰할 만한
573 ☐ hit-and-miss ⓐ 되는 대로 하는,
      마구잡이로 하는
574 ☐ remember ⓥ 기억하다, 기억나다
575 ☐ involve ⓥ 연관시키다
576 ☐ block ⓥ 차단하다
577 ☐ easily ⓐd 쉽게
578 ☐ growth ⓝ 성장
579 ☐ keep ⓥ 유지하다[유지하게 하다]
580 ☐ balance ⓝ 균형[평형]

43~45
581 ☐ passion ⓝ 열정
582 ☐ kingdom ⓝ 왕국
583 ☐ locate ⓥ 위치시키다
584 ☐ at the foot of ~의 기슭에, 하단부에
585 ☐ forest ⓝ 숲
586 ☐ preparation ⓝ 준비, 채비
587 ☐ set out for ~을 향해 나서다
588 ☐ season ⓝ 계절
589 ☐ pass by (시간이) 지나가다
590 ☐ previous ⓐ 이전의
591 ☐ deerskin ⓝ 사슴 가죽
592 ☐ fearlessly ⓐd 겁 없이, 대담하게

593 ☐ lick ⓥ 핥다
594 ☐ palace ⓝ 궁궐
595 ☐ spot ⓥ 알아채다, 발견하다
596 ☐ aim ⓝ 겨냥, 목표 ⓥ 겨누다
597 ☐ arrow ⓝ 화살
598 ☐ order ⓥ 명령하다
599 ☐ sight ⓝ 광경
600 ☐ servant ⓝ 신하
601 ☐ behavior ⓝ 행동
602 ☐ belong to ~의 것이다
603 ☐ mate ⓝ 짝
604 ☐ have a change of heart 마음을 바꾸다,
      심경의 변화가 생기다
605 ☐ realize ⓥ 깨닫다
606 ☐ pain ⓝ 고통
607 ☐ loss ⓝ 상실
608 ☐ promise ⓝ 약속

06회

TEST A-B 각 단어의 뜻을 [A] 영어는 우리말로, [B] 우리말은 영어로 쓰시오.

A	English	Korean	B	Korean	English
01	harmful		01	실망한	
02	massive		02	식욕	
03	rude		03	수용하다, 허용하다	
04	translate		04	성취	
05	aspect		05	납득시키다, 설득하다	
06	confident		06	전달하다	
07	gather		07	처리하다	
08	approximately		08	괴로움	
09	meanwhile		09	방정식, 등식	
10	worth		10	이전의	
11	fix		11	불편함	
12	properly		12	포함하다	
13	arise		13	눈에 띄는, 두드러지는	
14	joyfully		14	핵심적인	
15	instrument		15	유지하다	
16	complex		16	허용 가능한, 수용 가능한	
17	increasingly		17	거주하다, 살다	
18	entry		18	입학, 입장	
19	organ		19	법적으로	
20	adapt to		20	지나가다, 추월하다	

▶ A-D 정답 : 해설편 057쪽

TEST C-D 각 단어의 뜻을 골라 기호를 쓰시오.

C	English			Korean	D	Korean			English
01	observe	( )	ⓐ	~에 좌우되다	01	역으로	( )	ⓐ	unchecked
02	anxious	( )	ⓑ	인정하다	02	떨어지다, 감소하다	( )	ⓑ	amount
03	overestimate	( )	ⓒ	과대평가하다	03	확인되지 않은	( )	ⓒ	repetition
04	obvious	( )	ⓓ	겨냥, 목표	04	~을 극복하다	( )	ⓓ	distinguish
05	impress	( )	ⓔ	불안한	05	완전히, 전적으로	( )	ⓔ	permission
06	recognize	( )	ⓕ	돌리다, 바꾸다	06	탐구하다	( )	ⓕ	necessity
07	appropriate	( )	ⓖ	적절한	07	대표하다, 나타내다	( )	ⓖ	means
08	genuinely	( )	ⓗ	말하다, 관찰하다	08	불평등, 부당함	( )	ⓗ	instruction
09	internal	( )	ⓘ	애석한 일, 딱한 일	09	지침, 가르침	( )	ⓘ	injustice
10	artificial	( )	ⓙ	내적인	10	수단	( )	ⓙ	get over
11	spell out	( )	ⓚ	진정으로	11	실질적인, 효과적인	( )	ⓚ	explore
12	shame	( )	ⓛ	인상을 주다	12	구별하다	( )	ⓛ	conversely
13	ignore	( )	ⓜ	상세히 말하다	13	허락	( )	ⓜ	entirely
14	command	( )	ⓝ	준비, 채비	14	총액, 총계	( )	ⓝ	effective
15	depend on	( )	ⓞ	무시하다	15	필요성	( )	ⓞ	drop
16	present	( )	ⓟ	명령(어)	16	기기, 장비	( )	ⓟ	equipment
17	arise	( )	ⓠ	인공의	17	반복	( )	ⓠ	decline
18	preparation	( )	ⓡ	존재하는	18	(기분이) 어색한, 불편한	( )	ⓡ	remodel
19	aim	( )	ⓢ	발생하다, 일어나다	19	하락하다, 떨어지다	( )	ⓢ	awkward
20	shift	( )	ⓣ	명백한	20	개조하다	( )	ⓣ	represent

2020학년도 3월 고1 전국연합학력평가 문제지

영어 영역

제 3 교시

07회

1

● 문항수 45개 | 배점 100점 | 제한 시간 70분

● 점수 표시가 없는 문항은 모두 2점

07회

1번부터 17번까지는 듣고 답하는 문제입니다. 1번부터 15번까지는 한 번만 들려주고, 16번부터 17번까지는 두 번 들려줍니다. 방송을 잘 듣고 답을 하시기 바랍니다.

1. 다음을 듣고, 남자가 하는 말의 목적으로 가장 적절한 것을 고르시오.

① 미세 먼지 수치가 높을 때 대처 요령을 안내하려고
② 교실 내 공기 정화기 설치 일정을 알리려고
③ 체육 실기 시험 준비 방법을 설명하려고
④ 미세 먼지 방지용 마스크 배부 행사를 홍보하려고
⑤ 미세 먼지 감축을 위해 대중교통 이용을 독려하려고

2. 대화를 듣고, 여자의 의견으로 가장 적절한 것을 고르시오.

① 받는 사람에게 필요한 것을 선물해야 한다.
② 정성 어린 선물 포장은 선물의 가치를 높인다.
③ 선물 포장을 위해 다양한 재료를 활용해야 한다.
④ 선물을 받으면 적절한 감사 인사를 하는 것이 좋다.
⑤ 환경을 위해 선물 포장을 간소하게 할 필요가 있다.

3. 대화를 듣고, 두 사람의 관계를 가장 잘 나타낸 것을 고르시오.

① 정원사 – 집주인
② 출판사 직원 – 작가
③ 가구 판매원 – 손님
④ 관광 가이드 – 관광객
⑤ 인테리어 디자이너 – 잡지 기자

4. 대화를 듣고, 그림에서 대화의 내용과 일치하지 <u>않는</u> 것을 고르시오.

5. 대화를 듣고, 여자가 할 일로 가장 적절한 것을 고르시오.

① 악기 점검하기
② 연습 시간 확인하기
③ 단원들에게 연락하기
④ 관객용 의자 배치하기
⑤ 콘서트 포스터 붙이기

6. 대화를 듣고, 여자가 지불할 금액을 고르시오. [3점]

① $140 ② $180 ③ $200 ④ $220 ⑤ $280

7. 대화를 듣고, 남자가 이번 주말에 캠핑하러 갈 수 <u>없는</u> 이유를 고르시오.

① 계단을 수리해야 해서
② 캠프장을 예약할 수 없어서
③ 폭우로 인해 캠프장이 폐쇄되어서
④ 프로젝트를 마무리해야 해서
⑤ 어머니를 돌봐야 해서

8. 대화를 듣고, Pinewood Bake Sale에 관해 언급되지 <u>않은</u> 것을 고르시오.

① 개최 요일
② 시작 시간
③ 판매 제품
④ 수익금 기부처
⑤ 개최 장소

9. 2020 Global Village Festival에 관한 다음 내용을 듣고, 일치하지 <u>않는</u> 것을 고르시오. [3점]

① 이틀간 Green City Park에서 열린다.
② 음악 공연과 미술 전시회를 포함한다.
③ 현금이나 신용 카드로 음식을 구입할 수 있다.
④ 선착순 100명에게 특별 선물을 준다.
⑤ 차량당 주차비는 10달러이다.

10. 다음 표를 보면서 대화를 듣고, 두 사람이 예약할 방을 고르시오.

Wayne Island Hotel Rooms

	Room	View	Breakfast	Price
①	A	City	×	$70
②	B	Mountain	×	$80
③	C	Mountain	○	$95
④	D	Ocean	×	$105
⑤	E	Ocean	○	$120

11. 대화를 듣고, 남자의 마지막 말에 대한 여자의 응답으로 가장 적절한 것을 고르시오.

① No thanks. I'm already full.
② Sure. The onion soup is great here.
③ No idea. I've never been here before.
④ Yes. I recommend you be there on time.
⑤ I agree. Let's go to a Mexican restaurant.

12. 대화를 듣고, 여자의 마지막 말에 대한 남자의 응답으로 가장 적절한 것을 고르시오.

① I see. Thank you for letting me know.
② Unfortunately, I got caught in the rain.
③ Well, it's been raining since yesterday.
④ You're right. It'll be sunny this afternoon.
⑤ Yeah. These umbrellas are available online.

13. 대화를 듣고, 여자의 마지막 말에 대한 남자의 응답으로 가장 적절한 것을 고르시오. [3점]

Man: _____

① I have, but he didn't take it seriously.
② Don't worry. I have no problem with him.
③ Well, he always keeps the bathroom clean.
④ Sorry. I delayed moving out of the apartment.
⑤ Of course. I'll help you move into a new apartment.

14. 대화를 듣고, 남자의 마지막 말에 대한 여자의 응답으로 가장 적절한 것을 고르시오.

Woman: _____

① I'll text you how much it costs to fix the floor.
② Right. I don't think you can enter the competition.
③ Okay. I'll let you know as soon as the date is set.
④ But the auditorium was already repaired last week.
⑤ The competition will be held in the school gym instead.

15. 다음 상황 설명을 듣고, Billy의 어머니가 Billy에게 할 말로 가장 적절한 것을 고르시오.

Billy's mother: _____

① Make sure to answer the letters.
② Try to participate in school events often.
③ I'm sure you can make some good friends.
④ You need to prepare for the meeting.
⑤ Don't forget to bring me the letters.

[16 ~ 17] 다음을 듣고, 물음에 답하시오.

16. 여자가 하는 말의 주제로 가장 적절한 것은?

① major exporting countries of dairy products
② health benefits of drinking milk regularly
③ unique food cultures around the world
④ suitable environments for dairy animals
⑤ various milk sources in different countries

17. 언급된 나라가 아닌 것은?

① Canada　　② India　　③ Finland
④ Norway　　⑤ Romania

이제 듣기 문제가 끝났습니다. 18번부터는 문제지의 지시에 따라 답을 하시기 바랍니다.

18. 다음 글의 목적으로 가장 적절한 것은?

Dear Ms. Spadler,

　You've written to our company complaining that your toaster, which you bought only three weeks earlier, doesn't work. You were asking for a new toaster or a refund. Since the toaster has a year's warranty, our company is happy to replace your faulty toaster with a new toaster. To get your new toaster, simply take your receipt and the faulty toaster to the dealer from whom you bought it. The dealer will give you a new toaster on the spot. Nothing is more important to us than the satisfaction of our customers. If there is anything else we can do for you, please do not hesitate to ask.

Yours sincerely,
Betty Swan

*warranty: 품질 보증(서)

① 새로 출시한 제품을 홍보하려고
② 흔히 생기는 고장 사례를 알려주려고
③ 품질 보증서 보관의 중요성을 강조하려고
④ 고장 난 제품을 교환하는 방법을 안내하려고
⑤ 제품 만족도 조사에 참여해줄 것을 요청하려고

19. 다음 글에 드러난 'I'의 심경 변화로 가장 적절한 것은?

　I was diving alone in about 40 feet of water when I got a terrible stomachache. I was sinking and hardly able to move. I could see my watch and knew there was only a little more time on the tank before I would be out of air. It was hard for me to remove my weight belt. Suddenly I felt a prodding from behind me under the armpit. My arm was being lifted forcibly. Around into my field of vision came an eye. It seemed to be smiling. It was the eye of a big dolphin. Looking into that eye, I knew I was safe. I felt that the animal was protecting me, lifting me toward the surface.

*prodding: 쿡 찌르기

① excited → bored　　② pleased → angry
③ jealous → thankful　　④ proud → embarrassed
⑤ frightened → relieved

20. 다음 글에서 필자가 주장하는 바로 가장 적절한 것은?

Keeping good ideas floating around in your head is a great way to ensure that they won't happen. Take a tip from writers, who know that the only good ideas that come to life are the ones that get written down. Take out a piece of paper and record everything you'd love to do someday — aim to hit one hundred dreams. You'll have a reminder and motivator to get going on those things that are calling you, and you also won't have the burden of remembering all of them. When you put your dreams into words you begin putting them into action.

① 친구의 꿈을 응원하라.
② 하고 싶은 일을 적으라.
③ 신중히 생각한 후 행동하라.
④ 효과적인 기억법을 개발하라.
⑤ 실현 가능한 목표에 집중하라.

21. 밑줄 친 "rise to the bait"가 다음 글에서 의미하는 바로 가장 적절한 것은? [3점]

We all know that tempers are one of the first things lost in many arguments. It's easy to say one should keep cool, but how do you do it? The point to remember is that sometimes in arguments the other person is trying to get you to be angry. They may be saying things that are intentionally designed to annoy you. They know that if they get you to lose your cool you'll say something that sounds foolish; you'll simply get angry and then it will be impossible for you to win the argument. So don't fall for it. A remark may be made to cause your anger, but responding with a cool answer that focuses on the issue raised is likely to be most effective. Indeed, any attentive listener will admire the fact that you didn't "rise to the bait."

① stay calm
② blame yourself
③ lose your temper
④ listen to the audience
⑤ apologize for your behavior

22. 다음 글의 요지로 가장 적절한 것은?

Practically anything of value requires that we take a risk of failure or being rejected. This is the price we all must pay for achieving the greater rewards lying ahead of us. To take risks means you will succeed sometime but never to take a risk means that you will never succeed. Life is filled with a lot of risks and challenges and if you want to get away from all these, you will be left behind in the race of life. A person who can never take a risk can't learn anything. For example, if you never take the risk to drive a car, you can never learn to drive. If you never take the risk of being rejected, you can never have a friend or partner. Similarly, by not taking the risk of attending an interview, you will never get a job.

① 위험을 무릅쓰지 않으면 아무 것도 얻지 못한다.
② 자신이 잘하는 일에 집중하는 것이 효율적이다.
③ 잦은 실패 경험은 도전할 의지를 잃게 한다.
④ 위험 요소가 있으면 미리 피하는 것이 좋다.
⑤ 부탁을 자주 거절하면 신뢰를 잃는다.

23. 다음 글의 주제로 가장 적절한 것은?

Although individual preferences vary, touch (both what we touch with our fingers and the way things feel as they come in contact with our skin) is an important aspect of many products. Consumers like some products because of their feel. Some consumers buy skin creams and baby products for their soothing effect on the skin. In fact, consumers who have a high need for touch tend to like products that provide this opportunity. When considering products with material properties, such as clothing or carpeting, consumers like goods they can touch in stores more than products they only see and read about online or in catalogs.

* property: 속성

① benefits of using online shopping malls
② touch as an important factor for consumers
③ importance of sharing information among consumers
④ necessity of getting feedback from consumers
⑤ popularity of products in the latest styles

24. 다음 글의 제목으로 가장 적절한 것은?

In life, they say that too much of anything is not good for you. In fact, too much of certain things in life can kill you. For example, they say that water has no enemy, because water is essential to all life. But if you take in too much water, like one who is drowning, it could kill you. Education is the exception to this rule. You can never have too much education or knowledge. The reality is that most people will never have enough education in their lifetime. I am yet to find that one person who has been hurt in life by too much education. Rather, we see lots of casualties every day, worldwide, resulting from the lack of education. You must keep in mind that education is a long-term investment of time, money, and effort into humans.

* casualty: 피해자

① All Play and No Work Makes Jack a Smart Boy
② Too Much Education Won't Hurt You
③ Too Heads Are Worse than One
④ Don't Think Twice Before You Act
⑤ Learn from the Future, Not from the Past

25. 다음 도표의 내용과 일치하지 <u>않는</u> 것은?

The Most Spoken Languages Worldwide in 2015

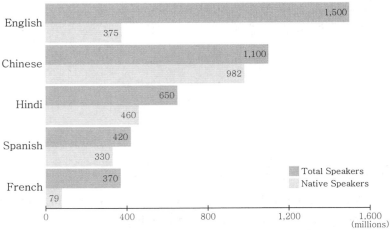

• Note: Total Speakers = Native Speakers + Non-native Speakers

The above graph shows the numbers of total speakers and native speakers of the five most spoken languages worldwide in 2015. ① English is the most spoken language worldwide, with 1,500 million total speakers. ② Chinese is second on the list with 1,100 million total speakers. ③ In terms of the number of native speakers, however, Chinese is the most spoken language worldwide, followed by Hindi. ④ The number of native speakers of English is smaller than that of Spanish. ⑤ French is the least spoken language among the five in terms of the number of native speakers.

26. Ellen Church에 관한 다음 글의 내용과 일치하지 <u>않는</u> 것은?

Ellen Church was born in Iowa in 1904. After graduating from Cresco High School, she studied nursing and worked as a nurse in San Francisco. She suggested to Boeing Air Transport that nurses should take care of passengers during flights because most people were frightened of flying. In 1930, she became the first female flight attendant in the U.S. and worked on a Boeing 80A from Oakland, California to Chicago, Illinois. Unfortunately, a car accident injury forced her to end her career after only eighteen months. Church started nursing again at Milwaukee County Hospital after she graduated from the University of Minnesota with a degree in nursing education. During World War II, she served as a captain in the Army Nurse Corps and received an Air Medal. Ellen Church Field Airport in her hometown, Cresco, was named after her.

① San Francisco에서 간호사로 일했다.
② 간호사가 비행 중에 승객을 돌봐야 한다고 제안했다.
③ 미국 최초의 여성 비행기 승무원이 되었다.
④ 자동차 사고로 다쳤지만 비행기 승무원 생활을 계속했다.
⑤ 고향인 Cresco에 그녀의 이름을 따서 붙인 공항이 있다.

27. Science Selfie Competition에 관한 다음 안내문의 내용과 일치하지 <u>않는</u> 것은?

Science Selfie Competition

For a chance to win science goodies, just submit a selfie of yourself enjoying science outside of school!

Deadline: Friday, March 20, 2020, 6 p.m.

Details:
• Your selfie should include a visit to any science museum or a science activity at home.
• Be as creative as you like, and write one short sentence about the selfie.
• Only one entry per person!
• Email your selfie with your name and class to mclara@oldfold.edu.

Winners will be announced on March 27, 2020.

Please visit www.oldfold.edu to learn more about the competition.

① 학교 밖에서 과학을 즐기는 셀카 사진을 출품한다.
② 셀카 사진에 관한 하나의 짧은 문장을 써야 한다.
③ 1인당 사진 여러 장을 출품할 수 있다.
④ 셀카 사진을 이름 및 소속 학급과 함께 이메일로 보내야 한다.
⑤ 수상자는 2020년 3월 27일에 발표될 것이다.

28. Toy & Gift Warehouse Sale에 관한 다음 안내문의 내용과 일치하는 것은?

Toy & Gift Warehouse Sale

at Wilson Square
from April 3 to April 16

We carry items that are in stock at bigger retailers for a cheaper price. You can expect to find toys for children from birth to teens. Ten toy companies will participate in the sale.

Wednesday – Friday: 10 a.m. – 6 p.m.
Saturday & Sunday: 11 a.m. – 5 p.m.
Closed on Monday & Tuesday

Returns must be made within one week of purchase.

For more information, please visit us at www.poptoy.com.

① 4월 16일부터 시작된다.
② 십 대를 위한 장난감은 판매하지 않는다.
③ 스무 개의 장난감 회사가 참여한다.
④ 월요일과 화요일에는 운영되지 않는다.
⑤ 반품은 구입 후 2주간 가능하다.

29. 다음 글의 밑줄 친 부분 중, 어법상 틀린 것은? [3점]

"You are what you eat." That phrase is often used to ① show the relationship between the foods you eat and your physical health. But do you really know what you are eating when you buy processed foods, canned foods, and packaged goods? Many of the manufactured products made today contain so many chemicals and artificial ingredients ② which it is sometimes difficult to know exactly what is inside them. Fortunately, now there are food labels. Food labels are a good way ③ to find the information about the foods you eat. Labels on food are ④ like the table of contents found in books. The main purpose of food labels ⑤ is to inform you what is inside the food you are purchasing.

* manufactured: (공장에서) 제조된
** table of contents: (책 등의) 목차

30. 다음 글의 밑줄 친 부분 중, 문맥상 낱말의 쓰임이 적절하지 않은 것은? [3점]

We often ignore small changes because they don't seem to ① matter very much in the moment. If you save a little money now, you're still not a millionaire. If you study Spanish for an hour tonight, you still haven't learned the language. We make a few changes, but the results never seem to come ② quickly and so we slide back into our previous routines. The slow pace of transformation also makes it ③ easy to break a bad habit. If you eat an unhealthy meal today, the scale doesn't move much. A single decision is easy to ignore. But when we ④ repeat small errors, day after day, by following poor decisions again and again, our small choices add up to bad results. Many missteps eventually lead to a ⑤ problem.

[31 ~ 34] 다음 빈칸에 들어갈 말로 가장 적절한 것을 고르시오.

31. Remember that _____ is always of the essence. If an apology is not accepted, thank the individual for hearing you out and leave the door open for if and when he wishes to reconcile. Be conscious of the fact that just because someone accepts your apology does not mean she has fully forgiven you. It can take time, maybe a long time, before the injured party can completely let go and fully trust you again. There is little you can do to speed this process up. If the person is truly important to you, it is worthwhile to give him or her the time and space needed to heal. Do not expect the person to go right back to acting normally immediately.

* reconcile: 화해하다

① curiosity　　　　② independence
③ patience　　　　④ creativity
⑤ honesty

32. Although many small businesses have excellent websites, they typically can't afford aggressive online campaigns. One way to get the word out is through an advertising exchange, in which advertisers place banners on each other's websites for free. For example, a company selling beauty products could place its banner on a site that sells women's shoes, and in turn, the shoe company could put a banner on the beauty product site. Neither company charges the other; they simply exchange ad space. Advertising exchanges are gaining in popularity, especially among marketers who do not have much money and who don't have a large sales team. By _____, advertisers find new outlets that reach their target audiences that they would not otherwise be able to afford.

* aggressive: 매우 적극적인　** outlet: 출구

① trading space
② getting funded
③ sharing reviews
④ renting factory facilities
⑤ increasing TV commercials

33. Motivation may come from several sources. It may be the respect I give every student, the daily greeting I give at my classroom door, the undivided attention when I listen to a student, a pat on the shoulder whether the job was done well or not, an accepting smile, or simply "I love you" when it is most needed. It may simply be asking how things are at home. For one student considering dropping out of school, it was a note from me after one of his frequent absences saying that he made my day when I saw him in school. He came to me with the note with tears in his eyes and thanked me. He will graduate this year. Whatever technique is used, the students must know that you _____. But the concern must be genuine — the students can't be fooled.

① care about them
② keep your words
③ differ from them
④ evaluate their performance
⑤ communicate with their parents

34. Say you normally go to a park to walk or work out. Maybe today you should choose a different park. Why? Well, who knows? Maybe it's because you need the connection to the different energy in the other park. Maybe you'll run into people there that you've never met before. You could make a new best friend simply by visiting a different park. You never know what great things will happen to you until you step outside the zone where you feel comfortable. If you're staying in your comfort zone and you're not pushing yourself past that same old energy, then you're not going to move forward on your path. By forcing yourself to do something different, you're awakening yourself on a spiritual level and you're forcing yourself to do something that will benefit you in the long run. As they say, _____. [3점]

① variety is the spice of life
② fantasy is the mirror of reality
③ failure teaches more than success
④ laziness is the mother of invention
⑤ conflict strengthens the relationship

[35 ~ 36] 주어진 글 다음에 이어질 글의 순서로 가장 적절한 것을 고르시오.

35.

> Ideas about how much disclosure is appropriate vary among cultures.

(A) On the other hand, Japanese tend to do little disclosing about themselves to others except to the few people with whom they are very close. In general, Asians do not reach out to strangers.

(B) Those born in the United States tend to be high disclosers, even showing a willingness to disclose information about themselves to strangers. This may explain why Americans seem particularly easy to meet and are good at cocktail-party conversation.

(C) They do, however, show great care for each other, since they view harmony as essential to relationship improvement. They work hard to prevent those they view as outsiders from getting information they believe to be unfavorable. [3점]

* disclosure: (정보의) 공개

① (A) − (C) − (B)　　② (B) − (A) − (C)
③ (B) − (C) − (A)　　④ (C) − (A) − (B)
⑤ (C) − (B) − (A)

36.

> A god called Moinee was defeated by a rival god called Dromerdeener in a terrible battle up in the stars. Moinee fell out of the stars down to Tasmania to die.

(A) He took pity on the people, gave them bendable knees and cut off their inconvenient kangaroo tails so they could all sit down at last. Then they lived happily ever after.

(B) Then he died. The people hated having kangaroo tails and no knees, and they cried out to the heavens for help. Dromerdeener heard their cry and came down to Tasmania to see what the matter was.

(C) Before he died, he wanted to give a last blessing to his final resting place, so he decided to create humans. But he was in such a hurry, knowing he was dying, that he forgot to give them knees; and he absent-mindedly gave them big tails like kangaroos, which meant they couldn't sit down.

① (A) − (C) − (B)　　② (B) − (A) − (C)
③ (B) − (C) − (A)　　④ (C) − (A) − (B)
⑤ (C) − (B) − (A)

07회

[37~38] 글의 흐름으로 보아, 주어진 문장이 들어가기에 가장 적절한 곳을 고르시오.

37.

> In the U.S. we have so many metaphors for time and its passing that we think of time as "a thing," that is "the weekend is almost gone," or "I haven't got the time."

There are some cultures that can be referred to as "people who live outside of time." The Amondawa tribe, living in Brazil, does not have a concept of time that can be measured or counted. (①) Rather they live in a world of serial events, rather than seeing events as being rooted in time. (②) Researchers also found that no one had an age. (③) Instead, they change their names to reflect their stage of life and position within their society, so a little child will give up their name to a newborn sibling and take on a new one. (④) We think such statements are objective, but they aren't. (⑤) We create these metaphors, but the Amondawa don't talk or think in metaphors for time. [3점]

* metaphor: 은유 ** sibling: 형제자매

38.

> Of course, within cultures individual attitudes can vary dramatically.

The natural world provides a rich source of symbols used in art and literature. (①) Plants and animals are central to mythology, dance, song, poetry, rituals, festivals, and holidays around the world. (②) Different cultures can exhibit opposite attitudes toward a given species. (③) Snakes, for example, are honored by some cultures and hated by others. (④) Rats are considered pests in much of Europe and North America and greatly respected in some parts of India. (⑤) For instance, in Britain many people dislike rodents, and yet there are several associations devoted to breeding them, including the National Mouse Club and the National Fancy Rat Club.

* pest: 유해 동물 ** rodent: (쥐, 다람쥐 등이 속한) 설치류

39. 다음 글에서 전체 흐름과 관계 <u>없는</u> 문장은?

Paying attention to some people and not others doesn't mean you're being dismissive or arrogant. ① It just reflects a hard fact: there are limits on the number of people we can possibly pay attention to or develop a relationship with. ② Some scientists even believe that the number of people with whom we can continue stable social relationships might be limited naturally by our brains. ③ The more people you know of different backgrounds, the more colorful your life becomes. ④ Professor Robin Dunbar has explained that our minds are only really capable of forming meaningful relationships with a maximum of about a hundred and fifty people. ⑤ Whether that's true or not, it's safe to assume that we can't be real friends with everyone.

* dismissive: 무시하는 ** arrogant: 거만한

40. 다음 글의 내용을 한 문장으로 요약하고자 한다. 빈칸 (A), (B)에 들어갈 말로 가장 적절한 것은?

> While there are many evolutionary or cultural reasons for cooperation, the eyes are one of the most important means of cooperation, and eye contact may be the most powerful human force we lose in traffic. It is, arguably, the reason why humans, normally a quite cooperative species, can become so noncooperative on the road. Most of the time we are moving too fast — we begin to lose the ability to keep eye contact around 20 miles per hour — or it is not safe to look. Maybe our view is blocked. Often other drivers are wearing sunglasses, or their car may have tinted windows. (And do you really want to make eye contact with those drivers?) Sometimes we make eye contact through the rearview mirror, but it feels weak, not quite believable at first, as it is not "face-to-face."

* tinted: 색이 옅게 들어간

↓

> While driving, people become _____(A)_____ , because they make _____(B)_____ eye contact.

	(A)		(B)
①	uncooperative	……	little
②	careful	……	direct
③	confident	……	regular
④	uncooperative	……	direct
⑤	careful	……	little

[41 ~ 42] 다음 글을 읽고, 물음에 답하시오.

Many high school students study and learn inefficiently because they insist on doing their homework while watching TV or listening to loud music. These same students also typically (a) interrupt their studying with repeated phone calls, trips to the kitchen, video games, and Internet surfing. Ironically, students with the greatest need to concentrate when studying are often the ones who surround themselves with the most distractions. These teenagers argue that they can study *better* with the TV or radio (b) playing. Some professionals actually (c) oppose their position. They argue that many teenagers can actually study productively under less-than-ideal conditions because they've been exposed repeatedly to "background noise" since early childhood. These educators argue that children have become (d) used to the sounds of the TV, video games, and loud music. They also argue that insisting students turn off the TV or radio when doing homework will not necessarily improve their academic performance. This position is certainly not generally shared, however. Many teachers and learning experts are (e) convinced by their own experiences that students who study in a noisy environment often learn inefficiently.

41. 윗글의 제목으로 가장 적절한 것은?

① Successful Students Plan Ahead
② Studying with Distractions: Is It Okay?
③ Smart Devices as Good Learning Tools
④ Parents & Teachers: Partners in Education
⑤ Good Habits: Hard to Form, Easy to Break

42. 밑줄 친 (a) ~ (e) 중에서 문맥상 낱말의 쓰임이 적절하지 <u>않은</u> 것은? [3점]

① (a)　② (b)　③ (c)　④ (d)　⑤ (e)

[43 ~ 45] 다음 글을 읽고, 물음에 답하시오.

(A)

Dorothy was home alone. She was busy with a school project, and suddenly wanted to eat French fries. She peeled two potatoes, sliced them up and put a pot with cooking oil on the stove. Then the telephone rang. It was her best friend Samantha. While chatting away on the phone, Dorothy noticed a strange light shining from the kitchen, and then (a) she remembered about the pot of oil on the stove!

(B)

A while later, after the wound had been treated, the family sat around the kitchen table and talked. "I learned a big lesson today," Dorothy said. Her parents expected (b) her to say something about the fire. But she talked about something different. "I have decided to use kind words more just like you." Her parents were very grateful, because Dorothy had quite a temper.

(C)

Dorothy dropped the phone and rushed to the kitchen. The oil was on fire. "Chill! Take a deep breath," (c) she said to herself. *What did they teach us not to do in a situation like this? Don't try to put it out by throwing water on it, because it will cause an explosion*, she remembered. She picked up the pot's lid and covered the pot with it to put out the flames. In the process she burned her hands. Dorothy felt dizzy and sat down at the kitchen table.

(D)

A couple of minutes later, her parents came rushing into the house. Samantha had suspected that something might be wrong after Dorothy dropped the phone just like that, and (d) she had phoned Dorothy's parents. Dorothy started to cry. Her mother hugged her tightly and looked at the wound. "Tell me what happened," she said. Dorothy told her, sobbing and sniffing. "Aren't you going to yell at me?" (e) she asked them through the tears. Her father answered with a smile, "I also put my lid on to keep me from exploding." Dorothy looked at him, relieved. "But be careful not to be so irresponsible again."

* sob: 흐느껴 울다　** sniff: 코를 훌쩍거리다

43. 주어진 글 (A)에 이어질 내용을 순서에 맞게 배열한 것으로 가장 적절한 것은?

① (B) − (D) − (C)　② (C) − (B) − (D)
③ (C) − (D) − (B)　④ (D) − (B) − (C)
⑤ (D) − (C) − (B)

44. 밑줄 친 (a) ~ (e) 중에서 가리키는 대상이 나머지 넷과 <u>다른</u> 것은?

① (a)　② (b)　③ (c)　④ (d)　⑤ (e)

45. 윗글의 Dorothy에 관한 내용으로 적절하지 <u>않은</u> 것은?

① 프렌치프라이를 만들려고 감자 두 개를 깎았다.
② 친절한 말을 더 많이 쓰겠다고 다짐했다.
③ 불붙은 기름에 물을 끼얹지 말아야 한다는 것을 기억했다.
④ 뚜껑으로 냄비를 덮어 불을 끄다가 손을 데었다.
⑤ 아버지의 말을 듣고 화를 냈다.

---

* 확인 사항

○ 답안지의 해당란에 필요한 내용을 정확히 기입(표기)했는지 확인하시오.

01
001 ☐ **fine dust** 미세 먼지
002 ☐ **serious** ⓐ 심각한
003 ☐ **explain** ⓥ 설명하다
004 ☐ **keep out** ~이 들어가지 않게 하다
005 ☐ **turn on** ~을 켜다
006 ☐ **air purifier** 공기 정화기
007 ☐ **as ~ as possible** 가능한 한 ~한[하게]

02
008 ☐ **wrap** ⓥ 싸다
009 ☐ **key chain** 열쇠고리
010 ☐ **fill A with B** A를 B로 채우다
011 ☐ **decorate** ⓥ 장식하다
012 ☐ **end up** 결국 ~하게 되다
013 ☐ **trash can** 쓰레기통
014 ☐ **packaging** ⓝ 포장(재)
015 ☐ **produce** ⓥ 만들다
016 ☐ **environment** ⓝ 환경
017 ☐ **reduce** ⓥ 줄이다

03
018 ☐ **last** ⓐ 마지막의, 지난
019 ☐ **prepare for** ~을 준비하다
020 ☐ **work on** ~에 노력을 들이다[착수하다]
021 ☐ **look forward to** ~을 고대하다
022 ☐ **wooden** ⓐ 나무로 된
023 ☐ **have ~ in mind** ~을 염두에 두다
024 ☐ **particular** ⓐ 특정한, 특별한
025 ☐ **plain** ⓐ 평범한, 단순한
026 ☐ **rectangular** ⓐ 직사각형의
027 ☐ **downstairs** ⓐ 아래층에

04
028 ☐ **take a look** (~을) 한번 보다
029 ☐ **locker** ⓝ 사물함
030 ☐ **in a row** 계속해서, 연이어
031 ☐ **star-shaped** ⓐ 별 모양의
032 ☐ **rug** ⓝ 깔개

05
033 ☐ **preparation** ⓝ 준비, 대비
034 ☐ **come along** (원하는 대로) 되어 가다[나아지다]
035 ☐ **instrument** ⓝ 악기, 도구
036 ☐ **practice** ⓝ 연습, 실습
037 ☐ **put up** ~을 붙이다[게시하다]
038 ☐ **hallway** ⓝ 복도
039 ☐ **arrange** ⓥ 배치하다
040 ☐ **audience** ⓝ 관객

06
041 ☐ **wireless** ⓐ 무선의
042 ☐ **pair** ⓝ (두 개로 된) 한 쌍
043 ☐ **portable** ⓐ 휴대용의
044 ☐ **discount** ⓝ 할인

07
045 ☐ **reserve** ⓥ 예약하다
046 ☐ **campsite** ⓝ 캠프장, 야영지
047 ☐ **surgery** ⓝ 수술
048 ☐ **get well** (병이) 낫다

08
049 ☐ **flyer** ⓝ 전단
050 ☐ **raise money** 모금하다, 돈을 마련하다
051 ☐ **product** ⓝ 상품, 제품
052 ☐ **profit** ⓝ 수익금
053 ☐ **in need** 어려움에 처한
054 ☐ **donate** ⓥ 기부하다

09
055 ☐ **performance** ⓝ 공연
056 ☐ **exhibition** ⓝ 전시회
057 ☐ **serve** ⓥ (음식·음료 등을) 내다 [제공하다]
058 ☐ **range from A to B** (범위가) A에서 B까지 이다

10
059 ☐ **book** ⓥ 예약하다
060 ☐ **summer vacation** 여름 휴가
061 ☐ **option** ⓝ 선택(할 수 있는 것)
062 ☐ **go with** ~을 선택하다

11
063 ☐ **favorite** ⓐ 특히 좋아하는
064 ☐ **recommend** ⓥ 권하다, 추천하다
065 ☐ **full** ⓐ 배부른

12
066 ☐ **weather forecast** 일기 예보
067 ☐ **get caught in the rain** 비를 맞다
068 ☐ **available** ⓐ 구할 수 있는

13
069 ☐ **rent** ⓥ 임차하다, 빌리다
070 ☐ **share** ⓥ 함께 쓰다, 공유하다
071 ☐ **move out** 이사 나가다
072 ☐ **get along with** ~와 잘 지내다
073 ☐ **bother** ⓥ 신경 쓰이게 하다
074 ☐ **messy** ⓐ 지저분한
075 ☐ **awful** ⓐ 끔찍한
076 ☐ **take ~ seriously** ~을 심각하게 받아들이다, ~을 진지하게 받아들이다
077 ☐ **delay** ⓥ 미루다, 연기하다

14
078 ☐ **competition** ⓝ (경연) 대회, 시합
079 ☐ **auditorium** ⓝ 강당
080 ☐ **repair** ⓥ 수리하다
081 ☐ **decide** ⓥ 결정하다
082 ☐ **exact** ⓐ 정확한
083 ☐ **set** ⓥ 정하다, 결정하다
084 ☐ **cost** ⓥ (비용이) 들다
085 ☐ **fix** ⓥ 수리하다
086 ☐ **gym** ⓝ 체육관

15
087 ☐ **enter** ⓥ 입학하다, 들어가다
088 ☐ **information** ⓝ 정보
089 ☐ **parent-teacher meeting** 학부모 교사 모임
090 ☐ **deliver** ⓥ 전하다, 배달하다
091 ☐ **miss** ⓥ 놓치다
092 ☐ **make sure** 반드시 ~하다

16~17
093 ☐ **participate in** ~에 참가하다
094 ☐ **prepare** ⓥ 준비하다

095 ☐ **guess** ⓥ 추측하다, 짐작하다
096 ☐ **wonder** ⓥ 궁금해하다
097 ☐ **water buffalo** ⓝ 물소
098 ☐ **consume** ⓥ 소비하다, 먹다, 마시다
099 ☐ **reindeer** ⓝ 순록
100 ☐ **dairy animal** 착유 동물
101 ☐ **survive** ⓥ 살아남다, 견뎌 내다
102 ☐ **fat** ⓝ 지방
103 ☐ **content** ⓝ 함량
104 ☐ **export** ⓥ 수출하다
105 ☐ **suitable** ⓐ 적합한, 적절한
106 ☐ **various** ⓐ 다양한, 여러 가지의

18
107 ☐ **write** ⓥ 편지를 쓰다[써서 보내다], 편지하다
108 ☐ **complain** ⓥ 불평하다
109 ☐ **buy** 사다[사 주다], 구입하다
110 ☐ **work** ⓥ 작동되다[기능하다]
111 ☐ **asking** ⓝ 질문; 의뢰, 부탁; 청구
112 ☐ **refund** ⓝ 환불
113 ☐ **warranty** ⓝ 보증기간
114 ☐ **replace A with B** A를 B로 교환[교체]하다
115 ☐ **faulty** ⓐ 결함이 있는
116 ☐ **receipt** ⓝ 영수증
117 ☐ **dealer** ⓝ 판매자
118 ☐ **on the spot** 현장에서
119 ☐ **satisfaction** ⓝ 만족
120 ☐ **customer** ⓝ 고객
121 ☐ **hesitate** ⓥ 망설이다
122 ☐ **sincerely** ⓐ 진심으로

19
123 ☐ **dive** ⓥ 잠수하다
124 ☐ **terrible** ⓐ 심한
125 ☐ **stomachache** ⓝ 복통
126 ☐ **sink** ⓥ 가라앉다
127 ☐ **hardly** ⓐ 거의 ~ 않다
128 ☐ **remove** ⓥ 벗다, 제거하다
129 ☐ **weight belt** 웨이트 벨트 (잠수, 운동 때 무게를 더하기 위해 착용하는 벨트, 재킷)
130 ☐ **suddenly** ⓐ 갑자기
131 ☐ **behind** ⓐ 뒤에, 뒤떨어져
132 ☐ **armpit** ⓝ 겨드랑이
133 ☐ **lift** ⓥ 들어 올리다, 들리다
134 ☐ **forcibly** ⓐ 강제로, 강력히
135 ☐ **field of vision** 시야, 가시 범위
136 ☐ **smiling** ⓐ 미소짓는
137 ☐ **dolphin** ⓝ 돌고래
138 ☐ **protecting** ⓐ 지키는, 보호하는, 방어하는
139 ☐ **toward** prep 쪽으로, ···을 향하여
140 ☐ **surface** ⓝ 표면
141 ☐ **excited** ⓐ 신이 난, 들뜬, 흥분한
142 ☐ **bored** ⓐ 지루해하는
143 ☐ **pleased** ⓐ 기쁜
144 ☐ **angry** ⓐ 화난, 성난
145 ☐ **jealous** ⓐ 질투하는, 질투가 나는
146 ☐ **thankful** ⓐ 감사하는
147 ☐ **proud** ⓐ 자랑스러워하는, 자랑스러운

148 ☐ **embarrassed** ⓐ 당황한
149 ☐ **frightened** ⓐ 겁먹은, 무서워하는
150 ☐ **relieved** ⓐ 안도하는, 다행으로 여기는

20
151 ☐ **float** ⓥ 뜨다
152 ☐ **ensure** ⓥ 보장하다
153 ☐ **happen** ⓥ (무엇의 결과로) 일어나다[되다]
154 ☐ **writer** ⓝ 작가, 문인, 저술가
155 ☐ **come to life** (사물이) 생명력을 얻다, 살아 움직이다
156 ☐ **take out** 꺼내다
157 ☐ **a piece of paper** 한 장의 종이
158 ☐ **record** ⓥ 기록하다
159 ☐ **aim** ⓥ 반드시 ~하다, 목표로 하다
160 ☐ **hit** ⓥ (특정 수량·수준에) 이르다
161 ☐ **reminder** ⓝ 상기시키는 것
162 ☐ **motivator** ⓝ 동기 요인, 동기를 부여하는 것
163 ☐ **get going** 시작하다, 착수하다
164 ☐ **remember** ⓥ 기억하다
165 ☐ **burden** ⓝ 부담
166 ☐ **put A into words** A를 글 [말]로 적다[하다]
167 ☐ **put into action** 실행에 옮기다

21
168 ☐ **temper** ⓝ (걸핏하면 화를 내는) 성질
169 ☐ **argument** ⓝ 논쟁
170 ☐ **keep** ⓥ 유지하다
171 ☐ **cool** ⓐ 차분한, 침착한
172 ☐ **intentionally** ⓐ 일부러, 의도적으로
173 ☐ **design** ⓥ 고안하다
174 ☐ **annoy** ⓥ 화나게 하다
175 ☐ **lose one's cool** 침착함을 잃다
176 ☐ **foolish** ⓐ 어리석은
177 ☐ **simply** ⓐ 그냥 (간단히), 그저 (단순히)
178 ☐ **impossible** ⓐ 불가능한
179 ☐ **fall for** ~에 속아넘어가다
180 ☐ **make a remark** 말을 하다
181 ☐ **respond** ⓥ 대응하다
182 ☐ **answer** ⓝ 대답, 회신, 대응
183 ☐ **focus** ⓝ 초점, 주목
184 ☐ **raise** ⓥ (문제 등을) 제기하다
185 ☐ **effective** ⓐ 효과적인
186 ☐ **indeed** ⓐ 정말로
187 ☐ **attentive** ⓐ 주의 깊은
188 ☐ **admire** ⓥ 감탄하다
189 ☐ **rise to the bait** 미끼를 물다
190 ☐ **stay calm** 차분함, 침착함을 유지하다
191 ☐ **blame oneself** 자신을 책망하다
192 ☐ **lose one's temper** 화를 내다
193 ☐ **apologize for** ~에 대해 사과하다
194 ☐ **behavior** ⓝ 행동, 태도

22
195 ☐ **practically** ⓐ 사실상, 거의
196 ☐ **value** ⓝ 가치
197 ☐ **require** ⓥ 요구하다
198 ☐ **take a risk** 위험을 무릅쓰다
199 ☐ **failure** ⓝ 실패
200 ☐ **reject** ⓥ 거절하다
201 ☐ **price** ⓝ (치러야 할) 대가
202 ☐ **achieve** ⓥ 성취하다

07회

VOCA LIST 07

203 □ greater ⓐ ~보다 큰
204 □ reward ⓝ 보상
205 □ lie ⓥ 있다, 놓여 있다
206 □ ahead of (공간·시간상으로) ~ 앞에
207 □ mean ⓥ ~라는 뜻[의미]이다, …을 뜻하다 [의미하다]
208 □ succeed ⓥ 성공하다
209 □ sometime ⓐⓓ 언젠가
210 □ filled with ~로 가득 찬
211 □ challenge ⓝ 도전
212 □ get away from ~에서 벗어나다[피하다]
213 □ be left behind 뒤처지다
214 □ race ⓝ 경주, 레이스
215 □ for example 예를 들어
216 □ similarly ⓐⓓ 마찬가지로
217 □ attend ⓥ 참석하다

23
218 □ individual ⓐ 개인의
219 □ preference ⓝ 선호
220 □ vary ⓥ 다양하다
221 □ both ⓟⓡⓞⓝ 둘 다
222 □ touch ⓝ 촉감, 감촉 ⓥ 만지다
223 □ come in contact with ~와 접촉하다
224 □ aspect ⓝ 측면
225 □ consumer ⓝ 소비자
226 □ feel ⓝ 촉감, 감촉
227 □ baby product 유아용품
228 □ soothing ⓐ 진정시키는
229 □ provide ⓥ 제공[공급]하다
230 □ opportunity ⓝ 기회
231 □ considering ⓟⓡⓔⓟ ~을 고려[감안]하면
232 □ material ⓝ 재료, 직물
233 □ property ⓝ 특성, 속성
234 □ clothing ⓝ 옷[의복]
235 □ carpeting ⓝ 카펫류, 카펫천
236 □ benefit ⓝ 혜택, 이득
237 □ factor ⓝ 요인
238 □ among ⓟⓡⓔⓟ ~중[사이]에
239 □ necessity ⓝ 필요성
240 □ popularity ⓝ 인기
241 □ latest ⓐ (가장) 최근의[최신의]

24
242 □ be good for ~에 좋다
243 □ enemy ⓝ 적
244 □ essential ⓐ 필수적인
245 □ take in ~을 섭취하다
246 □ drown ⓥ 물에 빠지다, 익사하다
247 □ education ⓝ 교육
248 □ exception ⓝ 예외
249 □ knowledge ⓝ 지식
250 □ in one's lifetime 평생
251 □ be yet to- 아직 ~하지 못하다
252 □ hurt ⓥ 피해를 보다
253 □ worldwide ⓐⓓ 전 세계에서
254 □ result from ~로 인해 생기다
255 □ lack ⓝ 부족, 결여
256 □ keep in mind ~을 명심하다, 염두에 두다
257 □ long-term ⓐ 장기적인
258 □ investment ⓝ 투자
259 □ effort ⓝ 노력, 공

260 □ worse ⓐ 더 나쁜[못한/엉망인]
261 □ twice ⓐⓓ 두 번

25
262 □ worldwide ⓐ 전 세계적인
263 □ native speaker 원어민
264 □ in terms of ~의 면에서
265 □ follow ~의 뒤를 잇다
266 □ least ⓐ 가장 적게
267 □ term ⓝ 용어, 말

26
268 □ graduate from ~을 졸업하다
269 □ nursing ⓝ 간호(학)
270 □ suggest ⓥ 제안하다
271 □ take care of ~을 돌보다
272 □ passenger ⓝ 승객
273 □ unfortunately ⓐⓓ 불행하게도, 유감스럽게도
274 □ accident ⓝ (특히 자동차) 사고[재해]
275 □ female ⓝ 여성[여자]인
276 □ flight attendant 항공 승무원
277 □ injury ⓝ 부상
278 □ force ⓥ 어쩔 수 없이 ~하게 하다, 강요하다
279 □ end one's career 일을 그만두다
280 □ degree ⓝ 학위
281 □ serve as ~로 복무하다, ~의 역할을 하다
282 □ captain ⓝ 대위
283 □ Army Nurse Corps 육군 간호 부대
284 □ Air Medal 항공 훈장
285 □ hometown ⓝ 고향
286 □ name after ~의 이름을 따서 짓다

27
287 □ selfie ⓝ 셀카 사진
288 □ chance ⓝ 기회
289 □ goody ⓝ 매력적인 것, 갖고 싶은 것
290 □ submit ⓥ 출품하다, 제출하다
291 □ yourself ⓟⓡⓞⓝ 직접, 자신
292 □ enjoy ⓥ 즐기다
293 □ outside of …의 바깥쪽에, 밖에[으로]
294 □ deadline ⓝ 마감 기한
295 □ detail ⓝ 세부 사항
296 □ include ⓥ 포함하다
297 □ activity ⓝ (취미나 특별한 목적을 위한) 활동
298 □ creative ⓐ 창의적인
299 □ sentence ⓝ 문장
300 □ entry ⓝ 출품작
301 □ announce ⓥ 발표하다, 안내하다

28
302 □ warehouse ⓝ 창고
303 □ carry ⓥ (상점이 상품을) 취급하다
304 □ item ⓝ 품목
305 □ in stock 재고로 있는
306 □ retailer ⓝ 소매상
307 □ cheaper ⓐ 값이 더 싼
308 □ company ⓝ 회사
309 □ participate ⓥ 참가[참여]하다
310 □ return ⓝ 반품
311 □ purchase ⓝ 구입

29
312 □ phrase ⓝ 구절
313 □ often ⓐⓓ 흔히, 보통
314 □ relationship ⓝ 관계
315 □ between ⓟⓡⓔⓟ 사이[중간]에
316 □ physical ⓐ 신체적인, 물리적인
317 □ processed ⓐ 가공된
318 □ canned ⓐ 통조림으로 된
319 □ packaged ⓐ 포장된
320 □ contain ⓥ 함유하다
321 □ chemical ⓝ 화학 물질
322 □ artificial ⓐ 인공의
323 □ ingredient ⓝ 재료
324 □ food label 식품 (영양 성분) 라벨
325 □ fortunately ⓐⓓ 다행스럽게도, 운 좋게도
326 □ main ⓐ 주된, 가장 중요한
327 □ purpose ⓝ 목적
328 □ inform ⓥ 알리다, 통지하다
329 □ inside ⓟⓡⓔⓟ …의 안[속/내부]에[으로]
330 □ purchasing ⓝ 구매 (행위)

30
331 □ ignore ⓥ 무시하다
332 □ change ⓝ 변화
333 □ matter ⓥ 중요하다
334 □ in the moment 당장, 지금
335 □ millionaire ⓝ 백만장자
336 □ slide back into ~로 돌아가다, 복귀하다
337 □ previous ⓐ 이전의
338 □ routine ⓝ 일상
339 □ pace ⓝ 속도
340 □ transformation ⓝ 변화
341 □ break a bad habit 나쁜 습관을 버리다
342 □ unhealthy ⓐ 몸에 좋지 않은, 건강하지 않은
343 □ meal ⓝ 식사[끼니]
344 □ scale ⓝ 체중계, 저울
345 □ decision ⓝ 결정
346 □ repeat ⓥ 반복[되풀이]하다
347 □ error ⓝ 오류
348 □ day after day 매일같이[날마다]
349 □ again and again 몇 번이고, 되풀이해서
350 □ add up to (합이) 결국 ~이 되다
351 □ misstep ⓝ 실수, 잘못된 조치
352 □ eventually ⓐⓓ 결국
353 □ lead to ~로 이어지다

31
354 □ be of the essence 가장 중요하다
355 □ apology ⓝ 사과
356 □ accept ⓥ 받아들이다
357 □ thank ⓥ 감사하다
358 □ individual ⓝ 개인
359 □ hear ~ out ~의 말을 끝까지 들어주다
360 □ leave ⓥ ~을 (어떤 상태) 그대로 두다
361 □ conscious ⓐ 알고 있는, 의식하는
362 □ fully ⓐⓓ 완전히, 충분히
363 □ forgive ⓥ 용서하다
364 □ take time 시간이 걸리다
365 □ before ⓒⓞⓝⓙ …하기까지
366 □ injured ⓐ 상처받은, 부상 당한
367 □ party ⓝ 당사자, 상대방

368 □ completely ⓐⓓ 완전히
369 □ let go (걱정·근심 등을) 떨쳐 버리다
370 □ speed up 빨라지게 하다
371 □ process ⓝ 과정
372 □ truly ⓐⓓ 진정으로
373 □ important ⓐ 중요한
374 □ be worthwhile to- ~하는 것이 가치가 있다
375 □ heal ⓥ 치유되다
376 □ go back to (이전 상황·상태)로 돌아가다
377 □ normally ⓐⓓ 정상적으로
378 □ immediately ⓐⓓ 즉시, 곧
379 □ curiosity ⓝ 호기심
380 □ independence ⓝ 자립, 독립
381 □ patience ⓝ 인내
382 □ honesty ⓝ 정직(성), 솔직함

32
383 □ business ⓝ 사업체
384 □ excellent ⓐ 훌륭한
385 □ typically ⓐⓓ 보통, 전형적으로
386 □ afford ⓥ ~할 여유가 있다
387 □ aggressive ⓐ 매우 적극적인
388 □ get the word out 말을 퍼뜨리다
389 □ advertising ⓝ 광고(하기), 광고업
390 □ exchange ⓝ 교환, 주고받음, 맞바꿈
391 □ advertiser ⓝ 광고주
392 □ place ⓥ (광고를) 게시하다[내다]
393 □ for free 공짜로, 무료로
394 □ selling ⓐ 판매하는
395 □ beauty product 미용 제품
396 □ in turn 차례로, 결국
397 □ neither ⓐ (둘 중) 어느 쪽의 …도 …아니다
398 □ charge ⓥ (요금을) 청구하다, 부과하다
399 □ gain in popularity 인기를 얻다
400 □ especially ⓐⓓ 특히
401 □ marketer ⓝ 마케팅 담당자
402 □ sales team 영업팀
403 □ outlet ⓝ 배출구, 출구
404 □ reach ⓥ ~와 접촉하다
405 □ target audience 목표 접속자
406 □ otherwise ⓐⓓ 그러지 않으면
407 □ trade ⓥ ~을 교환하다
408 □ fund ⓥ 기금을 지원하다 ⓝ 기금
409 □ facility ⓝ 시설
410 □ commercial ⓝ 광고 ⓐ 상업적인

33
411 □ motivation ⓝ 동기 부여
412 □ several ⓐ 여러 가지의, 몇몇의
413 □ source ⓝ 공급원
414 □ greeting ⓝ 인사
415 □ respect ⓝ 존중
416 □ undivided ⓐ 완전한, 전적인
417 □ attention ⓝ 집중, 주의
418 □ a pat on the shoulder (격려의 의미로) 어깨를 토닥임
419 □ accepting ⓐ 포용적인, 수용적인
420 □ drop out of school 학교를 중퇴하다
421 □ frequent ⓐ 잦은, 빈번한
422 □ absence ⓝ 결석
423 □ make one's day ~을 행복하게 만들다

424 technique ⓝ 기법, 기술
425 concern ⓝ 관심, 걱정
426 genuine ⓐ 진실한, 진짜의
427 fool ⓥ 속이다
428 keep one's words 약속을 지키다
429 differ from ~와 다르다
430 evaluate ⓥ 평가하다

34
431 work out 운동하다
432 connection ⓝ 연결
433 run into ~을 우연히 만나다
434 never A until B B하고 나서야 비로소 A하다
435 comfort zone 안락 지대
436 move forward 앞으로 나아가다
437 path ⓝ 진로
438 awaken ⓥ 깨우다
439 spiritual ⓐ 영적인, 정신적인
440 benefit ⓥ 이롭게 하다
441 in the long run 결국에는, 장기적으로
442 spice ⓝ 묘미, 향신료
443 laziness ⓝ 게으름
444 invention ⓝ 발명
445 conflict ⓝ 갈등
446 strengthen ⓥ 강화하다

35
447 appropriate ⓐ 적절한
448 vary ⓥ 다르다
449 tend to- ~하는 경향이 있다
450 except to ~을 제외하고
451 close ⓐ 친한, 가까운
452 in general 일반적으로
453 reach out to ~에게 관심을 보이다
454 stranger ⓝ 낯선[모르는] 사람
455 willingness ⓝ 기꺼이 ~하려는 마음
456 be good at ~에 능숙하다
457 view A as B A를 B로 간주하다
458 harmony ⓝ 조화
459 improvement ⓝ 발전, 개선
460 prevent A from ~ing A가 ~하지 못하게 막다
461 outsider ⓝ 외부인
462 unfavorable ⓐ 불리한, 호의적이 아닌

36
463 defeat ⓥ 패배시키다
464 rival ⓐ 경쟁하는
465 fall out of ~에서 떨어지다
466 take pity on ~을 불쌍히 여기다
467 bendable ⓐ 구부릴 수 있는
468 cut off ~을 잘라 내다
469 inconvenient ⓐ 불편한
470 at last 마침내
471 cry out for ~을 얻고자 외치다
472 matter ⓝ 문제
473 blessing ⓝ 축복
474 resting place 안식처
475 be in a hurry 서두르다
476 absent-mindedly ⓐ 아무 생각 없이, 멍하니

37
477 passing ⓝ (시간의) 흐름, 경과
478 think of A as B A를 B라고 간주하다
479 that is 즉, 다시 말해서
480 refer to A as B A를 B라고 부르다, 언급하다
481 tribe ⓝ 부족
482 concept ⓝ 개념
483 measure ⓥ 측정하다
484 serial ⓐ 연속되는
485 rooted in ~에 뿌리를 둔
486 reflect ⓥ 반영하다
487 stage ⓝ (발달상의) 단계
488 give up ~을 넘겨주다
489 newborn ⓐ 갓 태어난
490 take on ~을 갖게 되다, ~을 맡다
491 statement ⓝ 말, 진술
492 objective ⓐ 객관적인

38
493 attitude ⓝ 태도
494 dramatically ⓐ 극적으로
495 symbol ⓝ 상징
496 literature ⓝ 문학
497 central ⓐ 중심인, 중심의
498 mythology ⓝ 신화
499 poetry ⓝ 시
500 ritual ⓝ 의식
501 holiday ⓝ 기념일
502 exhibit ⓥ 보여주다, 전시하다
503 opposite ⓐ 정반대의
504 given ⓐ (이미)정해진; 특정한
505 species ⓝ 종(種)
506 honor ⓥ 존경하다
507 association ⓝ 협회, 연관
508 devoted to ~에 전념하는
509 breed ⓥ 기르다, 낳다

39
510 pay attention to ~에 주의를 기울이다
511 hard fact 명백한 사실
512 limit ⓝ 한계 ⓥ 제한하다
513 the number of 수(數)
514 possibly ⓐ 아마
515 develop ⓥ 발전하다
516 stable ⓐ 안정적인
517 social relationship 사회적 관계
518 background ⓝ 배경
519 colorful ⓐ 다채로운
520 be capable of doing ~할 수 있다
521 form ⓥ 형성하다
522 meaningful ⓐ 유의미한
523 assume ⓥ 가정하다

40
524 evolutionary ⓐ 진화적인
525 reason ⓝ 이유, 까닭, 사유
526 cooperation ⓝ 협동, 협력
527 means ⓝ 수단
528 eye contact 시선의 마주침
529 force ⓝ 힘
530 traffic ⓝ (차량) 운행, 교통

531 arguably ⓐ 주장컨대
532 quite ⓐ 꽤, 상당히
533 cooperative ⓐ 협동하는, 협조하는
534 noncooperative ⓐ 비협조적인
535 most of ~의 대부분
536 ability ⓝ 능력
537 block ⓥ 차단하다
538 weak ⓐ 약한, 힘이 없는
539 rearview mirror 백미러
540 believable ⓐ 믿을 수 있는
541 careful ⓐ 주의 깊은
542 direct ⓐ 직접적인
543 confident ⓐ 자신감 있는
544 regular ⓐ 정기적인

41~42
545 inefficiently ⓐ 비효율적으로
546 insist on ~을 고집하다, 주장하다
547 interrupt ⓥ 방해하다
548 trip ⓝ (어디까지의) 이동
549 surf ⓥ (인터넷을) 서핑하다 [검색하다]
550 ironically ⓐ 모순적이게도
551 concentrate ⓥ 집중하다
552 surround ⓥ 에워싸다
553 distraction ⓝ 주의를 산만하게 하는 것
554 argue ⓥ 주장하다
555 professional ⓝ 전문가
556 actually ⓐ 실제로
557 oppose ⓥ 반대하다
558 position ⓝ 견해
559 productively ⓐ 생산적으로
560 less-than-ideal ⓐ 결코 이상적이지 않은
561 condition ⓝ 상황, 조건
562 expose ⓥ 노출시키다
563 repeatedly ⓐ 반복적으로
564 background noise 배경 소음
565 educator ⓝ 교육 전문가
566 used to ~에 익숙한
567 not necessarily 반드시 ~인 것은 아니다
568 improve ⓥ 높이다, 향상시키다
569 academic performance 학업 성적
570 generally ⓐ 일반적으로
571 convinced ⓐ 확신하는
572 noisy ⓐ 시끄러운
573 successful ⓐ 성공한, 성공적인
574 plan ahead 미리 계획하다, 장래의 계획을 세우다

43~45
575 busy with ~로 바쁜
576 peel ⓥ 깎다, 껍질을 벗기다
577 slice up ~을 얇게 자르다
578 chat away 수다 떨다
579 notice ⓥ 알아차리다
580 strange ⓐ 이상한
581 pot ⓝ 냄비, 솥
582 wound ⓝ 상처
583 treat ⓥ 치료하다
584 sit around ~에 둘러앉다
585 lesson ⓝ 교훈
586 decide to~ ~하기로 결정하다, ~하기로 결심하다

587 kind words 친절한 말
588 grateful ⓐ 감사해하는
589 have quite a temper 성질이 보통이 아니다
590 drop ⓥ 떨어지다, 떨어뜨리다
591 chill ⓥ 진정하다
592 deep breath 심호흡
593 put out 불을 끄다
594 throw ⓥ 내던지다
595 explosion ⓝ 폭발
596 lid ⓝ 뚜껑
597 flame ⓝ 불길
598 burn ⓥ 불에 데다
599 dizzy ⓐ 어지러운
600 a couple of 몇 개의, 몇 사람의
601 rush into 급하게[무모하게] …하다
602 suspect ⓥ 의심하다
603 tightly ⓐ (쥐거나 안는 방식이) 꼭
604 yell at ~에게 고함지르다
605 explode ⓥ 폭발하다
606 irresponsible ⓐ 무책임한

TEST A-B 각 단어의 뜻을 [A] 영어는 우리말로, [B] 우리말은 영어로 쓰시오.

A	English	Korean
01	lose one's temper	
02	soothing	
03	keep in mind	
04	armpit	
05	scale	
06	genuine	
07	breed	
08	independence	
09	inefficiently	
10	in terms of	
11	run into	
12	grateful	
13	bendable	
14	vary	
15	convinced	
16	motivator	
17	routine	
18	conflict	
19	association	
20	assume	

B	Korean	English
01	결함이 있는	
02	인공의	
03	(문제 등을) 제기하다	
04	중요하다	
05	패배시키다	
06	요인	
07	인내	
08	구절	
09	거절하다	
10	잦은, 빈번한	
11	부상	
12	안정적인	
13	강화하다	
14	의식	
15	평가하다	
16	신체적인, 물리적인	
17	관심, 걱정	
18	완전한, 전적인	
19	결국에는, 장기적으로	
20	알리다, 통지하다	

▶ A-D 정답 : 해설편 71쪽

TEST C-D 각 단어의 뜻을 골라 기호를 쓰시오.

C	English			Korean
01	interrupt	(	)	ⓐ 투자
02	investment	(	)	ⓑ 재료
03	suspect	(	)	ⓒ 방해하다
04	in turn	(	)	ⓓ 차례로, 결국
05	evolutionary	(	)	ⓔ 약속을 지키다
06	float	(	)	ⓕ 강요하다
07	force	(	)	ⓖ (합이) 결국 ~이 되다
08	on the spot	(	)	ⓗ 의심하다
09	keep one's words	(	)	ⓘ 현장에서
10	add up to	(	)	ⓙ ~을 고집하다, 주장하다
11	selfie	(	)	ⓚ 진화적인
12	insist on	(	)	ⓛ 불리한, 호의적이 아닌
13	unfavorable	(	)	ⓜ 셀카 사진
14	reminder	(	)	ⓝ 상기시키는 것
15	ingredient	(	)	ⓞ 뜨다
16	reflect	(	)	ⓟ 모순적이게도
17	ironically	(	)	ⓠ 보장하다
18	filled with	(	)	ⓡ ~로 가득 찬
19	ensure	(	)	ⓢ 반영하다
20	conscious	(	)	ⓣ 알고 있는, 의식하는

D	Korean			English
01	광고; 상업적인	(	)	ⓐ spiritual
02	재고로 있는	(	)	ⓑ in stock
03	객관적인	(	)	ⓒ eventually
04	~할 여유가 있다	(	)	ⓓ hesitate
05	차단하다	(	)	ⓔ block
06	표면	(	)	ⓕ surface
07	집중하다	(	)	ⓖ commercial
08	폭발	(	)	ⓗ aspect
09	~에 주의를 기울이다	(	)	ⓘ concentrate
10	뒤처지다	(	)	ⓙ objective
11	결국	(	)	ⓚ pay attention to
12	측면	(	)	ⓛ afford
13	영적인, 정신적인	(	)	ⓜ explosion
14	망설이다	(	)	ⓝ be left behind
15	고안하다	(	)	ⓞ design
16	안식처	(	)	ⓟ arguably
17	주장컨대	(	)	ⓠ yell at
18	~할 수 있다	(	)	ⓡ resting place
19	높이다, 향상시키다	(	)	ⓢ be capable of doing
20	~에게 고함지르다	(	)	ⓣ improve

영어 영역

● 문항수 45개 | 배점 100점 | 제한 시간 70분   ● 점수 표시가 없는 문항은 모두 2점   ● 출처 : 고1 학력평가

1번부터 17번까지는 듣고 답하는 문제입니다. 1번부터 15번까지는 한 번만 들려주고, 16번부터 17번까지는 두 번 들려줍니다. 방송을 잘 듣고 답을 하시기 바랍니다.

1. 다음을 듣고, 남자가 하는 말의 목적으로 가장 적절한 것을 고르시오.

① 파손된 사물함 신고 절차를 안내하려고
② 사물함에 이름표를 부착할 것을 독려하려고
③ 사물함을 반드시 잠그고 다녀야 함을 강조하려고
④ 사물함 교체를 위해 사물함을 비울 것을 당부하려고
⑤ 사물함 사용에 대한 학생 설문 조사 참여를 요청하려고

2. 대화를 듣고, 여자의 의견으로 가장 적절한 것을 고르시오.

① 음식물을 들고 서점에 들어가면 안 된다.
② 서점에 의자를 비치하면 매출에 도움이 된다.
③ 서점은 책 외에 다양한 품목을 판매해야 한다.
④ 서점은 고객들에게 추천 도서 목록을 제공해야 한다.
⑤ 온라인 서점에서 책을 구매하는 것이 더 경제적이다.

3. 대화를 듣고, 두 사람의 관계를 가장 잘 나타낸 것을 고르시오.

① 미용사 – 고객
② 화방 점원 – 화가
③ 미술관장 – 방문객
④ 패션 디자이너 – 모델
⑤ 모자 가게 주인 – 손님

4. 대화를 듣고, 그림에서 대화의 내용과 일치하지 않는 것을 고르시오

5. 대화를 듣고, 남자가 여자를 위해 할 일로 가장 적절한 것을 고르시오

① 동아리 안내 책자 가져다주기
② 동아리 모임 장소 예약하기
③ 동아리 방에 함께 가기
④ 동아리 모임 일정 짜기
⑤ 동아리 가입 신청서 대신 제출하기

6. 대화를 듣고, 두 사람이 지불할 금액을 고르시오. [3점]

① $75   ② $80   ③ $85   ④ $105   ⑤ $110

7. 대화를 듣고, 여자가 뉴욕 여행을 취소한 이유를 고르시오.

① 부모님이 편찮으셔서
② 시골로 이사를 가게 되어서
③ 부모님 댁에서 휴가를 보내고 싶어서
④ 새로운 프로젝트를 맡게 되어서
⑤ 휴가 기간이 짧아져서

8. 대화를 듣고, Fun Town Amusement Park에 관해 언급되지 않은 것을 고르시오.

① 위치
② 도착 소요 시간
③ 개장 시간
④ 입장료
⑤ 특별 프로그램

9. 2019 Riverside High School Musical에 관한 다음 내용을 듣고, 일치하지 않는 것을 고르시오.

① 공연작은 Shrek이다.
② 공연을 위한 오디션은 작년 12월에 있었다.
③ 공연은 사흘간 진행된다.
④ 입장권은 1인당 8달러이다.
⑤ 입장권은 연극 동아리실에서 구입할 수 있다.

10. 다음 표를 보면서 대화를 듣고, 남자가 구매할 토스터를 고르시오.

Bestselling Toasters in K-Store

	Model	Number of Slices	Price	Color
①	A	1	$25	white
②	B	1	$30	silver
③	C	2	$40	white
④	D	4	$45	silver
⑤	E	4	$55	silver

11. 대화를 듣고, 여자의 마지막 말에 대한 남자의 응답으로 가장 적절한 것을 고르시오.

① Sorry, but I'd rather go to Spain by myself.
② No, I'm taking a class in the community center.
③ Yes, you need to eat healthy food for your brain.
④ Yeah, you don't have to worry about your brain.
⑤ Well, I'm not interested in learning Spanish.

12. 대화를 듣고, 남자의 마지막 말에 대한 여자의 응답으로 가장 적절한 것을 고르시오.

① But I haven't finished writing it.
② Yes, I can help you study history.
③ Okay, let's go to the teacher's office.
④ Well, take your time to write the essay.
⑤ Sorry, but I didn't bring my essay today.

13. 대화를 듣고, 남자의 마지막 말에 대한 여자의 응답으로 가장 적절한 것을 고르시오.

Woman: _____

① You're right. That's why I chose this book.
② That makes sense. I'll switch to an easier book.
③ Okay. I'll choose one from the bestseller list next time.
④ Don't worry. It's not too difficult for me to read.
⑤ Yeah. I'll join the book club to read more books.

14. 대화를 듣고, 여자의 마지막 말에 대한 남자의 응답으로 가장 적절한 것을 고르시오. [3점]

Man: _____

① Well, I'm not sure if your son likes it.
② No, it's dangerous to leave kids home alone.
③ Of course, they are not safe even for adults.
④ That's why it's difficult to find drones for kids.
⑤ Yes, as long as you get a right drone for his age.

15. 다음 상황 설명을 듣고, Lily가 John에게 할 말로 가장 적절한 것을 고르시오. [3점]

Lily: _____

① Why don't you run for class president?
② Please give me a hand putting up the poster.
③ How about changing your slogan in the poster?
④ Will you help me make a slogan for the election?
⑤ Tell me how to keep good relationships with classmates.

[16~17] 다음을 듣고, 물음에 답하시오.

16. 여자가 하는 말의 주제로 가장 적절한 것은?

① proverbs that have animals in them
② different proverbs in various cultures
③ why proverbs are difficult to understand
④ importance of studying animals' behavior
⑤ advantages of teaching values through proverbs

17. 언급된 동물이 <u>아닌</u> 것은?

① birds   ② mice   ③ cows   ④ chickens ⑤ dogs

┌───┐
│ 이제 듣기 문제가 끝났습니다. 18번부터는 문제지의 │
│ 지시에 따라 답을 하시기 바랍니다.   │
└───┘

18. 다음 글의 목적으로 가장 적절한 것은?

Dear Mrs. Coling,

My name is Susan Harris and I am writing on behalf of the students at Lockwood High School. Many students at the school have been working on a project about the youth unemployment problem in Lockwood. You are invited to attend a special presentation that will be held at our school auditorium on April 16th. At the presentation, students will propose a variety of ideas for developing employment opportunities for the youth within the community. As one of the famous figures in the community, we would be honored by your attendance. We look forward to seeing you there.

Sincerely,

Susan Harris

① 학생들이 준비한 발표회 참석을 부탁하려고
② 학생들을 위한 특별 강연을 해 준 것에 감사하려고
③ 청년 실업 문제의 해결 방안에 관한 강연을 의뢰하려고
④ 학생들의 발표회에 대한 재정적 지원을 요청하려고
⑤ 학생들의 프로젝트 심사 결과를 알려려고

19. 다음 글에 드러난 'I'의 심경 변화로 가장 적절한 것은?

On December 6th, I arrived at University Hospital in Cleveland at 10:00 a.m. I went through the process of admissions. I grew anxious because the time for surgery was drawing closer. I was directed to the waiting area, where I remained until my name was called. I had a few hours of waiting time. I just kept praying. At some point in my ongoing prayer process, before my name was called, in the midst of the chaos, an unbelievable peace embraced me. All my fear disappeared! An unbelievable peace overrode my emotions. My physical body relaxed in the comfort provided, and I looked forward to getting the surgery over with and working hard at recovery.

① cheerful → sad   ② worried → relieved
③ angry → ashamed   ④ jealous → thankful
⑤ hopeful → disappointed

20. 다음 글에서 필자가 주장하는 바로 가장 적절한 것은?

It can be tough to settle down to study when there are so many distractions. Most young people like to combine a bit of homework with quite a lot of instant messaging, chatting on the phone, updating profiles on social-networking sites, and checking emails. While it may be true that you can multi-task and can focus on all these things at once, try to be honest with yourself. It is most likely that you will be able to work best if you concentrate on your studies but allow yourself regular breaks — every 30 minutes or so — to catch up on those other pastimes.

① 공부할 때는 공부에만 집중하라.
② 평소 주변 사람들과 자주 연락하라.
③ 피로감을 느끼지 않게 충분한 휴식을 취하라.
④ 자투리 시간을 이용하여 숙제를 하라.
⑤ 학습에 유익한 취미 활동을 하라.

21. 밑줄 친 <u>information blinded</u>가 다음 글에서 의미하는 바로 가장 적절한 것은? [3점]

Technology has doubtful advantages. We must balance too much information versus using only the right information and keeping the decision-making process simple. The Internet has made so much free information available on any issue that we think we have to consider all of it in order to make a decision. So we keep searching for answers on the Internet. This makes us <u>information blinded</u>, like deer in headlights, when trying to make personal, business, or other decisions. To be successful in anything today, we have to keep in mind that in the land of the blind, a one-eyed person can accomplish the seemingly impossible. The one-eyed person understands the power of keeping any analysis simple and will be the decision maker when he uses his one eye of intuition.

* intuition: 직관

① unwilling to accept others' ideas
② unable to access free information
③ unable to make decisions due to too much information
④ indifferent to the lack of available information
⑤ willing to take risks in decision-making

22. 다음 글의 요지로 가장 적절한 것은?

Recent studies show some interesting findings about habit formation. In these studies, students who successfully acquired one positive habit reported less stress; less impulsive spending; better dietary habits; decreased caffeine consumption; fewer hours spent watching TV; and even fewer dirty dishes. Keep working on one habit long enough, and not only does it become easier, but so do other things as well. It's why those with the right habits seem to do better than others. They're doing the most important thing regularly and, as a result, everything else is easier.

① 참을성이 많을수록 성공할 가능성이 커진다.
② 한 번 들인 나쁜 습관은 쉽게 고쳐지지 않는다.
③ 나이가 들어갈수록 좋은 습관을 형성하기 힘들다.
④ 무리한 목표를 세우면 달성하지 못할 가능성이 크다.
⑤ 하나의 좋은 습관 형성은 생활 전반에 긍정적 효과가 있다.

23. 다음 글의 주제로 가장 적절한 것은?

While some sand is formed in oceans from things like shells and rocks, most sand is made up of tiny bits of rock that came all the way from the mountains! But that trip can take thousands of years. Glaciers, wind, and flowing water help move the rocky bits along, with the tiny travelers getting smaller and smaller as they go. If they're lucky, a river may give them a lift all the way to the coast. There, they can spend the rest of their years on the beach as sand.

① things to cause the travel of water
② factors to determine the size of sand
③ how most sand on the beach is formed
④ many uses of sand in various industries
⑤ why sand is disappearing from the beach

24. 다음 글의 제목으로 가장 적절한 것을 고르시오.

Studies from cities all over the world show the importance of life and activity as an urban attraction. People gather where things are happening and seek the presence of other people. Faced with the choice of walking down an empty or a lively street, most people would choose the street with life and activity. The walk will be more interesting and feel safer. Events where we can watch people perform or play music attract many people to stay and watch. Studies of benches and chairs in city space show that the seats with the best view of city life are used far more frequently than those that do not offer a view of other people.

① The City's Greatest Attraction: People
② Leave the City, Live in the Country
③ Make More Parks in the City
④ Feeling Lonely in the Crowded Streets
⑤ Ancient Cities Full of Tourist Attractions

25. 다음 도표의 내용과 일치하지 <u>않는</u> 것은?

News Video Consumption: on News Sites vs. via Social Networks

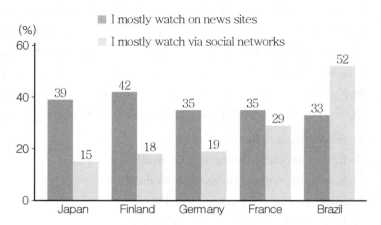

The above graph shows how people in five countries consume news videos: on news sites versus via social networks. ① Consuming news videos on news sites is more popular than via social networks in four countries. ② As for people who mostly watch news videos on news sites, Finland shows the highest percentage among the five countries. ③ The percentage of people who mostly watch news videos on news sites in France is higher than that in Germany. ④ As for people who mostly watch news videos via social networks, Japan shows the lowest percentage among the five countries. ⑤ Brazil shows the highest percentage of people who mostly watch news videos via social networks among the five countries.

26. chuckwalla에 관한 다음 글의 내용과 일치하지 <u>않는</u> 것은?

Chuckwallas are fat lizards, usually 20-25 cm long, though they may grow up to 45 cm. They weigh about 1.5 kg when mature. Most chuckwallas are mainly brown or black. Just after the annual molt, the skin is shiny. Lines of dark brown run along the back and continue down the tail. As the males grow older, these brown lines disappear and the body color becomes lighter; the tail becomes almost white. It is not easy to distinguish between male and female chuckwallas, because young males look like females and the largest females resemble males.

* molt: 탈피

① 길이가 45cm까지 자랄 수 있다.
② 대부분 갈색이거나 검은색이다.
③ 등을 따라 꼬리까지 짙은 갈색 선들이 나 있다.
④ 수컷의 몸통 색깔은 나이가 들수록 짙어진다.
⑤ 어린 수컷의 생김새는 암컷과 비슷하다.

27. L-19 Smart Watch 사용에 관한 다음 안내문의 내용과 일치하는 것은?

L-19 Smart Watch
User Guide

KEY FUNCTIONS

A Short press to confirm; long press to enter the sports mode.
B Short press to return to the 'home' menu; long press to send SOS location.
C Short press to turn on or off the background light; long press to turn on or off your watch.
D Press to go up. (In time, date or other settings, press the key to increase the value.)
E Press to go down. (In time, date or other settings, press the key to decrease the value.)

CAUTION

Make sure the battery level of your watch has at least two bars, in order to avoid an upgrading error.

* confirm: 설정값을 확정하다

① A를 짧게 누르면 스포츠 모드로 들어간다.
② B를 길게 누르면 '홈' 메뉴로 돌아간다.
③ C를 길게 누르면 배경 화면의 불빛이 켜지거나 꺼진다.
④ D를 누르면 설정값이 내려간다.
⑤ 업그레이드 오류를 피하려면 배터리 잔량 표시가 최소 두 칸은 되어야 한다.

28. 2017 Happy Voice Choir Audition에 관한 다음 안내문의 내용과 일치하지 <u>않는</u> 것은?

2017 Happy Voice Choir Audition

Do you love to sing? Happy Voice, one of the most famous school clubs, is holding an audition for you. Come and join us for some very exciting performances!

- Who: Any freshman
- When: Friday, March 24, 3 p.m.
- Where: Auditorium

All applicants should sing two songs:
 - 1st song: *Oh Happy Day!*
 - 2nd song: You choose your own.

To enter the audition, please email us at hvaudition@qmail.com.

For more information, visit the school website.

① 학교 동아리가 개최한다.
② 신입생이면 누구나 참가할 수 있다.
③ 3월 24일에 강당에서 열린다.
④ 지원자는 자신이 선택한 두 곡을 불러야 한다.
⑤ 참가하려면 이메일을 보내야 한다.

29. 다음 글의 밑줄 친 부분 중, 어법상 틀린 것은?

Bad lighting can increase stress on your eyes, as can light that is too bright, or light that shines ① <u>directly</u> into your eyes. Fluorescent lighting can also be ② <u>tiring</u>. What you may not appreciate is that the quality of light may also be important. Most people are happiest in bright sunshine — this may cause a release of chemicals in the body ③ <u>that</u> bring a feeling of emotional well-being. Artificial light, which typically contains only a few wavelengths of light, ④ <u>do</u> not seem to have the same effect on mood that sunlight has. Try experimenting with working by a window or ⑤ <u>using</u> full spectrum bulbs in your desk lamp. You will probably find that this improves the quality of your working environment.

* fluorescent lighting: 형광등

30. 다음 글의 밑줄 친 부분 중, 문맥상 낱말의 쓰임이 적절하지 않은 것은? [3점]

Painters have in principle an infinite range of colours at their disposal, especially in modern times with the chromatic ① <u>explosion</u> of synthetic chemistry. And yet painters don't use all the colours at once, and indeed many have used a remarkably ② <u>restrictive</u> selection. Mondrian limited himself mostly to the three primaries red, yellow and blue to fill his black-ruled grids, and Kasimir Malevich worked with similar self-imposed restrictions. For Yves Klein, one colour was ③ <u>enough</u>; Franz Kline's art was typically black on white. There was nothing ④ <u>new</u> in this: the Greeks and Romans tended to use just red, yellow, black and white. Why? It's impossible to generalize, but both in antiquity and modernity it seems likely that the ⑤ <u>expanded</u> palette aided clarity and comprehensibility, and helped to focus attention on the components that mattered: shape and form.

* chromatic: 유채색의   ** grid: 격자무늬

[31 ~ 34] 다음 빈칸에 들어갈 말로 가장 적절한 것을 고르시오.

31. In small towns the same workman makes chairs and doors and tables, and often the same person builds houses. And it is, of course, impossible for a man of many trades to be skilled in all of them. In large cities, on the other hand, because many people make demands on each trade, one trade alone — very often even less than a whole trade — is enough to support a man. For instance, one man makes shoes for men, and another for women. And there are places even where one man earns a living by only stitching shoes, another by cutting them out, and another by sewing the uppers together. Such skilled workers may have used simple tools, but their _____ did result in more efficient and productive work. [3점]

* trade: 직종

① specialization
② criticism
③ competition
④ diligence
⑤ imagination

32. All mammals need to leave their parents and set up on their own at some point. But human adults generally provide a comfortable existence — enough food arrives on the table, money is given at regular intervals, the bills get paid and the electricity for the TV doesn't usually run out. If teenagers didn't build up a fairly major disrespect for and conflict with their parents or carers, they'd never want to leave. In fact, _____ is probably a necessary part of growing up. Later, when you live independently, away from them, you can start to love them again because you won't need to be fighting to get away from them. And you can come back sometimes for a home-cooked meal. [3점]

① developing financial management skills
② learning from other people's experiences
③ figuring out your strengths and interests
④ managing relationship problems with your peers
⑤ falling out of love with the adults who look after you

33. What do advertising and map-making have in common? Without doubt the best answer is their shared need to communicate a limited version of the truth. An advertisement must create an image that's appealing and a map must present an image that's clear, but neither can meet its goal by _____. Ads will cover up or play down negative aspects of the company or service they advertise. In this way, they can promote a favorable comparison with similar products or differentiate a product from its competitors. Likewise, the map must remove details that would be confusing. [3점]

① reducing the amount of information
② telling or showing everything
③ listening to people's voices
④ relying on visual images only
⑤ making itself available to everyone

34. It is difficult to know how to determine whether one culture is better than another. What is the cultural rank order of rock, jazz, and classical music? When it comes to public opinion polls about whether cultural changes are for the better or the worse, looking forward would lead to one answer and looking backward would lead to a very different answer. Our children would be horrified if they were told they had to go back to the culture of their grandparents. Our parents would be horrified if they were told they had to participate in the culture of their grandchildren. Humans tend to _____. After a certain age, anxieties arise when sudden cultural changes are coming. Our culture is part of who we are and where we stand, and we don't like to think that who we are and where we stand are short-lived. [3점]

① seek cooperation between generations
② be forgetful of what they experienced
③ adjust quickly to the new environment
④ make efforts to remember what their ancestors did
⑤ like what they have grown up in and gotten used to

35. 다음 글에서 전체 흐름과 관계 없는 문장은?

Today car sharing movements have appeared all over the world. In many cities, car sharing has made a strong impact on how city residents travel. ① Even in strong car-ownership cultures such as North America, car sharing has gained popularity. ② In the U.S. and Canada, membership in car sharing now exceeds one in five adults in many urban areas. ③ Strong influence on traffic jams and pollution can be felt from Toronto to New York, as each shared vehicle replaces around 10 personal cars. ④ The best thing about driverless cars is that people won't need a license to operate them. ⑤ City governments with downtown areas struggling with traffic jams and lack of parking lots are driving the growing popularity of car sharing.

[36~37] 주어진 글 다음에 이어질 글의 순서로 가장 적절한 것을 고르시오.

36.

> Collaboration is the basis for most of the foundational arts and sciences.

(A) For example, his sketches of human anatomy were a collaboration with Marcantonio della Torre, an anatomist from the University of Pavia. Their collaboration is important because it marries the artist with the scientist.

(B) It is often believed that Shakespeare, like most playwrights of his period, did not always write alone, and many of his plays are considered collaborative or were rewritten after their original composition. Leonardo Da Vinci made his sketches individually, but he collaborated with other people to add the finer details.

(C) Similarly, Marie Curie's husband stopped his original research and joined Marie in hers. They went on to collaboratively discover radium, which overturned old ideas in physics and chemistry.

* anatomy: 해부학적 구조

① (A) - (C) - (B) ② (B) - (A) - (C)
③ (B) - (C) - (A) ④ (C) - (A) - (B)
⑤ (C) - (B) - (A)

37.

> Andrew Carnegie, the great early-twentieth-century businessman, once heard his sister complain about her two sons.

(A) Within days he received warm grateful letters from both boys, who noted at the letters' end that he had unfortunately forgotten to include the check. If the check had been enclosed, would they have responded so quickly?

(B) They were away at college and rarely responded to her letters. Carnegie told her that if he wrote them he would get an immediate response.

(C) He sent off two warm letters to the boys, and told them that he was happy to send each of them a check for a hundred dollars (a large sum in those days). Then he mailed the letters, but didn't enclose the checks.

* enclose: 동봉하다

① (A) − (C) − (B) 　② (B) − (A) − (C)
③ (B) − (C) − (A) 　④ (C) − (A) − (B)
⑤ (C) − (B) − (A)

39.

> However, if you tried to copy the original rather than your imaginary drawing, you might find your drawing now was a little better.

Imagine in your mind one of your favorite paintings, drawings, cartoon characters or something equally complex. (①) Now, with that picture in your mind, try to draw what your mind sees. (②) Unless you are unusually gifted, your drawing will look completely different from what you are seeing with your mind's eye. (③) Furthermore, if you copied the picture many times, you would find that each time your drawing would get a little better, a little more accurate. (④) Practice makes perfect. (⑤) This is because you are developing the skills of coordinating what your mind perceives with the movement of your body parts. [3점]

* coordinate ~ with ...: ~와 …을 조화시키다

40. 다음 글의 내용을 한 문장으로 요약하고자 한다. 빈칸 (A), (B)에 들어갈 말로 가장 적절한 것은?

> A large American hardware manufacturer was invited to introduce its products to a distributor with good reputation in Germany. Wanting to make the best possible impression, the American company sent its most promising young executive, Fred Wagner, who spoke fluent German. When Fred first met his German hosts, he shook hands firmly, greeted everyone in German, and even remembered to bow the head slightly as is the German custom. Fred, a very effective public speaker, began his presentation with a few humorous jokes to set a relaxed atmosphere. However, he felt that his presentation was not very well received by the German executives. Even though Fred thought he had done his cultural homework, he made one particular error. Fred did not win any points by telling a few jokes. It was viewed as too informal and unprofessional in a German business setting.
>
> * distributor: 배급 업체

⬇

> This story shows that using ___(A)___ in a business setting can be considered ___(B)___ in Germany.

　　(A)　　　　　(B)
① humor　　……　essential
② humor　　……　inappropriate
③ gestures　　……　essential
④ gestures　　……　inappropriate
⑤ first names　……　useful

[38 ~ 39] 글의 흐름으로 보아, 주어진 문장이 들어가기에 가장 적절한 곳을 고르시오.

38.

> When you hit puberty, however, sometimes these forever-friendships go through growing pains.

Childhood friends — friends you've known forever — are really special. (①) They know everything about you, and you've shared lots of firsts. (②) You find that you have less in common than you used to. (③) Maybe you're into rap and she's into pop, or you go to different schools and have different groups of friends. (④) Change can be scary, but remember: Friends, even best friends, don't have to be exactly alike. (⑤) Having friends with other interests keeps life interesting — just think of what you can learn from each other.

* puberty: 사춘기

[41 ~ 42] 다음 글을 읽고, 물음에 답하시오.

Researchers brought two groups of 11-year-old boys to a summer camp at Robbers Cave State Park in Oklahoma. The boys were strangers to one another and upon arrival at the camp, were randomly separated into two groups. The groups were kept apart for about a week. They swam, camped, and hiked. Each group chose a name for itself, and the boys printed their group's name on their caps and T-shirts. Then the two groups met. A series of athletic competitions were set up between them. Soon, each group considered the other an (a) enemy. Each group came to look down on the other. The boys started food fights and stole various items from members of the other group. Thus, under competitive conditions, the boys quickly (b) drew sharp group boundaries.

The researchers next stopped the athletic competitions and created several apparent emergencies whose solution (c) required cooperation between the two groups. One such emergency involved a leak in the pipe supplying water to the camp. The researchers assigned the boys to teams made up of members of both groups. Their job was to look into the pipe and fix the leak. After engaging in several such (d) cooperative activities, the boys started playing together without fighting. Once cooperation replaced competition and the groups (e) started to look down on each other, group boundaries melted away as quickly as they had formed.

* apparent: ~인 것으로 보이는

41. 윗글의 제목으로 가장 적절한 것은?

① How Are Athletic Competitions Helpful for Teens?
② Preparation: The Key to Preventing Emergencies
③ What Makes Group Boundaries Disappear?
④ Respect Individual Differences in Teams
⑤ Free Riders: Headaches in Teams

42. 밑줄 친 (a)~(e) 중에서 문맥상 낱말의 쓰임이 적절하지 않은 것은?

① (a)　② (b)　③ (c)　④ (d)　⑤ (e)

[43 ~ 45] 다음 글을 읽고, 물음에 답하시오.

(A)

Once in a village lived a rich man. He had many slaves and servants for work. The rich man was very unkind and cruel to them. One day one of the slaves made a mistake while cooking food. (a) He overcooked the food. When the rich man saw the food, he became angry and punished the slave. He kept the slave in a small room and locked it from outside.

(B)

After a few days the lion recovered. The slave and the lion became very close friends. A few days went by but one day the slave was caught by one of the guards of the rich man. The guard took (b) him to the rich man, who decided to punish him severely. The rich man ordered guards to put him in the lion's cage.

(C)

Somehow the slave escaped from that room and ran away. (c) He went to a forest. There he saw a lion. Instead of becoming afraid of the lion and running away, he went close to the lion. He saw the lion was injured and one of his legs was bleeding. The slave searched for herbs to cure the lion's wound and took care of the lion.

(D)

The whole village got the news about it and came to see. As soon as the slave was locked in the lion's cage, the lion came near (d) him and started licking his hand and hugged him. It was the same lion that the slave had helped in the forest. Seeing this, everyone was surprised. The rich man thought that the slave was such a great person that the lion didn't kill him. (e) He freed the slave, made him his friend and started to treat all his servants and slaves better.

43. 주어진 글 (A)에 이어질 내용을 순서에 맞게 배열한 것으로 가장 적절한 것은?

① (B) − (D) − (C)　② (C) − (B) − (D)
③ (C) − (D) − (B)　④ (D) − (B) − (C)
⑤ (D) − (C) − (B)

44. 밑줄 친 (a)~(e) 중에서 가리키는 대상이 나머지 넷과 다른 것은?

① (a)　② (b)　③ (c)　④ (d)　⑤ (e)

45. 윗글의 내용으로 적절하지 않은 것은?

① 부자는 노예가 요리한 음식을 보고 화가 났다.
② 노예는 부자의 경비병에게 잡혔다.
③ 노예는 사자를 보자 재빨리 달아났다.
④ 사자의 다리에서 피가 나고 있었다.
⑤ 노예는 사자 우리에 갇혔다.

* 확인 사항
○ 답안지의 해당란에 필요한 내용을 정확히 기입(표기)했는지 확인하시오.

01
001 □ vice principal 교감
002 □ announcement ⓝ 안내, 공고
003 □ complaint ⓝ 불평, 불만
004 □ decide ⓥ 결정하다
005 □ empty ⓥ 비우다
006 □ leave behind ~을 두고 가다
007 □ remove ⓥ 치우다, 제거하다
008 □ throw away 버리다

02
009 □ bookstore ⓝ 책방, 서점
010 □ downtown ⓐⓓ 시내에
011 □ cozy ⓐ 안락한, 편안한, 아늑한
012 □ actually ⓐⓓ 사실, 실제로
013 □ sell ⓥ 팔다, 팔리다
014 □ wonder ⓥ 궁금하다
015 □ attract ⓥ 끌어들이다, 끌어모으다
016 □ customer ⓝ 손님, 고객
017 □ go up (가격 등이) 오르다

03
018 □ long time no see. 오랜만이에요.
019 □ prepare for ~을 준비하다
020 □ suit ⓥ 어울리다(= go well with)
021 □ go well with ~와 잘 어울리다

04
022 □ flea market 벼룩시장
023 □ cart ⓝ 수레

05
024 □ fill out (양식 등을) 작성하다, 기입하다
025 □ application ⓝ 신청서, 지원서
026 □ belong to ~에 속하다
027 □ though ⓐⓓ (문미에서) 하지만, 그래도
028 □ brochure ⓝ 안내 책자
029 □ submit ⓥ 제출하다

06
030 □ tight ⓐ 꽉 끼는
031 □ originally ⓐⓓ 원래, 본래
032 □ enough ⓐⓓ 충분히

07
033 □ pack ⓥ (짐을) 싸다, 꾸리다, 챙기다
034 □ cancel ⓥ 취소하다
035 □ countryside ⓝ 시골 (지역), 전원 지대
036 □ miss ⓥ 보고 싶어 하다, 그리워하다

08
037 □ amusement park 놀이 공원
038 □ offer ⓥ 제공하다
039 □ feeding ⓝ 먹이 주기

09
040 □ invite ⓥ 초대하다
041 □ present ⓥ (연극·방송 등을) 공연하다
042 □ based on ~에 근거하여
043 □ be full of ~로 가득 차다
044 □ animated film 만화영화
045 □ cast ⓝ 출연자들, 배역진

046 □ crew ⓝ (특정한 기술을 가지고 함께 일을 하는) 팀, 반, 조
047 □ rehearse ⓥ 예행연습을 하다
048 □ hold ⓥ 개최하다
049 □ perfect ⓥ 완벽하게 하다
050 □ drama club 연극 동아리
051 □ detail ⓝ 세부 사항

10
052 □ slice ⓝ 조각
053 □ out of ~ 중에
054 □ price range 가격대
055 □ option ⓝ 선택지, 선택
056 □ go with ~을 고르다, ~을 받아들이다

11
057 □ foreign language 외국어
058 □ brain ⓝ 두뇌
059 □ by oneself 혼자
060 □ be good for ~에 좋다
061 □ healthy ⓐ 건강에 좋은

12
062 □ bring ⓥ 가져오다, 가져가다
063 □ how about ~? ~은 어때?
064 □ why don't we ~? ~하는 게 어때?
065 □ submit ⓥ 제출하다

13
066 □ review ⓝ 비평, 평론, 독후감
067 □ frankly ⓐⓓ 솔직히, 솔직히 말하면
068 □ challenging ⓐ 힘이 드는, 도전적인
069 □ though ⓒⓞⓝⓙ 그러나
070 □ What's the use of ~? ~하는 것이 무슨 소용이니?
071 □ switch ⓥ 바꾸다

14
072 □ drone ⓝ 드론, (지상에서 조종하는) 무인 항공기
073 □ be crazy about ~에 열광하다, ~을 몹시 좋아하다
074 □ quite ⓐⓓ 아주, 굉장히
075 □ as long as ~하기만 하면

15
076 □ freshman ⓝ 신입생
077 □ run for ~에 출마하다
078 □ class president 반장
079 □ election ⓝ 선거
080 □ slogan ⓝ 표어, 슬로건
081 □ impress ⓥ 깊은 인상을 주다
082 □ come up with 생각해 내다, 떠올리다
083 □ give a hand ~을 도와주다
084 □ relationship ⓝ 관계

16~17
085 □ proverb ⓝ 속담
086 □ feather ⓝ 털, 깃털
087 □ flock ⓥ 모이다, 떼 지어 가다
088 □ commonly ⓐⓓ 흔히, 일반적으로
089 □ appear ⓥ 나오다, 등장하다

090 □ mouse ⓝ 생쥐 (pl.) mice
091 □ guess ⓥ 추측하다
092 □ hatch ⓥ 부화하다
093 □ be around 존재하다
094 □ count 세다
095 □ life cycle 생애 주기
096 □ lesson ⓝ 교훈
097 □ hasty ⓐ 성급한, 서두른
098 □ decision ⓝ 결정
099 □ turn ⓝ 차례
100 □ Every dog has its day. 쥐구멍에도 볕 들 날이 있다.
101 □ advantage ⓝ 이점

18
102 □ on behalf of ~을 대신하여, ~을 대표하여
103 □ work on ~을 수행하다
104 □ unemployment ⓝ 실업
105 □ attend ⓥ 참석하다
106 □ hold ⓥ (행사 등을) 열다
107 □ auditorium ⓝ 강당
108 □ propose ⓥ 제안하다
109 □ opportunity ⓝ 기회
110 □ within ⓟⓡⓔⓟ ~의 이내에
111 □ figure ⓝ 인물

19
112 □ arrive ⓥ 도착하다
113 □ process ⓝ 절차
114 □ admission ⓝ 입원, 입장
115 □ anxious ⓐ 불안한
116 □ surgery ⓝ 수술
117 □ draw close 가까이 가다
118 □ direct ⓥ 길을 안내하다
119 □ waiting area 대기실
120 □ remain ⓥ (떠나지 않고) 남다
121 □ pray ⓥ 기도하다
122 □ ongoing ⓐ 진행 중인
123 □ midst ⓝ 중앙, 한가운데
124 □ chaos ⓝ 혼돈
125 □ embrace ⓥ 감싸다, 포옹하다
126 □ fear ⓝ 두려움
127 □ override ⓥ (~의 위로) 퍼지다
128 □ comfort ⓝ 편안함
129 □ look forward to 고대하다
130 □ get ~ over with ~을 끝마치다
131 □ recovery ⓝ 회복
132 □ cheerful ⓐ 활기찬
133 □ aschamed ⓐ 부끄러운

20
134 □ tough ⓐ 힘든, 어려운
135 □ settle down to 마음을 가라앉히고 ~하기 시작하다
136 □ distraction ⓝ 마음을 산만하게 하는 것, 집중력을 흐뜨리는 것
137 □ combine ⓥ 합치다
138 □ a bit of 약간의, 좀
139 □ quite ⓐⓓ 꽤, 상당히
140 □ a lot of 많은, 여러
141 □ instant ⓐ 즉각적인, 즉시의
142 □ profile ⓝ 신상 정보

143 □ multi-task 여러 가지 일을 동시에 처리하다
144 □ focus on ~에 집중하다
145 □ once ⓐⓓ 한번에
146 □ try to ~하려고 노력하다
147 □ honest ⓐ 솔직한
148 □ concentrate on ~에 집중하다
149 □ allow ⓥ 허락하다
150 □ regular ⓐ 규칙적인
151 □ break ⓝ 휴식
152 □ catch up on ~을 처리하다, 따라잡다, 만회하다
153 □ pastime ⓝ 소일거리, 취미

21
154 □ technology ⓝ 기술
155 □ doubtful ⓐ 의문의 여지가 있는, 의심스러운
156 □ balance ⓥ 균형을 유지하다
157 □ too much information 과도하게 많은 정보
158 □ versus ⓟⓡⓔⓟ ~에 비해
159 □ right ⓐ 정확한
160 □ decision-making process 의사 결정 과정
161 □ available ⓐ 이용 가능한
162 □ issue ⓝ 문제
163 □ consider ⓥ 고려하다
164 □ in order to (목적) 위하여
165 □ make a decision 결정을 하다
166 □ blind ⓐ 눈이 먼
167 □ deer ⓝ 사슴
168 □ headlight ⓝ (자동차) 전조등
169 □ personal ⓐ 사적인, 개인적인
170 □ keep in mind 명심하다
171 □ accomplish ⓥ 달성하다, 성취하다
172 □ seemingly ⓐⓓ 겉보기에
173 □ analysis ⓝ 분석
174 □ decision maker 의사 결정자
175 □ unwilling ⓐ (~하기를) 꺼리는, 마지못해 하는
176 □ unable ⓐ ~할 수 없는
177 □ due ⓐ ~ 때문에
178 □ access ⓥ 접근하다, 이용하다
179 □ indifferent ⓐ 무관심한
180 □ lack ⓝ 부족, 결여
181 □ willing ⓐ 기꺼이 하는
182 □ take a risk 위험을 감수하다

22
183 □ finding ⓝ 결과, 결론
184 □ habit ⓝ 버릇
185 □ formation ⓝ 형성
186 □ successfully ⓐⓓ 성공적으로
187 □ acquire ⓥ 습득하다, 얻다
188 □ dietary ⓐ 식사의
189 □ work on ~하려고 노력하다
190 □ regularly ⓐⓓ 규칙적으로

23
191 □ form ⓥ 형성하다, 만들다
192 □ shell ⓝ 조개껍데기
193 □ rock ⓝ 암석

194 ☐ sand ⓝ 모래
195 ☐ be made up of ~로 이루어지다
196 ☐ tiny ⓐ 작은
197 ☐ bit ⓝ (작은) 조각
198 ☐ all the way 내내, 멀리
199 ☐ glacier ⓝ 빙하
200 ☐ flow ⓥ 흐르다
201 ☐ rocky ⓐ 바위로 된
202 ☐ traveler ⓝ 여행자
203 ☐ give a lift ~을 실어다 주다, 태워주다, 들어 올리다
204 ☐ coast ⓝ 해안
205 ☐ spend ⓥ (시간을) 보내다
206 ☐ rest ⓝ (어떤 것의) 나머지
207 ☐ factor ⓝ 요인
208 ☐ determine ⓥ 결정하다
209 ☐ various ⓐ 다양한
210 ☐ industry ⓝ 산업, 제조업
211 ☐ disappear ⓥ 사라지다

24
212 ☐ urban ⓐ 도시의
213 ☐ attraction ⓝ 매력, 끌림, 명소
214 ☐ gather ⓥ 모이다
215 ☐ seek ⓥ 찾다, 구하다
216 ☐ presence ⓝ 존재
217 ☐ lively ⓐ 활기찬
218 ☐ perform ⓥ 공연하다, 연기하다, 수행하다
219 ☐ attract ⓥ 끌어들이다, 마음을 끌다
220 ☐ frequently ⓐⓓ 자주

25
221 ☐ consumption ⓝ 소비
222 ☐ via ⓟⓡⓔⓟ ~을 통하여, ~을 경유하여
223 ☐ consume ⓥ 소비하다, 쓰다
224 ☐ versus ⓟⓡⓔⓟ 대(對)
225 ☐ popular ⓐ 인기 있는
226 ☐ mostly ⓐⓓ 주로, 대개
227 ☐ highest ⓐ 가장 높은, 최고의
228 ☐ among ⓟⓡⓔⓟ ~사이에, ~중에
229 ☐ higher ⓐ 더 높은
230 ☐ as for ~에 있어서는
231 ☐ lowest ⓐ 최저의

26
232 ☐ lizard ⓝ 도마뱀
233 ☐ up to ~까지
234 ☐ weigh ⓥ 무게가 ~이다
235 ☐ mature ⓥ 다 자란, 성숙한
236 ☐ annual ⓐ 매년의, 1년의
237 ☐ disappear ⓥ 사라지다
238 ☐ distinguish ⓥ 구별하다
239 ☐ resemble ⓥ 닮다

27
240 ☐ user guide 사용 설명서
241 ☐ function ⓝ 기능
242 ☐ press ⓥ (기기를 작동시키기 위해 버튼 등을) 누르다
243 ☐ confirm ⓥ 확정하다
244 ☐ enter ⓥ 들어가다
245 ☐ return ⓥ 돌아가다

246 ☐ send ⓥ 보내다, 발송하다
247 ☐ sos ⓝ 조난[구조] 신호
248 ☐ location ⓝ 위치
249 ☐ background light 배경화면 불빛
250 ☐ go up 올라가다
251 ☐ setting ⓝ 설정, 환경
252 ☐ increase ⓥ 올리다, 증가시키다
253 ☐ value ⓝ 설정값
254 ☐ go down 내려가다
255 ☐ decrease ⓥ 줄이다, 감소시키다
256 ☐ caution ⓝ 주의 사항
257 ☐ make sure 반드시 ~하다
258 ☐ at least 적어도
259 ☐ avoid ⓥ 피하다

28
260 ☐ freshman ⓝ 신입생
261 ☐ auditorium ⓝ 강당, 방청석, 청중석
262 ☐ applicant ⓝ 지원자
263 ☐ enter ⓥ 참가하다, 들어가다, 입장하다
264 ☐ information ⓝ 정보, 자료

29
265 ☐ lighting ⓝ 조명, 빛
266 ☐ increase ⓥ 증가시키다
267 ☐ bright ⓐ 밝은
268 ☐ shine ⓥ 비추다
269 ☐ directly ⓐⓓ 곧장, 똑바로
270 ☐ tiring ⓐ 피곤한
271 ☐ appreciate ⓥ 이해하다
272 ☐ release ⓝ 분비, 방출
273 ☐ chemical ⓝ 화학 물질
274 ☐ emotional ⓐ 정서적인
275 ☐ artificial ⓐ 인공의
276 ☐ typically ⓐⓓ 일반적으로
277 ☐ contain ⓥ …이 들어[함유되어] 있다
278 ☐ wavelength ⓝ 파장, 주파수
279 ☐ effect ⓝ 효과
280 ☐ mood ⓝ 기분
281 ☐ experiment ⓥ 실험하다 ⓝ 실험
282 ☐ bulb ⓝ 전구
283 ☐ desk ⓝ 책상
284 ☐ lamp ⓝ 램프, 등
285 ☐ improve ⓥ 향상시키다, 개선하다
286 ☐ environment ⓝ 환경

30
287 ☐ in principle 원칙적으로, 이론상으로
288 ☐ infinite ⓐ 무한한
289 ☐ at one's disposal ~의 마음대로 이용할 수 있는
290 ☐ explosion ⓝ 폭발적 증가, 폭발
291 ☐ synthetic ⓐ 합성한
292 ☐ chemistry ⓝ 화학
293 ☐ at once 동시에
294 ☐ indeed ⓐⓓ 정말
295 ☐ remarkably ⓐⓓ 눈에 띄게, 두드러지게
296 ☐ restrictive ⓐ 제한적인
297 ☐ selection ⓝ 선택, 선발, 선정
298 ☐ limit ⓥ 제한하다
299 ☐ mostly ⓐⓓ 대부분, 대개
300 ☐ primary ⓝ 원색 ⓐ 주요한, 기본적인

301 ☐ fill ⓥ 채우다, 메우다
302 ☐ self-imposed 스스로 부과한, 자진해서 하는
303 ☐ typically ⓐⓓ 보통, 대개, 전형적으로
304 ☐ impossible ⓐ 불가능한
305 ☐ generalize ⓥ 일반화하다
306 ☐ antiquity ⓝ 고대, 아주 오래됨
307 ☐ modernity ⓝ 현대, 현대적임
308 ☐ it seems like ~인 것 같다
309 ☐ expand ⓥ 확장시키다
310 ☐ palette ⓝ 팔레트, 색
311 ☐ aid ⓥ (일이 수월해지도록) 돕다
312 ☐ clarity ⓝ 명확성
313 ☐ comprehensibility ⓝ 이해 가능성
314 ☐ focus ⓥ 집중하다
315 ☐ attention ⓝ 주의
316 ☐ component ⓝ 구성 요소
317 ☐ shape ⓝ 모양
318 ☐ form ⓝ 형태

31
319 ☐ workman ⓝ 일꾼, 노동자, 직공
320 ☐ impossible ⓐ 불가능한
321 ☐ skilled ⓐ 숙련된
322 ☐ place ⓝ 경우
323 ☐ stitch ⓥ 깁다, 꿰매다, 바느질하다
324 ☐ sew ⓥ 꿰매다, 깁다
325 ☐ result in ~로 이어지다, ~을 초래하다
326 ☐ efficient ⓐ 효율적인
327 ☐ productive ⓐ 생산적인
328 ☐ criticism ⓝ 비판
329 ☐ diligence ⓝ 근면

32
330 ☐ mammal ⓝ 포유동물
331 ☐ leave ⓥ 떠나다
332 ☐ set up on one's own 자립하다
333 ☐ point ⓝ 지점
334 ☐ generally ⓐⓓ 대개, 보통
335 ☐ existence ⓝ 생활, 생계, 존재, 현존
336 ☐ interval ⓝ 간격
337 ☐ bill ⓝ 청구서
338 ☐ get paid 봉급을 받다
339 ☐ electricity ⓝ 전기
340 ☐ usually ⓐⓓ 보통, 대개
341 ☐ run out (공급품 등이) 다 떨어지다
342 ☐ build up ~을 키우다, 쌓다
343 ☐ fairly ⓐⓓ 상당히, 꽤
344 ☐ major ⓐ 심각한
345 ☐ disrespect ⓝ 불손, 무례, 결례
346 ☐ conflict ⓝ 갈등, 충돌
347 ☐ carer ⓝ 보호자
348 ☐ in fact 사실
349 ☐ probably ⓐⓓ 아마
350 ☐ necessary ⓐ 필수적인
351 ☐ grow up 성장[성숙]하다
352 ☐ independently ⓐⓓ 독립하여
353 ☐ away from ~에서 떠나서
354 ☐ get away from ~로부터 벗어나다
355 ☐ home-cooked 가정에서 만든
356 ☐ financial ⓐ 재정적인, 금전적인
357 ☐ management ⓝ 관리, 처리

358 ☐ strength ⓝ 강점, 힘
359 ☐ peer ⓝ 동료, 친구
360 ☐ manage ⓥ 살아 나가다, 지내다
361 ☐ figure out ~을 알아내다
362 ☐ fall out of love with ~와 정을 떼다

33
363 ☐ advertising ⓝ 광고
364 ☐ map-making 지도 제작, 지도 만들기
365 ☐ have in common (관심사나 생각을) 공통적으로 지니다
366 ☐ communicate ⓥ 전달하다
367 ☐ appealing ⓐ 매력적인
368 ☐ present ⓥ 제시하다
369 ☐ meet ⓥ (목표나 기한 등을) 달성하다, 맞추다
370 ☐ play down 약화시키다, 낮추다
371 ☐ aspect ⓝ 측면
372 ☐ promote ⓥ 홍보하다, 촉진하다
373 ☐ favorable ⓐ 호의적인
374 ☐ comparison ⓝ 비교
375 ☐ differentiate ⓥ 차별화하다
376 ☐ competitor ⓝ 경쟁자, 경쟁 상대
377 ☐ confusing ⓐ 혼란을 주는, 혼란스러운

34
378 ☐ difficult ⓐ 어려운, 힘든
379 ☐ determine ⓥ 결정하다, 정하다
380 ☐ culture ⓝ 문화
381 ☐ rank ⓝ 순위
382 ☐ classical music 고전 음악, 클래식
383 ☐ when it comes to ~에 관해 이야기하면, ~에 관한 한
384 ☐ public opinion poll 여론 조사
385 ☐ forward ⓐⓓ (위치가) 앞으로
386 ☐ lead to ~로 이어지다
387 ☐ backward ⓐⓓ 뒤를 향해, 뒤쪽으로
388 ☐ horrified ⓐ 겁에 질린, 무서워하는
389 ☐ go back to (…로) 돌아가다
390 ☐ participate in ~에 참여하다
391 ☐ grandchildren ⓝ 손자
392 ☐ certain ⓐ 특정한, 일정한
393 ☐ anxiety ⓝ 불안, 걱정
394 ☐ arise ⓥ 생기다, 발생하다
395 ☐ sudden ⓐ 갑작스러운
396 ☐ short-lived 오래 가지 못하는, 단기적인
397 ☐ seek ⓥ 찾다
398 ☐ cooperation ⓝ 협력
399 ☐ generation ⓝ 세대
400 ☐ experienced ⓐ 경험[경력]이 있는
401 ☐ adjust ⓥ 적응하다
402 ☐ environment ⓝ (주변의) 환경
403 ☐ ancestor ⓝ 조상

35
404 ☐ have an impact on ~에 영향을 미치다
405 ☐ resident ⓝ 거주민, 거주자
406 ☐ ownership ⓝ 소유
407 ☐ popularity ⓝ 인기
408 ☐ membership ⓝ 회원 수, 회원들
409 ☐ exceed ⓥ 넘어서다, 능가하다
410 ☐ traffic jam 교통 체증

411 ☐ **vehicle** ⓝ 차량, 탈것

412 ☐ **replace** ⓥ 대체하다

413 ☐ **driverless car** 무인 자동차

414 ☐ **operate** ⓥ 조작하다, 가동하다

415 ☐ **struggle with** ~에 시달리다, ~로 고전하다

36

416 ☐ **collaboration** ⓝ 협업, 협동, 공동 작업

417 ☐ **basis** ⓝ 근거, 이유

418 ☐ **foundational** ⓐ 기초적인, 기본의

419 ☐ **sketch** ⓝ 개요

420 ☐ **anatomist** ⓝ 해부학자

421 ☐ **marry** ⓥ (서로 다른 두 가지 사상·사물을 성공적으로) 결합시키다

422 ☐ **playwright** ⓝ 극작가

423 ☐ **period** ⓝ 기간, 시기

424 ☐ **play** ⓝ 희곡

425 ☐ **consider** ⓥ (~을 ~로) 여기다

426 ☐ **rewrite** ⓥ 개작하다, 다시 쓰다

427 ☐ **composition** ⓝ 작성, 작곡, 작품

428 ☐ **individually** ⓐ𝖽 개인적으로, 따로

429 ☐ **fine** ⓐ 세밀한, 섬세한, 촘촘한

430 ☐ **join** ⓥ 합류하다

431 ☐ **radium** ⓝ 라듐

432 ☐ **overturn** ⓥ 뒤엎다, 전복시키다

433 ☐ **physics** ⓝ 물리학

434 ☐ **chemistry** ⓝ 화학

37

435 ☐ **businessman** ⓝ 사업가

436 ☐ **complain** ⓥ 불평하다

437 ☐ **grateful** ⓐ 감사해하는, 고마워하는

438 ☐ **note** ⓥ 언급하다, 말하다

439 ☐ **unfortunately** ⓐ𝖽 안타깝게도, 불행히도

440 ☐ **check** ⓝ 수표

441 ☐ **rarely** ⓐ𝖽 좀처럼 ~하지 않는

442 ☐ **immediate** ⓐ 즉각적인, 즉시의

443 ☐ **send off** 보내다, 발송하다

444 ☐ **mail** ⓥ (우편물을) 부치다, 보내다

38

445 ☐ **puberty** ⓝ 사춘기

446 ☐ **go through** ~을 겪다

447 ☐ **scary** ⓐ 무서운, 겁나는

448 ☐ **exactly** ⓐ𝖽 정확히

449 ☐ **alike** ⓐ (아주) 비슷한

450 ☐ **interest** ⓝ 관심사, 흥미

39

451 ☐ **copy** ⓥ 베끼다

452 ☐ **imaginary** ⓐ 상상의, 가상적인

453 ☐ **drawing** ⓝ (색칠을 하지 않은) 그림, 소묘, 데생

454 ☐ **favorite** ⓐ 마음에 드는, 매우 좋아하는

455 ☐ **painting** ⓝ (물감으로 그린) 그림

456 ☐ **cartoon** ⓝ 만화

457 ☐ **character** ⓝ 등장인물

458 ☐ **equally** ⓐ𝖽 똑같이

459 ☐ **complex** ⓐ 복잡한

460 ☐ **unless** 𝖼𝗈𝗇𝗃 ~하지 않는 한

461 ☐ **unusually** ⓐ𝖽 특별하게

462 ☐ **gifted** ⓐ 재능 있는에

463 ☐ **completely** ⓐ𝖽 완전히

464 ☐ **furthermore** ⓐ𝖽 게다가

465 ☐ **accurate** ⓐ 정확한

466 ☐ **practice** ⓝ 연습

467 ☐ **perceive** ⓥ 인지하다, 인식하다

468 ☐ **movement** ⓝ 움직임

469 ☐ **body parts** 신체부분

40

470 ☐ **manufacturer** ⓝ 제조 업체, 생산자

471 ☐ **introduce** ⓥ 소개하다, 도입하다

472 ☐ **distributor** ⓝ 배급 업체, 배급자

473 ☐ **reputation** ⓝ 명성

474 ☐ **impression** ⓝ 인상

475 ☐ **promising** ⓐ 촉망받는, 전도 유망한

476 ☐ **executive** ⓝ 임원, 중역

477 ☐ **firmly** ⓐ𝖽 굳게, 단단히, 단호히

478 ☐ **greet** ⓥ 인사하다, 환영하다

479 ☐ **bow** ⓥ (고개를) 숙이다

480 ☐ **slightly** ⓐ𝖽 약간, 조금

481 ☐ **custom** ⓝ 관습

482 ☐ **relaxed** ⓐ 편안한

483 ☐ **atmosphere** ⓝ 분위기

484 ☐ **particular** ⓐ 특정한

485 ☐ **informal** ⓐ 비격식적인, 허물없는

41~42

486 ☐ **arrival** ⓝ 도착

487 ☐ **randomly** ⓐ𝖽 무작위로

488 ☐ **separate** ⓥ 나누다, 분리하다

489 ☐ **apart** ⓐ𝖽 떨어져, 따로

490 ☐ **athletic** ⓐ 운동의, 육상의

491 ☐ **look down on** ~을 얕잡아보다, 깔보다

492 ☐ **competitive** ⓐ 경쟁적인

493 ☐ **boundary** ⓝ 경계

494 ☐ **apparent** ⓐ 명백한

495 ☐ **emergency** ⓝ 비상사태

496 ☐ **involve** ⓥ 포함하다

497 ☐ **leak** ⓝ (물이) 새는 곳, 구멍 ⓥ (물이나 기체가) 새다

498 ☐ **supply** ⓥ 공급하다

499 ☐ **assign** ⓥ 배정하다

500 ☐ **look into** ~을 조사하다

501 ☐ **replace** ⓥ 대체하다

502 ☐ **melt away** 차츰 사라지다

503 ☐ **preparation** ⓝ 대비, 준비

504 ☐ **free rider** 무임승차자

43~45

505 ☐ **cruel** ⓐ 잔인한

506 ☐ **punish** ⓥ 처벌하다

507 ☐ **recover** ⓥ 회복하다, 낫다

508 ☐ **close** ⓐ (사이가) 친한, 가까운

509 ☐ **punish** ⓥ 처벌하다

510 ☐ **severely** ⓐ𝖽 엄하게, 심하게

511 ☐ **order** ⓥ 명령하다

512 ☐ **escape** ⓥ 달아나다, 탈출하다

513 ☐ **instead of** ~ 대신에

514 ☐ **run away** 도망치다, 달아나다

515 ☐ **injure** ⓥ 상처를 입히다

516 ☐ **bleed** ⓥ 피를 흘리다, 출혈하다

517 ☐ **search for** ~을 찾다

518 ☐ **herb** ⓝ 약초

519 ☐ **cure** ⓥ 치료하다

520 ☐ **wound** ⓝ 상처, 부상

521 ☐ **whole** ⓐ 전체의, 모든

522 ☐ **lick** ⓥ 핥다

523 ☐ **free** ⓥ 풀어 주다 ⓐ 자유로운

524 ☐ **treat** ⓥ 대하다, 대접하다

08회

TEST A-B 각 단어의 뜻을 [A] 영어는 우리말로, [B] 우리말은 영어로 쓰시오.

A	English	Korean
01	on behalf of	
02	embrace	
03	catch up on	
04	indifferent	
05	finding	
06	give a lift	
07	consume	
08	mature	
09	at one's disposal	
10	generalize	
11	diligence	
12	run out	
13	interval	
14	competitor	
15	exceed	
16	note	
17	go through	
18	promising	
19	boundary	
20	bleed	

B	Korean	English
01	참석하다	
02	제안하다	
03	기도하다	
04	편안함	
05	마음을 산만하게 하는 것, 집중력을 흩뜨리는 것	
06	분석	
07	위험을 감수하다	
08	매력, 끌림, 명소	
09	사라지다	
10	이해하다	
11	눈에 띄게, 두드러지게	
12	~로 이어지다, ~를 초래하다	
13	(목표 등을) 달성하다, 맞추다	
14	조상	
15	대체하다	
16	명성	
17	(물이) 새는 곳, 새다	
18	잔인한	
19	처벌하다	
20	상처를 입히다	

▶ A-D 정답 : 해설편 **084**쪽

TEST C-D 각 단어의 뜻을 골라 기호를 쓰시오.

C	English			Korean
01	admission	(	)	ⓐ 습득하다, 얻다
02	seemingly	(	)	ⓑ 원색, 주요한
03	acquire	(	)	ⓒ 닮다
04	glacier	(	)	ⓓ 동료
05	urban	(	)	ⓔ 겁에 질린, 무서워하는
06	via	(	)	ⓕ 정서적인
07	resemble	(	)	ⓖ 재능 있는
08	emotional	(	)	ⓗ 빙하
09	infinite	(	)	ⓘ 배정하다
10	primary	(	)	ⓙ ~을 통하여, ~을 경유하여
11	sew	(	)	ⓚ 입원, 입장
12	peer	(	)	ⓛ 즉각적인
13	horrified	(	)	ⓜ 상상의, 가상의
14	driverless car	(	)	ⓝ 인상
15	immediate	(	)	ⓞ 회복하다
16	imaginary	(	)	ⓟ 꿰매다, 깁다
17	gifted	(	)	ⓠ 겉보기에
18	impression	(	)	ⓡ 무인 자동차
19	assign	(	)	ⓢ 무한한
20	recover	(	)	ⓣ 도시의

D	Korean			English
01	실업	(	)	ⓐ accomplish
02	절차	(	)	ⓑ regularly
03	즉각적인, 즉시의	(	)	ⓒ freshman
04	달성하다, 성취하다	(	)	ⓓ artificial
05	규칙적으로	(	)	ⓔ synthetic
06	나머지	(	)	ⓕ vehicle
07	존재	(	)	ⓖ unemployment
08	신입생	(	)	ⓗ wavelength
09	인공의	(	)	ⓘ puberty
10	합성한	(	)	ⓙ informal
11	효율적인	(	)	ⓚ process
12	포유류	(	)	ⓛ atmosphere
13	불안, 걱정	(	)	ⓜ severely
14	차량, 탈것	(	)	ⓝ mammal
15	사춘기	(	)	ⓞ efficient
16	~하지 않는 한	(	)	ⓟ instant
17	분위기	(	)	ⓠ rest
18	비격식적인, 허물없는	(	)	ⓡ anxiety
19	엄하게, 심하게	(	)	ⓢ presence
20	파장, 주파수	(	)	ⓣ unless

2023학년도 6월 고1 전국연합학력평가 문제지

제 3 교시

영어 영역

1

09회

● 문항수 45개 | 배점 100점 | 제한 시간 70분

● 점수 표시가 없는 문항은 모두 2점

1번부터 17번까지는 듣고 답하는 문제입니다. 1번부터 15번까지는 한 번만 들려주고, 16번부터 17번까지는 두 번 들려줍니다. 방송을 잘 듣고 답을 하시기 바랍니다.

1. 다음을 듣고, 여자가 하는 말의 목적으로 가장 적절한 것을 고르시오.

① 체육대회 종목을 소개하려고
② 대회 자원봉사자를 모집하려고
③ 학생 회장 선거 일정을 공지하려고
④ 경기 관람 규칙 준수를 당부하려고
⑤ 학교 홈페이지 주소 변경을 안내하려고

2. 대화를 듣고, 남자의 의견으로 가장 적절한 것을 고르시오.

① 산책은 창의적인 생각을 할 수 있게 돕는다.
② 식사 후 과격한 운동은 소화를 방해한다.
③ 지나친 스트레스는 집중력을 감소시킨다.
④ 독서를 통해 창의력을 증진할 수 있다.
⑤ 꾸준한 운동은 기초체력을 향상시킨다.

3. 대화를 듣고, 두 사람의 관계를 가장 잘 나타낸 것을 고르시오.

① 고객 – 우체국 직원   ② 투숙객 – 호텔 지배인
③ 여행객 – 여행 가이드   ④ 아파트 주민 – 경비원
⑤ 손님 – 옷가게 주인

4. 대화를 듣고, 그림에서 대화의 내용과 일치하지 않는 것을 고르시오.

5. 대화를 듣고, 남자가 할 일로 가장 적절한 것을 고르시오.

① 초대장 보내기   ② 피자 주문하기
③ 거실 청소하기   ④ 꽃다발 준비하기
⑤ 스마트폰 사러 가기

6. 대화를 듣고, 여자가 지불할 금액을 고르시오. [3점]

① $54   ② $60   ③ $72   ④ $76   ⑤ $80

7. 대화를 듣고, 남자가 록 콘서트에 갈 수 없는 이유를 고르시오.

① 일을 하러 가야 해서
② 피아노 연습을 해야 해서
③ 할머니를 뵈러 가야 해서
④ 친구의 개를 돌봐야 해서
⑤ 과제를 아직 끝내지 못해서

8. 대화를 듣고, Eco Day에 관해 언급되지 않은 것을 고르시오.

① 행사 시간   ② 행사 장소   ③ 참가비
④ 준비물   ⑤ 등록 방법

9. Eastville Dance Contest에 관한 다음 내용을 듣고, 일치하지 않는 것을 고르시오.

① 처음으로 개최되는 경연이다.
② 모든 종류의 춤이 허용된다.
③ 춤 영상을 8월 15일까지 업로드 해야 한다.
④ 학생들은 가장 좋아하는 영상에 투표할 수 있다.
⑤ 우승팀은 상으로 상품권을 받게 될 것이다.

10. 다음 표를 보면서 대화를 듣고, 두 사람이 구입할 정수기를 고르시오.

Water Purifiers

	Model	Price	Water Tank Capacity(liters)	Power-saving Mode	Warranty
①	A	$570	4	×	1 year
②	B	$650	5	○	1 year
③	C	$680	5	×	3 years
④	D	$740	5	○	3 years
⑤	E	$830	6	○	3 years

11. 대화를 듣고, 남자의 마지막 말에 대한 여자의 응답으로 가장 적절한 것을 고르시오.

① Great. We don't have to wait in line.
② All right. We can come back later.
③ Good job. Let's buy the tickets.
④ No worries. I will stand in line.
⑤ Too bad. I can't buy that car.

12. 대화를 듣고, 여자의 마지막 말에 대한 남자의 응답으로 가장 적절한 것을 고르시오.

① Yes. You can register online.
② Sorry. I can't see you next week.
③ Right. I should go to his office now.
④ Fantastic! I'll take the test tomorrow.
⑤ Of course. I can help him if he needs my help.

13. 대화를 듣고, 여자의 마지막 말에 대한 남자의 응답으로 가장 적절한 것을 고르시오. [3점]

Man: _____

① I agree. You can save a lot by buying secondhand.
② Great idea! Our message would make others smile.
③ Sorry. I forgot to write a message in the book.
④ Exactly. Taking notes during class is important.
⑤ Okay. We can arrive on time if we leave now.

14. 대화를 듣고, 남자의 마지막 말에 대한 여자의 응답으로 가장 적절한 것을 고르시오. [3점]

Woman: _____

① Why not? I can bring some food when we go camping.
② I'm sorry. That fishing equipment is not for sale.
③ I don't think so. The price is most important.
④ Really? I'd love to meet your family.
⑤ No problem. You can use my equipment.

15. 다음 상황 설명을 듣고, Violet이 Peter에게 할 말로 가장 적절한 것을 고르시오.

Violet: _____

① Will you join the science club together?
② Is it okay to use a card to pay for the drinks?
③ Why don't we donate our books to the library?
④ How about going to the cafeteria to have lunch?
⑤ Can you borrow the books for me with your card?

[16~17] 다음을 듣고, 물음에 답하시오.

16. 남자가 하는 말의 주제로 가장 적절한 것은?

① different causes of sleep disorders
② various ways to keep foods fresh
③ foods to improve quality of sleep
④ reasons for organic foods' popularity
⑤ origins of popular foods around the world

17. 언급된 음식이 <u>아닌</u> 것은?

① kiwi fruits   ② milk   ③ nuts
④ tomatoes   ⑤ honey

이제 듣기 문제가 끝났습니다. 18번부터는 문제지의 지시에 따라 답을 하시기 바랍니다.

---

18. 다음 글의 목적으로 가장 적절한 것은?

ACC Travel Agency Customers:

Have you ever wanted to enjoy a holiday in nature? This summer is the best time to turn your dream into reality. We have a perfect travel package for you. This travel package includes special trips to Lake Madison as well as massage and meditation to help you relax. Also, we provide yoga lessons taught by experienced instructors. If you book this package, you will enjoy all this at a reasonable price. We are sure that it will be an unforgettable experience for you. If you call us, we will be happy to give you more details.

① 여행 일정 변경을 안내하려고
② 패키지 여행 상품을 홍보하려고
③ 여행 상품 불만족에 대해 사과하려고
④ 여행 만족도 조사 참여를 부탁하려고
⑤ 패키지 여행 업무 담당자를 모집하려고

19. 다음 글에 드러난 'I'의 심경 변화로 가장 적절한 것은?

When I woke up in our hotel room, it was almost midnight. I didn't see my husband nor daughter. I called them, but I heard their phones ringing in the room. Feeling worried, I went outside and walked down the street, but they were nowhere to be found. When I decided I should ask someone for help, a crowd nearby caught my attention. I approached, hoping to find my husband and daughter, and suddenly I saw two familiar faces. I smiled, feeling calm. Just then, my daughter saw me and called, "Mom!" They were watching the magic show. Finally, I felt all my worries disappear.

① anxious   → relieved   ② delighted   → unhappy
③ indifferent   → excited   ④ relaxed   → upset
⑤ embarrassed → proud

20. 다음 글에서 필자가 주장하는 바로 가장 적절한 것은?

Research shows that people who work have two calendars: one for work and one for their personal lives. Although it may seem sensible, having two separate calendars for work and personal life can lead to distractions. To check if something is missing, you will find yourself checking your to-do lists multiple times. Instead, organize all of your tasks in one place. It doesn't matter if you use digital or paper media. It's okay to keep your professional and personal tasks in one place. This will give you a good idea of how time is divided between work and home. This will allow you to make informed decisions about which tasks are most important.

① 결정한 것은 반드시 실행하도록 노력하라.
② 자신이 담당한 업무에 관한 전문성을 확보하라.
③ 업무 집중도를 높이기 위해 책상 위를 정돈하라.
④ 좋은 아이디어를 메모하는 습관을 길러라.
⑤ 업무와 개인 용무를 한 곳에 정리하라.

21. 밑줄 친 become unpaid ambassadors가 다음 글에서 의미하는 바로 가장 적절한 것은?

Why do you care how a customer reacts to a purchase? Good question. By understanding post-purchase behavior, you can understand the influence and the likelihood of whether a buyer will repurchase the product (and whether she will keep it or return it). You'll also determine whether the buyer will encourage others to purchase the product from you. Satisfied customers can become unpaid ambassadors for your business, so customer satisfaction should be on the top of your to-do list. People tend to believe the opinions of people they know. People trust friends over advertisements any day. They know that advertisements are paid to tell the "good side" and that they're used to persuade them to purchase products and services. By continually monitoring your customer's satisfaction after the sale, you have the ability to avoid negative word-of-mouth advertising.

① recommend products to others for no gain
② offer manufacturers feedback on products
③ become people who don't trust others' words
④ get rewards for advertising products overseas
⑤ buy products without worrying about the price

22. 다음 글의 요지로 가장 적절한 것은?

The promise of a computerized society, we were told, was that it would pass to machines all of the repetitive drudgery of work, allowing us humans to pursue higher purposes and to have more leisure time. It didn't work out this way. Instead of more time, most of us have less. Companies large and small have off-loaded work onto the backs of consumers. Things that used to be done for us, as part of the value-added service of working with a company, we are now expected to do ourselves. With air travel, we're now expected to complete our own reservations and check-in, jobs that used to be done by airline employees or travel agents. At the grocery store, we're expected to bag our own groceries and, in some supermarkets, to scan our own purchases.

* drudgery: 고된 일

① 컴퓨터 기반 사회에서는 여가 시간이 더 늘어난다.
② 회사 업무의 전산화는 업무 능률을 향상시킨다.
③ 컴퓨터화된 사회에서 소비자는 더 많은 일을 하게 된다.
④ 온라인 거래가 모든 소비자들을 만족시키기에는 한계가 있다.
⑤ 산업의 발전으로 인해 기계가 인간의 일자리를 대신하고 있다.

23. 다음 글의 주제로 가장 적절한 것은?

We tend to believe that we possess a host of socially desirable characteristics, and that we are free of most of those that are socially undesirable. For example, a large majority of the general public thinks that they are more intelligent, more fair-minded, less prejudiced, and more skilled behind the wheel of an automobile than the average person. This phenomenon is so reliable and ubiquitous that it has come to be known as the "Lake Wobegon effect," after Garrison Keillor's fictional community where "the women are strong, the men are good-looking, and all the children are above average." A survey of one million high school seniors found that 70% thought they were above average in leadership ability, and only 2% thought they were below average. In terms of ability to get along with others, *all* students thought they were above average, 60% thought they were in the top 10%, and 25% thought they were in the top 1%!

* ubiquitous: 도처에 있는

① importance of having a positive self-image as a leader
② our common belief that we are better than average
③ our tendency to think others are superior to us
④ reasons why we always try to be above average
⑤ danger of prejudice in building healthy social networks

24. 다음 글의 제목으로 가장 적절한 것은?

Few people will be surprised to hear that poverty tends to create stress: a 2006 study published in the American journal *Psychosomatic Medicine*, for example, noted that a lower socioeconomic status was associated with higher levels of stress hormones in the body. However, richer economies have their own distinct stresses. The key issue is time pressure. A 1999 study of 31 countries by American psychologist Robert Levine and Canadian psychologist Ara Norenzayan found that wealthier, more industrialized nations had a faster pace of life — which led to a higher standard of living, but at the same time left the population feeling a constant sense of urgency, as well as being more prone to heart disease. In effect, fast-paced productivity creates wealth, but it also leads people to feel time-poor when they lack the time to relax and enjoy themselves.

* prone: 걸리기 쉬운

① Why Are Even Wealthy Countries Not Free from Stress?
② In Search of the Path to Escaping the Poverty Trap
③ Time Management: Everything You Need to Know
④ How Does Stress Affect Human Bodies?
⑤ Sound Mind Wins the Game of Life!

25. 다음 도표의 내용과 일치하지 <u>않는</u> 것은?

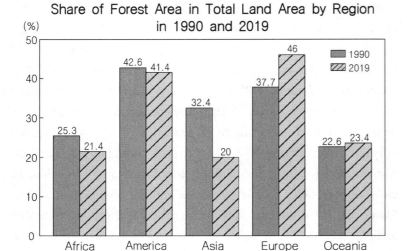

Share of Forest Area in Total Land Area by Region in 1990 and 2019

The above graph shows the share of forest area in total land area by region in 1990 and 2019. ① Africa's share of forest area in total land area was over 20% in both 1990 and 2019. ② The share of forest area in America was 42.6% in 1990, which was larger than that in 2019. ③ The share of forest area in Asia declined from 1990 to 2019 by more than 10 percentage points. ④ In 2019, the share of forest area in Europe was the largest among the five regions, more than three times that in Asia in the same year. ⑤ Oceania showed the smallest gap between 1990 and 2019 in terms of the share of forest area in total land area.

26. Gary Becker에 관한 다음 글의 내용과 일치하지 <u>않는</u> 것은?

Gary Becker was born in Pottsville, Pennsylvania in 1930 and grew up in Brooklyn, New York City. His father, who was not well educated, had a deep interest in financial and political issues. After graduating from high school, Becker went to Princeton University, where he majored in economics. He was dissatisfied with his economic education at Princeton University because "it didn't seem to be handling real problems." He earned a doctor's degree in economics from the University of Chicago in 1955. His doctoral paper on the economics of discrimination was mentioned by the Nobel Prize Committee as an important contribution to economics. Since 1985, Becker had written a regular economics column in *Business Week*, explaining economic analysis and ideas to the general public. In 1992, he was awarded the Nobel Prize in economic science.

* discrimination: 차별

① New York City의 Brooklyn에서 자랐다.
② 아버지는 금융과 정치 문제에 깊은 관심이 있었다.
③ Princeton University에서의 경제학 교육에 만족했다.
④ 1955년에 경제학 박사 학위를 취득했다.
⑤ *Business Week*에 경제학 칼럼을 기고했다.

27. 2023 Drone Racing Championship에 관한 다음 안내문의 내용과 일치하지 <u>않는</u> 것은?

2023 Drone Racing Championship

Are you the best drone racer? Then take the opportunity to prove you are the one!

When & Where
● 6 p.m. — 8 p.m., Sunday, July 9
● Lakeside Community Center

Requirements
● Participants: High school students only
● Bring your own drone for the race.

Prize
● $500 and a medal will be awarded to the winner.

Note
● The first 10 participants will get souvenirs.

For more details, please visit www.droneracing.com or call 313 - 6745 - 1189.

---

① 7월 9일 일요일에 개최된다.
② 고등학생만 참가할 수 있다.
③ 자신의 드론을 가져와야 한다.
④ 상금과 메달이 우승자에게 수여될 것이다.
⑤ 20명의 참가자가 기념품을 받을 것이다.

28. Summer Scuba Diving One-day Class에 관한 다음 안내문의 내용과 일치하는 것은?

Summer Scuba Diving One-day Class

Join our summer scuba diving lesson for beginners, and become an underwater explorer!

Schedule
● 10:00 - 12:00 Learning the basics
● 13:00 - 16:00 Practicing diving skills in a pool

Price
● Private lesson: $150
● Group lesson (up to 3 people): $100 per person
● Participants can rent our diving equipment for free.

Notice
● Participants must be 10 years old or over.
● Participants must register at least 5 days before the class begins.

For more information, please go to www.ssdiver.com.

---

① 오후 시간에 바다에서 다이빙 기술을 연습한다.
② 그룹 수업의 최대 정원은 4명이다.
③ 다이빙 장비를 유료로 대여할 수 있다.
④ 연령에 관계없이 참가할 수 있다.
⑤ 적어도 수업 시작 5일 전까지 등록해야 한다.

29. 다음 글의 밑줄 친 부분 중, 어법상 틀린 것은? [3점]

Although praise is one of the most powerful tools available for improving young children's behavior, it is equally powerful for improving your child's self-esteem. Preschoolers believe what their parents tell ① them in a very profound way. They do not yet have the cognitive sophistication to reason ② analytically and reject false information. If a preschool boy consistently hears from his mother ③ that he is smart and a good helper, he is likely to incorporate that information into his self-image. Thinking of himself as a boy who is smart and knows how to do things ④ being likely to make him endure longer in problem-solving efforts and increase his confidence in trying new and difficult tasks. Similarly, thinking of himself as the kind of boy who is a good helper will make him more likely to volunteer ⑤ to help with tasks at home and at preschool.

* profound: 뜻 깊은 ** sophistication: 정교화(함)

30. 다음 글의 밑줄 친 부분 중, 문맥상 낱말의 쓰임이 적절하지 않은 것은?

Advertisers often displayed considerable facility in ① adapting their claims to the market status of the goods they promoted. Fleischmann's yeast, for instance, was used as an ingredient for cooking homemade bread. Yet more and more people in the early 20th century were buying their bread from stores or bakeries, so consumer demand for yeast ② increased. The producer of Fleischmann's yeast hired the J. Walter Thompson advertising agency to come up with a different marketing strategy to ③ boost sales. No longer the "Soul of Bread," the Thompson agency first turned yeast into an important source of vitamins with significant health ④ benefits. Shortly thereafter, the advertising agency transformed yeast into a natural laxative. ⑤ Repositioning yeast helped increase sales.

* laxative: 완하제(배변을 쉽게 하는 약·음식·음료)

[31~34] 다음 빈칸에 들어갈 말로 가장 적절한 것을 고르시오.

31. Individuals who perform at a high level in their profession often have instant credibility with others. People admire them, they want to be like them, and they feel connected to them. When they speak, others listen — even if the area of their skill has nothing to do with the advice they give. Think about a world-famous basketball player. He has made more money from endorsements than he ever did playing basketball. Is it because of his knowledge of the products he endorses? No. It's because of what he can do with a basketball. The same can be said of an Olympic medalist swimmer. People listen to him because of what he can do in the pool. And when an actor tells us we should drive a certain car, we don't listen because of his expertise on engines. We listen because we admire his talent. _____ connects. If you possess a high level of ability in an area, others may desire to connect with you because of it.

* endorsement: (유명인의 텔레비전 등에서의 상품) 보증 선전

① Patience   ② Sacrifice
③ Honesty   ④ Excellence
⑤ Creativity

32. Think of the brain as a city. If you were to look out over a city and ask "where is the economy located?" you'd see there's no good answer to the question. Instead, the economy emerges from the interaction of all the elements — from the stores and the banks to the merchants and the customers. And so it is with the brain's operation: it doesn't happen in one spot. Just as in a city, no neighborhood of the brain _____. In brains and in cities, everything emerges from the interaction between residents, at all scales, locally and distantly. Just as trains bring materials and textiles into a city, which become processed into the economy, so the raw electrochemical signals from sensory organs are transported along superhighways of neurons. There the signals undergo processing and transformation into our conscious reality.

[3점]

* electrochemical: 전기화학의

① operates in isolation
② suffers from rapid changes
③ resembles economic elements
④ works in a systematic way
⑤ interacts with another

33. Someone else's body language affects our own body, which then creates an emotional echo that makes us feel accordingly. As Louis Armstrong sang, "When you're smiling, the whole world smiles with you." If copying another's smile makes us feel happy, the emotion of the smiler has been transmitted via our body. Strange as it may sound, this theory states that _____. For example, our mood can be improved by simply lifting up the corners of our mouth. If people are asked to bite down on a pencil lengthwise, taking care not to let the pencil touch their lips (thus forcing the mouth into a smile-like shape), they judge cartoons funnier than if they have been asked to frown. The primacy of the body is sometimes summarized in the phrase "I must be afraid, because I'm running." [3점]

* lengthwise: 길게 ** frown: 얼굴을 찡그리다

① language guides our actions
② emotions arise from our bodies
③ body language hides our feelings
④ what others say affects our mood
⑤ negative emotions easily disappear

34. _____ boosts sales. Brian Wansink, Professor of Marketing at Cornell University, investigated the effectiveness of this tactic in 1998. He persuaded three supermarkets in Sioux City, Iowa, to offer Campbell's soup at a small discount: 79 cents rather than 89 cents. The discounted soup was sold in one of three conditions: a control, where there was no limit on the volume of purchases, or two tests, where customers were limited to either four or twelve cans. In the unlimited condition shoppers bought 3.3 cans on average, whereas in the scarce condition, when there was a limit, they bought 5.3 on average. This suggests scarcity encourages sales. The findings are particularly strong because the test took place in a supermarket with genuine shoppers. It didn't rely on claimed data, nor was it held in a laboratory where consumers might behave differently. [3점]

* tactic: 전략

① Promoting products through social media
② Reducing the risk of producing poor quality items
③ Restricting the number of items customers can buy
④ Offering several options that customers find attractive
⑤ Emphasizing the safety of products with research data

35. 다음 글에서 전체 흐름과 관계 <u>없는</u> 문장은?

Although technology has the potential to increase productivity, it can also have a negative impact on productivity. For example, in many office environments workers sit at desks with computers and have access to the internet. ① They are able to check their personal e-mails and use social media whenever they want to. ② This can stop them from doing their work and make them less productive. ③ Introducing new technology can also have a negative impact on production when it causes a change to the production process or requires workers to learn a new system. ④ Using technology can enable businesses to produce more goods and to get more out of the other factors of production. ⑤ Learning to use new technology can be time consuming and stressful for workers and this can cause a decline in productivity.

[36~37] 주어진 글 다음에 이어질 글의 순서로 가장 적절한 것을 고르시오.

36.

Up until about 6,000 years ago, most people were farmers. Many lived in different places throughout the year, hunting for food or moving their livestock to areas with enough food.

(A) For example, priests wanted to know when to carry out religious ceremonies. This was when people first invented clocks — devices that show, measure, and keep track of passing time.

(B) There was no need to tell the time because life depended on natural cycles, such as the changing seasons or sunrise and sunset. Gradually more people started to live in larger settlements, and some needed to tell the time.

(C) Clocks have been important ever since. Today, clocks are used for important things such as setting busy airport timetables — if the time is incorrect, aeroplanes might crash into each other when taking off or landing! [3점]

① (A) − (C) − (B)　　② (B) − (A) − (C)
③ (B) − (C) − (A)　　④ (C) − (A) − (B)
⑤ (C) − (B) − (A)

37.

> Managers are always looking for ways to increase productivity, which is the ratio of costs to output in production. Adam Smith, writing when the manufacturing industry was new, described a way that production could be made more efficient, known as the "division of labor."

(A) Because each worker specializes in one job, he or she can work much faster without changing from one task to another. Now 10 workers can produce thousands of pins in a day — a huge increase in productivity from the 200 they would have produced before.

(B) One worker could do all these tasks, and make 20 pins in a day. But this work can be divided into its separate processes, with a number of workers each performing one task.

(C) Making most manufactured goods involves several different processes using different skills. Smith's example was the manufacture of pins: the wire is straightened, sharpened, a head is put on, and then it is polished.

* ratio: 비율

① (A) − (C) − (B)　　　② (B) − (A) − (C)
③ (B) − (C) − (A)　　　④ (C) − (A) − (B)
⑤ (C) − (B) − (A)

[38~39] 글의 흐름으로 보아, 주어진 문장이 들어가기에 가장 적절한 곳을 고르시오.

38.

> Yet we know that the face that stares back at us from the glass is not the same, cannot be the same, as it was 10 minutes ago.

Sometimes the pace of change is far slower. (①) The face you saw reflected in your mirror this morning probably appeared no different from the face you saw the day before — or a week or a month ago. (②) The proof is in your photo album: Look at a photograph taken of yourself 5 or 10 years ago and you see clear differences between the face in the snapshot and the face in your mirror. (③) If you lived in a world without mirrors for a year and then saw your reflection, you might be surprised by the change. (④) After an interval of 10 years without seeing yourself, you might not at first recognize the person peering from the mirror. (⑤) Even something as basic as our own face changes from moment to moment.

* peer: 응시하다

39.

> As children absorb more evidence from the world around them, certain possibilities become much more likely and more useful and harden into knowledge or beliefs.

According to educational psychologist Susan Engel, curiosity begins to decrease as young as four years old. By the time we are adults, we have fewer questions and more default settings. As Henry James put it, "Disinterested curiosity is past, the mental grooves and channels set." (①) The decline in curiosity can be traced in the development of the brain through childhood. (②) Though smaller than the adult brain, the infant brain contains millions more neural connections. (③) The wiring, however, is a mess; the lines of communication between infant neurons are far less efficient than between those in the adult brain. (④) The baby's perception of the world is consequently both intensely rich and wildly disordered. (⑤) The neural pathways that enable those beliefs become faster and more automatic, while the ones that the child doesn't use regularly are pruned away. [3점]

* default setting: 기본값 ** groove: 고랑 *** prune: 가지치기하다

40. 다음 글의 내용을 한 문장으로 요약하고자 한다. 빈칸 (A), (B)에 들어갈 말로 가장 적절한 것은?

> Nearly eight of ten U.S. adults believe there are "good foods" and "bad foods." Unless we're talking about spoiled stew, poison mushrooms, or something similar, however, no foods can be labeled as either good or bad. There are, however, combinations of foods that add up to a healthful or unhealthful diet. Consider the case of an adult who eats only foods thought of as "good" — for example, raw broccoli, apples, orange juice, boiled tofu, and carrots. Although all these foods are nutrient-dense, they do not add up to a healthy diet because they don't supply a wide enough variety of the nutrients we need. Or take the case of the teenager who occasionally eats fried chicken, but otherwise stays away from fried foods. The occasional fried chicken isn't going to knock his or her diet off track. But the person who eats fried foods every day, with few vegetables or fruits, and loads up on supersized soft drinks, candy, and chips for snacks has a bad diet.

↓

> Unlike the common belief, defining foods as good or bad is not __(A)__ ; in fact, a healthy diet is determined largely by what the diet is __(B)__ .

	(A)	(B)
①	incorrect	limited to
②	appropriate	composed of
③	wrong	aimed at
④	appropriate	tested on
⑤	incorrect	adjusted to

[41~42] 다음 글을 읽고, 물음에 답하시오.

Early hunter-gatherer societies had (a) <u>minimal</u> structure. A chief or group of elders usually led the camp or village. Most of these leaders had to hunt and gather along with the other members because the surpluses of food and other vital resources were seldom (b) <u>sufficient</u> to support a full-time chief or village council. The development of agriculture changed work patterns. Early farmers could reap 3-10 kg of grain from each 1 kg of seed planted. Part of this food/energy surplus was returned to the community and (c) <u>limited</u> support for nonfarmers such as chieftains, village councils, men who practice medicine, priests, and warriors. In return, the nonfarmers provided leadership and security for the farming population, enabling it to continue to increase food/energy yields and provide ever larger surpluses.

With improved technology and favorable conditions, agriculture produced consistent surpluses of the basic necessities, and population groups grew in size. These groups concentrated in towns and cities, and human tasks (d) <u>specialized</u> further. Specialists such as carpenters, blacksmiths, merchants, traders, and sailors developed their skills and became more efficient in their use of time and energy. The goods and services they provided brought about an (e) <u>improved</u> quality of life, a higher standard of living, and, for most societies, increased stability.

* reap: (농작물을) 베어들이다 ** chieftain: 수령, 두목

41. 윗글의 제목으로 가장 적절한 것은?

① How Agriculture Transformed Human Society
② The Dark Shadow of Agriculture: Repetition
③ How Can We Share Extra Food with the Poor?
④ Why Were Early Societies Destroyed by Agriculture?
⑤ The Advantages of Large Groups Over Small Groups in Farming

42. 밑줄 친 (a)~(e) 중에서 문맥상 낱말의 쓰임이 적절하지 <u>않은</u> 것은? [3점]

① (a)   ② (b)   ③ (c)   ④ (d)   ⑤ (e)

[43~45] 다음 글을 읽고, 물음에 답하시오.

(A)

A nurse took a tired, anxious soldier to the bedside. "Jack, your son is here," the nurse said to an old man lying on the bed. She had to repeat the words several times before the old man's eyes opened. Suffering from the severe pain because of heart disease, he barely saw the young uniformed soldier standing next to him. (a) <u>He</u> reached out his hand to the soldier.

(B)

Whenever the nurse came into the room, she heard the soldier say a few gentle words. The old man said nothing, only held tightly to (b) <u>him</u> all through the night. Just before dawn, the old man died. The soldier released the old man's hand and left the room to find the nurse. After she was told what happened, she went back to the room with him. The soldier hesitated for a while and asked, "Who was this man?"

(C)

She was surprised and asked, "Wasn't he your father?" "No, he wasn't. I've never met him before," the soldier replied. She asked, "Then why didn't you say something when I took you to (c) <u>him</u>?" He said, "I knew there had been a mistake, but when I realized that he was too sick to tell whether or not I was his son, I could see how much (d) <u>he</u> needed me. So, I stayed."

(D)

The soldier gently wrapped his fingers around the weak hand of the old man. The nurse brought a chair so that the soldier could sit beside the bed. All through the night the young soldier sat there, holding the old man's hand and offering (e) <u>him</u> words of support and comfort. Occasionally, she suggested that the soldier take a rest for a while. He politely said no.

43. 주어진 글 (A)에 이어질 내용을 순서에 맞게 배열한 것으로 가장 적절한 것은?

① (B) − (D) − (C)   ② (C) − (B) − (D)
③ (C) − (D) − (B)   ④ (D) − (B) − (C)
⑤ (D) − (C) − (B)

44. 밑줄 친 (a)~(e) 중에서 가리키는 대상이 나머지 넷과 <u>다른</u> 것은?

① (a)   ② (b)   ③ (c)   ④ (d)   ⑤ (e)

45. 윗글에 관한 내용으로 적절하지 <u>않은</u> 것은?

① 노인은 심장병으로 극심한 고통을 겪고 있었다.
② 군인은 간호사를 찾기 위해 병실을 나갔다.
③ 군인은 노인과 이전에 만난 적이 있다고 말했다.
④ 간호사는 군인이 앉을 수 있도록 의자를 가져왔다.
⑤ 군인은 잠시 쉬라는 간호사의 제안을 정중히 거절하였다.

★ 확인 사항

○ 답안지의 해당란에 필요한 내용을 정확히 기입(표기)했는지 확인하시오.

01
001 president ⓝ 회장
002 annual ⓐ 연마다 하는
003 e-sports ⓝ 게임, e-스포츠
004 competition ⓝ 대회, 경쟁
005 hold ⓥ 개최하다
006 set up 설치하다
007 fill out 작성하다
008 application form 신청서

02
009 work on ~을 작업하다
010 make progress 진전되다
011 waste ⓥ 낭비하다
012 take a walk 산책하다
013 active ⓐ 활동적인, 적극적인
014 have time for ~할 시간이 있다
015 tip ⓝ 조언

03
016 send ⓥ 보내다
017 breakable ⓐ 깨지기 쉬운
018 clothes 옷, 의류
019 package ⓝ 소포
020 express mail 급행 우편
021 extra charge 추가 비용
022 deliver ⓥ 배달하다
023 as soon as possible 최대한 빨리

04
024 busk ⓥ 버스킹하다, 거리 공연하다
025 amazing ⓐ 멋진, 근사한
026 next to ~의 옆에서
027 while ⓒⓞⓝⓙ ~하는 동안, 한편
028 leave open 열어두다
029 performance ⓝ 공연, 성과
030 recently ⓐⓓ 최근에
031 have fun 재미있게 보내다

05
032 invitation card 초대장
033 what about ~은 어때?
034 check ⓥ 확인하다
035 cook ⓥ 요리하다
036 order ⓥ 주문하다
037 present ⓝ 선물
038 forget to ~해야 하는 걸 잊다
039 right away 즉시
040 clean up 청소하다, 치우다

06
041 blanket ⓝ 담요
042 cushion ⓝ 쿠션
043 on sale 할인 중인
044 have a look 살펴보다
045 show ⓥ 보여주다
046 go well with ~와 잘 어울리다
047 credit card 신용 카드

07
048 art class 미술 수업
049 go to a concert 콘서트에 가다

050 I'm afraid I can't. 미안하지만 안 되겠어.
051 take care of ~을 돌보다
052 somewhere ⓐⓓ 어딘가
053 No problem. 문제 없어요, 괜찮아요. 그럼요.
054 visit ⓥ 방문하다

08
055 pick up 줍다
056 trash ⓝ 쓰레기
057 walk around ~을 돌아다니다
058 Why don't we ~? ~하면 어때?
059 environment ⓝ 환경
060 lately ⓐⓓ 최근에, 요즘
061 used to ~하곤 했다
062 sign up for ~에 등록하다, 신청하다
063 look forward to ~을 고대하다

09
064 pleased ⓐ 기쁜
065 participate in ~에 참가하다
066 as ⓟⓡⓔⓟ (자격) ~로서
067 all kinds of 모든 종류의
068 allow ⓥ 허용하다
069 vote for ~을 위해 투표하다
070 receive ⓥ 받다
071 show off 뽐내다, 보여주다
072 talent ⓝ 재능

10
073 water purifier 정수기
074 Good idea. (동의) 좋은 생각이에요.
075 budget ⓝ 예산
076 spend ⓥ 소비하다
077 capacity ⓝ 용량
078 perfect for ~에게 딱 적당한
079 power-saving mode 절전 모드
080 electricity ⓝ 전기
081 warranty ⓝ 보증 (기간)

11
082 get inside 안으로 들어가다
083 auto show 자동차 전시회
084 stand in line 줄 서서 기다리다
085 in advance 미리
086 Good job. (격려나 칭찬의 의미로) 잘했어.
087 No worries. 걱정 마.
088 Too bad. (하지 못해) 아깝네. (유감스러운 일에) 안됐네.

12
089 grade ⓝ 점수
090 take a test 시험을 치다
091 go ask 가서 물어보다
092 register ⓥ 등록하다
093 fantastic ⓐ 환상적인

13
094 note ⓝ 쪽지
095 secondhand bookstore 중고 서점
096 bookmark ⓝ 책갈피
097 sweet ⓐ 상냥한, 다정한

098 leave ⓥ 남기다
099 resell ⓥ 되팔다
100 take notes 필기하다
101 on time 제때

14
102 have a plan 계획이 있다, 일정이 있다
103 plan to ~할 계획이다
104 go camping 캠핑 가다
105 at least 적어도
106 close to ~와 가까운
107 hobby ⓝ 취미
108 relieve stress 스트레스를 풀다
109 fishing ⓝ 낚시

15
110 classmate ⓝ 반 친구
111 group assignment 팀 과제
112 public ⓐ 공립의, 공공의
113 library ⓝ 도서관
114 section ⓝ 구역
115 useful ⓐ 유용한
116 check out 대출하다, 빌리다
117 walk up to ~ 쪽으로 (걸어서) 다가오다
118 donate ⓥ 기부하다
119 cafeteria ⓝ 구내식당

16~17
120 sleep clinic 수면 클리닉
121 essential ⓐ 필수적인
122 daily life 일상
123 introduce ⓥ 소개하다, 도입하다
124 contain ⓥ 함유하다
125 fall asleep 잠들다
126 wake up 잠에서 깨다
127 rich in ~가 풍부한
128 nerve ⓝ 신경
129 get a good night's sleep 숙면하다
130 internal ⓐ 내부의
131 body clock 생체 시계
132 at the right time 제때, 적기에
133 awake ⓐ 깨어 있는
134 diet plan 식단
135 disorder ⓝ 장애, 질환
136 fresh ⓐ 신선한
137 popularity ⓝ 인기
138 origin ⓝ 기원

18
139 travel agency 여행사
140 customer ⓝ 고객
141 turn A into B A를 B로 바꾸다
142 reality ⓝ 현실
143 trip ⓝ 여행
144 A as well as B B뿐 아니라 A도
145 meditation ⓝ 명상
146 experienced ⓐ 경험 많은, 숙련된
147 instructor ⓝ 강사
148 book ⓥ 예약하다
149 reasonable ⓐ 적당한
150 unforgettable ⓐ 잊지 못할
151 detail ⓝ 세부, 구체적 내용, 상세

19
152 almost ⓐⓓ 거의
153 midnight ⓝ 자정
154 ring ⓥ 울리다
155 worried ⓐ 걱정한
156 decide ⓥ 결심하다, 정하다
157 ask for help 도움을 요청하다
158 crowd ⓝ 군중
159 catch one's attention 관심을 끌다
160 approach ⓥ 다가가다
161 suddenly ⓐⓓ 문득, 갑자기
162 familiar ⓐ 익숙한
163 calm ⓐ 평온한
164 magic show 마술 쇼
165 disappear ⓥ 사라지다
166 anxious ⓐ 불안한
167 delighted ⓐ 기쁜
168 embarrassed ⓐ 당황한

20
169 calendar ⓝ 달력
170 personal life 사생활
171 sensible ⓐ 분별 있는, 현명한
172 separate ⓐ 별개의
173 lead to ~로 이어지다
174 distraction ⓝ 주의 분산, 정신을 흩뜨리는 것
175 missing ⓐ 빠진, 실종된
176 to-do list 할 일 목록
177 multiple ⓐ 여럿의, 다수의
178 organize ⓥ 정리하다
179 task ⓝ 일, 과업
180 professional ⓐ 직업의, 전문적인
181 divide ⓥ 나누다, 분배하다
182 make an informed decision 잘 알고 결정하다

21
183 care ⓥ 신경 쓰다 ⓝ 관심, 신경
184 react to ~에 반응하다
185 purchase ⓝ 구매 ⓥ 사다
186 likelihood ⓝ 가능성, 확률
187 whether ⓒⓞⓝⓙ ~인지 아닌지
188 buyer ⓝ 구매자
189 return ⓥ 반품하다
190 encourage ⓥ 격려하다
191 satisfied ⓐ 만족한
192 unpaid ⓐ 무급의
193 ambassador ⓝ (외교 시 나라를 대표하는) 대사, 사절
194 on the top of ~의 맨 위에
195 opinion ⓝ 의견, 생각
196 advertisement ⓝ 광고
197 be paid to 돈을 받고 ~하다
198 continually ⓐⓓ 지속적으로
199 word-of-mouth ⓐ 구전의
200 for no gain 대가 없이
201 overseas ⓐⓓ 해외에

22
202 promise ⓝ 약속
203 computerize ⓥ 컴퓨터화하다
204 repetitive ⓐ 반복되는

09회

205 ☐ **drudgery** ⓝ 고된 일
206 ☐ **pursue** ⓥ 추구하다
207 ☐ **leisure** ⓝ 여가, 레저
208 ☐ **off-load** ⓥ 짐을 내리다, 떠넘기다
209 ☐ **as part of** ~의 일환으로
210 ☐ **be expected to** ~하도록 기대되다
211 ☐ **complete** ⓥ 완수하다 ⓐ 완전한
212 ☐ **reservation** ⓝ 예약
213 ☐ **check-in** ⓝ (호텔 등에) 체크인
214 ☐ **grocery store** 슈퍼, 식료품 가게
215 ☐ **scan** ⓥ 스캔하다, 찍다, 훑다

23
216 ☐ **possess** ⓥ 지니다, 소유하다
217 ☐ **a host of** 여러, 다수의
218 ☐ **socially** ⓐⓓ 사회적으로
219 ☐ **desirable** ⓐ 바람직한
220 ☐ **characteristic** ⓝ 특성
221 ☐ **be free of** ~가 없는
222 ☐ **general public** 일반 대중
223 ☐ **intelligent** ⓐ 지적인
224 ☐ **fair-minded** ⓐ 공정한
225 ☐ **prejudiced** ⓐ 고정 관념이 있는
226 ☐ **skilled** ⓐ 능숙한
227 ☐ **behind the wheel** 운전할 때, 핸들을 잡은
228 ☐ **automobile** ⓝ 자동차
229 ☐ **average** ⓐ 평균의 ⓝ 평균 ⓥ 평균을 내다
230 ☐ **phenomenon** ⓝ 현상
231 ☐ **reliable** ⓐ 믿을 만한
232 ☐ **ubiquitous** ⓐ 도처에 있는
233 ☐ **fictional** ⓐ 허구의
234 ☐ **good-looking** ⓐ 잘생긴
235 ☐ **million** ⓝ 100만
236 ☐ **high school senior** 고교 졸업반
237 ☐ **in terms of** ~의 면에서
238 ☐ **get along with** ~와 어울리다
239 ☐ **self-image** ⓝ 자아상(사람이 자기 자신에 대해 가진 이미지)
240 ☐ **superior to** ~보다 우월한
241 ☐ **social network** 사회적 네트워크

24
242 ☐ **poverty** ⓝ 가난
243 ☐ **create** ⓥ 만들어내다, 창출하다
244 ☐ **publish** ⓥ 출판하다
245 ☐ **socioeconomic** ⓐ 사회경제적인
246 ☐ **status** ⓝ 지위
247 ☐ **be associated with** ~와 연관되다
248 ☐ **distinct** ⓐ 특유의, 독특한, 뚜렷한
249 ☐ **time pressure** 시간 압박
250 ☐ **psychologist** ⓝ 심리학자
251 ☐ **wealthy** ⓐ 부유한
252 ☐ **industrialize** ⓥ 산업화하다
253 ☐ **nation** ⓝ 나라
254 ☐ **pace** ⓝ 속도
255 ☐ **standard of life** 생활 수준
256 ☐ **constant** ⓐ 지속적인
257 ☐ **urgency** ⓝ 다급함
258 ☐ **prone to** ~에 걸리기 쉬운
259 ☐ **productivity** ⓝ 생산성
260 ☐ **in search of** ~을 찾아서
261 ☐ **escape** ⓥ 탈출하다, 빠져나가다

262 ☐ **sound** ⓐ 건전한

25
263 ☐ **share** ⓝ 점유율, 몫
264 ☐ **forest** ⓝ 숲
265 ☐ **region** ⓝ 지역
266 ☐ **total** ⓐ 전체의
267 ☐ **decline** ⓥ 감소하다, 줄어들다
268 ☐ **percentage point** 퍼센트포인트(백분율 간 격차)
269 ☐ **more than** ~ 이상
270 ☐ **gap** ⓝ 격차, 차이

26
271 ☐ **well educated** 교육을 많이 받은
272 ☐ **interest** ⓝ 흥미, 관심
273 ☐ **financial** ⓐ 재정적인
274 ☐ **political** ⓐ 정치적인
275 ☐ **graduate from** ~을 졸업하다
276 ☐ **major in** ~을 전공하다
277 ☐ **handle** ⓥ 다루다, 대처하다
278 ☐ **earn** ⓥ 얻다, 취득하다
279 ☐ **doctor's degree** 박사 학위
280 ☐ **doctoral paper** 박사 논문
281 ☐ **discrimination** ⓝ 차별
282 ☐ **mention** ⓥ 언급하다
283 ☐ **contribution** ⓝ 기여, 이바지
284 ☐ **regular** ⓐ 주기적인, 정규적인
285 ☐ **analysis** ⓝ 분석
286 ☐ **award** ⓥ 상을 주다, 수여하다

27
287 ☐ **drone** ⓝ 드론, 무인 항공기
288 ☐ **championship** ⓝ 선수권
289 ☐ **take an opportunity** 기회를 잡다
290 ☐ **prove** ⓥ 증명하다
291 ☐ **community center** 주민센터
292 ☐ **requirement** ⓝ 필수 요건
293 ☐ **bring** ⓥ 가져오다, 지참하다
294 ☐ **winner** ⓝ 우승자
295 ☐ **souvenir** ⓝ 기념품

28
296 ☐ **one-day class** 일일 수업
297 ☐ **underwater** ⓐ 물속의, 수중의
298 ☐ **explorer** ⓝ 탐험가
299 ☐ **basics** ⓝ 기본, 필수적인 것들
300 ☐ **private lesson** 개인 레슨
301 ☐ **rent** ⓥ 대여하다
302 ☐ **equipment** ⓝ 장비

29
303 ☐ **praise** ⓥ 칭찬
304 ☐ **available** ⓐ 이용할 수 있는
305 ☐ **improve** ⓥ 개선하다, 향상시키다
306 ☐ **equally** ⓐⓓ 마찬가지로, 똑같이
307 ☐ **self-esteem** ⓝ 자존감
308 ☐ **preschooler** ⓝ 미취학 아동
309 ☐ **profound** ⓐ 뜻 깊은
310 ☐ **cognitive** ⓐ 인지적인
311 ☐ **sophistication** ⓝ 정교화(함)
312 ☐ **reason** ⓥ 추론하다

313 ☐ **analytically** ⓐⓓ 분석적으로
314 ☐ **reject** ⓥ 거부하다
315 ☐ **false** ⓐ 틀린, 잘못된
316 ☐ **consistently** ⓐⓓ 지속적으로
317 ☐ **be likely to** ~할 가능성이 크다
318 ☐ **incorporate A into B** A를 B로 통합시키다
319 ☐ **endure** ⓥ 지속하다, 참다
320 ☐ **problem-solving** ⓝ 문제 해결
321 ☐ **confidence** ⓝ 자신감
322 ☐ **volunteer** ⓥ 자원하다

30
323 ☐ **display** ⓥ 보이다, 전시하다
324 ☐ **considerable** ⓐ 상당한
325 ☐ **facility** ⓝ 능력, 재능
326 ☐ **claim** ⓥ 주장
327 ☐ **goods** ⓝ 상품, 재화
328 ☐ **yeast** ⓝ (반죽 발효에 쓰는) 효모, 이스트
329 ☐ **ingredient** ⓝ 재료
330 ☐ **century** ⓝ 100년, 세기
331 ☐ **demand** ⓝ 수요 ⓥ 요구하다
332 ☐ **hire** ⓥ 고용하다
333 ☐ **come up with** 떠올리다, 고안하다
334 ☐ **strategy** ⓝ 전략
335 ☐ **boost** ⓥ 촉진하다, 증진하다
336 ☐ **sale** ⓝ 매출, 판매
337 ☐ **significant** ⓐ 상당한, 중요한
338 ☐ **shortly thereafter** 그 후 얼마 안 되어
339 ☐ **transform** ⓥ 변모시키다
340 ☐ **laxative** ⓝ 완하제(배변을 쉽게 하는 약·음식·음료)
341 ☐ **reposition** ⓥ (제품의) 이미지를 바꾸다

31
342 ☐ **perform** ⓥ 수행하다
343 ☐ **profession** ⓝ 직업
344 ☐ **instant** ⓐ 즉각적인
345 ☐ **credibility** ⓝ 신뢰
346 ☐ **admire** ⓥ 존경하다
347 ☐ **connected to** ~에 연결된
348 ☐ **even if** 설령 ~일지라도
349 ☐ **have nothing to do with** ~와 관련이 없다
350 ☐ **advice** ⓝ 조언
351 ☐ **world-famous** ⓐ 세계적으로 유명한
352 ☐ **make money** 돈을 벌다
353 ☐ **endorsement** ⓝ (유명인의 텔레비전 등에서의 상품) 보증 선전
354 ☐ **knowledge** ⓝ 지식
355 ☐ **endorse** ⓥ (유명인이 광고에 나와 특정 상품을) 보증하다, 홍보하다
356 ☐ **medalist** ⓝ 메달리스트
357 ☐ **certain** ⓐ 특정한
358 ☐ **expertise** ⓝ 전문 지식
359 ☐ **desire** ⓥ 바라다, 열망하다
360 ☐ **patience** ⓝ 인내심
361 ☐ **sacrifice** ⓝ 희생
362 ☐ **honesty** ⓝ 정직

32
363 ☐ **think of A as B** A를 B로 여기다

364 ☐ **look out** ~을 내다보다
365 ☐ **instead** ⓐⓓ 대신에
366 ☐ **emerge** ⓥ 나타나다, 생겨나다
367 ☐ **element** ⓝ 요소
368 ☐ **merchant** ⓝ 상인
369 ☐ **operation** ⓝ 작동, 작용
370 ☐ **spot** ⓝ 지점
371 ☐ **neighborhood** ⓝ 근방, 이웃, 지역
372 ☐ **resident** ⓝ 주민
373 ☐ **scale** ⓝ 규모
374 ☐ **locally** ⓐⓓ 국지적으로
375 ☐ **distantly** ⓐⓓ 멀리, 원거리로
376 ☐ **textile** ⓝ 직물
377 ☐ **process** ⓥ 가공하다, 처리하다
378 ☐ **raw** ⓐ 원재료의, 날것의
379 ☐ **electrochemical** ⓐ 전기화학의
380 ☐ **sensory organ** 감각 기관
381 ☐ **transport** ⓥ 수송하다, 실어 나르다
382 ☐ **undergo** ⓥ 거치다, 겪다
383 ☐ **transformation** ⓝ 변화, 변모
384 ☐ **conscious** ⓐ 의식적인
385 ☐ **in isolation** 고립되어
386 ☐ **resemble** ⓥ ~와 닮다
387 ☐ **systematic** ⓐ 체계적인

33
388 ☐ **body language** 신체 언어, 몸짓 언어
389 ☐ **affect** ⓥ 영향을 미치다
390 ☐ **emotional** ⓐ 정서적인
391 ☐ **echo** ⓝ 메아리
392 ☐ **accordingly** ⓐⓓ 그에 따라
393 ☐ **copy** ⓥ 복사하다
394 ☐ **transmit** ⓥ 전달하다
395 ☐ **via** ⓟⓡⓔⓟ ~을 통해서
396 ☐ **strange** ⓐ 이상한
397 ☐ **theory** ⓝ 이론
398 ☐ **state** ⓥ 진술하다
399 ☐ **mood** ⓝ 기분, 분위기
400 ☐ **lift up** ~을 들어올리다
401 ☐ **be asked to** ~하도록 요청받다
402 ☐ **bite down on** ~을 깨물다
403 ☐ **lengthwise** ⓐⓓ 길게
404 ☐ **take care (not) to** ~(하지 않)도록 주의하다
405 ☐ **touch** ⓥ 닿다, 만지다
406 ☐ **judge** ⓥ 판단하다
407 ☐ **frown** ⓥ 얼굴을 찡그리다
408 ☐ **primacy** ⓝ 우선함
409 ☐ **summarize** ⓥ 요약하다
410 ☐ **arise from** ~에서 생겨나다
411 ☐ **hide** ⓥ 숨기다

34
412 ☐ **investigate** ⓥ 조사하다
413 ☐ **effectiveness** ⓝ 유효성, 효과 있음
414 ☐ **tactic** ⓝ 전략
415 ☐ **persuade** ⓥ 설득하다
416 ☐ **discount** ⓝ 할인
417 ☐ **rather than** ~ 대신에
418 ☐ **condition** ⓝ 조건
419 ☐ **control** ⓝ 통제 집단(실험에서 처치를 가하지 않고 둔 집단)

420 ☐ limit ⓝ 제한 ⓥ 제한하다
421 ☐ volume ⓝ 양
422 ☐ unlimited ⓐ 제한되지 않은, 무제한의
423 ☐ on average 평균적으로
424 ☐ scarcity ⓝ 희소성
425 ☐ genuine ⓐ 진짜의
426 ☐ rely on ~에 의존하다
427 ☐ laboratory ⓝ 실험실
428 ☐ behave ⓥ 행동하다
429 ☐ differently ⓐ 다르게
430 ☐ attractive ⓐ 매력적인
431 ☐ emphasize ⓥ 강조하다

35
432 ☐ potential ⓝ 잠재력
433 ☐ negative ⓐ 부정적인
434 ☐ impact ⓝ 영향, 충격
435 ☐ have access to ~에 접근하다, ~을 이용하다
436 ☐ whenever ⓒⓞⓝⓙ ~할 때마다
437 ☐ stop A from B A가 B하지 못하게 막다
438 ☐ production ⓝ 생산, 제조
439 ☐ cause ⓥ 야기하다
440 ☐ require ⓥ 요구하다
441 ☐ enable ⓥ ~할 수 있게 하다
442 ☐ get A out of B B에서 A를 얻어내다
443 ☐ factor ⓝ 요인, 요소
444 ☐ time-consuming ⓐ 시간이 많이 걸리는

36
445 ☐ up until ~에 이르기까지
446 ☐ throughout ⓟⓡⓔⓟ ~ 내내
447 ☐ hunt for ~을 사냥하다
448 ☐ livestock ⓝ 가축
449 ☐ carry out 수행하다
450 ☐ religious ⓐ 종교적인
451 ☐ ceremony ⓝ 의식
452 ☐ invent ⓥ 발명하다
453 ☐ device ⓝ 장치
454 ☐ measure ⓥ 측정하다
455 ☐ keep track of ~을 추적하다, 기록하다
456 ☐ natural cycle 자연적 주기
457 ☐ season ⓝ 계절
458 ☐ sunrise ⓝ 일출, 해돋이
459 ☐ sunset ⓝ 일몰, 해넘이
460 ☐ gradually ⓐ 점차
461 ☐ settlement ⓝ 정착(지)
462 ☐ tell the time 시간을 알다
463 ☐ ever since 그 이후로
464 ☐ timetable ⓝ 시간표
465 ☐ crash into ~에 충돌하다
466 ☐ take off 이륙하다
467 ☐ land ⓥ 착륙하다

37
468 ☐ manager ⓝ 관리자
469 ☐ ratio ⓝ 비율
470 ☐ cost ⓝ 비용
471 ☐ output ⓝ 산출
472 ☐ manufacturing industry 제조업
473 ☐ describe ⓥ 설명하다
474 ☐ efficient ⓐ 효율적인

475 ☐ known as ~라고 알려진
476 ☐ division of labor 분업
477 ☐ specialize in ~에 특화되다
478 ☐ thousands of 수천의
479 ☐ a number of 많은
480 ☐ involve ⓥ 포함하다, 수반하다
481 ☐ straighten ⓥ 곧게 펴다
482 ☐ sharpen ⓥ 뾰족하게 하다
483 ☐ put on 끼우다, 달다, 입다, 착용하다
484 ☐ polish ⓥ 다듬다

38
485 ☐ stare back at ~을 마주 보다
486 ☐ far ⓐⓓ (비교급 앞에서) 훨씬
487 ☐ reflect ⓥ 반사하다
488 ☐ mirror ⓝ 거울
489 ☐ probably ⓐⓓ 아마도
490 ☐ appear ⓥ ~인 것처럼 보이다
491 ☐ proof ⓝ 증거
492 ☐ clear ⓐ 명확한
493 ☐ snapshot ⓝ 스냅사진, 짧은 묘사
494 ☐ reflection ⓝ (물이나 거울에 비친) 그림자
495 ☐ surprised ⓐ 놀란
496 ☐ interval ⓝ 간격
497 ☐ at first 처음에
498 ☐ peer ⓥ 응시하다
499 ☐ basic ⓐ 기본적인
500 ☐ from moment to moment 시시각각

39
501 ☐ absorb ⓥ (정보를) 받아들이다
502 ☐ possibility ⓝ 가능성
503 ☐ harden ⓥ 굳어지다
504 ☐ belief ⓝ 믿음, 신념
505 ☐ educational ⓐ 교육의
506 ☐ curiosity ⓝ 호기심
507 ☐ decrease ⓥ 감소하다
508 ☐ default setting 기본값
509 ☐ disinterested ⓐ 무관심한
510 ☐ groove ⓝ 고랑
511 ☐ channel ⓝ 경로
512 ☐ development ⓝ 발달
513 ☐ childhood ⓝ 어린 시절
514 ☐ infant ⓝ 유아
515 ☐ neural ⓐ 신경의
516 ☐ mess ⓝ 엉망
517 ☐ perception ⓝ 지각, 인식
518 ☐ consequently ⓐⓓ 그 결과
519 ☐ intensely ⓐⓓ 대단히, 강렬하게
520 ☐ disordered ⓐ 무질서한
521 ☐ pathway ⓝ 경로
522 ☐ automatic ⓐ 자동적인
523 ☐ prune ⓥ 가지치기하다

40
524 ☐ nearly ⓐⓓ 거의
525 ☐ unless ⓒⓞⓝⓙ ~하지 않는 한
526 ☐ spoiled ⓐ 상한
527 ☐ poison mushroom 독버섯
528 ☐ label A as B A를 B라고 분류하다
529 ☐ either A or B A 또는 B
530 ☐ combination ⓝ 조합

531 ☐ add up to 결국 ~이 되다
532 ☐ healthful ⓐ 건강에 좋은
533 ☐ broccoli ⓝ 브로콜리
534 ☐ tofu ⓝ 두부
535 ☐ nutrient-dense ⓐ 영양이 풍부한
536 ☐ supply ⓥ 공급하다
537 ☐ a wide variety of 매우 다양한
538 ☐ nutrient ⓝ 영양분
539 ☐ occasionally ⓐⓓ 가끔
540 ☐ otherwise ⓐⓓ 그렇지 않으면, 다른 경우에는
541 ☐ stay away from ~을 멀리하다
542 ☐ off track 제 길에서 벗어난
543 ☐ load up on ~로 배를 가득 채우다
544 ☐ unlike ⓟⓡⓔⓟ ~와 달리
545 ☐ largely ⓐⓓ 대체로, 주로
546 ☐ composed of ~로 구성된

41~42
547 ☐ hunter-gatherer ⓝ 수렵 채집인
548 ☐ minimal ⓐ 최소한의
549 ☐ structure ⓝ 구조
550 ☐ chief ⓝ 추장, 족장, 우두머리
551 ☐ along with ~와 함께
552 ☐ surplus ⓝ 잉여, 흑자
553 ☐ vital ⓐ 필수적인, 매우 중요한
554 ☐ resource ⓝ 자원
555 ☐ seldom ⓐⓓ ~할 때가 드물다, 좀처럼 ~하지 않다
556 ☐ sufficient ⓐ 충분한
557 ☐ support ⓥ 지원하다, 부양하다
558 ☐ full-time ⓐ 전임의, 정규직의
559 ☐ agriculture ⓝ 농업
560 ☐ reap ⓥ (농작물을) 베어들이다
561 ☐ grain ⓝ 곡물
562 ☐ plant ⓥ (식물을) 심다
563 ☐ community ⓝ 지역 사회
564 ☐ chieftain ⓝ 수령, 두목
565 ☐ practice medicine 의사로 개업하다, 의술을 행하다
566 ☐ priest ⓝ 성직자
567 ☐ warrior ⓝ 전사
568 ☐ security ⓝ 안보
569 ☐ yield ⓝ 수확량
570 ☐ favorable ⓐ 우호적인
571 ☐ basic necessity 기본 필수품
572 ☐ grow in size 규모가 커지다
573 ☐ concentrate ⓥ 집중되다
574 ☐ further ⓐⓓ 더욱
575 ☐ carpenter ⓝ 목수
576 ☐ blacksmith ⓝ 대장장이
577 ☐ sailor ⓝ 선원
578 ☐ bring about ~을 야기하다, 초래하다, 가져오다
579 ☐ quality of life 삶의 질
580 ☐ stability ⓝ 안정성
581 ☐ shadow ⓝ 그림자

43~45
582 ☐ tired ⓐ 피곤한
583 ☐ anxious ⓐ 불안한, 걱정하는
584 ☐ bedside ⓝ 침대 옆, 머리맡

585 ☐ nurse ⓝ 간호사
586 ☐ lie on ~에 눕다
587 ☐ repeat ⓥ 반복하다
588 ☐ several ⓐ 몇몇의, 여럿의
589 ☐ severe ⓐ 극심한
590 ☐ heart disease 심장병
591 ☐ barely ⓐⓓ 간신히 ~하다, 거의 못 ~하다
592 ☐ uniformed ⓐ 유니폼을 입은
593 ☐ reach out one's hand 손을 뻗다
594 ☐ gentle ⓐ 부드러운, 다정한
595 ☐ tightly ⓐⓓ 꽉
596 ☐ through the night 밤새
597 ☐ dawn ⓝ 새벽
598 ☐ release ⓥ 놓다, 해방시키다
599 ☐ hesitate ⓥ 주저하다
600 ☐ for a while 잠시
601 ☐ take A to B A를 B에게 데려가다
602 ☐ mistake ⓝ 실수
603 ☐ wrap ⓥ 감싸다
604 ☐ take a rest 쉬다
605 ☐ politely ⓐⓓ 정중하게

09회

TEST A-B 각 단어의 뜻을 [A] 영어는 우리말로, [B] 우리말은 영어로 쓰시오.

A	English	Korean
01	meditation	
02	anxious	
03	likelihood	
04	superior to	
05	fictional	
06	status	
07	consistently	
08	ask for help	
09	facility	
10	emerge	
11	peer	
12	surplus	
13	hesitate	
14	endure	
15	region	
16	distinct	
17	phenomenon	
18	desirable	
19	pursue	
20	distraction	

B	Korean	English
01	익숙한	
02	지니다, 소유하다	
03	생산성	
04	경험 많은, 숙련된	
05	무급의	
06	감소하다, 줄어들다	
07	상을 주다, 수여하다	
08	고용하다	
09	진술하다	
10	강조하다	
11	호기심	
12	간신히 ~하다, 거의 ~ 못하다	
13	필수적인, 매우 중요한	
14	안정성	
15	기여	
16	당황한	
17	상당한	
18	~로 구성된	
19	~하지 않는 한	
20	반사하다	

▶ A-D 정답 : 해설편 098쪽

TEST C-D 각 단어의 뜻을 골라 기호를 쓰시오.

C	English			Korean
01	instructor	( )	ⓐ	관심을 끌다
02	word-of-mouth	( )	ⓑ	분별 있는, 현명한
03	drudgery	( )	ⓒ	잘 알고 결정하다
04	prejudiced	( )	ⓓ	직업
05	industrialize	( )	ⓔ	거치다, 겪다
06	financial	( )	ⓕ	초래하다, 야기하다
07	strategy	( )	ⓖ	(정보를) 받아들이다
08	profession	( )	ⓗ	강사
09	undergo	( )	ⓘ	얼굴을 찡그리다
10	frown	( )	ⓙ	무질서한
11	have access to	( )	ⓚ	전략
12	bring about	( )	ⓛ	극심한
13	severe	( )	ⓜ	미취학 아동
14	preschooler	( )	ⓝ	재정적인
15	catch one's attention	( )	ⓞ	구전의
16	sensible	( )	ⓟ	~에 접근하다, ~을 이용하다
17	make an informed decision	( )	ⓠ	산업화하다
18	absorb	( )	ⓡ	상한
19	spoiled	( )	ⓢ	고정 관념이 있는
20	disordered	( )	ⓣ	고된 일

D	Korean			English
01	기쁜	( )	ⓐ	prone to
02	많은	( )	ⓑ	analysis
03	자동차	( )	ⓒ	self-esteem
04	기념품	( )	ⓓ	ingredient
05	뜻깊은	( )	ⓔ	livestock
06	비율	( )	ⓕ	automobile
07	~에 걸리기 쉬운	( )	ⓖ	delighted
08	분석	( )	ⓗ	sophistication
09	인지적인	( )	ⓘ	sacrifice
10	요약하다	( )	ⓙ	genuine
11	차별	( )	ⓚ	ratio
12	자존감	( )	ⓛ	neural
13	재료	( )	ⓜ	summarize
14	변모시키다	( )	ⓝ	carry out
15	희생	( )	ⓞ	transform
16	진짜의	( )	ⓟ	cognitive
17	가축	( )	ⓠ	profound
18	신경의	( )	ⓡ	souvenir
19	수행하다	( )	ⓢ	discrimination
20	정교화	( )	ⓣ	a host of

제 3 교시

영어 영역

● 문항수 45개 | 배점 100점 | 제한 시간 70분

● 점수 표시가 없는 문항은 모두 2점

1번부터 17번까지는 듣고 답하는 문제입니다. 1번부터 15번까지는 한 번만 들려주고, 16번부터 17번까지는 두 번 들려줍니다. 방송을 잘 듣고 답을 하시기 바랍니다.

1. 다음을 듣고, 남자가 하는 말의 목적으로 가장 적절한 것을 고르시오.
① 사생활 보호의 중요성을 강조하려고
② 건물 벽 페인트 작업을 공지하려고
③ 회사 근무시간 변경을 안내하려고
④ 새로운 직원 채용을 공고하려고
⑤ 친환경 제품 출시를 홍보하려고

2. 대화를 듣고, 여자의 의견으로 가장 적절한 것을 고르시오.
① 운전자는 제한 속도를 지켜야 한다.
② 교통경찰을 더 많이 배치해야 한다.
③ 보행자의 부주의가 교통사고를 유발한다.
④ 교통사고를 목격하면 즉시 신고해야 한다.
⑤ 대중교통을 이용하면 이동시간을 줄일 수 있다.

3. 대화를 듣고, 두 사람의 관계를 가장 잘 나타낸 것을 고르시오.
① 작가 – 출판사 직원   ② 관람객 – 박물관 해설사
③ 손님 – 주방장   ④ 탑승객 – 항공 승무원
⑤ 학생 – 사서

4. 대화를 듣고, 그림에서 대화의 내용과 일치하지 않는 것을 고르시오

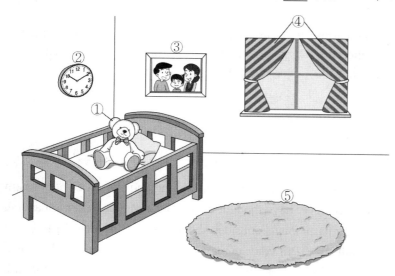

5. 대화를 듣고, 남자가 할 일로 가장 적절한 것을 고르시오.
① 보고서 제출하기   ② 티켓 예매하기
③ 자전거 수리하기   ④ 축구 연습하기
⑤ 팝콘 구입하기

6. 대화를 듣고, 여자가 지불할 금액을 고르시오. [3점]
① $40   ② $60   ③ $80   ④ $100   ⑤ $120

7. 대화를 듣고, 남자가 음식 부스에 갈 수 없는 이유로 가장 적절한 것을 고르시오.
① 밴드 오디션 연습을 해야 해서
② 보드게임 부스를 설치해야 해서
③ 영어 프로젝트를 끝내야 해서
④ 샌드위치를 준비해야 해서
⑤ 친구를 만나러 가야 해서

8. 대화를 듣고, Spanish culture class에 관해 언급되지 않은 것을 고르시오.
① 강사   ② 활동 종류   ③ 수업 요일
④ 준비물   ⑤ 수강료

9. Summer Flea Market에 관한 다음 내용을 듣고, 일치하지 않는 것을 고르시오. [3점]
① 일주일 동안 진행된다.
② 학교 주차장에서 열린다.
③ 장난감, 양초와 같은 물품을 살 수 있다.
④ 상태가 좋은 중고 물품을 판매할 수 있다.
⑤ 첫날 방문하면 할인 쿠폰을 선물로 받는다.

10. 다음 표를 보면서 대화를 듣고, 여자가 구입할 운동화를 고르시오.

Sneakers

	Model	Price	Style	Waterproof	Color
①	A	$50	casual	×	black
②	B	$60	active	×	white
③	C	$65	casual	○	black
④	D	$70	casual	○	white
⑤	E	$85	active	○	white

11. 대화를 듣고, 여자의 마지막 말에 대한 남자의 응답으로 가장 적절한 것을 고르시오.
① All children's books are 20% off.
② It takes time to write a good article.
③ I like to read action adventure books.
④ There are too many advertisements on TV.
⑤ The store has been closed since last month.

12. 대화를 듣고, 남자의 마지막 말에 대한 여자의 응답으로 가장 적절한 것을 고르시오.
① You're welcome. I'm happy to help you.
② That's not true. I made it with your help.
③ Okay. Good food always makes me feel better.
④ Really? You should definitely visit the theater later.
⑤ Never mind. You'll do better on the next presentation.

13. 대화를 듣고, 여자의 마지막 말에 대한 남자의 응답으로 가장 적절한 것을 고르시오.

Man: _____

① I'm excited to buy a new guitar.
② Summer vacation starts on Friday.
③ You can find it on the school website.
④ Let's go to the school festival together.
⑤ You can get some rest during the vacation.

14. 대화를 듣고, 남자의 마지막 말에 대한 여자의 응답으로 가장 적절한 것을 고르시오.

Woman: _____

① I agree. There are many benefits of exercising at the gym.
② You're right. Not all exercise is helpful for your brain.
③ Don't worry. It's not too difficult for me to exercise.
④ That sounds great. Can I join the course, too?
⑤ That's too bad. I hope you get well soon.

15. 다음 상황 설명을 듣고, Ted가 Monica에게 할 말로 가장 적절한 것을 고르시오. [3점]

Ted: _____

① Can I draw your club members on the poster?
② Are you interested in joining my drawing club?
③ Could you tell me how to vote in the election?
④ Can you help me make posters for the election?
⑤ Would you run in the next school president election?

[16~17] 다음을 듣고, 물음에 답하시오.

16. 여자가 하는 말의 주제로 가장 적절한 것은?

① downsides of fatty food
② healthy foods for breakfast
③ ways to avoid eating snacks
④ easy foods to cook in 5 minutes
⑤ the importance of a balanced diet

17. 언급된 음식이 <u>아닌</u> 것은?

① eggs   ② cheese   ③ potatoes
④ yogurt   ⑤ berries

> **이제 듣기 문제가 끝났습니다. 18번부터는 문제지의 지시에 따라 답을 하시기 바랍니다.**

18. 다음 글의 목적으로 가장 적절한 것은?

> Dear Boat Tour Manager,
>
> On March 15, my family was on one of your Glass Bottom Boat Tours. When we returned to our hotel, I discovered that I left behind my cell phone case. The case must have fallen off my lap and onto the floor when I took it off my phone to clean it. I would like to ask you to check if it is on your boat. Its color is black and it has my name on the inside. If you find the case, I would appreciate it if you would let me know.
>
> Sincerely,
> Sam Roberts

① 제품의 고장 원인을 문의하려고
② 분실물 발견 시 연락을 부탁하려고
③ 시설물의 철저한 관리를 당부하려고
④ 여행자 보험 가입 절차를 확인하려고
⑤ 분실물 센터 확장의 필요성을 건의하려고

19. 다음 글에 드러난 Matthew의 심경 변화로 가장 적절한 것은?

One Saturday morning, Matthew's mother told Matthew that she was going to take him to the park. A big smile came across his face. As he loved to play outside, he ate his breakfast and got dressed quickly so they could go. When they got to the park, Matthew ran all the way over to the swing set. That was his favorite thing to do at the park. But the swings were all being used. His mother explained that he could use the slide until a swing became available, but it was broken. Suddenly, his mother got a phone call and she told Matthew they had to leave. His heart sank.

① embarrassed → indifferent
② excited → disappointed
③ cheerful → ashamed
④ nervous → touched
⑤ scared → relaxed

20. 다음 글에서 필자가 주장하는 바로 가장 적절한 것은?

Meetings encourage creative thinking and can give you ideas that you may never have thought of on your own. However, on average, meeting participants consider about one third of meeting time to be unproductive. But you can make your meetings more productive and more useful by preparing well in advance. You should create a list of items to be discussed and share your list with other participants before a meeting. It allows them to know what to expect in your meeting and prepare to participate.

① 회의 결과는 빠짐없이 작성해서 공개해야 한다.
② 중요한 정보는 공식 회의를 통해 전달해야 한다.
③ 생산성 향상을 위해 정기적인 평가회가 필요하다.
④ 모든 참석자의 동의를 받아서 회의를 열어야 한다.
⑤ 회의에서 다룰 사항은 미리 작성해서 공유해야 한다.

21. 밑줄 친 <u>put the glass down</u>이 다음 글에서 의미하는 바로 가장 적절한 것은? [3점]

A psychology professor raised a glass of water while teaching stress management principles to her students, and asked them, "How heavy is this glass of water I'm holding?" Students shouted out various answers. The professor replied, "The absolute weight of this glass doesn't matter. It depends on how long I hold it. If I hold it for a minute, it's quite light. But, if I hold it for a day straight, it will cause severe pain in my arm, forcing me to drop the glass to the floor. In each case, the weight of the glass is the same, but the longer I hold it, the heavier it feels to me." As the class nodded their heads in agreement, she continued, "Your stresses in life are like this glass of water. If you still feel the weight of yesterday's stress, it's a strong sign that it's time to <u>put the glass down</u>."

① pour more water into the glass
② set a plan not to make mistakes
③ let go of the stress in your mind
④ think about the cause of your stress
⑤ learn to accept the opinions of others

22. 다음 글의 요지로 가장 적절한 것은?

Your emotions deserve attention and give you important pieces of information. However, they can also sometimes be an unreliable, inaccurate source of information. You may feel a certain way, but that does not mean those feelings are reflections of the truth. You may feel sad and conclude that your friend is angry with you when her behavior simply reflects that she's having a bad day. You may feel depressed and decide that you did poorly in an interview when you did just fine. Your feelings can mislead you into thinking things that are not supported by facts.

① 자신의 감정으로 인해 상황을 오해할 수 있다.
② 자신의 생각을 타인에게 강요해서는 안 된다.
③ 인간관계가 우리의 감정에 영향을 미친다.
④ 타인의 감정에 공감하는 자세가 필요하다.
⑤ 공동체를 위한 선택에는 보상이 따른다.

23. 다음 글의 주제로 가장 적절한 것은?

Every day, children explore and construct relationships among objects. Frequently, these relationships focus on how much or how many of something exists. Thus, children count — "One cookie, two shoes, three candles on the birthday cake, four children in the sandbox." Children compare — "Which has more? Which has fewer? Will there be enough?" Children calculate — "How many will fit? Now, I have five. I need one more." In all of these instances, children are developing a notion of quantity. Children reveal and investigate mathematical concepts through their own activities or experiences, such as figuring out how many crackers to take at snack time or sorting shells into piles.

① difficulties of children in learning how to count
② how children build mathematical understanding
③ why fingers are used in counting objects
④ importance of early childhood education
⑤ advantages of singing number songs

24. 다음 글의 제목으로 가장 적절한 것은?

Only a generation or two ago, mentioning the word *algorithms* would have drawn a blank from most people. Today, algorithms appear in every part of civilization. They are connected to everyday life. They're not just in your cell phone or your laptop but in your car, your house, your appliances, and your toys. Your bank is a huge web of algorithms, with humans turning the switches here and there. Algorithms schedule flights and then fly the airplanes. Algorithms run factories, trade goods, and keep records. If every algorithm suddenly stopped working, it would be the end of the world as we know it.

① We Live in an Age of Algorithms
② Mysteries of Ancient Civilizations
③ Dangers of Online Banking Algorithms
④ How Algorithms Decrease Human Creativity
⑤ Transportation: A Driving Force of Industry

25. 다음 도표의 내용과 일치하지 <u>않는</u> 것은?

Percent of U.S. Households with Pets

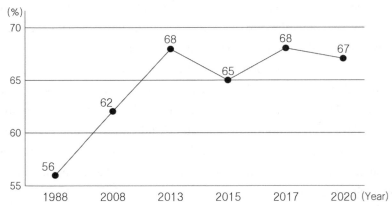

The graph above shows the percent of households with pets in the United States (U.S.) from 1988 to 2020. ① In 1988, more than half of U.S. households owned pets, and more than 6 out of 10 U.S. households owned pets from 2008 to 2020. ② In the period between 1988 and 2008, pet ownership increased among U.S. households by 6 percentage points. ③ From 2008 to 2013, pet ownership rose an additional 6 percentage points. ④ The percent of U.S. households with pets in 2013 was the same as that in 2017, which was 68 percent. ⑤ In 2015, the rate of U.S. households with pets was 3 percentage points lower than in 2020.

26. Claude Bolling에 관한 다음 글의 내용과 일치하지 <u>않는</u> 것은?

Pianist, composer, and big band leader, Claude Bolling, was born on April 10, 1930, in Cannes, France, but spent most of his life in Paris. He began studying classical music as a youth. He was introduced to the world of jazz by a schoolmate. Later, Bolling became interested in the music of Fats Waller, one of the most excellent jazz musicians. Bolling became famous as a teenager by winning the Best Piano Player prize at an amateur contest in France. He was also a successful film music composer, writing the music for more than one hundred films. In 1975, he collaborated with flutist Rampal and published *Suite for Flute and Jazz Piano Trio*, which he became most well-known for. He died in 2020, leaving two sons, David and Alexandre.

① 1930년에 프랑스에서 태어났다.
② 학교 친구를 통해 재즈를 소개받았다.
③ 20대에 Best Piano Player 상을 받았다.
④ 성공적인 영화 음악 작곡가였다.
⑤ 1975년에 플루트 연주자와 협업했다.

27. Kids Taekwondo Program에 관한 다음 안내문의 내용과 일치하지 <u>않는</u> 것은?

Kids Taekwondo Program
Enjoy our taekwondo program this summer vacation.

□ **Schedule**
• Dates: August 8th － August 10th
• Time: 9:00 a.m. － 11:00 a.m.

□ **Participants**
• Any child aged 5 and up

□ **Activities**
• Self-defense training
• Team building games to develop social skills

□ **Participation Fee**
• $50 per child (includes snacks)

□ **Notice**
• What to bring: water bottle, towel
• What not to bring: chewing gum, expensive items

① 8월 8일부터 3일간 운영한다.
② 5세 이상의 어린이가 참가할 수 있다.
③ 자기 방어 훈련 활동을 한다.
④ 참가비에 간식비가 포함되지 않는다.
⑤ 물병과 수건을 가져와야 한다.

28. Moonlight Chocolate Factory Tour에 관한 다음 안내문의 내용과 일치하는 것은?

Moonlight Chocolate Factory Tour
Take this special tour and have a chance to enjoy our most popular chocolate bars.

□ **Operating Hours**
• Monday － Friday, 2:00p.m. － 5:00 p.m.

□ **Activities**
• Watching our chocolate-making process
• Tasting 3 types of chocolate (dark, milk, and mint chocolate)

□ **Notice**
• Ticket price: $30
• Wearing a face mask is required.
• Taking pictures is not allowed inside the factory.

① 주말 오후 시간에 운영한다.
② 초콜릿 제조 과정을 볼 수 있다.
③ 네 가지 종류의 초콜릿을 시식한다.
④ 마스크 착용은 참여자의 선택 사항이다.
⑤ 공장 내부에서 사진 촬영이 가능하다.

29. 다음 글의 밑줄 친 부분 중, 어법상 틀린 것은?

Despite all the high-tech devices that seem to deny the need for paper, paper use in the United States ① has nearly doubled recently. We now consume more paper than ever: 400 million tons globally and growing. Paper is not the only resource ② that we are using more of. Technological advances often come with the promise of ③ using fewer materials. However, the reality is that they have historically caused more materials use, making us ④ dependently on more natural resources. The world now consumes far more "stuff" than it ever has. We use twenty-seven times more industrial minerals, such as gold, copper, and rare metals, than we ⑤ did just over a century ago. We also each individually use more resources. Much of that is due to our high-tech lifestyle.

* copper: 구리

30. 다음 글의 밑줄 친 부분 중, 문맥상 낱말의 쓰임이 적절하지 않은 것은? [3점]

Do you sometimes feel like you don't love your life? Like, deep inside, something is missing? That's because we are living someone else's life. We allow other people to ① influence our choices. We are trying to meet their expectations. Social pressure is deceiving — we are all impacted without noticing it. Before we realize we are losing ownership of our lives, we end up ② ignoring how other people live. Then, we can only see the greener grass — ours is never good enough. To regain that passion for the life you want, you must ③ recover control of your choices. No one but yourself can choose how you live. But, how? The first step to getting rid of expectations is to treat yourself ④ kindly. You can't truly love other people if you don't love yourself first. When we accept who we are, there's no room for other's ⑤ expectations.

[31~34] 다음 빈칸에 들어갈 말로 가장 적절한 것을 고르시오.

31. One of the big questions faced this past year was how to keep innovation rolling when people were working entirely virtually. But experts say that digital work didn't have a negative effect on innovation and creativity. Working within limits pushes us to solve problems. Overall, virtual meeting platforms put more constraints on communication and collaboration than face-to-face settings. For instance, with the press of a button, virtual meeting hosts can control the size of breakout groups and enforce time constraints; only one person can speak at a time; nonverbal signals, particularly those below the shoulders, are diminished; "seating arrangements" are assigned by the platform, not by individuals; and visual access to others may be limited by the size of each participant's screen. Such _____ are likely to stretch participants beyond their usual ways of thinking, boosting creativity.

① restrictions
② responsibilities
③ memories
④ coincidences
⑤ traditions

32. The law of demand is that the demand for goods and services increases as prices fall, and the demand falls as prices increase. *Giffen goods* are special types of products for which the traditional law of demand does not apply. Instead of switching to cheaper replacements, consumers demand more of giffen goods when the price increases and less of them when the price decreases. Taking an example, rice in China is a giffen good because people tend to purchase less of it when the price falls. The reason for this is, when the price of rice falls, people have more money to spend on other types of products such as meat and dairy and, therefore, change their spending pattern. On the other hand, as rice prices increase, people _____. [3점]

① order more meat
② consume more rice
③ try to get new jobs
④ increase their savings
⑤ start to invest overseas

33. In a study at Princeton University in 1992, research scientists looked at two different groups of mice. One group was made intellectually superior by modifying the gene for the glutamate receptor. Glutamate is a brain chemical that is necessary in learning. The other group was genetically manipulated to be intellectually inferior, also done by modifying the gene for the glutamate receptor. The smart mice were then raised in standard cages, while the inferior mice were raised in large cages with toys and exercise wheels and with lots of social interaction. At the end of the study, although the intellectually inferior mice were genetically handicapped, they were able to perform just as well as their genetic superiors. This was a real triumph for nurture over nature. Genes are turned on or off _____. [3점]

* glutamate: 글루타민산염 ** manipulate: 조작하다

① by themselves for survival
② free from social interaction
③ based on what is around you
④ depending on genetic superiority
⑤ so as to keep ourselves entertained

34. Researchers are working on a project that asks coastal towns how they are preparing for rising sea levels. Some towns have risk assessments; some towns even have a plan. But it's a rare town that is actually carrying out a plan. One reason we've failed to act on climate change is the common belief that _____. For decades, climate change was a prediction about the future, so scientists talked about it in the future tense. This became a habit — so that even today many scientists still use the future tense, even though we know that a climate crisis is ongoing. Scientists also often focus on regions most affected by the crisis, such as Bangladesh or the West Antarctic Ice Sheet, which for most Americans are physically remote. [3점]

① it is not related to science
② it is far away in time and space
③ energy efficiency matters the most
④ careful planning can fix the problem
⑤ it is too late to prevent it from happening

35. 다음 글에서 전체 흐름과 관계 <u>없는</u> 문장은?

According to Marguerite La Caze, fashion contributes to our lives and provides a medium for us to develop and exhibit important social virtues. ① Fashion may be beautiful, innovative, and useful; we can display creativity and good taste in our fashion choices. ② And in dressing with taste and care, we represent both self-respect and a concern for the pleasure of others. ③ There is no doubt that fashion can be a source of interest and pleasure which links us to each other. ④ Although the fashion industry developed first in Europe and America, today it is an international and highly globalized industry. ⑤ That is, fashion provides a sociable aspect along with opportunities to imagine oneself differently — to try on different identities.

* virtue: 가치

[36~37] 주어진 글 다음에 이어질 글의 순서로 가장 적절한 것을 고르시오.

36.

Mrs. Klein told her first graders to draw a picture of something to be thankful for. She thought that most of the class would draw turkeys or Thanksgiving tables. But Douglas drew something different.

(A) The class was so responsive that Mrs. Klein had almost forgotten about Douglas. After she had the others at work on another project, she asked Douglas whose hand it was. He answered softly, "It's yours. Thank you, Mrs. Klein."

(B) Douglas was a boy who usually spent time alone and stayed around her while his classmates went outside together during break time. What the boy drew was a hand. But whose hand? His image immediately attracted the other students' interest.

(C) So, everyone rushed to talk about whose hand it was. "It must be the hand of God that brings us food," said one student. "A farmer's," said a second student, "because they raise the turkeys." "It looks more like a police officer's," added another, "they protect us."

① (A) − (C) − (B)　　　② (B) − (A) − (C)
③ (B) − (C) − (A)　　　④ (C) − (A) − (B)
⑤ (C) − (B) − (A)

37.

According to legend, once a vampire bites a person, that person turns into a vampire who seeks the blood of others. A researcher came up with some simple math, which proves that these highly popular creatures can't exist.

(A) In just two-and-a-half years, the original human population would all have become vampires with no humans left. But look around you. Have vampires taken over the world? No, because there's no such thing.

(B) If the first vampire came into existence that day and bit one person a month, there would have been two vampires by February 1st, 1600. A month later there would have been four, the next month eight, then sixteen, and so on.

(C) University of Central Florida physics professor Costas Efthimiou's work breaks down the myth. Suppose that on January 1st, 1600, the human population was just over five hundred million. [3점]

① (A) − (C) − (B) ② (B) − (A) − (C)
③ (B) − (C) − (A) ④ (C) − (A) − (B)
⑤ (C) − (B) − (A)

[38~39] 글의 흐름으로 보아, 주어진 문장이 들어가기에 가장 적절한 곳을 고르시오.

38.

For example, if you rub your hands together quickly, they will get warmer.

Friction is a force between two surfaces that are sliding, or trying to slide, across each other. For example, when you try to push a book along the floor, friction makes this difficult. Friction always works in the direction opposite to the direction in which the object is moving, or trying to move. So, friction always slows a moving object down. (①) The amount of friction depends on the surface materials. (②) The rougher the surface is, the more friction is produced. (③) Friction also produces heat. (④) Friction can be a useful force because it prevents our shoes slipping on the floor when we walk and stops car tires skidding on the road. (⑤) When you walk, friction is caused between the tread on your shoes and the ground, acting to grip the ground and prevent sliding.

* skid: 미끄러지다 ** tread: 접지면, 바닥

39.

But, a blind person will associate the same friend with a unique combination of experiences from their non-visual senses that act to represent that friend.

Humans born without sight are not able to collect visual experiences, so they understand the world entirely through their other senses. (①) As a result, people with blindness at birth develop an amazing ability to understand the world through the collection of experiences and memories that come from these non-visual senses. (②) The dreams of a person who has been without sight since birth can be just as vivid and imaginative as those of someone with normal vision. (③) They are unique, however, because their dreams are constructed from the non-visual experiences and memories they have collected. (④) A person with normal vision will dream about a familiar friend using visual memories of shape, lighting, and colour. (⑤) In other words, people blind at birth have similar overall dreaming experiences even though they do not dream in pictures.

40. 다음 글의 내용을 한 문장으로 요약하고자 한다. 빈칸 (A), (B)에 들어갈 말로 가장 적절한 것은? [3점]

According to a study of Swedish adolescents, an important factor of adolescents' academic success is how they respond to challenges. The study reports that when facing difficulties, adolescents exposed to an authoritative parenting style are less likely to be passive, helpless, and afraid to fail. Another study of nine high schools in Wisconsin and northern California indicates that children of authoritative parents do well in school, because these parents put a lot of effort into getting involved in their children's school activities. That is, authoritative parents are significantly more likely to help their children with homework, to attend school programs, to watch their children in sports, and to help students select courses. Moreover, these parents are more aware of what their children do and how they perform in school. Finally, authoritative parents praise academic excellence and the importance of working hard more than other parents do.

↓

The studies above show that the children of authoritative parents often succeed academically, since they are more ___(A)___ to deal with their difficulties and are affected by their parents' ___(B)___ involvement.

	(A)		(B)
①	likely	......	random
②	willing	......	minimal
③	willing	......	active
④	hesitant	......	unwanted
⑤	hesitant	......	constant

[41~42] 다음 글을 읽고, 물음에 답하시오.

U.K. researchers say a bedtime of between 10 p.m. and 11 p.m. is best. They say people who go to sleep between these times have a (a) lower risk of heart disease. Six years ago, the researchers collected data on the sleep patterns of 80,000 volunteers. The volunteers had to wear a special watch for seven days so the researchers could collect data on their sleeping and waking times. The scientists then monitored the health of the volunteers. Around 3,000 volunteers later showed heart problems. They went to bed earlier or later than the (b) ideal 10 p.m. to 11 p.m. timeframe.

One of the authors of the study, Dr. David Plans, commented on his research and the (c) effects of bedtimes on the health of our heart. He said the study could not give a certain cause for their results, but it suggests that early or late bedtimes may be more likely to disrupt the body clock, with (d) positive consequences for cardiovascular health. He said that it was important for our body to wake up to the morning light, and that the worst time to go to bed was after midnight because it may (e) reduce the likelihood of seeing morning light which resets the body clock. He added that we risk cardiovascular disease if our body clock is not reset properly.

*disrupt: 혼란케 하다 **cardiovascular: 심장 혈관의

41. 윗글의 제목으로 가장 적절한 것은?

① The Best Bedtime for Your Heart
② Late Bedtimes Are a Matter of Age
③ For Sound Sleep: Turn Off the Light
④ Sleeping Patterns Reflect Personalities
⑤ Regular Exercise: A Miracle for Good Sleep

42. 밑줄 친 (a)~(e) 중에서 문맥상 낱말의 쓰임이 적절하지 <u>않은</u> 것은?

① (a)   ② (b)   ③ (c)   ④ (d)   ⑤ (e)

[43~45] 다음 글을 읽고, 물음에 답하시오.

(A)

Once, a farmer lost his precious watch while working in his barn. It may have appeared to be an ordinary watch to others, but it brought a lot of happy childhood memories to him. It was one of the most important things to (a) him. After searching for it for a long time, the old farmer became exhausted.

*barn: 헛간(곡물·건초 따위를 두는 곳)

(B)

The number of children looking for the watch slowly decreased and only a few tired children were left. The farmer gave up all hope of finding it and called off the search. Just when the farmer was closing the barn door, a little boy came up to him and asked the farmer to give him another chance. The farmer did not want to lose out on any chance of finding the watch so let (b) him in the barn.

(C)

After a little while the boy came out with the farmer's watch in his hand. (c) He was happily surprised and asked how he had succeeded to find the watch while everyone else had failed. He replied "I just sat there and tried listening for the sound of the watch. In silence, it was much easier to hear it and follow the direction of the sound." (d) He was delighted to get his watch back and rewarded the little boy as promised.

(D)

However, the tired farmer did not want to give up on the search for his watch and asked a group of children playing outside to help him. (e) He promised an attractive reward for the person who could find it. After hearing about the reward, the children hurried inside the barn and went through and round the entire pile of hay looking for the watch. After a long time searching for it, some of the children got tired and gave up.

43. 주어진 글 (A)에 이어질 내용을 순서에 맞게 배열한 것으로 가장 적절한 것은?

① (B) − (D) − (C)   ② (C) − (B) − (D)
③ (C) − (D) − (B)   ④ (D) − (B) − (C)
⑤ (D) − (C) − (B)

44. 밑줄 친 (a) ~ (e) 중에서 가리키는 대상이 나머지 넷과 <u>다른</u> 것은?

① (a)   ② (b)   ③ (c)   ④ (d)   ⑤ (e)

45. 윗글에 관한 내용으로 적절하지 <u>않은</u> 것은?

① 농부의 시계는 어린 시절의 행복한 기억을 불러일으켰다.
② 한 어린 소년이 농부에게 또 한 번의 기회를 달라고 요청했다.
③ 소년이 한 손에 농부의 시계를 들고 나왔다.
④ 아이들은 시계를 찾기 위해 헛간을 뛰쳐나왔다.
⑤ 아이들 중 일부는 지쳐서 시계 찾기를 포기했다.

* 확인 사항
○ 답안지의 해당란에 필요한 내용을 정확히 기입(표기)했는지 확인하시오.

VOCA LIST 10

01
- 001 □ building ⓝ 건물
- 002 □ manager ⓝ 관리인
- 003 □ paint ⓥ 페인트를 칠하다
- 004 □ next week 다음 주
- 005 □ surprise ⓥ 놀라게 하다
- 006 □ smell ⓥ 냄새가 나다
- 007 □ safe ⓐ 안전한
- 008 □ eco-friendly ⓐ 친환경적인
- 009 □ inconvenience ⓥ 불편하게 하다
- 010 □ cooperation ⓝ 협조

02
- 011 □ get a driver's license 운전면허를 따다
- 012 □ driving test 운전면허 시험
- 013 □ nervous ⓐ 불안해하는
- 014 □ speed limit 제한 속도
- 015 □ everywhere ⓐⓓ 어디에나, 도처에
- 016 □ driver ⓝ 운전자
- 017 □ terrible ⓐ 끔찍한, 소름끼치는
- 018 □ serious ⓐ 심각한
- 019 □ accident ⓝ 사고
- 020 □ dangerous ⓐ 위험한
- 021 □ follow ⓥ 지키다, 따르다

03
- 022 □ look good 좋아 보이다
- 023 □ any other 뭔가 다른
- 024 □ recommend ⓥ 추천하다
- 025 □ borrow ⓥ 빌리다
- 026 □ up to ~까지
- 027 □ return ⓥ 반납하다
- 028 □ on time 제때

04
- 029 □ toy bear 곰 인형
- 030 □ cute ⓐ 귀여운
- 031 □ round ⓐ 원형의
- 032 □ wall ⓝ 벽
- 033 □ go well with ~와 잘 어울리다
- 034 □ How do you like ~? ~이 어때요?
- 035 □ family picture 가족사진
- 036 □ striped ⓐ 줄무늬가 있는
- 037 □ What do you think of ~? ~을 어떻게 생각해요?

05
- 038 □ fix ⓥ 고치다
- 039 □ soccer practice 축구 연습
- 040 □ coach ⓝ 코치
- 041 □ tire ⓥ 피로[피곤]해지다
- 042 □ due ⓐ 기한인, ~하기로 되어 있는

06
- 043 □ amusement park 놀이공원
- 044 □ in total 전체로서, 통틀어
- 045 □ discount ⓝ 할인
- 046 □ print out ~을 출력하다
- 047 □ ID ⓝ 신분증
- 048 □ here you are 여기 (있어) (상대방에게 무엇을 주면서 하는 말)
- 049 □ original price 정가

07
- 050 □ finish ⓥ 끝내다, 완료하다
- 051 □ be busy ~ing ~하느라 바쁘다
- 052 □ booth ⓝ (칸을 막아 임시로 만든) 점포, 전시장
- 053 □ look forward to ~을 고대하다
- 054 □ terribly ⓐⓓ 너무, 대단히

08
- 055 □ teenage ⓐ 십대의
- 056 □ native speaker 원어민
- 057 □ activity ⓝ 활동
- 058 □ traditional ⓐ 전통적인
- 059 □ try on ~을 입어보다
- 060 □ class material 수업 자료

09
- 061 □ resident ⓝ 거주자, 주민
- 062 □ hold ⓥ 계속 유지하다
- 063 □ flea market 벼룩시장
- 064 □ parking lot 주차장
- 065 □ different ⓐ 여러 가지의, 가지가지의
- 066 □ such as ~와 같은
- 067 □ candle ⓝ 양초
- 068 □ reasonable ⓐ 합리적인, 적당한
- 069 □ used item 중고품
- 070 □ condition ⓝ 상태

10
- 071 □ sneakers ⓝ 스니커즈 운동화
- 072 □ budget ⓝ 예산
- 073 □ active ⓐ 활동적인
- 074 □ prefer ⓥ (다른 것보다) …을 좋아하다
- 075 □ match ⓥ 어울리다
- 076 □ waterproof ⓐ 방수의
- 077 □ rainy day 비 오는 날
- 078 □ take an advice 충고를 따르다

11
- 079 □ advertisement ⓝ 광고
- 080 □ special event 특별 행사
- 081 □ take time to ~하는 데 시간이 걸리다
- 082 □ article ⓝ 기사, 논문

12
- 083 □ worry ⓥ 걱정하다
- 084 □ do well on ~을 잘하다
- 085 □ presentation ⓝ 발표
- 086 □ take one's mind off of ~의 생각을 떨쳐내다
- 087 □ meal ⓝ 식사
- 088 □ definitely ⓐⓓ 꼭, 반드시

13
- 089 □ instead ⓐⓓ 대신에
- 090 □ exam ⓝ 시험
- 091 □ first grader 1학년생
- 092 □ improve ⓥ 향상시키다
- 093 □ get rest 휴식을 취하다

14
- 094 □ work out 운동하다

15
- 095 □ exercise ⓝ 운동
- 096 □ at home 집에서
- 097 □ alone ⓐⓓ 혼자
- 098 □ fitness ⓝ 신체 단련
- 099 □ benefit ⓝ 이점, 이득
- 100 □ helpful ⓐ 도움이 되는
- 101 □ get well (병 등이) 낫다

15
- 102 □ run for ~에 입후보하다
- 103 □ school president 전교 회장
- 104 □ election ⓝ 선거
- 105 □ effective ⓐ 효과적인
- 106 □ make an impression on ~에게 인상을 주다
- 107 □ draw ⓥ 그리다

16~17
- 108 □ host ⓝ 진행자
- 109 □ listener ⓝ 청취자
- 110 □ healthy ⓐ 건강한
- 111 □ excellent ⓐ 훌륭한, 탁월한
- 112 □ protein ⓝ 단백질
- 113 □ option ⓝ 선택
- 114 □ reduce ⓥ 줄이다
- 115 □ hunger ⓝ 배고픔
- 116 □ weight loss 체중 감량
- 117 □ contain ⓥ 함유하다, ~이 들어 있다
- 118 □ digestion ⓝ 소화
- 119 □ sugar ⓝ 당분, 당
- 120 □ fiber ⓝ 섬유소
- 121 □ tasty ⓐ 맛있는
- 122 □ downside ⓝ 단점
- 123 □ fatty ⓐ 기름진, 지방이 많은
- 124 □ importance ⓝ 중요성
- 125 □ balanced diet 균형식(영양의 균형을 갖춘 식사)

18
- 126 □ return ⓥ 돌아오다
- 127 □ discover ⓥ 발견하다
- 128 □ leave behind ~을 남겨놓고 오다
- 129 □ lap ⓝ 무릎
- 130 □ floor ⓝ 바닥
- 131 □ clean ⓥ 닦다
- 132 □ inside ⓐⓓ 안에
- 133 □ appreciate ⓥ 감사하다

19
- 134 □ take ⓥ 데리고 가다
- 135 □ dress ⓥ 옷을 입다
- 136 □ swing ⓝ 그네
- 137 □ favorite ⓐ 매우 좋아하는
- 138 □ slide ⓝ 미끄럼틀
- 139 □ available ⓐ 이용할 수 있는
- 140 □ sink ⓥ 가라앉다
- 141 □ embarrassed ⓐ 당황한
- 142 □ indifferent ⓐ 무관심한
- 143 □ disappointed ⓐ 실망한
- 144 □ ashamed ⓐ 수치스러운
- 145 □ nervous ⓐ 긴장한
- 146 □ touched ⓐ 감동한

20
- 147 □ scared ⓐ 겁에 질린
- 148 □ relaxed ⓐ 느긋한

20
- 149 □ encourage ⓥ 촉진하다, 격려하다
- 150 □ creative ⓐ 창의적인
- 151 □ on average 평균적으로
- 152 □ participant ⓝ 참가자
- 153 □ consider ⓥ 여기다
- 154 □ meeting time 회의 시간
- 155 □ unproductive ⓐ 비생산적인
- 156 □ productive ⓐ 생산적인
- 157 □ discuss ⓥ 논의하다
- 158 □ expect ⓥ 기대하다

21
- 159 □ psychology ⓝ 심리학
- 160 □ raise ⓥ (무엇을 위로) 들어 올리다
- 161 □ management ⓝ 관리
- 162 □ principle ⓝ 원칙, 원리
- 163 □ heavy ⓐ 무거운
- 164 □ shout ⓥ 외치다
- 165 □ various ⓐ 다양한
- 166 □ reply ⓥ 대답하다
- 167 □ absolute ⓐ (상대적이 아닌) 절대적인
- 168 □ matter ⓥ 중요하다
- 169 □ depend ⓥ ~에 달려 있다, 좌우되다
- 170 □ quite ⓐⓓ 꽤
- 171 □ straight ⓐⓓ 계속해서
- 172 □ severe ⓐ 심각한
- 173 □ pain ⓝ 아픔, 통증, 고통
- 174 □ case ⓝ 사례
- 175 □ nod ⓥ 끄덕이다
- 176 □ in agreement 동의하며
- 177 □ continue ⓥ 계속하다, 이어서 말하다
- 178 □ sign ⓝ 신호
- 179 □ put down ~을 내려놓다
- 180 □ pour ⓥ 쏟다, 붓다
- 181 □ mistake ⓝ 실수
- 182 □ let go of ~을 내려놓다, 버리다, 포기하다
- 183 □ opinion ⓝ 의견

22
- 184 □ emotion ⓝ 감정
- 185 □ deserve ⓥ ~을 받을 만하다
- 186 □ attention ⓝ 주목
- 187 □ unreliable ⓐ 믿을 만하지 않은
- 188 □ inaccurate ⓐ 부정확한
- 189 □ source of information 정보 출처
- 190 □ reflection ⓝ 반영
- 191 □ truth ⓝ 사실
- 192 □ conclude ⓥ 결론을 내리다
- 193 □ behavior ⓝ 행동, 태도
- 194 □ depressed ⓐ 우울한
- 195 □ decide ⓥ 결정하다
- 196 □ poorly ⓐⓓ 좋지 못하게
- 197 □ interview ⓝ 면접
- 198 □ mislead A into B A를 속여 B하게 하다
- 199 □ support ⓥ 뒷받침하다, 지지하다

23
- 200 □ explore ⓥ 탐구하다

10회

201 construct ⓥ 구성하다
202 relationship ⓝ 관계
203 object ⓝ 사물
204 frequently ⓐⓓ 자주, 종종, 빈번히
205 exist ⓥ 존재하다
206 thus ⓐⓓ 따라서
207 count ⓥ 세다
208 sandbox ⓝ (어린이가 안에서 노는) 모래 놀이 통
209 compare ⓥ 비교하다
210 calculate ⓥ 계산하다
211 one more 하나 더
212 instance ⓝ 예시, 사례
213 notion ⓝ 개념
214 quantity ⓝ (측정 가능한) 양, 수량
215 reveal ⓥ 밝히다, 드러내다
216 investigate ⓥ 연구하다, 조사하다
217 concept ⓝ 개념
218 such as 예를 들어
219 sort A into B A를 B로 분류하다
220 shell ⓝ (조개 등의) 껍데기
221 advantage ⓝ 이점

24
222 generation ⓝ 세대
223 mention ⓥ 말하다, 언급하다
224 algorithm ⓝ 알고리즘, 연산
225 draw a blank 아무 반응을 얻지 못하다
226 appear ⓥ 나타나다, 보이기 시작하다
227 civilization ⓝ 문명
228 connect ⓥ 이어지다, 연결되다
229 everyday life 일상생활
230 appliance ⓝ 가전 (제품)
231 huge ⓐ 거대한
232 here and there 여기저기에
233 flight ⓝ 비행
234 fly an airplane 비행기를 운항하다
235 run ⓥ (사업체 등을) 운영하다
236 factory ⓝ 공장
237 trade ⓥ 거래하다, 교역하다
238 ancient ⓐ 고대의
239 decrease ⓥ 줄다, 감소하다
240 driving force 원동력

25
241 pet ⓝ 반려동물, 애완동물
242 household ⓝ 가정, 가구
243 own ⓥ 보유하다, 소유하다
244 period ⓝ 기간, 시기
245 ownership ⓝ 보유, 소유(권)
246 rise ⓥ 오르다
247 additional ⓐ 추가의

26
248 composer ⓝ 작곡가
249 big band (재즈의) 빅 밴드
250 classical music 고전 음악
251 youth ⓝ 젊은 시절, 청춘
252 introduce ⓥ 소개하다
253 musician ⓝ 음악가
254 famous ⓐ 유명한
255 prize ⓝ 상(賞)

256 successful ⓐ 성공한
257 film music 영화 음악
258 collaborate with ~와 협업하다
259 flutist ⓝ 플루티스트
260 publish ⓥ 발매하다, 출간하다
261 well-known ⓐ 잘 알려진, 유명한

27
262 self-defense ⓝ 자기 방어
263 training ⓝ 교육, 훈련, 연수
264 social skill 사교성
265 water bottle 물병
266 expensive ⓐ 비싼

28
267 have a chance to ~할 기회를 갖다
268 operating hour 운영 시간
269 process ⓝ 과정
270 require ⓥ 필요로 하다

29
271 despite ⓟⓡⓔⓟ ~에도 불구하고
272 high-tech ⓐ 첨단 기술의
273 device ⓝ 장치, 기기
274 deny ⓥ 부인[부정]하다
275 paper ⓝ 종이
276 nearly ⓐⓓ 거의
277 recently ⓐⓓ 최근에
278 consume ⓥ 소비하다
279 globally ⓐⓓ 전 세계적으로
280 grow ⓥ 커지다, 늘다, 많아지다
281 resource ⓝ 자원
282 advance ⓝ 발전
283 promise ⓝ 가능성
284 material ⓝ 물질, 자재, 재료
285 historically ⓐⓓ 역사적으로
286 dependently ⓐⓓ 의존적으로, 남에게 의지하여
287 natural resources 천연자원
288 stuff ⓝ 재료
289 industrial ⓐ 산업의
290 mineral ⓝ 광물
291 copper ⓝ 구리
292 rare ⓐ 희귀한, 드문
293 ago ⓐⓓ (얼마의 시간) 전에
294 individually ⓐⓓ 개별적으로, 각각 따로
295 lifestyle ⓝ 생활 방식

30
296 sometimes ⓐⓓ 때때로, 가끔
297 missing ⓐ 빠진, 실종된
298 else ⓐⓓ 다른
299 influence ⓝ 영향 ⓥ 영향을 미치다
300 meet the expectation 기대를 충족하다
301 pressure ⓝ 압박, 압력
302 deceiving ⓐ 현혹시키는, 속이는
303 impact ⓥ 영향을 미치다
304 realize ⓥ 깨닫다, 알아차리다
305 lose ⓥ 잃어버리다
306 ignore ⓥ 무시하다
307 grass ⓝ 풀, 잔디
308 regain ⓥ 되찾다

309 passion ⓝ 열정
310 recover ⓥ 회복하다
311 get rid of ~을 없애다
312 expectation ⓝ 예상, 기대
313 treat ⓥ 대하다
314 accept ⓥ 받아들이다

31
315 face ⓥ 직면하다
316 innovation ⓝ 혁신
317 entirely ⓐⓓ 완전히
318 virtually ⓐⓓ (컴퓨터를 이용해) 가상으로
319 expert ⓝ 전문가
320 have a negative effect on ~에 부정적 영향을 미치다
321 solve ⓥ 해결하다
322 overall ⓐⓓ 전반적으로, 대체로
323 constraint ⓝ 제한, 한계, 통제
324 collaboration ⓝ 공동 작업, 협업
325 face-to-face ⓐ 대면하는
326 setting ⓝ 설정
327 for instance 예를 들어
328 press ⓥ 누르다
329 control ⓥ 제어하다
330 breakout group (전체에서 나누어진) 소집단
331 enforce ⓥ 시행하다
332 at a time 한 번에
333 nonverbal ⓐ 비언어적인
334 signal ⓝ 신호
335 particularly ⓐⓓ 특히
336 shoulder ⓝ 어깨
337 diminish ⓥ 줄이다
338 seating arrangement 좌석 배치
339 assign ⓥ 배정하다, 할당하다
340 access ⓝ 접근
341 screen ⓝ 화면
342 stretch ⓥ 늘이다, 확장하다
343 restriction ⓝ 제한점
344 responsibility ⓝ 책임
345 coincidence ⓝ 우연의 일치, 동시 발생
346 tradition ⓝ 전통
347 boost ⓥ 증진시키다

32
348 law ⓝ 법칙
349 demand ⓝ 수요 ⓥ 필요로 하다, 요구하다
350 increase ⓥ 증가하다
351 price ⓝ 값, 가격
352 fall ⓥ (값이) 떨어지다
353 type ⓝ 유형
354 apply for ~에 적용되다
355 instead ⓐⓓ 대신에
356 switch to ~로 바꾸다
357 cheaper ⓐ 값이 더 싼
358 replacement ⓝ 대체(품)
359 consumer ⓝ 소비자
360 decrease ⓥ 내리다
361 tend ⓥ 경향이 있다
362 purchase ⓥ 구입하다
363 reason ⓝ 이유
364 dairy ⓝ 유제품

365 pattern ⓝ (정형화된) 양식, 패턴
366 on the other hand 다른 한편으로는, 반면에
367 meat ⓝ 고기
368 invest ⓥ 투자하다
369 overseas ⓐⓓ 해외에

33
370 study ⓝ (특정 분야의 학문·과학·예술의) 연구
371 look ⓥ ~을 조사하다, 관찰하다
372 different ⓐ 다른
373 intellectually ⓐⓓ 지적으로
374 superior ⓐ 우수한
375 modify ⓥ 수정하다, 바꾸다
376 gene ⓝ 유전자
377 glutamate ⓝ 글루타민산염
378 receptor ⓝ 수용체
379 chemical ⓝ 화학 물질
380 necessary ⓐ 필요한
381 genetically ⓐⓓ 유전적으로
382 manipulate ⓥ 다루다, 조작하다
383 inferior ⓐ 열등한
384 cage ⓝ 우리
385 wheel ⓝ 바퀴
386 handicapped ⓐ 장애가 있는, 불리한 입장인
387 perform ⓥ 수행하다
388 as well as ~과 마찬가지로 잘
389 triumph ⓝ 승리
390 nurture ⓝ 양육
391 survival ⓝ 생존
392 free from ~ 없이, ~을 면하여
393 entertain ⓥ 즐겁게 해 주다

34
394 researcher ⓝ 연구원
395 coastal ⓐ 해안의
396 prepare ⓥ 준비하다
397 sea level 해수면
398 risk ⓝ 위험
399 assessment ⓝ 평가
400 actually ⓐⓓ 실제로
401 carry out ~을 수행[이행]하다
402 fail ⓥ 실패하다
403 climate change 기후 변화
404 belief ⓝ 믿음, 신념
405 decade ⓝ 10년간
406 prediction ⓝ 예측
407 tense ⓝ (문법) 시제
408 habit ⓝ 습관
409 future tense 미래 시제
410 ongoing ⓐ 진행 중인
411 region ⓝ 지방, 지역
412 affect ⓥ 영향을 미치다
413 crisis ⓝ 위기
414 Antarctic ⓐ 남극의
415 ice sheet 빙상
416 physically ⓐⓓ 물리적으로, 신체적으로
417 remote ⓐ 멀리 떨어진
418 relate ⓥ 관련시키다
419 far away 멀리

420 ☐ **energy efficiency** 에너지 효율
421 ☐ **careful** ⓐ 신중한
422 ☐ **prevent** ⓥ 막다

35
423 ☐ **contribute to** ~에 기여하다, ~의 원인이 되다
424 ☐ **provide** ⓥ 제공하다
425 ☐ **medium** ⓝ 수단
426 ☐ **exhibit** ⓥ 보여주다, 드러내다
427 ☐ **virtue** ⓝ 가치
428 ☐ **innovative** ⓐ 혁신적인
429 ☐ **useful** ⓐ 유용한
430 ☐ **display** ⓥ 드러내다
431 ☐ **taste** ⓝ 취향
432 ☐ **care** ⓝ 관심
433 ☐ **represent** ⓥ 나타내다, 표현하다
434 ☐ **self-respect** ⓝ 자기 존중, 자존심
435 ☐ **concern** ⓝ 관심, 우려
436 ☐ **pleasure** ⓝ 기쁨, 즐거움
437 ☐ **link A to B** A와 B를 연결하다
438 ☐ **highly** ⓐⓓ 매우
439 ☐ **sociable** ⓐ 사교적인, 사람들과 어울리기 좋아하는
440 ☐ **along with** ~와 더불어
441 ☐ **opportunity** ⓝ 기회
442 ☐ **identity** ⓝ 정체성

36
443 ☐ **thankful** ⓐ 고맙게 생각하는, 감사하는
444 ☐ **turkey** ⓝ 칠면조
445 ☐ **thanksgiving** ⓝ 추수감사절
446 ☐ **responsive** ⓐ 즉각 반응하는, 관심을 보이는
447 ☐ **forget** ⓥ 잊다
448 ☐ **softly** ⓐⓓ 부드럽게
449 ☐ **usually** ⓐⓓ 보통, 대개
450 ☐ **spend** ⓥ (시간을) 보내다
451 ☐ **stay** ⓥ 머무르다
452 ☐ **classmate** ⓝ 반 친구
453 ☐ **break time** 휴식 시간
454 ☐ **immediately** ⓐⓓ 즉시
455 ☐ **attract one's interest** ~의 관심을 끌다
456 ☐ **raise** ⓥ 기르다, 키우다
457 ☐ **police officer** 경찰관
458 ☐ **protect** ⓥ 보호하다, 지키다

37
459 ☐ **according** ⓐⓓ ~에 의하면
460 ☐ **legend** ⓝ 전설
461 ☐ **vampire** ⓝ 흡혈귀
462 ☐ **bite** ⓥ 물다
463 ☐ **turn** ⓥ (…한 상태로) 변하다
464 ☐ **seek** ⓥ 구하다
465 ☐ **prove** ⓥ 입증[증명]하다
466 ☐ **popular** ⓐ 인기 있는, 대중적인
467 ☐ **creature** ⓝ 생명이 있는 존재, 생물
468 ☐ **original** ⓐ 원래의
469 ☐ **human** ⓝ 인류
470 ☐ **look around** 둘러보다
471 ☐ **take over** ~을 지배하다, 장악하다
472 ☐ **no such thing** 그런 일은 없다

473 ☐ **come into existence** 생기다, 나타나다
474 ☐ **later** ⓐⓓ 후에
475 ☐ **break down** 무너뜨리다
476 ☐ **myth** ⓝ 미신, (잘못된) 통념

38
477 ☐ **rub** ⓥ 문지르다
478 ☐ **quickly** ⓐⓓ 빨리, 빠르게
479 ☐ **warm** ⓥ 따뜻해지다
480 ☐ **friction** ⓝ 마찰
481 ☐ **force** ⓝ 힘
482 ☐ **surface** ⓝ 표면
483 ☐ **slide** ⓥ 미끄러지다
484 ☐ **each other** 서로
485 ☐ **push** ⓥ 밀다
486 ☐ **direction** ⓝ 방향
487 ☐ **opposite** ⓐ 반대의
488 ☐ **slow down** ~을 느려지게 하다
489 ☐ **amount** ⓝ 양
490 ☐ **rough** ⓐ 거친
491 ☐ **slip** ⓥ (넘어지거나 넘어질 뻔하게) 미끄러지다
492 ☐ **skid** ⓥ 미끄러지다
493 ☐ **tread** ⓝ 접지면
494 ☐ **act** ⓥ 역할을 하다
495 ☐ **grip** ⓥ 붙잡다

39
496 ☐ **blind person** 맹인, 시각 장애인
497 ☐ **associate A with B** A와 B를 연결 짓다, 연상하다
498 ☐ **unique** ⓐ 독특한
499 ☐ **combination** ⓝ 조합
500 ☐ **experience** ⓝ 경험
501 ☐ **non-visual** 비시각적
502 ☐ **sense** ⓝ 감각
503 ☐ **sight** ⓝ 시력
504 ☐ **collect** ⓥ 모으다, 수집하다
505 ☐ **understand** ⓥ 이해하다
506 ☐ **entirely** ⓐⓓ 전적으로
507 ☐ **result** ⓝ 결과
508 ☐ **amazing** ⓐ 놀라운
509 ☐ **ability** ⓝ 능력
510 ☐ **collection** ⓝ 수집
511 ☐ **dream** ⓝ 꿈
512 ☐ **vivid** ⓐ 생생한
513 ☐ **imaginative** ⓐ 상상력이 풍부한
514 ☐ **normal** ⓐ 정상적인
515 ☐ **vision** ⓝ 시력
516 ☐ **familiar** ⓐ 익숙한, 친숙한
517 ☐ **shape** ⓝ 모양, 형태
518 ☐ **colour** ⓝ 색
519 ☐ **in other words** 다시 말해서
520 ☐ **similar** ⓐ 비슷한, 유사한

40
521 ☐ **adolescent** ⓝ 청소년
522 ☐ **important** ⓐ 중요한
523 ☐ **factor** ⓝ 요인
524 ☐ **success** ⓝ 성공
525 ☐ **respond** ⓥ 반응을 보이다
526 ☐ **authoritative** ⓐ 권위적인

527 ☐ **parenting** ⓝ 육아
528 ☐ **passive** ⓐ 수동적인, 소극적인
529 ☐ **afraid** ⓐ 두려워하는, 겁내는
530 ☐ **indicate** ⓥ 나타내다
531 ☐ **involve** ⓥ 관련시키다, 참여시키다
532 ☐ **helpless** ⓐ 무기력한
533 ☐ **put effort into** ~에 노력을 쏟다
534 ☐ **significantly** ⓐⓓ 상당히
535 ☐ **homework** ⓝ 숙제, 과제
536 ☐ **attend** ⓥ 참석하다, 참여하다
537 ☐ **watch** ⓥ 지켜보다
538 ☐ **select** ⓥ 선택하다
539 ☐ **course** ⓝ 강의, 과목
540 ☐ **moreover** ⓐⓓ 게다가, 더욱이
541 ☐ **aware** ⓐ 알고 있는
542 ☐ **praise** ⓥ 칭찬하다
543 ☐ **random** ⓐ 무작위적인
544 ☐ **hesitant** ⓐ 망설이는
545 ☐ **constant** ⓐ 지속적인

41~42
546 ☐ **bedtime** ⓝ 취침 시간
547 ☐ **heart disease** 심장병
548 ☐ **volunteer** ⓝ 지원자
549 ☐ **monitor** ⓥ 추적 관찰하다
550 ☐ **health** ⓝ 건강
551 ☐ **go to bed** 자다, 취침하다
552 ☐ **ideal** ⓐ 이상적인
553 ☐ **timeframe** ⓝ 기간, 시간
554 ☐ **author** ⓝ 저자
555 ☐ **comment** ⓥ 언급하다, 의견을 말하다
556 ☐ **effect** ⓝ 영향
557 ☐ **certain** ⓐ 확실한
558 ☐ **cause** ⓝ 원인
559 ☐ **suggest** ⓥ 암시하다, 시사하다
560 ☐ **late** ⓐ 늦은
561 ☐ **disrupt** ⓥ 혼란케 하다
562 ☐ **body clock** 생체 시계
563 ☐ **consequence** ⓝ 결과, 영향
564 ☐ **cardiovascular** ⓐ 심장 혈관의
565 ☐ **midnight** ⓝ 자정
566 ☐ **likelihood** ⓝ 가능성, 공산
567 ☐ **reset** ⓥ 다시 맞추다, 재설정하다
568 ☐ **disease** ⓝ 질환
569 ☐ **properly** ⓐⓓ 적절하게
570 ☐ **sound** ⓐ 좋은, 건전한
571 ☐ **personality** ⓝ 성격

43~45
572 ☐ **farmer** ⓝ 농부
573 ☐ **watch** ⓝ 시계
574 ☐ **while** ⓒⓞⓝⓙ ~하는 동안
575 ☐ **barn** ⓝ 헛간(곡물·건초 따위를 두는 곳)
576 ☐ **ordinary** ⓐ 평범한
577 ☐ **others** ⓝ 다른 사람들
578 ☐ **bring** ⓥ 가져다주다
579 ☐ **childhood** ⓝ 어린 시절
580 ☐ **search** ⓥ 찾아보다
581 ☐ **for a long time** 오랫동안
582 ☐ **exhaust** ⓥ 기진맥진하게 만들다
583 ☐ **slowly** ⓐⓓ 천천히, 서서히
584 ☐ **tired** ⓐ 지친

585 ☐ **give up** 포기하다
586 ☐ **hope** ⓝ 희망
587 ☐ **precious** ⓐ 소중한, 귀중한
588 ☐ **call off** ~을 중단하다, 멈추다
589 ☐ **chance** ⓝ 기회
590 ☐ **lose out on** ~을 놓치다, ~에게 지다
591 ☐ **delight** ⓥ 매우 기뻐하다
592 ☐ **reward** ⓥ 보상하다
593 ☐ **promise** ⓥ 약속하다
594 ☐ **attractive** ⓐ 매력적인
595 ☐ **pile** ⓝ 더미
596 ☐ **hay** ⓝ 건초

10회

TEST A-B 각 단어의 뜻을 [A] 영어는 우리말로, [B] 우리말은 영어로 쓰시오.

A	English	Korean
01	deceiving	
02	attractive	
03	principle	
04	self-defense	
05	discuss	
06	explore	
07	physically	
08	grip	
09	reflection	
10	unreliable	
11	coincidence	
12	prediction	
13	genetically	
14	unique	
15	ownership	
16	quantity	
17	consequence	
18	nurture	
19	touched	
20	publish	

B	Korean	English
01	과정	
02	해외에	
03	소비하다	
04	참가자	
05	표면	
06	수정하다, 바꾸다	
07	기르다, 키우다	
08	우수한	
09	가정, 가구	
10	구성하다	
11	회복하다	
12	부정확한	
13	평가	
14	가라앉다	
15	역사적으로	
16	소개하다	
17	소중한, 귀중한	
18	제한, 한계	
19	언급하다, 의견을 말하다	
20	관심, 우려	

▶ A-D 정답 : 해설편 111쪽

TEST C-D 각 단어의 뜻을 골라 기호를 쓰시오.

C	English			Korean
01	missing	(	)	ⓐ 즉각 반응하는, 관심을 보이는
02	embarrassed	(	)	ⓑ 개념
03	deserve	(	)	ⓒ 계산하다
04	responsive	(	)	ⓓ 청소년
05	pour	(	)	ⓔ 생생한
06	material	(	)	ⓕ 심각한
07	combination	(	)	ⓖ 거래하다, 교역하다
08	trade	(	)	ⓗ 문지르다
09	vivid	(	)	ⓘ 늘이다, 확장하다
10	investigate	(	)	ⓙ 빠진, 실종된
11	replacement	(	)	ⓚ 가전제품
12	notion	(	)	ⓛ ~을 받을 만하다
13	authoritative	(	)	ⓜ 쏟다, 붓다
14	adolescent	(	)	ⓝ 당황한
15	rub	(	)	ⓞ 열등한
16	appliance	(	)	ⓟ 물질, 자재, 재료
17	severe	(	)	ⓠ 연구하다, 조사하다
18	inferior	(	)	ⓡ 조합
19	calculate	(	)	ⓢ 권위적인
20	stretch	(	)	ⓣ 대체품

D	Korean			English
01	상상력이 풍부한	(	)	ⓐ reveal
02	사교적인	(	)	ⓑ immediately
03	줄이다	(	)	ⓒ support
04	미신, (잘못된) 통념	(	)	ⓓ imaginative
05	준비하다	(	)	ⓔ taste
06	산업의	(	)	ⓕ enforce
07	세대	(	)	ⓖ industrial
08	비생산적인	(	)	ⓗ dairy
09	가능성, 공산	(	)	ⓘ sociable
10	즉시	(	)	ⓙ slide
11	안에	(	)	ⓚ represent
12	유제품	(	)	ⓛ unproductive
13	미끄러지다	(	)	ⓜ author
14	나타내다, 표현하다	(	)	ⓝ prepare
15	취향	(	)	ⓞ diminish
16	밝히다, 드러내다	(	)	ⓟ creature
17	시행하다	(	)	ⓠ inside
18	저자	(	)	ⓡ likelihood
19	생명이 있는 존재, 생물	(	)	ⓢ generation
20	뒷받침하다, 지지하다	(	)	ⓣ myth

2021학년도 6월 고1 전국연합학력평가 문제지

제 3 교시

영어 영역

1

11회

● 문항수 45개 | 배점 100점 | 제한 시간 70분

● 점수 표시가 없는 문항은 모두 2점

1번부터 17번까지는 듣고 답하는 문제입니다. 1번부터 15번까지는 한 번만 들려주고, 16번부터 17번까지는 두 번 들려줍니다. 방송을 잘 듣고 답을 하시기 바랍니다.

1. 다음을 듣고, 남자가 하는 말의 목적으로 가장 적절한 것을 고르시오.
① 건강 검진 일정을 공지하려고
② 독감 예방 접종을 권장하려고
③ 개인 위생 관리를 당부하려고
④ 보건소 운영 기간을 안내하려고
⑤ 독감 예방 접종 부작용을 경고하려고

2. 대화를 듣고, 여자의 의견으로 가장 적절한 것을 고르시오.
① 독서 습관을 기르자.
② 지역 서점을 이용하자.
③ 지역 특산품을 애용하자.
④ 중고 서점을 활성화시키자.
⑤ 온라인을 통한 도서 구입을 늘리자.

3. 대화를 듣고, 두 사람의 관계를 가장 잘 나타낸 것을 고르시오.
① 호텔 직원 – 투숙객   ② 열쇠 수리공 – 집주인
③ 경비원 – 입주민   ④ 은행원 – 고객
⑤ 치과의사 – 환자

4. 대화를 듣고, 그림에서 대화의 내용과 일치하지 않는 것을 고르시오.

5. 대화를 듣고, 남자가 여자를 위해 할 일로 가장 적절한 것을 고르시오. [3점]
① 부엌 청소하기   ② 점심 준비하기
③ 카메라 구매하기   ④ 딸 데리러 가기
⑤ 요리법 검색하기

6. 대화를 듣고, 여자가 지불할 금액을 고르시오.
① $30   ② $50   ③ $63   ④ $65   ⑤ $70

7. 대화를 듣고, 남자가 공연장에 갈 수 없는 이유로 가장 적절한 것을 고르시오.
① 출장을 가야 해서
② 숙제를 끝내야 해서
③ 조카를 돌봐야 해서
④ 이사 준비를 해야 해서
⑤ 친구와 만날 약속을 해서

8. 대화를 듣고, 강아지 키우기에 관해 언급되지 않은 것을 고르시오.
① 산책시키기   ② 먹이 주기
③ 목욕시키기   ④ 배변 훈련시키기
⑤ 소변 패드 치우기

9. Sharing Friday Movement에 관한 다음 내용을 듣고, 일치하지 않는 것을 고르시오. [3점]
① 매주 금요일에 2달러씩 기부하는 운동이다.
② 2001년 핀란드에서 시작되었다.
③ 기부금은 가난한 지역에 깨끗한 물을 공급하는 데 쓰인다.
④ 올해 20명의 학생에게 장학금을 지급했다.
⑤ 추가 정보는 홈페이지를 통해 얻을 수 있다.

10. 다음 표를 보면서 대화를 듣고, 여자가 구입할 모델을 고르시오.

Selfie Sticks

	Model	Weight	Maximum Length	Bluetooth Remote Control	Price
①	A	150g	60cm	×	$ 10
②	B	150g	80cm	○	$ 30
③	C	180g	80cm	○	$ 20
④	D	180g	100cm	×	$ 15
⑤	E	230g	100cm	○	$ 25

11. 대화를 듣고, 남자의 마지막 말에 대한 여자의 응답으로 가장 적절한 것을 고르시오.
① Again? You've lost your bag twice.
② You're right. I'll take a warm jacket.
③ Why? I know you prefer cold weather.
④ What? I finished packing a present for you.
⑤ Sorry. But you can't join the trip at this point.

12. 대화를 듣고, 여자의 마지막 말에 대한 남자의 응답으로 가장 적절한 것을 고르시오.
① No thank you. I've had enough.
② Great. I'll book for five people at six.
③ That's a good choice. The food is wonderful.
④ Okay. I'll set a place and time for the meeting.
⑤ Sorry to hear that. I'll cancel the reservation now.

13. 대화를 듣고, 남자의 마지막 말에 대한 여자의 응답으로 가장 적절한 것을 고르시오.

Woman: _____

① I'm in charge of giving the presentation.
② I think you're the right person for that role.
③ It's important to choose your team carefully.
④ The assignment is due the day after tomorrow.
⑤ I hope we don't stay up late to finish the project.

14. 대화를 듣고, 여자의 마지막 말에 대한 남자의 응답으로 가장 적절한 것을 고르시오.

Man: _____

① I'm good at public speaking.
② I'm sorry for forgetting my assignment.
③ Unfortunately, my alarm doesn't wake me up.
④ The speech contest is just around the corner.
⑤ It helps me keep deadlines to complete specific tasks.

15. 다음 상황 설명을 듣고, Harold가 Kate에게 할 말로 가장 적절한 것을 고르시오. [3점]

Harold: _____

① Okay. You'd better put your best effort into the match.
② I see. You should play the match instead of her.
③ Take it easy. Take good care of yourself first.
④ You deserve it. Practice makes perfect.
⑤ Don't worry. You'll win this match.

[16~17] 다음을 듣고, 물음에 답하시오.

16. 여자가 하는 말의 주제로 가장 적절한 것은?

① problems with illegal hunting
② characteristics of migrating animals
③ effects of light pollution on wild animals
④ various ways to save endangered animals
⑤ animal habitat change due to water pollution

17. 언급된 동물이 <u>아닌</u> 것은?

① sea turtles ② fireflies ③ salmon
④ honey bees ⑤ tree frogs

이제 듣기 문제가 끝났습니다. 18번부터는 문제지의 지시에 따라 답을 하시기 바랍니다.

---

18. 다음 글의 목적으로 가장 적절한 것은?

Dear Mr. Jones,

I am James Arkady, PR Director of KHJ Corporation. We are planning to redesign our brand identity and launch a new logo to celebrate our 10th anniversary. We request you to create a logo that best suits our company's core vision, 'To inspire humanity.' I hope the new logo will convey our brand message and capture the values of KHJ. Please send us your logo design proposal once you are done with it. Thank you.

Best regards,
James Arkady

① 회사 로고 제작을 의뢰하려고
② 변경된 회사 로고를 홍보하려고
③ 회사 비전에 대한 컨설팅을 요청하려고
④ 회사 창립 10주년 기념품을 주문하려고
⑤ 회사 로고 제작 일정 변경을 공지하려고

19. 다음 글에 드러난 Cindy의 심경 변화로 가장 적절한 것은?

One day, Cindy happened to sit next to a famous artist in a café, and she was thrilled to see him in person. He was drawing on a used napkin over coffee. She was looking on in awe. After a few moments, the man finished his coffee and was about to throw away the napkin as he left. Cindy stopped him. "Can I have that napkin you drew on?", she asked. "Sure," he replied. "Twenty thousand dollars." She said, with her eyes wide-open, "What? It took you like two minutes to draw that." "No," he said. "It took me over sixty years to draw this." Being at a loss, she stood still rooted to the ground.

① relieved → worried ② indifferent → embarrassed
③ excited → surprised ④ disappointed → satisfied
⑤ jealous → confident

20. 다음 글에서 필자가 주장하는 바로 가장 적절한 것은?

Sometimes, you feel the need to avoid something that will lead to success out of discomfort. Maybe you are avoiding extra work because you are tired. You are actively shutting out success because you want to avoid being uncomfortable. Therefore, overcoming your instinct to avoid uncomfortable things at first is essential. Try doing new things outside of your comfort zone. Change is always uncomfortable, but it is key to doing things differently in order to find that magical formula for success.

① 불편할지라도 성공하기 위해서는 새로운 것을 시도해야 한다.
② 일과 생활의 균형을 맞추는 성공적인 삶을 추구해야 한다.
③ 갈등 해소를 위해 불편함의 원인을 찾아 개선해야 한다.
④ 단계별 목표를 설정하여 익숙한 것부터 도전해야 한다.
⑤ 변화에 적응하기 위해 직관적으로 문제를 해결해야 한다.

21. 밑줄 친 want to use a hammer가 다음 글에서 의미하는 바로 가장 적절한 것은? [3점]

We have a tendency to interpret events selectively. If we want things to be "this way" or "that way" we can most certainly select, stack, or arrange evidence in a way that supports such a viewpoint. Selective perception is based on what seems to us to stand out. However, what seems to us to be standing out may very well be related to our goals, interests, expectations, past experiences, or current demands of the situation — "with a hammer in hand, everything looks like a nail." This quote highlights the phenomenon of selective perception. If we want to use a hammer, then the world around us may begin to look as though it is full of nails!

① are unwilling to stand out
② make our effort meaningless
③ intend to do something in a certain way
④ hope others have a viewpoint similar to ours
⑤ have a way of thinking that is accepted by others

22. 다음 글의 요지로 가장 적절한 것은?

Rather than attempting to punish students with a low grade or mark in the hope it will encourage them to give greater effort in the future, teachers can better motivate students by considering their work as incomplete and then requiring additional effort. Teachers at Beachwood Middle School in Beachwood, Ohio, record students' grades as *A*, *B*, *C*, or *I* (Incomplete). Students who receive an *I* grade are required to do additional work in order to bring their performance up to an acceptable level. This policy is based on the belief that students perform at a failure level or submit failing work in large part because teachers accept it. The Beachwood teachers reason that if they no longer accept substandard work, students will not submit it. And with appropriate support, they believe students will continue to work until their performance is satisfactory.

① 학생에게 평가 결과를 공개하는 것은 학습 동기를 떨어뜨린다.
② 학생에게 추가 과제를 부여하는 것은 학업 부담을 가중시킨다.
③ 지속적인 보상은 학업 성취도에 장기적으로 부정적인 영향을 준다.
④ 학생의 자기주도적 학습 능력은 정서적으로 안정된 학습 환경에서 향상된다.
⑤ 학생의 과제가 일정 수준에 도달하도록 개선 기회를 주면 동기 부여에 도움이 된다.

23. 다음 글의 주제로 가장 적절한 것은?

Curiosity makes us much more likely to view a tough problem as an interesting challenge to take on. A stressful meeting with our boss becomes an opportunity to learn. A nervous first date becomes an exciting night out with a new person. A colander becomes a hat. In general, curiosity motivates us to view stressful situations as challenges rather than threats, to talk about difficulties more openly, and to try new approaches to solving problems. In fact, curiosity is associated with a less defensive reaction to stress and, as a result, less aggression when we respond to irritation.

* colander: (음식 재료의 물을 빼는 데 쓰는) 체

① importance of defensive reactions in a tough situation
② curiosity as the hidden force of positive reframes
③ difficulties of coping with stress at work
④ potential threats caused by curiosity
⑤ factors that reduce human curiosity

24. 다음 글의 제목으로 가장 적절한 것은?

When people think about the development of cities, rarely do they consider the critical role of vertical transportation. In fact, each day, more than 7 billion elevator journeys are taken in tall buildings all over the world. Efficient vertical transportation can expand our ability to build taller and taller skyscrapers. Antony Wood, a Professor of Architecture at the Illinois Institute of Technology, explains that advances in elevators over the past 20 years are probably the greatest advances we have seen in tall buildings. For example, elevators in the Jeddah Tower in Jeddah, Saudi Arabia, under construction, will reach a height record of 660m.

① Elevators Bring Buildings Closer to the Sky
② The Higher You Climb, the Better the View
③ How to Construct an Elevator Cheap and Fast
④ The Function of the Ancient and the Modern City
⑤ The Evolution of Architecture: Solutions for Overpopulation

25. 다음 도표의 내용과 일치하지 <u>않는</u> 것은?

Health Spending as a Share of GDP for Selected OECD Countries [2018]

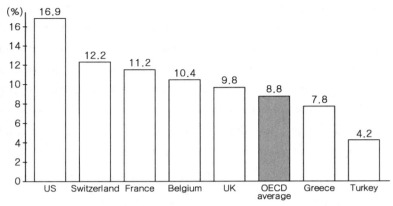

The above graph shows health spending as a share of GDP for selected OECD countries in 2018. ① On average, OECD countries were estimated to have spent 8.8 percent of their GDP on health care. ② Among the given countries above, the US had the highest share, with 16.9 percent, followed by Switzerland at 12.2 percent. ③ France spent more than 11 percent of its GDP, while Turkey spent less than 5 percent of its GDP on health care. ④ Belgium's health spending as a share of GDP sat between that of France and the UK. ⑤ There was a 3 percentage point difference in the share of GDP spent on health care between the UK and Greece.

26. Lithops에 관한 다음 글의 내용과 일치하지 <u>않는</u> 것은?

　Lithops are plants that are often called 'living stones' on account of their unique rock-like appearance. They are native to the deserts of South Africa but commonly sold in garden centers and nurseries. Lithops grow well in compacted, sandy soil with little water and extreme hot temperatures. Lithops are small plants, rarely getting more than an inch above the soil surface and usually with only two leaves. The thick leaves resemble the cleft in an animal's foot or just a pair of grayish brown stones gathered together. The plants have no true stem and much of the plant is underground. Their appearance has the effect of conserving moisture.

*cleft: 갈라진 틈

① 살아있는 돌로 불리는 식물이다.
② 원산지는 남아프리카 사막 지역이다.
③ 토양의 표면 위로 대개 1인치 이상 자란다.
④ 줄기가 없으며 땅속에 대부분 묻혀 있다.
⑤ 겉모양은 수분 보존 효과를 갖고 있다.

27. "Go Green" Writing Contest에 관한 다음 안내문의 내용과 일치하지 <u>않는</u> 것은?

"Go Green" Writing Contest
Share your talents & conserve the environment

☐ **Main Topic:** Save the Environment

☐ **Writing Categories**
　・Slogan　・Poem　・Essay

☐ **Requirements:**
● Participants: High school students
● Participate in one of the above categories (only one entry per participant)

☐ **Deadline: July 5th, 2021**
● Email your work to apply@gogreen.com.

☐ **Prize for Each Category**
　・1st place: $80　・2nd place: $60　・3rd place: $40

☐ The winners will be announced only on the website on July 15th, 2021. No personal contact will be made.

☐ For more information, visit www.gogreen.com.

① 대회 주제는 환경 보호이다.
② 참가자는 한 부문에만 참가해야 한다.
③ 마감 기한은 7월 5일이다.
④ 작품은 이메일로 제출해야 한다.
⑤ 수상자는 개별적으로 연락받는다.

28. Virtual Idea Exchange에 관한 다음 안내문의 내용과 일치하는 것은?

Virtual Idea Exchange

Connect in real time and have discussions about the upcoming school festival.

☐ **Goal**
・Plan the school festival and share ideas for it.

☐ **Participants:** Club leaders only

☐ **What to Discuss**
・Themes　・Ticket sales　・Budget

☐ **Date & Time:** 5 to 7 p.m. on Friday, June 25th, 2021

☐ **Notes**
・Get the access link by text message 10 minutes before the meeting and click it.
・Type your real name when you enter the chatroom.

① 동아리 회원이라면 누구나 참여 가능하다.
② 티켓 판매는 논의 대상에서 제외된다.
③ 회의는 3시간 동안 열린다.
④ 접속 링크를 문자로 받는다.
⑤ 채팅방 입장 시 동아리명으로 참여해야 한다.

29. 다음 글의 밑줄 친 부분 중, 어법상 틀린 것은? [3점]

There have been occasions ① in which you have observed a smile and you could sense it was not genuine. The most obvious way of identifying a genuine smile from an insincere ② one is that a fake smile primarily only affects the lower half of the face, mainly with the mouth alone. The eyes don't really get involved. Take the opportunity to look in the mirror and manufacture a smile ③ using the lower half your face only. When you do this, judge ④ how happy your face really looks — is it genuine? A genuine smile will impact on the muscles and wrinkles around the eyes and less noticeably, the skin between the eyebrow and upper eyelid ⑤ are lowered slightly with true enjoyment. The genuine smile can impact on the entire face.

30. 다음 글의 밑줄 친 부분 중, 문맥상 낱말의 쓰임이 적절하지 않은 것은? [3점]

Detailed study over the past two or three decades is showing that the complex forms of natural systems are essential to their functioning. The attempt to ① straighten rivers and give them regular cross-sections is perhaps the most disastrous example of this form-and-function relationship. The natural river has a very ② irregular form: it curves a lot, spills across floodplains, and leaks into wetlands, giving it an ever-changing and incredibly complex shoreline. This allows the river to ③ prevent variations in water level and speed. Pushing the river into tidy geometry ④ destroys functional capacity and results in disasters like the Mississippi floods of 1927 and 1993 and, more recently, the unnatural disaster of Hurricane Katrina. A $50 billion plan to "let the river loose" in Louisiana recognizes that the ⑤ controlled Mississippi is washing away twenty-four square miles of that state annually.

* geometry: 기하학 ** capacity: 수용능력

[31~34] 다음 빈칸에 들어갈 말로 가장 적절한 것을 고르시오.

31. In a culture where there is a belief that you can have anything you truly want, there is no problem in choosing. Many cultures, however, do not maintain this belief. In fact, many people do not believe that life is about getting what you want. Life is about doing what you are *supposed* to do. The reason they have trouble making choices is they believe that what they may want is not related to what they are supposed to do. The weight of outside considerations is greater than their _____. When this is an issue in a group, we discuss what makes for good decisions. If a person can be unburdened from their cares and duties and, just for a moment, consider what appeals to them, they get the chance to sort out what is important to them. Then they can consider and negotiate with their external pressures.

① desires ② merits ③ abilities
④ limitations ⑤ worries

32. Research has confirmed that athletes are less likely to participate in unacceptable behavior than are non-athletes. However, moral reasoning and good sporting behavior seem to decline as athletes progress to higher competitive levels, in part because of the increased emphasis on winning. Thus winning can be _____ in teaching character development. Some athletes may want to win so much that they lie, cheat, and break team rules. They may develop undesirable character traits that can enhance their ability to win in the short term. However, when athletes resist the temptation to win in a dishonest way, they can develop positive character traits that last a lifetime. Character is a learned behavior, and a sense of fair play develops only if coaches plan to teach those lessons systematically.

* trait: 특성

① a piece of cake
② a one-way street
③ a bird in the hand
④ a fish out of water
⑤ a double-edged sword

33. Due to technological innovations, music can now be experienced by more people, for more of the time than ever before. Mass availability has given individuals unheard-of control over their own sound-environment. However, it has also confronted them with the simultaneous availability of countless genres of music, in which they have to orient themselves. People start filtering out and organizing their digital libraries like they used to do with their physical music collections. However, there is the difference that the choice lies in their own hands. Without being restricted to the limited collection of music-distributors, nor being guided by the local radio program as a 'preselector' of the latest hits, the individual actively has to _____.
The search for the right song is thus associated with considerable effort. [3점]

* simultaneous: 동시의

① choose and determine his or her musical preferences
② understand the technical aspects of recording sessions
③ share unique and inspiring playlists on social media
④ interpret lyrics with background knowledge of the songs
⑤ seek the advice of a voice specialist for better performances

34. It is common to assume that creativity concerns primarily the relation between actor(creator) and artifact(creation). However, from a sociocultural standpoint, the creative act is never "complete" in the absence of a second position — that of an audience. While the actor or creator him/herself is the first audience of the artifact being produced, this kind of distantiation can only be achieved by _____.
This means that, in order to be an audience to your own creation, a history of interaction with others is needed. We exist in a social world that constantly confronts us with the "view of the other." It is the view we include and blend into our own activity, including creative activity. This outside perspective is essential for creativity because it gives new meaning and value to the creative act and its product. [3점]

* artifact: 창작물

① exploring the absolute truth in existence
② following a series of precise and logical steps
③ looking outside and drawing inspiration from nature
④ internalizing the perspective of others on one's work
⑤ pushing the audience to the limits of its endurance

35. 다음 글에서 전체 흐름과 관계 <u>없는</u> 문장은? [3점]

Health and the spread of disease are very closely linked to how we live and how our cities operate. The good news is that cities are incredibly resilient. Many cities have experienced epidemics in the past and have not only survived, but advanced. ① The nineteenth and early-twentieth centuries saw destructive outbreaks of cholera, typhoid, and influenza in European cities. ② Doctors such as Jon Snow, from England, and Rudolf Virchow, of Germany, saw the connection between poor living conditions, overcrowding, sanitation, and disease. ③ A recognition of this connection led to the replanning and rebuilding of cities to stop the spread of epidemics. ④ In spite of reconstruction efforts, cities declined in many areas and many people started to leave. ⑤ In the mid-nineteenth century, London's pioneering sewer system, which still serves it today, was built as a result of understanding the importance of clean water in stopping the spread of cholera.

* resilient: 회복력이 있는 ** sewer system: 하수 처리 시스템

[36~37] 주어진 글 다음에 이어질 글의 순서로 가장 적절한 것을 고르시오.

36.

Starting from birth, babies are immediately attracted to faces. Scientists were able to show this by having babies look at two simple images, one that looks more like a face than the other.

(A) These changes help the organisms to survive, making them alert to enemies. By being able to recognize faces from afar or in the dark, humans were able to know someone was coming and protect themselves from possible danger.

(B) One reason babies might like faces is because of something called evolution. Evolution involves changes to the structures of an organism(such as the brain) that occur over many generations.

(C) By measuring where the babies looked, scientists found that the babies looked at the face-like image more than they looked at the non-face image. Even though babies have poor eyesight, they prefer to look at faces. But why?

① (A) − (C) − (B) ② (B) − (A) − (C)
③ (B) − (C) − (A) ④ (C) − (A) − (B)
⑤ (C) − (B) − (A)

37.

> People spend much of their time interacting with media, but that does not mean that people have the critical skills to analyze and understand it.

(A) Research from New York University found that people over 65 shared seven times as much misinformation as their younger counterparts. All of this raises a question: What's the solution to the misinformation problem?

(B) One well-known study from Stanford University in 2016 demonstrated that youth are easily fooled by misinformation, especially when it comes through social media channels. This weakness is not found only in youth, however.

(C) Governments and tech platforms certainly have a role to play in blocking misinformation. However, every individual needs to take responsibility for combating this threat by becoming more information literate.

* counterpart: 상대방

① (A) − (C) − (B)
② (B) − (A) − (C)
③ (B) − (C) − (A)
④ (C) − (A) − (B)
⑤ (C) − (B) − (A)

[38~39] 글의 흐름으로 보아, 주어진 문장이 들어가기에 가장 적절한 곳을 고르시오.

38.

> As the sticks approach each other, the air immediately in front of them is compressed and energy builds up.

Sound and light travel in waves. An analogy often given for sound is that of throwing a small stone onto the surface of a still pond. Waves radiate outwards from the point of impact, just as sound waves radiate from the sound source. (①) This is due to a disturbance in the air around us. (②) If you bang two sticks together, you will get a sound. (③) When the point of impact occurs, this energy is released as sound waves. (④) If you try the same experiment with two heavy stones, exactly the same thing occurs, but you get a different sound due to the density and surface of the stones, and as they have likely displaced more air, a louder sound. (⑤) And so, a physical disturbance in the atmosphere around us will produce a sound.

* analogy: 비유 ** radiate: 사방으로 퍼지다

39.

> It has been observed that at each level of transfer, a large proportion, 80 − 90 percent, of the potential energy is lost as heat.

Food chain means the transfer of food energy from the source in plants through a series of organisms with the repeated process of eating and being eaten. (①) In a grassland, grass is eaten by rabbits while rabbits in turn are eaten by foxes. (②) This is an example of a simple food chain. (③) This food chain implies the sequence in which food energy is transferred from producer to consumer or higher trophic level. (④) Hence the number of steps or links in a sequence is restricted, usually to four or five. (⑤) The shorter the food chain or the nearer the organism is to the beginning of the chain, the greater the available energy intake is. [3점]

* trophic: 영양의

40. 다음 글의 내용을 한 문장으로 요약하고자 한다. 빈칸 (A), (B)에 들어갈 말로 가장 적절한 것은?

A woman named Rhonda who attended the University of California at Berkeley had a problem. She was living near campus with several other people — none of whom knew one another. When the cleaning people came each weekend, they left several rolls of toilet paper in each of the two bathrooms. However, by Monday all the toilet paper would be gone. It was a classic tragedy-of-the-commons situation: because some people took more toilet paper than their fair share, the public resource was destroyed for everyone else. After reading a research paper about behavior change, Rhonda put a note in one of the bathrooms asking people not to remove the toilet paper, as it was a shared item. To her great satisfaction, one roll reappeared in a few hours, and another the next day. In the other note-free bathroom, however, there was no toilet paper until the following weekend, when the cleaning people returned.

↓

A small ____(A)____ brought about a change in the behavior of the people who had taken more of the ____(B)____ goods than they needed.

	(A)		(B)
①	reminder	······	shared
②	reminder	······	recycled
③	mistake	······	stored
④	mistake	······	borrowed
⑤	fortune	······	limited

[41~42] 다음 글을 읽고, 물음에 답하시오.

If you were afraid of standing on balconies, you would start on some lower floors and slowly work your way up to higher ones. It would be easy to face a fear of standing on high balconies in a way that's totally controlled. Socializing is (a) trickier. People aren't like inanimate features of a building that you just have to be around to get used to. You have to interact with them, and their responses can be unpredictable. Your feelings toward them are more complex too. Most people's self-esteem isn't going to be affected that much if they don't like balconies, but your confidence can (b) suffer if you can't socialize effectively.

It's also harder to design a tidy way to gradually face many social fears. The social situations you need to expose yourself to may not be (c) available when you want them, or they may not go well enough for you to sense that things are under control. The progression from one step to the next may not be clear, creating unavoidable large (d) decreases in difficulty from one to the next. People around you aren't robots that you can endlessly experiment with for your own purposes. This is not to say that facing your fears is pointless when socializing. The principles of gradual exposure are still very (e) useful. The process of applying them is just messier, and knowing that before you start is helpful.

41. 윗글의 제목으로 가장 적절한 것은?

① How to Improve Your Self-Esteem
② Socializing with Someone You Fear: Good or Bad?
③ Relaxation May Lead to Getting Over Social Fears
④ Are Social Exposures Related with Fear of Heights?
⑤ Overcoming Social Anxiety Is Difficult; Try Gradually!

42. 밑줄 친 (a) ~ (e) 중에서 문맥상 낱말의 쓰임이 적절하지 <u>않은</u> 것은?

① (a)　　② (b)　　③ (c)　　④ (d)　　⑤ (e)

[43~45] 다음 글을 읽고, 물음에 답하시오.

(A)

When I was 17, I discovered a wonderful thing. My father and I were sitting on the floor of his study. We were organizing his old papers. Across the carpet I saw a fat paper clip. Its rust dusted the cover sheet of a report of some kind. I picked it up. I started to read. Then I started to cry.

(B)

"Daddy," I said, handing him the pages, "this speech — how did you ever get permission to give it? And weren't you scared?" "Well, honey," he said, "I didn't ask for permission. I just asked myself, 'What is the most important challenge facing my generation?' I knew immediately. Then (a) I asked myself, 'And if I weren't afraid, what would I say about it in this speech?'"

(C)

It was a speech he had written in 1920, in Tennessee. Then only 17 himself and graduating from high school, he had called for equality for African Americans. (b) I marvelled, proud of him, and wondered how, in 1920, so young, so white, and in the deep South, where the law still separated black from white, (c) he had had the courage to deliver it. I asked him about it.

(D)

"I wrote it. And I delivered it. About half way through I looked out to see the entire audience of teachers, students, and parents stand up — and walk out. Left alone on the stage, (d) I thought to myself, 'Well, I guess I need to be sure to do only two things with my life: keep thinking for myself, and not get killed.'" He handed the speech back to me, and smiled. "(e) You seem to have done both," I said.

43. 주어진 글 (A)에 이어질 내용을 순서에 맞게 배열한 것으로 가장 적절한 것은?

① (B) − (D) − (C)　　② (C) − (B) − (D)
③ (C) − (D) − (B)　　④ (D) − (B) − (C)
⑤ (D) − (C) − (B)

44. 밑줄 친 (a) ~ (e) 중에서 가리키는 대상이 나머지 넷과 <u>다른</u> 것은?

① (a)　　② (b)　　③ (c)　　④ (d)　　⑤ (e)

45. 윗글에 관한 내용으로 적절하지 <u>않은</u> 것은?

① 아버지와 나는 서류를 정리하고 있었다.
② 나는 서재에서 발견한 것을 읽고 나서 울기 시작했다.
③ 아버지는 연설을 하기 위한 허락을 구하지 않았다.
④ 아버지가 연설문을 썼을 당시 17세였다.
⑤ 교사, 학생, 학부모 모두 아버지의 연설을 끝까지 들었다.

* 확인 사항
○ 답안지의 해당란에 필요한 내용을 정확히 기입(표기)했는지 확인하시오.

01
001 school nurse 보건 교사
002 get sick with ~에 걸리다
003 seasonal influenza 계절성 독감
004 lead to ~로 이어지다, ~을 낳다
005 hospitalization ⓝ 입원
006 recommend ⓥ 권유하다
007 flu vaccine 독감 예방주사
008 keep ~ from ... ~가 …하지 못하게 하다
009 update ⓥ 갱신하다
010 protect against ~로부터 지키다
011 doctor's office 의원, (개인) 병원
012 health department 보건부

02
013 convenient ⓐ 편리한
014 flip through ~을 훑어보다 [휙휙 넘기다]
015 shut down 문을 닫다
016 pity ⓝ 안타까움, 불쌍히 여김
017 go out of business 폐업하다
018 next time 다음번에

03
019 lock out of 열쇠가 없어서 ~에 못 들어가다
020 respond ⓥ 응답하다
021 electric ⓐ 전기의
022 fix ⓝ 수리
023 cost ⓥ 비용이 들다
024 service charge 봉사료

04
025 crowded ⓐ 어수선한, 붐비는
026 electric keyboard 전기 키보드
027 microphone ⓝ 마이크
028 hobby ⓝ 취미
029 star-shaped ⓐ 별 모양의
030 incredible ⓐ 믿을 수 없는, 대단한
031 practice ⓥ 연습하다

05
032 recipe ⓝ 요리법
033 a little bit 약간
034 promise ⓥ 약속하다
035 by the way 그나저나
036 remember ⓥ 기억하다
037 pick up (~을 차로) 데려오다
038 forget 잊어버리다

06
039 laptop ⓝ 노트북 컴퓨터
040 original price 정가
041 USB charging port USB 충전 단자
042 budget ⓝ 예산
043 bargain ⓝ (정상가보다) 싸게 사는 물건

07
044 business trip 출장
045 be busy -ing ~하느라 바쁘다
046 prepare ⓥ 준비하다
047 turn down ~을 거절하다
048 take care of ~을 돌보다
049 niece 여자 조카

08
050 raise ⓥ 키우다, 기르다
051 walk ⓥ 산책시키다
052 feed ⓥ 먹이를 주다
053 toilet train 배변 훈련을 시키다
054 pee pad 소변 패드
055 responsibility ⓝ 책임, 책임감

09
056 donate ⓥ 기부하다
057 fund ⓝ 기금
058 movement ⓝ 운동
059 do good 선행하다
060 scholarship ⓝ 장학금

10
061 selfie stick 셀카봉, 셀피스틱
062 prefer ⓥ 선호하다
063 length ⓝ 길이
064 extend ⓥ 늘어나다, 확장하다
065 at least 적어도

11
066 pack ⓥ (짐을) 싸다[꾸리다]
067 had better (~하는 것이) 좋을 것이다

12
068 eat out 외식하다
069 book ⓥ 예약하다
070 important ⓐ 중요한
071 I've had enough. 이제 됐어요.

13
072 work on ~을 작업하다, ~에 공을 들이다
073 climate change 기후 변화
074 responsible ⓐ 책임감이 있는
075 research ⓝ 조사
076 in charge of ~을 담당하는, 책임지는
077 assignment ⓝ 과제
078 stay up late 늦게까지 깨어 있다

14
079 slip one's mind 깜박 잊다
080 forgetful ⓐ 잘 잊어버리는, 건망증이 있는
081 work ⓥ 효과가 있다
082 time management application 시간 관리 앱
083 around the corner 코앞에, 목전에
084 complete ⓥ 마치다, 완수하다
085 specific ⓐ 특정한, 구체적인

15
086 talented ⓐ 재능 있는
087 passionate ⓐ 열정적인
088 upcoming ⓐ 다가오는
089 match ⓝ 시합, 경기
090 injure ⓥ 부상을 입다
091 elbow ⓝ 팔꿈치
092 insist on ~을 주장하다
093 heartbroken ⓐ 마음이 아픈
094 be concerned about ~에 대해 걱정하다
095 recover ⓥ 회복하다

096 persuade ⓥ 설득하다
097 calm down 진정하다
098 put effort into ~에 공을 들이다
099 Take it easy. 쉬엄쉬엄해. 진정해.
100 Practice makes perfect. 자꾸 연습하다 보면 잘하게 된다. 연습이 완벽을 만든다.

16~17
101 light pollution 빛 공해
102 wildlife ⓝ 야생 동물
103 lay ⓥ (알을) 낳다
104 with the help of ~의 도움으로, ~ 덕분에
105 artificial ⓐ 인공적인
106 confuse ⓥ 혼란스럽게 하다
107 firefly ⓝ 반딧불이
108 disappear ⓥ 사라지다
109 disturb ⓥ 방해하다, 지장을 주다
110 attract ⓥ 끌다, 유인하다
111 salmon ⓝ 연어
112 migrate ⓥ 이동하다
113 randomly ⓐ 무작위로, 닥치는 대로
114 threaten ⓥ 위협하다
115 survival ⓝ 생존
116 interrupt ⓥ 방해하다
117 mating call 짝짓기 울음소리
118 tree frog 청개구리
119 reproduce ⓥ 번식하다
120 illegal ⓐ 불법의
121 characteristic ⓝ 특성, 특징
122 endangered ⓐ 멸종 위기에 처한
123 habitat ⓝ 서식지

18
124 PR director 홍보부 이사
125 corporation ⓝ 기업, 회사
126 redesign ⓥ 다시 설계하다
127 identity ⓝ 정체성
128 launch ⓥ 시작하다, 런칭하다
129 logo ⓝ (회사·조직을 나타내는) 상징[로고]
130 celebrate ⓥ 기념하다
131 anniversary ⓝ 기념일
132 request ⓥ 요청하다
133 suit ⓥ ~에 적합하다
134 core ⓝ 핵심
135 inspire ⓥ 고무시키다
136 humanity ⓝ 인류애
137 convey ⓥ 전달하다
138 capture ⓥ (사진이나 글로 감정·분위기 등을) 정확히 담아내다
139 proposal ⓝ 제안, 제의

19
140 thrilled ⓐ 몹시 기쁜, 황홀해하는
141 in person 직접
142 draw ⓥ 그리다
143 look on (관여하지는 않고) 구경하다[지켜보다]
144 awe ⓝ 경외심
145 throw away 버리다
146 reply ⓥ 대답하다
147 at a loss (무슨 말을 해야 할지) 모르는
148 rooted ⓐ (~에) 붙박인
149 relieved ⓐ 안도하는

150 worried ⓐ 걱정하는
151 indifferent ⓐ 무관심한
152 embarrassed ⓐ 당황한
153 surprised ⓐ 놀라는
154 disappointed ⓐ 실망한
155 satisfied ⓐ 만족하는
156 jealous ⓐ 질투하는
157 confident ⓐ 자신감 있는

20
158 avoid ⓥ 피하다
159 discomfort ⓝ 불편함
160 extra ⓐ 추가의
161 actively ⓐ 적극적으로
162 shut out ~을 차단하다[가로막다]
163 uncomfortable ⓐ 불편한
164 therefore ⓐ 따라서
165 overcome ⓥ 극복하다
166 instinct ⓝ 본능
167 essential ⓐ 필수적인, 본질적인
168 comfort zone 안전지대, 일을 적당히 하거나 요령을 피우는 상태
169 magical ⓐ 마법의
170 formula ⓝ 공식, 제조법

21
171 tendency ⓝ 경향
172 interpret ⓥ 해석하다
173 selectively ⓐ 선택적으로
174 certainly ⓐ 틀림없이, 분명히
175 select ⓥ 선택하다
176 stack ⓥ 쌓다, 포개다
177 arrange ⓥ 정리하다, 배열하다
178 evidence ⓝ 증거
179 support ⓥ 뒷받침하다
180 viewpoint ⓝ 관점
181 perception ⓝ 지각, 인식
182 be based on ~에 기초하다, 근거하다
183 stand out 두드러지다
184 be related to ~와 관련이 있다
185 interest ⓝ 관심, 관심사
186 expectation ⓝ 기대
187 demand ⓝ 요구
188 hammer ⓝ 망치
189 nail ⓝ 못
190 quote ⓝ 인용구
191 highlight ⓥ 강조하다
192 phenomenon ⓝ 현상
193 unwilling ⓐ (~하기를) 꺼리는, 마지못해 하는
194 meaningless ⓐ 무의미한
195 intend ⓥ 의도하다, 하려고 하는
196 similar ⓐ 비슷한

22
197 punish ⓥ 처벌하다
198 encourage ⓥ 격려하다, 용기를 주다
199 motivate ⓥ 동기를 부여하다
200 incomplete ⓐ 미완성된
201 additional ⓐ 추가적인
202 record ⓥ 기록하다
203 receive ⓥ 받다

VOCA LIST 11

204	in order to	(목적) 위하여
205	up to	~까지
206	acceptable	ⓐ 수용 가능한
207	belief	ⓝ 믿음
208	submit	ⓥ 제출하다
209	in large part	대체로
210	reason	ⓥ 추론하다, 생각하다
211	substandard	ⓐ 수준 이하의, 열악한
212	appropriate	ⓐ 적절한
213	satisfactory	ⓐ 만족스러운

23

214	curiosity	ⓝ 호기심
215	view ~ as ...	~을 ...로 여기다
216	challenge	ⓝ 도전
217	take on	(책임이나 일을) 맡다, 지다
218	opportunity	ⓝ 기회
219	in general	일반적으로
220	threat	ⓝ 위협
221	approach	ⓝ 접근법
222	be associated with	~와 관련이 있다
223	defensive	ⓐ 방어적인
224	aggression	ⓝ 공격
225	irritation	ⓝ 짜증
226	reaction	ⓝ 반응
227	tough	ⓐ 힘든, 어려운
228	hidden	ⓐ 숨은
229	cope with	~에 대처하다
230	potential	ⓐ 잠재적인
231	factor	ⓝ 요인
232	reduce	ⓥ 감소시키다

24

233	development	ⓝ 발전
234	rarely	ⓐⓓ 거의 ~하지 않는
235	critical	ⓐ 중요한
236	vertical	ⓐ 수직의
237	transportation	ⓝ 운송, 수송
238	journey	ⓝ 이동
239	efficient	ⓐ 능률적인, 유능한; 효율적인
240	expand	ⓥ 확장하다
241	skyscraper	ⓝ 고층 건물
242	architecture	ⓝ 건축
243	probably	ⓐⓓ 아마도
244	under construction	건설 중인
245	closer	ⓐ 가까워
246	construct	ⓥ 건설하다
247	cheap	ⓐ (값이) 싼
248	function	ⓝ 기능
249	ancient	ⓐ 고대의
250	modern	ⓐ 현대의, 근대의
251	evolution	ⓝ 진화
252	solution	ⓝ 해결책
253	overpopulation	ⓝ 인구 과잉

25

254	spending	ⓝ (정부·조직체의) 지출
255	share	ⓝ 점유율
256	selected	ⓐ 선택된, 선발된
257	on average	평균적으로
258	estimate	ⓥ 추정하다, 추산하다
259	difference	ⓝ 차이

26

260	on account of	~ 때문에
261	rock-like	ⓐ 바위 같은
262	appearance	ⓝ 겉모습
263	native to	~이 원산지인
264	desert	ⓝ 사막
265	commonly	ⓐⓓ 일반적으로
266	garden center	식물원
267	nursery	ⓝ 종묘원
268	compacted	ⓐ 빽빽한, 탄탄한
269	extreme	ⓐ 극도의
270	temperature	ⓝ 온도
271	surface	ⓝ 표면
272	resemble	ⓥ 닮다, 비슷[유사]하다
273	gather	ⓥ 모으다, 모이다
274	stem	ⓝ 줄기
275	conserve	ⓥ 보존하다
276	moisture	ⓝ 습기

27

277	go green	친환경적이 되다
278	share	ⓥ 나누다, 공유하다
279	talent	ⓝ 재능
280	environment	ⓝ 환경
281	category	ⓝ 부문, 분야
282	slogan	ⓝ 구호, 표어
283	poem	ⓝ (한 편의) 시
284	essay	ⓝ 에세이
285	requirement	ⓝ 요구 사항
286	participant	ⓝ 참가자
287	entry	ⓝ 출품작
288	deadline	ⓝ 기한, 마감 시간[일자]
289	announce	ⓥ 공지하다, 발표하다

28

290	virtual	ⓐ 가상의
291	real time	실시간
292	discussion	ⓝ 토론
293	upcoming	ⓐ 다가오는
294	goal	ⓝ 목표
295	plan	ⓥ 계획하다
296	theme	ⓝ 주제
297	access	ⓝ 접속
298	text message	문자 메시지
299	type	ⓥ (타자기·컴퓨터로) 타자 치다[입력하다]
300	chatroom	ⓝ 채팅방, 대화방

29

301	occasion	ⓝ 경우
302	observe	ⓥ 목격하다, 관찰하다
303	sense	ⓥ 이해하다
304	genuine	ⓐ 진짜인
305	obvious	ⓐ 명백한, 분명한
306	identify	ⓥ 알아보다, 식별하다
307	insincere	ⓐ 진실하지 않은
308	primarily	ⓐⓓ 주로
309	affect	ⓥ 영향을 미치다
310	lower	ⓐ 아래쪽의
311	mainly	ⓐⓓ 주로
312	involved	ⓐ 관련이 있는
313	manufacture	ⓥ 만들다
314	judge	ⓥ 판단하다

315	impact	ⓥ 영향을 미치다
316	wrinkle	ⓝ 주름
317	noticeably	ⓐⓓ 눈에 띄게, 두드러지게
318	eyebrow	ⓝ 눈썹
319	eyelid	ⓝ 눈꺼풀
320	slightly	ⓐⓓ 살짝, 약간
321	enjoyment	ⓝ 즐거움
322	entire	ⓐ 전체의

30

323	detailed	ⓐ 자세한
324	decade	ⓝ 10[십]년
325	functioning	ⓝ 기능, 작용
326	attempt	ⓝ 노력, 시도
327	straighten	ⓥ 바로 펴다, 똑바르게 하다
328	regular	ⓐ 규칙적인
329	cross-section	ⓝ 횡단면
330	perhaps	ⓐⓓ 아마, 어쩌면
331	disastrous	ⓐ 처참한, 피해가 막심한
332	relationship	ⓝ 관계
333	irregular	ⓐ 불규칙한
334	curve	ⓝ 굽이치다
335	spill	ⓥ 흐르다, 쏟아지다
336	floodplain	ⓝ 범람원
337	leak into	~에 새어 들어가다
338	wetland	ⓝ 습지
339	incredibly	ⓐⓓ 엄청나게, 믿을 수 없게
340	shoreline	ⓝ 강가
341	prevent	ⓥ 막다[예방/방지하다]
342	variation	ⓝ 변이, 변화
343	destroy	ⓥ 파괴하다
344	disaster	ⓝ 재난, 재앙
345	controlled	ⓐ 통제된
346	square mile	제곱마일
347	annually	ⓐⓓ 매년, 연마다

31

348	maintain	ⓥ 유지하다
349	be supposed to	~하기로 되어 있다
350	reason	ⓝ 이유
351	have trouble ~ing	~하는 데 어려움을 겪다
352	consideration	ⓝ 고려 사항
353	decision	ⓝ 결정, 판단
354	unburden	ⓥ 벗어나게 하다
355	sort out	~을 가려내다
356	negotiate	ⓥ 협상하다
357	external	ⓐ 외부적인
358	desire	ⓝ 욕망
359	merit	ⓝ 장점
360	limitation	ⓝ 한계

32

361	confirm	ⓥ (맞다고) 확인하다
362	athlete	ⓝ 운동선수
363	less	ⓐⓓ 더 적게, 덜하게
364	unacceptable	ⓐ 받아들여지지 않는, 용인되지 않는
365	moral	ⓐ 도덕적인
366	reasoning	ⓝ 추론 (능력)
367	decline	ⓥ 감소하다
368	progress	ⓝ (앞으로 무엇을 향해) 감[나아감]

369	competitive	ⓐ 경쟁하는, 경쟁력 있는
370	emphasis	ⓝ 강조
371	character	ⓝ 인격, 인성
372	cheat	ⓥ 속이다
373	undesirable	ⓐ 바람직하지 않은
374	enhance	ⓥ 강화하다
375	short term	단기의, 비교적 단기간의
376	resist	ⓥ 저항하다
377	temptation	ⓝ 유혹
378	dishonest	ⓐ 부정직한
379	learned	ⓐ 학습된, 후천적인
380	systematically	ⓐⓓ 체계적으로
381	a piece of cake	식은 죽 먹기, 아주 쉬운 일
382	a one-way street	일방 통행로
383	a bird in the hand	수중에 든 새, 확실한 일
384	a fish out of water	물 밖에 나온 고기, 낯선 환경에서 불편해 하는 사람
385	a double-edged sword	양날의 검, 양면성을 가진 상황

33

386	innovation	ⓝ 혁신
387	availability	ⓝ 이용 가능성
388	individual	ⓝ 개인
389	unheard-of	ⓐ 전례 없는
390	confront A with B	A를 B와 대면시키다
391	countless	ⓐ 헤아릴 수 없는, 무수한
392	orient	ⓥ 적응하다, 익숙해지다, 자기 위치를 알다
393	filter out	~을 걸러 내다
394	collection	ⓝ 수집
395	lie	ⓥ 있다, 존재하다
396	restrict	ⓥ 국한시키다, 제한하다
397	distributor	ⓝ 배급 업자
398	considerable	ⓐ 상당한
399	determine	ⓥ 결정하다
400	preferences	ⓝ 선호
401	aspect	ⓝ 측면
402	knowledge	ⓝ 지식

34

403	common	ⓐ 일반적인
404	assume	ⓥ 가정하다, 추정하다
405	concern	ⓥ 관련되다
406	relation	ⓝ 관계
407	actor	ⓝ 행위자
408	sociocultural	ⓐ 사회문화적인
409	standpoint	ⓝ 관점
410	in the absence of	~이 없을 때에
411	position	ⓝ 입장
412	audience	ⓝ 관객, 청중
413	distantiation	ⓝ 거리두기
414	interaction	ⓝ 상호 작용
415	constantly	ⓐⓓ 지속적으로
416	confront	ⓥ 직면하다, 맞서다
417	blend into	~에 뒤섞다
418	include	ⓥ 포함하다
419	perspective	ⓝ 관점
420	absolute	ⓐ 절대적인
421	in existence	현존하는
422	precise	ⓐ 정확한

423 ☐ **logical** ⓐ 논리적인
424 ☐ **internalize** ⓥ 내면화하다
425 ☐ **endurance** ⓝ 인내심, 참을성

35
426 ☐ **spread** ⓝ 확산 ⓥ 퍼지다
427 ☐ **disease** ⓝ 질병
428 ☐ **be linked to** ~와 연관되다[관련이 있다]
429 ☐ **operate** ⓥ 작동되다
430 ☐ **epidemic** ⓝ 전염병
431 ☐ **advance** ⓝ 발전
432 ☐ **destructive** ⓐ 파괴적인
433 ☐ **outbreak** ⓝ 발발, 창궐
434 ☐ **typhoid** ⓝ 장티푸스
435 ☐ **overcrowding** ⓝ 과밀 거주, 초만원
436 ☐ **sanitation** ⓝ 위생 (관리)
437 ☐ **recognition** ⓝ 인식
438 ☐ **in spite of** 불구하고
439 ☐ **reconstruction** ⓝ 재건
440 ☐ **pioneering** ⓐ 선구적인
441 ☐ **as a result of** ~의 결과로

36
442 ☐ **be attracted to** ~에 끌리다
443 ☐ **immediately** ⓐⓓ 즉시, 즉각
444 ☐ **organism** ⓝ 유기체
445 ☐ **survive** ⓥ 살아남다, 생존하다
446 ☐ **alert** ⓐ 경계하는
447 ☐ **enemy** ⓝ 적
448 ☐ **recognize** ⓥ 알아보다
449 ☐ **afar** ⓐⓓ 멀리
450 ☐ **coming** ⓐ 다가오는, 다음의
451 ☐ **protect** ⓥ 보호하다, 지키다
452 ☐ **possible** ⓐ 할 수 있는
453 ☐ **danger** ⓝ 위험
454 ☐ **involve** ⓥ 수반하다
455 ☐ **structure** ⓝ 구조
456 ☐ **occur** ⓥ 발생하다
457 ☐ **generation** ⓝ 세대
458 ☐ **measure** ⓥ 측정하다, 유심히 바라보다
459 ☐ **eyesight** ⓝ 시력
460 ☐ **prefer to** B보다 A를 더 좋아하다

37
461 ☐ **interact with** ~와 상호 작용하다
462 ☐ **analyze** ⓥ 분석하다
463 ☐ **misinformation** ⓝ 오보, 잘못된 정보
464 ☐ **raise a question** 의문을 제기하다
465 ☐ **well-known** ⓐ 잘 알려진
466 ☐ **demonstrate** ⓥ 입증하다
467 ☐ **fool** ⓥ 속이다
468 ☐ **especially** ⓐⓓ 특히
469 ☐ **weakness** ⓝ 약점
470 ☐ **youth** ⓝ 젊은이
471 ☐ **government** ⓝ 정부
472 ☐ **tech** ⓝ 기술
473 ☐ **role** ⓝ 역할
474 ☐ **block** ⓥ 막다, 차단하다
475 ☐ **take responsibility for** ~을 책임지다
476 ☐ **combat** ⓥ 싸우다
477 ☐ **literate** ⓐ ~을 다룰 줄 아는, 글을 읽고 쓸 줄 아는

38
478 ☐ **approach** ⓥ 다가가다[오다]
479 ☐ **immediately** ⓐⓓ 바로 옆에[가까이에]
480 ☐ **compress** ⓥ 압축하다
481 ☐ **build up** 축적되다
482 ☐ **travel** ⓥ 이동하다
483 ☐ **wave** ⓝ 파장
484 ☐ **often** ⓐⓓ 자주
485 ☐ **onto** ⓟⓡⓔⓟ (이동을 나타내는 동사와 함께 쓰여) 위에
486 ☐ **pond** ⓝ 연못
487 ☐ **outward** ⓐ (중심·특정 지점에서) 밖으로 향하는
488 ☐ **impact** ⓝ 충격, 여파
489 ☐ **due to** ~때문에
490 ☐ **disturbance** ⓝ 교란, 방해
491 ☐ **bang** ⓥ 쾅 하고 치다
492 ☐ **release** ⓥ 방출하다
493 ☐ **experiment** ⓝ 실험 ⓥ 실험하다
494 ☐ **density** ⓝ 밀도
495 ☐ **displace** ⓥ 대체하다, (평소의 위치에서) 옮겨 놓다
496 ☐ **atmosphere** ⓝ (지구의) 대기
497 ☐ **produce** ⓥ 만들다

39
498 ☐ **each** ⓐ 각
499 ☐ **transfer** ⓝ 이동
500 ☐ **proportion** ⓝ 비율
501 ☐ **potential** ⓐ 잠재적
502 ☐ **food chain** 먹이 사슬
503 ☐ **transfer** ⓥ 이동하다
504 ☐ **plant** ⓝ 식물
505 ☐ **a series of** 일련의
506 ☐ **repeated** ⓐ 반복[되풀이]되는
507 ☐ **process** ⓝ 과정
508 ☐ **grassland** ⓝ 풀밭, 초원
509 ☐ **in turn** 이윽고, 차례로
510 ☐ **imply** ⓥ 암시하다
511 ☐ **sequence** ⓝ 연쇄, 사슬
512 ☐ **consumer** ⓝ 소비자
513 ☐ **hence** ⓐⓓ 이런 이유로
514 ☐ **sequence** ⓝ 배열
515 ☐ **usually** ⓐⓓ 보통
516 ☐ **intake** ⓝ 섭취량

40
517 ☐ **attend** ⓥ 다니다, 참석하다
518 ☐ **problem** ⓝ 문제
519 ☐ **near** ⓐⓓ 근처
520 ☐ **several** ⓟⓡⓞⓝ (몇)몇의
521 ☐ **toilet paper** 화장실 휴지
522 ☐ **classic** ⓐ 고전적인
523 ☐ **tragedy of the commons** 공유지의 비극
524 ☐ **fair** ⓐ 공평한
525 ☐ **share** ⓝ 몫
526 ☐ **public** ⓐ 공공의
527 ☐ **resource** ⓝ 자원, 재원
528 ☐ **research paper** 연구 논문
529 ☐ **behavior change** 행동 변화
530 ☐ **note** ⓝ 쪽지
531 ☐ **remove** ⓥ 없애다

532 ☐ **satisfaction** ⓝ 만족(감), 흡족; 만족(감을 주는 것)
533 ☐ **reappear** ⓥ 다시 나타나다
534 ☐ **note-free** ⓐ 쪽지가 없는
535 ☐ **following** ⓐ (시간상으로) 그다음의
536 ☐ **bring about** ~을 야기하다
537 ☐ **behavior** ⓝ 행동
538 ☐ **reminder** ⓝ (잊고 있었던 것을) 상기시켜 주는 것
539 ☐ **recycle** ⓥ 재활용[재생]하다
540 ☐ **mistake** ⓝ 실수, 잘못
541 ☐ **stored** ⓐ 축적된
542 ☐ **borrowed** ⓐ 빌린, 빌려온
543 ☐ **fortune** ⓝ 행운
544 ☐ **limited** ⓐ 제한된

41~42
545 ☐ **afraid** ⓥ 두려워[무서워]하는
546 ☐ **standing** ⓐ 서 있는
547 ☐ **face** ⓥ 직면하다
548 ☐ **socialize** ⓥ (사람과) 사귀다, 사회화하다
549 ☐ **tricky** ⓐ 까다로운, 다루기 힘든
550 ☐ **inanimate** ⓐ 무생물의
551 ☐ **get used to** ~에 익숙해지다
552 ☐ **interact** ⓥ 상호 작용을 하다
553 ☐ **response** ⓝ 반응
554 ☐ **unpredictable** ⓐ 예측 불가한
555 ☐ **complex** ⓐ 복잡한
556 ☐ **self-esteem** ⓝ 자존감
557 ☐ **affected** ⓐ 영향받는
558 ☐ **suffer** ⓥ 고통을 받다
559 ☐ **effectively** ⓐⓓ 효과적으로
560 ☐ **confidence** ⓝ 자신감
561 ☐ **tidy** ⓐ 깔끔한
562 ☐ **gradually** ⓐⓓ 점차적으로
563 ☐ **social fear** 사회적 공포
564 ☐ **social situation** 사회적 상황
565 ☐ **expose** ⓥ 노출시키다
566 ☐ **sense** ⓥ 감지하다, 알아차리다
567 ☐ **under control** 통제되는
568 ☐ **progression** ⓝ 진전
569 ☐ **clear** ⓐ 분명한
570 ☐ **unavoidable** ⓐ 피할 수 없는
571 ☐ **decrease** ⓥ 줄다[감소하다]
572 ☐ **difficulty** ⓝ 어려움
573 ☐ **endlessly** ⓐⓓ 끝없이
574 ☐ **purpose** ⓝ 목적
575 ☐ **pointless** ⓐ 의미 없는
576 ☐ **principle** ⓝ 원칙, 원리
577 ☐ **exposure** ⓝ (유해한 환경 등에의) 노출
578 ☐ **messy** ⓐ 어수선한, 지저분한
579 ☐ **improve** ⓥ 높아지다
580 ☐ **relaxation** ⓝ 휴식
581 ☐ **get over something** ~을 극복[처리]하다
582 ☐ **fear of heights** 고소 공포증
583 ☐ **anxiety** ⓝ 불안(감), 염려

43~45
584 ☐ **discover** ⓥ 발견하다
585 ☐ **wonderful** ⓐ 놀라운
586 ☐ **study** ⓝ 서재
587 ☐ **organize** ⓥ 정리하다, 조직하다

588 ☐ **paper** ⓝ 서류
589 ☐ **rust** ⓝ 녹
590 ☐ **dust** ⓥ ~을 먼지투성이로 만들다
591 ☐ **handing** ⓝ 건네주다, 넘겨주다
592 ☐ **permission** ⓝ 허락
593 ☐ **scared** ⓐ 두려운, 무서운
594 ☐ **graduate from** ~을 졸업하다
595 ☐ **call for** ~을 요구하다, 필요로 하다
596 ☐ **equality** ⓝ 평등
597 ☐ **marvel** ⓥ 놀라다
598 ☐ **separate** ⓥ 분리시키다
599 ☐ **courage** ⓝ 용기
600 ☐ **deliver** ⓥ (연설이나 강연을) 하다

11회

● 채점 : 맞은 개수 _____ / 80

TEST A-B 각 단어의 뜻을 [A] 영어는 우리말로, [B] 우리말은 영어로 쓰시오.

A	English	Korean
01	gather	
02	build up	
03	intake	
04	spread	
05	appropriate	
06	limitation	
07	decline	
08	quote	
09	aggression	
10	analyze	
11	pointless	
12	equality	
13	blend into	
14	occasion	
15	awe	
16	identity	
17	considerable	
18	proportion	
19	reappear	
20	vertical	

B	Korean	English
01	겉모습	
02	유혹	
03	진전	
04	흐르다, 쏟아지다	
05	본능	
06	허락	
07	입증하다	
08	호기심	
09	관점	
10	인류애	
11	강화하다	
12	충격, 여파	
13	위생 (관리)	
14	추가적인	
15	복잡한, 엉망진창인	
16	다가가다[오다]	
17	고층 건물	
18	자존감	
19	협상하다	
20	유지하다	

▶ A-D 정답 : 해설편 124쪽

TEST C-D 각 단어의 뜻을 골라 기호를 쓰시오.

C	English			Korean
01	undesirable	(	)	ⓐ 현존하는
02	celebrate	(	)	ⓑ 녹
03	restrict	(	)	ⓒ 해석하다
04	classic	(	)	ⓓ 처참한, 피해가 막심한
05	slightly	(	)	ⓔ 처벌하다
06	conserve	(	)	ⓕ 위협
07	in existence	(	)	ⓖ 싸우다
08	interpret	(	)	ⓗ 식은 죽 먹기
09	thrilled	(	)	ⓘ 살짝, 약간
10	a piece of cake	(	)	ⓙ 보존하다
11	manufacture	(	)	ⓚ 바람직하지 않은
12	inanimate	(	)	ⓛ 무생물의
13	distantiation	(	)	ⓜ 몹시 기쁜, 황홀해하는
14	disastrous	(	)	ⓝ 만들다
15	phenomenon	(	)	ⓞ 현상
16	threat	(	)	ⓟ 기념하다
17	punish	(	)	ⓠ 국한시키다, 제한하다
18	alert	(	)	ⓡ 고전적인
19	rust	(	)	ⓢ 경계하는
20	combat	(	)	ⓣ 거리두기

D	Korean			English
01	파괴적인	(	)	ⓐ upcoming
02	내면화하다	(	)	ⓑ acceptable
03	노력, 시도	(	)	ⓒ attempt
04	쌓다, 포개다	(	)	ⓓ insincere
05	다가오는	(	)	ⓔ bring about
06	시력	(	)	ⓕ cope with
07	절대적인	(	)	ⓖ weight
08	이윽고, 차례로	(	)	ⓗ disastrous
09	이용 가능성	(	)	ⓘ embarrassed
10	~을 야기하다	(	)	ⓙ eyesight
11	당황한	(	)	ⓚ absolute
12	처참한, 피해가 막심한	(	)	ⓛ indifferent
13	~에 대처하다	(	)	ⓜ availability
14	인구 과잉	(	)	ⓝ internalize
15	피할 수 없는	(	)	ⓞ noticeably
16	비중, 무게	(	)	ⓟ overpopulation
17	진실하지 않은	(	)	ⓠ stack
18	무관심한	(	)	ⓡ unavoidable
19	눈에 띄게, 두드러지게	(	)	ⓢ in turn
20	수용 가능한	(	)	ⓣ destructive

※ 답안지 작성(표기)은 반드시 검은색 컴퓨터용 사인펜만을 사용하고, 연필 또는 샤프 등의 필기구를 절대 사용하지 마십시오.

결시자 확인 (수험생은 표기하지 말것.)

검은색 컴퓨터용 사인펜을 사용하여 수험번호란과 옆란을 표기	○

※ 문제지 표지에 안내된 필적 확인 문구를 아래 '필적 확인란'에 정자로 반드시 기재하여야 합니다.

필 적 확인란	

성 명	

수 험 번 호

문형

홀수형 ○

짝수형 ○

※문제의 문형을 확인 후 표기

감독관 확인 (수험생은 표기하지 말것) — 서 명 또는 날 인 — 본인 여부, 수험번호 및 문형의 표기가 정확한지 확인, 옆란에 서명 또는 날인

문번	답 란	문번	답 란	문번	답 란
1	① ② ③ ④ ⑤	21	① ② ③ ④ ⑤	41	① ② ③ ④ ⑤
2	① ② ③ ④ ⑤	22	① ② ③ ④ ⑤	42	① ② ③ ④ ⑤
3	① ② ③ ④ ⑤	23	① ② ③ ④ ⑤	43	① ② ③ ④ ⑤
4	① ② ③ ④ ⑤	24	① ② ③ ④ ⑤	44	① ② ③ ④ ⑤
5	① ② ③ ④ ⑤	25	① ② ③ ④ ⑤	45	① ② ③ ④ ⑤
6	① ② ③ ④ ⑤	26	① ② ③ ④ ⑤		
7	① ② ③ ④ ⑤	27	① ② ③ ④ ⑤		
8	① ② ③ ④ ⑤	28	① ② ③ ④ ⑤		
9	① ② ③ ④ ⑤	29	① ② ③ ④ ⑤		
10	① ② ③ ④ ⑤	30	① ② ③ ④ ⑤		
11	① ② ③ ④ ⑤	31	① ② ③ ④ ⑤		
12	① ② ③ ④ ⑤	32	① ② ③ ④ ⑤		
13	① ② ③ ④ ⑤	33	① ② ③ ④ ⑤		
14	① ② ③ ④ ⑤	34	① ② ③ ④ ⑤		
15	① ② ③ ④ ⑤	35	① ② ③ ④ ⑤		
16	① ② ③ ④ ⑤	36	① ② ③ ④ ⑤		
17	① ② ③ ④ ⑤	37	① ② ③ ④ ⑤		
18	① ② ③ ④ ⑤	38	① ② ③ ④ ⑤		
19	① ② ③ ④ ⑤	39	① ② ③ ④ ⑤		
20	① ② ③ ④ ⑤	40	① ② ③ ④ ⑤		

리얼 오리지널 I 예비 고1 《반배치고사＋3월·6월 모의고사》

✂ 절취선

[　　회] 리얼 오리지널 모의고사 답안지

③교시 영어영역

※ 답안지 작성(표기)은 반드시 검은색 컴퓨터용 사인펜만을 사용하고, 연필 또는 샤프 등의 필기구를 절대 사용하지 마십시오.

결시자 확인 (수험생은 표기하지 말것.)

검은색 컴퓨터용 사인펜을 사용하여 수험번호란과 옆란을 표기 ○

※ 문제지 표지에 안내된 필적 확인 문구를 아래 '필적 확인란'에 정자로 반드시 기재하여야 합니다.

필 적 확인란

성 명

수 험 번 호

문형

홀수형 ○

짝수형 ○

※문제의 문형을 확인 후 표기

감독관 확인 (수험생은 표기하지 말것) 서 명 또는 날 인 본인 여부, 수험번호 및 문형의 표기가 정확한지 확인, 옆란에 서명 또는 날인

문번	답 란	문번	답 란	문번	답 란
1	① ② ③ ④ ⑤	21	① ② ③ ④ ⑤	41	① ② ③ ④ ⑤
2	① ② ③ ④ ⑤	22	① ② ③ ④ ⑤	42	① ② ③ ④ ⑤
3	① ② ③ ④ ⑤	23	① ② ③ ④ ⑤	43	① ② ③ ④ ⑤
4	① ② ③ ④ ⑤	24	① ② ③ ④ ⑤	44	① ② ③ ④ ⑤
5	① ② ③ ④ ⑤	25	① ② ③ ④ ⑤	45	① ② ③ ④ ⑤
6	① ② ③ ④ ⑤	26	① ② ③ ④ ⑤		
7	① ② ③ ④ ⑤	27	① ② ③ ④ ⑤		
8	① ② ③ ④ ⑤	28	① ② ③ ④ ⑤		
9	① ② ③ ④ ⑤	29	① ② ③ ④ ⑤		
10	① ② ③ ④ ⑤	30	① ② ③ ④ ⑤		
11	① ② ③ ④ ⑤	31	① ② ③ ④ ⑤		
12	① ② ③ ④ ⑤	32	① ② ③ ④ ⑤		
13	① ② ③ ④ ⑤	33	① ② ③ ④ ⑤		
14	① ② ③ ④ ⑤	34	① ② ③ ④ ⑤		
15	① ② ③ ④ ⑤	35	① ② ③ ④ ⑤		
16	① ② ③ ④ ⑤	36	① ② ③ ④ ⑤		
17	① ② ③ ④ ⑤	37	① ② ③ ④ ⑤		
18	① ② ③ ④ ⑤	38	① ② ③ ④ ⑤		
19	① ② ③ ④ ⑤	39	① ② ③ ④ ⑤		
20	① ② ③ ④ ⑤	40	① ② ③ ④ ⑤		

리얼 오리지널 I 예비 고1 《반배치고사＋3월·6월 모의고사》

[　　회] 리얼 오리지널 모의고사 답안지

③ 교시 영어영역

결시자 확인 (수험생은 표기하지 말것.)

| 검은색 컴퓨터용 사인펜을 사용하여 수험번호란과 옆란을 표기 | ○ |

※ 문제지 표지에 안내된 필적 확인 문구를 아래 '필적 확인란'에 정자로 반드시 기재하여야 합니다.

| 필 적 확인란 | |

| 성 명 | |

수 험 번 호

문형

홀수형 ○

짝수형 ○

※문제의 문형을 확인 후 표기

감독관 확인 (수험생은 표기 하지 말것)

(서 명 또는 날 인)

본인 여부, 수험번호 및 문형의 표기가 정확한지 확인, 옆란에 서명 또는 날인

문번	답 란
1	① ② ③ ④ ⑤
2	① ② ③ ④ ⑤
3	① ② ③ ④ ⑤
4	① ② ③ ④ ⑤
5	① ② ③ ④ ⑤
6	① ② ③ ④ ⑤
7	① ② ③ ④ ⑤
8	① ② ③ ④ ⑤
9	① ② ③ ④ ⑤
10	① ② ③ ④ ⑤
11	① ② ③ ④ ⑤
12	① ② ③ ④ ⑤
13	① ② ③ ④ ⑤
14	① ② ③ ④ ⑤
15	① ② ③ ④ ⑤
16	① ② ③ ④ ⑤
17	① ② ③ ④ ⑤
18	① ② ③ ④ ⑤
19	① ② ③ ④ ⑤
20	① ② ③ ④ ⑤

문번	답 란
21	① ② ③ ④ ⑤
22	① ② ③ ④ ⑤
23	① ② ③ ④ ⑤
24	① ② ③ ④ ⑤
25	① ② ③ ④ ⑤
26	① ② ③ ④ ⑤
27	① ② ③ ④ ⑤
28	① ② ③ ④ ⑤
29	① ② ③ ④ ⑤
30	① ② ③ ④ ⑤
31	① ② ③ ④ ⑤
32	① ② ③ ④ ⑤
33	① ② ③ ④ ⑤
34	① ② ③ ④ ⑤
35	① ② ③ ④ ⑤
36	① ② ③ ④ ⑤
37	① ② ③ ④ ⑤
38	① ② ③ ④ ⑤
39	① ② ③ ④ ⑤
40	① ② ③ ④ ⑤

문번	답 란
41	① ② ③ ④ ⑤
42	① ② ③ ④ ⑤
43	① ② ③ ④ ⑤
44	① ② ③ ④ ⑤
45	① ② ③ ④ ⑤

✂ 절취선

[　　회] 리얼 오리지널 모의고사 답안지

③ 교시 영어영역

결시자 확인 (수험생은 표기하지 말것.)

| 검은색 컴퓨터용 사인펜을 사용하여 수험번호란과 옆란을 표기 | ○ |

※ 문제지 표지에 안내된 필적 확인 문구를 아래 '필적 확인란'에 정자로 반드시 기재하여야 합니다.

| 필 적 확인란 | |

| 성 명 | |

수 험 번 호

문형

홀수형 ○

짝수형 ○

※문제의 문형을 확인 후 표기

감독관 확인 (수험생은 표기 하지 말것)

(서 명 또는 날 인)

본인 여부, 수험번호 및 문형의 표기가 정확한지 확인, 옆란에 서명 또는 날인

※ 답안지 작성(표기)은 반드시 검은색 컴퓨터용 사인펜만을 사용하고, 연필 또는 샤프 등의 필기구를 절대 사용하지 마십시오.

문번	답 란
1	① ② ③ ④ ⑤
2	① ② ③ ④ ⑤
3	① ② ③ ④ ⑤
4	① ② ③ ④ ⑤
5	① ② ③ ④ ⑤
6	① ② ③ ④ ⑤
7	① ② ③ ④ ⑤
8	① ② ③ ④ ⑤
9	① ② ③ ④ ⑤
10	① ② ③ ④ ⑤
11	① ② ③ ④ ⑤
12	① ② ③ ④ ⑤
13	① ② ③ ④ ⑤
14	① ② ③ ④ ⑤
15	① ② ③ ④ ⑤
16	① ② ③ ④ ⑤
17	① ② ③ ④ ⑤
18	① ② ③ ④ ⑤
19	① ② ③ ④ ⑤
20	① ② ③ ④ ⑤

문번	답 란
21	① ② ③ ④ ⑤
22	① ② ③ ④ ⑤
23	① ② ③ ④ ⑤
24	① ② ③ ④ ⑤
25	① ② ③ ④ ⑤
26	① ② ③ ④ ⑤
27	① ② ③ ④ ⑤
28	① ② ③ ④ ⑤
29	① ② ③ ④ ⑤
30	① ② ③ ④ ⑤
31	① ② ③ ④ ⑤
32	① ② ③ ④ ⑤
33	① ② ③ ④ ⑤
34	① ② ③ ④ ⑤
35	① ② ③ ④ ⑤
36	① ② ③ ④ ⑤
37	① ② ③ ④ ⑤
38	① ② ③ ④ ⑤
39	① ② ③ ④ ⑤
40	① ② ③ ④ ⑤

문번	답 란
41	① ② ③ ④ ⑤
42	① ② ③ ④ ⑤
43	① ② ③ ④ ⑤
44	① ② ③ ④ ⑤
45	① ② ③ ④ ⑤

리얼 오리지널 I 예비 고1 〈반배치고사＋3월·6월 모의고사〉

③ 교시 영어영역

※ 답안지 작성(표기)은 반드시 검은색 컴퓨터용 사인펜만을 사용하고, 연필 또는 샤프 등의 필기구를 절대 사용하지 마십시오.

결시자 확인 (수험생은 표기하지 말것.)

| 검은색 컴퓨터용 사인펜을 사용하여 수험번호란과 옆란을 표기 | ○ |

※ 문제지 표지에 안내된 필적 확인 문구를 아래 '필적 확인란'에 정자로 반드시 기재하여야 합니다.

| 필 적 확인란 | |

| 성 명 | |

수 험 번 호

문형

홀수형 ○

짝수형 ○

※문제의 문형을 확인 후 표기

감독관 확인
(수험생은 표기 하지 말것)
(서 명 또는 날 인)
본인 여부, 수험번호 및 문형의 표기가 정확한지 확인, 옆란에 서명 또는 날인

문번	답 란	문번	답 란	문번	답 란
1	① ② ③ ④ ⑤	21	① ② ③ ④ ⑤	41	① ② ③ ④ ⑤
2	① ② ③ ④ ⑤	22	① ② ③ ④ ⑤	42	① ② ③ ④ ⑤
3	① ② ③ ④ ⑤	23	① ② ③ ④ ⑤	43	① ② ③ ④ ⑤
4	① ② ③ ④ ⑤	24	① ② ③ ④ ⑤	44	① ② ③ ④ ⑤
5	① ② ③ ④ ⑤	25	① ② ③ ④ ⑤	45	① ② ③ ④ ⑤
6	① ② ③ ④ ⑤	26	① ② ③ ④ ⑤		
7	① ② ③ ④ ⑤	27	① ② ③ ④ ⑤		
8	① ② ③ ④ ⑤	28	① ② ③ ④ ⑤		
9	① ② ③ ④ ⑤	29	① ② ③ ④ ⑤		
10	① ② ③ ④ ⑤	30	① ② ③ ④ ⑤		
11	① ② ③ ④ ⑤	31	① ② ③ ④ ⑤		
12	① ② ③ ④ ⑤	32	① ② ③ ④ ⑤		
13	① ② ③ ④ ⑤	33	① ② ③ ④ ⑤		
14	① ② ③ ④ ⑤	34	① ② ③ ④ ⑤		
15	① ② ③ ④ ⑤	35	① ② ③ ④ ⑤		
16	① ② ③ ④ ⑤	36	① ② ③ ④ ⑤		
17	① ② ③ ④ ⑤	37	① ② ③ ④ ⑤		
18	① ② ③ ④ ⑤	38	① ② ③ ④ ⑤		
19	① ② ③ ④ ⑤	39	① ② ③ ④ ⑤		
20	① ② ③ ④ ⑤	40	① ② ③ ④ ⑤		

리얼 오리지널 l 예비 고1 〈반배치고사+3월·6월 모의고사〉

✂ ─ 절취선

[회] 리얼 오리지널 모의고사 답안지

③ 교시 영어영역

※ 답안지 작성(표기)은 반드시 검은색 컴퓨터용 사인펜만을 사용하고, 연필 또는 샤프 등의 필기구를 절대 사용하지 마십시오.

결시자 확인 (수험생은 표기하지 말것.)

| 검은색 컴퓨터용 사인펜을 사용하여 수험번호란과 옆란을 표기 | ○ |

※ 문제지 표지에 안내된 필적 확인 문구를 아래 '필적 확인란'에 정자로 반드시 기재하여야 합니다.

| 필 적 확인란 | |

| 성 명 | |

수 험 번 호

문형

홀수형 ○

짝수형 ○

※문제의 문형을 확인 후 표기

감독관 확인
(수험생은 표기 하지 말것)
(서 명 또는 날 인)
본인 여부, 수험번호 및 문형의 표기가 정확한지 확인, 옆란에 서명 또는 날인

문번	답 란	문번	답 란	문번	답 란
1	① ② ③ ④ ⑤	21	① ② ③ ④ ⑤	41	① ② ③ ④ ⑤
2	① ② ③ ④ ⑤	22	① ② ③ ④ ⑤	42	① ② ③ ④ ⑤
3	① ② ③ ④ ⑤	23	① ② ③ ④ ⑤	43	① ② ③ ④ ⑤
4	① ② ③ ④ ⑤	24	① ② ③ ④ ⑤	44	① ② ③ ④ ⑤
5	① ② ③ ④ ⑤	25	① ② ③ ④ ⑤	45	① ② ③ ④ ⑤
6	① ② ③ ④ ⑤	26	① ② ③ ④ ⑤		
7	① ② ③ ④ ⑤	27	① ② ③ ④ ⑤		
8	① ② ③ ④ ⑤	28	① ② ③ ④ ⑤		
9	① ② ③ ④ ⑤	29	① ② ③ ④ ⑤		
10	① ② ③ ④ ⑤	30	① ② ③ ④ ⑤		
11	① ② ③ ④ ⑤	31	① ② ③ ④ ⑤		
12	① ② ③ ④ ⑤	32	① ② ③ ④ ⑤		
13	① ② ③ ④ ⑤	33	① ② ③ ④ ⑤		
14	① ② ③ ④ ⑤	34	① ② ③ ④ ⑤		
15	① ② ③ ④ ⑤	35	① ② ③ ④ ⑤		
16	① ② ③ ④ ⑤	36	① ② ③ ④ ⑤		
17	① ② ③ ④ ⑤	37	① ② ③ ④ ⑤		
18	① ② ③ ④ ⑤	38	① ② ③ ④ ⑤		
19	① ② ③ ④ ⑤	39	① ② ③ ④ ⑤		
20	① ② ③ ④ ⑤	40	① ② ③ ④ ⑤		

리얼 오리지널 l 예비 고1 〈반배치고사+3월·6월 모의고사〉

[회] 리얼 오리지널 모의고사 답안지

※ 답안지 작성(표기)은 반드시 검은색 컴퓨터용 사인펜만을 사용하고, 연필 또는 샤프 등의 필기구를 절대 사용하지 마십시오.

③ 교시 영어영역

결시자 확인 (수험생은 표기하지 말것.)

검은색 컴퓨터용 사인펜을 사용하여 수험번호란과 옆란을 표기	○

※ 문제지 표지에 안내된 필적 확인 문구를 아래 '필적 확인란'에 정자로 반드시 기재하여야 합니다.

필 적 확인란	

성 명

수 험 번 호

문형

홀수형 ○

짝수형 ○

※문제의 문형을 확인 후 표기

감독관 확인 (수험생은 표기하지 말것) (서 명 또는 날 인)

본인 여부, 수험번호 및 문형의 표기가 정확한지 확인, 옆란에 서명 또는 날인

문번	답 란
1	① ② ③ ④ ⑤
2	① ② ③ ④ ⑤
3	① ② ③ ④ ⑤
4	① ② ③ ④ ⑤
5	① ② ③ ④ ⑤
6	① ② ③ ④ ⑤
7	① ② ③ ④ ⑤
8	① ② ③ ④ ⑤
9	① ② ③ ④ ⑤
10	① ② ③ ④ ⑤
11	① ② ③ ④ ⑤
12	① ② ③ ④ ⑤
13	① ② ③ ④ ⑤
14	① ② ③ ④ ⑤
15	① ② ③ ④ ⑤
16	① ② ③ ④ ⑤
17	① ② ③ ④ ⑤
18	① ② ③ ④ ⑤
19	① ② ③ ④ ⑤
20	① ② ③ ④ ⑤

문번	답 란
21	① ② ③ ④ ⑤
22	① ② ③ ④ ⑤
23	① ② ③ ④ ⑤
24	① ② ③ ④ ⑤
25	① ② ③ ④ ⑤
26	① ② ③ ④ ⑤
27	① ② ③ ④ ⑤
28	① ② ③ ④ ⑤
29	① ② ③ ④ ⑤
30	① ② ③ ④ ⑤
31	① ② ③ ④ ⑤
32	① ② ③ ④ ⑤
33	① ② ③ ④ ⑤
34	① ② ③ ④ ⑤
35	① ② ③ ④ ⑤
36	① ② ③ ④ ⑤
37	① ② ③ ④ ⑤
38	① ② ③ ④ ⑤
39	① ② ③ ④ ⑤
40	① ② ③ ④ ⑤

문번	답 란
41	① ② ③ ④ ⑤
42	① ② ③ ④ ⑤
43	① ② ③ ④ ⑤
44	① ② ③ ④ ⑤
45	① ② ③ ④ ⑤

✂ 절취선

[회] 리얼 오리지널 모의고사 답안지

※ 답안지 작성(표기)은 반드시 검은색 컴퓨터용 사인펜만을 사용하고, 연필 또는 샤프 등의 필기구를 절대 사용하지 마십시오.

③ 교시 영어영역

결시자 확인 (수험생은 표기하지 말것.)

검은색 컴퓨터용 사인펜을 사용하여 수험번호란과 옆란을 표기	○

※ 문제지 표지에 안내된 필적 확인 문구를 아래 '필적 확인란'에 정자로 반드시 기재하여야 합니다.

필 적 확인란	

성 명

수 험 번 호

문형

홀수형 ○

짝수형 ○

※문제의 문형을 확인 후 표기

감독관 확인 (수험생은 표기하지 말것) (서 명 또는 날 인)

본인 여부, 수험번호 및 문형의 표기가 정확한지 확인, 옆란에 서명 또는 날인

문번	답 란
1	① ② ③ ④ ⑤
2	① ② ③ ④ ⑤
3	① ② ③ ④ ⑤
4	① ② ③ ④ ⑤
5	① ② ③ ④ ⑤
6	① ② ③ ④ ⑤
7	① ② ③ ④ ⑤
8	① ② ③ ④ ⑤
9	① ② ③ ④ ⑤
10	① ② ③ ④ ⑤
11	① ② ③ ④ ⑤
12	① ② ③ ④ ⑤
13	① ② ③ ④ ⑤
14	① ② ③ ④ ⑤
15	① ② ③ ④ ⑤
16	① ② ③ ④ ⑤
17	① ② ③ ④ ⑤
18	① ② ③ ④ ⑤
19	① ② ③ ④ ⑤
20	① ② ③ ④ ⑤

문번	답 란
21	① ② ③ ④ ⑤
22	① ② ③ ④ ⑤
23	① ② ③ ④ ⑤
24	① ② ③ ④ ⑤
25	① ② ③ ④ ⑤
26	① ② ③ ④ ⑤
27	① ② ③ ④ ⑤
28	① ② ③ ④ ⑤
29	① ② ③ ④ ⑤
30	① ② ③ ④ ⑤
31	① ② ③ ④ ⑤
32	① ② ③ ④ ⑤
33	① ② ③ ④ ⑤
34	① ② ③ ④ ⑤
35	① ② ③ ④ ⑤
36	① ② ③ ④ ⑤
37	① ② ③ ④ ⑤
38	① ② ③ ④ ⑤
39	① ② ③ ④ ⑤
40	① ② ③ ④ ⑤

문번	답 란
41	① ② ③ ④ ⑤
42	① ② ③ ④ ⑤
43	① ② ③ ④ ⑤
44	① ② ③ ④ ⑤
45	① ② ③ ④ ⑤

리얼 오리지널 I 예비 고1 〈반배치고사＋3월·6월 모의고사〉

절취선

SPEED 정답 체크

반 배치고사+3월·6월 전국연합 모의고사 | 예비 고1·영어

| 신입생 학급 배치고사 |

01회 고등학교 신입생 학급 배치고사

01③ 02③ 03④ 04① 05⑤ 06① 07④ 08③ 09③ 10⑤
11④ 12③ 13⑤ 14④ 15⑤ 16③ 17④ 18⑤ 19② 20⑤
21② 22③ 23③ 24⑤ 25② 26② 27② 28③ 29④ 30④

02회 고등학교 신입생 학급 배치고사

01② 02② 03⑤ 04① 05① 06① 07② 08② 09③ 10③
11④ 12③ 13② 14② 15③ 16④ 17⑤ 18④ 19③ 20④
21⑤ 22① 23⑤ 24④ 25③ 26① 27⑤ 28③ 29⑤ 30③

03회 고등학교 신입생 학급 배치고사

01⑤ 02④ 03③ 04① 05② 06③ 07⑤ 08③ 09⑤ 10①
11④ 12① 13⑤ 14③ 15④ 16③ 17③ 18④ 19⑤ 20①
21③ 22③ 23③ 24⑤ 25② 26① 27③ 28③ 29② 30⑤

| 3월 전국연합학력평가 |

04회 2023학년도 3월 전국연합학력평가

01⑤ 02⑤ 03③ 04⑤ 05② 06② 07① 08③ 09④ 10②
11② 12① 13③ 14① 15③ 16③ 17④ 18③ 19② 20⑤
21⑤ 22① 23① 24② 25⑤ 26② 27③ 28④ 29⑤ 30④
31① 32③ 33① 34② 35④ 36④ 37② 38④ 39③ 40①
41① 42③ 43③ 44④ 45④

05회 2022학년도 3월 전국연합학력평가

01① 02③ 03② 04④ 05④ 06③ 07① 08③ 09⑤ 10③
11① 12⑤ 13② 14② 15① 16④ 17④ 18② 19③ 20⑤
21⑤ 22① 23④ 24② 25⑤ 26③ 27⑤ 28⑤ 29③ 30⑤
31② 32③ 33① 34① 35④ 36③ 37② 38④ 39② 40①
41⑤ 42⑤ 43② 44④ 45⑤

06회 2021학년도 3월 전국연합학력평가

01④ 02④ 03① 04③ 05④ 06③ 07① 08② 09⑤ 10②
11① 12⑤ 13② 14③ 15④ 16② 17④ 18④ 19① 20⑤
21② 22⑤ 23① 24⑤ 25③ 26⑤ 27⑤ 28④ 29③ 30③
31⑤ 32④ 33① 34⑤ 35⑤ 36② 37③ 38② 39④ 40②
41① 42⑤ 43③ 44④ 45②

07회 2020학년도 3월 전국연합학력평가

01① 02⑤ 03③ 04④ 05⑤ 06② 07⑤ 08② 09④ 10②
11② 12① 13① 14③ 15⑤ 16⑤ 17④ 18④ 19⑤ 20②
21③ 22① 23② 24② 25④ 26④ 27③ 28④ 29② 30③
31③ 32① 33① 34① 35② 36⑤ 37④ 38⑤ 39③ 40①
41② 42③ 43③ 44④ 45⑤

08회 2024학년도 3월 대비 모의고사 [특별 부록]

01④ 02② 03⑤ 04④ 05① 06① 07③ 08④ 09③ 10④
11② 12③ 13① 14⑤ 16① 17③ 18① 19② 20①
21③ 22⑤ 23③ 24① 25③ 26④ 27⑤ 28④ 29④ 30⑤
31① 32⑤ 33② 34⑤ 35④ 36② 37③ 38② 39④ 40②
41③ 42⑤ 43② 44⑤ 45③

| 6월 전국연합학력평가 |

09회 2023학년도 6월 전국연합학력평가

01② 02① 03④ 04⑤ 05③ 06④ 07④ 08③ 09⑤ 10④
11① 12③ 13② 14⑤ 15⑤ 16③ 17④ 18② 19① 20⑤
21① 22③ 23② 24① 25④ 26② 27⑤ 28⑤ 29④ 30②
31④ 32① 33② 34① 35④ 36② 37⑤ 38② 39⑤ 40②
41① 42③ 43④ 44② 45③

10회 2022학년도 6월 전국연합학력평가

01② 02① 03⑤ 04⑤ 05① 06③ 07① 08⑤ 09⑤ 10④
11① 12③ 13③ 14④ 15④ 16② 17③ 18② 19② 20⑤
21② 22① 23② 24① 25⑤ 26③ 27④ 28② 29④ 30②
31① 32② 33③ 34② 35④ 36③ 37⑤ 38④ 39⑤ 40③
41① 42④ 43④ 44② 45④

11회 2021학년도 6월 전국연합학력평가

01② 02② 03② 04④ 05④ 06① 07③ 08② 09④ 10③
11② 12⑤ 13① 14⑤ 15③ 16③ 17④ 18① 19③ 20①
21③ 22⑤ 23② 24① 25⑤ 26③ 27⑤ 28④ 29⑤ 30③
31① 32⑤ 33① 34④ 35④ 36⑤ 37② 38③ 39④ 40①
41⑤ 42④ 43② 44② 45⑤

※ 절취선을 따라 잘라서 쓸 수 있습니다.

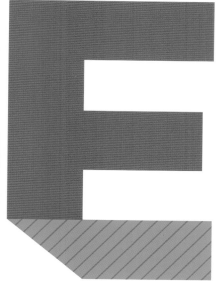
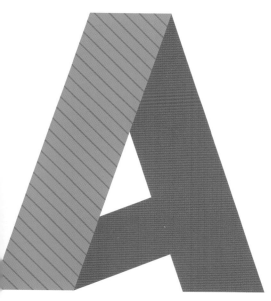

2024 리얼 오리지널

www.ipsifly.com

REAL

The Real series ipsifly provide questions in previous real test and you can practice as real college scholastic ability test.

545만권 베스트셀러
리얼 오리지널 시리즈 누적 판매
2006~2023

2 0 2 4 반 배 치 고 사 + 학 평 대 비

반 배치고사 +3월·6월 전국연합 모의고사

11회 [반 배치고사 3회 3월 5회 + 6월 3회]

반 배치+3월은 중3 과정! 6월 모의고사는 고1 1학기!

- 2024학년도 신입생 **반 배치고사** 대비 기출 모의고사 3회
- 최신 4개년 고1 [3월] 전국연합 학력평가 기출 4회
- 최신 3개년 고1 [6월] 전국연합 학력평가 기출 3회
- 고1 [1학기] 6월 모의고사까지 풀어 볼 수 있는 특별 구성
- 핵심 단어를 모두 수록한 **VOCA LIST & VOCA TEST**
- 입체적 해설로 [직독직해 · 구문 풀이 · 고난도 꿀팁] 수록
- 듣기 파일 [QR 코드] 수록 & MP3 파일 제공
- [특별 부록] 3월 대비 실전 모의고사 1회

예비 고1 영어

· 해 설 편 ·

수능 모의고사 전문 출판

| 신입생 학급 배치고사 |

01회 고등학교 신입생 학급 배치고사

01③ 02③ 03④ 04① 05⑤ 06① 07④ 08③ 09③ 10⑤
11④ 12② 13⑤ 14④ 15③ 16③ 17④ 18⑤ 19② 20⑤
21② 22③ 23③ 24⑤ 25② 26② 27③ 28③ 29④ 30④

02회 고등학교 신입생 학급 배치고사

01② 02② 03⑤ 04① 05① 06① 07② 08② 09③ 10③
11④ 12③ 13② 14② 15③ 16④ 17⑤ 18④ 19③ 20④
21⑤ 22① 23⑤ 24④ 25③ 26① 27⑤ 28③ 29⑤ 30③

03회 고등학교 신입생 학급 배치고사

01⑤ 02④ 03③ 04① 05② 06③ 07⑤ 08③ 09⑤ 10①
11④ 12② 13⑤ 14③ 15④ 16③ 17③ 18④ 19⑤ 20①
21③ 22③ 23③ 24⑤ 25② 26① 27③ 28③ 29② 30⑤

| 3월 전국연합학력평가 |

04회 2023학년도 3월 전국연합학력평가

01⑤ 02⑤ 03④ 04⑤ 05② 06② 07① 08③ 09④ 10②
11② 12① 13③ 14① 15③ 16③ 17④ 18③ 19② 20⑤
21⑤ 22① 23① 24② 25⑤ 26⑤ 27③ 28④ 29⑤ 30④
31① 32③ 33① 34④ 35④ 36④ 37② 38④ 39⑤ 40①
41② 42③ 43④ 44④ 45④

05회 2022학년도 3월 전국연합학력평가

01① 02③ 03② 04④ 05④ 06③ 07① 08③ 09⑤ 10③
11① 12⑤ 13② 14② 15① 16④ 17④ 18② 19③ 20⑤
21⑤ 22① 23④ 24② 25⑤ 26③ 27④ 28⑤ 29③ 30⑤
31② 32③ 33① 34① 35④ 36③ 37② 38④ 39② 40①
41⑤ 42⑤ 43② 44④ 45⑤

06회 2021학년도 3월 전국연합학력평가

01④ 02④ 03① 04③ 05④ 06③ 07① 08② 09⑤ 10②
11① 12① 13① 14③ 15④ 16② 17④ 18④ 19① 20③
21② 22⑤ 23① 24⑤ 25③ 26⑤ 27⑤ 28④ 29③ 30③
31⑤ 32④ 33① 34⑤ 35③ 36② 37⑤ 38② 39④ 40②
41① 42⑤ 43④ 44⑤ 45②

07회 2020학년도 3월 전국연합학력평가

01① 02⑤ 03③ 04④ 05⑤ 06② 07⑤ 08② 09④ 10②
11② 12① 13① 14③ 15⑤ 16⑤ 17④ 18④ 19⑤ 20②
21③ 22① 23② 24② 25④ 26④ 27③ 28④ 29② 30③
31③ 32① 33① 34① 35② 36⑤ 37④ 38⑤ 39③ 40①
41② 42③ 43③ 44④ 45⑤

08회 2024학년도 3월 대비 모의고사 [특별 부록]

01④ 02② 03⑤ 04④ 05① 06① 07③ 08④ 09③ 10④
11② 12③ 13② 14⑤ 15④ 16① 17③ 18① 19② 20①
21③ 22⑤ 23③ 24① 25③ 26④ 27⑤ 28④ 29④ 30⑤
31① 32⑤ 33② 34⑤ 35④ 36② 37③ 38② 39③ 40②
41③ 42⑤ 43④ 44⑤ 45③

| 6월 전국연합학력평가 |

09회 2023학년도 6월 전국연합학력평가

01② 02② 03① 04④ 05⑤ 06③ 07④ 08③ 09⑤ 10④
11② 12③ 13② 14⑤ 15⑤ 16③ 17④ 18② 19① 20⑤
21① 22③ 23④ 24① 25④ 26③ 27⑤ 28⑤ 29④ 30②
31④ 32① 33② 34③ 35④ 36① 37⑤ 38② 39⑤ 40②
41① 42③ 43④ 44② 45③

10회 2022학년도 6월 전국연합학력평가

01② 02① 03⑤ 04⑤ 05① 06③ 07① 08⑤ 09⑤ 10④
11① 12③ 13③ 14④ 15④ 16② 17③ 18② 19② 20⑤
21③ 22① 23② 24① 25⑤ 26③ 27④ 28② 29④ 30②
31① 32② 33③ 34② 35④ 36③ 37⑤ 38④ 39⑤ 40③
41① 42④ 43④ 44② 45④

11회 2021학년도 6월 전국연합학력평가

01② 02② 03② 04④ 05④ 06① 07③ 08③ 09④ 10③
11② 12⑤ 13① 14④ 15③ 16③ 17④ 18① 19③ 20①
21③ 22⑤ 23② 24① 25⑤ 26③ 27⑤ 28④ 29⑤ 30③
31① 32⑤ 33① 34④ 35④ 36⑤ 37② 38③ 39④ 40①
41⑤ 42④ 43② 44② 45⑤

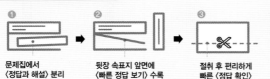

〈빠른 정답 보기〉 활용 안내

① 문제집에서 〈정답과 해설〉 분리

② 뒷장 속표지 앞면에 〈빠른 정답 보기〉 수록

③ 절취 후 편리하게 빠른 〈정답 확인〉

정답을 빨리 확인하고 채점할 수 있도록 〈**빠른 정답 보기**〉를 제공합니다.
❶ 문제집에서 책속의 책 〈정답과 해설〉을 분리하세요.
❷ 뒷장 속표지 앞면에 〈빠른 정답 보기〉가 있습니다.
❸ 절취선을 따라 자른 후 정답 확인할 때 사용하고, 책갈피처럼 사용하시면 분실을 예방할 수 있습니다.

반 배치고사 + 3월·6월
전국연합 모의고사

예비 고1 영어 [해설편]

Contents

Ⅰ 신입생 학급 배치고사

01회 고등학교 신입생 반배치 기출 002쪽

02회 고등학교 신입생 반배치 기출 007쪽

03회 고등학교 신입생 반배치 기출 012쪽

Ⅱ [3월] 전국연합학력평가

04회 2023학년도 3월 전국연합학력평가 017쪽

05회 2022학년도 3월 전국연합학력평가 031쪽

06회 2021학년도 3월 전국연합학력평가 044쪽

07회 2020학년도 3월 전국연합학력평가 058쪽

08회 2024학년도 3월 대비 실전 모의고사 [특별 부록] 071쪽

Ⅲ [6월] 전국연합학력평가

09회 2023학년도 6월 전국연합학력평가 085쪽

10회 2022학년도 6월 전국연합학력평가 098쪽

11회 2021학년도 6월 전국연합학력평가 111쪽

※ 수록된 정답률은 실제와 차이가 있을 수 있습니다.
   문제 난도를 파악하는데 참고용으로 활용하시기
   바랍니다.

· 정답 ·

01 ③ 02 ③ 03 ④ 04 ① 05 ⑤ 06 ① 07 ④ 08 ③ 09 ③ 10 ⑤ 11 ④ 12 ② 13 ⑤ 14 ④ 15 ③
16 ③ 17 ④ 18 ⑤ 19 ② 20 ⑤ 21 ② 22 ③ 23 ④ 24 ⑤ 25 ② 26 ② 27 ② 28 ③ 29 ④ 30 ④

---

01 악수의 의미 정답 ③

밑줄 친 This[this]가 가리키는 것으로 가장 적절한 것은? [2점]

① smiling – 미소 　② knocking – 노크 　✔③ handshaking – 악수
④ arm wrestling – 팔씨름 　⑤ crossing fingers – 손가락 겹치기

이것은 당신이 누군가를 만났을 때 "Hello"라고 인사하는 것의 옛날 방식이다. 먼 옛날에, 남자들은 "당신은 나를 신뢰해도 됩니다."라고 말하는 방법으로써 이것을 했다. 그가 칼을 뽑아 들 준비가 되어있지 않다는 것을 보여주기 위해서 남자는 그의 손을 다른 이에게 내밀었다. 서로는 상대편이 자신의 손에 어떤 무기도 없다는 것을 보고, 상대방을 신뢰할 수 있다고 알았다. 오늘날, 사람들은 "만나서 반갑습니다." 혹은 "환영합니다."를 의미하는 다정한 제스처로써 이것을 한다. 기네스북(1977)에 따르면, 애틀랜틱시티 시장인 Joseph Lazarow는 단 하루에 악수를 11,000번 이상 했다.

Why? 왜 정답일까?

요즘, 사람들은 "만나서 반갑습니다." 또는 "환영합니다."라는 표현을 하기 위해 우호적인 몸짓으로 이것을 한다(Today, people do this as a friendly gesture that means "Nice to meet you," or "Welcome.")고 말한다. 따라서 밑줄 친 This[this]가 가리키는 것으로 가장 적절한 것은 ③ 'handshaking(악수)'이다.

● ancient 고대의
● hold out(과거형 held out) 내밀다
● weapon 무기
● form 방식, 유형
● pull out 꺼내다
● according to ~에 따르면, ~에 따라

---

02 허리케인 피해자들을 돕기 위한 기부요청 정답 ③

다음 글의 목적으로 가장 적절한 것은? [3점]

① 자연재해의 위험성을 경고하려고
② 재난 사고 시 대처 요령을 안내하려고
✔③ 재난 피해자를 위한 기부를 요청하려고
④ 자원봉사 활동의 일정 변경을 공지하려고
⑤ 재난 피해자를 도운 것에 대해 감사하려고

시민 여러분께,

여러분께서 모두 텔레비전과 신문에서 사진을 보아서 아시는 바와 같이, 중앙아메리카가 일련의 허리케인으로 심하게 피해를 당했습니다. 수만 명의 사람들이 집을 잃었으며 먹을 것과 옷 같은 기본적인 생필품이 없습니다. 저는 우리가 그곳을 돕기 위해 어떤 일을 해야 한다고 느낍니다. 그래서 우리는 여러분께 통조림 제품, 따뜻한 옷, 담요, 그리고 돈을 기부하도록 부탁드립니다. 9월 10일 토요일 오전 10시에서 오후 4시 사이에 지역 센터로 모든 기부 물품을 가져와 주십시오. 그들이 도움을 절실하게 필요로 할 때에 여러분의 동료들을 도와주셔서 감사합니다.

George Anderson 올림

Why? 왜 정답일까?

중앙아메리카가 일련의 허리케인에 의해 심하게 피해를 당해서(~ Central America has been hit hard by a series of hurricanes.), 통조림 제품, 따뜻한 옷, 담요, 그리고 돈을 기부하도록 부탁드립니다(So, we are asking you to donate canned goods, warm clothes, blankets, and money.), 에서 허리케인 피해자를 위해서 기부를 부탁한다는 내용이 언급되어 있다. 따라서 글의 목적으로는 ③ '재난 피해자를 위한 기부를 요청하려고'가 가장 적절하다.

● a series of 일련의
● necessities 생필품
● blanket 담요
● in one's(소유격) time of ~의 시기에
● tens of thousands of 수만의
● donate 기부하다
● fellow 동료
● desperate 절실한

---

03 실수에서 배우는 점 정답 ④

다음 글의 밑줄 친 부분 중, 어법상 틀린 것은? [4점]

다음에 당신이 까다로운 난제를 마주쳤을 때, "내가 이 사안을 해결하기 위해서, 나는 9번 실패해야할 것이지만, 10번째 시도에서, 나는 성공할 것이다"라고 마음속으로 생각하라. 이러한 태도는 당신이 실패에 대한 두려움 없이 창의적으로 생각할 수 있게 해줄 것이다. 이것은 실패로부터의 배움이 성공을 향한 일보전진이라는 것을 당신이 이해하기 때문이다. 위험을 감수하라, 그리고 당신이 실패할 때 더 이상 "맙소사, 얼마나 시간과 노력 낭비인가!"라고 생각하지 마라. 대신에, 그 실수에서 배워라, 그리고 "멋진데! 한 번 넘어졌고, 아홉 번 남았어 ― 나는 앞으로 전진 하고 있는 거야!"라고 제대로 생각하라. 그리고 정말로 당신은 그렇다. 당신의 첫 번째 실패 이후에, "좋아, 10% 끝났어."라고 생각하라. 실수와 상실과 실패는 모두 더 깊은 이해와 창의적인 해결책으로의 길을 명확하게 가리키는 반짝이는 빛이다.

Why? 왜 정답일까?

④는 동사원형 learn으로 시작하는 명령문이고 and로 이어지는 병렬구조이므로 thinking을 동사원형 think로 고쳐야 한다. 따라서 어법상 틀린 것은 ④이다.

Why? 왜 오답일까?

① 'in order + to부정사'는 '~하기 위하여'의 의미로 ①이 포함된 문장에선 '문제를 해결하기 위해서'의 의미이므로 어법상 적절하다.
② understand 뒤에 that은 that 이하(목적어)를 이끄는 접속사이므로 어법상 적절하다.
③ 'what + a(an) + (형용사) + 명사 + (주어) + (동사)'의 감탄문 형태이므로 어법상 적절하다.
⑤ 주어가 복수형인 'Mistakes, loss and failure'이므로 복수 동사 are이 온 것은 어법상 적절하다.

● challenge 도전
● issue 문제, 쟁점
● attitude 태도
● make forward progress 앞으로 나아가다, 도약하다
● indeed 정말, 사실로
● resolve 해결하다
● attempt 시도
● misstep 실수

---

04 화가 난 상황에서 벗어나는 방법 정답 ①

(A), (B), (C)의 각 네모 안에서 문맥에 맞는 날말로 가장 적절한 것은? [4점]

	(A)	(B)	(C)
✔①	tied 연결된	disappear 사라지다	bothering 괴롭히고 있는
②	tied 연결된	disappear 사라지다	pleasing 즐거운
③	tied 연결된	appear 나타나다	bothering 괴롭히고 있는
④	unrelated 관련 없는	disappear 사라지다	pleasing 즐거운
⑤	unrelated 관련 없는	appear 나타나다	pleasing 즐거운

대부분의 사람에게 감정은 상황적이다. 현 시점의 뭔가가 여러분을 화나게 한다면 그 감정 자체는 그것이 일어나는 상황과 (A) 연결되어 있다. 여러분이 그 감정의 상황 속에 남아있는 한 화가 난 상태에 머물기 쉽다. 여러분이 그 상황을 '떠나면', 정반대가 사실이 된다. 여러분이 그 상황에서 벗어나자마자 그 감정은 (B) 사라지기 시작한다. 그 상황에서 벗어나게 되면 그것(상황)은 여러분을 제어하지 못한다. 상담원은 (상담) 의뢰인에게 그들을 (C) 괴롭히고 있는 그 어떤 것과도 약간의 감정적 거리를 두라고 자주 충고한다. 그것을 하는 한 가지 쉬운 방법은 여러분이 화의 근원에서 여러분 자신을 '지리적으로' 떼어놓는 것이다.

Why? 왜 정답일까?

(A) 사람에게 있어 감정은 상황적이라 뭔가가 여러분을 화나게 하면(Something in the here and now makes you mad,) 그 상황과 연결되어 있다고 하는 것이 자연스럽기 때문에 (A)에 적절한 어휘는 tied(연결된)이다.
(B) 여러분이 그 상황을 떠나면 정반대가 사실이 된다(If you leave the situation, the opposite is true.)는 앞 문장을 통해 감정이 사라진다고 해야 자연스럽다. 따라서 (B)에 적절한 어휘는 disappear(사라지다)이다.
(C) 상담원이 의뢰인에게 어떤 것과 감정적 거리를 두라고 자주 충고한다(Counselors often advise clients to get some emotional distance from whatever is ~.)라는 문장을 통해 (C)에 적절한 어휘는 bothering(괴롭히고 있는)이다. 따라서 정답은 ①이다.

● situational 상황에 따른
● unrelated 관련이 없는
● remain 계속하다, 유지하다
● opposite 반대의
● prevent 막다, 방해하다
● counselor 상담원
● geographically 지리적으로
● source 출처, 근원
● the here and now 현 시점, 현재
● as long as ~인 한
● be likely to ~할 것 같다
● move away from ~에서 벗어나다
● take hold of ~을 제어하다(붙잡다)
● client 의뢰인, 고객
● separate A from B A와 B를 구별하다

---

05 발을 바깥 쪽으로 해서 대화할 때 발이 뜻하는 것 정답 ⑤

다음 빈칸에 들어갈 말로 가장 적절한 것을 고르시오. [3점]

① talk – 이야기하다 　② join – 함께하다 　③ argue – 주장하다
④ follow – 따르다 　✔⑤ escape – 도망치다

두 사람이 서로에게 이야기 할 때, 그들은 대개 정면으로 마주보고 말한다. 하지만 만약 두 사람 중 한 명이 그의 발을 약간 돌리거나 발 한 짝을 반복적으로 바깥방향으로 움직인다면 (발 한 짝은 당신 쪽으로 하고 다른 한 짝은 당신에서 떨어져 있는 L 대형으로), 당신은 그가 벗어나고 싶거나 혹은 그가 어딘가 다른 곳에 있기를 바란다고 확신할 수도 있다. 사람의 몸통은 예의상 여전히 당신을 마주 본채로 남아있을 수도 있지만, 발은 도망치고 싶은 두뇌의 필요나 욕구를 더욱 정직하게 반영하는지도 모른다.

Why? 왜 정답일까?

두 사람이 대화를 할 때 보통 마주보고 이야기 한다고 말하면서 그러나 한명이 발을 꼬아서 돌리거나 하는 상대를 외면하는 형태로 움직인다면 그가 벗어나고 싶거나 어딘가 다른 장소로 도망치기를 바란다(the brain's need or desire to escape.)는 것을 알 수 있다는 내용의 글이다. 따라서 문맥상 적절한 어휘는 ⑤ '도망치다'이다.

● normally 보통, 정상적으로
● slightly 약간
● outward 밖으로 향하는, 표면상의
● out of politeness 예의상
● toe to toe 마주보며, 정면에서
● repeatedly 반복적으로
● formation 형태, 형성
● reflect 비추다, 반영하다

---

06 용기 있게 도전하기 정답 ①

다음 빈칸에 들어갈 말로 가장 적절한 것을 고르시오. [4점]

✔① being courageous – 용기를 내는 것
② helping others – 다른 사람을 돕는 것
③ making friends – 친구를 사귀는 것
④ recovering health – 건강을 되찾는 것
⑤ encouraging patients – 환자를 격려하는 것

용기 있는 것에 대해 여러분의 마음을 바꿀 만한 충고를 하나 하겠다. 의사가 당신에게 이제 살 수 있는 날이 6개월뿐이고, 이제껏 하고 싶었던 모든 일을 해보라고 권했다고 가정해 보자. 무엇을 하겠는가? 스카이다이빙이나 절벽 등반을 하거나, 혹은 한 달 동안 숲 속에서 혼자 살아 보기를 늘 원했지만 다칠까 두려웠는가? 지금 그 일들을 시도한다고 뭐가 달라지겠는가? 거의 틀림없이 그것을 헤쳐 나갈 것이고, 그것이 당신에게 남아 있는 시간을 풍요롭게 해 줄 것이다. 밖으로 나가서 모든 두려움에 용감하게 맞섰노라고 말하는 게 낫지 않겠는가? 왜 사형 선고를 받을 때까지 기다리는가? 그것이 당신에게 그렇게 중요하다면, 지금 하라.

Why? 왜 정답일까?

필자는 당신에게 이제 살 수 있는 날이 6개월뿐임을 가정해 보라(Suppose that your doctor said that you have six months to live ~.)고 하며 하고 싶지만 두려워서 하지 못했던 일에 도전하라는 내용이다. 따라서 빈칸에 들어갈 말로 가장 적절한 것은 ① '용기를 내는 것'이다.

- **suppose** 가정하다
- **sky dive** 스카이다이빙을 하다
- **cliff** 절벽
- **attempt** 시도하다
- **live through** ~을 헤쳐 나가다
- **face** 맞서다
- **recommend** 권하다
- **climb** 등반하다, 오르다
- **harm** 다치게 하다
- **certainly** 틀림없이
- **enrich** 풍요롭게 하다

---

07 부모가 자녀들과 독서를 해야 하는 이유 정답 ④

다음 빈칸에 들어갈 말로 가장 적절한 것을 고르시오. [3점]

① visual aids – 시각적인 도움
② word memorization – 단어 암기
③ competition with others – 다른 이들과 하는 경쟁
④ the input of both parents – 양쪽 부모의 개입
⑤ the experience of writing – 글쓰기 경험

아이들에게 독서를 위한 배움의 중요한 요소는 양쪽 부모의 개입이다. 국립 독서 재단의 리포트는 아버지들의 40%가 그들 자신이 그럴 것보다 자신의 배우자가 아이들과 함께 독서를 더 많이 할 것 같다고 믿는다는 것을 강조했다. 더한 것은, 아이들 중 25%에 이르기까지 자신들의 아빠가 독서하는 것을 본 적이 없었다. 하지만 만약 아버지들이 그들의 아이들과 함께 독서할 시간을 마련한다면, 그것은 그들 아이들의 삶에 막대한 영향을 끼칠 것이다. 아버지 협회에 따르면, 독서는 더욱 친밀한 아버지-아이 관계를 낳고 향상된 아이의 행동과 높은 성취로 이어질 수 있다.

Why? 왜 정답일까?

아버지가 그들의 자녀들과 독서할 시간을 낸다면, 그것은 자녀들의 삶에 큰 영향을 끼칠 것(But if fathers could find the time to read with their children, it would have a huge impact on the lives of their children.)이라고 한다. 따라서 빈칸에 들어갈 말로 적절한 것은 ④ '양쪽 부모의 개입'이다.

- **be likely to** ~할 것 같다
- **according to** ~에 따르면
- **impact on** ~에 영향을 주다
- **achievement** 성취, 달성

---

08 신생아가 있을 때 음식을 잘 먹기 위한 방법 정답 ③

다음 빈칸에 들어갈 말로 가장 적절한 것을 고르시오. [4점]

① your baby cries to be fed at night – 아기가 밤에 먹을 것을 달라고 울어대다
② you find a new recipe for your meal – 식사를 위한 새로운 요리법을 찾아내다
③ you are really hungry to think about eating – 먹고 싶은 생각이 들 정도로 매우 배고프다
④ your kids finish all the food on their plates – 자녀들이 접시 위에 있는 모든 음식을 다 먹다
⑤ you feel like taking a nap after a heavy meal – 음식을 많이 먹은 후 낮잠을 자고 싶은 기분이 들다

신생아가 생기면 잘 먹는 것이 항상 쉬운 것은 아니다. 맛있고 영양가 많은 식사를 준비할 시간, 혹은 심지어 그것을 먹을 시간조차 없는 것처럼 보일 수도 있다. 다음 요령을 배울 필요가 있을 것이다. 먹고 싶은 생각이 들 정도로 매우 배고파질 때까지 기다리려고 하지 마라. 신생아가 있으면, 음식을 준비하는 일이 평상시보다 아마 시간이 더 오래 걸릴 것이다. 이미 배고픔을 느낄 때 (음식 준비를) 시작하게 되면, 음식이 준비되기 전에 대단히 배가 고플 것이다. 배가 몹시 고프고 피곤하면, 건강하게 먹는 것이 어렵다. 기름진 패스트푸드, 초콜릿, 쿠키 혹은 감자 칩을 먹고 싶어질 수도 있다. 이런 종류의 음식은 가끔은 괜찮겠지만, 매일 그렇지는 않다.

Why? 왜 정답일까?

신생아가 있을 땐 잘 먹는 것이 어려우므로 잘 먹을 수 있는 방법을 나열하고 있다. 신생아가 있으면 음식을 준비하는 데 시간이 더 오래 걸리고(When you have a newborn baby, preparing food will probably take longer than usual.) 음식이 준비되기 전에 배가 몹시 고파서(~ you will be absolutely starving before the food is ready.) 음식이 다 될 때까지 참지 못하고 건강에 나쁜 음식을 먹게 되니 배가 고플 때까지 기다리지 말고 음식을 미리 준비하라는 내용이다. 따라서 빈칸에 들어갈 내용으로 가장 적절한 것은 ③ '먹고 싶은 생각이 들 정도로 매우 배고프다'이다.

- **newborn baby** 신생아
- **nutritious** 영양가 많은
- **probably** 아마
- **starve** 매우 배고프다, 굶주리다
- **chip** (감자튀김 따위의) 얇은 조각
- **recipe** 요리법
- **take a nap** 낮잠을 자다
- **prepare** 준비하다
- **trick** 요령, 비결
- **absolutely** 대단히, 절대적으로
- **fatty** 기름진
- **feed** 먹을 것을 주다, 먹이다
- **feel like -ing** ~하고 싶은 기분이 들다

---

09 육지의 다양한 특징 정답 ③

다음 글의 밑줄 친 부분 중, 문맥상 낱말의 쓰임이 적절하지 <u>않은</u> 것은? [3점]

당신은 아마도 땅의 여러 가지 ① 다른 지형을 본 적이 있을 것이다. 아마도 당신은 산의 정

상으로 하이킹하러 간 적이 있을 것이다. 산은 지형이다. 지형은 모종의 형태를 가지고 자연적으로 형성된 지구 표면의 한 부분이다. 지구는 여러 종류의 지형으로 이루어져 있다. 산은 가장 ② 눈에 띄는 지형이다. 산은 땅의 ③ 하강한(→ 높아진) 부분이며, 대개 뾰족한 측면을 가지고, 그것 주변 지역 위로 솟아 있다. 어떤 산들은 높고, 암석으로 되어 있고, 눈으로 ④ 덮여있다. 다른 것들은 나무로 덮여있다. 또 다른 지구의 지형은 평원이다. 그것은 대부분 ⑤ 납작한 넓은 대지 구역이다. 평원은 종종 풍부한 토양으로 이루어져 있고 양질의 농지를 만든다.

Why? 왜 정답일까?

산은 보통 뾰족한 측면을 가지고 주변 지역 위로 솟아올라 있다(~ usually with sharp sides, that rises above the area around it.)고 했으므로 육지의 낮아진 부분이 아니라 높아진 부분이라고 해야 자연스럽다. 따라서 문맥상 낱말의 쓰임이 적절하지 않은 것은 ③이다.

- **probably** 아마도
- **landform** 지형
- **plain** 평원, 평야
- **feature** 특색
- **be covered with** ~으로 덮이다

---

10 레이저 포인터의 단점 정답 ⑤

(A), (B), (C)의 각 네모 안에서 문맥에 맞는 낱말로 가장 적절한 것은? [4점]

	(A)		(B)		(C)
①	strengths 강점	……	shown 드러난	……	inferior 열등한
②	strengths 강점	……	hidden 감춰진	……	superior 우세한
③	weaknesses 약점	……	shown 드러난	……	superior 우세한
④	weaknesses 약점	……	hidden 감춰진	……	superior 우세한
⑤	weaknesses 약점	……	shown 드러난	……	inferior 열등한

1990년대에 인기를 끌었던 레이저 포인터는 처음에는 대체로 손에 쥐기에 두꺼웠다. 오래지 않아, 이 포인터는 더 얇은 주머니형 모델이 출시되면서 다루기가 더 쉬워졌다. 그럼에도 불구하고, 레이저 포인터에는 그 자체의 (A) 약점이 있었다. 건전지가 필요했고 이를 교체해야 했으며, 긴장한 강연자의 떨리는 손동작이 반짝이는 붉은 점의 갑작스런 움직임 속에 (B) 드러났다. 더욱이, 이 붉은 점은 특정 배경에서는 보기 어려워서 레이저 포인터를 심지어 단순한 지시봉보다 (C) 열등하게 만들었다. 이 문제를 바로잡기 위해 더 발전된, 그래서 더 비싼 초록빛 레이저 포인터가 도입되게 되었다.

Why? 왜 정답일까?

(A) 처음에 두꺼워서 불편했던 것이 얇아졌다는 내용 바로 뒤에 '그럼에도 불구하고'라는 접속부사가 쓰였으므로 '약점'의 의미인 weaknesses가 자연스럽다.
(B) 레이저 포인터의 약점에 대해 설명하고 있고, 긴장한 강연자의 떨리는 손동작이 붉은 점에 드러났다고 해야 문맥상 자연스러우므로 '드러난'의 의미인 shown이 들어가야 한다.
(C) 붉은 색 레이저 포인터의 단점에 대해 계속해서 설명하고 있으므로 '열등한'이라는 의미인 inferior가 적절하다. 따라서 정답은 ⑤이다.

- **thick** 두꺼운
- **strength** 강점
- **lecturer** 강연자
- **inferior** 열등한
- **correct** 바로잡다
- **introduce** 도입하다, 소개하다
- **handle** 다루다
- **weakness** 약점
- **glowing** 반짝이는
- **superior** 우세한
- **advanced** 발전된, 고급의

---

11 고등학생들이 수면이 부족한 이유 정답 ④

다음 도표의 내용과 일치하지 <u>않는</u> 것은? [3점]

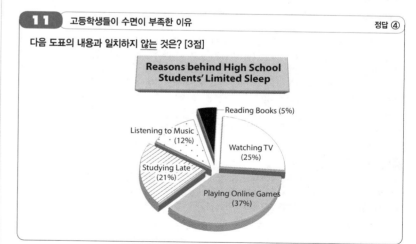

고등학생들이 수면이 부족한 이유

작년 한국의 고등학생들은 하룻밤 평균 5시간 27분 잤다. 원인을 찾기 위해 설문 조사가 행해졌다. 위의 차트는 왜 대부분의 고등학생들이 충분히 잘 수 없었는지를 보여주고 있다. ① 온라인 게임을 하는 것이 수면 부족의 첫 번째 이유였다. ② 학생 4분의 1은 그들이 TV를 봤거나 때문에 충분히 잠을 잘 수 없었다고 응답했다. ③ 밤늦게 공부하는 것은 이번 조사에서 세 번째로 높은 비율을 차지했다. ④ 음악 감상은 밤늦게 공부하는 것보다 높은 순위를 차지했다. ⑤ 학생 중 단지 5%만이 책을 읽느라 충분히 자지 못했다고 응답했다.

Why? 왜 정답일까?

늦게까지 공부하는 비율은 21%이고 음악 듣기는 12%이므로 늦게까지 공부하는 비율이 음악 듣기보다 더 높다. 따라서 도표의 내용과 일치하지 않는 것은 ④이다.

- **reason** 이유
- **average** 평균(의)
- **reply** 대답하다
- **per** ~마다, ~당
- **survey** 조사

12 비가 그친 후 활기찬 분위기   정답 ②

다음 글의 분위기로 가장 적절한 것은? [2점]

① sad and gloomy
슬프고 우울한
② ✔ merry and lively
즐겁고 활기 넘치는
③ tense and urgent
긴장되고 긴급한
④ funny and humorous
재미있고 유머러스한
⑤ boring and monotonous
지루하고 단조로운

비가 그쳤다. 도로는 깨끗했고, 나무에서 먼지가 씻겨 나갔다. 땅에서는 새로운 기운이 돋아났다. 개구리들은 연못에서 시끄럽게 울어댔다. 그들은 몸집이 컸고 목구멍이 즐거움으로 부풀어 있었다. 풀은 작은 물방울들로 인해 반짝이고 있었다. 몇몇 남자아이들이 비가 와서 만들어진 길 옆 작은 개울에서 놀고 있었다. 그들과 그들의 밝은 눈을 보는 것은 흐뭇한 일이었다. 그들은 이제까지 없던 재미를 맛보고 있었으며, 나는 그들이 매우 행복하다는 것을 알 수 있었다. 누군가 그들에게 뭔가를 말했을 때, 비록 그들은 한 마디 말도 이해하지 못했지만, 즐거워서 웃음을 터뜨렸다.

Why? 왜 정답일까?

땅에서 새로운 기운이 돋아나고, 개구리가 울고, 풀은 반짝였고, 아이들은 즐거워서 웃음을 터뜨렸다는 내용에서 ② '즐겁고 활기 넘치는' 분위기를 느낄 수 있다.

- dust 먼지
- pond 연못
- swell(– swelled – swollen) 부풀리다
- stream 개울
- have the time of one's life 이제까지 없던 재미를 맛보다
- refresh 새롭게 하다, 기운나게 하다
- throat 목구멍, 목청
- sparkle 반짝이다

13 배우자 선택 시 후각이 미치는 영향   정답 ⑤

글의 흐름으로 보아, 주어진 문장이 들어가기에 가장 적절한 곳을 고르시오. [4점]

어떤 과학자들은 우리의 배우자 선택이 우리의 후각을 따르는 단순한 문제라고 설명한다. ① 스위스 Lausanne 대학의 Claus Wedekind는 젖은 티셔츠를 가지고 재미있는 실험을 실시했다. ② 그는 49명의 여성들에게 이전에 다양한 신원미상의 남자들이 입었던 티셔츠의 냄새를 맡아 달라고 부탁했다. ③ 그는 그 후 여성들에게 어떤 티셔츠가 가장 냄새가 좋고 어떤 것이 가장 나빴는지 순위를 매겨 달라고 부탁했다. ④ 그는 여성은 자신과 가장 유전적으로 차이 나는 남성이 입었던 티셔츠의 냄새를 선호한다는 것을 발견했다. ⑤ 이러한 유전적인 차이는 그 남성의 면역 체계가 여성에게 없는 어떤 것을 지니고 있을 것 같다는 걸 의미한다. 그를 그녀 아이의 아버지로 선택함으로써, 그녀는 그녀 아이가 건강할 가능성을 높인다.

Why? 왜 정답일까?

그는 여성들이 자신과 가장 유전적으로 다른 남성이 입은 티셔츠의 냄새를 선호한다는 것을 알았다고 (He found that women preferred the smell of a T-shirt worn by a man who was the most genetically different from her.) 말한 뒤에 주어진 문장이 위치하고 난 후 아이의 아버지를 그렇게 선택함으로써 아이들이 건강할 가능성을 높이는 것이라는 말로 이어지고 있다. 따라서 주어진 문장이 들어가기에 가장 적절한 곳은 ⑤이다.

- immune 면역성이 있는
- experiment 실험
- prefer ~을 (더) 좋아하다
- increase 증가하다
- possess 소유하다
- unidentified 정체 불명의
- genetically 유전적으로

14 쇼핑 정보 검색   정답 ④

글의 흐름으로 보아, 주어진 문장이 들어가기에 가장 적절한 곳을 고르시오. [4점]

쇼핑객들은 보통 지출할 수 있는 돈의 양이 한정되어 있고, 쇼핑할 수 있는 시간도 한정되어 있다. ① 쇼핑이 사실 정보 검색이라고 깨닫는 것은 중요하다. ② 여러분은 광고, 친구, 판매원, 라벨, 잡지 기사, 인터넷, 또는 몇몇 다른 출처에서 정보를 얻을 수 있다. ③ 여러분은 또한 옷을 입어보거나, 자동차 시험 운전을 해보거나, 헬스클럽에서 판촉 행사를 이용하는 것 같이 그 제품을 직접 사용하는 것에서 정보를 얻을 수도 있다. ④ 그러나 쇼핑객들은 이러한 정보의 출처 중에서 어떤 것을 얻는 것에는 비용이 든다는 것을 이해해야 한다. 이러한 비용에는 교통비와 시간이 포함될 수 있다. ⑤ 오직 여러분만이 그 비용을 감수할지 말지를 결정할 수 있다.

Why? 왜 정답일까?

④ 뒤에 나오는 문장의 These costs는 주어진 문장의 costs를 가리키고, 주어진 문장의 these sources of information은 ②와 ③ 다음에 나오는 문장에서 설명하고 있는 정보의 출처를 가리키므로 ④에 들어가는 것이 자연스럽다. 따라서 주어진 문장이 들어가기에 가장 적절한 곳은 ④이다.

- source 출처
- amount 양
- obtain 얻다
- product 제품
- include 포함하다
- limited 한정된, 제한된
- search 검색, 탐색
- article 기사
- take advantage of ~을 이용하다
- decide 결정하다

15 가상의 물   정답 ③

다음 글에서 전체 흐름과 관계 없는 문장을 고르시오. [4점]

우리의 음식과 제품에 내포된 물은 '가상의 물(공산품·농축산물의 제조·재배에 드는 물)'이라고 불린다. 예를 들어 2파운드의 밀을 생산하기 위해서 약 265갤런의 물이 필요하다. ① 그래서 이 2파운드의 밀이 필요한 가상의 물은 265갤런이다. ② 가상의 물은 또한 유제품, 수프, 음료, 그리고 액체로 된 약에도 있다. ③ 하지만 건강을 유지하기 위해 가능한 한 많은 물을 마시는 것이 필요하다. ④ 매일 인간은 다양한 가상의 물을 소비하는데 가상의 물의 함유량은 제품에 따라 다르다. ⑤ 예를 들어 2파운드의 고기를 생산하려면 2파운드의 채소를 생산하는 것의 약 5배에서 10배의 물이 필요하다.

Why? 왜 정답일까?

가상의 물이 무엇인지 언급하며 그것이 들어있는 식품 등의 예를 나열하며 설명하는 글인데 ③에서 건강을 유지하기 위한 물의 필요성을 얘기하고 있다. 따라서 글의 전체 흐름과 관계 없는 문장은 ③이다.

- embedded 내포된, 포함된
- virtual 가상의
- dairy product 유제품
- liquid medicine 물약
- consume 소비하다
- vary 다르다, 차이가 있다
- manufacture 제조하다
- wheat 밀
- beverage 음료
- as ~ as possible 가능한 ~한
- content 함유량, 내용물, 만족하다
- require 필요하다

16 초기 아메리카 원주민들의 생활 방식   정답 ③

다음 글에서 전체 흐름과 관계 없는 문장을 고르시오. [3점]

초기 아메리카 원주민들은 필요한 모든 것을 만들어야 했다. ① 각 부족이 도구, 옷, 장난감, 주거, 음식을 만드는 데 사용한 각종 재료들은 주변에서 발견한 것에 달려 있었다. ② 또한, 그들이 만든 것은 자신의 생활 방식에 적합했다. ③ 대부분의 부족은 고유 언어를 사용하고 있었지만, 다른 부족들과 의사소통할 수 있었다. ④ 예를 들면, 대초원에서 이동을 많이 하며 사는 부족은 점토로 된 그릇을 만들지 않았다. ⑤ 점토 그릇은 너무 무겁고 운반할 때 깨지기 쉬워서 그들은 동물 가죽으로 된 용기를 만들었다.

Why? 왜 정답일까?

초기 아메리카 원주민들이 생활이 필요한 것들을 삶의 방식에 맞게 만들어야 했다(Early native Americans had to make everything they needed.)고 설명하는 글이다. 따라서 글의 흐름과 관계 없는 문장은 ③이다.

- native 타고난, 원래의
- clothing 의류
- depend upon(on) ~에 의존하다
- travel 이동하다
- container 용기
- tribe 부족
- shelter 주거
- the Plains 대초원
- clay 진흙

17 생산적인 질문하기   정답 ④

다음 글의 빈칸 (A), (B)에 들어갈 말로 가장 적절한 것은? [3점]

	(A)		(B)
①	Therefore 그러므로	……	Similarly 비슷하게
②	For example 예를 들어	……	Instead 대신에
③	However 하지만	……	Similarly 비슷하게
✔④	However 하지만	……	Instead 대신에
⑤	For example 예를 들어	……	By contrast 그에 반해서

당신이 고통스럽게 느린 속도로 움직이고 있는 꼬리를 문 교통정체 안에 있는 동안, 당신은 "어떻게 이 교통 체증이 정리될 수 있을까?"라고 궁금해 한다. 그 답변은 쉽지만 실용적이지는 않다. 즉, 도로를 넓히거나 추가의 고속도로를 건설함으로써 유동을 증대시키는 것이다. (A) 하지만, 현실은 만약 당신이 대통령이나 주지사가 아니라면, 해결책 또한 일어나게 만들 수 없다는 것이다. 따라서 당신의 스트레스 지수는 당신의 혈압과 함께 상승한다, 당신의 질문이 잘못된 것은 아니다. (B) 대신에, "이 교통체증에서의 여분의 40분을 가지고, 그 시간을 어떻게 효과적으로 사용할 수 있을까?"를 물어라. 이제 당신은 생산적인 질문을 하고 있는 것이다. 당신을 즐겁게 하는 음악이나 당신을 교육할 오디오 책을 듣는 것을 고려할 수 있다.

Why? 왜 정답일까?

교통 정체 안에 있다면 도로를 넓히거나 추가로 고속도로를 만들어서 흐름을 확대하는 것이라고 말하고 있는데 (A) 뒤에서는 이 방안이 대통령이나 통치자가 아니면 그 해결책대로 해결할 수도 없다고 말하면서 내용이 역전되기 때문에 '하지만'인 'However'가 오는 것이 적절하다. (B)의 앞에서는 그런 질문이 답은 쉽지만 스트레스 지수와 혈압이 올라간다고 말했고 (B) 뒤에 이 교통체증의 시간을 효과적으로 어떻게 쓸 수 있을지를 물으라는 내용의 이야기가 나오므로 빈칸에는 '~대신에'의 의미를 나타내는 'Instead'가 오는 것이 적절하다. 따라서 빈칸에 들어갈 말로 적절한 것은 ④ '하지만(However) – 대신에(Instead)'이다.

- traffic 교통(량)
- additional 추가의
- president 대통령
- blood pressure 혈압
- painfully 극도로
- unless …하지 않는 한
- governor 총독
- entertain 접대하다

18 농장 체험에 대한 안내문   정답 ⑤

Farm Experience Days에 관한 다음 안내문의 내용과 일치하지 않는 것은? [2점]

① 소, 양, 돼지에게 먹이를 줄 수 있다.
② 날씨에 따라 당일 체험 활동이 달라질 수 있다.
③ 점심 비용이 참가비에 포함되어 있다.
④ 예약이 필요하다.
✔⑤ 주말에도 이용할 수 있다.

농장 체험의 날

오셔서 저희의 '농장 체험의 날'을 즐기세요.

여기 여러분이 즐길 수 있는 몇 가지 활동이 있습니다.

■ 암탉의 달걀을 수거할 수 있습니다.

■ 「소, 양, 돼지에게 먹이를 줄 수 있습니다.」←「」: ①의 근거일치

■ 농장을 돌아보며 동물에 대해 배울 수 있습니다.

– 「날씨에 따라서 당일 (체험) 활동이 달라질 수 있습니다.」 ┌「」: ②의 근거(일치)

– 「참가비는 1인당 50달러입니다. 여기에는 정성을 들여 손수 만든 점심이 포함되어 있습니다.」
└「」: ③의 근거(일치)

– 「예약이 필요합니다.」 ┌「」: ④의 근거(일치)

– 「평일에만 문을 엽니다.」 ──「」: ⑤의 근거(불일치)

추가 정보를 원하시면 5252-7088로 전화 주십시오.

Why? 왜 정답일까?

'We're only open on weekdays.'라는 문장을 통해 평일에만 '농장 체험의 날'이 열린다는 것을 알 수 있다. 따라서 안내문의 내용과 일치하지 않는 것은 ⑤ '주말에도 이용할 수 있다.'이다.

Why? 왜 오답일까?

① 'Feed the cows, sheep, and pigs'의 내용과 일치한다.
② 'The activities of the day may change according to the weather.'의 내용과 일치한다.
③ 'The fee is $50 per person. This includes a hearty, homemade lunch.'의 내용과 일치한다.
④ 'Reservations are required.'의 내용과 일치한다.

- experience 체험, 경험
- collect 수거하다
- according to ~에 따라서
- per ~당, ~마다
- hearty 정성을 들인, 진심이 담긴
- reservation 예약
- information 정보
- activity 활동
- feed 먹이를 주다
- weather 날씨
- include 포함하다
- homemade 손수 만든
- require 필요로 하다, 요구하다

---

19 Maria Montessori의 일생 정답 ②

Maria Montessori에 관한 다음 글의 내용과 일치하는 것은? [3점]
① 1870년 로마에서 태어났다.
☑ 이탈리아에서 최초의 여성 의사가 되었다.
③ 주로 상류층 아동을 치료했다.
④ 1925년 Children's House라 불리는 첫 교실을 열었다.
⑤ 2차 세계대전이 끝난 후 인도로 갔다.

「Maria Montessori는 1870년 8월 31일에 이탈리아 Chiaravalle에서 태어났다.」 그녀가 14살일 때, 그녀의 가족은 로마로 이사했다. 「그녀는 1896년 로마 대학의 의학 대학에서 공부를 마치고 이탈리아 최초의 여의사가 되었다.」 ─「」: ②의 근거(일치) 한 명의 의사로서, 「그녀는 주로 많은 가난한 노동자 계층의 아이들을 치료했고, 초기 아동 발달과 교육을 연구하기 시작했다.」 「1907년에 그녀는 └「」: ③의 근거(일치) Children's House라고 불리는 그녀의 첫 번째 교실을 열었다.」 1925년까지 미국에서 1,000개 └「」: ④의 근거(불일치) 가 넘는 몬테소리 학교가 개설되었다. 「제2차 세계 대전이 시작되자, 몬테소리는 그녀가 평화를 위한 교육이라 불린 프로그램을 개발했던 인도로 갔다.」 그녀는 1952년 5월 6일에 사망 └「」: ⑤의 근거(불일치) 했다.

Why? 왜 정답일까?

Maria Montessori는 주로 많은 가난한 노동자 계급의 아이들을 치료했고 유아 발달과 교육을 연구하기 시작했다(~ she mainly treated many poor and working-class children ~)고 말하고 있다. 따라서 글의 내용과 일치하는 것은 ②이다.

Why? 왜 오답일까?

① 'Maria Montessori was born on August 31, 1870, in Chiaravalle, Italy.'의 내용과 일치하지 않는다.
③ 'As a doctor, she mainly treated many poor and working-class children ~'의 내용과 일치하지 않는다.
④ 'In 1907, she opened her first classroom called Children's House.'의 내용과 일치하지 않는다.
⑤ 'Once World War II began, Montessori went to India, where she developed a program called Education for Peace.'의 내용과 일치하지 않는다.

- medical school 의과 대학
- treat 대하다
- development 발달
- female 여성
- childhood 어린 시절
- develop 성장(발달)하다

---

20 아이들에게 음식 결정권 가르치기 정답 ⑤

다음 글의 제목으로 가장 적절한 것은? [3점]
① Be a Role Model to Your Children – 자녀들에게 역할 모델이 되어라
② Hunger: The Best Sauce for Children – 허기: 아이들에게 최고의 반찬
③ Table Manners: Are They Important? – 식사 예절: 그것이 중요한가?
④ Good Nutrition: Children's Brain Power – 충분한 영양 섭취: 아이들의 지력
☑ Teach Children Food Independence – 아이들에게 음식 독립성을 가르쳐라

아이들에게 선택권을 주고 그들이 얼마나 많이 먹기를 원할지, 그들이 먹고 싶어 할지 또는 아닐지, 그리고 그들이 무엇을 먹기를 원할지에 대해 자신이 결정하게 허락하라. 예를 들어 "Lisa야, 파스타와 미트볼을 먹고 싶니, 아니면 닭고기와 구운 감자를 먹고 싶니?"라고 여러분이 저녁 식사를 위해 만들려고 생각 중인 것에 대한 의사결정 과정에 그들을 포함시켜라. 그들이 저녁 식사 하는 동안 얼마나 먹어야 하는지를 의논할 때, 그들에게 적당량의 음식을 차려 줘라. 만약 그들이 (식사를) 끝낸 후에도 여전히 '배고프다'고 주장하면, 그들에게 5분에서 10분 동안 기다리라고 요청하고, 만약 그들이 계속 허기를 느끼면, 그때 그들은 또 한 접시의 음식을 먹을 수 있다. 제대로 배우면, 이것들은 훌륭한 자신감과 자기통제를 가르쳐 주는 멋진 행동이다.

Why? 왜 정답일까?

아이들에게 음식 선택권을 주고 스스로 결정하게 하라(Give children options and allow them

[문제편 p.005]

---

to make their own decisions ~.)며 저녁 식사 준비와 식사 중에 아이들을 어떤 방식으로 의사 결정 과정에 포함시켜야 하는지 예를 들며 이야기하고 있다. 따라서 글의 제목으로 가장 적절한 것은 ⑤ '아이들에게 음식 독립성을 가르쳐라.'이다.

- option 선택권, 선택의 자유
- discuss 회의하다, 의논하다
- reasonable 적당한, 알맞은
- be through 끝내다, 마치다
- properly 제대로, 올바르게
- self-confidence 자신감
- nutrition 영양 섭취
- decision 결정, 판단
- serve (음식을) 차려내다
- claim 주장하다
- behavior 행동
- brilliant 훌륭한, 찬란히 빛나는
- self-control 자기통제

---

21 수력 발전 댐의 부정적 효과 정답 ②

다음 글의 주제로 가장 적절한 것은? [4점]
① necessity of saving energy – 에너지 절약의 필요성
☑ dark sides of hydroelectric dams – 수력 발전 댐의 부정적 측면
③ types of hydroelectric power plants – 수력 발전소의 유형
④ popularity of renewable power sources – 재생 가능한 에너지원의 인기
⑤ importance of protecting the environment – 환경 보호의 중요성

수력 발전은 깨끗하고 재생 가능한 에너지원이다. 하지만 댐에 관해 알아두어야 할 중요한 몇 가지가 있다. 수력 발전 댐을 건설하기 위해서, 댐 뒤의 넓은 지역이 반드시 물에 잠겨야 한다. 때때로 지역 사회 전체가 다른 지역으로 이주되어야 한다. 숲 전체가 물에 잠길 수도 있다. 댐에서 방류된 물은 평소보다 더 차서 이것이 강 하류의 생태계에 영향을 미칠 수 있다. 그것은 강기슭을 유실되게 하고 강바닥의 생물을 파괴할 수도 있다. 댐의 가장 나쁜 영향은 알을 낳기 위해 흐름을 거슬러 올라가야 하는 연어에게 관찰되어 왔다. 댐으로 막히면, 연어의 생활 주기는 완결될 수 없다.

Why? 왜 정답일까?

수력 발전 댐을 건설할 때 알아두어야 할 중요한 몇 가지가 있다(~ there are a few things about dams that are important to know.)고 말한 후, 수력 발전 댐 건설이 지역 사회와 생태계에 나쁜 영향을 끼친다는 이야기를 하고 있다. 따라서 글의 주제로 가장 적절한 것은 ② '수력 발전 댐의 부정적 측면'이다.

- renewable 재생 가능한
- flood 홍수
- drown (물에) 잠기게 하다
- affect 영향을 미치다
- wash away ~을 유실되게 하다
- destroy 파괴하다
- effect 영향, 결과
- salmon 연어
- lay an egg 알을 낳다
- life cycle 생활 주기
- power source 에너지원
- entire 전체의, 전부의
- release 방류(방출)하다
- downstream 하류의, 하류에
- riverbank 강기슭, 강둑
- bottom (밑)바닥, 하부
- observe 관찰하다
- upstream 흐름을 거슬러 올라가, 상류로
- block 막다, 차단하다
- complete 완결하다, 완수하다

---

22 애완동물의 개별적 욕구 존중의 필요성 정답 ③

다음 글의 요지로 가장 적절한 것은? [4점]
① 애완동물에게는 적절한 운동이 필요하다.
② 애완동물도 다양한 감정을 느낄 수 있다.
☑ 애완동물의 개별적 특성을 존중해야 한다.
④ 자신의 상황에 맞는 애완동물을 선택해야 한다.
⑤ 훈련을 통해 애완동물의 행동을 교정할 수 있다.

애완동물의 특별한 욕구를 인식하고 그것을 존중해 주는 것이 중요하다. 예를 들어, 여러분의 애완동물이 운동을 좋아하고, 에너지가 넘치는 개라면 매일 밖으로 데리고 나가 한 시간 동안 공을 쫓아다니게 하면 실내에서 다루기가 훨씬 더 쉬워질 것이다. 여러분의 고양이가 수줍음을 타고 겁이 많다면 의상을 차려입고 고양이 품평회 쇼에 나가서 자신의 모습을 보여 주는 것을 원치 않을 것이다. 이와 비슷하게, 여러분은 마코 앵무새가 항상 조용하고 가만히 있기를 기대해서는 안 된다. 그들은 천성적으로 시끄럽고 감정에 사로잡히기 쉬운 동물이며 여러분의 아파트가 열대우림만큼 소리를 잘 흡수하지 못하는 것은 그들의 잘못이 아니다.

Why? 왜 정답일까?

애완동물의 특별한 욕구를 인식하고 존중하는 것이 중요하다(It is important to recognize your pet's particular needs and respect them.)고 말한 후 개, 고양이, 마코 앵무새 등 각 애완동물의 특성을 예로 제시하고 있다. 따라서 글의 요지로 가장 적절한 것은 ③ '애완동물의 개별적 특성을 존중해야 한다.'이다.

- recognize 인식하다
- needs 욕구
- athletic 운동을 좋아하는
- timid 겁이 많은, 소심한
- still 고요한
- by nature 천성적으로
- creature 동물, 생물
- absorb 흡수하다
- particular 특정한, 특별한
- respect 존중, 정중
- manageable 다루기 쉬운
- display 보여주다
- all the time 항상
- emotional 감정적인
- fault 잘못
- A as well as B B 뿐만 아니라 A도

---

23 야간 근무 중에 한 가족과의 식사 정답 ③

주어진 글 다음에 이어질 글의 순서로 가장 적절한 것은? [3점]
① (A) – (C) – (B)
② (B) – (A) – (C)
☑ (B) – (C) – (A)
④ (C) – (A) – (B)
⑤ (C) – (B) – (A)

나는 (야간 근무의) 보수가 훨씬 더 나았기 때문에 야간에 근무하는 일을 맡았다.

(B) 불행히도, 밤에 일하는 것은 내가 더는 아내와 아이들과 함께 저녁을 먹을 수 없다는 것을 의미했다. 구내식당의 샌드위치는 집의 따뜻한 식사와 완전히 똑같은 것은 아니다.

(C) 어느 날 밤, 아내는 아이들을 챙기고 저녁을 싸서 직장에 있는 나를 보러 와 나를 놀라게 했다. 우리 다섯은 구내식당의 식탁에 둘러앉았고 그것은 한동안 내가 했던 식사 중 최고의 식사였다.

(A) 나는 평소보다 약간 더 긴 휴식을 했는데 상사는 그것에 대해 그리 좋아하지 않았다. 그래서 우리는 그것을 아주 자주 할 수는 없었지만, 그들이 올 때는 매우 좋았다.

보수가 좋아서 야간 근무를 시작했다는 주어진 글 다음에 가족과의 따뜻한 식사를 할 수 없는 야간 근무의 단점을 설명하는 (B)가 이어지고, 가족들이 저녁을 싸서 직장에서 함께한 내용인 (C)가 이어지는 것이 자연스럽다. 하지만 가족들과 함께하는 저녁은 평소보다 더 긴 휴식을 의미했고, 상사가 그 휴식을 좋아하지 않는다는 내용의 (A)가 맨 마지막에 오는 것이 흐름상 자연스럽다. 따라서 글의 순서로 가장 적절한 것은 ③ '(B) – (C) – (A)'이다.

- slightly 약간
- than usual 평소보다
- mean 의미하다
- cafeteria 구내식당
- meal 식사
- pack up ～을 싸다, 꾸리다
- break 휴식
- unfortunately 불행하게도
- no longer 더는 ～ 아니다
- exactly 정확히
- surprise 놀라게 하다
- in a long time 한동안

---

24 생일 선물 사는 대신 자선단체에 기부하기   정답 ⑤

다음 글에서 필자가 주장하는 바로 가장 적절한 것은? [3점]

① 생일 파티를 간소하게 하자.
② 부모님께 감사하는 마음을 갖자.
③ 사용하지 않는 물건을 자선단체에 기부하자.
④ 값비싼 선물보다는 정성이 담긴 편지를 쓰자.
☑ 생일 선물에 드는 비용으로 어려운 사람을 돕자.

어떤 사람들은 우리보다 돈을 더 필요로 한다. 예를 들어, 어떤 사람들은 자연재해나 전쟁 때문에 집을 잃었고, 한편 다른 사람들은 음식이나 의복이 충분하지 않다. 그러므로 올해 우리 생일을 위해 선물을 사는 대신 자선 단체에 돈을 기부하라고 친구와 가족에게 말하자. 어떤 아이들은 생일 선물을 포기하고 싶어 하지 않을지도 모른다는 것을 알며, 나는 이해한다. 그러나 누군가가 음식, 의복, 주거지 없이 살 수 있는 것보다 우리가 새 장난감이나 게임 없이 사는 것이 더 쉽다는 것을 기억하라. 그러므로 올해 생일에는 우리가 다른 사람들에게 기부하고 싶다고 친구와 가족에게 말해야 한다.

올해에는 생일 선물을 사는 대신에, 음식이나 의복, 주거지가 없는 사람들을 돕는 자선 단체에 기부하자(So this year, for our birthdays, let's tell our friends and family to donate money to a charity instead of buying us presents.)고 친구와 가족에게 말하라고 권유하는 내용이다. 따라서 필자의 주장으로 가장 적절한 것은 ⑤ '생일 선물에 드는 비용으로 어려운 사람을 돕자.'이다.

- due to ～때문에
- war 전쟁
- donate 기부하다
- instead of ～대신에
- give up 포기하다
- shelter 주거지, 집, 피난처
- natural disaster 자연재해
- clothing 의복
- charity 자선단체
- present 선물
- live without ～없이 살다

---

25 숲에 때로는 이로운 화재와 홍수   정답 ②

다음 글의 내용을 한 문장으로 요약하고자 한다. 빈칸 (A)와 (B)에 들어갈 말로 가장 적절한 것은? [4점]

	(A)		(B)
①	support 지지하다	…….	beneficial 이로운
☑	harm 피해를 주다	…….	beneficial 이로운
③	protect 보호하다	…….	unsafe 안전하지 못한
④	harm 피해를 주다	…….	terrible 끔찍한
⑤	support 지지하다	…….	terrible 끔찍한

어떻게 화재가 숲을 변화시킬까? 몇몇 동물들이 먹는 작은 식물들은 파괴된다. 주거지를 제공하던 두터운 덤불들은 사라질지도 모른다. 하지만 몇몇 생물들에게 해로운 변화가 다른 이들에게는 좋을 수 있다. 화재는 새로운 서식지를 만들어 낼 수 있다. 서식지는 생물이 거주하는 장소이다. 홍수 이후에, 사람들과 동물들은 그들의 집을 잃을지도 모른다. 흙탕물이 뒤덮고 빛을 차단하면 식물들은 죽는다. 하지만 물이 바싹 마르면, 비옥한 토지가 남는다. 홍수 이전에는 그들이 생장하지 못했을지도 모르는 그 장소에서 새로운 식물들은 생장할 수 있다.

➡ 숲의 화재와 홍수는 처음에는 서식지에 (A) 해를 끼치지만 이후에 그것들을 새로운 식물과 동물이 살 수 있게 하는 (B) 이로운 환경을 만들어 낼 수 있다.

화재가 숲의 동물들이 먹는 작은 식물을 파괴시킬 수도 있지만 이런 변화가 다른 이들에게는 좋을 수도 있다(But a change that is harmful to some organisms can be good for others.)고 말하고 있다. 마지막에는 홍수가 나기 이전에는 자라지 못했던 장소에서 새로운 식물들이 자랄 수 있다고 말하고 있다. 따라서 빈칸에 가장 적절한 것은 ② '(A) harm(피해를 주다) – (B) beneficial(이로운)'이다.

- provide 제공(공급)하다
- disappear 사라지다
- organism 유기체
- shelter 주거지
- harmful 해로운
- habitat 서식지

26-27 모든 것으로부터 새로운 것을 배울 수 있다는 할아버지의 말씀

어느 날 나는 할아버지가 덤불을 보고 계신 것을 보았다. 할아버지는 30분 동안, 말없이 가만히 서 계셨다. 더 가까이 다가갔을 때, 난 할아버지가 일종의 새를 보고 계신다는 것을 알 수 있었지만 어떤 종류의 새인지는 알 수 없었다. 내가 막 할아버지에게 여쭤보려고 했을 때, 흔한 울새가 덤불에서 날아갔다. 나는 할아버지께 무엇을 보고 계셨는지 여쭤보았다. 할아버지는 미소를 지으시면서 "울새란다."라고 대답하셨다. 나는 "하지만 할아버지, 그냥 흔한 울새잖아요. 울새가 뭐가 그렇게 흥미로우세요?"라고 말했다. 그는 "그냥 울새라고?" 말씀하셨다. 그 다음, 그는 땅에 막대기로 새 그림을 그리시고는 나에게 막대기를 건네주시면서, "울새의 검은 반점이 있는 자리가 모두 어디인지 그려 봐라."라고 말씀하셨다. 난 "잘 모르겠는데요."라고 말했다. 할아버지께서는 계속해서 말씀하셨다. "봐라, 각각의 새는 너와 나처럼 서로 다르단다. 그 어떤 새도 다른 새와 같지 않아. 울새를 볼 때마다 항상 새로운 것을 배울 수 있어. 그건 모든 경험, 모든 상황, 모든 새, 나무, 바위, 물, 나뭇잎과 같은 삶의 다른 모든 것에도 마찬가지야. 어떤 것이든 더 배울 점이 있어." 할아버지는 계속하셨다. "그러니, 동물을 만져보고, 그 동물의 마음을 느껴야 그 동물을 알기 시작하는 거야. 그런 다음에야, 오직 그래야만 알기 시작할 수 있단다."

- bush 덤불
- a sort of 일종의
- robin 울새
- located ～에 위치한
- spirit 영혼
- silent 조용히
- be about to 막 ～하려고 하다
- mark 반점
- observe 관찰하다
- attitude 태도

---

26 글의 제목   정답 ②

위 글의 제목으로 가장 적절한 것은? [3점]

① Share Your Experiences with Other People – 경험을 다른 사람들과 나눠라
☑ Learn Something New from Everything – 모든 것으로부터 새로운 것을 배워라
③ Touch Others with Kind Words – 친절한 말로 다른 사람들을 감동시켜라
④ Be Happy Where You Are – 어디에 있든지 행복하라
⑤ Have a Positive Attitude – 긍정적인 태도를 가져라

어떤 것이든 그로부터 새로운 것을 배울 수 있다(We can always learn something new every time we observe a robin. That is also true of everything else in life, every experience, every situation, every bird, tree, rock, water, and leaf.)고 말하고 있으므로, 글의 제목으로 가장 적절한 것은 ② '모든 것으로부터 새로운 것을 배워라'이다.

---

27 빈칸 추론   정답 ②

위 글의 빈칸에 들어갈 말로 가장 적절한 것은? [4점]

① hardworking – 열심히 일하는   ☑ different – 다른   ③ friendly – 친절한
④ active – 활동적인   ⑤ free – 자유로운

빈칸의 바로 다음 문장에서 어떠한 새도 서로 같지 않다(No single bird is the same as another.)고 말하였다. 따라서 빈칸에 들어갈 말로 가장 적절한 것은 ② '다른'이다.

28-30 Robby의 피아노 연주

(A)
Robby는 어머니와 함께 사는 어린 소년이었다. 「그의 어머니는 그의 아들이 그녀를 위해 피아노 연주하는 것을 듣고 싶어 했고, 그래서 그녀의 아들을 피아노 선생님에게 보냈지만」 거기에는 작은 문제가 하나 있었다. (a) 그는 음악적으로 재능이 없었고 그러니 배우는 데 무척 느렸다. 하지만, 그의 어머니는 그녀 아들의 연주를 간절히 듣고 싶어 해서 매주 Robby를 선생님에게 보내곤 했다.

(C)
어느 날 Robby는 피아노 수업에 다니는 것을 그만두었다. 피아노 선생님은 그가 포기해버렸다고 생각했다. 오래 지나지 않아, 선생님은 시에서 열리는 피아노 콘서트를 조직하는 업무를 맡았다. 갑자기, 선생님은 그 콘서트에 참가하겠다고 말하는 Robby의 전화를 받았다. 선생님은 그에게 그가 부족했다는 것과 그가 수업에 나오는 것을 그만두었기 때문에 (c) 그는 더 이상 학생이 아니라고 말했다. 「Robby는 선생님께 기회를 달라고 애원하며 그를 실망시키지 않겠다고 약속했다.」 `— 「」: 30번 ③의 근거(일치)`

`「」: 30번 ④의 근거(불일치)`
(D)
「결국, (d) 그는 Robby을 연주하게 하는 것에 동의했지만, 마지막 순간에 그의 마음을 바꾸길 바라며, 그를 맨 뒤에 넣었다.」 드디어, Robby가 연주할 차례였고 (e) 그의 이름이 발표됐을 때, 그는 걸어 들어갔다. Robby가 연주를 시작하면서, 관객들은 이 작은 소년의 기량에 경탄했다. 사실, 그는 그날 저녁 최고의 공연을 선사했다. 「그의 연주 끝에 관객들과 피아노 선생님은 그에게 큰 박수를 보냈다.」 `「」: 30번 ⑤의 근거(일치)` 관객들은 Robby에게 어떻게 그렇게 훌륭하게 연주를 해냈는지 물어봤다.

(B)
자신 앞에 있는 마이크에, (b) 그는 "저희 어머니가 암으로 아프셨기 때문에" 저를 보내줄 사람이 아무도 없어서 매주 피아노 수업에 나올 수 없었습니다. 그녀는 바로 오늘 아침에 돌아가셨고 그녀가 제가 연주하는 것을 듣기를 바랐습니다. 아시겠지만, 그녀가 살아계셨을 때 청각 장애인이셨기 때문에 이번이 제가 연주하는 것을 그녀가 들을 수 있는 처음이었고 이제 저는 그녀가 저의 연주를 듣고 있다는 것을 알고 있습니다. 저는 그녀를 위해 최선을 다해 연주해야 합니다!"라고 말했다. `— 「」: 30번 ②의 근거(일치)`

- organize 준비(조직)하다
- brilliantly 찬란히
- enough 필요한 만큼의(충분한)

28 글의 순서 찾기 정답 ③

주어진 글 (A)에 이어질 내용을 순서에 맞게 배열한 것으로 가장 적절한 것은? [4점]

① (B) — (C) — (D) ② (C) — (B) — (D)
✔③ (C) — (D) — (B) ④ (D) — (B) — (C)
⑤ (D) — (C) — (B)

Why? 왜 정답일까?

(A)에서 어머니는 Robby의 피아노 연주를 듣고 싶어서 매주 피아노 선생님에게 보냈다는 내용 뒤에 어느 날 Robby가 피아노 수업을 더 이상 오지 않았고 선생님도 Robby를 본인의 학생이 아니라고 생각하던 중 Robby에게서 콘서트에 참가하고 싶어 한다는 내용의 전화가 왔다는 내용의 (C)가 온후 (D)에서 선생님은 Robby가 연주하는 것에 동의했지만 그의 마음이 바뀌기를 바라며 제일 마지막 순번에 Robby를 넣었다는 내용이 온다. 그러나 Robby는 연주를 훌륭히 해냈고 사람들이 Robby에게 어떻게 그렇게 훌륭한 연주를 해냈는지를 물었다. 마지막에 청각 장애인이던 어머니께서 암으로 아프셨는데 오늘 아침에 돌아 가셨고 이제는 어머니께서 본인의 연주를 들으실 수 있다는 걸 알기에 앞으로 최선을 다할 것이라는 내용의 (B)가 오는 게 적절하다. 따라서 이어질 내용을 순서에 맞게 배열한 것은 ③ '(C) — (D) — (B)'이다.

29 지칭 추론 정답 ④

위 글 (a) ~ (e) 중 가리키는 대상이 나머지 넷과 다른 것은? [3점]

① (a) ② (b) ③ (c) ✔④ (d) ⑤ (e)

Why? 왜 정답일까?

(d)는 피아노 선생님을 가리키고 (a), (b), (c), (e)는 모두 Robby를 가리킨다. 따라서 대상이 다른 것은 ④ '(d)'이다.

30 세부 내용 파악 정답 ④

위 글에 관한 내용과 일치하지 않는 것은? [3점]

① Robby의 어머니는 아들의 피아노 연주를 듣고 싶었다.
② Robby의 어머니는 암으로 아팠다.
③ Robby는 피아노 선생님에게 기회를 달라고 간청했다.
✔④ Robby는 콘서트에서 첫 순서로 연주했다.
⑤ 청중들은 Robby에게 큰 박수를 보냈다.

Why? 왜 정답일까?

선생님께서는 Robby가 콘서트에서 연주 하는 것에 동의 했지만 마지막 순간에 그의 마음이 바뀌길 바라며 그를 맨 뒤에 넣었다(~ but put him last, hoping that he would change his mind at the last minute.)고 했다. 따라서 글의 내용과 일치하지 않는 것은 ④이다.

Why? 왜 오답일까?

① 'His mother wanted to hear her son play the piano for her, so she sent her son to a piano teacher but there was one small problem.'의 내용과 일치한다.
② '~ my mother was sick with cancer.'의 내용과 일치한다.
③ 'Robby begged him for a chance and promised that he would not let him down.'의 내용과 일치한다.
⑤ 'At the end of his presentation the crowd and the piano teacher gave him a big hand.'의 내용과 일치한다.

02회 | 신입생 학급 배치고사 | 정답과 해설 | 예비 고1

• 정답 •

01 ② 02 ② 03 ⑤ 04 ① 05 ① 06 ① 07 ② 08 ② 09 ③ 10 ③ 11 ④ 12 ③ 13 ③ 14 ② 15 ③
16 ④ 17 ⑤ 18 ④ 19 ④ 20 ④ 21 ⑤ 22 ① 23 ⑤ 24 ④ 25 ③ 26 ① 27 ⑤ 28 ③ 29 ⑤ 30 ③

01 이야기 속 갈등 정답 ②

밑줄 친 This[this]가 가리키는 것으로 가장 적절한 것은? [2점]

① title - 제목 ✔② conflict - 갈등 ③ theme - 주제
④ setting - 배경 ⑤ motivation - 동기

이것은 극에 있어서 그리고 줄거리를 짜는 데 필수적이다. 이는 주요 인물들이 해결을 향해 노력해야 하는 문제로 여겨진다. 인물들이 싸우는 것이 이야기의 일면일 수는 있지만, 이것은 인물들이 서로 싸우는 데 특히 국한되지 않는다. 더 큰 의미에서, 이것은 이야기의 결말 이전에 주요 인물 또는 인물들이 반드시 극복해야 하나의 장애물이다.

Why? 왜 정답일까?

글에 따르면 '이것'은 극이나 이야기에 필수적이며 주인공들이 해결하기 위해 노력할 문제로 여겨지고, 단순히 인물끼리 '싸우는(arguing with the other)' 것을 넘어 결말 이전까지 필히 넘어야 할 장애물을 나타낸다고 하였다. 이러한 맥락을 고려할 때 밑줄 친 This[this]가 가리키는 것으로 가장 적절한 것은 ② '갈등'이다.

● form 짜다, 구성하다, 형성하다 ● plot 줄거리, 이야기
● resolve 해결하다 ● aspect 면, 양상
● obstacle 장애물 ● overcome 극복하다

02 병을 극복한 친구의 일화 정답 ②

밑줄 친 He[his]가 가리키는 대상이 나머지 넷과 다른 것은? [3점]

몇 년 전, 내 친구 중 한 명이 아프게 되었다. 시간이 지나면서 ① 그는 상태가 점점 악화되었고 수술을 위해 병원으로 실려 갔다. 의사는 내가 그를 다시 볼 가능성이 희박하다고 경고했지만, ② 그는 틀렸다. 내 친구가 (바퀴 달린 침대에) 실려서 멀어져 가기 직전, 그는 속삭였다. "심란해 하지 마. 며칠이면 난 여기서 나갈 거야." 담당 간호사가 나를 연민 어린 눈으로 보았다. 하지만, ③ 그는 정말로 무사히 극복해 냈다. 모든 게 다 끝나고, 의사는 말했다. "그 무엇도 아닌, 살고자 하는 ④ 그의 열망이 그를 살렸습니다. ⑤ 그가 만일 죽음의 가능성을 받아들이길 거부하지 않았더라면 그는 결코 회복하지 못했을 겁니다."

Why? 왜 정답일까?

①, ③, ④, ⑤는 'One of my friends', ②는 'The doctor'를 각각 지칭하므로, 밑줄 친 He[his]가 가리키는 대상이 나머지 넷과 다른 것은 ②이다.

● operation 수술 ● attending nurse 담당 간호사
● pity 연민, 동정 ● come through 극복하다, 해 내다, 회복하다
● pull through (심한 병·수술 뒤에) 회복하다 ● refuse 거부하다, 거절하다
● accept 받아들이다, 수용하다

03 체중 감량을 위한 아침 식사의 중요성 정답 ⑤

다음 글의 목적으로 가장 적절한 것은? [3점]

① 건강에 좋은 요리법을 추천하려고
② 기상 시간과 성적 향상의 관계를 설명하려고
③ 식료품을 신선하게 보관하는 방법을 소개하려고
④ 아침형 인간과 저녁형 인간의 특성을 비교하려고
✔⑤ 아침 식사를 챙겨먹을 수 있는 요령을 알려주려고

아침을 먹는 사람들은 더 활기 있고 살찔 확률도 더 낮다. 그러므로 아침을 굶는 것은 썩 훌륭한 체중 감량법이 아니다. 다이어트에 관심이 있다면, 당신은 등교 전에 간단한 식사를 할 수 있는 이 몇 가지 방법을 시도해보고 싶을지도 모른다. 먼저, 그릭 요거트나 달걀 완숙, 과일처럼 아침으로 가지고 갈 만한 메뉴로 냉장고를 채워 두라. 학교에 도착한 후 배가 더 고플 때 먹을 수 있도록 아침을 싸 가라. 바로 전날 밤에 다음날 먹을 아침을 계획하라. 부모님께 준비해 달라고 부탁드려라. 아침에 피곤하지 않도록, 30분 일찍 잠자리에 들라. 몸이 깨고 배고파질 시간을 좀 더 갖도록 10분 먼저 일어나라.

Why? 왜 정답일까?

'If you are concerned about your diet, you might want to try some of these methods to grab a quick bite to eat before school.'에서 아침 식사를 간단히 챙겨먹을 수 있는 몇 가지 방법을 소개하겠다고 말하므로, 글의 목적으로 가장 적절한 것은 ⑤ '아침 식사를 챙겨먹을 수 있는 요령을 알려주려고'이다.

● lose weight 체중을 감량하다, 살을 빼다
● be concerned about ~에 관심이 있다, ~을 걱정하다
● grab a bite 간단히 먹다 ● hard-boiled (달걀이) 완숙인, 완숙의

04 스마트폰을 통한 농작물 관리 정답 ①

다음 글의 밑줄 친 부분 중, 어법상 틀린 것은? [4점]

모든 농작물을 확인하러 한밤중에 농장으로 뛰어가는 것은 옛일이 되었다. 오늘날 농부들이

해야할 것은 그저 침대에 있으면서 스마트폰 화면을 누르는 것이다. 이는 모두 '스마트농장' 신기술 덕분이다. 이런 스마트농업 앱은 온실 내 기온 및 습도, 햇빛의 양을 측정 및 분석할 수 있는 다양한 기술인 '사물 인터넷(IoT)'으로 이어진다. 모든 데이터는 농부들이 실시간으로 그들의 온실 상황을 확인하고 통제할 수 있는 스마트폰으로 전송된다. 새로운 시스템은 생산성과 농작물의 질을 높여주는 반면, 인력과 필요 에너지 투입량은 줄여준다.

Why? 왜 정답일까?

주어는 'All farmers have to do'인데 이는 목적격 관계대명사가 중간에 생략된 구조이다. 즉 원래는 'All (that) farmers have to do'인데 that이 생략되고 'farmers have to do'라는 불완전한 절이 대명사 'All(~한 모든 것)'을 꾸미고 있다. 이 대명사 All은 단수 취급하므로 ①의 복수 동사 are는 is로 고쳐야 적절하다. 따라서 어법상 틀린 것은 ①이다.

Why? 왜 오답일까?

② 'thanks to'는 '~ 덕분에'라는 뜻의 전치사구로서 뒤에 명사를 받는다. 여기서도 'the new "smartfarm" technology'라는 명사구가 나온다.
③ 앞에 선행사 'a range of technologies'가 나오고 뒤에 주어 없이 동사로 시작하는 불완전한 문장이 이어지므로 주격 관계대명사 that을 쓴 것은 적절하다.
④ 문맥상 farmers라는 복수 명사의 소유격을 나타내야 하므로 their는 적절하다.
⑤ 접속사 while 뒤에는 '주어 + be 동사'가 생략된 채 분사나 전명구가 곧바로 이어질 수 있다. 따라서 while 뒤에 현재분사인 reducing이 이어진 것은 적절하다.

- thanks to ~ 덕분에
- measure 측정하다, 재다
- humidity 습도, 습기
- in real time 실시간으로, 즉시
- a range of 다양한
- analyze 분석하다
- transfer 전송하다, 옮기다
- productivity 생산성

---

05 개선의 여지가 있는 피드백 정답 ①

(A), (B), (C)의 각 네모 안에서 어법에 맞는 낱말로 가장 적절한 것은? [4점]

	(A)	(B)	(C)
✓①	where	turns	colorblind
②	where	turns	colorblindly
③	where	turned	colorblind
④	of which	turned	colorblindly
⑤	of which	turned	colorblind

피드백은 많은 활동에서 개선될 수 있다. 천장에 페인트를 칠하는 단순 작업을 생각해 보라. 이 일은 보이는 것보다 어려운데 천장은 거의 항상 흰색으로 칠해지며 어디에 칠을 했는지 정확히 보기 힘들기 때문이다. 나중에 페인트가 마를 때, 오래된 페인트 부분이 짜증나게도 눈에 보인다. 이 문제를 어떻게 해결할 수 있는가? 어떤 똑똑한 사람이 젖었을 때는 분홍색을 띠다가 마르고 나면 흰색이 되는 천장 페인트 종류를 개발했다. 칠하는 사람이 심한 색맹이라 분홍색과 흰색의 차이를 못 구별하지 않고서야. 이는 문제를 해결해 준다.

Why? 왜 정답일까?

(A) see의 목적어로 명사절이 와야 하므로 간접의문문을 만드는 의문사 where가 적절하다.
(B) 선행사 'a type of ceiling paint' 뒤에 주격 관계대명사 that이 나오는데 이 뒤에는 등위접속사 but으로 연결된 2개의 동사가 나온다. 즉 but 앞에 나오는 현재형 동사 goes on과 병렬을 이루는 동사가 필요하므로 (B)에는 turns가 적절하다.
(C) be동사인 is의 주격 보어 역할을 할 형용사가 필요하므로, colorblind가 적절하다. '형용사+ly'는 부사이다. 정답은 ①이다.

- patch 부분, 조각
- visible 눈에 보이는, 가시적인
- tell (차이를) 구별하다, 식별하다
- annoyingly 짜증나게, 성가시게
- go on (색이나 특징을) 띠다

---

06 다른 사람들의 행동을 모방하는 인간들 정답 ①

다음 빈칸에 들어갈 말로 가장 적절한 것을 고르시오. [4점]

✓① copied – 따라 하던   ② blamed – 비난하던   ③ ignored – 무시하던
④ corrected – 바로잡던   ⑤ controlled – 통제하던

5만 년 전 당신이 수렵 채집인 친구들과 세렝게티를 돌아다니다가, 갑자기 모두가 뛰기 시작했다고 가정해 보라. 당신은 당신이 보고 있는 것이 사자인지 아니면 고기가 될 무해한 동물인지 생각하면서 가만히 서 있었을까? 아니다, 당신은 친구들을 따라 뛰었을 것이다. 우리는 다른 사람들의 행동을 따라 하던 이들의 직계 후손이다. 이러한 패턴은 우리 안에 너무 깊이 뿌리내려서, 심지어 더 이상 생존상의 이득이 없는 지금도 우리는 이 패턴을 따른다. 예를 들어, 당신이 외국 도시에서 배가 고픈데 좋은 식당을 모른다면, 현지인들이 몰려 있는 식당을 고르는 게 타당하다. 다시 말해, 당신은 현지인들의 행동을 모방하는 것이다.

Why? 왜 정답일까?

글의 결론인 마지막 문장 'In other words, you imitate the local's behavior.'에서 우리는 수렵 채집인 시절부터 남을 모방하여 행동하였고 이러한 행동 특성이 현대에 이르러서도 유지되고 있다는 점을 언급하므로, 빈칸에 들어갈 말로 가장 적절한 것은 ① '따라 하던'이다. 'copied'와 'imitate'가 서로 재서술 관계에 있음을 파악한다.

- suppose 가정하다
- motionless 가만히 있는, 움직이지 않는
- serve as ~의 역할을 하다
- root 뿌리내리게 하다
- local 현지인
- hunter-gatherer 수렵 채집인
- harmless 무해한, 해가 없는
- heir 후손, 계승자, 상속자
- advantage 이득, 이점

---

07 리더의 특징 정답 ②

다음 빈칸에 들어갈 말로 가장 적절한 것을 고르시오. [3점]

① to give up – 포기하는   ✓ to speak up – 소신을 말하는

---

③ to keep secrets – 비밀을 지키는   ④ to praise others – 남들을 칭찬하는
⑤ to refuse a favor – 호의를 거절하는

변화가 필요한 모든 교회나 회사, 또는 비영리 단체 내에는, 일어나야 할 변화를 아는 내부자 무리가 존재한다. 그들은 휴게실에 모여서 서로에게 불평을 한다. 하지만 매일같이 그들은 아무것도 변하지 않을 것이라 생각하며 일을 시작한다. 그래서 그들은 입다물고 있는다. 어떤 일이 일어나야 하는지에 대한 통찰이 없는 게 아니다. 그들은 그저 그것에 대해 무언가 해볼 용기가 없을 뿐이다. 리더는 모두가 남몰래 속삭일 때 공개적으로 말할 용기가 있는 사람이다. 그의 통찰력이 군중으로부터 그를 돋보이게 하는 것이 아니다. 자기가 본 것에 대한 조치를 취하고 모두가 침묵할 때 소신을 말하는 그의 용기가 그렇게 한다(그를 돋보이게 한다).

Why? 왜 정답일까?

군중은 변화가 필요하다는 것을 몰라서가 아니라 용기가 없기에 숨어서 불평을 하지만, 리더는 공개적으로 말할 수 있는 용기를 갖춘 사람임(A leader is someone who has the courage to say publicly ~)을 설명하는 글이다. 빈칸은 리더가 '공개적으로 말할 줄 안다'는 내용을 반복하는 부분에 있으므로, 이에 들어갈 말로 가장 적절한 것은 ② '소신을 말하는'이다.

- nonprofit organization 비영리 단체
- go about ~을 시작하다, ~에 착수하다
- courage 용기
- privately 남몰래, 사적으로
- set ~ apart ~을 돋보이게 하다
- take place 일어나다, 발생하다
- lack ~이 없다, 결여되다
- whisper 속삭이다
- insight 통찰
- act on ~에 대해 조치를 취하다

---

08 선물을 주는 사람과 받는 사람의 관점 차이 정답 ②

다음 빈칸에 들어갈 말로 가장 적절한 것을 고르시오. [4점]

① shows the giver's taste – 주는 사람의 취향을 보여주는
✓ provides value over time – 시간이 지남에 따라 가치를 주는
③ is well-wrapped in ribbons – 리본에 잘 싸인
④ can impress his or her friends – 자신의 친구를 감동시킬 수 있는
⑤ remains in the giver's memory – 주는 사람의 기억에 남는

한 마케팅 연구원 집단에서 나쁜 선물은 정확히 무엇이며 왜 사람들은 그런 선물을 사는지 연구했다. 연구원들은 주는 사람과 받는 사람이 서로 다른 것에 초점을 맞추는 것이 나쁜 선물의 한 가지 이유라고 말했다. 주는 사람은 받는 사람을 깜짝 놀라게 하거나 감명시키고 싶어 교환의 순간에 초점을 맞추는 반면에 받는 사람은 선물의 장기적인 유용성에 초점을 맞춘다. "우리가 알아낸 것은 주는 사람은 받는 사람에게 '큰 감동을 주길' 원해서 당장 즐길 수 있는 선물을 주지만, 받는 사람은 시간이 지남에 따라 가치를 주는 선물에 더 관심이 있다는 것입니다."라고 연구원 Jeff Galak이 말했다.

Why? 왜 정답일까?

'The giver focuses on the moment of the exchange, wanting to surprise or impress the recipient, while the recipient focuses on the long-term usefulness of the gift.'에서 주는 사람은 교환의 순간 그 자체(의 즐거움)에, 받는 사람은 선물의 장기적 유용성에 관심이 있다고 말하는데, 빈칸은 '받는 사람'을 설명하는 부분에 있으므로 이에 들어갈 말로 가장 적절한 것은 ② '시간이 지남에 따라 가치를 주는'이다.

- focus on ~에 집중하다, ~에 초점을 맞추다
- usefulness 유용성
- immediately 당장, 즉시
- impress 감명시키다, 감동을 주다
- wow 큰 감동을 주다, 열광시키다

---

09 통증이 통증의 근원지가 아닌 다른 곳에서 느껴지는 이유 정답 ③

다음 빈칸에 들어갈 말로 가장 적절한 것을 고르시오. [4점]

① the lower back and upper legs – 등 아래 부분과 다리 위쪽
② the farthest part from the heart – 심장에서 가장 먼 부분
✓ a place other than its true source – 진정한 근원지가 아닌 곳
④ the skin and muscles, not the bones – 뼈가 아닌 피부와 근육
⑤ the mind made up by the imagination – 상상으로 만들어진 생각

가슴이 아픈 것 같은 느낌을 주는 소화불량으로 인한 고통을 느껴본 적이 있는가? 이런 종류의 혼란은 내부 장기 속 고통을 느끼는 모든 신경들이 신체 표면으로 정보를 보내는, 똑같은 척수 내 통로를 통하여 신호를 보내기 때문에 생긴다. 이는 뇌가 무엇이 잘못되었는가를 확신하지 못하는 상태로 있게 만든다. 사실, 고통은 진정한 근원지가 아닌 곳에서 느껴진다. 이러한 이유로, 의사들은 환자들이 왼쪽 팔에서 통증을 호소하면 그것이 심장마비를 나타낼 수 있다는 것을 알게 된다. 마찬가지로, 신장결석으로 인한 고통은 위통처럼 느껴질 수 있다.

Why? 왜 정답일까?

첫 두 문장에서 소화불량인데 가슴이 아픈 경우를 예로 들어 고통을 감지하는 모든 신경은 결국 같은 통로를 이용하여 몸 표면으로 신호를 보내기 때문에 어느 한 곳이 아프더라도 정작 병의 근원은 다른 곳일 수 있다는 내용을 설명하고 있다. 빈칸 뒤의 두 문장에서도 팔이 아플 때 심장마비, 위가 아플 때 신장결석이 의심되는 예(For this reason, doctors learn that when patients complain about pain in their left arm, it may indicate a heart attack. Similarly, pain from a kidney stone may feel like a stomachache.)를 통해 병이 있는 장소와 고통이 느껴지는 장소는 '전혀 다를' 수 있음을 이야기하므로, 빈칸에 들어갈 말로 가장 적절한 것은 ③ '진정한 근원지가 아닌 곳'이다.

- indigestion 소화불량
- nerve 신경
- internal 내부의
- surface 표면
- confusion 혼란
- sense 느끼다, 감지하다
- organ 장기
- indicate 나타내다, 보여 주다

---

10 일급과 물값의 상대적 비교 정답 ③

다음 도표의 내용과 일치하지 않는 것은? [3점]

The Cost of Water & Typical Daily Low Salary

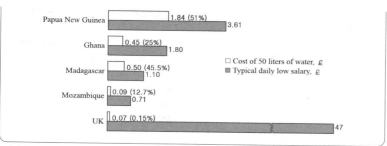

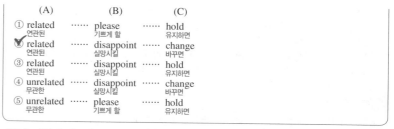

	(A)	(B)	(C)
①	related 연관된	please 기쁘게 할	hold 유지하면
✓②	related 연관된	disappoint 실망시킬	change 바꾸면
③	related 연관된	disappoint 실망시킬	hold 유지하면
④	unrelated 무관한	disappoint 실망시킬	change 바꾸면
⑤	unrelated 무관한	please 기쁘게 할	hold 유지하면

*Water Aid*의 보고에 따르면, 몇몇 사람들은 통상의 낮은 일급에 비하여 더 많은 돈을 물에 지불한다. ① 파푸아뉴기니에서 물 50리터의 비용은 그 나라 노동자 일급의 50퍼센트 이상이다. ② 가나에서 물 50리터의 비용은 그 나라 노동자 일급의 1/4을 차지한다. ③ 마다가스카르에서 물 50리터의 비용은 파푸아뉴기니에서보다 그 나라 노동자의 일급에서 더 큰 비중을 차지한다. ④ 모잠비크의 물 50리터 비용은 영국을 제외한 모든 국가 중 가장 적은 비율을 차지한다. ⑤ 영국 사람들은 물 50리터에 그들의 일급 중 1퍼센트도 안 되는 비용을 낸다.

Why? 왜 정답일까?

도표에 따르면 파푸아뉴기니에서 물 50리터의 비용은 노동자 일급의 51%, 마다가스카르에서 같은 양의 물 비용은 노동자 일급의 45.5%이다. 즉 마다가스카르의 물값은 노동자 임금에 대한 비율로 따질 때 파푸아뉴기니의 물값보다 더 '적은' 비율을 차지하므로, 도표와 일치하지 않는 것은 ③이다.

- daily salary 일급
- account for ~을 차지하다
- take up ~을 차지하다

---

11 상어의 실제 특징   정답 ④

다음 글의 밑줄 친 부분 중, 문맥상 낱말의 쓰임이 적절하지 않은 것은? [3점]

영화에서 상어는 위험한 포식자이다. 상어들은 사람을 보자마자 ① 공격할 준비가 되어 있다. 하지만 경력이 풍부한 많은 상어 잠수부들이 말하듯이, 실제 상어는 그런 영화상의 이미지에 대체로 ② 맞지 않는다. 대부분의 상어는 먹어치울 사람을 찾아다니지 않는다. 다양한 상어 종을 일반화할 수는 있겠으나, 각 개체로서 상어들은 굉장히 ③ 다양한 특성을 지니고 있는 것은 사실이다. 상어들은 사람을 만나더라도 공격적으로 변하지 않는다. 다른 상어들은 지극히 ④ 환영하면서(→ 적대적이어서), 외부인이 자기 영역에 들어오면 쉽게 몹시 화가 난다. 하지만 전반적으로, 대부분의 상어들은 사람을 꽤 ⑤ 두려워한다.

Why? 왜 정답일까?

'~, so they are quick to be very upset by an outsider entering their area.'에서 상어들은 자신의 영역에 침입해 들어온 외부인에게 쉽게 화를 느낀다고 하였으므로 ④의 welcoming은 반의어인 'hostile(적대적인)'로 바뀌어야 한다. 따라서 문맥상 적절하지 않은 것은 ④이다.

- predator 포식자
- fit ~에 맞다
- aggressive 공격적인
- more ~ than not 꽤 ~, 매우 ~
- experienced 경력이 풍부한
- personality 특성, 성격
- on the whole 전반적으로, 대체로

---

12 공기 오염으로 인한 피해   정답 ③

주어진 글 다음에 이어질 글의 순서로 가장 적절한 것은? [4점]

① (A) – (C) – (B)   ② (B) – (A) – (C)
✓③ (B) – (C) – (A)   ④ (C) – (A) – (B)
⑤ (C) – (B) – (A)

새로운 보고서에서는 2060년 무렵 바깥 공기 오염이 전 세계적으로 한 해에 9백만 명의 죽음을 유발할 것이라고 한다. 이는 오염이 사람들을 직접 아프게 한다는 뜻이 아닐 수도 있다. 이는 암과 심장병 같은 다른 질환을 야기할 수 있다.

(B) 이 위협적인 질병들은 사람이 많고 유해 먼지 및 가스 수준이 높은 지역에 큰 영향을 미칠 것이다. 이러한 지역 중 많은 곳은 중국 및 인도의 도시들일 것이다. 사람들은 동유럽 및 중동 일부 지역, 아시아 기타 지역에도 문제가 있음을 알 것이다.

(C) 공기 오염의 결과는 종종 달러(돈)의 관점에서 논의된다. 2060년 무렵, 국가들은 많은 돈을 잃게 될 것이다. 이러한 손실은 공기 오염과 관련된 건강 문제 때문일 것이다. 노동 생산성 저하, 건강 비용 증가, 작물 수확 감소 등이 모두 손실을 야기할 것이다.

(A) 하지만, 큰 달러 액수가 공기 오염의 진정한 비용을 반영하지는 않는다. 유독성 공기가 원인인 고통, 괴로움, 예방 가능한 죽음에는 가격이라는 것이 없다. 단지 밖에 나가서 놀려고 마스크를 써야 하는 일에도 마찬가지다. 이러한 문제는 돈보다 더 중요하다.

Why? 왜 정답일까?

공기 오염이 암과 심장병 같은 질환을 야기할 수 있다는 내용의 주어진 글 뒤에는, 이 병들을 'These threatening diseases'라는 말로 받으며 특히 어느 지역에 큰 여파가 갈 것인지를 설명하는 (B)가 나와야 적절하다. 이 뒤로는 공기 오염이 '돈'의 관점에서 설명되기도 한다는 내용의 (C), 하지만 이 관점이 공기 오염이 미치는 손실을 다 설명하지는 못한다는 내용의 (A)가 차례로 이어지는 것이 자연스럽다. 따라서 주어진 글 다음에 이어질 글의 순서로 가장 적절한 것은 ③ '(B) – (C) – (A)'이다.

- pollution 오염, 공해
- disease 질환, 병
- suffering 괴로움, 고통
- threatening 위협적인
- productivity 생산성
- result in ~을 야기하다, ~을 초래하다
- cancer 암
- reflect 반영하다
- avoidable 예방 가능한, 피할 수 있는
- poisonous 유해한, 유독한
- harvest 수확(량)

---

13 개 훈련 시 주의사항   정답 ②

(A), (B), (C)의 각 네모 안에서 문맥에 맞는 낱말로 가장 적절한 것은? [4점]

개들은 당신이 가르치는 맥락 안에서 배운다. 만일 부엌에서 어떤 행동을 개에게 가르친다면, 개는 그 행동이 부엌과 (A) 연관된 것이라 생각할 것이다. 만일 당신이 늘 거실에서 개를 가르치고 친구들이 왔을 때 개가 복도에서도 그 행동을 할 것이라 가정한다면, 개는 아마 당신을 (B) 실망시킬 것이다. 당신은 개에게 그 행동을 복도에서 가르치지 않았고, 거실에서 가르쳤다! 당신은 어떤 행동이 발생하기를 원하는 환경에서 그 행동을 가르쳐야 한다. 개를 훈련시킬 때, 환경을 (C) 바꾸면 당신이 생각하기에 개가 알고 있는 것도 다시 가르쳐야 할 수 있다는 점을 기억하라.

Why? 왜 정답일까?

(A) 'You have to teach a behavior in the environment in which you want it to occur.'에서 개에게 어떤 행동을 가르칠 때 그 행동이 일어나기를 바라는 환경에서 가르쳐야 한다는 것은 개가 행동을 배우는 장소와 행동을 서로 연관시킨다는 의미를 나타내므로 (A)에는 'related'가 적절하다.

(B) 'You didn't teach him the behavior in the hallway—you taught him in the living room!'을 통해 개가 거실에서 배운 행동은 복도에서는 하지 않을 것임을 알 수 있어 (B)에는 'disappoint'가 적절하다.

(C) 'You have to teach a behavior in the environment in which you want it to occur.'을 통해 만일 개가 원래 어떤 행동을 배운 곳이 아닌 다른 곳으로 장소를 '이동'하면 같은 행동을 다시 가르쳐야 할 수도 있다는 내용을 유추할 수 있으므로, (C)에는 'change'가 적절하다. 정답은 ② '연관된 – 실망시킬 – 바꾸면'이다.

- context 맥락, 상황
- assume 가정하다
- environment 환경
- behavior 행동, 행위
- hallway 복도
- occur 발생하다, 일어나다

---

14 미국인들이 영국을 여행할 때 주의할 점   정답 ②

다음 글에서 전체 흐름과 관계 없는 문장은? [2점]

미국에서 런던에 오는 방문객들은 안전한 보행자가 되는 데 어려움이 있다. 그들은 일생을 차들이 왼쪽으로 올 것이라 예상하며 살았다. ① 하지만 영국에서는 차가 왼쪽 차선에서 달리기 때문에, 위험은 오른쪽에서 온다. ② 거리에 차가 더 적으면 교통사고가 덜 난다는 것을 뜻한다. ③ 그 결과, 미국 여행자들에게 많은 보행자 사고가 근사한 디자인으로 이들을 도울 방법을 떠올렸다. ⑤ 많은 길 모퉁이, 특히 여행자들이 자주 방문하는 지역에, 보도에는 "오른쪽을 보세요!"라고 쓰여 있는 표지판이 있다.

Why? 왜 정답일까?

이 글은 미국에서 온 보행자들이 길을 건널 때 좌측에서 오는 차들에 익숙해져 있어 통행 방향이 반대인 런던에 가면 사고를 당하기 쉽다(But in the United Kingdom automobiles drive on the left-hand side of the road, so the danger often comes from the right.)는 내용을 다룬다. ②는 차가 적으면 교통사고가 덜 난다는 내용을 다루고 있어 흐름과 맞지 않다. 따라서 전체 흐름과 관계 없는 문장은 ②이다.

- pedestrian 보행자
- expect 예상하다, 기대하다
- especially 특히
- sidewalk 인도
- entire life 일생, 평생
- automobile 자동차
- frequently 자주

---

15 오로라의 근원에 대한 과거 사람들의 생각   정답 ③

글의 흐름으로 보아, 주어진 문장이 들어가기에 가장 적절한 곳을 고르시오. [4점]

북극에서 긴 겨울밤 중에 돌아다니다가, 갑자기 하늘에서 환하고 번쩍이는 빛을 본다면, 당황하지 마라. ① 이 장관의 극광은 오로라라고 불린다. ② 이는 전기 미립자가 태양에서 흘러나와 지구의 대기에 있는 기체에 부딪치면서 생긴다. ③ 과거에 사람들은 무엇이 기막히게 멋진 오로라를 유발하는지 전혀 몰랐다. 그래서 그들은 무슨 일이 있는 것인지 이해하기 위해 이야기를 지어냈다. ④ 캐나다의 이누이트 족은 하늘이 지구에 펼쳐진 반구형 지붕이고 그 지붕에 있는 구멍이 빛을 받아들이고 망자들의 영혼은 내보낸다고 생각했다. ⑤ 그들은 오로라가 영혼을 천국으로 인도하는 타오르는 횃불이라고 믿었다.

Why? 왜 정답일까?

③ 앞의 문장에서 오로라가 어떻게 생겨나는지에 관해 설명한 데 이어, 주어진 문장에서는 '과거의 경우' 사람들은 무엇이 오로라의 원인인지를 전혀 알지 못했다고 지적하고, ③ 뒤의 문장에서는 그래서 그들(they)이 오로라의 근원에 대한 이야기를 지어내게 되었다고 이야기한다. 따라서 주어진 문장이 들어가기에 가장 적절한 곳은 ③이다.

- spectacular 장관의, 극적인
- awesome 기막히게 멋진, 어마어마한
- flash 번쩍이다, 잠깐 비치다
- atmosphere 대기
- spirit 영혼
- not have a clue 전혀 모르다
- out and about 돌아다니다
- panic (겁을 먹어) 허둥대다
- dome 반구형 지붕
- torch 횃불

---

16 디지털 카메라의 셔터 소리   정답 ④

글의 흐름으로 보아, 주어진 문장이 들어가기에 가장 적절한 곳을 고르시오. [3점]

디지털 카메라는 일반적으로 필름 카메라보다 그 사용자들에게 더 나은 피드백을 제공해 준다. ① 매번의 촬영 후에, 사진사는 방금 찍힌 사진을 작은 형태로 볼 수 있다. ② 이는 필름 시대에 흔했던 모든 오류를 제거해 준다. ③ 그 오류는 필름을 제대로 넣지 못한 것에서부터 중심인물의 머리를 잘라먹는 것에 이른다. ④ 하지만 초기의 디지털 카메라는 한 가지 중요한 피드백에 있어 실패하였다. 사진이 찍혔을 때, 이미지가 찍혔다는 것을 알려주는 소리 신호가 없었다. ⑤ 오늘날의 (카메라) 모델은 이제 사진이 찍혔을 때 매우 만족스럽지만 완전히 가짜인, "셔터가 찰칵대는" 소리를 포함하고 있다.

Why? 왜 정답일까?

④ 앞에서 디지털 카메라는 필름 카메라에 비해 더 나은 피드백을 제공해 주어서, 디지털 카메라를 통해 사람들은 기존에는 알지 못했던 오류들에 관해 파악할 수 있었다고 이야기하는데, 주어진 문장에서는 '초기 디지털 카메라의 경우' 한 가지 피드백을 주는 데 실패하였다고 설명하며 흐름을 전환한다. ④ 뒤의 문장에서는 (필름 카메라가 사진을 찍으면 찰칵 소리가 난 것에 반해) 디지털 카메라의 경우에는 이미지가 찍혔을 때 소리 신호를 주지 못하는 한계가 있었음을 말하며 주어진 문장에서 말한 '한 가지 실패'의 구체적인 내용을 설명한다. 따라서 주어진 문장이 들어가기에 가장 적절한 곳은 ④이다.

- **crucial** 중요한, 중대한
- **era** 시대
- **properly** 제대로, 적절히
- **fake** 가짜인, 꾸며낸
- **remove** 제거하다
- **load** (필름을) 넣다
- **indicate** 알려주다, 나타내다

---

17 단편 소설 대회 개최 안내 　　　　정답 ⑤

다음 Annual Teen Short Story Competition에 대한 내용과 일치하지 <u>않는</u> 것은? [2점]
① 13세에서 19세의 십대들을 대상으로 한다.
② 작품 분량은 2,500단어 이하여야 한다.
③ 지원서는 이메일로 접수 가능하다.
④ 작품은 가장 가까운 Baunt Books에 제출 가능하다.
✓ 수상작은 결과 발표 후 그 다음 해에 출판된다.

연례 십 대 단편 소설 대회

올해의 십 대 단편 공모전에 지금 참가하세요!
• 『13세부터 19세까지 모든 십 대 참가 가능』—「」: ①의 근거(일치)
• 『2,500단어 이하의 직접 작성한 이야기여야 합니다!』—「」: ②의 근거(일치)

📖 등록 방법:
「연락처와 함께 소설과 신청서를 shortstory@tmail.com으로 보내주셔야 합니다.」「또한 가장 가까운 Baunt Books 지점에 (작성 완료된 문서 사본과 함께) 소설을 직접 제출해주셔야 합니다.」 반드시 한 줄씩 여백을 두고 타이핑하여 단면 인쇄해 오셔야 합니다.　「」: ③의 근거(일치)　「」: ④의 근거(일치)

대회는 2017년 1월 8일 일요일까지 진행됩니다. 『결과는 2017년 4월에 발표될 것이며, 수상작은 2017년 5월에 출판될 것입니다.』—「」: ⑤의 근거(불일치)

Why? 왜 정답일까?

'Results will be announced in April 2017, and winning stories will be published in May 2017.'에서 결과 발표와 수상작 출간 모두 2017년에 이루어진다는 사실을 알 수 있으므로, Annual Teen Short Story Competition에 대한 내용과 일치하지 않는 것은 ⑤ '수상작은 결과 발표 후 그 다음 해에 출판된다.'이다.

Why? 왜 오답일까?

① 'Open to all teens aged thirteen to nineteen'의 내용과 일치한다.
② 'Stories should be 2,500 words or less written in your own words!'의 내용과 일치한다.
③ 'You can email your story and the application form, along with your contact details, to shortstory@tmail.com.'의 내용과 일치한다.
④ 'You can also hand in your story in person to the nearest Baunt Books (along with a completed copy of the form).'의 내용과 일치한다.

- **application form** 신청서, 지원서
- **hand in** 제출하다
- **single-sided** 단면의
- **along with** ~와 함께
- **double-spaced** 한 줄씩 여백을 둔
- **publish** 출판하다, 게재하다

---

18 장님뱀의 특징 　　　　정답 ④

blind snake에 관한 다음 글의 내용과 일치하는 것은? [3점]
① 시력을 잃어 명암을 구분할 수 없다.
② 주로 땅 위에서 생활한다.
③ 머리와 꼬리를 구분하기 쉽다.
✓ 현재까지 수컷이 발견되지 않았다.
⑤ 완전히 자라면 모두 같은 색이 된다.

장님뱀은 주로 아프리카와 아시아에서 발견되는 무해한 뱀이다. 『이들은 완전히 눈이 멀지는 않았지만, 빛과 어둠을 구별할 수 있을 뿐이다.』「이 뱀들은 대부분의 일생을 지하에서 보낸다.」 이들을 지렁이로 착각하기는 아주 쉽다. 장님뱀은 확실히 세계에서 가장 작은 뱀일 것이다. 다 자란 뱀도 아주 작고 가늘다. 『장님뱀의 머리와 꼬리를 쉽게 구별할 수는 없다.』 이들은 가는 목을 지니고 있다. 『이 뱀들은 단성이며 현재까지 그 어떤 수컷 뱀도 발견된 적이 없다.』 『다 자란 뱀은 보라색, 회색부터 빛나는 은백색에 이르는 다양한 색을 띤다.』　「」: ①의 근거(불일치)　「」: ②의 근거(불일치)　「」: ③의 근거(불일치)　「」: ④의 근거(일치)　「」: ⑤의 근거(불일치)

Why? 왜 정답일까?

'These snakes are unisexual and no males of the species have been discovered till now.'에서 장님뱀 가운데 수컷은 발견되지 않았다고 하므로, 장님뱀에 관한 글의 내용과 일치하는 것은 ④ '현재까지 수컷이 발견되지 않았다.'이다.

Why? 왜 오답일까?

① 'They are not totally blind, but they can only tell light from dark.'에서 눈이 완전히 멀지는 않았고 빛과 어둠의 구별 정도는 가능하다고 하였다.
② 'These snakes spend most of their life underground.'에서 장님뱀은 일생 대부분을 지하에서 보낸다고 하였다.

③ 'You cannot easily tell the head of the blind snake from its tail.'에서 장님뱀의 머리와 꼬리를 구별하기는 어렵다고 하였다.
⑤ 'The adult snakes have varied colors ranging from purple, charcoal gray to shining silver-gray.'에서 다 자란 장님뱀은 다양한 색깔을 띨 수 있다고 하였다.

- **harmless** 무해한, 해가 없는
- **underground** 지하에서
- **unisexual** 단성의, 성별이 하나인
- **varied** 다양한
- **mainly** 주로
- **earthworm** 지렁이
- **discover** 발견하다
- **range from** ~에 이르다

---

19 물 절약의 필요성 　　　　정답 ③

다음 글의 제목으로 가장 적절한 것은? [3점]
① Recycling Water for a Low Price – 싼 가격에 물 재활용하기
② Various Factors of Water Pollution – 수질 오염의 다양한 요인
✓ Why We Should Not Waste Water – 왜 우리는 물을 낭비하지 말아야 하는가
④ Water as the Future Energy Resource – 미래 에너지 근원으로서의 물
⑤ Want Water? Sea Water Is the Answer! – 물을 원하는가? 바닷물이 정답이다!

선진국에서는 물이 수도꼭지에서 쉽게 흘러나오기 때문에 물을 당연하게 여기는 경향이 있다. 하지만 우리는 담수(민물)의 전 세계 공급량을 빠르게 소진하고 있고, 이러한 현실은 잠재적으로 심각한 결과를 가져올 수 있다. Water.org에 따르면, 지구상의 물 중 1퍼센트도 안 되는 양이 사람이 쓸 수 있도록 바로 이용 가능한데, 말인즉 이는 소금이 들어있다기보다 담수인 것이며 꽤 깨끗하다. 소금은 특별한 과정을 거치면 바닷물에서 제거되어 나올 수 있지만, 이는 너무 비싸서 물 부족 문제를 위한 실질적인 해결책으로 잘 이용되지 않는다. 물 절약은 담수를 최대한 사용할 수 있는 직접적이고 합리적인 방법이다.

Why? 왜 정답일까?

'Saving water is a straightforward, reasonable way to make the most of the fresh water.'에서 지구상의 물을 최대한 잘 활용하려면 물을 절약해야 한다고 이야기하므로, 글의 제목으로 가장 적절한 것은 ③ '왜 우리는 물을 낭비하지 말아야 하는가'이다.

- **developed nation** 선진국
- **flow** 흐르다
- **use up** 소진하다, 다 써버리다
- **readily** 선뜻, 기꺼이
- **shortage** 부족
- **take ~ for granted** ~을 당연하게 여기다
- **tap** 수도꼭지
- **potentially** 잠재적으로
- **practical** 실질적인, 실제적인
- **straightforward** 직접적, 간단한

---

20 자기만의 책을 소유해야 하는 이유 　　　　정답 ④

다음 글의 주제로 가장 적절한 것은? [3점]
① benefits of putting books in order – 책을 순서대로 놓는 것의 이점
② ways we can read a book a week – 한 주에 한 권씩 책을 읽는 방법
③ things to consider when writing a book – 책을 쓸 때 고려할 사항들
✓ the reason we should possess our own books – 자기만의 책을 소유해야 하는 이유
⑤ the importance of reading various kinds of books – 다양한 종류의 책을 읽는 것의 중요성

독서 습관은 인류의 가장 위대한 자원 중 하나이다. 그리고 우리는 빌린 책보다 우리가 소유한 책을 읽는 것을 훨씬 더 즐긴다. 빌린 책은 집에 온 손님과 같아서, 예의 바르게 그리고 정식으로 취급되어야 한다. 그 책이 손상되지 않는지 지켜보고 있어야 한다. 그 책을 무심하게 놓아둘 수도 없고, 책에 표시를 할 수도 없으며, 페이지를 접어둘 수도 없고, 편하게 이용할 수도 없다. 그러다가, 언젠가는 정말로 그것을 돌려주어야 한다. 하지만 당신 소유의 책은 당신의 것이어서 편하게 취급할 수 있다. 책에 표시를 하거나, 책을 탁자에 놓거나, 펼쳐놓고 엎어놓고 하는 데 겁을 먹을 필요가 없다.

Why? 왜 정답일까?

'But your own books belong to you; you treat them with familiarity.'에서 자기 소유의 책은 훨씬 더 편하게 다룰 수 있다고 이야기하며 책을 빌리기보다 직접 소유하는 것이 좋다는 내용을 제시하므로, 글의 주제로 가장 적절한 것은 ④ '자기만의 책을 소유해야 하는 이유'이다.

- **mankind** 인류
- **properly** 예의 바르게, 적절히
- **carelessly** 무심하게, 부주의하게
- **turn down** (옷깃이나 종이를) 접다
- **treat** 취급하다, 다루다
- **formally** 정식으로, 공식적으로
- **mark** 표시하다
- **familiarly** 편하게, 친근하게

---

21 가족 계획에 십 대를 참여시키는 방법 　　　　정답 ⑤

다음 글의 요지로 가장 적절한 것은? [4점]
① 부모는 자녀의 또래 관계에 관심을 가져야 한다.
② 자녀와 함께 보내는 시간은 양보다 질이 중요하다.
③ 부모의 대화 방식이 자녀의 성격에 영향을 미친다.
④ 부모의 지나친 간섭은 자녀의 정체성 확립에 방해된다.
✓ 가족 활동 계획 시 자녀를 독립된 인격체로 참여시켜야 한다.

십 대들은 자기 또래 집단과 무언가 신나는 것을 계획하고 자기 부모와 어울리고 싶어 하지 않는다. 부모는 이를 거절 또는 가족과 함께 하려는 욕구의 부족으로 여긴다. 하지만, 만일 부모가 십 대 아이를 한 명의 사람(독립심과 자기 정체성을 가진 누군가)으로 인식하고 계획 단계에서 함께 상의한다면, 십 대 아이는 가족과 함께하는 데 매우 관심을 가졌을 것이다. 우리가 십 대들을 아이로 인식하고 그들을 위해 계획을 짜줄 때야말로 우리가 그들이 가족과 함께하고 싶어 하지 않는다는 인상을 받게 되는 때이다.

Why? 왜 정답일까?

'However, if the parents had recognized the teenager as a person (someone with independence and self-identity) and had consulted with the teenager at the planning stage, the teenager may have been very interested in joining the family.'에서 십 대 아이를 독립적인 개체로 인정하고 가족 활동을 계획하는 단계에서 아이와 함께 상의하라는 조

언을 간접적으로 제시하므로, 글의 요지로 가장 적절한 것은 ⑤ '가족 활동 계획 시 자녀를 독립된 인격체로 참여시켜야 한다.'이다.

- go with ～와 어울리다
- lack 부족, 결여
- independence 독립(심)
- consult with ～와 상의하다
- rejection 거절, 거부
- recognize 인정하다
- self-identity 자기 정체성
- impression 인상, 느낌

22 비행기 추락 후 고립된 소년들 · 정답 ①

다음 글의 상황에 나타난 분위기로 가장 적절한 것은? [3점]

✓ hopeless – 절망적인   ② cheerful – 쾌활한   ③ noisy – 시끄러운
④ peaceful – 평화로운   ⑤ humorous – 우스운

Bill은 안경을 벗어 셔츠로 닦았다. "우리가 여기 있다는 걸 누가 알겠어? 우리 행방을 아무도 모를 걸." Bill이 말했다. 그는 전보다 창백했고 숨이 가빴다. "어쩌면 사람들은 우리가 어디로 가려고 했는지 알았을 수도 있고, 몰랐을 수도 있어. 하지만 우리가 아예 도착을 못했기 때문에 사람들은 우리가 어디 있는지 몰라." Bill은 다른 소년들을 쳐다보았다. "그게 내가 하려는 말이었어." Ralph가 말했다. 그는 다른 소년들의 심각한 얼굴을 보며 덧붙였다. "우리 비행기는 격추되어 불에 휩싸였어. 누구도 우리가 어디 있는지 몰라. 우린 아마 오랫동안 여기 갇혀있게 될 거야." 너무 완전한 침묵이어서 그들은 서로의 숨소리를 들을 수 있었다. 누구도 어떤 말도 하지 않았다.

Why? 왜 정답일까?

'"Our plane was shot down in flames. Nobody knows where we are. We might be stuck here for a long time."'을 통해 비행기가 격추된 상황에서 소년들이 고립을 예감하고 불안함과 절망에 휩싸인 장면을 묘사하므로, 상황에 나타난 분위기로 가장 적절한 것은 ① '절망적인'이다.

- take off (옷 등을) 벗다
- breathless 숨이 가쁜, 숨이 찬
- in flames 불에 휩싸인, 활활 타올라
- wipe out 닦다
- shot down ～을 격추시키다, 총으로 쏘아 넘어뜨리다

23 아이들에게 정기적으로 봉사를 경험하게 할 필요성 · 정답 ⑤

다음 글에서 필자가 주장하는 바로 가장 적절한 것은? [4점]

① 봉사자는 수용적인 태도를 갖추어야 한다.
② 수혜자들에게 필요한 자원봉사가 이루어져야 한다.
③ 자원봉사 관련 프로그램을 다양하게 개발해야 한다.
④ 어릴 때부터 봉사와 관련된 책을 많이 읽어야 한다.
✓ 아이들에게 정기적으로 봉사를 경험할 수 있게 해야 한다.

1년에 한 번 있는 자원봉사 날은 아이들이 인정 많은 사고방식을 취하는 데 좀처럼 충분하지 않다. 외로운 이웃을 위해 여분의 쿠키를 굽는 것, 작은 기쁨을 보태고자 양로원에서 노래를 부르는 것과 같이, 당신의 아이가 정기적으로 주는 것의 기쁨을 경험하도록 도울 방법을 찾아라. 아이를 자선 활동에 참여시키는 목적은 노벨상을 타는 것이 아닌, 그들에게 선을 체험할 기회를 주는 데 있다. 사실은, 아이들은 교과서에서 선행에 대해 읽는 것을 통해 친절해지는 법을 배우는 것이 아니라, 착한 행동을 하는 것으로부터 배운다. 더 많은 아이들이 정기적인 방법으로 주는 것이 어떤 기분인지 경험할수록, 그들은 자선 정신을 키워나갈 가능성이 더 높다.

Why? 왜 정답일까?

'Look for ways to help your children experience the joy of giving on a regular basis.'에서 아이들에게 정기적으로 선행을 할 기회를 갖도록 하라고 이야기하므로, 필자가 주장하는 바로 가장 적절한 것은 ⑤ '아이들에게 정기적으로 봉사를 경험할 수 있게 해야 한다.'이다.

- rarely 좀처럼 ～않다
- charitable 인정 많은, 자비로운
- opportunity 기회
- adopt 취하다, 채택하다
- on a regular basis 정기적으로, 규칙적으로
- goodness 선(善)

24 창의적인 통찰을 얻는 방법 · 정답 ④

다음 글의 빈칸 (A), (B)에 들어갈 말로 가장 적절한 것은? [4점]

	(A)	(B)		(A)	(B)
①	however 하지만	Besides 게다가	②	moreover 더욱이	However 하지만
③	moreover 더욱이	In addition 더구나	✓④	for example 예를 들어	However 하지만
⑤	for example 예를 들어	In addition 더구나			

자기 주제에 집중하는 것은 창의적인 통찰을 얻는 데 중요한 요인이다. (A) 예를 들어, 뉴튼은 일 내내 그 문제에 대해 생각하여 중력의 법칙에 이르렀다. 창의적인 통찰은 우리가 많은 지식과 경험을 갖고 있는 분야에서 가장 얻기 쉬운 듯하다. (B) 하지만 여기에는 모순이 있는데, 왜냐하면 우리는 우리가 이미 알고 있다고 생각하는 것에 관해서는 잘 생각하지 않는 경향이 있기 때문이다. 이미 있는 생각은 우리가 새로운 가능성을 깨닫지 못하게 만드는 경향이 있다. 이는 잘 알고 있다고 믿는 활동에 많은 노력을 기울이지 않는다면 창의적인 생각이 우리에게 다가오지 않을 것임을 뜻한다.

Why? 왜 정답일까?

(A) 빈칸 앞에서 자기 주제에 집중하는 것은 창의적인 통찰을 얻는 데 중요한 요인이라는 일반화된 내용을 말한 데 이어, 뒤에서는 '뉴튼'이라는 구체적인 학자의 경우가 예시로 나오므로, (A)에 들어갈 말로 적절한 것은 'for example'이다.

(B) 빈칸 앞에서 창의적인 통찰은 자기가 정통한 분야에서 가장 얻기 쉽다고 이야기하는데, 뒤에서는 이 말에 '모순'이 있다고 지적하면서 사람들은 자기가 알고 있다고 생각하는 것에 관해서는 잘 생각하지 않기 때문이라는 이유를 든다. 즉 빈칸 앞뒤로 서로 상반된 내용이 연결되므로, (B)에 들어갈 말로 적절한 것은 'However'이다. 정답은 ④ '예를 들어 – 하지만'이다.

- factor 요인
- insight 통찰
- paradox 모순
- realize 깨닫다
- gain 얻다
- gravitation 중력, 만유인력
- existing 이미 있는, 현존하는

25 비교할 만한 대안의 존재가 선택에 미치는 영향 · 정답 ③

다음 글의 내용을 한 문장으로 요약하고자 한다. 빈칸 (A)와 (B)에 들어갈 말로 가장 적절한 것은? [4점]

	(A)	(B)		(A)	(B)
①	creative 창의적인	a better deal 더 좋은 거래	②	creative 창의적인	a bad decision 나쁜 결정
✓③	attractive 매력적인	a better deal 더 좋은 거래	④	attractive 매력적인	a difficult choice 어려운 선택
⑤	objective 객관적인	a difficult choice 어려운 선택			

잠재적 고객들이 두 가지의 정기 구독 가입 제안을 받았는데, 56달러에 "온라인만" 이용, 125달러에 "온라인 + 인쇄본" 이용이 그것이었다. 대다수의 고객들이 첫 번째 안(56달러)를 골랐다. 그러고 나서 출판사에서는 그들이 알기로 누구도 선호하지 않을 것이었던 세 번째 안을 내놓았다. "인쇄본만 이용하는 데 125달러." 예상한 대로, 누구도 세 번째 안을 고르지 않았지만, 마법 같은 일이 일어났다! 다수가 이제 두 번째 안(온라인 + 인쇄본 이용에 125달러)을 골랐던 것이다! 이 세 번째 안의 도입은 2안을 괜찮은 거래처럼 보이게 만들었다. 온라인 버전을 무료로 얻게 되니 말이다! 여기에 무슨 일이 있던 걸까? 두 가지 안이 있는 첫 번째 시나리오는 각 안을 비교해 볼 대상이 아무것도 없었다. 하지만 세 번째 안의 도입으로, 2안과 3안이 비교 가능해졌고 2안이 이겼다. 1안은 비교 대상이 없으므로 제쳐졌다.

→ 딜 (A) 매력적인 세 번째 안의 도입은 비슷한 안(2안)을 상대적으로 (B) 더 좋은 거래처럼 보이게 만들었다.

Why? 왜 정답일까?

'The introduction of this third option made option 2 seem like a good bargain.'과 마지막 세 문장에서, 기존의 안과 비교가 가능하되 덜 매력적인 새로운 안을 도입하면 사람들이 기존 안을 더 많이 선택하도록 유도할 수 있다는 내용이 나오므로, 빈칸 (A)와 (B)에 들어갈 말로 적절한 것은 ③ (A) 'attractive(매력적인), (B) a better deal(더 좋은 거래)'이다.

- potential 잠재적인, (～이 될) 가능성이 있는
- majority 다수
- introduction 도입, 소개
- comparable 비교 가능한, 비교할 수 있는
- subscription 정기 구독
- publisher 출판사, 출판인
- for free 무료로
- left out 제쳐진, 버려진

26-27 타인을 위해 돈을 쓰면 커지는 행복

어떤 사람들은 많은 돈을 갖고 있으면 더 행복해질 거라고 믿는다. 예를 들어, 많은 사람들은 그들이 복권에 당첨되면 행복해질 거라고 생각한다. 하지만, 많은 복권 당첨자는 돈을 많이 써서 많은 빚을 진다. 또한, 그들은 친구와 가족이 선물이나 돈, 융자를 원하여 재정적 문제를 겪는다. 이러한 것들은 사람들을 불행하게 만든다. 복권 당첨자에 대한 이 예시는 "돈으로 행복을 살 수는 없다"는 것을 보여준다. 하지만, 이게 항상 사실일까?

경영대학원 교수 Michael Norton은 사람들이 돈을 가지고 어떻게 처신하는지에 대한 실험을 진행했다. 한 실험에서, 몇몇 대학생들은 자기 자신에게 돈을 썼고 몇몇 학생들은 다른 사람에게 돈을 썼다. 이후에, 모든 학생들은 기분에 대해 질문을 받았다. 자기 자신을 위해 돈을 쓴 학생들은 불행하다고 느끼지는 않았지만, 더 행복해 보이지도 않았다. 하지만 연구에서는 남들을 위해 돈을 쓴 학생들이 더 행복하다고 느꼈음을 보여주었다. Michael Norton은 전 세계에서 모든 연령대의 사람들을 데리고 이 유형의 돈 실험을 진행했다. 매번 결과는 똑같았다. 남을 위해 돈을 쓰는 것은 (돈을) 주는 사람의 행복감을 높였다.

- lottery 복권
- debt 빚
- financial 재정적인, 금융의
- experiment 실험
- overspend 너무 많이 쓰다
- loan 융자, 대출
- behave 처신하다, 행동하다

26 빈칸 추론 · 정답 ①

윗글의 빈칸에 들어갈 말로 가장 적절한 것은? [4점]

✓ improved – 높였다   ② blinded – 가렸다   ③ reduced – 감소시켰다
④ destroyed – 파괴했다   ⑤ bothered – 괴롭혔다

Why? 왜 정답일까?

실험의 예를 들어 그 결과를 주제로 제시한 글이다. 'However, the research shows that students that spent money on others felt happier.'에서 남을 위해 돈을 쓴 학생들이 더 큰 행복감을 느꼈다는 연구 결과가 제시되므로, 빈칸에 들어갈 말로 가장 적절한 것은 ① '높였다'이다.

27 제목 파악 · 정답 ⑤

윗글의 제목으로 가장 적절한 것은? [3점]

① A Wealthy Life is a Healthy Life – 부유한 삶이 건강한 삶이다
② The Key to Making Other People Feel Happy – 타인을 행복하게 만드는 비결
③ Managing Your Finance after Winning the Lottery – 복권 당첨 후 재정 관리하기
④ Saving Money Will Save You from Your Troubles – 저축이 당신을 문제로부터 지켜줄 것이다
✓ Happiness Gained from Spending Money on Others – 남을 위해 돈을 쓰는 행위에서 얻어지는 행복

Why? 왜 정답일까?

'However, the research shows that students that spent money on others felt happier.'에서 사람들은 남을 위해 돈을 쓸 때 더한 행복감을 느낀다는 내용을 제시하므로, 글의 제목으로 가장 적절한 것은 ⑤ '남을 위해 돈을 쓰는 행위에서 얻어지는 행복'이다.

(A)

┌ :30번 ①의 근거(불일치)
「6년 전 내 아들 Nick은 학교 축제에서 금붕어 한 마리를 들고 돌아왔다.」작은 용기를 찾아 나는 무신경하게 그것을 던져놓았다. Nick은 자기가 Fred라고 이름 붙여준 외톨이에게 곧 흥미를 잃어버렸다. 나는 돌보는 사람 역할을 떠맡았다.「최소한으로 필요한 음식과 신선한 물 외에, 나는 (a) 물고기의 집을 더 흥미롭게 만들어줄 그 어떤 일도 하지 않았다. 아치형 장식도, 식물도, 돌도 없었다.」 ┘ :30번 ②의 근거(불일치)

(C)

하지만 시간이 지나면서 나는 Fred와 가까워졌다. 그가 많이 움직여 다니지 않을 때면 나는 걱정이 되었다.「그가 죽어간다는 생각이 들었고, (d) 그를 움직이게 하려고 6인치짜리 어항을 크게 두드리곤 했다. 그는 활기를 찾았고 나는 안심이 되었다. 아침이면 나는 그가 거기 있는 것을 보고 안도하곤 했다.」 ┘ :30번 ④의 근거(불일치)

(D)

┌ :30번 ⑤의 근거(불일치)
지난여름, 남편과 나는 Nick이 캠프에 가 있는 동안 Montana로 갔다.「우리는 우리 19살짜리 아들 John에게 집과 Fred를 맡겼다.「나도 모르는 새에 그는 Fred를 놓아주겠다고 결심한 상태였다.」(e) 그는 하루하루 그렇게 작고 외로운 환경에 갇혀 있는 Fred를 더 이상 두고 볼 수 없었다.

(B)

┌ :30번 ③의 근거(일치)
「그래서 그는 (b) 그를 우리 근처의 작은 교회로 데려갔는데, 거기에는 아름다운 연못이 있었다. 덩치가 더 큰 다른 물고기 한 마리가 거기 혼자 있었다.」John이 Fred를 물에 놓아주자, 그는 어찌할 바 모르는 채 거기 누워 있었고, John은 (c) 그가 빠져 죽을까 걱정이 되었다. 하지만 갑자기 그 큰 물고기가 다가와서 Fred를 부드럽게 쳤고, 천천히 그들은 함께 자리를 떴다.

- goldfish 금붕어
- carelessly 부주의하게
- take over 떠맡다, 넘겨받다
- pond 연못
- tap 두드리다
- reassured 안도한, 마음이 놓인
- bear 참다, 두고 ~하다
- container 용기, 그릇
- dump 던져놓다, 버리다
- caretaker 돌보는 사람, 관리인
- lie(-lay-lain) 눕다, (놓여) 있다
- lively 활기찬
- no longer 더 이상 ~ 않는

28 글의 순서 찾기 정답 ③

주어진 글 (A)에 이어질 내용을 순서에 맞게 배열한 것으로 가장 적절한 것은? [3점]
① (B) - (D) - (C)
② (C) - (B) - (D)
✓ (C) - (D) - (B)
④ (D) - (B) - (C)
⑤ (D) - (C) - (B)

Why? 왜 정답일까?

아들인 Nick이 학교 축제에서 금붕어를 들고 왔고 처음에는 필자가 이 물고기에 큰 관심을 두지 않았다는 내용의 (A) 뒤에는, 날이 갈수록 이 물고기에 정을 느꼈다는 내용의 (C)가 이어져야 적절하다. 이 뒤로는 시간이 바뀌어 '지난여름'이 되었고 필자 부부가 Montana로 떠나 있는 새에 또 다른 아들인 John이 물고기를 놓아주기로 결심했다는 내용의 (D), 실제로 물고기를 교회 연못에 놓아주었다는 내용의 (B)가 차례로 이어져야 자연스럽다. 따라서 주어진 글 (A) 뒤에 이어질 내용을 순서에 맞게 배열한 것으로 가장 적절한 것은 ③ '(C) - (D) - (B)'이다.

29 지칭 추론 정답 ⑤

밑줄 친 (a) ~ (e) 중 가리키는 대상이 나머지 넷과 다른 것은? [3점]
① (a) ② (b) ③ (c) ④ (d) ✓ (e)

Why? 왜 정답일까?

(a), (b), (c), (d)는 'Fred'를, (e)는 'John'을 지칭하므로, 밑줄 친 (a) ~ (e) 중 가리키는 대상이 나머지 넷과 다른 것은 ⑤ '(e)'이다.

30 세부 내용 파악 정답 ③

윗글의 내용과 일치하는 것은? [3점]
① Nick은 시장에서 금붕어 한 마리를 사왔다.
② Nick의 가족은 Fred의 집에 식물과 돌을 넣어주었다.
✓ 교회 연못에는 커다란 물고기 한 마리가 살고 있었다.
④ Nick은 아침마다 Fred가 움직이는지 확인했다.
⑤ John은 Fred를 놓아주겠다고 엄마에게 알렸다.

Why? 왜 정답일까?

'One other fish, a larger one, was there alone.'을 통해 Fred를 놓아주러 간 교회 연못에는 덩치가 더 큰 물고기가 먼저 살고 있었음을 알 수 있으므로, 내용과 일치하는 것은 ③ '교회 연못에는 커다란 물고기 한 마리가 살고 있었다.'이다.

Why? 왜 오답일까?

① 'Six years ago, my son, Nick, brought home a goldfish from the school festival.'에서 Nick은 시장이 아닌 학교 축제에서 금붕어를 가져왔음을 알 수 있다.
② 'Not an arch, plant, or rock.'에서 Fred의 집에 아치형 장식, 식물, 돌을 아무것도 넣어주지 않았다고 하였다.
④ 'Mornings, I'd see him there and feel reassured.'에서 Fred가 잘 있는지 아침마다 확인한 사람은 Nick이 아닌 필자였음을 알 수 있다.
⑤ 'Unknown to me he'd made the decision to set Fred free.'에서 John은 엄마인 필자도 모르게 Fred를 놓아주겠다고 결심했음을 알 수 있다.

• 정답 •

01 ⑤ 02 ④ 03 ③ 04 ① 05 ② 06 ③ 07 ⑤ 08 ③ 09 ⑤ 10 ① 11 ④ 12 ② 13 ⑤ 14 ③ 15 ④ 16 ③ 17 ③ 18 ④ 19 ⑤ 20 ① 21 ③ 22 ③ 23 ③ 24 ⑤ 25 ② 26 ① 27 ③ 28 ③ 29 ② 30 ⑤

01 Pablo Picasso가 그림을 그리게 된 계기 정답 ⑤

밑줄 친 He[him/his]가 가리키는 대상이 나머지 넷과 다른 것은? [2점]

1881년 10월 25일에, 남부 스페인 말라가에서 한 미술교사와 그의 아내는 남자 아이를 낳았다. 몇 년 후에 그 아이는 위대한 예술가, Pablo Picasso로 알려지게 되었다. Pablo의 부모는 ① 그가 화가가 되기를 바랐다. 소년시절에, ② 그는 종종 그의 아버지와 투우경기에 갔었다. Pablo의 첫 번째 알려진 그림은 투우에 관한 것이었다. 그가 그것을 그렸을 때 ③ 그는 고작 8살 정도였다. 모든 이들은 그가 미술에 재능이 있다고 생각했고 그들이 옳았다. Pablo가 13살일 때, ④ 그는 그의 첫 미술 전시회를 가졌다. 그 즈음에 그의 아버지는 Pablo가 자신이 하는 것보다 더 잘 그린다는 것을 알아챘다. 그래서 Pablo의 아버지는 ⑤ 그의 아들에게 그의 모든 붓과 물감을 주었고, 다시는 그림을 그리지 않았다.

Why? 왜 정답일까?

①, ②, ③, ④는 Pablo Picasso를 가리키지만 ⑤는 Pablo Picasso의 아버지를 가리킨다. 따라서 밑줄 친 He[him / his]가 가리키는 대상이 나머지 넷과 다른 것은 ⑤이다.

- southern 남쪽(남부)에 위치한
- gift (재능 등을) 부여하다, 재주
- bullfight 투우

02 손상된 공중화장실 수리 요청 정답 ④

다음 글의 목적으로 가장 적절한 것은? [3점]
① 공원 화장실 이용 수칙을 안내하려고
② 학교 운동장 개방 시간을 공지하려고
③ 학생 안전교육의 필요성을 강조하려고
✓ 손상된 공중화장실 시설 수리를 요청하려고
⑤ 체계적인 공중시설 관리 방안을 제시하려고

우리는 중심가 Grand Park에 있는 화장실 시설들에 관한 염려를 표하고 싶습니다. 공원의 편리한 위치 덕분에, 우리 이웃 아이들은 방과 후 놀이 시설에서 노는 데에 많은 시간을 보냅니다. 우리들 중 일부는 그 시설을 오늘 아침에 방문했고, 그것들의 상태를 보고 섬뜩했습니다. 고장 난 변기에서 물이 흘러 바닥이 잠겨있었습니다. 아이들은 그렇게 된지 몇 주가 지났다고 말합니다. 이것은 사용자들에게 확연한 위험입니다. 부탁입니다. 그것을 당장 수리해주십시오. 우리는 당신의 사무소가 가능한 빨리 조치를 취해주길 요청합니다.

Why? 왜 정답일까?

중심가 Grand Park에 있는 화장실에 있는 변기가 고장이 나 이용객들에게 위험하니 수리할 것을 요청하는(It is clearly a danger to the users. Please, repair them immediately.) 글이다. 따라서 글의 목적으로 적절한 것은 ④ '손상된 공중화장실 시설 수리를 요청하려고'이다.

- express 표현하다, 나타내다
- convenient 편리한
- equipment 장비, 용품
- toilet 변기, 화장실
- take action 조치를 취하다
- facility 시설, 설비
- location 위치, 장소
- horrify 소름 끼치게(무섭게) 하다
- immediately 즉시

03 시행착오를 통해 배우는 용돈 관리의 필요성 정답 ③

다음 글의 밑줄 친 부분 중, 어법상 틀린 것은? [4점]

여러분의 부모는 여러분이 용돈을 현명하게 쓰지 않을 것을 걱정할 수도 있다. 여러분이 돈을 쓰는 데 몇 가지 어리석은 선택을 할 수도 있지만, 만일 여러분이 그렇게 한다면 그 결정은 여러분 자신의 결정이고 바라건대 여러분은 자신의 실수로 배울 것이다. 배움의 많은 부분이 시행착오를 거쳐서 일어난다. 돈은 여러분이 평생 동안 처리해 나가야 할 어떤 것임을 여러분의 부모에게 설명해라. 삶에서 나중보다 이른 시기에 실수를 저지르는 것이 더 낫다. 여러분이 언젠가는 가정을 갖게 될 것이라는 것과, 자신의 돈을 관리하는 법을 알 필요가 있다는 것을 설명해라. 학교에서 모든 것을 가르쳐 주는 것은 아니다!

Why? 왜 정답일까?

'It is better what you make your mistakes early on rather than later in life.'에서 what 이하가 주어, 동사, 목적어가 있는 완전한 문장이므로, 형식상의 주어 It에 대응하는 내용상의 주어인 명사절을 이끄는 that으로 고쳐야 한다. 따라서 ③의 what을 that으로 고쳐야 한다.

Why? 왜 오답일까?

① 'do'는 앞의 'make ~ choices'를 가리키는 대동사이다.
② 주어가 'Much'이므로 단수 동사 'occurs'가 쓰였다.
④ 'how to manage your money'가 'know'의 목적어 역할을 하고 있다.
⑤ 'everything'은 단수 취급을 하고 주어진 문장에선 '모든 것이 가르쳐지다'의 의미이기 때문에 수동태로 쓰였다.

- allowance 수당, 용돈
- through ~을 통해
- rather than ~보다는, 차라리
- hopefully 바라건대
- trial and error 시행착오
- manage 관리하다

04 가르치기의 중요성　　　　　　　　　　　정답 ①

(A), (B), (C)의 각 네모 안에서 어법에 맞는 낱말로 가장 적절한 것은? [4점]

	(A)	(B)	(C)
✓①	is	take	call
②	is	taken	call
③	is	take	calling
④	are	taken	calling
⑤	are	take	call

당신이 무엇인가 통달했는지를 아는 최선의 방법 중 하나는 그것을 가르쳐보는 것이다. 학생들에게 그 기회를 줘라. 교실 각각의 학생에게 당신이 공부하고 있는 광범위한 주제의 다른 양상을 알려주고 그 후에 그들이 배운 것을 다른 학우들에게 교대로 가르치게 해봐라. 그리고 일단 그것에 능숙해지면, 그들이 가르쳐야하는 것을 배우기 위해 그들에게 다른 학급이나 선생님들 혹은 부모를 초대하여 더 폭넓은 청중을 제공해봐라. 또한, 학기를 시작할 때, 학생들 개인의 관심사에 관해 물어봐라. 당신의 전문가 목록을 만들고, 학기 내내 필요에 따라 그들에게 요청하라. 가르치는 사람들의 교실은 배우는 사람들의 교실이다.

Why? 왜 정답일까?

(A)가 포함된 문장에서 주어는 'One of the best ways'로, One에 수를 일치시켜서 단수 동사 is가 쓰인 것은 어법상 적절하다.

(B)가 포함된 문장에서 '~ and then have them ~' 부분을 보면 have는 사역 동사, them은 목적어이고 그 다음은 목적격 보어가 오는 5형식 문형이다. 해석상 '그들이 교대하는' 능동의 의미이므로 동사원형 take가 오는 것이 적절하다.

(C) 동사원형 Keep으로 시작하는 명령문 형태로 접속사 and로 연결되어 있으므로 동사원형 call이 오는 것이 적절하다. 따라서 (A), (B), (C)의 각 네모 안에서 어법에 맞는 낱말로 가장 적절한 것은 ① '(A) is – (B) take – (C) call'이다.

- **opportunity** 기회
- **broader** 광범위한, 넓은
- **individual** 각각(개개)의
- **call upon** ~에게 요청하다(부탁하다)
- **aspect** 측면, 양상
- **take turns** 교대로 ~하다
- **expert** 전문가
- **throughout** ~내내, 도처에

05 Debbie가 항공사의 특별 대우를 받은 이유　　정답 ②

다음 빈칸에 들어갈 말로 가장 적절한 것을 고르시오. [4점]

① courageous – 용기 있는　✓② loyal – 충실한　③ complaining – 불평하는
④ dangerous – 위험한　⑤ temporary – 일시적인

최근에 아시아로 가는 비행에서 나는 Debbie를 만났는데, 그녀는 승무원 모두에게 따뜻한 인사를 받았으며 심지어 기장에게도 탑승에 대한 환영을 받았다. 그녀에게 쏟아지고 있는 그 모든 관심에 놀라서 나는 그녀가 그 항공사에 근무하는지 물어보았다. 그녀는 그렇지는 않았지만, 그 관심을 받을 자격이 있었는데, 이 비행이 그녀가 이 동일한 항공사로 400만 마일 넘게 비행하는 획기적인 기록을 세웠기 때문이다. 비행 동안에 나는 그 항공사의 최고 경영자가 그녀에게 직접 전화를 걸어 그녀가 오랫동안 그들의 서비스를 이용한 것에 감사했으며, 그녀가 선택할 수 있도록 멋진 고급 선물 목록을 받았다는 것을 알게 되었다. Debbie는 한 가지 매우 중요한 이유 때문에 이러한 특별 대우를 받을 수 있었는데, 그녀는 그 항공사에 충실한 고객이었기 때문이었다.

Why? 왜 정답일까?

'나'는 아시아행 비행기에서 Debbie를 만났고, 그녀가 승무원, 기장에게 탑승에 대한 환영을 받는 걸 보고 궁금해 했는데 Debbi이 이 항공사로 400만 마일 넘게 비행하는 놀라운 기록을 세운 것(~ but she deserved the attention, for this flight marked the milestone of her flying over 4 million miles with this same airline.)을 알게 됐다. 따라서 Debbie가 오랫동안 이 항공사의 고객이었다는 것을 알 수 있으므로 빈칸에 들어갈 말로 가장 적절한 것은 ② 'loyal(충실한)'이다.

- **recently** 최근에
- **flight attendant** 비행기 승무원
- **deserve** ~을 받을 자격이 있다
- **receive** 받다
- **treatment** 대우, 취급
- **customer** 고객
- **greet** 맞다, 환영하다
- **aboard** 탑승한
- **milestone** 획기적인 사건
- **acquire** 얻다, 획득하다
- **reason** 이유, 이성
- **loyal** 충실한

06 3D 프린트 기술　　　　　　　　　　　　　정답 ③

다음 빈칸에 들어갈 말로 가장 적절한 것을 고르시오. [3점]

① mix – 섞다　② open – 열다　✓③ draw – 그리다
④ move – 움직이다　⑤ taste – 맛보다

오늘날, 3D 프린트 기술은 회사와 대학에서만 사용되지만, 이제 가격은 더 낮아지고 질은 더 좋아지고 있다. 모든 가정이 미래에 3D 프린터를 보유하는 것을 상상해 볼 수 있다. 3D 프린트 기술은 복제할 원래의 물건을 필요로 하지 않는다는 점에 주목하라. 즉, 그 물체를 정확하게 묘사하는 한, 어떤 그림이라도 충분할 것이다. 머지않아 누군가 적절한 디자인을 만들어 내는 가정용 스케치 도구를 사용할 수 있고, 그 다음에는 가정용 프린터가 진짜 물건을 만들어 낼 수 있을 것이다. 그릴 수 있으면 만들 수 있다. 예를 들어 손님을 위한 정찬용 접시가 충분하지 않다면, 스케치로부터 실제 접시 몇 개를 '출력(제작)'할 수 있다.

Why? 왜 정답일까?

3D 프린터를 이용하면, 스케치 도구로 그림을 그려 진짜 물건을 만들어 낼 수 있을 것이라(Soon anyone can use a home sketching tool to produce the proper design, and then the home printer will be able to create the actual physical object.) 하고 있다. 따라서 빈칸에 들어갈 단어로 적절한 것은 ③ '그리다'이다.

- **technology** (과학)기술
- **require** 요구하다, 필요로 하다
- **quality** 질, 고급
- **describe** 묘사하다

- **original** 원래의
- **proper** 적당한, 적절한
- **actual** 실제의, 사실의
- **precisely** 정확하게
- **create** 창조하다, 만들어내다
- **physical object** 물체

07 집중하기와 먹는 양 사이의 관계　　　　　　정답 ⑤

다음 빈칸에 들어갈 말로 가장 적절한 것을 고르시오. [4점]

① make us talk with others – 우리가 다른 사람들과 대화하게 하다
② improve students' creativity – 학생들의 창의력을 증진시키다
③ take some time to disappear – 사라지는 데 시간이 걸리다
④ turn bad ideas into good ones – 형편없는 생각을 좋은 생각으로 변화시키다
✓⑤ encourage people to consume more – 사람들이 더 많이 먹도록 조장하다

사람들은 그들이 식사시간에 산만해져 음식에 주의를 기울이고 있지 않을 때 상당히 더 많이 먹는다. 한 실험에서, 영화 팬이 영화에 쏟는 관심의 양은 얼마나 많이 그들이 팝콘을 먹었는지와 관련이 있었다. 영화에 더욱 몰입했던 사람들은 확연하게 많은 양을 먹었다. 또 다른 실험에서, 점심시간 동안 재밌는 이야기를 들었던 사람들은 말없이 앉아 있었던 사람들보다 15% 더 많은 음식을 먹었다. TV를 보거나 잡지를 읽는 것 같이, 먹는 동안에 집중을 방해하는 것들은 사람들이 더 많이 먹도록 조장한다.

Why? 왜 정답일까?

사람들이 식사 시간에 산만해져 음식에 집중하지 못할 때 상당히 더 많이 먹고 영화에 몰입한 사람이 상당히 더 많은 양을 먹었다(Those who were more absorbed by the movie ate significantly larger amounts.)는 내용에서 식사 하는 동안 집중을 방해하는 것은 사람들이 더 많이 먹게 된다는 것을 알 수 있다. 따라서 빈칸에 들어갈 말로 가장 적절한 것은 ⑤ '사람들이 더 많이 먹도록 조장하다'이다.

- **significantly** 상당히
- **relate** 관련(결부)시키다
- **encourage** 격려(고무)하다
- **attention** 주의(집중)
- **disappear** 사라지다
- **consume** 소모하다

08 공정한 대우 받기를 기대하는 원숭이　　　　정답 ③

다음 빈칸에 들어갈 말로 가장 적절한 것을 고르시오. [4점]

① the taste of a grape is sour – 포도의 맛이 시다
② female monkeys tend to be patient – 암컷 원숭이들이 참는 경향이 있다
✓③ they expect to receive fair treatment – 그들이 공정한 대우 받기를 기대한다
④ writing letters is impossible for monkeys – 원숭이들에게 글자 쓰는 것은 불가능하다
⑤ the leader of the monkeys is treated better – 원숭이들의 우두머리는 좀 더 좋은 대우를 받는다

연구 책임자 Sarah Brosnan은 암컷 눈목꼬리감기 원숭이들을 둘씩 짝을 지었다. 이 연구원은 원숭이들이 작은 돌멩이를 연구원과 교환하도록 훈련시켰다. 원숭이가 돌멩이를 연구원과 60초 안에 교환했을 때, 그 원숭이는 보상을 받았다. 대게 보상은 오이 한 조각이었다. 교환했던 눈목꼬리감기 원숭이의 파트너도 보상을 받았다. 가끔 그 파트너는 동일한 보상을 받았지만 어떤 때에는 그 파트너가 더 나은 보상(포도)을 받았다. Brosnan은 이 불공평한 대우에 대한 반응이 놀라웠다고 말했다. 파트너가 더 나은 대우를 받는 것을 눈목꼬리감기 원숭이가 봤을 때, 그 원숭이는 불만족스러워했다. 몇몇 눈목꼬리감기 원숭이는 그 테스트를 계속하거나 그들이 받았던 오이 먹기를 원하지 않았다. 몇몇은 그들의 음식을 연구원에게 던져버렸다. Brosnan은 그들이 공정한 대우 받기를 기대한다고 깨달았다.

Why? 왜 정답일까?

원숭이들을 대상으로 한 실험에서 원숭이가 자신의 짝꿍이 더 나은 보상을 받는 것에 만족하지 않았다(When a capuchin saw its partner get better treatment, it was unhappy.)는 내용에서 원숭이들은 공평한 대우 받기를 원한다는 걸 유추할 수 있다. 따라서 빈칸에 들어갈 말로 가장 적절한 것은 ③ '그들이 공정한 대우 받기를 기대한다'이다.

- **researcher** 연구원, 조사원
- **response** 대답, 응답
- **within** (특정한 기간) 이내에, 안에
- **treatment** 대우

09 다른 나라의 언어로 의사소통하려는 노력　　정답 ⑤

다음 글의 밑줄 친 부분 중, 문맥상 낱말의 쓰임이 적절하지 않은 것은? [4점]

세상은 좁고, 사업은 모든 문화권의 사람들을 함께 모이게 한다. ① 외국 방문객이 있는 회의에 참석할 수도 있고, 이해하지 못하는 언어를 쓰는 국가로 파견될 수도 있다. 언어의 ② 차이는 훌륭한 예절이 빛을 발하기 좋은 기회이다. 취해야 하는 가장 좋은 일련의 행동은 ③ (언어) 준비를 좀 하는 것이다. 상용 회화집을 구하여 "안녕하세요." "부탁합니다." "고맙습니다." "만나서 반갑습니다." "안녕히 가세요."와 같은 몇 가지 ④ 기본 표현을 배울 수 있다. 다른 사람의 언어로 의사소통하려고 노력하는 것은 그 사람에 대한 ⑤ 무례함(→ 존중)을 보여준다.

Why? 왜 정답일까?

필자는 언어가 다를지라도 기본 표현으로 소통함으로써 외국인에게 예절을 보여줄 수 있다 말하고 있다. 따라서 ⑤의 disrespect를 respect로 고쳐야 한다.

- **culture** 문화
- **send off** ~을 파견하다, ~을 발송하다
- **obtain** 얻다, 획득하다
- **disrespect** 무례
- **attend** 참석하다
- **gap** 차이
- **expression** 표현
- **shine** 빛나다

10 대체 에너지로 쓰이는 태양력　　　　　　　정답 ①

(A), (B), (C)의 각 네모 안에서 문맥에 맞는 낱말로 가장 적절한 것은? [3점]

	(A)	(B)	(C)
✓①	cleaner 더 깨끗한	useful 유용한	catch 받다, 잡다
②	cleaner 더 깨끗한	useless 소용없는	release 놓아주다

③ cleaner ····· useful ····· release
　더 깨끗한　유용한　놓아주다
④ cheaper ····· useless ····· catch
　더 저렴한　소용없는　받다, 잡다
⑤ cheaper ····· useful ····· release
　더 저렴한　유용한　놓아주다

전 세계 에너지의 대부분은 석탄과 석유에서 나온다. 그러나 그것들을 태우는 것은 오염된 가스를 방출한다. 이것이 세계의 가장 주된 오염원이다. 그래서 과학자들은 에너지를 만드는 (A) 더 깨끗한 방법들을 찾아 오고 있는 중이다. 그들은 몇몇 해답이 햇빛에서 빛나는 것을 발견했다. "태양열은 지구에게 (B) 도움이 됩니다."라고 신종 에너지를 연구하는 단체에서 일하는 Nancy Hazard는 말한다. 예를 들어, 호주의 Tindo 버스는 그것의 조명과 난방과 에어컨을 위해 태양열을 이용한다. 게다가, 일본에서 사람들은 일광을 (C) 붙잡아주는 특수 지붕 타일이 달린 집을 짓고 있다. 타일에 의해 남겨진 에너지는 한 가족 전체를 위한 충분한 전기를 생산할 수 있다. 앞으로 몇 년 내로 이런 집 약 70,000여 채가 지어질 것이다.

Why? 왜 정답일까?

(A)에서 석탄과 석유를 태우는 건 더러운 가스를 방출하고 이것이 세계 오염의 가장 큰 원인이므로 과학자들은 에너지를 만드는 데 더 깨끗한 방법을 찾아오고 있다는 것이 자연스럽다. 따라서 (A)에는 'cleaner(더 깨끗한)'이 들어가는 것이 적절하다.
(B)의 앞부분에서 과학자들은 햇빛에서 몇 가지 뛰어난 해답을 찾았다고 했으므로 태양력이 도움이 되는 에너지임을 유추할 수 있다. 따라서 (B)에는 'useful(유용한)'이 들어가는 것이 적절하다.
(C)의 앞부분에서 호주의 Tindo 버스가 태양력을 이용하는 예를 들며 첨가를 뜻하는 'In addition'으로 시작하므로 일본에서도 태양빛을 이용하는 경우를 말할 것임을 유추할 수 있다. 따라서 (C)에는 'catch(받다, 잡다)'가 들어가는 것이 적절하다. 따라서 (A), (B), (C)의 각 네모 안에서 문맥에 맞는 낱말로 가장 적절한 것은 ① '(A) cleaner – (B) useful – (C) catch'이다.

- coal 석탄
- pollution 오염, 공해
- give off 풍기다, 내뿜다
- entire 전체의

---

11 2014년 세계 최상위 국제 관광 소비 국가 　　정답 ④

다음 도표의 내용과 일치하지 <u>않는</u> 것은? [3점]

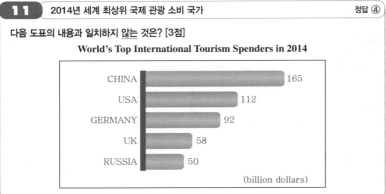

World's Top International Tourism Spenders in 2014

- CHINA 165
- USA 112
- GERMANY 92
- UK 58
- RUSSIA 50

(billion dollars)

위 도표는 2014년의 세계 최상위 국제 관광 소비 국가를 보여준다. ① 중국은 총 1,650억 달러로 목록의 최상위에 있었다. ② 세계에서 두 번째로 돈을 많이 소비한 국가인 미국은 국제 관광에 러시아의 두 배보다 더 많이 돈을 소비했다. ③ 미국보다 200억 달러가 적은 돈을 소비한 독일은 3위를 차지했다. ④ <u>영국은 580억 달러를 소비했는데, 그것은 미국이 소비한 금액의 절반보다 더 적었다.</u> ⑤ 다섯 개의 소비 국가 중에서, 러시아는 국제 관광에 가장 적은 금액의 돈을 소비했다.

Why? 왜 정답일까?

국제 관광에 미국은 1,120억 달러를 소비했고, 영국은 미국이 소비한 금액의 절반(560억 달러)보다 많은 580억 달러를 소비했다. 따라서 도표의 내용과 일치하지 않는 진술은 ④ '영국은 580억 달러를 소비했는데, 그것은 미국이 소비한 금액의 절반보다 더 적었다.'이다.

- above (편지·책에서) 위의
- international tourism 국제 관광
- take third place 3위를 차지하다
- half 반
- spender 소비자, 소비국가
- billion 10억
- spend 쓰다
- amount 총액

---

12 비 오는 스산한 거리 묘사 　　정답 ②

다음 글의 상황에 나타난 분위기로 가장 적절한 것은? [2점]

① lively – 생기 있는　　✓ lonely – 외로운　　③ colorful – 파란만장한
④ cheerful – 쾌활한　　⑤ festive – 축제의

"안녕히 주무세요, 선생님." 거리를 내려가며, 떠나면서 문을 열려 했던, 경찰관이 말했다. 약하게 차가운 비가 떨어지고 있었고, 바람은 세차게 되어, 지금은 끊임없이 불었다. 거리 위에 몇 안 되는 사람들이 외투 깃을 높이 올리고 손을 주머니에 넣은 채 슬프고 말없이 길을 재촉했다. 그리고 철물점의 문 앞에, 자신의 어린 시절 친구들과의 약속을 지키기 위해 수천 마일을 왔던 남자가 홀로 기다리고 있었다.

Why? 왜 정답일까?

약간씩 찬비가 내리고 있었고, 바람이 점차 강해졌고, 끊임없이 불고 있었다(There was now a slight, cold rain falling, and the wind had become stronger, so now it blew steadily.)고 말하면서 몇몇 사람들은 외투 깃을 올리고 손을 주머니에 넣은 채 슬프고 조용히 길을 재촉했다고 말하고 있다. 따라서 분위기로 가장 적절한 것은 ② '외로운(lonely)'이다.

- slight 약간의
- appointment 약속
- steadily 끊임없이
- boyhood 어린 시절

---

13 거북의 체온 조절 방법 　　정답 ⑤

글의 흐름으로 보아, 주어진 문장이 들어가기에 가장 적절한 곳을 고르시오. [3점]

거북은 조류와 포유류처럼 체온을 자동으로 조절하는 능력이 없다. ① 거북의 체온은 주위

환경에 따라 변한다. ② 날씨가 너무 추워지면, 거북은 연못 바닥의 진흙이나 숲의 흙 속 깊이 구멍을 판다. ③ 흙 속에 묻히면 거북은 어떻게 숨을 쉴 수 있을까? ④ 거북은 코와 입으로 숨 쉬는 것을 멈춘다. ⑤ 대신 거북은 피부와 꼬리 아래에 있는 구멍을 통해 공기를 받아들인다. 그리고 봄이 와서 땅이 따뜻해지면, 거북은 땅을 파고 나와 다시 평소대로 숨 쉬기 시작한다.

Why? 왜 정답일까?

③의 뒷부분부터는 거북이의 숨쉬기에 대해 설명하고 있는데 ⑤의 직전 문장에서 거북이가 코와 입으로 숨쉬는 것을 멈춘다고 말하고 있다. 따라서, 대안으로 어떤 방식을 취하는지에 대해 설명하는 주어진 문장은 ⑤의 위치로 연결되어야 한다. 따라서 정답은 ⑤이다.

- instead 대신에
- through ~을 통해
- automatic 자동적인
- according to ~에 따르면
- breath 입김, 숨
- dig 파다
- take in 받아들이다, 흡수하다
- opening 구멍
- temperature 온도
- bury 묻다
- warm up 적당히 열이 오르다
- normally 보통 때는, 정상적으로

---

14 자신을 응원해 주는 사람이 없을 때, 스스로를 격려하기 　　정답 ③

글의 흐름으로 보아, 주어진 문장이 들어가기에 가장 적절한 곳을 고르시오. [3점]

여러분의 인생에서 여러분을 믿고 응원하는 사람들이 있다는 것은 좋은 일이다. (①) 그들은 여러분이 성취하려고 노력하고 있는 것에 진심으로 관심을 가지며 여러분의 모든 목표와 노력을 지지한다. (②) 우리는 각자 우리의 인생에서 자신의 능력을 확신하고 자신의 목표를 향해 앞으로 나아가기 위해 우리를 격려해 주는 사람들이 필요하다. ③ <u>하지만 여러분의 인생에서 누군가가 일어나 응원하는 사람이 주변에 아무도 없을 때가 있을 것이다.</u> 이런 일이 일어날 때, 우울하지 마라. (④) 대신에 여러분 자신의 치어리더가 되라. (⑤) 어느 누구도 여러분의 장점과 소질을 여러분보다 더 잘 알지 못하고 그 어느 누구도 여러분에게 여러분보다 더 잘 동기를 부여할 수 없으므로, 동기를 부여하는 격려의 말을 여러분 자신에게 하라.

Why? 왜 정답일까?

주어진 문장은 우리의 인생에서 우리를 응원하고 지지하는 사람이 없을 때가 있다는 부정적인 내용을 이야기하고 있다. ③ 이후의 문장들이 '이런 일이 일어날 때, 우울하지 마라.' 내용이 있으므로 앞에 부정적인 내용이 나와야 한다. 따라서 주어진 문장의 위치는 ③이 적절하다.

- achieve 성취하다
- goal 목표
- encourage 격려하다
- capability 능력, 역량
- instead 대신에
- pep talk 격려 연설, 격려의 말
- motivate 동기를 부여하다
- support 지지하다, 힘을 돋우다
- effort 수고
- confident 자신이 있는
- depressed 우울한, 풀이 죽은
- motivational 동기를 부여하는
- strength 장점

---

15 빛과 색 사이의 관계 　　정답 ④

다음 글에서 전체 흐름과 관계 <u>없는</u> 문장을 모두 고르시오. [3점]

빛이 유리 수정을 통과해 빛날 때, 당신은 나타나기 시작하는 색의 줄(무늬)들을 관찰할 수 있을 것이다. 이것은 빛이 무지개 모든 색으로 구성되어 있다는 것을 보여준다. ① 빛이 채색된 물체 위에 비칠 때, 그 물체의 표면은 그것에 부딪치는 빛 파동들 중 일부를 흡수하거나 받아들인다. ② 그 물체는 색의 일부를 흡수하고 다른 색은 반사한다. ③ 당신은 반사된 색을 보지 흡수된 색을 보는 것이 아니다. ④ 빛은 파동으로 이동하며 빈 공간을 지나갈 수 있다. ⑤ 바나나는 노란 빛을 반사하고 다른 색을 흡수하기 때문에 노란색으로 보인다.

Why? 왜 정답일까?

빛이 물체 위로 비칠 때, 색이 나타나게 되는 이치를 설명하고 있는데 ④에서 뜬금 없이 빛은 파동 안에서 이동하며 빈 공간을 지나갈 수 있다고 말하고 있다. 따라서 글에서 전체 흐름과 관계 없는 문장은 ④이다.

- be made up of ~로 이루어져 있다
- surface 표면
- take in 흡수하다
- pass through ~을 빠져나가다
- object 물건, 물체
- absorb 빨아들이다, 흡수하다
- reflect 반사하다, 반영하다

---

16 음악 공부의 이점 　　정답 ③

다음 글에서 전체 흐름과 관계 <u>없는</u> 문장을 모두 고르시오. [4점]

음악 공부는 아이들이 학교에서 하는 읽기, 수학, 그리고 다른 과목에서의 모든 학습의 질을 높여준다. ① 그것은 또한 언어와 의사소통 기술을 발달시키는 데 도움이 된다. ② 아이들이 자라면서 음악 훈련은 아이들이 학교에서 성과를 이루는 데 필요한 자제력과 자신감을 계발하도록 계속 도움을 준다. ③ <u>음악을 들으면서 공부하는 것은 학생들이 자료를 배우는 데 어려움을 갖게 한다.</u> ④ 목표를 세우고 달성하는 것과 더불어 매일 행해지는 음악 연습은 자기절제와 인내심, 그리고 책임감을 계발한다. ⑤ 그러한 자제력은 숙제나 다른 학교 과제를 제시간에 해내고 자료 정리하기와 같은 다른 영역으로 옮겨간다.

Why? 왜 정답일까?

이 글은 음악 공부가 다른 과목에서 학습의 질을 높여준다는 '음악의 긍정적 기능'에 대해 설명하고 있는데, ③은 음악을 들으면서 공부하는 것에 대한 부정적 효과를 이야기하고 있다. 따라서 글의 전체 흐름과 관계 없는 문장은 ③이다.

- enrich 질을 높이다
- communication 의사소통
- self-confidence 자신감
- cause ~하게 하다, 일으키다
- material 자료, 재료
- along with ~와 더불어
- responsibility 책임감
- organize 정리하다, 조직하다
- develop 계발하다, 개발하다
- continue 계속하다
- achieve 성과를 이루다, 성취하다
- have a difficult time -ing ~하는 데 어려움을 갖다
- day-to-day 매일 행해지는, 그날그날의
- patience 인내심
- carry over to ~로 옮겨가다

17 부모와 십 대 자녀와의 신체 접촉

정답 ③

다음 글의 빈칸 (A), (B)에 들어갈 말로 가장 적절한 것은? [3점]

	(A)		(B)
①	In addition 게다가	……	However 그러나
②	In other words 다시 말해서	……	In short 간단히 말해서
✓③	For instance 예를 들어	……	However 하지만
④	For instance 예를 들어	……	In short 간단히 말해서
⑤	In addition 게다가	……	Similarly 유사하게

부모의 신체적 접촉이 십 대에게 자신들의 애정을 전달하는가? 대답은 예, 아니오 모두이다. 그것은 모두 언제, 어디서, 그리고 어떻게 하느냐에 달려 있다. (A) 예를 들면, 십 대 자녀가 친구들과 함께 있을 때 하는 포옹은 당황스러울 것이다. 그것은 십 대 자녀로 하여금 부모를 밀치거나 "하지 마세요."라고 말하게 할 것이다. (B) 하지만, 시합 후 집으로 돌아온 십 대 자녀의 어깨를 마사지하는 것은 애정을 깊이 전달할 수 있다. 학교에서의 실망스러운 하루 후에 사랑이 담긴 접촉은 진실한 부모의 사랑으로 환영받을 것이다.

Why? 왜 정답일까?

부모의 신체적 접촉은 상황에 따라 아이들에게 긍정적일 수도 있고 부정적일 수도 있다는 요지를 먼저 언급하고, (A) 뒤에서는 구체적인 예를 들고 있으므로, (A)에는 '예를 들면'이 오는 것이 적절하다. 또한, (B)의 뒤부터는 앞의 내용과는 달리 신체적 접촉이 긍정적으로 작용하는 예를 이야기하고 있으므로, (B)에는 역접의 접속부사인 '하지만'이 들어가야 한다. 따라서 정답은 ③ '예를 들어 – 하지만'이다.

- physical 육체의
- communicate 의사소통을 하다
- answer 답하다
- hug 껴안다
- parent 부모
- massage 마사지
- deeply 깊게
- welcome 맞이하다
- touch 만지다
- teenager 10대
- depend on ~에 의존하다
- embarrass 당황스럽게 만들다
- push away 밀어젖히다
- shoulder 어깨
- disappointing 실망스러운

18 중고 서적 시장 안내

정답 ④

다음 광고의 내용과 일치하지 않는 것은? [2점]

① 행사의 목적은 자선기금 모금이다.
② 개인당 최대 40권을 판매할 수 있다.
③ 판매자는 수익의 10%를 기부하도록 요구받는다.
✓④ 참가 신청서는 당일 행사 장소에서 제출해야 한다.
⑤ 행사는 2월 27일 오후 5시까지 열린다.

〈서적 시장〉

「인천 글로벌 센터는 아동 자선 단체를 위한 기금을 모금하기 위해 특별한 중고 서적 시장을 개최하고 있습니다.」「중고 책을 팔기 원하는 누구나 이 행사에 참여할 수 있습니다.」「1인당 40권의 책을 팔도록 제한됩니다.」「게다가, 판매자들은 그들 수익의 10%를 자선 단체에 기부할 것이 요구됩니다.」「이 행사에 참여하기 위해서 2월 25일까지 온라인 지원서를 제출해야 합니다.」

언제 : 2월 27일, 오전 10시에서 오후 5시
어디서 : 센트럴 파크
판매 물품 : 중고 책
더 많은 정보를 원한다면 www.gloabalabc.com을 방문해 주세요.

Why? 왜 정답일까?

인천 글로벌 센터는 아동 자선 단체를 위한 기금을 모금하기 위해 특별한 중고 서적 시장에 대해 안내하는 내용이다. 이 중고 서적 시장에 참여하려면 2월 25일까지 온라인으로 지원서를 제출해야 한다(To join this event, you should submit your application form online by Feb. 25.)고 말하고 있다. 따라서 내용과 일치 하지 않는 것은 ④이다.

Why? 왜 오답일까?

① 'The Incheon Global Center is holding a special market for used books to raise funds for a children's charity.'의 내용과 일치한다.
② 'Each person is limited to selling 40 books.'의 내용과 일치한다.
③ '~ sellers are required to give 10 percent of their earnings to the charity.'의 내용과 일치한다.
⑤ 'When: Feb. 27, 10 a.m. to 5 p.m.'의 내용과 일치한다.

- raise 들어올리다
- limit 한계
- require 필요(요구)하다
- application 지원서
- charity 자선(구호) 단체
- in addition 게다가
- submit 제출하다

19 아프리카산 흑멧돼지

정답 ⑤

warthog에 관한 다음 글의 내용과 일치하지 않는 것은? [3점]

① 아프리카에서만 볼 수 있다.
② 물을 마시지 않고 몇 달 동안 버틸 수 있다.
③ 수컷이 암컷보다 무게가 더 많이 나간다.
④ 달릴 때 꼬리를 위로 세운다.
✓⑤ 시력은 좋지만 청력은 좋지 않다.

(아프리카산) 흑멧돼지는 돼지과에 속한다. 「이 동물은 아프리카에서만 볼 수 있다.」대부분의 동물과는 달리, 흑멧돼지는 「물을 마시지 않고도 몇 달 동안 건조한 지역에서 살 수 있다.」

흑멧돼지의 몸길이는 4피트에서 6피트에 달하고 무게는 110파운드에서 260파운드까지 나갈 수 있다. 「수컷이 암컷보다 20파운드에서 50파운드 더 무겁다.」「흑멧돼지는 달리고 있을 때 꼬리를 위로 세운 자세를 유지한다.」이 자세에서는 꼬리가 바람에 흔들리는 깃발처럼 보인다. 「흑멧돼지는 시력은 좋지 않지만, 후각과 청각은 탁월하다.」

Why? 왜 정답일까?

마지막 문장에서 시력은 좋지 않지만, 청력은 좋다(Warthogs have poor eyesight, but excellent senses of smell and hearing.)고 언급하였다. 따라서 글의 내용과 일치하지 않는 것은 ⑤이다.

Why? 왜 오답일까?

① 'This animal can be found only in Africa.'의 내용과 일치한다.
② '~ warthogs can survive in dry areas without drinking water for several months.'의 내용과 일치한다.
③ 'Males are 20 to 50 pounds heavier than females.'의 내용과 일치한다.
④ 'Warthogs keep their tails in the upright position when they are running.'의 내용과 일치한다.

- warthog (아프리카산) 흑멧돼지
- survive 살아남다
- in length 길이에 있어서
- female 여자
- upright 곧게 선
- sense 감각
- flag 깃발
- unlike ~와 달리
- reach 도달하다
- male 남자
- position 위치
- eyesight 시력
- hearing 청력
- excellent 훌륭한

20 마음씨가 따뜻한 Dr. John Ross

정답 ①

다음 글의 제목으로 가장 적절한 것은? [4점]

✓① A Warm-Hearted Doctor – 마음씨가 따뜻한 의사
② Folk Medicine Really Works – 민간요법은 정말로 효과가 있다
③ The Importance of Family Love – 가족 사랑의 중요성
④ A Little Knowledge Is Dangerous – 제대로 알지 못하는 지식은 위험하다(선무당이 사람 잡는다)
⑤ A Doctor Who Couldn't Cure Himself – 자신의 병을 치료할 수 없었던 의사

Dr. John Ross는 환자들을 돕기로 잘 알려져 있었다. 그의 환자 중 다수가 가난한 농부들이어서, 그들은 Dr. Ross의 얼마 안 되는 진료비를 항상 지불할 수 있는 것은 아니었다. 그 훌륭한 의사는 채소나 달걀, 심지어는 "감사합니다"라는 간단한 인사말을 진료비로 받곤 했다. 어느 겨울날 오후에, 그는 열이 있는 한 아이를 진료하러 어느 집에 갔다. 그 소녀의 가족은 그들의 작은 집을 따뜻하게 하는 데 필요한 장작을 다 써 버렸다. Dr. Ross는 자기 차에서 여분의 담요를 가져다주고는 아빠에게 찬물로 딸의 이마를 적셔주라고 말했다. 그런 다음 Dr. Ross는 다른 환자들을 돌보러 떠났다. 부러진 다리를 맞추고, 아기의 출산을 돕고, 감염된 손가락을 소독한 다음 그는 한 무더기 장작을 가지고 아픈 아이의 집으로 돌아왔다. 그는 어린 소녀와 그녀의 가족을 위해 불을 지폈다.

Why? 왜 정답일까?

가난한 사람들에게 진료비 대신 채소나 달걀, 또는 감사 인사를 받으며(The good doctor would accept vegetables, eggs, or even a simple "thank you" in payment.) 환자를 잘 돕는 한 의사가 아픈 소녀와 가난한 소녀의 가족을 위해 취한 행동에 대한 내용이다. 따라서 글의 제목으로 가장 적절한 것은 ① '마음씨가 따뜻한 의사'이다.

- well-known 잘 알려진, 유명한
- can afford to ~할 수 있다
- firewood 장작
- blanket 담요
- daughter 딸
- take care of ~을 보살피다, 돌보다
- load 짐
- patient 환자
- run out of ~을 다 써 버리다
- spare 여분의
- bathe 적시다, 씻다
- forehead 이마
- infect 감염시키다
- build a fire 불을 피우다

21 더 주기, 행복하게 지내는 방법

정답 ③

다음 글의 주제로 가장 적절한 것은? [3점]

① how to save money effectively – 돈을 효과적으로 아끼는 방법
② disadvantages of wasting your money – 돈을 쓰는 데 있어서의 단점
✓③ giving more as a way to stay in happiness – 행복하게 지내기 위한 방법으로의 더 주는 것
④ suggestions for choosing appropriate presents – 적절한 선물 선택을 위한 제안
⑤ significance of spending money on your future – 앞으로 쓸 돈에 대한 중요성

자신들에게 돈을 쓰고 나서 더 행복할지 타인에게 쓴 후에 더 행복할지 사람들에게 물어보라. 그러면 압도적인 다수는 '나(에게)' 칸을 체크할 것이다. 과학은 정확하게 그 반대가 사실이라는 것을 보여준다. 사람들은 자신보다 남을 위해 베푼 이후에 훨씬 더 행복해진다. 좋은 소식은 여러분이 친구나 가족을 위해 수입의 상당 부분을 따로 떼어 놓을 필요는 없다는 것이다. 사실, 최소의 선물이 행복에 있어서 놀랄 만큼 크고 오래 지속되는 변화를 빠르게 낳을 수 있다. 다른 사람들에게 쓰인 몇 달러가 여러분이 했었던 최고의 투자 중 하나일지도 모른다. 그리고 만약 여러분이 정말로 당신의 현금을 나눠줄 여유가 없다면, 하루에 5번의 비금전적인 친절한 행동을 실천하는 것 또한 상당한 행복의 증가를 제공해준다는 것을 기억하라.

Why? 왜 정답일까?

사람들은 자기 자신보다 남을 위해 베푼 후에 훨씬 더 행복해 진다고 말하면서(People become much happier after providing for others rather than themselves.), 꼭 돈이 드는 것이 아니어도 사소한 선물이 행복에 커다란 변화를 줄 수 있다는 내용의 글이다. 따라서 글의 주제로 가장 적절한 것은 ③ '행복하게 지내기 위한 방법으로의 더 주는 것'이다.

- majority 가장 많은 수
- provide 제공(공급)하다
- proportion 부분
- opposite 다른 편
- rather than …보다는
- income 소득

- investment 투자
- kindness 친절
- afford 여유(형편)가 되다
- significant 중요한

- expressive 나타내는
- incorporating 결합시키는
- conversation 대화
- behavior 행동

22 교육적인 장난감 활용법　　정답 ③

다음 글의 요지로 가장 적절한 것은? [4점]
① 장난감 구입 시 제품의 안전성을 고려해야 한다.
② 아이는 자주 가지고 노는 장난감에 애착을 가진다.
☑ 모든 장난감은 활용 방법에 따라 교육적일 수 있다.
④ 아이의 발달단계를 고려한 장난감을 제공해야 한다.
⑤ 학습에 도움이 되는 장난감을 더 많이 개발해야 한다.

당신의 자녀가 또 다른 장난감 자동차 때문에 조를 때, 'no'라고 말하는 것은 쉽다. 그러나 그가 수학을 돕는 장난감을 부탁할 때, 항복할 겁니까? 사실, 모든 장난감은 교육적일 수 있다. 즉, 가장 교육적인 것들은 대개 자동차나 인형과 같이 가장 단순한 것이다. 이것은 어떻게 그들이 거래되느냐 대한 것이 아니고, 당신이 그것들을 어떻게 가지고 노느냐에 대한 것이다. 배움은 반드시 비싼 발달 장난감에서 나와야 하는 것은 아니다. 만약 당신의 자녀가 자동차나 기차를 가지고 지속적으로 놀고 있다면, 그는 읽기와 쓰기를 연습하기 위해 그것들을 사용할 수 있다. 분필을 가지고, 당신의 자녀가 씨름하던 글자나 단어 모양의 길을 만들어라 그리고 그것의 게임을 만들어라. 즉, 그것들을 지나가는 동안 글자나 단어를 큰소리로 말하라. 이 게임은 당신의 자녀가 몇몇 중요한 단어를 인식하는 것을 도와주는 재미있는 방법이다.

Why? 왜 정답일까?
글의 초반에 장난감이 수학을 푸는데 도움이 된다면 어떨까 하는 질문과(But when he asks for a toy that helps with math, do you give in?) 함께 아이들이 갖고 노는 장난감을 어떻게 학습에 활동하는 지를 말하고 있다. 따라서 글의 요지로 가장 적절한 것은 ③ '모든 장난감은 활용방법에 따라 교육적일 수 있다.'이다.

- simple 간단한
- developmental 발달(개발)상의
- struggle 투쟁(고투)하다
- necessarily 어쩔 수 없이
- constantly 끊임없이
- recognize 알아보다

23 산업 발전에 따른 노동조합 결성　　정답 ③

주어진 글 다음에 이어질 글의 순서로 가장 적절한 것은? [4점]
① (A) – (C) – (B)
② (B) – (A) – (C)
☑ (B) – (C) – (A)
④ (C) – (A) – (B)
⑤ (C) – (B) – (A)

산업이 발달하면서, 사람들의 삶은 변화하기 시작했다. 공장들은 새로운 일자리를 많이 창출했고, 따라서 많은 근로자들이 필요했다.
(B) 시골에는 일자리가 거의 없었기 때문에, 사람들은 공장에서 근로하기 위해 멀리서 왔다. 공장 주위에 새로운 도시들이 성장하기 시작했다.
(C) 그러나 이런 도시에서의 생활 여건은 끔찍했다. 몇몇 사람들은 오랜 시간 위험한 여건에서 근로해야만 했다. 그들은 매우 적은 보수를 지불받았다. 많은 여성들과 아이들도 근로해야만 했다. 근로자들은 상황이 불공평하다고 느꼈다.
(A) 그래서 그들은 노동조합이라 불리는 단체들을 결성했다. 다수의 끔찍한 여건들은 시정되었고 근무 환경은 나아졌다. 오늘날 미국에는 노동조합에 속한 약 1,600만 명의 근로자들이 있다.

Why? 왜 정답일까?
산업이 발전하면서 사람들의 삶은 변하기 시작했고 공장들이 많은 일자리를 창출했기 때문에 근로자들도 많이 필요해졌다고 말하고 있다(The factories created many new jobs, so many workers were needed.)는 내용으로, 그 다음에는 일자리가 별로 없는 시골에서 도시로 많이 이동했고 그래서 공장 주변으로 새 도시들이 성장했다는 (B)의 내용이 온다. 그 후에 도시의 생활 여건이 끔찍했다는 (C)의 내용이 이어지고 그래서 노동조합이라는 단체가 결성되었다는 (A)의 내용으로 마무리 된다. 따라서 글의 순서로 가장 적절한 것은 ③ '(B) – (C) – (A)'이다.

- labor unions 노동조합
- belong to ~에 속하다
- unfair 부당한
- condition 상태
- situation 상황

24 다양하게 움직이는 행복한 사람들　　정답 ⑤

다음 글에서 필자가 주장하는 바로 가장 적절한 것은? [3점]
① 지킬 수 있는 약속을 해라.
② 대화 중 지나친 몸짓을 피해라.
③ 친구의 애정 어린 충고에 귀 기울여라.
④ 건강을 지키기 위해 규칙적인 생활 습관을 가져라.
☑ 행복하기 위해 행복한 사람이 행동하는 것처럼 행동해라.

행복한 사람들은 불행한 사람들이 하는 거와는 매우 다른 방식으로 움직인다는 것을 연구는 밝혀냈다. 더욱 편안한 방식으로 걸으며, 팔을 약간 더 가볍게 흔들고, 걸음에 생기를 넣어봐라. 또한, 대화 중에 좀 더 표현력이 있는 제스처를 하고, 더 화사한 옷을 입고, 적극적으로 감동적인 감정 단어들, 특히 "사랑하다"와 "좋아하다"와 "다정한"을 사용하고, 목소리의 음조에 더 다양한 변화를 주고, 그리고 약간 더 빠르게 말하라. 이런 행위를 당신의 평소의 행동에 포함시키는 것은 당신의 행복을 증가시킬 것이다.

Why? 왜 정답일까?
연구에서 행복한 사람들은 불행한 사람들이 하는 거와는 매우 다른 방식으로 움직인다는 것을 밝혔다(Research has revealed that happy people move in a very different way than unhappy people do.)고 말하면서 편안한 방식으로 걸으며, 대화 중에 좀 더 표현력이 있는 제스처를 하며 감동적인 감정 단어들을 사용하라고 권하고 있다. 따라서 필자의 주장으로 적절한 것은 ⑤ '행복하기 위해 행복한 사람이 행동하는 것처럼 행동해라.'이다.

25 강이 국가 간의 경계일 때 문제점　　정답 ②

다음 글의 내용을 한 문장으로 요약하고자 한다. 빈칸 (A)와 (B)에 들어갈 말로 가장 적절한 것은? [4점]

　　(A)　　　　　　(B)
① establishing ······ invisible
　확립하는　　　　눈에 보이지 않는
☑ establishing ······ changeable
　확립하는　　　　변하기 쉬운
③ removing ······ fixed
　제거하는　　　　고정된
④ linking ······ fixed
　연결하는　　　　고정된
⑤ linking ······ changeable
　연결하는　　　　변하기 쉬운

주나 국가 사이의 자연적 경계는 강, 호수, 사막 그리고 산맥을 따라 나타난다. 그것 중에 강을 따라 형성된 경계가 가장 이상적인 것처럼 보인다. 왜냐하면, 그것들이 분명한 구분을 해주고, 그것들은 확립되고 인정된 물리적 특징이기 때문이다. 하지만 실제로 강을 따라 형성된 경계는 강이 경로를 바꿈에 따라 변할 수 있다. 홍수 후에 강의 경로가 변하여 주나 국가 사이의 경계를 바꿀 수 있다. 예를 들어, 미국과 멕시코를 구분 짓는 Rio Grande 강은 경로를 빈번하게 바꾸어, 국가 간 경계의 정확한 위치를 결정하는 데 문제를 일으켰다.

➡ 강은 경계를 (A) 확립하기에 이상적인 것처럼 보이지만, 사실은 그렇지 않은데, 그 이유는 그것의 경로가 (B) 변할 수도 있기 때문이다.

Why? 왜 정답일까?
강은 자연적 경계 중 하나로 분명한 구분을 해주어 경계를 확립하기 때문에 이상적인 것처럼 보이지만, 실제로 강은 경로가 바뀔 수 있기 때문에 문제를 일으키기도 한다는 내용이므로 (A)에는 '확립하는'의 의미인 establishing, (B)에는 '변하기 쉬운'이란 의미의 changeable이 적절하다. 따라서 정답은 ②이다.

- natural 자연적인
- ideal 이상적인
- establish 확립하다
- feature 특징
- shift 변화하다, 바꾸다
- frequently 빈번하게
- location 위치
- mountain range 산맥
- separation 구분
- recognize 인정하다
- in reality 실제로
- alter 바꾸다
- determine 결정하다

26-27 거짓말에 대해 아이들을 처벌하는 것은 효과가 있나?

McGill 대학의 연구원들은 372명의 아이들을 참여시킨 한 실험을 통해 흥미로운 결과를 발견했다. 그들은 각각의 아이를 그들 뒤쪽 테이블 위에 놓인 장난감 하나와 같이 1분 동안 혼자 남겨두었고, 그 아이들에게 자신들이 없는 동안 그것을 쳐다보지 말라고 말해주었다. 그들이 방에 나가 있는 동안, 비밀 비디오카메라가 무엇이 일어났는지 기록했다. 그 결과는 66%가 약간 넘는 아이들이 장난감을 쳐다본 것을 보여주었다. 그 아이들이 장난감을 쳐다봤는지 아닌지 질문을 받았을 때, 다시 약 66%의 아이들이 거짓말을 했다. 더욱 흥미로운 것은, 그들이 어른들을 기쁘게 할 것이기 때문에 사실을 말해 달라고 요청 받았을 때보다 그들이 벌을 받은 것을 두려워했다면 아이들은 사실을 말할 가능성이 더 적다는 것이다. "요점은 벌은 사실을 말하기를 장려하지 않는다는 겁니다."라고 그 연구의 책임자인 Victoria Talwar는 말한다. "사실, 벌에 대한 위협은 아이들이 진실을 말할 가능성을 감소시킴으로써 반대의 효과를 가질 수 있다."

- discover 발견하다
- involve 수반(포함)하다
- interestingly 흥미 있게
- punishment 처벌
- reduce 줄이다
- experiment 실험
- absence 결석
- punish 처벌하다
- promote 촉진(고취)하다
- likelihood 가능성

26 빈칸 추론　　정답 ①

위 글의 빈칸에 들어갈 말로 가장 적절한 것은? [4점]
☑ reverse – 반대의
② desirable – 바람직한
③ productive – 생산적인
④ profitable – 수익성 있는
⑤ educational – 교육적인

Why? 왜 정답일까?
아이들은 어른을 기쁘게 하기 위해서 진실을 이야기해 달라는 요청을 받을 때보다 처벌에 대한 두려움이 있을 때 진실을 말할 가능성이 더 적다(~ children were less likely to tell the truth if they were afraid of being punished than if they were asked to tell the truth because it would please the adult.)고 말하면서 처벌에 대한 두려움은 아이들이 진실을 말하게 하는 가능성을 줄이는 역효과 즉 'reverse'를 가질 수 있다는 내용으로 마무리 되는 게 적절하다. 따라서 빈칸에 들어갈 말로 가장 적절한 것은 ① 'reverse(반대의)'이다.

27 제목 파악　　정답 ③

위 글의 제목으로 가장 적절한 것은? [3점]
① Why Are Children Crazy for Toys? – 아이들은 장난감에 왜 열광할까?
② Can Telling a Lie Be a Good Excuse? – 거짓말이 좋은 변명이 될 수 있을까?
☑ Does Punishing Children for Lying Work? – 거짓말하는 것에 대해 아이들을 처벌하는 것은 효과가 있는가?
④ Curiosity: The Key to Improving Creativity – 호기심: 창의력 향상의 비법
⑤ Truth: The Essential Value to Respect Parents – 진실: 부모님을 존경하기 위한 중요한 가치

Why? 왜 정답일까?
처벌에 대한 두려움은 아이들이 진실을 말하게 하는 가능성을 줄이는 역효과를 가질 수 있다(In fact, the threat of punishment can have the reverse effect by reducing the likelihood that

children will tell the truth.)고 말하고 있다. 따라서 제목으로 가장 적절한 것은 ③ '거짓말하는 것에 대해 아이들을 처벌하는 것은 효과가 있는가?'이다.

28-30 **가정을 위해 야구선수로서의 경력을 포기한 Tim Burke**

(A)
부모가 가정을 위해 소중한 시간을 투자하지 않으면 가정은 강해지지 않는다. 'New Man'에서 Gary Oliver는 프로 야구 선수였던 Tim Burke가 자신의 가정에 관해 내렸던 어려운 결정에 대해 적고 있다. 맨 처음 Tim이 기억할 수 있는 그 때부터 그의 꿈은 프로 야구 선수가 되는 것이었다. 『다년간의 노력 끝에 (a) 그는 그 꿈을 이뤘다.』┌─ :30번 ①의 근거(일치)

(C)
『그가 Montreal Expos 팀에서 성공한 투수로 활동하는 동안』 (c) 그와 그의 아내는 가정을 꾸리고 싶었지만, 아이를 가질 수 없다는 것을 알게 되었다. 『심사숙고 끝에 그들은 특수 장애가 있는 네 명의 해외 아이를 입양하기로 했다.』 이것은 Tim이 인생에서 가장 힘든 결정 중 하나를 하게 이르렀다.
└─ 『 』:30번 ④의 근거(일치)

(D)
그는 (장거리를) 이동하며 다니는 자신의 삶이 훌륭한 남편과 아버지가 되는 능력과 상충된다는 것을 발견했다. 시간이 흐르면서 (d) 그가 일과 가정에서 모두 잘할 수 없다는 것이 명확해졌다. 심사숙고 끝에 그는 많은 사람이 믿을 수 없다고 여기는 결정을 내렸다. 즉 『그는 프로야구를 포기하기로 결정했다.』 ┌─ :30번 ⑤의 근거(불일치)

┌─ 『 』:30번 ②의 근거(일치)
(B)
『Tim이 마지막으로 경기장을 떠날 때 한 기자가 그를 멈춰 세웠다. 그러고 나서 (b) 그는 그가 왜 은퇴하려고 하는지 물었다.』 "야구는 제가 없어도 별 문제 없이 잘 돌아갈 겁니다. 그것은 잠시도 중단되지 않을 겁니다. 하지만 저는 우리 아이들의 유일한 아버지이자 제 아내의 유일한 남편입니다. 그리고 그들은 야구가 저를 필요로 하는 것보다 훨씬 더 저를 필요로 합니다."라고 그는 그 기자에게 말했다.

- **invest** 투자하다
- **through years of** ~의 수년을 거쳐
- **miss a beat** 잠시 중단되다
- **start a family** 가정을 꾸리다, 첫 아이를 보다
- **adopt** 입양하다
- **conflict** 상충되다, 충돌하다
- **thought** 생각, 사고
- **unbelievable** 믿을 수 없는
- **precious** 소중한, 귀중한
- **retire** 은퇴하다
- **pitcher** 투수
- **discover** 발견하다, 알아내다
- **special-needs** (장애인의) 특수 요구
- **quality** 훌륭한, 양질의
- **consider** 잘 생각하다, 숙고하다

28 글의 순서 찾기 정답 ③

주어진 글 (A)에 이어질 내용을 순서에 맞게 배열한 것으로 가장 적절한 것은? [3점]
① (B) − (D) − (C)
② (C) − (B) − (D)
✓③ (C) − (D) − (B)
④ (D) − (B) − (C)
⑤ (D) − (C) − (B)

Why? 왜 정답일까?
(A)의 마지막 문장에서 열심히 노력해서 Tim이 꿈을 이뤘다는 내용이 나오므로 투수로서 성공한 이야기가 나오는 (C)가 다음에 이어져야 한다. 그리고 (C)의 마지막 부분에 'difficult decisions'가 나오므로 그에 해당하는 내용이 나오는 (D)가 이어지고 그 어려운 결정을 한 이유가 (B)에 나오고 있다. 따라서 글의 순서로 가장 적절한 것은 ③ '(C) − (D) − (B)'이다.

29 지칭 추론 정답 ②

밑줄 친 (a) ~ (e) 중에서 가리키는 대상이 나머지 넷과 다른 것은? [3점]
① (a) ✓② (b) ③ (c) ④ (d) ⑤ (e)

Why? 왜 정답일까?
(a), (c), (d), (e)는 'Tim'이며 (b)는 'reporter'이므로 가리키는 대상이 나머지 넷과 다른 것은 ② '(b)'이다.

30 내용 불일치 정답 ⑤

윗글의 Tim Burke에 관한 내용과 일치하지 않는 것은? [4점]
① 열심히 노력하여 프로 야구 선수가 되었다.
② 마지막 경기 후에 기자로부터 질문을 받았다.
③ Montreal Expos 팀의 투수였다.
④ 네 명의 아이를 입양하기로 했다.
✓⑤ 가정을 위해 프로 야구를 계속하기로 했다.

Why? 왜 정답일까?
(D)에서 '~ he decided to give up professional baseball.'을 통해서 Tim이 야구를 포기한 것을 알 수 있다. 따라서 글의 내용과 일치하지 않는 것은 ⑤이다.

Why? 왜 오답일까?
① (A) 'Through years of hard work he achieved that goal.'의 내용과 일치한다.
② (B) 'When Tim left the stadium for the last time, a reporter stopped him. And then he asked why he was retiring.'의 내용과 일치한다.
③ (C) 'While he was a successful pitcher for the Montreal Expos, ~.'의 내용과 일치한다.
④ (C) 'After much thought, they decided to adopt four special-needs international children.'의 내용과 일치한다.

04회 | 2023학년도 3월 학력평가 고1

| 정답 |
01 ⑤ 02 ⑤ 03 ③ 04 ⑤ 05 ② 06 ② 07 ① 08 ③ 09 ④ 10 ② 11 ② 12 ① 13 ① 14 ① 15 ③
16 ③ 17 ④ 18 ③ 19 ② 20 ⑤ 21 ⑤ 22 ① 23 ① 24 ② 25 ⑤ 26 ⑤ 27 ③ 28 ④ 29 ⑤ 30 ④
31 ① 32 ③ 33 ① 34 ② 35 ④ 36 ④ 37 ② 38 ④ 39 ⑤ 40 ① 41 ② 42 ④ 43 ④ 44 ④ 45 ④

★ 표시된 문항은 [등급을 가르는 문제]에 해당하는 문항입니다.

01 아이스하키 리그 첫 경기 관람 독려 정답률 85% | 정답 ⑤

다음을 듣고, 남자가 하는 말의 목적으로 가장 적절한 것을 고르시오.
① 아이스하키부의 우승을 알리려고
② 아이스하키부 훈련 일정을 공지하려고
③ 아이스하키부 신임 감독을 소개하려고
④ 아이스하키부 선수 모집을 안내하려고
✓⑤ 아이스하키부 경기의 관람을 독려하려고

M : Hello, Villeford High School students.
안녕하세요, Villeford 고등학교 학생 여러분.
This is principal Aaron Clark.
저는 교장인 Aaron Clark입니다.
As a big fan of the Villeford ice hockey team, I'm very excited about the upcoming National High School Ice Hockey League.
Villeford 아이스하키 팀의 열렬한 팬으로서, 저는 다가오는 전국 고교 아이스하키 리그를 몹시 기대하고 있습니다.
As you all know, the first game will be held in the Central Rink at 6 p.m. this Saturday.
여러분 모두가 알다시피, 첫 경기는 이번 주 토요일 저녁 6시에 Central Rink에서 열립니다.
I want as many of you as possible to come and cheer our team to victory.
최대한 많이 와서 우리 팀의 승리를 응원해주기 바랍니다.
I've seen them put in an incredible amount of effort to win the league.
선수들이 이번 리그를 이기려고 엄청난 노력을 기울이는 것을 보았습니다.
It will help them play better just to see you there cheering for them.
여러분이 거기서 응원해주는 것을 선수들이 보기만 해도 경기를 더 잘하는 데 도움이 될 겁니다.
I really hope to see you at the rink. Thank you.
여러분을 링크장에서 만날 수 있기를 진심으로 바랍니다. 고맙습니다.

Why? 왜 정답일까?
'I want as many of you as possible to come and cheer our team to victory.'에서 아이스하키 리그 경기 관람을 독려하는 담화임을 알 수 있으므로, 남자가 하는 말의 목적으로 가장 적절한 것은 ⑤ '아이스하키부 경기의 관람을 독려하려고'이다.

- **principal** ⓝ 교장
- **put in effort** 노력을 기울이다
- **amount** ⓝ 양
- **excited** ⓐ 기대하는, 신나는
- **incredible** 엄청난, 믿을 수 없는

02 약을 새로 처방 받기를 권하기 정답률 89% | 정답 ⑤

대화를 듣고, 여자의 의견으로 가장 적절한 것을 고르시오.
① 과다한 항생제 복용을 자제해야 한다.
② 오래된 약을 함부로 폐기해서는 안 된다.
③ 약을 복용할 때는 정해진 시간을 지켜야 한다.
④ 진료 전에 자신의 증상을 정확히 확인해야 한다.
✓⑤ 다른 사람에게 처방된 약을 복용해서는 안 된다.

W : Honey, are you okay?
여보, 괜찮아요?
M : I'm afraid I've caught a cold. I've got a sore throat.
나 감기에 걸린 것 같아요. 인후통이 있어요.
W : Why don't you go see a doctor?
병원에 가는 게 어때요?
M : Well, I don't think it's necessary. I've found some medicine in the cabinet. I'll take it.
음, 그게 필요한 것 같지는 않아요. 찬장에서 약을 좀 찾았어요. 그걸 먹겠어요.
W : You shouldn't take that medicine. That's what I got prescribed last week.
그 약을 먹으면 안 돼요. 그거 내가 지난주에 처방받은 거예요.
M : My symptoms are similar to yours.
내 증상도 당신 증상이랑 비슷해요.
W : Honey, you shouldn't take medicine prescribed for others.
여보, 다른 사람한테 처방된 약을 먹으면 안 돼요.
M : It's just a cold. I'll get better if I take your medicine.
그냥 감기인걸요. 당신 약을 먹으면 나을 거예요.
W : It could be dangerous to take someone else's prescription.
다른 사람의 처방약을 먹는 것은 위험할 수도 있어요.
M : Okay. Then I'll go see a doctor this afternoon.
알겠어요. 그럼 오늘 오후에 병원에 갈게요.

Why? 왜 정답일까?
'Honey, you shouldn't take medicine prescribed for others.'와 'It could be dangerous to take someone else's prescription.'에서 여자는 다른 사람에게 처방된 약을 먹어서는 안 된다는 의견을 말하고 있다. 따라서 여자의 의견으로 가장 적절한 것은 ⑤ '다른 사람에게 처방된 약을 복용해서는 안 된다.'이다.

- **catch a cold** 감기에 걸리다
- **see a doctor** 병원에 가다
- **prescribe** ⓥ 처방하다
- **prescription** ⓝ 처방(전)
- **sore throat** 인후통
- **cabinet** ⓝ 찬장, 캐비닛
- **symptom** ⓝ 증상

대화를 듣고, 두 사람의 관계를 가장 잘 나타낸 것을 고르시오.
① 관람객 - 박물관 관장
② 세입자 - 건물 관리인
☑ 화가 - 미술관 직원
④ 고객 - 전기 기사
⑤ 의뢰인 - 건축사

W : Hi, Mr. Thomson. How are your preparations going?
안녕하세요. Thomson 씨. 준비 어떻게 돼 가세요?
M : You arrived at the right time. I have something to tell you.
마침 잘 오셨어요. 말씀드릴 게 있어요.
W : Okay. What is it?
네, 뭔가요?
M : Well, I'm afraid that we have to change the exhibition room for your paintings.
음, 죄송하지만 선생님 그림을 둘 전시실을 바꿔야 할 것 같아요.
W : May I ask why?
이유를 여쭤봐도 될까요?
M : Sure. We have some electrical problems there.
물론이죠. 거기 전기 문제가 좀 있어서요.
W : I see. Then where are you going to exhibit my works?
그렇군요. 그럼 제 작품을 어디에 전시하실 예정인가요?
M : Our gallery is going to exhibit your paintings in the main hall.
우리 갤러리에서는 선생님 작품을 메인 홀에 전시할 계획이에요.
W : Okay. Can I see the hall now?
그렇군요. 지금 홀을 봐도 될까요?
M : Sure. Come with me.
물론이죠. 같이 가시죠.

Why? 왜 정답일까?

'~ we have to change the exhibition room for your paintings.', 'Then where are you going to exhibit my works?', 'Our gallery is going to exhibit your paintings in the main hall.'에서 여자가 화가이고, 남자가 미술관 직원임을 알 수 있다. 따라서 두 사람의 관계로 가장 적절한 것은 ③ '화가 - 미술관 직원'이다.

● preparation ⓝ 준비, 대비
● exhibition ⓝ 전시
● electrical ⓐ 전기의
● exhibit ⓥ 전시하다

대화를 듣고, 그림에서 대화의 내용과 일치하지 않는 것을 고르시오.

M : Hi, Grace. What are you looking at on your phone?
안녕, Grace. 핸드폰으로 뭐 보고 있어?
W : Hi, James. It's a photo I took when I did some volunteer work. We painted pictures on a street wall.
안녕, James. 내가 봉사활동 좀 하면서 찍었던 사진이야. 거리 벽에다 그림을 그렸어.
M : Let me see. 「Wow, I like the whale with the flower pattern.」 ①의 근거 일치
나도 좀 보자. 와, 꽃무늬가 있는 고래 그림이 마음에 들어.
W : I like it, too. 「How do you like the house under the whale?」 ②의 근거 일치
나도 그게 좋아. 고래 밑에 있는 집은 어때?
M : It's beautiful. 「What are these two chairs for?」 ③의 근거 일치
예쁘다. 이 의자 두 개는 왜 있는 거야?
W : You can take a picture sitting there. The painting becomes the background.
거기 앉아서 사진을 찍을 수 있어. 그림이 배경이 되는 거지.
M : Oh, I see. 「Look at this tree! It has heart-shaped leaves.」 ④의 근거 일치
오, 그렇구나. 이 나무 좀 봐! 하트 모양 잎이 있어.
W : That's right. We named it the Love Tree.
맞아. 우린 그걸 '사랑의 나무'라고 이름 지었어.
M : 「The butterfly on the tree branch is lovely, too.」 ⑤의 근거 불일치
나뭇가지 위의 나비도 귀엽다.
W : I hope a lot of people enjoy the painting.
많은 사람들이 그림을 즐겨주면 좋겠어.

Why? 왜 정답일까?

대화에서 나뭇가지 위에 나비가 있다고 하는데(The butterfly on the tree branch is lovely, too.), 그림 속 나뭇가지 위에는 새가 있다. 따라서 그림에서 대화의 내용과 일치하지 않는 것은 ⑤이다.

● volunteer work 봉사활동
● How do you like ~? ~는 어때?

대화를 듣고, 남자가 할 일로 가장 적절한 것을 고르시오.
① 티켓 디자인하기
☑ 포스터 게시하기
③ 블로그 개설하기
④ 밴드부원 모집하기
⑤ 콘서트 장소 대여하기

M : Hi, Stella. How are you doing these days?
안녕, Stella. 요즘 뭐 하고 있어?

W : Hi, Ryan. I've been busy helping my granddad with his concert. He made a rock band with his friends.
안녕, Ryan. 난 요새 우리 할아버지 콘서트 준비를 돕느라 바빴어. 친구분들하고 록 밴드를 만드셨거든.
M : There must be a lot of things to do.
할 게 많겠구나.
W : Yeah. I reserved a place for the concert yesterday.
응. 난 어제 콘서트 장소를 예약했어.
M : What about posters and tickets?
포스터랑 티켓은?
W : Well, I've just finished designing a poster.
음, 포스터 디자인은 방금 다 했어.
M : Then I think I can help you.
그럼 내가 널 도와줄 수 있을 거 같아.
W : Really? How?
정말? 어떻게?
M : Actually, I have a music blog. I think I can upload the poster there.
사실, 난 음악 블로그를 하고 있어. 거기다 포스터를 올려줄 수 있을 것 같아.
W : That's great!
그거 좋네!
M : Just send the poster to me, and I'll post it online.
나한테 포스터를 보내주기만 하면, 내가 온라인에 그걸 올릴게.
W : Thanks a lot.
정말 고마워.

Why? 왜 정답일까?

남자는 할아버지의 콘서트 준비를 도와 포스터를 만들었다는 여자에게 포스터를 보내주기만 하면 자신이 운영하는 음악 블로그에 게시해 주겠다고 한다(Just send the poster to me, and I'll post it online.). 따라서 남자가 할 일로 가장 적절한 것은 ② '포스터 게시하기'이다.

● be busy ~ing ~하느라 바쁘다
● reserve ⓥ 예약하다

대화를 듣고, 여자가 지불할 금액을 고르시오. [3점]
① $70　☑ $90　③ $100　④ $110　⑤ $120

M : Good morning. How may I help you?
안녕하세요. 무엇을 도와드릴까요?
W : Hi. I want to buy a coffee pot.
안녕하세요. 전 커피포트를 사고 싶어요.
M : Okay. You can choose from these coffee pots.
알겠습니다. 여기 포트들 중에서 선택하시면 돼요.
W : I like this one. How much is it?
이거 마음에 드네요. 얼마인가요?
M : It was originally $60, but it's now on sale for $50.
원래는 60달러인데, 지금 50달러로 세일 중이에요.
W : Okay, I'll buy it. I'd also like to buy this red tumbler.
그렇군요. 이걸 사겠어요. 그리고 이 빨간색 텀블러도 사고 싶어요.
M : Actually, it comes in two sizes. This smaller one is $20 and a bigger one is $30.
사실, 이것은 두 개 사이즈로 나옵니다. 이 작은 것은 20달러이고 더 큰 것은 30달러예요.
W : The smaller one would be easier to carry around. I'll buy two smaller ones.
작은 게 들고 다니기 더 편하겠네요. 작은 거로 두 개 사겠어요.
M : All right. Is there anything else you need?
알겠습니다. 더 필요하신 건 없으신가요?
W : No, that's all. Thank you.
이거면 돼요. 고맙습니다.
M : Okay. How would you like to pay?
알겠습니다. 어떻게 지불하시겠습니까?
W : I'll pay by credit card. Here you are.
신용 카드로 지불할게요. 여기 있습니다.

Why? 왜 정답일까?

대화에 따르면 여자는 본래 60달러이지만 현재 50달러로 세일 중인 커피포트를 하나 사고, 하나에 20달러인 작은 텀블러도 두 개 샀다. 이를 식으로 나타내면 '50+(20×2)=90'이므로, 여자가 지불할 금액은 ② '$90'이다.

● come in (사이즈나 색상이) 나오다
● carry around 들고 다니다

대화를 듣고, 남자가 지갑을 구매하지 못한 이유를 고르시오.
☑ 해당 상품이 다 팔려서
② 브랜드명을 잊어버려서
③ 계산대의 줄이 길어서
④ 공항에 늦게 도착해서
⑤ 면세점이 문을 닫아서

[Cell phone rings.]
[휴대전화가 울린다.]
W : Hi, Brian.
안녕, Brian.
M : Hi, Mom. I'm in line to get on the plane.
엄마, 저 비행기 타려고 줄 서 있어요.
W : Okay. By the way, did you drop by the duty free shop in the airport?
그래. 그나저나 너 공항 면세점에는 들렀니?
M : Yes, but I couldn't buy the wallet you asked me to buy.
네, 그런데 엄마가 사달라고 부탁하신 지갑은 못 샀어요.
W : Did you forget the brand name?
브랜드 이름을 잊어버린 거야?
M : No. I remembered that. I took a memo.
아니요. 그건 기억했어요. 메모했는걸요.
W : Then did you arrive late at the airport?
그럼 공항에 늦게 도착했어?
M : No, I had enough time to shop.
아니요, 쇼핑할 시간은 충분했어요.

W : Then why couldn't you buy the wallet?
그럼 왜 지갑을 못 산 거니?

M : Actually, because they were all sold out.
사실, 그게 품절이 됐더라고요.

W : Oh, really?
오, 정말?

M : Yeah. The wallet must be very popular.
네, 그 지갑 무척 인기가 많은가봐요.

W : Okay. Thanks for checking anyway.
알겠어. 그래도 확인해줘서 고마워.

Why? 왜 정답일까?

대화에서 남자는 여자가 부탁한 지갑을 사지 못한 이유로 그것이 품절이었기 때문(Actually, because they were all sold out.)임을 언급한다. 따라서 남자가 지갑을 구매하지 못한 이유로 가장 적절한 것은 ① '해당 상품이 다 팔려서'이다.

- in line 줄을 선, 줄 서서
- duty free shop 면세점
- drop by ~에 들르다

---

08 합창단 오디션 | 정답률 88% | 정답 ③

대화를 듣고, Youth Choir Audition에 관해 언급되지 않은 것을 고르시오.
① 지원 가능 연령 ② 날짜 ☑③ 심사 기준
④ 참가비 ⑤ 지원 방법

M : Lucy, look at this.
Lucy, 이것 좀 봐.

W : Wow. It's about the Youth Choir Audition.
와, Youth Choir Audition에 관한 거구나.

M : Yes. 『It's open to anyone aged 13 to 18.』 ①의근거 일치
응. 13~18세인 누구나 참가할 수 있어.

W : I'm interested in joining the choir. 『When is it?
난 합창단에 드는 데 관심이 있어. 언제 해?

M : April 2nd, from 9 a.m. to 5 p.m.』 ②의근거 일치
4월 2일 아침 9시부터 오후 5시까지래.

W : The place for the audition is the Youth Training Center. It's really far from here.
오디션 장소는 Youth Training Center네. 여기서 아주 멀어.

M : I think you should leave early in the morning.
너 아침 일찍 출발해야겠네.

W : That's no problem. 『Is there an entry fee?
그건 괜찮아. 참가비가 있니?

M : No, it's free.』 ④의근거 일치
아니, 무료래.

W : Good. I'll apply for the audition.
좋아, 난 오디션에 지원하겠어.

M : 『Then you should fill out an application form on this website.』 ⑤의근거 일치
그럼 이 웹 사이트에서 신청서를 작성해야 해.

W : All right. Thanks.
알겠어. 고마워.

Why? 왜 정답일까?

대화에서 남자와 여자는 Youth Choir Audition의 지원 가능 연령, 날짜, 참가비, 지원 방법을 언급하므로, 언급되지 않은 것은 ③ '심사 기준'이다.

Why? 왜 오답일까?

① 'It's open to anyone aged 13 to 18.'에서 '지원 가능 연령'이 언급되었다.
② 'April 2nd, from 9 a.m. to 5 p.m.'에서 '날짜'가 언급되었다.
④ 'No, it's free.'에서 '참가비'가 언급되었다.
⑤ '~ you should fill out an application form on this website.'에서 '지원 방법'이 언급되었다.

- choir ⓝ 합창단
- apply for ~에 신청하다, 지원하다
- entry fee 참가비
- fill out (서류를) 작성하다

---

09 진로 관련 특별 행사 안내 | 정답률 90% | 정답 ④

2023 Career Week에 관한 다음 내용을 듣고, 일치하지 않는 것을 고르시오.
① 5일 동안 열릴 것이다.
② 미래 직업 탐색을 돕는 프로그램이 있을 것이다.
③ 프로그램 참가 인원에 제한이 있다.
☑④ 특별 강연이 마지막 날에 있을 것이다.
⑤ 등록은 5월 10일에 시작된다.

W : Hello, Rosehill High School students!
안녕하세요, Rosehill 고등학교 학생 여러분!
I'm your school counselor, Ms. Lee.
저는 진로 상담 교사인 Ms. Lee입니다.
I'm so happy to announce a special event, the 2023 Career Week.
특별행사인 2023 Career Week에 관해 알려드리게 되어 기쁩니다.
『It'll be held from May 22nd for five days.』 ①의근거 일치
이것은 5월 22일부터 5일간 개최됩니다.
『There will be many programs to help you explore various future jobs.』 ②의근거 일치
여러분이 다양한 미래 직업을 탐색하도록 도와줄 많은 프로그램이 있을 겁니다.
『Please kindly note that the number of participants for each program is limited to 20.』 ③의근거 일치
프로그램마다 참가자 수가 20명으로 제한된다는 것을 유념해 주세요.
『A special lecture on future career choices will be presented on the first day.』 ④의근거 불일치
미래 직업 선택에 대한 특별 강연이 첫날 제공될 예정입니다.
『Registration begins on May 10th.』 ⑤의근거 일치
등록은 5월 10일부터 시작됩니다.
For more information, please visit our school website.
더 많은 정보를 원하시면, 우리 학교 웹 사이트를 방문해주세요.
I hope you can come and enjoy the 2023 Career Week!
여러분이 2023 Career Week에 와서 즐길 수 있기를 바랍니다!

Why? 왜 정답일까?

'A special lecture on future career choices will be presented on the first day.'에서 미래 직업 선택에 관한 특강은 첫날 있을 것이라고 하므로, 내용과 일치하지 않는 것은 '④ 특별 강연이 마지막 날에 있을 것이다.'이다.

Why? 왜 오답일까?

① 'It'll be held from May 22nd for five days.'의 내용과 일치한다.
② 'There will be many programs to help you explore various future jobs.'의 내용과 일치한다.
③ 'Please kindly note that the number of participants for each program is limited to 20.'의 내용과 일치한다.
⑤ 'Registration begins on May 10th.'의 내용과 일치한다.

- announce ⓥ 안내하다
- note ⓥ 주목하다, 유념하다
- registration ⓝ 등록, 신청
- explore ⓥ 탐색하다
- be limited to ~로 제한되다

---

10 프라이팬 고르기 | 정답률 90% | 정답 ②

다음 표를 보면서 대화를 듣고, 여자가 구입할 프라이팬을 고르시오.

Frying Pans

	Model	Price	Size (inches)	Material	Lid
①	A	$30	8	Aluminum	○
☑②	B	$32	9.5	Aluminum	○
③	C	$35	10	Stainless Steel	×
④	D	$40	11	Aluminum	×
⑤	E	$70	12.5	Stainless Steel	○

M : Jessica, what are you doing?
Jessica, 뭐 하고 있어?

W : I'm trying to buy one of these five frying pans.
이 다섯 개 프라이팬 중 하나 사려고 해.

M : Let me see. This frying pan seems pretty expensive.
좀 보자. 이 프라이팬은 꽤 비싸 보이는걸.

W : Yeah. 『I don't want to spend more than $50.』 근거1 Price 조건
응. 난 50달러 넘게 쓰고 싶지 않아.

M : Okay. 『And I think 9 to 12-inch frying pans will work for most of your cooking.』 근거2 Size 조건
그래. 그리고 내 생각에 9인치에서 12인치 크기의 프라이팬이 대부분의 요리에 적합할 거야.

W : I think so, too. An 8-inch frying pan seems too small for me.
나도 그렇게 생각해. 8인치는 나한테 너무 작아 보여.

M : What about the material? Stainless steel pans are good for fast cooking.
소재는 어때? 스테인리스 팬이 빨리 요리하는 데 좋아.

W : I know, but they are heavier. 『I'll buy an alumium pan.』 근거3 Material 조건
나도 알지만, 그건 더 무거워. 알루미늄 팬을 살 거야.

M : Then you have two options left. 『Do you need a lid?』 근거4 Lid 조건
그럼 선택권이 두 개 남았네. 너 뚜껑 필요해?

W : Of course. A lid keeps the oil from splashing. I'll buy this one.
물론이지. 뚜껑은 기름이 안 튀게 막아줘. 난 이걸 살래.

M : Good choice.
좋은 선택이야.

Why? 왜 정답일까?

대화에 따르면 여자는 가격이 50달러를 넘지 않고, 크기는 9~12인치이며, 소재는 알루미늄으로 되어 있고, 뚜껑이 딸려 있는 프라이팬을 사려고 한다. 따라서 여자가 구입할 프라이팬은 ② 'B'이다.

- work for ~에 적합하다
- lid ⓝ 뚜껑
- splash ⓥ (물 등을) 튀기다, 철벅거리다
- material ⓝ 소재, 재료, 자재
- keep A from B A가 B하지 못하게 막다

---

11 단편 영화 프로젝트 | 정답률 85% | 정답 ②

대화를 듣고, 남자의 마지막 말에 대한 여자의 응답으로 가장 적절한 것을 고르시오.
① I don't think I can finish editing it by then. – 내가 그때까지 편집을 끝낼 수 있을 거 같지 않아.
☑② I learned it by myself through books. – 책 보고 독학했어.
③ This short movie is very interesting. – 이 단편영화 무척 재밌어.
④ You should make another video clip. – 넌 다른 영상을 만들어야 해.
⑤ I got an A⁺ on the team project. – 난 팀 프로젝트에서 A⁺를 받았어.

M : Have you finished your team's short-movie project?
너네 팀 단편 영화 프로젝트 끝냈어?

W : Not yet. I'm still editing the video clip.
아직. 난 아직 영상을 편집하고 있어.

M : Oh, you edit? How did you learn to do that?
오, 네가 편집해? 그거 어디서 배웠어?

W : I learned it by myself through books.
책 보고 독학했어.

Why? 왜 정답일까?

여자가 영상을 직접 편집하고 있다는 말에 남자는 어떻게 배웠는지(How did you learn to do that?) 물으며 관심을 보인다. 따라서 여자의 응답으로 가장 적절한 것은 ② '책 보고 독학했어.'이다.

- video clip (짧은) 영상
- learn by oneself 독학하다

---

12 차로 데리러 와달라고 부탁하기 | 정답률 83% | 정답 ①

대화를 듣고, 여자의 마지막 말에 대한 남자의 응답으로 가장 적절한 것을 고르시오.
☑① All right. I'll come pick you up now. – 그래. 내가 지금 태우러 가마.
② I'm sorry. The library is closed today. – 미안해. 도서관은 오늘 닫았어.

③ No problem. You can borrow my book. – 물론이지. 내 책을 빌려가도 된다.
④ Thank you so much. I'll drop you off now. – 무척 고맙구나. 지금 내가 널 내려줄게.
⑤ Right. I've changed the interior of my office. – 맞아. 내 사무실 인테리어를 바꿨어.

[Cell phone rings.]
[휴대전화가 울린다.]
W : Daddy, are you still working now?
　아빠, 아직 일하고 계세요?
M : No, Emma. I'm about to get in my car and drive home.
　아니, Emma. 지금 차에 타서 집으로 가려던 참이야.
W : Great. Can you give me a ride? I'm at the City Library near your office.
　잘됐네요. 저 좀 태워주실래요? 저 아빠 사무실 근처 시립 도서관에 있어요.
M : All right. I'll come pick you up now.
　그래. 내가 지금 태우러 가마.

Why? 왜 정답일까?

남자가 집으로 가려던 참이라고 말하자 여자는 남자 사무실 근처에 있는 시립 도서관으로 태우러 와달라고 부탁하고 있다(**Can you give me a ride? I'm at the City Library near your office.**). 따라서 남자의 응답으로 가장 적절한 것은 ① '그래. 내가 지금 태우러 가마.'이다.

● be about to ~할 참이다
● pick up ~을 (차에) 태우다
● drop off ~을 (차에서) 내려주다

---

13 농장에 함께 가도 될지 묻기　　　정답률 83% | 정답 ③

대화를 듣고, 남자의 마지막 말에 대한 여자의 응답으로 가장 적절한 것을 고르시오.
Woman:
① Try these tomatoes and cucumbers. – 이 토마토랑 오이 좀 먹어봐.
② I didn't know peppers are good for skin. – 난 고추가 피부에 좋은 줄 몰랐어.
✔ Just wear comfortable clothes and shoes. – 그냥 편한 옷이랑 신발만 있으면 돼.
④ You can pick tomatoes when they are red. – 토마토가 빨간색이면 따도 돼.
⑤ I'll help you grow vegetables on your farm. – 너희 농장에서 채소 기르는 걸 도와줄게.

M : Claire, how's your farm doing?
　Claire, 너네 농장 어때?
W : Great! I harvested some cherry tomatoes and cucumbers last weekend. Do you want some?
　아주 좋아! 난 방울토마토랑 오이를 지난 주말에 좀 수확했어. 너 좀 줄까?
M : Of course. I'd like some very much.
　물론이지. 주면 아주 좋아.
W : Okay. I'll bring you some tomorrow.
　그래. 내가 내일 좀 가져다줄게.
M : Thanks. Are you going to the farm this weekend too?
　고마워. 너 이번 주말에도 농장 가?
W : Yes. The peppers are almost ready to be picked.
　응. 고추 딸 때가 거의 다 됐어.
M : Can I go with you? I'd like to look around your farm and help you pick the peppers.
　나도 가도 돼? 나도 너네 농장 좀 둘러보고 고추 따는 거 도와주고 싶어.
W : Sure. It would be fun to work on the farm together.
　물론이지. 같이 농장에서 일하면 재미있을 거야.
M : Sounds nice. Is there anything I need to prepare?
　근사할 거 같아. 내가 준비해야 할 게 있어?
W : Just wear comfortable clothes and shoes.
　그냥 편한 옷이랑 신발만 있으면 돼.

Why? 왜 정답일까?

여자네 농장에 따라가려는 남자가 준비물을 물으므로(**Is there anything I need to prepare?**), 여자의 응답으로 가장 적절한 것은 ③ '그냥 편한 옷이랑 신발만 있으면 돼.'이다.

● harvest ⓥ 수확하다
● cucumber ⓝ 오이

---

14 싸운 친구에게 직접 만나 사과하라고 권하기　　　정답률 89% | 정답 ①

대화를 듣고, 여자의 마지막 말에 대한 남자의 응답으로 가장 적절한 것을 고르시오. [3점]
Man:
✔ You're right. I'll meet her and apologize. – 네 말이 맞아, 걔를 만나서 사과하겠어.
② I agree with you. That's why I did it. – 네 말에 동의해. 그래서 내가 그렇게 했어.
③ Thank you. I appreciate your apology. – 고마워. 네 사과 고맙게 받을게.
④ Don't worry. I don't think it's your fault. – 걱정 마. 난 그게 네 잘못이라고 생각하지 않아.
⑤ Too bad. I hope the two of you get along. – 안됐네. 둘이 잘 지내길 바라.

W : Daniel, what's wrong?
　Daniel, 무슨 일이야?
M : Hi, Leila. I had an argument with Olivia.
　안녕, Leila. 나 Olivia랑 싸웠어.
W : Was it serious?
　진짜로 싸웠어?
M : I'm not sure, but I think I made a mistake.
　잘 모르겠어, 그런데 내가 실수를 한 것 같아.
W : So that's why you have a long face.
　그래서 네 얼굴이 우울하구나.
M : Yeah. I want to get along with her, but she's still angry at me.
　응. 난 걔랑 잘 지내고 싶은데, 걘 아직 나한테 화가 나 있어.
W : Did you say you're sorry to her?
　미안하다고 말했어?
M : Well, I texted her saying that I'm sorry.
　음, 미안하다고 말하는 문자를 보냈어.
W : I don't think it's a good idea to express your apology through a text message.
　문자 메시지로 사과를 표현하는 게 좋은 생각인 것 같지는 않아.
M : Do you think so? Now I know why I haven't received any response from her yet.
　그래? 이제 왜 내가 걔한테 아직 아무 답도 못 받았는지 알겠네.

020　예비 고1 · 반배치 + 3월 · 6월 영어 [리얼 오리지널]

W : I think it'd be best to go and talk to her in person.
　내 생각에 걔한테 가서 직접 말해보는 게 최선일 거 같아.
M : You're right. I'll meet her and apologize.
　네 말이 맞아. 걔를 만나서 사과하겠어.

Why? 왜 정답일까?

친구에게 문자로 사과했으나 답을 받지 못했다는 남자에게 여자는 직접 만나 사과하는 것이 가장 좋겠다고 충고하고 있다(**I think it'd be best to go and talk to her in person.**). 따라서 남자의 응답으로 가장 적절한 것은 ① '네 말이 맞아. 걔를 만나서 사과하겠어.'이다.

● have a long face 우울한 얼굴을 하다
● in person 직접
● appreciate ⓥ 감사하다
● get along with ~와 잘 지내다
● apologize ⓥ 사과하다

---

15 해돋이를 보기 위한 기상 시간 정하기　　　정답률 80% | 정답 ③

다음 상황 설명을 듣고, John이 Ted에게 할 말로 가장 적절한 것을 고르시오. [3점]
John: _____
① How can we find the best sunrise spot? – 최고의 해돋이 장소는 어떻게 찾지?
② Why do you go mountain climbing so often? – 넌 왜 그렇게 자주 등산을 가니?
✔ What time should we get up tomorrow morning? – 우리 내일 아침 몇 시에 일어나야 하지?
④ When should we come down from the mountain top? – 우리 산 정상에서 언제 내려가야 할까?
⑤ Where do we have to stay in the mountain at night? – 우리 밤에는 산 어디에 있어야 할까?

M : Ted and John are college freshmen.
　Ted와 John은 대학 신입생이다.
They are climbing Green Diamond Mountain together.
그들은 Green Diamond Mountain에 함께 오른다.
Now they have reached the campsite near the mountain top.
이제 그들은 산 정상 근처의 캠핑장에 이르렀다.
After climbing the mountain all day, they have a relaxing time at the campsite.
하루 종일 산을 오른 뒤, 그들은 캠핑장에서 여유로운 시간을 보내고 있다.
While drinking coffee, Ted suggests to John that they watch the sunrise at the mountain top the next morning.
커피를 마시던 중, Ted는 John에게 다음날 아침 산 정상에서 해돋이를 보자고 제안한다.
John thinks it's a good idea.
John은 그게 좋은 생각인 것 같다.
So, now John wants to ask Ted how early they should wake up to see the sunrise.
그래서, 이제 John은 Ted에게 해돋이를 보려면 얼마나 일찍 일어나야 할지 물어보려고 한다.
In this situation, what would John most likely say to Ted?
이 상황에서, John은 Ted에게 뭐라고 말할 것인가?
John : What time should we get up tomorrow morning?
　우리 내일 아침 몇 시에 일어나야 하지?

Why? 왜 정답일까?

상황에 따르면 John은 Ted의 제안에 따라 다음 날 산 정상에서 해돋이를 보려면 몇 시에 일어나야 할지 Ted에게 물어보려 한다(~ John wants to ask Ted how early they should wake up to see the sunrise.). 따라서 John이 Ted에게 할 말로 가장 적절한 것은 ③ '우리 내일 아침 몇 시에 일어나야 하지?'이다.

● relaxing ⓐ 여유로운, 느긋한
● sunrise ⓝ 일출, 해돋이

16-17 가족끼리 즐길 수 있는 운동

W : Good morning, everyone.
　안녕하세요, 여러분.
Do you spend a lot of time with your family?
여러분은 가족과 시간을 보내시나요?
One of the best ways to spend time with your family is to enjoy sports together.
가족과 시간을 보내는 최고의 방법 중 하나는 함께 운동을 즐기는 것입니다.
『Today, I will share some of the best sports that families can play together.』 16번의 근거
오늘, 저는 가족들이 함께할 수 있는 몇 가지 최고의 스포츠를 공유드리려고 합니다.
『The first one is badminton.』 17번 ①의 근거 일치
첫 번째는 배드민턴입니다.
The whole family can enjoy the sport with minimal equipment.
가족 모두가 최소의 장비로 스포츠를 즐길 수 있습니다.
『The second one is basketball.』 17번 ②의 근거 일치
두 번째는 농구입니다.
You can easily find a basketball court near your house.
집 근처에서 농구장을 쉽게 찾아볼 수 있죠.
『The third one is table tennis.』 17번 ③의 근거 일치
세 번째는 탁구입니다.
It can be played indoors anytime.
이것은 실내에서 언제든 할 수 있죠.
『The last one is bowling.』 17번 ⑤의 근거 일치
마지막으로 볼링입니다.
Many families have a great time playing it together.
많은 가족들은 볼링을 함께하며 멋진 시간을 보냅니다.
When you go home today, how about playing one of these sports with your family?
오늘 집에 가시면, 이 운동 중 하나를 가족들과 해보시면 어떨까요?

● whole ⓐ 전체의
● equipment ⓝ 장비
● the elderly 연세 드신 분들, 노인들
● traditional ⓐ 전통적인
● minimal ⓐ 최소의
● table tennis 탁구
● useful ⓐ 유용한

---

16 주제 파악　　　정답률 96% | 정답 ③

여자가 하는 말의 주제로 가장 적절한 것은?
① indoor sports good for the elderly – 노인층에 좋은 실내 스포츠
② importance of learning rules in sports – 스포츠에서 규칙을 익히는 것의 중요성
✔ best sports for families to enjoy together – 가족이 함께 즐길 수 있는 최고의 운동

④ useful tips for winning a sports game – 운동 경기를 이기기 위한 유용한 조언
⑤ history of traditional family sports – 전통 가족 스포츠의 역사

Why? 왜 정답일까?

'Today, I will share some of the best sports that families can play together.'에서 여자는 가족이 함께 즐기기 좋은 운동을 몇 가지 소개하겠다고 하므로, 여자가 하는 말의 주제로 가장 적절한 것은 ③ '가족이 함께 즐길 수 있는 최고의 운동'이다.

---

17 언급 유무 파악　　　　　　　정답률 96% | 정답 ④

언급된 스포츠가 **아닌** 것은?

① badminton – 배드민턴　② basketball – 농구　③ table tennis – 탁구
✔ soccer – 축구　⑤ bowling – 볼링

Why? 왜 정답일까?

담화에서 여자는 가족끼리 즐기기 좋은 스포츠의 예시로 배드민턴, 농구, 탁구, 볼링을 언급한다. 따라서 언급되지 않은 것은 ④ '축구'이다.

Why? 왜 오답일까?

① 'The first one is badminton.'에서 '배드민턴'이 언급되었다.
② 'The second one is basketball.'에서 '농구'가 언급되었다.
③ 'The third one is table tennis.'에서 '탁구'가 언급되었다.
⑤ 'The last one is bowling.'에서 '볼링'이 언급되었다.

---

18 아파트 놀이터 시설 수리 요청　　　정답률 93% | 정답 ③

다음 글의 목적으로 가장 적절한 것은?

① 아파트의 첨단 보안 설비를 홍보하려고
② 아파트 놀이터의 임시 폐쇄를 공지하려고
✔ 아파트 놀이터 시설의 수리를 요청하려고
④ 아파트 놀이터 사고의 피해 보상을 촉구하려고
⑤ 아파트 공용 시설 사용 시 유의 사항을 안내하려고

To whom it may concern,
관계자분께
I am a resident of the Blue Sky Apartment.
저는 Blue Sky 아파트의 거주자입니다.
Recently I observed / that the kid zone is in need of repairs.
최근에 저는 알게 되었습니다. / 아이들을 위한 구역이 수리가 필요하다는 것을
I want you to pay attention / to the poor condition of the playground equipment in the zone.
저는 귀하께서 관심을 기울여 주시기를 바랍니다. / 그 구역 놀이터 설비의 열악한 상태에
The swings are damaged, / the paint is falling off, / and some of the bolts on the slide are missing.
그네가 손상되었고, / 페인트가 떨어져 나가고 있고, / 미끄럼틀의 볼트 몇 개가 빠져 있습니다.
The facilities have been in this terrible condition / since we moved here.
시설들은 이렇게 형편없는 상태였습니다. / 우리가 이곳으로 이사 온 이후로
They are dangerous / to the children playing there.
이것들은 위험합니다. / 거기서 노는 아이들에게
Would you please have them repaired?
이것들을 수리해 주시겠습니까?
I would appreciate your immediate attention / to solve this matter.
즉각적인 관심을 보여주시면 감사하겠습니다. / 이 문제를 해결하기 위해
Yours sincerely, / Nina Davis
Nina Davis 드림

관계자분께

저는 Blue Sky 아파트의 거주자입니다. 최근에 저는 아이들을 위한 구역이 수리가 필요하다는 것을 알게 되었습니다. 저는 귀하께서 그 구역 놀이터 설비의 열악한 상태에 관심을 기울여 주시기를 바랍니다. 그네가 손상되었고, 페인트가 떨어져 나가고 있고, 미끄럼틀의 볼트 몇 개가 빠져 있습니다. 시설들은 우리가 이곳으로 이사 온 이후로 이렇게 형편없는 상태였습니다. 이것들은 거기서 노는 아이들에게 위험합니다. 이것들을 수리해 주시겠습니까? 이 문제를 해결하기 위한 즉각적인 관심을 보여주시면 감사하겠습니다.

Nina Davis 드림

Why? 왜 정답일까?

'I want you to pay attention to the poor condition of the playground equipment in the zone.'와 'Would you please have them repaired?'에 놀이터 시설 수리를 요청하는 필자의 목적이 잘 드러나 있다. 따라서 글의 목적으로 가장 적절한 것은 ③ '아파트 놀이터 시설의 수리를 요청하려고'이다.

● **to whom it may concern** 담당자 귀하, 관계자 귀하
● **in need of** ~이 필요한　　● **pay attention to** ~에 주의를 기울이다
● **equipment** ⓝ 장비　　● **damaged** ⓐ 손상된
● **fall off** 벗겨지다, 떨어져 나가다　　● **facility** ⓝ 시설
● **immediate** ⓐ 즉각적인

구문 풀이

6행 The facilities have been in this terrible condition since we moved here.
　　　　　　현재완료　　　　　　접속사(~ 이후로)　과거

---

19 야생에서 회색곰을 만난 필자　　　정답률 82% | 정답 ②

다음 글에 드러난 'I'의 심경 변화로 가장 적절한 것은?

① sad → angry　　　✔ delighted → scared
　슬픈　　화난　　　　　기쁜　　겁에 질린

---

③ satisfied → jealous
　만족하는　질투하는
⑤ frustrated → excited
　좌절한　　신난
④ worried → relieved
　걱정하는　안도한

On a two-week trip in the Rocky Mountains, / I saw a grizzly bear in its native habitat.
로키산맥에서 2주간의 여행 중, / 나는 자연 서식지에서 회색곰 한 마리를 보았다.
At first, / I felt joy / as I watched the bear walk across the land.
처음에 / 나는 기쁨을 느꼈다. / 내가 그 곰이 땅을 가로질러 걸어가는 모습을 보았을 때
He stopped every once in a while / to turn his head about, / sniffing deeply.
그것은 이따금 멈춰 서서 / 고개를 돌려 / 깊게 코를 킁킁거렸다.
He was following the scent of something, / and slowly I began to realize / that this giant animal was smelling me!
그것은 무언가의 냄새를 따라가고 있었고, / 나는 서서히 깨닫기 시작했다! / 거대한 이 동물이 내 냄새를 맡고 있다는 것을
I froze.
나는 얼어붙었다.
This was no longer a wonderful experience; / it was now an issue of survival.
이것은 더는 멋진 경험이 아니었고, / 이제 그것은 생존의 문제였다.
The bear's motivation was to find meat to eat, / and I was clearly on his menu.
그 곰의 동기는 먹을 고기를 찾는 것이었고, / 나는 분명히 그의 메뉴에 올라 있었다.

로키산맥에서 2주간의 여행 중, 나는 자연 서식지에서 회색곰 한 마리를 보았다. 처음에 나는 그 곰이 땅을 가로질러 걸어가는 모습을 보았을 때 기분이 좋았다. 그것은 이따금 멈춰 서서 고개를 돌려 깊게 코를 킁킁거렸다. 그것은 무언가의 냄새를 따라가고 있었고, 나는 서서히 거대한 이 동물이 내 냄새를 맡고 있다는 것을 깨닫기 시작했다! 나는 얼어붙었다. 이것은 더는 멋진 경험이 아니었고, 이제 생존의 문제였다. 그 곰의 동기는 먹을 고기를 찾는 것이었고, 나는 분명히 그의 메뉴에 올라 있었다.

Why? 왜 정답일까?

처음에 회색곰을 발견하고 기분이 좋았던(At first, I felt joy as I watched the bear walk across the land.) 필자가 곰이 자신을 노린다는 것을 알고 겁에 질렸다(I froze.)는 내용이다. 따라서 'I'의 심경 변화로 가장 적절한 것은 ② '기쁜 → 겁에 질린'이다.

● **grizzly bear** (북미·러시아 일부 지역에 사는) 회색곰　● **habitat** ⓝ 서식지
● **walk across** ~을 횡단하다　　● **every once in a while** 이따금
● **turn about** 뒤돌아보다, 방향을 바꾸다　　● **sniff** ⓥ 킁킁거리다
● **scent** ⓝ 냄새　　● **freeze** ⓥ 얼어붙다
● **no longer** 더 이상 ~않다　　● **motivation** ⓝ (행동의) 이유, 동기 (부여)
● **jealous** ⓐ 질투하는　　● **frustrated** ⓐ 좌절한

구문 풀이

3행 He stopped every once in a while to turn his head about, sniffing deeply.
　　　　　　　　　　　　　　　　목적(~하려고)　　　분사구문(~하면서)

---

20 신체 리듬이 정점일 때를 파악해 활용하기　정답률 81% | 정답 ⑤

다음 글에서 필자가 주장하는 바로 가장 적절한 것은?

① 부정적인 감정에 에너지를 낭비하지 말라.
② 자신의 신체 능력에 맞게 운동량을 조절하라.
③ 자기 성찰을 위한 아침 명상 시간을 확보하라.
④ 생산적인 하루를 보내려면 일을 균등하게 배분하라.
✔ 자신의 에너지가 가장 높은 시간을 파악하여 활용하라.

It is difficult for any of us / to maintain a constant level of attention / throughout our working day.
우리 중 누구라도 어렵다. / 일정한 수준의 주의 집중을 유지하기는 / 근무일 내내
We all have body rhythms / characterised by peaks and valleys of energy and alertness.
우리 모두 신체 리듬을 가지고 있다. / 에너지와 기민함의 정점과 저점을 특징으로 하는
You will achieve more, / and feel confident as a benefit, / if you schedule your most demanding tasks / at times when you are best able to cope with them.
여러분은 더 많은 것을 이루고, / 이득으로 자신감을 느낄 것이다. / 여러분이 가장 힘든 작업을 하도록 계획을 잡으면 / 가장 잘 처리할 수 있는 시간에
If you haven't thought about energy peaks before, / take a few days to observe yourself.
만약 여러분이 전에 에너지 정점에 관해 생각해 본 적이 없다면, / 며칠 자신을 관찰할 시간을 가지라.
Try to note the times / when you are at your best.
때를 알아차리도록 노력하라. / 여러분이 상태가 제일 좋을
We are all different.
우리는 모두 다르다.
For some, / the peak will come first thing in the morning, / but for others / it may take a while to warm up.
어떤 사람에게는 / 정점이 아침에 제일 먼저 오지만, / 다른 사람에게는 / 준비되는 데 얼마간의 시간이 걸릴 수도 있다.

우리 중 누구라도 근무일 내내 일정한 수준의 주의 집중을 유지하기는 어렵다. 우리 모두 에너지와 기민함의 정점과 저점을 특징으로 하는 신체 리듬을 가지고 있다. 가장 힘든 작업을 가장 잘 처리할 수 있는 시간에 하도록 계획을 잡으면, 더 많은 것을 이루고, 이득으로 자신감을 느낄 것이다. 만약 전에 에너지 정점에 관해 생각해 본 적이 없다면, 며칠 동안 자신을 관찰하라. 상태가 제일 좋을 때를 알아차리도록 노력하라. 우리는 모두 다르다. 어떤 사람에게는 정점이 아침에 제일 먼저 오지만, 다른 사람에게는 준비되는 데 얼마간의 시간이 걸릴 수도 있다.

Why? 왜 정답일까?

힘든 작업을 분배할 수 있도록 하루 중 신체 리듬이 가장 좋은 시간을 찾아보라(Try to note the times when you are at your best.)고 조언하는 글이므로, 필자의 주장으로 가장 적절한 것은 ⑤ '자신의 에너지가 가장 높은 시간을 파악하여 활용하라.'이다.

● **maintain** ⓥ 유지하다　　● **constant** ⓐ 지속적인
● **throughout** prep ~ 내내　　● **characterise** ⓥ ~을 특징으로 하다
● **peaks and valleys** 정점과 저점, 부침, 성쇠　● **alertness** ⓝ 기민함
● **achieve** ⓥ 성취하다　　● **confident** ⓐ 자신감 있는
● **benefit** ⓝ 이득　　● **demanding** ⓐ 까다로운, 힘든
● **cope with** ~을 처리하다　　● **warm up** 준비가 되다, 몸을 풀다

7행 Try to note the times when you are at your best.
선행사(시간) 관계부사

---

21 더 많은 기술을 받아들인 대가 정답률 55% | 정답 ⑤

밑줄 친 The divorce of the hands from the head가 다음 글에서 의미하는 바로 가장 적절한 것은? [3점]

① ignorance of modern technology
현대 기술에 대한 무지
② endless competition in the labor market
노동 시장에서의 끝없는 경쟁
③ not getting along well with our coworkers
동료와 잘 지내지 않는 것
④ working without any realistic goals for our career
경력을 위한 아무 현실적 목표도 없이 일하는 것
☑ our increasing use of high technology in the workplace
우리가 직장에서 고도의 기술을 점점 더 많이 사용하는 것

If we adopt technology, / we need to pay its costs.
만약 우리가 기술을 받아들이면, / 우리는 그것의 비용을 치러야 한다.
Thousands of traditional livelihoods / have been pushed aside by progress, / and the lifestyles around those jobs / removed.
수천 개의 전통적인 생계 수단이 / 발전 때문에 밀려났으며, / 그 직업과 관련된 생활 방식이 / 없어졌다.
Hundreds of millions of humans today / work at jobs they hate, / producing things they have no love for.
오늘날 수억 명의 사람들이 / 자기가 싫어하는 일자리에서 일한다 / 그들이 아무런 애정을 느끼지 못하는 것들을 생산하면서
Sometimes / these jobs cause physical pain, disability, or chronic disease.
때때로 / 이러한 일자리는 육체적 고통, 장애 또는 만성 질환을 유발한다.
Technology creates many new jobs / that are certainly dangerous.
기술은 많은 새로운 일자리를 창출한다. / 확실히 위험한
At the same time, / mass education and media train humans / to avoid low-tech physical work, / to seek jobs working in the digital world.
동시에, / 대중 교육과 대중 매체는 인간을 훈련시킨다 / 낮은 기술의 육체노동을 피하고 / 디지털 세계에서 일하는 직업을 찾도록
The divorce of the hands from the head / puts a stress on the human mind.
손이 머리로부터 단절돼 있는 것은 / 인간의 정신에 부담을 준다.
Indeed, / the sedentary nature of the best-paying jobs / is a health risk / — for body and mind.
실제로, / 가장 보수가 좋은 직업이 주로 앉아서 하는 특성을 지녔다는 것은 / 건강상 위험 요소이다. / 신체와 정신에

만약 우리가 기술을 받아들이면, 우리는 그것의 비용을 치러야 한다. 수천 개의 전통적인 생계 수단이 발전 때문에 밀려났으며, 그 직업과 관련된 생활 방식이 없어졌다. 오늘날 수억 명의 사람들이 자기가 싫어하는 일자리에서 일하면서 아무런 애정을 느끼지 못하는 것들을 생산한다. 때때로 이러한 일자리는 육체적 고통, 장애 또는 만성 질환을 유발한다. 기술은 확실히 위험한 많은 새로운 일자리를 창출한다. 동시에, 대중 교육과 대중 매체는 인간이 낮은 기술의 육체노동을 피하고 디지털 세계에서 일하는 직업을 찾도록 훈련시킨다. 손이 머리로부터 단절돼 있는 것은 인간의 정신에 부담을 준다. 실제로, 가장 보수가 좋은 직업이 주로 앉아서 하는 특성을 지녔다는 것은 신체 및 정신 건강의 위험 요소이다.

Why? 왜 정답일까?

첫 두 문장에서 우리는 더 많은 기술을 받아들이면서 더 많은 전통적 방식을 포기하게 되었다고 말한다. 특히 밑줄이 포함된 문장 앞에서는 현대 인간이 육체노동을 덜 찾고 앉아서 하는 일을 찾도록(to avoid low-tech physical work, to seek jobs working in the digital world) 훈련되면서 더 많은 건강 위험에 노출되었다고 설명한다. 이러한 흐름으로 보아, 밑줄 부분은 결국 '인간이 기술을 더 많이 받아들인 대가로' 육체와 정신의 건강을 잃게 되었다는 뜻으로 볼 수 있다. 따라서 밑줄 친 부분의 의미로 가장 적절한 것은 ⑤ '우리가 직장에서 고도의 기술을 점점 더 많이 사용하는 것'이다.

- **adopt** ⓥ 수용하다, 받아들이다
- **livelihood** ⓝ 생계
- **progress** ⓝ 진보
- **million** ⓝ 100만
- **have love for** ~에 애정을 갖다
- **disability** ⓝ 장애
- **certainly** ⓐ 분명히, 확실히
- **seek** ⓥ 찾다, 추구하다
- **divorce A from B** A와 B의 분리, A를 B로부터 분리시키다
- **put a stress on** ~에 스트레스[부담]를 주다
- **nature** ⓝ 본성, 특성
- **ignorance** ⓝ 무지
- **competition** ⓝ 경쟁
- **get along (well) with** ~와 잘 지내다
- **cost** ⓝ 비용 ⓥ (~의 비용을) 치르게 하다
- **push aside** 밀어치우다
- **remove** ⓥ 제거하다
- **produce** ⓥ 만들어내다
- **physical** ⓐ 신체적인
- **chronic** ⓐ 만성의
- **mass** ⓝ (일반) 대중 ⓐ 대중의, 대량의
- **sedentary** ⓐ 주로 앉아서 하는
- **health risk** 건강상 위험
- **endless** ⓐ 끝없는
- **labor market** 노동 시장
- **realistic** ⓐ 현실적인

구문 풀이

3행 Hundreds of millions of humans today work at jobs (that) they hate,
수식어 / 목적격 관계대명사
producing things [they have no love for.]
선행사

---

22 숙련된 학습자의 융통성 정답률 83% | 정답 ①

다음 글의 요지로 가장 적절한 것은?

☑ 숙련된 학습자는 상황에 맞는 학습 전략을 사용할 줄 안다.
② 선다형 시험과 논술 시험은 평가의 형태와 목적이 다르다.
③ 문화마다 특정 행사와 상황에 맞는 복장 규정이 있다.
④ 학습의 양보다는 학습의 질이 학업 성과를 좌우한다.
⑤ 학습 목표가 명확할수록 성취 수준이 높아진다.

When students are starting their college life, / they may approach every course, test, or learning task the same way, / using what we like to call "the rubber-stamp approach."
학생들이 대학 생활을 시작할 때 / 그들은 모든 과목, 시험, 또는 학습 과제를 똑같은 방식으로 접근할지도 모른다. / 우리가 '고무도장 방식'이라고 부르고자 하는 방법을 이용하여

Think about it this way: / Would you wear a tuxedo to a baseball game? / A colorful dress to a funeral? / A bathing suit to religious services?
그것을 이렇게 생각해 보라. / 여러분은 야구 경기에 턱시도를 입고 가겠는가? / 장례식에 화려한 드레스를 입고 가겠는가? / 종교 예식에 수영복을 입고 가겠는가?
Probably not.
아마 아닐 것이다.
You know / there's appropriate dress for different occasions and settings.
여러분은 안다 / 다양한 행사와 상황마다 적합한 옷이 있음을
Skillful learners know / that "putting on the same clothes" / won't work for every class.
숙련된 학습자는 알고 있다. / '같은 옷을 입는 것'이 / 모든 수업에 효과가 있지 않을 것이라는 걸
They are flexible learners.
그들은 유연한 학습자이다.
They have different strategies / and know when to use them.
그들은 다양한 전략을 갖고 있으며 / 그것을 언제 사용해야 하는지 안다.
They know / that you study for multiple-choice tests differently / than you study for essay tests.
그들은 안다. / 여러분이 선다형 시험은 다르게 학습한다는 것을 / 여러분이 논술 시험을 위해 학습하는 것과는
And they not only know what to do, / but they also know how to do it.
그리고 그들은 무엇을 해야 하는지 알고 있을 뿐만 아니라, / 그것을 어떻게 해야 하는지도 알고 있다.

대학 생활을 시작할 때 학생들은 우리가 '고무도장 방식(잘 살펴보지도 않고 무조건 승인 또는 처리하는 방식)'이라고 부르고자 하는 방법을 이용하여 모든 과목, 시험, 또는 학습 과제를 똑같은 방식으로 접근할지도 모른다. 그것을 이렇게 생각해 보라. 여러분은 야구 경기에 턱시도를 입고 가겠는가? 장례식에 화려한 드레스를 입고 가겠는가? 종교 예식에 수영복을 입고 가겠는가? 아마 아닐 것이다. 다양한 행사와 상황마다 적합한 옷이 있음을 여러분은 알고 있다. 숙련된 학습자는 '같은 옷을 입는 것'이 모든 수업에 효과가 있지 않을 것이라는 걸 알고 있다. 그들은 유연한 학습자이다. 그들은 다양한 전략을 갖고 있으며 그것을 언제 사용해야 하는지 안다. 그들은 선다형 시험은 논술 시험을 위해 학습하는 것과는 다르게 학습한다는 것을 안다. 그리고 그들은 무엇을 해야 하는지 알고 있을 뿐만 아니라, 그것을 어떻게 해야 하는지도 알고 있다.

Why? 왜 정답일까?

숙련된 학습자는 상황마다 적절한 학습 전략이 있음을 알고 이를 융통성 있게 사용한다(Skillful learners know that "putting on the same clothes" won't work for every class. They are flexible learners. They have different strategies and know when to use them.)는 내용이다. 따라서 글의 요지로 가장 적절한 것은 ① '숙련된 학습자는 상황에 맞는 학습 전략을 사용할 줄 안다.'이다.

- **course** ⓝ 수업, 강좌
- **rubber-stamp** ⓥ 고무도장, 잘 살펴보지도 않고 무조건 허가하는 사람
- **colorful** ⓐ 화려한, 색색의
- **bathing suit** 수영복
- **appropriate** ⓐ 적절한
- **skillful** ⓐ 숙련된
- **strategy** ⓝ 전략
- **funeral** ⓝ 장례식
- **religious service** 종교 의식
- **occasion** ⓝ 상황, 경우
- **flexible** ⓐ 융통성 있는
- **multiple-choice test** 객관식 시험, 선다형 시험

구문 풀이

1행 When students are starting their college life, they may approach every course, test, or learning task the same way, using what we like to call "the rubber-stamp approach."
분사구문 / 관계대명사 / └불완전한 문장 (to call의 목적어가 없음)
to call의 보어

★★★ 등급을 가르는 문제!
23 관광 산업이 성장한 배경 정답률 39% | 정답 ①

다음 글의 주제로 가장 적절한 것은?

☑ factors that caused tourism expansion – 관광 산업의 확장을 일으킨 요인
② discomfort at a popular tourist destination – 유명한 여행지에서의 불편
③ importance of tourism in society and economy – 사회와 경제에서 관광 산업이 갖는 중요성
④ negative impacts of tourism on the environment – 관광 산업이 환경에 미치는 부정적 영향
⑤ various types of tourism and their characteristics – 다양한 유형의 관광 산업과 그 특징

As the social and economic situation of countries got better, / wage levels and working conditions improved.
국가들의 사회적 및 경제적 상황이 더 나아지면서, / 임금 수준과 근로 여건이 개선되었다.
Gradually / people were given more time off.
점차 / 사람들은 더 많은 휴가를 받게 되었다.
At the same time, / forms of transport improved / and it became faster and cheaper / to get to places.
동시에, / 운송 형태가 개선되었고 / 더 빠르고 더 저렴해졌다. / 장소를 이동하는 것이
England's industrial revolution / led to many of these changes.
영국의 산업 혁명이 / 이러한 변화 중 많은 것을 일으켰다.
Railways, / in the nineteenth century, / opened up now famous seaside resorts / such as Blackpool and Brighton.
철도는 / 19세기에, / 현재 유명한 해안가 리조트를 개업시켰다. / Blackpool과 Brighton 같은
With the railways / came many large hotels.
철도가 생기면서 / 많은 대형 호텔이 생겨났다.
In Canada, for example, / the new coast-to-coast railway system made possible / the building of such famous hotels / as Banff Springs and Chateau Lake Louise in the Rockies.
예를 들어, 캐나다에서는 / 새로운 대륙 횡단 철도 시스템이 가능하게 했다. / 그런 유명한 호텔 건설을 / 로키산맥의 Banff Springs와 Chateau Lake Louise 같은
Later, / the arrival of air transport / opened up more of the world / and led to tourism growth.
이후에 / 항공 운송의 출현은 / 세계의 더 많은 곳을 열어 주었고 / 관광 산업의 성장을 이끌었다.

국가들의 사회적 및 경제적 상황이 더 나아지면서, 임금 수준과 근로 여건이 개선되었다. 점차 사람들은 더 많은 휴가를 받게 되었다. 동시에, 운송 형태가 개선되었고 장소를 이동하는 것이 더 빠르고 더 저렴해졌다. 영국의 산업 혁명이 이러한 변화 중 많은 것을 일으켰다. 19세기에, 철도로 인해 Blackpool과 Brighton 같은 현재 유명한 해안가 리조트가 들어서게 되

었다. 철도가 생기면서 많은 대형 호텔이 생겨났다. 예를 들어, 캐나다에서는 새로운 대륙 횡단 철도 시스템이 로키산맥의 Banff Springs와 Chateau Lake Louise 같은 유명한 호텔 건설을 가능하게 했다. 이후에 항공 운송의 출현은 세계의 더 많은 곳(으로 가는 길)을 열어 주었고 관광 산업의 성장을 이끌었다.

24 성공적인 직업의 함정   정답률 67% | 정답 ②

다음 글의 제목으로 가장 적절한 것은?

① Don't Compete with Yourself – 자기 자신과 경쟁하지 말라
✔ A Trap of a Successful Career – 성공적인 직업의 함정
③ Create More Jobs for Young People – 젊은이들을 위해 더 많은 일자리를 창출하라
④ What Difficult Jobs Have in Common – 어려운 직업에는 어떤 공통점이 있는가
⑤ A Road Map for an Influential Employer – 영향력이 큰 고용주를 위한 지침

Success can lead you / off your intended path / and into a comfortable rut.
성공은 여러분을 이끌 수 있다. / 의도된 길에서 벗어나 / 틀에 박힌 편안한 생활로 들어가도록
If you are good at something / and are well rewarded for doing it, / you may want to keep doing it / even if you stop enjoying it.
여러분이 어떤 일을 잘하고 / 그 일을 하는 데 대한 보상을 잘 받는다면, / 여러분은 그걸 계속하고 싶을 수도 있다. / 여러분이 그것을 즐기지 않게 되더라도
The danger is / that one day you look around and realize / you're so deep in this comfortable rut / that you can no longer see the sun or breathe fresh air; / the sides of the rut have become so slippery / that it would take a superhuman effort / to climb out; / and, effectively, you're stuck.
위험한 점은 ~이다. / 어느 날 여러분이 주변을 둘러보고 깨닫게 된다는 것 / 여러분이 틀에 박힌 이 편안한 생활에 너무나 깊이 빠져 있어서 / 더는 태양을 보거나 신선한 공기를 호흡할 수 없다고 / 그 틀에 박힌 생활의 양쪽 면이 너무나 미끄럽게 되어 / 초인적인 노력이 필요할 것이라고 / 기어올라 나오려면 / 그리고 사실상 여러분이 꼼짝할 수 없다는 것
And it's a situation / that many working people worry / they're in now.
그리고 이는 상황이다. / 많은 근로자가 걱정하는 / 현재 자신이 처해 있는
The poor employment market / has left them feeling locked / in what may be a secure, or even well-paying — but ultimately unsatisfying — job.
열악한 고용 시장은 / 이들이 갇혀 있다고 느끼게 했다. / 안정적이거나 심지어 보수가 좋을 수도 있지만 궁극적으로는 만족스럽지 못한 일자리에

성공은 여러분이 의도한 길에서 벗어나 틀에 박힌 편안한 생활로 들어가도록 이끌 수 있다. 여러분이 어떤 일을 잘하고 그 일을 하는 데 대한 보상을 잘 받는다면, 그것을 즐기지 않게 되더라도 계속하고 싶을 수도 있다. 위험한 점은 어느 날 여러분이 주변을 둘러보고, 자신이 틀에 박힌 이 편안한 생활에 너무나 깊이 빠져 있어서 더는 태양을 보거나 신선한 공기를 호흡할 수 없으며, 그 틀에 박힌 생활의 양쪽 면이 너무나 미끄럽게 되어 기어올라 나오려면 초인적인 노력이 필요할 것이고, 사실상 자신이 꼼짝할 수 없다는 것을 깨닫게 된다는 것이다. 그리고 이는 많은 근로자가 현재 자신이 처해 있다고 걱정하는 상황이다. 열악한 고용 시장은 이들이 안정적이거나 심지어 보수가 좋을 수도 있지만 궁극적으로는 만족스럽지 못한 일자리에 갇혀 있다고 느끼게 했다.

구문 풀이

8행 The poor employment market has left them feeling locked in [what may be a secure, or even well-paying — but ultimately unsatisfying — job].
동사 ／ 목적어 ／ 목적격 보어(현재분사) ／ [ ]: in의 목적절
may be의 주격 보어

25 국내 출생자 수와 사망자 수의 변화 추이   정답률 74% | 정답 ⑤

다음 도표의 내용과 일치하지 않는 것은?

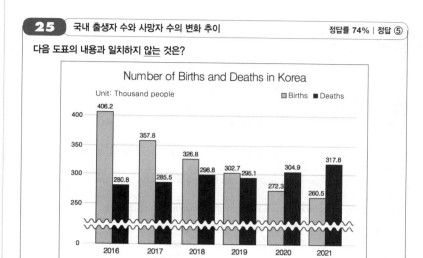

Number of Births and Deaths in Korea
Unit: Thousand people ■ Births ■ Deaths

	2016	2017	2018	2019	2020	2021
Births	406.2	357.8	326.8	302.7	272.3	260.5
Deaths	280.8	285.5	298.8	295.1	304.9	317.8

The above graph shows the number of births and deaths in Korea / from 2016 to 2021.
위 그래프는 한국에서의 출생자 수와 사망자 수를 보여 준다. / 2016년부터 2021년까지
① The number of births / continued to decrease / throughout the whole period.
출생자 수는 / 계속 감소했다. / 전체 기간 내내
② The gap between the number of births and deaths / was the largest in 2016.
출생자 수와 사망자 수 사이의 차이는 / 2016년에 가장 컸다.
③ In 2019, / the gap between the number of births and deaths / was the smallest, / with the number of births slightly larger than that of deaths.
2019년에는 / 출생자 수와 사망자 수 사이의 차이가 / 가장 작았는데, / 출생자 수가 사망자 수보다 약간 더 컸다.
④ The number of deaths / increased steadily during the whole period, / except the period from 2018 to 2019.
사망자 수는 / 전체 기간 동안 꾸준히 증가했다. / 2018년과 2019년까지의 기간을 제외하고
✔ In 2021, / the number of deaths / was larger than that of births / for the first time.
2021년에는 / 사망자 수가 / 출생자 수보다 더 컸다. / 처음으로

위 그래프는 2016년부터 2021년까지 한국에서의 출생자 수와 사망자 수를 보여 준다. ① 출생자 수는 전체 기간 내내 계속 감소했다. ② 출생자 수와 사망자 수 사이의 차이는 2016년에 가장 컸다. ③ 2019년에는 출생자 수와 사망자 수 사이의 차이가 가장 작았는데, 출생자 수가 사망자 수보다 약간 더 컸다. ④ 사망자 수는 2018년과 2019년까지의 기간을 제외하고 전체 기간 동안 꾸준히 증가했다. ⑤ 2021년에는 처음으로 사망자 수가 출생자 수보다 더 컸다.

26 Lilian Bland의 생애   정답률 91% | 정답 ⑤

Lilian Bland에 관한 다음 글의 내용과 일치하지 않는 것은?

① 승마와 사냥 같은 모험적인 활동을 즐겼다.
② 스포츠와 야생 동물 사진작가로 경력을 시작했다.
③ 자신의 비행기를 설계하고 제작했다.
④ 자동차 판매원으로 일하기도 했다.
✔ 캐나다에서 생의 마지막 기간을 보냈다.

Lilian Bland was born in Kent, England in 1878.
Lilian Bland는 1878년 잉글랜드 Kent에서 태어났다.
『Unlike most other girls at the time / she wore trousers / and spent her time enjoying adventurous activities / like horse riding and hunting.』 ①의 근거 일치
당시 대부분의 다른 여자아이와 달리 / 그녀는 바지를 입었고, / 모험적인 활동을 즐기며 시간을 보냈다. / 승마와 사냥 같은
『Lilian began her career / as a sports and wildlife photographer for British newspapers.』
Lilian은 경력을 시작했다. / 영국 신문사의 스포츠와 야생 동물 사진작가로 ②의 근거 일치
『In 1910 / she became the first woman / to design, build, and fly her own airplane.』
1910년 / 그녀는 최초의 여성이 되었다. / 자신의 비행기를 설계하고 제작하고 비행한 ③의 근거 일치
In order to persuade her / to try a slightly safer activity, / Lilian's dad bought her a car.
그녀가 ~하도록 설득하고자 / 약간 더 안전한 활동을 하도록 / Lilian의 아버지는 그녀에게 자동차를 사주었다.
『Soon Lilian was a master driver / and ended up working as a car dealer.』 ④의 근거 일치
곧 Lilian은 뛰어난 운전자가 되었고 / 결국 자동차 판매원으로 일하게 되었다.
She never went back to flying / but lived a long and exciting life nonetheless.
그녀는 비행에 결코 다시 복귀하지 않았지만, / 그렇기는 해도 오랫동안 흥미진진한 삶을 살았다.
She married, moved to Canada, and had a kid.
그녀는 결혼하여 캐나다로 이주했고, 아이를 낳았다.
『Eventually, / she moved back to England, / and lived there for the rest of her life.』
결국 / 그녀는 잉글랜드로 돌아와 / 거기서 생의 마지막 기간을 보냈다. ⑤의 근거 불일치

Lilian Bland는 1878년 잉글랜드 Kent에서 태어났다. 당시 대부분의 다른 여자아이와 달리 그녀는 바지를 입었고, 승마와 사냥 같은 모험적인 활동을 즐기며 시간을 보냈다. Lilian은 영국 신문사의 스포츠와 야생 동물 사진작가로 경력을 시작했다. 1910년에 그녀는 자신의 비행기를 설계하고 제작하고 비행한 최초의 여성이 되었다. 그녀가 약간 더 안전한 활동을 하도록 설득하고자, Lilian의 아버지는 그녀에게 자동차를 사주었다. 곧 Lilian은 뛰어난 운전자가 되었고 결국 자동차 판매원으로 일하게 되었다. 그녀는 비행에 결코 다시 복귀하지 않았지만, 그렇기는 해도 오랫동안 흥미진진한 삶을 살았다. 그녀는 결혼하여 캐나다로 이주했고, 아이를 낳았다. 결국 그녀는 잉글랜드로 돌아와 거기서 생의 마지막 기간을 보냈다.

- **unlike** prep ~와 달리
- **wildlife** n 야생 동물
- **persuade** v 설득하다
- **car dealer** 자동차 판매상
- **have a kid** 자식을 낳다
- **adventurous** a 모험적인
- **photographer** n 사진 작가
- **end up ~ing** 결국 ~하다
- **nonetheless** ad 그럼에도 불구하고
- **the rest of** ~의 나머지

구문 풀이

6행 In order to persuade her to try a slightly safer activity, Lilian's dad bought her a car.
→ 간접목적어 목적(~하기 위해서) 동사 직접목적어

---

27 **잡지 기사 공모**   정답률 93% | 정답 ③

Call for Articles에 관한 다음 안내문의 내용과 일치하지 <u>않는</u> 것은?
① 13세에서 18세까지의 누구나 참여할 수 있다.
② 기사는 고화질 컬러 사진을 포함해야 한다.
✓ ③ 사진 한 장에 5센트씩 지급한다.
④ 전화번호를 원고와 함께 보내야 한다.
⑤ 원고를 이메일로 제출해야 한다.

Call for Articles
기사 모집
Do you want to get your stories published?
여러분의 이야기가 출간되기를 원하시나요?
New Dream Magazine is looking for future writers!
*New Dream Magazine*은 미래의 작가를 찾고 있습니다!
「This event is open to anyone aged 13 to 18.」 ①의근거 일치
이 행사는 13세에서 18세까지 누구나 참여할 수 있습니다.
Articles
기사
Length of writing: 300 – 325 words
원고 길이: 300 ~ 325단어
「Articles should also include high-quality color photos.」 ②의근거 일치
기사에는 또한 고화질 컬러 사진이 포함되어야 합니다.
Rewards
사례금
Five cents per word
단어당 5센트
「Five dollars per photo」 ③의근거 불일치
사진당 5달러
Notes
주의 사항
「You should send us your phone number / together with your writing.」 ④의근거 일치
여러분의 전화번호를 보내주셔야 합니다. / 원고와 함께
「Please email your writing to us / at article@ndmag.com.」 ⑤의근거 일치
여러분의 원고를 저희에게 보내주세요. / 이메일 article@ndmag.com으로

기사 모집

여러분의 이야기가 출간되기를 원하시나요? *New Dream Magazine*은 미래의 작가를 찾고 있습니다! 이 행사는 13세에서 18세까지 누구나 참여할 수 있습니다.

기사
● 원고 길이: 300 ~ 325단어
● 기사에는 또한 고화질 컬러 사진이 포함되어야 합니다.

사례금
● 단어당 5센트
● 사진당 5달러

주의 사항
● 여러분의 전화번호를 원고와 함께 보내주셔야 합니다.
● 원고를 이메일 article@ndmag.com으로 보내주세요.

- **publish** v 출간하다
- **high-quality** a 고품질의
- **article** n 기사

---

28 **롤러스케이팅장 이용 안내**   정답률 90% | 정답 ④

Greenhill Roller Skating에 관한 다음 안내문의 내용과 일치하는 것은?
① 오전 9시부터 오후 9시까지 운영한다.
② 이용료는 시간 제한 없이 1인당 8달러이다.
③ 입장하려면 예약이 필요하다.
✓ ④ 10세 미만 어린이는 어른과 동행해야 한다.
⑤ 추가 요금을 내면 롤러스케이트를 빌려준다.

Greenhill Roller Skating
Greenhill 롤러스케이팅
Join us for your chance / to enjoy roller skating!
기회를 함께 해요! / 롤러스케이팅을 즐길
Place: Greenhill Park, 351 Cypress Avenue
장소: Cypress Avenue 351번지 Greenhill Park
Dates: Friday, April 7 – Sunday, April 9
일자: 4월 7일 금요일 ~ 4월 9일 일요일
「Time: 9 a.m. – 6 p.m.」 ①의근거 불일치
시간: 오전 9시 ~ 오후 6시
「Fee: $8 per person for a 50-minute session」 ②의근거 불일치
요금: 50분간 1인당 8달러
Details
세부 사항
「Admission will be on a first-come, first-served basis / with no reservations.」 ③의근거 불일치
입장은 선착순입니다. / 예약 없이
「Children under the age of 10 / must be accompanied by an adult.」 ④의근거 일치
10세 미만의 어린이는 / 어른과 동행해야 합니다.
「We will lend you our roller skates for free.」 ⑤의근거 불일치
롤러스케이트는 무료로 빌려드립니다.
Contact the Community Center for more information at 013-234-6114.
더 많은 정보를 위해서 주민센터 013-234-6114로 연락하세요.

Greenhill 롤러스케이팅

롤러스케이팅을 즐길 기회를 함께 해요!

● 장소: Cypress Avenue 351번지 Greenhill Park
● 일자: 4월 7일 금요일 ~ 4월 9일 일요일
● 시간: 오전 9시 ~ 오후 6시
● 요금: 50분간 1인당 8달러

세부 사항
– 입장은 예약 없이 선착순입니다.
– 10세 미만의 어린이는 어른과 동행해야 합니다.
– 롤러스케이트는 무료로 빌려드립니다.

더 많은 정보를 위해서 주민센터 013-234-6114로 연락하세요.

- **first-come, first-served** 선착순
- **for free** 공짜로
- **accompany** v 동반하다

---

29 **동물에게 투영된 인간의 특징**   정답률 62% | 정답 ⑤

다음 글의 밑줄 친 부분 중, 어법상 틀린 것은? [3점]

The most noticeable human characteristic / projected onto animals / is ① that they can talk in human language.
가장 눈에 띄는 인간의 특징은 / 동물에게 투영된 / 동물이 인간의 언어로 대화할 수 있다는 점이다.
Physically, / animal cartoon characters and toys ② made after animals / are also most often deformed / in such a way as to resemble humans.
신체적으로도, / 동물 만화 캐릭터와 동물을 본떠 만든 장난감은 / 또한 변형되는 경우가 아주 많다. / 인간을 닮은 그런 방식으로
This is achieved / by ③ showing them / with humanlike facial features / and deformed front legs to resemble human hands.
이것은 이뤄진다. / 그들을 보여줌으로써 / 인간과 같은 얼굴 특징을 갖고 있는 / 그리고 사람의 손을 닮게 변형된 앞다리를
In more recent animated movies / the trend has been / to show the animals in a more "natural" way.
더 최근의 만화 영화에서 / 추세는 ~였다. / 동물을 '자연스러운' 방식으로 묘사하는 것

However, / they still use their front legs / ④ <u>like</u> human hands / (for example, lions can pick up and lift small objects with one paw), / and they still talk with an appropriate facial expression.
그러나 / 이 동물들은 여전히 앞다리를 사용하고, / 사람 손처럼 (가령 사자가 한 발로 작은 물체를 집어들 수 있는 것처럼) / 그리고 그들은 여전히 적절한 표정을 지으며 이야기한다.

A general strategy / that is used to make the animal characters more emotionally appealing, / both to children and adults, / ☑ <u>is</u> to give them enlarged and deformed childlike features.
일반적인 전략은 / 동물 캐릭터를 더 감정적으로 매력적으로 만들기 위해 이용하는 / 아이와 어른 모두에게 / 그것들에 확대되고 변형된 어린이 같은 특징을 부여하는 것이다.

동물에게 투영된 가장 눈에 띄는 인간의 특징은 동물이 인간의 언어로 대화할 수 있다는 점이다. 신체적으로도, 동물 만화 캐릭터와 동물을 본떠 만든 장난감은 또한 인간을 닮도록 변형되는 경우가 아주 많다. 이것은 그들이 인간과 같은 얼굴 특징과 사람의 손을 닮게 변형된 앞다리를 갖고 있는 모습을 보여줌으로써 이뤄진다. 더 최근의 만화 영화에서 추세는 동물을 더 '자연스러운' 방식으로 묘사하는 것이었다. 그러나 이 동물들은 여전히 사람 손처럼 (가령 사자가 한 발로 작은 물체를 집어들 수 있는 것처럼) 앞다리를 사용하고, 여전히 적절한 표정을 지으며 이야기한다. 동물 캐릭터를 아이와 어른 모두에게 더 감정적으로 매력적으로 만들기 위해 이용하는 일반적인 전략은 그것들에 확대되고 변형된 어린이 같은 특징을 부여하는 것이다.

Why? 왜 정답일까?
핵심 주어가 단수 명사인 **A general strategy**이므로, 동사 또한 복수형인 **are** 대신 단수형인 **is**를 쓰는 것이 적합하다. 따라서 어법상 틀린 것은 ⑤이다.

Why? 왜 오답일까?
① 주격 보어 역할의 명사절을 이끌기 위해 접속사 **that**을 썼다.
② **animal cartoon characters and toys**가 '만들어지는' 대상이므로 과거분사 **made**를 사용해 꾸몄다.
③ 전치사 **by** 뒤에 목적어로 동명사 **showing**을 썼다.
④ 뒤에 명사구인 **human hands**가 나오는 것으로 보아 전치사 **like**(~처럼)가 적절하게 쓰였다.

- **noticeable** ⓐ 눈에 띄는, 두드러지는
- **project onto** ~에게 투영시키다
- **deform** ⓥ 변형하다
- **resemble** ⓥ ~와 닮다
- **natural** ⓐ 자연스러운
- **emotionally** ⓐd 정서적으로
- **enlarge** ⓥ 확대하다
- **characteristic** ⓝ 특징
- **cartoon character** 만화 캐릭터
- **in such a way as to** ~한 방식으로
- **humanlike** ⓐ 인간 같은
- **paw** ⓝ (동물의) 발
- **appealing** ⓐ 매력적인
- **feature** ⓝ 특징, 이목구비

구문 풀이

2행 Physically, animal cartoon characters and toys made after animals
   [주어] *[과거분사구]*
are also most often deformed in such a way as to resemble humans.
[동사구(수동태)] *[~하는 (그런) 식으로]*

★★★ 등급을 가르는 문제!
30 생산이 곧 수요 창출과 이득으로 이어지지 않는 시대   정답률 39% | 정답 ④

다음 글의 밑줄 친 부분 중, 문맥상 낱말의 쓰임이 적절하지 <u>않은</u> 것은? [3점]

The major philosophical shift in the idea of selling / came / when industrial societies became more affluent, / more competitive, / and more geographically spread out / during the 1940s and 1950s.
판매 개념에서의 주요한 철학적 변화가 / 일어났다. / 산업 사회가 더 부유해지고, / 더 경쟁적이 되고, / 지리적으로 더 확산되면서 / 1940년대와 1950년대 동안

This forced business / to develop ① <u>closer</u> relations with buyers and clients, / which in turn made business realize / that it was not enough / to produce a quality product at a reasonable price.
이로 인해 기업은 ~해야 했고, / 구매자 및 고객과 더 긴밀한 관계를 발전시켜야 / 이것은 결과적으로 기업이 깨닫게 했다. / 충분하지 않다는 것을 / 합리적인 가격에 양질의 제품을 생산하는 것으로는

In fact, / it was equally ② <u>essential</u> / to deliver products / that customers actually wanted.
사실, / 마찬가지로 매우 중요했다. / 제품을 내놓는 것이 / 고객이 실제로 원하는

Henry Ford produced his best-selling T-model Ford / in one color only (black) / in 1908, / but in modern societies / this was no longer ③ <u>possible</u>.
Henry Ford는 가장 많이 팔렸던 T-모델 Ford를 생산했지만, / 한 가지 색상(검은색)으로만 / 1908년에 / 현대 사회에서는 / 이것이 더 이상 가능하지 않았다.

The modernization of society / led to a marketing revolution / that ☑ <u>destroyed</u> the view / that production would create its own demand.
사회의 현대화는 / 마케팅 혁명으로 이어졌다. / 견해를 파괴한 / 생산이 그 자체의 수요를 창출할 것이라는

Customers, / and the desire to ⑤ <u>meet</u> their diverse and often complex needs, / became the focus of business.
고객 / 그리고 이들의 다양한 흔히 복잡한 욕구를 충족하고자 하는 욕망이 / 기업의 초점이 되었다.

산업 사회가 1940년대와 1950년대 동안 더 부유해지고, 더 경쟁적이 되고, 지리적으로 더 확산되면서 판매 개념에 주요한 철학적 변화가 일어났다. 이로 인해 기업은 구매자 및 고객과 ① 더 긴밀한 관계를 발전시켜야 했고, 이것은 결과적으로 기업이 합리적인 가격에 양질의 제품을 생산하는 것으로는 충분하지 않다는 것을 깨닫게 했다. 사실, 고객이 실제로 원하는 제품을 내놓는 것이 마찬가지로 ② 매우 중요했다. 1908년에 Henry Ford는 가장 많이 팔렸던 T-모델 Ford를 한 가지 색상(검은색)으로만 생산했지만, 현대 사회에서는 이것이 더 이상 ③ 가능하지 않았다. 사회의 현대화는 생산이 그 자체의 수요를 창출할 것이라는 견해를 ④ 강화한(→ 파괴한) 마케팅 혁명으로 이어졌다. 고객과 이들의 다양하고 흔히 복잡한 욕구를 ⑤ 충족하고자 하는 욕망이 기업의 초점이 되었다.

Why? 왜 정답일까?
현대 사회에 이르러 사람들이 전체적으로 풍족해지고 기업 간 경쟁은 치열해지면서, 합리적인 비용의 대량 생산으로 이득을 보던 시대는 지나고 고객마다 다양한 수요에 부응할 필요성이 커졌다는 내용이다. ④가 포함된 문장 앞에서, 과거에는 Ford 사처럼 한 가지 색상만으로 제품을 생산해도 괜찮았지만 현대 사회에서 이것이 '가능하지' 않다고 한다. 이 뒤에는 생산만으로 수요가 창출되리라는 기대가 '무너졌

[문제편 p.029]

다'가 설명이 이어져야 적합하므로, ④의 **strengthened**를 **destroyed**로 고쳐야 한다. 따라서 문맥상 낱말의 쓰임이 적절하지 않은 것은 ④이다.

- **philosophical** ⓐ 철학적인
- **industrial** ⓐ 산업의
- **geographically** ⓐd 지리적으로
- **in turn** 결과적으로
- **best-selling** ⓐ 가장 많이 팔리는, 베스트셀러인
- **revolution** ⓝ 혁명
- **complex** ⓐ 복잡한
- **shift** ⓝ 변화, 전환 ⓥ 바뀌다
- **affluent** ⓐ 부유한
- **spread** ⓥ 퍼지다
- **essential** ⓐ 매우 중요한
- **modernization** ⓝ 현대화
- **strengthen** ⓥ 강화하다

구문 풀이

3행 [This forced business to develop closer relations with buyers and clients],
   [ ]: 선행사
which in turn made business realize that it was not enough to produce a quality
계속적 용법 *사역동사* *원형부정사* *가주어* *진주어*
product at a reasonable price.

★★ 문제 해결 꿀~팁 ★★

▶ 많이 틀린 이유는?
T-model Ford가 한 가지 색상으로 출시된 것이 어떤 예시인지 파악해야 한다. 색상을 한 가지로만 출시해도 차가 잘 팔렸다는 것은, 과거에는 '그저 질 좋은 제품을 합리적인 가격에 제공하는 것으로 족했다'는 의미와 같다. 하지만 지금은 상황이 달라져서, 이러한 전략이 더 이상(no longer) '가능하지' 않다는 의미로 ③은 자연스럽다.
▶ 문제 해결 방법은?
Ford 차의 예시를 일반화한 표현이 바로 'production would create its own demand'이다. 즉 '생산만으로 수요가 만들어지고 제품이 팔리는' 상황을 가리키는 것이다. 오늘날에는 이런 상황이나 견해가 '강화되는' 것이 아니라 점점 '깨지고' 있다는 것이 글의 주제이다.

31 비행 방향에 따른 시차 피로 차이   정답률 55% | 정답 ①

다음 빈칸에 들어갈 말로 가장 적절한 것을 고르시오.
☑ direction – 방향
② purpose – 목적
③ season – 계절
④ length – 길이
⑤ cost – 비용

People differ / in how quickly they can reset their biological clocks / to overcome jet lag, / and the speed of recovery depends on the <u>direction</u> of travel.
사람마다 서로 다르며, / 체내 시계를 얼마나 빨리 재설정할 수 있는지에 있어서 / 시차로 인한 피로감을 극복하기 위해서 / 그 회복 속도는 이동의 방향에 달려 있다.

Generally, / it's easier / to fly westward and lengthen your day / than it is to fly eastward and shorten it.
일반적으로 / 더 쉽다. / 서쪽으로 비행해 여러분의 하루를 연장하는 것이 / 동쪽으로 비행하여 하루를 단축하는 것보다

This east-west difference in jet lag / is sizable enough / to have an impact on the performance of sports teams.
시차로 인한 피로감에 있어 이러한 동서의 차이는 / 충분히 크다. / 스포츠 팀의 경기력에 영향을 미칠 만큼

Studies have found / that teams flying westward perform significantly better / than teams flying eastward / in professional baseball and college football.
연구는 밝혔다. / 서쪽으로 비행하는 팀이 상당히 더 잘한다는 / 동쪽으로 비행하는 팀보다 / 프로 야구와 대학 미식 축구에서

A more recent study of more than 46,000 Major League Baseball games / found additional evidence / that eastward travel is tougher than westward travel.
46,000건 이상의 메이저 리그 야구 경기에 관한 더 최근의 연구에서는 / 추가적인 증거를 발견했다. / 동쪽으로 이동하는 것이 서쪽으로 이동하는 것보다 더 힘들다는

시차로 인한 피로감을 극복하기 위해서 체내 시계를 얼마나 빨리 재설정할 수 있는지는 사람마다 서로 다르며, 그 회복 속도는 이동의 방향에 달려 있다. 일반적으로 동쪽으로 비행하여 하루를 단축하는 것보다 서쪽으로 비행해 하루를 연장하는 것이 더 쉽다. 시차로 인한 피로감에서 이러한 동서의 차이는 스포츠 팀의 경기력에 영향을 미칠 만큼 충분히 크다. 연구에 따르면 서쪽으로 비행하는 팀이 동쪽으로 비행하는 팀보다 프로 야구와 대학 미식 축구에서 상당히 더 잘한다. 46,000건 이상의 메이저 리그 야구 경기에 관한 더 최근의 연구에서는 동쪽으로 이동하는 것이 서쪽으로 이동하는 것보다 더 힘들다는 추가적인 증거를 발견했다.

Why? 왜 정답일까?
빈칸 뒤에서 동쪽으로 이동해 하루를 줄이게 되는 경우보다 서쪽으로 이동해 하루를 연장하게 되는 경우 시차 회복이 더 쉽다고 한다(Generally, it's easier to fly westward and lengthen your day than it is to fly eastward and shorten it.). 즉, 이동의 '방향'이 중요하다는 글이므로, 빈칸에 들어갈 말로 가장 적절한 것은 ① '방향'이다.

- **biological clock** 체내 시계
- **jet lag** 시차로 인한 피로감
- **lengthen** ⓥ 연장하다
- **sizable** ⓐ 꽤 큰, 상당한
- **performance** ⓝ (선수의) 경기력, 수행, 성과
- **additional** ⓐ 추가적인
- **overcome** ⓥ 극복하다
- **depend on** ~에 좌우되다
- **shorten** ⓥ 단축하다
- **have an impact on** ~에 영향을 주다
- **significantly** ⓐd 상당히, 현저히

구문 풀이

4행 This east-west difference in jet lag is sizable enough to have an impact
on the performance of sports teams.
「형/부+enough+to부정사: ~할 만큼 충분히 …한」

32 일 처리에 걸리는 시간 제대로 파악하기   정답률 54% | 정답 ③

다음 빈칸에 들어갈 말로 가장 적절한 것을 고르시오.
① what benefits you can get – 여러분이 어떤 이득을 얻을 수 있는지
② how practical your tasks are – 여러분의 과업이 얼마나 현실성 있는지
☑ how long things are going to take – 일에 시간이 얼마나 오래 걸릴지
④ why failures are meaningful in life – 실패가 왜 인생에서 의미가 있는지
⑤ why your leisure time should come first – 왜 여러분의 여가 시간이 가장 우선이어야 하는지

If you want the confidence / that comes from achieving / what you set out to do each day, / then it's important / to understand how long things are going to take.
만약 여러분이 자신감을 원한다면 / 성취해 얻어지는 / 매일 여러분이 하고자 착수하는 일을 / 그러면 중요하다. / 일에 시간이 얼마나 오래 걸릴지 아는 것이

Over-optimism about what can be achieved / within a certain time frame / is a problem.
성취될 수 있는 것에 대한 지나친 낙관주의는 / 어떤 특정 기간 내에 / 문제다.

So work on it. // Make a practice of estimating the amount of time needed / alongside items on your 'things to do' list, / and learn by experience / when tasks take a greater or lesser time than expected.
그러므로 그것을 개선하려고 노력하라. / 필요한 시간의 양을 추산하는 것을 습관화하고, / '해야 할 일' 목록에 있는 항목과 함께, / 경험을 통해 배우라. / 언제 과제가 예상보다 더 많은 시간 또는 더 적은 시간을 필요로 하는지

Give attention / also to fitting the task to the available time.
주의를 기울이라. / 그 이용 가능한 시간에 과제를 맞추는 것에도 또한

There are some tasks / that you can only set about / if you have a significant amount of time available.
몇몇 과제가 있다. / 여러분이 비로소 시작할 수 있는 / 여러분이 이용할 시간이 상당히 많아야만

There is no point / in trying to gear up for such a task / when you only have a short period available.
무의미하다. / 그런 과제를 위해 준비하려 애쓰는 것은 / 여러분에게 이용 가능한 시간이 얼마 없을 때

So schedule the time / you need for the longer tasks / and put the short tasks into the spare moments in between.
그러므로 시간을 계획하라, / 여러분이 시간이 더 오래 걸리는 과제에 필요로 하는 / 그리고 그 사이 남는 시간에 시간이 짧게 걸리는 과제를 배치하라.

___

만약 매일 하고자 착수하는 일을 성취해 얻어지는 자신감을 원한다면 일에 시간이 얼마나 오래 걸릴지 아는 것이 중요하다. 어떤 특정 기간 내에 성취될 수 있는 것에 대한 지나친 낙관주의는 문제다. 그러므로 그것을 개선하려고 노력하라. '해야 할 일' 목록에 있는 항목과 함께, 필요한 시간의 양을 추산하는 것을 습관화하고, 언제 과제에 예상보다 더 많고 또 더 적은 시간이 걸리는지 경험을 통해 배우라. 그 이용 가능한 시간에 과제를 맞추는 것에도 또한 주의를 기울이라. 이용할 시간이 상당히 많아야만 시작할 수 있는 몇몇 과제가 있다. 여러분에게 이용 가능한 시간이 얼마 없을 때 그런 과제를 위해 준비하려 애쓰는 것은 무의미하다. 그러므로 시간이 더 오래 걸리는 과제에 필요한 시간을 계획하고, 그 사이 남는 시간에 시간이 짧게 걸리는 과제를 배치하라.

Why? 왜 정답일까?

과업을 끝내는 데 걸리는 시간을 정확히 추산하고 계획할 줄 알아야 한다(Make a practice of estimating the amount of time needed ~)는 내용의 글이므로, 빈칸에 들어갈 말로 가장 적절한 것은 ③ '일에 시간이 얼마나 오래 걸릴지'이다.

- confidence ⓝ 자신감
- time frame (어떤 일에 쓸 수 있는) 시간(대)
- make a practice of ~을 습관으로 하다
- learn by experience 경험을 통해 배우다
- set about ~을 시작하다
- gear up 준비를 갖추다, 대비하다
- set out 착수하다
- work on ~에 공을 들이다
- estimate ⓥ 추산하다
- fit ⓥ ~에 맞추다
- there is no point in ~하는 것은 의미가 없다
- practical ⓐ 현실성 있는, 타당한

구문 풀이

10행 There is no point in trying to gear up for such a task when you only have a short period available.
「there is no point in + 동명사」: ~해봐야 의미가 없다

___

★★★ 등급을 가르는 문제!

33 진화가 거듭되어도 상황이 변하지 않는 까닭 정답률 47% | 정답 ①

다음 빈칸에 들어갈 말로 가장 적절한 것을 고르시오. [3점]

✓ just stay in place – 제자리에 머무를 뿐이다
② end up walking slowly – 결국 느리게 걷게 된다
③ never run into each other – 결코 서로 마주치지 않는다
④ won't be able to adapt to changes – 변화에 적응할 수 없을 것이다
⑤ cannot run faster than their parents – 자기 부모보다 더 빨리 달릴 수 없다

In Lewis Carroll's *Through the Looking-Glass*, / the Red Queen takes Alice / on a race through the countryside.
Lewis Carroll의 *Through the Looking-Glass*에서 / 붉은 여왕은 Alice를 데리고 간다. / 시골을 통과하는 한 경주에

They run and they run, / but then Alice discovers / that they're still under the same tree / that they started from.
그들은 달리고 또 달리는데, / 그러다 Alice는 발견한다. / 그들이 나무 아래에 여전히 있음을 / 자신들이 출발했던

The Red Queen explains to Alice: / "*here*, you see, / it takes all the running you can do, / to keep in the same place."
붉은 여왕은 Alice에게 설명한다. / "*여기서는* 네가 보다시피 / 네가 할 수 있는 모든 뜀박질을 해야 한단다. / 같은 장소에 머물러 있으려면"이라고

Biologists sometimes use this Red Queen Effect / to explain an evolutionary principle.
생물학자들은 때때로 이 '붉은 여왕 효과'를 사용한다 / 진화의 원리를 설명하기 위해.

If foxes evolve to run faster / so they can catch more rabbits, / then only the fastest rabbits will live long enough / to make a new generation of bunnies / that run even faster / — in which case, of course, / only the fastest foxes will catch enough rabbits / to thrive and pass on their genes.
만약 여우가 더 빨리 달리게 진화한다면 / 그들이 더 많은 토끼를 잡기 위해 / 그러면 가장 빠른 토끼만이 충분히 오래 살아 / 새로운 세대의 토끼를 낳을 텐데, / 훨씬 더 빨리 달리는 / 이 경우 당연히도 / 가장 빠른 여우만이 충분한 토끼를 잡을 것이다 / 번성하여 자신들의 유전자를 물려줄 만큼.

Even though they might run, / the two species just stay in place.
그들이 달린다 해도 / 그 두 종은 제자리에 머무를 뿐이다.

___

Lewis Carroll의 *Through the Looking-Glass*에서, 붉은 여왕은 Alice를 데리고 시골을 통과하는 한 경주에 간다. 그들은 달리고 또 달리는데, 그러다 Alice는 자신들이 출발했던 나무 아래에 여전히 있음을 발견한다. 붉은 여왕은 Alice에게 "*여기서는* 보다시피 같은 장소에 머물러 있으려면 네가 할 수 있는 모든 뜀박질을 해야 한단다."라고 설명한다. 생물학자들은 때때로 이 '붉은 여왕 효과'를 사용해 진화의 원리를 설명한다. 만약 여우가 더 많은 토끼를 잡기 위해 더 빨리 달리게 진화한다면, 가장 빠른 토끼만이 충분히 오래 살아 훨씬 더 빨리 달리는

새로운 세대의 토끼를 낳을 텐데, 이 경우 당연히도 가장 빠른 여우만이 충분한 토끼를 잡아 번성하여 자신들의 유전자를 물려줄 것이다. 그 두 종은 달린다 해도 제자리에 머무를 뿐이다.

Why? 왜 정답일까?

원래 있던 자리를 유지하기 위해 전력 질주해야 하는(~ it takes all the running you can do, to keep in the same place.) 소설 속 상황에 빗대어 진화의 원리를 설명하는 글이다. 마지막 문장 앞에 제시된 여우와 토끼의 예시에 따르면, 여우가 토끼를 더 많이 잡기 위해 달리기가 빨라지도록 진화하면, 그 여우보다도 빠른 토끼만이 살아남아 번식하게 되므로 토끼 또한 더 빨라지도록 진화하게 된다. 이것은 다시 여우의 달리기가 더 빨라지게 하는 원인으로 작용하므로, 결과적으로 두 종의 상황은 시간이 지나도 차이가 없다. 따라서 빈칸에 들어갈 말로 가장 적절한 것은 ① '제자리에 머무를 뿐이다'이다.

- discover ⓥ 발견하다
- evolutionary ⓐ 진화적인
- generation ⓝ 세대
- pass on 물려주다
- species ⓝ (생물) 종
- adapt to ~에 적응하다
- biologist ⓝ 생물학자
- principle ⓝ 원리
- thrive ⓥ 번성하다
- gene ⓝ 유전자
- run into ~을 우연히 만나다

구문 풀이

2행 They run and they run, but then Alice discovers that they're still under the same tree that they started from.
접속사 / 선행사(the same + 명) | → 목적격 관계대명사

★★ 문제 해결 꿀~팁 ★★

▶ 많이 틀린 이유는?
여우가 토끼를 더 많이 잡기 위해 더 빨리 뛰도록 진화해도, 토끼 또한 똑같이 진화하기 때문에 결국 둘 다 '제자리에 있는' 셈이라는 것이 글의 결론이다. ③은 두 동물이 '서로 절대 우연히 만나지 않는다'는 의미로, run이 있어 혼동될 수 있지만 의미상 연관이 없다.

▶ 문제 해결 방법은?
글에 인용구가 나오면 주제와 연관되는 경우가 많다. 여기서도 인용구 안의 **to keep in the same place**가 주제를 가리키는 핵심 표현이다.

___

34 머릿속 아이디어일 때 이미 완성된 미래 정답률 53% | 정답 ②

다음 빈칸에 들어갈 말로 가장 적절한 것을 고르시오. [3점]

① didn't even have the potential to accomplish – 성취할 잠재력조차 지니고 있지 않았던
✓ have mentally concluded about the future – 미래에 대해 머릿속에서 완성한
③ haven't been able to picture in our mind – (전에는) 머릿속에 그릴 수 없었던
④ considered careless and irresponsible – 조심성 없고 무책임하다고 여겼던
⑤ have observed in some professionals – 몇몇 전문가에게서 관찰해 낸

Everything in the world around us / was finished in the mind of its creator / before it was started.
우리 주변 세상의 모든 것은 / 그것을 만들어 낸 사람의 마음속에서 완성되었다. / 그것이 시작되기 전에

The houses we live in, / the cars we drive, / and our clothing — / all of these began with an idea.
우리가 사는 집, / 우리가 운전하는 자동차, / 우리 옷, / 이 모든 것이 아이디어에서 시작했다.

Each idea was then studied, refined and perfected / before the first nail was driven / or the first piece of cloth was cut.
각각의 아이디어는 그런 다음 연구되고, 다듬어지고, 완성되었다. / 첫 번째 못이 박히거나 / 첫 번째 천 조각이 재단되기에 앞서

Long before the idea was turned into a physical reality, / the mind had clearly pictured the finished product.
그 아이디어가 물리적 실체로 바뀌기 훨씬 전에 / 마음은 완제품을 분명하게 그렸다.

The human being designs his or her own future / through much the same process.
인간은 자신의 미래를 설계한다. / 거의 똑같은 과정을 통해

We begin with an idea / about how the future will be.
우리는 아이디어로 시작한다. / 미래가 어떨지에 대한

Over a period of time / we refine and perfect the vision.
일정 기간에 걸쳐 / 우리는 그 비전을 다듬어 완성한다.

Before long, / our every thought, decision and activity / are all working in harmony / to bring into existence / what we have mentally concluded about the future.
머지않아, / 우리의 모든 생각, 결정, 활동은 / 모두 조화롭게 작용하게 된다. / 생겨나게 하려고 / 우리가 미래에 대해 머릿속에서 완성한 것을

___

우리 주변 세상의 모든 것은 시작되기 전에 그것을 만들어 낸 사람의 마음속에서 완성되었다. 우리가 사는 집, 우리가 운전하는 자동차, 우리 옷, 이 모든 것이 아이디어에서 시작했다. 각각의 아이디어는 그런 다음 첫 번째 못이 박히거나 첫 번째 천 조각이 재단되기에 앞서 연구되고, 다듬어지고, 완성되었다. 그 아이디어가 물리적 실체로 바뀌기 훨씬 전에 마음은 완제품을 분명하게 그렸다. 인간은 거의 똑같은 과정을 통해 자신의 미래를 설계한다. 우리는 미래가 어떨지에 대한 아이디어로 시작한다. 일정 기간에 걸쳐서 우리는 그 비전을 다듬어 완성한다. 머지않아, 우리의 모든 생각, 결정, 활동은 우리가 미래에 대해 머릿속에서 완성한 것을 생겨나게 하려고 모두 조화롭게 작용하게 된다.

Why? 왜 정답일까?

첫 문장에서 세상 모든 것은 실체가 있기 이전에 머릿속에서 이미 완성된 아이디어(finished in the mind of its creator)였다고 설명하는데, 글 중반부에서 우리 미래 역시 같은 식으로 설계된다고 말한다. 즉, 처음에 '이미 머릿속에서 만들어진' 아이디어가 다듬어지고 구현되는 과정이 똑같이 진행된다는 의미로, 빈칸에 들어갈 말로 가장 적절한 것은 ② '미래에 대해 머릿속에서 완성한'이다.

- clothing ⓝ 옷, 의복
- perfect ⓥ 완성하다, 완벽하게 하다
- turn A into B A를 B로 바꾸다
- process ⓝ 과정
- before long 머지않아
- bring into existence ~을 생겨나게 하다
- careless ⓐ 조심성 없는
- professional ⓝ 전문가 ⓐ 전문적인
- refine ⓥ 다듬다
- nail ⓝ 못
- picture ⓥ 상상하다, 그리다
- over a period of time 일정 기간에 걸쳐서
- in harmony 조화롭게
- mentally ⓐⓓ 머릿속에, 마음속으로
- irresponsible ⓐ 무책임한

구문 풀이

1행 Everything in the world around us was finished in the mind of its creator
주어(every-) 　　　　　　　　　　　　동사(단수)
before it was started.

---

35 서술자에 따라 다르게 이해되는 이야기　　　정답률 61% | 정답 ④

다음 글에서 전체 흐름과 관계 없는 문장은?

Whose story it is / affects *what* the story is.
누구의 이야기인지가 / 무슨 이야기인지에 영향을 미친다.

Change the main character, / and the focus of the story must also change.
주인공을 바꿔보라, / 그러면 이야기의 초점도 틀림없이 바뀐다.

If we look at the events through another character's eyes, / we will interpret them differently.
만약 우리가 다른 등장인물의 눈을 통해 사건을 본다면, / 우리는 그것을 다르게 해석할 것이다.

① We'll place our sympathies with someone new.
우리는 새로운 누군가에게 공감할 것이다.

② When the conflict arises / that is the heart of the story, / we will be praying for a different outcome.
갈등이 발생할 때, / 이야기의 핵심인, / 우리는 다른 결과를 간절히 바랄 것이다.

③ Consider, for example, / how the tale of Cinderella would shift / if told from the viewpoint of an evil stepsister.
예컨대, 생각해 보라, / 신데렐라 이야기가 어떻게 바뀔지 / 사악한 의붓자매의 관점에서 이야기된다면

✓ We know / Cinderella's kingdom does not exist, / but we willingly go there anyway.
우리는 알지만, / 신데렐라의 왕국이 존재하지 않는다는 것을 / 어쨌든 우리는 기꺼이 그곳에 간다.

⑤ *Gone with the Wind* is Scarlett O'Hara's story, / but what if we were shown the same events / from the viewpoint of Rhett Butler or Melanie Wilkes?
*Gone with the Wind*는 Scarlett O'Hara의 이야기이지만, / 만약 같은 사건이 우리에게 제시된다면 어떠할 것인가? / Rhett Butler나 Melanie Wilkes의 관점에서

누구의 이야기인지가 무슨 이야기인지에 영향을 미친다. 주인공을 바꾸면, 이야기의 초점도 틀림없이 바뀐다. 만약 우리가 다른 등장인물의 눈을 통해 사건을 본다면, 우리는 그것을 다르게 해석할 것이다. ① 우리는 새로운 누군가에게 공감할 것이다. ② 이야기의 핵심인 갈등이 발생할 때, 우리는 다른 결과를 간절히 바랄 것이다. ③ 예컨대, 신데렐라 이야기가 사악한 의붓자매의 관점에서 이야기된다면 어떻게 바뀔지 생각해 보라. ④ 우리는 신데렐라의 왕국이 존재하지 않는다는 것을 알지만, 어쨌든 기꺼이 그곳에 간다. ⑤ *Gone with the Wind*는 Scarlett O'Hara의 이야기이지만, 만약 같은 사건이 Rhett Butler나 Melanie Wilkes의 관점에서 우리에게 제시된다면 어떠할 것인가?

Why? 왜 정답일까?

이야기의 주인공이 누구인가에 따라 이야기 내용이 다르게 받아들여진다는 내용인데, ④는 Cinderella의 왕국에 관해서만 지엽적으로 언급하고 있다. 따라서 전체 흐름과 관계 없는 문장은 ④이다.

- **affect** ⓥ 영향을 미치다
- **sympathy** ⓝ 공감
- **arise** ⓥ 발생하다
- **outcome** ⓝ 결과
- **shift** ⓥ 바꾸다
- **evil** ⓐ 사악한 ⓝ 악
- **kingdom** ⓝ 왕국
- **interpret** ⓥ 해석하다, 이해하다
- **conflict** ⓝ 갈등
- **pray for** ~을 위해 기도하다
- **tale** ⓝ 이야기
- **viewpoint** ⓝ 관점
- **stepsister** ⓝ 의붓자매
- **willingly** ⓐ 기꺼이

구문 풀이

6행 Consider, for example, [how the tale of Cinderella would shift if told from
명령문(~하라)　　　　　[ ]: 목적어　　　　　접속사 + 과거분사(~한다면)
the viewpoint of an evil stepsister].

★★★ 등급을 가르는 문제!
36 농경 생활로 인한 인간 사회의 변화　　　정답률 36% | 정답 ④

주어진 글 다음에 이어질 글의 순서로 가장 적절한 것을 고르시오.

① (A) - (C) - (B)　　　② (B) - (A) - (C)
③ (B) - (C) - (A)　　　✓ (C) - (A) - (B)
⑤ (C) - (B) - (A)

In the Old Stone Age, / small bands of 20 to 60 people / wandered from place to place / in search of food.
구석기 시대에는 / 20 ~ 60명의 작은 무리가 / 여기저기 돌아다녔다 / 먹을 것을 찾아

Once people began farming, / they could settle down near their farms.
일단 사람들이 농사를 짓기 시작하면서, / 그들은 자신의 농경지 근처에 정착할 수 있었다.

(C) As a result, / towns and villages grew larger.
그 결과, / 도시와 마을이 더 커졌다

Living in communities / allowed people / to organize themselves more efficiently.
공동체 생활은 / 사람들이 ~하게 했다 / 더 효율적으로 조직되게

They could divide up the work / of producing food and other things they needed.
그들은 일을 나눌 수 있었다 / 식량과 자신들에게 필요한 다른 것들을 생산하는

(A) While some workers grew crops, / others built new houses and made tools.
어떤 노동자들은 농작물을 재배하는 한편, / 다른 노동자들은 새로운 집을 짓고 도구를 만들었다.

Village dwellers also learned to work together / to do a task faster.
마을 거주자들은 또한 함께 일하는 법을 익혔다. / 일을 더 빨리 하려고

(B) For example, / toolmakers could share the work / of making stone axes and knives.
예를 들어, / 도구 제작자들은 작업을 함께 할 수 있었다 / 돌도끼와 돌칼을 만드는

By working together, / they could make more tools / in the same amount of time.
함께 일하여 / 그들은 더 많은 도구를 만들 수 있었다. / 같은 시간 안에

구석기 시대에는 20 ~ 60명의 작은 무리가 먹을 것을 찾아 여기저기 돌아다녔다. 일단 농사를 짓기 시작하면서, 사람들은 자신의 농경지 근처에 정착할 수 있었다.

(C) 그 결과, 도시와 마을이 더 커졌다. 공동체 생활을 통해 사람들은 더 효율적으로 조직될 수 있었다. 그들은 식량과 자신들에게 필요한 다른 것들을 생산하는 일을 나눌 수 있었다.

(A) 어떤 노동자들은 농작물을 재배하는 한편, 다른 노동자들은 새로운 집을 짓고 도구를 만들었다. 마을 거주자들은 또한 일을 더 빨리 하려고 함께 일하는 법도 익혔다.

(B) 예를 들어, 도구 제작자들은 돌도끼와 돌칼을 만드는 작업을 함께 할 수 있었다. 그들은 함께 일하여 같은 시간 안에 더 많은 도구를 만들 수 있었다.

Why? 왜 정답일까?

농경이 시작되면서 사람들이 정착할 수 있었다는 내용의 주어진 글 뒤로, '그 결과' 도시와 마을이 생기고 사람들이 일을 분배할 수 있게 되었다고 설명하는 (C)가 먼저 연결된다. 이어서 (A)는 (C)에서 언급된 '분업'이 어떻게 이루어졌는지 언급하며, 사람들이 함께 일하는 법 또한 배우게 되었다고 이야기한다. (B)에서는 '함께 작업'하는 상황의 예를 제시하며 (A)를 보충 설명한다. 따라서 글의 순서로 가장 적절한 것은 ④ '(C) - (A) - (B)'이다.

- **Old Stone Age** 구석기 시대
- **wander** ⓥ 돌아다니다, 배회하다
- **settle down** 정착하다
- **dweller** ⓝ 거주자
- **community** ⓝ 공동체, 지역사회
- **efficiently** ⓐ 효율적으로
- **band** ⓝ (소규모) 무리
- **in search of** ~을 찾아서
- **crop** ⓝ 작물
- **axe** ⓝ 도끼
- **organize** ⓥ 조직하다, 정리하다
- **divide up** ~을 나누다

구문 풀이

2행 Once people began farming, they could settle down near their farms.
접속사(일단 ~한다면)

★★ 문제 해결 꿀~팁 ★★

▶ 많이 틀린 이유는?

글을 자세히 읽지 않고 연결어 중심으로만 보면, (B)가 주어진 글의 예시(For example)이고 (C)가 전체 글의 결론(As a result)일 것이라고 잘못 추론할 수 있다. 하지만, 내용적 단서가 중요하다. 주어진 글은 사람들이 농경을 시작하며 정착했다는 내용인데, (B)는 갑자기 '도구 제작자'를 언급하며, 이들이 업무를 분업해 담당하였다는 설명을 제시하고 있다. 서로 전혀 다른 키워드로 보아 (B)가 주어진 글에 대한 예시라고 보기 어렵기 때문에 ②를 답으로 고르는 것은 적절하지 않다.

▶ 문제 해결 방법은?

사람들이 농경지 근처에 정착하여 살게 되면서, 마을이 성장하고 분업화가 일어나(C), 누구는 농사를 짓고 누구는 도구를 만드는 한편 공동 작업도 활성화되었으며(A), 공동 작업으로 더 쉽고 빠른 작업이 가능해졌다(B)는 흐름이다.

★★★ 등급을 가르는 문제!
37 광물의 형성　　　정답률 42% | 정답 ②

주어진 글 다음에 이어질 글의 순서로 가장 적절한 것을 고르시오. [3점]

① (A) - (C) - (B)　　　✓ (B) - (A) - (C)
③ (B) - (C) - (A)　　　④ (C) - (A) - (B)
⑤ (C) - (B) - (A)

Natural processes form minerals in many ways.
자연 과정은 많은 방법으로 광물을 형성한다.

For example, / hot melted rock material, / called magma, / cools / when it reaches the Earth's surface, / or even if it's trapped below the surface.
예를 들어, / 뜨거운 용암 물질은 / 마그마라고 불리는 / 식는다. / 그것이 지구의 표면에 도달할 때, / 또는 그것이 심지어 표면 아래에 갇혔을 때도

As magma cools, / its atoms lose heat energy, / move closer together, / and begin to combine into compounds.
마그마가 식으면서 / 마그마의 원자는 열에너지를 잃고, / 서로 더 가까이 이동해 / 화합물로 결합하기 시작한다.

(B) During this process, / atoms of the different compounds / arrange themselves into orderly, repeating patterns.
이 과정 동안, / 서로 다른 화합물의 원자가 / 질서 있고 반복적인 패턴으로 배열된다.

The type and amount of elements / present in a magma / partly determine / which minerals will form.
원소의 종류와 양이 / 마그마에 존재하는 / 부분적으로 결정한다. / 어떤 광물이 형성될지를

(A) Also, / the size of the crystals that form / depends partly / on how rapidly the magma cools.
또한, / 형성되는 결정의 크기는 / 부분적으로는 달려 있다. / 마그마가 얼마나 빨리 식냐에

When magma cools slowly, / the crystals that form / are generally large enough / to see with the unaided eye.
마그마가 천천히 식으면, / 형성되는 결정은 / 대개 충분히 크다. / 육안으로 볼 수 있을 만큼

(C) This is because the atoms have enough time / to move together and form into larger crystals.
이것은 원자가 충분한 시간을 가지기 때문이다. / 함께 이동해 더 큰 결정을 형성할

When magma cools rapidly, / the crystals that form / will be small.
마그마가 빠르게 식으면, / 형성되는 결정은 / 작을 것이다.

In such cases, / you can't easily see individual mineral crystals.
이런 경우에는 / 여러분은 개별 광물 결정을 쉽게 볼 수 없다.

자연 과정은 많은 방법으로 광물을 형성한다. 예를 들어, 마그마라고 불리는 뜨거운 용암 물질은 지구의 표면에 도달할 때, 또는 심지어 표면 아래에 갇혔을 때도 식는다. 마그마가 식으면서 마그마의 원자는 열에너지를 잃고, 서로 더 가까이 이동해 화합물로 결합하기 시작한다.

(B) 이 과정 동안, 서로 다른 화합물의 원자가 질서 있고 반복적인 패턴으로 배열된다. 마그마에 존재하는 원소의 종류와 양이 어떤 광물이 형성될지를 부분적으로 결정한다.

(A) 또한, 형성되는 결정의 크기는 부분적으로는 마그마가 얼마나 빨리 식냐에 달려 있다. 마그마가 천천히 식으면, 형성되는 결정은 대개 육안으로 볼 수 있을 만큼 충분히 크다.

(C) 이것은 원자가 함께 이동해 더 큰 결정을 형성할 충분한 시간을 가지기 때문이다. 마그마가 빠르게 식으면, 형성되는 결정은 작을 것이다. 이런 경우에는 개별 광물 결정을 쉽게 볼 수 없다.

Why? 왜 정답일까?

마그마가 식을 때 광물이 형성될 수 있다는 내용의 주어진 글 뒤로, '이 식어가는 과정' 동안 마그마 속 원

소의 종류나 양에 따라 어떤 종류의 광물이 형성될지 결정된다고 설명하는 **(B)**가 먼저 연결된다. 이어서 **Also**로 시작하는 **(A)**는 추가로 마그마가 식는 속도에 따라 광물의 크기가 결정된다고 언급한다. 마지막으로 **(C)**는 **(A)** 후반부에서 언급되었듯이 마그마가 천천히 식을 때 광물의 크기가 커지는 이유에 관해 보충 설명한다. 따라서 글의 순서로 가장 적절한 것은 ② '**(B) – (A) – (C)**'이다.

- **form** ⓥ 형성하다
- **melt** ⓥ 녹이다, 녹다
- **trap** ⓥ 가두다
- **combine with** ~로 결합되다
- **partly** ⓐⓓ 부분적으로
- **with the unaided eye** 육안으로
- **orderly** ⓐ 질서 있는
- **in such cases** 이런 경우에
- **mineral** ⓝ 광물
- **surface** ⓝ 표면
- **atom** ⓝ 원자
- **compound** ⓝ 화합물
- **rapidly** ⓐⓓ 빠르게
- **arrange** ⓥ 배열하다
- **element** ⓝ 원소, 구성요소

구문 풀이

6행 Also, the size of the crystals that form depends partly on how rapidly the magma cools.
「how + 형/부 + 주어 + 동사 : 얼마나 ~한지」

★★ 문제 해결 꿀~팁 ★★

▶ 많이 틀린 이유는?
(B)는 마그마가 식는 속도에 따라 그로 인해 만들어지는 결정의 종류가 달라질 수 있다는 내용으로 끝나는데, **(C)**를 보면 갑자기 결정의 '크기'가 커지는 이유를 언급한다. **(C)**에 앞서 '크기'를 처음 언급하는 단락은 **Also**로 시작하는 **(A)**이다. **(A)**에서 먼저 size를 언급해야 크기가 커지는 '이유'를 설명하는 **(C)**가 자연스럽게 연결된다.
▶ 문제 해결 방법은?
(A)와 **(C)**가 둘 다 '크기'를 언급하고 있지만, **(B)**에는 '크기'에 관한 언급이 없다. 따라서 **Also**가 있는 **(A)**를 먼저 연결해 '크기'에 관한 내용을 추가한다는 뜻을 밝히고, 뒤이어 **(C)**를 연결해야 논리적 흐름이 자연스러워진다.

---

38 탄수화물의 종류　　　　정답률 57% | 정답 ④

글의 흐름으로 보아, 주어진 문장이 들어가기에 가장 적절한 곳을 고르시오.

All carbohydrates are basically sugars.
모든 탄수화물은 기본적으로 당이다.
① Complex carbohydrates are the good carbohydrates for your body.
복합 탄수화물은 몸에 좋은 탄수화물이다.
② These complex sugar compounds / are very difficult to break down / and can trap other nutrients / like vitamins and minerals / in their chains.
이러한 복당류 화합물은 / 분해하기 매우 어렵고 / 다른 영양소를 가두어 둘 수 있다 / 비타민과 미네랄 같은 / 그것의 사슬 안에
③ As they slowly break down, / the other nutrients are also released into your body, / and can provide you with fuel for a number of hours.
그것들이 천천히 분해되면서, / 다른 영양소도 여러분의 몸으로 방출되고, / 많은 시간 동안 여러분에게 연료를 공급할 수 있다.
✔ Bad carbohydrates, / on the other hand, / are simple sugars.
나쁜 탄수화물은 / 반면에 / 단당류이다.
Because their structure is not complex, / they are easy to break down / and hold few nutrients for your body / other than the sugars from which they are made.
그것의 구조는 복잡하지 않기 때문에 / 그것은 분해되기 쉬우며, / 몸을 위한 영양소를 거의 가지고 있지 않다 / 그것을 구성하는 당 말고는
⑤ Your body breaks down these carbohydrates rather quickly / and what it cannot use / is converted to fat and stored in the body.
여러분의 몸은 이러한 탄수화물을 상당히 빨리 분해하며, / 몸이 사용하지 못하는 것은 / 지방으로 바뀌어 몸에 저장된다.

모든 탄수화물은 기본적으로 당이다. ① 복합 탄수화물은 몸에 좋은 탄수화물이다. ② 이러한 복당류 화합물은 분해하기 매우 어렵고, 비타민과 미네랄 같은 다른 영양소를 그것의 사슬 안에 가두어 둘 수 있다. ③ 그것들이 천천히 분해되면서, 다른 영양소도 여러분의 몸으로 방출되고, 많은 시간 동안 여러분에게 연료를 공급할 수 있다. ④ 반면에 나쁜 탄수화물은 단당류이다. 그것의 구조는 복잡하지 않기 때문에 분해되기 쉬우며, 그것을 구성하는 당 말고는 몸을 위한 영양소를 거의 가지고 있지 않다. ⑤ 여러분의 몸은 이러한 탄수화물을 상당히 빨리 분해하며, 몸이 사용하지 못하는 것은 지방으로 바뀌어 몸에 저장된다.

Why? 왜 정답일까?

복합 탄수화물과 단당류의 차이점을 설명하는 글이다. ④ 앞은 복합당의 경우 구조가 복잡하기 때문에 분해 시간이 느리고 오랜 시간 몸에 연료를 공급한다는 내용이다. 한편 주어진 문장은 '나쁜 탄수화물'인 단당류를 언급하고, ④ 뒤에서는 이 단당류를 they로 받아 이것이 분해되기 쉽고 당 외에는 다른 영양소를 가지고 있지도 않아서 몸에서 다 쓰지 못하면 지방이 되어 쌓인다는 설명을 이어 간다. 따라서 주어진 문장이 들어가기에 가장 적절한 곳은 ④이다.

- **carbohydrate** ⓝ 탄수화물
- **break down** 분해하다
- **release** ⓥ 방출하다
- **a number of** 많은
- **be made from** ~로 구성되다
- **basically** ⓐⓓ 기본적으로
- **nutrient** ⓝ 영양소
- **provide A with B** A에게 B를 공급하다
- **structure** ⓝ 구조
- **convert** ⓥ 바꾸다

구문 풀이

4행 These complex sugar compounds are very difficult to break down and can trap other nutrients like vitamins and minerals in their chains.
보어(형용사구)　　부사 용법(~하기에)

---

39 초기 정보와 기대의 영향　　　　정답률 48% | 정답 ⑤

글의 흐름으로 보아, 주어진 문장이 들어가기에 가장 적절한 곳을 고르시오. [3점]

People commonly make the mistaken assumption / that because a person has one type of characteristic, / then they automatically have other characteristics / which go with it.
흔히 사람들은 잘못된 가정을 한다. / 어떤 사람이 어떤 특성 하나를 가지고 있으므로 / 그러면 그들은 자동으로 다른 특성을 지니고 있다는 / 그것과 어울리는

---

① In one study, / university students were given descriptions of a guest lecturer / before he spoke to the group.
한 연구에서, / 대학생들은 어떤 초청 강사에 대한 설명을 들었다. / 그가 그들 집단 앞에서 강연하기 전
② Half the students received a description / containing the word 'warm', / the other half were told / the speaker was 'cold'.
학생들 절반은 설명을 들었고, / '따뜻하다'라는 단어가 포함된 / 나머지 절반은 들었다. / 그 강사가 '차갑다'는 말을
③ The guest lecturer then led a discussion, / after which the students were asked / to give their impressions of him.
그러고 나서 그 초청 강사가 토론을 이끌었고, / 이후 학생들은 요청받았다. / 강사에 대한 인상을 말해 달라고
④ As expected, / there were large differences / between the impressions formed by the students, / depending upon their original information of the lecturer.
예상한 대로, / 큰 차이가 있었다. / 학생들에 의해 형성된 인상 간에는 / 그 강사에 대한 학생들의 최초 정보에 따라
✔ It was also found / that those students / who expected the lecturer to be warm / tended to interact with him more.
또한 밝혀졌다. / 그런 학생들은 / 그 강사가 따뜻할 거라고 기대했던 / 그와 더 많이 소통하는 경향이 있었다는 것이
This shows / that different expectations / not only affect the impressions we form / but also our behaviour and the relationship which is formed.
이것은 보여준다. / 서로 다른 기대가 / 우리가 형성하는 인상뿐 아니라 (~에도) 영향을 미친다는 것을 / 우리의 행동 및 형성되는 관계에도

흔히 사람들은 어떤 사람이 어떤 특성 하나를 가지고 있으면 자동으로 그것과 어울리는 다른 특성을 지니고 있다는 잘못된 가정을 한다. ① 한 연구에서, 대학생들은 어떤 초청 강사가 그들 집단 앞에서 강연하기 전 그 강사에 대한 설명을 들었다. ② 학생들 절반은 '따뜻하다'라는 단어가 포함된 설명을 들었고, 나머지 절반은 그 강사가 '차갑다'는 말을 들었다. ③ 그러고 나서 그 초청 강사가 토론을 이끌었고, 이후 학생들은 강사에 대한 인상을 말해 달라고 요청받았다. ④ 예상한 대로, 학생들에 의해 형성된 인상 간에는 그 강사에 대한 학생들의 최초 정보에 따라 큰 차이가 있었다. ⑤ 또한, 그 강사가 따뜻할 거라고 기대했던 학생들은 그와 더 많이 소통하는 경향이 있었다는 것이 밝혀졌다. 이것은 서로 다른 기대가 우리가 형성하는 인상뿐 아니라 우리의 행동 및 형성되는 관계에도 영향을 미친다는 것을 보여준다.

Why? 왜 정답일까?

대학생들 집단을 대상으로 초기 정보의 영향력을 연구한 실험을 소개하는 글이다. ① 이후로 ⑤ 앞까지 대학생들 두 집단이 똑같은 강사에 관해 상반된 정보를 들었고, 이에 따라 동일한 사람에 대해 서로 다른 인상을 갖게 되었다는 실험 내용이 소개된다. 이어서 주어진 문장은 추가적인 결과(was also found)로 각 집단에 따라 강사와 소통하는 정도에도 영향이 있었다는 내용을 제시한다. 마지막으로 ⑤ 뒤에서는 서로 다른 초기 정보와 기대로 인해 강사에 대한 인상뿐 아니라 관계 맺음에도 차이가 생겼다는 최종적 결론을 제시한다. 따라서 주어진 문장이 들어가기에 가장 적절한 곳은 ⑤이다.

- **lecturer** ⓝ 강사, 강연자
- **commonly** ⓐⓓ 흔히
- **assumption** ⓝ 가정, 추정
- **description** ⓝ 설명
- **be told** ~을 듣다
- **impression** ⓝ 인상
- **original** ⓐ 최초의, 원래의
- **relationship** ⓝ 관계
- **interact with** ~와 상호작용하다
- **mistaken** ⓐ 잘못된, 틀린
- **automatically** ⓐⓓ 자동으로, 저절로
- **contain** ⓥ 포함하다, (~이) 들어 있다
- **discussion** ⓝ 토론, 논의
- **as expected** 예상된 대로
- **expectation** ⓝ 기대, 예상

---

40 사회적 증거의 위력　　　　정답률 49% | 정답 ①

다음 글의 내용을 한 문장으로 요약하고자 한다. 빈칸 (A), (B)에 들어갈 말로 가장 적절한 것은?

	(A)		(B)
✔ ①	numbers 숫자	……	uncertain 불확실한
②	numbers 숫자	……	unrealistic 비현실적인
③	experiences 경험	……	unrealistic 비현실적인
④	rules 규칙	……	uncertain 불확실한
⑤	rules 규칙	……	unpleasant 불쾌한

To help decide what's risky and what's safe, / who's trustworthy and who's not, / we look for *social evidence*.
무엇이 위험하고 무엇이 안전한지 결정하는 것을 돕고자 / 누구를 신뢰할 수 있고 없는지를 / 우리는 *사회적 증거*를 찾는다.
From an evolutionary view, / following the group is almost always positive / for our prospects of survival.
진화의 관점에서 볼 때, / 집단을 따르는 것은 거의 항상 긍정적이다. / 우리의 생존 전망에
"If everyone's doing it, / it must be a sensible thing to do," / explains / famous psychologist and best selling writer of *Influence*, / Robert Cialdini.
"모든 사람이 그것을 하고 있다면, / 그것은 분별 있는 행동임에 틀림없다."라고 / 설명한다 / 저명한 심리학자이자 *Influence*를 쓴 베스트셀러 작가 / Robert Cialdini는
While we can frequently see this today in product reviews, / even subtler cues within the environment / can signal trustworthiness.
오늘날 우리가 상품평에서 이를 자주 볼 수 있지만, / 환경 내의 훨씬 더 미묘한 신호가 / 신뢰성을 나타낼 수 있다.
Consider this: / when you visit a local restaurant, / are they busy?
다음을 생각해보라. / 여러분이 어느 현지 음식점을 방문할 때, / 그들이 바쁜가?
Is there a line outside / or is it easy to find a seat?
밖에 줄이 있는가, / 아니면 자리를 찾기 쉬운가?
It is a hassle to wait, / but a line can be a powerful cue / that the food's tasty, / and these seats are in demand.
기다리기는 성가시지만, / 줄이라는 것은 강력한 신호일 수 있다. / 음식이 맛있다는 / 그리고 이곳의 좌석이 수요가 많다는
More often than not, / it's good / to adopt the practices of those around you.
대개는 / 좋다. / 주변 사람들의 행동을 따르는 것이
➡ We tend to feel safe and secure in (A) numbers / when we decide how to act, / particularly when faced with (B) uncertain conditions.
우리는 숫자에서 안전함과 안도감을 느끼는 경향이 있다. / 어떻게 행동할지 결정할 때 / 특히 불확실한 상황에 직면해 있다면

무엇이 위험하고 무엇이 안전하며, 누구를 신뢰할 수 있고 없는지를 결정하는 것을 돕고자, 우리는 *사회적 증거*를 찾는다. 진화의 관점에서 볼 때, 집단을 따르는 것은 거의 항상 우리의 생존 전망에 긍정적이다. "모든 사람이 그것을 하고 있다면, 그것은 분별 있는 행동임에 틀림없다."라고 저명한 심리학자이자 *Influence*를 쓴 베스트셀러 작가인 Robert Cialdini는 설명한다. 오늘날 상품평에서 이를 자주 볼 수 있지만, 환경 내의 훨씬 더 미묘한 신호가 신뢰성을 나타낼 수 있다. 다음을 생각해보라. 여러분이 어느 현지 음식점을 방문할 때, 그들(식당 사람들)이 바쁜가? 밖에 줄이 있는가, 아니면 (사람이 없어서) 자리를 찾기 쉬운가? 기다리

기는 성가시지만, 줄이라는 것은 음식이 맛있고 이곳의 좌석이 수요가 많다는 강력한 신호일 수 있다. 대개는 주변 사람들의 행동을 따르는 것이 좋다.

➡ 우리는 어떻게 행동할지 결정할 때 특히 (B) 불확실한 상황에 직면해 있다면 (A) 숫자에서 안전함과 안도감을 느끼는 경향이 있다.

Why? 왜 정답일까?

불확실한 상황에서 결정을 내려야 할 때 우리는 주변 집단의 행동을 따라 안전하게 선택하려 한다(~ following the group is almost always positive for our prospects of survival. / More often than not, it's good to adopt the practices of those around you.)는 내용의 글이다. 따라서 요약문의 빈칸 (A), (B)에 들어갈 말로 가장 적절한 것은 ① '(A) numbers(숫자), (B) uncertain(불확실한)'이다.

- **risky** ⓐ 위험한
- **evidence** ⓝ 근거, 증거
- **sensible** ⓐ 분별 있는, 현명한
- **subtle** ⓐ 미묘한
- **tasty** ⓐ 맛있는
- **more often than not** 대개
- **faced with** ~와 직면한
- **unrealistic** ⓐ 비현실적인
- **unpleasant** ⓐ 불쾌한
- **trustworthy** ⓐ 신뢰할 만한
- **prospect** ⓝ 예상, 가망성
- **frequently** ⓐᵈ 자주, 빈번히
- **hassle** ⓝ 성가신 일
- **in demand** 수요가 많은
- **practice** ⓝ 관례, 실행
- **uncertain** ⓐ 불확실한
- **rule** ⓝ 규칙 ⓥ 지배하다

구문 풀이

1행 To help decide what's risky and what's safe, who's trustworthy and who's not, we look for *social evidence*.
목적(~하려며) 원형부정사 / 의문사절1 / 의문사절2

41-42 익숙한 정보에 대한 전문가의 유리함

Chess masters shown a chess board / in the middle of a game for 5 seconds / with 20 to 30 pieces still in play / can immediately reproduce the position of the pieces from memory.
체스판을 본 체스의 달인들은 / 게임 중간에 5초 동안 / 20 ~ 30개의 말들이 아직 놓여 있는 상태로 / 그 말들의 위치를 외워서 즉시 재현할 수 있다.

Beginners, / of course, / are able to place only a few.
초보자들은 / 물론 / 겨우 몇 개만 기억해 낼 수 있다.

Now take the same pieces / and place them on the board randomly / and the (a) difference is much reduced.
이제 똑같은 말들을 가져다가 / 체스판에 무작위로 놓으라 / 그러면 그 차이는 크게 줄어든다.

『The expert's advantage is only for familiar patterns / — those previously stored in memory.』 42번의 근거
전문가의 유리함은 익숙한 패턴에 대해서만이다. / 즉 이전에 기억에 저장된 패턴

Faced with unfamiliar patterns, / even when it involves the same familiar domain, / the expert's advantage (b) disappears.
익숙하지 않은 패턴에 직면하면, / 그것이 같은 익숙한 분야와 관련 있는 경우라도 / 전문가의 유리함은 사라진다.

『The beneficial effects of familiar structure on memory』 / have been observed for many types of expertise, / including music.
익숙한 구조가 기억에 미치는 유익한 효과는 / 여러 전문 지식 유형에서 관찰되어 왔다 / 음악을 포함해

People with musical training / can reproduce short sequences of musical notation more accurately / than those with no musical training / when notes follow (c) conventional sequences, / but the advantage is much reduced / when the notes are ordered randomly.
음악 훈련을 받은 사람이 / 연속적 짧은 악보를 더 정확하게 재현할 수 있다 / 음악 훈련을 안 받은 사람보다 / 음표가 전형적인 순서를 따를 때는 / 하지만 그 유리함은 훨씬 줄어든다 / 음표가 무작위로 배열될 때는

Expertise also improves memory for sequences of (d) movements.
전문 지식은 또한 연속 동작에 대한 기억을 향상시킨다.

Experienced ballet dancers are able to repeat longer sequences of steps / than less experienced dancers, / and they can repeat a sequence of steps making up a routine better / than steps ordered randomly.
숙련된 발레 무용수가 더 긴 연속 스텝을 반복할 수 있다 / 경험이 적은 무용수보다 / 그리고 그들은 정해진 춤 동작을 이루는 연속 스텝을 더 잘 반복할 수 있다 / 무작위로 배열된 스텝보다

In each case, / memory range is (e) increased / by the ability to recognize familiar sequences and patterns.
각각의 경우, / 기억의 범위는 늘어난다 / 익숙한 순서와 패턴을 인식하는 능력에 의해

체스판을 게임 중간에 20 ~ 30개의 말들이 아직 놓여 있는 상태로 5초 동안 본 체스의 달인들은 그 말들의 위치를 외워서 즉시 재현할 수 있다. 물론 초보자들은 겨우 몇 개만 기억해 낼 수 있다. 이제 똑같은 말들을 가져다가 체스판에 무작위로 놓으면 그 (a) 차이는 크게 줄어든다. 전문가의 유리함은 익숙한 패턴, 즉 이전에 기억에 저장된 패턴에 대해서만 있다. 익숙하지 않은 패턴에 직면하면, 같은 익숙한 분야와 관련 있는 경우라도 전문가의 유리함은 (b) 사라진다. 익숙한 구조가 기억에 미치는 유익한 효과는 음악을 포함해 여러 전문 지식 유형에서 관찰되어 왔다. 음표가 (c) 특이한(→ 전형적인) 순서를 따를 때는 음악 훈련을 받은 사람이 음악 훈련을 안 받은 사람보다 연속적 짧은 악보를 더 정확하게 재현할 수 있지만, 음표가 무작위로 배열되면 그 유리함이 훨씬 줄어든다. 전문 지식은 또한 연속 (d) 동작에 대한 기억을 향상시킨다. 숙련된 발레 무용수가 경험이 적은 무용수보다 더 긴 연속 스텝을 반복할 수 있고, 무작위로 배열된 스텝보다 정해진 춤 동작을 이루는 연속 스텝을 더 잘 반복할 수 있다. 각각의 경우, 기억의 범위는 익숙한 순서와 패턴을 인식하는 능력에 의해 (e) 늘어난다.

- **in the middle of** ~의 한가운데에
- **reproduce** ⓥ 재현하다
- **beginner** ⓝ 초심자
- **randomly** ⓐᵈ 무작위로
- **advantage** ⓝ 유리함, 이점
- **previously** ⓐᵈ 이전에, 사전에
- **domain** ⓝ 영역, 분야
- **beneficial** ⓐ 유익한, 이로운
- **sequence** ⓝ 연속, 순서
- **accurately** ⓐᵈ 정확하게
- **experienced** ⓐ 숙련된, 경험 많은
- **guarantee** ⓥ 보장하다
- **in play** 시합 중인
- **from memory** 외워서, 기억하여
- **only a few** 몇 안 되는 (것)
- **reduce** ⓥ 줄이다, 감소시키다
- **familiar** ⓐ 익숙한, 친숙한
- **unfamiliar** ⓐ 익숙지 않은, 낯선
- **disappear** ⓥ 사라지다
- **expertise** ⓝ 전문 지식
- **musical notation** 악보
- **unusual** ⓐ 특이한
- **routine** ⓝ 습관, (정해진) 춤 동작, 루틴

구문 풀이

1행 Chess masters shown a chess board in the middle of a game for 5 seconds with 20 to 30 pieces still in play can immediately reproduce the position of the pieces from memory.
주어 / 과거분사 shown의 직접목적어 / 동사구

---

41 제목 파악 정답률 64% | 정답 ②

윗글의 제목으로 가장 적절한 것은?

① How Can We Build Good Routines? – 어떻게 하면 좋은 습관을 들일 수 있을까?
✓② Familiar Structures Help Us Remember – 익숙한 구조는 우리가 기억하는 것을 돕는다
③ Intelligence Does Not Guarantee Expertise – 지능이 전문 지식을 보장하는 것은 아니다
④ Does Playing Chess Improve Your Memory? – 체스를 하는 것이 기억력을 향상시킬까?
⑤ Creative Art Performance Starts from Practice – 창의적인 예술 공연은 연습에서 시작된다

Why? 왜 정답일까?

익숙한 정보가 기억력에 미치는 좋은 영향(The beneficial effects of familiar structure on memory)을 설명하는 글로, 전문가의 경우 익숙하고 패턴화된 정보는 더 잘 기억하지만 무작위적인 정보는 전문 분야라고 하더라도 기억력 면에서 초심자와 큰 차이를 보이지 못한다는 예시를 다루고 있다. 따라서 글의 제목으로 가장 적절한 것은 ② '익숙한 구조는 우리가 기억하는 것을 돕는다'이다.

42 어휘 추론 정답률 48% | 정답 ③

밑줄 친 (a) ~ (e) 중에서 문맥상 낱말의 쓰임이 적절하지 않은 것은?

① (a)   ② (b)   ✓③ (c)   ④ (d)   ⑤ (e)

Why? 왜 정답일까?

'The expert's advantage is only for familiar patterns ~'에서 전문가의 유리함, 즉 전문가들이 자기 분야의 정보를 더 잘 기억할 수 있는 까닭은 바로 정보의 '익숙한 구조'에 있다고 한다. 이를 음악 전문가들의 사례에 적용하면, 음표에 대한 전문가들의 기억이 비전문가들을 넘어설 수 있는 경우는 음표가 '익숙한' 패턴으로 배열된 때일 것이므로, (c)에는 unusual 대신 conventional을 써야 한다. 따라서 문맥상 낱말의 쓰임이 적절하지 않은 것은 ③ '(c)'이다.

43-45 친절로 없어진 괴물

(A)

Once upon a time, / there was a king / who lived in a beautiful palace.
옛날 옛적에, / 한 왕이 있었다. / 아름다운 궁전에 사는

『While the king was away, / a monster approached the gates of the palace.』 45번 ①의 근거 일치
왕이 없는 동안, / 한 괴물이 궁전 문으로 접근했다.

The monster was so ugly and smelly / that the guards froze in shock.
그 괴물이 너무 추하고 냄새가 나서 / 경비병들은 충격으로 얼어붙었다.

He passed the guards / and sat on the king's throne.
괴물은 경비병들을 지나 / 왕의 왕좌에 앉았다.

The guards soon came to their senses, / went in, / and shouted at the monster, / demanding that (a) he get off the throne.
경비병들은 곧 정신을 차리고 / 안으로 들어가 / 괴물을 향해 소리치며 / 그에게 왕좌에서 내려올 것을 요구했다.

(D)

With each bad word the guards used, / the monster grew more ugly and smelly.
경비병들이 나쁜 말을 사용할 때마다, / 그 괴물은 더 추해졌고, 더 냄새가 났다.

『The guards got even angrier — / they began to brandish their swords / to scare the monster away from the palace.』 45번 ⑤의 근거 일치
경비병들은 한층 더 화가 났다. / 그들은 칼을 휘두르기 시작했다. / 그 괴물을 겁주어 궁전에서 쫓아내려고

But (e) he just grew bigger and bigger, / eventually taking up the whole room.
하지만 그는 그저 점점 더 커져서 / 결국 방 전체를 차지했다.

He grew more ugly and smelly than ever.
그는 그 어느 때보다 더 추해졌고, 더 냄새가 났다.

(B)

Eventually the king returned.
마침내 왕이 돌아왔다.

He was wise and kind / and saw what was happening.
그는 현명하고 친절했으며, / 무슨 일이 일어나고 있는지 알았다.

He knew what to do.
그는 어떻게 해야 할지 알고 있었다.

『He smiled and said to the monster, / "Welcome to my palace!"』 45번 ②의 근거 일치
그는 미소를 지으며 그 괴물에게 말했다. / "나의 궁전에 온 것을 환영하오!"라고

He asked the monster / if (b) he wanted a cup of coffee.
왕은 그 괴물에게 물었다. / 그가 커피 한 잔을 원하는지

The monster began to grow smaller / as he drank the coffee.
괴물은 더 작아지기 시작했다. / 그가 그 커피를 마시면서

(C)

The king offered (c) him some take-out pizza and fries.
왕은 그에게 약간의 테이크아웃 피자와 감자튀김을 제안했다.

The guards immediately called for pizza.
경비병들은 즉시 피자를 시켰다.

『The monster continued to get smaller / with the king's kind gestures.』 45번 ③의 근거 일치
그 괴물은 몸이 계속 더 작아졌다. / 왕의 친절한 행동에

(d) He then offered the monster a full body massage.
그러고 나서 그는 괴물에게 전신 마사지를 제공해 주었다.

『As the guards helped with the relaxing massage, / the monster became tiny.』
경비병들이 편안한 마사지를 도와주자 / 그 괴물은 매우 작아졌다. 45번 ④의 근거 불일치

With another act of kindness to the monster, / he just disappeared.
그 괴물에게 또 한 번의 친절한 행동을 베풀자, / 그는 바로 사라졌다.

(A)

옛날 옛적에, 아름다운 궁전에 사는 한 왕이 있었다. 왕이 없는 동안, 한 괴물이 궁전 문으로

[문제편 p.032] [04회] 2023학년도 3월 029

접근했다. 그 괴물이 너무 추하고 냄새가 나서 경비병들은 충격으로 얼어붙었다. 괴물은 경비병들을 지나 왕의 왕좌에 앉았다. 경비병들은 곧 정신을 차리고 안으로 들어가 괴물을 향해 소리치며 (a) 그에게 왕좌에서 내려올 것을 요구했다.

(D)
경비병들이 나쁜 말을 사용할 때마다, 그 괴물은 더 추해졌고, 더 냄새가 났다. 경비병들은 한층 더 화가 났다. 그들은 그 괴물을 겁주어 궁전에서 쫓아내려고 칼을 휘두르기 시작했다. 하지만 (e) 그는 그저 점점 더 커져서 결국 방 전체를 차지했다. 그는 그 어느 때보다 더 추해졌고, 더 냄새가 났다.

(B)
마침내 왕이 돌아왔다. 그는 현명하고 친절했으며, 무슨 일이 일어나고 있는지 알았다. 그는 어떻게 해야 할지 알고 있었다. 그는 미소를 지으며 그 괴물에게 "나의 궁전에 온 것을 환영하오!"라고 말했다. 왕은 그 괴물에게 (b) 그가 커피 한 잔을 원하는지 물었다. 괴물은 그 커피를 마시면서 더 작아지기 시작했다.

(C)
왕은 (c) 그에게 약간의 테이크아웃 피자와 감자튀김을 제안했다. 경비병들은 즉시 피자를 시켰다. 그 괴물은 왕의 친절한 행동에 몸이 계속 더 작아졌다. 그리고 나서 (d) 그는 괴물에게 전신 마사지를 제공해 주었다. 경비병들이 편안한 마사지를 도와주자 그 괴물은 매우 작아졌다. 그 괴물에게 또 한 번의 친절한 행동을 베풀자, 그는 바로 사라졌다.

- approach ⓥ 다가오다, 접근하다
- ugly ⓐ 추한
- in shock 충격을 받아
- come to one's senses 정신을 차리다
- get off ~을 떠나다
- take-out ⓐ 사서 가지고 가는
- gesture ⓝ 몸짓, (감정의) 표시, 표현
- brandish ⓥ 휘두르다
- take up ~을 차지하다
- gate ⓝ 문
- smelly ⓐ 냄새 나는, 악취가 나는
- throne ⓝ 왕좌
- shout at ~을 향해 소리치다
- wise ⓐ 현명한
- call for ~을 시키다, ~을 요구하다
- tiny ⓐ 아주 작은
- scare away ~을 겁주어 쫓아버리다
- than ever 그 어느 때보다

구문 풀이
(A) 5행 The guards soon came to their senses, went in, and shouted at the monster, demanding that he (should) get off the throne.
요구 동사 / 생략 / 동사원형
(D) 4행 But he just grew bigger and bigger, eventually taking up the whole room.
「비교급＋and＋비교급 : 점점 더 ~한」 / 분사구문(그리고 ~하다)

---

43 글의 순서 파악   정답률 77% | 정답 ④

주어진 글 (A)에 이어질 내용을 순서에 맞게 배열한 것으로 가장 적절한 것은?
① (B) - (D) - (C)
② (C) - (B) - (D)
③ (C) - (D) - (B)
✔④ (D) - (B) - (C)
⑤ (D) - (C) - (B)

Why? 왜 정답일까?

왕이 없을 때 어느 괴물이 왕좌에 대신 앉아버렸다는 내용의 **(A)** 뒤에는, 경비병들이 괴물을 위협하며 쫓아내려 했으나 오히려 괴물의 몸집이 점점 커질 뿐이었다는 내용의 **(D)**, 왕이 돌아와서는 사태를 파악하고 괴물에게 친절을 베풀기 시작했다는 내용의 **(B)**, 왕이 음식과 마사지 등 친절한 행동을 보탤 때마다 괴물이 점점 작아져서 마침내는 없어졌다는 내용의 **(C)**가 차례로 연결되어야 한다. 따라서 글의 순서로 가장 적절한 것은 ④ '**(D) - (B) - (C)**'이다.

---

44 지칭 추론   정답률 75% | 정답 ④

밑줄 친 (a)~(e) 중에서 가리키는 대상이 나머지 넷과 다른 것은?
① (a)   ② (b)   ③ (c)   ✔④ (d)   ⑤ (e)

Why? 왜 정답일까?

(a), (b), (c), (e)는 the monster, (d)는 the king을 가리키므로, (a)~(e) 중에서 가리키는 대상이 다른 하나는 ④ '(d)'이다.

---

45 세부 내용 파악   정답률 83% | 정답 ④

윗글에 관한 내용으로 적절하지 <u>않은</u> 것은?
① 왕이 없는 동안 괴물이 궁전 문으로 접근했다.
② 왕은 미소를 지으며 괴물에게 환영한다고 말했다.
③ 왕의 친절한 행동에 괴물의 몸이 계속 더 작아졌다.
✔④ 경비병들은 괴물을 마사지해 주기를 거부했다.
⑤ 경비병들은 겁을 주어 괴물을 쫓아내려 했다.

Why? 왜 정답일까?

(C) 'As the guards helped with the relaxing massage, ~'에서 경비병들은 괴물을 마사지해주기를 거부하지 않고, 오히려 마사지를 도와줬음을 알 수 있다. 따라서 내용과 일치하지 않는 것은 ④ '경비병들은 괴물을 마사지해 주기를 거부했다.'이다.

Why? 왜 오답일까?

① (A) 'While the king was away, a monster approached the gates of the palace.'의 내용과 일치한다.
② (B) 'He smiled and said to the monster, "Welcome to my palace!"'의 내용과 일치한다.
③ (C) 'The monster continued to get smaller with the king's kind gestures.'의 내용과 일치한다.
⑤ (D) 'The guards ~ began to brandish their swords to scare the monster away from the palace.'의 내용과 일치한다.

A	B	C	D
01 갈등	01 settle down	01 ⓒ	01 ⓗ
02 광물	02 efficiently	02 ⓗ	02 ⓢ
03 탄수화물	03 contain	03 ⓑ	03 ⓔ
04 토론	04 scare away	04 ⓜ	04 ⓜ
05 불쾌한	05 discover	05 ⓘ	05 ⓕ
06 다가오다, 접근하다	06 gene	06 ⓐ	06 ⓘ
07 보장하다	07 randomly	07 ⓘ	07 ⓞ
08 ~을 차지하다	08 constant	08 ⓡ	08 ⓕ
09 기꺼이	09 species	09 ⓙ	09 ⓚ
10 방출하다	10 organize	10 ⓞ	10 ⓑ
11 냄새	11 jealous	11 ⓠ	11 ⓐ
12 좌절한	12 motivation	12 ⓘ	12 ⓒ
13 자신감 있는	13 estimate	13 ⓚ	13 ⓓ
14 발생하다	14 wander	14 ⓟ	14 ⓘ
15 ~로 결합되다	15 principle	15 ⓔ	15 ⓖ
16 ~을 처리하다	16 impression	16 ⓕ	16 ⓘ
17 수용하다, 받아들이다	17 empathy	17 ⓝ	17 ⓘ
18 ~에 적응하다	18 habitat	18 ⓢ	18 ⓟ
19 유지하다	19 expectation	19 ⓖ	19 ⓠ
20 ~을 시키다, 요구하다	20 structure	20 ⓘ	20 ⓝ

• 정답 •

01 ① 02 ③ 03 ② 04 ④ 05 ④ 06 ③ 07 ① 08 ③ 09 ⑤ 10 ③ 11 ① 12 ⑤ 13 ② 14 ② 15 ①
16 ④ 17 ④ 18 ② 19 ③ 20 ⑤ 21 ⑤ 22 ② 23 ④ 24 ② 25 ⑤ 26 ③ 27 ④ 28 ⑤ 29 ③ 30 ★⑤
31 ② 32 ③ 33 ① 34 ★① 35 ④ 36 ③ 37 ② 38 ④ 39 ② 40 ① 41 ⑤ 42 ⑤ 43 ② 44 ④ 45 ⑤

★ 표기된 문항은 [등급을 가르는 문제]에 해당하는 문항입니다.

---

01 농구 리그 등록 방법 변경 안내
정답률 86% | 정답 ①

다음을 듣고, 남자가 하는 말의 목적으로 가장 적절한 것을 고르시오.
☑ 농구 리그 참가 등록 방법의 변경을 알리려고
② 확정된 농구 리그 시합 일정을 발표하려고
③ 농구 리그의 심판을 추가 모집하려고
④ 농구 리그 경기 관람을 권장하려고
⑤ 농구 리그 우승 상품을 안내하려고

M : Good afternoon, everybody.
안녕하세요, 여러분.
This is Student President Sam Wilson.
저는 학생회장인 Sam Wilson입니다.
As you know, the lunch basketball league will begin soon.
여러분도 알다시피, 점심시간 농구 리그가 곧 시작됩니다.
Many students are interested in joining the league and waiting for the sign-up sheet to be handed out at the gym.
많은 학생들이 리그 참가에 관심을 보이고 있고 체육관에서 신청서가 배부되기를 기다리고 있습니다.
For easier access, we've decided to change the registration method.
보다 쉽게 접근할 수 있도록, 저희는 등록 방법을 바꾸기로 했습니다.
Instead of going to the gym to register, simply log into the school website and fill out the registration form online.
체육관에 가서 등록하는 대신, 학교 웹 사이트에 로그인해서 온라인 신청서를 작성하기만 해 주세요.
Thank you for listening and let's have a good league.
들어주셔서 감사합니다, 좋은 리그 경기를 합시다.

Why? 왜 정답일까?
'For easier access, we've decided to change the registration method. Instead of going to the gym to register, simply log into the school website and fill out the registration form online.'에서 남자는 점심시간 농구 리그 참가 등록이 온라인 등록으로 바뀌었음을 공지하고 있다. 따라서 남자가 하는 말의 목적으로 가장 적절한 것은 ① '농구 리그 참가 등록 방법의 변경을 알리려고'이다.

● **hand out** 배부하다, 나눠주다
● **registration** ⑩ 등록
● **access** ⑩ 접근, 이용

---

02 손으로 얼굴을 만지지 말라고 권하기
정답률 96% | 정답 ③

대화를 듣고, 여자의 의견으로 가장 적절한 것을 고르시오.
① 평소에 피부 상태를 잘 관찰할 필요가 있다.
② 여드름을 치료하려면 피부과 병원에 가야 한다.
☑ 얼굴을 손으로 만지는 것은 얼굴 피부에 해롭다.
④ 지성 피부를 가진 사람은 자주 세수를 해야 한다.
⑤ 손을 자주 씻는 것은 감염병 예방에 도움이 된다.

W : Daniel, what are you doing in front of the mirror?
Daniel, 거울 앞에서 뭐 하고 있어?
M : I have skin problems these days. I'm trying to pop these pimples on my face.
요새 피부에 문제가 있어. 얼굴에 난 이 여드름들을 짜려는 중이야.
W : Pimples are really annoying, but I wouldn't do that.
여드름은 정말 거슬리긴 하는데, 나라면 짜지 않겠어.
M : Why not?
왜?
W : When you pop them with your hands, you're touching your face.
네가 그걸 손으로 짜면, 얼굴을 만지게 되잖아.
M : Are you saying that I shouldn't touch my face?
내가 얼굴을 만지면 안 된다는 얘기야?
W : Exactly. You know our hands are covered with bacteria, right?
바로 그거야. 우리 손은 세균으로 뒤덮여 있는 거 알잖아, 그렇지?
M : So?
그래서?
W : You'll be spreading bacteria all over your face with your hands. It could worsen your skin problems.
넌 손으로 얼굴 전체에 세균을 퍼뜨리게 될 거야. 그건 피부 문제를 더 나빠지게 만들 수 있지.
M : Oh, I didn't know that.
오, 난 그건 몰랐어.
W : Touching your face with your hands is bad for your skin.
손으로 얼굴을 만지는 것은 피부에 해로워.
M : Okay, I got it.
그래, 알았어.

Why? 왜 정답일까?
얼굴에 난 여드름을 손으로 짜려는 남자에게 여자는 세균이 뒤덮인 손으로 얼굴을 만지는 것이 피부에 좋지 않다(Touching your face with your hands is bad for your skin.)는 것을 설명해주고 있다. 따라서 여자의 의견으로 가장 적절한 것은 ③ '얼굴을 손으로 만지는 것은 얼굴 피부에 해롭다.'이다.

● **pop a pimple** 여드름을 짜다
● **spread** ⑨ 퍼뜨리다
● **annoying** ⑨ 거슬리는, 짜증나게 하는
● **worsen** ⑨ 악화시키다

---

03 만화가와 환경 운동가의 우연한 만남
정답률 91% | 정답 ②

대화를 듣고, 두 사람의 관계를 가장 잘 나타낸 것을 고르시오.
① 방송 작가 − 연출자
☑ 만화가 − 환경 운동가
③ 촬영 감독 − 동화 작가
④ 토크쇼 진행자 − 기후학자
⑤ 제품 디자이너 − 영업 사원

M : Excuse me. You're Chloe Jones, aren't you?
실례합니다. Chloe Jones 씨 맞으시죠?
W : Yes, I am. Have we met before?
네, 맞아요. 전에 뵈었었나요?
M : No, but I'm a big fan of yours. I've watched your speeches on climate change, and they're very inspiring.
아니요, 하지만 전 당신의 열성팬이에요. 기후 변화에 대한 당신의 연설을 보았고, 그것은 매우 고무적이었어요.
W : Thank you. I'm so glad to hear that.
고맙습니다. 그 말씀을 들으니 몹시 기쁘네요.
M : And, I also think your campaign about plastic pollution has been very successful.
그리고, 플라스틱 오염에 관한 당신의 캠페인 또한 아주 성공적이었다고 생각해요.
W : As an environmental activist, that means a lot to me.
환경 운동가로서, 그것은 제게 많은 의미가 있죠.
M : May I make a suggestion? I thought it'd be nice if more children could hear your ideas.
제안을 하나 해도 될까요? 더 많은 어린이들이 당신의 생각을 접할 수 있으면 좋을 것 같아요.
W : That's what I was thinking. Do you have any good ideas?
저도 그렇게 생각했답니다. 좋은 아이디어가 있으신가요?
M : Actually, I'm a cartoonist. Perhaps I can make comic books based on your work.
사실, 전 만화가예요. 어쩌면 제가 당신의 작업에 기반해 만화책을 만들 수 있을 거예요.
W : That is a wonderful idea. Can I contact you later to discuss it more?
멋진 생각이네요. 좀 더 논의하기 위해 나중에 연락드려도 될까요?
M : Sure. By the way, my name is Jack Perse. Here's my business card.
그럼요. 참, 제 이름은 Jack Perse입니다. 여기 제 명함이요.

Why? 왜 정답일까?
'Actually, I'm a cartoonist.'에서 남자는 만화가이고, 'As an environmental activist, that means a lot to me.'에서 여자는 환경 운동가임을 알 수 있다. 따라서 두 사람의 관계로 가장 적절한 것은 ② '만화가 − 환경 운동가'이다.

● **climate change** 기후 변화
● **pollution** ⑩ 오염, 공해
● **make a suggestion** 제안하다
● **business card** 명함
● **inspiring** ⑧ 고무하는
● **environmental activist** 환경 운동가
● **discuss** ⑨ 상의하다

---

04 새로 꾸민 수조 사진 구경하기
정답률 76% | 정답 ④

대화를 듣고, 그림에서 대화의 내용과 일치하지 않는 것을 고르시오.

W : Yesterday, I decorated my fish tank like a beach.
어제 난 내 수조를 바닷가처럼 꾸몄어.
M : I'd like to see it. Do you have a picture?
나도 보고 싶다. 사진 있어?
W : Sure. Here. [Pause] 「Do you recognize the boat in the bottom left corner?」①의 근거 일치
응, 여기. [잠시 멈춤] 왼쪽 아래 구석에 배 알아보겠어?
M : Yes. It's the one I gave you, isn't it?
응, 내가 너한테 준 거네, 그렇지?
W : Right. It looks good in the fish tank, doesn't it?
맞아. 수조에 넣어두니 근사하지, 그렇지?
M : It does. 「I love the beach chair in the center.」②의 근거 일치
그러네. 가운데 있는 해변용 의자 마음에 든다.
W : Yeah. I like it, too.
응. 나도 그게 마음에 들어.
M : 「I see a starfish next to the chair.」③의 근거 일치
의자 옆에 불가사리가 있네.
W : Isn't it cute? 「And do you see these two surf boards on the right side of the picture?」④의 근거 불일치
귀엽지 않아? 그리고 사진 오른쪽에 서핑 보드 두 개가 있는 거 보여?
M : Yeah. I like how you put both of them side by side.
응. 두 개를 나란히 배치해둔 게 좋네.
W : I thought that'd look cool.
그게 멋져 보이는 것 같더라고.
M : 「Your fish in the top left corner looks happy with its new home.」⑤의 근거 일치
왼쪽 위 구석에 있는 네 물고기도 새로운 집에 만족한 것 같네.
W : I hope so.
그러길 바라.

Why? 왜 정답일까?
대화에 따르면 사진 오른쪽에 서핑 보드가 두 개 있다(And do you see these two surf boards on the right side of the picture?)고 하는데, 그림에서는 서핑 보드가 하나 뿐이다. 따라서 그림에서 대화의 내용과 일치하지 않는 것은 ④이다.

● **fish tank** 수조
● **side by side** 나란히
● **starfish** ⑩ 불가사리

대화를 듣고, 여자가 남자에게 부탁한 일로 가장 적절한 것을 고르시오.

① 장난감 사 오기
② 풍선 달기
③ 케이크 가져오기
✔ 탁자 옮기기
⑤ 아이들 데려오기

[Cell phone rings.]
[휴대전화가 울린다.]
M : Hello, honey. I'm on the way home. How's setting up Mike's birthday party going?
여보세요, 여보. 나 집에 가고 있어요. Mike의 생일 파티 준비는 어떻게 돼 가요?
W : Good, but I still have stuff to do. Mike and his friends will get here soon.
잘돼 가는데, 아직 할 일이 있어요. Mike와 친구들이 곧 이리로 올 거예요.
M : Should I pick up the birthday cake?
내가 생일 케익을 찾으러 갈까요?
W : No, that's okay. I already did that.
아니, 괜찮아요. 내가 이미 찾아왔어요.
M : Then, do you want me to put up the balloons around the doorway when I get there?
그럼, 내가 도착해서 현관문 주변에 풍선을 달아놓을까요?
W : I'll take care of it. Can you take the table out to the front yard?
그건 내가 할게요. 탁자를 앞마당으로 옮겨줄 수 있어요?
M : Sure. Are we having the party outside?
물론이죠. 우리 야외 파티를 하는 건가요?
W : Yes. The weather is beautiful so I made a last minute change.
네, 날씨가 좋아서 막판에 바꿨어요.
M : Great. The kids can play with water guns in the front yard.
좋아요. 애들은 앞마당에서 물총을 갖고 놀아도 되겠네요.
W : Good idea. I'll go to the garage and grab the water guns.
좋은 생각이에요. 내가 차고에 가서 물총을 가져와야겠어요.

Why? 왜 정답일까?

아들의 생일 파티를 밖에서 하기로 마음을 바꾼 여자는 남자에게 탁자를 밖으로 옮겨달라고 하므로(Can you take the table out to the front yard?), 여자가 부탁한 일로 가장 적절한 것은 ④ '탁자 옮기기'이다.

● put up 달다, 올리다, 게시하다
● make a last minute change 마지막 순간에 바꾸다
● grab ⓥ 집다, 잡다

대화를 듣고, 남자가 지불할 금액을 고르시오. [3점]

① $14　　② $16　　✔ $18　　④ $20　　⑤ $22

W : Welcome to Green Eco Shop. How can I help you?
Green Eco Shop에 잘 오셨어요. 무엇을 도와드릴까요?
M : Hi, do you sell eco-friendly toothbrushes?
안녕하세요, 친환경 칫솔 파시나요?
W : Yes, we have a few types over here. Which do you like?
네, 이쪽에 몇 가지 종류가 있습니다. 어떤 것이 마음에 드세요?
M : Hmm.... How much are these?
흠... 이건 얼마인가요?
W : They're $2 each. They are made from bamboo.
하나에 2달러입니다. 대나무로 만들었어요.
M : All right. I'll take four of them.
좋아요. 이거 네 개 살게요.
W : Excellent choice. Anything else?
탁월한 선택입니다. 다른 거 필요하신 건요?
M : I also need bath sponges.
목욕용 스펀지도 필요해요.
W : They're right behind you. They're plastic-free and only $3 each.
바로 뒤쪽에 있어요. 플라스틱이 안 들어간 제품이고 하나에 3달러밖에 안 합니다.
M : Okay. I'll also take four of them. That'll be all.
그럼요. 이것도 네 개 살게요. 이거면 됐어요.
W : If you have a store membership, you can get a 10% discount off the total price.
매장 회원이시면, 총 가격에서 10퍼센트 할인을 받으실 수 있어요.
M : Great. I'm a member. Here are my credit and membership cards.
좋네요. 전 회원이에요. 여기 제 신용카드랑 회원 카드요.

Why? 왜 정답일까?

대화에 따르면 남자는 하나에 2달러인 대나무 칫솔을 네 개 사고, 하나에 3달러인 목욕용 스펀지도 네 개 산 뒤, 총 가격에서 회원 할인 10퍼센트를 받았다. 이를 식으로 나타내면 '$(2 \times 4 + 3 \times 4) \times 0.9 = 18$'이므로, 남자가 지불할 총 금액은 ③ '$18'이다.

● eco-friendly ⓐ 친환경적인
● bamboo ⓝ 대나무
● plastic-free ⓐ 플라스틱이 들어가지 않은

대화를 듣고, 두 사람이 오늘 실험을 할 수 없는 이유를 고르시오.

✔ 실험용 키트가 배달되지 않아서
② 실험 주제를 변경해야 해서
③ 과학실을 예약하지 못해서
④ 보고서를 작성해야 해서
⑤ 남자가 감기에 걸려서

[Cell phone rings.]
[휴대전화가 울린다.]
M : Hey, Suji. Where are you?
안녕, Suji. 어디 있어?
W : I'm in the library checking out books. I'll be heading out to the science lab for our experiment in a couple of minutes.
도서관에서 책 빌리고 있어. 몇 분 있다가 우리 실험하는 과학실로 갈게.
M : I guess you haven't checked my message yet. We can't do the experiment today.
너 내 메시지 아직 못 확인했나 보구나. 우리 오늘 실험 못해.

W : Really? Isn't the lab available today?
진짜? 실험실 오늘 쓸 수 있는 거 아니었어?
M : Yes, it is, but I canceled our reservation.
맞는데, 내가 예약을 취소했어.
W : Why? Are you still suffering from your cold?
왜? 너 아직도 감기로 아픈 거야?
M : No, I'm fine now.
아니, 이제 괜찮아.
W : That's good. Then why aren't we doing the experiment today? We need to hand in the science report by next Monday.
다행이다. 그럼 왜 오늘 실험을 안 하는 거야? 다음 주 월요일까지 과학 보고서 내야 하잖아.
M : Unfortunately, the experiment kit hasn't been delivered yet. It'll arrive tomorrow.
안타깝게도, 실험용 키트가 아직 배달되지 않았어. 그게 내일 도착할 거야.
W : Oh, well. The experiment has to wait one more day, then.
오, 그렇구나. 그럼 하루 더 기다렸다가 실험해야겠네.

Why? 왜 정답일까?

대화에 따르면 남자는 실험용 키트를 아직 배송받지 못했기에 (Unfortunately, the experiment kit hasn't been delivered yet.) 예약된 실험을 취소했다고 하므로, 두 사람이 오늘 실험을 할 수 없는 이유로 가장 적절한 것은 ① '실험용 키트가 배달되지 않아서'이다.

● check out (책 등을) 대출하다
● a couple of 몇몇의, 둘의
● deliver ⓥ 배송하다
● science lab 과학실
● hand in 제출하다

대화를 듣고, Stanville Free-cycle에 관해 언급되지 않은 것을 고르시오.

① 참가 대상
② 행사 장소
✔ 주차 가능 여부
④ 행사 시작일
⑤ 금지 품목

W : Honey, did you see the poster about the Stanville Free-cycle?
여보, Stanville Free-cycle에 관한 포스터 봤어요?
M : Free-cycle? What is that?
프리사이클요? 그게 뭐예요?
W : It's another way of recycling. You give away items you don't need and anybody can take them for free.
재활용의 또 다른 방법이에요. 필요하지 않은 물품을 버리면 누군가 그것을 공짜로 가져가는 거죠.
M : Oh, it's like one man's garbage is another man's treasure. 「Who can participate?
오, 어떤 사람의 쓰레기가 다른 사람의 보물이라는 것 같군요. 누가 참여할 수 있나요?
W : It's open to everyone living in Stanville.」 ①의근거 일치
Stanville에 사는 누구나 참여할 수 있어요.
M : Great. 「Where is it taking place?
좋네요. 어디서 열려요?
W : At Rose Park on Second Street.」 ②의근거 일치
Second Street에 있는 Rose Park에서요.
M : 「When does the event start?
행사는 언제 시작해요?
W : It starts on April 12 and runs for a week.」 ④의근거 일치
4월 12일에 시작해서 일주일 동안 운영돼요.
M : Let's see what we can free-cycle, starting from the cupboard.
우리가 뭘 프리사이클할 수 있는지 찬장부터 살펴보죠.
W : Okay. 「But breakable items like glass dishes or cups won't be accepted.」 ⑤의근거 일치
좋아요. 하지만 유리 접시나 컵처럼 깨지기 쉬운 물품은 허용되지 않을 거예요.
M : I see. I'll keep that in mind.
알겠어요. 그 점을 기억할게요.

Why? 왜 정답일까?

대화에서 남자와 여자는 Stanville Free-cycle의 참가 대상, 행사 장소, 행사 시작일, 금지 품목에 관해 언급한다. 따라서 언급되지 않은 것은 ③ '주차 가능 여부'이다.

Why? 왜 오답일까?

① 'It's open to everyone living in Stanville.'에서 '참가 대상'이 언급된다.
② 'At Rose Park on Second Street.'에서 '행사 장소'가 언급된다.
④ 'It starts on April 12 ～'에서 '행사 시작일'이 언급된다.
⑤ 'But breakable items like glass dishes or cups won't be accepted.'에서 '금지 품목'이 언급되었다.

● give away 버리다, 거저 주다
● treasure ⓝ 보물
● for free 공짜로
● breakable ⓐ 깨지기 쉬운

River Valley Music Camp에 관한 다음 내용을 듣고, 일치하지 않는 것을 고르시오.

① 4월 11일부터 5일 동안 진행된다.
② 학교 오케스트라 단원이 아니어도 참가할 수 있다.
③ 자신의 악기를 가져오거나 학교에서 빌릴 수 있다.
④ 마지막 날에 공연을 촬영한다.
✔ 참가 인원에는 제한이 없다.

M : Hello, River Valley High School students.
안녕하세요, River Valley 고등학교 학생 여러분.
This is your music teacher, Mr. Stailor.
저는 음악 교사인 Stailor 선생님입니다.
「Starting on April 11, we are going to have the River Valley Music Camp for five days.」 ①의근거 일치
4월 11일부터, River Valley Music Camp가 5일 동안 열립니다.
「You don't need to be a member of the school orchestra to join the camp.」 ②의근거 일치
캠프에 참여하기 위해 학교 오케스트라 단원일 필요는 없습니다.
「You may bring your own instrument or you can borrow one from the school.」
자신의 악기를 가져오거나, 학교에서 하나 빌리면 됩니다. ③의근거 일치
「On the last day of camp, we are going to film our performance and play it on screen

at the school summer festival.」 **④의 근거 일치**
캠프 마지막 날, 우리는 공연을 촬영하여 그것을 학교 여름 축제에서 스크린으로 재생할 예정입니다.
「Please keep in mind the camp is limited to 50 students.」 **⑤의 근거 불일치**
캠프 참가 인원은 50명으로 제한되어 있다는 점 유의해 주세요.
Sign-ups start this Friday, on a first-come-first-served basis.
신청은 이번 주 금요일부터 선착순으로 이루어집니다.
Come and make music together!
오셔서 함께 음악을 즐깁시다!

Why? 왜 정답일까?

'Please keep in mind the camp is limited to 50 students.'에서 참가 인원은 50명으로 제한된다고 하므로, 내용과 일치하지 않는 것은 ⑤ '참가 인원에는 제한이 없다.'이다.

Why? 왜 오답일까?

① 'Starting on April 11, we are going to have the River Valley Music Camp for five days.'의 내용과 일치한다.
② 'You don't need to be a member of the school orchestra to join the camp.'의 내용과 일치한다.
③ 'You may bring your own instrument or you can borrow one from the school.'의 내용과 일치한다.
④ 'On the last day of camp, we are going to film our performance ~'의 내용과 일치한다.

- instrument ⓝ 악기
- be limited to ~로 제한되다
- performance ⓝ 공연
- on a first-come-first-served basis 선착순으로

---

10 소형 진공청소기 구매하기 정답률 85% | 정답 ③

다음 표를 보면서 대화를 듣고, 여자가 주문할 소형 진공청소기를 고르시오.

Handheld Vacuum Cleaners

	Model	Price	Working Time	Weight	Washable Filter
①	A	$50	8 minutes	2.5 kg	×
②	B	$80	12 minutes	2.0 kg	○
✓③	C	$100	15 minutes	1.8 kg	○
④	D	$120	20 minutes	1.8 kg	×
⑤	E	$150	25 minutes	1.6 kg	○

W : Ben, do you have a minute?
　Ben, 잠깐 시간 돼?
M : Sure. What is it?
　응. 왜?
W : I'm trying to buy a handheld vacuum cleaner among these five models. Could you help me choose one?
　난 소형 진공청소기를 이 다섯 개 제품 중에 사려고 해. 내가 하나 고르는 걸 도와줄래?
M : Okay. 「How much are you willing to spend?
　그래. 얼마나 쓸 생각이야?
W : No more than $130.」 **근거1** Price 조건
　130달러 이하로.
M : Then we can cross this one out. 「What about the working time?
　그럼 이거는 빼야겠다. 작동 시간은?
W : I think it should be longer than 10 minutes.」 **근거2** Working Time 조건
　10분 이상은 돼야 할 것 같아.
M : Then that narrows it down to these three.
　그럼 이 세 개로 좁혀지네.
W : 「Should I go with one of the lighter ones?
　내가 좀 가벼운 것 중에 골라야 할까?
M : Yes. Lighter ones are easier to handle while cleaning.」 **근거3** Weight 조건
　응, 더 가벼운 게 청소할 때 들고 있기 더 편하니까.
W : All right. 「What about the filter?
　그래. 필터는 어쩌지?
M : The one with a washable filter would be a better choice.」 **근거4** Washable Filter 조건
　씻어 쓸 수 있는 필터가 더 좋은 선택일 거야.
W : I got it. Then I'll order this one.
　알겠어. 그럼 이걸로 주문할래.

Why? 왜 정답일까?

대화에 따르면 여자는 가격이 130달러를 넘지 않으면서, 작동 시간은 10분 이상이고 무게는 가벼운 것으로, 필터는 씻어 쓸 수 있는 청소기를 고르려고 한다. 따라서 여자가 주문할 소형 진공청소기는 ③ 'C'이다.

- handheld ⓐ 손에 들고 쓰는
- narrow down to ~로 좁히다
- cross out (선을 그어) 지우다

---

11 먼지로 눈이 아플 때 어떻게 할지 묻기 정답률 76% | 정답 ①

대화를 듣고, 남자의 마지막 말에 대한 여자의 응답으로 가장 적절한 것을 고르시오.

✓① Why don't you rinse your eyes with clean water? – 깨끗한 물로 눈을 좀 헹구면 어때?
② Can you explain more about the air pollution? – 대기 오염에 대해 더 설명해 줄래?
③ I need to get myself a new pair of glasses. – 나는 새 안경을 하나 사야겠어.
④ I agree that fine dust is a serious problem. – 나는 미세먼지는 심각한 문제라는 데 동의해.
⑤ We should go outside and take a walk. – 우리는 밖에 좀 나가서 산책을 해야겠어.

M : My eyes are sore today.
　오늘 눈이 따갑네.
W : Too bad. Maybe some dust got in your eyes.
　딱해라. 아마 눈에 먼지가 좀 들어갔나봐.
M : You're probably right. What should I do?
　네 말이 맞을 수도 있겠네. 어떻게 하지?
W : Why don't you rinse your eyes with clean water?
　깨끗한 물로 눈을 좀 헹구면 어때?

Why? 왜 정답일까?

눈에 먼지가 들어가서 따가운가보다는 여자의 말에 남자는 어떻게 해야 할지 묻고 있으므로(What should I do?), 여자의 응답으로 가장 적절한 것은 ① '깨끗한 물로 눈을 좀 헹구면 어때?'이다.

- sore ⓐ 따가운, 아픈, 화끈거리는
- rinse ⓥ 헹구다

---

12 옆자리가 비었는지 물어보기 정답률 77% | 정답 ⑤

대화를 듣고, 여자의 마지막 말에 대한 남자의 응답으로 가장 적절한 것을 고르시오.

① That's not fair. I booked this seat first. – 공평하지 않아. 내가 이 자리를 먼저 예약했어요.
② Thank you. My friend will be glad to know it. – 고맙습니다. 제 친구가 알면 좋아할 거예요.
③ You're welcome. Feel free to ask me anything. – 천만에요. 어떤 것이든 편하게 물어보세요.
④ Not at all. I don't mind changing seats with you. – 아니에요. 당신과 자리를 바꿔도 괜찮아요.
✓⑤ That's okay. I think the seat next to it is available. – 괜찮아요. 그 옆자리는 비어 있는 것 같아요.

W : Excuse me. Would you mind if I sit here?
　실례합니다. 여기 좀 앉아도 될까요?
M : I'm sorry, but it's my friend's seat. He'll be back in a minute.
　죄송하지만, 제 친구 자리예요. 조금 있으면 돌아올 거예요.
W : Oh, I didn't know that. Sorry for bothering you.
　오, 제가 몰랐네요. 귀찮게 해 드려서 죄송해요.
M : That's okay. I think the seat next to it is available.
　괜찮아요. 그 옆자리는 비어 있는 것 같아요.

Why? 왜 정답일까?

여자는 남자의 옆자리에 앉으려고 했다가 친구 자리라는 답을 듣고 귀찮게 해 미안하다며(Sorry for bothering you.) 사과하고 있다. 따라서 남자의 응답으로 가장 적절한 것은 ⑤ '괜찮아요. 그 옆자리는 비어 있는 것 같아요.'이다.

- Would you mind if~? ~해도 괜찮을까요?
- feel free to 편하게 ~하다
- bother ⓥ 귀찮게 하다, 성가시게 하다

---

13 야구 경기 함께 보기로 약속하기 정답률 93% | 정답 ②

대화를 듣고, 남자의 마지막 말에 대한 여자의 응답으로 가장 적절한 것을 고르시오.
Woman:

① Smells good. Can I try the pizza? – 냄새 좋네. 나 피자 좀 먹어도 돼?
✓② Great. I'll bring chips and popcorn. – 좋아. 내가 과자랑 팝콘 좀 가져갈게.
③ No problem. I'll cancel the tickets. – 문제 없어. 내가 표를 취소할게.
④ Sorry. I don't like watching baseball. – 미안해. 난 야구 보는 거 안 좋아해.
⑤ Sure. Here's the hammer I borrowed. – 물론이지. 여기 내가 빌려갔던 망치야.

M : Hey, Jasmine.
　안녕, Jasmine.
W : Hi, Kurt. Are you going to be at home tomorrow afternoon?
　안녕, Kurt. 너 내일 오후에 집에 있을 거야?
M : Yeah, I'm going to watch the baseball game with my friends at home.
　응, 내 친구들이랑 집에서 야구 경기 볼 거야.
W : Good. Can I drop by your house and give you back the hammer I borrowed?
　잘됐다. 나 너네 집에 들러서 내가 빌려갔던 망치 돌려줘도 돼?
M : Sure. Come over any time. By the way, why don't you join us and watch the game?
　물론이지. 아무 때나 들러. 그런데, 우리랑 함께 경기 보면 어때?
W : I'd love to. Which teams are playing?
　좋지. 어느 팀이 경기해?
M : Green Thunders and Black Dragons.
　Green Thunders랑 Black Dragons 경기야.
W : That'll be exciting. What time should I come?
　재미있겠네. 몇 시에 갈까?
M : Come at five. We'll have pizza before the game.
　5시에 와. 우린 경기 전에 피자를 먹을 거야.
W : Perfect. Do you want me to bring anything?
　완벽해. 내가 뭐 좀 가져갈까?
M : Maybe some snacks to eat while watching the game.
　경기 보면서 먹을 간식이 좋을 것 같아.
W : Great. I'll bring chips and popcorn.
　좋아. 내가 과자랑 팝콘 좀 가져갈게.

Why? 왜 정답일까?

남자네 집에 들러서 야구를 함께 보기로 한 여자에게 남자는 간식 거리를 좀 가져오면 좋겠다고 하므로(Maybe some snacks to eat while watching the game.), 여자의 응답으로 가장 적절한 것은 ② '좋아. 내가 과자랑 팝콘 좀 가져갈게.'이다.

- drop by ~에 들르다
- give back ~을 돌려주다
- by the way (화제를 전환하며) 그나저나, 그런데

---

14 독서 동아리 가입 권하기 정답률 93% | 정답 ②

대화를 듣고, 여자의 마지막 말에 대한 남자의 응답으로 가장 적절한 것을 고르시오. [3점]
Man: _____

① Exactly. This is a best-selling novel. – 바로 그거야. 그건 베스트셀러 소설이야.
✓② Sounds cool. I'll join a book club, too. – 괜찮을 것 같다. 나도 독서 동아리에 들래.
③ Not really. Books make good presents. – 별로 그렇지 않아. 책은 좋은 선물이 되지.
④ New year's resolutions are hard to keep. – 새해 다짐은 지키기 힘들어.
⑤ Let's buy some books for your book club. – 너네 독서 동아리를 위해 책을 좀 사자.

W : Hi, Tom.
　안녕, Tom.
M : Hi, Jane. What are you reading?
　안녕, Jane. 뭘 읽고 있어?

W : It's a novel by Charles Dickens. I'm going to talk about it with my book club members this weekend.
Charles Dickens의 소설이야. 이번 주말에 우리 독서 동아리 회원들하고 이 책에 대해서 이야기할 거야.

M : Oh, you're in a book club?
오, 너 독서 동아리였어?

W : Yes. I joined it a few months ago. And now I read much more than before.
응. 몇 달 전에 가입했어. 그래서 요새 전보다 훨씬 많은 책을 읽고 있어.

M : Really? Actually one of my new year's resolutions is to read more books.
진짜? 사실 내 새해 결심 중 하나가 책을 더 많이 읽는 거야.

W : Then, joining a book club will surely help.
그럼 독서 동아리 드는 게 분명 도움이 될 거야.

M : Hmm.... What other benefits can I get if I join one?
흠... 내가 동아리에 들면 얻을 수 있는 이점이 또 뭐가 있지?

W : You can also share your reading experiences with others.
네 독서 경험을 다른 사람들하고 공유할 수도 있어.

M : That'd be nice.
그거 괜찮네.

W : Yeah, it really broadens your mind. I really recommend you to join a book club.
응. 그건 정말 시각을 넓혀 줘. 난 네가 독서 동아리에 드는 걸 정말 추천해.

M : Sounds cool. I'll join a book club, too.
괜찮을 것 같다. 나도 독서 동아리에 들래.

Why? 왜 정답일까?

여자는 독서 동아리에 들었을 때의 장점을 열거하면서 남자에게 동아리에 들 것을 권하므로(I really recommend you to join a book club.), 남자의 응답으로 가장 적절한 것은 ② '괜찮을 것 같다. 나도 독서 동아리에 들래.'이다.

- resolution ⓝ 다짐, 결심
- broaden ⓥ 넓히다, 확장하다
- benefit ⓝ 이점

---

15 안내견을 함부로 만지지 않기 정답률 89% | 정답 ①

다음 상황 설명을 듣고, Brian이 Sally에게 할 말로 가장 적절한 것을 고르시오. [3점]
Brian:
✔ You shouldn't touch a guide dog without permission. – 안내견을 허락 없이 만져서는 안 돼.
② The dog would be happy if we give it some food. – 우리가 음식을 좀 주면 개가 좋아할 거야.
③ I'm sure it's smart enough to be a guide dog. – 분명 이 개는 안내견이 될 만큼 충분히 똑똑한가봐.
④ I suggest that you walk your dog every day. – 너희 개를 매날 산책시키라고 제안하겠어.
⑤ I'm afraid that dogs are not allowed in here. – 유감이지만 개는 여기 들일 수 없어.

M : Brian and Sally are walking down the street together.
Brian과 Sally는 함께 거리를 걷고 있다.
A blind man and his guide dog are walking towards them.
시각 장애인과 안내견이 그들을 향해 걸어오고 있다.
Sally likes dogs very much, so she reaches out to touch the guide dog.
Sally는 개를 무척 좋아해서, 안내견을 만지려고 손을 뻗는다.
Brian doesn't think that Sally should do that.
Brian은 Sally가 그렇게 하면 안 된다고 생각한다.
The guide dog needs to concentrate on guiding the blind person.
안내견은 시각 장애인을 안내하는 데 집중해야 한다.
If someone touches the dog, the dog can lose its focus.
만일 누군가 그 개를 만지면, 개는 집중력이 흐트러질 수 있다.
So Brian wants to tell Sally not to touch the guide dog without the permission of the dog owner.
그래서 Brian은 Sally에게 개 주인의 허락 없이 안내견을 만지지 말라고 말하고 싶다.
In this situation, what would Brian most likely say to Sally?
이 상황에서, Brian은 Sally에게 뭐라고 말할 것인가?
Brian : You shouldn't touch a guide dog without permission.
안내견을 허락 없이 만져서는 안 돼.

Why? 왜 정답일까?

상황에 따르면 Brian은 안내견을 만지려는 Sally에게 주인의 허락 없이 만져서는 안 된다고 말해 주려 한다(So Brian wants to tell Sally not to touch the guide dog without the permission of the dog owner.). 따라서 Brian이 Sally에게 할 말로 가장 적절한 것은 ① '안내견을 허락 없이 만져서는 안 돼.'이다.

- reach out (손을) 뻗다
- lose one's focus 집중력을 잃다, 초점을 잃다
- concentrate on ~에 집중하다
- permission ⓝ 허락

16-17 관절에 무리가 되지 않는 운동 소개

W : Hello, everybody. Welcome to the health workshop.
안녕하세요, 여러분. 헬스 워크숍에 잘 오셨습니다.
I'm Alanna Reyes, the head trainer from Eastwood Fitness Center.
저는 Eastwood Fitness Center의 수석 트레이너 Alanna Reyes입니다.
As you know, joints are body parts that link bones together.
아시다시피, 관절은 뼈를 함께 연결해주는 신체 부위입니다.
And doing certain physical activities puts stress on the joints.
그리고 특정한 신체 활동을 하는 것은 관절에 무리를 줍니다.
「But the good news is that people with bad joints can still do certain exercises.」
하지만 좋은 소식은 관절이 안 좋은 사람들도 여전히 특정 운동을 할 수 있다는 겁니다.
They have relatively low impact on the joints.
그것들은 관절에 상대적으로 적은 충격을 줍니다.
Here are some examples.」 **16번의 근거**
여기 몇 가지 예가 있습니다.
「The first is swimming.」 **17번 ①의 근거** 일치
첫째는 수영입니다.
While swimming, the water supports your body weight.
수영 중에는, 물이 여러분의 체중을 받쳐줍니다.
「The second is cycling.」 **17번 ②의 근거** 일치
두 번째는 사이클입니다.
You put almost no stress on the knee joints when you pedal smoothly.

페달을 부드럽게 밟을 때에는 무릎 관절에 거의 무리가 가지 않습니다.
「Horseback riding is another exercise that puts very little stress on your knees.」 **17번 ③의 근거** 일치
승마도 무릎에 거의 무리가 가지 않는 또 하나의 운동입니다.
「Lastly, walking is great because it's low-impact, unlike running.」 **17번 ⑤의 근거** 일치
마지막으로 걷기도 좋은데, 뛰는 것과는 달리 충격이 적기 때문입니다.
If you have bad joints, don't give up exercising.
관절이 나빠도, 운동을 포기하지 마세요.
Instead, stay active and stay healthy!
그 대신, 계속 활동하고 건강을 유지하세요!

- joint ⓝ 관절
- relatively ⓐⓓ 상대적으로, 비교적
- smoothly ⓐⓓ 부드럽게
- put stress on ~에 무리를 주다
- impact ⓝ 충격, 영향

---

16 주제 파악 정답률 76% | 정답 ④

여자가 하는 말의 주제로 가장 적절한 것은?
① activities that help build muscles – 근육을 키우는 데 도움이 되는 활동
② ways to control stress in daily life – 일상 스트레스를 다스리는 방법
③ types of joint problems in elderly people – 노년층에서 나타나는 관절 문제의 종류
✔ low-impact exercises for people with bad joints – 관절이 약한 사람들을 위한 충격이 적은 운동
⑤ importance of daily exercise for controlling weight – 체중 조절을 위한 매일 운동의 중요성

Why? 왜 정답일까?

'But the good news is that people with bad joints can still do certain exercises.'와 'Here are some examples.'를 통해, 여자가 관절에 무리가 되지 않는 운동을 소개하려 함을 알 수 있으므로, 여자가 하는 말의 주제로 가장 적절한 것은 ④ '관절이 약한 사람들을 위한 충격이 적은 운동'이다.

---

17 언급 유무 파악 정답률 92% | 정답 ④

언급된 운동이 아닌 것은?
① swimming – 수영
② cycling – 사이클
③ horseback riding – 승마
✔ bowling – 볼링
⑤ walking – 걷기

Why? 왜 정답일까?

담화에서 여자는 관절에 무리가 되지 않는 운동의 예로 수영, 사이클, 승마, 걷기를 언급하므로, 언급되지 않은 것은 ④ '볼링'이다.

Why? 왜 오답일까?

① 'The first is swimming.'에서 '수영'이 언급되었다.
② 'The second is cycling.'에서 '사이클'이 언급되었다.
③ 'Horseback riding is another exercise ~'에서 '승마'가 언급되었다.
⑤ 'Lastly, walking is great ~'에서 '걷기'가 언급되었다.

---

18 모금 음악회 참석 요청 정답률 87% | 정답 ②

다음 글의 목적으로 가장 적절한 것은?
① 합창 대회 결과를 공지하려고
② ✔ 모금 음악회 참석을 요청하려고
③ 음악회 개최 장소를 예약하려고
④ 합창곡 선정에 조언을 구하려고
⑤ 기부금 사용 내역을 보고하려고

Dear Ms. Robinson,
Robinson 씨께,
The Warblers Choir is happy to announce / that we are invited to compete in the International Young Choir Competition.
Warblers 합창단은 알려드리게 되어 기쁩니다. / 저희가 국제 청년 합창 대회에서 실력을 겨루도록 초청받은 사실을
The competition takes place in London on May 20.
대회는 5월 20일 런던에서 열립니다.
Though we wish to participate in the event, / we do not have the necessary funds to travel to London.
비록 저희는 대회에 참가하고 싶지만, / 저희에게는 런던에 가는 데 필요한 자금이 없습니다.
So we are kindly asking you to support us / by coming to our fundraising concert.
그래서 귀하께서 저희를 후원해 주시기를 정중하게 부탁드립니다. / 저희 모금 음악회에 참석하셔서
It will be held on March 26.
음악회는 3월 26일에 개최될 것입니다.
In this concert, / we shall be able to show you / how big our passion for music is.
이 음악회에서 / 저희는 귀하께 보여드릴 수 있을 것입니다. / 음악에 대한 저희의 열정이 얼마나 큰지
Thank you in advance / for your kind support and help.
미리 감사드립니다. / 귀하의 친절한 후원과 도움에 대해
Sincerely, // Arnold Reynolds
Arnold Reynolds 드림

Robinson 씨께,
저희 Warblers 합창단이 국제 청년 합창 대회에서 실력을 겨루도록 초청받은 사실을 알려드리게 되어 기쁩니다. 대회는 5월 20일 런던에서 열립니다. 비록 저희는 대회에 참가하고 싶지만, 런던에 가는 데 필요한 자금이 없습니다. 그래서 귀하께서 저희 모금 음악회에 참석하셔서 저희를 후원해 주시기를 정중하게 부탁드립니다. 음악회는 3월 26일에 개최될 것입니다. 이 음악회에서 음악에 대한 저희의 열정이 얼마나 큰지 귀하께 보여드릴 수 있을 것입니다. 귀하의 친절한 후원과 도움에 대해 미리 감사드립니다.

Arnold Reynolds 드림

Why? 왜 정답일까?

'So we are kindly asking you to support us by coming to our fundraising concert.'에서 모금 음악회에 참석하여 후원을 해주기를 바란다는 내용이 제시되므로, 글의 목적으로 가장 적절한 것은 ② '모금 음악회 참석을 요청하려고'이다.

- **compete in** ~에서 경쟁하다
- **support** ⓥ 후원하다 ⓝ 지지, 후원
- **passion** ⓝ 열정
- **take place** (행사 등이) 열리다
- **fundraising** ⓝ 모금
- **in advance** 미리

구문 풀이

8행 In this concert, we shall be able to show you how big our passion for music is.
4형식 동사 / 간접 목적어 / 직접목적어(간접의문문)

---

19 학업 최우수상을 받게 되어 기뻐하는 Zoe　　정답률 80% | 정답 ③

다음 글에 드러난 Zoe의 심경 변화로 가장 적절한 것은?

① hopeful → disappointed
　기대하는　실망한
✓③ nervous → delighted
　긴장한　기쁜
⑤ relaxed → proud
　느긋한　자랑스러운
② guilty → confident
　죄책감을 느끼는　자신 있는
④ angry → calm
　화난　평온한

The principal stepped on stage.
교장 선생님이 무대 위로 올라갔다.

"Now, I present this year's top academic award / to the student who has achieved the highest placing."
"이제, 저는 올해의 학업 최우수상을 수여합니다. / 최고 등수를 차지한 학생에게"

He smiled at the row of seats / where twelve finalists had gathered.
그는 좌석 열을 향해 미소를 지었다. / 열두 명의 최종 입상 후보자가 모여 있는

Zoe wiped a sweaty hand on her handkerchief / and glanced at the other finalists.
Zoe는 땀에 젖은 손을 손수건에 문질러 닦고는 / 나머지 다른 최종 입상 후보자들을 힐끗 보았다.

They all looked as pale and uneasy as herself.
그들은 모두 그녀만큼 창백하고 불안해 보였다.

Zoe and one of the other finalists / had won first placing in four subjects / so it came down / to how teachers ranked their hard work and confidence.
Zoe와 나머지 다른 최종 입상 후보자 중 한 명이 / 네 개 과목에서 1위를 차지했으므로, / 이제 그것은 좁혀졌다. / 그들의 노력과 자신감을 선생님들이 어떻게 평가하는가로

"The Trophy for General Excellence / is awarded to Miss Zoe Perry," / the principal declared.
"전체 최우수상을 위한 트로피는 / Zoe Perry 양에게 수여됩니다."라고 / 교장 선생님이 공표했다.

"Could Zoe step this way, please?"
"Zoe는 이리로 나와 주시겠습니까?"

Zoe felt as if she were in heaven.
Zoe는 마치 천국에 있는 기분이었다.

She walked into the thunder of applause with a big smile.
그녀는 활짝 웃음을 지으며 우레와 같은 박수갈채를 받으며 걸어갔다.

교장 선생님이 무대 위로 올라갔다. "이제, 최고 등수를 차지한 학생에게 올해의 학업 최우수상을 수여하겠습니다." 그는 열두 명의 최종 입상 후보자가 모여 있는 좌석 열을 향해 미소를 지었다. Zoe는 땀에 젖은 손을 손수건에 문질러 닦고는 나머지 다른 최종 입상 후보자들을 힐끗 보았다. 그들은 모두 그녀만큼 창백하고 불안해 보였다. Zoe와 나머지 다른 최종 입상 후보자 중 한 명이 네 개 과목에서 1위를 차지했으므로, 선생님들이 그들의 노력과 자신감을 어떻게 평가하는가로 좁혀졌다. "전체 최우수상 트로피는 Zoe Perry 양에게 수여됩니다."라고 교장 선생님이 공표했다. "Zoe는 이리로 나와 주시겠습니까?" Zoe는 마치 천국에 있는 기분이었다. 그녀는 활짝 웃음을 지으며 우레와 같은 박수갈채를 받으며 걸어갔다.

Why? 왜 정답일까?

학업 최우수상 수상자 발표를 앞두고 긴장했던(Zoe wiped a sweaty hand ~. ~ pale and uneasy as herself.) Zoe가 수상자로 호명된 뒤 기뻐했다(Zoe felt as if she were in heaven. She ~ with a big smile.)는 내용의 글이므로, Zoe의 심경 변화로 가장 적절한 것은 ③ '긴장한 → 기쁜'이다.

- **row** ⓝ 줄, 열
- **gather** ⓥ 모이다
- **sweaty** ⓐ 땀에 젖은
- **pale** ⓐ 창백한
- **confidence** ⓝ 자신감
- **finalist** ⓝ 최종 후보자, 결승 진출자
- **wipe** ⓥ 닦다
- **glance at** ~을 흘긋 보다
- **uneasy** ⓐ 불안한
- **applause** ⓝ 박수 갈채

구문 풀이

10행 Zoe felt as if she were in heaven.
「as if + 주어 + 과거 동사 : (실제로 ~이지 않지만) 마치 ~인 것처럼」

---

20 작은 일부터 잘 처리하기　　정답률 87% | 정답 ⑤

다음 글에서 필자가 주장하는 바로 가장 적절한 것은?

① 숙면을 위해서는 침대를 깔끔하게 관리해야 한다.
② 일의 효율성을 높이려면 협동심을 발휘해야 한다.
③ 올바른 습관을 기르려면 정해진 규칙을 따라야 한다.
④ 건강을 유지하기 위해서는 기상 시간이 일정해야 한다.
✓⑤ 큰일을 잘 이루려면 작은 일부터 제대로 수행해야 한다.

When I was in the army, / my instructors would show up in my barracks room, / and the first thing they would inspect / was our bed.
내가 군대에 있을 때, / 교관들이 나의 병영 생활관에 모습을 드러내곤 했었는데, / 그들이 맨 먼저 검사하곤 했던 것은 / 우리의 침대였다.

It was a simple task, / but every morning / we were required / to make our bed to perfection.
단순한 일이었지만, / 매일 아침 / 우리는 요구받았다. / 침대를 완벽하게 정돈하도록

It seemed a little ridiculous at the time, / but the wisdom of this simple act / has been proven to me many times over.
그것은 그 당시에는 약간 우스꽝스럽게 보였지만, / 이 단순한 행위의 지혜는 / 여러 차례 거듭하여 나에게 증명되었다.

If you make your bed every morning, / you will have accomplished the first task of the day.
그것은 여러분이 매일 아침 침대를 정돈한다면, / 여러분은 하루의 첫 번째 과업을 성취한 것이 된다.

It will give you a small sense of pride / and it will encourage you to do another task and another.
그것은 여러분에게 작은 자존감을 주고, / 그것은 또 다른 과업을 잇따라 이어가도록 용기를 줄 것이다.

By the end of the day, / that one task completed / will have turned into many tasks completed.
하루가 끝날 때쯤에는, / 완수된 그 하나의 과업이 / 여러 개의 완수된 과업으로 변해 있을 것이다.

If you can't do little things right, / you will never do the big things right.
여러분이 작은 일들을 제대로 할 수 없으면, / 여러분은 결코 큰일들을 제대로 할 수 없을 것이다.

내가 군대에 있을 때, 교관들이 나의 병영 생활관에 모습을 드러내곤 했었는데, 그들이 맨 먼저 검사하곤 했던 것은 우리의 침대였다. 단순한 일이었지만, 매일 아침 우리는 침대를 완벽하게 정돈하도록 요구받았다. 그 당시에는 약간 우스꽝스럽게 보였지만, 이 단순한 행위의 지혜는 여러 차례 거듭하여 나에게 증명되었다. 여러분이 매일 아침 침대를 정돈한다면, 여러분은 하루의 첫 번째 과업을 성취한 것이 된다. 그것은 여러분에게 작은 자존감을 주고, 또 다른 과업을 잇따라 이어가도록 용기를 줄 것이다. 하루가 끝날 때쯤에는, 완수된 그 하나의 과업이 여러 개의 완수된 과업으로 변해 있을 것이다. 작은 일들을 제대로 할 수 없으면, 여러분은 결코 큰일들을 제대로 할 수 없을 것이다.

Why? 왜 정답일까?

매일 잠자리 정돈부터 잘해야 했던 군대 시절 이야기를 토대로 작은 일부터 잘 해내야 큰일을 처리할 수 있다(If you can't do little things right, you will never do the big things right.)는 결론을 이끌어내는 글이다. 따라서 필자의 주장으로 가장 적절한 것은 ⑤ '큰일을 잘 이루려면 작은 일부터 제대로 수행해야 한다.'이다.

- **inspect** ⓥ 조사하다
- **make the bed** 잠자리를 정돈하다
- **wisdom** ⓝ 지혜
- **turn into** ~로 바뀌다
- **task** ⓝ 일, 과업, 과제
- **ridiculous** ⓐ 우스꽝스러운
- **complete** ⓥ 완수하다

구문 풀이

6행 If you make your bed every morning, you will have accomplished the first task of the day.
접속사(조건) / 동사(현재) / 동사(미래완료)

---

21 적극적으로 구직 활동하기　　정답률 58% | 정답 ⑤

밑줄 친 Leave those activities to the rest of the sheep이 다음 글에서 의미하는 바로 가장 적절한 것은? [3점]

① Try to understand other job-seekers' feelings.
　다른 구직자들의 심정을 이해하려고 노력해보라.
② Keep calm and stick to your present position.
　평정심을 유지하고 현재 입장을 지켜라.
③ Don't be scared of the job-seeking competition.
　구직 경쟁을 두려워하지 말라.
④ Send occasional emails to your future employers.
　미래 고용주들에게 가끔 이메일을 보내라.
✓⑤ Be more active to stand out from other job-seekers.
　다른 구직자들보다 두드러지기 위해 더 적극적으로 하라.

A job search is not a passive task.
구직 활동은 수동적인 일이 아니다.

When you are searching, / you are not browsing, / nor are you "just looking".
여러분이 구직 활동을 할 때, / 여러분은 이것저것 훑어보고 다니지 않으며 / '그냥 구경만 하지'도 않는다.

Browsing is not an effective way / to reach a goal / you claim to want to reach.
훑어보고 다니는 것은 효과적인 방법이 아니다. / 목표에 도달할 수 있는 / 여러분이 도달하기를 원한다고 주장하는

If you are acting with purpose, / if you are serious about anything you chose to do, / then you need to be direct, / focused / and whenever possible, / clever.
만약 여러분이 목적을 가지고 행동한다면, / 만약 여러분이 하고자 선택한 어떤 것에 대해 진지하다면, / 여러분은 직접적이고, / 집중해야 하며, / 가능한 모든 경우에, / 영리해야 한다.

Everyone else searching for a job / has the same goal, / competing for the same jobs.
일자리를 찾는 다른 모든 사람이 / 같은 목표를 지니고 있으며, / 같은 일자리를 얻기 위해 경쟁한다.

You must do more than the rest of the herd.
여러분은 그 무리의 나머지 사람들보다 더 많은 것을 해야 한다.

Regardless of how long it may take you / to find and get the job you want, / being proactive will logically get you results faster / than if you rely only on browsing online job boards / and emailing an occasional resume.
여러분에게 얼마나 오랜 시간이 걸리든 간에, / 원하는 직업을 찾아서 얻는 데 / 진취적인 것이 논리적으로 여러분에게 더 빨리 결과를 가져다줄 것이다. / 여러분이 온라인 취업 게시판을 검색하는 것보다는 / 그리고 가끔 이력서를 이메일로 보내는 것

Leave those activities to the rest of the sheep.
그런 활동들은 나머지 양들이 하도록 남겨 두라.

구직 활동은 수동적인 일이 아니다. 구직 활동을 할 때, 여러분은 이것저것 훑어보고 다니지 않으며 '그냥 구경만 하지'도 않는다. 훑어보고 다니는 것은 여러분이 도달하기를 원한다고 주장하는 목표에 도달할 수 있는 효과적인 방법이 아니다. 만약 여러분이 목적을 가지고 행동한다면, 하고자 선택한 어떤 것에 대해 진지하다면, 여러분은 직접적이고, 집중해야 하며, 가능한 한 영리해야 한다. 일자리를 찾는 다른 모든 사람이 같은 목표를 지니고 있으며, 같은 일자리를 얻기 위해 경쟁한다. 여러분은 그 무리의 나머지 사람들보다 더 많은 것을 해야 한다. 원하는 직업을 찾아서 얻는 데 얼마나 오랜 시간이 걸리든 간에, 온라인 취업 게시판을 검색하고 가끔 이력서를 이메일로 보내는 것에만 의존하는 것보다는 진취적인 것이 논리적으로 여러분이 더 빨리 결과를 얻도록 해줄 것이다. 그런 활동들은 나머지 양들이 하도록 남겨 두라.

Why? 왜 정답일까?

마지막 문장 바로 앞에서 온라인 취업 게시판을 검색하고 가끔 이메일을 보내는 것보다 더 적극적인 행동을 해야 한다(being proactive will ~ get you results faster)고 언급한 뒤, 마지막 문장에서는 비교적 소극적인 행동은 남들더러 하게 두라고 말하며 적극적인 행동의 필요성을 다시금 주장한다. 따라서 밑줄 친 부분의 의미로 가장 적절한 것은 ⑤ '다른 구직자들보다 두드러지기 위해 더 적극적으로 하라.'이다.

- **passive** ⓐ 수동적인
- **herd** ⓝ 무리
- **proactive** ⓐ 상황을 앞서서 주도하는
- **occasional** ⓐ 가끔씩의
- **stand out from** ~에서 두드러지다
- **claim** ⓥ 주장하다
- **regardless of** ~와 상관없이
- **logically** ad 논리적으로
- **resume** ⓝ 이력서

1행 When you are searching, you are not browsing, nor are you "just looking".
「nor + 동사 + 주어 : ~도 않다(도치 구문)」

---

22 수면의 중요한 기능 정답률 92% | 정답 ①

다음 글의 요지로 가장 적절한 것은?
☑ 수면은 건강 유지와 최상의 기능 발휘에 도움이 된다.
② 업무량이 증가하면 필요한 수면 시간도 증가한다.
③ 균형 잡힌 식단을 유지하면 뇌 기능이 향상된다.
④ 불면증은 주위 사람들에게 부정적인 영향을 미친다.
⑤ 꿈의 내용은 깨어 있는 시간 동안의 경험을 반영한다.

Many people view sleep as merely a "down time" / when their brain shuts off and their body rests.
많은 사람이 수면을 그저 '가동되지 않는 시간'으로 본다. / 그들의 뇌는 멈추고 신체는 쉬는

In a rush to meet work, school, family, or household responsibilities, / people cut back on their sleep, / thinking it won't be a problem, / because all of these other activities seem much more important.
일, 학교, 가족, 또는 가정의 책임을 다하기 위해 서두르는 와중에, / 사람들은 수면 시간을 줄이고, / 그것이 문제가 되지 않을 것으로 생각하는데, / 왜냐하면 이러한 모든 다른 활동들이 훨씬 더 중요해 보이기 때문이다.

But research reveals / that a number of vital tasks carried out during sleep / help to maintain good health / and enable people to function at their best.
하지만 연구는 밝히고 있다. / 수면 중에 수행되는 많은 매우 중요한 과업이 / 건강을 유지하는 데 도움이 되고 / 사람들이 최상의 수준으로 기능할 수 있게 해 준다는 것

While you sleep, / your brain is hard at work / forming the pathways / necessary for learning and creating memories and new insights.
여러분이 잠을 자는 동안, / 여러분의 뇌는 열심히 일하고 있다. / 경로를 형성하느라 / 학습하고 기억과 새로운 통찰을 만드는 데 필요한

Without enough sleep, / you can't focus and pay attention / or respond quickly.
충분한 수면이 없다면, / 여러분은 정신을 집중하고 주의를 기울이거나 / 빠르게 반응할 수 없다.

A lack of sleep may even cause mood problems.
수면 부족은 심지어 감정 문제를 일으킬 수도 있다.

In addition, / growing evidence shows / that a continuous lack of sleep / increases the risk for developing serious diseases.
게다가, / 점점 더 많은 증거가 보여 준다. / 계속된 수면 부족이 / 심각한 질병의 발생 위험을 증가시킨다는 것

많은 사람이 수면을 그저 뇌는 멈추고 신체는 쉬는 '가동되지 않는 시간'으로 본다. 일, 학교, 가족, 또는 가정의 책임을 다하기 위해 서두르는 와중에, 사람들은 수면 시간을 줄이고, 그것이 문제가 되지 않을 것으로 생각하는데, 왜냐하면 이러한 모든 다른 활동들이 훨씬 더 중요해 보이기 때문이다. 하지만 연구는 수면 중에 수행되는 매우 중요한 여러 과업이 건강을 유지하는 데 도움이 되고 사람들이 최상의 수준으로 기능할 수 있게 해 준다는 것을 밝히고 있다. 잠을 자는 동안, 여러분의 뇌는 학습하고 기억과 새로운 통찰을 만드는 데 필요한 경로를 형성하느라 열심히 일하고 있다. 충분한 수면이 없다면, 여러분은 정신을 집중하고 주의를 기울이거나 빠르게 반응할 수 없다. 수면이 부족하면 심지어 감정 (조절) 문제를 일으킬 수도 있다. 게다가, 계속된 수면 부족이 심각한 질병의 발생 위험을 증가시킨다는 것을 점점 더 많은 증거가 보여 준다.

Why? 왜 정답일까?
주제를 제시하는 'But ~ a number of vital tasks carried out during sleep help to maintain good health and enable people to function at their best.'에서 수면 중 이루어지는 많은 일이 건강 및 기능 유지에 도움이 된다고 하므로, 글의 요지로 가장 적절한 것은 ① '수면은 건강 유지와 최상의 기능 발휘에 도움이 된다.'이다.

● view A as B A를 B로 보다
● down time 정지 시간, 휴식 시간
● carry out ~을 수행하다
● develop a disease 병을 키우다
● merely ad 그저, 단순히
● cut back on ~을 줄이다
● insight n 통찰력

5행 But research reveals that a number of vital tasks carried out during sleep help to maintain good health and enable people to function at their best.
접속사(~것) 주어(a number of + 복수 명사 : 많은 ~) 과거분사구
동사1 목적어 동사2 목적어 목적격 보어

---

23 미래 날씨 예측에 영향을 받는 인간의 생활 정답률 63% | 정답 ④

다음 글의 주제로 가장 적절한 것은? [3점]
① new technologies dealing with climate change
기후 변화에 대처하는 신기술
② difficulties in predicting the weather correctly
정확한 날씨 예측의 어려움
③ weather patterns influenced by rising temperatures
온도 상승에 영향을 받는 날씨 패턴
☑ knowledge of the climate widely affecting our lives
우리 삶에 광범위하게 영향을 미치는 기후에 관한 지식
⑤ traditional wisdom helping our survival in harsh climates
혹독한 기후에서 우리의 생존을 돕는 전통적 지혜

The whole of human society / operates on knowing the future weather.
전체 인간 사회는 / 미래의 날씨를 아는 것을 기반으로 운영된다.

For example, / farmers in India know / when the monsoon rains will come next year / and so they know when to plant the crops.
예를 들어, / 인도의 농부들은 알고, / 내년에 몬순 장마가 올 시기를 / 그래서 그들은 작물을 심을 시기를 안다.

Farmers in Indonesia know / there are two monsoon rains each year, / so next year they can have two harvests.
인도네시아의 농부들은 알고, / 매년 몬순 장마가 두 번 있다는 것을 / 그래서 이듬해에 그들은 수확을 두 번 할 수 있다.

This is based on their knowledge of the past, / as the monsoons have always come / at about the same time each year in living memory.
이것은 과거에 대한 그들의 지식에 기반을 두고 있는데, / 몬순은 항상 왔기 때문이다. / 살아 있는 기억 속에서 매년 거의 같은 시기에

But the need to predict goes deeper than this; / it influences every part of our lives.

그러나 예측할 필요는 이것보다 더욱더 깊어지는데 / 그것은 우리 생활의 모든 부분에 영향을 미치기 때문이다.

Our houses, roads, railways, airports, offices, and so on / are all designed for the local climate.
우리의 집, 도로, 철도, 공항, 사무실 등은 / 모두 지역의 기후에 맞추어 설계된다.

For example, / in England all the houses have central heating, / as the outside temperature is usually below 20℃, / but no air-conditioning, / as temperatures rarely go beyond 26℃, / while in Australia the opposite is true: / most houses have air-conditioning but rarely central heating.
예를 들어, / 영국에서는 모든 집은 중앙 난방을 갖추고 있지만, / 외부의 기온이 대체로 섭씨 20도 미만이기 때문에 / 냉방기는 없는 / 기온이 섭씨 26도 위로 올라가는 일은 거의 없어서 / 호주에서는 그 정반대가 사실인 반면에 / 대부분의 집은 냉방기를 갖추었지만 중앙 난방은 거의 없다.

전체 인간 사회는 미래의 날씨를 아는 것을 기반으로 운영된다. 예를 들어, 인도의 농부들은 내년에 몬순 장마가 올 시기를 알고, 그래서 그들은 작물을 심을 시기를 안다. 인도네시아의 농부들은 매년 몬순 장마가 두 번 있다는 것을 알고, 그래서 이듬해에 그들은 수확을 두 번 할 수 있다. 이것은 과거에 대한 그들의 지식에 기반을 두고 있는데, 살아 있는 기억 속에서 몬순은 매년 항상 거의 같은 시기에 왔기 때문이다. 그러나 예측할 필요는 이것보다 더욱더 깊어지는데, 그것은 우리 생활의 모든 부분에 영향을 미치기 때문이다. 우리의 집, 도로, 철도, 공항, 사무실 등은 모두 지역의 기후에 맞추어 설계된다. 예를 들어, 영국에서는 외부의 기온이 대체로 섭씨 20도 미만이기 때문에 모든 집은 중앙 난방을 갖추고 있지만, 기온이 섭씨 26도 위로 올라가는 일은 거의 없어서 냉방기는 없는 반면, 호주에서는 그 정반대가 사실이어서, 대부분의 집은 냉방기를 갖추었지만 중앙 난방은 거의 없다.

Why? 왜 정답일까?
첫 문장에서 인간 사회는 미래 날씨 예측에 기반하여 운영된다(The whole of human society operates on knowing the future weather.)는 중심 내용을 제시하는 것으로 보아, 글의 주제로 가장 적절한 것은 ④ '우리 삶에 광범위하게 영향을 미치는 기후에 관한 지식'이다.

● monsoon n (동남아 여름철의) 몬순, 우기, 장마
● predict v 예측하다
● harsh a 혹독한
● harvest n 수확
● influence v 영향을 미치다

2행 For example, farmers in India know when the monsoon rains will come next year and so they know when to plant the crops.
주어1 동사1 목적어1(간접의문문)
주어2 동사2 목적어2(의문사 + to부정사)

---

24 감정을 인식하고 명명할 수 있는 능력 정답률 64% | 정답 ②

다음 글의 제목으로 가장 적절한 것은?
① True Friendship Endures Emotional Arguments – 진정한 우정은 감정적인 다툼을 견뎌낸다
☑ Detailed Labeling of Emotions Is Beneficial – 감정에 상세하게 이름을 붙이는 것은 이롭다
③ Labeling Emotions: Easier Said Than Done – 감정에 이름 붙이기: 말하기는 쉬워도 행하기는 어렵다
④ Categorize and Label Tasks for Efficiency – 효율성을 위해 작업을 분류하고 이름 붙여라
⑤ Be Brave and Communicate Your Needs – 용기를 갖고 여러분의 요구를 전달하라

Our ability to accurately recognize and label emotions / is often referred to as *emotional granularity*.
감정을 정확히 인식하고 그것에 이름을 붙일 수 있는 우리의 능력은 / 흔히 감정 입자도라고 불린다.

In the words of Harvard psychologist Susan David, / "Learning to label emotions / with a more nuanced vocabulary / can be absolutely transformative."
Harvard 대학의 심리학자인 Susan David의 말에 의하면, / "이름을 붙이는 법을 배우는 것은 / 감정에 더 미묘한 차이가 있는 어휘로 / 절대적으로 변화시킬 수 있다."

David explains / that if we don't have a rich emotional vocabulary, / it is difficult / to communicate our needs / and to get the support that we need from others.
David는 설명한다. / 우리가 풍부한 감정적인 어휘를 갖고 있지 않으면, / 어렵다고 / 우리의 욕구를 전달하는 것이 / 그리고 우리가 필요로 하는 지지를 다른 사람들로부터 얻는 것이

But those / who are able to distinguish between a range of various emotions / "do much, much better / at managing the ups and downs of ordinary existence / than those who see everything in black and white."
그러나 사람들은 / 광범위한 다양한 감정을 구별할 수 있는 / "훨씬, 훨씬 더 잘한다. / 평범한 존재로 사는 중에 겪는 좋은 일들과 궂은 일들을 다스리는 일을 / 모든 것을 흑백 논리로 보는 사람들보다"

In fact, / research shows / that the process of labeling emotional experience / is related to greater emotion regulation and psychosocial well-being.
사실, / 연구 결과가 보여 준다. / 감정적인 경험에 이름을 붙이는 과정은 / 더 큰 감정 통제 및 심리 사회적인 행복과 관련되어 있다는 것

감정을 정확하게 인식하고 그것에 이름을 붙일 수 있는 우리의 능력은 흔히 *감정 입자도*라고 불린다. Harvard 대학의 심리학자인 Susan David의 말에 의하면, "감정에 더 미묘한 차이가 있는 어휘로 이름을 붙이는 법을 배우는 것은 절대적으로 (사람을) 변화시킬 수 있다." David는 우리가 풍부한 감정적인 어휘를 갖고 있지 않으면, 우리의 욕구를 전달하고 다른 사람들로부터 우리가 필요로 하는 지지를 얻는 것이 어렵다고 설명한다. 그러나 광범위한 다양한 감정을 구별할 수 있는 사람들은 "모든 것을 흑백 논리로 보는 사람들보다 평범한 존재로 사는 중에 겪는 좋은 일들과 궂은 일들을 다스리는 일을 훨씬, 훨씬 더 잘한다." 사실, 감정적인 경험에 이름을 붙이는 과정은 더 큰 감정 통제 및 심리 사회적인 행복과 관련되어 있다는 것을 연구 결과가 보여 준다.

Why? 왜 정답일까?
마지막 문장에 따르면 감정적인 경험에 이름을 붙이는 것은 감정을 더 잘 통제하고 심리 사회적으로 더 큰 행복감을 느끼는 것과 관련되어 있다(~ the process of labeling emotional experience is related to greater emotion regulation and psychosocial well-being.)고 하므로, 글의 제목으로 가장 적절한 것은 ② '감정에 상세하게 이름을 붙이는 것은 이롭다'이다.

● accurately ad 정확하게
● absolutely ad 절대적으로
● communicate v 전달하다
● ups and downs 좋은 일과 궂은 일, 오르락내리락
● regulation n 통제
● refer to A as B A를 B라고 부르다
● transformative a 변화시키는
● distinguish v 구별하다
● existence n 존재
● psychosocial a 심리사회적인

구문 풀이

1행 Our ability to accurately recognize and label emotions is often referred to
주어 　형용사적 용법　　　　 동사(refer to A as B의 수동태)
as *emotional granularity*.

---

25 온라인 강의와 학습 자료를 이용한 영국인들의 비율
정답률 68% | 정답 ⑤

다음 도표의 내용과 일치하지 <u>않는</u> 것은?

Percentage of UK People
Who Used Online Course and Online Learning Material
(in 2020, by age group)

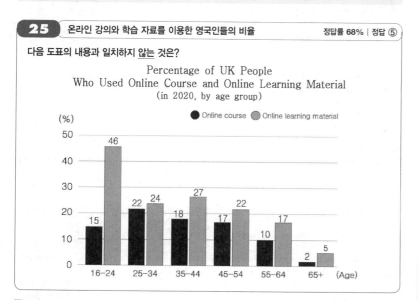

The above graph shows the percentage of people in the UK / who used online courses and online learning materials, / by age group / in 2020.
위 도표는 영국 사람들의 비율을 보여 준다. / 온라인 강의와 온라인 학습 자료를 이용한 / 연령 집단별로 / 2020년도에
① In each age group, / the percentage of people / who used online learning materials / was higher than that of people / who used online courses.
각 연령 집단에서, / 사람들의 비율이 / 온라인 학습 자료를 이용한 / 사람들의 비율보다 더 높았다. / 온라인 강의를 이용한
② The 25 − 34 age group / had the highest percentage of people / who used online courses / in all the age groups.
25세에서 34세 연령 집단에서, / 차이는 / 사람들의 비율과 / 온라인 강의를 이용한 / 모든 연령 집단 중
③ Those aged 65 and older / were the least likely to use online courses / among the six age groups.
65세 이상인 사람들이 / 온라인 강의를 이용할 가능성이 가장 낮았다. / 여섯 개의 연령 집단 가운데서
④ Among the six age groups, / the gap / between the percentage of people / who used online courses / and that of people who used online learning materials / was the greatest in the 16 − 24 age group.
여섯 개의 연령 집단 가운데서, / 차이는 / 사람들의 비율과 / 온라인 강의를 이용한 / 그리고 온라인 학습 자료를 이용한 사람들의 비율 사이의 / 16세와 24세 연령 집단에서 가장 컸다.
☑ In each of the 35 − 44, 45 − 54, and 55 − 64 age groups, / more than one in five people / used online learning materials.
35세에서 44세, 45세에서 54세, 55세에서 64세의 각 연령 집단에서 / 다섯 명 중 한 명이 넘는 비율의 사람들이 / 온라인 학습 자료를 이용했다.

위 도표는 2020년도에 온라인 강의와 온라인 학습 자료를 이용한 영국 사람들의 비율을 연령 집단별로 보여 준다. ① 각 연령 집단에서 온라인 학습 자료를 이용한 사람들의 비율이 온라인 강의를 이용한 사람들의 비율보다 더 높았다. ② 모든 연령 집단 중, 25세에서 34세 연령 집단에서 온라인 강의를 이용한 사람들의 비율이 가장 높았다. ③ 여섯 개의 연령 집단 가운데서, 65세 이상인 사람들이 온라인 강의를 이용할 가능성이 가장 낮았다. ④ 여섯 개의 연령 집단 가운데서, 온라인 강의를 이용한 사람들의 비율과 온라인 학습 자료를 이용한 사람들의 비율 차이는 16세에서 24세 연령 집단에서 가장 컸다. ⑤ 35세에서 44세, 45세에서 54세, 55세에서 64세의 각 연령 집단에서 다섯 명 중 한 명이 넘는 비율로 온라인 학습 자료를 이용했다.

Why? 왜 정답일까?
도표에 따르면 55~64세 집단에서 온라인 학습 자료를 이용한 비율은 17%로, 전체의 5분의 1에 미치지 못했다. 따라서 도표와 일치하지 않는 것은 ⑤이다.

● learning material 학습 자료　　　● be the least likely to ~할 가능성이 가장 낮다

---

26 Antonie van Leeuwenhoek의 생애
정답률 91% | 정답 ③

Antonie van Leeuwenhoek에 관한 다음 글의 내용과 일치하지 <u>않는</u> 것은?

① 세포 연구로 잘 알려진 과학자였다.
② 22살에 Delft로 돌아왔다.
☑ 여러 개의 언어를 알았다.
④ 유리로 물건을 만드는 방법을 알고 있었다.
⑤ 화가를 고용하여 설명하는 것을 그리게 했다.

『Antonie van Leeuwenhoek was a scientist / well known for his cell research.』 ①의 근거 일치
Antonie van Leeuwenhoek은 과학자였다. / 세포 연구로 잘 알려진
He was born in Delft, the Netherlands, / on October 24, 1632.
그는 네덜란드 Delft에서 태어났다. / 1632년 10월 24일에
At the age of 16, / he began to learn job skills in Amsterdam.
16살에 / 그는 Amsterdam에서 직업 기술을 배우기 시작했다.
『At the age of 22, / Leeuwenhoek returned to Delft.』 ②의 근거 일치
22살에 / Leeuwenhoek은 Delft로 돌아왔다.
It wasn't easy for Leeuwenhoek to become a scientist.
Leeuwenhoek이 과학자가 되기는 쉽지 않았다.
『He knew only one language — Dutch —』 ③의 근거 불일치 / which was quite unusual for scientists of his time.
그는 오직 한 가지 언어, 즉 네덜란드어만을 알고 있었는데, / 그것은 그 당시 과학자들에게는 상당히 드문 것이었다.
But his curiosity was endless, / and he worked hard.
하지만 그의 호기심은 끝이 없었고, / 그는 열심히 노력했다.
He had an important skill.
그에게는 중요한 기술이 있었다.

『He knew how to make things out of glass.』 ④의 근거 일치
그는 유리로 물건을 만드는 법을 알고 있었다.
This skill came in handy / when he made lenses for his simple microscope.
이 기술은 도움이 되었다. / 그가 자신의 간단한 현미경에 쓰일 렌즈를 만들 때
He saw tiny veins / with blood flowing through them.
그는 미세한 혈관을 보았다. / 그 속에 피가 흐르고 있는
He also saw living bacteria in pond water.
그는 또한 연못 물 속에서 살아 있는 박테리아를 보았다.
He paid close attention to the things he saw / and wrote down his observations.
그는 자신이 본 것들에 세심한 주의를 기울였고 / 그가 관찰한 것을 기록했다.
『Since he couldn't draw well, / he hired an artist / to draw pictures of what he described.』 ⑤의 근거 일치
그가 그림을 잘 그릴 수 없었기 때문에, / 그는 화가를 고용하여 / 자신이 설명하는 것을 그림으로 그리게 했다.

Antonie van Leeuwenhoek은 세포 연구로 잘 알려진 과학자였다. 그는 1632년 10월 24일 네덜란드 Delft에서 태어났다. 그는 16살에 Amsterdam에서 직업 기술을 배우기 시작했다. Leeuwenhoek은 22살에 Delft로 돌아왔다. Leeuwenhoek이 과학자가 되기는 쉽지 않았다. 그는 오직 한 가지 언어, 즉 네덜란드어만을 알고 있었는데, 그것은 그 당시 과학자들에게는 상당히 드문 것이었다. 하지만 그의 호기심은 끝이 없었고, 그는 열심히 노력했다. 그에게는 중요한 기술이 있었다. 그는 유리로 물건을 만드는 법을 알고 있었다. 이 기술은 그가 자신의 간단한 현미경에 쓰일 렌즈를 만들 때 도움이 되었다. 그는 피가 흐르고 있는 미세한 혈관을 보았다. 그는 또한 연못 물속에서 살아 있는 박테리아를 보았다. 그는 자신이 본 것들에 세심한 주의를 기울였고 관찰한 것을 기록했다. 그는 그림을 잘 그릴 수 없었기 때문에, 화가를 고용하여 자신이 설명하는 것을 그림으로 그리게 했다.

Why? 왜 정답일까?
'He knew only one language—Dutch ~'에서 Antonie van Leeuwenhoek는 오직 네덜란드어만 알았다고 하므로, 내용과 일치하지 않는 것은 ③ '여러 개의 언어를 알았다.'이다.

Why? 왜 오답일까?
① 'Antonie van Leeuwenhoek was a scientist well known for his cell research.'의 내용과 일치한다.
② 'At the age of 22, Leeuwenhoek returned to Delft.'의 내용과 일치한다.
④ 'He knew how to make things out of glass.'의 내용과 일치한다.
⑤ '~ he hired an artist to draw pictures of what he described.'의 내용과 일치한다.

● curiosity ⓝ 호기심　　　　　　　　● endless ⓐ 끝이 없는
● make A out of B B로 A를 만들다　　● microscope ⓝ 현미경
● pond ⓝ 연못　　　　　　　　　　　● observation ⓝ 관찰

구문 풀이

5행 He knew only one language — Dutch — which was quite unusual for
선행사(문장)　　　　　　 계속적 용법
scientists of his time.

---

27 꽃 교실 안내
정답률 95% | 정답 ④

Rachel's Flower Class에 관한 다음 안내문의 내용과 일치하지 <u>않는</u> 것은?

① 플라워 박스 만들기 수업은 오후 1시에 시작된다.
② 수강료에 꽃값과 다른 재료비가 포함된다.
③ 수강생은 가위와 가방을 가져와야 한다.
☑ 수업 등록은 전화로만 할 수 있다.
⑤ 수업 당일 취소 시 환불을 받을 수 없다.

Rachel's Flower Class
Rachel의 꽃 교실
Make Your Life More Beautiful!
인생을 더 아름답게 만드세요!
Class Schedule (Every Monday to Friday)
수업 일정 (매주 월요일부터 금요일까지)

Flower Arrangement 꽃꽂이	11 a.m. – 12 p.m. 오전 11시 ~ 정오
『Flower Box Making 플라워 박스 만들기	1 p.m. – 2 p.m. ①의 근거 일치 오후 1시 ~ 오후 2시

Price
가격
『$50 for each class (flowers and other materials included)』 ②의 근거 일치
각 수업당 $50 (꽃값과 다른 재료비 포함)
『Bring your own scissors and a bag.』 ③의 근거 일치
본인의 가위와 가방을 가져오세요.
Other Info.
다른 정보
『You can sign up for classes / either online or by phone.』 ④의 근거 불일치
수업 등록을 할 수 있습니다. / 온라인이나 전화로
『No refund for cancellations on the day of your class』 ⑤의 근거 일치
수업 당일 취소 시 환불 불가
To contact, / visit www.rfclass.com or call 03-221-2131.
연락하시려면, / www.rfclass.com을 방문하시거나 03-221-2131로 전화주세요.

Rachel의 꽃 교실

인생을 더 아름답게 만드세요!

수업 일정 (매주 월요일부터 금요일까지)

꽃꽂이	오전 11시 ~ 정오
플라워 박스 만들기	오후 1시 ~ 오후 2시

가격
• 각 수업당 $50 (꽃값과 다른 재료비 포함)

- 본인의 가위와 가방을 가져오세요.

다른 정보
- 온라인이나 전화로 수업 등록을 할 수 있습니다.
- 수업 당일 취소 시 환불 불가

연락하시려면, www.rfclass.com을 방문하시거나 03-221-2131로 전화주세요.

Why? 왜 정답일까?

'You can sign up for classes either online or by phone.'에서 수업 등록은 전화뿐 아니라 온라인으로도 가능하다고 하므로, 안내문의 내용과 일치하지 않는 것은 ④ '수업 등록은 전화로만 할 수 있다.'이다.

Why? 왜 오답일까?

① 'Flower Box Making / 01 p.m. – 02 p.m.'의 내용과 일치한다.
② '$50 for each class (flowers and other materials included)'의 내용과 일치한다.
③ 'Bring your own scissors and a bag.'의 내용과 일치한다.
⑤ 'No refund for cancellations on the day of your class'의 내용과 일치한다.

- flower arrangement 꽃꽂이
- sign up for ~에 등록하다

---

28 야간 궁궐 투어 안내 　　　　정답률 91% | 정답 ⑤

Nighttime Palace Tour에 관한 다음 안내문의 내용과 일치하는 것은?
① 금요일에는 하루에 두 번 투어가 운영된다.
② 8세 미만 어린이의 티켓은 5달러이다.
③ 예약은 투어 하루 전까지만 가능하다.
④ 투어 가이드의 안내 없이 궁궐을 둘러본다.
✔ 추가 비용 없이 전통 의상을 입어 볼 수 있다.

Nighttime Palace Tour
야간 궁궐 투어
Date: Friday, April 29 – Sunday, May 15
날짜: 4월 29일 금요일 ~ 5월 15일 일요일
Time
시간

『Friday』 금요일	7 p.m. – 8:30 p.m.』①의 근거 불일치 오후 7시 ~ 오후 8시 30분
Saturday & Sunday 토요일과 일요일	6 p.m. – 7:30 p.m. 오후 6시 ~ 오후 7시 30분
	8 p.m. – 9:30 p.m. 오후 8시 ~ 오후 9시 30분

Tickets & Booking
티켓과 예약
$15 per person 『free for kids under 8)』②의 근거 불일치
1인당 15달러 (8세 미만 어린이는 무료)
『Bookings will be accepted / up to 2 hours before the tour starts.』③의 근거 불일치
예약은 가능합니다. / 투어가 시작되기 2시간 전까지
Program Activities
프로그램 활동
『Group tour with a tour guide (1 hour)』④의 근거 불일치
투어 가이드와 단체 투어 (1시간)
Trying traditional foods and drinks (30 minutes)
전통 음식 시식 및 음료 시음 (30분)
『You can try on traditional clothes / with no extra charge.』⑤의 근거 일치
전통 의상을 입어 볼 수 있습니다. / 추가 비용 없이
For more information, / please visit our website, www.palacenighttour.com.
더 많은 정보를 원하시면, / 저희 웹 사이트 www.palacenighttour.com에 방문하세요.

야간 궁궐 투어

날짜: 4월 29일 금요일 ~ 5월 15일 일요일

시간

금요일	오후 7시 ~ 오후 8시 30분
토요일과 일요일	오후 6시 ~ 오후 7시 30분
	오후 8시 ~ 오후 9시 30분

티켓과 예약
- 1인당 15달러 (8세 미만 어린이는 무료)
- 예약은 투어 시작 2시간 전까지 가능합니다.

프로그램 활동
- 투어 가이드와 단체 투어 (1시간)
- 전통 음식 시식 및 음료 시음 (30분)

※ 추가 비용 없이 전통 의상을 입어 볼 수 있습니다.
※ 더 많은 정보를 원하시면, 저희 웹 사이트 www.palacenighttour.com에 방문하세요.

Why? 왜 정답일까?

'You can try on traditional clothes with no extra charge.'에서 전통 의상 착용은 추가 비용 없이도 가능하다고 하므로, 안내문의 내용과 일치하는 것은 ⑤ '추가 비용 없이 전통 의상을 입어 볼 수 있다.'이다.

Why? 왜 오답일까?

① 'Friday / 7 p.m. – 8:30 p.m.'에서 금요일 투어는 한 번만 열린다고 하였다.
② '(free for kids under 8)'에서 8세 미만 어린이는 무료 입장이라고 하였다.
③ 'Bookings will be accepted up to 2 hours before the tour starts.'에서 투어 예약은 투어 시작 2시간 전까지 가능하다고 하였다.

④ 'Group tour with a tour guide (1 hour)'에서 투어 가이드와 함께 1시간 동안 그룹 투어를 하게 된다고 하였다.

- palace ⓝ 궁전
- accept ⓥ 접수하다, 수용하다

---

29 비슷한 대상과 어울리기를 선호하는 경향 　　　　정답률 63% | 정답 ③

다음 글의 밑줄 친 부분 중, 어법상 틀린 것은?

We usually get along best with people / who we think are like us.
우리는 보통 사람들과 가장 잘 지낸다. / 우리가 같다고 생각하는
In fact, we seek them out.
사실, 우리는 그들을 찾아낸다.
It's why places like Little Italy, Chinatown, and Koreatown ① exist.
이 이유로 리틀 이탈리아, 차이나타운, 코리아타운과 같은 장소들이 존재한다.
But I'm not just talking about race, skin color, or religion.
하지만 나는 인종, 피부색, 또는 종교만을 말하는 것이 아니다.
I'm talking about people / who share our values / and look at the world / the same way we ② do.
나는 사람들을 말하는 것이다. / 우리의 가치관을 공유하고 / 세상을 바라보는 / 우리와 같은 방식으로
As the saying goes, / birds of a feather flock together.
속담에서처럼, / 같은 깃털을 가진 새가 함께 무리 짓는다.
This is a very common human tendency / ✔ that is rooted in how our species developed.
이것은 매우 흔한 인간의 경향이다. / 우리 종이 발전한 방식에 깊게 뿌리박혀 있는
Imagine you are walking out in a forest.
여러분이 숲에 나가 걷는다고 상상해 보라.
You would be conditioned / to avoid something unfamiliar or foreign / because there is a high likelihood / that ④ it would be interested in killing you.
여러분은 조건화되어 있을 것이다. / 친숙하지 않거나 낯선 것을 피하도록 / 가능성이 커서 / 그런 것이 여러분을 죽이는 데 관심이 있을
Similarities make us ⑤ relate better to other people / because we think / they'll understand us on a deeper level than other people.
유사점은 우리가 다른 사람들과 마음이 더 잘 통할 수 있도록 하는데, / 우리가 생각하기 때문이다. / 그들이 우리를 다른 사람들보다 더 깊이 있는 수준으로 이해할 것이라고

우리는 보통 우리와 같다고 생각하는 사람들과 가장 잘 지낸다. 사실, 우리는 그들을 찾아낸다. 이 이유로 리틀 이탈리아, 차이나타운, 코리아타운과 같은 장소들이 존재한다. 하지만 나는 인종, 피부색, 또는 종교만을 말하는 것이 아니다. 우리의 가치관을 공유하고 우리와 같은 방식으로 세상을 바라보는 사람들을 말하는 것이다. 속담에서처럼, 같은 깃털을 가진 새가 함께 무리 짓는다(유유상종이다). 이것은 우리 종이 발전한 방식에 깊게 뿌리박혀 있는 매우 흔한 인간의 경향이다. 여러분이 숲에 나가 걷는다고 상상해 보라. 친숙하지 않거나 낯선 것은 여러분을 죽이는 데 관심이 있을 가능성이 커 여러분은 그런 것을 피하도록 조건화되어 있을 것이다. 유사점(을 갖고 있는 것)은 우리가 다른 사람들과 마음이 더 잘 통할 수 있도록 하는데, 그들이 우리를 다른 사람들보다 더 깊이 있는 수준으로 이해할 것으로 생각하기 때문이다.

Why? 왜 정답일까?

관계대명사 what은 선행사를 포함하고 있는데, ③ 앞에는 선행사 a very common human tendency가 있으므로 what을 that 또는 which로 고쳐야 한다. 따라서 어법상 틀린 것은 ③이다.

Why? 왜 오답일까?

① 주어가 복수 명사인 places이므로 복수 동사 exist가 바르게 쓰였다. like Little Italy, Chinatown, and Koreatown은 주어 places를 꾸미는 전명구이다.
② 앞의 일반동사구 look at을 가리키는 대동사 do가 바르게 쓰였다.
④ something unfamiliar or foreign을 받는 단수 대명사로 it이 바르게 쓰였다.
⑤ 사역동사 make의 목적격 보어로 원형부정사 relate가 바르게 쓰였다.

- get along with ~와 잘 지내다, 어울리다
- race ⓝ 인종
- be rooted in ~에 뿌리박고 있다, ~에 원인이 있다
- relate to ~을 이해하다, ~에 공감하다
- seek out (오랫동안 공들여) 찾아다니다
- as the saying goes 속담에서 말하듯이, 옛말처럼
- condition ⓥ 조건화하다

구문 풀이

1행 We usually get along best with people [who (we think) are like us].
　　　　　　　　　선행사　주격 관·대　(　): 삽입절

★★★ 등급을 가르는 문제!
30 거절에 대한 두려움 극복하기 　　　　정답률 45% | 정답 ⑤

다음 글의 밑줄 친 부분 중, 문맥상 낱말의 쓰임이 적절하지 않은 것은? [3점]

Rejection is an everyday part of our lives, / yet most people can't handle it well.
거절은 우리 삶의 일상적인 부분이지만, / 대부분의 사람은 그것을 잘 감당하지 못한다.
For many, / it's so painful / that they'd rather not ask for something at all / than ask and ① risk rejection.
많은 사람에게 / 거절이 너무 고통스러워서 / 그들은 아예 무언가를 요청하지 않으려 한다. / 요청하고 거절의 위험을 감수하기보다는
Yet, as the old saying goes, / if you don't ask, / the answer is always no.
하지만 옛말처럼, / 여러분이 요청하지 않으면 / 대답은 항상 '아니오'이다.
Avoiding rejection / ② negatively affects many aspects of your life.
거절을 피하는 것은 / 여러분의 삶의 많은 측면에 부정적으로 영향을 준다.
All of that happens / only because you're not ③ tough enough to handle it.
이 모든 것은 일어난다. / 단지 여러분이 거절을 감당할 만큼 강하지 않기 때문에
For this reason, / consider rejection therapy.
이러한 이유로 / 거절 요법을 고려해 보라.
Come up with a ④ request or an activity / that usually results in a rejection.
요청이나 활동을 생각해 내라. / 일반적으로 거절당할 만한
Working in sales is one such example.
판매 분야에서 일하는 것이 그러한 사례 중 하나이다.
Asking for discounts at the stores / will also work.
매장에서 할인을 요청하는 것은 / 또한 효과가 있을 것이다.
By deliberately getting yourself ✔ rejected / you'll grow a thicker skin / that will allow you to take on much more in life, / thus making you more successful / at dealing with unfavorable circumstances.

의도적으로 스스로를 거절당할 상황에 놓이게 함으로써 / 여러분은 더한 둔감함을 키우게 될 것이다. / 여러분이 인생에서 훨씬 더 많은 것을 떠맡을 수 있게 해준다. / 그리하여 여러분은 더 성공적이 될 것이다. / 호의적이지 않은 상황에 대처하는 것에

거절은 우리 삶의 일상적인 부분이지만, 대부분의 사람은 그것을 잘 감당하지 못한다. 많은 사람에게 거절이 너무 고통스러워서, 그들은 요청하고 거절의 ① 위험을 감수하기보다는 아예 무언가를 요청하지 않으려 한다. 하지만 옛말처럼, 요청하지 않으면 대답은 항상 '아니오'이다. 거절을 피하는 것은 여러분의 삶의 많은 측면에 ② 부정적으로 영향을 준다. 이 모든 것은 단지 여러분이 거절을 감당할 만큼 ③ 강하지 않기 때문에 일어난다. 이러한 이유로 거절 요법을 (시도하는 것을) 고려해 보라. 일반적으로 거절당할 만한 ④ 요청이나 활동을 생각해 내라. 판매 분야에서 일하는 것이 그러한 사례 중 하나이다. 매장에서 할인을 요청하는 것 또한 효과가 있을 것이다. 의도적으로 스스로를 ⑤ 환영받는(→ 거절당할) 상황에 놓이게 함으로써 여러분은 더 둔감해지고, 인생에서 훨씬 더 많은 것을 떠맡을 수 있게 되며, 그리하여 호의적이지 않은 상황에 더 성공적으로 대처할 수 있게 될 것이다.

Why? 왜 정답일까?
⑤ 앞에서 판매 분야에서 일하는 등 거절을 경험할 법한 요청이나 활동에 참여해보라고 언급하는데, 이는 거절을 부르는 상황의 예시이므로 ⑤의 welcomed는 rejected로 바뀌어야 적절하다. 따라서 문맥상 낱말의 쓰임이 적절하지 않은 것은 ⑤이다.

- **rejection** ⓝ 거절
- **grow a thick skin** 무덤덤해지다, 둔감해지다
- **circumstance** ⓝ 상황, 환경
- **come up with** ~을 생각해내다, 떠올리다
- **unfavorable** ⓐ 호의적이지 않은

구문 풀이
2행 For many, it's so painful that they'd rather not ask for something at all
「so ~ that …: 너무 ~해서 …하다」 「차라리 ~ 않다」 동사원형1
than ask and risk rejection.
동사원형2

★★ 문제 해결 꿀~팁 ★★
▶ 많이 틀린 이유는?
오답 중 ③이 포함된 문장은 우리가 거절을 왜 피하려 하는지 그 이유를 설명하는 문장이다. 우리가 거절에 잘 대처할 만큼 '충분히 강하지' 않기 때문이라는 것이다. 그렇기에 훈련이 필요하다는 결론까지 자연스럽게 연결되므로, ③은 문맥상 어색하지 않다.
▶ 문제 해결 방법은?
정답인 ⑤가 포함된 문장은 예시 앞의 'Come up with a request or an activity that usually results in a rejection.'과 같은 의미이다. '일부러 거절이라는 결과를 초래할' 수 있는 상황은 '환영받는' 상황이 아니라 그야말로 '거부당하는' 상황이다.

★★★ 등급을 가르는 문제!
31 세밀한 묘사의 필요성 | 정답률 46% | 정답 ②

다음 빈칸에 들어갈 말로 가장 적절한 것을 고르시오.
① similarities – 유사점 ✓② particulars – 세부 사항 ③ fantasies – 환상
④ boredom – 지루함 ⑤ wisdom – 지혜

Generalization without specific examples / that humanize writing / is boring to the listener and to the reader.
구체적인 사례가 없는 일반화는 / 글을 인간미 있게 하는 / 듣는 사람과 읽는 사람에게 지루하다.
Who wants to read platitudes all day?
누가 상투적인 말을 온종일 읽고 싶어 하겠는가?
Who wants to hear the words / great, greater, best, smartest, finest, humanitarian, on and on and on / without specific examples?
누가 듣고 싶어 하겠는가? / 위대한, 더 위대한, 최고의, 제일 똑똑한, 가장 훌륭한, 인도주의적인, 이런 말들을 계속해서 끊임없이 / 구체적인 사례가 없이
Instead of using these 'nothing words,' / leave them out completely / and just describe the particulars.
이런 '공허한 말들'을 사용하는 대신에, / 그것들을 완전히 빼고 / 세부 사항만을 서술하라.
There is nothing worse than reading a scene in a novel / in which a main character is described up front / as heroic or brave or tragic or funny, / while thereafter, the writer quickly moves on to something else.
소설 속 장면을 읽는 것보다 더 끔찍한 것은 없다. / 주인공이 대놓고 묘사되는 / 영웅적이다, 용감하다, 비극적이다, 혹은 웃긴다고 / 한편 그 후 작가가 다른 것으로 빠르게 넘어가는
That's no good, no good at all.
그건 좋지 않으며, 전혀 좋지 않다.
You have to use less one word descriptions / and more detailed, engaging descriptions / if you want to make something real.
여러분은 한 단어 묘사는 덜 사용하고 / 세밀하고 마음을 끄는 묘사를 더 많이 사용해야 한다. / 여러분이 어떤 것을 실감 나는 것으로 만들고 싶다면

글을 인간미 있게 하는 구체적인 사례가 없는 일반화는 듣는 사람에게도 읽는 사람에게도 지루하다. 누가 상투적인 말을 온종일 읽고 싶어 하겠는가? 구체적인 사례가 없이 위대한, 더 위대한, 최고의, 제일 똑똑한, 가장 훌륭한, 인도주의적인, 이런 말들을 누가 계속해서 끊임없이 듣고 싶어 하겠는가? 이런 '공허한 말들'을 사용하는 대신에, 그것들을 완전히 빼고 세부 사항만을 서술하라. 주인공을 대놓고 영웅적이다, 용감하다, 비극적이다, 혹은 웃긴다고 묘사한 후 작가가 다른 것으로 빠르게 넘어가는 소설 속 장면을 읽는 것보다 더 끔찍한 것은 없다. 그건 좋지 않으며, 전혀 좋지 않다. 어떤 것을 실감 나는 것으로 만들고 싶다면, 한 단어 짜리 묘사는 덜 사용하고, 세밀하고 마음을 끄는 묘사를 더 많이 사용해야 한다.

Why? 왜 정답일까?
마지막 문장에서 장면을 실감 나게 만들려면 세밀하고 마음을 끄는 묘사를 사용해야 한다(You have to use less one word descriptions and more detailed, engaging descriptions if you want to make something real.)고 언급하는 것으로 보아, 빈칸에 들어갈 말로 가장 적절한 것은 ② '세부 사항'이다. 이는 빈칸 앞의 specific examples을 재진술한 말이기도 하다.

- **specific** ⓐ 구체적인
- **humanitarian** ⓐ 인도주의적인
- **engaging** ⓐ 마음을 끄는, 몰입시키는
- **humanize** ⓥ 인간적으로 만들다
- **leave out** ~을 빼다

05회

구문 풀이
6행 There is nothing worse than reading a scene in a novel [in which a main
「nothing + 비교급 + than : ~보다 더 …한 것은 없다(최상급 의미)」 선행사 = where
character is described up front as heroic or brave or tragic or funny, while thereafter, the writer quickly moves on to something else].

★★ 문제 해결 꿀~팁 ★★
▶ 많이 틀린 이유는?
첫 문장의 Generalization만 보고 ①을 고르면 안 된다. '특별한' 사례의 공통점을 찾아 '일반화'하라는 내용은 글 어디에도 없기 때문이다.
▶ 문제 해결 방법은?
빈칸이 주제문인 명령문에 있으므로, 마찬가지로 '~해야 한다'라는 당위의 의미를 나타내는 마지막 문장을 잘 읽어야 한다. more detailed, engaging와 같은 의미의 단어를 빈칸에 넣으면 된다.

★★★ 등급을 가르는 문제!
32 정보 공유에 있어 대면 상호작용의 중요성 | 정답률 49% | 정답 ③

다음 빈칸에 들어갈 말로 가장 적절한 것을 고르시오.
① natural talent – 천부적 재능 ② regular practice – 규칙적인 연습
✓③ personal contact – 개인적인 접촉 ④ complex knowledge – 복잡한 지식
⑤ powerful motivation – 강력한 동기

Face-to-face interaction / is a uniquely powerful — and sometimes the only — way / to share many kinds of knowledge, / from the simplest to the most complex.
대면 상호 작용은 / 유례 없이 강력한 — 때로는 유일한 — 방법이다. / 많은 종류의 지식을 공유하는 / 가장 간단한 것부터 가장 복잡한 것까지
It is one of the best ways / to stimulate new thinking and ideas, / too.
그것은 가장 좋은 방법의 하나이다. / 새로운 생각과 아이디어를 자극하는 / 또한
Most of us would have had difficulty learning / how to tie a shoelace only from pictures, / or how to do arithmetic from a book.
우리 대부분이 배웠다면 어려움을 겪었을 것이다. / 그림만으로 신발 끈 묶는 법 / 또는 책으로부터 계산하는 방법을
Psychologist Mihàly Csikszentmihàlyi found, / while studying high achievers, / that a large number of Nobel Prize winners / were the students of previous winners: / they had access to the same literature as everyone else, / but personal contact made a crucial difference / to their creativity.
심리학자 Mihàly Csikszentmihàlyi는 발견했다. / 높은 성취도를 보이는 사람들을 연구하면서 / 다수의 노벨상 수상자가 / 이전 수상자들의 학생들이라는 것을 / 그들은 다른 모든 사람들과 똑같은 문헌에 접근할 수 있었지만, / 개인적인 접촉이 결정적인 차이를 만들었다. / 이들의 창의성에
Within organisations / this makes conversation / both a crucial factor for high-level professional skills / and the most important way of sharing everyday information.
조직 내에서 / 이것은 대화를 만든다. / 고급 전문 기술을 위한 매우 중요한 요소이자 / 일상 정보를 공유하는 가장 중요한 방식으로

대면 상호 작용은 가장 간단한 것부터 가장 복잡한 것까지 많은 종류의 지식을 공유하는 유례 없이 강력한 — 때로는 유일한 — 방법이다. 그것은 새로운 생각과 아이디어를 자극하는 최고의 방법 중 하나이기도 하다. 우리 대부분이 그림으로만 신발 끈 묶는 법을 배웠거나, 책으로 셈법을 배웠다면 어려움을 겪었을 것이다. 심리학자 Mihàly Csikszentmihàlyi는 높은 성취도를 보이는 사람들을 연구하면서 다수의 노벨상 수상자가 이전 (노벨상) 수상자들의 학생들이라는 것을 발견했다. 그들은 다른 모든 사람들과 똑같은 (연구) 문헌에 접근할 수 있었지만, 개인적인 접촉이 이들의 창의성에 결정적인 차이를 만들었다. 이로 인해 조직 내에서 대화는 고급 전문 기술을 위한 매우 중요한 요소이자 일상 정보를 공유하는 가장 중요한 방식이 된다.

Why? 왜 정답일까?
첫 문장과 마지막 문장에서 정보를 공유하는 가장 중요한 방법으로 대면 상호 작용(Face-to-face interaction) 또는 대화(conversation)를 언급하고 있다. 따라서 빈칸에 들어갈 말로 가장 적절한 것은 ③ '개인적인 접촉'이다.

- **stimulate** ⓥ 자극하다
- **crucial** ⓐ 아주 중요한

구문 풀이
4행 Most of us would have had difficulty learning {how to tie a shoelace} only
「have difficulty + 동명사 : ~하는 데 어려움을 겪다」
from pictures, or {how to do arithmetic} from a book.
{ } : 명사구(how + to부정사 : ~하는 방법)

★★ 문제 해결 꿀~팁 ★★
▶ 많이 틀린 이유는?
글 처음과 마지막에 many kinds of knowledge, from the simplest to the most complex 또는 high-level professional skills와 같은 표현이 등장하므로 얼핏 보면 ④가 적절해 보인다. 하지만 빈칸은 이러한 정보 공유나 전문 능력 개발에 '무엇이 영향을 미치는지' 그 요인을 밝히는 것이므로 ④를 빈칸에 넣기는 부적절하다.
▶ 문제 해결 방법은?
첫 문장의 Face-to-face interaction과 마지막 문장의 conversation이 키워드이다. 이 둘을 일반화할 수 있는 표현이 바로 '빈칸'이다.

33 영화 속 외국어 대화에 자막이 없을 때의 효과 | 정답률 59% | 정답 ①

다음 빈칸에 들어갈 말로 가장 적절한 것을 고르시오. [3점]
✓① seeing the film from her viewpoint – 그녀의 시각에서 영화를 보고 있게
② impressed by her language skills – 그녀의 언어 능력에 감명받게
③ attracted to her beautiful voice – 그녀의 아름다운 목소리에 이끌리게
④ participating in a heated debate – 열띤 토론에 참여하게
⑤ learning the language used in the film – 영화에서 사용된 언어를 배우고 있게

Most times a foreign language is spoken in film, / subtitles are used / to translate the dialogue for the viewer.
영화에서 외국어가 사용되는 대부분의 경우 / 자막이 사용된다. / 관객을 위해 대화를 통역하려고
However, / there are occasions / when foreign dialogue is left unsubtitled / (and thus incomprehensible to most of the target audience).
하지만, / 경우가 있다. / 외국어 대화가 자막 없이 처리되는 / (그리하여 대부분의 주요 대상 관객이 이해하지 못하게)
This is often done / if the movie is seen / mainly from the viewpoint of a particular character / who does not speak the language.
흔히 이렇게 처리된다. / 영화가 보여지는 경우에 / 주로 특정한 등장인물의 관점에서 / 그 언어를 할 줄 모르는
Such absence of subtitles / allows the audience / to feel a similar sense of incomprehension and alienation / that the character feels.
그러한 자막의 부재는 / 관객이 ~하게 한다. / 비슷한 몰이해와 소외의 감정을 / 그 등장인물이 느끼는
An example of this / is seen in *Not Without My Daughter*.
이것의 한 예는 / *Not Without My Daughter*에서 볼 수 있다.
The Persian language dialogue / spoken by the Iranian characters / is not subtitled / because the main character Betty Mahmoody does not speak Persian / and the audience is seeing the film from her viewpoint.
페르시아어 대화는 / 이란인 등장인물들이 하는 / 자막 없이 처리되며 / 왜냐하면 주인공 Betty Mahmoody가 페르시아어를 하지 못하기 때문에 / 관객은 그녀의 시각에서 영화를 보고 있게 된다.

영화에서 외국어가 사용되는 대부분의 경우 관객을 위해 대화를 통역하려고 자막이 사용된다. 하지만 외국어 대화가 자막 없이 (그리하여 대부분의 주요 대상 관객이 이해하지 못하게) 처리되는 경우가 있다. 영화가 그 언어를 할 줄 모르는 특정한 등장인물의 관점에서 주로 보여지는 경우에 흔히 이렇게 처리된다. 그러한 자막의 부재는 관객이 그 등장인물이 느끼는 것과 비슷한 몰이해와 소외의 감정을 느끼게 한다. 이것의 한 예를 *Not Without My Daughter*에서 볼 수 있다. 주인공 Betty Mahmoody가 페르시아어를 하지 못하기 때문에 이란인 등장인물들이 하는 페르시아어 대화에는 자막이 없으며, 관객은 그녀의 시각에서 영화를 보고 있게 된다.

Why? 왜 정답일까?
외국어 대화가 자막 없이 사용되는 경우는 그 언어를 할 줄 모르는 특정 등장인물의 시점에서 사건을 보게 만든다(~ if the movie is seen mainly from the viewpoint of a particular character who does not speak the language.)는 설명으로 보아, 빈칸에 들어갈 말로 가장 적절한 것은 ① '그녀의 시각에서 영화를 보고 있게'이다.

● translate ⓥ 번역하다, 통역하다
● viewpoint ⓝ 관점, 시점
● occasion ⓝ 경우, 때
● absence ⓝ 부재

구문 풀이

2행 However, there are occasions [when foreign dialogue is left unsubtitled (and thus incomprehensible to most of the target audience)].
선행사(경우) 관계부사 5형식 수동태 보어1(과거분사) 보어2(형용사)

★★★ 등급을 가르는 문제! ★★★

34 홈 이점이 발휘되지 못하는 경우   정답률 19% | 정답 ①

다음 빈칸에 들어갈 말로 가장 적절한 것을 고르시오. [3점]
☑ often welcome a road trip – 길을 떠나는 것을 흔히 반길
② avoid international matches – 국제적 경기를 피할
③ focus on increasing ticket sales – 티켓 매출을 높이는 데 집중할
④ want to have an eco-friendly stadium – 친환경적인 경기장을 갖기를 원할
⑤ try to advertise their upcoming games – 다가오는 경기를 광고하려 애쓸

One dynamic that can change dramatically in sport / is the concept of the home-field advantage, / in which perceived demands and resources seem to play a role.
스포츠에서 극적으로 바뀔 수 있는 한 가지 역학은 / 홈 이점이라는 개념으로, / 여기에는 인식된 부담과 자원이 역할을 하는 것처럼 보인다.
Under normal circumstances, / the home ground would appear / to provide greater perceived resources / (fans, home field, and so on).
일반적인 상황에서, / 홈그라운드는 보일 것이다. / 인식된 자원을 더 많이 제공하는 것처럼 / (팬, 홈 경기장 등)
However, / researchers Roy Baumeister and Andrew Steinhilber / were among the first / to point out / that these competitive factors can change; / for example, / the success percentage for home teams / in the final games of a playoff or World Series / seems to drop.
하지만, / 연구원 Roy Baumeister와 Andrew Steinhilber는 / 최초의 사람들 중 하나였다. / 지적한 / 이러한 경쟁력이 있는 요소들이 바뀔 수도 있다고 / 예를 들어, / 홈 팀들의 성공률은 / 우승 결정전이나 미국 프로 야구 선수권의 마지막 경기에서 / 떨어지는 것처럼 보인다.
Fans can become part of the perceived demands / rather than resources / under those circumstances.
팬들은 인식된 부담의 일부가 될 수 있다. / 자원보다는 / 이러한 상황에서
This change in perception can also explain / why a team that's struggling at the start of the year / will often welcome a road trip / to reduce perceived demands and pressures.
이러한 인식의 변화는 또한 설명할 수 있다. / 왜 연초에 고전하는 팀이 / 길을 떠나는 것을 흔히 반길 것인지 / 인식된 부담과 압박을 줄이기 위해

스포츠에서 극적으로 바뀔 수 있는 한 가지 역학은 홈 이점이라는 개념으로, 여기에는 인식되는 부담과 자원이 일조하는 것처럼 보인다. 일반적인 상황에서, 홈그라운드는 인식되는 자원(팬, 홈 경기장 등)을 더 많이 제공하는 것처럼 보일 것이다. 하지만, 연구원 Roy Baumeister와 Andrew Steinhilber는 이러한 경쟁력이 있는 요소들이 바뀔 수도 있다고 처음으로 지적한 사람 중 하나이다. 예를 들어, 우승 결정전이나 미국 프로 야구 선수권의 마지막 경기에서 홈 팀들의 성공률은 떨어지는 것처럼 보인다. 이러한 상황에서 팬들은 자원보다는 인식되는 부담의 일부가 될 수 있다. 이러한 인식의 변화는 왜 연초에 고전하는 팀이 인식되는 부담과 압박을 줄이기 위해 길을 떠나는 것(원정 경기를 가는 것)을 흔히 반길 것인지 또한 설명할 수 있다.

Why? 왜 정답일까?
홈그라운드의 이점은 부담에 대한 인식이나 자원에 의해 뒤집힐 수 있다(~ the concept of the home-field advantage, in which perceived demands and resources seem to play a

role.)는 내용의 글이다. for example 뒤로 결승전 등 중요한 경기에서 팬들은 선수들에게 자원이 아닌 부담일 수 있기에 도리어 홈 팀의 성적이 부진해질 수 있다고 한다. 이를 근거로 볼 때, 마지막 문장은 부진하는 팀이 도리어 부담을 피하고 '홈그라운드에서의 경기를 피한다'는 내용일 것이다. 따라서 빈칸에 들어갈 말로 가장 적절한 것은 ① '길을 떠나는 것을 흔히 반길'이다.

● play a role in ~에 역할을 하다. 일조하다
● perception ⓝ 인식
● competitive ⓐ 경쟁력 있는
● struggle ⓥ 고전하다, 분투하다

구문 풀이

1행 One dynamic [that can change dramatically in sport] is the concept of
주어(선행사) 주격 관계대명사 동사(단수) 보어(선행사)
the home-field advantage, in which perceived demands and resources seem to
전치사 + 관계대명사
play a role.

★★ 문제 해결 꿀~팁 ★★

▶ 많이 틀린 이유는?
home-field advantage만 보면 정답과 정반대되는 의미의 ②를 고르기 쉽다. 하지만 사실 이 글은 '홈 구장의 이점'을 긍정하는 글이 아니라 이 이점이 '없을 수도 있는' 경우에 대한 글이다.
▶ 문제 해결 방법은?
for example 뒤에서, 홈 팀의 결승전 승률이 '떨어지는' 것처럼 보인다는 예를 제시한다. 이 점이 어떤 결과를 불러올까 생각해보면, 연초에 고전 중인 팀은 오히려 '홈 팀에서 경기하기를 꺼릴' 수도 있다는 추론이 가능하다.

35 커피의 부정적 영향 주의하기   정답률 60% | 정답 ④

다음 글에서 전체 흐름과 관계 없는 문장은?
Who hasn't used a cup of coffee / to help themselves stay awake while studying?
커피 한 잔을 이용해 보지 않은 사람이 있을까? / 공부하는 동안 깨어 있는 것을 돕기 위해
Mild stimulants / commonly found in tea, coffee, or sodas / possibly make you more attentive / and, thus, better able to remember.
가벼운 자극제는 / 차, 커피 또는 탄산음료에서 흔히 발견되는 / 아마도 여러분을 더 주의 깊게 만들고, / 따라서 더 잘 기억할 수 있게 한다.
① However, / you should know / that stimulants are as likely / to have negative effects on memory / as they are to be beneficial.
하지만, / 여러분은 알아야 한다. / 자극제가 ~할 수도 있다는 것을 / 기억력에 부정적인 영향을 미칠 / 그것들이 이로울 수 있는 만큼
② Even if they could improve performance at some level, / the ideal doses are currently unknown.
비록 그것이 특정 수준에서 수행을 향상할 수 있다고 할지라도, / 이상적인 복용량은 현재 알려지지 않았다.
③ If you are wide awake and well-rested, / mild stimulation from caffeine can do little / to further improve your memory performance.
만약 여러분이 완전히 깨어 있고 잘 쉬었다면, / 카페인으로부터의 가벼운 자극은 거의 영향을 주지 못할 수 있다. / 여러분의 기억력을 더욱 향상하는 데
☑ In contrast, / many studies have shown / that drinking tea is healthier than drinking coffee.
반면에, / 많은 연구에서 밝혀졌다. / 커피를 마시는 것보다 차를 마시는 것이 건강에 더 좋다는 것이
⑤ Indeed, / if you have too much of a stimulant, / you will become nervous, / find it difficult to sleep, / and your memory performance will suffer.
실제로 / 만약 여러분이 자극제를 너무 많이 섭취하면, / 여러분은 신경이 과민해지고, / 잠을 자기 어려워지며, / 기억력도 저하될 것이다.

공부하는 동안 깨어 있는 것을 돕기 위해 커피 한 잔을 이용해 보지 않은 사람이 있을까? 차, 커피 또는 탄산음료에서 흔히 발견되는 가벼운 자극제는 아마도 여러분을 더 주의 깊게 만들고, 따라서 더 잘 기억할 수 있게 한다. ① 하지만, 자극제가 기억력에 이로울 수 있는 만큼 부정적인 영향을 미칠 수도 있다는 것을 알아야 한다. ② 비록 그것이 특정 수준에서 수행을 향상할 수 있다고 할지라도, (자극제의) 이상적인 복용량은 현재 알려지지 않았다. ③ 만약 여러분이 완전히 깨어 있고 잘 쉬었다면, 카페인으로부터의 가벼운 자극은 여러분의 기억력을 더욱 향상하는 데 거의 영향을 주지 못할 수 있다. ④ 반면에, 많은 연구에서 커피를 마시는 것보다 차를 마시는 것이 건강에 더 좋다는 것이 밝혀졌다. ⑤ 실제로 만약 여러분이 자극제를 너무 많이 섭취하면, 신경이 과민해지고, 잠을 자기 어려워지며, 기억력도 저하될 것이다.

Why? 왜 정답일까?
커피를 지나치게 많이 마시면 부정적 영향이 나타날 수 있다는 내용의 글인데, ④는 커피보다 차가 몸에 좋다는 무관한 설명을 제시하고 있다. 따라서 전체 흐름과 관계 없는 문장은 ④이다.

● attentive ⓐ 주의 깊은
● ideal ⓐ 이상적인
● have an effect on ~에 영향을 미치다
● suffer ⓥ 악화되다

구문 풀이

4행 However, you should know that stimulants are as likely to have negative
접속사(~것) 'as + 원급 + as : ~만큼 …한'
effects on memory as they are to be beneficial.
be to 용법(~할 수 있다)

36 과거 시골 건축업자들의 건축 양식   정답률 58% | 정답 ③

주어진 글 다음에 이어질 글의 순서로 가장 적절한 것을 고르시오.
① (A) – (C) – (B)
② (B) – (A) – (C)
☑ (B) – (C) – (A)
④ (C) – (A) – (B)
⑤ (C) – (B) – (A)

Toward the end of the 19th century, / a new architectural attitude emerged.
19세기 말이 되면서, / 새로운 건축학적 사고방식이 나타났다.
Industrial architecture, / the argument went, / was ugly and inhuman; / past styles had more to do with pretension / than what people needed in their homes.
산업 건축은 / 그 주장에 따르면, / 추하고 비인간적이었다. / 과거의 스타일은 허세와 더욱 관련이 있었다 / 사람들이 자기 집에서 필요로 했던 것보다는

(B) Instead of these approaches, / why not look at the way / ordinary country builders worked in the past?
이러한 접근 대신에, / 방식을 살펴보는 것은 어떠한가? / 평범한 시골 건축업자들이 과거에 일했던

They developed their craft skills over generations, / demonstrating mastery of both tools and materials.
그들은 세대를 거쳐 공예 기술을 발전시켰다. / 도구와 재료 둘 다에 숙달한 기술을 보이며

(C) Those materials were local, / and used with simplicity — / houses built this way / had plain wooden floors and whitewashed walls inside.
그 재료는 지역적이고, / 단순하게 사용되었는데, / 이러한 방식으로 건축된 집들은 / 실내가 평범한 나무 바닥과 회반죽을 칠한 벽으로 되어 있었다.

(A) But they supplied people's needs perfectly / and, at their best, had a beauty / that came from the craftsman's skill / and the rootedness of the house in its locality.
그러나 그것들은 사람들의 필요를 완벽하게 충족시켰고, / 가장 좋은 경우 아름다움을 갖추고 있었다. / 장인의 솜씨에서 비롯된 / 그리고 그 집이 그 지역에 뿌리내림으로써 비롯된

19세기 말이 되면서, 새로운 건축학적 사고방식이 나타났다. 그 주장에 따르면, 산업 건축은 추하고 비인간적이었다. 과거의 스타일은 사람들이 자기 집에서 필요로 했던 것보다는 허세와 더욱 관련이 있었다.

(B) 이러한 접근 대신, 평범한 시골 건축업자들이 과거에 일했던 방식을 살펴보는 것은 어떠한가? 그들은 도구와 재료 둘 다에 숙달한 기술을 보이며, 세대를 거쳐 공예 기술을 발전시켰다.

(C) 그 재료는 지역적이었고, 단순하게 사용되었는데, 이러한 방식으로 건축된 집들은 실내가 평범한 나무 바닥과 회반죽을 칠한 벽으로 되어 있었다.

(A) 그러나 그것들은 사람들의 필요를 완벽하게 충족시켰고, 가장 좋은 경우 장인의 솜씨와 집이 그 지역에 뿌리내리며 비롯된 아름다움을 갖추고 있었다.

Why? 왜 정답일까?

산업 건축 양식을 언급하는 주어진 글 뒤로, '이 접근법' 대신 평범한 시골 건축업자들의 작업 방식을 살펴보겠다고 언급하는 (B), (B)에서 언급된 재료를 Those materials로 받으며 이것들이 단순하게 사용되었다고 설명하는 (C), '그래도' 이렇게 건축된 집들은 사람들의 필요만큼은 완벽하게 충족시켰다는 내용의 (A)가 차례로 연결된다. 따라서 글의 순서로 가장 적절한 것은 ③ '(B) – (C) – (A)'이다.

- **architectural** ⓐ 건축의
- **inhuman** ⓐ 비인간적인
- **rootedness** ⓝ 뿌리내림, 고착, 정착
- **demonstrate** ⓥ 입증하다
- **plain** ⓐ 평범한, 단순한
- **emerge** ⓥ 나타나다, 출현하다
- **craftsman** ⓝ 장인
- **locality** ⓝ (~이 존재하는) 지역, 곳
- **mastery** ⓝ 숙달한 기술

구문 풀이

2행 Industrial architecture, (the argument went), was ugly and inhuman;
　주어1　( ): 삽입절　동사1
past styles had more to do with pretension than {what people needed in their
주어2　동사2(~와 더 관련이 있었다)　관계대명사(~것)
homes}.

---

37 | 좋은 음악과 나쁜 음악 | 정답률 61% | 정답 ②

주어진 글 다음에 이어질 글의 순서로 가장 적절한 것을 고르시오. [3점]

① (A) – (C) – (B)　　② (B) – (A) – (C) ✔
③ (B) – (C) – (A)　　④ (C) – (A) – (B)
⑤ (C) – (B) – (A)

Robert Schumann once said, / "The laws of morals are those of art."
Robert Schumann은 언젠가 말했다. / "도덕의 법칙은 예술의 법칙이다."라고

What the great man is saying here / is that there is good music and bad music.
여기서 이 위인이 말하고 있는 것은 / 좋은 음악과 나쁜 음악이 있다는 것이다.

(B) The greatest music, / even if it's tragic in nature, / takes us to a world higher than ours; / somehow the beauty uplifts us.
가장 위대한 음악은, / 심지어 그것이 사실상 비극적일지라도, / 우리의 세상보다 더 높은 세상으로 우리를 데려간다. / 어떻게든지 아름다움은 우리를 고양시킨다.

Bad music, on the other hand, degrades us.
반면에 나쁜 음악은 우리를 격하시킨다.

(A) It's the same with performances: / a bad performance isn't necessarily the result of incompetence.
연주도 마찬가지다. / 나쁜 연주가 반드시 무능의 결과는 아니다.

Some of the worst performances occur / when the performers, / no matter how accomplished, / are thinking more of themselves / than of the music they're playing.
최악의 연주 중 일부는 발생한다. / 연주자들이 ~할 때 / 아무리 숙달되었더라도 / 자기 자신을 더 생각하고 있는 / 연주하고 있는 곡보다

(C) These doubtful characters aren't really listening / to what the composer is saying / — they're just showing off, / hoping that they'll have a great 'success' with the public.
이 미덥지 못한 사람들은 정말로 듣고 있는 것이 아니다. / 작곡가가 말하는 것을 / 그들은 그저 뽐내고 있을 뿐이다. / 그들이 대중적으로 큰 '성공'을 거두기를 바라며

The performer's basic task / is to try to understand the meaning of the music, / and then to communicate it honestly to others.
연주자의 기본 임무는 / 음악의 의미를 이해하려고 노력하고서, / 그것을 다른 사람들에게 정직하게 전달하는 것이다.

Robert Schumann은 "도덕의 법칙은 예술의 법칙이다."라고 말한 적이 있다. 여기서 이 위인이 말하고 있는 것은 좋은 음악과 나쁜 음악이 있다는 것이다.

(B) 가장 위대한 음악은, 심지어 그것이 사실상 비극적일지라도, 우리의 세상보다 더 높은 세상으로 우리를 데려가며, 아름다움은 어떻게든지 우리를 고양시킨다. 반면에 나쁜 음악은 우리를 격하시킨다.

(A) 연주도 마찬가지다. 나쁜 연주가 반드시 무능의 결과는 아니다. 최악의 연주 중 일부는 연주자들이 아무리 숙달되더라도 연주하고 있는 곡보다 자기 자신을 더 생각하고 있을 때 발생한다.

(C) 이 미덥지 못한 사람들은 작곡가가 말하는 것을 정말로 듣고 있는 것이 아니다. 그들은 대중적으로 큰 '성공'을 거두기를 바라며 그저 뽐내고 있을 뿐이다. 연주자의 기본 임무는

는 음악의 의미를 이해하려고 노력하고서, 그것을 다른 사람들에게 정직하게 전달하는 것이다.

Why? 왜 정답일까?

음악에 좋은 음악과 나쁜 음악이 있음을 언급하는 주어진 글 뒤로, 두 음악의 특징을 풀어 설명하는 (B), 연주에도 나쁜 연주와 좋은 연주가 있음을 덧붙이는 (A), (A)에서 언급된 최악의 연주자를 These doubtful characters로 가리키는 (C)가 차례로 연결된다. 따라서 글의 순서로 가장 적절한 것은 ② '(B) – (A) – (C)'이다.

- **accomplished** ⓐ 숙달된, 기량이 뛰어난
- **doubtful** ⓐ 미심쩍은
- **show off** 과시하다, 뽐내다
- **uplift** ⓥ 고양시키다, 들어올리다
- **composer** ⓝ 작곡가

구문 풀이

5행 Some of the worst performances occur when the performers, no matter
　주어　　　　　동사(복수)
how accomplished (they are), are thinking more of themselves than of the music
「no matter how + 형/부 + 주어 + 동사 : 아무리 ~할지라도」
they're playing.

---

38 | 생물 다양성으로 인한 이득 | 정답률 52% | 정답 ④

글의 흐름으로 보아, 주어진 문장이 들어가기에 가장 적절한 곳을 고르시오. [3점]

When an ecosystem is biodiverse, / wildlife have more opportunities / to obtain food and shelter.
생태계에 생물 종이 다양할 때, / 야생 생물들은 더 많은 기회를 얻는다. / 먹이와 서식지를 얻을

Different species react and respond / to changes in their environment / differently.
다양한 종들은 작용하고 반응한다. / 그들의 환경 변화에 / 다르게

① For example, / imagine a forest with only one type of plant in it, / which is the only source of food and habitat / for the entire forest food web.
예를 들어, / 단 한 종류의 식물만 있는 숲을 상상해 보라 / 그 식물은 유일한 먹이원이자 서식지이다. / 숲의 먹이 그물 전체에게 있어

② Now, / there is a sudden dry season / and this plant dies.
이제, / 갑작스러운 건기가 오고 / 이 식물이 죽는다.

③ Plant-eating animals / completely lose their food source and die out, / and so do the animals / that prey upon them.
초식 동물은 / 그들의 먹이원을 완전히 잃고 죽게 되고, / 동물들도 그렇게 된다. / 그들을 먹이로 삼는

✔ But, when there is biodiversity, / the effects of a sudden change / are not so dramatic.
하지만 종 다양성이 있을 때, / 갑작스러운 변화의 영향은 / 그렇게 극적이지 않다.

Different species of plants / respond to the drought differently, / and many can survive a dry season.
다양한 종의 식물들이 / 가뭄에 다르게 반응하고, / 많은 식물이 건기에 살아남을 수 있다.

⑤ Many animals have a variety of food sources / and don't just rely on one plant; / now our forest ecosystem is no longer at the death!
많은 동물은 다양한 먹이원을 가지고 있으며 / 그저 한 식물에 의존하지는 않는다. / 그래서 이제 우리의 숲 생태계는 더는 종말에 처해 있지 않다!

생태계에 생물 종이 다양할 때, 야생 생물들은 먹이와 서식지를 얻을 더 많은 기회를 얻는다. 다양한 종들은 그들의 환경 변화에 다르게 작용하고 반응한다. ① 예를 들어, 단 한 종류의 식물만 있는 숲을 상상해 보면, 그 식물은 숲의 먹이 그물 전체의 유일한 먹이원이자 서식지이다. ② 이제, 갑작스러운 건기가 오고 이 식물이 죽는다. ③ 초식 동물은 그들의 먹이원을 완전히 잃고 죽게 되고, 그들을 먹이로 삼는 동물들도 그렇게 된다. ④ 하지만 종 다양성이 있을 때, 갑작스러운 변화의 영향은 그렇게 극적이지 않다. 다양한 종의 식물들이 가뭄에 다르게 반응하고, 많은 식물이 건기에 살아남을 수 있다. ⑤ 많은 동물은 다양한 먹이원을 가지고 있으며 한 식물에만 의존하지 않기에, 이제 우리의 숲 생태계는 더는 종말에 처해 있지 않다!

Why? 왜 정답일까?

생물 다양성이 보장되면 환경 변화에 대처하기가 더 좋다는 내용의 글로, ④ 앞에서는 식물이 한 종류만 있는 숲의 예를 들어 이 경우 갑작스러운 건기라도 찾아와 식물이 죽으면 숲 전체 생태계가 망가진다는 내용을 제시한다. 한편 주어진 문장은 But으로 흐름을 반전시키며 생물 다양성이 있으면 상황이 다르다는 것을 언급한다. ④ 뒤에서는 '다양한 식물 종'을 언급하며, 이것들이 건기에 대처하는 방식이 모두 다르기에 많은 수가 살아남아 생태계가 유지될 수 있음을 설명한다. 따라서 주어진 문장이 들어가기에 가장 적절한 곳은 ④이다.

- **ecosystem** ⓝ 생태계
- **die out** 멸종되다, 자취를 감추다
- **food web** 먹이 그물, 먹이 사슬 체계
- **prey upon** ~을 잡아먹다, 괴롭히다

구문 풀이

5행 For example, imagine a forest with only one type of plant in it, which is
　　　　　　　　　선행사　　　　계속적 용법
the only source of food and habitat for the entire forest food web.

★★★ 등급을 가르는 문제!

39 | 우리 생활의 다방면에 연관된 밤하늘 | 정답률 34% | 정답 ②

글의 흐름으로 보아, 주어진 문장이 들어가기에 가장 적절한 곳을 고르시오.

We are connected to the night sky in many ways.
우리는 많은 방식으로 밤하늘과 연결되어 있다.

① It has always inspired people / to wonder and to imagine.
그것은 항상 사람들에게 영감을 주었다. / 궁금해하고 상상하도록

✔ Since the dawn of civilization, / our ancestors created myths / and told legendary stories / about the night sky.
문명의 시작부터, / 우리 선조들은 신화를 만들었고 / 전설적 이야기를 했다. / 밤하늘에 대해

Elements of those narratives became embedded / in the social and cultural identities of many generations.
그러한 이야기들의 요소들은 깊이 새겨졌다. / 여러 세대의 사회 · 문화적 정체성에

③ On a practical level, / the night sky helped past generations / to keep track of time and create calendars / — essential to developing societies / as aids to farming and seasonal gathering.

실용적인 수준에서, / 밤하늘은 과거 세대들이 ~하도록 도왔고 / 시간을 기록하고 달력을 만들도록 / 이는 사회를 발전시키는 데 필수적이었다. / 농업과 계절에 따른 수확의 보조 도구로서

④ For many centuries, / it also provided a useful navigation tool, / vital for commerce and for exploring new worlds.
수 세기 동안, / 그것은 또한 유용한 항해 도구를 제공했다. / 무역과 새로운 세계를 탐험하는 데 필수적인

⑤ Even in modern times, / many people in remote areas of the planet / observe the night sky / for such practical purposes.
심지어 현대에도, / 지구의 외딴 지역에 있는 많은 사람이 / 밤하늘을 관찰한다. / 그러한 실용적인 목적을 위해

우리는 많은 방식으로 밤하늘과 연결되어 있다. ① 그것은 항상 사람들이 궁금해하고 상상하도록 영감을 주었다. ② 문명의 시작부터, 우리 선조들은 밤하늘에 대해 신화를 만들었고 전설적 이야기를 했다. 그러한 이야기들의 요소들은 여러 세대의 사회·문화적 정체성에 깊이 새겨졌다. ③ 실용적인 수준에서, 밤하늘은 과거 세대들이 시간을 기록하고 달력을 만들도록 도왔고 이는 농업과 계절에 따른 수확의 보조 도구로서 사회를 발전시키는 데 필수적이었다. ④ 수 세기 동안, 그것은 또한 무역과 새로운 세계를 탐험하는 데 필수적인 유용한 항해 도구를 제공했다. ⑤ 심지어 현대에도, 지구의 외딴 지역에 있는 많은 사람이 그러한 실용적인 목적을 위해 밤하늘을 관찰한다.

Why? 왜 정답일까?

② 앞에서 인류는 밤하늘을 궁금해했다고 언급한 후, 주어진 문장은 인류가 거의 문명이 시작되던 시기부터 밤하늘에 대한 다양한 전설과 신화를 만들어냈다고 설명한다. 그리고 ② 뒤의 문장은 주어진 문장의 myths and legendary stories를 those narratives로 가리킨다. 따라서 주어진 문장이 들어가기에 가장 적절한 곳은 ②이다.

- keep track of ~을 기록하다
- vital ⓐ 필수적인, 매우 중요한
- gathering ⓝ 수집, 수확
- remote ⓐ 멀리 떨어진

구문 풀이

6행 On a practical level, the night sky helped past generations to keep track of
동사 목적어 목적격 보어1
time and (to) create calendars — (which are) essential to developing societies as
목적격 보어2 선행사 생략
aids to farming and seasonal gathering.

★★ 문제 해결 꿀~팁 ★★

▶ 많이 틀린 이유는?
③ 앞에서 밤하늘에 대한 이야기는 '사회문화적 정체성에 깊이 새겨졌다'고 하는데, ③ 뒤에서는 '실용적으로 살펴보면' 밤하늘 연구가 달력 제작 등에 영향을 미쳤다고 한다. 즉 On a practical level 앞뒤로 일반적 논의에서 더 구체적인 내용으로 나아가는 내용이 자연스럽게 연결된다.
▶ 문제 해결 방법은?
② 앞에서는 '이야기'로 볼 만한 내용이 없는데, ② 뒤에서는 갑자기 those narratives를 언급하므로 논리적 공백이 발생한다. 이때 주어진 문장을 보면 myths와 legendary stories가 있으므로, 이것을 ② 뒤에서 those narratives로 연결했다는 것을 알 수 있다.

---

40 경쟁자 제거에 망가니즈를 활용하는 식물   정답률 55% | 정답 ①

다음 글의 내용을 한 문장으로 요약하고자 한다. 빈칸 (A), (B)에 들어갈 말로 가장 적절한 것은?

	(A)		(B)
✓	increase 증가시키다	………	deadly 치명적인
②	increase 증가시키다	………	advantageous 이로운
③	indicate 보여주다	………	nutritious 영양가 있는
④	reduce 줄이다	………	dry 건조한
⑤	reduce 줄이다	………	warm 따뜻한

The common blackberry (*Rubus allegheniensis*) / has an amazing ability / to move manganese from one layer of soil to another / using its roots.
common blackberry(*Rubus allegheniensis*)는 / 놀라운 능력이 있다. / 토양의 망가니즈를 한 층에서 다른 층으로 옮기는 / 뿌리를 이용하여

This may seem like a funny talent / for a plant to have, / but it all becomes clear / when you realize the effect / it has on nearby plants.
이것은 기이한 재능처럼 보일 수도 있지만, / 식물이 가지기에는 / 전부 명확해진다. / 여러분이 영향을 깨닫고 나면 / 그것이 근처의 식물에 미치는

Manganese can be very harmful to plants, / especially at high concentrations.
망가니즈는 식물에 매우 해로울 수 있으며, / 특히 고농도일 때 그렇다.

Common blackberry is unaffected by damaging effects of this metal / and has evolved two different ways of using manganese to its advantage.
common blackberry는 이 금속 원소의 해로운 효과에 영향을 받지 않으며, / 망가니즈를 자신에게 유리하게 사용하는 두 가지 다른 방법을 발달시켰다.

First, / it redistributes manganese / from deeper soil layers to shallow soil layers / using its roots as a small pipe.
첫째로, / 그것은 망가니즈를 재분배한다. / 깊은 토양층으로부터 얕은 토양층으로 / 그것의 뿌리를 작은 관으로 사용하여

Second, / it absorbs manganese as it grows, / concentrating the metal in its leaves.
둘째로, / 그것은 성장하면서 망가니즈를 흡수하여 / 그 금속 원소를 잎에 농축한다.

When the leaves drop and decay, / their concentrated manganese deposits / further poison the soil around the plant.
잎이 떨어지고 부패할 때, / 그것의 농축된 망가니즈 축적물은 / 그 식물 주변의 토양을 독성 물질로 더욱 오염시킨다.

For plants / that are not immune to the toxic effects of manganese, / this is very bad news.
식물에게 / 망가니즈의 유독한 영향에 면역이 없는 / 이것은 매우 나쁜 소식이다.

Essentially, / the common blackberry eliminates competition / by poisoning its neighbors with heavy metals.
본질적으로, / common blackberry는 경쟁자를 제거한다. / 중금속으로 그것의 이웃을 중독시켜

➡ The common blackberry has an ability / to (A) increase the amount of manganese / in the surrounding upper soil, / which makes the nearby soil / quite (B) deadly for other plants.
common blackberry는 능력이 있는데, / 망가니즈의 양을 증가시키는 / 주변의 위쪽 토양에 / 그것은 근처의 토양을 ~하게 만든다. / 다른 식물에게 상당히 치명적이게

---

common blackberry(*Rubus allegheniensis*)는 뿌리를 이용하여 토양의 한 층에서 다른 층으로 망가니즈를 옮기는 놀라운 능력이 있다. 이것은 식물이 가지기에는 기이한 재능처럼 보일 수도 있지만, 그것이 근처의 식물에 미치는 영향을 깨닫고 나면 전부 명확해진다. 망가니즈는 식물에 매우 해로울 수 있으며, 특히 고농도일 때 그렇다. common blackberry는 이 금속 원소의 해로운 효과에 영향을 받지 않으며, 망가니즈를 자신에게 유리하게 사용하는 두 가지 다른 방법을 발달시켰다. 첫째로, 그것은 뿌리를 작은 관으로 사용하여 망가니즈를 깊은 토양층으로부터 얕은 토양층으로 재분배한다. 둘째로, 그것은 성장하면서 망가니즈를 흡수하여 그 금속 원소를 잎에 농축한다. 잎이 떨어지고 부패할 때 그것의 농축된 망가니즈 축적물은 그 식물 주변의 토양을 독성 물질로 더욱 오염시킨다. 망가니즈의 유독한 영향에 면역이 없는 식물에게 이것은 매우 나쁜 소식이다. 본질적으로, common blackberry는 중금속으로 그것의 이웃을 중독시켜 경쟁자를 제거한다.

➡ common blackberry는 주변 위쪽 토양에 있는 망가니즈의 양을 (A) 증가시키는 능력이 있는데, 그것은 근처의 토양이 다른 식물에게 상당히 (B) 치명적이게 만든다.

Why? 왜 정답일까?

첫 문장과 마지막 세 문장에 따르면 common blackberry는 뿌리를 이용해 망가니즈를 끌어올리거나 이동시킬 수 있어서 주변 토양에 망가니즈가 더 많아지게 할 수 있는데, 이것은 경쟁자 제거에 도움이 된다고 한다. 따라서 요약문의 빈칸 (A), (B)에 들어갈 말로 가장 적절한 것은 ① '(A) increase(증가시키다), (B) deadly(치명적인)'이다.

- concentration ⓝ 농도, 농축
- absorb ⓥ 흡수하다
- eliminate ⓥ 제거하다
- shallow ⓐ 얕은
- be immune to ~에 면역이 있다

구문 풀이

3행 This may seem like a funny talent for a plant to have, but it all becomes
주어1 동사1 주격 보어 의미상 주어 형용사적 용법 주어2 동사2
clear when you realize the effect [it has on nearby plants].
주격 보어2 선행사

41-42 우리를 가로막는 이들을 이해하기

The longest journey we will make / is the eighteen inches between our head and heart.
우리가 갈 가장 긴 여정은 / 우리의 머리에서 가슴까지의 18인치이다.

「If we take this journey, / it can shorten our (a) misery in the world.」 41번의 근거
우리가 이 여행을 한다면, / 그것은 세상에서 우리의 비참함을 줄일 수 있다.

Impatience, judgment, frustration, and anger / reside in our heads.
조급함, 비난, 좌절, 그리고 분노가 / 우리 머릿속에 있다.

When we live in that place too long, / it makes us (b) unhappy.
우리가 그 장소에서 너무 오래 살면, / 그것은 우리를 불행하게 만든다.

But when we take the journey from our heads to our hearts, / something shifts (c) inside.
그러나 우리가 머리부터 가슴까지의 여행을 하면, / 내면에서 무엇인가 바뀐다.

What if we were able to love everything / that gets in our way?
만일 모든 것을 우리가 사랑할 수 있다면 어떻게 될까? / 우리를 가로막는

What if we tried loving the shopper / who unknowingly steps in front of us in line, / the driver who cuts us off in traffic, / the swimmer who splashes us with water during a belly dive, / or the reader who pens a bad online review of our writing?
만일 우리가 그 쇼핑객을 사랑하려고 노력한다면 어떨까? / 줄을 서 있는 우리 앞에 무심코 들어온 / 차량 흐름에서 우리 앞에 끼어든 그 운전자를, / 배 쪽으로 다이빙하면서 우리에게 물을 튀긴 수영하는 그 사람을, / 우리의 글에 대해 나쁜 온라인 후기를 쓴 독자를?

「Every person who makes us miserable / is (d) like us」 42번의 근거 — / a human being, / most likely doing the best they can, / deeply loved by their parents, a child, or a friend.
우리를 비참하게 만드는 모든 사람은 / 우리와 같다. / 인간, / 아마도 분명히 최선을 다하고 있으며, / 부모, 자녀, 또는 친구로부터 깊이 사랑받는

And how many times have we unknowingly stepped / in front of someone in line?
그리고 우리는 몇 번이나 무심코 들어갔을까? / 줄을 서 있는 누군가의 앞에

Cut someone off in traffic?
차량 흐름에서 누군가에게 끼어든 적은?

Splashed someone in a pool?
수영장에서 누군가에게 물을 튀긴 적은?

Or made a negative statement / about something we've read?
혹은 부정적인 진술을 한 적은 몇 번이었을까? / 우리가 읽은 것에 대해

It helps to (e) remember / that a piece of us resides in every person we meet.
기억하는 것은 도움이 된다. / 우리가 만나는 모든 사람 속에 우리의 일부가 있다는 것을

우리가 갈 가장 긴 여정은 우리의 머리에서 가슴까지의 18인치이다. 우리가 이 여행을 한다면, 그것은 세상에서 우리의 (a) 비참함을 줄일 수 있다. 조급함, 비난, 좌절, 그리고 분노가 우리 머릿속에 있다. 우리가 그 장소에서 너무 오래 살면, 그것은 우리를 (b) 불행하게 만든다. 그러나 우리가 머리부터 가슴까지의 여행을 하면, (c) 내면에서 무엇인가 바뀐다. 만일 우리를 가로막는 모든 것을 우리가 사랑할 수 있다면 어떻게 될까? 만일 줄을 서 있는 우리 앞에 무심코 들어온 그 쇼핑객을, 차량 흐름에서 우리 앞에 끼어든 그 운전자를, 배 쪽으로 다이빙하면서 우리에게 물을 튀긴 수영하는 그 사람을, 우리의 글에 대해 나쁜 온라인 후기를 쓴 그 독자를 우리가 사랑하려고 노력한다면 어떨까?

우리를 비참하게 만드는 모든 사람은 우리와 (d) 같다. 그들은 아마도 분명히 최선을 다하고 있으며, 부모, 자녀, 또는 친구로부터 깊이 사랑받는 인간일 것이다. 그리고 우리는 몇 번이나 무심코 줄을 서 있는 누군가의 앞에 끼어 들어갔을까? 차량 흐름에서 누군가에게 끼어든 적은? 수영장에서 누군가에게 물을 튀긴 적은? 혹은 우리가 읽은 것에 대해 부정적인 진술을 한 적은 몇 번이었을까? 우리가 만나는 모든 사람 속에 우리의 일부가 있다는 것을 (e) 부정하는(→기억하는) 것은 도움이 된다.

- misery ⓝ 불행, 비참함
- frustration ⓝ 좌절
- cut off ~을 가로막다
- deny ⓥ 부인하다
- impatience ⓝ 조급함
- get in one's way ~를 방해하다
- splash ⓥ (물을) 튀기다, 끼얹다

구문 풀이

6행 What if we were able to love everything [that gets in our way]?
「what if + 주어 + 과거 동사 ~? : 가정법 과거(실제로 ~하지 않지만 만일 ~한다면 어떨까?)」

41 제목 파악
정답률 52% | 정답 ⑤

윗글의 제목으로 가장 적절한 것은?

① Why It Is So Difficult to Forgive Others – 다른 사람을 용서하기란 왜 그토록 어려울까
② Even Acts of Kindness Can Hurt Somebody – 친절한 행동조차도 누군가를 상처 입힐 수 있다
③ Time Is the Best Healer for a Broken Heart – 실연에는 시간이 가장 좋은 약이다
④ Celebrate the Happy Moments in Your Everyday Life – 매일의 일상에서 행복한 순간을 축복하라
☑ Understand Others to Save Yourself from Unhappiness – 타인을 이해하여 스스로를 불행에서 구하라

Why? 왜 정답일까?

첫 두 문장인 'The longest journey we will make is the eighteen inches between our head and heart. If we take this journey, it can shorten our misery in the world.'에서 남을 이해하는 과정을 '머리부터 가슴까지의 여행'에 빗대어, 이 여행은 우리에게 가장 멀게 느껴지지만 잘 이뤄지면 우리를 불행에서 구해줄 수 있다고 한다. 따라서 글의 제목으로 가장 적절한 것은 ⑤ '타인을 이해하여 스스로를 불행에서 구하라'이다.

42 어휘 추론
정답률 54% | 정답 ⑤

밑줄 친 (a)~(e) 중에서 문맥상 낱말의 쓰임이 적절하지 않은 것은?

① (a)   ② (b)   ③ (c)   ④ (d)   ☑ (e)

Why? 왜 정답일까?

'Every person who makes us miserable is like us ~'에서 우리를 비참하게 하는 사람들에게도 우리 자신의 모습이 있다고 설명하는 것으로 보아, 이 점을 우리가 '기억하고' 있을 때 우리 마음속의 불행이 걷어진다는 결론이 적절하다. 즉 (e)의 deny를 remember로 고쳐야 한다. 따라서 문맥상 낱말의 쓰임이 적절하지 않은 것은 ⑤ '(e)'이다.

43-45 여행자들과 수도승의 대화

(A)

One day / a young man was walking along a road on his journey / from one village to another.
어느 날 / 한 젊은이가 여행 중에 길을 따라 걷고 있었다. / 한 마을로부터 다른 마을로
『As he walked / he noticed a monk working in the fields.』 45번①의 근거 일치
그가 걸어갈 때 / 그는 들판에서 일하는 한 수도승을 보게 되었다.
The young man turned to the monk and said, / "Excuse me.
그 젊은이는 그 수도승을 향해 돌아보며 말했다. / "실례합니다.
Do you mind if I ask (a) you a question?"
제가 스님께 질문을 하나 드려도 되겠습니까?"라고
"Not at all," replied the monk.
"물론입니다."라고 그 수도승은 대답했다.

(C)

"I am traveling / from the village in the mountains / to the village in the valley / and I was wondering / if (c) you knew what it is like in the village in the valley."
"저는 가고 있는데 / 산속의 마을로부터 / 골짜기의 마을로 / 저는 궁금합니다. / 스님께서 골짜기의 마을은 어떤지 아시는지"
"Tell me," / said the monk, / "what was your experience of the village in the mountains?"
"저에게 말해 보십시오." / 수도승은 말했다. / "산속의 마을에서의 경험은 어땠는지"라고
"Terrible," replied the young man.
그 젊은이는 "끔찍했습니다."라고 대답했다.
"I am glad to be away from there.
"그곳을 벗어나게 되어 기쁩니다.
I found the people most unwelcoming.
저는 그곳 사람들이 정말로 불친절하다고 생각했습니다.
So tell (d) me, / what can I expect in the village in the valley?"
그러니 저에게 말씀해 주십시오. / 제가 골짜기의 마을에서 무엇을 기대할 수 있을까요?"
"I am sorry to tell you," / said the monk, / "but I think / your experience will be much the same there."
"말씀드리기에 유감이지만," / 수도승은 말했다. / "제 생각에 선생님의 경험은 그곳에서도 거의 같을 것 같다고 생각합니다."
『The young man lowered his head helplessly / and walked on.』 45번④의 근거 일치
그 젊은이는 힘없이 고개를 숙이고 / 계속 걸어갔다.

(B)

A while later / a middle-aged man journeyed down the same road / and came upon the monk.
잠시 후 / 한 중년 남자가 같은 길을 걸어와서 / 그 수도승을 만났다.
"'I am going to the village in the valley,'" / said the man. 45번②의 근거 일치
"저는 골짜기의 마을로 가고 있습니다." / 그 남자는 말했다.
"'Do you know what it is like?'" 45번③의 근거 일치
"그곳이 어떤지 아십니까?"라고
"I do," / replied the monk, / "but first tell (b) me about the village where you came from."
"알고 있습니다만," / 그 수도승은 대답했다. / "먼저 저에게 선생님께서 떠나오신 마을에 관해 말해 주십시오."라고
"I've come from the village in the mountains," / said the man.
"저는 산속의 마을로부터 왔습니다." / 그 남자는 말했다.
"It was a wonderful experience.
"그것은 멋진 경험이었습니다.
I felt / as though I was a member of the family in the village."
저는 느꼈습니다. / 마치 제가 그 마을의 가족의 일원인 것처럼"

(D)

"Why did you feel like that?" asked the monk.
그 수도승은 "왜 그렇게 느끼셨습니까?"라고 물었다.
"The elders gave me much advice, / and people were kind and generous.
"어르신들은 저에게 많은 조언을 해 주셨고, / 사람들은 친절하고 너그러웠습니다.
『I am sad to have left there.』 45번⑤의 근거 불일치
저는 그곳을 떠나서 슬픕니다.
And what is the village in the valley like?" / he asked again.
그런데 골짜기의 마을은 어떻습니까?"라고 / 그는 다시 물었다.
"(e) I think you will find it much the same," / replied the monk.
"저는 선생님은 그곳이 거의 같다고 여기실 거로 생각합니다."라고 / 수도승은 대답했다.
"I'm glad to hear that," / the middle-aged man said smiling and journeyed on.
"그 말씀을 들으니 기쁩니다." / 그 중년 남자는 미소를 지으며 말하고서 여행을 계속했다.

- come upon ~을 우연히 만나다
- unwelcoming ⓐ 불친절한, 환영하지 않는
- generous ⓐ 관대한
- valley ⓝ 골짜기
- helplessly ⓐⓓ 힘없이, 무기력하게

구문 풀이

[B] 6행 I felt as though I was a member of the family in the village.
접속사(마치 ~인 것처럼)

[C] 6행 I found the people most unwelcoming.
5형식 동사 / 목적어 / 목적격 보어(형용사)

[D] 2행 I am sad to have left there.
완료부정사(am보다 과거에 일어난 일 묘사)

43 글의 순서 파악
정답률 66% | 정답 ②

주어진 글 (A)에 이어질 내용을 순서에 맞게 배열한 것으로 가장 적절한 것은?

① (B) – (D) – (C)   ☑ (C) – (B) – (D)
③ (C) – (D) – (B)   ④ (D) – (B) – (C)
⑤ (D) – (C) – (B)

Why? 왜 정답일까?

여행 중이던 젊은이가 수도승을 만나 물어볼 것이 있다고 말했다는 (A) 뒤에는, 젊은이가 산속 마을에 대한 자신의 부정적 감상을 말하며 골짜기의 마을이 어떠한지 묻자 수도승이 산속 마을과 차이가 없을 것이라고 답했다는 내용의 (C)가 연결된다. 이어서 (B)에서는 똑같이 산속 마을에서 출발한 중년 남자가 수도승과 비슷한 대화를 나누며 산속 마을에 관해 좋은 감상을 이야기했다는 내용이 나오고, (D)에서는 수도승이 그렇다면 골짜기 마을도 좋게 느껴질 것이라 답해주었다고 한다. 따라서 글의 순서로 가장 적절한 것은 ② '(C) – (B) – (D)'이다.

44 지칭 추론
정답률 64% | 정답 ④

밑줄 친 (a)~(e) 중에서 가리키는 대상이 나머지 넷과 다른 것은?

① (a)   ② (b)   ③ (c)   ☑ (d)   ⑤ (e)

Why? 왜 정답일까?

(a), (b), (c), (e)는 the monk, (d)는 the young man이므로, (a)~(e) 중에서 가리키는 대상이 다른 하나는 ④ '(d)'이다.

45 세부 내용 파악
정답률 72% | 정답 ⑤

윗글에 관한 내용으로 적절하지 않은 것은?

① 한 수도승이 들판에서 일하고 있었다.
② 중년 남자는 골짜기에 있는 마을로 가는 중이었다.
③ 수도승은 골짜기에 있는 마을에 대해 질문받았다.
④ 수도승의 말을 듣고 젊은이는 고개를 숙였다.
☑ 중년 남자는 산속에 있는 마을을 떠나서 기쁘다고 말했다.

Why? 왜 정답일까?

(D) 'I am sad to have left there.'에 따르면 중년 남자는 산속 마을을 떠나서 슬펐다고 말했으므로, 내용과 일치하지 않는 것은 ⑤ '중년 남자는 산속에 있는 마을을 떠나서 기쁘다고 말했다.'이다.

Why? 왜 오답일까?

① (A) 'As he walked he noticed a monk working in the fields.'의 내용과 일치한다.
② (B) "I am going to the village in the valley," said the man.'의 내용과 일치한다.
③ (B) "Do you know what it is like?"'의 내용과 일치한다.
④ (C) 'The young man lowered his head helplessly and walked on.'의 내용과 일치한다.

A	B	C	D
01 발표하다, 알리다	01 maintain	01 ⓕ	01 ⓟ
02 책임	02 communicate	02 ⓟ	02 ⓘ
03 열정	03 regulation	03 ⓚ	03 ⓘ
04 모이다	04 flow	04 ⓡ	04 ⓗ
05 일, 과업, 과제	05 foreign	05 ⓘ	05 ⓡ
06 완수하다	06 engaging	06 ⓜ	06 ⓘ
07 진지한	07 competitive	07 ⓞ	07 ⓣ
08 통찰력	08 necessarily	08 ⓔ	08 ⓔ
09 기온	09 material	09 ⓐ	09 ⓝ
10 인식하다	10 influence	10 ⓝ	10 ⓠ
11 호기심	11 traditional	11 ⓘ	11 ⓢ
12 감당하다	12 reply	12 ⓘ	12 ⓕ
13 구체적인	13 indeed	13 ⓒ	13 ⓐ
14 이전의	14 observe	14 ⓓ	14 ⓒ
15 관점, 시점	15 civilization	15 ⓘ	15 ⓚ
16 줄이다	16 currently	16 ⓖ	16 ⓓ
17 나타나다, 출현하다	17 claim	17 ⓢ	17 ⓖ
18 생태계	18 factor	18 ⓑ	18 ⓑ
19 살아남다	19 plain	19 ⓗ	19 ⓞ
20 제거하다	20 mainly	20 ⓠ	20 ⓜ

---

06 회 | 2021학년도 3월 학력평가   고1

| 정답과 해설 |

• 정답 •

01 ④ 02 ④ 03 ① 04 ③ 05 ④　06 ③ 07 ① 08 ② 09 ⑤ 10 ②　11 ① 12 ① 13 ③ 14 ③ 15 ④
16 ② 17 ④ 18 ④ 19 ① 20 ③　21 ② 22 ⑤ 23 ① 24 ⑤ 25 ③　26 ⑤ 27 ⑤ 28 ④ 29 ③ 30 ③
★31 ⑤ 32 ④ 33 ① 34 ⑤ 35 ③　★36 ② 37 ③ ★38 ② 39 ④ ★40 ②　41 ① 42 ⑤ 43 ② 44 ⑤ 45 ②

★ 표기된 문항은 [등급을 가르는 문제]에 해당하는 문항입니다.

01 젖은 바닥을 다닐 때 주의하도록 당부하기   정답률 96% | 정답 ④

다음을 듣고, 남자가 하는 말의 목적으로 가장 적절한 것을 고르시오.
① 교내 청소 일정을 공지하려고
② 학교 시설 공사의 지연에 대해 사과하려고
③ 하교 시 교실 창문을 닫을 것을 요청하려고
✓ 교내의 젖은 바닥을 걸을 때 조심하도록 당부하려고
⑤ 깨끗한 교실 환경 조성을 위한 아이디어를 공모하려고

M : Good morning, students.
　안녕하세요, 학생 여러분.
This is Mr. Lewis from the school administration office.
　학교 행정실의 Lewis 선생입니다.
Last night there was a heavy rainstorm.
　어젯밤 심한 폭우가 있었습니다.
The pouring rain left some of the school's hallways wet and slippery.
　억수같은 비로 학교 복도 몇 곳이 젖었고 미끄럽습니다.
The first floor hallway and the central stairway are especially dangerous to walk on.
　1층 복도와 중앙 계단은 특히 걸어다니기 위험합니다.
Please be extra careful when you walk through these areas.
　이 구역들을 통과할 때 특별히 조심해 주세요.
You could get seriously hurt if you slip on the wet floor.
　젖은 바닥에 미끄러지면 심하게 다칠 수 있습니다.
We're doing our best to take care of the situation.
　저희는 상황을 처리하기 위해 최선을 다하겠습니다.
Thank you.
　감사합니다.

Why? 왜 정답일까?

'The first floor hallway and the central stairway are especially dangerous to walk on. Please be extra careful when you walk through these areas.'에서 간밤의 폭우로 인해 1층 복도와 중앙 계단이 젖고 미끄러워졌으니 걸어다닐 때 각별히 주의할 것을 당부하고 있다. 따라서 남자가 하는 말의 목적으로 가장 적절한 것은 ④ '교내의 젖은 바닥을 걸을 때 조심하도록 당부하려고'이다.

● **administration office** 행정실
● **pour** ⓥ 쏟다, 퍼붓다
● **slippery** ⓐ 미끄러운
● **seriously** ⓐ 심하게
● **rainstorm** ⓝ 폭우
● **hallway** ⓝ 복도
● **stairway** ⓝ 계단
● **take care of** ～을 처리하다

02 수면 문제 해결을 위한 조언   정답률 95% | 정답 ④

대화를 듣고, 여자의 의견으로 가장 적절한 것을 고르시오.
① 짧은 낮잠은 업무 효율을 높인다.
② 야식은 숙면에 방해가 될 수 있다.
③ 사람마다 최적의 수면 시간이 다르다.
✓ 베개를 바꾸면 숙면에 도움이 될 수 있다.
⑤ 숙면을 위해 침실을 서늘하게 하는 것이 좋다.

W : Mike, you look very tired today.
　Mike, 너 오늘 되게 피곤해 보인다.
M : I am. I'm having trouble sleeping at night these days.
　맞아. 난 요새 잠드는 데 어려움이 있어.
W : What's the matter?
　무슨 일이야?
M : I don't know. I just can't fall asleep until late at night.
　나도 몰라. 그냥 밤 늦게까지 잠이 안 와.
W : I feel bad for you.
　안됐구나.
M : I need to find a way to sleep better.
　난 잠을 더 잘 잘 수 있는 방법을 찾아야 해.
W : Can I share how I handled my sleeping problem?
　내가 수면 문제를 어떻게 해결했는지 알려줘도 될까?
M : Sure.
　물론이지.
W : After I changed my pillow, I was able to sleep much better. Changing your pillow can help you with your sleeping problem.
　내가 베개를 바꾸고 나서 나는 훨씬 더 잘 잘 수 있었어. 베개를 바꾸는 것은 수면 문제를 해결하는 데 도움이 될 수 있어.
M : Thanks for the tip. I hope that works for me, too.
　조언 고마워. 나한테도 효과가 있으면 좋겠다.

Why? 왜 정답일까?

'Changing your pillow can help you with your sleeping problem.'에서 여자는 베개를 바꾼 것이 수면 문제를 해결하는 데 도움이 되었다고 하므로, 여자의 의견으로 가장 적절한 것은 ④ '베개를 바꾸면 숙면에 도움이 될 수 있다.'이다.

● **have trouble ~ing** ～하는 데 문제가 있다
● **handle** ⓥ 다루다, 처리하다
● **work for** ～에 효과가 있다
● **fall asleep** 잠들다
● **pillow** ⓝ 베개

03 파티 음식 부탁하기
정답률 96% | 정답 ①

대화를 듣고, 두 사람의 관계를 가장 잘 나타낸 것을 고르시오.

✓ 파티 주최자 - 요리사
② 슈퍼마켓 점원 - 손님
③ 배달 기사 - 음식점 주인
④ 영양학자 - 식품 제조업자
⑤ 인테리어 디자이너 - 의뢰인

M : Hi, I'm Daniel Jones. I'm glad to finally meet you.
안녕하세요, 전 Daniel Jones입니다. 마침내 뵙게 되어 기쁘네요.

W : Welcome. Mr. Harvey told me you're coming.
잘 오셨어요. Harvey 씨가 제게 당신이 오실 거라고 얘기해 줬어요.

M : He told me nice things about you.
그에게서 좋은 말씀 많이 들었습니다.

W : Thanks. I hear that you're holding a party at your house in two weeks.
고맙습니다. 2주 뒤에 댁에서 파티를 여실 예정이라고 들었어요.

M : That's right. I'm hoping you could take charge of the food for my party.
맞습니다. 제 파티에서 음식을 담당해 주시기를 바라고 있어요.

W : Sure. You can always depend on a chef like me.
물론이죠. 저 같은 요리사라면 늘 믿으셔도 됩니다.

M : Great. Is there anything I need to prepare for you?
아주 좋아요. 제가 준비해 드릴 게 있을까요?

W : No need. I'll be taking care of the party food from start to finish.
그러실 것 없습니다. 제가 처음부터 끝까지 파티 음식을 담당하겠습니다.

M : Sounds fantastic.
환상적으로 들리는군요.

W : Now let's talk about the menu.
이제 메뉴에 관해 이야기하시죠.

Why? 왜 정답일까?

'I hear that you're holding a party at your house in two weeks.'에서 남자가 파티를 주최하는 사람임을, 'You can always depend on a chef like me.'에서 여자가 요리사임을 알 수 있다. 따라서 두 사람의 관계로 가장 적절한 것은 ① '파티 주최자 - 요리사'이다.

● hold a party 파티를 열다
● take charge of ~을 담당하다, 책임지다
● depend on ~을 믿다, 의지하다
● No need. 그러실 것 없습니다.

04 온라인 강의 촬영 스튜디오 확인하기
정답률 81% | 정답 ③

대화를 듣고, 그림에서 대화의 내용과 일치하지 <u>않는</u> 것을 고르시오.

W : Is that the photo of our school's new studio?
이게 우리 학교의 새 스튜디오 사진인가요?

M : Yes. We can shoot online lectures here.
네. 우린 여기서 온라인 강의를 찍을 수 있어요.

W : Can I have a look?
제가 봐도 돼요?

M : Sure. 『Do you see that camera facing the chair?』 ①의근거 일치 It's the latest model.
그럼요. 『의자 맞은편에 있는 카메라 보여요?』 최신 제품이에요.

W : I see. 『What is that ring on the stand next to the camera?』 ②의근거 일치
그렇군요. 『카메라 옆 스탠드에 있는 링은 뭔가요?』

M : That's the lighting. It's to brighten the teacher's face.
그건 조명이에요. 선생님의 얼굴을 비추기 위한 것이죠.

W : Hmm.... 『The round clock on the wall looks simple and modern.』 ③의근거 불일치
흠... 『벽에 있는 동그란 시계가 심플하고 모던해 보이네요.』

M : Teachers can check the time on the clock while shooting.
선생님들께서 촬영 중 시계로 시간을 확인하실 수 있어요.

W : 『The microphone on the table looks very professional.』 ④의근거 일치
『테이블 위의 마이크는 굉장히 전문적으로 보여요.』

M : It really does. 『Also, I like the tree in the corner.』 ⑤의근거 일치 It goes well with the studio.
정말로 그렇습니다. 『그리고, 저는 구석에 있는 나무도 마음에 들어요.』 스튜디오와 잘 어울려요.

Why? 왜 정답일까?

대화에 따르면 벽에 걸린 시계는 동그란 모양인데(**The round clock on the wall looks simple and modern.**), 그림에는 네모 모양 시계가 걸려 있다. 따라서 그림에서 대화의 내용과 일치하지 않는 것은 ③이다.

● lecture ⓝ 강의
● latest ⓐ 최신의
● go well with ~와 잘 어울리다

05 영화 약속 확인하기
정답률 94% | 정답 ④

대화를 듣고, 남자가 할 일로 가장 적절한 것을 고르시오.

① 영화 예매하기
② 지갑 가져오기
③ 시간표 출력하기
✓ 학생증 재발급받기
⑤ 영화 감상문 제출하기

M : Hi, Jamie. You remember we're going to the movies later today, right?
안녕, Jamie. 우리 오늘 이따 영화 보러 가는 거 기억하지, 그렇지?

W : Of course. I'll see you after class.
물론이지. 수업 끝나고 봐.

M : Didn't you say there's a student discount on the movie ticket?
영화 표에 학생 할인이 있다고 말하지 않았어?

W : Yes, I did. Don't forget to bring your student ID card.
응. 네 학생증 들고 오는 것 잊지 마.

M : But I've lost my ID. Is there any other way to get the discount?
그런데 난 학생증을 잃어버렸어. 할인을 받을 다른 방법 뭐 없을까?

W : Probably not. Why don't you go get a new ID card from the school office?
아마 없을걸. 학교 사무실에서 새로운 학생증을 받으면 어때?

M : Do you know where the office is?
사무실이 어디인지 알아?

W : Yes. It's on the first floor.
응. 1층에 있어.

M : Okay. I'll go there right away.
알겠어. 바로 거기 가볼게.

Why? 왜 정답일까?

남자는 여자와 영화를 볼 예정인데 영화표를 할인받을 수 있는 학생증을 잃어버렸다. 여자는 남자에게 사무실로 가서 다시 학생증을 발급받는 것이 어떤지 제안하며 1층에 사무실이 있다고 알려준다. 이에 남자는 바로 사무실에 가보겠다(**I'll go there right away.**)고 하므로, 남자가 할 일로 가장 적절한 것은 ④ '학생증 재발급받기'이다.

● go to the movies 영화 보러 가다
● get a discount 할인을 받다

06 캠핑용품 구매하기
정답률 81% | 정답 ③

대화를 듣고, 여자가 지불할 금액을 고르시오. [3점]

① $72
② $80
✓ $90
④ $100
⑤ $110

W : Hi, I'm looking for camping chairs. Can you recommend one?
안녕하세요, 전 캠핑 의자를 찾고 있어요. 하나 추천해 주실래요?

M : Good morning. This is our best-selling chair. They're $20 each.
안녕하세요. 이게 제일 잘 나가는 의자입니다. 하나에 20달러예요.

W : That sounds good. I'll take it.
좋은 것 같네요. 이걸 살게요.

M : How many do you need?
몇 개가 필요하신가요?

W : I need four chairs.
전 의자 4개가 필요해요.

M : Okay. Is there anything else you need?
알겠습니다. 더 필요한 것은 없으세요?

W : I also need a camping knife.
캠핑용 칼도 필요해요.

M : How about this one? It's $20.
이건 어떠세요? 20달러입니다.

W : That looks convenient. I'll buy one. Do you offer any discounts?
편리해 보이네요. 하나 살게요. 할인도 해주시나요?

M : Yes. Since your total purchase is over $80, we'll give you a 10% discount on the total amount.
네. 총 구매 금액이 80달러를 넘어서, 총액에서 10퍼센트를 할인해 드릴게요.

W : That sounds nice. I'll pay with my credit card.
좋네요. 신용 카드로 계산할게요.

Why? 왜 정답일까?

대화에 따르면 여자는 20달러짜리 캠핑 의자 4개와, 역시 20달러인 캠핑용 칼을 한 자루 사고, 총 금액에서 10%를 할인받았다. 이를 식으로 나타내면 '(20×4 + 20)×0.9 = 90'이므로, 여자가 지불할 금액은 ③ '$90'이다.

● convenient ⓐ 편리한
● purchase ⓝ 구매

07 과학 보고서를 끝내지 못한 이유
정답률 74% | 정답 ①

대화를 듣고, 남자가 보고서를 완성하지 <u>못한</u> 이유를 고르시오.

✓ 실험을 다시 해서
② 제출일을 착각해서
③ 주제가 변경되어서
④ 컴퓨터가 고장 나서
⑤ 심한 감기에 걸려서

M : Hi, Rebecca. What's up?
안녕, Rebecca. 무슨 일이야?

W : Hey, Tom. Can I borrow your laptop today?
안녕, Tom. 내가 오늘 네 노트북을 빌려도 될까?

M : Yes, but I have to finish my science report first.
응, 그런데 난 과학 보고서를 먼저 끝내야 해.

W : Really? Wasn't the science report due last week?
정말? 과학 보고서는 지난 주가 마감 아니었어?

M : Yes, it was. But I couldn't finish it.
맞아. 그런데 내가 그걸 마칠 수가 없었어.

W : What happened? I thought your experiment went well.
무슨 일이 있었던 거야? 난 네 실험이 잘되었다고 생각했는데.

M : Actually, it didn't. I made a mistake in the experimental process.
사실은 그렇지 않았어. 난 실험 과정에서 실수를 했어.

W : Oh, no. Did you have to do the experiment all over again?
오, 이런. 실험을 다 다시 해야 했던 거야?

M : Yes, it took a lot of time. So I haven't finished my report yet.
응, 시간이 오래 걸렸어. 그래서 아직 내 보고서를 끝내지 못했어.

W : I see. Let me know when you're done.
알겠어. 네가 다 하면 알려줘.

Why? 왜 정답일까?

대화에 따르면 남자는 과학 실험을 처음부터 다시 해야 했기에(**Did you have to do the experiment** all over again? / Yes, it took a lot of time.) 과학 보고서를 제때 완성하지 못했다. 따라서 남자가 보고서를 완성하지 못한 이유로 가장 적절한 것은 ① '실험을 다시 해서'이다.

- laptop ⓝ 노트북 컴퓨터
- experimental ⓐ 실험의
- due ⓐ 마감인, 예정인

---

08 달리기 행사 등록하기
정답률 93% | 정답 ②

대화를 듣고, Spring Virtual Run에 관해 언급되지 <u>않은</u> 것을 고르시오.
① 달리는 거리 ✔ 참가 인원 ③ 달리는 장소
④ 참가비 ⑤ 기념품

W : Hi, Asher. What are you doing on the computer?
안녕, Asher. 컴퓨터로 뭐 하고 있어?
M : I'm signing up for an event called the Spring Virtual Run.
난 Spring Virtual Run이라는 행사에 등록하고 있어.
W : The Spring Virtual... Run?
Spring Virtual... Run이라고?
M : It's a race. 『Participants upload their record after running either a three-mile race or a ten-mile race.』 ①의근거 일치
경주야. 『참가자들은 3마일짜리 또는 10마일짜리 경주 중 하나를 뛰고 나서 자기 기록을 올리는 거야.』
W : 『Can you run at any location?』
『아무 장소에서든 달릴 수 있어?』
M : Yes. I can choose any place in the city.』 ③의근거 일치
응. 시내 아무 장소나 선택하면 돼.』
W : That sounds interesting. I want to participate, too.
재미있겠다. 나도 참여하고 싶어.
M : 『Then you should sign up online and pay the registration fee. It's twenty dollars.』 ④의근거 일치
『그럼 온라인으로 등록하고 나서 참가비를 내야 해. 20달러야.』
W : Twenty dollars? That's pretty expensive.
20달러라고? 꽤 비싸네.
M : But souvenirs are included in the fee. 『All participants will get a T-shirt and a water bottle.』 ⑤의근거 일치
하지만 참가비 안에 기념품이 포함되어 있어. 『모든 참가자들은 티셔츠와 물병을 받게 돼.』
W : That's reasonable. I'll sign up.
적당하네. 나도 등록할래.

Why? 왜 정답일까?
대화에서 남자와 여자는 Spring Virtual Run의 달리는 거리, 달리는 장소, 참가비, 기념품에 관해 언급하였다. 따라서 언급되지 않은 것은 ② '참가 인원'이다.

Why? 왜 오답일까?
① 'Participants upload their record after running either a three-mile race or a ten-mile race.'에서 '달리는 거리'가 언급되었다.
③ 'Yes. I can choose any place in the city.'에서 '달리는 장소'가 언급되었다.
④ 'It's twenty dollars.'에서 '참가비'가 언급되었다.
⑤ 'All participants will get a T-shirt and a water bottle.'에서 '기념품'이 언급되었다.

- sign up 등록하다, 가입하다
- souvenir ⓝ 기념품
- registration fee 참가비
- reasonable ⓐ (가격 등이) 적당한, 합리적인

---

09 자연사 박물관 가족의 밤 행사 안내
정답률 82% | 정답 ⑤

Family Night at the Museum에 관한 다음 내용을 듣고, 일치하지 <u>않는</u> 것을 고르시오.
① 박물관 정규 운영 시간 종료 후에 열린다.
② 행사과 별 모형 아래에서 잠을 잔다.
③ 참가자들에게 침낭이 제공된다.
④ 6세부터 13세까지를 위한 프로그램이다.
✔ 사전 등록 없이 현장에서 참가할 수 있다.

W : Do your children love adventures?
여러분의 아이들이 모험을 좋아하나요?
Here's a great adventure for you and your children.
여기 여러분과 아이들을 위한 근사한 모험이 있습니다.
The Museum of Natural History is starting a special program — Family Night at the Museum.
자연사 박물관에서 특별 프로그램인 Family Night at the Museum을 시작할 예정입니다.
『When the regular museum hours are over, you and your children get to walk around the museum with a flashlight.』 ①의근거 일치
『박물관 정규 운영 시간이 끝나면, 여러분과 아이들은 플래시를 들고 박물관을 돌아다닙니다.』
『After your adventure is complete, you will sleep under the amazing models of planets and stars.』 ②의근거 일치
『모험이 끝나면, 여러분은 근사한 행성 및 별 모형 아래에서 잠을 잘 것입니다.』
『Sleeping bags, snacks, and water will be provided.』 ③의근거 일치
『침낭, 간식, 그리고 물이 제공될 것입니다.』
『This program is for children ages 6 to 13.』 ④의근거 일치
『이 프로그램은 6세부터 13세까지의 어린이들을 위한 것입니다.』
All those who want to join must register in advance.
참여하고 싶으신 분들은 꼭 사전에 등록하셔야 합니다.
『On-site registration is not accepted.』 ⑤의근거 불일치
『현장 등록은 불가능합니다.』
Why not call today and sign up?
오늘 전화해서 등록하시는 게 어떠세요?

Why? 왜 정답일까?
'On-site registration is not accepted.'에서 현장 등록은 불가하다고 하므로, 내용과 일치하지 않는 것은 ⑤ '사전 등록 없이 현장에서 참가할 수 있다.'이다.

Why? 왜 오답일까?
① 'When the regular museum hours are over, you and your children get to walk around the museum with a flashlight.'의 내용과 일치한다.

② 'After your adventure is complete, you will sleep under the amazing models of planets and stars.'의 내용과 일치한다.
③ 'Sleeping bags, snacks, and water will be provided.'의 내용과 일치한다.
④ 'This program is for children ages 6 to 13.'의 내용과 일치한다.

- natural history 자연사, 박물학
- in advance 사전에, 미리
- complete ⓐ 완료된
- on-site ⓐ 현장의, 현지의

---

10 스마트 워치 사기
정답률 84% | 정답 ②

다음 표를 보면서 대화를 듣고, 여자가 구매할 스마트 워치를 고르시오.

Smart Watches

	Model	Waterproof	Warranty	Price
①	A	×	2 years	$90
✔②	B	○	3 years	$110
③	C	○	1 year	$115
④	D	×	2 years	$120
⑤	E	○	4 years	$125

M : Hi, how can I help you today?
안녕하세요, 오늘 무엇을 도와드릴까요?
W : Hi, I'm looking for a smart watch.
안녕하세요, 전 스마트 워치를 찾고 있습니다.
M : Sure. We have these five models.
그러시군요. 여기 다섯 가지 제품이 있습니다.
W : Hmm.... I want to wear it when I swim.
흠... 전 그것을 수영할 때 차고 싶어요.
M : 『Then you're looking for one that's waterproof.』 근거1 Waterproof 조건
『그럼 방수가 되는 제품을 찾으시는 거군요.』
W : That's right. Do you think a one-year warranty is too short?
맞아요. 1년짜리 보증은 너무 짧다고 생각하세요?
M : Yes. 『I recommend one that has a warranty longer than one year.』 근거2 Warranty 조건
네. 『보증기간이 1년보다 더 긴 제품을 추천드려요.』
W : Okay. I'll take your advice.
알겠습니다. 조언을 따를게요.
M : That leaves you with these two options. 『I'd get the cheaper one because it's as good as the other one.』
그럼 이 두 가지 선택권이 남습니다. 『싼 것도 다른 제품에 못지않게 좋기 때문에 저라면 싼 것을 사겠어요.』
W : I see. Then I'll go with the cheaper one.』 근거3 Price 조건
그렇군요. 그럼 더 싼 것으로 살게요.』
M : Good choice.
좋은 선택입니다.

Why? 왜 정답일까?
대화에 따르면 여자는 수영할 때 찰 수 있도록 방수가 되고, 보증기간이 1년 이상이면서, 가격이 더 싼 스마트 워치를 사려고 한다. 따라서 여자가 구매할 스마트 워치는 ② 'B'이다.

- waterproof ⓐ 방수의
- recommend ⓥ 추천하다, 권장하다
- warranty ⓝ 보증
- go with ~을 선택하다

---

11 새로 산 셔츠 구경하기
정답률 87% | 정답 ①

대화를 듣고, 여자의 마지막 말에 대한 남자의 응답으로 가장 적절한 것을 고르시오.
✔① Oh, I should get it exchanged. – 오, 교환 받아야겠어요.
② Sure. I'll order a shirt for you. – 물론이죠. 제가 셔츠를 하나 주문해 드릴게요.
③ Well, it's too expensive for me. – 음, 저한테는 너무 비싸요.
④ No. Please find me a smaller size. – 아니에요. 제게 더 작은 사이즈를 찾아주세요.
⑤ Sorry, but this shirt is not on sale. – 죄송하지만, 이 셔츠는 세일 품목이 아닙니다.

W : Liam, how did your shopping go?
Liam, 쇼핑 어땠니?
M : It was good, Mom. I got this shirt at a good price.
좋았어요, 엄마. 전 이 셔츠를 좋은 가격에 샀어요.
W : It looks nice. Wait! It's missing a button.
근사해 보이네. 잠깐! 단추가 하나 없구나.
M : Oh, I should get it exchanged.
오, 교환 받아야겠어요.

Why? 왜 정답일까?
남자가 쇼핑을 가서 사온 셔츠를 보던 여자는 셔츠에 단추가 하나 없는 것을 발견한다(Wait! It's missing a button.). 따라서 남자의 응답으로 가장 적절한 것은 ① '오, 교환 받아야겠어요.'이다.

- miss ⓥ 빠뜨리다, 빼놓다
- exchange ⓥ 교환하다

---

12 도넛 가게 소개받기
정답률 82% | 정답 ①

대화를 듣고, 남자의 마지막 말에 대한 여자의 응답으로 가장 적절한 것을 고르시오.
✔① Good. Let's meet around six. – 좋지. 여섯시쯤 만나자.
② That's okay. I don't like donuts. – 괜찮아. 난 도넛 안 좋아해.
③ I want to open my own donut shop. – 난 내 도넛 가게를 열고 싶어.
④ Don't worry. I can do that by myself. – 걱정 마. 나 혼자서 할 수 있어.
⑤ Thanks for sharing your donut recipe. – 네 도넛 레시피를 공유해줘서 고마워.

M : Alicia, these donuts are delicious. Can you tell me where you bought them?
Alicia, 이 도넛 맛있다. 어디서 샀는지 말해줄 수 있어?

W : They're from a new donut shop. I can take you there if you want.
새로 연 도넛 가게에서 산 거야. 네가 원하면 데려다줄 수 있어.

M : That'd be nice. How's today after work?
그럼 좋지. 오늘 일 끝나고는 어때?

W : Good. Let's meet around six.
좋지. 여섯시쯤 만나자.

Why? 왜 정답일까?

새로 연 도넛 가게에 데려다줄 수 있다는 여자의 말에 남자는 오늘 일이 끝난 후 가면 어떨지(How's today after work?) 제안하고 있으므로, 여자의 응답으로 가장 적절한 것은 ① '좋지. 여섯시쯤 만나자.'이다.

- around [ad] 약, ∼쯤
- by oneself 혼자서

---

13 플라스틱 발자국을 줄이기 위한 노력   정답률 82% | 정답 ②

대화를 듣고, 여자의 마지막 말에 대한 남자의 응답으로 가장 적절한 것을 고르시오. [3점]

Man:

① This coffee place is very popular. – 이 커피집 정말 인기 많아.
✓ You can stop using plastic straws. – 넌 플라스틱 빨대를 그만 쓸 수 있어.
③ I'll order drinks when you're ready. – 네가 준비되면 음료 시킬게.
④ Your drink will be ready in a minute. – 네 음료가 1분 뒤에 준비될 거야.
⑤ The cups come in various colors and shapes. – 이 컵은 다양한 색과 모양으로 나와.

W : Brandon, I'm sorry I'm late.
Brandon, 늦어서 미안해.

M : That's okay. Let's order our drinks. I'll get my coffee in my personal cup.
괜찮아. 우리 마실 거 주문하자. 내 커피는 내 개인 컵에 받을래.

W : Oh, you brought your own cup?
오, 네 컵을 가져온 거야?

M : Yes, it is a reusable cup. I'm trying to reduce my plastic footprint.
응, 이건 재사용 가능한 컵이야. 난 내 플라스틱 발자국을 줄이려고 노력 중이야.

W : What is plastic footprint?
플라스틱 발자국이 뭐야?

M : It is the total amount of plastic a person uses and throws away.
한 사람이 쓰고서 버리는 플라스틱의 총량이야.

W : You care a lot about the environment.
넌 환경을 많이 생각하는구나.

M : I do. Plastic waste is a huge environmental problem.
맞아. 플라스틱 쓰레기는 엄청난 환경 문제야.

W : I should use a reusable cup, too. What else can I do to reduce my plastic footprint?
나도 재사용 가능한 컵을 써야겠다. 내가 내 탄소 발자국을 줄이기 위해 할 수 있는 게 또 뭐가 있니?

M : You can stop using plastic straws.
넌 플라스틱 빨대를 그만 쓸 수 있어.

Why? 왜 정답일까?

남자가 개인 컵을 사용하며 플라스틱 사용량을 줄이기 위해 노력하고 있다는 말에 여자는 자신도 동참해야겠다고 말하며 플라스틱을 덜 쓰기 위해 할 수 있는 일이 또 없는지(What else can I do to reduce my plastic footprint?) 물어보고 있다. 따라서 남자의 응답으로 가장 적절한 것은 ② '넌 플라스틱 빨대를 그만 쓸 수 있어.'이다.

- reusable [a] 재사용 가능한
- huge [a] 엄청난, 거대한
- reduce [v] 줄이다
- environmental [a] 환경의

---

14 자전거를 타고 등교하기   정답률 90% | 정답 ③

대화를 듣고, 남자의 마지막 말에 대한 여자의 응답으로 가장 적절한 것을 고르시오. [3점]

Woman:

① Luckily, I didn't get hurt in the accident. – 다행히 난 사고에서 다치지 않았어.
② I have enough money to get a new bike. – 난 새 자전거를 사기에 충분한 돈이 있어.
✓ You really need one for your own safety. – 네 자신의 안전을 위해 꼭 하나 있어야 해.
④ You may feel sleepy after biking to school. – 학교에 자전거를 타고 오면 졸릴 수도 있어.
⑤ We can put our bikes in the school parking lot. – 우린 자전거를 학교 주차장에 두면 돼.

M : Good morning, Kathy. That's a cool helmet.
안녕, Kathy. 헬멧 근사하네.

W : Hi, Alex. It's for biking. I rode my bike to school.
안녕, Alex. 자전거 탈 때 쓰는 거야. 난 학교에 자전거를 타고 왔어.

M : How often do you ride your bike to school?
얼마나 자주 자전거로 등교해?

W : I try to do it every day. It's very refreshing.
매일 하려고 노력해. 아주 상쾌하거든.

M : Sounds nice. I'm thinking of riding to school, too.
좋을 것 같다. 나도 학교에 타고 다닐까 생각 중이야.

W : Good! We should ride together.
좋아! 우리 같이 타고 오자.

M : Let's do that, but I'm not very good at biking.
그러자, 그런데 난 자전거를 잘 못 타.

W : It's okay. We can go slowly. Also, remember to wear your helmet.
괜찮아, 천천히 다니면 되지. 그리고 헬멧을 잊지 말고 써.

M : But I don't have a helmet yet.
하지만 난 아직 헬멧이 없어.

W : You really need one for your own safety.
네 자신의 안전을 위해 꼭 하나 있어야 해.

Why? 왜 정답일까?

자전거로 등교할 때 꼭 헬멧을 써야 한다는 여자의 말에 남자는 아직 헬멧이 없다(But I don't have a helmet yet.)고 말하고 있으므로, 여자의 응답으로 가장 적절한 것은 ③ '네 자신의 안전을 위해 꼭 하나 있어야 해.'이다.

[문제편 p.050]

- refreshing [a] 상쾌한
- safety [n] 안전
- be good at ∼을 잘하다

---

15 밴드의 리드 보컬 찾기   정답률 89% | 정답 ④

다음 상황 설명을 듣고, Jasper가 Mary에게 할 말로 가장 적절한 것을 고르시오.

Jasper: _____

① Where is the audition being held? – 오디션이 어디서 열릴 거래?
② How about writing your own song? – 네 노래를 직접 써보는 건 어때?
③ Let's play a different song this time. – 이번에는 다른 노래를 연주해 보자.
✓ I think you should be our lead singer. – 난 네가 우리 리드 보컬이 되어야 할 것 같아.
⑤ Don't you think we need more practice? – 우리가 더 연습이 필요하다고 생각하지 않니?

W : Jasper and Mary are trying to form a rock band for the school band competition.
Jasper와 Mary는 학교 밴드 경연대회를 위해 록 밴드를 만들려고 한다.

Mary plays the guitar, and Jasper is the drummer.
Mary는 기타를 치고, Jasper는 드러머이다.

They pick a keyboard player through an audition.
그들은 오디션을 통해 키보드 연주자를 고른다.

Now, they need a lead singer.
이제 리드 보컬이 필요하다.

Although the band is not completely formed, they begin their first practice today.
비록 밴드가 다 결성된 것은 아니지만, 그들은 오늘 첫 연습을 시작한다.

Since they don't have a lead singer yet, Mary sings while playing the guitar.
아직 리드 보컬이 없기 때문에, Mary가 기타를 치면서 노래를 부른다.

Hearing her sing, the other members are amazed.
그녀가 노래하는 것을 들었을 때, 다른 멤버들은 놀란다.

Mary has the perfect voice for rock music!
Mary는 록 음악에 딱 맞는 목소리를 갖고 있었다!

So Jasper wants to tell Mary to be the lead singer for their band.
그래서 Jasper는 Mary에게 밴드의 리드 보컬이 되어 달라고 말하고 싶다.

In this situation, what would Jasper most likely say to Mary?
이 상황에서, Jasper는 Mary에게 뭐라고 말하겠는가?

Jasper : I think you should be our lead singer.
난 네가 우리 리드 보컬이 되어야 할 것 같아.

Why? 왜 정답일까?

상황에 따르면 Jasper는 Mary와 함께 밴드의 리드 보컬을 찾던 중 기타를 치며 노래하는 Mary의 멋진 목소리를 듣고 Mary에게 직접 리드 보컬이 되어줄 것을 제안하고 싶어 한다(So Jasper wants to tell Mary to be the lead singer for their band.). 따라서 Jasper가 Mary에게 할 말로 가장 적절한 것은 ④ '난 네가 우리 리드 보컬이 되어야 할 것 같아.'이다.

- form [v] 만들다, 형성하다
- completely [ad] 완전히
- How about ~ing ∼하는 게 어때?
- competition [n] 경연, 경쟁
- amazed [a] 놀란

16-17 반려동물의 행복에 있어 장난감의 역할

M : Good afternoon, everybody.
안녕하세요, 여러분.

Today, we'll talk about what our animal companions love: Toys.
오늘 우리는 우리 동물 친구들이 정말 좋아하는 것, 즉 장난감에 관해 이야기해볼 거예요.

『How do toys help our pets?』 **16번의 근거**
『장난감이 반려동물에게 어떻게 도움이 될까요?』

First, toys play a very important role in keeping your pet happy.
첫째, 장난감은 여러분의 반려동물을 행복한 상태로 유지해주는 데 아주 중요한 역할을 해요.

『A toy like a scratcher helps to reduce your cat's stress.』 **17번 ①의 근거** 일치
『스크래처 같은 장난감은 여러분의 고양이의 스트레스를 줄이는 데 도움이 됩니다.』

Second, toys are a great tool for a pet to get exercise.
둘째, 장난감은 반려동물이 운동하게 해주는 훌륭한 도구입니다.

『For example, a hamster loves to run on a wheel toy.』 **17번 ②의 근거** 일치
『예를 들어, 햄스터는 쳇바퀴 장난감 위에서 달리는 것을 좋아합니다.』

Third, toys build a bond between you and your pet.
셋째, 장난감은 여러분과 반려동물 사이에 유대감을 형성해 줍니다.

『Playing with a small soft ball will give you and your dog a joyful experience.』 **17번 ③의 근거** 일치
『작고 부드러운 공을 갖고 노는 것은 여러분과 개에게 즐거운 경험을 줍니다.』

Lastly, toys help keep your pet entertained.
마지막으로, 장난감은 여러분의 반려동물을 계속 즐겁게 해줍니다.

『A small hiding tent will make your parrot feel less bored when you are not around.』 **17번 ⑤의 근거** 일치
『자그마한 숨바꼭질 텐트는 여러분이 주변에 없을 때 여러분의 앵무새가 덜 지루하게 해줍니다.』

Now let's watch a video of pets playing with their toys.
이제 반려동물들이 장난감을 갖고 노는 영상을 봅시다.

- companion [n] 친구, 동반자
- reduce [v] 줄이다
- joyful [a] 즐거운
- parrot [n] 앵무새
- play a role in ∼에 역할을 하다, 일조하다
- bond [n] 유대
- entertain [v] 즐겁게 해주다

---

16 주제 파악   정답률 84% | 정답 ②

남자가 하는 말의 주제로 가장 적절한 것은?

① eco-friendly toys for pets – 반려동물들을 위한 친환경 장난감
✓ roles of toys in pets' well-being – 반려동물의 행복에 있어 장난감의 역할
③ types of pets' unusual behaviors – 반려동물의 특이한 행동의 종류
④ foods that are dangerous to pets – 반려동물에게 위험한 음식
⑤ difficulties in raising children with pets – 아이를 반려동물과 함께 키우는 것의 어려움

Why? 왜 정답일까?

'How do toys help our pets?'에서 남자는 장난감이 반려동물에 어떤 식으로 도움이 되는지 자문

한 뒤 장난감의 역할을 열거하고 있다. 따라서 남자가 하는 말의 주제로 가장 적절한 것은 ② '반려동물의 행복에 있어 장난감의 역할'이다.

<table>
<tr><td>**17**</td><td>언급 유무 파악</td><td>정답률 91% | 정답 ④</td></tr>
</table>

언급된 동물이 아닌 것은?
① cat – 고양이　　② hamster – 햄스터　　③ dog – 개
✓ turtle – 바다거북　　⑤ parrot – 앵무새

Why? 왜 정답일까?

담화에서 남자는 장난감이 반려동물에게 어떻게 도움이 되는지 열거하며 고양이, 햄스터, 개, 앵무새를 언급하였다. 따라서 언급되지 않은 것은 ④ '바다거북'이다.

Why? 왜 오답일까?

① 'A toy like a scratcher helps to reduce your cat's stress.'에서 '고양이'가 언급되었다.
② 'For example, a hamster loves to run on a wheel toy.'에서 '햄스터'가 언급되었다.
③ 'Playing with a small soft ball will give you and your dog a joyful experience.'에서 '개'가 언급되었다.
⑤ 'A small hiding tent will make your parrot feel less bored when you are not around.'에서 '앵무새'가 언급되었다.

<table>
<tr><td>**18**</td><td>도서관 공사 자원봉사 모집</td><td>정답률 90% | 정답 ④</td></tr>
</table>

다음 글의 목적으로 가장 적절한 것은?
① 도서관 임시 휴관의 이유를 설명하려고
② 도서관 자원봉사자 교육 일정을 안내하려고
③ 도서관 보수를 위한 모금 행사를 제안하려고
✓ 도서관 공사에 참여할 자원봉사자를 모집하려고
⑤ 도서관에서 개최하는 글쓰기 대회를 홍보하려고

Dear members of Eastwood Library,
Eastwood 도서관 회원들께,
Thanks to the Friends of Literature group, / we've successfully raised enough money / to remodel the library building.
Friends of Literature 모임 덕분에, / 우리는 충분한 돈을 성공적으로 모았습니다. / 도서관 건물을 리모델링하기 위한
John Baker, our local builder, / has volunteered to help us with the remodelling / but he needs assistance.
우리 지역의 건축업자인 John Baker 씨가 / 우리의 리모델링을 돕기로 자원했지만, / 그는 도움이 필요합니다.
By grabbing a hammer or a paint brush / and donating your time, / you can help with the construction.
망치나 페인트 붓을 쥐고 / 시간을 기부함으로써, / 여러분은 공사를 도울 수 있습니다.
Join Mr. Baker in his volunteering team / and become a part of making Eastwood Library a better place!
Baker 씨의 자원봉사 팀에 동참하여 / Eastwood 도서관을 더 좋은 곳으로 만드는 데 참여하십시오!
Please call 541-567-1234 for more information.
더 많은 정보를 원하시면 541-567-1234로 전화해 주십시오.
Sincerely, // Mark Anderson
Mark Anderson 드림

Eastwood 도서관 회원들께,

Friends of Literature 모임 덕분에, 우리는 도서관 건물을 리모델링하기 위한 충분한 돈을 성공적으로 모았습니다. 우리 지역의 건축업자인 John Baker 씨가 우리의 리모델링을 돕기로 자원했지만, 그는 도움이 필요합니다. 망치나 페인트 붓을 쥐고 시간을 기부함으로써, 여러분은 공사를 도울 수 있습니다. Baker 씨의 자원봉사 팀에 동참하여 Eastwood 도서관을 더 좋은 곳으로 만드는 데 참여하십시오! 더 많은 정보를 원하시면 541-567-1234로 전화해 주십시오.

Mark Anderson 드림

Why? 왜 정답일까?

'By grabbing a hammer or a paint brush and donating your time, you can help with the construction. Join Mr. Baker in his volunteering team ~'에서 자원봉사 팀에 참여하여 도서관 공사에 도움이 되어 달라고 언급하는 것으로 볼 때, 글의 목적으로 가장 적절한 것은 ④ '도서관 공사에 참여할 자원봉사자를 모집하려고'이다.

● raise ⓥ (돈을) 모으다
● assistance ⓝ 도움
● construction ⓝ 공사, 건설
● volunteer ⓥ 자원하다
● grab ⓥ 쥐다

구문 풀이

5행 By grabbing a hammer or a paint brush and donating your time, you can
「by + 동명사1 + 동명사2 : ~하고 …함으로써」
help with the construction.

<table>
<tr><td>**19**</td><td>새 친구가 생길 것이라는 기대감에 들뜬 Shirley</td><td>정답률 93% | 정답 ①</td></tr>
</table>

다음 글에 드러난 Shirley의 심경으로 가장 적절한 것은?
✓ curious and excited – 궁금하고 신난
② sorry and upset – 미안하고 언짢은
③ jealous and annoyed – 질투 나고 짜증 난
④ calm and relaxed – 평온하고 여유로운
⑤ disappointed and unhappy – 실망하고 불행한

On the way home, / Shirley noticed a truck parked / in front of the house across the street.
집에 오는 길에, / Shirley는 트럭 한 대가 주차된 것을 알아차렸다. / 길 건너편 집 앞에

New neighbors!
새 이웃이었다!
Shirley was dying to know about them.
Shirley는 그들에 대해 알고 싶어 죽을 지경이었다.
"Do you know anything about the new neighbors?" / she asked Pa at dinner.
"새 이웃에 대해 뭔가 알고 계셔요?"라고 / 저녁 식사 시간에 그녀는 아빠에게 물었다.
He said, / "Yes, and there's one thing / that may be interesting to you."
그는 말했다. / "그럼, 그리고 한 가지 있지. / 네 흥미를 끌 만한 것이"라고
Shirley had a billion more questions.
Shirley는 더 묻고 싶은 게 엄청나게 많았다.
Pa said joyfully, / "They have a girl just your age.
아빠는 기쁘게 말했다. / "딱 네 나이의 여자아이가 한 명 있어.
Maybe she wants to be your playmate."
아마 그 애가 네 놀이 친구가 되고 싶어 할 수도 있어."라고
Shirley nearly dropped her fork on the floor.
Shirley는 포크를 바닥에 떨어뜨릴 뻔했다.
How many times had she prayed for a friend?
그녀가 친구를 달라고 얼마나 많이 기도했던가?
Finally, her prayers were answered!
마침내 그녀의 기도가 응답받았다!
She and the new girl could go to school together, / play together, / and become best friends.
그녀와 새로 온 여자아이는 함께 학교에 가고, / 함께 놀고, / 그리고 제일 친한 친구가 될 수 있을지도 모른다.

집에 오는 길에, Shirley는 트럭 한 대가 길 건너편 집 앞에 주차된 것을 알아차렸다. 새 이웃이었다! Shirley는 그들에 대해 알고 싶어 죽을 지경이었다. 저녁 식사 시간에 그녀는 "새 이웃에 대해 뭔가 알고 계셔요?"라고 아빠에게 물었다. 그는 "그럼. 그리고 네 흥미를 끌 만한 것이 한 가지 있지."라고 말했다. Shirley는 더 묻고 싶은 게 엄청나게 많았다. 아빠는 "딱 네 나이의 여자아이가 한 명 있어. 아마 그 애가 네 놀이 친구가 되고 싶어 할 수도 있어."라고 기쁘게 말했다. Shirley는 포크를 바닥에 떨어뜨릴 뻔했다. 그녀가 친구를 달라고 얼마나 많이 기도했던가? 마침내 그녀의 기도가 응답받았다! 그녀와 새로 온 여자아이는 함께 학교에 가고, 함께 놀고, 그리고 제일 친한 친구가 될 수 있을지도 모른다.

Why? 왜 정답일까?

새 이웃이 이사온 것을 본 Shirley가 새 친구에 대한 호기심과 설렘으로 기뻐하는 모습(Shirley was dying to know about them. / How many times had she prayed for a friend? Finally, her prayers were answered!)을 주로 묘사한 글이다. 따라서 Shirley의 심경으로 가장 적절한 것은 ① '궁금하고 신난'이다.

● notice ⓥ 알아차리다
● be dying to 간절히 ~하고 싶어 하다
● curious ⓐ 호기심이 많은
● disappointed ⓐ 실망한
● across the street 길 건너에
● joyfully ⓐⓓ 즐겁게
● jealous ⓐ 질투 나는

구문 풀이

1행 On the way home, Shirley noticed a truck parked in front of the house
지각 동사　목적어　목적격 보어
across the street.　　　　　　　(과거분사)

<table>
<tr><td>**20**</td><td>이메일을 보내기 전 꼭 최종 검토하기</td><td>정답률 91% | 정답 ③</td></tr>
</table>

다음 글에서 필자가 주장하는 바로 가장 적절한 것은?
① 중요한 이메일은 출력하여 보관해야 한다.
② 글을 쓸 때에는 개요 작성부터 시작해야 한다.
✓ 이메일을 전송하기 전에 반드시 검토해야 한다.
④ 업무와 관련된 컴퓨터 기능을 우선 익혀야 한다.
⑤ 업무상 중요한 내용은 이메일보다는 직접 전달해야 한다.

At a publishing house and at a newspaper / you learn the following:
출판사와 신문사에서 / 다음과 같이 알게 된다:
It's not a mistake / if it doesn't end up in print.
그것은 실수가 아니다. / 결국 인쇄물로 나오지 않으면
It's the same for email.
그것은 이메일에서도 마찬가지다.
Nothing bad can happen / if you haven't hit the Send key.
어떤 나쁜 일도 일어날 수 없다. / 여러분이 전송 버튼을 눌러 버리기 전까지는
What you've written / can have misspellings, errors of fact, rude comments, obvious lies, / but it doesn't matter.
여러분이 쓴 글에는 / 잘못 쓴 철자, 사실의 오류, 무례한 말, 명백한 거짓말이 있을 수 있지만, / 그것은 문제가 되지 않는다.
If you haven't sent it, / you still have time to fix it.
여러분이 그것을 전송하지 않았다면, / 여러분에게는 아직 그것을 고칠 시간이 있다.
You can correct any mistake / and nobody will ever know the difference.
여러분은 어떤 실수도 수정할 수 있고 / 누구도 결코 그 변화를 모를 것이다.
This is easier said than done, of course.
물론, 이것은 말은 쉽지만 행하기는 어렵다.
Send is your computer's most attractive command.
전송은 여러분 컴퓨터의 가장 매력적인 명령어이다.
But before you hit the Send key, / make sure that you read your document carefully one last time.
그러나 여러분이 그 전송 버튼을 누르기 전에, / 반드시 문서를 마지막으로 한 번 주의 깊게 읽어 보라.

출판사와 신문사에서 다음과 같이 알게 된다. *결국 인쇄물로 나오지 않으면 그것은 실수가 아니다.* 그것은 이메일에서도 마찬가지다. 전송 버튼을 눌러 버리기 전까지는 어떤 나쁜 일도 일어날 수 없다. 여러분이 쓴 글에는 잘못 쓴 철자, 사실의 오류, 무례한 말, 명백한 거짓말이 있을 수 있지만, 그것은 문제가 되지 않는다. 그것을 전송하지 않았다면, 아직 그것을 고칠 시간이 있다. 어떤 실수라도 수정할 수 있고 누구도 결코 그 변화를 모를 것이다. 물론, 이것은 말은 쉽지만 행하기는 어렵다. 전송은 여러분 컴퓨터의 가장 매력적인 명령어이다. 그러나 그 전송 버튼을 누르기 전에, 반드시 문서를 마지막으로 한 번 주의 깊게 읽어 보라.

Why? 왜 정답일까?

마지막 문장인 '~ before you hit the Send key, make sure that you read your document carefully one last time.'에서 이메일의 전송 버튼을 누르기 전 꼭 마지막으로 주의 깊게 읽어보라고 언급하는 것으로 볼 때, 필자가 주장하는 바로 가장 적절한 것은 ③ '이메일을 전송하기 전에 반드시 검토해야 한다.'이다.

- **in print** 출간되는, 발표되는
- **rude** ⓐ 무례한
- **fix** ⓥ 고치다
- **command** ⓝ 명령(어) ⓥ 명령하다
- **misspelling** ⓝ 오탈자
- **obvious** ⓐ 명백한
- **easier said than done** 행동보다 말이 쉽다

구문 풀이

9행 But before you hit the Send key, make sure that you read your document
접속사(~ 전에)   명령문(~하라)   접속사(~것)
carefully one last time.

---

21 과거의 후회를 극복하고 미래를 기약하기   정답률 73% | 정답 ②

밑줄 친 translate it from the past tense to the future tense가 다음 글에서 의미하는 바로 가장 적절한 것은? [3점]

① look for a job linked to your interest – 흥미와 관련된 일을 찾을
☑ get over regrets and plan for next time – 후회를 극복하고 다음을 계획할
③ surround yourself with supportive people – 힘을 주는 사람들로 주변을 채울
④ study grammar and write clear sentences – 문법을 공부하여 명확한 문장을 쓸
⑤ examine your way of speaking and apologize – 말하는 방법을 돌아보고 사과할

Get past the 'I wish I hadn't done that!' reaction.
'내가 그것을 하지 말았어야 했는데!'라는 반응을 넘어서라.
If the disappointment you're feeling / is linked to an exam you didn't pass / because you didn't study for it, / or a job you didn't get / because you said silly things at the interview, / or a person you didn't impress / because you took entirely the wrong approach, / accept that it's *happened* now.
만일 여러분이 느끼는 실망이 / 통과하지 못한 시험과 연관되어 있다면, / 여러분이 시험공부를 하지 않았기 때문에 / 또는 여러분이 얻지 못한 일자리 / 여러분이 면접에서 바보 같은 말을 했기 때문에 / 또는 여러분이 좋은 인상을 주지 못한 사람 / 여러분이 완전히 잘못된 접근 방법을 택했기 때문에 / 이제는 그 일이 *일어나* 버렸다는 것을 받아들여라.
The only value of 'I wish I hadn't done that!' / is that you'll know better what to do next time.
'내가 그것을 하지 말았어야 했는데'의 유일한 가치는 / 여러분이 다음에 무엇을 할지 더 잘 알게 되리라는 점이다.
The learning pay-off is useful and significant.
배움으로 얻게 되는 이득은 유용하고 의미가 있다.
This 'if only I ...' agenda is virtual.
이러한 '내가 …하기만 했더라면'이라는 의제는 가상의 것이다.
Once you have worked that out, / it's time to translate it / from the past tense to the future tense:
여러분이 그것을 파악했다면, / 이제 그것을 바꿀 때이다. / 과거 시제에서 미래 시제로
'Next time I'm in this situation, I'm going to try to ...'.
'다음에 내가 이 상황일 때 나는 …하려고 할 것이다.'

'내가 그것을 하지 말았어야 했는데!'라는 반응을 넘어서라. 만일 여러분이 느끼는 실망이 시험공부를 하지 않았기 때문에 통과하지 못한 시험, 면접에서 바보 같은 말을 해서 얻지 못한 일자리, 또는 완전히 잘못된 접근 방법을 택하는 바람에 좋은 인상을 주지 못한 사람과 연관되어 있다면, 이제는 그 일이 *일어나* 버렸다는 것을 받아들여라. '내가 그것을 하지 말았어야 했는데!'의 유일한 가치는 다음에 무엇을 할지 더 잘 알게 되리라는 점이다. 배움으로 얻게 되는 이득은 유용하고 의미가 있다. 이러한 '내가 …하기만 했더라면'이라는 의제는 가상의 것이다. 여러분이 그것을 파악했다면, 이제 그것을 과거 시제에서 미래 시제로 바꿀 때이다. '다음에 내가 이 상황일 때 나는 …하려고 할 것이다.'

Why? 왜 정답일까?

'The only value of 'I wish I hadn't done that!' is that you'll know better what to do next time.'에서 과거에 이미 해버린 일을 하지 말았어야 한다는 후회는 다음에 할 일을 더 잘 알게 된다는 점에서만 의의가 있다고 한다. 이를 근거로 볼 때, '과거 시제 대신 미래 시제를 쓰라'는 뜻의 밑줄 친 부분은 후회되는 상황을 거울로 삼아 앞으로 같은 상황이 벌어질 때 할 일에 대한 대책을 세우라는 의미로 이해할 수 있다. 따라서 밑줄 친 부분이 의미하는 바로 가장 적절한 것은 ② '후회를 극복하고 다음을 계획할'이다.

- **get past** 지나가다, 추월하다
- **impress** ⓥ 인상을 주다
- **pay-off** ⓝ 이득, 보상
- **translate** ⓥ 바꾸다, 번역하다
- **supportive** ⓐ 힘이 되는, 지지를 주는
- **disappointment** ⓝ 실망
- **entirely** ⓐⓓ 완전히, 전적으로
- **virtual** ⓐ 가상의
- **get over** ~을 극복하다
- **examine** ⓥ 검토하다, 조사하다

구문 풀이

1행 If the disappointment [you're feeling] is linked to an exam [you didn't
접속사(~한다면) 주어   동사구   to의 목적어1
pass because you didn't study for it], or a job [you didn't get because you said
            to의 목적어2
silly things at the interview], or a person [you didn't impress because you took
                                to의 목적어3
entirely the wrong approach], accept that it's *happened* now.
                            명령문(~하라) 접속사 └→ has

---

22 스트레스와 괴로움의 원천인 자기 의심   정답률 67% | 정답 ⑤

다음 글의 요지로 가장 적절한 것은?
① 비판적인 시각은 객관적인 문제 분석에 도움이 된다.
② 성취 욕구는 스트레스를 이겨 낼 원동력이 될 수 있다.
③ 적절한 수준의 스트레스는 과제 수행의 효율을 높인다.
④ 실패의 경험은 자존감을 낮추고, 타인에 의존하게 한다.
☑ 자기 의심은 스트레스를 유발하고, 객관적 판단을 흐린다.

If you care deeply about something, / you may place greater value on your ability / to succeed in that area of concern.
여러분이 무언가에 깊이 관심을 두면, / 여러분은 여러분의 능력에 더 큰 가치를 둘지 모른다. / 그 관심 영역에서 성공하기 위한
The internal pressure / you place on yourself / to achieve or do well socially / is normal and useful, / but when you doubt your ability / to succeed in areas / that are important to you, / your self-worth suffers.
내적인 압박은 / 여러분이 스스로에게 가하는 / 성취하거나 사회적으로 성공하기 위해 / 정상적이고 유용하지만, / 여러분이 여러분의 능력을 의심하면, / 영역에서 성공하기 위한 / 자신에게 중요한 / 여러분의 자아 존중감은 상처를 입는다.
Situations are uniquely stressful for each of us / based on whether or not they activate our doubt.
상황은 우리 각각에게 저마다 다른 방식으로 스트레스를 준다. / 그것이 우리의 의심을 활성화하는지 여부에 따라
It's not the pressure to perform / that creates your stress.
결코 수행에 대한 압박이 아니다. / 여러분의 스트레스를 일으키는 것은
Rather, it's the self-doubt / that bothers you.
오히려, 바로 자기 의심이다. / 여러분을 괴롭히는 것은
Doubt causes you / to see positive, neutral, and even genuinely negative experiences / more negatively / and as a reflection of your own shortcomings.
의심은 여러분이 ~하게 한다. / 긍정적인 경험, 중립적인 경험, 그리고 심지어 진짜로 부정적인 경험을 보게 / 더 부정적으로 / 그리고 여러분 자신의 단점을 반영한 것으로
When you see situations and your strengths more objectively, / you are less likely to have doubt / as the source of your distress.
여러분이 상황과 여러분의 강점을 더 객관적으로 바라볼 때, / 여러분은 의심을 덜 가질 것이다. / 괴로움의 원천인

무언가에 깊이 관심을 두면, 그 관심 영역에서 성공하기 위한 여러분의 능력에 더 큰 가치를 둘지도 모른다. 성취하거나 사회적으로 성공하기 위해 스스로에게 가하는 내적인 압박은 정상적이고 유용하지만, 자신에게 중요한 영역에서 성공하기 위한 여러분의 능력을 의심하면, 여러분의 자아 존중감은 상처를 입는다. 상황이 우리의 의심을 활성화하는지 여부에 따라 그것은 우리 각각에게 저마다 다른 방식으로 스트레스를 준다. 여러분의 스트레스를 일으키는 것은 결코 수행에 대한 압박이 아니다. 오히려, 여러분을 괴롭히는 것은 바로 자기 의심이다. 의심은 긍정적인 경험, 중립적인 경험, 그리고 심지어 진짜로 부정적인 경험을 더 부정적으로 보게 하고, 여러분 자신의 단점을 반영한 것으로 (그것들을) 보게 한다. 상황과 여러분의 강점을 더 객관적으로 바라볼 때, 여러분은 괴로움의 원천인 의심을 덜 가질 것이다.

Why? 왜 정답일까?

'Rather, it's the self-doubt that bothers you.' 이후로 수행에 대한 압박이 아닌 자기 의심이야말로 우리에게 스트레스를 주며 우리가 스스로를 실제보다 더 부정적으로 바라보도록 만든다는 내용이 제시된다. 따라서 글의 요지로 가장 적절한 것은 ⑤ '자기 의심은 스트레스를 유발하고, 객관적 판단을 흐린다.'이다.

- **concern** ⓝ 관심, 걱정
- **doubt** ⓝ 의심 ⓥ 의심하다
- **uniquely** ⓐⓓ 특유의 방법으로, 독특하게
- **neutral** ⓐ 중립적인
- **reflection** ⓝ 반영
- **objectively** ⓐⓓ 객관적으로
- **internal** ⓐ 내적인
- **self-worth** ⓝ 자아 존중감, 자기 가치감
- **activate** ⓥ 활성화하다
- **genuinely** ⓐⓓ 진정으로
- **shortcoming** ⓝ 단점

구문 풀이

2행 The internal pressure [(that) you place on yourself to achieve or do well
                  주어1(선행사)   목적격 관계대명사   부사적 용법(~하기 위해)
socially] is normal and useful, but when you doubt your ability to succeed in areas
        동사1(단수)   접속사(~ 할 때)   └→ 형용사적 용법 선행사
[that are important to you] your self-worth suffers.
주격 관계대명사   주어2   동사2

---

23 대화 중 거짓말을 할 때의 특징   정답률 68% | 정답 ①

다음 글의 주제로 가장 적절한 것은?
☑ delayed responses as a sign of lying – 거짓말의 징후인 늦어지는 대답
② ways listeners encourage the speaker – 청자가 화자를 격려하는 방식
③ difficulties in finding useful information – 유용한 정보를 찾는 데 있어서의 어려움
④ necessity of white lies in social settings – 사회적 상황에서 선의의 거짓말의 필요성
⑤ shared experiences as conversation topics – 대화 주제로서의 공유된 경험

When two people are involved in an honest and open conversation, / there is a back and forth flow of information.
두 사람이 솔직하고 진실한 대화에 참여하면 / 정보가 왔다 갔다 하며 흘러간다.
It is a smooth exchange.
그것은 순조로운 대화이다.
Since each one is drawing on their past personal experiences, / the pace of the exchange is as fast as memory.
각자가 자신의 개인적인 과거 경험에 의존하고 있기 때문에, / 주고받는 속도가 기억만큼 빠르다.
When one person lies, / their responses will come more slowly / because the brain needs more time / to process the details of a new invention / than to recall stored facts.
한 사람이 거짓말하면, / 그 사람의 반응이 더 느리게 나올 텐데, / 뇌는 더 많은 시간이 필요하기 때문이다. / 새로 꾸며 낸 이야기의 세부 사항을 처리하는 데에 / 저장된 사실을 기억해 내는 데 비해
As they say, "Timing is everything."
사람들이 말하듯 "타이밍이 가장 중요하다."
You will notice the time lag / when you are having a conversation with someone / who is making things up as they go.
여러분은 시간의 지연을 알아차릴 것이다. / 여러분이 누군가와 이야기를 하고 있으면, / 말을 하면서 이야기를 꾸며 내고 있는
Don't forget / that the other person may be reading your body language as well, / and if you seem to be disbelieving their story, / they will have to pause / to process that information, too.
잊지 말라. / 상대가 여러분의 몸짓 언어 역시 읽고 있을지도 모른다는 것과 / 만약 여러분이 그 사람의 이야기를 믿지 않고 있는 것처럼 보이면, / 그 사람은 잠시 멈춰야 할 것임을 / 그 정보 또한 처리하기 위해

두 사람이 솔직하고 진술한 대화에 참여하면 정보가 왔다 갔다 하며 흘러간다. 그것은 순조로운 대화이다. 각자가 자신의 개인적인 과거 경험에 의존하고 있기 때문에, 주고받는 속도가 기억만큼 빠르다. 한 사람이 거짓말하면, 그 사람의 반응이 더 느리게 나올 텐데, 뇌는 저장된 사실을 기억해 내는 데 비해 새로 꾸며 낸 이야기의 세부 사항을 처리하는 데에 더 많은

시간이 필요하기 때문이다. 사람들이 말하듯 "타이밍이 가장 중요하다." 말을 하면서 이야기를 꾸며 내고 있는 누군가와 이야기를 하고 있으면, 여러분은 시간의 지연을 알아차릴 것이다. 상대가 여러분의 몸짓 언어 역시 읽고 있을지도 모른다는 것과, 만약 여러분이 그 사람의 이야기를 믿지 않고 있는 것처럼 보이면 그 사람은 그 정보 또한 처리하기 위해 잠시 멈춰야 할 것임을 잊지 말아야 한다.

Why? 왜 정답일까?

'When one person lies, their responses will come more slowly ~'와 'You will notice the time lag when you are having a conversation with someone who is making things up as they go.'에서 두 사람이 모두 솔직하게 임하는 대화와는 달리 한 사람이 거짓말을 하고 있는 대화에서는 거짓말을 하고 있는 사람의 반응이 느려진다고 한다. 따라서 글의 주제로 가장 적절한 것은 ① '거짓말의 징후인 늦어지는 대답'이다.

- exchange ⓝ 대화, 주고받음, 교환
- process ⓥ 처리하다
- make up 만들어내다, 꾸며내다
- necessity ⓝ 필요성
- draw on ~에 의존하다, ~을 이용하다
- recall ⓥ 회상하다
- disbelieve ⓥ 불신하다, 믿지 않다

구문 풀이

5행 When one person lies, their responses will come more slowly because the brain needs more time to process the details of a new invention than to recall stored facts.

---

24 산 이후 사용하지 않아 낭비가 되어버리는 물건들   정답률 77% | 정답 ⑤

다음 글의 제목으로 가장 적절한 것은?

① Spending Enables the Economy – 소비가 경제를 가능하게 한다
② Money Management: Dos and Don'ts – 돈 관리: 해야 할 일과 하지 말아야 할 일
③ Too Much Shopping: A Sign of Loneliness – 너무 많은 쇼핑: 외로움의 신호
④ 3R's of Waste: Reduce, Reuse, and Recycle – 쓰레기의 3R: 줄이고, 다시 쓰고, 재활용하자
✔ What You Buy Is Waste Unless You Use It – 당신이 사는 것은 당신이 그것을 이용하지 않는 한 낭비이다

Think, for a moment, / about something you bought / that you never ended up using.
잠시 생각해 봐라. / 여러분이 산 물건에 대해 / 여러분이 결국 한 번도 사용하지 않았던

An item of clothing / you never ended up wearing?
옷 한 벌? / 여러분이 결국 한 번도 입지 않은

A book you never read?
여러분이 한 번도 읽지 않은 책 한 권?

Some piece of electronic equipment / that never even made it out of the box?
어떤 전자 기기? / 심지어 상자에서 꺼내 보지도 않은

It is estimated / that Australians alone / spend on average $10.8 billion AUD (approximately $9.99 billion USD) every year / on goods they do not use / — more than the total government spending on universities and roads.
추산되는데, / 호주인들만 봐도 / 매년 평균 108억 호주 달러(약 99억 9천 미국 달러)를 쓰는 것으로 / 그들이 사용하지 않는 물건에 / 이는 대학과 도로에 사용하는 정부 지출 총액을 넘는 금액이다

That is an average of $1,250 AUD (approximately $1,156 USD) / for each household.
그 금액은 평균 1,250 호주 달러(약 1,156 미국 달러)이다. / 각 가구당

All the things we buy / that then just sit there gathering dust / are waste / — a waste of money, / a waste of time, / and waste in the sense of pure rubbish.
우리가 산 모든 물건은 / 그러고 나서 제자리에서 먼지를 뒤집어쓰고 있는 / 낭비인데, / 돈 낭비, / 시간 낭비, / 그리고 순전히 쓸모없는 물건이라는 의미로 낭비이다.

As the author Clive Hamilton observes, / 'The difference / between the stuff we buy and what we use / is waste.'
작가인 Clive Hamilton이 말하는 것처럼, / "뺀 것은 / 우리가 사는 물건에서 우리가 사용하는 것을 / 낭비이다".

여러분이 사 놓고 결국 한 번도 사용하지 않았던 물건에 대해 잠시 생각해 봐라. 결국 한 번도 입지 않은 옷 한 벌? 한 번도 읽지 않은 책 한 권? 심지어 상자에서 꺼내 보지도 않은 어떤 전자 기기? 호주인들만 봐도 사용하지 않는 물건에 매년 평균 108억 호주 달러(약 99억 9천 미국 달러)를 쓰는 것으로 추산되는데, 이는 대학과 도로에 사용하는 정부 지출 총액을 넘는 금액이다. 그 금액은 각 가구당 평균 1,250 호주 달러(약 1,156 미국 달러)이다. 우리가 사고 나서 제자리에서 먼지를 뒤집어쓰고 있는 모든 물건은 낭비인데, 돈 낭비, 시간 낭비, 그리고 순전히 쓸모없는 물건이라는 의미로 낭비이다. 작가인 Clive Hamilton이 말하는 것처럼 "우리가 사는 물건에서 우리가 사용하는 것을 뺀 것은 낭비이다".

Why? 왜 정답일까?

사고 나서 한 번도 사용하지 않아 먼지만 쌓이고 있는 물건은 모두 낭비라는 내용의 글로, 마지막 두 문장이 주제를 잘 제시한다(All the things we buy that then just sit there gathering dust are waste ~. ~ 'The difference between the stuff we buy and what we use is waste.') 따라서 글의 제목으로 가장 적절한 것은 ⑤ '당신이 사는 것은 당신이 그것을 이용하지 않는 한 낭비이다'이다.

- end up 결국 ~하다
- equipment ⓝ 기기, 장비
- gather ⓥ 모으다
- rubbish ⓝ 쓰레기
- difference ⓝ 뺀 것, (양의) 차이
- electronic ⓐ 전자의
- approximately ⓐⓓ 대략
- waste ⓝ 낭비, 쓰레기
- observe ⓥ 말하다, 관찰하다

구문 풀이

9행 All the things [(that) we buy] [that then just sit there gathering dust] are waste — a waste of money, a waste of time, and waste in the sense of pure rubbish.

---

25 교육용 콘텐츠를 이용하기 위해 기기를 사용한 학생들의 비율   정답률 80% | 정답 ③

다음 도표의 내용과 일치하지 않는 것은?

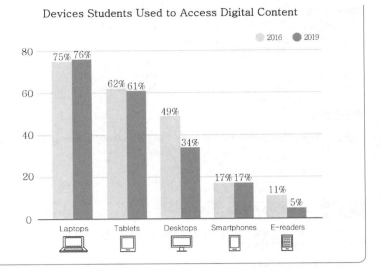

Devices Students Used to Access Digital Content

2016 ● 2019

	Laptops	Tablets	Desktops	Smartphones	E-readers
2016	75%	62%	49%	17%	11%
2019	76%	61%	34%	17%	5%

The above graph shows / the percentage of students from kindergarten to 12th grade / who used devices / to access digital educational content / in 2016 and in 2019.
위 그래프는 보여 준다. / 유치원에서 12학년까지의 학생들의 비율을 / 기기를 사용한, / 교육용 디지털 콘텐츠를 이용하기 위해 / 2016년과 2019년에

① Laptops were the most used device / for students to access digital content / in both years.
노트북은 가장 많이 사용된 기기였다. / 학생들이 디지털 콘텐츠를 이용하기 위해 / 두 해 모두

② Both in 2016 and in 2019, / more than 6 out of 10 students used tablets.
2016년과 2019년 모두 / 10명 중 6명이 넘는 학생들이 태블릿을 사용했다.

✔ More than half the students used desktops / to access digital content / in 2016, / and more than a third used desktops in 2019.
절반이 넘는 학생들이 데스크톱을 사용하여 / 디지털 콘텐츠를 이용했고, / 2016년에는 / 2019년에는 3분의 1이 넘는 학생들이 데스크톱을 사용했다.

④ The percentage of smartphones in 2016 / was the same as that in 2019.
2016년 스마트폰의 비율은 / 2019년 스마트폰의 비율과 같았다.

⑤ E-readers ranked the lowest in both years, / with 11 percent in 2016 and 5 percent in 2019.
전자책 단말기는 두 해 모두 가장 낮은 순위를 차지했는데, / 2016년에는 11퍼센트였고 2019년에는 5퍼센트였다.

위 그래프는 2016년과 2019년에 교육용 디지털 콘텐츠를 이용하기 위해 기기를 사용한, 유치원에서 12학년까지의 학생들의 비율을 보여 준다. ① 두 해 모두 노트북은 학생들이 디지털 콘텐츠를 이용하기 위해 가장 많이 사용한 기기였다. ② 2016년과 2019년 모두 10명 중 6명이 넘는 학생들이 태블릿을 사용했다. ③ 2016년에는 절반이 넘는 학생들이 데스크톱을 사용하여 디지털 콘텐츠를 이용했고, 2019년에는 3분의 1이 넘는 학생들이 데스크톱을 사용했다. ④ 2016년 스마트폰의 비율은 2019년 스마트폰의 비율과 같았다. ⑤ 전자책 단말기는 두 해 모두 가장 낮은 순위를 차지했는데, 2016년에는 11퍼센트였고 2019년에는 5퍼센트였다.

Why? 왜 정답일까?

도표에 따르면 2016년 교육용 디지털 콘텐츠 이용 목적으로 데스크톱을 사용했던 학생들의 비율은 49%로 절반을 넘지 못했다. 따라서 도표와 일치하지 않는 것은 ③이다.

- kindergarten ⓝ 유치원
- educational ⓐ 교육의
- access ⓥ 이용하다, 접근하다, 접속하다

---

26 Elizabeth Catlett의 생애   정답률 91% | 정답 ⑤

Elizabeth Catlett에 관한 다음 글의 내용과 일치하지 않는 것은?

① 할머니로부터 노예 이야기를 들었다.
② Carnegie Institute of Technology로부터 입학을 거절당했다.
③ University of Iowa에서 석사 학위를 취득했다.
④ 미국과 멕시코에서 많은 상을 받았다.
✔ 멕시코 시민권을 결국 받지 못했다.

Elizabeth Catlett was born in Washington, D.C. in 1915.
Elizabeth Catlett은 1915년 Washington, D.C.에서 태어났다.

「As a granddaughter of slaves, / Catlett heard the stories of slaves from her grandmother.」 ①의근거 일치
노예의 손녀로서 / Catlett은 할머니로부터 노예 이야기를 들었다.

「After being disallowed entrance / from the Carnegie Institute of Technology / because she was black, / Catlett studied design and drawing at Howard University.」 ②의근거 일치
입학을 거절당한 이후, / Carnegie Institute of Technology로부터 / 그녀가 흑인이라는 이유로 / Catlett은 Howard 대학에서 디자인과 소묘를 공부했다.

「She became one of the first three students / to earn a master's degree in fine arts / at the University of Iowa.」 ③의근거 일치
그녀는 첫 세 명의 학생들 중 한 명이 되었다. / 순수 미술 석사 학위를 취득한 / Iowa 대학에서

Throughout her life, / she created art / representing the voices of people / suffering from social injustice.
평생 동안 / 그녀는 예술 작품을 창작했다. / 사람들의 목소리를 대변하는 / 사회적 불평등으로 고통받는

「She was recognized with many prizes and honors / both in the United States and in Mexico.」 ④의근거 일치
그녀는 많은 상과 표창으로 인정받았다. / 미국과 멕시코 모두에서

「She spent over fifty years in Mexico, / and she took Mexican citizenship in 1962.」 ⑤의근거 불일치
그녀는 멕시코에서 50년이 넘는 세월을 보냈고, / 1962년에 멕시코 시민권을 받았다.

Catlett died in 2012 at her home in Mexico.
Catlett은 2012년에 멕시코에 있는 자신의 집에서 생을 마쳤다.

Elizabeth Catlett은 1915년 Washington, D.C.에서 태어났다. 노예의 손녀로서 Catlett은 할머니로부터 노예 이야기를 들었다. 흑인이라는 이유로 Carnegie Institute of Technology로부터 입학을 거절당한 이후, Catlett은 Howard 대학에서 디자인과 소묘를 공부했다. 그녀는 Iowa 대학에서 순수 미술 석사 학위를 취득한 첫 세 명의 학생 중 한 명이 되었다. 평생 동안 그녀는 사회적 불평등으로 고통받는 사람들의 목소리를 대변하는 예술 작품을 창작했다. 그녀는 미국과 멕시코 모두에서 많은 상과 표창으로 인정받았다. 그녀는 멕시코에서 50년이

넘는 세월을 보냈고, 1962년에 멕시코 시민권을 받았다. Catlett은 2012년에 멕시코에 있는 자신의 집에서 생을 마쳤다.

Why? 왜 정답일까?

'~ she took Mexican citizenship in 1962.'에 따르면 Elizabeth Catlett은 1962년에 멕시코 시민권을 취득하였다. 따라서 내용과 일치하지 않는 것은 ⑤ '멕시코 시민권을 결국 받지 못했다.'이다.

Why? 왜 오답일까?

① 'As a granddaughter of slaves, Catlett heard the stories of slaves from her grandmother.'의 내용과 일치한다.
② 'After being disallowed entrance from the Carnegie Institute of Technology because she was black, ~'의 내용과 일치한다.
③ 'She became one of the first three students to earn a master's degree in fine arts at the University of Iowa.'의 내용과 일치한다.
④ 'She was recognized with many prizes and honors both in the United States and in Mexico.'의 내용과 일치한다.

- slave ⓝ 노예
- entrance ⓝ 입학, 입장
- fine arts 순수 미술
- injustice ⓝ 불평등, 부당함
- citizenship ⓝ 시민권
- disallow ⓥ (공식적으로) 거절하다, 인정하지 않다
- earn ⓥ 얻다, 취득하다
- represent ⓥ 대표하다, 나타내다
- recognize ⓥ 인정하다

구문 풀이

3행 After being disallowed entrance from the Carnegie Institute of Technology
전치사(~ 후에)   수동동명사
because she was black, Catlett studied design and drawing at Howard University.
접속사(~ 때문에)   주어   동사

---

27 봄 농장 캠프 안내   정답률 95% | 정답 ⑤

Spring Farm Camp에 관한 다음 안내문의 내용과 일치하지 <u>않는</u> 것은?
① 6세 ~ 10세 어린이가 참가할 수 있다.
② 참가비에 점심과 간식이 포함되어 있다.
③ 염소젖으로 치즈를 만드는 활동을 한다.
④ 딸기잼을 만들어 집으로 가져갈 수 있다.
☑ 비가 오면 운영하지 않는다.

Spring Farm Camp
봄 농장 캠프

Our one-day spring farm camp / gives your kids true, hands-on farm experience.
우리의 일일 봄 농장 캠프는 / 여러분의 자녀에게 진정한 농장 체험을 제공합니다.

When: Monday, April 19 – Friday, May 14
기간: 4월 19일 월요일 ~ 5월 14일 금요일

Time: 9 a.m. – 4 p.m.
시간: 오전 9시 ~ 오후 4시

『Ages: 6 – 10』 ①의근거 일치
나이: 6세 ~ 10세

『Participation Fee: $70 per person (lunch and snacks included)』 ②의근거 일치
참가비: 개인당 70달러 (점심과 간식 포함)

Activities:
활동:
『making cheese from goat's milk』 ③의근거 일치
염소젖으로 치즈 만들기
picking strawberries
딸기 따기
『making strawberry jam to take home』 ④의근거 일치
집으로 가져갈 딸기잼 만들기
『We are open rain or shine.』 ⑤의근거 불일치
날씨에 상관없이 운영합니다.
For more information, / go to www.b_orchard.com.
더 많은 정보를 원하시면 / www.b_orchard.com에 접속하세요.

봄 농장 캠프

우리의 일일 봄 농장 캠프는 여러분의 자녀에게 진정한 농장 체험을 제공합니다.

기간: 4월 19일 월요일 ~ 5월 14일 금요일
시간: 오전 9시 ~ 오후 4시
나이: 6세 ~ 10세
참가비: 개인당 70달러 (점심과 간식 포함)
활동:
• 염소젖으로 치즈 만들기
• 딸기 따기
• 집으로 가져갈 딸기잼 만들기
날씨에 상관없이 운영합니다.
더 많은 정보를 원하시면 www.b_orchard.com에 접속하세요.

Why? 왜 정답일까?

'We are open rain or shine.'에서 농장 체험 행사는 날씨에 상관없이 열린다고 하므로, 안내문의 내용과 일치하지 않는 것은 ⑤ '비가 오면 운영하지 않는다.'이다.

Why? 왜 오답일까?

① 'Ages: 6 – 10'의 내용과 일치한다.
② 'Participation Fee: $70 per person / (lunch and snacks included)'의 내용과 일치한다.
③ 'making cheese from goat's milk'의 내용과 일치한다.
④ 'making strawberry jam to take home'의 내용과 일치한다.

- hands-on ⓐ 직접 해 보는, 체험의
- rain or shine 날씨에 상관없이

---

28 수족관 이용 안내   정답률 92% | 정답 ④

Great Aquarium에 관한 다음 안내문의 내용과 일치하는 것은?
① 마지막 입장 시간은 오후 6시이다.
② 물고기 먹이 주기는 오후 1시에 시작한다.
③ 60세 이상의 티켓 가격은 33달러이다.
☑ 티켓 소지자는 무료 음료 쿠폰을 받는다.
⑤ 예약은 입장 30분 전까지 가능하다.

Great Aquarium
Great 수족관

Opening Hours: 10 a.m. – 6 p.m., daily
개장 시간: 매일 오전 10시 ~ 오후 6시
『Last entry is at 5 p.m.』 ①의근거 불일치
마지막 입장은 오후 5시입니다.
Events
행사

Fish Feeding 물고기 먹이 주기	『10 a.m. – 11 a.m.』 ②의근거 불일치 오전 10시 ~ 오전 11시
Penguin Feeding 펭귄 먹이 주기	1 p.m. – 2 p.m. 오후 1시 ~ 오후 2시

Ticket Prices
티켓 가격

Age 나이	Price 가격
Kids (12 and under) 어린이(12세 이하)	$25 25달러
Adults (20 – 59) 성인(20세 ~ 59세)	$33 33달러
Teens (13 – 19) 십 대(13세 ~ 19세)	$30 ③의근거 불일치 30달러
『Seniors (60 and above) 노인(60세 이상)	

『Ticket holders will receive a free drink coupon.』 ④의근거 일치
티켓 소지자는 무료 음료 쿠폰을 받습니다.
Booking Tickets
티켓 예약
ALL visitors are required to book online.
'모든' 방문객은 온라인으로 예약해야 합니다.
『Booking will be accepted up to 1 hour before entry.』 ⑤의근거 불일치
예약은 입장 1시간 전까지 받습니다.

Great 수족관

개장 시간: 매일 오전 10시 ~ 오후 6시
마지막 입장은 오후 5시입니다.

행사

물고기 먹이 주기	오전 10시 ~ 오전 11시
펭귄 먹이 주기	오후 1시 ~ 오후 2시

티켓 가격

나이	가격
어린이(12세 이하)	25달러
성인(20세 ~ 59세)	33달러
십 대(13세 ~ 19세) 노인(60세 이상)	30달러

* 티켓 소지자는 무료 음료 쿠폰을 받습니다.

티켓 예약
• '모든' 방문객은 온라인으로 예약해야 합니다.
• 예약은 입장 1시간 전까지 받습니다.

Why? 왜 정답일까?

'Ticket holders will receive a free drink coupon.'에서 티켓 소지자는 무료 음료 쿠폰을 받게 된다고 하므로, 안내문의 내용과 일치하는 것은 ④ '티켓 소지자는 무료 음료 쿠폰을 받는다.'이다.

Why? 왜 오답일까?

① 'Last entry is at 5 p.m.'에서 마지막 입장 시간은 오후 5시라고 하였다.
② 'Fish Feeding / 10 a.m. – 11 a.m.'에서 물고기 먹이 주기는 오전 10시에 시작한다고 하였다.
③ 'Seniors (60 and above) / $30'에서 60세 이상 노인의 티켓 가격은 십 대와 마찬가지로 30달러라고 하였다.
⑤ 'Booking will be accepted up to 1 hour before entry.'에서 예약은 입장 1시간 전까지 가능하다고 하였다.

- entry ⓝ 입장
- accept ⓥ 수용하다, 허용하다
- book ⓥ 예약하다
- up to ~까지

---

29 악기 연주를 배우기 전 악기를 탐구할 시간 주기   정답률 61% | 정답 ③

다음 글의 밑줄 친 부분 중, 어법상 틀린 것은? [3점]

Although there is usually a correct way / of holding and playing musical instruments, / the most important instruction to begin with / is ① that they are not toys / and that they must be looked after.

비록 정확한 방법이 대체로 있다고 해도 / 악기를 잡고 연주하는 / 우선적으로 가장 중요한 가르침은 / 악기가 장난감이 아니라는 것과 / 악기를 관리해야 한다는 것이다.

② Allow children time / to explore ways of handling and playing the instruments for themselves / before showing them.
아이들에게 시간을 주어라. / 악기를 직접 다루고 연주하는 방법을 탐구할 / 그것을 알려 주기 전에

Finding different ways to produce sounds / ✔ is an important stage of musical exploration.
소리를 만들어 내는 여러 가지 방법을 찾는 것은 / 음악적 탐구의 중요한 단계이다.

Correct playing comes from the desire / ④ to find the most appropriate sound quality / and find the most comfortable playing position / so that one can play with control over time.
정확한 연주는 욕구에서 나온다. / 가장 알맞은 음질을 찾고 / 가장 편안한 연주 자세를 찾으려는 / 오랜 시간 동안 잘 다루면서 연주할 수 있도록

As instruments and music become more complex, / learning appropriate playing techniques / ⑤ increasingly relevant.
악기와 음악이 더 복잡해짐에 따라, / 알맞은 연주 기술을 알게 되는 것은 / 점점 더 유의미해진다.

비록 악기를 잡고 연주하는 정확한 방법이 대체로 있다고 해도 우선적으로 가장 중요한 가르침은 악기가 장난감이 아니라는 것과 악기를 관리해야 한다는 것이다. 아이들에게 (악기를 다루고 연주하는) 방법을 알려 주기 전에 직접 악기를 다루고 연주하는 방법을 탐구할 시간을 주어라. 소리를 만들어 내는 여러 가지 방법을 찾는 것은 음악적 탐구의 중요한 단계이다. 정확한 연주는 가장 알맞은 음질을 찾고 오랜 시간 동안 잘 다루면서 연주할 수 있도록 가장 편안한 연주 자세를 찾으려는 욕구에서 나온다. 악기와 음악이 더 복잡해짐에 따라, 알맞은 연주 기술을 알게 되는 것은 점점 더 유의미해진다.

Why? 왜 정답일까?
'Finding different ways ~'는 동명사구 주어이므로 단수 취급한다. 따라서 are 대신 is를 써야 한다. 어법상 틀린 것은 ③이다.

Why? 왜 오답일까?
① 뒤에 'they are not toys'라는 완전한 2형식 문장이 나오므로 앞에 접속사 that을 쓴 것은 적절하다. 참고로 that절은 동사 is의 주격 보어이다.
② 앞에 주어 You가 생략된 명령문으로 동사 Allow가 원형으로 바르게 쓰였다.
④ the desire를 꾸미는 말로 to부정사가 바르게 쓰였다. ability, attempt, chance, desire, opportunity 등은 to부정사의 꾸밈을 받는 명사임을 기억해 둔다.
⑤ 2형식 동사 becomes의 보어인 형용사 relevant를 꾸미기 위해 앞에 부사인 increasingly가 적절하게 쓰였다.

- instrument ⓝ 악기, 도구
- look after ~을 관리하다, 돌보다
- appropriate ⓐ 적절한
- increasingly ⓐd 점점 더
- instruction ⓝ 지침, 가르침
- explore ⓥ 탐구하다
- complex ⓐ 복잡한
- relevant ⓐ 유의미한, 적절한, 관련 있는

구문 풀이
1행 Although there is usually a correct way of holding and playing musical
접속사(~에도 불구하고) 동사(단수)   주어
instruments, the most important instruction to begin with is {that they are not toys}
주어   동사 접속사1
and {that they must be looked after}.
접속사2   [   ]: is의 보어

---

30 인공 조명의 가격 하락에 따른 결과   정답률 59% | 정답 ③

다음 글의 밑줄 친 부분 중, 문맥상 낱말의 쓰임이 적절하지 않은 것은? [3점]

When the price of something fundamental / drops greatly, / the whole world can change.
기본적인 어떤 것의 가격이 / 크게 하락할 때, / 온 세상이 바뀔 수 있다.

Consider light.
조명을 생각해 보자.

Chances are / you are reading this sentence / under some kind of artificial light.
아마 ~일 것이다. / 여러분은 이 문장을 읽고 있을 / 어떤 유형의 인공조명 아래에서

Moreover, / you probably never thought about / whether using artificial light for reading was worth it.
또한, / 여러분은 ~에 대해 아마 생각해 본 적이 없을 것이다. / 독서를 위해 인공조명을 이용하는 것이 그럴 만한 가치가 있는지

Light is so ① cheap / that you use it without thinking.
조명이 너무 싸서 / 여러분은 생각 없이 그것을 이용한다.

But in the early 1800s, / it would have cost you four hundred times / what you are paying now / for the same amount of light.
하지만 1800년대 초반에는, / 여러분에게 400배만큼의 비용이 들었을 것이다. / 여러분이 오늘날 지불하고 있는 것의 / 같은 양의 조명에 대해

At that price, / you would ② notice the cost / and would think twice / before using artificial light to read a book.
그 가격이면, / 여러분은 비용을 의식할 것이고 / 다시 한 번 생각할 것이다. / 책을 읽기 위해 인공조명을 이용하기 전에

The ✔ drop in the price of light / lit up the world.
조명 가격의 하락은 / 세상을 밝혔다.

Not only did it turn night into day, / but it allowed us to live and work in big buildings / that ④ natural light could not enter.
그것은 밤을 낮으로 바꾸었을 뿐 아니라, / 그것은 큰 건물에서 우리가 살고 일할 수 있게 해 주었다. / 자연의 빛이 들어올 수 없는

Nearly nothing we have today / would be ⑤ possible / if the cost of artificial light had not dropped to almost nothing.
우리가 오늘날 누리는 것 중에 거의 아무것도 없다. / 가능한 것은 / 만약 인공조명의 비용이 거의 공짜 수준으로 하락하지 않았더라면

기본적인 어떤 것의 가격이 크게 하락할 때, 온 세상이 바뀔 수 있다. 조명을 생각해 보자. 아마 여러분은 어떤 유형의 인공조명 아래에서 이 문장을 읽고 있을 것이다. 또한, 여러분은 독서를 위해 인공조명을 이용하는 것이 그럴 만한 가치가 있는지에 대해 아마 생각해 본 적이 없을 것이다. 조명이 너무 ① 싸서 여러분은 생각 없이 그것을 이용한다. 하지만 1800년대 초반에는, 같은 양의 조명에 대해 오늘날 지불하고 있는 것의 400배만큼의 비용이 들었을 것이다. 그 가격이면, 여러분은 비용을 ② 의식할 것이고 책을 읽기 위해 인공조명을 이용하기 전에 다시 한 번 생각할 것이다. 조명 가격의 ③ 증가(→ 하락)는 세상을 밝혔다. 그것은 밤을 낮으로 바꾸었을 뿐 아니라, ④ 자연의 빛(자연광)이 들어올 수 없는 큰 건물에서 우리가 살고 일할 수 있게 해 주었다. 만약 인공조명의 비용이 거의 공짜 수준으로 하락하지 않았더라면 우리가 오늘날 누리는 것 중에 ⑤ 가능한 것은 거의 아무것도 없을 것이다.

Why? 왜 정답일까?
마지막 두 문장에서 인공조명의 비용이 거의 공짜 수준으로 떨어졌기 때문에 오늘날 우리는 자연광이 들어올 수 없는 건물에서도 살고 일하며 많은 것들을 누릴 수 있게 되었다고 언급하고 있다. 이를 근거로 볼 때, ③이 포함된 문장은 한때는 몹시 높았던 인공조명의 가격이 '떨어지면서' 세상이 밝아졌다는 의미가 되어야 한다. 따라서 increase를 drop으로 고쳐야 한다. 문맥상 낱말의 쓰임이 적절하지 않은 것은 ③이다.

- fundamental ⓐ 기본적인
- artificial ⓐ 인공의
- cost ⓥ (~에게 …의 비용을) 요하다. 치르게 하다 ⓝ 비용
- drop ⓥ 하락하다, 떨어지다 ⓝ 하락
- worth ⓐ ~의 가치가 있는

구문 풀이
11행 Not only did it turn night into day, but it allowed us to live and work in
「동사+주어+동사원형」: 도치 구문」   「allow+목적어+to부정사: ~이 …하게 해 주다」
big buildings [that natural light could not enter].
선행사   「not only+A+but (also)+B : A뿐 아니라 B도(A, B 자리에 문장)」

★★★ 등급을 가르는 문제!
31 동물을 보살필 때 일관적이고 예측 가능한 환경을 만들어줄 필요성   정답률 51% | 정답 ⑤

다음 빈칸에 들어갈 말로 가장 적절한 것을 고르시오.
① silent - 고요하도록
② natural - 자연스럽도록
③ isolated - 고립되도록
④ dynamic - 역동적이도록
✔ predictable - 예측 가능하도록

One of the most important aspects of providing good care / is making sure / that an animal's needs are being met consistently and predictably.
좋은 보살핌을 제공하는 것의 가장 중요한 측면 중에 한 가지는 / 반드시 ~하는 것이다. / 동물의 욕구가 일관되고도 예측 가능하게 충족되도록

Like humans, / animals need a sense of control.
사람과 마찬가지로, / 동물은 통제감이 필요하다.

So an animal / who may get enough food / but doesn't know when the food will appear / and can see no consistent schedule / may experience distress.
그러므로 동물은 / 충분한 음식을 제공받고 있을지라도 / 음식이 언제 눈에 보일지 모르고 / 일관된 일정을 알 수 없는 / 괴로움을 겪을지도 모른다.

We can provide a sense of control / by ensuring that our animal's environment is predictable: / there is always water available / and always in the same place.
우리는 통제감을 줄 수 있다. / 우리 동물의 환경이 예측 가능하도록 보장함으로써 / 즉, 마실 수 있는 물이 늘 있고, / 늘 같은 곳에 있다.

There is always food / when we get up in the morning / and after our evening walk.
늘 음식이 있다. / 우리가 아침에 일어날 때 / 그리고 저녁 산책을 한 후에

There will always be a time and place to eliminate, / without having to hold things in to the point of discomfort.
변을 배설할 수 있는 시간과 장소가 늘 있을 것이다. / 불편할 정도로 참을 필요 없이

Human companions can display consistent emotional support, / rather than providing love one moment / and withholding love the next.
사람 친구는 일관된 정서적 지지를 보이는 것이 좋다. / 한순간에는 애정을 주다가 / 그다음에는 애정을 주지 않기보다는

When animals know what to expect, / they can feel more confident and calm.
동물이 기대할 수 있는 것이 무엇인지 알고 있을 때, / 그들은 자신감과 차분함을 더 많이 느낄 수 있다.

좋은 보살핌을 제공하는 것의 가장 중요한 측면 중에 한 가지는 반드시 동물의 욕구가 일관되고도 예측 가능하게 충족되도록 하는 것이다. 사람과 마찬가지로, 동물은 통제감이 필요하다. 그러므로 충분한 음식을 제공받고 있을지라도 음식이 언제 눈에 보일지 모르고 일관된 일정을 알 수 없는 동물은 괴로움을 겪을지도 모른다. 우리 동물의 환경이 예측 가능하도록 보장함으로써 우리는 통제감을 줄 수 있다. 즉, 마실 수 있는 물이 늘 있고, 늘 같은 곳에 있다. 아침에 일어날 때 그리고 저녁 산책을 한 후에 늘 음식이 있다. 불편할 정도로 참을 필요 없이 변을 배설할 수 있는 시간과 장소가 늘 있을 것이다. 사람 친구는 한순간에는 애정을 주다가 그다음에는 애정을 주지 않기보다는 일관된 정서적 지지를 보이는 것이 좋다. 기대할 수 있는 것이 무엇인지 알고 있을 때, 동물은 자신감과 차분함을 더 많이 느낄 수 있다.

Why? 왜 정답일까?
첫 문장인 'One of the most important aspects of providing good care is making sure that an animal's needs are being met consistently and predictably.'에서 동물을 잘 보살피기 위해서는 동물의 욕구가 일관적이고도 예측 가능한 방식으로 충족되게 해줄 필요가 있다고 언급하고 있다. 따라서 빈칸에 들어갈 말로 가장 적절한 것은 동물의 환경을 '예측 가능하게' 만들어 주어야 한다는 의미를 완성하는 ⑤ '예측 가능하도록'이다.

- aspect ⓝ 측면
- consistently ⓐd 일관되게
- sense of control 통제감
- ensure ⓥ 반드시 ~하다, 보장하다
- discomfort ⓝ 불편함
- confident ⓐ 자신감 있는
- make sure 반드시 ~하다
- predictably ⓐd 예측 가능하게
- distress ⓝ 괴로움
- to the point of ~할 수 있을 정도로
- withhold ⓥ 주지 않다
- isolated ⓐ 고립된

구문 풀이
4행 So an animal [who may get enough food but doesn't know when the food
주어(선행사) 주격 관·대 동사구1   동사구2   의문사(언제 ~할지)
will appear and can see no consistent schedule] may experience distress.
동사구3   동사

★★ 문제 해결 꿀~팁 ★★

▶ 많이 틀린 이유는?
빈칸 뒤에서 반려동물에게 정해진 장소와 시간에 따라 어떤 것을 기대할 수 있는 안정적인 환경을 제공할 필요가 있다는 내용이 주를 이루고 있다. 이 안정된 환경이 꼭 '자연스러운' 것이라고 볼 수는 없으므로 ②는 답으로 부적절하다.

▶ 문제 해결 방법은?
첫 문장에서 '일관되고 예측 가능한' 환경의 중요성을 언급한 데 이어, 마지막 문장에서도 동물에게 '무엇을 기대할 수 있는지'가 분명한 환경을 주는 것이 좋다는 내용을 제시하고 있으므로 ⑤가 답으로 가장 적절하다.

32 음식으로 아이의 기분을 달래주는 것의 장단기적 영향 정답률 74% | 정답 ④

다음 빈칸에 들어갈 말로 가장 적절한 것을 고르시오.

① make friends – 친구를 사귀는
② learn etiquettes – 예절을 배우는
③ improve memory – 기억을 향상시키는
✓④ manage emotions – 감정을 다스리는
⑤ celebrate achievements – 성취를 축하하는

When a child is upset, / the easiest and quickest way to calm them down / is to give them food.
아이가 화를 낼 때, / 아이를 진정시키는 가장 쉽고 가장 빠른 방법은 / 아이에게 음식을 주는 것이다.

This acts as a distraction / from the feelings they are having, / gives them something to do with their hands and mouth / and shifts their attention / from whatever was upsetting them.
이것은 주의를 돌리는 것으로 작용하고, / 아이가 가지고 있는 감정으로부터 / 손과 입으로 할 수 있는 무언가를 아이에게 제공하며, / 아이의 주의를 옮겨 가게 한다. / 화나게 하고 있는 것이 무엇이든 그것으로부터

If the food chosen is also seen as a treat / such as sweets or a biscuit, / then the child will feel 'treated' and happier.
또한 선택된 음식이 특별한 먹거리로 여겨지면, / 사탕이나 비스킷 같은 / 그 아이는 '특별한 대접을 받았다'고 느끼고 기분이 더 좋을 것이다.

In the shorter term / using food like this is effective.
단기적으로는 / 이처럼 음식을 이용하는 것은 효과적이다.

But in the longer term / it can be harmful / as we quickly learn / that food is a good way to manage emotions.
하지만 장기적으로는 / 그것은 해로울 수 있다. / 우리가 곧 알게 되기 때문에 / 음식이 감정을 다스리는 좋은 방법이라는 것을

Then as we go through life, / whenever we feel annoyed, anxious or even just bored, / we turn to food to make ourselves feel better.
그러면 우리가 삶을 살아가면서, / 짜증이 나거나, 불안하거나, 심지어 그저 지루함을 느낄 때마다, / 우리 자신의 기분을 더 좋게 만들기 위해 우리는 음식에 의존한다.

아이가 화를 낼 때, 아이를 진정시키는 가장 쉽고 가장 빠른 방법은 음식을 주는 것이다. 이것은 아이가 가지고 있는 감정으로부터 주의를 돌리는 것으로 작용하고, 손과 입으로 할 수 있는 무언가를 아이에게 제공하며, 화나게 하고 있는 것이 무엇이든 그것으로부터 아이의 주의를 옮겨 가게 한다. 또한 선택된 음식이 사탕이나 비스킷 같은 특별한 먹거리로 여겨지면, 그 아이는 '특별한 대접을 받았다'고 느끼고 기분이 더 좋을 것이다. 이처럼 음식을 이용하는 것은 단기적으로는 효과적이다. 하지만 음식이 감정을 다스리는 좋은 방법이라는 것을 우리가 곧 알게 되기 때문에 그것은 장기적으로는 해로울 수 있다. 그러면 우리가 삶을 살아가면서, 짜증이 나거나, 불안하거나, 심지어 그저 지루함을 느낄 때마다, 우리 자신의 기분을 더 좋게 만들기 위해 우리는 음식에 의존한다.

Why? 왜 정답일까?

화난 아이의 기분을 음식으로 달래주는 것이 단기적으로는 효과가 있지만 장기적으로는 아이가 기분이 좋지 않을 때 음식에 의존하게 하는 결과를 낳기 때문에 좋지 않을 수 있다는 내용을 다룬 글이다. 두 번째 문장과 세 번째 문장에서, 음식은 아이가 기분이 나쁠 때 주의를 돌려주는 효과가 있으며, 특히 그 음식이 특별한 먹거리로 여겨지는 경우 아이를 특히 더 기분 좋게 한다고 설명하고 있다. 또한 마지막 문장에서는 그리하여 우리가 장기적으로 '기분을 나아지게' 하고자 할 때 음식에 의존하는 결과가 나타날 수 있다고 한다. 따라서 빈칸에 들어갈 말로 가장 적절한 것은 ④ '감정을 다스리는'이다.

● distraction ⓝ 정신을 분산시키는 것, 주의를 돌리는 것
● shift ⓥ 돌리다, 바꾸다
● treat ⓝ 간식 ⓥ 대접하다
● anxious ⓐ 불안한
● celebrate ⓥ 축하하다
● see A as B A를 B로 간주하다
● harmful ⓐ 해로운
● turn to ∼에 의지하다
● achievement ⓝ 성취

구문 풀이

10행 Then as we go through life, whenever we feel annoyed, anxious or even
접속사(∼함에 따라) 복합관계부사(∼할 때마다) 2형식 동사 보어1 보어2
just bored, we turn to food to make ourselves feel better.
보어3 주어 동사 목적어 부사적 용법(목적) 목적어 원형부정사

33 수생 생물의 특성을 유지하며 발달한 개구리 정답률 60% | 정답 ①

다음 빈칸에 들어갈 말로 가장 적절한 것을 고르시오. [3점]

✓① still kept many ties to the water – 여전히 물과의 여러 인연을 유지했다
② had almost all the necessary organs – 필요한 신체 기관을 거의 모두 갖추고 있었다
③ had to develop an appetite for new foods – 새로운 음식에 대한 식욕을 발달시켜야 했다
④ often competed with land-dwelling species – 땅에 사는 생물 종들과 종종 경쟁했다
⑤ suffered from rapid changes in temperature – 기온의 급격한 변화로 고생했다

Scientists believe / that the frogs' ancestors were water-dwelling, fishlike animals.
과학자들은 믿는다. / 개구리의 조상이 물에 사는, 물고기 같은 동물이었다고

The first frogs and their relatives / gained the ability / to come out on land / and enjoy the opportunities for food and shelter there.
최초의 개구리와 그들의 친척은 / 능력을 얻었다. / 육지로 나와 / 그곳에서 먹을 것과 살 곳에 대한 기회를 누릴 수 있는

But they still kept many ties to the water.
하지만 개구리는 여전히 물과의 여러 인연을 유지했다.

A frog's lungs do not work very well, / and it gets part of its oxygen / by breathing through its skin.
개구리의 폐는 그다지 기능을 잘하지 않고, / 개구리는 산소를 일부 얻는다. / 피부를 통해 호흡함으로써

But for this kind of "breathing" to work properly, / the frog's skin must stay moist.
하지만 이런 종류의 '호흡'이 제대로 이뤄지기 위해서는, / 개구리의 피부가 촉촉하게 유지되어야 한다.

And so the frog must remain near the water / where it can take a dip every now and then / to keep from drying out.
그래서 개구리는 물의 근처에 있어야 한다. / 이따금 몸을 잠깐 담글 수 있는 / 건조해지는 것을 막기 위해

Frogs must also lay their eggs in water, / as their fishlike ancestors did.
개구리 역시 물속에 알을 낳아야 한다. / 물고기 같은 조상이 그랬던 것처럼,

And eggs laid in the water / must develop into water creatures, / if they are to survive.
그리고 물속에 낳은 알은 / 물에 사는 생물로 발달해야 한다. / 그것들이 살아남으려면

For frogs, / metamorphosis thus provides the bridge / between the water-dwelling young forms and the land-dwelling adults.
개구리에게 있어서, / 따라서 탈바꿈은 다리를 제공한다. / 물에 사는 어린 형체와 육지에 사는 성체를 이어주는

과학자들은 개구리의 조상이 물에 사는, 물고기 같은 동물이었다고 믿는다. 최초의 개구리와 그들의 친척은 육지로 나와 그곳에서 먹을 것과 살 곳에 대한 기회를 누릴 수 있는 능력을 얻었다. 하지만 개구리는 여전히 물과의 여러 인연을 유지했다. 개구리의 폐는 그다지 기능을 잘하지 않고, 개구리는 피부를 통해 호흡함으로써 산소를 일부 얻는다. 하지만 이런 종류의 '호흡'이 제대로 이뤄지기 위해서는, 개구리의 피부가 촉촉하게 유지되어야 한다. 그래서 개구리는 건조해지는 것을 막기 위해 이따금 몸을 잠깐 담글 수 있는 물의 근처에 있어야 한다. 물고기 같은 조상들이 그랬던 것처럼, 개구리 역시 물속에 알을 낳아야 한다. 그리고 물속에 낳은 알이 살아남으려면, 물에 사는 생물로 발달해야 한다. 따라서, 개구리에게 있어서 탈바꿈은 물에 사는 어린 형체와 육지에 사는 성체를 이어주는 다리를 제공한다.

Why? 왜 정답일까?

개구리는 당초 물고기 같은 동물로 기원하여 육지에서 생활하도록 진화했지만 여전히 '물에 사는' 생물로서의 특징을 지니고 있다는 내용의 글이다. 빈칸 뒤에서 개구리는 폐가 그다지 발달해 있지 않아 피부를 이용해 호흡하는데, 호흡이 원활하기 위해서는 피부가 늘 젖어 있어야 하고, 따라서 물을 가까이 해야 하며, 알 또한 물속에 낳아 번식해야 하기에 '물에 살기 적합한' 생물로 발달할 수밖에 없는 운명임을 설명하고 있다. 이러한 흐름을 근거로 볼 때, 빈칸에 들어갈 말로 가장 적절한 것은 개구리가 '물고기다운' 특성을 완전히 포기하지 않았다는 의미의 ① '여전히 물과의 여러 인연을 유지했다'이다.

● ancestor ⓝ 조상
● relative ⓝ 친척
● moist ⓐ 촉촉한
● dry out 건조하다, 바짝 마르다
● tie ⓝ 관계, 연결
● appetite ⓝ 식욕
● dwell ⓥ 거주하다, 살다
● properly ⓐd 적절히
● take a dip 잠깐 수영을 하다
● lay ⓥ (알을) 낳다
● organ ⓝ (신체) 기관
● compete with ∼와 경쟁하다

구문 풀이

7행 But for this kind of "breathing" to work properly, the frog's skin must stay
의미상 주어 부사적 용법(∼하려면) 2형식 동사
moist.
보어

★★★ 등급을 가르는 문제!

34 실질적 자유에 영향을 주는 요소 정답률 34% | 정답 ⑤

다음 빈칸에 들어갈 말로 가장 적절한 것을 고르시오. [3점]

① respecting others' rights to freedom
다른 사람들의 자유권을 존중하는
② protecting and providing for the needy
궁핍한 사람들을 보호하고 돕는
③ learning what socially acceptable behaviors are
사회적으로 수용 가능한 행동이 무엇인지 아는
④ determining how much they can expect from others
다른 사람들에게 얼마나 많은 것을 기대할 수 있는지를 정하는
✓⑤ having the means and ability to do what they choose
그들이 선택하는 것을 할 수 있는 수단과 능력을 갖추고 있는가

It is important / to distinguish between being legally allowed to do something, / and actually being able to go and do it.
중요하다. / 어떤 일을 할 수 있도록 법적으로 허용되는 것을 구별하는 것은 / 실제로 그것을 해 버릴 수 있는 것과

A law could be passed / allowing everyone, / if they so wish, / to run a mile in two minutes.
법이 통과될 수도 있다. / 모든 사람에게 허용하는 / 그들이 그러기를 원한다면, / 2분 안에 1마일을 달릴 수 있도록

That would not, however, increase their effective freedom, / because, although allowed to do so, / they are physically incapable of it.
그러나 그것이 그들의 실질적 자유를 증가시키지는 않을 것이다. / 그렇게 하는 것이 허용되더라도, / 그들이 물리적으로 그렇게 할 수 없기 때문에

Having a minimum of restrictions and a maximum of possibilities / is fine.
최소한의 제약과 최대한의 가능성을 두는 것은 / 괜찮다.

But in the real world / most people will never have the opportunity / either to become all that they are allowed to become, / or to need to be restrained from doing everything / that is possible for them to do.
하지만 현실 세계에서, / 대부분의 사람에게는 가능성이 없다. / 그들이 되어도 된다는 모든 것이 될 / 혹은 모든 것을 하지 못하게 저지당해야 할 / 그들이 하는 것이 가능한

Their effective freedom depends on / actually having the means and ability / to do what they choose.
그들의 실질적 자유는 달려 있다. / 실제로 수단과 능력을 갖추고 있는가에 / 그들이 선택하는 것을 할 수 있는

어떤 일을 할 수 있도록 법적으로 허용되는 것과 실제로 그것을 해 버릴 수 있는 것을 구별하는 것은 중요하다. 원한다면, 모든 사람이 2분 안에 1마일을 달릴 수 있도록 허용하는 법이 통과될 수도 있다. 그러나 그렇게 하는 것이 허용되더라도, 물리적으로 그렇게 할 수 없기 때문에, 그것이 그들의 실질적 자유를 증가시키지는 않을 것이다. 최소한의 제약과 최대한의 가능성을 두는 것은 괜찮다. 하지만 현실 세계에서, 대부분의 사람에게는 그들이 되어도 된다는 모든 것이 될 가능성이 없고, 할 수 있는 모든 것을 하지 못하게 저지당해야 할 가능성도 없을 것이다. 그들의 실질적 자유는 실제로 그들이 선택하는 것을 할 수 있는 수단과 능력을 갖추고 있는가에 달려 있다.

Why? 왜 정답일까?

첫 문장에서 어떤 것을 법적으로 해도 되는 상태와 실제로 그것을 행할 수 있는지를 구별하는 것이 중요하다고 언급한 데 이어, 2분 안에 1마일을 달리도록 허용하는 법이 통과되는 경우가 예시로 나온다. 예시에 따르면 2분 안에 1마일을 뛰는 것이 법적으로 가능해질지라도 '실제로 그렇게 할 수 있는' 사람들이 없기에 사람들의 실질적 자유가 증가되지 않는다고 한다. 이를 근거로 볼 때, 사람들의 '실질적' 자유란 '법으로 허용되는 행위를 실제 행할 능력이 있는지'에 따라 좌우된다는 결론을 도출할 수 있다. 따라서 빈칸에 들어갈 말로 가장 적절한 것은 ⑤ '그들이 선택하는 것을 할 수 있는 수단과 능력을 갖추고 있는가'이다.

● distinguish ⓥ 구별하다
● allowed ⓐ 허가받은, 허용된
● be incapable of ∼을 할 수 없다
● physically ⓐd 신체적으로, 물리적으로
● needy ⓐ (경제적으로) 어려운, 궁핍한
● means ⓝ 수단
● legally ⓐd 법적으로
● effective ⓐ 실질적인, 효과적인
● restrain ⓥ 저지[제지]하다
● depend on ∼에 좌우되다
● acceptable ⓐ 허용 가능한, 수용 가능한

4행 That would not, however, increase their *effective* freedom, because,

주어(=앞 문장) 조동사 　동사원형 　접속사(~ 때문에)

(although (they are) allowed to do so), they are physically incapable of it.

( ): 삽입구 　생략 　주어 　동사구(~할 수 없다)

★★ 문제 해결 꿀~팁 ★★

▶ 많이 틀린 이유는?

실제로 행할 수 있는 행동이 법적으로 허용될 때 실질적 자유가 커질 수 있다는 내용의 글이다. 타인의 자유권을 존중하는 것에 관한 내용은 언급되지 않으므로 ①은 답으로 부적절하다.

▶ 문제 해결 방법은?

첫 문장에서 어떤 일이 법적으로 허용되는 것과 그 일을 실제 할 수 있는가는 다른 개념이라고 언급한다. 이어서 법적으로 허용되더라도 실제로는 할 수 없는 일일 때 사람들의 실질적 자유는 증가하지 않는다는 것을 뒷받침하는 예시가 나온다. 이를 토대로 볼 때, 자유에 있어 중요한 것은 어떤 일이 법적으로 허용되는 것을 넘어서 '그 일을 실제로 할 수 있는지' 여부임을 알 수 있다.

---

35 뮤지션들이 홀로 많은 것을 할 수 있게 된 오늘날의 음악 시장 　정답률 65% | 정답 ③

다음 글에서 전체 흐름과 관계 없는 문장은?

Today's music business / has allowed musicians / to take matters into their own hands.
오늘날의 음악 사업은 / 뮤지션들이 ~하게 해 주었다. / 스스로 일을 처리할 수 있게

① Gone are the days of musicians / waiting for a gatekeeper / (someone / who holds power / and prevents you from being let in) / at a label or TV show / to say they are worthy of the spotlight.
뮤지션들의 시대는 지났다. / 문지기를 기다리던 / (사람 / 권력을 쥔 / 그리고 여러분이 들어가는 것을 막는) / 음반사나 TV 프로그램의 / 그들이 스포트라이트를 받을 만하다고 말해주기를

② In today's music business, / you don't need to ask for permission / to build a fanbase / and you no longer need to pay thousands of dollars to a company / to do it.
오늘날의 음악 사업에서는 / 여러분은 허락을 요청할 필요가 없으며, / 팬층을 만들기 위해 / 여러분은 회사에 수천 달러를 지불할 필요도 더 이상 없다. / 그렇게 하려고

☑ There are rising concerns / over the marketing of child musicians / using TV auditions.
우려가 증가하고 있다. / 나이 어린 뮤지션들을 마케팅하는 데에 대한 / TV 오디션을 이용하여

④ Every day, / musicians are getting their music out / to thousands of listeners / without any outside help.
매일 / 뮤지션들은 자신들의 음악을 내놓고 있다. / 수천 명의 청취자에게 / 어떤 외부의 도움 없이

⑤ They simply deliver it to the fans directly, / without asking for permission or outside help / to receive exposure or connect with thousands of listeners.
그들은 그저 그것을 팬들에게 직접 전달한다. / 허락이나 외부의 도움을 요청하지 않고, / 노출을 얻거나 수천 명의 청취자와 관계를 형성하기 위해

오늘날의 음악 사업은 뮤지션들이 스스로 일을 처리할 수 있게 해 주었다. ① 뮤지션들이 음반사나 TV 프로그램의 문지기(권력을 쥐고 사람들이 들어가는 것을 막는 사람)가 그들이 스포트라이트를 받을 만하다고 말해주기를 기다리던 시대는 지났다. ② 오늘날의 음악 사업에서는 팬층을 만들기 위해 허락을 요청할 필요가 없으며, 그렇게 하려고 회사에 수천 달러를 지불할 필요도 더 이상 없다. ③ TV 오디션을 이용하여 나이 어린 뮤지션들을 마케팅하는 데에 대한 우려가 증가하고 있다. ④ 매일 뮤지션들은 어떤 외부의 도움도 없이 수천 명의 청취자에게 자신들의 음악을 내놓고 있다. ⑤ 그들은 노출을 얻거나 수천 명의 청취자와 관계를 형성하기 위해 허락이나 외부의 도움을 요청하지 않고, 그저 자신들의 음악을 팬들에게 직접 전달한다.

Why? 왜 정답일까?

오늘날 뮤지션들은 음반사 등에 크게 의지할 필요 없이 직접 대중에게 음악을 전달하고 스스로 마케팅할 수 있는 시장 환경에서 활동한다는 내용을 다룬 글이다. ①, ②, ④, ⑤는 주제에 부합하지만, ③은 **TV 오디션**을 통한 어린 뮤지션들의 마케팅에 관해 언급하고 있어 흐름에서 벗어난다. 따라서 전체 흐름과 관계 없는 문장은 ③이다.

- take matters into one's own hands 스스로 일을 추진하다, 일을 독자적으로 하다
- gatekeeper ⓝ 문지기, 수위
- permission ⓝ 허락
- deliver ⓥ 전달하다
- be worthy of ~을 받을 만하다, ~의 가치가 있다
- concern ⓝ 우려

구문 풀이

2행 Gone are the days of musicians waiting for a gatekeeper (someone [who

「보어＋동사＋주어 : 도치 구문」　현재분사「wait＋　의미상 주어＝a gatekeeper

holds power and prevents you from being let in]) at a label or TV show to say they

동사1 　동사2 　　　　　　　　　　　to부정사 : ~이 …하도록 기다리다」

are worthy of the spotlight.

---

36 스포츠에 활용되는 공의 특징 　정답률 56% | 정답 ②

주어진 글 다음에 이어질 글의 순서로 가장 적절한 것을 고르시오.

① (A) - (C) - (B) 　　　　☑ (B) - (A) - (C)
③ (B) - (C) - (A) 　　　　④ (C) - (A) - (B)
⑤ (C) - (B) - (A)

Almost all major sporting activities / are played with a ball.
거의 모든 주요 스포츠 활동은 / 공을 갖고 행해진다.

(B) The rules of the game / always include rules / about the type of ball that is allowed, / starting with the size and weight of the ball.
경기의 규칙들은 / 규칙들을 늘 포함하고 있다. / 허용되는 공의 유형에 관한 / 공의 크기와 무게부터 시작해서

The ball must also have a certain stiffness.
공은 또한 특정 정도의 단단함을 갖추어야 한다.

(A) A ball might have the correct size and weight / but if it is made as a hollow ball of steel / it will be too stiff / and if it is made from light foam rubber with a heavy center / it will be too soft.

공이 적절한 크기와 무게를 갖출 수 있으나 / 그것이 속이 빈 강철 공으로 만들어지면 / 그것은 너무 단단할 것이고, / 그것이 무거운 중심부를 가진 가벼운 발포 고무로 만들어지면 / 그 공은 너무 물렁할 것이다.

(C) Similarly, along with stiffness, / a ball needs to bounce properly.
마찬가지로, 단단함과 더불어 / 공은 적절히 튈 필요가 있다.

A solid rubber ball / would be too bouncy for most sports, / and a solid ball made of clay / would not bounce at all.
순전히 고무로만 된 공은 / 대부분의 스포츠에 지나치게 잘 튈 것이고, / 순전히 점토로만 만든 공은 / 전혀 튀지 않을 것이다.

거의 모든 주요 스포츠 활동은 공을 갖고 행해진다.

(B) 경기의 규칙들은 공의 크기와 무게부터 시작해서 허용되는 공의 유형에 관한 규칙들을 늘 포함하고 있다. 공은 또한 특정 정도의 단단함을 갖추어야 한다.

(A) 공이 적절한 크기와 무게를 갖출 수 있으나 속이 빈 강철 공으로 만들어지면 그것은 너무 단단할 것이고, 무거운 중심부를 가진 가벼운 발포 고무로 만들어지면 그 공은 너무 물렁할 것이다.

(C) 마찬가지로, 공은 단단함과 더불어 적절히 튈 필요가 있다. 순전히 고무로만 된 공은 대부분의 스포츠에 지나치게 잘 튈 것이고, 순전히 점토로만 만든 공은 전혀 튀지 않을 것이다.

Why? 왜 정답일까?

스포츠에 활용되는 공이 갖추어야 할 특징에 관해 설명하는 글이다. 먼저 주어진 글에서 공이 스포츠에서 널리 쓰인다는 내용을 제시한 데 이어, **(B)**에서는 경기 규칙을 보면 어떤 공이 사용되어야 하는지를 명시하고 있다는 내용과 함께 공이 단단함을 갖추어야 한다는 점을 언급한다. 이어서 **(A)**는 공이 적절한 크기나 무게를 갖추더라도 강철로 되어 있다면 지나치게 단단할 것이고, 역으로 (매트리스에 주로 활용되는) 발포 고무로 만들어진다면 너무 물렁할 것이라는 보충 설명을 제시한다. 이러한 **(A)**의 내용에 Similarly 로 연결되는 **(C)**는 단단함과 더불어 필요한 특징으로서 잘 튀어오르는 속성을 언급하고 있다. 따라서 글의 순서로 가장 적절한 것은 ② '(B) - (A) - (C)'이다.

- major ⓐ 주요한
- steel ⓝ 강철
- rubber ⓝ 고무
- bounce ⓥ 튀어오르다
- solid ⓐ 순수한(다른 물질이 섞이지 않은)
- hollow ⓐ (속이) 빈
- stiff ⓐ 단단한
- certain ⓐ 확실한, 틀림없는
- properly [ad] 적절히
- clay ⓝ 점토

구문 풀이

3행 A ball might have the correct size and weight but if it is made as a hollow

주어 　동사 　　　　　　　　조건 접속사1 ←　현재시제1 전치사(~로서)

ball of steel it will be too stiff and if it is made from light foam rubber with a heavy

미래시제1 조건 접속사2 ←　현재시제2(~으로 만들어지다)

center it will be too soft.

미래시제2

---

37 수학과 화학에서의 기호 사용 　정답률 61% | 정답 ③

주어진 글 다음에 이어질 글의 순서로 가장 적절한 것을 고르시오. [3점]

① (A) - (C) - (B) 　　　　② (B) - (A) - (C)
☑ (B) - (C) - (A) 　　　　④ (C) - (A) - (B)
⑤ (C) - (B) - (A)

If you had to write a math equation, / you probably wouldn't write, / "Twenty-eight plus fourteen equals forty-two."
만일 여러분이 수학 등식을 써야 한다면, / 여러분은 아마 쓰지 않을 것이다. / '스물여덟 더하기 열넷은 마흔둘과 같다.'라고

It would take too long to write / and it would be hard to read quickly.
그것은 쓰는 데 너무 오래 걸리고 / 빨리 읽기가 어려울 것이다.

(B) You would write, "28 + 14 = 42."
여러분은 '28 + 14 = 42'라고 쓸 것이다.

Chemistry is the same way.
화학도 마찬가지이다.

Chemists have to write chemical equations all the time, / and it would take too long to write and read / if they had to spell everything out.
화학자들은 항상 화학 방정식을 써야 하고, / 쓰고 읽는 데 너무 오래 걸릴 것이다. / 만약 그들이 모든 것을 상세히 다 써야 한다면

(C) So chemists use symbols, / just like we do in math.
그래서 화학자들은 기호를 사용한다. / 우리가 수학에서 하는 것처럼

A chemical formula lists all the elements / that form each molecule / and uses a small number / to the bottom right of an element's symbol / to stand for the number of atoms of that element.
화학식은 모든 원소를 나열하고 / 각 분자를 구성하는 / 작은 숫자를 사용한다. / 원소 기호의 오른쪽 아래에 / 그 원소의 원자 수를 나타내기 위해

(A) For example, / the chemical formula for water is H_2O.
예를 들어, / 물의 화학식은 H_2O이다.

That tells us / that a water molecule is made up / of two hydrogen ("H" and "2") atoms / and one oxygen ("O") atom.
그것은 우리에게 말해 준다. / 하나의 물 분자는 이루어져 있다는 것을 / 두 개의 수소 원자('H'와 '2')와 / 하나의 산소 원자('O')로

만일 여러분이 수학 등식을 써야 한다면, 여러분은 아마 '스물여덟 더하기 열넷은 마흔둘과 같다.'라고 쓰지 않을 것이다. 그것은 쓰는 데 너무 오래 걸리고 빨리 읽기가 어려울 것이다.

(B) 여러분은 '28 + 14 = 42'라고 쓸 것이다. 화학도 마찬가지이다. 화학자들은 항상 화학 방정식을 써야 하고, 만약 그들이 모든 것을 상세히 다 써야 한다면 쓰고 읽는 데 너무 오래 걸릴 것이다.

(C) 그래서 화학자들은 우리가 수학에서 하는 것처럼 기호를 사용한다. 화학식은 각 분자를 구성하는 모든 원소를 나열하고 그 원소의 원자 수를 나타내기 위해 원소 기호의 오른쪽 아래에 작은 숫자를 사용한다.

(A) 예를 들어, 물의 화학식은 H_2O이다. 그것은 우리에게 하나의 물 분자는 두 개의 수소 원자('H'와 '2')와 하나의 산소 원자('O')로 이루어져 있다는 것을 말해 준다.

Why? 왜 정답일까?

주어진 글에서 우리가 수학 등식을 쓸 때 말로 풀어쓰지 않을 것이라 언급한 데 이어, **(B)**에서는 우리가 '28 + 14 = 42'와 같이 '기호'를 사용할 것이라고 설명한다. 이어서 **(C)**는 **(B)**의 후반부에 이어 화학에서

도 기호 사용이 필요하다고 언급하며, 특히 화학식의 경우 원소 기호 아래 작은 숫자를 사용하여 원자 수를 나타낸다는 내용을 덧붙인다. **For example**로 시작하는 **(A)**는 **(C)**에서 언급한 아래 첨자 사용을 보여줄 수 있는 예로 H_2O를 제시한다. 따라서 글의 순서로 가장 적절한 것은 ③ '(B) − (C) − (A)'이다.

- **equation** ⓝ 방정식, 등식
- **hydrogen** ⓝ 수소
- **spell out** 상세히 말하다
- **element** ⓝ 원소, 요소
- **be made up of** ~으로 구성되다, 이루어지다
- **atom** ⓝ 원자
- **symbol** ⓝ 기호
- **stand for** ~을 나타내다[대표하다]

구문 풀이

1행 If you had to write a math equation, you probably wouldn't write,
「if + 주어 + 과거 동사 ~,   주어 + 조동사 과거형 + 동사원형 : 가정법 과거(현재 사실의 반대 가정)」
"Twenty-eight plus fourteen equals forty-two."

★★★ 등급을 가르는 문제!
38 작은 발전으로 이루는 큰 변화   정답률 36% | 정답 ②

글의 흐름으로 보아, 주어진 문장이 들어가기에 가장 적절한 곳을 고르시오.

It is so easy / to overestimate the importance of one defining moment / and underestimate the value of making small improvements on a daily basis.
매우 쉽다. / 결정적인 한순간의 중요성을 과대평가하고 / 매일 작은 발전을 이루는 것의 가치를 과소평가하는
Too often, / we convince ourselves / that massive success requires massive action.
너무 자주 / 우리는 스스로를 납득시킨다 / 거대한 성공에는 거대한 행동이 필요하다고
① Whether it is losing weight, / winning a championship, / or achieving any other goal, / we put pressure on ourselves / to make some earthshaking improvement / that everyone will talk about.
그것이 체중을 줄이는 것이든, / 결승전에서 이기는 것이든, / 혹은 어떤 다른 목표를 달성하는 것이든 간에, / 우리는 우리 스스로에게 압력을 가한다. / 지축을 흔들 만한 발전을 이루도록 / 모두가 이야기하게 될
✔Meanwhile, / improving by 1 percent isn't particularly notable, / but it can be far more meaningful in the long run.
한편, / 1퍼센트 발전하는 것은 특별히 눈에 띄지는 않지만, / 그것은 장기적으로는 훨씬 더 의미가 있을 수 있다.
The difference / this tiny improvement can make over time / is surprising.
변화는 / 시간이 지남에 따라 이 작은 발전이 이룰 수 있는 / 놀랍다.
③ Here's how the math works out: / if you can get 1 percent better each day for one year, / you'll end up thirty-seven times better / by the time you're done.
다음과 같이 계산이 이루어지는데, / 만일 여러분이 1년 동안 매일 1퍼센트씩 더 나아질 수 있다면, / 여러분은 결국 37배 더 나아질 것이다. / 여러분이 끝마칠 때 즈음
④ Conversely, if you get 1 percent worse each day for one year, / you'll decline nearly down to zero.
역으로, / 여러분이 1년 동안 매일 1퍼센트씩 나빠지면 / 여러분은 거의 0까지 떨어질 것이다.
⑤ What starts as a small win or a minor failure / adds up to something much more.
작은 승리나 사소한 패배로 시작한 것은 / 쌓여서 훨씬 더 큰 무언가가 된다.

결정적인 한순간의 중요성을 과대평가하고 매일 작은 발전을 이루는 것의 가치를 과소평가하기는 매우 쉽다. 너무 자주 우리는 거대한 성공에는 거대한 행동이 필요하다고 스스로를 납득시킨다. ① 체중을 줄이는 것이든, 결승전에서 이기는 것이든, 혹은 어떤 다른 목표를 달성하는 것이든 간에, 우리는 모두가 이야기하게 될 지축을 흔들 만한 발전을 이루도록 우리 스스로에게 압력을 가한다. ② 한편, 1퍼센트 발전하는 것은 특별히 눈에 띄지는 않지만, 장기적으로는 훨씬 더 의미가 있을 수 있다. 시간이 지남에 따라 이 작은 발전이 이룰 수 있는 변화는 놀랍다. ③ 다음과 같이 계산이 이루어지는데, 만일 여러분이 1년 동안 매일 1퍼센트씩 더 나아질 수 있다면, 끝마칠 때 즈음 여러분은 결국 37배 더 나아질 것이다. ④ 역으로, 1년 동안 매일 1퍼센트씩 나빠지면 여러분은 거의 0까지 떨어질 것이다. ⑤ 작은 승리나 사소한 패배로 시작한 것은 쌓여서 훨씬 더 큰 무언가가 된다.

Why? 왜 정답일까?

② 앞에서는 우리가 작은 변화의 가치를 과소평가하고 거대한 발전에 맞는 거대한 행동을 해나가도록 스스로를 압박한다는 내용이 주를 이룬다. 이에 이어 주어진 문장은 Meanwhile로 흐름을 전환하며 '1퍼센트만큼' 작게 발전하는 것이 당장은 눈에 띄지 않아도 장기적으로는 큰 의미를 가질 수 있다고 설명한다. ② 뒤의 문장은 주어진 문장에서 언급한 '1퍼센트의 발전'을 this tiny improvement라는 말로 바꾸며 '작은 발전'으로 인한 변화가 시간이 지난 후에는 놀라울 수 있음을 환기시킨다. 따라서 주어진 문장이 들어가기에 가장 적절한 곳은 ②이다.

- **meanwhile** ⓐⓓ 한편
- **in the long run** 장기적으로
- **underestimate** ⓥ 과소평가하다
- **convince** ⓥ 납득시키다, 설득하다
- **put pressure on** ~에 압박을 가하다
- **tiny** ⓐ 극히 작은
- **decline** ⓥ 떨어지다, 감소하다
- **notable** ⓐ 눈에 띄는, 두드러지는
- **overestimate** ⓥ 과대평가하다
- **on a daily basis** 매일
- **massive** ⓐ 거대한
- **earthshaking** ⓐ 극히 중대한, 세상을 떠들썩하게 하는
- **conversely** ⓐⓓ 역으로

구문 풀이

7행 (Whether it is losing weight, winning a championship, or achieving any
주어   동사 동명사 보어1   동명사 보어2   동명사 보어3
other goal), we put pressure on ourselves to make some earthshaking improvement
( ): 부사절(~이든 …이든)   선행사
[that everyone will talk about].
목적격 관계대명사

★★ 문제 해결 꿀~팁 ★★

▶ 많이 틀린 이유는?
최다 오답인 ④ 앞뒤는 Conversely를 기점으로 매일 조금씩 1년 동안 발전하는 경우와 나빠지는 경우가 적절히 대비를 이루는 맥락이다. 따라서 ④에 주어진 문장을 넣기에는 부적절하다.
▶ 문제 해결 방법은?
② 앞에서는 거창한 결과를 이룩하려면 거창한 행동이 필요하다고 생각한다는 내용이 주를 이루는데,
② 뒤에서는 '이 작은 발전(this tiny improvement)'에 관해 언급한다.
즉 ② 앞뒤 내용이 서로 상충하므로 Meanwhile(한편)으로 시작하며 흐름을 반전하는 주어진 문장이 ②에 들어가야 한다.

06회

★★★ 등급을 가르는 문제!
39 현지 환경을 미리 조사하고 대비하기   정답률 54% | 정답 ④

글의 흐름으로 보아, 주어진 문장이 들어가기에 가장 적절한 곳을 고르시오. [3점]

The continued survival of the human race / can be explained / by our ability to adapt to our environment.
인류의 지속적인 생존은 / 설명될 수 있을 것이다. / 환경에 적응하는 우리의 능력으로
① While we may have lost some of our ancient ancestors' survival skills, / we have learned new skills / as they have become necessary.
우리가 고대 조상들의 생존 기술 중 일부를 잃어버렸을지도 모르지만, / 우리는 새로운 기술을 배웠다. / 새로운 기술이 필요해지면서
② Today, / the gap / between the skills we once had / and the skills we now have / grows ever wider / as we rely more heavily on modern technology.
오늘날 / 간극이 / 한때 우리가 가졌던 기술과 / 현재 우리가 가진 기술 사이의 / 어느 때보다 더 커졌다. / 우리가 현대 기술에 크게 의존함에 따라
③ Therefore, / when you head off into the wilderness, / it is important / to fully prepare for the environment.
그러므로, / 여러분이 미지의 땅으로 향할 때에는 / 중요하다. / 그 환경에 대해 충분히 준비하는 것이
✔Before a trip, / research / how the native inhabitants dress, work, and eat.
떠나기 전에, / 조사하라. / 토착 주민들이 어떻게 옷을 입고 일하고 먹는지를
How they have adapted to their way of life / will help you to understand the environment / and allow you to select the best gear / and learn the correct skills.
그들이 어떻게 자신들의 생활 방식에 적응했는가는 / 여러분이 그 환경을 이해하도록 도울 것이고, / 여러분이 최선의 장비를 선별하도록 해 줄 것이다. / 그리고 적절한 기술을 배우도록
⑤ This is crucial / because most survival situations arise / as a result of a series of events / that could have been avoided.
이것은 중요하다. / 생존이 걸린 대부분의 상황이 발생하기 때문에 / 일련의 사건의 결과로 / 피할 수도 있었던

인류의 지속적인 생존은 환경에 적응하는 우리의 능력으로 설명될 수 있을 것이다. ① 우리가 고대 조상들의 생존 기술 중 일부를 잃어버렸을지도 모르지만, 새로운 기술이 필요해지면서 우리는 새로운 기술을 배웠다. ② 오늘날 우리가 현대 기술에 더 크게 의존함에 따라 한때 우리가 가졌던 기술과 현재 우리가 가진 기술 사이의 간극이 어느 때보다 더 커졌다. ③ 그러므로, 미지의 땅으로 향할 때에는 그 환경에 대해 충분히 준비하는 것이 중요하다. ④ 떠나기 전에, 토착 주민들이 어떻게 옷을 입고 일하고 먹는지를 조사하라. 그들이 어떻게 자신들의 생활 방식에 적응했는가는 여러분이 그 환경을 이해하도록 도울 것이고, 여러분이 최선의 장비를 선별하고 적절한 기술을 배우도록 해 줄 것이다. ⑤ 생존이 걸린 대부분의 상황이 피할 수도 있었던 일련의 사건의 결과로 발생하기 때문에 이것은 중요하다.

Why? 왜 정답일까?

④ 앞의 두 문장에서 현대 기술에 대한 우리의 의존도가 높아짐에 따라 과거의 기술과 오늘날의 기술 간에 격차가 더 벌어졌으므로 잘 모르는 곳에 갈 때에는 그 환경에 대한 충분한 준비가 필요하다고 언급한다. 이에 대한 구체적인 조언으로서 주어진 문장은 떠나기 전 '토착 주민'의 옷, 음식, 일하는 문화 등을 조사하라고 언급한다. ④ 뒤의 문장은 주어진 문장의 '토착 주민'을 they로 언급하며 이들이 나름의 삶의 방식에 어떻게 적응해 있는지를 파악하면 그 환경을 이해하는 데 도움이 될 것이라고 설명한다. 따라서 주어진 문장이 들어가기에 가장 적절한 곳은 ④이다.

- **adapt to** ~에 적응하다
- **rely on** ~에 의존하다
- **wilderness** ⓝ 황무지
- **arise** ⓥ 발생하다, 일어나다
- **ancestor** ⓝ 조상
- **heavily** ⓐⓓ 심하게, 많이
- **crucial** ⓐ 매우 중요한
- **as a result of** ~의 결과로

구문 풀이

11행 How they have adapted to their way of life will help you to understand the
주어(간접의문문 : 어떻게 ~하는지)   「help + 목적어 + to부정사 : ~이 …하는 데 도움이 되다」
environment and allow you to select the best gear and (to) learn the correct skills.
                「allow + 목적어 + to부정사 : ~이 …하게 하다」

★★ 문제 해결 꿀~팁 ★★

▶ 많이 틀린 이유는?
인간은 환경에 맞추어 계속 적응하고 변하는데, 오늘날 인간은 기술에 대한 의존도가 커서 과거와의 간극이 더욱 벌어졌기에 미지의 땅으로 나아갈 때에는 항상 환경에 대한 대비와 조사가 필요하다는 내용의 글이다. 특히 최다 오답인 ③ 앞뒤로 '과거 기술과 현대 기술의 간극이 커져서 → 새로운 땅으로 갈 때 환경을 잘 알아봐야 한다'라는 내용이 적절한 인과 관계로 연결되어 있다. 따라서 주어진 문장을 ③에 넣는 것은 부적절하다.
▶ 문제 해결 방법은?
④ 뒤의 문장에 they가 나오므로 앞에서 they로 받을 만한 복수 명사가 언급되어야 한다. ④ 앞의 문장에는 적절한 복수 명사가 없는 반면, 주어진 문장에는 the native inhabitants가 있다. 따라서 이 they에 '토착 주민'을 넣어서 읽어 보고 맥락이 자연스러운지 확인해 보면 답을 찾을 수 있다.

★★★ 등급을 가르는 문제!
40 존재만으로 관계를 상하게 하는 휴대폰   정답률 52% | 정답 ②

다음 글의 내용을 한 문장으로 요약하고자 한다. 빈칸 (A), (B)에 들어갈 말로 가장 적절한 것은?

	(A)		(B)		(A)		(B)
①	weakens 약화시킨다	……	answered 응대되고	✔	weakens 약화시킨다	……	ignored 무시되고
③	renews 새롭게 한다	……	answered 응대되고	④	maintains 유지시킨다	……	ignored 무시되고
⑤	maintains 유지시킨다	……	updated 업데이트되고				

In one study, / researchers asked pairs of strangers / to sit down in a room and chat.
한 연구에서, / 연구자들은 서로 모르는 사람들끼리 짝을 지어 ~하게 했다. / 한 방에 앉아서 이야기하도록
In half of the rooms, / a cell phone was placed on a nearby table; / in the other half, / no phone was present.
절반의 방에는 / 근처 탁자 위에 휴대폰이 놓여 있었고, / 나머지 절반에는 / 휴대폰이 없었다.
After the conversations had ended, / the researchers asked the participants / what they thought of each other.
대화가 끝난 후, / 연구자들은 참가자들에게 물었다. / 그들이 서로에 대해 어떻게 생각하는지를

Here's what they learned: / when a cell phone was present in the room, / the participants reported / the quality of their relationship was worse / than those who'd talked in a cell phone-free room.
여기에 그들이 알게 된 것이 있다. / 방에 휴대폰이 있을 때 / 참가자들은 말했다. / 자신들의 관계의 질이 더 나빴다고 / 휴대폰이 없는 방에서 대화했던 참가자들에 비해

The pairs who talked in the rooms with cell phones / thought / their partners showed less empathy.
휴대폰이 있는 방에서 대화한 짝들은 / 생각했다. / 자신의 상대가 공감을 덜 보여 주었다고

Think of all the times / you've sat down / to have lunch with a friend / and set your phone on the table.
모든 순간을 떠올려 보라. / 여러분이 자리에 앉아 / 친구와 점심을 먹기 위해 / 탁자 위에 휴대폰을 놓았던

You might have felt good about yourself / because you didn't pick it up / to check your messages, / but your unchecked messages / were still hurting your connection / with the person sitting across from you.
여러분은 잘했다고 느꼈을지 모르지만, / 여러분이 휴대폰을 집어 들지 않았으므로 / 메시지를 확인하려고 / 여러분의 확인하지 않은 메시지는 / 여전히 관계를 상하게 하고 있었다 / 맞은편에 앉아 있는 사람과의

➡ The presence of a cell phone / (A) weakens the connection / between people involved in conversations, / even when the phone is being (B) ignored.
휴대폰의 존재는 / 관계를 약화시킨다. / 대화에 참여하는 사람들 간의 / 심지어 휴대폰이 무시되고 있을 때조차

한 연구에서, 연구자들은 서로 모르는 사람들끼리 짝을 지어 한 방에 앉아서 이야기하도록 했다. 절반의 방에는 근처 탁자 위에 휴대폰이 놓여 있었고, 나머지 절반에는 휴대폰이 없었다. 대화가 끝난 후, 연구자들은 참가자들에게 서로에 대해 어떻게 생각하는지를 물었다. 여기에 그들이 알게 된 것이 있다. 방에 휴대폰이 있을 때 참가자들은 휴대폰이 없는 방에서 대화했던 참가자들에 비해 자신들의 관계의 질이 더 나빴다고 말했다. 휴대폰이 있는 방에서 대화한 짝들은 자신의 상대가 공감을 덜 보여 주었다고 생각했다. 친구와 점심을 먹기 위해 자리에 앉아 탁자 위에 휴대폰을 놓았던 모든 순간을 떠올려 보라. 메시지를 확인하려고 휴대폰을 집어 들지 않았으므로 잘했다고 느꼈을지 모르지만, 여러분의 확인하지 않은 메시지는 여전히 맞은편에 앉아 있는 사람과의 관계를 상하게 하고 있었다.

➡ 휴대폰의 존재는 심지어 휴대폰이 (B) 무시되고 있을 때조차 대화에 참여하는 사람들 간의 관계를 (A) 약화시킨다.

- **present** ⓐ 존재하는
- **unchecked** ⓐ 확인되지 않은
- **weaken** ⓥ 약화시키다
- **renew** ⓥ 새롭게 하다, 갱신하다, 재개하다
- **participant** ⓝ 참가자
- **hurt** ⓥ 손상시키다, 다치게 하다
- **ignore** ⓥ 무시하다
- **maintain** ⓥ 유지하다

구문 풀이

13행 You might have felt good about yourself because you didn't pick it up to check your messages, but your unchecked messages were still hurting your connection with the person sitting across from you.
might have + p.p.: ~했을지도 모른다 / 접속사(~ 때문에) / 주어 / 동사(과거진행) / 현재분사

★★ 문제 해결 꿀~팁 ★★

▶ 많이 틀린 이유는?
마지막 문장에서 '확인하지 않은(unchecked)' 휴대폰 메시지가 관계에 악영향을 미치고 있었다는 결론이 제시된다. 즉 요약문의 (B)에는 휴대전화에 '응답하고 있지 않은' 상황에조차 관계가 약화되고 있었다는 의미를 완성하는 말이 들어가야 한다. ①의 answered는 휴대전화에 '응답하는' 상황에조차 관계가 나빠지고 있었다는 의미를 나타내므로 부적절하다.

▶ 문제 해결 방법은?
요약문에서 '실험 – 결과' 구조의 글이 나오면 바로 결과가 제시되는 문장을 찾아 요약문을 그 문장과 일치시킨다는 느낌으로 문제를 풀면 된다. 이 문제에서도 실험의 결론을 제시하는 마지막 문장과 요약문의 내용이 서로 같아야 한다.

41-42 반복의 중요성

As kids, / we worked hard at learning to ride a bike; / when we fell off, / we got back on again, / until it became second nature to us.
아이였을 때, / 우리는 열심히 자전거 타기를 배웠고, / 우리가 넘어지면, / 우리는 다시 올라탔는데, / 그것이 우리에게 제2의 천성이 될 때까지 그렇게 했다.

But when we try something new in our adult lives / we'll usually make just one attempt / before judging whether it's (a) worked.
그러나 우리가 어른으로 살면서 새로운 것을 시도해 볼 때 / 우리는 대체로 단 한 번만 시도해 본다. / 그것이 잘되었는지 판단하기 전에

If we don't succeed the first time, / or if it feels a little awkward, / we'll tell ourselves / it wasn't a success / rather than giving it (b) another shot.
만일 우리가 처음에 성공하지 못하거나 / 혹은 그것이 약간 어색하게 느껴지면, / 우리는 스스로에게 말할 것이다. / 그것이 성공이 아니었다고 / 또 한번 시도해 보기보다는

『That's a shame, / because repetition is central / to the process of rewiring our brains.』
그것은 애석한 일인데, / 반복이 핵심적이기 때문이다. / 우리 뇌를 재연결하는 과정에서 **41번의 근거**

Consider the idea / that your brain has a network of neurons.
개념을 생각해 보라. / 여러분의 뇌가 뉴런의 연결망을 가지고 있다는

They will (c) connect with each other / whenever you remember to use a brain-friendly feedback technique.
그것들은 서로 연결될 것이다. / 여러분이 뇌 친화적인 피드백 기술을 잊지 않고 사용할 때마다

Those connections aren't very (d) reliable at first, / which may make your first efforts a little hit-and-miss.
그 연결은 처음에는 그리 신뢰할 만하지 않고, / 여러분의 첫 번째 시도가 다소 마구잡이가 되도록 할 수도 있다.

You might remember one of the steps involved, / and not the others.
여러분은 연관된 단계 중 하나를 기억하고, / 다른 것들을 기억하지 못할 수도 있다. **42번의 근거**

『But scientists have a saying: / "neurons that fire together, wire together."』
그러나 과학자들은 말한다. / "함께 활성화되는 뉴런들은 함께 연결된다."라고

In other words, / repetition of an action / (e) strengthens the connections / between the neurons involved in that action.
다시 말하자면, / 어떤 행동의 반복은 / 연결을 강화한다. / 그 행동에 연관된 뉴런들 사이의

『That means / the more times you try using that new feedback technique, / the more easily it will come to you / when you need it.』 **41번의 근거**
그것은 의미한다. / 여러분이 그 새로운 피드백 기술을 더 여러 차례 사용해 볼수록, / 그것이 더 쉽게 여러분에게 다가올 것을 / 여러분이 그것을 필요로 할 때

아이였을 때, 우리는 열심히 자전거 타기를 배웠고, 넘어지면 다시 올라탔는데, 그것이 우리에게 제2의 천성이 될 때까지 그렇게 했다. 그러나 어른으로 살면서 새로운 것을 시도해 볼 때 우리는 대체로 단 한 번만 시도해 보고 나서 그것이 (a) 잘되었는지 판단하려 한다. 만일 우리가 처음에 성공하지 못하거나 혹은 약간 어색한 느낌이 들면, (b) 또 한번 시도해 보기보다는 그것이 성공이 아니었다고 스스로에게 말할 것이다. 그것은 애석한 일인데, 우리 뇌를 재연결하는 과정에서 반복이 핵심적이기 때문이다. 여러분의 뇌가 뉴런의 연결망을 가지고 있다는 개념을 생각해 보라. 여러분이 뇌 친화적인 피드백 기술을 잊지 않고 사용할 때마다 그것들은 서로 (c) 연결될 것이다. 그 연결은 처음에는 그리 (d) 신뢰할 만하지 않고, 여러분의 첫 번째 시도가 다소 마구잡이가 되도록 할 수도 있다. 여러분은 연관된 단계 중 하나를 기억하고, 다른 것들을 기억하지 못할 수도 있다. 그러나 과학자들은 "함께 활성화되는 뉴런들은 함께 연결된다."라고 말한다. 다시 말하자면, 어떤 행동의 반복은 그 행동에 연관된 뉴런들 사이의 연결을 (e) 차단한다(→ 강화한다). 그것은 여러분이 그 새로운 피드백 기술을 더 여러 차례 사용해 볼수록, 필요할 때 그것이 더 쉽게 여러분에게 다가올 것을 의미한다.

- **work hard at** ~을 들이다, 열심히 하다
- **nature** ⓝ 본성, 천성
- **awkward** ⓐ (기분이) 어색한, 불편한
- **shame** ⓝ 애석한 일, 딱한 일
- **central** ⓐ 핵심적인
- **hit-and-miss** 되는 대로 하는, 마구잡이로 하는
- **curious** ⓐ 호기심이 많은
- **fall off** 넘어지다
- **make an attempt** 시도하다
- **give it a shot** 시도하다
- **repetition** ⓝ 반복
- **reliable** ⓐ 신뢰할 만한
- **block** ⓥ 차단하다

구문 풀이

10행 They will connect with each other whenever you remember to use a brain-friendly feedback technique.
복합관계부사 'remember + to부정사: ~할 것을 기억하다(~할 때마다)'

18행 That means the more times you try using that new feedback technique, the more easily it will come to you when you need it.
the + 비교급 ~, the + 비교급 ...: ~할수록 더 ...하다

---

41 제목 파악 | 정답률 72% | 정답 ①

윗글의 제목으로 가장 적절한 것은?
✓① Repeat and You Will Succeed – 반복하면 성공할 것이다
② Be More Curious, Be Smarter – 더 호기심을 가지고, 더 똑똑해져라
③ Play Is What Makes Us Human – 놀이는 우리를 인간답게 만드는 것이다
④ Stop and Think Before You Act – 행동하기 전에 가만히 생각하라
⑤ Growth Is All About Keeping Balance – 성장은 전적으로 균형 유지에 관한 것이다

42 어휘 추론 | 정답률 60% | 정답 ⑤

밑줄 친 (a) ~ (e) 중에서 문맥상 낱말의 쓰임이 적절하지 않은 것은?
① (a) ② (b) ③ (c) ④ (d) ✓⑤ (e)

43-45 동물도 상실의 고통을 느낀다는 것을 깨달은 사냥꾼 왕

(A)
Once upon a time, / there lived a young king / who had a great passion for hunting.
옛날 옛적에, / 젊은 왕이 살았다. / 사냥에 대해 엄청난 열정을 가진

His kingdom was located at the foot of the Himalayas.
그의 왕국은 히말라야 산기슭에 위치해 있었다.

『Once every year, / he would go hunting in the nearby forests.』 **45번 ①의 근거 일치**
매년 한 번씩, / 그는 근처의 숲으로 사냥하러 가는 했다.

(a) He would make all the necessary preparations, / and then set out for his hunting trip.
그는 모든 필요한 준비를 하고 / 자신의 사냥 여행을 떠나고는 했다.

(C)
Like all other years, / the hunting season had arrived.
여느 해처럼, / 사냥철이 왔다.

Preparations began in the palace / and the king got ready for (c) his hunting trip.
궁궐에서 준비가 시작되었고 왕은 자신의 사냥 여행을 갈 준비를 했다.

Deep in the forest, / he spotted a beautiful wild deer.
숲속 깊은 곳에서 / 그는 아름다운 야생 사슴을 발견했다.

It was a large stag.
그것은 큰 수사슴이었다.

His aim was perfect.
그의 겨냥은 완벽했다.

『When he killed the deer with just one shot of his arrow, / the king was filled with pride.』
그가 단 한 발의 화살로 그 사슴을 잡고서 / 왕은 의기양양했다.
45번 ③의 근거 일치

(d) The proud hunter ordered a hunting drum / to be made out of the skin of the deer.
그 의기양양한 사냥꾼은 사냥용 북이 ~되도록 명령했다. / 그 사슴의 가죽으로 만들어지도록

(B)

Seasons changed.
계절이 바뀌었다.

A year passed by.
1년이 지나갔다.

And it was time to go hunting once again.
그리고 또 다시 사냥하러 갈 때가 되었다.

The king went to the same forest as the previous year.
왕은 작년과 같은 숲으로 갔다.

(b) He used his beautiful deerskin drum / to round up animals.
그는 아름다운 사슴 가죽으로 만든 북을 사용하여 / 동물을 몰았다.

But none came.
그러나 아무도 오지 않았다.

All the animals ran for safety, / except one doe.
모든 동물이 안전한 곳으로 도망쳤는데, / 암사슴 한 마리는 예외였다.

『She came closer and closer to the drummer.』 45번 ②의 근거 불일치
암사슴은 북 치는 사람에게 점점 더 가까이 다가왔다.

Suddenly, / she started fearlessly licking the deerskin drum.
갑자기, / 암사슴은 두려움 없이 사슴 가죽으로 만든 북을 핥기 시작했다.

(D)

The king was surprised by this sight.
이 광경을 보고 왕은 놀랐다.

『An old servant had an answer / to this strange behavior.』 45번 ④의 근거 일치
한 나이 든 신하가 답을 알고 있었다. / 이 이상한 행동에 대한

"The deerskin used to make this drum / belonged to her mate, / the deer who we hunted last year.
"이 북을 만드는 데 사용된 사슴 가죽은 / 암사슴의 짝의 것인데, / 우리가 작년에 사냥한 그 사슴입니다.

This doe is mourning the death of her mate," / (e) the man said.
이 암사슴은 짝의 죽음을 애도하고 있는 것입니다."라고 / 그 남자는 말했다.

Upon hearing this, / the king had a change of heart.
이 말을 듣자마자, / 왕의 마음이 바뀌었다.

He had never realized / that an animal, too, felt the pain of loss.
그는 전혀 몰랐다. / 동물도 역시 상실의 고통을 느낀다는 것을

『He made a promise, / from that day on, / to never again hunt wild animals.』 45번 ⑤의 근거 일치
그는 약속했다. / 그날 이후 / 다시는 결코 야생 동물을 사냥하지 않겠다고

(A)

옛날 옛적에 사냥에 대해 엄청난 열정을 가진 젊은 왕이 살았다. 그의 왕국은 히말라야 산기슭에 위치해 있었다. 매년 한 번씩, 그는 근처의 숲으로 사냥하러 가고는 했다. (a) 그는 모든 필요한 준비를 하고 자신의 사냥 여행을 떠나고는 했다.

(C)

여느 해처럼, 사냥철이 왔다. 궁궐에서 준비가 시작되었고 왕은 (c) 자신의 사냥 여행을 갈 준비를 했다. 숲속 깊은 곳에서 그는 아름다운 야생 사슴을 발견했다. 그것은 큰 수사슴이었다. 그의 겨냥은 완벽했다. 단 한 발의 화살로 그 사슴을 잡고서 왕은 의기양양했다. (d) 그 의기양양한 사냥꾼은 그 사슴의 가죽으로 사냥용 북을 만들도록 명령했다.

(B)

계절이 바뀌었다. 1년이 지나갔다. 그리고 또 다시 사냥하러 갈 때가 되었다. 왕은 작년과 같은 숲으로 갔다. (b) 그는 아름다운 사슴 가죽으로 만든 북을 사용하여 동물을 몰았다. 그러나 아무도 오지 않았다. 모든 동물이 안전한 곳으로 도망쳤는데, 암사슴 한 마리는 예외였다. 암사슴은 북 치는 사람에게 점점 더 가까이 다가왔다. 갑자기, 암사슴은 두려움 없이 사슴 가죽으로 만든 북을 핥기 시작했다.

(D)

이 광경을 보고 왕은 놀랐다. 한 나이 든 신하가 이 이상한 행동의 이유를 알고 있었다. "이 북을 만드는 데 사용된 사슴 가죽은 암사슴의 짝의 것인데, 우리가 작년에 사냥한 그 사슴입니다. 이 암사슴은 짝의 죽음을 애도하고 있는 것입니다."라고 (e) 그 남자는 말했다. 이 말을 듣자마자, 왕의 마음이 바뀌었다. 그는 동물도 역시 상실의 고통을 느낀다는 것을 전혀 몰랐었다. 그는 그날 이후 다시는 결코 야생 동물을 사냥하지 않겠다고 약속했다.

- **passion** ⓝ 열정
- **preparation** ⓝ 준비, 채비
- **previous** ⓐ 이전의
- **lick** ⓥ 핥다
- **aim** ⓝ 겨냥, 목표 ⓥ 겨누다
- **have a change of heart** 마음을 바꾸다, 심경의 변화가 생기다
- **loss** ⓝ 상실
- **at the foot of** ~의 기슭에, 하단부에
- **set out for** ~을 향해 나서다
- **fearlessly** ⓐ 겁 없이, 대담하게
- **spot** ⓥ 알아채다, 발견하다

구문 풀이

(A) 1행 Once upon a time, there lived a young king [who had a great passion for hunting].
동사 / 주어 / 주격 관계대명사

(C) 6행 The proud hunter ordered a hunting drum to be made out of the skin of the deer.
「order + 목적어 + to부정사 : ~이 …하게 명령하다」

(D) 2행 The deerskin used to make this drum belonged to her mate, the deer
주어 / 과거분사 부사적 용법(목적) / 동사 / 동격(= her mate)
[who(m) we hunted last year].

(D) 7행 He made a promise, from that day on, to never again hunt wild animals.
「to + 부사 + 동사원형 : 분리부정사(부정사를 수식하는 부사를 to와 동사원형 사이에 삽입한 형태)」

---

43 글의 순서 파악 　　　　정답률 82% | 정답 ②

주어진 글 (A)에 이어질 내용을 순서에 맞게 배열한 것으로 가장 적절한 것은?
① (B) - (D) - (C)　　　✔② (C) - (B) - (D)
③ (C) - (D) - (B)　　　④ (D) - (B) - (C)
⑤ (D) - (C) - (B)

Why? 왜 정답일까?

시간적 단서를 잘 활용해야 하는 순서 문제이다. 옛날에 어느 한 왕이 사냥에 대한 열정이 있어 매년 사냥 여행을 떠났다는 내용의 (A) 뒤에는, 다른 모든 해처럼 사냥철이 와서 왕이 사냥을 떠났고 아름다운 야생 사슴 한 마리를 잡아 그 기념으로 북을 만들었다는 내용의 (C)가 이어져야 한다. 이어서 (B)에서는 '1년 후' 다시 사냥하러 갈 때가 되어 길을 떠난 왕이 북소리에 피하지 않고 도리어 가까이 오는 암사슴 한 마리를 발견했다는 내용이 전개된다. 마지막으로 (D)는 '이 광경'에 왕이 놀라자, 한 신하가 상황을 설명해 주었다는 내용으로 마무리된다. 따라서 글의 순서로 가장 적절한 것은 ② '(C) - (B) - (D)'이다.

44 지칭 추론 　　　　정답률 81% | 정답 ⑤

밑줄 친 (a) ~ (e) 중에서 가리키는 대상이 나머지 넷과 다른 것은?
① (a)　　② (b)　　③ (c)　　④ (d)　　✔⑤ (e)

Why? 왜 정답일까?

(a), (b), (c), (d)는 the king을, (e)는 An old servant를 가리키므로, (a) ~ (e) 중에서 가리키는 대상이 다른 하나는 ⑤ '(e)'이다.

45 세부 내용 파악 　　　　정답률 80% | 정답 ②

윗글에 관한 내용으로 적절하지 않은 것은?
① 왕은 매년 근처의 숲으로 사냥 여행을 갔다.
✔② 암사슴은 북 치는 사람으로부터 도망갔다.
③ 왕은 화살로 단번에 수사슴을 맞췄다.
④ 한 나이 든 신하가 암사슴의 행동의 이유를 알고 있었다.
⑤ 왕은 다시는 야생 동물을 사냥하지 않겠다고 약속했다.

Why? 왜 정답일까?

(B) 'She came closer and closer to the drummer.'에서 모든 동물들이 북소리를 듣고는 안전한 곳으로 피신하는 가운데 암사슴 한 마리는 북 치는 사람에게 가까이 다가왔다고 하므로, 내용과 일치하지 않는 것은 ② '암사슴은 북 치는 사람으로부터 도망갔다.'이다.

Why? 왜 오답일까?

① (A) 'Once every year, he would go hunting in the nearby forests.'의 내용과 일치한다.
③ (C) 'When he killed the deer with just one shot of his arrow, ~'의 내용과 일치한다.
④ (D) 'An old servant had an answer to this strange behavior.'의 내용과 일치한다.
⑤ (D) 'He made a promise, from that day on, to never again hunt wild animals.'의 내용과 일치한다.

어휘 Review Test 06 　　　　문제편 060쪽

A	B	C	D
01 해로운	01 disappointed	01 ⓗ	01 ①
02 거대한	02 appetite	02 ⓔ	02 ⓠ
03 무례한	03 accept	03 ⓒ	03 ⓐ
04 바꾸다, 번역하다	04 achievement	04 ①	04 ①
05 측면	05 convince	05 ①	05 ⓜ
06 자신감 있는	06 deliver	06 ⓑ	06 ⓚ
07 모으다	07 process	07 ⓖ	07 ①
08 대략	08 distress	08 ⓚ	08 ①
09 한편	09 equation	09 ①	09 ⓗ
10 ~의 가치가 있는	10 previous	10 ⓠ	10 ⓖ
11 고치다	11 discomfort	11 ⓜ	11 ⓗ
12 적절히	12 include	12 ①	12 ⓓ
13 발생하다, 일어나다	13 notable	13 ⓞ	13 ⓔ
14 즐겁게	14 central	14 ⓟ	14 ⓑ
15 악기, 도구	15 maintain	15 ⓐ	15 ①
16 복잡한	16 acceptable	16 ①	16 ⓟ
17 점점 더	17 dwell	17 ⓢ	17 ⓒ
18 입장	18 entrance	18 ⓝ	18 ⓢ
19 (신체) 기관	19 legally	19 ⓓ	19 ⓞ
20 ~에 적응하다	20 get past	20 ①	20 ⓡ

• 정답 •

01 ① 02 ⑤ 03 ③ 04 ④ 05 ⑤ 06 ② 07 ⑤ 08 ② 09 ④ 10 ② 11 ② 12 ① 13 ① 14 ③ 15 ⑤
16 ⑤ 17 ④ 18 ④ 19 ⑤ 20 ② 21 ③ 22 ① 23 ② 24 ② 25 ④ 26 ④ 27 ③ 28 ④ 29 ③ 30 ③
31 ③ 32 ① 33 ① 34 ① 35 ② 36 ⑤ 37 ④ 38 ⑤ 39 ③ 40 ① 41 ② 42 ③ 43 ③ 44 ④ 45 ⑤

★ 표기된 문항은 [등급을 가르는 문제]에 해당하는 문항입니다.

---

01 미세 먼지 수치가 높을 때의 대처 요령 　　정답률 94% | 정답 ①

다음을 듣고, 남자가 하는 말의 목적으로 가장 적절한 것을 고르시오.
☑ 미세 먼지 수치가 높을 때 대처 요령을 안내하려고
② 교실 내 공기 정화기 설치 일정을 알리려고
③ 체육 실기 시험 준비 방법을 설명하려고
④ 미세 먼지 방지용 마스크 배부 행사를 홍보하려고
⑤ 미세 먼지 감축을 위해 대중교통 이용을 독려하려고

M : Hello, students.
안녕하세요, 학생 여러분.
This is Mike Smith, your P.E. teacher.
저는 여러분의 체육 선생님인 Mike Smith입니다.
These days, the fine dust problem is getting serious.
요즘 미세 먼지 문제가 심각해지고 있습니다.
So, I'd like to explain what you should do when the fine dust level is high.
그래서 미세 먼지 수치가 높을 때 어떻게 해야 하는지 설명하려고 합니다.
First, close all the classroom windows to keep out the dust.
첫째로, 먼지가 들어오지 못하게 하기 위해 교실 창문을 모두 닫으세요.
Second, turn on the air purifier in the classroom.
둘째로, 교실에 있는 공기 청정기를 켜세요.
The air purifier will help keep the air clean.
공기 청정기는 공기를 청결하게 유지하는 데 도움을 줄 것입니다.
Third, drink water and wash your hands as often as possible.
셋째로, 물을 마시고 가능한 한 자주 손을 씻으세요.
Last, it's important to wear a mask when you're outside.
마지막으로, 실외에서는 마스크를 착용하는 것이 중요합니다.
Thank you for listening.
들어주셔서 고맙습니다.

Why? 왜 정답일까?

'So, I'd like to explain what you should do when the fine dust level is high.'에서 남자는 미세 먼지 수치가 높을 때 학생들이 어떻게 해야 할지 알려주겠다고 말하므로, 남자가 하는 말의 목적으로 가장 적절한 것은 ① '미세 먼지 수치가 높을 때 대처 요령을 안내하려고'이다.

• as ~ as possible 가능한 한 ~한[하게]　　• fine dust ⓝ 미세 먼지
• serious ⓐ 심각한　　• explain ⓥ 설명하다
• keep out ⓥ ~이 들어오지 못하게 하다　　• turn on ~을 켜다
• air purifier ⓝ 공기 청정기

---

02 선물 포장 간소화 　　정답률 94% | 정답 ⑤

대화를 듣고, 여자의 의견으로 가장 적절한 것을 고르시오.
① 받는 사람에게 필요한 것을 선물해야 한다.
② 정성 어린 선물 포장은 선물의 가치를 높인다.
③ 선물 포장을 위해 다양한 재료를 활용해야 한다.
④ 선물을 받으면 적절한 감사 인사를 하는 것이 좋다.
☑ 환경을 위해 선물 포장을 간소하게 할 필요가 있다.

W : Look at all the shiny paper and ribbons! What are you doing, Tom?
이 온갖 반짝거리는 종이와 리본들 좀 봐! 뭐 하고 있어, Tom?
M : I'm wrapping a birthday present for my friend Laura.
난 내 친구 Laura를 위한 생일 선물을 포장하고 있어.
W : What are you going to give her?
그 애에게 뭘 줄 거야?
M : A key chain. I hope she likes it.
열쇠고리. 그 애가 이것을 맘에 들어하면 좋겠어.
W : That's a pretty big box for a key chain, isn't it?
그건 열쇠고리를 위한 것치고는 꽤 큰 상자네, 안 그래?
M : Yes, I filled it with paper flowers. Now I'm going to wrap the box with shiny paper and decorate it with ribbons.
응, 난 이걸 종이꽃으로 채웠어. 이제 나는 상자를 반짝이는 포장지로 싸고 리본으로 장식할 거야.
W : I think it's a little too much. Most of the paper and ribbons will end up in the trash can.
약간 과한 것 같아. 대부분의 포장지와 리본은 결국엔 쓰레기통에 가게 되잖아.
M : Hmm.... You're right. My packaging will produce a lot of trash.
흠.... 네 말이 맞아. 내 포장은 많은 쓰레기를 만들어 낼 거야.
W : Yeah. We need to make gift packaging simple for the environment.
응. 우리는 환경을 위해 선물 포장을 간소하게 해야 해.
M : I agree. I'll try to reduce the packaging then.
동의해. 그럼 포장을 줄이도록 노력할게.
W : Good thinking.
좋은 생각이야.

Why? 왜 정답일까?

'We need to make gift packaging simple for the environment.'에서 여자는 환경을 위해 선물 포장을 간소하게 해야 한다고 말하므로, 여자의 의견으로 가장 적절한 것은 ⑤ '환경을 위해 선물 포장을 간소하게 할 필요가 있다.'이다.

• wrap ⓥ 싸다　　• decorate ⓥ 장식하다
• end up ⓥ 결국 ~하다　　• reduce ⓥ 줄이다

---

03 나무 책상 사기 　　정답률 79% | 정답 ③

대화를 듣고, 두 사람의 관계를 가장 잘 나타낸 것을 고르시오.
① 정원사 – 집주인　　② 출판사 직원 – 작가
☑ 가구 판매원 – 손님　　④ 관광 가이드 – 관광객
⑤ 인테리어 디자이너 – 잡지 기자

M : Come on in, Ms. Miller. It's been a while since your last visit.
들어오세요, Miller 씨. 마지막 방문 이후로 오랜만이네요.
W : Good morning, Mr. Stevens. I've been in Europe for the last two months.
안녕하세요, Stevens 씨. 전 지난 두 달 동안 유럽에 있었어요.
M : Wow. Are you preparing for your second book?
와. 두 번째 책을 준비하고 계신 거예요?
W : Yes, I'm working on it.
네, 작업하고 있어요.
M : I'm looking forward to it. So, what brings you here today?
기대되는군요. 그럼, 오늘은 무슨 일로 오셨나요?
W : I'd like to buy a wooden desk.
전 나무 책상을 사고 싶어요.
M : I see. Do you have a particular design in mind?
그렇군요. 특별히 염두에 둔 디자인이 있나요?
W : Just a plain rectangular one would be great.
그냥 평범한 직사각형 책상이면 좋을 것 같아요.
M : Okay. What color would you like?
알겠습니다. 어떤 색을 원하시나요?
W : I was thinking dark brown.
짙은 갈색을 생각하고 있었어요.
M : Great. We have a perfect one for you downstairs. Come this way.
좋습니다. 아래층에 당신께 딱 맞는 것이 있어요. 이쪽으로 오세요.
W : All right.
좋아요.

Why? 왜 정답일까?

'I'd like to buy a wooden desk.', 'We have a perfect one for you downstairs.' 등에서 남자가 가구를 판매하는 직원이며, 여자가 손님임을 알 수 있다. 따라서 두 사람의 관계로 가장 적절한 것은 ③ '가구 판매원 – 손님'이다.

• work on ~에 노력을 들이다[착수하다]　　• look forward to ⓥ ~을 고대하다
• plain ⓐ 평범한, 단순한　　• rectangular ⓐ 직사각형의

---

04 새로 꾸민 동아리방 사진 구경하기 　　정답률 81% | 정답 ④

대화를 듣고, 그림에서 대화의 내용과 일치하지 않는 것을 고르시오.

W : James, have you been to our new club room?
James, 우리 새 동아리방에 가 봤어?
M : Unfortunately, I haven't.
안타깝게도 못 가봤어.
W : I have a picture of it. Do you want to take a look?
나한테 사진이 있어. 한번 볼래?
M : Sure. [Pause] 「Wow, I see lockers on the left side of the picture.」①의 근거 일치
그래. [잠시 멈춤] 「와, 사진 왼쪽에 사물함이 보이네.」
W : Yes. We finally have our own lockers. 「Do you see the trophies on the lockers?」
그래. 드디어 우리만의 사물함이 생겼어. 「사물함 위에 있는 트로피 보여?」
M : Yeah. There are two trophies.」②의 근거 일치 Are they the ones we won in the National School Band Contest?
응. 트로피가 두 개 있네. 이게 우리가 National School Band Contest에서 우승했을 때 탔던 건가?
W : Right. We won two years in a row. I'm so proud of our band.
맞아. 우리는 2년 연속으로 우승했지. 우리 밴드가 너무 자랑스러워.
M : Me, too. 「And the drums are under the clock.」③의 근거 일치
나도 그래. 「그리고 드럼이 시계 아래에 있구나.」
W : Yes. 「And on the right side of the picture is a round table with chairs.」④의 근거 불일치
응. 「그리고 사진 오른쪽에는 둥근 테이블과 의자가 있어.」
M : Looks great. 「I also love the star-shaped rug in front of the drums.」⑤의 근거 일치
멋져 보인다. 「난 드럼 앞에 별 모양 깔개도 몹시 마음에 들구나.」
W : I like it, too. We're really going to enjoy our new club room.
나도 그래. 우리는 새로운 동아리방에 가는 것이 정말 즐거울 거야.

Why? 왜 정답일까?

대화에서는 사진 오른쪽에 둥근 테이블이 의자와 함께 놓여있다고 하는데(And on the right side of the picture is a round table with chairs.), 그림의 테이블은 사각형이다. 따라서 그림에서 대화의 내용과 일치하지 않는 것은 ④이다.

• take a look (~을) 한번 보다　　• locker ⓝ 사물함
• in a row 계속해서, 연이어　　• star-shaped ⓐ 별 모양의

05 오케스트라 공연 준비 　　　　　정답률 87% | 정답 ⑤

대화를 듣고, 여자가 할 일로 가장 적절한 것을 고르시오.
① 악기 점검하기　　　　　　② 연습 시간 확인하기
③ 단원들에게 연락하기　　　④ 관객용 의자 배치하기
☑ 콘서트 포스터 붙이기

M : Ellie, the school orchestra's concert is just three days away. How's the preparation coming along?
Ellie, 학교 오케스트라 연주회가 딱 3일 앞으로 다가왔구나. 준비는 어떻게 되어 가니?
W : Great, Mr. Brown. All of our orchestra members are very excited.
아주 좋아요, Brown 선생님. 우리 오케스트라 단원들 모두가 몹시 들떠있어요.
M : Good. Did everyone check their instruments?
좋아. 다들 악기 점검은 했니?
W : Of course. Everything sounded fine in practice today.
물론이죠. 오늘 연습에서는 모든 소리가 좋게 들렸어요.
M : I heard the posters were ready.
포스터가 준비되었다고 들었어.
W : Yes. Here they are. One of the orchestra members designed them.
네, 여기 있어요. 오케스트라 단원 중 한 명이 그것들을 디자인했어요.
M : They look pretty nice. When are you going to put the posters up in the hallway?
아주 근사해 보이는구나. 복도에 포스터를 언제 붙일 거니?
W : I'm going to do that now.
지금 하려고 해요.
M : You're doing a great job as the leader of the school orchestra. Have you arranged the chairs for the audience?
넌 학교 오케스트라 단장 역할을 아주 잘하고 있어. 청중들을 위해 의자를 준비해 뒀니?
W : I already did it with some of the members.
몇몇 단원들과 이미 끝내 두었어요.
M : Perfect.
완벽해.

Why? 왜 정답일까?
오케스트라 공연을 준비하고 있는 여자는 선생님인 남자가 공연 포스터를 언제 붙일 것인지 묻자(When are you going to put the posters up in the hallway?) 지금 붙일 예정이라고 답한다(I'm going to do that now.). 따라서 여자가 할 일로 가장 적절한 것은 ⑤ '콘서트 포스터 붙이기'이다.

● **preparation** ⓝ 준비, 대비
● **put up** ~을 붙이다[게시하다]
● **come along** ⓥ (원하는 대로) 되어 가다
● **arrange** ⓥ 준비하다, 배치하다

06 무선 이어폰과 휴대용 스피커 구매하기 　정답률 90% | 정답 ②

대화를 듣고, 여자가 지불할 금액을 고르시오. [3점]
① $140　　☑ $180　　③ $200　　④ $220　　⑤ $280

M : Good afternoon. How can I help you?
안녕하세요. 무엇을 도와드릴까요?
W : I'd like to buy some wireless earphones for my children. How much is this pair?
저희 아이들을 위해 무선 이어폰을 사고 싶어요. 이건 얼마인가요?
M : It's $60 for a pair. It's a very popular model.
한 쌍에 60달러입니다. 아주 인기 있는 제품이에요.
W : Great. I'll take two pairs.
좋아요. 전 두 쌍을 사겠어요.
M : I see. Is there anything else you need?
알겠습니다. 더 필요한 건 없으십니까?
W : Oh, I also need a portable speaker.
오, 휴대용 스피커도 필요해요.
M : These two are the latest models.
이 두 가지가 최신 모델입니다.
W : How much are they?
얼마인가요?
M : This black one is $80 and the pink one is $100.
이 검은색은 80달러이고 분홍색은 100달러입니다.
W : I'll take the black one.
검은색을 사겠어요.
M : Okay. Is that all you need?
알겠습니다. 이게 필요하신 것 전부인가요?
W : Yes. Oh, I have this discount coupon. Can I use it?
네. 아, 전 이 할인 쿠폰이 있어요. 이것을 제가 쓸 수 있나요?
M : Sure. You can get 10% off the total price with this coupon.
물론이죠. 이 쿠폰으로 총 가격의 10%를 할인받으실 수 있어요.
W : Great. Here's the coupon and here's my credit card.
아주 좋아요. 여기 쿠폰이 있고 신용 카드는 여기 있어요.

Why? 왜 정답일까?
대화에 따르면 여자는 아이들을 위해 60달러짜리 이어폰을 두 개 사고, 80달러짜리 휴대용 스피커를 추가로 구매한 뒤, 총 가격에서 10퍼센트를 할인받았다. 이를 식으로 나타내면 '(60×2＋80)×0.9＝180'이므로, 여자가 지불할 금액은 ② '$180'이다.

● **wireless** ⓐ 무선의
● **portable** ⓐ 휴대용의, 가지고 다닐 수 있는

07 남자가 캠핑에 갈 수 없는 이유 　　정답률 94% | 정답 ⑤

대화를 듣고, 남자가 이번 주말에 캠핑하러 갈 수 없는 이유를 고르시오.
① 계단을 수리해야 해서　　　② 캠프장을 예약할 수 없어서
③ 폭우로 인해 캠프장이 폐쇄되어서　④ 프로젝트를 마무리해야 해서
☑ 어머니를 돌봐야 해서

W : Jason, you're going camping this weekend, right?
Jason, 너 이번 주말에 캠핑 가지, 그렇지?
M : I reserved a campsite, but I'm afraid I can't go.
난 캠핑장을 예약했는데, 못 갈 것 같아.

W : Why not? Is it going to rain?
왜? 비 온대?
M : No. It'll be sunny this weekend.
아니. 이번 주말에는 날씨가 맑을 거야.
W : Then do you have to work this weekend? You said you're busy with your project.
그럼 이번 주말에 일해야 하니? 프로젝트 때문에 바쁘다고 했잖아.
M : No, I finished the project last week.
아니, 프로젝트는 지난주에 끝냈어.
W : Then why can't you go camping?
그럼 왜 캠핑을 못 가?
M : My mother fell down the stairs and broke her arm.
우리 엄마가 계단에서 넘어져서 팔이 부러졌어.
W : Oh, no. Is she all right?
오, 세상에. 엄마는 괜찮으시니?
M : Well, she had surgery. So I have to take care of her in the hospital this weekend.
음, 엄마는 수술을 받으셨어. 그래서 난 이번 주말에 병원에서 엄마를 돌봐야 해.
W : I see. I hope she'll get better soon.
그렇구나. 엄마가 빨리 나으시길 바랄게.
M : Thanks.
고마워.

Why? 왜 정답일까?
남자는 주말에 캠핑을 갈 예정이었지만 팔을 다쳐 수술을 받은 어머니를 병원에서 돌봐야 하기에(So I have to take care of her in the hospital this weekend.) 캠핑을 갈 수 없게 되었다고 설명하고 있다. 따라서 남자가 캠핑하러 갈 수 없는 이유로 가장 적절한 것은 ⑤ '어머니를 돌봐야 해서'이다.

● **busy with** ~ 때문에 바쁜
● **get well** ⓥ (건강이) 나아지다, 좋아지다
● **take care of** ⓥ ~을 돌보다

08 빵 바자회 　　　　　　　　　정답률 92% | 정답 ②

대화를 듣고, Pinewood Bake Sale에 관해 언급되지 않은 것을 고르시오.
① 개최 요일　　☑ 시작 시간　　③ 판매 제품
④ 수익금 기부처　　⑤ 개최 장소

W : Hi, Ross. What's on the flyer?
안녕, Ross. 전단지에 뭐가 있어?　①의근거 일치
M : 『The Pinewood Bake Sale is this Friday.』 Would you like to go with me?
『Pinewood Bake Sale(빵 바자회)이 이번 주 금요일이래.』 나랑 같이 갈래?
W : A bake sale? What's that?
빵 바자회? 그게 뭐야?
M : In a bake sale, people raise money by selling bakery products. 『At the Pinewood Bake Sale, people will be selling doughnuts and cupcakes.』 ③의근거 일치
빵 바자회에서 사람들은 제과 제품을 팔아서 돈을 모아. 『Pinewood Bake Sale에서 사람들은 도넛과 컵케이크를 팔 거야.』
W : Sounds delicious. So all profits go to people in need, right?
맛있겠다. 그럼 모든 수익은 불우이웃에 돌아가는 거지, 맞지?
M : That's right. 『The flyer says the profits will be donated to Pinewood Children's Hospital.』 ④의근거 일치
맞아. 『전단지에서 말하길 수익금은 Pinewood 어린이 병원에 기부될 거래.』
W : I'd love to join you. Where is it going to be held?
나도 너랑 같이 가고 싶어. 어디서 열리는 거야?
M : 『In the Pinewood High School gym.』 ⑤의근거 일치
『Pinewood 고등학교 체육관에서.』
W : Okay. Let's go together.
알았어. 같이 가자.

Why? 왜 정답일까?
대화에서 남자와 여자는 Pinewood Bake Sale의 개최 요일, 판매 제품, 수익금 기부처, 개최 장소를 언급하였다. 따라서 언급되지 않은 것은 ② '시작 시간'이다.

Why? 왜 오답일까?
① 'The Pinewood Bake Sale is this Friday.'에서 '개최 요일'이 언급되었다.
③ 'At the Pinewood Bake Sale, people will be selling doughnuts and cupcakes.'에서 '판매 제품'이 언급되었다.
④ 'The flyer says the profits will be donated to Pinewood Children's Hospital.'에서 '수익금 기부처'가 언급되었다.
⑤ 'In the Pinewood High School gym.'에서 '개최 장소'가 언급되었다.

● **raise** ⓥ (돈을) 모으다
● **in need** 불우한, 어려운 처지에 있는
● **profit** ⓝ 수익
● **donate** ⓥ 기부하다

09 지역 사회 축제 안내 　　　　　정답률 92% | 정답 ④

2020 Global Village Festival에 관한 다음 내용을 듣고, 일치하지 않는 것을 고르시오. [3점]
① 이틀간 Green City Park에서 열린다.
② 음악 공연과 미술 전시회를 포함한다.
③ 현금이나 신용 카드로 음식을 구입할 수 있다.
☑ 선착순 100명에게 특별 선물을 준다.
⑤ 차량당 주차비는 10달러이다.

W : Hello, Green City residents.
안녕하세요, Green City 주민 여러분.
This is Rachel White, the head of the Community Services Department.
저는 사회 복지부장인 Rachel White입니다.
Are you ready to enjoy the 2020 Global Village Festival?
2020 Global Village Festival을 즐길 준비가 되셨습니까?
『It'll be held on March 28 and 29 at Green City Park.』 ①의근거 일치
『그것은 3월 28일과 29일에 Green City 공원에서 열릴 것입니다.』
『This two-day festival includes music performances and art exhibitions.』 ②의근거 일치
『이 이틀간의 축제에는 음악 공연과 미술 전시회가 포함됩니다.』
Samples of food from around the world will be served.
세계 각국의 음식 시식도 제공될 것입니다.　③의근거 일치
『Prices of the food range from $2 to $5 and you can pay by cash or credit card.』

「음식의 가격은 2달러에서 5달러로, 현금이나 신용 카드로 지불할 수 있습니다.」
「The first 50 visitors will get special gifts.」 ④의 근거 불일치
「선착순 50명의 방문객들은 특별한 선물을 받으실 것입니다.」
「Parking will be available for $10 a car.」 ⑤의 근거 일치
「주차비는 차량 한 대당 10달러입니다.」
For more information, visit the festival website.
더 많은 정보를 보시려면, 축제 웹 사이트를 방문해 주세요.
Thank you.
감사합니다.

Why? 왜 정답일까?

'The first 50 visitors will get special gifts.'에서 선착순 100명이 아닌 50명에게 특별한 선물을 줄 것이라고 하므로, 내용과 일치하지 않는 것은 ④ '선착순 100명에게 특별한 선물을 준다.'이다.

Why? 왜 오답일까?

① 'It'll be held on March 28 and 29 at Green City Park.'의 내용과 일치한다.
② 'This two-day festival includes music performances and art exhibitions.'의 내용과 일치한다.
③ '~ you can pay by cash or credit card.'의 내용과 일치한다.
⑤ 'Parking will be available for $10 a car.'의 내용과 일치한다.

- **performance** ⓝ 공연, 연주
- **exhibition** ⓝ 전시
- **range A from B** ⓥ 범위가 A부터 B에 이르다

---

10 여름 휴가 동안 묵을 호텔 예약하기 정답률 80% | 정답 ②

다음 표를 보면서 대화를 듣고, 두 사람이 예약할 방을 고르시오.

Wayne Island Hotel Rooms

	Room	View	Breakfast	Price
①	A	City	×	$70
✓②	B	Mountain	×	$80
③	C	Mountain	○	$95
④	D	Ocean	×	$105
⑤	E	Ocean	○	$120

M : Honey, what are you doing on your computer?
여보, 컴퓨터로 뭐 하고 있어요?
W : I'm trying to book a room at Wayne Island Hotel for our summer vacation.
우리 여름 휴가를 위해 Wayne Island Hotel에 방을 예약하려고 해요.
M : Our summer vacation? Isn't it a bit early?
우리 여름 휴가요? 좀 이르지 않아요?
W : We can get a room much cheaper if we book early.
일찍 예약하면 방을 훨씬 더 싸게 잡을 수 있어요.
M : I see. Which room do you have in mind?
알겠어요. 당신은 어떤 방을 마음에 두고 있어요?
W : I was thinking a room with a city view. What do you think?
난 도시 경관을 볼 수 있는 방을 생각하고 있었어요. 어떻게 생각해요?
M : 「Well, a room with a mountain view or an ocean view would be better.」 근거1 View 조건
음, 산이나 바다가 보이는 방이 더 좋을 것 같아요.
W : I agree.」「Shall we have breakfast in the hotel?」 근거2 Breakfast 조건
그래요.「호텔에서 아침을 먹을까요?
M : I don't think we need to.」 I heard there are some good restaurants near the hotel.
그럴 필요는 없을 것 같아요.」 호텔 근처에 좋은 레스토랑이 몇 군데 있다고 들었어요.
W : Okay. Then we have two options left. 「I'd like to go with the cheaper one.」 근거3 Price 조건
알겠어요. 그럼 두 가지 선택지가 남았어요.「난 더 싼 걸로 하고 싶어요.
M : Sounds good.」 Let's book this room then.
좋아요.」 그럼 이 방을 예약합시다.

Why? 왜 정답일까?

대화에 따르면 남자와 여자는 산이나 바다 경관이 보이면서, 조식은 포함되지 않고, 가격이 더 싼 방을 예약하려고 한다. 따라서 두 사람이 예약할 방은 ② 'B'이다.

- **book** ⓥ 예약하다
- **summer vacation** ⓝ 여름 휴가
- **have ~ in mind** ⓥ ~을 마음에 두다

---

11 메뉴 추천하기 정답률 89% | 정답 ②

대화를 듣고, 남자의 마지막 말에 대한 여자의 응답으로 가장 적절한 것을 고르시오.

① No thanks. I'm already full. – 사양할게. 난 벌써 배가 불러.
✓② Sure. The onion soup is great here. – 물론이지. 여긴 양파 수프가 훌륭해.
③ No idea. I've never been here before. – 모르겠어. 난 여기 한 번도 와 본 적이 없어.
④ Yes. I recommend you be there on time. – 응. 난 네가 제시간에 거기 가길 권해.
⑤ I agree. Let's go to a Mexican restaurant. – 동의해. 멕시코 음식점으로 가자.

M : This restaurant looks great. Have you been here before?
이 식당 정말 근사해 보인다. 전에 여기에 와 본 적 있어?
W : Yeah, it's one of my favorite restaurants. Let's see the menu.
응, 여긴 내가 가장 좋아하는 식당 중 하나야. 메뉴판을 보자.
M : Everything looks so good. Can you recommend anything?
모든 게 아주 좋아 보여. 뭐 좀 추천해 줄래?
W : Sure. The onion soup is great here.
물론이지. 여긴 양파 수프가 훌륭해.

Why? 왜 정답일까?

대화에서 남자는 여자와 함께 간 식당의 메뉴가 모두 근사해 보인다면서 여자에게 메뉴를 추천해줄 수 있는지 묻는다(Can you recommend anything?). 따라서 여자의 응답으로 가장 적절한 것은 ② '물론이지. 여긴 양파 수프가 훌륭해.'이다.

- **recommend** ⓥ 추천하다, 권장하다

---

12 우산 챙겨 가라고 말해주기 정답률 87% | 정답 ①

대화를 듣고, 여자의 마지막 말에 대한 남자의 응답으로 가장 적절한 것을 고르시오.

✓① I see. Thank you for letting me know. – 그렇군요. 알려줘서 고마워요.
② Unfortunately, I got caught in the rain. – 안타깝게도 난 비를 만났어요.
③ Well, it's been raining since yesterday. – 음, 어제부터 비가 계속 오고 있어요.
④ You're right. It'll be sunny this afternoon. – 당신 말이 맞네요. 오후에는 날이 갤 거예요.
⑤ Yeah. These umbrellas are available online. – 네. 이 우산들은 지금 온라인에서 살 수 있어요.

W : Honey, don't forget to bring your umbrella to work today.
여보, 오늘 출근길에 우산 가져가는 거 잊지 말아요.
M : Umbrella? The sky is clear now.
우산이요? 지금 하늘은 맑아요.
W : The weather forecast said it'd rain this afternoon.
일기예보에서 오늘 오후에 비가 온다고 했어요.
M : I see. Thank you for letting me know.
그렇군요. 알려줘서 고마워요.

Why? 왜 정답일까?

여자는 남자에게 오후에 비가 온다는 일기예보가 있었다면서(The weather forecast said it'd rain this afternoon.) 남자에게 출근길에 우산을 가져가도록 권하고 있다. 따라서 남자의 응답으로 가장 적절한 것은 ① '그렇군요. 알려줘서 고마워요.'이다.

- **get caught in the rain** ⓥ (가는 길에) 비를 만나다
- **available** ⓐ 이용 가능한

---

13 룸메이트와의 문제로 이사를 고민하는 남자 정답률 82% | 정답 ①

대화를 듣고, 여자의 마지막 말에 대한 남자의 응답으로 가장 적절한 것을 고르시오. [3점]
Man: _____

✓① I have, but he didn't take it seriously.
했지, 하지만 그는 그것을 심각하게 받아들이지 않아.
② Don't worry. I have no problem with him.
걱정 마, 난 그와 문제가 없어.
③ Well, he always keeps the bathroom clean.
음, 그는 항상 화장실을 깨끗하게 유지해.
④ Sorry. I delayed moving out of the apartment.
미안. 난 이사 나가는 것을 미뤘어.
⑤ Of course. I'll help you move into a new apartment.
물론이지. 네가 새 아파트로 이사가는 걸 내가 도와줄게.

W : Hey, Chris. What are you looking at on your cell phone?
안녕, Chris. 핸드폰으로 뭘 보고 있어?
M : I'm looking for an apartment to rent.
나는 세를 들어갈 아파트를 찾고 있어.
W : Aren't you sharing an apartment with William?
William과 아파트를 같이 쓰는 거 아니었어?
M : Yeah, but I'm thinking about moving out.
응, 근데 이사를 나갈까 생각 중이야.
W : Why? I thought you two get along well with each other.
왜? 난 너희 둘이 서로 잘 지내는 줄 알았어.
M : There have been a lot of problems between us. One thing especially bothers me.
우리 사이에는 많은 문제가 있었어. 특히 한 가지가 나를 성가시게 해.
W : Oh, what is it?
오, 그게 뭔데?
M : Actually, he never cleans up. The kitchen and the bathroom are always messy.
사실, 그는 절대 청소를 안 해, 부엌과 화장실이 항상 지저분해.
W : That's awful. Have you talked about this issue with him?
끔찍하구나. 이 문제에 대해 그와 이야기해 봤어?
M : I have, but he didn't take it seriously.
했지, 하지만 그는 그것을 심각하게 받아들이지 않아.

Why? 왜 정답일까?

룸메이트가 좀처럼 청소를 하지 않아 이사를 나갈까 고민 중이라는 남자에게 여자는 룸메이트와 이 문제에 대해 이야기를 해보는지 묻고 있다(Have you talked about this issue with him?). 따라서 남자의 응답으로 가장 적절한 것은 ① '했지, 하지만 그는 그것을 심각하게 받아들이지 않아.'이다.

- **bother** ⓥ 성가시게 하다, 귀찮게 하다
- **messy** ⓐ 지저분한

---

14 과학 경연대회 일정 변경 정답률 84% | 정답 ③

대화를 듣고, 남자의 마지막 말에 대한 여자의 응답으로 가장 적절한 것을 고르시오.
Woman: _____

① I'll text you how much it costs to fix the floor.
바닥 수리에 얼마가 드는지 네게 문자해 줄게.
② Right. I don't think you can enter the competition.
맞아. 난 네가 대회에 참가할 수 있다고 생각하지 않아.
✓③ Okay. I'll let you know as soon as the date is set.
알겠어. 날짜가 정해지는 대로 알려줄게.
④ But the auditorium was already repaired last week.
하지만 강당은 이미 지난주에 수리되었어.
⑤ The competition will be held in the school gym instead.
대회는 대신 학교 체육관에서 열릴 거야.

M : Ms. Peterson! I heard you were looking for me.
Peterson 선생님! 절 찾으셨다고 들었어요.
W : Yes, Louis. I need to tell you about the science competition scheduled for next week.
그래, Louis. 다음 주에 예정된 과학 경연대회에 대해 네게 말해줄 게 있단다.
M : Okay. What's it about?
네, 무슨 일이에요?
W : As you know, it'll be held in the school auditorium, but part of the floor needs repairing.
너도 알다시피, 그것은 학교 강당에서 열릴 건데, 바닥 일부가 수리되어야 해.
M : Then is it going to be held somewhere else?
그럼 다른 곳에서 열리는 거예요?
W : No, but the competition will be delayed.
아니, 하지만 대회가 연기될 거야.

M : Then when is it going to be held?
그럼 언제 열려요?

W : The date hasn't been decided yet, but it'll take at least two weeks to repair the floor. I'll text you the exact date later.
아직 날짜는 정해지지 않았지만, 바닥을 수리하는 데 적어도 2주가 걸릴 거야. 정확한 날짜는 나중에 네게 문자로 보내줄게.

M : I see. I'll wait for your text message.
그렇군요. 문자를 기다리고 있을게요.

W : Okay. I'll let you know as soon as the date is set.
알겠어. 날짜가 정해지는 대로 알려줄게.

Why? 왜 정답일까?

대화에서 여자는 남자에게 과학 경연대회가 강당 바닥 수리로 인해 연기되었으므로 정확한 날짜는 추후 문자를 보내 알려주겠다(I'll text you the exact date later.)고 한다. 이에 남자는 대화 말미에서 문자를 기다리고 있겠다(I see. I'll wait for your text message.)고 말하므로, 여자의 응답으로 가장 적절한 것은 ③ '알겠어. 날짜가 정해지는 대로 알려줄게.'이다.

- auditorium ⓝ 강당
- repair ⓥ 수리하다

---

15 가정통신문을 잊지 말고 가져오도록 당부하기 정답률 80% | 정답 ⑤

다음 상황 설명을 듣고, Billy의 어머니가 Billy에게 할 말로 가장 적절한 것을 고르시오.

Billy's mother: _____

① Make sure to answer the letters. – 꼭 편지에 답을 하도록 해.
② Try to participate in school events often. – 학교 행사에 종종 참여하도록 노력해 보렴.
③ I'm sure you can make some good friends. – 난 네가 좋은 친구들을 몇몇 사귈 수 있을 거라고 확신해.
④ You need to prepare for the meeting. – 넌 회의 준비를 할 필요가 있어.
✔ Don't forget to bring me the letters. – 나한테 편지 가져다주는 것을 잊지 마.

M : Billy entered high school this year.
Billy는 올해 고등학교에 입학했다.

In Billy's school, letters to parents are given to the students.
Billy의 학교에서는 부모님께 보내는 편지를 학생들에게 주었다.

The letters include a lot of information about school events such as parent-teacher meetings.
편지에는 학부모 교사 모임 등 학교 행사에 대한 많은 정보가 들어 있다.

Students have to deliver them to their parents, but Billy often forgets to bring them to his mother.
학생들은 그것들을 부모님에게 전달해야 하지만, Billy는 종종 그것들을 어머니에게 가져다 드리는 것을 잊곤 한다.

Billy's mother is worried that she may not get important information about school events.
Billy의 어머니는 자신이 학교 행사에 대한 중요한 정보를 얻지 못할까 봐 걱정하고 있다.

She even missed some of them because she didn't get the letters.
그녀는 편지를 받지 못해서 심지어 몇몇 행사를 놓치기도 했다.

So she wants to tell Billy that he must give them to her.
그래서 그녀는 Billy에게 그것들을 꼭 가지고 오라고 말하고 싶어 한다.

In this situation, what would Billy's mother most likely say to Billy?
이 상황에서, Billy의 어머니는 Billy에게 뭐라고 말하겠는가?

Billy's mother : Don't forget to bring me the letters.
나한테 편지 가져다주는 것을 잊지 마.

Why? 왜 정답일까?

상황에 따르면 아들인 Billy가 가정통신문을 제대로 가져다주지 않아 학교 행사에 대한 정보를 놓칠까봐 걱정하고 있는 Billy의 어머니는 아들에게 꼭 잊지 말고 통신문을 가져다 줄 것을 당부하고 싶어 한다(So she wants to tell Billy that he must give them to her.). 따라서 Billy의 어머니가 Billy에게 할 말로 가장 적절한 것은 ⑤ '나한테 편지 가져다주는 것을 잊지 마.'이다.

- parent-teacher meeting ⓝ 학부모 교사 모임
- make sure ⓥ 반드시 ~하다

16-17 우유의 다양한 원천

W : Good morning, class.
안녕하세요, 학생 여러분.

What did you have for breakfast?
아침으로 무엇을 먹었나요?

I guess some of you had your favorite cereal with milk.
여러분 중 몇몇은 여러분이 가장 좋아하는 시리얼을 우유와 함께 먹었을 겁니다.

「Have you ever wondered where milk comes from?」 16번의 근거
「우유가 어디에서 나오는지 궁금해 본 적이 있나요?」

Most people would say it's from cows, and they're right.
대부분의 사람들은 그것이 젖소에서 나온 것이라고 말하는데, 그 말이 맞습니다.

「Around ninety percent of milk in Canada and the U.S. comes from cows.」 17번 ①의 근거 일치
「캐나다와 미국에서 약 90퍼센트의 우유는 젖소에서 나옵니다.」

But cows are not the only source of milk.
그러나 젖소만이 우유의 원천인 것은 아닙니다.

「People around the world get milk from different animals.」 16번의 근거
「전 세계 사람들은 다른 동물에서 우유를 얻기도 합니다.」

「Water buffalos are the main source of milk in India.」 17번 ②의 근거 일치
「물소는 인도에서 우유의 주된 공급원입니다.」

They produce half the milk consumed in the country.
그 소들은 그 나라에서 소비되는 우유의 절반을 생산합니다.

「Some people in the northern part of Finland drink reindeer milk」 17번 ③의 근거 일치 because they are the only dairy animals that can survive such a cold environment.
「핀란드 북부에 있는 일부 사람들은 순록의 우유를 마시는데」, 순록이 그토록 추운 환경에서 살아남을 수 있는 유일한 낙농 동물이기 때문입니다.

「People in Romania get milk from sheep and use it to make cheese.」 17번 ⑤의 근거 일치
「루마니아 사람들은 양으로부터 우유를 얻어 치즈를 만드는 데 씁니다.」

It has twice the fat content of cow milk.
그것은 젖소에서 나온 우유보다 지방 함량이 두 배입니다.

Now let's watch a video about these animals.
이제 이 동물들에 대한 영상을 봅시다.

- consume ⓥ 소비하다, 먹다, 마시다
- dairy ⓐ 낙농의, 유제품의
- content ⓝ 함량

---

16 주제 파악 정답률 89% | 정답 ⑤

여자가 하는 말의 주제로 가장 적절한 것은?

① major exporting countries of dairy products – 유제품의 주요 수출국
② health benefits of drinking milk regularly – 우유를 정기적으로 마시는 것의 건강상 이득
③ unique food cultures around the world – 세계 각지의 독특한 식문화
④ suitable environments for dairy animals – 낙농 동물을 위한 적절한 환경
✔ various milk sources in different countries – 각국의 우유의 다양한 원천

Why? 왜 정답일까?

'Have you ever wondered where milk comes from?'에서 여자는 우유의 원천이라는 화제를 던지고, 'People around the world get milk from different animals.'를 통해 소 말고도 우유를 제공하는 동물이 있다고 언급하며 지역마다 어떤 동물들이 있는지 예를 들어 설명한다. 따라서 여자가 하는 말의 주제로 가장 적절한 것은 ⑤ '각국의 우유의 다양한 원천'이다.

---

17 언급 유무 파악 정답률 89% | 정답 ④

언급된 나라가 아닌 것은?

① Canada – 캐나다
② India – 인도
③ Finland – 핀란드
✔ Norway – 노르웨이
⑤ Romania – 루마니아

Why? 왜 정답일까?

담화에서 여자는 다양한 우유의 원천과 관련된 지역들의 예로 캐나다, 인도, 핀란드, 루마니아를 언급하였다. 따라서 언급되지 않은 것은 ④ '노르웨이'이다.

Why? 왜 오답일까?

① 'Around ninety percent of milk in Canada and the U.S. comes from cows.'에서 '캐나다'가 언급되었다.
② 'Water buffalos are the main source of milk in India.'에서 '인도'가 언급되었다.
③ 'Some people in the northern part of Finland drink reindeer milk ~'에서 '핀란드'가 언급되었다.
⑤ 'People in Romania get milk from sheep and use it to make cheese.'에서 '루마니아'가 언급되었다.

---

18 토스터기 교환 요청 대응 정답률 83% | 정답 ④

다음 글의 목적으로 가장 적절한 것은?

① 새로 출시한 제품을 홍보하려고
② 흔히 생기는 고장 사례를 알려주려고
③ 품질 보증서 보관의 중요성을 강조하려고
✔ 고장 난 제품을 교환하는 방법을 안내하려고
⑤ 제품 만족도 조사에 참여해줄 것을 요청하려고

Dear Ms. Spadler,
Spadler씨께.

You've written to our company / complaining / that your toaster, which you bought only three weeks earlier, / doesn't work.
귀하는 저희 회사에 편지를 쓰셨습니다. / 불평하는 / 불과 3주 전에 구입한 귀하의 토스터가 / 작동하지 않는다고

You were asking for a new toaster or a refund.
귀하는 새 토스터나 환불을 요구하셨습니다.

Since the toaster has a year's warranty, / our company is happy / to replace your faulty toaster with a new toaster.
그 토스터는 1년의 품질 보증 기간이 있기 때문에, / 저희 회사는 기쁩니다. / 귀하의 고장 난 토스터를 새 토스터로 교환해 드리게 되어

To get your new toaster, / simply take your receipt and the faulty toaster / to the dealer from whom you bought it.
새 토스터를 받으시려면, / 귀하의 영수증과 고장 난 토스터를 가져가시기만 하면 됩니다. / 귀하가 그것을 구매했던 판매인에게

The dealer will give you a new toaster on the spot.
그 판매인이 그 자리에서 바로 새 토스터를 드릴 것입니다.

Nothing is more important to us / than the satisfaction of our customers.
저희에게 더 중요한 것은 없습니다. / 저희 고객의 만족보다

If there is anything else we can do for you, / please do not hesitate to ask.
만약 저희가 귀하를 위해 할 수 있는 기타 어떤 일이 있다면, / 주저하지 말고 요청하십시오.

Yours sincerely, // Betty Swan
Betty Swan 드림

Spadler씨께,

귀하는 불과 3주 전에 구입한 토스터가 작동하지 않는다고 저희 회사에 불평하는 편지를 쓰셨습니다. 귀하는 새 토스터나 환불을 요구하셨습니다. 그 토스터는 1년의 품질 보증 기간이 있기 때문에, 저희 회사는 귀하의 고장 난 토스터를 새 토스터로 기꺼이 교환해 드리겠습니다. 새 토스터를 받으시려면, 귀하의 영수증과 고장 난 토스터를 구매했던 판매인에게 가져가시기만 하면 됩니다. 그 판매인이 그 자리에서 바로 새 토스터를 드릴 것입니다. 저희에게 고객의 만족보다 더 중요한 것은 없습니다. 만약 저희가 귀하를 위해 할 수 있는 기타 어떤 일이 있다면, 주저하지 말고 요청하십시오.

Betty Swan 드림

Why? 왜 정답일까?

글 중간에서 필자는 편지를 받는 고객이 불만을 제기했던 토스터를 기꺼이 교환해주겠다면서, 영수증을 함께 챙겨 구매처로 찾아가면 교환이 가능할 것(To get your new toaster, simply take your receipt and the faulty toaster to the dealer from whom you bought it.)임을 알려주고 있다. 따라서 글의 목적으로 가장 적절한 것은 ④ '고장 난 제품을 교환하는 방법을 안내하려고'이다.

- complain ⓥ 불평하다
- refund ⓝ 환불
- warranty ⓝ 보증기간
- faulty ⓐ 결함이 있는
- dealer ⓝ 판매자
- on the spot 현장에서
- satisfaction ⓝ 만족
- hesitate ⓥ 망설이다

6행 To get your new toaster, simply take your receipt and the faulty toaster to
부사적 용법(~하기 위해, 하려면)   명령문   목적어
the dealer [from whom you bought it].
선행사   「전치사＋관계대명사」

9행 Nothing is more important to us than the satisfaction of our customers.
「부정 주어＋비교급＋than : 최상급 대용(~보다 …한 것은 없다)」

---

19 잠수 도중 곤경에 처했다가 돌고래를 만나 구조된 필자   정답률 79% | 정답 ⑤

다음 글에 드러난 'I'의 심경 변화로 가장 적절한 것은?

① excited → bored
   신난   지루한
② pleased → angry
   기쁜   화난
③ jealous → thankful
   질투 나는   감사한
④ proud → embarrassed
   자랑스러운   당황한
✓⑤ frightened → relieved
   겁에 질린   안도한

I was diving alone in about 40 feet of water / when I got a terrible stomachache.
나는 40피트 정도의 물속에서 혼자 잠수하고 있었다. / 내가 배가 몹시 아팠을 때

I was sinking and hardly able to move.
나는 가라앉고 있었고 거의 움직일 수가 없었다.

I could see my watch / and knew there was only a little more time on the tank / before I would be out of air.
나는 시계를 볼 수 있었고 / (공기) 탱크 잔여 시간이 조금밖에 없다는 것을 알았다. / 내가 공기가 떨어지기 전까지

It was hard for me to remove my weight belt.
나는 웨이트 벨트를 벗기가 힘들었다.

Suddenly I felt a prodding from behind me / under the armpit.
갑자기 나는 뒤에서 쿡 찌르는 것을 느꼈다. / 겨드랑이 밑으로

My arm was being lifted forcibly.
내 팔이 강제로 들어 올려지고 있었다.

Around into my field of vision / came an eye.
내 시야 안으로 / 눈이 하나 들어왔다.

It seemed to be smiling.
그것은 웃고 있는 것 같았다.

It was the eye of a big dolphin.
그것은 큰 돌고래의 눈이었다.

Looking into that eye, / I knew I was safe.
그 눈을 들여다보니, / 나는 안전하다는 것을 알았다.

I felt / that the animal was protecting me, / lifting me toward the surface.
나는 느꼈다. / 그 동물이 나를 보호해 주고 있다고 / 나를 수면으로 들어 올려

40피트 정도의 물속에서 혼자 잠수하고 있었을 때, 나는 배가 몹시 아팠다. 나는 가라앉고 있었고 거의 움직일 수가 없었다. 나는 시계를 볼 수 있었고 공기가 떨어지기 전까지 (공기) 탱크 잔여 시간이 조금밖에 없다는 것을 알았다. 웨이트 벨트를 벗기가 힘들었다. 갑자기 나는 뒤에서 겨드랑이 밑으로 쿡 찌르는 것을 느꼈다. 내 팔이 강제로 들어 올려지고 있었다. 내 시야 안으로 눈이 하나 들어왔다. 그것은 웃고 있는 것 같았다. 그것은 큰 돌고래의 눈이었다. 그 눈을 들여다보니, 나는 안전하다는 것을 알았다. 나는 그 동물이 수면으로 나를 들어 올려 보호해 주고 있다고 느꼈다.

Why? 왜 정답일까?

'I was diving alone in about 40 feet of water when I got a terrible stomachache. I was sinking and hardly able to move.'에서 잠수하던 중 배가 아팠던 필자가 생명이 위험할 수도 있는 상황에 놓였음을 알 수 있고, 'Looking into that eye, I knew I was safe. I felt that the animal was protecting me, lifting me toward the surface.'에서 돌고래의 구조를 받게 된 필자가 위기를 벗어났음을 알 수 있다. 따라서 이를 통해 유추할 수 있는 'I'의 심경 변화로 가장 적절한 것은 ⑤ '겁에 질린 → 안도한'이다.

- **armpit** ⓝ 겨드랑이
- **field of vision** ⓝ 시야, 가시 범위
- **embarrassed** ⓐ 당황한
- **forcibly** ⓐⓓ 강제로, 강력히
- **surface** ⓝ 표면

구문 풀이

6행 Around into my field of vision came an eye.
「장소 부사구＋동사＋주어 : 도치 구문」

---

20 하고 싶은 일을 적어보기   정답률 80% | 정답 ②

다음 글에서 필자가 주장하는 바로 가장 적절한 것은?

① 친구의 꿈을 응원하라.
✓② 하고 싶은 일을 적으라.
③ 신중히 생각한 후 행동하라.
④ 효과적인 기억법을 개발하라.
⑤ 실현 가능한 목표에 집중하라.

Keeping good ideas floating around in your head / is a great way / to ensure that they won't happen.
좋은 생각을 머릿속에서 떠돌게 하는 것은 / 좋은 방법이다. / 반드시 그것이 이루어지지 않게 하는

Take a tip from writers, / who know / that the only good ideas that come to life / are the ones that get written down.
작가들로부터 조언을 얻으라, / 이들은 안다. / 생명력을 얻게 되는 좋은 생각은 / 오로지 종이에 적어둔 것들뿐임을

Take out a piece of paper / and record everything you'd love to do someday / — aim to hit one hundred dreams.
종이 한 장을 꺼내 / 언젠가 여러분이 하고 싶은 모든 것을 기록하고, / 꿈이 100개에 이르는 것을 목표로 해라.

You'll have a reminder and motivator / to get going on those things that are calling you, / and you also won't have the burden / of remembering all of them.
여러분은 상기시키고 동기를 부여해주는 것을 갖게 될 테고, / 자신을 부르고 있는 것들을 시작하도록 / 또한 여러분은 부담을 갖지 않을 것이다. / 그 모든 것을 기억해야 한다는

When you put your dreams into words / you begin putting them into action.
여러분이 꿈을 글로 적을 때 / 여러분은 그것을 실행하기 시작하는 것이다.

좋은 생각을 머릿속에서만 떠돌게 하는 것은 그것이 이루어지지 않게 하는 확실한 방법이다. 작가들로부터 조언을 얻어야 하는데, 이들은 생명력을 얻게 되는 좋은 생각은 오로지 종이에

적어둔 것들뿐임을 안다. 종이 한 장을 꺼내 언젠가 하고 싶은 모든 것을 기록하고, 꿈이 100개에 이르는 것을 목표로 해라. 여러분은 자신을 부르고 있는 것들을 시작하도록 (스스로에게) 상기시키고 동기를 부여해주는 것을 갖게 될 테고, 또한 그 모든 것을 기억해야 한다는 부담을 갖지 않을 것이다. 꿈을 글로 적을 때 여러분은 그것을 실행하기 시작하는 것이다.

Why? 왜 정답일까?

'When you put your dreams into words you begin putting them into action.'에서 필자는 꿈을 글로 적는 것이 실행의 첫걸음임을 언급하며 꿈을 써 나가는 것의 중요성을 상기시키고 있다. 따라서 필자의 주장으로 가장 적절한 것은 ② '하고 싶은 일을 적으라.'이다.

- **float** ⓥ 뜨다
- **aim** ⓥ 반드시 ~하다, 목표로 하다
- **motivator** ⓝ 동기 요인, 동기를 부여하는 것
- **put into action** ⓥ 실행에 옮기다
- **ensure** ⓥ 보장하다
- **reminder** ⓝ 상기시키는 것
- **burden** ⓝ 부담

구문 풀이

1행 Keeping good ideas floating around in your head is a great way to ensure
동명사구 주어   동사(단수)   주격 보어   형용사적 용법
{that they won't happen}.
[ ] : 명사절(~것)

---

21 논쟁에서 화내지 않기   정답률 61% | 정답 ③

밑줄 친 "rise to the bait"가 다음 글에서 의미하는 바로 가장 적절한 것은? [3점]

① stay calm – 침착함을 유지하다
② blame yourself – 스스로를 비난하다
✓③ lose your temper – 화를 내다
④ listen to the audience – 청중의 말을 듣다
⑤ apologize for your behavior – 자신의 행동에 대해 사과하다

We all know / that tempers are one of the first things / lost in many arguments.
우리 모두 안다. / 화는 첫 번째 것들 중 하나임을 / 많은 논쟁에서 내게 되는

It's easy to say one should keep cool, / but how do you do it?
침착함을 유지해야 한다고 말하는 것은 쉽지만, / 그러나 어떻게 그렇게 하는가?

The point to remember is / that sometimes in arguments the other person / is trying to get you to be angry.
기억해야 할 점은 / 때로는 논쟁에서 상대방은 / 여러분을 화나게 하려고 한다는 것이다.

They may be saying things / that are intentionally designed to annoy you.
그들은 말을 하고 있을지도 모른다. / 여러분을 화나게 하기 위해 의도적으로 고안한

They know / that if they get you to lose your cool, / you'll say something that sounds foolish; / you'll simply get angry / and then it will be impossible for you to win the argument.
그들은 안다. / 만약 그들이 여러분의 침착함을 잃게 한다면, / 여러분이 바보 같은 말을 할 것이고 / 여러분이 그저 화를 낼 것이고 / 그러면 여러분이 그 논쟁에서 이기란 불가능할 것임을

So don't fall for it.
그러니 속아넘어가지 마라.

A remark may be made to cause your anger, / but responding with a cool answer / that focuses on the issue raised / is likely to be most effective.
어떤 말이 여러분의 화를 불러일으키기 위해 언급될지도 모르지만, / 침착한 답변으로 대응하는 것이 / 제기된 문제에 초점을 맞춘 / 가장 효과적인 것 같다.

Indeed, any attentive listener will admire the fact / that you didn't "rise to the bait."
정말로, 주의 깊은 청자라면 누구라도 사실에 감탄할 것이다. / 여러분이 '미끼를 물지' 않았다는

많은 논쟁에서 첫 번째로 저지르는 것 중에 하나가 화를 내는 것임을 우리 모두 안다. 침착함을 유지하라고 말하는 것은 쉽지만, 어떻게 침착함을 유지하는가? 기억해야 할 점은 때로는 논쟁에서 상대방은 여러분을 화나게 하려고 한다는 것이다. 그들은 여러분을 화나게 하기 위해 의도적으로 고안한 말을 하고 있을지도 모른다. 그들은 만약 자신들이 여러분의 침착함을 잃게 한다면 여러분은 바보 같은 말을 하고 그저 화를 낼 것이고 그러면 여러분이 그 논쟁에서 이기란 불가능할 것임을 안다. 그러니 속아넘어가지 마라. 어떤 말이 여러분의 화를 불러일으키기 위해 언급될지도 모르지만, 제기된 문제에 초점을 맞춘 침착한 답변으로 대응하는 것이 가장 효과적인 것 같다. 정말로, 주의 깊은 청자라면 누구라도 여러분이 '미끼를 물지' 않았다는 사실에 감탄할 것이다.

Why? 왜 정답일까?

글에 따르면 논쟁에서 화가 나려 할 때 기억해야 할 점은 상대방이 우리를 화나게 하기 위해 일부러 어떤 말을 했을 수도 있다는 것이다(The point to remember is that sometimes in arguments the other person is trying to get you to be angry.). 마지막 두 문장에서는 그리하여 쉽게 화를 내지 않고 침착함을 유지하며 문제에만 초점을 맞춘 답변을 하면 상대방은 우리가 '화를 내지' 않았다는 바로 그 점에 감탄할 것이라는 결론을 도출하고 있다. 따라서 밑줄 친 부분이 의미하는 바로 가장 적절한 것은 ③ '화를 내다'이다.

- **lose one's temper** ⓥ 화를 내다
- **intentionally** ⓐⓓ 일부러, 의도적으로
- **lose one's cool** ⓥ 침착함을 잃다
- **remark** ⓝ 말, 언급
- **admire** ⓥ 감탄하다
- **apologize for** ⓥ ~에 대해 사과하다
- **argument** ⓝ 논쟁
- **design** ⓥ 고안하다
- **fall for** ⓥ ~에 속아넘어가다
- **raise** ⓥ (문제 등을) 제기하다
- **rise to the bait** ⓥ 미끼를 물다

구문 풀이

8행 A remark may be made to cause your anger, but responding with a cool
주어1   동사1(조동사 수동태)   ~하기 위해   주어2(동명사구)   선행사
answer [that focuses on the issue raised] is likely to be most effective.
주격 관계대명사   과거분사   동사2(~할 것 같다)

---

22 위험을 감수할 필요성   정답률 89% | 정답 ①

다음 글의 요지로 가장 적절한 것은?

✓① 위험을 무릅쓰지 않으면 아무것도 얻지 못한다.
② 자신이 잘하는 일에 집중하는 것이 효율적이다.

③ 잦은 실패 경험은 도전할 의지를 잃게 한다.
④ 위험 요소가 있으면 미리 피하는 것이 좋다.
⑤ 부탁을 자주 거절하면 신뢰를 잃는다.

Practically anything of value requires / that we take a risk of failure or being rejected.
사실상 어떤 가치 있는 것은 요구한다. / 우리가 실패나 거절당할 위험을 무릅쓸 것을

This is the price / we all must pay / for achieving the greater rewards lying ahead of us.
이것은 대가이다. / 우리 모두가 지불해야 하는 / 우리 앞에 놓인 더 큰 보상을 성취하기 위해

To take risks / means you will succeed sometime / but never to take a risk / means that you will never succeed.
위험을 무릅쓴다는 것은 / 여러분이 언젠가 성공할 것이라는 것을 의미하지만 / 위험을 전혀 무릅쓰지 않는 것은 / 여러분이 결코 성공하지 못할 것임을 의미한다.

Life is filled with a lot of risks and challenges / and if you want to get away from all these, / you will be left behind in the race of life.
인생은 많은 위험과 도전으로 가득 차 있으며, / 여러분이 이 모든 것에서 벗어나기를 원하면 / 인생이라는 경주에서 뒤처지게 될 것이다.

A person who can never take a risk / can't learn anything.
결코 위험을 무릅쓰지 못하는 사람은 / 아무것도 배울 수 없다.

For example, if you never take the risk to drive a car, / you can never learn to drive.
예를 들어, 만약 여러분이 차를 운전하기 위해 위험을 무릅쓰지 않는다면, / 여러분은 결코 운전을 배울 수 없다.

If you never take the risk of being rejected, / you can never have a friend or partner.
여러분이 거절당할 위험을 무릅쓰지 않는다면 / 여러분은 친구나 파트너를 절대 얻을 수 없다.

Similarly, by not taking the risk of attending an interview, / you will never get a job.
마찬가지로 면접에 참석하는 위험을 무릅쓰지 않음으로써, / 여러분은 결코 일자리를 얻지 못할 것이다.

사실상 모든 가치 있는 것은 우리가 실패나 거절당할 위험을 무릅쓸 것을 요구한다. 이것은 우리 앞에 놓인 더 큰 보상을 성취하기 위해 우리 모두가 지불해야 하는 대가이다. 위험을 무릅쓴다는 것은 언젠가 성공할 것이라는 것을 의미하지만 위험을 전혀 무릅쓰지 않는 것은 결코 성공하지 못할 것임을 의미한다. 인생은 많은 위험과 도전으로 가득 차 있으며, 이 모든 것에서 벗어나기를 원하면 인생이라는 경주에서 뒤처지게 될 것이다. 결코 위험을 무릅쓰지 못하는 사람은 아무것도 배울 수 없다. 예를 들어, 만약 차를 운전하기 위해 위험을 무릅쓰지 않는다면, 여러분은 결코 운전을 배울 수 없다. 거절당할 위험을 무릅쓰지 않는다면 친구나 파트너를 절대 얻을 수 없다. 마찬가지로 면접에 참석하는 위험을 무릅쓰지 않음으로써, 여러분은 결코 일자리를 얻지 못할 것이다.

Why? 왜 정답일까?

예시 앞에 나와 주제를 제시하는 'A person who can never take a risk can't learn anything.'에서 위험을 감수하지 않는 사람은 그 어떤 것도 배울 수 없다는 논지를 말하고 있다. 따라서 글의 요지로 가장 적절한 것은 ① '위험을 무릅쓰지 않으면 아무 것도 얻지 못한다.'이다.

- **practically** ⓐ 사실상, 거의
- **reject** ⓥ 거절하다
- **filled with** ~로 가득 찬
- **take a risk** ⓥ 위험을 무릅쓰다
- **reward** ⓝ 보상
- **be left behind** ⓥ 뒤처지다

구문 풀이

1행 Practically anything of value requires that we (should) take a risk of failure or being rejected.
주어 =valuable 동사(요구) 생략 전치사 목적어1
목적어2(수동 동명사)

---

23 소비자에게 중요한 요소인 촉감   정답률 77% | 정답 ②

다음 글의 주제로 가장 적절한 것은?

① benefits of using online shopping malls – 온라인 쇼핑몰 이용의 이점
✔ touch as an important factor for consumers – 소비자에게 중요한 요소인 촉감
③ importance of sharing information among consumers – 소비자 간 정보 공유의 중요성
④ necessity of getting feedback from consumers – 소비자 피드백을 수렴할 필요성
⑤ popularity of products in the latest styles – 최신 스타일 제품의 인기

Although individual preferences vary, / touch / (both what we touch with our fingers / and the way things feel as they come in contact with our skin) / is an important aspect of many products.
개인의 선호는 다양하지만, / 촉감은 / (우리가 손가락으로 만지는 것과 / 물건이 우리의 피부에 접촉될 때 느껴지는 방식 모두) / 많은 제품의 중요한 측면이다.

Consumers like some products / because of their feel.
소비자들은 어떤 제품을 좋아한다. / 그것들의 그 감촉 때문에

Some consumers buy skin creams and baby products / for their soothing effect on the skin.
일부 소비자들은 피부용 크림과 유아용품을 구입한다. / 피부를 진정시키는 그것들의 효과 때문에

In fact, consumers who have a high need for touch / tend to like products / that provide this opportunity.
실제로, 촉감에 대한 욕구가 많은 소비자는 / 제품을 좋아하는 경향이 있다. / 이런 기회를 제공하는

When considering products with material properties, / such as clothing or carpeting, / consumers like goods they can touch in stores more / than products they only see and read about online or in catalogs.
재료 속성과 함께 제품을 고려할 때, / 의류나 카펫과 같은 / 소비자들은 상점에서 만져볼 수 있는 제품을 더 좋아한다. / 그들이 온라인이나 카탈로그에서 보고 읽기만 하는 제품보다

개인의 선호는 다양하지만, 촉감(우리가 손가락으로 만지는 것과 물건이 우리의 피부에 접촉될 때 느껴지는 방식 모두)은 많은 제품의 중요한 측면이다. 소비자들은 어떤 제품을 그 감촉 때문에 좋아한다. 일부 소비자들은 피부 진정 효과 때문에 피부용 크림과 유아용품을 구입한다. 실제로, 촉감에 대한 욕구가 많은 소비자는 이런 기회를 제공하는 제품을 좋아하는 경향이 있다. 의류나 카펫과 같은 제품을 재료의 속성과 함께 고려할 때, 소비자들은 온라인이나 카탈로그에서 보고 읽기만 하는 제품보다 상점에서 만져볼 수 있는 제품을 더 좋아한다.

Why? 왜 정답일까?

'Although individual preferences vary, touch ~ is an important aspect of many products.'에서 소비자의 개인적 선호가 비록 다양하지만 촉감이 많은 제품에 있어 중요한 측면임을 언급하므로, 글의 주제로 가장 적절한 것은 ② '소비자에게 중요한 요소인 촉감'이다.

- **preference** ⓝ 선호
- **come in contact with** ⓥ ~와 접촉하다

- **aspect** ⓝ 측면
- **opportunity** ⓝ 기회
- **factor** ⓝ 요인
- **soothing** ⓐ 진정시키는
- **material** ⓝ 재료, 직물
- **necessity** ⓝ 필요성

구문 풀이

1행 Although individual preferences vary, touch (both what we touch with our
양보 접속사(비록 ~이지만)   자동사   주어   both+A+and+B
fingers and the way [things feel] as they come in contact with our skin) is an
동사(단수)
important aspect of many products.

---

24 아무리 많이 해도 지나침이 없는 교육   정답률 73% | 정답 ②

다음 글의 제목으로 가장 적절한 것은?

① All Play and No Work Makes Jack a Smart Boy
놀기만 하고 일하지 않는 것은 Jack(일반 사람을 나타냄)을 똑똑한 아이로 만든다
✔ Too Much Education Won't Hurt You
너무 많은 정보라고 해도 당신을 해하지 않을 것이다
③ Too Heads Are Worse than One
너무 (많은) 두뇌는 하나만 못하다
④ Don't Think Twice Before You Act
행동하기 전에 두 번 생각하지 마라
⑤ Learn from the Future, Not from the Past
과거가 아닌 미래로부터 배우라

In life, they say / that too much of anything is not good for you.
삶에서는 사람들이 말하기를 / 어떤 것이든 과하면 이롭지 않다고 한다.

In fact, too much of certain things in life / can kill you.
실제로, 삶에서 과하게 많은 어떤 것들은 / 당신을 죽일 수 있다.

For example, they say / that water has no enemy, / because water is essential to all life.
예를 들어, 사람들은 말하기를 / 물은 적이 없다고 한다. / 물은 모든 생물에게 필수적이기 때문에

But if you take in too much water, / like one who is drowning, / it could kill you.
그러나 당신이 만일 너무 많은 물을 마시면, / 물에 빠진 사람처럼 / 그것은 당신을 죽게 할 수 있다.

Education is the exception to this rule.
교육은 이 규칙에서 예외이다.

You can never have too much education or knowledge.
당신은 교육이나 지식을 결코 지나치게 많이 지닐 수 없다.

The reality is / that most people will never have enough education in their lifetime.
실상은 / 대부분의 사람은 평생 충분한 교육을 받지 못하리라는 것이다.

I am yet to find that one person / who has been hurt in life by too much education.
나는 그런 한 사람을 아직 본 적이 없다. / 교육을 너무 받아서 삶에서 피해를 본

Rather, we see lots of casualties every day, worldwide, / resulting from the lack of education.
오히려 우리는 매일, 전 세계에서 수많은 피해자들을 본다. / 교육의 부족으로 인해 생긴

You must keep in mind / that education is a long-term investment / of time, money, and effort into humans.
당신은 명심해야 한다. / 교육이 장기 투자임을 / 인간에 대한 시간, 돈, 그리고 노력의

삶에서는 어떤 것이든 과하면 이롭지 않다고 한다. 실제로, 삶에서 어떤 것은 과하면 위험할 수 있다. 예를 들어, 물은 모든 생물에게 필수적이기 때문에 물에 빠진 사람처럼 너무 많은 물을 마시면, 이는 당신을 죽게 할 수 있다. 교육은 이 규칙에서 예외이다. 교육이나 지식은 아무리 많이 있어도 지나치지 않다. 실상은 대부분의 사람은 평생 충분한 교육을 받지 못하리라는 것이다. 나는 교육을 너무 받아서 삶에서 피해를 본 사람을 아직 본 적이 없다. 오히려 우리는 매일, 전 세계에서 교육의 부족으로 인해 생긴 수많은 피해자들을 본다. 교육이 인간에게 시간, 돈, 그리고 노력을 장기 투자하는 것임을 명심해야 한다.

Why? 왜 정답일까?

'Education is the exception to this rule.' 앞뒤로 인생에서 무엇이든 과하면 좋지 않다는 내용과, 교육은 이 규칙에서 예외라는 내용이 상반되고 있다. 특히 'You can never have too much education or knowledge.'에서 교육이나 정보는 아무리 많이 주어지더라도 지나침이 없다고 언급하는 것으로 볼 때, 글의 제목으로 가장 적절한 것은 ② '너무 많은 정보라고 해도 당신을 해하지 않을 것이다'이다.

- **essential** ⓐ 필수적인
- **drown** ⓥ 물에 빠지다, 익사하다
- **lack** ⓝ 부족, 결여
- **investment** ⓝ 투자
- **take in** ⓥ ~을 섭취하다
- **exception** ⓝ 예외
- **keep in mind** ⓥ ~을 명심하다, 염두에 두다

구문 풀이

8행 I am yet to find that one person [who has been hurt in life by too much
아직 ~하지 못하다   선행사   주격 관·대 현재완료 수동태
education].

---

25 세계에서 가장 많이 사용된 언어의 총 사용자 및 원어민 수   정답률 84% | 정답 ④

다음 도표의 내용과 일치하지 않는 것은?

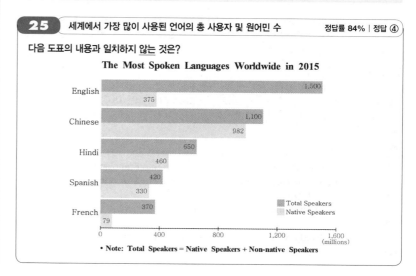

The Most Spoken Languages Worldwide in 2015

English: 1,500 / 375
Chinese: 1,100 / 982
Hindi: 650 / 460
Spanish: 420 / 330
French: 370 / 79

■ Total Speakers
■ Native Speakers

0   400   800   1,200   1,600 (millions)

• Note: Total Speakers = Native Speakers + Non-native Speakers

The above graph / shows the numbers of total speakers and native speakers / of the five most spoken languages worldwide in 2015.
위 그래프는 / 총 사용자 수와 원어민 수를 보여 준다. / 2015년에 전 세계에서 가장 많이 사용된 다섯 개 언어의

① English is the most spoken language worldwide, / with 1,500 million total speakers.
영어는 전 세계에서 가장 많이 사용되는 언어로, / 15억 명의 총 사용자가 있다.

② Chinese is second on the list / with 1,100 million total speakers.
중국어는 목록에서 2위로 / 11억 명의 총 사용자가 있다.

③ In terms of the number of native speakers, however, / Chinese is the most spoken language worldwide, / followed by Hindi.
하지만 원어민 수라는 면에서는, / 중국어가 전 세계에서 가장 많이 사용되는 언어이며, / 힌디어가 그 뒤를 잇는다.

☑ The number of native speakers of English / is smaller than that of Spanish.
영어의 원어민 수는 / 스페인어의 원어민 수보다 더 적다.

⑤ French is the least spoken language among the five / in terms of the number of native speakers.
프랑스어는 다섯 개 언어 중 가장 적게 사용되는 언어이다. / 원어민 수라는 면에서

위 그래프는 2015년에 전 세계에서 가장 많이 사용된 다섯 개 언어의 총 사용자 수와 원어민 수를 보여 준다. ① 영어는 전 세계에서 가장 많이 사용되는 언어로, 15억 명의 총 사용자가 있다. ② 중국어는 목록에서 2위로 11억 명의 총 사용자가 있다. ③ 하지만 원어민 수라는 면에서는, 중국어가 전 세계에서 가장 많이 사용되는 언어이며, 힌디어가 그 뒤를 잇는다. ④ 영어의 원어민 수는 스페인어의 원어민 수보다 더 적다. ⑤ 프랑스어는 원어민 수라는 면에서 다섯 개 언어 중 가장 적게 사용되는 언어이다.

Why? 왜 정답일까?

도표에 따르면 영어 원어민의 수는 3억 7천 5백만 명으로 스페인어 원어민의 수인 3억 3천 3백만 명보다 많다. 따라서 도표와 일치하지 않는 것은 ④이다.

- native speaker ⓝ 원어민
- follow ⓥ ~의 뒤를 잇다
- in terms of ~의 면에서
- term ⓝ 용어, 말

---

26 Ellen Church의 생애 정답률 84% | 정답 ④

Ellen Church에 관한 다음 글의 내용과 일치하지 않는 것은?
① San Francisco에서 간호사로 일했다.
② 간호사가 비행 중에 승객을 돌봐야 한다고 제안했다.
③ 미국 최초의 여성 비행기 승무원이 되었다.
☑ 자동차 사고로 다쳤지만 비행기 승무원 생활을 계속했다.
⑤ 고향인 Cresco에 그녀의 이름을 따서 붙인 공항이 있다.

Ellen Church was born in Iowa in 1904.
Ellen Church는 1904년에 Iowa에서 태어났다.

「After graduating from Cresco High School, / she studied nursing and worked as a nurse in San Francisco.」 ①의 근거 일치
Cresco 고등학교를 졸업한 후, / 그녀는 간호학을 공부했고 San Francisco에서 간호사로 일했다.

「She suggested to Boeing Air Transport / that nurses should take care of passengers during flights / because most people were frightened of flying.」 ②의 근거 일치
그녀는 Boeing Air Transport에 제안했다. / 간호사가 비행 중에 승객을 돌봐야 한다고 / 대부분의 사람이 비행을 무서워했기 때문에

「In 1930, she became the first female flight attendant in the U.S. / and worked on a Boeing 80A from Oakland, California to Chicago, Illinois.」 ③의 근거 일치
1930년에 그녀는 미국 최초의 여성 비행기 승무원이 되었고 / California 주 Oakland에서 Illinois 주 Chicago까지 가는 Boeing 80A에서 근무했다.

「Unfortunately, a car accident injury / forced her to end her career after only eighteen months.」
불행하게도, 자동차 사고 부상은 / 그녀가 겨우 18개월 후에 어쩔 수 없이 일을 그만두게 만들었다. ④의 근거 불일치

Church started nursing again at Milwaukee County Hospital / after she graduated from the University of Minnesota / with a degree in nursing education.
Church는 Milwaukee County 병원에서 다시 간호사 일을 시작했다. / 그녀가 Minnesota 대학을 졸업한 후 / 간호 교육학 학위와 함께

During World War Ⅱ, / she served as a captain in the Army Nurse Corps / and received an Air Medal.
제2차 세계대전 중 / 그녀는 육군 간호 부대에서 대위로 복무했고 / 항공 훈장을 받았다.

「Ellen Church Field Airport in her hometown, Cresco, / was named after her.」 ⑤의 근거 일치
그녀의 고향인 Cresco에 있는 Ellen Church Field 공항은 / 그녀의 이름을 따서 붙여졌다.

Ellen Church는 1904년에 Iowa에서 태어났다. Cresco 고등학교를 졸업한 후, 그녀는 간호학을 공부했고 San Francisco에서 간호사로 일했다. 그녀는 대부분의 사람이 비행을 무서워하기 때문에 간호사가 비행 중에 승객을 돌봐야 한다고 Boeing Air Transport에 제안했다. 1930년에 그녀는 미국 최초의 여성 비행기 승무원이 되어 California 주 Oakland에서 Illinois 주 Chicago까지 가는 Boeing 80A에서 근무했다. 불행하게도, 자동차 사고 부상으로 그녀는 겨우 18개월 후에 일을 그만두어야 했다. Church는 간호 교육학 학위를 받으며 Minnesota 대학을 졸업한 후 Milwaukee County 병원에서 다시 간호사 일을 시작했다. 제2차 세계대전 중 그녀는 육군 간호 부대에서 대위로 복무했고 항공 훈장을 받았다. 그녀의 고향인 Cresco에 있는 Ellen Church Field 공항은 그녀의 이름을 따서 붙여졌다.

Why? 왜 정답일까?

'Unfortunately, a car accident injury forced her to end her career after only eighteen months.'에서 자동차 사고 부상으로 인해 Ellen Church는 18개월 만에 승무원 일을 그만두어야 했다고 하므로, 내용과 일치하지 않는 것은 ④ '자동차 사고로 다쳤지만 비행기 승무원 생활을 계속했다.'이다.

Why? 왜 오답일까?

① '~ she studied nursing and worked as a nurse in San Francisco.'의 내용과 일치한다.
② 'She suggested to Boeing Air Transport that nurses should take care of passengers during flights ~'의 내용과 일치한다.
③ 'In 1930, she became the first female flight attendant in the U.S. ~'의 내용과 일치한다.
⑤ 'Ellen Church Field Airport in her hometown, Cresco, was named after her.'의 내용과 일치한다.

- graduate from ⓥ ~을 졸업하다
- passenger ⓝ 승객
- flight attendant ⓝ 항공 승무원
- force ⓥ 어쩔 수 없이 ~하게 하다, 강요하다
- name after ⓥ ~의 이름을 따서 짓다
- take care of ⓥ ~을 돌보다
- frightened ⓐ 무서워하는, 겁에 질린
- injury ⓝ 부상
- serve as ⓥ ~로 복무하다, ~의 역할을 하다

구문 풀이

3행 She suggested to Boeing Air Transport that nurses should take care of
「제안 동사 + that + 주어 + (should) 동사원형: ~해야 한다고 제안하다」
passengers during flights because most people were frightened of flying.
이유 접속사

---

27 과학 셀카 사진 대회 정답률 88% | 정답 ③

Science Selfie Competition에 관한 다음 안내문의 내용과 일치하지 않는 것은?
① 학교 밖에서 과학을 즐기는 셀카 사진을 출품한다.
② 셀카 사진에 관한 하나의 짧은 문장을 써야 한다.
☑ 1인당 사진 여러 장을 출품할 수 있다.
④ 셀카 사진을 이름 및 소속 학급과 함께 이메일로 보내야 한다.
⑤ 수상자는 2020년 3월 27일에 발표될 것이다.

Science Selfie Competition
과학 셀카 사진 대회
For a chance to win science goodies, / just submit a selfie of yourself enjoying science outside of school! ①의 근거 일치
상으로 좋은 과학 용품을 받을 기회를 얻으려면, / 학교 밖에서 과학을 즐기는 자신의 셀카 사진을 출품하기만 하면 됩니다!
Deadline: Friday, March 20, 2020, 6 p.m.
마감 기한: 2020년 3월 20일 금요일 오후 6시
Details:
세부 사항:
Your selfie / should include a visit to any science museum / or a science activity at home.
여러분의 셀카 사진은 / 아무 과학 박물관 방문을 포함해야 합니다. / 혹은 집에서 하는 과학 활동을
Be as creative as you like, / and write one short sentence about the selfie. ②의 근거 일치
마음껏 창의력을 발휘하고, / 셀카 사진에 관한 하나의 짧은 문장을 쓰세요.
Only one entry per person! ③의 근거 불일치
1인당 한 장의 출품작만!
Email your selfie with your name and class to mclara@oldfold.edu. ④의 근거 일치
셀카 사진을 이름 및 소속 학급과 함께 mclara@oldfold.edu로 이메일로 보내세요.
Winners will be announced on March 27, 2020. ⑤의 근거 일치
수상자는 2020년 3월 27일에 발표될 것입니다.
Please visit www.oldfold.edu / to learn more about the competition.
www.oldfold.edu를 방문하세요. / 대회에 대해 더 자세히 알아보려면

과학 셀카 사진 대회

상으로 좋은 과학 용품을 받을 기회를 얻으려면, 학교 밖에서 과학을 즐기는 셀카 사진을 출품하기만 하면 됩니다!

마감 기한: 2020년 3월 20일 금요일 오후 6시

세부 사항:
• 셀카 사진에는 과학 박물관 방문이나 집에서 하는 과학 활동이 포함되어야 합니다.
• 마음껏 창의력을 발휘하고, 셀카 사진에 관한 하나의 짧은 문장을 쓰세요.
• 1인당 한 장의 출품작만!
• 셀카 사진을 이름 및 소속 학급과 함께 mclara@oldfold.edu로 이메일로 보내세요.

수상자는 2020년 3월 27일에 발표될 것입니다.

대회에 대해 더 자세히 알아보려면 www.oldfold.edu를 방문하세요.

Why? 왜 정답일까?

'Only one entry per person!'에서 출품작은 1인당 한 장만 낼 수 있다고 하므로, 안내문의 내용과 일치하지 않는 것은 ③ '1인당 사진 여러 장을 출품할 수 있다.'이다.

Why? 왜 오답일까?

① '~, just submit a selfie of yourself enjoying science outside of school!'의 내용과 일치한다.
② '~ write one short sentence about the selfie.'의 내용과 일치한다.
④ 'Email your selfie with your name and class to mclara@oldfold.edu.'의 내용과 일치한다.
⑤ 'Winners will be announced on March 27, 2020.'의 내용과 일치한다.

- selfie ⓝ 셀카 사진
- entry ⓝ 출품작
- goody ⓝ 매력적인 것, 갖고 싶은 것
- announce ⓥ 발표하다, 안내하다

---

28 장난감 창고 세일 정답률 89% | 정답 ④

Toy & Gift Warehouse Sale에 관한 다음 안내문의 내용과 일치하는 것은?
① 4월 16일부터 시작된다.
② 십 대를 위한 장난감은 판매하지 않는다.
③ 스무 개의 장난감 회사가 참여한다.
☑ 월요일과 화요일에는 운영되지 않는다.
⑤ 반품은 구입 후 2주간 가능하다.

Toy & Gift Warehouse Sale
장난감과 선물 창고 세일
at Wilson Square
Wilson Square에서
「from April 3 to April 16」 ①의 근거 불일치
4월 3일부터 4월 16일까지

We carry items / that are in stock at bigger retailers / for a cheaper price.
우리는 품목들을 취급합니다. / 더 큰 소매상에 재고로 있는 / 더 싼 가격에
「You can expect to find toys / for children from birth to teens.」②의근거 불일치
여러분은 장난감을 찾아볼 수 있습니다. / 신생아부터 십 대까지의 아이들을 위한
「Ten toy companies will participate in the sale.」③의근거 불일치
열 개의 장난감 회사가 이 판매에 참여할 것입니다.
Wednesday – Friday: 10 a.m. – 6 p.m.
수요일 ~ 금요일: 오전 10시 ~ 오후 6시
Saturday & Sunday: 11 a.m. – 5 p.m.
토요일과 일요일: 오전 11시 ~ 오후 5시
「Closed on Monday & Tuesday」④의근거 일치
월요일과 화요일에는 운영되지 않음
「Returns must be made within one week of purchase.」⑤의근거 불일치
반품은 구입 후 1주일 이내에 하셔야 합니다.
For more information, / please visit us at www.poptoy.com.
더 많은 정보를 원하시면, / www.poptoy.com을 방문하십시오.

장난감과 선물 창고 세일

Wilson Square에서
4월 3일부터 4월 16일까지

우리는 더 큰 소매상에 재고로 있는 품목들을 더 싼 가격에 취급합니다. 여러분은 신생아부터 십 대까지의 아이들을 위한 장난감을 찾아볼 수 있습니다. 열 개의 장난감 회사가 이 판매에 참여할 것입니다.

수요일 ~ 금요일: 오전 10시 ~ 오후 6시
토요일과 일요일: 오전 11시 ~ 오후 5시
월요일과 화요일에는 운영되지 않음

반품은 구입 후 1주일 이내에 하셔야 합니다.
더 많은 정보를 원하시면, www.poptoy.com을 방문하십시오.

Why? 왜 정답일까?

'Closed on Monday & Tuesday'에서 월요일과 화요일에는 문을 닫는다고 하므로, 안내문의 내용과 일치하는 것은 ④ '월요일과 화요일에는 운영되지 않는다.'이다.

Why? 왜 오답일까?

① 'from April 3 to April 16'에서 4월 3일이 시작일이고, 4월 16일이 종료일이라고 하였다.
② 'You can expect to find toys for children from birth to teens.'에서 신생아부터 십 대를 위한 장난감이 있다고 하였다.
③ 'Ten toy companies will participate in the sale.'에서 열 개의 장난감 회사가 세일에 참여한다고 하였다.
⑤ 'Returns must be made within one week of purchase.'에서 반품은 구입 후 1주일 안에 가능하다고 하였다.

- **warehouse** ⓝ 창고
- **in stock** 재고로 있는
- **return** ⓝ 반품
- **carry** ⓥ (상점이 상품을) 취급하다
- **retailer** ⓝ 소매상
- **purchase** ⓝ 구입

★★★ 등급을 가르는 문제!

29 식품 라벨을 통한 식품 정보 습득   정답률 51% | 정답 ②

다음 글의 밑줄 친 부분 중, 어법상 틀린 것은? [3점]

"You are what you eat."
'당신이 먹는 것이 바로 당신이다.'
That phrase is often used to ① show the relationship / between the foods you eat and your physical health.
그 구절은 흔히 관계를 보여주기 위해 사용된다. / 여러분이 먹는 음식과 여러분의 신체적 건강 사이의
But do you really know what you are eating / when you buy processed foods, canned foods, and packaged goods?
하지만 여러분은 자신이 무엇을 먹고 있는지 정말 아는가? / 가공식품, 통조림 식품, 포장 판매 식품을 살 때
Many of the manufactured products made today / contain so many chemicals and artificial ingredients / ②✓ that it is sometimes difficult / to know exactly what is inside them.
오늘날 만들어진 제조 식품 중 다수가 / 너무 많은 화학물질과 인공적인 재료를 함유하고 있어서 / 때로는 어렵다 / 정확히 그 안에 무엇이 들어 있는지 알기가
Fortunately, now there are food labels.
다행히도, 이제는 식품 라벨이 있다.
Food labels are a good way / ③ to find the information about the foods you eat.
식품 라벨은 좋은 방법이다. / 여러분이 먹는 식품에 관한 정보를 알아내는
Labels on food are ④ like the table of contents / found in books.
식품 라벨은 목차와 같다. / 책에서 볼 수 있는
The main purpose of food labels / ⑤ is to inform you / what is inside the food you are purchasing.
식품 라벨의 주된 목적은 / 여러분에게 알려주는 것이다. / 여러분이 구입하고 있는 식품 안에 무엇이 들어 있는지

'당신이 먹는 것이 바로 당신이다(사람은 먹는 대로 이루어진다).' 그 구절은 흔히 여러분이 먹는 음식과 여러분의 신체적 건강 사이의 관계를 보여주기 위해 사용된다. 하지만 여러분은 가공식품, 통조림 식품, 포장 판매 식품을 살 때 자신이 무엇을 먹고 있는지 정말 아는가? 오늘날 만들어진 제조 식품 중 다수가 너무 많은 화학물질과 인공적인 재료를 함유하고 있어서 때로는 정확히 그 안에 무엇이 들어 있는지 알기가 어렵다. 다행히도, 이제는 식품 라벨이 있다. 식품 라벨은 여러분이 먹는 식품에 관한 정보를 알아내는 좋은 방법이다. 식품 라벨은 책에서 볼 수 있는 목차와 같다. 식품 라벨의 주된 목적은 여러분이 구입하고 있는 식품 안에 무엇이 들어 있는지 여러분에게 알려주는 것이다.

Why? 왜 정답일까?

'~ it is sometimes difficult ~'가 완전한 문장이므로 뒤에 불완전한 절이 나올 때 쓰는 관계대명사 which는 ② 자리에 나올 수 없다. 앞에 so many가 나오는 것으로 볼 때, 전체 문장은 'so ~ that … (너무 ~해서 …하다)' 구문임을 알 수 있다. 따라서 which를 결과의 부사절을 이끄는 접속사 that으로 고쳐야 한다. 어법상 틀린 것은 ②이다.

Why? 왜 오답일까?

① 'be used＋to부정사(~하기 위해 사용되다)' 구문이 바르게 쓰였다.
③ a good way를 꾸미는 형용사적 용법으로 to부정사구인 to find가 바르게 쓰였다.
④ be동사 뒤에서 보어 역할을 하는 전명구를 이루기 위해 전치사 like(~처럼)가 바르게 쓰였다.
⑤ 주어가 The main purpose라는 단수 명사이므로 단수 동사 is가 바르게 쓰였다.

- **phrase** ⓝ 구절
- **processed** ⓐ 가공된
- **packaged** ⓐ 포장된
- **artificial** ⓐ 인공의
- **purpose** ⓝ 목적
- **physical** ⓐ 신체적인, 물리적인
- **canned** ⓐ 통조림으로 된
- **contain** ⓥ 함유하다
- **ingredient** ⓝ 재료

구문 풀이

4행 Many of the manufactured products made today contain so many
　　　　　　　주어　　　　　　　과거분사　　　동사(복수)　'so ~'
chemicals and artificial ingredients that it is sometimes difficult to know exactly
　　　　　　　　　　　　　　　　　that … : 너무 ~해서 …하다)
what is inside them.

★★ 문제 해결 꿀~팁 ★★

▶ 많이 틀린 이유는?
④의 like는 동사뿐 아니라 '~처럼'이라는 의미의 전치사로 쓰여 뒤에 명사구를 수반할 수 있다는 점을 기억해 둔다. 또한 ⑤는 주어와 동사의 수 일치를 묻는 경우로 핵심 주어와 수식어구를 구별하는 것이 풀이의 관건이다.
▶ 문제 해결 방법은?
② 'which vs. that'은 빈출되는 어법 사항이다. 둘 다 관계대명사로서 뒤에 불완전한 절을 수반할 수 있지만, that의 경우 접속사로도 쓰일 수 있기 때문에 뒤에 완전한 문장이 나오면 which가 아닌 that을 쓴다는 데 주의한다.

---

30 작은 변화를 무시하기 쉬운 이유   정답률 61% | 정답 ③

다음 글의 밑줄 친 부분 중, 문맥상 낱말의 쓰임이 적절하지 않은 것은? [3점]

We often ignore small changes / because they don't seem to ① matter very much in the moment.
우리는 흔히 작은 변화들을 무시한다. / 그것들이 당장은 크게 중요한 것 같지 않아서
If you save a little money now, / you're still not a millionaire.
여러분이 지금 돈을 약간 모아도, / 여러분은 여전히 백만장자가 아니다.
If you study Spanish for an hour tonight, / you still haven't learned the language.
여러분이 오늘 밤에 스페인어를 한 시간 동안 공부해도, / 여러분은 여전히 그 언어를 익힌 것은 아니다.
We make a few changes, / but the results never seem to come ② quickly / and so we slide back into our previous routines.
우리는 약간의 변화를 만들어 보지만, / 그러나 그 결과는 결코 빨리 오지 않는 것 같고 / 그래서 우리는 이전의 일상으로 다시 빠져든다.
The slow pace of transformation / also makes it ✓ difficult to break a bad habit.
변화의 느린 속도는 / 또한 나쁜 습관을 버리기 어렵게 만든다.
If you eat an unhealthy meal today, / the scale doesn't move much.
여러분이 오늘 몸에 좋지 않은 음식을 먹어도, / 체중계는 크게 움직이지 않는다.
A single decision is easy to ignore.
하나의 결정은 무시하기 쉽다.
But when we ④ repeat small errors, / day after day, / by following poor decisions again and again, / our small choices add up to bad results.
하지만 우리가 작은 오류를 반복한다면, / 날마다 / 잘못된 결정을 반복적으로 따르면서 / 우리의 작은 선택들이 모여 좋지 않은 결과를 만들어낸다.
Many missteps eventually lead to a ⑤ problem.
많은 실수는 결국 문제로 이어진다.

우리는 흔히 작은 변화들이 당장은 크게 ① 중요한 것 같지 않아서 그것들을 무시한다. 지금 돈을 약간 모아도, 여러분은 여전히 백만장자가 아니다. 오늘 밤에 스페인어를 한 시간 동안 공부해도, 여러분은 여전히 그 언어를 익힌 것은 아니다. 우리는 약간의 변화를 만들어 보지만, 그 결과는 결코 ② 빨리 오지 않는 것 같고 그래서 우리는 이전의 일상으로 다시 ✓빠져든다. 변화의 느린 속도는 또한 나쁜 습관을 버리기 ③ 쉽게(→ 어렵게) 만든다. 오늘 몸에 좋지 않은 음식을 먹어도 체중계는 크게 움직이지 않는다. 하나의 결정은 무시하기 쉽다. 하지만 우리가 잘못된 결정을 반복적으로 따라 작은 오류를 날마다 ④ 반복한다면, 우리의 작은 선택들이 모여 좋지 않은 결과를 만들어낸다. 많은 실수는 결국 ⑤ 문제로 이어진다.

Why? 왜 정답일까?

'We make a few changes, but the results never seem to come quickly and so we slide back into our previous routines.'에서 우리가 변화를 시도하더라도 바로 변화가 나타나는 것이 아니기에 우리는 다시 변화 이전의 일상으로 돌아가게 된다고 설명한다. 이에 비추어 볼 때, 변화가 느리게 찾아오는 점은 나쁜 습관을 버리기 '어렵게' 만든다는 의미가 되도록 ③의 easy를 difficult로 바꾸어야 한다. 문맥상 낱말의 쓰임이 적절하지 않은 것은 ③이다.

- **ignore** ⓥ 무시하다
- **in the moment** 당장, 지금
- **slide back into** ~로 돌아가다, 복귀하다
- **routine** ⓝ 일상
- **break a bad habit** 나쁜 습관을 버리다
- **scale** ⓝ 체중계, 저울
- **misstep** ⓝ 실수, 잘못된 조치
- **matter** ⓥ 중요하다
- **millionaire** ⓝ 백만장자
- **previous** ⓐ 이전의
- **transformation** ⓝ 변화
- **unhealthy** ⓐ 몸에 좋지 않은, 건강하지 않은
- **add up to** (합이) 결국 ~이 되다
- **eventually** ⓐ㉯ 결국

구문 풀이

6행 The slow pace of transformation also makes it easy to break a bad habit.
　　　　　　　　　　　　　　　5형식 동사　목적격 보어　진목적어
　　　　　　　　　　　　　　　　　　　　　　　　　　　↳가목적어

---

31 상처 받은 상대방에게 시간을 주며 기다려주기   정답률 56% | 정답 ③

다음 빈칸에 들어갈 말로 가장 적절한 것을 고르시오.

Remember that patience is always of the essence.
인내가 항상 가장 중요하다는 것을 기억해라.

If an apology is not accepted, / thank the individual for hearing you out / and leave the door open / for if and when he wishes to reconcile.
사과가 받아들여지지 않으면, / 그 사람이 여러분의 말을 끝까지 들어줬다는 것에 감사하고, / 문(가능성)을 열어 두어라. / 그 사람이 화해하고 싶 을 경우와 시기를 위해

Be conscious of the fact / that just because someone accepts your apology / does not mean she has fully forgiven you.
사실을 알고 있어라. / 단지 누군가가 여러분의 사과를 받아들인다고 해서 / 그 사람이 여러분을 온전히 용서했다는 뜻이 아니라는

It can take time, maybe a long time, / before the injured party can completely let go / and fully trust you again.
시간이 걸릴 수 있고, 어쩌면 오래 걸릴 수 있다. / 상처받은 당사자가 완전히 떨쳐 버리기까지 / 그리고 여러분을 온전히 다시 믿기까지

There is little you can do / to speed this process up.
여러분이 할 수 있는 것은 거의 없다. / 이 과정을 빨리하게 하기 위해

If the person is truly important to you, / it is worthwhile / to give him or her the time and space needed to heal.
그 사람이 여러분에게 진정으로 중요하다면, / 가치가 있다. / 그 사람에게 치유되는 데 필요한 시간과 공간을 주는 것이

Do not expect the person / to go right back to acting normally immediately.
그 사람에게 기대하지 마라. / 즉시 평상시처럼 행동하는 것으로 바로 돌아갈 것이라고

인내가 항상 가장 중요하다는 것을 기억해라. 사과가 받아들여지지 않으면, 그 사람이 여러분의 말을 끝까지 들어줬다는 것에 감사하고, 그 사람이 화해하고 싶을 경우와 시기를 위해 문(가능성)을 열어 두어라. 단지 누군가가 여러분의 사과를 받아들인다고 해서 그 사람이 여러분을 온전히 용서했다는 뜻이 아니라는 사실을 알고 있어라. 상처받은 당사자가 완전히 떨쳐 버리고 여러분을 온전히 다시 믿기까지 시간이 걸릴 수 있고, 어쩌면 오래 걸릴 수 있다. 이 과정을 빨리하게 하기 위해 여러분이 할 수 있는 것은 거의 없다. 그 사람이 여러분에게 진정으로 중요하다면, 그 사람에게 치유되는 데 필요한 시간과 공간을 주는 것이 가치가 있다. 그 사람이 즉시 평상시의 행동으로 바로 돌아갈 것이라고 기대하지 마라.

Why? 왜 정답일까?

마지막 세 문장에서 용서의 과정을 빨리하게 할 방법은 없고, 상대방에게 시간을 줄 필요가 있으므로 상대방이 곧바로 평상시대로 돌아갈 것이라는 기대를 하지 말라(~ it is worthwhile to give him or her the time and space needed to heal. Do not expect the person to go right back to acting normally immediately.)고 조언하고 있다. 이는 상대방을 기다려주며 인내심을 발휘하라는 내용으로 요약할 수 있으므로, 빈칸에 들어갈 말로 가장 적절한 것은 ③ '인내'이다.

- essence ⓝ 본질
- hear ~ out ⓥ ~의 말을 끝까지 들어주다
- injured ⓐ 상처받은, 부상 당한
- worthwhile ⓐ 가치 있는
- independence ⓝ 자립, 독립
- apology ⓝ 사과
- conscious ⓐ 알고 있는, 의식하는
- speed up ⓥ 빨리하게 하다
- normally ⓐ 정상적으로
- patience ⓝ 인내

구문 풀이

3행 Be conscious of the fact that just because someone accepts your apology
　　　　　　　　　　　　　동격 접속사　　　　　주어(부사절이 명사절처럼 쓰임)
does not mean she has fully forgiven you.
　동사　　　　　목적어

---

32 광고 교환   정답률 58% | 정답 ①

다음 빈칸에 들어갈 말로 가장 적절한 것을 고르시오.

✔ trading space - 공간을 교환함
② getting funded - 자금을 지원받음
③ sharing reviews - 상품평을 공유함
④ renting factory facilities - 공장 시설을 빌림
⑤ increasing TV commercials - TV 광고를 늘림

Although many small businesses have excellent websites, / they typically can't afford aggressive online campaigns.
비록 많은 작은 사업체들이 훌륭한 웹 사이트를 가지고 있지만, / 보통 그들은 매우 적극적인 온라인 캠페인을 할 여유가 없다.

One way to get the word out / is through an advertising exchange, / in which advertisers place banners on each other's websites for free.
소문나게 하는 한 가지 방법은 / 광고 교환을 통해서이다. / 광고주들이 서로의 웹 사이트에 무료로 배너를 게시하는

For example, / a company selling beauty products / could place its banner on a site that sells women's shoes, / and in turn, / the shoe company could put a banner on the beauty product site.
예를 들어, / 미용 제품을 판매하는 회사는 / 여성 신발을 판매하는 사이트에 자신의 배너를 게시할 수 있고, / 그다음에는 / 그 신발 회사가 미용 제품 사이트에 배너를 게시할 수 있다.

Neither company charges the other; / they simply exchange ad space.
두 회사 모두 상대에게 비용을 청구하지 않는데, / 그들은 그저 광고 공간을 교환하는 것이다.

Advertising exchanges are gaining in popularity, / especially among marketers / who do not have much money / and who don't have a large sales team.
광고 교환은 인기를 얻고 있다. / 특히 마케팅 담당자들 사이에서 / 돈이 많지 않거나 / 대규모 영업팀이 없는

By trading space, / advertisers find new outlets / that reach their target audiences / that they would not otherwise be able to afford.
공간을 교환함으로써, / 광고주들은 새로운 (광고의) 출구를 찾는다. / 자신의 목표 고객과 접촉할 수 있는 / 그러지 않으면 그들이 접촉할 여유가 없는

비록 많은 작은 사업체들이 훌륭한 웹 사이트를 가지고 있지만, 그들은 보통 매우 적극적인 온라인 캠페인을 할 여유가 없다. 소문나게 하는 한 가지 방법은 광고주들이 서로의 웹 사이트에 무료로 배너를 게시하는 광고 교환을 통해서이다. 예를 들어, 미용 제품을 판매하는 회사는 여성 신발을 판매하는 사이트에 자신의 배너를 게시할 수 있고, 그다음에는 그 신발 회사가 미용 제품 사이트에 배너를 게시할 수 있다. 두 회사 모두 상대에게 비용을 청구하지 않는데, 그들은 그저 광고 공간을 교환하는 것이다. 광고 교환은 특히 돈이 많지 않거나 대규모 영업팀이 없는 마케팅 담당자들 사이에서 인기를 얻고 있다. 공간을 교환함으로써, 광고주들

은 그러지 않으면 접촉할 여유가 없는 자신의 목표 고객과 접촉할 수 있는 새로운 (광고의) 출구를 찾는다.

Why? 왜 정답일까?

예시 앞의 주제문 'One way to get the word out is through an advertising exchange, in which advertisers place banners on each other's websites for free.'에서 작은 사업체들은 서로 웹 사이트에 무료로 배너를 게시하는 광고 교환을 통해 사업체를 홍보한다는 내용을 제시하므로, 빈칸에 들어갈 말로 가장 적절한 것은 ① '공간을 교환함'이다.

- typically ⓐ 보통, 전형적으로
- get the word out ⓥ 말을 퍼뜨리다
- charge ⓥ (요금을) 청구하다, 부과하다
- fund ⓥ 기금을 지원하다 ⓝ 기금
- commercial ⓝ 광고 ⓐ 상업적인
- afford ⓥ ~할 여유가 있다
- in turn 차례로, 결국
- gain in popularity ⓥ 인기를 얻다
- facility ⓝ 시설

구문 풀이

2행 One way to get the word out is through an advertising exchange, in which
　　　　주어　　　형용사적 용법　　　동사　　　　　　　보어(전명구)　　　　계속적 용법
advertisers place banners on each other's websites for free.

---

33 관심의 표현을 통한 동기 부여   정답률 59% | 정답 ①

다음 빈칸에 들어갈 말로 가장 적절한 것을 고르시오.

✔ care about them - 그들에 대해 신경 쓴다
② keep your words - 약속을 지킨다
③ differ from them - 그들과 다르다
④ evaluate their performance - 그들의 수행을 평가한다
⑤ communicate with their parents - 그들의 부모와 소통한다

Motivation may come from several sources.
동기 부여는 여러 원천에서 올 수 있다.

It may be the respect / I give every student, / the daily greeting I give at my classroom door, / the undivided attention when I listen to a student, / a pat on the shoulder whether the job was done well or not, / an accepting smile, / or simply "I love you" when it is most needed.
그것은 존중일 수 있다. / 내가 모든 학생에게 하는 / 내가 우리반 교실 문에서 매일 하는 인사, / 내가 학생의 말을 들을 때의 완전한 집중, / 일을 잘했든 못했든 어깨를 토닥여주는 것, / 포용적인 미소, / 혹은 "사랑해"라는 말이 가장 필요할 때 그저 그 말을 해주는 것(일 수도 있다.)

It may simply be asking how things are at home.
그것은 그저 집에 별일이 없는지를 물어보는 것일지도 모른다.

For one student considering dropping out of school, / it was a note from me after one of his frequent absences / saying that he made my day when I saw him in school.
학교를 중퇴하는 것을 고려하던 한 학생에게, / 그것은 그 학생의 잦은 결석 중 어느 한 결석 후에 쓴 나의 짧은 편지였다. / 내가 그 학생을 학교에서 보았을 때 그가 나를 매우 기쁘게 해주었다는 내용의

He came to me with the note with tears in his eyes / and thanked me.
그 학생은 눈물을 글썽이며 그 편지를 들고 내게 와서 / 고맙다고 했다.

He will graduate this year.
그 학생은 올해 졸업할 것이다.

Whatever technique is used, / the students must know that you care about them.
어떤 기법이 사용되든, / 학생들은 여러분이 그들에 대해 신경 쓴다는 것을 틀림없이 알 것이다.

But the concern must be genuine / — the students can't be fooled.
그런데 그 관심은 진심이어야 하는데 / 학생들이 속을 리가 없기 때문이다.

동기 부여는 여러 원천에서 올 수 있다. 그것은 내가 모든 학생에게 하는 존중, 교실 문에서 매일 하는 인사, 학생의 말을 들을 때의 완전한 집중, 일을 잘했든 못했든 어깨를 토닥여주는 것, 포용적인 미소, 혹은 "사랑해"라는 말이 가장 필요할 때 그저 그 말을 해주는 것일 수도 있다. 그것은 그저 집에 별일이 없는지를 물어보는 것일지도 모른다. 학교를 중퇴하는 것을 고려하던 한 학생에게, 그것은 그 학생의 잦은 결석 중 어느 한 결석 후에 그 학생을 학교에서 보니 매우 기뻤다고 쓴 나의 짧은 편지였다. 그 학생은 눈물을 글썽이며 그 편지를 들고 내게 와서 고맙다고 했다. 그 학생은 올해 졸업할 것이다. 어떤 기법이 사용되든, 학생들은 여러분이 그들에 대해 신경 쓴다는 것을 틀림없이 알 것이다. 그런데 그 관심은 진심이어야 하는데 학생들이 속을 리가 없기 때문이다.

Why? 왜 정답일까?

학생들에게 동기를 부여하는 방식은 여러 가지가 있으며, 어떤 행위이든 학생에 대한 관심(concern)을 진실로 보여줄 수 있어야 한다는 내용을 다룬 글이다. 따라서 빈칸에 들어갈 말로 가장 적절한 것은 '관심'의 의미를 담은 ① '그들에 대해 신경 쓴다'이다.

- undivided ⓐ 완전한, 전적인
- a pat on the shoulder ⓝ (격려의 의미로) 어깨를 토닥임
- accepting ⓐ 포용적인, 수용적인
- frequent ⓐ 잦은, 빈번한
- concern ⓝ 관심, 걱정
- fool ⓥ 속이다
- evaluate ⓥ 평가하다
- attention ⓝ 집중, 주의
- drop out of school ⓥ 학교를 중퇴하다
- make one's day ⓥ ~을 행복하게 만들다
- genuine ⓐ 진실한, 진짜의
- keep one's words ⓥ 약속을 지키다

구문 풀이

1행 It may be the respect [I give every student], the daily greeting [I give at
　　　　　　　　　　　　보어1　　　　　　　　　　　　　　보어2
my classroom door], the undivided attention when I listen to a student, a pat on
　　　　　　　　　　　　　　보어3
the shoulder whether the job was done well or not, an accepting smile, or simply
　　　　　　　　　　～이든 아니든　　　　　　　　　　　　보어5
"I love you" when it is most needed.
　보어6

★★★ 등급을 가르는 문제!

34 삶에 다양함을 주기   정답률 54% | 정답 ①

다음 빈칸에 들어갈 말로 가장 적절한 것을 고르시오. [3점]

☑ variety is the spice of life – 다양성은 인생의 묘미이다
② fantasy is the mirror of reality – 공상은 현실의 거울이다
③ failure teaches more than success – 실패는 성공보다 더 많은 것을 가르쳐준다
④ laziness is the mother of invention – 게으름은 발명의 어머니이다
⑤ conflict strengthens the relationship – 갈등은 관계를 강화한다

Say you normally go to a park to walk or work out.
여러분이 보통 어떤 공원에 산책이나 운동을 하러 간다고 하자.
Maybe today you should choose a different park.
어쩌면 오늘 여러분은 다른 공원을 선택해야겠다.
Why?
왜?
Well, who knows?
글쎄, 누가 알겠는가?
Maybe it's because you need the connection to the different energy / in the other park.
어쩌면 여러분이 다른 기운과 연결되는 것이 필요하기 때문일 것이다. / 다른 공원에서
Maybe you'll run into people there / that you've never met before.
어쩌면 여러분은 거기서 사람들을 만나게 될 것이다. / 여러분이 전에 만난 적이 없는
You could make a new best friend / simply by visiting a different park.
여러분은 새로운 가장 친한 친구를 사귈 수 있다. / 그저 다른 공원을 방문함으로써
You never know what great things will happen to you / until you step outside the zone where you feel comfortable.
여러분은 결코 자신에게 어떤 대단한 일이 일어날지 알지 못한다. / 여러분이 편안함을 느끼는 지대 밖으로 나가기 전까지
If you're staying in your comfort zone / and you're not pushing yourself past that same old energy, / then you're not going to move forward on your path.
여러분이 안락 지대에 머무르고 있다면, / 그리고 자신을 밀어붙여 늘 똑같은 기운에서 벗어나도록 하지 않는다면, / 그러면 여러분은 자신의 진로에서 앞으로 나아가지 못할 것이다.
By forcing yourself to do something different, / you're awakening yourself on a spiritual level / and you're forcing yourself to do something / that will benefit you in the long run.
자신에게 다른 어떤 것을 하게 함으로써, / 여러분은 영적인 차원에서 자신을 깨우치고, / 여러분은 스스로 어떤 일을 하게 만들고 있다. / 결국에는 자신을 이롭게 할
As they say, variety is the spice of life.
사람들이 말하듯이, 다양성은 인생의 묘미이다.

보통 어떤 공원에 산책이나 운동을 하러 간다고 하자. 어쩌면 오늘 여러분은 다른 공원을 선택해야겠다. 왜? 글쎄, 누가 알겠는가? 어쩌면 여러분이 다른 공원에서 다른 기운과 연결되는 것이 필요하기 때문일 것이다. 어쩌면 여러분은 거기서 전에 만난 적이 없는 사람들을 만나게 될 것이다. 여러분은 그저 다른 공원을 방문함으로써 새로운 가장 친한 친구를 사귈 수 있다. 여러분은 편안함을 느끼는 지대 밖으로 나가고 나서야 비로소 자신에게 어떤 대단한 일이 일어날지 안다. 여러분이 안락 지대에 머무르고 있고, 자신을 밀어붙여 늘 똑같은 기운에서 벗어나도록 하지 않는다면, 자신의 진로에서 앞으로 나아가지 못할 것이다. 자신에게 다른 어떤 것을 하게 만듦으로써, 여러분은 영적인 차원에서 자신을 깨우치고, 결국에는 자신을 이롭게 할 어떤 일을 할 수 밖에 없다. 사람들이 말하듯이, 다양성은 인생의 묘미이다.

Why? 왜 정답일까?

항상 익숙하고 편안한 안락 지대를 벗어나 새로운 무언가를 시도할 때 깨달음이 일어나고 스스로를 이롭게 할 수 있다(By forcing yourself to do something different, you're awakening yourself on a spiritual level and you're forcing yourself to do something that will benefit you in the long run.)는 내용의 글이다. 따라서 빈칸에 들어갈 말로 가장 적절한 것은 '새롭고 다양한 것을 시도해보면 좋다'는 의미를 담은 ① '다양성은 인생의 묘미이다'이다.

● run into ⓥ ~을 우연히 만나다
● spiritual ⓐ 영적인, 정신적인
● spice ⓝ 묘미, 향신료
● invention ⓝ 발명
● strengthen ⓥ 강화하다
● force ⓥ (어쩔 수 없이) ~하게 하다
● in the long run 결국에는, 장기적으로
● laziness ⓝ 게으름
● conflict ⓝ 갈등

구문 풀이

6행 You never know what great things will happen to you until you step outside
「not[never]+A+   until+B : B하고 나서야 비로소 A하다」
the zone [where you feel comfortable].
선행사 관계부사

★★ 문제 해결 꿀~팁 ★★

▶ 많이 틀린 이유는?
글 마지막 문장에 빈칸이 나오면 보통 주제를 요약하므로, 글에서 언급되지 않은 내용은 답으로 고르지 않도록 주의한다. ②의 fantasy와 reality는 본문에서 언급된 바 없고, ③의 failure과 success 또한 글의 중심 소재가 아니다.
▶ 문제 해결 방법은?
이 글에서는 different라는 형용사가 곳곳에 등장하며 '다양한 것'을 시도하라는 주장을 펼치고 있으므로 이 형용사를 variety라는 명사로 바꾼 ①이 답으로 적절하다.

35 정보 공개에 관한 문화별 견해 차이   정답률 65% | 정답 ②

주어진 글 다음에 이어질 글의 순서로 가장 적절한 것을 고르시오. [3점]
① (A) – (C) – (B)   ☑ (B) – (A) – (C)
③ (B) – (C) – (A)   ④ (C) – (A) – (B)
⑤ (C) – (B) – (A)

Ideas about how much disclosure is appropriate / vary among cultures.
얼마나 많은 정보를 공개하는 것이 적절한지에 관한 생각은 / 문화마다 다르다.
(B) Those born in the United States / tend to be high disclosers, / even showing a willingness / to disclose information about themselves to strangers.
미국에서 태어난 사람들은 / 정보를 많이 공개하려는 경향이 있고, / 기꺼이 의향을 보이기까지 한다 / 자기 자신에 관한 정보를 낯선 이에게 공개하려는
This may explain / why Americans seem particularly easy to meet / and are good at cocktail-party conversation.
이것은 설명할 수 있다 / 왜 미국인들이 특히 만나기 편해 보이고 / 칵테일 파티에서 대화하는 데에 능숙한지를

(A) On the other hand, / Japanese tend to do little disclosing about themselves to others / except to the few people with whom they are very close.
반면에, / 일본인들은 타인에게 자신에 관한 정보를 거의 공개하지 않는 경향이 있다. / 자신과 매우 친한 소수의 사람들을 제외하고는
In general, Asians do not reach out to strangers.
일반적으로 아시아인들은 낯선 이에게 관심을 내보이지 않는다.
(C) They do, however, show great care for each other, / since they view harmony as essential to relationship improvement.
그러나 그들은 서로를 매우 배려하는 모습을 보인다. / 그들이 조화를 관계 발전에 필수적이라고 간주하기 때문에
They work hard / to prevent those they view as outsiders / from getting information they believe to be unfavorable.
그들은 열심히 노력한다. / 그들이 외부인이라고 간주하는 사람들이 (~하지) 못하게 하려고 / 자신이 불리하다고 생각하는 정보를 얻는 것을

얼마나 많은 정보를 공개하는 것이 적절한지에 관한 생각은 문화마다 다르다.
(B) 미국에서 태어난 사람들은 정보를 많이 공개하려는 경향이 있고, 자기 자신에 관한 정보를 낯선 이에게 기꺼이 공개하려는 의향을 보이기까지 한다. 이것은 왜 미국인들이 특히 만나기 편해 보이고 칵테일 파티에서 대화하는 데에 능숙한지를 설명할 수 있다.
(A) 반면에, 일본인들은 자신과 매우 친한 소수의 사람들을 제외하고는 타인에게 자신에 관한 정보를 거의 공개하지 않는 경향이 있다. 일반적으로 아시아인들은 낯선 이에게 관심을 내보이지 않는다.
(C) 그러나 그들은 조화를 관계 발전에 필수적이라고 간주하기 때문에 서로를 매우 배려하는 모습을 보인다. 그들은 자신이 불리하다고 생각하는 정보를 외부인이라고 간주되는 사람들이 얻지 못하게 하려고 열심히 노력한다.

Why? 왜 정답일까?

정보 공개에 대한 생각이 문화마다 다르다고 언급한 주어진 글 뒤에는, 미국인들의 예를 들기 시작하는 (B), 일본인의 예를 대조하는 (A), 일본인들이 자신에 대한 정보를 공개하려 하지는 않지만 조화를 중시하기 때문에 서로 배려를 하기 위해 애쓴다는 내용을 덧붙이는 (C)가 차례로 이어져야 한다. 따라서 글의 순서로 가장 적절한 것은 ② '(B) – (A) – (C)'이다.

● appropriate ⓐ 적절한   ● vary ⓥ 다르다
● close ⓐ 친한, 가까운   ● reach out to ⓥ ~에게 관심을 보이다
● willingness ⓝ 기꺼이 ~하려는 마음   ● essential ⓐ 필수적인, 본질적인
● unfavorable ⓐ 불리한, 호의적이 아닌

구문 풀이

13행 They work hard to prevent those [they view as outsiders] from getting
「prevent+A+   from+동명사 : A가 ~하지 못하게 하다」
information [they believe to be unfavorable].
선행사

36 인간 창조에 관한 신화   정답률 60% | 정답 ⑤

주어진 글 다음에 이어질 글의 순서로 가장 적절한 것을 고르시오.
① (A) – (C) – (B)   ② (B) – (A) – (C)
③ (B) – (C) – (A)   ④ (C) – (A) – (B)
☑ (C) – (B) – (A)

A god called Moinee was defeated / by a rival god called Dromerdeener / in a terrible battle up in the stars.
Moinee라는 신이 패배했다. / Dromerdeener이라는 이름의 라이벌 신에게 / 하늘 위 별에서 벌어진 끔찍한 전투에서
Moinee fell out of the stars down to Tasmania to die.
Moinee는 별에서 Tasmania로 떨어져 죽었다.
(C) Before he died, / he wanted to give a last blessing to his final resting place, / so he decided to create humans.
그가 죽기 전에 / 그는 최후의 안식처에 마지막 축복을 해주고 싶어서 / 인간을 창조하기로 결심했다.
But he was in such a hurry, / knowing he was dying, / that he forgot to give them knees; / and he absent-mindedly gave them big tails like kangaroos, / which meant they couldn't sit down.
그러나 그는 매우 서둘렀기에 / 자신이 죽어가고 있다는 것을 알고 / 그들에게 무릎을 만들어 주는 것을 잊었고, / 그는 아무 생각 없이 캥거루처럼 큰 꼬리를 만들어 주었는데, / 그것은 그들이 앉을 수 없다는 것을 의미했다.
(B) Then he died.
그리고 나서 그는 죽었다.
The people hated having kangaroo tails and no knees, / and they cried out to the heavens for help.
사람들은 캥거루 같은 꼬리가 있고 무릎이 없는 것을 싫어했고, / 그들은 도움을 얻고자 하늘에 외쳤다.
Dromerdeener heard their cry / and came down to Tasmania to see what the matter was.
Dromerdeener는 그들의 외침을 듣고 / 무엇이 문제인지 보려고 Tasmania로 내려왔다.
(A) He took pity on the people, / gave them bendable knees / and cut off their inconvenient kangaroo tails / so they could all sit down at last.
그는 사람들을 불쌍히 여겨서 / 그들에게 구부러지는 무릎을 만들어 주고, / 그들의 불편한 캥거루 꼬리를 잘라냈다. / 마침내 그들이 모두 앉을 수 있도록
Then they lived happily ever after.
그 후 사람들은 영원히 행복하게 살았다.

Moinee라는 신이 하늘 위 별에서 벌어진 끔찍한 전투에서 Dromerdeener이라는 이름의 라이벌 신에게 패배했다. Moinee는 별에서 Tasmania로 떨어져 죽었다.
(C) 죽기 전에 그는 최후의 안식처에 마지막 축복을 해주고 싶어서 인간을 창조하기로 결심했다. 그러나 그는 자신이 죽어가고 있다는 것을 알고 매우 서둘렀기에 그들에게 무릎을 만들어 주는 것을 잊고, 아무 생각 없이 캥거루처럼 큰 꼬리를 만들어 주었는데, 그것은 그들이 앉을 수 없다는 것을 의미했다.
(B) 그리고 나서 그는 죽었다. 사람들은 캥거루 같은 꼬리가 있고 무릎이 없는 것을 싫어했고, 도움을 얻고자 하늘에 외쳤다. Dromerdeener는 그들의 외침을 듣고 무엇이 문제인지 보려고 Tasmania로 내려왔다.
(A) 그는 사람들을 불쌍히 여겨서 그들에게 구부러지는 무릎을 만들어 주고, 마침내 그들이 모두 앉을 수 있도록 불편한 캥거루 꼬리를 잘라냈다. 그 후 사람들은 영원히 행복하게 살았다.

Why? 왜 정답일까?

Moinee라는 신이 Dromerdeener와의 싸움에서 패배해서 죽게 되었다는 내용의 주어진 글 뒤에는, Moinee가 죽기 전에 서둘러 인간을 만들었는데 무릎이 없고 대신에 꼬리가 달린 형태였다는 내용의 (C), 그의 사후 사람들이 불편함을 해결하고자 하늘에 도움을 요청했다는 내용의 (B), Dromerdeener가 이 외침을 듣고 내려와 꼬리를 없애고 무릎을 만들어 주었다는 내용의 (A)가 차례로 이어져야 한다. 따라서 글의 순서로 가장 적절한 것은 ⑤ '(C) – (B) – (A)'이다.

- **defeat** ⓥ 패배시키다
- **fall out of** ~에서 떨어지다
- **bendable** ⓐ 구부릴 수 있는
- **blessing** ⓝ 축복
- **absent-mindedly** ⓐⓓ 아무 생각 없이, 멍하니
- **take pity on** ⓥ ~을 불쌍히 여기다
- **inconvenient** ⓐ 불편한
- **resting place** ⓝ 안식처

구문 풀이

12행 But he was in such a hurry, knowing he was dying, that he forgot to give 「such ~ that … : 너무 ~해서 …하다」 ~할 것을 잊다
them knees; and he absent-mindedly gave them big tails like kangaroos, which 선행사 계속적 용법
meant they couldn't sit down.

★★★ 등급을 가르는 문제!

37 Amondawa 부족의 독특한 시간 관념　　　정답률 38% | 정답 ④

글의 흐름으로 보아, 주어진 문장이 들어가기에 가장 적절한 곳을 고르시오. [3점]

There are some cultures / that can be referred to as "people who live outside of time."
어떤 문화가 있다. / '시간 밖에서 사는 사람들'이라고 부를 수 있는
The Amondawa tribe, living in Brazil, / does not have a concept of time / that can be measured or counted.
브라질에 사는 Amondawa 부족에게는 / 시간이라는 개념이 없다. / 측정되거나 셀 수 있는
① Rather they live in a world of serial events, / rather than seeing events as being rooted in time.
오히려 그들은 연속되는 사건의 세상에서 산다. / 사건이 시간에 뿌리를 두고 있다고 간주하기보다는
② Researchers also found that no one had an age.
연구자들은 또한 나이가 있는 사람이 아무도 없다는 것을 알아냈다.
③ Instead, they change their names / to reflect their stage of life and position within their society, / so a little child will give up their name to a newborn sibling / and take on a new one.
대신에 그들은 이름을 바꾼다. / 자신들의 생애 단계와 사회 내 위치를 반영하기 위해 / 그래서 어린아이는 자신의 이름을 갓 태어난 형제자매에게 넘겨주고 / 새로운 이름을 갖는다.
✔ In the U.S. we have so many metaphors for time and its passing / that we think of time as "a thing," / that is "the weekend is almost gone," or "I haven't got the time."
미국에는 시간과 시간의 흐름에 관한 매우 많은 은유가 있어서 / 우리는 시간을 '물건'으로 간주하는데, / 즉 "주말이 거의 다 지나갔다."라거나 "나는 시간이 없다."라는 식이다.
We think such statements are objective, / but they aren't.
우리는 그러한 말들이 객관적이라고 생각하지만, / 그것들은 그렇지 않다.
⑤ We create these metaphors, / but the Amondawa don't talk or think in metaphors for time.
우리는 이런 은유를 만들어 내지만, / Amondawa 사람들은 시간을 은유적으로 말하거나 생각하지 않는다.

'시간 밖에서 사는 사람들'이라고 부를 수 있는 어떤 문화가 있다. 브라질에 사는 Amondawa 부족에게는 측정되거나 셀 수 있는 시간이라는 개념이 없다. ① 오히려 그들은 사건이 시간에 뿌리를 두고 있다고 간주하기보다는 연속되는 사건의 세상에서 산다. ② 연구자들은 또한 나이가 있는 사람이 아무도 없다는 것을 알아냈다. ③ 대신에 그들은 자신들의 생애 단계와 사회 내 위치를 반영하기 위해 이름을 바꾸어서 어린아이는 자신의 이름을 갓 태어난 형제자매에게 넘겨주고 새로운 이름을 갖는다. ④ 미국에는 시간과 시간의 흐름에 관한 매우 많은 은유가 있어서 우리는 시간을 '물건'으로 간주하는데, 즉 "주말이 거의 다 지나갔다."라거나 "나는 시간이 없다."라는 식이다. 우리는 그러한 말들이 객관적이라고 생각하지만, 그렇지 않다. ⑤ 우리는 이런 은유를 만들어 내지만, Amondawa 사람들은 시간을 은유적으로 말하거나 생각하지 않는다.

Why? 왜 정답일까?

Amondawa 부족의 독특한 시간 관념을 소개한 글이다. ④ 앞에서는 이들이 사건을 시간별로 파악하기보다는 그저 연속된 사건 속에 살며 나이도 세지 않는다는 내용을 제시한다. 반면 주어진 문장은 미국의 예를 들어 시간과 시간의 흐름을 물건처럼 느끼게 하는 많은 은유가 있다고 언급하는데, ④ 뒤에서는 '이러한 은유적인 말들'이 객관적으로 보이더라도 Amondawa 부족의 관점에는 적용될 수 없다는 이야기임을 덧붙이고 있다. 따라서 주어진 문장이 들어가기에 가장 적절한 곳은 ④이다.

- **passing** ⓝ (시간의) 흐름, 경과
- **refer to A as B** ⓥ A를 B라고 부른다, 언급하다
- **measure** ⓥ 측정하다
- **reflect** ⓥ 반영하다
- **objective** ⓐ 객관적인
- **think of A as B** ⓥ A를 B라고 간주하다
- **tribe** ⓝ 부족
- **rooted in** ~에 뿌리를 둔
- **statement** ⓝ 말, 진술

구문 풀이

1행 In the U.S. we have so many metaphors for time and its passing that we 「so ~ that … : 너무 ~해서 …하다」
think of time as "a thing," that is "the weekend is almost gone," or "I haven't got 「think of A as B : A를 B라고 간주하다」 └→ 즉, 다시 말해
the time."

★★ 문제 해결 꿀~팁 ★★

▶ 많이 틀린 이유는?
⑤의 these metaphors가 주어진 문장의 따옴표 구절과 이어진다고 보면 ⑤을 답으로 고르기 쉽지만, 앞에 나오는 such statements 또한 가리키는 바가 불분명함을 염두에 두어야 한다.
▶ 문제 해결 방법은?
④ 뒤의 such statements가 가리키는 바에 주목해야 한다. 앞에 '진술'로 받을만한 말이 따로 나오지 않았는데 바로 '이러한 진술'이라는 언급을 이어가는 것은 부적절하며, 마침 주어진 문장이 따옴표로 다양한 구절을 제시하고 있는 것으로 볼 때, such statement 앞에 주어진 문장이 나와야 함을 알 수 있다.

★★★ 등급을 가르는 문제!

38 각종 동식물에 대한 태도 차이　　　정답률 39% | 정답 ⑤

글의 흐름으로 보아, 주어진 문장이 들어가기에 가장 적절한 곳을 고르시오.

The natural world provides a rich source of symbols / used in art and literature.
자연계는 상징의 풍부한 원천을 제공한다. / 예술과 문학에서 사용되는
① Plants and animals are central / to mythology, dance, song, poetry, rituals, festivals, and holidays around the world.
식물과 동물은 중심에 있다. / 전 세계의 신화, 춤, 노래, 시, 의식, 축제 그리고 기념일의
② Different cultures can exhibit opposite attitudes / toward a given species.
각기 다른 문화는 상반되는 태도를 보일 수 있다. / 주어진 종에 대해
③ Snakes, for example, / are honored by some cultures / and hated by others.
예를 들어, 뱀은 / 일부 문화에서는 존경의 대상이고 / 다른 문화에서는 증오를 받는다.
④ Rats are considered pests in much of Europe and North America / and greatly respected in some parts of India.
쥐는 유럽과 북아메리카의 많은 지역에서 유해 동물로 여겨지고, / 인도의 일부 지역에서는 매우 중시된다.
✔ Of course, within cultures / individual attitudes can vary dramatically.
물론 (같은) 문화 내에서 / 개인의 태도는 극적으로 다를 수 있다.
For instance, in Britain many people dislike rodents, / and yet there are several associations / devoted to breeding them, / including the National Mouse Club and the National Fancy Rat Club.
예를 들어, 영국에서는 많은 사람들이 설치류를 싫어하지만, / 여러 협회들이 있다. / 그들을 기르는 데 전념하는 / National Mouse Club과 National Fancy Rat Club을 포함해서

자연계는 예술과 문학에서 사용되는 상징의 풍부한 원천을 제공한다. ① 식물과 동물은 전 세계의 신화, 춤, 노래, 시, 의식, 축제 그리고 기념일의 중심에 있다. ② 각기 다른 문화는 주어진 종에 대해 상반되는 태도를 보일 수 있다. ③ 예를 들어, 뱀은 일부 문화에서는 존경의 대상이고 다른 문화에서는 증오를 받는다. ④ 쥐는 유럽과 북아메리카의 많은 지역에서 유해 동물로 여겨지고, 인도의 일부 지역에서는 매우 중시된다. ⑤ 물론 (같은) 문화 내에서 개인의 태도는 극적으로 다를 수 있다. 예를 들어, 영국에서는 많은 사람들이 설치류를 싫어하지만, National Mouse Club과 National Fancy Rat Club을 포함해서 설치류를 기르는 데 전념하는 여러 협회들이 있다.

Why? 왜 정답일까?

각종 자연물에 대한 태도 차이를 설명한 글로, ⑤ 앞의 문장에서는 쥐가 유럽과 북미 등지에서는 유해한 동물로, 인도 일부 지역에서는 매우 귀중한 동물로 여겨진다는 점을 대조하여 설명하고 있다. 주어진 문장은 이에 추가적으로 같은 문화권 내에서 개인의 태도 또한 다를 수 있다는 점을 언급하고, ⑤ 뒤에서는 영국의 예를 들어 많은 사람들이 설치류를 싫어하지만 설치류를 기르기 위해 전념하는 여러 협회가 또한 있다는 내용을 부연한다. 따라서 주어진 문장이 들어가기에 가장 적절한 곳은 ⑤이다.

- **dramatically** ⓐⓓ 극적으로
- **mythology** ⓝ 신화
- **exhibit** ⓥ 보여주다, 전시하다
- **given** ⓐ (이미) 정해진, 특정한
- **association** ⓝ 협회, 연관
- **literature** ⓝ 문학
- **ritual** ⓝ 의식
- **opposite** ⓐ 정반대의
- **honor** ⓥ 존경하다
- **breed** ⓥ 기르다, 낳다

구문 풀이

8행 Rats are considered pests in much of Europe and North America and (are) 「A + be considered + B : A가 B로 간주되다」 생략
greatly respected in some parts of India.

★★ 문제 해결 꿀~팁 ★★

▶ 많이 틀린 이유는?
② 앞의 두 문장은 자연계의 대상들이 세계 각지의 예술과 문학에 핵심적인 역할을 했다는 넓은 내용을, ② 뒤의 문장은 특히 한 자연물에 대해서도 문화권마다 시각이 다르다는 좁은 내용을 제시한다. ③ 뒤의 문장은 이 좁혀진 내용에 대한 예를 제시하므로, ②와 ③ 앞뒤는 흐름이 자연스럽게 이어진다.
▶ 문제 해결 방법은?
Of course로 시작하는 주어진 문장은 '물론 한 문화권 내에서도' 사람따라 반응이 다르다는 내용을 이어 가고 있다. 따라서 앞에서 각 문화권의 시각 차이에 대한 언급이 마무리되고, 한 나라 안에서도 같은 대상에 대한 서로 다른 입장이 존재한다는 예로 넘어가는 ⑤에 주어진 문장이 들어가야 한다.

39 관계 맺음의 수적 한계　　　정답률 66% | 정답 ③

다음 글에서 전체 흐름과 관계 없는 문장은?

Paying attention to some people and not others / doesn't mean / you're being dismissive or arrogant.
일부 사람들에게 주의를 기울이고 다른 사람들에게 그렇게 하지 않는 것이 / 의미하지는 않는다. / 여러분이 남을 무시하고 있다거나 거만하게 굴고 있다는 것을
① It just reflects a hard fact: / there are limits on the number of people / we can possibly pay attention to or develop a relationship with.
그것은 단지 명백한 사실을 반영할 뿐인데, / 사람의 수에 한계가 있다는 것이다. / 우리가 아마 주의를 기울이거나 관계를 발전시킬 수 있는
② Some scientists even believe / that the number of people with / whom we can continue stable social relationships / might be limited naturally by our brains.
일부 과학자는 심지어 믿는다. / 사람의 수가 / 우리가 안정된 사회적 관계를 지속할 수 있는 / 우리의 뇌에 의해 자연스럽게 제한되는 것일지도 모른다고
✔ The more people you know of different backgrounds, / the more colorful your life becomes.
여러분이 다른 배경의 사람들을 더 많이 알수록, / 여러분의 삶은 더 다채로워진다.
④ Professor Robin Dunbar has explained / that our minds are only really capable of forming meaningful relationships / with a maximum of about a hundred and fifty people.
Robin Dunbar 교수는 설명했다. / 우리의 마음은 의미 있는 관계를 진정 형성할 수 있을 뿐이라고 / 최대 약 150명의 사람과
⑤ Whether that's true or not, / it's safe to assume / that we can't be real friends with everyone.
그것이 사실이든 아니든, / 가정하는 것이 안전하다. / 우리가 모든 사람과 진정한 친구가 될 수 있는 것은 아니라고

일부 사람들에게 주의를 기울이고 다른 사람들에게 그렇게 하지 않는 것이 여러분이 남을 무시하고 있다거나 거만하게 굴고 있다는 것을 의미하지는 않는다. ① 그것은 단지 명백한 사실을 반영할 뿐인데, 우리가 아마 주의를 기울이거나 관계를 발전시킬 수 있는 사람의 수에 한계가 있다는 것이다. ② 일부 과학자는 우리가 안정된 사회적 관계를 지속할 수 있는 사람의 수가 우리의 뇌에 의해 자연스럽게 제한되는 것일지도 모른다고까지 믿는다. ③ 여러분이 다른 배경의 사람들을 더 많이 알수록, 여러분의 삶은 더 다채로워진다. ④ Robin Dunbar 교수는 우리의 마음은 최대 약 150명의 사람과 의미 있는 관계를 진정 형성할 수 있을 뿐이라고 설명했다. ⑤ 그것이 사실이든 아니든, 우리가 모든 사람과 진정한 친구가 될 수 있는 것은 아니라고 가정하는 것이 안전하다.

Why? 왜 정답일까?

사람은 타인과 무한정 관계를 맺어갈 수 있는 것이 아니며, 유의미한 관계를 맺을 수 있는 수에 제한이 있다는 내용을 다룬 글이다. 하지만 ③은 우리가 다양한 배경을 지닌 사람들과 더 많이 관계를 맺을수록 좋다는 내용을 언급하고 있어 주제에서 벗어나 있다. 따라서 전체 흐름과 관계 없는 문장은 ③이다.

- **pay attention to** ⓥ ~에 주의를 기울이다
- **hard fact** 명백한 사실
- **social relationship** 사회적 관계
- **background** ⓝ 배경
- **maximum** ⓝ 최대
- **reflect** ⓥ 반영하다
- **stable** ⓐ 안정적인
- **limited** ⓐ 제한된
- **meaningful** ⓐ 유의미한
- **assume** ⓥ 가정하다

구문 풀이

4행 Some scientists even believe that the number of people [with whom we can continue stable social relationships] might be limited naturally by our brains.

---

40 사람들이 운전하는 동안 비협조적인 이유

정답률 59% | 정답 ①

다음 글의 내용을 한 문장으로 요약하고자 한다. 빈칸 (A), (B)에 들어갈 말로 가장 적절한 것은?

	(A)	(B)		(A)	(B)
✓	uncooperative 비협조적인	little 거의 없는	②	careful 주의하는	direct 직접적인
③	confident 자신이 있는	regular 정기적인	④	uncooperative 비협조적인	direct 직접적인
⑤	careful 주의하는	little 거의 없는			

While there are many evolutionary or cultural reasons for cooperation, / the eyes are one of the most important means of cooperation, / and eye contact may be the most powerful human force / we lose in traffic.
협동을 하는 진화적이거나 문화적인 많은 이유가 있지만, / 눈은 가장 중요한 협동 수단 중 하나이고, / 눈 맞춤은 가장 강력한 인간의 힘일지도 모른다. / 우리가 차량 운행 중에 잃고 마는

It is, arguably, the reason / why humans, normally a quite cooperative species, / can become so noncooperative on the road.
그것은 이유라고 주장할 수 있다. / 보통은 꽤 협동적인 종인 인간이 / 도로에서 그렇게 비협조적이 될 수 있는

Most of the time we are moving too fast / — we begin to lose the ability / to keep eye contact around 20 miles per hour — / or it is not safe to look.
대부분의 시간에 우리는 너무 빨리 움직이고 있어서, / 우리는 능력을 잃기 시작하거나, / 시속 20마일 정도에서 시선을 마주치는 / 혹은 (서로를) 보는 것이 안전하지 않다.

Maybe our view is blocked.
어쩌면 우리의 시야가 차단되어 있을 수도 있다.

Often other drivers are wearing sunglasses, / or their car may have tinted windows.
흔히 다른 운전자들이 선글라스를 끼고 있기도 하고, / 혹은 그들의 차에는 색이 옅게 들어가 있는 창문이 있을 수 있다.

(And do you really want to make eye contact with those drivers?)
(그리고 당신은 정말로 그러한 운전자들과 시선을 마주치고 싶은가?)

Sometimes we make eye contact through the rearview mirror, / but it feels weak, not quite believable at first, / as it is not "face-to-face."
때로는 우리는 백미러를 통해 시선을 마주치지만, / 이것은 약하게, 처음에는 별로 믿을 수 없게 느껴진다. / 이것은 '얼굴을 마주하고 있는 것'이 아니기 때문에

➡ While driving, / people become (A) uncooperative, / because they make (B) little eye contact.
운전하는 동안, / 사람들은 비협조적이 되는데 / 왜냐하면 그들이 시선을 거의 마주치지 않기 때문이다.

협동을 하는 진화적이거나 문화적인 많은 이유가 있지만, 눈은 가장 중요한 협동 수단 중 하나이고, 눈 맞춤은 우리가 차량 운행 중에 잃고 마는 가장 강력한 인간의 힘일지도 모른다. 그것은 보통은 꽤 협동적인 종인 인간이 도로에서 그렇게 비협조적이 될 수 있는 이유라고 주장할 수 있다. 대부분의 시간에 우리는 너무 빨리 움직이고 있어서, 시속 20마일 정도에서 시선을 마주치는 능력을 잃기 시작하거나, 혹은 (서로를) 보는 것이 안전하지 않다. 어쩌면 우리의 시야가 차단되어 있을 수도 있다. 흔히 다른 운전자들이 선글라스를 끼고 있기도 하고, 혹은 그들의 차 창문 색깔이 옅게 들어가 있을 수도 있다. (그리고 당신은 정말로 그러한 운전자들과 시선을 마주치고 싶은가?) 때로는 우리는 백미러를 통해 시선을 마주치지만, '얼굴을 마주하고 있는 것'이 아니기 때문에 약하게, 처음에는 별로 믿을 수 없게 느껴진다.

➡ 운전하는 동안, 사람들은 (A) 비협조적이 되는데, 왜냐하면 그들이 (B) 거의 시선을 마주치지 않기 때문이다.

Why? 왜 정답일까?

첫 두 문장에서 눈은 사람이 협동하게 하는 가장 강력한 수단 중 하나인데, 운전하는 동안 우리는 상대방과 눈을 맞추지 못하므로 더 비협조적이 되고 만다(~ **eye contact may be the most powerful human force we lose in traffic. It is, arguably, the reason why humans, normally a quite cooperative species, can become so noncooperative on the road.**)는 주제를 소개하고 있다. 따라서 요약문의 빈칸 (A), (B)에 들어갈 말로 가장 적절한 것은 ① '(A) uncooperative(비협조적인), (B) little(거의 없는)'이다.

- **evolutionary** ⓐ 진화적인
- **force** ⓝ 힘
- **quite** ⓐ 꽤, 상당히
- **noncooperative** ⓐ 비협조적인
- **rearview mirror** ⓝ 백미러
- **believable** ⓐ 믿을 수 있는
- **eye contact** 눈 맞춤
- **arguably** ⓐ 주장컨대
- **normally** ⓐ 보통
- **block** ⓥ 차단하다
- **weak** ⓐ 약한
- **confident** ⓐ 자신감 있는

구문 풀이

4행 It is, arguably, the reason [why humans, (normally a quite cooperative species), can become so noncooperative on the road].

41-42 배경 소음이 공부에 미치는 영향에 대한 논란

Many high school students study and learn inefficiently / because they insist on doing their homework / while watching TV or listening to loud music.
많은 고등학생은 비효율적으로 공부하고 학습한다. / 그들이 숙제를 하겠다고 고집하기 때문에 / TV를 보거나 시끄러운 음악을 들으면서

These same students also typically (a) interrupt their studying / with repeated phone calls, trips to the kitchen, video games, and Internet surfing.
이 학생들은 또한 보통 자신의 공부를 방해한다. / 반복적인 전화 통화, 부엌에 들르기, 비디오 게임, 인터넷 서핑으로

Ironically, / students with the greatest need to concentrate when studying / are often the ones / who surround themselves with the most distractions.
모순적이게도, / 공부할 때 집중할 필요가 가장 큰 학생들은 / 흔히 학생들이다. / 주의를 산만하게 하는 것들로 가장 많이 자신을 에워싸는

『These teenagers argue / that they can study *better* with the TV or radio (b) playing.』 **41번의 근거**
이런 십 대들은 주장한다. / 그들이 TV나 라디오를 켜 둔 채로 공부를 더 잘 할 수 있다고

Some professionals actually (c) support their position.
일부 전문가는 실제로 그들의 견해를 지지한다.

『They argue / that many teenagers can actually study productively under less-than-ideal conditions / because they've been exposed repeatedly to "background noise" / since early childhood.』 **42번의 근거**
그들은 주장한다. / 많은 십 대들이 전혀 이상적이지 않은 상황에서 실제로 생산적으로 공부할 수 있다고 / 그들이 '배경 소음'에 반복적으로 노출되어 왔기 때문에 / 어린 시절부터

These educators argue / that children have become (d) used / to the sounds of the TV, video games, and loud music.
이 교육 전문가들은 주장한다. / 아이들이 익숙해졌다고 / TV, 비디오 게임, 그리고 시끄러운 음악 소리에

They also argue / that insisting students turn off the TV or radio / when doing homework / will not necessarily improve their academic performance.
그들은 또한 주장한다. / 학생들이 TV나 라디오를 꺼야 한다고 주장하는 것이 / 숙제를 할 때 / 반드시 그들의 학업 성적을 높이는 것은 아니라고

This position is certainly not generally shared, however.
그러나 이 견해는 분명히 일반적으로 공유되는 것은 아니다.

『Many teachers and learning experts / are (e) convinced by their own experiences / that students who study in a noisy environment / often learn inefficiently.』 **41번의 근거**
많은 교사와 학습 전문가는 / 스스로의 경험으로 확신한다. / 시끄러운 환경에서 공부하는 학생들이 / 흔히 비효율적으로 학습한다는 것을

많은 고등학생은 TV를 보거나 시끄러운 음악을 들으면서 숙제를 하겠다고 고집하기 때문에 비효율적으로 공부하고 학습한다. 이 학생들은 또한 반복적인 전화 통화, 부엌에 들르기, 비디오 게임, 인터넷 서핑으로 보통 자신의 공부를 (a) 방해한다. 모순적이게도, 공부할 때 집중할 필요가 가장 큰 학생들은 흔히 주의를 산만하게 하는 것들로 가장 많이 자신을 에워싸는 학생들이다. 이런 십 대들은 TV나 라디오를 (b) 켜 둔 채로 공부를 더 잘 할 수 있다고 주장한다. 일부 전문가는 실제로 그들의 견해에 (c) 반대한다(→ 지지한다). 그들은 많은 십 대들이 어린 시절부터 '배경 소음'에 반복적으로 노출되어 왔기 때문에 전혀 이상적이지 않은 상황에서 실제로 생산적으로 공부할 수 있다고 주장한다. 이 교육 전문가들은 아이들이 TV, 비디오 게임, 그리고 시끄러운 음악 소리에 (d) 익숙해졌다고 주장한다. 그들은 또한 숙제를 할 때 학생들이 TV나 라디오를 꺼야 한다고 주장하는 것이 반드시 그들의 학업 성적을 높이는 것은 아니라고 주장한다. 그러나 이 견해는 분명히 일반적으로 공유되는 것은 아니다. 많은 교사와 학습 전문가는 시끄러운 환경에서 공부하는 학생들이 흔히 비효율적으로 학습한다는 것을 스스로의 경험으로 (e) 확신한다.

- **inefficiently** ⓐ 비효율적으로
- **interrupt** ⓥ 방해하다
- **concentrate** ⓥ 집중하다
- **distraction** ⓝ 주의를 산만하게 하는 것
- **productively** ⓐ 생산적으로
- **repeatedly** ⓐ 반복적으로
- **improve** ⓥ 높이다, 향상시키다
- **convinced** ⓐ 확신하는
- **insist on** ⓥ ~을 고집하다, 주장하다
- **ironically** ⓐ 모순적이게도
- **surround** ⓥ 에워싸다
- **professional** ⓝ 전문가 ⓐ 전문적인
- **less-than-ideal** ⓐ 결코 이상적이지 않은
- **not necessarily** 반드시 ~인 것은 아니다
- **generally** ⓐ 일반적으로

구문 풀이

19행 Many teachers and learning experts are convinced by their own experiences that students [who study in a noisy environment] often learn inefficiently.

---

41 제목 파악

정답률 70% | 정답 ②

윗글의 제목으로 가장 적절한 것은?

① Successful Students Plan Ahead – 성공하는 학생은 미리 계획한다
✓ Studying with Distractions: Is It Okay? – 주의를 산만하게 만드는 것과 함께 공부하기: 괜찮을까?
③ Smart Devices as Good Learning Tools – 좋은 학습 도구로서의 스마트 기기
④ Parents & Teachers: Partners in Education – 부모와 교사: 교육에서의 파트너
⑤ Good Habits: Hard to Form, Easy to Break – 좋은 습관: 형성하기는 어렵고 버리기는 쉽다

Why? 왜 정답일까?

학생들은 음악, TV 소리 등 각종 배경 소음이나 공부에 방해가 되는 활동들이 학습에 별 방해가 되지 않는다고 주장하지만, 실상 많은 교사들과 학습 전문가들의 경험에 따르면 이 주장은 반박될 수 있다(~ **students who study in a noisy environment often learn inefficiently.**)는 내용을 다룬 글이다. 따라서 글의 제목으로 가장 적절한 것은 ② '주의를 산만하게 만드는 것과 함께 공부하기: 괜찮을까?'이다.

42 어휘 추론   정답률 44% | 정답 ③

밑줄 친 (a)~(e) 중에서 문맥상 낱말의 쓰임이 적절하지 않은 것은? [3점]

① (a)   ② (b)   ✓③ (c)   ④ (d)   ⑤ (e)

Why? 왜 정답일까?

③이 포함된 문장 뒤에서 일부 전문가들은 십 대들이 어렸을 때부터 배경 소음이 있는 환경에 익숙해져 왔기 때문에 소음이 있어도 능률적으로 공부할 수 있다(They argue that many teenagers can actually study productively under less-than-ideal conditions because they've been exposed repeatedly to "background noise" since early childhood)고 주장한다는 내용이 나온다. 이는 전문가들이 TV나 라디오를 켜 놓고도 공부를 더 잘할 수 있다고 주장하는 십 대들을 지지 또는 옹호한 것으로 볼 수 있으므로, ③의 oppose는 support로 고쳐야 한다. 따라서 문맥상 낱말의 쓰임이 적절하지 않은 것은 ③ '(c)'이다.

★★ 문제 해결 꿀~팁 ★★

▶ 많이 틀린 이유는?
(b)의 playing은 TV나 라디오가 자동사인 play의 행위 주체임을 나타내는 현재분사로 '재생되고 있는, 켜져 있는'이라는 의미를 나타낸다. 한편 (d)의 used는 become used to(~에 익숙해지다)라는 의미의 관용 표현으로 바르게 쓰였다.

▶ 문제 해결 방법은?
상식이나 배경지식에 기초해서 풀면 (c)의 oppose가 적절해 보이지만, 바로 뒤의 'They argue ~'를 근거로 보면 Some professionals가 '배경 소음이 있어도 공부를 잘할 수 있다'는 입장을 옹호하는 이들임을 알 수 있다.

43-45 집안에 불을 낼 뻔했던 Dorothy가 부모님의 반응을 보고 배운 교훈

(A)

Dorothy was home alone.
Dorothy는 집에 혼자 있었다.
「She was busy with a school project, / and suddenly wanted to eat French fries.
그녀는 학교 프로젝트로 바빴고, / 갑자기 프렌치프라이가 먹고 싶었다.
She peeled two potatoes, / sliced them up / and put a pot with cooking oil on the stove.」 45번 ①의근거 일치
그녀는 감자 두 개를 깎아 / 그것들을 얇게 썰고 / 식용유를 넣은 냄비를 스토브에 올렸다.
Then the telephone rang.
그때 전화벨이 울렸다.
It was her best friend Samantha.
그녀의 가장 친한 친구 Samantha였다.
While chatting away on the phone, / Dorothy noticed a strange light shining from the kitchen, / and then (a) she remembered about the pot of oil on the stove!
전화로 수다를 떨다 / Dorothy는 부엌에서 비치는 이상한 불빛을 알아차렸고 / 그때 그녀는 기름을 넣은 냄비를 스토브에 올려 둔 것이 기억났다!

(C)

Dorothy dropped the phone and rushed to the kitchen.
Dorothy는 전화기를 떨어뜨리고 부엌으로 달려 갔다.
The oil was on fire.
기름에 불이 붙어 있었다.
"Chill! Take a deep breath," (c) she said to herself.
"진정해! 심호흡해."라고 그녀는 혼잣말을 했다.
What did they teach us not to do in a situation like this?
이런 상황에서 하지 말라고 배운 것은 뭐였지?
「*Don't try to put it out by throwing water on it, / because it will cause an explosion*, / she remembered.」 45번 ③의근거 일치
물을 끼얹어서 불을 끄려고 하지 마라, / 왜냐하면 그렇게 하면 폭발이 일어날 테니까 / 그녀는 기억했다.
「She picked up the pot's lid / and covered the pot with it / to put out the flames.
그녀는 냄비 뚜껑을 집어 들었고 / 그것으로 냄비를 덮어 / 불을 껐다.
In the process she burned her hands.」 45번 ④의근거 일치
그 과정에서 그녀는 손을 데었다.
Dorothy felt dizzy and sat down at the kitchen table.
Dorothy는 머리가 어질어질해서 부엌 식탁에 앉았다.

(D)

A couple of minutes later, / her parents came rushing into the house.
몇 분 후 / 그녀의 부모님이 집으로 급히 들어왔다.
Samantha had suspected / that something might be wrong / after Dorothy dropped the phone just like that, / and (d) she had phoned Dorothy's parents.
Samantha는 의심했다. / 뭔가 잘못된 것이 아닌가 하고 / Dorothy가 그렇게 전화기를 떨어뜨린 후에 / 그리고 그녀는 Dorothy의 부모님께 전화를 걸었다.
Dorothy started to cry.
Dorothy는 울기 시작했다.
Her mother hugged her tightly and looked at the wound.
그녀의 어머니는 그녀를 꼭 껴안고 상처를 봤다.
"Tell me what happened," she said.
"무슨 일이 있었는지 말해봐."라고 어머니가 말했다.
Dorothy told her, sobbing and sniffing.
Dorothy는 흐느껴 울면서 코를 훌쩍거리며 어머니에게 말했다.
"Aren't you going to yell at me?" / (e) she asked them through the tears.
"저한테 고함치지 않으실 건가요?" / 그녀는 눈물을 흘리며 그들에게 물었다.
「Her father answered with a smile, / "I also put my lid on to keep me from exploding."
그녀의 아버지는 미소를 지으며 대답했다. / "나도 (감정이) 폭발하지 않게 내 뚜껑을 덮었어."
Dorothy looked at him, relieved.」 45번 ⑤의근거 불일치
Dorothy는 안심한 채 그를 바라보았다.
"But be careful not to be so irresponsible again."
"하지만 다시는 그렇게 무책임하게 행동하지 않도록 조심해라."

(B)

A while later, after the wound had been treated, / the family sat around the kitchen table and talked.
잠시 후 그 상처가 치료된 뒤에, / 가족들은 부엌에 둘러앉아 이야기를 나누었다.

"I learned a big lesson today," Dorothy said.
"저는 오늘 큰 교훈을 배웠어요."라고 Dorothy는 말했다.
Her parents expected (b) her to say something about the fire.
그녀의 부모님은 그녀가 불에 대해 뭐라고 말할 것이라고 예상했다.
But she talked about something different.
하지만 그녀는 다른 것에 관해 말했다.
「"I have decided to use kind words more just like you."」 45번 ②의근거 일치
"저도 딱 엄마와 아빠처럼 친절한 말을 더 많이 쓰기로 했어요."
Her parents were very grateful, / because Dorothy had quite a temper.
그녀의 부모님은 매우 감사함을 느꼈다. / Dorothy는 꽤나 욱하는 성질이 있었기 때문에

(A)

Dorothy는 집에 혼자 있었다. 그녀는 학교 프로젝트로 바빴고, 갑자기 프렌치프라이가 먹고 싶었다. 그녀는 감자 두 개를 깎아 얇게 썰고 식용유를 넣은 냄비를 스토브에 올렸다. 그때 전화벨이 울렸다. 그녀의 가장 친한 친구 Samantha였다. 전화로 수다를 떨다가 Dorothy는 부엌에서 비치는 이상한 불빛을 알아차렸고 그때 (a) 그녀는 기름을 넣은 냄비를 스토브에 올려 둔 것이 기억났다!

(C)

Dorothy는 전화기를 떨어뜨리고 부엌으로 달려 갔다. 기름에 불이 붙어 있었다. "진정해! 심호흡해."라고 (c) 그녀는 혼잣말을 했다. 이런 상황에서 하지 말라고 배운 것은 뭐였지? 물을 끼얹어서 불을 끄려고 하지 마라, 왜냐하면 그렇게 하면 폭발이 일어날 테니까.라고 그녀는 기억했다. 그녀는 냄비 뚜껑을 집어 들었고 그것으로 냄비를 덮어 불을 껐다. 그 과정에서 그녀는 손을 데었다. Dorothy는 머리가 어질어질해서 부엌 식탁에 앉았다.

(D)

몇 분 후 그녀의 부모님이 집으로 급히 들어왔다. Samantha는 Dorothy가 그렇게 전화기를 떨어뜨린 후에 뭔가 잘못된 것이 아닌가 하고 의심하여 (d) 그녀는 Dorothy의 부모님께 전화를 걸었다. Dorothy는 울기 시작했다. 그녀의 어머니는 그녀를 꼭 껴안고 상처를 봤다. "무슨 일이 있었는지 말해봐."라고 어머니가 말했다. Dorothy는 흐느껴 울면서 코를 훌쩍거리며 어머니에게 말했다. "저한테 고함치지 않으실 건가요?"라고 (e) 그녀는 눈물을 흘리며 부모님에게 물었다. 그녀의 아버지는 미소를 지으면서 "나도 (감정이) 폭발하지 않게 내 뚜껑을 덮었어."라고 대답했다. Dorothy는 안심한 채 그를 바라보았다. "하지만 다시는 그렇게 무책임하게 행동하지 않도록 조심하렴."

(B)

잠시 후 그 상처를 치료한 뒤에, 가족들은 부엌 식탁에 둘러앉아 이야기를 나누었다. "저는 오늘 큰 교훈을 배웠어요."라고 Dorothy는 말했다. 그녀의 부모님은 (b) 그녀가 불이 난 것에 대해 뭐라고 말할 것이라고 예상했다. 하지만 그녀는 다른 것에 관해 말했다. "저도 딱 엄마와 아빠처럼 친절한 말을 더 많이 쓰기로 했어요." Dorothy는 꽤나 욱하는 성질이 있었기 때문에 그녀의 부모님은 매우 감사함을 느꼈다.

- busy with ~로 바쁜
- chat away ⓥ 수다 떨다
- treat ⓥ 치료하다
- have quite a temper ⓥ 성질이 보통이 아니다
- rush to ⓥ ~로 달려가다
- explosion ⓝ 폭발
- flame ⓝ 불꽃
- suspect ⓥ 의심하다
- yell at ⓥ ~에게 고함지르다
- slice up ⓥ ~을 얇게 자르다
- wound ⓝ 상처
- grateful ⓐ 감사해하는
- drop ⓥ 떨어뜨리다
- put out ⓥ 불을 끄다
- lid ⓝ 뚜껑
- dizzy ⓐ 어지러운
- tightly ⓐⓓ 꼭, 단단히
- irresponsible ⓐ 무책임한

구문 풀이

(A) 5행 While chatting away on the phone, Dorothy noticed a strange light shining
(분사구문(~하는 동안)) (지각 동사) (목적어)
from the kitchen, and then she remembered about the pot of oil on the stove!
(목적격 보어(현재분사))

(D) 2행 Samantha had suspected that something might be wrong after Dorothy
(주어1) (동사1) (접속사(~것)) (시간 접속사(~한 후에))
dropped the phone just like that, and she had phoned Dorothy's parents.
(주어2) (동사2)

43 글의 순서 파악   정답률 75% | 정답 ③

주어진 글 (A)에 이어질 내용을 순서에 맞게 배열한 것으로 가장 적절한 것은?

① (B) - (D) - (C)   ② (C) - (B) - (D)
✓③ (C) - (D) - (B)   ④ (D) - (B) - (C)
⑤ (D) - (C) - (B)

Why? 왜 정답일까?

Dorothy가 프렌치프라이를 해 먹으려고 냄비를 올렸다가 깜빡 잊고 불을 낼 위기에 처했다는 내용의 (A) 뒤에는, Dorothy가 냄비를 뚜껑으로 덮어 불을 끄다가 다쳤다는 내용의 (C), 친구의 전화를 받고 달려온 Dorothy의 부모님이 Dorothy를 나무라는 대신 잘 타일렀다는 내용의 (D), 상처를 치료한 뒤 Dorothy가 앞으로 부모님처럼 친절한 말을 많이 써야겠다는 각오를 언급했다는 내용의 (B)가 차례로 이어져야 한다. 따라서 글의 순서로 가장 적절한 것은 ③ '(C) - (D) - (B)'이다.

44 지칭 추론   정답률 69% | 정답 ④

밑줄 친 (a)~(e) 중에서 가리키는 대상이 나머지 넷과 다른 것은?

① (a)   ② (b)   ③ (c)   ✓④ (d)   ⑤ (e)

Why? 왜 정답일까?

(a), (b), (c), (e)는 Dorothy를, (d)는 같은 문장의 주어 Samantha를 가리키므로, (a)~(e) 중에서 가리키는 대상이 다른 하나는 ④ '(d)'이다.

45 세부 내용 파악   정답률 77% | 정답 ⑤

윗글의 Dorothy에 관한 내용으로 적절하지 않은 것은?

① 프렌치프라이를 만들려고 감자 두 개를 깎았다.
② 친절한 말을 더 많이 쓰겠다고 다짐했다.
③ 불붙은 기름에 물을 끼얹지 말아야 한다는 것을 기억했다.
④ 뚜껑으로 냄비를 덮어 불을 끄다가 손을 데었다.
☑ 아버지의 말을 듣고 화를 냈다.

Why? 왜 정답일까?

(D) 'Her father answered with a smile, "I also put my lid on to keep me from exploding." Dorothy looked at him, relieved.'에서 Dorothy는 '감정이 터지지 않게 뚜껑을 닫았다'는 아버지의 말을 듣고 안도했음을 알 수 있다. 따라서 내용과 일치하지 않는 것은 ⑤ '아버지의 말을 듣고 화를 냈다.'이다.

Why? 왜 오답일까?

① (A) 'She ~ suddenly wanted to eat French fries. She peeled two potatoes. ~'의 내용과 일치한다.
② (B) '"I have decided to use kind words more just like you."'의 내용과 일치한다.
③ (C) '~ Don't try to put it out by throwing water on it, because it will cause an explosion.'의 내용과 일치한다.
④ (C) 'She picked up the pot's lid and covered the pot with it to put out the flames. In the process she burned her hands.'의 내용과 일치한다.

어휘 Review Test 07

문제편 072쪽

A	B	C	D
01 화를 내다	01 faulty	01 ⓒ	01 ⑨
02 진정시키는	02 artificial	02 ⓐ	02 ⓑ
03 ~을 명심하다, 염두에 두다	03 raise	03 ⓗ	03 ⓘ
04 겨드랑이	04 matter	04 ⓓ	04 ⓘ
05 체중계, 저울	05 defeat	05 ⓚ	05 ⓔ
06 진실한, 진짜의	06 factor	06 ⓞ	06 ⓕ
07 기르다, 낳다	07 patience	07 ⓕ	07 ⓘ
08 자립, 독립	08 phrase	08 ⓘ	08 ⓜ
09 비효율적으로	09 reject	09 ⓔ	09 ⓚ
10 ~의 면에서	10 frequent	10 ⑨	10 ⓒ
11 ~을 우연히 만나다	11 injury	11 ⓜ	11 ⓒ
12 감사해하는	12 stable	12 ⓙ	12 ⓗ
13 구부릴 수 있는	13 strengthen	13 ⓘ	13 ⓐ
14 다르다	14 ritual	14 ⓝ	14 ⓓ
15 확신하는	15 evaluate	15 ⓑ	15 ⓞ
16 동기 요인, 동기를 부여 하는 것	16 physical	16 ⓢ	16 ⓡ
17 일상	17 concern	17 ⓟ	17 ⓟ
18 갈등	18 undivided	18 ⓡ	18 ⓢ
19 협회, 연관	19 in the long run	19 ⓠ	19 ⓘ
20 가정하다	20 inform	20 ⓘ	20 ⓠ

• 정답 •

01 ④ 02 ② 03 ⑤ 04 ④ 05 ① 06 ① 07 ③ 08 ④ 09 ③ 10 ④ 11 ② 12 ③ 13 ② 14 ⑤ 15 ④ 16 ① 17 ③ 18 ① 19 ② 20 ① 21 ④ 22 ⑤ 23 ③ 24 ① 25 ③ 26 ④ 27 ⑤ 28 ④ 29 ④ 30 ⑤ 31 ① 32 ⑤ 33 ② 34 ⑤ 35 ④ 36 ② 37 ③ 38 ② 39 ④ 40 ② 41 ④ 42 ⑤ 43 ④ 44 ⑤ 45 ③

★ 표기된 문항은 [등급을 가르는 문제]에 해당하는 문항입니다.

01 사물함 교체 안내

정답률 89% | 정답 ④

다음을 듣고, 남자가 하는 말의 목적으로 가장 적절한 것을 고르시오.

① 파손된 사물함 신고 절차를 안내하려고
② 사물함에 이름표를 부착할 것을 독려하려고
③ 사물함을 반드시 잠그고 다녀야 함을 강조하려고
☑ 사물함 교체를 위해 사물함을 비울 것을 당부하려고
⑤ 사물함 사용에 대한 학생 설문 조사 참여를 요청하려고

M : Hello, students.
안녕하세요, 학생 여러분.
This is your vice principal Mike Westwood.
저는 교감인 Mike Westwood입니다.
I have an important announcement today.
오늘 중요한 안내 사항이 있습니다.
As the student lockers are getting old, we've been receiving complaints from many of you.
학생 사물함이 노후화되어, 우리는 여러분 중 다수로부터 불만을 접수해 왔습니다.
So we've decided to replace the lockers over the weekend.
그래서 우리는 주말 동안 사물함을 교체하기로 결정했습니다.
We ask that you empty your lockers and leave them open by this Friday, March 22.
우리는 여러분이 이번 주 금요일인 3월 22일까지 사물함을 비우고 그것들을 열어두기를 요청합니다.
Make sure to take all the items from your lockers and leave nothing behind.
꼭 사물함에서 모든 물품들을 챙겨가고 아무것도 남겨두지 않도록 하세요.
Any items that are not removed will be thrown away.
치우지 않은 물건들은 버려질 것입니다.
Thank you for your cooperation.
여러분의 협조에 고맙습니다.

Why? 왜 정답일까?

'So we've decided to replace the lockers over the weekend. We ask that you empty your lockers and leave them open by this Friday, March 22.'에서 주말 동안 사물함을 교체하기로 결정되었으므로 이번 금요일까지 사물함을 비우고 문을 연 채로 두기를 요청한다는 내용이 나오므로, 남자가 하는 말의 목적으로 가장 적절한 것은 ④ '사물함 교체를 위해 사물함을 비울 것을 당부하려고'이다.

- **vice principal** 교감
- **decide** ⓥ 결정하다
- **leave behind** ~을 두고 가다
- **throw away** 버리다
- **complaint** ⓝ 불평, 불만
- **empty** ⓥ 비우다
- **remove** ⓥ 치우다, 제거하다

02 서점 의자에 대한 의견 나누기

정답률 92% | 정답 ②

대화를 듣고, 여자의 의견으로 가장 적절한 것을 고르시오.

① 음식물을 들고 서점에 들어가면 안 된다.
☑ 서점에 의자를 비치하면 매출에 도움이 된다.
③ 서점은 책 외에 다양한 품목을 판매해야 한다.
④ 서점은 고객들에게 추천 도서 목록을 제공해야 한다.
⑤ 온라인 서점에서 책을 구매하는 것이 더 경제적이다.

W : Paul, what did you do on the weekend?
Paul, 주말에 뭐 했어?
M : I went to the new bookstore downtown. Have you been there?
시내에 새로 생긴 서점에 갔었어. 너 거기 가봤어?
W : Yes. They put lots of cozy chairs in the bookstore. I like that.
응. 서점에 안락한 의자가 많이 있던데. 마음에 들더라.
M : Actually, I wonder why they did that.
사실, 난 왜 그랬는지 궁금해.
W : I think it helps the bookstore sell more.
난 그게 서점이 장사가 더 잘되게 도와줄 거라고 생각하는데.
M : Really? What if people just read books sitting on the chairs without buying them?
정말? 만일 사람들이 책을 사지는 않고 의자에 앉아서 그냥 읽기만 하면?
W : I heard that the longer people stay, the more they're likely to buy.
내가 듣기론 사람들이 더 오래 있을수록, 살 가능성이 더 높대.
M : That makes sense.
일리가 있네.
W : More chairs can attract more customers and the sales will go up.
의자가 더 많이 있으면 더 많은 손님을 끌어모을 수 있고 매출이 올라갈 거야.
M : You're right.
네 말이 맞아.

Why? 왜 정답일까?

남자가 시내에 새로 생긴 서점에 편안한 의자가 왜 많은지 모르겠다고 말하자, 여자는 그렇게 하면 장사에 도움이 될 것(I think it helps the bookstore sell more.)이라고 말하며 그 구체적인 이유를 설명하고 있다. 따라서 여자의 의견으로 가장 적절한 것은 ② '서점에 의자를 비치하면 매출에 도움이 된다.'이다.

- **bookstore** Ⓝ 책방, 서점
- **cozy** Ⓐ 안락한, 편안한, 아늑한
- **sell** Ⓥ 팔다, 팔리다
- **attract** Ⓥ 끌어들이다, 끌어모으다
- **go up** (가격 등이) 오르다
- **downtown** ⓐⓓ 시내에
- **actually** ⓐⓓ 사실, 실제로
- **wonder** Ⓥ 궁금하다
- **customer** Ⓝ 손님, 고객

---

03 모자 가게 주인과 손님의 대화 정답률 84% | 정답 ⑤

대화를 듣고, 두 사람의 관계를 가장 잘 나타낸 것을 고르시오.

① 미용사 - 고객
② 화방 점원 - 화가
③ 미술관장 - 방문객
④ 패션 디자이너 - 모델
☑ 모자 가게 주인 - 손님

M : Hello, Ally! Long time no see.
　안녕하세요, Ally! 오랜만이네요.
W : Hi, Robert. It's been a long time since I came to your store.
　안녕하세요, Robert. 당신의 가게에 방문한 후로 오랜 시간이 지났네요.
M : You must have been busy.
　바빴나봐요.
W : Yeah. Did I tell you that I had to prepare for an exhibition?
　네. 제가 전시회를 준비해야 한다고 말씀 드렸나요?
M : Oh, yeah. I remember. How did it go?
　오, 네. 기억나요. 어떻게 되었나요?
W : It went well. It was finally over last week.
　잘 되었어요. 그것은 지난주에 마침내 끝났어요.
M : Good. So what kind of hat are you looking for today?
　좋네요. 그럼 오늘은 어떤 종류의 모자를 찾고 계신가요?
W : Actually I've changed my hair style, so I'm not sure which hat will suit me.
　사실 저는 머리 스타일을 바꿔서, 어떤 모자가 제게 어울릴지 확신이 들지 않아요.
M : Oh, you cut your hair short! Why don't you try this hat? It goes well with short hair.
　오, 당신은 머리를 짧게 자르셨군요! 이 모자를 써 보시는 게 어때요? 그것은 짧은 머리와 잘 어울려요.
W : Let me try. [Pause] I love it!
　써 볼게요. [잠시 멈춤] 마음에 들어요!
M : It looks great on you.
　당신에게 근사해 보여요.
W : Thanks. I'll take it.
　고맙습니다. 그걸 살게요.

Why? 왜 정답일까?

'So what kind of hat are you looking for today?', 'Why don't you try this hat?'에서 남자가 모자 가게 주인임을, 'It's been a long time since I came to your store.', 'I'm not sure which hat will suit me.', 'Let me try.'에서 여자가 손님임을 알 수 있으므로, 두 사람의 관계로 가장 적절한 것은 ⑤ '모자 가게 주인 - 손님'이다.

- **long time no see.** 오랜만이에요.
- **suit** Ⓥ 어울리다(= go well with)
- **prepare for** ~을 준비하다
- **go well with** ~와 잘 어울리다

---

04 벼룩시장에서 찍은 사진에 대해 이야기하기 정답률 86% | 정답 ④

대화를 듣고, 그림에서 대화의 내용과 일치하지 <u>않는</u> 것을 고르시오.

W : Harry, have a look at this picture. It's from the flea market yesterday.
　Harry, 이 사진 좀 봐. 어제 벼룩시장에서 찍은 거야.
M : Wow! 「There's a heart-shaped balloon in the air.」 ①의 근거 일치
　우와! 공중에 하트 모양 풍선이 있네.
W : Yeah. 「Look at the man playing the guitar on the left.」 ②의 근거 일치 He's selling old guitars.
　그래. 왼쪽에 기타 연주하고 있는 남자를 봐. 그는 낡은 기타를 팔고 있어.
M : Interesting. This boy must be your brother Kevin. 「He's playing with a yoyo!」 ③의 근거 일치
　흥미로운데. 이 남자애는 네 동생인 Kevin이구나. 요요를 갖고 놀고 있네!
W : Right. He bought it there.
　맞아. 저기서 그걸 샀어.
M : I see. 「Oh, you're wearing a hat with flowers.」 ④의 근거 불일치 It's pretty.
　그렇구나. 아, 너는 꽃이 달린 모자를 쓰고 있네. 모자 예쁘다.
W : Thanks. I got it there for just one dollar.
　고마워. 저기서 단 1달러에 그걸 샀어.
M : Great. You're eating ice cream. 「Did you buy it from the ice cream cart on the right?」 ⑤의 근거 일치
　훌륭한데. 넌 아이스크림을 먹고 있네. 오른쪽에 있는 아이스크림 수레에서 산 거야?
W : Yes. It was delicious.
　응. 맛있었어.
M : It looks like you had a good time there.
　거기서 즐거운 시간을 보낸 것 같네.

Why? 왜 정답일까?

대화에서 남자는 여자가 꽃이 달린 모자를 쓰고 있다(Oh, you're wearing a hat with flowers.)고

말하는데, 그림에 따르면 여자는 리본이 달린 모자를 쓰고 있다. 따라서 그림에서 대화의 내용과 일치하지 않는 것은 ④이다.

- **flea market** 벼룩시장
- **cart** Ⓝ 수레

---

05 영화 동아리 가입 정답률 55% | 정답 ①

대화를 듣고, 남자가 여자를 위해 할 일로 가장 적절한 것을 고르시오.

☑ 동아리 안내 책자 가져다주기
② 동아리 모임 장소 예약하기
③ 동아리 방에 함께 가기
④ 동아리 모임 일정 짜기
⑤ 동아리 가입 신청서 대신 제출하기

W : What are you doing, Sam?
　Sam, 뭐 하고 있어?
M : I'm filling out an application to join the school movie club.
　학교 영화 동아리에 가입하려고 신청서를 작성하고 있어.
W : Really? I'm also interested in that club.
　정말? 나도 그 동아리에 관심이 있어.
M : Let's join together then.
　그럼 같이 가입하자.
W : I'd love to, but I already belong to the science club.
　그러고 싶은데, 이미 과학 동아리에 들었어.
M : You can join both.
　둘 다 가입할 수 있어.
W : You're right. I'll have to check the movie club's meeting schedule first, though.
　네 말이 맞아. 하지만 동아리 모임 스케줄을 먼저 체크해봐야 해.
M : Then I'll pick up the movie club's brochure for you from the club room later.
　그럼 나중에 내가 동아리 방에서 영화 동아리 안내 책자를 가지고 올게.
W : That'll be great. Thanks.
　그러면 정말 좋겠다. 고마워.
M : No problem. I'll have to go submit this application form anyway.
　고맙기는. 아무튼 난 이 신청서를 내러 가야겠어.

Why? 왜 정답일까?

여자가 영화 동아리에 관심을 보이자 남자는 함께 가입할 것을 권유하는데, 여자는 이미 영화 동아리에 들어 있어서 모임 일정이 어떻게 되는지를 먼저 체크해야 한다고 답한다. 이에 남자는 동아리 방에서 책자를 가져다주겠다(Then I'll pick up the movie club's brochure for you from the club room later.)고 제안하므로, 남자가 여자를 위해 할 일로 가장 적절한 것은 ① '동아리 안내 책자 가져다주기'이다.

- **fill out** (양식 등을) 작성하다, 기입하다
- **belong to** ~에 속하다
- **brochure** Ⓝ 안내 책자
- **application** Ⓝ 신청서, 지원서
- **though** ⓐⓓ (문미에서) 하지만, 그래도
- **submit** Ⓥ 제출하다

---

06 아들을 위한 새 신발 사기 정답률 76% | 정답 ①

대화를 듣고, 두 사람이 지불할 금액을 고르시오. [3점]

☑ $75
② $80
③ $85
④ $105
⑤ $110

M : Honey, I think Paul needs new shoes.
　여보, 제 생각에 Paul에게 새 신발이 필요한 것 같아요.
W : You're right. His shoes are getting too tight for his feet.
　당신 말이 맞아요. 그의 신발은 그의 발에 너무 꽉 끼어요.
M : Let's buy a pair online. I know a good store. [Clicking sound] Have a look.
　온라인으로 한 켤레 사죠. 내가 좋은 매장을 알아요. [클릭하는 소리] 한 번 봐요.
W : Oh, how about these shoes? They're originally $100 a pair, but they're 30% off now.
　오, 이 신발 어때요? 이건 원래는 한 켤레에 100달러인데, 지금은 30퍼센트 세일을 하네요.
M : That's a good deal. Let's buy a pair.
　괜찮은 거래네요. 한 켤레 사죠.
W : Oh, there are shoe bags, too. Why don't we buy one?
　오, 신발주머니도 있네요. 하나 사는 게 어때요?
M : Okay. There are two kinds, a $10 bag and a $15 bag. Which one do you like?
　그래요. 10달러짜리 주머니와 15달러짜리 주머니, 이렇게 두 종류가 있네요. 어떤 것이 좋아요?
W : The $10 one looks good enough.
　10달러짜리가 충분히 좋아 보이네요.
M : Then let's take it. Is that all we need?
　그럼 그것을 사죠. 이게 우리가 필요한 전부인가요?
W : Yes. Oh, here it says that if you're a member of this online store, you'll get $5 off.
　네. 오, 이 온라인 매장 회원이면 5달러를 할인받는다고 여기 쓰여 있네요.
M : That's good. I'm a member. Let's buy them now.
　좋네요. 난 회원이에요. 그것들을 지금 사죠.
W : Okay.
　그래요.

Why? 왜 정답일까?

대화에 따르면 남자와 여자는 원래 한 켤레에 100달러인 신발을 30퍼센트 할인된 가격에 사고, 10달러짜리 신발주머니를 추가로 구매한 뒤, 전체 가격에서 5달러를 할인받았다. 이를 식으로 나타내면 '(100×0.7)+10−5=75'이므로, 두 사람이 지불할 금액은 ① '$75'이다.

- **tight** Ⓐ 꽉 끼는
- **enough** ⓐⓓ 충분히
- **originally** ⓐⓓ 원래, 본래

---

07 Sabina가 뉴욕 여행을 취소한 이유 정답률 92% | 정답 ③

대화를 듣고, 여자가 뉴욕 여행을 취소한 이유를 고르시오.

① 부모님이 편찮으셔서
② 시골로 이사를 가게 되어서
☑ 부모님 댁에서 휴가를 보내고 싶어서
④ 새로운 프로젝트를 맡게 되어서
⑤ 휴가 기간이 짧아져서

M : Sabina, have you finished packing for your trip?
Sabina, 여행을 위해 짐은 다 썼니?

W : You mean the trip to New York?
뉴욕 여행 말하는 거야?

M : Yes, you're leaving this weekend, right?
응. 너 이번 주말에 떠나잖아, 맞지?

W : Oh, actually I canceled the trip.
아, 사실 나 그 여행 취소했어.

M : Why? Do you have a new project coming up?
왜? 다가오는 새 프로젝트라도 있어?

W : No. It's just because of my parents.
아니. 그냥 우리 부모님 때문에.

M : Is there something wrong with them?
부모님께 무슨 문제라도 있는 거야?

W : Not really. I just want to spend my vacation at my parents' house.
그렇진 않아. 그냥 휴가를 부모님 댁에서 보내고 싶어서.

M : Oh, right. They moved to the countryside last year.
아, 맞다. 작년에 시골로 이사 가셨지.

W : Yeah. I miss them a lot. It'll be great to stay with them.
응. 무척 보고 싶어. 부모님과 함께 있으면 아주 좋을 거야.

M : Sure. They'll be happy to have you there.
물론이지. 부모님은 네가 거기에 가면 행복하실 거야.

Why? 왜 정답일까?

여자가 뉴욕 여행을 취소했다는 말에 남자가 이유를 묻자 여자는 휴가를 부모님 집에서 보내고 싶기 때문(I just want to spend my vacation at my parents' house.)이라고 답한다. 따라서 답으로 적절한 것은 ③ '부모님 댁에서 휴가를 보내고 싶어서'이다.

- pack ⓥ (짐을) 싸다, 꾸리다, 챙기다
- cancel ⓥ 취소하다
- countryside ⓝ 시골 (지역), 전원 지대
- miss ⓥ 보고 싶어 하다, 그리워하다

---

08 놀이공원 특징 설명하기 　　정답률 93% | 정답 ④

대화를 듣고, Fun Town Amusement Park에 관해 언급되지 <u>않은</u> 것을 고르시오.
① 위치
② 도착 소요 시간
③ 개장 시간
☑ 입장료
⑤ 특별 프로그램

W : Honey, what are you looking at?
여보, 뭘 보고 있어요?

M : It's the website of the Fun Town Amusement Park. How about taking the kids there this weekend?
Fun Town 놀이공원 웹 사이트예요. 이번 주말에 애들을 데리고 여기 가는 건 어때요?

W : Good idea. 『It's located in Southern California, right?』 ①의 근거 일치
좋은 생각이에요. 남부 캘리포니아에 있는 것 맞죠?

M : Yes. 『It'll take about one hour to get there by car.』 ②의 근거 일치
그래요. 거기까지 차로 가려면 한 시간 정도 걸릴 거예요.

W : What time shall we leave here?
여기서 언제 출발해야 하나요?

M : About 8 in the morning. 『The park is open from 9 a.m. to 8 p.m.』 ③의 근거 일치
아침 8시 정도요. 공원은 오전 9시부터 오후 8시까지 열어요.

W : Okay. Are there any programs that our kids will find interesting?
알겠어요. 우리 애들이 재밌어 할 프로그램이라도 있어요?

M : 『Yeah, they offer many special programs including animal feeding.』 ⑤의 근거 일치
있어요, 동물들 먹이 주기를 포함해서 많은 특별 프로그램을 제공해요.

W : Great. I'll go tell the kids now.
아주 좋네요. 아이들한테 지금 가서 말할게요.

M : Go ahead. They'll be excited to hear that.
그렇게 해요. 그 말을 들으면 아주 신나할 거예요.

Why? 왜 정답일까?

대화에서 남자와 여자는 Fun Town Amusement Park의 위치, 도착 소요 시간, 개장 시간, 특별 프로그램에 대해서 언급하였다. 따라서 Fun Town Amusement Park에 관해 언급되지 않은 것은 ④ '입장료'이다.

Why? 왜 오답일까?

① 'It's located in Southern California, right?'에서 '위치'가 언급되었다.
② 'It'll take about one hour to get there by car.'에서 '도착 소요 시간'이 언급되었다.
③ 'The park is open from 9 a.m. to 8 p.m.'에서 '개장 시간'이 언급되었다.
⑤ 'Yeah, they offer many special programs including animal feeding.'에서 '특별 프로그램'이 언급되었다.

- amusement park 놀이 공원
- offer ⓥ 제공하다
- feeding ⓝ 먹이 주기

---

09 교내 뮤지컬 상연 안내 　　정답률 87% | 정답 ③

2019 Riverside High School Musical에 관한 다음 내용을 듣고, 일치하지 <u>않는</u> 것을 고르시오.
① 공연작은 Shrek이다.
② 공연을 위한 오디션은 작년 12월에 있었다.
☑ 공연은 사흘간 진행된다.
④ 입장권은 1인당 8달러이다.
⑤ 입장권은 연극 동아리실에서 구입할 수 있다.

W : Hello, students.
안녕하세요, 학생 여러분.

This is Janice Hawkins, your drama teacher.
저는 여러분의 연극 선생님인 Janice Hawkins입니다.

I'm happy to invite you and your family to the 2019 Riverside High School Musical.
여러분과 여러분의 가족을 2019 Riverside High School Musical에 초대하게 되어 기쁩니다.

『This year we're presenting Shrek, based on the famous animated film.』 ①의 근거 일치
올해 저희는 유명한 만화영화에 바탕을 둔 Shrek을 상연합니다.

It's full of singing, dancing, romance and lots of fun.
그것은 노래와 춤, 로맨스와 많은 재미로 가득합니다.

『The auditions for the show were in December last year.』 ②의 근거 일치
공연을 위한 오디션은 작년 12월에 있었습니다.

The cast and crew have been rehearsing for months to perfect their performance.
출연진들과 제작진들이 그들의 공연을 완벽하게 만들기 위해 몇 달 리허설을 해 왔습니다.

『The musical will be held in the auditorium for two days on March 15 and 16.』 ③의 근거 불일치
뮤지컬은 3월 15일과 16일 이틀 동안 강당에서 열립니다.

『Tickets are $8 per person.』 ④의 근거 일치
입장권은 1인당 8달러입니다.

『You can buy tickets in the drama club room.』 ⑤의 근거 일치
연극 동아리실에서 입장권을 구입할 수 있습니다.

For more details, visit the school website.
더 많은 세부사항을 위해서는, 학교 웹 사이트를 방문해주세요.

Thank you.
고맙습니다.

Why? 왜 정답일까?

'The musical will be held in the auditorium for two days on March 15 and 16.'에서 공연은 3월 15일과 16일 이틀에 걸쳐 진행된다고 하므로, 내용과 일치하지 않는 것은 ③ '공연은 사흘간 진행된다.'이다.

Why? 왜 오답일까?

① 'This year we're presenting Shrek, based on the famous animated film.'의 내용과 일치한다.
② 'The auditions for the show were in December last year.'의 내용과 일치한다.
④ 'Tickets are $8 per person.'의 내용과 일치한다.
⑤ 'You can buy tickets in the drama club room.'의 내용과 일치한다.

- invite ⓥ 초대하다
- present ⓥ (연극·방송 등을) 공연하다
- based on ~에 근거하여
- be full of ~로 가득 차다
- animated film 만화영화
- cast ⓝ 출연자들, 배역진
- crew ⓝ (특정한 기술을 가지고 함께 일을 하는) 팀, 반, 조
- rehearse ⓥ 예행연습을 하다
- hold ⓥ 개최하다
- perfect ⓥ 완벽하게 하다
- drama club 연극 동아리
- detail ⓝ 세부 사항

---

10 토스터 구매하기 　　정답률 78% | 정답 ④

다음 표를 보면서 대화를 듣고, 남자가 구매할 토스터를 고르시오.

Bestselling Toasters in K-Store

	Model	Number of Slices	Price	Color
①	A	1	$25	white
②	B	1	$30	silver
③	C	2	$40	white
☑	D	4	$45	silver
⑤	E	4	$55	silver

W : Hello. How may I help you, sir?
안녕하세요. 어떻게 도와드릴까요, 손님?

M : I'm looking for a toaster.
토스터를 찾고 있어요.

W : Okay. These five are our bestsellers. How about this one-slice toaster?
그러시군요. 이 다섯 개가 저희 베스트셀러입니다. 이 한 조각짜리 토스터는 어때요?

M : It's nice. 『But I want to toast at least two slices at a time.』 근거1 Number of Slices 조건
좋은데요. 그런데 저는 한 번에 적어도 두 장을 굽고 싶어요.

W : Then you need to choose one out of these three models. May I ask your price range?
그러면 이 세 개 모델 중에 하나를 선택하셔야겠네요. 가격대를 여쭤봐도 될까요?

M : 『Well, I don't want to spend more than fifty dollars.』 근거2 Price 조건
음, 저는 50달러 이상을 쓰고 싶지는 않아요.

W : You have two options left then. Which color do you like better?
그러면 두 개 선택지가 남으시네요. 어떤 색을 더 좋아하세요?

M : 『I'll go with the silver one.』 근거3 Color 조건
은색으로 할게요.

W : Okay. Good choice.
알겠습니다. 잘 고르셨어요.

Why? 왜 정답일까?

대화에 따르면 남자는 한 번에 적어도 두 장 이상의 빵을 구울 수 있으면서, 가격이 50달러를 넘지 않고, 색깔은 은색인 토스터기를 선택하고자 한다. 따라서 남자가 구매할 토스터로 적절한 것은 ④ 'D'이다.

- slice ⓝ 조각
- out of ~ 중에
- price range 가격대
- option ⓝ 선택지, 선택
- go with ~을 고르다, ~을 받아들이다

---

11 스페인어 공부 　　정답률 78% | 정답 ②

대화를 듣고, 여자의 마지막 말에 대한 남자의 응답으로 가장 적절한 것을 고르시오.
① Sorry, but I'd rather go to Spain by myself. – 미안하지만, 난 차라리 혼자 스페인에 가겠어.
☑ No, I'm taking a class in the community center. – 아니, 나는 주민 센터에서 수업을 듣고 있어.
③ Yes, you need to eat healthy food for your brain. – 응, 넌 두뇌를 위해 건강에 좋은 음식을 먹어야 해.
④ Yeah, you don't have to worry about your brain. – 그래, 넌 네 뇌에 대해 걱정할 필요가 없어.
⑤ Well, I'm not interested in learning Spanish. – 음, 난 스페인어를 배우는 데 관심이 없어.

W : Grandpa, is that a Spanish book you're reading?
할아버지, 읽고 계시는 게 스페인어 책인가요?

M : Yes, I just started to learn Spanish. You know learning a foreign language is good for your brain.
응, 난 막 스페인어를 배우기 시작했단다. 외국어를 배우는 게 두뇌에 좋다는 걸 너도 알지.

W : Sounds great. Are you learning it by yourself?
좋네요. 독학하시는 거예요?

M : No, I'm taking a class in the community center.
아니, 나는 주민 센터에서 수업을 듣고 있어.

Why? 왜 정답일까?

여자는 스페인어 책을 보고 있는 남자에게 혼자서 스페인어를 공부하는지 묻고 있으므로(Are you learning it by yourself?), 남자의 응답으로 가장 적절한 것은 ② '아니, 나는 주민 센터에서 수업을 듣고 있어.'이다.

- foreign language 외국어
- brain ⓝ 두뇌
- by oneself 혼자
- be good for ~에 좋다
- healthy ⓐ 건강에 좋은

---

12 역사 에세이 제출   정답률 79% | 정답 ③

대화를 듣고, 남자의 마지막 말에 대한 여자의 응답으로 가장 적절한 것을 고르시오.

① But I haven't finished writing it. – 그치만 난 그걸 다 못 썼는 걸.
② Yes, I can help you study history. – 그래, 내가 네 역사 공부를 도와줄게.
✓③ Okay, let's go to the teacher's office. – 그래, 교무실로 가자.
④ Well, take your time to write the essay. – 그럼, 천천히 에세이를 써.
⑤ Sorry, but I didn't bring my essay today. – 미안, 그런데 내가 오늘 에세이를 안 가져 왔어.

M : Lydia, have you finished writing the history essay?
Lydia, 역사 에세이 쓰는 것 다 했니?

W : Yes, I have. I brought it today. How about you?
응, 다 했어. 오늘 난 그걸 가져왔어. 너는 어때?

M : Me, too. Why don't we go submit the essay now?
나도. 우리 지금 가서 에세이를 내는 게 어때?

W : Okay, let's go to the teacher's office.
그래, 교무실로 가자.

Why? 왜 정답일까?

남자가 여자에게 역사 에세이를 다 썼는지 묻자 여자는 다 써서 에세이를 가지고 왔다며 남자의 진행 상황은 어떤지를 묻는다. 이에 남자는 자신도 마찬가지라며 가서 에세이를 내자(Why don't we go submit the essay now?)고 말하고 있으므로, 남자의 마지막 말에 대한 여자의 응답으로 가장 적절한 것은 ③ '그래, 교무실로 가자.'이다.

- bring ⓥ 가져오다, 가져가다
- how about ~? ~은 어때?
- why don't we ~? ~하는 게 어때?
- submit ⓥ 제출하다

---

13 서평 과제를 위한 책 고르기   정답률 59% | 정답 ②

대화를 듣고, 남자의 마지막 말에 대한 여자의 응답으로 가장 적절한 것을 고르시오.

Woman: _____

① You're right. That's why I chose this book.
아빠 말씀이 맞아요. 그것이 제가 이 책을 골랐던 이유예요.
✓② That makes sense. I'll switch to an easier book.
그 말씀이 맞네요. 더 쉬운 책으로 바꿀게요.
③ Okay. I'll choose one from the bestseller list next time.
알겠어요. 다음에는 베스트셀러 목록에서 한 권을 고를게요.
④ Don't worry. It's not too difficult for me to read.
걱정 마세요. 그것은 제가 읽기에 너무 어렵지 않아요.
⑤ Yeah. I'll join the book club to read more books.
그래요. 책을 더 많이 읽기 위해 독서 동아리에 들 거예요.

M : What are you reading, Lily?
뭘 읽고 있니, Lily?

W : It's a book for my English class, Dad. We have to read a book and write a review.
제 영어 수업을 위한 책이에요, 아빠. 저희는 책 한 권을 읽고 서평을 써야 해요.

M : Do you like the book?
그 책이 마음에 드니?

W : Well, I'm not sure. Frankly it's too difficult for me.
음, 잘 모르겠어요. 솔직히 말하면 저한테 너무 어려워요.

M : Why did you choose to read that book then?
그럼 왜 그 책을 읽기로 결정했니?

W : It was on the bestseller list and it looked interesting. It's very challenging, though.
이게 베스트셀러 목록에 있었고 재미있어 보였거든요. 그런데 무척 어려워요.

M : Maybe you should try another book that suits your level.
아마 넌 네 수준에 맞는 다른 책을 시도해보겠구나.

W : I know what you mean, but wouldn't I learn more from reading a difficult book?
무슨 말씀이신지 알지만, 전 어려운 책을 읽어서 더 많은 걸 배우게 되지 않을까요?

M : Well, what's the use of reading it if you can't understand it?
글쎄, 네가 이해를 할 수 없다면 그것을 읽어서 무슨 소용이 있니?

W : That makes sense. I'll switch to an easier book.
그 말씀이 맞네요. 더 쉬운 책으로 바꿀게요.

Why? 왜 정답일까?

여자가 서평을 쓰기 위해 고른 책이 너무 어렵다고 말하자 남자는 수준에 맞는 책을 다시 고를 것을 권하며(Maybe you should try another book that suits your level.) 이해하지 못하는 책을 읽는 것은 소용이 없다고 이야기한다(Well, what's the use of reading it if you can't understand it?). 따라서 여자의 응답으로 가장 적절한 것은 ② '그 말씀이 맞네요. 더 쉬운 책으로 바꿀게요.'이다.

- review ⓝ 비평, 평론, 독후감
- frankly ad 솔직히, 솔직히 말하면
- challenging ⓐ 힘이 드는, 도전적인
- though conj 그러나
- What's the use of ~? ~하는 것이 무슨 소용이니?
- switch ⓥ 바꾸다

---

14 생일 선물 고르기   정답률 78% | 정답 ⑤

대화를 듣고, 여자의 마지막 말에 대한 남자의 응답으로 가장 적절한 것을 고르시오. [3점]

Man: _____

① Well, I'm not sure if your son likes it.
음, 아드님이 좋아할지는 잘 모르겠어요.
② No, it's dangerous to leave kids home alone.
아뇨, 아이들을 집에 혼자 두는 것은 위험해요.
③ Of course, they are not safe even for adults.
물론이죠, 드론은 심지어 어른들에게도 안전하지 않아요.
④ That's why it's difficult to find drones for kids.
그게 아이들을 위한 드론을 찾기 어려운 이유죠.
✓⑤ Yes, as long as you get a right drone for his age.
그럼요, 아이 나이에 맞는 드론을 사 주기만 하면요.

M : What are you looking at, Monica?
뭘 보고 있어, Monica?

W : Oh, I'm looking for a birthday gift for my son Willy.
아, 제 아들 Willy를 위한 생일선물을 찾고 있어요.

M : I see. Did you find anything good?
그렇군요. 뭔가 좋은 걸 찾았나요?

W : Not yet. Do you have any ideas?
아직이요. 아이디어라도 있으세요?

M : Hmm. Why don't you get him a drone?
흠. 드론을 사주시는 건 어때요?

W : A drone? I'm not sure if he'll like it.
드론요? 아들이 좋아할지 모르겠네요.

M : Of course, he will. Boys are crazy about drones these days.
당연히 좋아할 거예요. 남자애들은 요새 드론에 열광하는 걸요.

W : Willy is just nine years old. Do you think he can fly a drone?
Willy는 아직 겨우 9살인걸요. 드론을 날릴 수 있을 거라고 생각하세요?

M : I guess so. There are quite a lot of drones for kids.
그럴 거예요. 아이들을 위한 드론이 아주 많아요.

W : Are you sure they're safe enough for a nine-year-old?
드론이 아홉 살짜리 아이들에게도 충분히 안전하다고 확신하나요?

M : Yes, as long as you get a right drone for his age.
그럼요, 아이 나이에 맞는 드론을 사 주기만 하면요.

Why? 왜 정답일까?

여자가 아들의 생일 선물로 무엇을 주면 좋을지 모르겠다고 말하자 남자는 드론을 추천하는데, 여자는 아이 나이가 아홉 살로 아직 어린데 드론이 괜찮을지 모르겠다며 확실히 안전한지(Are you sure they're safe enough for a nine-year-old?)를 되묻고 있다. 이에 대한 남자의 응답으로 가장 적절한 것은 ⑤ '그럼요, 아이 나이에 맞는 드론을 사 주기만 하면요.'이다.

- drone ⓝ 드론, (지상에서 조종하는) 무인 항공기
- quite ad 아주, 굉장히
- be crazy about ~에 열광하다, ~을 몹시 좋아하다
- as long as ~하기만 하면

---

15 선거 표어 만드는 데 도움 요청하기   정답률 74% | 정답 ④

다음 상황 설명을 듣고, Lily가 John에게 할 말로 가장 적절한 것을 고르시오. [3점]

Lily: _____

① Why don't you run for class president?
너 반장 선거에 출마하는 게 어때?
② Please give me a hand putting up the poster.
포스터 붙이는 것을 도와줘.
③ How about changing your slogan in the poster?
네 포스터 표어를 바꾸는 게 어때?
✓④ Will you help me make a slogan for the election?
선거를 위한 표어를 만드는 것을 도와줄래?
⑤ Tell me how to keep good relationships with classmates.
반 친구들과 어떻게 좋은 관계를 유지하는지 말해줘.

M : Lily is a freshman in high school.
Lily는 고등학교 신입생이다.

She is planning to run for class president this year.
그녀는 올해 반장에 출마할 계획이다.

She really wants to win the election.
그녀는 선거에서 정말 이기고 싶다.

She thinks she needs a poster with a cool slogan to impress her classmates.
그녀는 반 친구들에게 인상을 남길 수 있는 멋진 표어가 담긴 포스터가 필요하다고 생각한다.

But she has difficulty coming up with a good slogan.
하지만 그녀는 좋은 표어를 생각해 내는 데 어려움이 있다.

Lily knows her friend John is very creative and has a lot of great ideas.
Lily는 친구인 John이 굉장히 창의적이고 좋은 아이디어가 많다는 것을 안다.

So she wants to ask him for help.
그래서 그녀는 그에게 도움을 구하고 싶다.

In this situation, what would Lily most likely say to John?
이 상황에서, Lily는 John에게 뭐라고 말할 것인가?

Lily : Will you help me make a slogan for the election?
선거를 위한 표어를 만드는 것을 도와줄래?

Why? 왜 정답일까?

Lily는 반장 선거를 위한 포스터를 만들고 싶어하는데 마땅한 표어가 떠오르지 않아서(But she has difficulty coming up with a good slogan.) 반 친구들 중 창의적인 친구인 John에게 표어 고안에 대한 도움을 요청하려고 한다(So she wants to ask him for help.). 따라서 Lily가 John에게 할 말로 가장 적절한 것은 ④ '선거를 위한 표어를 만드는 것을 도와줄래?'이다.

- freshman ⓝ 신입생
- class president 반장
- slogan ⓝ 표어, 슬로건
- come up with 생각해 내다, 떠올리다
- relationship ⓝ 관계
- run for ~에 출마하다
- election ⓝ 선거
- impress ⓥ 깊은 인상을 주다
- give a hand ~을 도와주다

16-17 동물이 나오는 속담

W : Hello, class.
안녕하세요, 여러분.

『You must have heard of the proverb, 'Birds of a feather flock together.'』
여러분은 '같은 깃털의 새들이 함께 모인다(유유상종)'이라는 속담을 분명 들어봤을 겁니다. 17번 ①의 근거 일치
We all know what this proverb means because it's commonly used.
이것은 흔히 쓰이기 때문에 우리는 모두 이 속담이 무슨 뜻인지 알고 있습니다.
『Like this, there are many proverbs in which animals appear.
이 속담처럼, 동물들이 나오는 많은 속담이 있습니다.
Let's talk about them today.』 16번의 근거
오늘은 그것들에 관해 이야기해 봅시다.
『First one is, 'When the cat's away, the mice will play.'』 17번 ②의 근거 일치
첫 번째 속담은, '고양이가 없으면 생쥐가 살맛 난다'입니다.
It is using the fun relationship between the two animals.
이것은 두 동물들의 재미있는 관계를 이용한 것입니다.
We can easily guess the meaning of this proverb: the weaker do whatever they want when the stronger are not around.
우리는 이 속담의 의미를 쉽게 추측할 수 있는데, 강자가 주변에 없으면 약자는 자기가 원하는 무엇이든 한다는 것입니다.
『The next one is, 'Don't count your chickens before they're hatched.'』 17번 ④의 근거 일치
다음 속담은, '병아리가 부화하기 전에 닭의 수를 헤아리지 마라(김칫국부터 마시지 마라)'입니다.
It's using a chicken's life cycle.
이것은 닭의 생애 주기를 이용하고 있습니다.
From this proverb, we can learn the lesson that we should not make hasty decisions.
이 속담으로부터, 우리는 섣부른 결정을 내려서는 안 된다는 교훈을 배울 수 있습니다.
Now it's your turn to talk about a few proverbs like these.
이제 여러분이 이런 몇 가지 속담에 대해 이야기를 해볼 차례입니다.
『You may have already thought about one with dogs, like 'Every dog has its day.'』 17번 ⑤의 근거 일치
여러분은 '모든 개들은 자기 날을 갖는다(쥐구멍에도 볕들 날이 있다)'와 같이 개에 관한 것을 이미 하나 생각해봤을 것입니다.
Let's talk about some together.
몇 가지를 함께 이야기해 봅시다.

- proverb ⓝ 속담
- flock ⓥ 모이다, 떼 지어 가다
- appear ⓥ 나오다, 등장하다
- guess ⓥ 추측하다
- be around 존재하다
- life cycle 생애 주기
- hasty ⓐ 성급한, 서두른
- turn ⓝ 차례
- Every dog has its day. 쥐구멍에도 볕 들 날이 있다.
- advantage ⓝ 이점

- feather ⓝ 털, 깃털
- commonly ⓐd 흔히, 일반적으로
- mouse ⓝ 생쥐 (pl.) mice
- hatch ⓥ 부화하다
- count ⓥ 세다
- lesson ⓝ 교훈
- decision ⓝ 결정

16 주제 파악 정답률 79% | 정답 ①

여자가 하는 말의 주제로 가장 적절한 것은?
☑ proverbs that have animals in them – 동물이 나오는 속담
② different proverbs in various cultures – 여러 문화 속의 다양한 속담
③ why proverbs are difficult to understand – 속담을 이해하기 어려운 이유
④ importance of studying animals' behavior – 동물의 행동을 연구하는 것의 중요성
⑤ advantages of teaching values through proverbs – 속담을 통해 가치관을 가르치는 것의 이점

Why? 왜 정답일까?

'Like this, there are many proverbs in which animals appear. Let's talk about them today.'에서 여자는 동물들이 나오는 속담이 많이 있다고 말하며 이에 관해 이야기해보자고 하므로, 여자가 하는 말의 주제로 가장 적절한 것은 ① '동물이 나오는 속담'이다.

17 언급 유무 파악 정답률 83% | 정답 ③

언급된 동물이 아닌 것은?
① birds – 새
② mice – 생쥐
☑ cows – 소
④ chickens – 닭
⑤ dogs – 개

Why? 왜 정답일까?

담화에서 여자는 속담에 등장하는 동물의 예로 새, 생쥐, 닭, 개를 언급하였다. 따라서 언급되지 않은 것은 ③ '소'이다.

Why? 왜 오답일까?

① 'Birds of a feather flock together.'에서 '새'가 언급되었다.
② 'When the cat's away, the mice will play.'에서 '생쥐'가 언급되었다.
④ 'Don't count your chickens before they're hatched.'에서 '닭'이 언급되었다.
⑤ 'Every dog has its day.'에서 '개'가 언급되었다.

18 특별 발표회 참석 부탁하기 정답률 79% | 정답 ①

다음 글의 목적으로 가장 적절한 것은?
☑ 학생들이 준비한 발표회 참석을 부탁하려고
② 학생들을 위한 특별 강연을 해 준 것에 감사하려고
③ 청년 실업 문제의 해결 방안에 관한 강연을 의뢰하려고
④ 학생들의 발표회에 대한 재정적 지원을 요청하려고
⑤ 학생들의 프로젝트 심사 결과를 알리려고

Dear Mrs. Coling,
Coling 선생님께,
My name is Susan Harris / and I am writing on behalf of the students / at Lockwood High School.
제 이름은 Susan Harris이고 / 학생들을 대표하여 이 글을 씁니다. / Lockwood 고교의
Many students at the school / have been working on a project / about the youth unemployment problem in Lockwood.
저희 학교의 많은 학생들은 / 프로젝트를 수행해 왔습니다. / Lockwood 지역의 청년 실업 문제에 관한
You are invited to attend a special presentation / that will be held at our school auditorium on April 16th.

특별 발표회에 귀하를 초대합니다. / 저희 학교 강당에서 4월 16일 열리는
At the presentation, / students will propose a variety of ideas / for developing employment opportunities / for the youth within the community.
발표회에서 / 학생들은 여러 가지 안을 제안할 것입니다. / 고용 기회를 늘리는 / 지역 사회 내 청년들을 위한
As one of the famous figures in the community, / we would be honored by your attendance.
지역 사회의 유명인사 중 한 분으로서, / 귀하가 참석하시면 영광일 것입니다.
We look forward to seeing you there.
거기서 귀하를 뵙기를 고대합니다.
Sincerely, // Susan Harris
Susan Harris 드림

Coling 선생님께,

제 이름은 Susan Harris이고 Lockwood 고교 학생들을 대표하여 이 글을 씁니다. 저희 학교의 많은 학생들은 Lockwood 지역의 청년 실업 문제를 해결하기 위한 프로젝트를 수행해 왔습니다. 저희 학교 강당에서 4월 16일 열리는 특별 발표회에 귀하를 초대합니다. 발표회에서 학생들은 지역 사회 내 청년들을 위한 고용 기회를 늘리는 여러 가지 안을 제안할 것입니다. 지역 사회의 유명인사 중 한 분으로서, 귀하가 참석하시면 영광일 것입니다. 거기서 귀하를 뵙기를 고대합니다.

Susan Harris 드림

Why? 왜 정답일까?

글 중간에서 청년 실업과 관련된 특별 발표회에 초대하겠다(You are invited to attend a special presentation that will be held at our school auditorium on April 16th.)는 뜻을 밝힌 데 이어, 마지막 두 문장에서는 참석해주면 영광일 것이고 발표회 자리에서 보게 되기를 바란다며 편지를 맺고 있으므로, 글의 목적으로 가장 적절한 것은 ① '학생들이 준비한 발표회 참석을 부탁하려고'이다.

- on behalf of ~을 대신하여, ~을 대표하여
- unemployment ⓝ 실업
- hold ⓥ (행사 등을) 열다
- propose ⓥ 제안하다
- within prep ~의 이내에
- work on ~을 수행하다
- attend ⓥ 참석하다
- auditorium ⓝ 강당
- opportunity ⓝ 기회
- figure ⓝ 인물

구문 풀이

5행 You are invited to attend a special presentation [that will be held at our school auditorium on April 16th].
be invited to + 동사원형 : ~하도록 초청되다 ← 주격 관계대명사

19 수술 대기 중 경험한 안도감 정답률 86% | 정답 ②

다음 글에 드러난 'I'의 심경 변화로 가장 적절한 것은?
① cheerful → sad
  활기찬   슬픈
☑ worried → relieved
  걱정하는   안도하는
③ angry → ashamed
  화난   부끄러운
④ jealous → thankful
  질투하는   고마워하는
⑤ hopeful → disappointed
  희망찬   실망하는

On December 6th, / I arrived at University Hospital in Cleveland / at 10:00 a.m.
12월 6일 / 나는 클리블랜드에 있는 University 병원에 도착했다. / 오전 10시에
I went through the process of admissions.
나는 입원 수속을 밟았다.
I grew anxious / because the time for surgery was drawing closer.
나는 점점 불안해졌다. / 수술 시간이 다가오고 있어
I was directed to the waiting area, / where I remained until my name was called.
나는 대기실로 안내되었고 / 거기서 내 이름이 불릴 때까지 있었다.
I had a few hours of waiting time.
나는 몇 시간 동안 기다렸다.
I just kept praying.
나는 계속 기도만 했다.
At some point in my ongoing prayer process, / before my name was called, / in the midst of the chaos, / an unbelievable peace embraced me.
계속 기도하는 어느 시점에선가, / 내 이름이 불리기 전, / 혼돈 한가운데서 / 믿을 수 없는 평화가 나를 감쌌다.
All my fear disappeared!
나의 모든 두려움이 사라졌다!
An unbelievable peace overrode my emotions.
믿을 수 없는 평화가 내 감정 위로 퍼졌다.
My physical body relaxed in the comfort provided, / and I looked forward to getting the surgery over with / and working hard at recovery.
주어진 편안함 속에 몸의 긴장이 풀렸고, / 나는 수술을 끝마치기를 고대하였다. / 그리고 회복을 위해 열심히 노력하기를

12월 6일 오전 10시에 나는 클리블랜드에 있는 University 병원에 도착했다. 나는 입원 수속을 밟았다. 수술 시간이 다가오고 있어 나는 점점 불안해졌다. 나는 대기실로 안내되었고 거기서 내 이름이 불릴 때까지 있었다. 나는 몇 시간 동안 기다렸다. 나는 계속 기도만 했다. 계속 기도하는 어느 시점에선가, 내 이름이 불리기 전, 혼돈 한가운데서 믿을 수 없는 평화가 나를 감쌌다. 나의 모든 두려움이 사라졌다! 믿을 수 없는 평화가 내 감정 위로 퍼졌다. 주어진 편안함 속에 몸의 긴장이 풀렸고, 나는 수술을 끝마치고 회복을 위해 열심히 노력하기를 고대하였다.

Why? 왜 정답일까?

'I grew anxious because the time for surgery was drawing closer.'에서 수술을 기다리며 걱정하던 필자가 '~ an unbelievable peace embraced me. All my fear disappeared! An unbelievable peace overrode my emotions.' 이후로 문득 마음의 평화를 찾았음을 알 수 있으므로, 'I'의 심경 변화로 가장 적절한 것은 ② '걱정하는 → 안도하는'이다.

- process ⓝ 절차
- surgery ⓝ 수술
- pray ⓥ 기도하다
- admission ⓝ 입원, 입장
- direct ⓥ 길을 안내하다
- ongoing ⓐ 진행 중인

- **chaos** ⓝ 혼돈
- **override** ⓥ (~의 위로) 퍼지다
- **get ~ over with** ~을 끝마치다
- **embrace** ⓥ 감싸다, 포옹하다
- **comfort** ⓝ 편안함

구문 풀이

8행 My physical body relaxed in the comfort provided, / and I looked forward
주어1 　　　　동사1(과거)　　　　　과거분사　　　　　　동사2 「look forward
to getting the surgery over with and working hard at recovery.
to + 동명사1 + 　　　　　　　　동명사2 : ~하고 …하기를 고대하다」

---

20 공부 시간과 휴식 시간을 나누기 　　　　정답률 71% | 정답 ①

다음 글에서 필자가 주장하는 바로 가장 적절한 것은?
☑ 공부할 때는 공부에만 집중하라.
② 평소 주변 사람들과 자주 연락하라.
③ 피로감을 느끼지 않게 충분한 휴식을 취하라.
④ 자투리 시간을 이용하여 숙제를 하라.
⑤ 학습에 유익한 취미 활동을 하라.

It can be tough to settle down to study / when there are so many distractions.
공부에 전념하는 것은 힘들 수 있다. / 마음을 산만하게 하는 것들이 너무 많이 있을 때
Most young people like to combine a bit of homework / with quite a lot of instant
messaging, / chatting on the phone, / updating profiles on social-networking sites, / and
checking emails.
많은 젊은이들이 숙제를 찔끔하는 것과 함께 하고 싶어 한다. / 즉각적으로 메시지 주고받기, / 전화로 잡담하기, / SNS에 신상 정보
업데이트하기, / 그리고 이메일 확인하기를 잔뜩 하는 것
While it may be true / that you can multi-task / and can focus on all these things at once, /
try to be honest with yourself.
사실일지도 모르지만, / 여러분이 동시에 여러 가지 일을 처리할 수 있고 / 이러한 모든 일들에 집중할 수 있다는 것이 / 자신에게 솔
직해지려고 노력해라.
It is most likely that you will be able to work best / if you concentrate on your studies / but
allow yourself regular breaks / — every 30 minutes or so — / to catch up on those other
pastimes.
여러분은 아마도 가장 잘 공부할 수 있을 것이다. / 여러분이 공부에 집중하되 / 규칙적인 휴식을 허락한다면 / 30분 정도마다 / (앞
서 못했던) 그런 다른 소일거리를 하기 위해

마음을 산만하게 하는 것들이 너무 많이 있을 때, 공부에 전념하는 것은 힘들 수 있다. 많은
젊은이들이 숙제를 찔끔하는 것과 즉각적으로 메시지 주고받기, 전화로 잡담하기, SNS에 신
상 정보 업데이트하기, 그리고 이메일 확인하기를 잔뜩 하는 것을 함께 하고 싶어 한다. 여러
분이 동시에 여러 가지 일을 처리할 수 있고 이러한 모든 일들에 집중할 수 있다는 것이 사실
일지도 모르지만, 자신에게 솔직해지려고 노력해라. 여러분이 공부에 집중하되 (공부를 하느
라 못했던) 그런 다른 소일거리를 하기 위해 규칙적인 휴식을 — 30분 정도마다 — 허락한다
면 여러분은 아마도 가장 잘 공부할 수 있을 것이다.

Why? 왜 정답일까?

첫 문장에서 마음을 산만하게 하는 것이 많으면 공부에 집중하기는 어렵다는 점을 언급한 뒤, 마지막 문
장에서는 공부를 할 때에는 공부에 집중하되 다른 소일거리는 규칙적인 휴식시간을 두어 처리하라고(It is
most likely that you will be able to work best if you concentrate on your studies
but allow yourself regular breaks — every 30 minutes or so — to catch up on those
other pastimes.)는 결론을 내리고 있다. 따라서 필자가 주장하는 바로 가장 적절한 것은 ① '공부할
때는 공부에만 집중하라.'이다.

- **tough** ⓐ 힘든, 어려운
- **distraction** ⓝ 마음을 산만하게 하는 것, 집중력을 흩뜨리는 것
- **combine** ⓥ 합치다
- **instant** ⓐ 즉각적인, 즉시의
- **once** adv 한번에
- **allow** ⓥ 허락하다
- **catch up on** ~을 처리하다, 따라잡다, 만회하다
- **settle down to** 마음을 가라앉히고 ~하기 시작하다
- **quite** adv 꽤, 상당히
- **multi-task** 여러 가지 일을 동시에 처리하다
- **concentrate on** ~에 집중하다
- **regular** ⓐ 규칙적인
- **pastime** ⓝ 소일거리, 취미

구문 풀이

6행 It is most likely {that you will be able to work best / if you concentrate on
가주어　　　　　　　접속사　　주어　　　동사(~할 수 있을 것이다)　　조건 접속사　　　　　동사1
your studies but allow yourself regular breaks — every 30 minutes or so — to catch
동사2　　간접목적어　　　　직접목적어　　　　　　　　　　　　　　　　　　　　~하기 위해
up on those other pastimes}.
{ } : 진주어

---

21 정보 과잉의 역설 　　　　정답률 58% | 정답 ③

밑줄 친 information blinded가 다음 글에서 의미하는 바로 가장 적절한 것은? [3점]
① unwilling to accept others' ideas
다른 사람들의 생각을 수용하기 꺼려하는
② unable to access free information
무료 정보에 접근할 수 없는
☑ unable to make decisions due to too much information
너무나 많은 정보 때문에 의사 결정을 할 수 없는
④ indifferent to the lack of available information
이용 가능한 정보의 부족에 무관심한
⑤ willing to take risks in decision-making
의사 결정에서 기꺼이 위험을 무릅쓰는

Technology has doubtful advantages.
기술은 의문의 여지가 있는 이점을 지니고 있다.
We must balance too much information / versus using only the right information / and
keeping the decision-making process simple.
우리는 너무 많은 정보는 조절해야 한다. / 정확한 정보만 사용해서 / 의사 결정 과정을 간소하게 하는 것에 맞추어
The Internet has made / so much free information available / on any issue / that we think /
we have to consider all of it / in order to make a decision.
인터넷은 만들어서 / 너무 많은 무료 정보를 이용 가능하게 / 어떤 문제에 대해서도 / 우리는 생각한다 / 그 모든 정보를 고려해야 한
다고 / 어떤 결정을 하기 위해서

So / we keep searching for answers / on the Internet.
그래서 / 우리는 계속 답을 검색한다. / 인터넷에서
This makes us information blinded, / like deer in headlights, / when trying to make
personal, business, or other decisions.
이것이 우리를 정보에 눈멀게 만든다. / 전조등 불빛에 노출된 사슴처럼, / 우리가 개인적, 사업적, 혹은 다른 결정을 하려고 애쓸 때
To be successful in anything today, / we have to keep in mind / that in the land of the blind,
/ a one-eyed person can accomplish the seemingly impossible.
오늘날 어떤 일에 있어서 성공하기 위해서는, / 우리는 명심해야 한다 / 눈먼 사람들의 세계에서는 / 한 눈으로 보는 사람이 불가능해
보이는 일을 이룰 수 있다는 것을
The one-eyed person understands / the power of keeping any analysis simple / and will be
the decision maker / when he uses his one eye of intuition.
한 눈으로 보는 사람은 이해하고, / 어떤 분석이든 단순하게 하는 것의 힘을 / 의사 결정자가 될 것이다. / 직관이라는 한 눈을 사용할 때

기술은 의문의 여지가 있는 이점을 지니고 있다. 우리는 정확한 정보만 사용해서 의사 결정
과정을 간소하게 하는 것에 맞추어 너무 많은 정보는 조절해야 한다. 인터넷은 어떤 문제에
대해서든 너무 많은 무료 정보를 이용 가능하게 만들어서 우리는 어떤 결정을 하기 위해서
그 모든 정보를 고려해야 한다고 생각한다. 그래서 우리는 계속 인터넷에서 답을 검색한다.
이것이 우리가 개인적, 사업적, 혹은 다른 결정을 하려고 애쓸 때, 전조등 불빛에 노출된 사
슴처럼 우리를 정보에 눈멀게 만든다. 오늘날 어떤 일에 있어서 성공하기 위해서는, 우리는
눈먼 사람들의 세계에서는 한 눈으로 보는 사람이 불가능해 보이는 일을 이룰 수 있다는 것
을 명심해야 한다. 한 눈으로 보는 사람은 어떤 분석이든 단순하게 하는 것의 힘을 이해하고,
직관이라는 한 눈을 사용할 때 의사 결정자가 될 것이다.

Why? 왜 정답일까?

너무 많은 정보는 의사결정에 도리어 방해가 된다는 정보의 역설을 소재로 한 글이다. 밑줄 앞의 두 문장
에서 우리는 오늘날 선택의 상황에서 관련된 모든 정보를 고려하려고 애쓴다는 것을 지적하고, 글의 마지
막 두 문장에서는 직관을 이용하여 상황을 단순하게 바라볼 때 불가능한 일이 가능해지고 의사결정이 촉
진된다는 결론을 제시한다. 따라서 정보에 눈멀게 된다는 뜻의 밑줄 친 부분은 정보의 과잉으로 인해 의
사결정이 어려워지는 상황을 빗댄 표현으로 볼 수 있어, 답으로 가장 적절한 것은 ③ '너무나 많은 정보
때문에 의사 결정을 할 수 없는'이다.

- **doubtful** ⓐ 의문의 여지가 있는, 의심스러운
- **available** ⓐ 이용 가능한
- **deer** ⓝ 사슴
- **accomplish** ⓥ 달성하다, 성취하다
- **analysis** ⓝ 분석
- **access** ⓥ 접근하다, 이용하다
- **lack** ⓝ 부족, 결여
- **versus** prep ~에 비해
- **blind** ⓐ 눈이 먼
- **personal** ⓐ 사적인, 개인적인
- **seemingly** adv 겉보기에
- **unwilling** ⓐ (~하기를) 꺼리는, 마지못해 하는
- **indifferent** ⓐ 무관심한
- **take a risk** 위험을 감수하다

구문 풀이

3행 The Internet has made so much free information available on any issue
「so + 형용사 +
that we think we have to consider all of it in order to make a decision.
that + 주어 + 동사 : 너무 ~해서 …하다」　　　　　　　　　　~하기 위해

---

22 좋은 습관 형성의 긍정적 영향 　　　　정답률 82% | 정답 ⑤

다음 글의 요지로 가장 적절한 것은?
① 참을성이 많을수록 성공할 가능성이 커진다.
② 한 번 들인 나쁜 습관은 쉽게 고쳐지지 않는다.
③ 나이가 들어갈수록 좋은 습관을 형성하기 힘들다.
④ 무리한 목표를 세우면 달성하지 못할 가능성이 크다.
☑ 하나의 좋은 습관 형성은 생활 전반에 긍정적 효과가 있다.

Recent studies show some interesting findings / about habit formation.
최근의 연구에서는 몇 가지 흥미로운 결과를 보여준다. / 습관 형성에 대한
In these studies, / students who successfully acquired one positive habit / reported less
stress; / less impulsive spending; / better dietary habits; / decreased caffeine consumption;
/ fewer hours spent watching TV; / and even fewer dirty dishes.
이런 연구들에서, / 한 가지 긍정적인 습관을 성공적으로 습득한 학생들은 / 더 적은 스트레스와 / 더 적은 충동적 소비, / 더 좋은 식
습관, / 카페인 소비 감소, / TV 시청 시간 감소, / 그리고 심지어 (설거지를 안 한) 더러운 접시 수의 감소를 보고했다.
Keep working on one habit long enough, / and not only does it become easier, / but so do
other things as well.
한 가지 습관에 충분히 오랜 시간을 들여 노력하라, / 그러면 그것이 쉬워질 뿐 아니라, / 다른 것들 또한 쉬워질 것이다.
It's why / those with the right habits / seem to do better than others.
이 때문에 / 올바른 습관을 가진 사람들은 / 다른 사람들보다 더 뛰어나 보이는 것이다.
They're doing the most important thing regularly / and, as a result, everything else is
easier.
그들은 가장 중요한 것을 규칙적으로 하고 있고 / 그 결과로 다른 모든 것이 더 쉬워진다.

최근의 연구에서는 습관 형성에 대한 몇 가지 흥미로운 결과를 보여준다. 이런 연구들에서,
한 가지 긍정적인 습관을 성공적으로 습득한 학생들은 더 적은 스트레스와 충동적 소비, 더
좋은 식습관, 카페인 소비 감소, TV 시청 시간 감소, 그리고 심지어 (설거지를 안 한) 더러운
접시 수의 감소를 보고했다. 한 가지 습관에 충분히 오랜 시간을 들여 노력하면, 그것이 쉬워
질 뿐 아니라, 다른 것들 또한 쉬워질 것이다. 이 때문에 올바른 습관을 가진 사람들은 다른
사람들보다 더 뛰어나 보이는 것이다. 그들은 가장 중요한 것을 규칙적으로 하고 있고 그 결
과로 다른 모든 것이 더 쉬워진다.

Why? 왜 정답일까?

글 중간의 명령문에서 충분히 오랜 시간 노력하여 한 가지 습관을 들이면 그 습관을 행하는 것이 쉬워질
뿐 아니라 나머지 다른 것들 또한 쉽게 할 수 있을 것(Keep working on one habit long enough,
and not only does it become easier, but so do other things as well.)이라 이야기하며
좋은 습관을 형성하는 것의 긍정적 영향에 대해 말하고 있으므로, 글의 요지로 가장 적절한 것은 ⑤ '하나
의 좋은 습관 형성은 생활 전반에 긍정적 효과가 있다.'이다.

- **finding** ⓝ 결과, 결론
- **formation** ⓝ 형성
- **acquire** ⓥ 습득하다, 얻다
- **work on** ~하려고 노력하다
- **habit** ⓝ 버릇
- **successfully** adv 성공적으로
- **dietary** ⓐ 식사의
- **regularly** adv 규칙적으로

구문 풀이

5행 Keep working on one habit long enough, / and not only does it become
「keep + 동명사 : 계속해서 ~하다」 「not only + A(도치) +
easier, but so do other things as well.
but + B(긍정 동의) as well : A뿐 아니라 B도」

---

23 바닷가 모래의 형성
정답률 71% | 정답 ③

다음 글의 주제로 가장 적절한 것은?

① things to cause the travel of water – 물의 이동을 유발하는 것
② factors to determine the size of sand – 모래의 크기를 결정하는 요인
✓③ how most sand on the beach is formed – 대부분의 바닷가 모래가 형성되는 방법
④ many uses of sand in various industries – 다양한 산업에서의 모래의 많은 용도
⑤ why sand is disappearing from the beach – 해변에서 모래가 사라지고 있는 이유

While some sand is formed in oceans / from things like shells and rocks, / most sand is made up of tiny bits of rock / that came all the way from the mountains!
어떤 모래는 바다에서 만들어지기도 하지만, / 조개껍데기나 암초 같은 것들로부터 / 대부분의 모래는 암석의 작은 조각들로 이루어져 있다! / 멀리 산맥에서 온
But that trip can take thousands of years.
그런데 그 여정은 수천 년이 걸릴 수 있다.
Glaciers, wind, and flowing water / help move the rocky bits along, / with the tiny travelers getting smaller and smaller / as they go.
빙하, 바람 그리고 흐르는 물은 / 이 암석 조각들을 운반하는 데 도움이 되고, / 작은 여행자들(암석 조각들)은 점점 더 작아진다. / 이동하면서
If they're lucky, / a river may give them a lift / all the way to the coast.
만약 운이 좋다면, / 강물이 그것들을 실어다 줄지도 모른다. / 해안까지 내내
There, / they can spend the rest of their years / on the beach as sand.
거기서, / 그것들은 여생을 보낼 수 있다. / 해변에서 모래가 되어

어떤 모래는 바다에서 조개껍데기나 암초 같은 것들로부터 만들어지기도 하지만, 대부분의 모래는 저 멀리 산맥에서 온 작은 암석 조각들로 이루어져 있다! 그런데 그 여정은 수천 년이 걸릴 수 있다. 빙하, 바람 그리고 흐르는 물은 이 암석 조각들의 운반을 돕고, 작은 여행자들(암석 조각들)은 이동하면서 점점 더 작아진다. 만약 운이 좋다면, 강물이 그것들을 해안까지 내내 실어다 줄지도 모른다. 거기서, 그것들은 해변에서 모래로 여생을 보낼 수 있다.

Why? 왜 정답일까?

첫 문장에서 대부분의 바닷가 모래는 멀리 산맥에서 온 작은 암석 조각들로 이루어져 있다고 말한 뒤(~ most sand is made up of tiny bits of rock that came all the way from the mountains!), 이어지는 문장은 산맥의 모래가 바다에 이르는 여정이 수천 년에 달할 수도 있는 긴 과정임을 언급한다(But that trip can take thousands of years.). 즉 바닷가의 모래가 어떻게 바다까지 오는지를 설명하는 것이 글의 주제이므로, 답으로 가장 적절한 것은 ③ '대부분의 바닷가 모래가 형성되는 방법'이다.

● **form** ⓥ 형성하다, 만들다
● **be made up of** ~로 이루어지다
● **glacier** ⓝ 빙하
● **rocky** ⓐ 바위로 된
● **coast** ⓝ 해안
● **shell** ⓝ 조개껍데기
● **bit** ⓝ (작은) 조각
● **flow** ⓥ 흐르다
● **give a lift** ~을 실어다 주다, 태워주다, 들어 올리다
● **rest** ⓝ (어떤 것의) 나머지

구문 풀이

4행 Glaciers, wind, and flowing water help move the rocky bits along, /
주어(복수 취급) 동사 목적어(원형부정사)
with the tiny travelers getting smaller and smaller as they go.
「with + 목적어 + 현재분사 : ~하면서」 비교급 형용사(getting의 보어) └→~함에 따라

---

24 도시 생활의 매력
정답률 69% | 정답 ①

다음 글의 제목으로 가장 적절한 것을 고르시오.

✓① The City's Greatest Attraction: People – 도시의 가장 큰 매력: 사람들
② Leave the City, Live in the Country – 도시를 떠나 시골에서 살라
③ Make More Parks in the City – 도시에 더 많은 공원 만들기
④ Feeling Lonely in the Crowded Streets – 사람 많은 거리에서 고독함 느끼기
⑤ Ancient Cities Full of Tourist Attractions – 관광명소로 가득한 고대 도시들

Studies from cities all over the world / show the importance of life and activity / as an urban attraction.
전 세계 도시에서 이루어진 연구는 / 생활과 활동의 중요성을 보여준다. / 도시의 매력으로서
People gather where things are happening / and seek the presence of other people.
사람들은 일이 일어나고 있는 곳에 모여들고 / 타인의 존재를 찾아나선다.
Faced with the choice of walking down an empty or a lively street, / most people would choose the street with life and activity.
비어있는 거리 또는 활기찬 거리를 걷는 것에 관한 선택에 직면했을 때, / 대부분의 사람들은 활기와 활동이 있는 거리를 선택한다.
The walk will be more interesting and feel safer.
(활기찬 곳에서의) 걷기는 더 즐겁고 더 안전하게 느껴질 것이다.
Events where we can watch people perform or play music / attract many people to stay and watch.
다른 사람들이 공연하거나 음악을 연주하는 것을 볼 수 있는 행사는 / 많은 사람들을 끌어들여 자리에 머물러 보게 한다.
Studies of benches and chairs in city space / show / that the seats with the best view of city life / are used far more frequently / than those that do not offer a view of other people.
도시 공간 내 벤치나 의자에 관한 연구는 / 보여준다. / 도시 생활을 가장 잘 관망할 수 있는 자리가 / 훨씬 더 자주 이용된다는 것을 / 다른 사람의 풍경을 잘 볼 수 없는 곳보다

전 세계 도시에서 이루어진 연구는 도시의 매력으로서 생활과 활동의 중요성을 보여준다. 사람들은 일이 일어나고 있는 곳에 모여들고 타인의 존재를 찾아나선다. 비어있는 거리 또는 활기찬 거리를 걷는 것에 관한 선택에 직면했을 때, 대부분의 사람들은 활기와 활동이 있는 거리를 선택한다. (활기찬 곳에서의) 걷기는 더 즐겁고 더 안전하게 느껴질 것이다. 다른 사

람들이 공연하거나 음악을 연주하는 것을 볼 수 있는 행사는 많은 사람들을 끌어들여 자리에 머물러 보게 한다. 도시 공간 내 벤치나 의자에 관한 연구는 도시 생활을 가장 잘 관망할 수 있는 자리가 다른 사람의 풍경을 잘 볼 수 없는 곳보다 훨씬 더 자주 이용된다는 것을 보여준다.

Why? 왜 정답일까?

첫 문장에서 전 세계 도시에서 이루어진 연구가 도시의 매력으로서 생활과 활동이 중요하다는 것을 보여준다(Studies from cities all over the world show the importance of life and activity as an urban attraction.)고 이야기한 후 활기찬 거리, 길거리 행사, 의자나 벤치 등의 내용을 예로 제시한 글이다. 따라서 글의 제목으로 가장 적절한 것은 ① '도시의 가장 큰 매력: 사람들'이다.

● **urban** ⓐ 도시의
● **gather** ⓥ 모이다
● **presence** ⓝ 존재
● **perform** ⓥ 공연하다, 연기하다, 수행하다
● **frequently** ⓪ 자주
● **attraction** ⓝ 매력, 끌림, 명소
● **seek** ⓥ 찾다, 구하다
● **lively** ⓐ 활기찬
● **attract** ⓥ 끌어들이다, 마음을 끌다

구문 풀이

6행 Events [where we can watch people perform or play music] attract many
주어 관계부사 지각 동사 목적어 목적격 보어1 목적격 보어2 동사
people to stay and watch.

---

25 5개 국가에서의 뉴스 영상 소비
정답률 81% | 정답 ③

다음 도표의 내용과 일치하지 않는 것은?

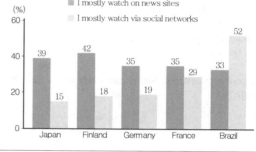

News Video Consumption: on News Sites vs. via Social Networks

	Japan	Finland	Germany	France	Brazil
I mostly watch on news sites	39	42	35	35	33
I mostly watch via social networks	15	18	19	29	52

The above graph shows / how people in five countries consume news videos: / on news sites versus via social networks.
위 그래프는 보여준다. / 다섯 개 국가에서 사람들이 뉴스 영상을 소비하는 방식. / 즉 뉴스 사이트에서의 뉴스 영상 소비 대 소셜 네트워크를 통한 뉴스 영상 소비를
① Consuming news videos on news sites / is more popular than via social networks / in four countries.
뉴스 영상 사이트에서의 뉴스 영상 소비는 / 소셜 네트워크를 통한 것보다 더 인기가 있다. / 네 개 국가에서
② As for people / who mostly watch news videos on news sites, / Finland shows the highest percentage / among the five countries.
사람들에 있어서는 / 주로 뉴스 사이트에서 뉴스 영상을 시청하는 / 핀란드가 가장 높은 비율을 보여 준다. / 다섯 개 국가 중에서
✓③ The percentage of people / who mostly watch news videos on news sites in France / is higher than that in Germany.
사람들의 비율은 / 프랑스에서 주로 뉴스 사이트에서 뉴스 영상을 시청하는 / 독일에서의 비율보다 더 높다.
④ As for people / who mostly watch news videos via social networks, / Japan shows the lowest percentage / among the five countries.
사람들에 있어서는 / 주로 소셜 네트워크를 통해 뉴스 영상을 시청하는 / 일본이 가장 낮은 비율을 보여 준다. / 다섯 개 국가 중에서
⑤ Brazil shows the highest percentage of people / who mostly watch news videos via social networks / among the five countries.
브라질 사람들의 가장 높은 비율을 보여 준다. / 주로 소셜 네트워크를 통해 뉴스 영상을 시청하는 / 다섯 개 국가 중에서

위 그래프는 다섯 개 국가에서 사람들이 뉴스 영상을 소비하는 방식, 즉 뉴스 사이트에서의 뉴스 영상 소비 대 소셜 네트워크를 통한 뉴스 영상 소비를 보여준다. ① 뉴스 영상 사이트에서의 뉴스 영상 소비는 네 개 국가에서 소셜 네트워크를 통한 것보다 더 인기가 있다. ② 주로 뉴스 사이트에서 뉴스 영상을 시청하는 사람들에 있어서는 핀란드가 다섯 개 국가 중에서 가장 높은 비율을 보여 준다. ③ 프랑스에서 주로 뉴스 사이트에서 뉴스 영상을 시청하는 사람들의 비율은 독일에서의 비율보다 더 높다. ④ 주로 소셜 네트워크를 통해 뉴스 영상을 시청하는 사람들에 있어서는 다섯 개 국가 중에서 일본이 가장 낮은 비율을 보여 준다. ⑤ 브라질은 다섯 개 국가 중에서 주로 소셜 네트워크를 통해 뉴스 영상을 시청하는 사람들의 가장 높은 비율을 보여 준다.

Why? 왜 정답일까?

도표에 따르면 프랑스에서 뉴스 사이트에서 뉴스 영상을 보는 사람들의 비율은 35%인데, 독일 또한 같은 항목에서 동일한 비율을 보이므로, 도표와 일치하지 않는 것은 ③이다.

● **consume** ⓝ 소비하다, 쓰다
● **among** prep ~사이에, ~중에
● **via** prep ~을 통하여, ~을 경유하여
● **mostly** ⓪ 주로, 대개

---

26 chuckwalla의 특징
정답률 90% | 정답 ④

chuckwalla에 관한 다음 글의 내용과 일치하지 않는 것은?

① 길이가 45cm까지 자랄 수 있다.
② 대부분 갈색이거나 검은색이다.
③ 등을 따라 꼬리까지 짙은 갈색 선들이 나 있다.
✓④ 수컷의 몸통 색깔은 나이가 들수록 짙어진다.
⑤ 어린 수컷의 생김새는 암컷과 비슷하다.

「Chuckwallas are fat lizards, usually 20-25 cm long, / though they may grow up to 45 cm.」
Chuckwalla는 보통 20~25cm 길이의 통통한 도마뱀이다. / 비록 그들이 45cm까지 자랄 수도 있지만 **①의 근거 일치**
They weigh about 1.5kg / when mature.
무게는 1.5kg 정도 나간다. / 다 크면

『Most chuckwallas are mainly brown or black.』 ②의근거 일치
대부분의 Chuckwalla는 주로 갈색 또는 검정색이다.
Just after the annual molt, / the skin is shiny.
매년의 탈피 직후에, / 피부는 윤이 난다.
『Lines of dark brown run along the back / and continue down the tail.』 ③의근거 일치
짙은 갈색 선들이 등을 따라 / 꼬리까지 이어져 있다.
『As the males grow older, / these brown lines disappear / and the body color becomes
lighter;』 / the tail becomes almost white.   ④의근거 불일치
수컷은 자라면서 / 이 갈색 선이 사라지고 / 몸의 색깔이 밝아진다. / 꼬리는 거의 흰색이 된다.
『It is not easy / to distinguish between male and female chuckwallas, / because young
males look like females / and the largest females resemble males.』 ⑤의근거 일치
쉽지 않은데, / chuckwalla 수컷과 암컷을 구별하는 거는 / 어린 수컷은 암컷처럼 생겼고 / 가장 큰 암컷은 수컷을 닮기 때문에 그렇다.

Chuckwalla는 보통 20 ~ 25cm 길이의 뚱뚱한 도마뱀이지만, 45cm까지 자랄 수도 있다. 무게는 다 크면 1.5kg 정도 나간다. 대부분의 Chuckwalla는 주로 갈색 또는 검정색이다. 매년의 탈피 직후에, 피부는 윤이 난다. 짙은 갈색 선들이 등을 따라 꼬리까지 이어져 있다. 수컷은 자라면서 이 갈색 선이 사라지고 몸의 색깔이 밝아진다. 꼬리는 거의 흰색이 된다. chuckwalla 수컷과 암컷의 구별은 쉽지 않은데, 어린 수컷은 암컷처럼 생겼고 가장 큰 암컷은 수컷을 닮기 때문에 그렇다.

Why? 왜 정답일까?
'As the males grow older, these brown lines disappear and the body color becomes lighter,'에서 수컷은 자라면서 몸 색깔이 짙어지지 않고 도리어 밝아진다는 내용을 확인할 수 있다. 따라서 chuckwalla에 관한 글의 내용과 일치하지 않는 것은 ④ '수컷의 몸통 색깔은 나이가 들수록 짙어진다.'이다.

Why? 왜 오답일까?
① 'Chuckwallas are fat lizards, usually 20–25cm long, though they may grow up to 45cm.'의 내용과 일치한다.
② 'Most chuckwallas are mainly brown or black.'의 내용과 일치한다.
③ 'Lines of dark brown run along the back and continue down the tail.'의 내용과 일치한다.
⑤ '~. because young males look like females and the largest females resemble males.'의 내용과 일치한다.

- lizard ⓝ 도마뱀
- weigh ⓥ 무게가 ~이다
- annual ⓐ 매년의, 1년의
- distinguish ⓥ 구별하다
- up to ~까지
- mature ⓐ 다 자란, 성숙한
- disappear ⓥ 사라지다
- resemble ⓥ 닮다

구문 풀이
> 7행 It is not easy to distinguish between male and female chuckwallas, /
> 가주어   진주어   「between A and B : A와 B 사이」
> because young males look like females and the largest females resemble males.
>   ~처럼 보이다   ~을 닮다(타동사)

---

27 스마트 워치 기능 소개   정답률 75% | 정답 ⑤

L-19 Smart Watch 사용에 관한 다음 안내문의 내용과 일치하는 것은?
① A를 짧게 누르면 스포츠 모드로 들어간다.
② B를 길게 누르면 '홈' 메뉴로 돌아간다.
③ C를 길게 누르면 배경 화면의 불빛이 커지거나 꺼진다.
④ D를 누르면 설정값이 내려간다.
☑ 업그레이드 오류를 피하려면 배터리 잔량 표시가 최소 두 칸은 되어야 한다.

L-19 Smart Watch
L-19 Smart Watch
User Guide
사용 설명서
KEY FUNCTIONS
주요 기능
『A Short press to confirm; / long press to enter the sports mode.』 ①의근거 불일치
설정값을 확정하려면 짧게 누르시오; / 스포츠 모드로 들어가려면 길게 누르시오.
『B Short press to return to the 'home' menu; / long press to send SOS location.』
'홈' 메뉴로 돌아가려면 짧게 누르시오; / 구조 요청 위치 정보를 보내려면 길게 누르시오. ②의근거 불일치
『C Short press to turn on or off the background light; / long press to turn on or off your
watch.』 ③의근거 불일치
배경 화면의 불빛을 켜거나 끄려면 짧게 누르시오; / 시계를 켜거나 끄려면 길게 누르시오.
『D Press to go up. / (In time, date or other settings, / press the key to increase the value.)』
설정값을 올리려면 누르시오. / (시간, 날짜, 혹은 다른 설정에서 / 값을 올리려면 키를 누르시오.) ④의근거 불일치
E Press to go down. / (In time, date or other settings, / press the key to decrease the
value.)
설정값을 내리려면 누르시오. / (시간, 날짜, 혹은 다른 설정에서 / 값을 내리려면 키를 누르시오.)
CAUTION
주의 사항
『Make sure / the battery level of your watch / has at least two bars, / in order to avoid an
upgrading error.』 ⑤의근거 일치
반드시 하십시오. / 시계의 배터리 잔량 표시가 / 최소 두 칸은 되도록 / 업그레이드 오류를 피하려면

L-19 Smart Watch

사용 설명서

주요 기능
A 설정값을 확정하려면 짧게 누르시오; 스포츠 모드로 들어가려면 길게 누르시오.
B '홈' 메뉴로 돌아가려면 짧게 누르시오; 구조 요청 위치 정보를 보내려면 길게 누르시오.
C 배경 화면의 불빛을 켜거나 끄려면 짧게 누르시오; 시계를 켜거나 끄려면 길게 누르시오.
D 설정값을 올리려면 누르시오. (시간, 날짜, 혹은 다른 설정에서 값을 올리려면 키를 누르시오.)

E 설정값을 내리려면 누르시오. (시간, 날짜, 혹은 다른 설정에서 값을 내리려면 키를 누르시오.)
주의 사항
업그레이드 오류를 피하기 위하여, 반드시 시계의 배터리 잔량 표시가 최소 두 칸은 되도록 하십시오.

Why? 왜 정답일까?
'Make sure the battery level of your watch has at least two bars, in order to avoid an upgrading error.'에서 업그레이드 오류를 피하려면 시계의 배터리 잔량 표시가 반드시 최소 두 칸은 되도록 해야 한다는 내용이 나오므로, 안내문의 내용과 일치하는 것은 ⑤ '업그레이드 오류를 피하려면 배터리 잔량 표시가 최소 두 칸은 되어야 한다.'이다.

Why? 왜 오답일까?
① 'A ~ long press to enter the sports mode.'에서 스포츠 모드로 들어가려면 A를 길게 누르라고 하였다.
② 'B Short press to return to the 'home' menu; ~'에서 '홈' 메뉴로 돌아가려면 B를 짧게 누르라고 하였다.
③ 'C Short press to turn on or off the background light; ~'에서 배경화면의 불빛을 켜거나 끄려면 C를 짧게 누르라고 하였다.
④ 'D Press to go up. (In time, date or other settings, press the key to increase the value.)'에서 설정값을 올리려면 D를 누르라고 하였다.

- function ⓝ 기능
- background light 배경화면 불빛

---

28 합창단 오디션 안내   정답률 83% | 정답 ④

2017 Happy Voice Choir Audition에 관한 다음 안내문의 내용과 일치하지 않는 것은?
① 학교 동아리가 개최한다.
② 신입생이면 누구나 참가할 수 있다.
③ 3월 24일에 강당에서 열린다.
☑ 지원자는 자신이 선택한 두 곡을 불러야 한다.
⑤ 참가하려면 이메일을 보내야 한다.

2017 Happy Voice Choir Audition
2017 Happy Voice 합창단 오디션
Do you love to sing?
노래 부르는 것을 좋아하세요?
『Happy Voice, one of the most famous school clubs, / is holding an audition for you.』
가장 인기 있는 학교 동아리 중 하나인 Happy Voice에서 / 여러분을 위한 오디션을 개최합니다. ①의근거 일치
Come and join us for some very exciting performances!
오셔서 몇 가지 아주 즐거운 공연에 함께 하세요!
『Who: Any freshman』 ②의근거 일치
대상: 신입생 누구나
『When: Friday, March 24, 3 p.m.』
일시: 3월 24일 금요일 오후 3시
Where: Auditorium』 ③의근거 일치
장소: 강당
『All applicants should sing two songs:』
모든 지원자 분들은 두 곡의 노래를 부르셔야 합니다.
1st song: *Oh Happy Day!*
첫 곡: *Oh Happy Day!*
2nd song: You choose your own.』 ④의근거 불일치
두 번째 곡: 직접 선택하세요.
『To enter the audition, / please email us at hvaudition@qmail.com.』 ⑤의근거 일치
오디션에 참가하려면, / hvaudition@qmail.com으로 이메일을 보내주세요.
For more information, / visit the school website.
더 많은 정보를 얻으려면 학교 웹 사이트를 방문해 주세요.

2017 Happy Voice 합창단 오디션

노래 부르는 것을 좋아하세요? 가장 인기 있는 학교 동아리 중 하나인 Happy Voice에서 여러분을 위한 오디션을 개최합니다. 오셔서 몇 가지 아주 즐거운 공연에 함께 하세요!

- 대상: 신입생 누구나
- 일시: 3월 24일 금요일 오후 3시
- 장소: 강당

모든 지원자 분들은 두 곡의 노래를 부르셔야 합니다.
– 첫 곡: *Oh Happy Day!*
– 두 번째 곡: 직접 선택하세요.

오디션에 참가하시려면, hvaudition @ qmail.com으로 이메일을 보내주세요.

더 많은 정보를 얻으시려면 학교 웹 사이트를 방문해 주세요.

Why? 왜 정답일까?
'All applicants should sing two songs:' 문장을 통해 한 곡은 *Oh Happy Day!*라는 지정곡을, 나머지는 본인이 선택한 곡을 부른다는 것을 알 수 있으므로, 2017 Happy Voice Choir Audition에 관한 안내문의 내용과 일치하지 않는 것은 ④ '지원자는 자신이 선택한 두 곡을 불러야 한다.'이다.

Why? 왜 오답일까?
① 'Happy Voice, one of the most famous school clubs, is holding an audition for you.'의 내용과 일치한다.
② 'Who: Any freshman'의 내용과 일치한다.
③ 'When: Friday, March 24, 3 p.m. / Where: Auditorium'의 내용과 일치한다.
⑤ 'To enter the audition, please email us at hvaudition@qmail.com.'의 내용과 일치한다.

- freshman ⓝ 신입생
- applicant ⓝ 지원자
- information ⓝ 정보, 자료
- auditorium ⓝ 강당, 방청석, 청중석
- enter ⓥ 참가하다, 들어가다. 입장하다

구문 풀이

1행 Happy Voice, one of the most famous school clubs, is holding an audition for you.
주어 / 동격구 / 동사

★★★ 등급을 가르는 문제!

29 정서에 영향을 미치는 조명　　　정답률 49% | 정답 ④

다음 글의 밑줄 친 부분 중, 어법상 틀린 것은?

Bad lighting can increase stress on your eyes, / as can light that is too bright, / or light that shines ① directly into your eyes.
좋지 못한 조명은 여러분의 눈에 스트레스를 증가시킬 수 있다. / 너무 밝은 빛이나 / 눈에 직선으로 들어오는 빛과 마찬가지로

Fluorescent lighting can also be ② tiring.
형광등 또한 피로감을 줄 수 있다.

What you may not appreciate is / that the quality of light may also be important.
여러분이 모를 수도 있는 것은 / 빛의 질 또한 중요할 수 있다는 것이다.

Most people are happiest in bright sunshine / — this may cause a release of chemicals in the body / ③ that bring a feeling of emotional well-being.
대부분의 사람들은 밝은 햇빛 속에서 가장 행복하다 / 이것은 아마 체내 화학물질을 분비시킬지도 모른다. / 정서적인 행복감을 주는

Artificial light, / which typically contains only a few wavelengths of light, / ④ does not seem to have the same effect on mood / that sunlight has.
인공조명이 / 전형적으로 몇 개 안 되는 빛 파장만 포함하는 / 기분에 미치는 효과는 똑같지 않을 / 햇빛이 미치는 효과와

Try experimenting / with working by a window / or ⑤ using full spectrum bulbs in your desk lamp.
실험해 보아라. / 창가에서 작업하거나 / 책상 전등에 있는 모든 파장이 있는 전구를 사용하여

You will probably find / that this improves the quality / of your working environment.
아마도 알게 될 것이다. / 이것이 질을 향상시킨다는 것을 / 여러분의 작업 환경의

너무 밝은 빛이나 눈에 직선으로 들어오는 빛과 마찬가지로 좋지 못한 조명은 여러분의 눈에 스트레스를 증가시킬 수 있다. 형광등 또한 피로감을 줄 수 있다. 여러분이 모를 수도 있는 것은 빛의 질 또한 중요할 수 있다는 것이다. 대부분의 사람들은 밝은 햇빛 속에서 가장 행복하다 — 이것은 아마 정서적인 행복감을 주는 체내 화학물질을 분비시킬지도 모른다. 전형적으로 몇 개 안 되는 빛 파장만 포함하는 인공 조명이 기분에 미치는 효과는 햇빛과 똑같지 않을 수 있다. 창가에서 작업하거나 책상 전등에 있는 모든 파장이 있는 전구를 사용하여 실험해 보아라. 이것이 여러분의 작업 환경의 질을 향상시킨다는 것을 아마도 알게 될 것이다.

Why? 왜 정답일까?

주어가 불가산명사인 Artificial light이므로 동사는 단수인 does로 쓰는 것이 적절하다. 따라서 어법상 틀린 것은 ④이다.

Why? 왜 오답일까?

① 동사 shines를 꾸미는 말로서 부사 directly의 쓰임은 어법상 맞다.
② 주어인 Fluorescent lighting이 피로감을 주는 주체이므로 능동의 현재분사 tiring의 쓰임은 어법상 맞다.
③ 선행사 chemicals를 꾸미고 뒤에 복수 동사 bring를 연결하는 말로서 주격 관계대명사 that의 쓰임은 어법상 맞다.
⑤ 등위접속사 or 앞에 동명사 experimenting이 나오므로, 이와 병렬을 이루도록 동명사인 using을 쓴 것은 어법상 맞다. 두 동명사는 명령문 동사 Try의 목적어이다.

- lighting ⓝ 조명, 빛
- directly ⓐⓓ 곧장, 똑바로
- release ⓝ 분비, 방출
- emotional ⓐ 정서적인
- typically ⓐⓓ 일반적으로
- experiment ⓥ 실험하다 ⓝ 실험
- bright ⓐ 밝은
- appreciate ⓥ 이해하다
- chemical ⓝ 화학 물질
- artificial ⓐ 인공의
- wavelength ⓝ 파장, 주파수
- improve ⓥ 향상시키다, 개선하다

구문 풀이

1행 Bad lighting can increase stress on your eyes, / as can light [that is too bright], or light [that shines directly into your eyes].
「as + 동사 + 주어: ~이 …하듯이(도치 구문)」

★★ 문제 해결 꿀~팁 ★★

▶ 많이 틀린 이유는?
최다 오답인 ②는 감정 유발 동사의 태를 묻고 있다. 감정 유발 동사를 분사로 바꿀 때에는 분사가 설명하는 명사에 따라 태를 결정한다. 즉 명사가 감정을 유발하는 주체라면 현재분사를, 감정을 느끼게 되는 대상이라면 과거분사를 쓴다. 여기서는 분사가 주어인 '형광등'을 설명하는데 이는 피로감을 유발하는 주체로 보는 것이 타당하다. 따라서 tiring의 쓰임은 어법상 맞다.

▶ 문제 해결 방법은?
④에서 묻는 수 일치 개념은 어법 최빈출 포인트 중 하나이다. 뒤에 관계절을 수반하는 긴 주어가 나오면 관계절이 어디에서 시작되고 끝나는지, 주어의 핵심부는 무엇인지 눈여겨보고 동사의 단복수 여부를 결정하도록 한다.

30 화가들의 제한적인 색상 선택　　　정답률 50% | 정답 ⑤

다음 글의 밑줄 친 부분 중, 문맥상 낱말의 쓰임이 적절하지 않은 것은? [3점]

Painters have in principle / an infinite range of colours at their disposal, / especially in modern times / with the chromatic ① explosion of synthetic chemistry.
이론상으로 화가들은 사용할 수 있는데, / 무한한 범위의 색을 마음대로 / 현대에 특히 그렇다. / 합성 화학을 통한 유채색의 폭발적 증가를 이룬

And yet / painters don't use all the colours at once, / and indeed many have used / a remarkably ② restrictive selection.
그러나 / 화가들이 모든 색을 동시에 사용하는 것은 아닌데, / 사실 많은 화가들은 사용해 왔다. / 눈에 띄게 제한적으로 색을 선택하여

Mondrian limited himself / mostly to the three primaries red, yellow and blue / to fill his black-ruled grids, / and Kasimir Malevich worked / with similar self-imposed restrictions.
Mondrian은 스스로를 제한했고, / 대개 빨강, 노랑, 그리고 파랑의 3원색으로 / 자신의 검정색 선이 그려진 격자무늬를 채우기 위해 / Kasimir Malevich는 작업했다. / 비슷하게 스스로 부과한 제한에 따라

For Yves Klein, one colour was ③ enough; / Franz Kline's art was typically black on white.
Yves Klein에게는 한 가지 색이면 충분했고, / Franz Klein의 예술(작품)은 보통 흰색 바탕 위에 검정색이었다.

There was nothing ④ new in this: / the Greeks and Romans tended to use / just red, yellow, black and white.
여기에는 새로울 것이 없었는데, / 그리스와 로마 사람들은 사용하는 경향이 있었다. / 단지 빨간색, 노란색, 검정색 그리고 흰색만을

Why?
왜 그랬을까?

It's impossible to generalize, / but both in antiquity and modernity / it seems likely / that the ⑤ limited palette aided clarity and comprehensibility, / and helped to focus attention / on the components that mattered: / shape and form.
일반화할 수는 없지만, / 고대와 현대에 모두 / ~했을 것 같다. / (범위가) 제한된 팔레트가 [색이] 명확성과 이해 가능성에 도움을 주고 / 주의를 집중할 수 있도록 도움을 주었을 / 중요한 구성요소인 / 모양과 형태에

이론상으로 화가들은 무한한 범위의 색을 마음대로 사용할 수 있는데, 합성 화학에서 유채색의 ① 폭발적 증가를 이룬 현대에 특히 그렇다. 그러나 화가들이 모든 색을 동시에 사용하는 것은 아닌데, 사실 많은 화가들은 눈에 띄게 ② 제한적으로 색을 선택하여 사용해 왔다. Mondrian은 자신의 검정색 선이 그려진 격자무늬를 채우기 위해 대개 빨강, 노랑, 그리고 파랑의 3원색으로 스스로를 제한했고, Kasimir Malevich는 비슷하게 스스로 부과한 제한에 따라 작업했다. Yves Klein에게는 한 가지 색이면 ③ 충분했고, Franz Klein의 예술(작품)은 보통 흰색 바탕 위에 검정색이었다. 여기에는 ④ 새로울 것이 없었는데, 그리스와 로마 사람들은 단지 빨간색, 노란색, 검정색 그리고 흰색만을 사용하는 경향이 있었다. 왜 그랬을까? 일반화할 수는 없지만, 고대와 현대에서 모두 (범위가) ⑤ 확대된(→ 제한된) 팔레트가[색이] 명확성과 이해 가능성에 도움을 주고 중요한 구성 요소인 모양과 형태에 주의를 집중할 수 있도록 도움을 주었던 것 같다.

Why? 왜 정답일까?

다양한 색을 이용할 수 있게 된 현대에 이르러서도 많은 화가들은 고대 시절 화가들이 그랬듯이 제한된 색을 쓰곤 하는데(And yet painters don't use all the colours at once, and indeed many have used a remarkably restrictive selection.) 이것이 모양과 형태에 보다 주의를 기울이게 도와줄 것임을 설명한 글이다. 즉 색이 '제한적으로' 선택되는 이유를 언급하는 것이 글의 핵심이므로, ⑤의 expanded를 limited로 고쳐야 한다. 따라서 낱말의 쓰임이 적절하지 않은 것은 ⑤이다.

- in principle 원칙적으로, 이론상으로
- at one's disposal ~의 마음대로 이용할 수 있는
- synthetic ⓐ 합성인
- restrictive ⓐ 제한적인
- self-imposed 스스로 부과한, 자진해서 하는
- generalize ⓥ 일반화하다
- modernity ⓝ 현대, 현대적임
- aid ⓥ (일이 수월해지도록) 돕다
- comprehensibility ⓝ 이해 가능성
- infinite ⓐ 무한한
- explosion ⓝ 폭발적 증가, 폭발
- remarkably ⓐⓓ 눈에 띄게, 두드러지게
- primary ⓝ 원색 ⓐ 주요한, 기본적인
- typically ⓐⓓ 보통, 대개, 전형적으로
- antiquity ⓝ 고대, 아주 오래됨
- expand ⓥ 확장시키다
- clarity ⓝ 명확성
- component ⓝ 구성 요소

구문 풀이

10행 It's impossible to generalize, but both in antiquity and modernity it seems
가주어 / 진주어 / 주어 동사
likely {that the limited palette aided clarity and comprehensibility, and helped to
보어 [ ]: 명사절 / 동사1 / 동사2
focus attention on the components [that mattered]: shape and form}.
= the components

31 대도시의 분업　　　정답률 48% | 정답 ①

다음 빈칸에 들어갈 말로 가장 적절한 것을 고르시오. [3점]

✓ ① specialization – 전문화
② criticism – 비판
③ competition – 경쟁
④ diligence – 근면
⑤ imagination – 상상

In small towns / the same workman makes chairs and doors and tables, / and often the same person builds houses.
작은 마을에서는 / 똑같은 일꾼이 의자와 문, 탁자를 만들고, / 바로 같은 사람이 종종 집도 짓는다.

And it is, of course, impossible / for a man of many trades / to be skilled in all of them.
그리고 물론 불가능하다. / 많은 직업을 가진 한 사람이 / 그 모든 데 능하기는

In large cities, on the other hand, / because many people make demands on each trade, / one trade alone / — very often even less than a whole trade — / is enough to support a man.
반면에 대도시에서는, / 많은 사람들이 각 직종을 필요로 하기에, / 한 가지 직종만으로도, / 아주 흔하게 전체 직종에 훨씬 못 미치는 / 한 사람이 먹고 사는 데 충분하다.

For instance, / one man makes shoes for men, / and another for women.
예를 들어, / 한 사람은 남자 신발을 만들고, / 다른 사람은 여자 신발을 만든다.

And there are places / even where one man earns a living / by only stitching shoes, / another by cutting them out, / and another by sewing the uppers together.
그리고 경우까지도 있다. / 어떤 사람은 생계를 꾸려가는 / 신발을 깁기만 하여 / 다른 사람은 자르기만 하고, / 또 다른 사람은 신발 윗부분을 꿰매기만 하여

Such skilled workers may have used simple tools, / but their specialization / did result in more efficient and productive work.
그런 숙련된 노동자들은 간단한 도구만을 썼을지도 모르지만, / 그들의 전문화는 / 정말로 더 효율적이고 생산적인 작업으로 이어졌다.

작은 마을에서는 똑같은 일꾼이 의자와 문, 탁자를 만들고, 바로 같은 사람이 종종 집도 짓는다. 그리고 물론 많은 직업을 가진 한 사람이 그 모든 데 능하기는 불가능하다. 반면에 대도시에서는, 많은 사람들이 각 직종을 필요로 하기에, 아주 흔하게 전체 직종에 훨씬 못 미치는 한 가지 직종만으로도, 한 사람이 먹고 사는 데 충분하다. 예를 들어, 한 사람은 남자 신발을 만들고, 다른 사람은 여자 신발을 만든다. 그리고 어떤 사람은 신발을 깁기만 하고, 다른 사람은 자르기만 하고, 또 다른 사람은 신발 윗부분을 꿰매기만 하여 생계를 꾸려가는 경우까지도 있다. 그런 숙련된 노동자들은 간단한 도구만을 썼을지도 모르지만, 그들의 전문화는 정말로 더 효율적이고 생산적인 작업으로 이어졌다.

Why? 왜 정답일까?

작은 마을과 대도시의 업무 방식을 대조한 글이다. 작은 마을에서는 한 사람이 여러 가지 일을 하게 되지만, 대도시에서는 한 사람이 한 가지 직종만 갖고서도 먹고 사는 데 충분하여 분업이 이루어진다(In large cities, ~, because many people make demands on each trade, one trade alone—very often even less than a whole trade—is enough to support a man.)고 이야기하므로, 빈칸에 들어갈 말로 적절한 것은 '분업'과 대응될 수 있는 ① '전문화'이다.

- **workman** ⓝ 일꾼, 노동자, 직공
- **skilled** ⓐ 숙련된
- **stitch** ⓥ 깁다, 꿰매다, 바느질하다
- **result in** ~로 이어지다, ~을 초래하다
- **productive** ⓐ 생산적인
- **diligence** ⓝ 근면
- **impossible** ⓐ 불가능한
- **place** ⓝ 경우
- **sew** ⓥ 꿰매다, 깁다
- **efficient** ⓐ 효율적인
- **criticism** ⓝ 비판

구문 풀이

7행 And there are places [even where one man earns a living by only stitching shoes, another by cutting them out, and another by sewing the uppers together].
동사 / 주어 / 관계부사 / 생계를 꾸리다 / 'by + 동명사: ~함으로써' / (earns a living 생략)

---

32 성장 과정의 일부인 자립 정답률 45% | 정답 ⑤

다음 빈칸에 들어갈 말로 가장 적절한 것을 고르시오. [3점]

① developing financial management skills – 금전 관리 기술을 발달시키는 것
② learning from other people's experiences – 다른 사람의 경험에서 배우는 것
③ figuring out your strengths and interests – 여러분의 강점과 흥미를 알아내는 것
④ managing relationship problems with your peers – 동료와의 인간관계 문제를 관리하는 것
✔ falling out of love with the adults who look after you – 자신을 보살펴 주는 어른과 정을 떼는 것

All mammals need to leave their parents / and set up on their own / at some point.
모든 포유동물은 부모를 떠나서 / 스스로 자립해야 한다 / 어느 시점에서는

But human adults generally provide a comfortable existence / — enough food arrives on the table, / money is given at regular intervals, / the bills get paid / and the electricity for the TV doesn't usually run out.
하지만 성인 인간은 대개 안락한 생활을 제공하는데, / 충분한 음식이 식탁 위에 차려지고, / 일정한 기간마다 돈이 지급되며, / 청구서가 지불되고, / TV 전기가 대개 끊기지 않는다.

If teenagers didn't build up / a fairly major disrespect for and conflict with / their parents or carers, / they'd never want to leave.
십 대 아이가 키우지 않는다면, / 매우 심각한 불손과 갈등을 / 부모나 보호자에 대한 / 그들은 결코 떠나고 싶어 하지 않을 것이다.

In fact, / falling out of love with the adults / who look after you / is probably a necessary part of growing up.
사실, / 어른과의 정을 떼는 것은 / 보살펴 주는 / 아마도 성장의 필수적인 부분일 것이다.

Later, / when you live independently, away from them, / you can start to love them again / because you won't need to be fighting / to get away from them.
나중에, / 여러분이 그들과 떨어져서 독립적으로 생활하게 되면, / 그들을 다시 사랑하기 시작할 수 있다 / 싸울 필요가 없을 것이기 때문에 / 그들에게서 벗어나기 위해서

And you can come back sometimes / for a home-cooked meal.
그리고 여러분은 돌아올 수 있다 / 가끔 집 밥을 먹기 위해

모든 포유동물은 어느 시점에서는 부모를 떠나서 자립해야 한다. 하지만 성인 인간은 대개 안락한 생활을 제공하여, 충분한 음식이 식탁 위에 차려지고, 일정한 기간마다 돈이 지급되며, 청구서가 지불되고, TV 전기가 대개 끊기지 않는다. 십 대 아이가 부모나 보호자에 대한 매우 심각한 불손과 갈등을 키우지 않는다면, 그들은 결코 떠나고 싶어 하지 않을 것이다. 사실, 자신을 보살펴 주는 어른과 정을 떼는 것은 아마도 성장의 필수적인 부분일 것이다. 나중에, 여러분이 그들과 떨어져서 독립적으로 생활하게 되면, 그들에게서 벗어나기 위해서 싸울 필요가 없을 것이기 때문에 그들을 다시 사랑하기 시작할 수 있을 것이다. 그리고 여러분은 가끔 집 밥을 먹기 위해 돌아올 수 있다.

Why? 왜 정답일까?

첫 문장에서 모든 포유류는 어느 시점이 되면 부모를 떠나 자립해야 한다(All mammals need to leave their parents and set up on their own at some point.)는 핵심 내용이 나오므로, 강조의 연결어인 In fact 뒤의 빈칸 또한 '자립'에 관련된 내용을 언급할 것임을 유추할 수 있다. 따라서 빈칸에 들어갈 말로 가장 적절한 것은 ⑤ '자신을 보살펴 주는 어른과 정을 떼는 것'이다.

- **mammal** ⓝ 포유동물
- **existence** ⓝ 생활, 생계, 존재, 현존
- **run out** (공급품 등이) 다 떨어지다
- **disrespect** ⓝ 불손, 무례, 결례
- **independently** ⓐd 독립하여
- **financial** ⓐ 재정적인, 금전적인
- **peer** ⓝ 동료, 친구
- **fall out of love with** ~와 정을 떼다
- **point** ⓝ 지점
- **interval** ⓝ 간격
- **fairly** ⓐd 상당히, 꽤
- **conflict** ⓝ 갈등, 충돌
- **home-cooked** 가정에서 만든
- **strength** ⓝ 강점, 힘
- **manage** ⓥ 살아 나가다, 지내다

구문 풀이

2행 But human adults generally provide a comfortable existence / {— enough food arrives on the table, money is given at regular intervals, the bills get paid and the electricity for the TV doesn't usually run out}.
: a comfortable existence의 내용 설명 / 주어1 / 동사1(자동사) / 주어2 / 동사2(수동태) / 주어3 / 동사3(수동태) / 주어4 / 동사4(자동사)

★★★ 등급을 가르는 문제!
33 광고와 지도 제작의 공통된 특성 정답률 39% | 정답 ②

다음 빈칸에 들어갈 말로 가장 적절한 것을 고르시오. [3점]

① reducing the amount of information – 정보의 양을 줄여서
✔ telling or showing everything – 모든 것을 말하거나 보여줌
③ listening to people's voices – 사람들의 목소리에 귀 기울여서
④ relying on visual images only – 시각 이미지에만 의존해서
⑤ making itself available to everyone – 자체로 모두가 이용 가능하게 만들어서

What do advertising and map-making have in common?
광고와 지도 제작은 무슨 공통점이 있을까?

Without doubt / the best answer is their shared need / to communicate a limited version of the truth.
의심할 여지없이 / 최고의 대답은 공통된 필요성에 있다 / 제한된 형태의 사실을 전달하는

An advertisement must create an image / that's appealing / and a map must present an image that's clear, / but neither can meet its goal / by telling or showing everything.
광고는 이미지를 만들어내야 하고 / 매력적인 / 지도는 명백한 이미지를 제시해야 하지만, / 둘 다 목표를 달성할 수는 없다 / 모든 것을 말하거나 보여줌으로써

Ads will cover up or play down / negative aspects of the company or service / they advertise.
광고는 가리거나 약화시킬 것이다. / 회사나 서비스의 부정적인 측면을 / 그들이 광고하는

In this way, / they can promote a favorable comparison with similar products / or differentiate a product from its competitors.
이런 식으로, / 그들은 유사 상품과의 유리한 비교를 홍보하거나 / 제품을 그 경쟁 제품과 차별화할 수 있다.

Likewise, the map must remove details / that would be confusing.
마찬가지로, 지도는 세부사항을 지워야 한다. / 혼란을 줄 수 있는

광고와 지도 제작은 무슨 공통점이 있을까? 의심할 여지없이 최고의 대답은 제한된 형태의 사실을 전달하는 공통된 필요성에 있다. 광고는 매력적인 이미지를 만들어내야 하고 지도는 명백한 이미지를 제시해야 하지만, 둘 다 모든 것을 말하거나 보여줌으로써 목표를 달성할 수는 없다. 광고는 그들이 광고하는 회사나 서비스의 부정적인 측면을 가리거나 약화시킬 것이다. 이런 식으로, 그들은 유사 상품과의 유리한 비교를 홍보하거나 제품을 그 경쟁 제품과 차별화할 수 있다. 마찬가지로, 지도는 혼란을 줄 수 있는 세부사항을 지워야 한다.

Why? 왜 정답일까?

광고와 지도는 서로 제한된 형태의 사실만을 전달하여 목적을 달성한다(Without doubt the best answer is their shared need to communicate a limited version of the truth.)는 내용이다. 광고가 제품의 약점을 숨기거나 축소하여 말하듯이, 지도 또한 혼란을 줄 수 있는 세부사항을 나타내지 않는다는 것을 말하고 있다. 이를 통해 오히려 '모든 것을 말하면' 광고든 지도든 목적을 달성할 수 없으리라는 내용을 유추할 수 있어, 빈칸에 들어갈 말로 가장 적절한 것은 ② '모든 것을 말하거나 보여줌'이다.

- **advertising** ⓝ 광고
- **have in common** (관심사나 생각을) 공통적으로 지니다
- **communicate** ⓥ 전달하다
- **present** ⓥ 제시하다
- **play down** 약화시키다, 낮추다
- **promote** ⓥ 홍보하다, 촉진하다
- **comparison** ⓝ 비교
- **competitor** ⓝ 경쟁자, 경쟁 상대
- **map-making** 지도 제작, 지도 만들기
- **appealing** ⓐ 매력적인
- **meet** ⓥ (목표나 기한 등을) 달성하다, 맞추다
- **aspect** ⓝ 측면
- **favorable** ⓐ 호의적인
- **differentiate** ⓥ 차별화하다
- **confusing** ⓐ 혼란을 주는, 혼란스러운

구문 풀이

2행 Without doubt / the best answer is their shared need to communicate a limited version of the truth.
의심할 여지없이 / 형용사적 용법

★★ 문제 해결 꿀~팁 ★★

▶ 많이 틀린 이유는?
빈칸 문제이니만큼 주제문을 찾으면 쉽게 답에 접근할 수 있으나, 빈칸 문장에 neither라는 부정어가 있으므로 주제를 거꾸로 뒤집은 내용이 답이 된다는 점에서 어려운 문제였다.

▶ 문제 해결 방법은?
글의 주제는 광고와 지도가 공통적으로 제한된 진실만을 담는다는, 즉 '다 말하지 않는' 특성이 있다는 것이다. 이를 빈칸 문장의 맥락에 맞게 뒤집어 생각하면 '다 말하면 광고나 지도가 제 기능을 못한다'는 내용을 유추할 수 있다. 최다 오답인 ①은 '정보 양의 제한'이라는 핵심 내용을 그대로 담고 있기에, 빈칸에 넣으면 오히려 '정보를 제한할 때 광고나 지도 제작의 목적이 달성되지 않는다'는, 주제와 정반대되는 내용을 나타내게 된다.

★★★ 등급을 가르는 문제!
34 문화적 변화에 대한 인간의 태도 정답률 36% | 정답 ⑤

다음 빈칸에 들어갈 말로 가장 적절한 것을 고르시오. [3점]

① seek cooperation between generations – 세대 간 협력을 추구하는
② be forgetful of what they experienced – 그들이 경험한 것을 잘 잊어버리는
③ adjust quickly to the new environment – 새로운 환경에 빠르게 적응하는
④ make efforts to remember what their ancestors did – 자신의 조상이 했던 것을 기억하려고 노력하는
✔ like what they have grown up in and gotten used to – 자신이 자라고 익숙해진 것을 좋아하는

It is difficult to know how to determine / whether one culture is better than another.
방법을 알기는 어렵다. / 한 문화가 다른 문화보다 나은지를 결정하는

What is the cultural rank order / of rock, jazz, and classical music?
문화적인 순위는 어떻게 될까? / 록, 재즈, 고전 음악의

When it comes to public opinion polls / about whether cultural changes are for the better or the worse, / looking forward would lead to one answer / and looking backward would lead to a very different answer.
여론 조사에 관한 한, / 문화적 변화가 더 나아지는 것인지 더 나빠지는 것인지에 관한 / 앞을 내다보는 것과 / 뒤돌아보는 것은 아주 다른 대답으로 이어진다.

Our children would be horrified / if they were told / they had to go back to the culture of their grandparents.
우리 아이들은 겁이 날 것이다. / 말을 들으면 / 조부모의 문화로 되돌아가야 한다는

Our parents would be horrified / if they were told / they had to participate in the culture of their grandchildren.
우리 부모님은 겁이 날 것이다. / 들으면 / 손주의 문화에 참여해야 한다고

Humans tend to like / what they have grown up in / and gotten used to.
인간은 좋아하는 경향이 있다. / 자신이 자라고 / 익숙해진 것을

After a certain age, / anxieties arise / when sudden cultural changes are coming.
특정한 나이 이후에는 / 불안감이 생긴다. / 갑작스러운 문화적 변화가 다가오고 있을 때

Our culture is part of / who we are and where we stand, / and we don't like to think / that who we are and where we stand / are short-lived.
우리 문화는 일부이고, / 우리의 정체성과 우리의 입지의 / 우리는 생각하고 싶어 하지 않는다. / 우리의 정체성과 우리의 입지가 / 오래가지 못한다고

한 문화가 다른 문화보다 더 나은지를 결정하는 방법을 알기는 어렵다. 록, 재즈, 고전 음악의 문화적인 순위는 어떻게 될까? 문화적 변화가 더 나아지는 것인지 더 나빠지는 것인지에 관한 여론 조사에 관한 한, 앞을 내다보는 것과 뒤를 돌아보는 것은 아주 다른 대답으로 이어진다. 우리 아이들은 조부모의 문화로 되돌아가야 한다는 말을 들으면 겁이 날 것이다. 우리 부모님은 손주의 문화에 참여해야 한다고 들으면 겁이 날 것이다. 인간은 자신이 자라고 익숙해진 것을 좋아하는 경향이 있다. 특정한 나이 이후에는 갑작스러운 문화적 변화가 다가오고 있을 때 불안감이 생긴다. 우리 문화는 우리의 정체성과 우리의 입지의 일부이고, 우리는 우리의 정체성과 우리의 입지가 오래가지 못한다고 생각하고 싶어 하지 않는다.

Why? 왜 정답일까?
인간은 특정한 나이가 지나면 갑작스러운 문화의 변화에 불안감을 느끼는데 이는 우리의 문화가 우리 정체성과 입지의 일부로 여겨지기 때문이라는(Our culture is part of who we are and where we stand, ~) 내용을 다룬 글이다. 우리는 우리 자신의 문화가 오래가지 못한다고 여기고 싶어 하지 않는다는 내용의 마지막 문장을 근거로 볼 때, 빈칸 앞의 두 문장에서 언급하듯이 우리가 다른 세대의 문화에 참여해야 한다고 생각하면 겁을 내는 이유는 우리가 우리 자신의 문화를 가장 편하게 여기고 좋아하기 때문임을 유추할 수 있으므로, 빈칸에 들어갈 말로 가장 적절한 것은 ⑤ '자신이 자라고 익숙해진 것을 좋아하는'이다.

- determine ⓥ 결정하다, 정하다
- public opinion poll 여론 조사
- participate in ~에 참여하다
- certain ⓐ 특정한, 일정한
- arise ⓥ 생기다, 발생하다
- seek ⓥ 찾다
- adjust ⓥ 적응하다
- culture ⓝ 문화
- horrified ⓐ 겁에 질린, 무서워하는
- grandchildren ⓝ 손자
- anxiety ⓝ 불안, 걱정
- short-lived 오래 가지 못하는, 단기적인
- cooperation ⓝ 협력
- ancestor ⓝ 조상

구문 풀이
[3행] When it comes to public opinion polls about {whether cultural changes
　　　 ~에 관한 한　　　　 명사구　　　　　　 ~인지 아닌지
are for the better or the worse}, looking forward would lead to one answer and
[ ]: 명사절(about의 목적어)　　 동명사구 주어1　　　 동사1
looking backward would lead to a very different answer.
동명사구 주어2　　　 동사2

★★ 문제 해결 꿀~팁 ★★
▶ 많이 틀린 이유는?
인간은 자신이 익숙하게 느끼는 문화를 좋아한다는 내용의 글로, 빈칸 앞의 예시와 뒤의 결론 내용을 종합하면 답을 고를 수 있다. 최다 오답인 ④는 사람들이 조상의 행동을 기억하려고 애쓴다는 뜻인데 이는 본문의 내용과 관계가 없다. 새로운 환경에 대한 적응력을 언급하는 ③은 우리가 새로운 문화에 잘 적응한다는 뜻으로 이해될 수 있으므로 주제와 상반된다.
▶ 문제 해결 방법은?
결론이 다소 추상적이므로 예시를 통해 글을 이해하면 쉽다. 아이이든 노인이든 서로 다른 세대의 문화에 참여해야 한다면 겁부터 날 것이라는 언급을 통해, 익숙한 것을 좋게 여기는 인간의 특성을 유추하도록 한다.

35　차량 공유 운동의 인기　　　　정답률 53% | 정답 ④

다음 글에서 전체 흐름과 관계 없는 문장은?

Today car sharing movements / have appeared all over the world.
오늘날 차량 공유 운동이 / 전 세계에서 일어났다.
In many cities, / car sharing has made a strong impact / on how city residents travel.
많은 도시에서, / 차량 공유는 강한 영향을 미쳤다. / 도시 거주민의 이동 방식에
① Even in strong car-ownership cultures / such as North America, / car sharing has gained popularity.
심지어 차량 소유의 문화가 강한 지역에서도 / 북미 같은, / 차량 공유는 인기를 얻었다.
② In the U.S. and Canada, / membership in car sharing / now exceeds one in five adults in many urban areas.
미국과 캐나다에서, / 차량 공유 회원 수는 / 현재 많은 도시 지역에서 성인 5명 중 1명을 넘어섰다.
③ Strong influence on traffic jams and pollution / can be felt from Toronto to New York, / as each shared vehicle replaces around 10 personal cars.
교통 체증 및 오염에 대한 강한 영향력은 / 토론토부터 뉴욕까지 느껴질 수 있다. / 공유된 차량 한 대가 10대의 개인 차량을 대체함에 따라
✔The best thing about driverless cars / is that people won't need a license / to operate them.
무인 자동차에 관한 가장 좋은 점은 / 사람들이 면허증을 필요로 하지 않는다는 것이다. / 차를 몰기 위해
⑤ City governments with downtown areas / struggling with traffic jams and lack of parking lots / are driving the growing popularity of car sharing.
시내 지역이 있는 시 정부에서는 / 교통 체증과 주차 공간 부족으로 시달리고 있는 / 차량 공유의 인기 증가를 부추기고 있다.

오늘날 차량 공유 운동이 전 세계에서 일어났다. 많은 도시에서 차량 공유는 도시 거주민의 이동 방식에 강한 영향을 미쳤다. ① 심지어 차량 소유의 문화가 강한 북미 같은 지역에서도 차량 공유는 인기를 얻었다. ② 미국과 캐나다에서 차량 공유 회원 수는 현재 많은 도시 지역에서 성인 5명 중 1명을 넘어섰다. ③ 공유된 차량 한 대가 10대의 개인 차량을 대체함에 따라 교통 체증 및 오염에 대한 강한 영향력을 토론토부터 뉴욕까지 느낄 수 있다. ④ 무인 자동차에 관한 가장 좋은 점은 사람들이 차를 몰기 위해 면허증을 필요로 하지 않는다는 것이다. ⑤ 시내의 교통 체증과 주차 공간 부족에 시달리고 있는 시 정부에서는 차량 공유의 인기 증가를 부추기고 있다.

Why? 왜 정답일까?
이 글은 차량 공유 운동이 전 세계에 걸쳐, 특히 차량 소유 문화가 강한 북미 지역에서까지 인기를 누리고 있다는 내용을 설명한다. ① ~ ③에서는 미국과 캐나다에서 차량 공유의 인기를 확인할 수 있다는 내용을, ⑤에서는 교통 체증 및 주차 공간 부족에 시달리는 시 정부이 차량 공유를 장려하고 있다는 내용을 이야기한다. 하지만 ④는 '무인 자동차'에 관해 언급하고 있어 흐름에 맞지 않는다. 따라서 전체 흐름과 관계 없는 문장은 ④이다.

[문제편 p.078]

- have an impact on ~에 영향을 미치다
- ownership ⓝ 소유
- membership ⓝ 회원 수, 회원들
- traffic jam 교통 체증
- replace ⓥ 대체하다
- operate ⓥ 조작하다, 가동하다
- resident ⓝ 거주민, 거주자
- popularity ⓝ 인기
- exceed ⓥ 넘어서다, 능가하다
- vehicle ⓝ 차량, 탈것
- driverless car 무인 자동차
- struggle with ~에 시달리다, ~로 고전하다

구문 풀이
[10행] City governments with downtown areas [struggling with traffic jams and
　　　　　　 주어　　　　　　　　　　　　　　 고전하는가 명사구1
lack of parking lots] are driving the growing popularity of car sharing.
명사구2　　　　　 동사(현재진행)　　 현재분사 ↗

36　과학과 예술의 근간인 협업　　　　정답률 58% | 정답 ②

주어진 글 다음에 이어질 글의 순서로 가장 적절한 것을 고르시오.

① (A) – (C) – (B)　　　　　　 ✔ (B) – (A) – (C)
③ (B) – (C) – (A)　　　　　　 ④ (C) – (A) – (B)
⑤ (C) – (B) – (A)

Collaboration is the basis / for most of the foundational arts and sciences.
협업은 기반이다. / 대부분의 기초 예술과 과학의
(B) It is often believed / that Shakespeare, like most playwrights of his period, / did not always write alone, / and many of his plays are considered collaborative / or were rewritten after their original composition.
흔히 믿어지고, / 셰익스피어는, 당대 대부분의 극작가처럼, / 늘 혼자 작품을 썼던 것은 아니라고 / 그의 희곡 중 다수가 협업을 한 것으로 여겨지거나 / 최초의 창작 후에 개작되었다.
Leonardo Da Vinci made his sketches individually, / but he collaborated with other people / to add the finer details.
레오나르도 다빈치는 혼자서 스케치를 그렸지만, / 다른 사람들과 협업했다. / 더 세밀한 세부 묘사를 더 하기 위해
(A) For example, / his sketches of human anatomy / were a collaboration with Marcantonio della Torre, / an anatomist from the University of Pavia.
예를 들어, / 인체의 해부학적 구조를 그린 그의 스케치는 / Marcantonio della Torre와 협업한 것이었다. / Pavia 대학의 해부학자인
Their collaboration is important / because it marries the artist with the scientist.
그들의 협업은 중요하다. / 예술가와 과학자가 결합한 것이어서
(C) Similarly, / Marie Curie's husband stopped his original research / and joined Marie in hers.
마찬가지로, / Marie Curie의 남편은 원래 자신이 하던 연구를 중단하고 / Marie의 연구를 함께 했다.
They went on to collaboratively discover radium, / which overturned old ideas / in physics and chemistry.
그들은 더 나아가 협업으로 라듐을 발견했고, / 그것은 기존 개념들을 뒤집었다. / 물리학과 화학에서의

협업은 대부분의 기초 예술과 과학의 기반이다.
(B) 셰익스피어는, 당대 대부분의 극작가처럼, 늘 혼자 작품을 썼던 것은 아니라고 흔히 믿어지고, 그의 희곡 중 다수가 협업을 한 것으로 여겨지거나 최초의 창작 후에 개작되었다. 레오나르도 다빈치는 혼자서 스케치를 했지만, 더 세밀한 세부 묘사를 더하기 위해 다른 사람들과 협업했다.
(A) 예를 들어, 그의 인체 해부 구조 스케치는 Pavia 대학의 해부학자인 Marcantonio della Torre와 협업한 것이었다. 그들의 협업은 예술가와 과학자가 결합한 것이어서 중요하다.
(C) 마찬가지로, Marie Curie의 남편은 원래 자신이 하던 연구를 중단하고 Marie의 연구를 함께 했다. 그들은 더 나아가 협업으로 라듐을 발견했고, 그것은 물리학과 화학의 오래된 개념들을 뒤집었다.

Why? 왜 정답일까?
협업이 기초 예술과 과학의 기반임을 언급한 주어진 글 뒤에는, 셰익스피어와 레오나르도 다빈치의 예를 제시하는 (B), 다빈치를 단락 초반에서 his로 받아 그의 스케치 중 협동 작업의 사례를 언급하는 (A), 이어서 추가 사례를 제시하는 Similarly 뒤로 과학에서의 예로서 퀴리 부부를 언급하는 (C)가 차례로 연결되는 것이 자연스럽다. 따라서 글의 순서로 가장 적절한 것은 ② '(B) – (A) – (C)'이다.

- collaboration ⓝ 협업, 협동, 공동 작업
- foundational ⓐ 기초적인, 기본의
- anatomist ⓝ 해부학자
- marry ⓥ (서로 다른 두 가지 사상·사물을 성공적으로) 결합시키다
- playwright ⓝ 극작가
- rewrite 개작하다, 다시 쓰다
- individually ⓐⓓ 개인적으로, 따로
- join ⓥ 합류하다
- basis ⓝ 근거, 이유
- sketch ⓝ 개요
- period ⓝ 기간, 시기
- composition ⓝ 작성, 작곡, 작품
- fine ⓐ 세밀한, 섬세한, 촘촘한
- overturn ⓥ 뒤엎다, 전복시키다

구문 풀이
[7행] It is often believed {that Shakespeare, like most playwrights of his period,
　　　 주어(가주어) 동사1 　　　 주어 　　　　　　　[ ]: 진주어
did not always write alone}, and many of his plays are considered collaborative
　 동사1 　　　　　　　　　　　　　 주어2　　　　　　 동사2 　　　 보어(형용사)
or were rewritten after their original composition.
　 동사3

37　조카에게 빠른 답장을 받은 Carnegie　　　　정답률 54% | 정답 ③

주어진 글 다음에 이어질 글의 순서로 가장 적절한 것을 고르시오.

① (A) – (C) – (B)　　　　　　 ② (B) – (A) – (C)
✔ (B) – (C) – (A)　　　　　　 ④ (C) – (A) – (B)
⑤ (C) – (B) – (A)

Andrew Carnegie, the great early-twentieth-century businessman, / once heard his sister complain about her two sons.
20세기 초반의 위대한 사업가 Andrew Carnegie는 / 언젠가 누이가 자기 두 아들에 대해 불평하는 것을 들었다.
(B) They were away at college / and rarely responded to her letters.
그들은 멀리서 대학을 다니면서 / 어머니의 편지에 좀처럼 답장을 하지 않고 있었다.

Carnegie told her / that if he wrote them / he would get an immediate response.
Carnegie는 그녀에게 이야기했다. / 자신이 그들에게 편지를 쓰면 / 자신이 즉각적인 답장을 받을 것이라고

(C) He sent off two warm letters to the boys, / and told them / that he was happy / to send each of them a check for a hundred dollars / (a large sum in those days).
그는 다정한 편지 두 통을 조카들에게 보냈고, / 이야기했다. / 그가 기쁘다는 것을 / 그들 각각에게 100달러짜리 수표를 보내게 되어 / (당시 큰 액수였던)

Then he mailed the letters, / but didn't enclose the checks.
그런 다음 그는 편지를 부쳤지만, / 수표를 동봉하지는 않았다.

(A) Within days / he received warm grateful letters from both boys, / who noted at the letters' end / that he had unfortunately forgotten to include the check.
며칠 안에 / 그는 두 조카에게서 다정한 감사 편지를 받았는데, / 그들은 편지 말미에 언급했다. / 삼촌이 안타깝게도 수표를 함께 보내는 것을 잊었음을

If the check had been enclosed, / would they have responded so quickly?
만일 수표가 동봉되었더라면, / 그들이 그토록 빨리 답장을 보냈을까?

20세기 초반의 위대한 사업가 Andrew Carnegie는 언젠가 누이가 자기 두 아들에 대해 불평하는 것을 들었다.

(B) 그들은 멀리서 대학을 다니면서 어머니의 편지에 좀처럼 답장을 하지 않고 있었다. Carnegie는 자신이 그들에게 편지를 쓰면 자신은 즉각적인 답장을 받을 것이라고 이야기했다.

(C) 그는 다정한 편지 두 통을 조카들에게 보냈고, 그들 각각에게 (당시 큰 액수였던) 100달러짜리 수표를 보내게 되어 기쁘다는 것을 이야기했다. 그런 다음 그는 편지를 부쳤지만, 수표를 동봉하지는 않았다.

(A) 며칠 안에 그는 두 조카에게서 다정한 감사 편지를 받았는데, 그들은 편지 말미에 삼촌이 안타깝게도 수표를 함께 보내는 것을 잊었음을 언급했다. 만일 수표가 동봉되었더라면, 그들이 그토록 빨리 답장을 보냈을까?

Why? 왜 정답일까?

주어진 글에서는 Carnegie가 누이가 두 아들에 대해 불평하는 것을 들었다는 이야기가 나오는데 (B)에서는 이 '두 아들'을 They로 받아 이들이 어머니의 편지에 좀처럼 답을 하지 않았다는 이야기를 이어 간다. 한편 (B)의 마지막 부분에는 Carnegie가 자신이 편지를 쓴다면 바로 답을 받을 수 있다고 말했다는 내용이 나오는데 (C)에서는 Carnegie가 조카에게 '수표를 보내게 되어 기쁘다'라고 편지를 쓰면서 수표는 보내지 않았다는 내용을 이어서 제시한다. 마지막으로 (A)에서는 Carnegie가 며칠만에 조카들로부터 답장을 받고 이는 수표를 동봉한다고 말했으면서 실제로 동봉하지는 않았기 때문이었다는 내용을 말한다. 따라서 주어진 글 다음에 이어질 글의 순서로 가장 적절한 것은 ③ '(B) – (C) – (A)'이다.

- businessman ⓝ 사업가
- grateful ⓐ 감사해하는, 고마워하는
- unfortunately ⓐⓓ 안타깝게도, 불행히도
- rarely ⓐⓓ 좀처럼 ~하지 않는
- complain ⓥ 불평하다
- note ⓥ 언급하다, 말하다
- check ⓝ 수표
- immediate ⓐ 즉각적인, 즉시의

구문 풀이

3행 Within days / he received warm grateful letters from both boys, who noted (at the letters' end) that he had unfortunately forgotten to include the check.
접속사 「forget to + 동사원형 : (미래에) ~하는 것을 잊다」

★★★ 등급을 가르는 문제! ★★★

38 어린 시절의 친구가 주는 이점   정답률 41% | 정답 ②

글의 흐름으로 보아, 주어진 문장이 들어가기에 가장 적절한 곳을 고르시오.

Childhood friends — friends you've known forever — / are really special.
당신이 평생 동안 알아왔던 어린 시절의 친구는 / 정말로 특별하다.

① They know everything about you, / and you've shared lots of firsts.
그들은 당신에 대해서 모든 것을 알고, / 당신은 그들과 많은 것들을 처음으로 함께 했다.

☑ When you hit puberty, however, / sometimes these forever-friendships go through growing pains.
하지만 사춘기가 되면, / 때때로 이런 영원한 우정은 성장통을 겪는다.

You find / that you have less in common than you used to.
당신은 알게 된다. / 과거보다 공유하는 것이 적다는 것을

③ Maybe you're into rap and she's into pop, / or you go to different schools / and have different groups of friends.
아마 당신은 랩을 좋아하는데 친구는 팝을 좋아한다거나, / 학교가 달라지고 / 서로 다른 친구 무리와 어울리게 될 수 있다.

④ Change can be scary, but remember:
변화는 무서울 수 있지만, 기억하라.

Friends, even best friends, / don't have to be exactly alike.
심지어 가장 친한 친구더라도 친구들이 / 완전히 똑같을 필요는 없다.

⑤ Having friends with other interests / keeps life interesting / — just think of what you can learn from each other.
다른 관심사를 가진 친구를 두는 것은 / 삶을 흥미롭게 만들 수 있다. / 그저 서로에게 무엇을 배울 수 있겠는지 생각해 보라.

당신이 평생 동안 알아왔던 어린 시절의 친구는 정말로 특별하다. ① 그들은 당신에 대해서 모든 것을 알고, 당신은 그들과 많은 것들을 처음으로 함께 했다. ② 하지만 사춘기가 되면, 때때로 이런 영원한 우정은 성장통을 겪는다. 당신은 과거보다 공유하는 것이 적다는 것을 알게 된다. ③ 아마 당신은 랩을 좋아하는데 친구는 팝을 좋아한다거나, 학교가 달라지고 서로 다른 친구 무리와 어울리게 될 수 있다. ④ 변화는 무서울 수 있지만, 기억하라. 심지어 가장 친한 친구더라도 친구들이 완전히 똑같을 필요는 없다. ⑤ 다른 관심사를 가진 친구를 두는 것은 삶을 흥미롭게 만들 수 있다. 그저 서로에게 무엇을 배울 수 있겠는지 생각해 보라.

Why? 왜 정답일까?

② 앞의 문장에서는 어린 시절의 친구가 모든 것을 서로 공유하고 많은 처음을 함께 나눈 '특별한 사이'임을 말하는데, 주어진 문장은 이를 however로 뒤집으며 사춘기가 되면 이러한 우정에 '성장통'이 찾아온다는 내용을 제시한다. ② 뒤의 문장에서는 주어진 문장에 이어 사춘기 이후에 사람들은 어린 시절의 친구와 서로 공유하는 것이 적어지고 관심사가 달라지게 된다는 내용을 말한다. 따라서 주어진 문장이 들어가기에 가장 적절한 곳은 ②이다.

- puberty ⓝ 사춘기
- scary ⓐ 무서운, 겁나는
- alike ⓐ (아주) 비슷한
- go through ~을 겪다
- exactly ⓐⓓ 정확히
- interest ⓝ 관심사, 흥미

구문 풀이

9행 Having friends with other interests keeps life interesting / — just think of
주어(동명사)   동사(단수) 목적어 ↳목적격 보어(현재분사)
what you can learn from each other.
의문사(무엇)

★★ 문제 해결 꿀~팁 ★★

▶ 많이 틀린 이유는?
주어진 문장에 however라는 역접의 연결어가 있으므로 본문에서 앞뒤가 서로 다른 말을 하는 지점에 주어진 문장을 넣어야 한다. 최다 오답은 ④인데 ④의 앞뒤 모두 '어린 시절의 친구가 시간이 지나서 서로 안 맞게 될 수 있지만 괜찮다'는 내용으로 요약될 수 있으므로 ④를 흐름 반전의 지점으로 보기는 어렵다.

▶ 문제 해결 방법은?
주어진 문장 넣기 유형에서 주어진 문장은 보통 흐름 반전의 연결사를 포함하고 있기 마련이다. 본문을 읽을 때 각 번호 앞뒤 문장이 요약했을 때 서로 같은 말인지 다른 말인지를 계속 비교해 보면 오답을 피할 수 있다.

39 그림을 나아지게 할 방법   정답률 54% | 정답 ③

글의 흐름으로 보아, 주어진 문장이 들어가기에 가장 적절한 곳을 고르시오. [3점]

Imagine in your mind / one of your favorite paintings, drawings, cartoon characters / or something equally complex.
마음으로 그려 보라. / 좋아하는 회화, 소묘, 만화의 등장인물이나 / 그 정도로 복잡한 어떤 것 중 하나를

① Now, / with that picture in your mind, / try to draw what your mind sees.
이제 / 그 그림을 염두에 두고 / 마음이 본 것을 그리려고 애써 보라.

② Unless you are unusually gifted, / your drawing will look completely different / from what you are seeing / with your mind's eye.
특별하게 재능이 있는 게 아니라면 / 여러분이 그린 그림은 완전히 다르게 보일 것이다. / 여러분이 보고 있는 것과 / 마음의 눈으로

☑ However, / if you tried to copy the original / rather than your imaginary drawing, / you might find / your drawing now was a little better.
하지만 / 원본을 베끼려고 애쓴다면 / 마음속에 존재하는 그림보다 / 알게 될 것이다. / 여러분의 그림은 이제 조금 더 나아졌다는 것을

Furthermore, / if you copied the picture many times, / you would find / that each time your drawing would get a little better, / a little more accurate.
게다가 / 그 그림을 여러 번 베낀다면 / 알게 될 것이다. / 매번 여러분의 그림이 조금 더 나아지고 / 조금 더 정확해질 거라는 것을

④ Practice makes perfect.
연습하면 완벽해진다.

⑤ This is because you are developing the skills / of coordinating what your mind perceives / with the movement of your body parts.
이것은 능력이 발달되고 있기 때문이다. / 마음이 인식한 것을 조화시키는 / 신체 부위의 움직임과

좋아하는 회화, 소묘, 만화의 등장인물이나 그 정도로 복잡한 어떤 것 중 하나를 마음속으로 그려 보라. ① 이제 그 그림을 염두에 두고 마음이 보는 것을 그리려고 애써 보라. ② 특별하게 재능이 있는 게 아니라면 여러분이 그린 그림은 여러분이 마음의 눈으로 보고 있는 것과 완전히 다르게 보일 것이다. ③ 하지만 상상 속 그림보다 원본을 베끼려고 애쓴다면 여러분은 그림이 이제 조금 더 나아졌다는 것을 알게 될 것이다. 게다가 그 그림을 여러 번 베낀다면 매번 여러분의 그림이 조금 더 나아지고 조금 더 정확해질 거라는 것을 알게 될 것이다. ④ 연습하면 완벽해진다. ⑤ 이것은 마음이 인식한 것을 신체 부위의 움직임과 조화시키는 능력이 발달되고 있기 때문이다.

Why? 왜 정답일까?

어떤 원본을 마음으로 상상하며 재현하려 하기보다 실제로 두고 따라 그리는 연습을 할 때 그림이 좋아질 수 있다는 내용을 다룬 글이다. ③ 앞의 문장에서 원본을 마음으로 생각하고 그리면 실제 그림은 원본과 달라진다는 내용을 말한 데 이어, However로 시작하는 주어진 문장은 실제 원본을 놓고 베끼려고 애쓴다면 그림이 나아진다는 반전된 내용을 제시한다. ③ 뒤에서는 보고 그리기를 여러 번 반복할수록 그림이 더 정확해질 것이라는 내용을 이어 간다. 따라서 주어진 문장이 들어가기에 가장 적절한 곳은 ③이다.

- copy ⓥ 베끼다
- drawing ⓝ (색칠을 하지 않은) 그림, 소묘, 데생
- complex ⓐ 복잡한
- unusually ⓐⓓ 특별하게
- completely ⓐⓓ 완전히
- practice ⓝ 연습
- imaginary ⓐ 상상의, 가상적인
- equally ⓐⓓ 똑같이
- unless ⓒⓞⓝ ~하지 않는 한
- gifted ⓐ 재능 있는
- accurate ⓐ 정확한
- perceive ⓥ 인지하다, 인식하다

구문 풀이

7행 Unless you are unusually gifted, your drawing will look completely different
조건 접속사(~하지 않으면) 현재시제   주어   미래시제   형용사 보어
from what you are seeing with your mind's eye.
관계대명사(~것)

40 문화 차이로 인해 야기된 비즈니스 실패   정답률 54% | 정답 ②

다음 글의 내용을 한 문장으로 요약하고자 한다. 빈칸 (A), (B)에 들어갈 말로 가장 적절한 것은?

	(A)		(B)		(A)		(B)
①	humor 유머	......	essential 본질적으로	☑	humor 유머	......	inappropriate 부적절하게
③	gestures 제스처	......	essential 본질적으로	④	gestures 제스처	......	inappropriate 부적절하게
⑤	first names 이름	......	useful 유용하게				

A large American hardware manufacturer / was invited to introduce its products / to a distributor with good reputation in Germany.
미국의 큰 하드웨어 제조 업체가 / 자사 제품을 소개하도록 초청받았다. / 독일에서 평판이 좋은 배급 업체에

Wanting to make the best possible impression, / the American company sent its most promising young executive, Fred Wagner, / who spoke fluent German.
최고의 인상을 심어주고 싶은 생각에, / 미국의 회사는 가장 촉망받는 젊은 임원 Fred Wagner를 보냈는데, / 그는 독일어를 유창하게 말하였다.

When Fred first met his German hosts, / he shook hands firmly, / greeted everyone in German, / and even remembered to bow the head slightly / as is the German custom.
Fred가 그를 초대한 독일 쪽 사람들을 처음 만났을 때, / 그는 굳게 악수를 하고, / 독일어로 모두에게 인사를 했으며, / 고개를 살짝 숙여 인사하는 것도 잊지 않았다 / 독일의 관습대로

Fred, a very effective public speaker, / began his presentation with a few humorous jokes / to set a relaxed atmosphere.
유능한 대중 연설가인 Fred는 / 몇 가지 우스운 농담으로 발표를 시작했다. / 편안한 분위기를 조성하기 위해

However, he felt / that his presentation was not very well received / by the German executives.
하지만, 그는 느꼈다. / 자기가 아주 잘 받아들여지지 않는다고 / 독일 임원들에게

Even though Fred thought / he had done his cultural homework, / he made one particular error.
Fred는 비록 생각했지만, / 자기가 문화적인 숙제를 마쳤다고 / 그는 한 가지 특정한 실수를 저질렀다

Fred did not win any points / by telling a few jokes.
Fred는 그 어떤 점수도 얻지 못했다. / 몇 가지 농담을 이야기하여서

It was viewed as too informal and unprofessional / in a German business setting.
이는 너무 비격식적이고 비전문적인 것으로 여겨졌다. / 독일 비즈니스 상황에서는

➡ This story shows / that using (A) humor in a business setting / can be considered (B) inappropriate / in Germany.
이 이야기는 보여준다. / 비즈니스 상황에서 유머를 쓰는 것이 / 부적절하게 여겨질 수 있다는 것을 / 독일에서

미국의 큰 하드웨어 제조 업체가 독일에서 평판이 좋은 배급 업체에 자사 제품을 소개하도록 초청받았다. 최고의 인상을 심어주고 싶은 생각에, 미국의 회사는 가장 촉망받는 젊은 임원 Fred Wagner를 보냈는데, 그는 독일어를 유창하게 말하였다. Fred가 그를 초대한 독일 쪽 사람들을 처음 만났을 때, 그는 굳게 악수를 하고, 독일어로 모두에게 인사를 했으며, 독일의 관습대로 고개를 살짝 숙여 인사하는 것도 잊지 않았다. 대중 연설을 매우 유능하게 하는 Fred는 편안한 분위기를 조성하기 위해 몇 가지 우스운 농담으로 발표를 시작했다. 하지만, 그는 발표가 독일 임원들에게 아주 잘 받아들여지지 않는다고 느꼈다. Fred는 비록 자기가 문화적인 숙제를 마쳤다고 생각했지만(독일 문화에 대한 대비를 열심히 했다고 생각했지만), 한 가지 특정한 실수를 저질렀다. Fred는 몇 가지 농담을 이야기하여서 그 어떤 점수도 얻지 못했다. 이는 독일 비즈니스 상황에서는 너무 비격식적이고 비전문적인 것으로 여겨졌다.

➡ 이 이야기는 비즈니스 상황에서 (A) 유머를 쓰는 것이 독일에서 (B) 부적절하게 여겨질 수 있다는 것을 보여준다.

Why? 왜 정답일까?

마지막 두 문장을 통해 Fred가 발표 초반에 농담을 꺼낸 것은 독일 임원들에게 도리어 비격식적이고 비전문적인 것으로 비쳐져(Fred did not win any points by telling a few jokes. It was viewed as too informal and unprofessional in a German business setting.) 비즈니스 실패로 이어지고 말았다는 것을 알 수 있으므로, 빈칸 (A)와 (B)에 들어갈 말로 적절한 것은 ② 'A) humor(유머), (B) inappropriate(부적절하게)'이다.

- **manufacturer** ⓝ 제조 업체, 생산자
- **distributor** ⓝ 배급 업체, 배급자
- **impression** ⓝ 인상
- **executive** ⓝ 임원, 중역
- **greet** ⓥ 인사하다, 환영하다
- **slightly** ⓐⓓ 약간, 조금
- **relaxed** ⓐ 편안한
- **particular** ⓐ 특정한
- **introduce** ⓥ 소개하다, 도입하다
- **reputation** ⓝ 명성
- **promising** ⓐ 촉망받는, 전도 유망한
- **firmly** ⓐⓓ 굳게, 단단히, 단호히
- **bow** ⓥ (고개를) 숙이다
- **custom** ⓝ 관습
- **atmosphere** ⓝ 분위기
- **informal** ⓐ 비격식적인, 허물없는

구문 풀이

5행 When Fred first met his German hosts, / he shook hands firmly, greeted
접속사(~할 때) 동사1 동사2
everyone in German, and even remembered to bow the head slightly as is the
동사3 'remember to+동사원형 : ~하는 것을 잊지 않다' 접속사(~대로)
German custom.

41-42 그룹 간의 경계심을 사라지게 하는 협동

Researchers brought two groups of 11-year-old boys to a summer camp / at Robbers Cave State Park in Oklahoma.
연구자들은 두 그룹의 11세 소년들을 주립 공원의 여름 캠프에 데려왔다. / Oklahoma에 있는 Robbers Cave

The boys were strangers to one another / and upon arrival at the camp, / were randomly separated into two groups.
그 소년들은 서로 몰랐고 / 캠프에 도착하자마자 / 무작위로 두 그룹으로 나뉘었다.

The groups were kept apart / for about a week.
그 그룹들은 서로 떨어져 있었다. / 약 1주일 동안

They swam, camped, and hiked.
그들은 수영하고, 야영하고, 하이킹을 했다.

Each group chose a name for itself, / and the boys printed their group's name / on their caps and T-shirts.
각 그룹은 자기 그룹의 이름을 지었고, / 소년들은 자신의 그룹 이름을 새겼다. / 모자와 티셔츠에

Then the two groups met.
그 후 두 그룹이 만났다.

A series of athletic competitions / were set up between them.
일련의 운동 시합이 마련되었다. / 그들 사이에

Soon, / each group considered the other an (a) enemy.
곧, / 각 그룹은 서로를 적으로 여겼다.

Each group came to look down on the other.
각 그룹은 서로를 얕잡아 보게 되었다.

The boys started food fights / and stole various items / from members of the other group.
소년들은 먹을 것을 가지고 싸우기 시작하고 / 여러 물건을 훔쳤다. / 상대 그룹의 구성원으로부터

Thus, / under competitive conditions, / the boys quickly (b) drew sharp group boundaries.
그래서 / 경쟁적인 환경에서 / 소년들은 재빨리 뚜렷한 그룹 경계를 그었다.

The researchers / next stopped the athletic competitions / and created several apparent emergencies / whose solution (c) required cooperation between the two groups.
연구자들은 / 그런 다음 운동 시합을 멈추고, / 몇 가지 비상사태로 보이는 상황을 만들었다. / 해결에는 두 그룹 사이의 협력이 필요한

One such emergency involved a leak in the pipe / supplying water to the camp.
그러한 비상사태 중 하나는 파이프가 새는 경우를 포함했다. / 캠프에 물을 공급하는

The researchers assigned the boys to teams / made up of members of both groups.
연구자들은 소년들을 팀에 배정했다. / 두 그룹의 일원들로 구성된

Their job was / to look into the pipe / and fix the leak.
그들의 임무는 / 파이프를 조사하고 / 새는 곳을 고치는 것이었다.

After engaging in several such (d) cooperative activities, / the boys started playing together / without fighting.
그러한 협력적인 활동을 몇 차례 한 후에, / 소년들은 함께 놀기 시작했다. / 싸우지 않고

「Once cooperation replaced competition / and the groups (e) ceased to look down on each other, / group boundaries melted away / as quickly as they had formed.」 41번의 근거
일단 협력이 경쟁을 대체하고 / 그룹들이 서로를 얕잡아 보기를 중단하자, / 그룹 경계가 사라져 간다. / 형성되었던 것만큼 빠르게

연구자들은 두 그룹의 11세 소년들을 Oklahoma에 있는 Robbers Cave 주립 공원의 여름 캠프에 데려왔다. 그 소년들은 서로 몰랐고 캠프에 도착하자마자 무작위로 두 그룹으로 나뉘었다. 그 그룹들은 약 1주일 동안 서로 떨어져 있었다. 그들은 수영하고, 야영하고, 하이킹을 했다. 각 그룹은 자기 그룹의 이름을 지었고, 소년들은 자신의 그룹 이름을 모자와 티셔츠에 새겼다. 그 후 두 그룹이 만났다. 그들 사이에 일련의 운동 시합이 마련되었다. 곧, 각 그룹은 서로를 (a) 적으로 여겼다. 각 그룹은 서로를 얕잡아 보게 되었다. 소년들은 먹을 것을 가지고 싸우기 시작했고 상대 그룹 구성원의 여러 물건을 훔쳤다. 그래서 경쟁적인 환경에서 소년들은 재빨리 뚜렷한 그룹 경계를 (b) 그었다. 그런 다음, 연구자들은 운동 시합을 멈추고, 해결에 두 그룹 사이의 협력이 (c) 필요한, 몇 가지 비상사태로 보이는 상황을 만들었다. 그러한 비상사태 중 하나는 캠프에 물을 공급하는 파이프가 새는 경우를 포함했다. 연구자들은 소년들을 두 그룹 모두의 일원으로 구성된 팀에 배정했다. 그들의 임무는 파이프를 조사하고 새는 곳을 고치는 것이었다. 그러한 (d) 협력적인 활동을 몇 차례 한 후에, 소년들은 싸우지 않고 함께 놀기 시작했다. 일단 협력이 경쟁을 대체하고 그룹들이 서로를 얕잡아 보기를 (e) 시작하자(→ 중단하자), 그룹 경계가 형성되었던 것만큼 빠르게 사라져 갔다.

- **randomly** ⓐⓓ 무작위로
- **apart** ⓐⓓ 떨어져, 따로
- **look down on** ~을 얕잡아보다, 깔보다
- **boundary** ⓝ 경계
- **leak** ⓝ (물이) 새는 곳, 구멍 ⓥ (물이나 기체가) 새다
- **replace** ⓥ 대체하다
- **separate** ⓥ 나누다, 분리하다
- **athletic** ⓐ 운동의, 육상의
- **competitive** ⓐ 경쟁적인
- **emergency** ⓝ 비상사태
- **assign** ⓥ 배정하다
- **melt away** 차츰 사라지다

구문 풀이

14행 The researchers next stopped the athletic competitions and created
동사1 동사2
several apparent emergencies [whose solution required cooperation between the
선행사 소유격 관계대명사
two groups].

41 제목 파악 　　　　　　　　정답률 49% | 정답 ③

윗글의 제목으로 가장 적절한 것은?
① How Are Athletic Competitions Helpful for Teens? – 운동 시합은 어떻게 십 대에게 도움이 되는가?
② Preparation: The Key to Preventing Emergencies – 대비: 비상사태 예방의 비결
③ What Makes Group Boundaries Disappear? – 무엇이 그룹 경계를 사라지게 하는가?
④ Respect Individual Differences in Teams – 팀 내 개인차를 존중하라
⑤ Free Riders: Headaches in Teams – 무임승차자: 팀의 골칫거리

Why? 왜 정답일까?

소년들을 두 그룹으로 나누어 일련의 경쟁을 하도록 했을 때에는 그룹 간에 적개심과 경계가 형성되었지만, 그룹 간의 협력이 필요한 활동에 참여하게 하자 그 경계가 쉽게 사라졌다(Once cooperation replaced competition ~, group boundaries melted away as quickly as they had formed.)는 내용의 실험을 소개하는 글이다. 따라서 글의 제목으로 가장 적절한 것은 ③ '무엇이 그룹 경계를 사라지게 하는가?'이다.

★★★ 등급을 가르는 문제!

42 어휘 추론 　　　　　　　　정답률 35% | 정답 ⑤

밑줄 친 (a)~(e) 중에서 문맥상 낱말의 쓰임이 적절하지 않은 것은?
① (a)　　② (b)　　③ (c)　　④ (d)　　✔ (e)

Why? 왜 정답일까?

마지막 문장의 and 앞에서 협력이 경쟁을 대체하였다(cooperation replaced competition)는 내용이 언급되는 것으로 보아, and 뒤에는 그룹들이 경쟁 관계에서 벗어나 서로를 얕잡아 보기를 '그만두었다'는 내용이 이어지는 것이 적절하므로, (e)의 started는 반의어인 ceased로 고쳐야 한다. 따라서 문맥상 낱말의 쓰임이 적절하지 않은 것은 ⑤ '(e)'이다.

★★ 문제 해결 꿀~팁 ★★

▶ 많이 틀린 이유는?
문장이 어렵지는 않지만 길이로 인한 압박이 있어 전체 맥락을 파악하는 데 부담이 따르는 지문이다. 최다 오답인 ②는 앞에서 소년들이 팀 별로 경계심을 키웠음을 보여주는 사례가 나오는 것으로 볼 때 맥락상 적절하다. (b) 바로 앞의 문장을 주의 깊게 읽도록 한다.

▶ 문제 해결 방법은?
첫 단락과 두 번째 단락이 '소년들 간 반목 vs. 협동'이라는 키워드로 대조를 이루므로, 이 점에 주의하여 선택지 문장의 맥락을 파악해야 한다.

43-45 사자와의 우정으로 목숨을 건진 노예

(A)

Once in a village lived a rich man.
옛날 한 마을에 어떤 부자가 살았다.

He had many slaves and servants for work.
그는 일을 해 주는 많은 노예와 하인이 있었다.

The rich man was very unkind and cruel to them.
그 부자는 그들에게 매우 불친절하고 잔인했다.

One day one of the slaves made a mistake / while cooking food.
어느 날 노예 중 한 명이 실수를 했다. / 요리를 하다가

(a) He overcooked the food.
그는 음식을 너무 익혀버렸다.

「When the rich man saw the food, / he became angry and punished the slave.」 **45번 ①의 근거** 일치
부자가 그 음식을 보았을 때, / 그는 화가 나서 노예에게 벌을 주었다.

He kept the slave in a small room / and locked it from outside.
그는 작은 방에 노예를 가두고 / 밖에서 문을 잠가버렸다.

(C)

Somehow the slave escaped from that room / and ran away.
어찌찌 노예는 그 방에서 탈출해서 / 도망을 쳤다.

(c) He went to a forest.
그는 숲으로 갔다.

There he saw a lion.
거기서 그는 사자 한 마리를 보았다.

「Instead of becoming afraid of the lion and running away, / he went close to the lion.」
사자를 무서워하며 도망치는 대신, / 그는 사자에게 가까이 다가섰다. **45번 ③의 근거** 불일치

「He saw / the lion was injured / and one of his legs was bleeding.」 **45번 ④의 근거** 일치
그는 보았다. / 사자가 상처를 입은 것을 / 그리고 그의 다리 중 하나에서 피가 흐르는 것을

The slave searched for herbs / to cure the lion's wound / and took care of the lion.
그 노예는 약초를 찾아나섰고 / 사자의 상처를 치료하기 위한 / 사자를 돌봐주었다.

(B)

After a few days the lion recovered.
며칠 뒤 사자는 회복했다.

The slave and the lion became very close friends.
노예와 사자는 매우 친한 친구 사이가 되었다.

「A few days went by / but one day the slave was caught / by one of the guards of the rich man.」 **45번 ②의 근거** 일치
며칠이 흘렀는데 / 어느 날 노예는 붙잡혔다. / 부자의 경비병 중 한 명에게

The guard took (b) him to the rich man, / who decided to punish him severely.
그 경비병은 그를 부자에게 데려갔고, / 부자는 그를 엄하게 처벌하기로 마음먹었다.

The rich man ordered guards / to put him in the lion's cage.
부자는 경비병들에게 명령했다. / 그를 사자 우리 안에 집어넣으라고

(D)

The whole village got the news about it / and came to see.
마을 전체가 이 소식을 듣고 / 보러 왔다.

「As soon as the slave was locked in the lion's cage, / the lion came near (d) him / and started licking his hand and hugged him.」 **45번 ⑤의 근거** 일치
노예가 사자 우리에 갇히자마자, / 사자가 그에게 다가가 / 그의 손을 핥기 시작했고 그를 껴안았다.

It was the same lion / that the slave had helped in the forest.
이 사자는 바로 / 노예가 숲에서 도와주었던 사자였다.

Seeing this, / everyone was surprised.
이것을 보고, / 모든 사람들이 놀랐다.

The rich man thought / that the slave was such a great person / that the lion didn't kill him.
부자는 생각했다. / 노예가 너무 대단한 사람이어서 / 사자가 그를 죽이지 않는다고

(e) He freed the slave, / made him his friend / and started to treat all his servants and slaves better.
그는 노예를 풀어주고 / 자기 친구로 삼았으며 / 모든 하인과 노예를 더 잘 대해주기 시작했다.

(A)

옛날 한 마을에 어떤 부자가 살았다. 그는 일을 해 주는 많은 노예와 하인이 있었다. 그 부자는 그들에게 매우 불친절하고 잔인했다. 어느날 노예 중 한 명이 요리를 하다가 실수를 했다. (a) 그는 음식을 너무 익혀버렸다. 부자가 그 음식을 보았을 때, 그는 화가 나서 노예에게 벌을 주었다. 그는 작은 방에 노예를 가두고 밖에서 문을 잠가버렸다.

(C)

어찌찌 노예는 그 방에서 탈출해서 도망을 쳤다. (c) 그는 숲으로 갔다. 거기서 그는 사자 한 마리를 보았다. 사자를 무서워하며 도망치는 대신, 그는 사자에게 가까이 다가섰다. 그는 사자가 상처를 입고 한쪽 다리에서 피를 흘리고 있는 것을 보았다. 그 노예는 사자의 상처를 치료하기 위한 약초를 찾아나섰고 사자를 돌봐주었다.

(B)

며칠 뒤 사자는 회복했다. 노예와 사자는 매우 친한 친구 사이가 되었다. 며칠이 흘렀는데 어느 날 노예는 부자의 경비병 중 한 명에게 붙잡혔다. 그 경비병은 (b) 그를 부자에게 데려갔고, 부자는 그를 엄하게 처벌하기로 마음먹었다. 부자는 경비병들에게 그를 사자 우리 안에 집어넣으라고 명령했다.

(D)

마을 전체가 이 소식을 듣고 보러 왔다. 노예가 사자 우리에 갇히자마자, 사자가 (d) 그에게 다가가 그의 손을 핥기 시작했고 그를 껴안았다. 이 사자는 노예가 숲에서 도와주었던 바로 그 사자였다. 이것을 보고, 모든 사람들이 놀랐다. 부자는 노예가 너무 대단한 사람이어서 사자가 그를 죽이지 않는다고 생각했다. (e) 그는 노예를 풀어주고 자기 친구로 삼았으며 모든 하인과 노예를 더 잘 대해주기 시작했다.

- cruel ⓐ 잔인한
- recover ⓥ 회복하다, 낫다
- punish ⓥ 처벌하다
- order ⓥ 명령하다
- instead of ~ 대신에
- injure ⓥ 상처를 입히다
- search for ~을 찾다
- cure ⓥ 치료하다
- whole ⓐ 전체의, 모든
- free ⓥ 풀어 주다 ⓐ 자유로운
- punish ⓥ 처벌하다
- close ⓐ (사이가) 친한, 가까운
- severely [ad] 엄하게, 심하게
- escape ⓥ 달아나다, 탈출하다
- run away 도망치다, 달아나다
- bleed ⓥ 피를 흘리다, 출혈하다
- herb ⓝ 약초
- wound ⓝ 상처, 부상
- lick ⓥ 핥다
- treat ⓥ 대하다, 대접하다

구문 풀이

[A] 3행 One day / one of the slaves made a mistake / while cooking food.
「one of the+복수명사」: ~ 중 하나 (he was 생략)

[B] 5행 The rich man ordered guards to put him in the lion's cage.
동사 / 목적어 / 목적격 보어(to부정사)

[D] 1행 As soon as the slave was locked in the lion's cage, / the lion came near
접속사「~하자마자」 / 동사1
him and started licking his hand and hugged him.
동사2「start+동명사」:~하기 시작하다 / 동사3

[문제편 p.080]

---

43 글의 순서 파악 정답률 73% | 정답 ②

주어진 글 (A)에 이어질 내용을 순서에 맞게 배열한 것으로 가장 적절한 것은?

① (B) - (D) - (C)   ✔ (C) - (B) - (D)
③ (C) - (D) - (B)   ④ (D) - (B) - (C)
⑤ (D) - (C) - (B)

Why? 왜 정답일까?

어느 날 노예가 실수로 음식을 너무 익혀버리자 주인인 부자가 그를 작은 방에 가두고 말았다는 내용을 제시한 (A) 뒤에는, 노예가 방에서 가까스로 탈출하여 숲으로 향했고 거기서 다친 사자를 만나 도와주게 되었다는 내용의 (C)가 나와야 적절하다. 이어서는 사자가 며칠 뒤 회복을 하였는데 노예는 주인인 부자에게 붙잡히게 되어 사자 우리에 집어넣어질 위기에 처했다는 내용의 (B)가 나와야 하고, 마지막에는 노예를 집어넣은 우리 안에 있던 사자가 사실은 노예가 며칠 전 구해준 사자였고 이 때문에 사자는 노예를 해치지 않았다는 결말을 말한 (D)가 나와야 자연스럽다. 따라서 (A)에 이어질 글의 순서로 가장 적절한 것은 ② '(C) - (B) - (D)'이다.

44 지칭 추론 정답률 67% | 정답 ⑤

밑줄 친 (a) ~ (e) 중에서 가리키는 대상이 나머지 넷과 다른 것은?

① (a)   ② (b)   ③ (c)   ④ (d)   ✔ (e)

Why? 왜 정답일까?

(a), (b), (c), (d)는 'the slave', (e)는 'the rich'를 나타낸다. 따라서 (a) ~ (e) 중에서 가리키는 대상이 나머지 넷과 다른 것은 ⑤ '(e)'이다.

45 세부 내용 파악 정답률 70% | 정답 ③

윗글의 내용으로 적절하지 않은 것은?

① 부자는 노예가 요리한 음식을 보고 화가 났다.
② 노예는 부자의 경비병에게 잡혔다.
✔ 노예는 사자를 보자 재빨리 달아났다.
④ 사자의 다리에서 피가 나고 있었다.
⑤ 노예는 사자 우리에 갇혔다.

Why? 왜 정답일까?

'Instead of becoming afraid of the lion and running away, he went close to the lion.'에서 노예는 사자를 보고 겁에 질려 도망가지 않고 사자에게 가까이 다가갔다는 내용을 확인할 수 있으므로, 윗글의 내용으로 적절하지 않은 것은 ③ '노예는 사자를 보자 재빨리 달아났다.'이다.

Why? 왜 오답일까?

① 'When the rich man saw the food, he became angry and punished the slave.'와 일치한다.
② 'A few days went by but one day the slave was caught by one of the guards of the rich man.'과 일치한다.
④ 'He saw the lion was injured and one of his legs was bleeding.'과 일치한다.
⑤ 'As soon as the slave was locked in the lion's cage, the lion came near him and started licking his hand and hugged him.'과 일치한다.

어휘 Review Test 08 문제편 084쪽

A		B		C		D	
01	~을 대신하여, 대표하여	01	attend	01	ⓚ	01	⓰
02	감싸다, 포옹하다	02	propose	02	ⓠ	02	ⓚ
03	~을 처리하다, 따라잡다, 만회하다	03	pray	03	ⓐ	03	ⓟ
04	무관심한	04	comfort	04	ⓗ	04	ⓐ
05	결과, 결론	05	distraction	05	ⓛ	05	ⓑ
06	~을 실어다 주다, 태워주다	06	analysis	06	ⓙ	06	⓰
07	소비하다, 쓰다	07	take a risk	07	ⓒ	07	ⓢ
08	다 자란, 성숙한	08	attraction	08	ⓕ	08	ⓒ
09	~의 마음대로 이용할 수 있는	09	disappear	09	ⓢ	09	ⓓ
10	일반화하다	10	appreciate	10	ⓑ	10	ⓔ
11	근면	11	remarkably	11	ⓟ	11	ⓞ
12	다 떨어지다	12	result in	12	ⓓ	12	ⓝ
13	간격	13	meet	13	ⓔ	13	ⓛ
14	경쟁자	14	ancestor	14	ⓕ	14	ⓕ
15	넘어서다, 능가하다	15	replace	15	ⓛ	15	ⓘ
16	언급하다, 말하다	16	reputation	16	ⓜ	16	ⓡ
17	~을 겪다	17	leak	17	ⓖ	17	ⓣ
18	촉망받는, 전도유망한	18	cruel	18	ⓗ	18	ⓘ
19	경계	19	punish	19	ⓘ	19	ⓜ
20	피를 흘리다	20	injure	20	ⓞ	20	ⓗ

· 정답 ·

01 ② 02 ① 03 ① 04 ④ 05 ⑤　06 ③ 07 ④ 08 ③ 09 ⑤ 10 ④　11 ① 12 ③ 13 ② 14 ⑤ 15 ⑤
16 ③ 17 ④ 18 ② 19 ① 20 ⑤　21 ① 22 ③ 23 ② 24 ① 25 ④　26 ② 27 ⑤ 28 ⑤ 29 ④ 30 ②
31 ④ 32 ① 33 ② 34 ③ 35 ④　36 ② 37 ⑤ 38 ② 39 ⑤ 40 ②　41 ① 42 ③ 43 ④ 44 ② 45 ③

★ 표기된 문항은 [등급을 가르는 문제]에 해당하는 문제입니다.

01　연례 게임 대회 자원봉사자 모집　정답률 92% | 정답 ②

다음을 듣고, 여자가 하는 말의 목적으로 가장 적절한 것을 고르시오.
① 체육대회 종목을 소개하려고
☑ 대회 자원봉사자를 모집하려고
③ 학생 회장 선거 일정을 공지하려고
④ 경기 관람 규칙 준수를 당부하려고
⑤ 학교 홈페이지 주소 변경을 안내하려고

W : Good afternoon, everybody.
　안녕하세요, 여러분.
This is your student council president, Monica Brown.
　저는 학생회장 Monica Brown입니다.
Our school's annual e-sports competition will be held on the last day of the semester.
　우리 학교가 매년 하는 게임 대회가 이번 학기 마지막 날에 열릴 예정입니다.
For the competition, we need some volunteers to help set up computers.
　대회를 위해, 우리는 컴퓨터 설치를 도와줄 자원봉사자가 좀 필요합니다.
If you're interested in helping us make the competition successful, please fill out the volunteer application form and email it to me.
　만일 여러분이 우리가 대회를 성공적으로 이끌도록 돕고 싶으시다면, 자원봉사자 신청서를 작성해서 제게 이메일로 보내주세요.
For more information, please visit our school website.
　더 많은 정보를 보려면, 학교 웹 사이트를 방문해주세요.
I hope many of you will join us. Thank you for listening.
　여러분들이 많이 함께해주시길 바랍니다. 들어주셔서 고맙습니다.

Why? 왜 정답일까?
게임 대회를 맞아 자원봉사자가 필요하다는(For the competition, we need some volunteers to help set up computers.) 내용이므로, 여자가 하는 말의 목적으로 가장 적절한 것은 ② '대회 자원봉사자를 모집하려고'이다.

● annual ⓐ 연마다 하는
● competition ⓝ 대회, 경쟁
● application form 신청서
● e-sports ⓝ 게임, e–스포츠
● fill out 작성하다

02　산책으로 창의력 높이기　정답률 90% | 정답 ①

대화를 듣고, 남자의 의견으로 가장 적절한 것을 고르시오.
☑ 산책은 창의적인 생각을 할 수 있게 돕는다.
② 식사 후 과격한 운동은 소화를 방해한다.
③ 지나친 스트레스는 집중력을 감소시킨다.
④ 독서를 통해 창의력을 증진할 수 있다.
⑤ 꾸준한 운동은 기초체력을 향상시킨다.

M : Hannah, how's your design project going?
　Hannah, 네 디자인 프로젝트는 어떻게 돼 가?
W : Hey, Aiden. I'm still working on it, but I'm not making much progress.
　안녕, Aiden. 아직 작업 중인데, 그다지 진전이 안 되네.
M : Can you tell me what the problem is?
　문제가 뭔지 말해줄래?
W : Hmm... [Pause] It's hard to think of creative ideas. I feel like I'm wasting my time.
　흠… [잠시 멈춤] 창의적인 아이디어를 생각하기가 어려워. 난 시간 낭비 중인 거 같아.
M : I understand. Why don't you take a walk?
　이해해. 산책을 해보면 어때?
W : How can that help me to improve my creativity?
　그게 내 창의력을 높이는 데 어떻게 도움이 되지?
M : It will actually make your brain more active. Then you'll see things differently.
　그건 실제로 네 뇌를 더 활동적이게 만들어. 그럼 넌 사물을 다르게 볼 수 있지.
W : But I don't have time for that.
　그런데 나 그럴 시간이 없어.
M : You don't need a lot of time. Even a short walk will help you to come up with creative ideas.
　시간이 많이 필요한 게 아냐. 잠깐 산책하는 것만으로도 창의적인 생각을 하는 데 도움이 될 거야.
W : Then I'll try it. Thanks for the tip.
　그럼 시도해봐야겠어. 조언 고마워.

Why? 왜 정답일까?
창의적인 생각을 떠올리기가 어렵다는 여자에게 남자는 산책을 권하며, 짧은 산책일지라도 창의력 증진에 도움이 된다고 조언한다(Even a short walk will help you to come up with creative ideas.). 따라서 남자의 의견으로 가장 적절한 것은 ① '산책은 창의적인 생각을 할 수 있게 돕는다.'이다.

● work on ~을 작업하다
● waste ⓥ 낭비하다
● have time for ~할 시간이 있다
● make progress 진전되다
● take a walk 산책하다

03　우체국에서 물건 부치기　정답률 88% | 정답 ①

대화를 듣고, 두 사람의 관계를 가장 잘 나타낸 것을 고르시오.

☑ 고객 – 우체국 직원
③ 여행객 – 여행 가이드
⑤ 손님 – 옷가게 주인
② 투숙객 – 호텔 지배인
④ 아파트 주민 – 경비원

W : Excuse me. Could you please tell me where I can put this box?
　실례합니다. 제가 이 박스를 어디에 놓으면 될지 말해주실래요?
M : Right here on this counter. How can I help you today?
　여기 이 카운터에 놔주세요. 오늘은 뭘 도와드릴까요?
W : I'd like to send this to Jeju Island.
　이걸 제주도로 보내고 싶어요.
M : Sure. Are there any breakable items in the box?
　알겠습니다. 상자 안에 깨지기 쉬운 물건이라도 들어 있나요?
W : No, there are only clothes in it.
　아뇨, 옷밖에 없어요.
M : Then, there should be no problem.
　그럼, 아무 문제가 없을 겁니다.
W : I see. What's the fastest way to send it?
　네, 제일 빠른 배송 방법이 뭔가요?
M : You can send the package by express mail, but there's an extra charge.
　급행 우편으로 보내실 수 있는데, 추가 비용이 있습니다.
W : That's okay. I want it to be delivered as soon as possible. When will it arrive in Jeju if it goes out today?
　괜찮아요. 최대한 빨리 보내고 싶어요. 오늘 배송 나가면 언제 제주도에 도착할까요?
M : If you send it today, it will be there by this Friday.
　오늘 보내시면 이번 주 금요일이면 도착할 겁니다.
W : Oh, Friday will be great. I'll do the express mail.
　오, 금요일이면 아주 좋겠네요. 급행 우편 할게요.

Why? 왜 정답일까?
'I'd like to send this to Jeju Island.', 'Sure. Are there any breakable items in the box?', 'What's the fastest way to send it?', 'You can send the package by express mail, but there's an extra charge.', 'I'll do the express mail.'에서 여자는 물건을 부치는 고객이고, 남자는 이를 처리해주는 우체국 직원임을 알 수 있다. 따라서 두 사람의 관계로 가장 적절한 것은 ① '고객 – 우체국 직원'이다.

● breakable ⓐ 깨지기 쉬운
● express mail 급행 우편
● deliver ⓥ 배달하다
● package ⓝ 소포
● extra charge 추가 비용

04　버스킹 사진 구경하기　정답률 87% | 정답 ④

대화를 듣고, 그림에서 대화의 내용과 일치하지 않는 것을 고르시오.

M : Kayla, I heard you went busking on the street last weekend.
　Kayla, 나 네가 지난 주말에 거리에 버스킹하러 갔다고 들었어.
W : It was amazing! I've got a picture here. Look!
　아주 멋졌어! 여기 사진이 있어. 봐봐!
M : 「Oh, you're wearing the hat I gave you.」 ①의근거 일치
　오, 내가 준 모자를 쓰고 있구나.
W : Yeah, I really like it.
　응, 나 그거 아주 마음에 들어.
M : Looks great. 「This boy playing the guitar next to you must be your brother Kevin.」 ②의근거 일치
　잘 어울리네. 네 옆에서 기타 치는 이 남자애는 네 남동생 Kevin이겠구나.
W : You're right. He played while I sang.
　맞아. 내가 노래하는 동안 걔는 연주를 했어.
M : Cool. 「Why did you leave the guitar case open?」 ③의근거 일치
　근사한걸. 기타 케이스는 왜 열어둔 거야?
W : That's for the audience. If they like our performance, they give us some money.
　관객을 때문에. 우리 공연이 마음에 들면 돈을 좀 주라고.
M : 「Oh, and you set up two speakers!」 ④의근거 불일치
　오, 그리고 너네 스피커도 두 개 설치해 뒀구나!
W : I did. I recently bought them.
　응. 최근에 샀어.
M : I see. 「And did you design that poster on the wall?」 ⑤의근거 일치
　그렇구나. 그리고 벽에 있는 저 포스터는 네가 디자인했어?
W : Yeah. My brother and I worked on it together.
　응, 내 남동생이랑 나랑 같이 작업했어.
M : It sounds like you really had a lot of fun!
　둘이 되게 재미있었겠다!

Why? 왜 정답일까?
대화에서 스피커는 두 개였다고 하는데(Oh, and you set up two speakers!), 그림 속 스피커는 하나뿐이다. 따라서 그림에서 대화의 내용과 일치하지 않는 것은 ④이다.

● busk ⓥ 버스킹하다, 거리 공연하다
● leave open 열어두다
● recently ⓐⓓ 최근에
● amazing ⓐ 멋진, 근사한
● performance ⓝ 공연, 성과

05 | 아들의 생일 파티 준비하기 정답률 90% | 정답 ⑤

대화를 듣고, 남자가 할 일로 가장 적절한 것을 고르시오.
① 초대장 보내기　　　② 피자 주문하기
③ 거실 청소하기　　　④ 꽃다발 준비하기
✓ 스마트폰 사러 가기

W : Honey, are we ready for Jake's birthday party tomorrow?
　여보, 우리 내일 Jake의 생일 파티 준비가 다 되었나요?
M : I sent the invitation cards last week. What about other things?
　내가 지난주에 초대장을 보냈어요. 다른 건요?
W : I'm not sure. Let's check.
　모르겠어요. 확인해보죠.
M : We are expecting a lot of guests. How about the dinner menu?
　손님이 많이 올 거예요. 저녁 메뉴는 뭐죠?
W : I haven't decided yet.
　아직 결정 못했어요.
M : We won't have much time to cook, so let's just order pizza.
　우린 요리할 시간이 많지 않을 테니, 그냥 피자를 주문하죠.
W : Okay. I'll do it tomorrow. What about the present?
　알겠어요. 내가 내일 할게요. 선물은 어떡하죠?
M : Oh, you mean the smartphone? I forgot to get it!
　오, 스마트폰 말하는 거죠? 그걸 사는 걸 잊었네요!
W : That's alright. Can you go to the electronics store and buy it now?
　괜찮아요. 지금 전자제품 가게 좀 가서 사올래요?
M : No problem. I'll do it right away.
　문제 없어요. 바로 할게요.
W : Good. Then, I'll clean up the living room while you're out.
　알겠어요. 그럼 당신이 외출한 동안 내가 거실을 치울게요.

Why? 왜 정답일까?
아들의 생일 선물인 스마트폰을 깜빡 잊고 못 샀다는 남자에게 여자는 지금 사 와달라고 부탁한다(Can you go to the electronics store and buy it now? / No problem. I'll do it right away.). 따라서 남자가 할 일로 가장 적절한 것은 ⑤ '스마트폰 사러 가기'이다.

● invitation card 초대장　　● present ⓝ 선물
● forget to ~해야 하는 걸 잊다　● clean up 청소하다, 치우다

06 | 쇼파에 놓을 담요와 쿠션 구매하기 정답률 80% | 정답 ③

대화를 듣고, 여자가 지불할 금액을 고르시오. [3점]
① $54　② $60　✓ $72　④ $76　⑤ $80

M : Good morning! How can I help you?
　안녕하세요! 뭘 도와드릴까요?
W : Hi. I'm looking for a blanket and some cushions for my sofa.
　안녕하세요. 전 소파에 놓을 담요랑 쿠션을 좀 찾고 있어요.
M : Okay. We've got some on sale. Would you like to have a look?
　알겠어요. 세일하는 제품이 좀 있습니다. 살펴보시겠어요?
W : Yes. How much is this green blanket?
　네. 이 녹색 담요는 얼만가요?
M : That's $40.
　40달러입니다.
W : Oh, I love the color green. Can you also show me some cushions that go well with this blanket?
　오, 전 녹색을 좋아해요. 이 담요랑 잘 어울리는 쿠션도 좀 보여주실래요?
M : Sure! How about these?
　물론이죠! 이건 어때요?
W : They look good. I need two of them. How much are they?
　좋아 보이네요. 두 개 필요합니다. 얼만가요?
M : The cushions are $20 each.
　쿠션은 하나에 20달러입니다.
W : Okay. I'll take one green blanket and two cushions. Can I use this coupon?
　알겠어요. 전 녹색 담요 하나랑 쿠션 두 개를 사겠어요. 제가 이 쿠폰을 사용해도 되나요?
M : Sure. It will give you 10% off the total.
　물론이죠. 총액에서 10퍼센트 할인됩니다.
W : Thanks! Here's my credit card.
　고맙습니다! 여기 제 신용 카드요.

Why? 왜 정답일까?
대화에 따르면 여자는 40달러짜리 담요 한 장과 20달러짜리 쿠션을 두 개 구입하고, 총액에서 10퍼센트를 할인받기로 했다. 이를 식으로 나타내면 '(40 + 20×2)×0.9 = 72'이므로, 여자가 지불할 금액은 ③ '$72'이다.

● blanket ⓝ 담요　　　● on sale 할인 중인
● have a look 살펴보다　● go well with ~와 잘 어울리다

07 | 록 콘서트에 가자고 제안하기 정답률 92% | 정답 ④

대화를 듣고, 남자가 록 콘서트에 갈 수 없는 이유를 고르시오.
① 일을 하러 가야 해서
② 피아노 연습을 해야 해서
③ 할머니를 뵈러 가야 해서
✓ 친구의 개를 돌봐야 해서
⑤ 과제를 아직 끝내지 못해서

W : Hello, Justin. What are you doing?
　안녕, Justin. 뭐 하고 있어?
M : Hi, Ellie. I'm doing my project for art class.
　안녕, Ellie. 나 미술 수업 프로젝트 하고 있어.
W : Can you go to a rock concert with me this Saturday? My sister gave me two tickets!
　너 이번 주 토요일에 나랑 록 콘서트 갈래? 우리 언니가 표를 두 장 줬어!
M : I'd love to! [Pause] But I'm afraid I can't.
　나도 가고 싶어! [잠시 멈춤] 근데 미안하지만 안 되겠어.
W : Do you have to work that day?
　그날 일해야 돼?
M : No, I don't work on Saturdays.
　아니, 나 토요일에 일 안 하지.
W : Then, why not? I thought you really like rock music.
　그럼 왜? 너 록 음악 되게 좋아하는 줄 알았는데.
M : Of course I do. But I have to take care of my friend's dog this Saturday.
　물론 좋아하지. 근데 이번 주 토요일엔 내 친구네 개를 돌봐줘야 해.
W : Oh, really? Is your friend going somewhere?
　오, 그래? 네 친구 어디 가는 거야?
M : He's visiting his grandmother that day.
　그날 자기 할머니를 뵈러 간대.
W : Okay, no problem. I'm sure I can find someone else to go with me.
　알겠어. 괜찮아. 난 같이 갈 다른 사람 찾을 수 있겠지.

Why? 왜 정답일까?
남자는 토요일에 할머니를 뵈러 가는 친구네 개를 돌봐주기로 해서(But I have to take care of my friend's dog this Saturday.) 여자와 함께 콘서트에 갈 수 없다고 한다. 따라서 남자가 록 콘서트에 갈 수 없는 이유로 가장 적절한 것은 ④ '친구의 개를 돌봐야 해서'이다.

● I'm afraid I can't. 미안하지만 안 되겠어.　● take care of ~을 돌보다
● somewhere ⓐⓓ 어딘가

08 | 환경의 날 행사 정답률 93% | 정답 ③

대화를 듣고, Eco Day에 관해 언급되지 않은 것을 고르시오.
① 행사 시간　　② 행사 장소　　✓ 참가비
④ 준비물　　　⑤ 등록 방법

W : Scott, did you see this Eco Day poster?
　Scott, 너 이 Eco Day(환경의 날) 포스터 봤어?
M : No, not yet. Let me see. [Pause] It's an event for picking up trash while walking around a park.
　아니, 아직. 나 볼래. [잠시 멈춤] 공원을 걸으면서 쓰레기를 줍는 행사구나.
W : Why don't we do it together? 「It's next Sunday from 10 a.m. to 5 p.m.」 ①의 근거 일치
　우리 이거 같이 하면 어때? 다음 주 토요일 아침 10시부터 오후 5시까지야.
M : Sounds good. I've been thinking a lot about the environment lately.
　좋네. 난 최근에 환경 생각을 많이 하고 있어.
W : Me, too. 「Also, the event will be held in Eastside Park.」 You know, we often used to go there. ②의 근거 일치
　나도 그래. 게다가, 이 행사는 Eastside Park에서 열린대. 알다시피 우리 자주 거기 갔잖아.
M : That's great. Oh, look at this. 「We have to bring our own gloves and small bags for the trash.」 ④의 근거 일치
　아주 좋네. 오, 이거 봐. 우린 장갑이랑 쓰레기 담을 작은 가방을 가져가야 해.
W : No problem. I have extra. I can bring some for you as well.
　문제 없어. 나 남는 거 있어. 내가 네 것도 좀 가져올 수 있어.
M : Okay, thanks. 「Do we have to sign up for the event?」
　알겠어, 고마워. 우리 행사 등록해야 하나?
W : Yes. The poster says we can do it online. ⑤의 근거 일치
　응. 포스터에 온라인으로 하면 된다고 적혀 있어.
M : Let's do it right now. I'm looking forward to it.
　지금 바로 하자. 기대된다.

Why? 왜 정답일까?
대화에서 남자와 여자는 Eco Day의 행사 시간, 행사 장소, 준비물, 등록 방법을 언급하므로, 언급되지 않은 것은 ③ '참가비'이다.

Why? 왜 오답일까?
① 'It's next Sunday from 10 a.m. to 5 p.m.'에서 '행사 시간'이 언급되었다.
② 'Also, the event will be held in Eastside Park.'에서 '행사 장소'가 언급되었다.
④ 'We have to bring our own gloves and small bags for the trash.'에서 '준비물'이 언급되었다.
⑤ 'The poster says we can do it online.'에서 '등록 방법'이 언급되었다.

● pick up 줍다　　　　　● trash ⓝ 쓰레기
● Why don't we ~? ~하면 어때?　● sign up for ~에 등록하다, 신청하다
● look forward to ~을 고대하다

09 | 교내 팀 댄스 대회 안내 정답률 80% | 정답 ⑤

Eastville Dance Contest에 관한 다음 내용을 듣고, 일치하지 않는 것을 고르시오.
① 처음으로 개최되는 경연이다.
② 모든 종류의 춤이 허용된다.
③ 춤 영상을 8월 15일까지 업로드 해야 한다.
④ 학생들은 가장 좋아하는 영상에 투표할 수 있다.
✓ 우승팀은 상으로 상품권을 받게 될 것이다.

M : Hello, Eastville High School students. This is your P.E. teacher, Mr. Wilson.
　안녕하세요, Eastville 고교 학생 여러분. 체육 교사 Wilson 선생님이에요.
　「I'm pleased to let you know that we're hosting the first Eastville Dance Contest.」 ①의 근거 일치
　여러분께 제 1회 Eastville Dance Contest가 개최된다는 것을 알리게 되어 기쁩니다.
　Any Eastville students who love dancing can participate in the contest as a team.
　춤추는 것을 좋아하는 모든 Eastville 학생들은 팀으로 대회에 참가할 수 있습니다.
　「All kinds of dance are allowed.」 ②의 근거 일치
　모든 종류의 춤이 허용됩니다.
　「If you'd like to participate, please upload your team's dance video to our school website by August 15th.」 ③의 근거 일치
　참가하고 싶다면, 8월 15일까지 여러분 팀의 댄스 영상을 우리 학교 웹 사이트에 업로드 해주세요.
　「Students can vote for their favorite video from August 16th to 20th.」 ④의 근거 일치
　학생들은 8월 16일부터 20일까지 가장 좋아하는 영상에 투표할 수 있습니다.

『The winning team will receive a trophy as a prize.』 **⑤의 근거** 불일치
우승팀은 상으로 트로피를 받게 됩니다.

Don't miss this great opportunity to show off your talents!
여러분의 재능을 뽐낼 이 대단한 기회를 놓치지 마세요!

- **pleased** ⓐ 기쁜
- **all kinds of** 모든 종류의
- **vote for** ~을 위해 투표하다
- **participate in** ~에 참가하다
- **allow** ⓥ 허용하다
- **show off** 뽐내다, 보여주다

---

10 새집에 놓을 정수기 사기 정답률 87% | 정답 ④

다음 표를 보면서 대화를 듣고, 두 사람이 구입할 정수기를 고르시오.

Water Purifiers

	Model	Price	Water Tank Capacity(liters)	Power-saving Mode	Warranty
①	A	$570	4	×	1 year
②	B	$650	5	○	1 year
③	C	$680	5	×	3 years
④	D	$740	5	○	3 years
⑤	E	$830	6	○	3 years

M : Honey, we need a water purifier for our new house.
여보, 우리 새집에 둘 정수기가 필요해요.

W : You're right. Let's order one online.
당신 말이 옳아요. 온라인에서 하나 주문하죠.

M : Good idea. *[Clicking Sound]* Look! These are the five bestsellers.
좋은 생각이에요. *[클릭하는 소리]* 이거 봐요! 이게 베스트셀러 다섯 개예요.

W : I see. 『What's our budget?』
그렇군요. 우리 예산이 얼마죠?

M : Well, I don't want to spend more than 800 dollars.』 **근거1** Price 조건
음, 800달러 넘게 쓰고 싶지 않군요.

W : 『Okay, how about the water tank capacity?』
알겠어요. 물 탱크 용량은요?

M : I think the five-liter tank would be perfect for us.』 **근거2** Water Tank Capacity 조건
5리터짜리 탱크면 우리한테 딱 좋겠어요.

W : I think so, too. 『And I like the ones with a power-saving mode.』
나도 그렇게 생각해요. 그리고 난 절전 모드가 있는 게 좋아요. **근거3** Power-saving Mode 조건

M : Okay, then we can save electricity. Now, there are just two options left.
그래요. 그럼 우린 전기를 절약할 수 있겠죠. 이제, 두 가지 선택권이 남았군요.

W : 『Let's look at the warranties. The longer, the better.』 **근거4** Warranty 조건
보증 기간을 보죠. 길수록 좋죠.

M : I agree. We should order this model.
동의해요. 이 제품으로 주문해야겠어요.

- **water purifier** 정수기
- **power-saving mode** 절전 모드
- **warranty** ⓝ 보증 (기간)
- **capacity** ⓝ 용량
- **electricity** ⓝ 전기

---

11 자동차 전시회 정답률 72% | 정답 ①

대화를 듣고, 남자의 마지막 말에 대한 여자의 응답으로 가장 적절한 것을 고르시오.

① Great. We don't have to wait in line. – 좋아. 우린 줄 서서 기다릴 필요가 없네.
② All right. We can come back later. – 알겠어. 다음에 다시 오면 돼.
③ Good job. Let's buy the tickets. – 잘했어. 표를 사자.
④ No worries. I will stand in line. – 걱정 마. 내가 줄 서 있을게.
⑤ Too bad. I can't buy that car. – 아깝네. 난 그 차를 살 수 없어.

M : Let's get inside. I'm so excited to see this auto show.
들어가자. 난 이 자동차 전시회 보게 돼서 무척 신나.

W : Look over there. So many people are already standing in line to buy tickets.
저기 봐. 엄청 많은 사람들이 벌써 표를 사려고 줄을 서 있어.

M : Fortunately, I bought our tickets in advance.
다행히도 난 우리 표를 미리 사뒀어.

W : Great. We don't have to wait in line.
좋아. 우린 줄 서서 기다릴 필요가 없네.

- **auto show** 자동차 전시회
- **in advance** 미리
- **stand in line** 줄 서서 기다리다

---

12 역사 시험 점수 확인 정답률 72% | 정답 ③

대화를 듣고, 여자의 마지막 말에 대한 남자의 응답으로 가장 적절한 것을 고르시오.

① Yes. You can register online.
응. 온라인으로 등록하면 돼.
② Sorry. I can't see you next week.
미안. 나 다음 주에 너 못 만나.
③ Right. I should go to his office now.
맞아. 지금 선생님 교무실로 가야겠어.
④ Fantastic! I'll take the test tomorrow.
환상적이네! 내일 테스트를 쳐야겠다.
⑤ Of course. I can help him if he needs my help.
물론이지. 그분께서 도움이 필요하시면 내가 도와드릴 수 있어.

W : Hi, Chris. Did you check your grade for the history test we took last week?
안녕, Chris. 너 지난주 우리 본 역사 시험 점수 확인해 봤어?

M : Yes. But I think there's something wrong with my grade.
응. 근데 내 성적에 뭔가 잘못된 것 같아.

W : Don't you think you should go ask Mr. Morgan about it?
너 Morgan 선생님께 가서 그거 여쭤봐야 한다고 생각하지 않아?

M : Right. I should go to his office now.
맞아. 지금 선생님 교무실로 가야겠어.

- **grade** ⓝ 점수
- **go ask** 가서 물어보다
- **take a test** 시험을 치다
- **register** ⓥ 등록하다

---

13 중고 책 안에 들어 있던 쪽지 정답률 79% | 정답 ②

대화를 듣고, 여자의 마지막 말에 대한 남자의 응답으로 가장 적절한 것을 고르시오. [3점]

Man: _____

① I agree. You can save a lot by buying secondhand.
같은 생각이에요. 중고 사면 돈을 많이 아낄 수 있죠.
② Great idea! Our message would make others smile.
좋은 생각이에요! 우리 메시지가 남들을 웃게 할 거예요.
③ Sorry. I forgot to write a message in the book.
죄송해요. 전 책 안에 메시지를 써놓는 걸 까먹었어요.
④ Exactly. Taking notes during class is important.
바로 그거예요. 수업 중에 필기하는 것은 중요해요.
⑤ Okay. We can arrive on time if we leave now.
알겠어요. 우리가 지금 떠나면 제때 도착할 수 있어요.

M : Mom, did you write this note?
엄마, 엄마가 이 쪽지 쓰셨어요?

W : What's that?
그게 뭔데?

M : I found this in the book you gave me.
엄마가 주신 책에서 이걸 찾았어요.

W : Oh, the one I bought for you at the secondhand bookstore last week?
오, 내가 지난 주 너한테 중고 서점에서 사다준 거 말이구나?

M : Yes. At first I thought it was a bookmark, but it wasn't. It's a note with a message!
네. 처음엔 책갈피인 줄 알았는데, 아니더라고요. 메시지가 적힌 쪽지였어요!

W : What does it say?
뭐라고 써 있는데?

M : It says, "I hope you enjoy this book."
'이 책을 재밌게 읽기 바랍니다.'라고 적혀 있어요.

W : How sweet! That really brings a smile to my face.
상냥해라! 정말 얼굴에 웃음이 지어지게 하네.

M : Yeah, mom. I love this message so much.
그러게요, 엄마. 전 이 메시지가 정말 마음에 들어요.

W : Well, then, why don't we leave a note if we resell this book later?
음, 그럼, 우리가 이 책을 나중에 다시 팔 때 쪽지를 남겨두면 어떨까?

M : Great idea! Our message would make others smile.
좋은 생각이에요! 우리 메시지가 남들을 웃게 할 거예요.

- **secondhand bookstore** 중고 서점
- **take notes** 필기하다
- **resell** ⓥ 되팔다

---

14 가족과 캠핑 가기 정답률 85% | 정답 ⑤

대화를 듣고, 남자의 마지막 말에 대한 여자의 응답으로 가장 적절한 것을 고르시오. [3점]

Woman: _____

① Why not? I can bring some food when we go camping.
왜 안 되겠어? 우리 캠핑갈 때 내가 음식을 좀 가져갈 수 있어.
② I'm sorry. That fishing equipment is not for sale.
미안해. 그 낚시 도구는 파는 게 아냐.
③ I don't think so. The price is most important.
난 그렇게 생각 안 해. 가격이 제일 중요해.
④ Really? I'd love to meet your family.
정말? 난 너희 가족을 만나보고 싶어.
⑤ No problem. You can use my equipment.
문제 없어. 내 장비를 쓰면 돼.

M : Do you have any plans for this weekend, Sandy?
이번 주말 계획 있어, Sandy?

W : Hey, Evan. I'm planning to go camping with my family.
안녕, Evan. 가족하고 캠핑 갈 계획이야.

M : I've never gone before. Do you go camping often?
난 한 번도 가본 적이 없어. 넌 캠핑 자주 가?

W : Yes. Two or three times a month at least.
응, 적어도 한 달에 두세 번 가.

M : That's cool. Why do you like it so much?
근사하네. 왜 그걸 그렇게 좋아해?

W : I like spending time in nature with my family. It makes me feel closer to them.
가족들하고 자연에서 시간 보내는 게 좋아. 가족들과 더 가까워지는 느낌이 들게 하거든.

M : I understand. It's like a family hobby, right?
그렇구나. 가족 취미 같은 거구나, 그치?

W : Yes, you're right. Camping helps me relieve all my stress, too.
응, 맞아. 캠핑은 내 스트레스를 다 푸는 데도 도움이 돼.

M : Sounds interesting. I'd love to try it.
재미있겠다. 나도 해보고 싶어.

W : If you go camping with your family, you'll see what I mean.
가족들하고 캠핑 가보면, 내 말이 무슨 말인지 알 거야.

M : I wish I could, but I don't have any equipment for it.
나도 가보고 싶은데, 난 장비가 하나도 없어.

W : No problem. You can use my equipment.
문제 없어. 내 장비를 쓰면 돼.

Why? 왜 정답일까?

가족과 캠핑을 가보고 싶지만 장비가 하나도 없다(I wish I could, but I don't have any equipment for it.)는 남자의 말에 대한 여자의 응답으로 가장 적절한 것은 ⑤ '문제 없어. 내 장비를 쓰면 돼.'이다.

● go camping 캠핑 가다　　● relieve stress 스트레스를 풀다

---

15 책 대신 빌려달라고 부탁하기　　정답률 91% | 정답 ⑤

다음 상황 설명을 듣고, Violet이 Peter에게 할 말로 가장 적절한 것을 고르시오.
Violet:

① Will you join the science club together? – 너 과학 동아리 같이 할래?
② Is it okay to use a card to pay for the drinks? – 음료 계산에 카드를 써도 될까?
③ Why don't we donate our books to the library? – 우리 책을 도서관에 기부하면 어때?
④ How about going to the cafeteria to have lunch? – 구내식당 가서 점심 먹는 거 어때?
☑ Can you borrow the books for me with your card? – 네 카드로 나 대신 책을 빌려줄 수 있어?

W : Violet and Peter are classmates.
Violet과 Peter는 반 친구이다.

They're doing their science group assignment together.
그들은 과학 팀 과제를 함께 하는 중이다.

On Saturday morning, they meet at the public library.
토요일 아침, 그들은 공립 도서관에서 만난다.

They decide to find the books they need in different sections of the library.
그들은 도서관 각기 다른 구역에서 필요한 책을 찾기로 한다.

Violet finds two useful books and tries to check them out.
Violet은 유용한 책을 두 권 찾아서 대출하려고 한다.

Unfortunately, she suddenly realizes that she didn't bring her library card.
안타깝게도, 그녀는 문득 도서관 카드를 가져오지 않았음을 깨닫는다.

At that moment, Peter walks up to Violet.
그때, Peter가 Violet에게 다가온다.

So, Violet wants to ask Peter to check out the books for her because she knows he has his library card.
Peter는 도서관 카드를 갖고 있다는 것을 알기에 Violet은 그에게 자기 대신 책을 빌려달라고 부탁하려 한다.

In this situation, what would Violet most likely say to Peter?
이 상황에서, Violet은 Peter에게 뭐라고 말할 것인가?

Violet : Can you borrow the books for me with your card?
네 카드로 나 대신 책을 빌려줄 수 있어?

Why? 왜 정답일까?

상황에 따르면 Violet은 필요한 책을 찾았지만 도서관 카드가 없어 못 빌리므로, Peter에게 책을 대신 빌려달라고 부탁하려 한다(So, Violet wants to ask Peter to check out the books for her because she knows he has his library card.). 따라서 Violet이 Peter에게 할 말로 가장 적절한 것은 ⑤ '네 카드로 나 대신 책을 빌려줄 수 있어?'이다.

● group assignment 팀 과제　　● public ⓐ 공립의, 공공의
● section ⓝ 구역　　● check out 대출하다, 빌리다

16-17 숙면에 도움이 되는 음식

M : Hello, everyone. I'm Shawn Collins, a doctor at Collins Sleep Clinic.
안녕하세요, 여러분. 저는 Collins Sleep Clinic의 의사 Shawn Collins입니다.

Sleep is one of the most essential parts of our daily lives.
수면은 우리의 일상에서 가장 중요한 부분 중 하나죠.

『So today, I'm going to introduce the best foods for helping you sleep better.』 **16번의 근거**
그래서 오늘, 저는 여러분께 더 잘 잠드는 데 도움이 되는 최고의 음식을 소개해 드리려고 합니다.

『First, kiwi fruits contain a high level of hormones that help you fall asleep more quickly, sleep longer, and wake up less during the night.』 **17번①의 근거 일치**
첫 번째로, 키위는 더 빨리 잠들고, 더 오래 자고, 밤 시간 동안 덜 깨게 도와주는 호르몬이 많이 함유되어 있습니다.

『Second, milk is rich in vitamin D and it calms the mind and nerves.』 **17번②의 근거 일치**
둘째로, 우유는 비타민 D가 풍부하고 정신과 신경을 안정시켜 줍니다.

If you drink a cup of milk before you go to bed, it will definitely help you get a good night's sleep.
잠자리에 들기 전 우유 한 컵을 드시면, 확실히 숙면하는 데 도움이 될 것입니다.

『Third, nuts can help to produce the hormone that controls your internal body clock and sends signals for the body to sleep at the right time.』 **17번③의 근거 일치**
세 번째로, 견과류는 생체 시계를 조절하는 호르몬을 만드는 것을 도와주고, 몸이 제때 잠자리에 들도록 신호를 보냅니다.

『The last one is honey. Honey helps you sleep well because it reduces the hormone that keeps the brain awake!』 **17번⑤의 근거 일치**
마지막은 꿀입니다. 꿀은 뇌를 깨어있게 만드는 호르몬을 줄여줘서 잠을 잘 자게 도와주죠!

Now, I'll show you some delicious diet plans using these foods.
이제, 이 음식들을 이용한 맛 좋은 식단을 알려드리겠습니다.

● essential ⓐ 필수적인
● nerve ⓝ 신경
● internal ⓐ 내부의
● disorder ⓝ 장애, 질환
● contain ⓥ 함유하다
● get a good night's sleep 숙면하다
● body clock 생체 시계

---

16 주제 파악　　정답률 93% | 정답 ③

남자가 하는 말의 주제로 가장 적절한 것은?
① different causes of sleep disorders – 수면 장애의 다양한 원인
② various ways to keep foods fresh – 음식을 신선하게 보관하는 여러 방법
☑ foods to improve quality of sleep – 수면의 질을 높여주는 음식
④ reasons for organic foods' popularity – 유기농 음식이 인기 있는 이유
⑤ origins of popular foods around the world – 세계의 인기 있는 음식의 기원

Why? 왜 정답일까?

잠을 더 잘 자게 해주는 음식을 소개하는 내용(So today, I'm going to introduce the best foods for helping you sleep better.)이므로, 남자가 하는 말의 주제로 가장 적절한 것은 ③ '수면의 질을 높여주는 음식들'이다.

---

17 언급 유무 파악　　정답률 92% | 정답 ④

언급된 음식이 아닌 것은?
① kiwi fruits – 키위
② milk – 우유
③ nuts – 견과류
☑ tomatoes – 토마토
⑤ honey – 꿀

Why? 왜 정답일까?

담화에서 남자는 잠에 도움이 되는 음식으로 키위, 우유, 견과류, 꿀을 언급하므로, 언급되지 않은 것은 ④ '토마토'이다.

Why? 왜 오답일까?

① 'First, kiwi fruits contain a high level of hormones that help you fall asleep more quickly, sleep longer, and wake up less during the night.'에서 '키위'가 언급되었다.
② 'Second, milk is rich in vitamin D and it calms the mind and nerves.'에서 '우유'가 언급되었다.
③ 'Third, nuts can help to produce the hormone that controls your internal body clock and sends signals for the body to sleep at the right time.'에서 '견과류'가 언급되었다.
⑤ 'The last one is honey.'에서 '꿀'이 언급되었다.

---

18 여름 휴가 패키지 홍보　　정답률 93% | 정답 ②

다음 글의 목적으로 가장 적절한 것은?
① 여행 일정 변경을 안내하려고
☑ 패키지 여행 상품을 홍보하려고
③ 여행 상품 불만족에 대해 사과하려고
④ 여행 만족도 조사 참여를 부탁하려고
⑤ 패키지 여행 업무 담당자를 모집하려고

ACC Travel Agency Customers:
ACC 여행사 고객님께

Have you ever wanted / to enjoy a holiday in nature?
당신은 원한 적이 있습니까? / 자연 속에서 휴가를 즐기기를

This summer is the best time / to turn your dream into reality.
이번 여름이 최고의 시간입니다. / 당신의 꿈을 현실로 바꿀

We have a perfect travel package for you.
우리에게는 당신을 위한 완벽한 패키지 여행 상품이 있습니다.

This travel package / includes special trips to Lake Madison / as well as massage and meditation to help you relax.
이 패키지 여행 상품은 / Lake Madison으로의 특별한 여행을 포함합니다. / 당신이 편히 쉴 수 있도록 돕는 마사지와 명상뿐만 아니라

Also, / we provide yoga lessons / taught by experienced instructors.
또한, / 우리는 요가 강의도 제공합니다. / 숙련된 강사에 의해 지도되는

If you book this package, / you will enjoy all this at a reasonable price.
만약 당신이 이 패키지를 예약한다면, / 당신은 이 모든 것을 합리적인 가격으로 즐길 것입니다.

We are sure / that it will be an unforgettable experience for you.
우리는 확신합니다. / 그것이 당신에게 잊지 못할 경험이 될 것이라고

If you call us, / we will be happy to give you more details.
당신이 우리에게 전화하시면, / 우리는 당신에게 더 많은 세부 사항을 기꺼이 알려드리겠습니다.

ACC 여행사 고객님께

자연 속에서 휴가를 즐기는 것을 원한 적이 있습니까? 이번 여름이 당신의 꿈을 현실로 바꿀 최고의 시간입니다. 우리에게는 당신을 위한 완벽한 패키지 여행 상품이 있습니다. 이 패키지 여행 상품은 당신이 편히 쉴 수 있도록 돕는 마사지와 명상뿐만 아니라 Lake Madison으로의 특별한 여행을 포함합니다. 또한, 우리는 숙련된 강사의 요가 강의도 제공합니다. 만약 당신이 이 패키지를 예약한다면, 당신은 이 모든 것을 합리적인 가격으로 즐길 것입니다. 우리는 그것이 당신에게 잊지 못할 경험이 될 것이라고 확신합니다. 우리에게 전화하시면, 우리는 당신에게 더 많은 세부 사항을 기꺼이 알려드리겠습니다.

Why? 왜 정답일까?

여름 휴가에 적합한 패키지 여행 상품이 있음을 홍보하는 글(We have a perfect travel package for you.)이므로, 글의 목적으로 가장 적절한 것은 ② '패키지 여행 상품을 홍보하려고'이다.

● travel agency 여행사
● experienced ⓐ 경험 많은, 숙련된
● unforgettable ⓐ 잊지 못할
● meditation ⓝ 명상
● instructor ⓝ 강사

구문 풀이

4행 This travel package includes special trips to Lake Madison as well as
「A + as well as + B : B뿐 아니라 A도」
massage and meditation to help you relax.
「help + 목적어 + 원형부사: ~이 …하는 데 도움이 되다」

---

19 남편과 딸이 없어진 줄 알았다가 다시 찾고는 안도한 필자 　정답률 88% | 정답 ①

다음 글에 드러난 'I'의 심경 변화로 가장 적절한 것은?

✓① anxious → relieved
　불안한 → 안도한
② delighted → unhappy
　기쁜 → 불행한
③ indifferent → excited
　무관심한 → 신난
④ relaxed → upset
　안도한 → 언짢은
⑤ embarrassed → proud
　당황한 → 자랑스러운

When I woke up in our hotel room, / it was almost midnight.
내가 호텔 방에서 깨어났을 때는 / 거의 자정이었다.

I didn't see my husband nor daughter.
남편과 딸이 보이지 않았다.

I called them, / but I heard their phones ringing in the room.
나는 그들에게 전화를 걸었지만, / 나는 그들의 전화가 방에서 울리는 것을 들었다.

Feeling worried, I went outside and walked down the street, / but they were nowhere to be found.
걱정이 되어, / 나는 밖으로 나가 거리를 걸어 내려갔지만, / 그들을 어디에서도 찾을 수 없었다.

When I decided / I should ask someone for help, / a crowd nearby caught my attention.
내가 마음 먹었을 때 / 내가 누군가에게 도움을 요청해야겠다고 / 근처에 있던 군중이 내 주의를 끌었다.

I approached, / hoping to find my husband and daughter, / and suddenly I saw two familiar faces.
나는 다가갔고, / 남편과 딸을 찾으려는 희망을 안고 / 갑자기 낯익은 두 얼굴이 보였다.

I smiled, feeling calm.
나는 안도하며 웃었다.

Just then, / my daughter saw me and called, / "Mom!"
바로 그때, / 딸이 나를 보고 외쳤다. / "엄마!"라고

They were watching the magic show.
그들은 마술 쇼를 보고 있는 중이었다.

Finally, / I felt all my worries disappear.
마침내, 나는 내 모든 걱정이 사라지는 것을 느꼈다.

내가 호텔 방에서 깨어났을 때는 거의 자정이었다. 남편과 딸이 보이지 않았다. 나는 그들에게 전화를 걸었지만, 나는 그들의 전화가 방에서 울리는 것을 들었다. 걱정이 되어, 나는 밖으로 나가 거리를 걸어 내려갔지만, 그들을 어디에서도 찾을 수 없었다. 내가 누군가에게 도움을 요청하려고 했을 때, 근처에 있던 군중이 내 주의를 끌었다. 나는 남편과 딸을 찾으려는 희망을 안고 다가갔고, 갑자기 낯익은 두 얼굴이 보였다. 나는 안도하며 웃었다. 바로 그때, 딸이 나를 보고 "엄마!"라고 외쳤다. 그들은 마술 쇼를 보고 있는 중이었다. 마침내, 나는 내 모든 걱정이 사라지는 것을 느꼈다.

Why? 왜 정답일까?

호텔 방에서 잠을 자다가 깬 필자가 남편과 딸이 없어져 걱정했다가(Feeling worried, ~) 둘이 마술 쇼를 보고 있었다는 것을 알고 안도했다는(I smiled, feeling calm. / Finally, I felt all my worries disappear.)는 글이다. 따라서 'I'의 심경 변화로 가장 적절한 것은 ① '불안한 → 안도한'이다.

● worried ⓐ 걱정한
● ask for help 도움을 요청하다
● approach ⓥ 다가가다
● disappear ⓥ 사라지다
● delighted ⓐ 기쁜
● decide ⓥ 결심하다, 정하다
● catch one's attention 관심을 끌다
● familiar ⓐ 익숙한
● anxious ⓐ 불안한
● embarrassed ⓐ 당황한

구문 풀이

3행 Feeling worried, I went outside and walked down the street, but they
분사구문(~하면서)
were nowhere to be found.
수동 부정사(they 보충 설명)

---

20 업무와 개인 용무를 한 곳에 정리하기 　정답률 78% | 정답 ⑤

다음 글에서 필자가 주장하는 바로 가장 적절한 것은?

① 결정한 것은 반드시 실행하도록 노력하라.
② 자신이 담당한 업무에 관한 전문성을 확보하라.
③ 업무 집중도를 높이기 위해 책상 위를 정돈하라.
④ 좋은 아이디어를 메모하는 습관을 길러라.
✓⑤ 업무와 개인 용무를 한 곳에 정리하라.

Research shows / that people who work have two calendars: / one for work and one for their personal lives.
연구는 보여준다. / 일하는 사람들이 두 개의 달력을 가지고 있다는 것을 / 업무를 위한 달력 하나와 개인적인 삶을 위한 달력 하나

Although it may seem sensible, / having two separate calendars for work and personal life / can lead to distractions.
비록 이것이 현명해 보일지도 모르지만, / 업무와 개인적인 삶을 위한 두 개의 별도의 달력을 갖는 것은 / 주의를 산만하게 할 수 있다.

To check if something is missing, / you will find yourself / checking your to-do lists multiple times.
누락된 것이 있는지를 확인하고자 / 당신은 자신이 ~한다는 것을 깨닫게 될 것이다. / 당신의 할 일 목록을 여러 번 확인하고 있는 것을

Instead, / organize all of your tasks in one place.
그렇게 하는 대신에, / 당신의 모든 일들을 한 곳에 정리하라.

It doesn't matter / if you use digital or paper media.
중요하지 않다. / 당신이 디지털 매체를 사용하든 종이 매체를 사용하든

It's okay / to keep your professional and personal tasks in one place.
괜찮다. / 당신의 업무와 개인 용무를 한 곳에 둬도

This will give you / a good idea of how time is divided between work and home.
이것은 당신에게 줄 것이다. / 일과 가정 사이에 시간이 어떻게 나뉘는지에 관한 좋은 생각을

This will allow you / to make informed decisions / about which tasks are most important.
이것은 당신이 ~하게 할 것이다. / 잘 알고 결정하게 / 어떤 일이 가장 중요한지에 대해

연구는 일하는 사람들이 두 개의 달력을 가지고 있다는 것을 보여준다. 하나는 업무를 위한 달력이고 하나는 개인적인 삶을 위한 달력이다. 비록 이것이 현명해 보일지도 모르지만, 업무와 개인적인 삶을 위한 두 개의 별도의 달력을 갖는 것은 주의를 산만하게 할 수 있다. 누락된 것이 있는지를 확인하고자 당신은 자신이 할 일 목록을 여러 번 확인하고 있다는 것을 깨닫게 될 것이다. 그렇게 하는 대신에, 당신의 모든 일들을 한 곳에 정리하라. 당신이 디지털 매체를 사용하든 종이 매체를 사용하든 중요하지 않다. 당신의 업무와 개인 용무를 한 곳에 둬도 괜찮다. 이것은 당신에게 일과 가정 사이에 시간이 어떻게 나눠지는지에 대해 잘 알게 해줄 것이다. 이것은 어떤 일이 가장 중요한지에 대해 잘 알고 결정하게 할 것이다.

Why? 왜 정답일까?

개인 용무와 일을 한 곳에 정리하라고(~ keep your professional and personal tasks in one place.) 조언하는 글이므로, 필자가 주장하는 바로 가장 적절한 것은 ⑤ '업무와 개인 용무를 한 곳에 정리하라.'이다.

● sensible ⓐ 분별 있는, 현명한
● distraction ⓝ 주의 분산, 정신을 흩뜨리는 것
● organize ⓥ 정리하다
● make an informed decision 잘 알고 결정하다
● separate ⓐ 별개의
● multiple ⓐ 여럿의, 다수의
● divide ⓥ 나누다, 분배하다

구문 풀이

4행 To check if something is missing, you will find yourself checking your
목적(~하려면) 접속사(~인지 아닌지)　　　　동사　　목적어　목적격 보어
to-do lists multiple times.

---

21 고객의 구매 후 행동을 관찰할 필요성 　정답률 56% | 정답 ①

밑줄 친 become unpaid ambassadors가 다음 글에서 의미하는 바로 가장 적절한 것은?

✓① recommend products to others for no gain – 대가 없이 다른 사람들에게 제품을 추천할
② offer manufacturers feedback on products – 제조업자들에게 제품에 대한 피드백을 제공할
③ become people who don't trust others' words – 다른 사람들의 말을 믿지 않는 사람이 될
④ get rewards for advertising products overseas – 해외에 광고를 해주고 보상을 받을
⑤ buy products without worrying about the price – 가격에 대해 걱정하지 않고 제품을 살

Why do you care / how a customer reacts to a purchase?
왜 당신은 신경 쓰는가? / 고객이 구매품에 어떻게 반응하는지

Good question.
좋은 질문이다.

By understanding post-purchase behavior, / you can understand the influence / and the likelihood of whether a buyer will repurchase the product / (and whether she will keep it or return it).
구매 후 행동을 이해함으로써, / 당신은 그 영향력을 이해할 수 있다. / 그리고 구매자가 제품을 재구매할지 하는 가능성을 / (그리고 그 사람이 제품을 계속 가질지 반품할지)

You'll also determine / whether the buyer will encourage others / to purchase the product from you.
또한 당신은 알아낼 것이다. / 구매자가 다른 사람들에게 권할지 아닐지를 / 당신으로부터 제품을 구매하도록

Satisfied customers can become unpaid ambassadors for your business, / so customer satisfaction should be on the top of your to-do list.
만족한 고객은 당신의 사업을 위한 무급 대사가 될 수 있으므로, / 고객 만족이 할 일 목록의 최상단에 있어야 한다.

People tend to believe the opinions of people they know.
사람들은 자기가 아는 사람들의 의견을 믿는 경향이 있다.

People trust friends over advertisements any day.
사람들은 언제든 광고보다 친구를 더 신뢰한다.

They know / that advertisements are paid to tell the "good side" / and that they're used / to persuade them to purchase products and services.
그들은 알고 있다. / 광고는 '좋은 면'을 말하도록 돈을 지불받고, / 그것은 이용된다는 것을 / 그들더러 제품과 서비스를 구매하게 설득하려고

By continually monitoring your customer's satisfaction after the sale, / you have the ability / to avoid negative word-of-mouth advertising.
판매 후 고객의 만족을 지속적으로 관찰하여 / 당신은 능력을 얻는다. / 부정적인 입소문 광고를 피할 수 있는

왜 당신은 고객이 구매품에 어떻게 반응하는지 신경 쓰는가? 좋은 질문이다. 구매 후 행동을 이해함으로써, 당신은 그 영향력과 구매자가 제품을 재구매할지(그리고 그 사람이 제품을 계속 가질지 반품할지) 하는 가능성을 이해할 수 있다. 또한 당신은 구매자가 다른 사람들에게 당신으로부터 제품을 구매하도록 권할지 아닐지를 알아낼 수 있다. 만족한 고객은 당신의 사업을 위한 무급 대사가 될 수 있으므로, 고객 만족이 할 일 목록의 최상단에 있어야 한다. 사람들은 아는 사람들의 의견을 믿는 경향이 있다. 사람들은 언제든 광고보다 친구를 더 신뢰한다. 그들은 광고는 '좋은 면'을 말하도록 돈을 지불받고, 그것은 그들더러 제품과 서비스를 구매하게 설득하려고 이용된다는 것을 알고 있다. 판매 후 고객의 만족을 지속적으로 관찰하여 당신은 부정적인 입소문 광고를 피할 수 있는 능력을 얻는다.

Why? 왜 정답일까?

구매 후 행동을 관찰하면 구매자들이 다른 사람들에게 제품을 권해줄지(~ whether the buyer will encourage others to purchase the product from you.) 알 수 있다는 내용으로 보아, 밑줄 친 부분의 의미로 가장 적절한 것은 ① '대가 없이 다른 사람들에게 제품을 추천할'이다.

● purchase ⓝ 구매 ⓥ 사다
● return ⓥ 반품하다
● unpaid ⓐ 무급의
● ambassador ⓝ (외교 시 나라를 대표하는) 대사, 사절
● advertisement ⓝ 광고
● word-of-mouth ⓐ 구전의
● likelihood ⓝ 가능성, 확률
● satisfied ⓐ 만족한
● continually ⓐⓓ 지속적으로
● overseas ⓐⓓ 해외에

구문 풀이

10행 They know {that advertisements are paid to tell the "good side"} and {that they're used to persuade them to purchase products and services}.
「be used to + 동사원형 : ~하기 위해 사용되다」　　　　　{ }: know의 목적어

22 컴퓨터화된 사회에서 오히려 일이 늘어난 소비자들   정답률 54% | 정답 ③

다음 글의 요지로 가장 적절한 것은?
① 컴퓨터 기반 사회에서는 여가 시간이 더 늘어난다.
② 회사 업무의 전산화는 업무 능률을 향상시킨다.
☑ 컴퓨터화된 사회에서 소비자는 더 많은 일을 하게 된다.
④ 온라인 거래가 모든 소비자들을 만족시키기에는 한계가 있다.
⑤ 산업의 발전으로 인해 기계가 인간의 일자리를 대신하고 있다.

The promise of a computerized society, / we were told, / was / that it would pass to machines all of the repetitive drudgery of work, / allowing us humans / to pursue higher purposes / and to have more leisure time.
컴퓨터화된 사회의 약속은 / 우리가 듣기로 / ~이었다 / 그것이 모든 반복적인 고된 일을 기계에 넘겨 / 우리 인간들이 ~하게 해준다는 것 / 더 높은 목적을 추구하고 / 더 많은 여가 시간을 가질 수 있게

It didn't work out this way.
일은 이런 식으로 되지는 않았다.

Instead of more time, / most of us have less.
더 많은 시간 대신에, / 우리 대부분은 더 적은 시간을 가지고 있다.

Companies large and small / have off-loaded work onto the backs of consumers.
크고 작은 회사들은 / 일을 소비자들의 등에 떠넘겼다.

Things that used to be done for us, / as part of the value-added service of working with a company, / we are now expected to do ourselves.
우리를 위해 행해지던 일들을 / 회사에 맡겨 해결하던 부가가치 서비스의 일환으로, / 우리는 이제 스스로 하도록 기대받는다.

With air travel, / we're now expected / to complete our own reservations and check-in, / jobs that used to be done by airline employees or travel agents.
항공 여행의 경우, / 이제는 우리는 기대된다 / 예약과 체크인을 직접 완수하도록 / 항공사 직원이나 여행사 직원이 하던 일인

At the grocery store, / we're expected to bag our own groceries / and, in some supermarkets, / to scan our own purchases.
식료품점에서는, / 우리가 우리 자신의 식료품을 직접 봉지에 넣도록 기대받는다. / 그리고 일부 슈퍼마켓에서는 / 우리가 직접 구매한 물건을 스캔하도록

우리가 듣기로, 컴퓨터화된 사회의 약속은 그것이 모든 반복적인 고된 일을 기계에 넘겨 우리 인간들이 더 높은 목적을 추구하고 더 많은 여가 시간을 가질 수 있게 해준다는 것이었다. 일은 이런 식으로 되지는 않았다. 더 많은 시간 대신에, 우리 대부분은 더 적은 시간을 가지고 있다. 크고 작은 회사들은 일을 소비자들의 등에 떠넘겼다. 우리는 회사에 맡겨 해결하던 부가가치 서비스의 일환으로 우리를 위해 행해지던 일들을 이제 스스로 하도록 기대받는다. 항공 여행의 경우, 항공사 직원이나 여행사 직원들이 하던 일인 예약과 체크인을 이제는 우리가 직접 완수하도록 기대된다. 식료품점에서는, 우리가 우리 자신의 식료품을 직접 봉지에 넣도록, 그리고 일부 슈퍼마켓에서는 우리가 직접 구매한 물건을 스캔하도록 기대받는다.

Why? 왜 정답일까?
컴퓨터화된 사회가 도래하면 개인은 더 많은 여가 시간을 누릴 것으로 기대되었지만, 실상은 반대로 더 많은 일을 하게 되었다(Instead of more time, most of us have less. Companies large and small have off-loaded work onto the backs of consumers.)는 내용이다. 따라서 글의 요지로 가장 적절한 것은 ③ '컴퓨터화된 사회에서 소비자는 더 많은 일을 하게 된다.'이다.

- repetitive ⓐ 반복되는
- pursue ⓥ 추구하다
- as part of ~의 일환으로
- drudgery ⓝ 고된 일
- off-load ⓥ 짐을 내리다, 떠넘기다
- grocery store 슈퍼, 식료품 가게

구문 풀이

6행 Things [that used to be done for us], (as part of the value-added service
       to do의 목적어   ~하곤 했다   ( ): 삽입구
of working with a company), we are now expected to do ourselves.
                 주어 「be expected + to부정사: ~하도록 기대되다」

23 자신을 평균 이상으로 보는 경향   정답률 66% | 정답 ②

다음 글의 주제로 가장 적절한 것은?
① importance of having a positive self-image as a leader
    리더로서 긍정적인 자아상을 갖는 것의 중요성
☑ our common belief that we are better than average
    우리가 평균보다 낫다는 일반적인 믿음
③ our tendency to think others are superior to us
    남들이 우리보다 낫다고 생각하는 우리의 경향성
④ reasons why we always try to be above average
    우리가 늘 평균보다 나아지려고 노력하는 이유
⑤ danger of prejudice in building healthy social networks
    건전한 사회적 네트워크를 구축할 때 편견의 위험성

We tend to believe / that we possess a host of socially desirable characteristics, / and that we are free of most of those / that are socially undesirable.
우리는 믿는 경향이 있다. / 우리가 사회적으로 바람직한 특성들을 많이 지니고 있고, / 우리가 특성 대부분은 지니고 있지 않다고 / 사회적으로 바람직하지 않은

For example, / a large majority of the general public thinks / that they are more intelligent, / more fair-minded, / less prejudiced, / and more skilled behind the wheel of an automobile / than the average person.
예를 들어, / 대다수의 일반 대중들은 생각한다. / 자신이 더 지적이고, / 더 공정하고, / 편견을 덜 가지고, / 자동차를 운전할 때 더 능숙하다고 / 보통 사람보다

This phenomenon is so reliable and ubiquitous / that it has come to be known as the "Lake Wobegon effect," / after Garrison Keillor's fictional community / where "the women are strong, / the men are good-looking, / and all the children are above average."
이 현상은 너무 신뢰할 수 있고 어디서나 볼 수 있기 때문에 / 그것은 'Lake Wobegon effect'라고 알려지게 되었다. / Garrison Keillor의 허구적인 공동체의 이름을 따서 / '여성들은 강하고, / 남성들은 잘생겼으며, / 모든 아이들은 평균 이상'인

A survey of one million high school seniors found / that 70% thought they were above average in leadership ability, / and only 2% thought they were below average.
고등학교 졸업반 학생 100만 명을 대상으로 한 설문조사는 밝혔다. / 70%는 자신이 리더십 능력에 있어 평균 이상이라고 생각했고, / 2%만이 자신이 평균 이하라고 생각했다는 것을

In terms of ability to get along with others, / all students thought they were above average, / 60% thought they were in the top 10%, / and 25% thought they were in the top 1%!
다른 사람들과 잘 지내는 능력에 있어서, / 모든 학생들은 자신이 평균 이상이라고 생각했고, / 60%는 자신이 상위 10%에 속한다고 생각했고, / 25%는 자신이 상위 1%에 속한다고 생각했다!

우리는 우리가 사회적으로 바람직한 특성들을 많이 지니고 있고, 사회적으로 바람직하지 않은 특성들 대부분은 지니고 있지 않다고 믿는 경향이 있다. 예를 들어, 대다수의 일반 대중들은 자신이 보통 사람보다 더 지적이고, 더 공정하고, 편견을 덜 가지고, 자동차를 운전할 때 더 능숙하다고 생각한다. 이 현상은 너무 신뢰할 수 있고 어디서나 볼 수 있기 때문에 '여성들은 강하고, 남성들은 잘생겼으며, 모든 아이들은 평균 이상'인 Garrison Keillor의 허구적인 공동체의 이름을 따서 'Lake Wobegon effect'라고 알려지게 되었다. 고등학교 졸업반 학생 100만 명을 대상으로 한 설문조사에서, (학생들의) 70%는 자신이 리더십 능력에 있어 평균 이상이라고 생각했고, 2%만이 자신이 평균 이하라고 생각했다는 것을 발견했다. 다른 사람들과 잘 지내는 능력에 있어서, 모든 학생들은 자신이 평균 이상이라고 생각했고, 60%는 자신이 상위 10%에 속한다고 생각했고, 25%는 자신이 상위 1%에 속한다고 생각했다!

Why? 왜 정답일까?
사람들은 스스로 바람직한 특성은 더 많이 가지고 있고, 바람직하지 않은 특성은 덜 가지고 있다고 믿는 경향이 있음(We tend to believe that we possess a host of socially desirable characteristics, and that we are free of most of those that are socially undesirable.)을 설명하는 글이다. 뒤에 이어지는 여러 예시에도 사람들이 스스로를 특정 항목에서 '평균 이상'이라고 생각한다는 내용이 주를 이룬다. 따라서 글의 주제로 가장 적절한 것은 ② '우리가 평균보다 낫다는 일반적인 믿음'이다.

- possess ⓥ 지니다, 소유하다
- desirable ⓐ 바람직한
- fair-minded ⓐ 공정한
- skilled ⓐ 능숙한
- automobile ⓝ 자동차
- reliable ⓐ 믿을 만한
- fictional ⓐ 허구의
- million ⓝ 100만
- self-image ⓝ 자아상(사람이 자기 자신에 대해 가진 이미지)
- superior to ~보다 우월한
- a host of 여러, 다수의
- characteristic ⓝ 특성
- prejudiced ⓐ 고정 관념이 있는
- behind the wheel 운전할 때, 핸들을 잡은
- phenomenon ⓝ 현상
- ubiquitous ⓐ 도처에 있는
- good-looking ⓐ 잘생긴

구문 풀이

1행 We tend to believe {that we possess a host of socially desirable
              { }: to believe의 목적절
characteristics}, and {that we are free of most of those that are socially
                              대명사(= characteristics)
undesirable}.

24 부유한 국가의 스트레스 요소   정답률 64% | 정답 ①

다음 글의 제목으로 가장 적절한 것은?
☑ Why Are Even Wealthy Countries Not Free from Stress?
    왜 심지어 부유한 국가들도 스트레스에서 자유롭지 못한 걸까?
② In Search of the Path to Escaping the Poverty Trap
    가난의 덫을 벗어나기 위한 길을 찾아서
③ Time Management: Everything You Need to Know
    시간 관리: 당신이 알아야 할 모든 것
④ How Does Stress Affect Human Bodies?
    스트레스는 우리 몸에 어떤 영향을 미칠까?
⑤ Sound Mind Wins the Game of Life!
    건전한 정신이 인생이란 게임에서 이긴다!

Few people will be surprised / to hear that poverty tends to create stress: / a 2006 study / published in the American journal *Psychosomatic Medicine*, / for example, / noted / that a lower socioeconomic status / was associated with higher levels of stress hormones in the body.
놀랄 사람은 거의 없을 것이다. / 가난이 스트레스를 유발하는 경향이 있다는 것을 듣고 / 2006년 연구는 / 미국의 저널 *Psychosomatic Medicine*에 발표된 / 예를 들어, / 언급했다. / 더 낮은 사회 경제적 지위가 / 체내의 더 높은 수치의 스트레스 호르몬과 관련이 있다고

However, / richer economies have their own distinct stresses.
하지만, / 더 부유한 국가는 그들만의 독특한 스트레스를 가지고 있다.

The key issue is time pressure.
핵심 쟁점은 시간 압박이다.

A 1999 study of 31 countries / by American psychologist Robert Levine and Canadian psychologist Ara Norenzayan / found / that wealthier, more industrialized nations had a faster pace of life / — which led to a higher standard of living, / but at the same time / left the population feeling a constant sense of urgency, / as well as being more prone to heart disease.
31개국을 대상으로 한 1999년 연구 / 미국 심리학자 Robert Levine과 캐나다 심리학자 Ara Norenzayan에 의한 / 알아냈다. / 더 부유하고 더 산업화된 국가들이 더 빠른 삶의 속도를 가지고 있다는 것, / 그리고 이것이 더 높은 생활 수준으로 이어졌지만, / 동시에 / 사람들에게 지속적인 촉박함을 느끼게 했다는 것을 / 심장병에 걸리기 더 쉽게 했을 뿐 아니라

In effect, / fast-paced productivity creates wealth, / but it also leads people to feel time-poor / when they lack the time / to relax and enjoy themselves.
사실, / 빠른 속도의 생산력은 부를 창출하지만, / 이는 또한 사람들이 시간이 부족하다고 느끼게 한다. / 그들이 시간이 부족할 때 / 긴장을 풀고 즐겁게 지낼

가난이 스트레스를 유발하는 경향이 있다는 것을 듣고 놀랄 사람은 거의 없을 것이다. 예를 들어, 미국의 저널 *Psychosomatic Medicine*에 발표된 2006년 연구는 더 낮은 사회 경제적 지위가 체내의 더 높은 수치의 스트레스 호르몬과 관련이 있다고 언급했다. 하지만, 더 부유한 국가는 그들 특유의 스트레스를 가지고 있다. 핵심 쟁점은 시간 압박이다. 미국 심리학자 Robert Levine과 캐나다 심리학자 Ara Norenzayan이 31개국을 대상으로 한 1999년 연구는 더 부유하고 더 산업화된 국가들이 더 빠른 삶의 속도를 가지고 있다는 것, 그리고 이것이 더 높은 생활 수준으로 이어졌지만, 동시에 사람들이 심장병에 걸리기 더 쉽게 했을 뿐 아니라 지속적인 촉박함을 느끼게 했다는 것을 알아냈다. 사실, 빠른 속도의 생산력은 부를 창출하지만, 이는 또한 사람들이 긴장을 풀고 즐겁게 지낼 시간이 없을 때 시간이 부족하다고 느끼게 한다.

Why? 왜 정답일까?
부유한 국가에 사는 사람들이 시간 압박이라는 스트레스에 시달린다(However, richer economies have their own distinct stresses. The key issue is time pressure.)는 내용이므로, 글의 제목으로 가장 적절한 것은 ① '왜 심지어 부유한 국가들도 스트레스에서 자유롭지 못한 걸까?'이다.

- poverty ⓝ 가난
- socioeconomic ⓐ 사회경제적인

- **status** ⓝ 지위
- **psychologist** ⓝ 심리학자
- **industrialize** ⓥ 산업화하다
- **urgency** ⓝ 다급함
- **productivity** ⓝ 생산성
- **distinct** ⓐ 특유의, 독특한, 뚜렷한
- **wealthy** ⓐ 부유한
- **constant** ⓐ 지속적인
- **prone to** ~에 걸리기 쉬운

구문 풀이

1행 Few people will be surprised to hear that poverty tends to create stress: ~
감정 형용사   원인(~해서)

---

25   지역별 산림 면적 점유율 비교   정답률 80% | 정답 ④

다음 도표의 내용과 일치하지 <u>않는</u> 것은?

Share of Forest Area in Total Land Area by Region in 1990 and 2019

The above graph shows / the share of forest area / in total land area by region / in 1990 and 2019.
위 도표는 보여준다. / 산림 면적의 점유율을 / 지역별 총 토지 면적에서 / 1990년과 2019년의

① Africa's share of forest area in total land area / was over 20% in both 1990 and 2019.
아프리카의 전체 토지 면적에서 산림 면적의 점유율이 / 1990년과 2019년 둘 다 20%를 넘었다.

② The share of forest area in America / was 42.6% in 1990, / which was larger than that in 2019.
아메리카의 산림 면적 점유율은 / 1990년에 42.6%였고, / 이는 2019년보다 더 컸다.

③ The share of forest area in Asia / declined from 1990 to 2019 / by more than 10 percentage points.
아시아의 산림 면적 점유율은 / 1990년부터 2019년까지 감소했다. / 10퍼센트포인트 이상만큼

✔ In 2019, / the share of forest area in Europe / was the largest among the five regions, / more than three times that in Asia in the same year.
2019년 / 유럽의 산 면적 점유율은 / 다섯 개 지역 중 가장 컸고, / 같은 해 아시아의 세 배가 넘었다.

⑤ Oceania showed the smallest gap between 1990 and 2019 / in terms of the share of forest area in total land area.
오세아니아는 1990년과 2019년 사이에 가장 작은 차이를 보였다. / 총 토지 면적에서 산림 면적의 점유율에 있어

위 도표는 1990년과 2019년의 지역별 총 토지 면적에서 산림 면적의 점유율을 보여준다. ① 아프리카의 전체 토지 면적에서 산림 면적의 점유율이 1990년과 2019년 둘 다 20%를 넘었다. ② 1990년 아메리카의 산림 면적 점유율은 42.6%였고, 이는 2019년보다 더 컸다. ③ 아시아의 산림 면적 점유율은 1990년부터 2019년까지, 10퍼센트포인트 이상 감소했다. ④ 2019년 유럽의 산 면적 점유율은 다섯 개 지역 중 가장 컸고, 같은 해 아시아의 세 배가 넘었다. ⑤ 오세아니아는 1990년과 2019년 사이에 총 토지 면적에서 산림 면적의 점유율에 있어 가장 작은 차이를 보였다.

Why? 왜 정답일까?

도표에 따르면 2019년 아시아의 산림 면적 점유율은 20%인데, 유럽의 점유율은 46%이므로 두 비율은 3배 이상 차이 나지 않는다. 따라서 도표와 일치하지 않는 것은 ④이다.

- **region** ⓝ 지역
- **decline** ⓥ 감소하다, 줄어들다

---

26   Gary Becker의 생애   정답률 86% | 정답 ③

Gary Becker에 관한 다음 글의 내용과 일치하지 <u>않는</u> 것은?

① New York City의 Brooklyn에서 자랐다.
② 아버지는 금융과 정치 문제에 깊은 관심이 있었다.
✔ Princeton University에서의 경제학 교육에 만족했다.
④ 1955년에 경제학 박사 학위를 취득했다.
⑤ Business Week에 경제학 칼럼을 기고했다.

「Gary Becker was born in Pottsville, Pennsylvania in 1930 / and grew up in Brooklyn, New York City.」 ①의근거 일치
Gary Becker는 1930년 Pennsylvania 주 Pottsville에서 태어났고 / New York City의 Brooklyn에서 자랐다.

「His father, who was not well educated, / had a deep interest in financial and political issues.」 ②의근거 일치
그의 아버지는, / 교육을 제대로 받지 못했는데 / 금융과 정치 문제에 깊은 관심이 있었다.

After graduating from high school, / Becker went to Princeton University, / where he majored in economics.
고등학교를 졸업한 후, / Becker는 Princeton University로 진학했고, / 거기서 그는 경제학을 전공했다.

「He was dissatisfied / with his economic education at Princeton University / because "it didn't seem to be handling real problems."」 ③의근거 불일치
그는 불만족했다. / Princeton University에서의 경제학 교육에 / '그것이 현실적인 문제를 다루고 있는 것처럼 보이지 않았기' 때문에

「He earned a doctor's degree in economics / from the University of Chicago / in 1955.」 ④의근거 일치
그는 경제학 박사 학위를 취득했다. / University of Chicago에서 / 1955년에

His doctoral paper on the economics of discrimination / was mentioned by the Nobel Prize Committee / as an important contribution to economics.
차별의 경제학에 대한 그의 박사 논문은 / 노벨상 위원회에 의해 언급되었다 / 경제학에 대한 중요한 기여로

「Since 1985, / Becker had written a regular economics column in Business Week, / explaining economic analysis and ideas to the general public.」 ⑤의근거 일치

1985년부터, / Becker는 Business Week에 경제학 칼럼을 정기적으로 기고했다. / 경제학적 분석과 아이디어를 일반 대중에게 설명하는

In 1992, / he was awarded / the Nobel Prize in economic science.
1992년에, / 그는 수상했다. / 노벨 경제학상을

Gary Becker는 1930년 Pennsylvania 주 Pottsville에서 태어났고 New York City의 Brooklyn에서 자랐다. 교육을 제대로 받지 못한 그의 아버지는 금융과 정치 문제에 깊은 관심이 있었다. 고등학교를 졸업한 후, Becker는 Princeton University로 진학했고, 거기서 그는 경제학을 전공했다. 'Princeton University에서의 경제학 교육이 현실적인 문제를 다루고 있는 것처럼 보이지 않았기' 때문에 그는 그것에 불만족했다. 그는 1955년에 University of Chicago에서 경제학 박사 학위를 취득했다. 차별의 경제학에 대한 그의 박사 논문은 노벨상 위원회에 의해 경제학에 대한 중요한 기여로 언급되었다. 1985년부터, Becker는 Business Week에 경제학적 분석과 아이디어를 일반 대중에게 설명하는 경제학 칼럼을 정기적으로 기고했다. 1992년에, 그는 노벨 경제학상을 수상했다.

Why? 왜 정답일까?

'He was dissatisfied with his economic education at Princeton University ~'에서 Gary Becker는 Princeton University에서의 경제학 교육에 불만족했다고 하므로, 내용과 일치하지 않는 것은 ③ 'Princeton University에서의 경제학 교육에 만족했다.'이다.

Why? 왜 오답일까?

① 'Gary Becker ~ grew up in Brooklyn, New York City.'의 내용과 일치한다.
② 'His father, who was not well educated, had a deep interest in financial and political issues.'의 내용과 일치한다.
④ 'He earned a doctor's degree in economics from the University of Chicago in 1955.'의 내용과 일치한다.
⑤ 'Since 1985, Becker had written a regular economics column in Business Week, ~'의 내용과 일치한다.

- **financial** ⓐ 재정적인
- **doctoral paper** 박사 논문
- **mention** ⓥ 언급하다
- **analysis** ⓝ 분석
- **handle** ⓥ 다루다, 대처하다
- **discrimination** ⓝ 차별
- **contribution** ⓝ 기여, 이바지
- **award** ⓥ 상을 주다, 수여하다

구문 풀이

13행 In 1992, he was awarded the Nobel Prize in economic science.
4형식 수동태   직접목적어

---

27   드론 레이싱 선수권   정답률 94% | 정답 ⑤

2023 Drone Racing Championship에 관한 다음 안내문의 내용과 일치하지 <u>않는</u> 것은?

① 7월 9일 일요일에 개최된다.
② 고등학생만 참가할 수 있다.
③ 자신의 드론을 가져와야 한다.
④ 상금과 메달이 우승자에게 수여될 것이다.
✔ 20명의 참가자가 기념품을 받을 것이다.

2023 Drone Racing Championship
2023 드론 레이싱 선수권

Are you the best drone racer?
여러분은 최고의 드론 레이서인가요?

Then take the opportunity / to prove you are the one!
그렇다면 기회를 잡으세요! / 여러분이 바로 그 사람이라는 것을 증명할

When & Where
일시 & 장소

「6 p.m. – 8 p.m., Sunday, July 9」 ①의근거 일치
7월 9일 일요일 오후 6시부터 오후 8시까지

Lakeside Community Center
Lakeside 주민센터

Requirements
필수 조건

「Participants: High school students only」 ②의근거 일치
참가자: 고등학생만

「Bring your own drone for the race.」 ③의근거 일치
레이스를 위해 당신의 드론을 가져 오세요.

Prize
부상

「$500 and a medal will be awarded to the winner.」 ④의근거 일치
500달러와 메달이 우승자에게 수여될 것입니다.

Note
참고 사항

「The first 10 participants will get souvenirs.」 ⑤의근거 불일치
선착순 10명의 참가자들은 기념품을 받게 될 것입니다.

For more details, / please visit www.droneracing.com / or call 313-6745-1189.
더 많은 세부 정보를 원하시면, / www.droneracing.com을 방문하거나 / 313-6745-1189로 전화하세요.

2023 Drone Racing Championship(2023 드론 레이싱 선수권)

여러분은 최고의 드론 레이서인가요? 그렇다면 여러분이 바로 그 사람이라는 것을 증명할 기회를 잡으세요!

일시 & 장소
• 7월 9일 일요일 오후 6시부터 오후 8시까지
• Lakeside 주민센터

필수 조건
• 참가자: 고등학생만
• 레이스를 위해 당신의 드론을 가져 오세요.

부상
• 500달러와 메달이 우승자에게 수여될 것입니다.

참고 사항
• 선착순 10명의 참가자들은 기념품을 받게 될 것입니다.

더 많은 세부 정보를 원하시면, www.droneracing.com을 방문하거나 313-6745-1189로 전화하세요.

Why? 왜 정답일까?

'The first 10 participants will get souvenirs.'에서 선착순 10명의 참가자에게 기념품을 준다고 하므로, 안내문의 내용과 일치하지 않는 것은 ⑤ '20명의 참가자가 기념품을 받을 것이다.'이다.

Why? 왜 오답일까?

① '6 p.m. – 8 p.m., Sunday, July 9'의 내용과 일치한다.
② 'Participants: High school students only'의 내용과 일치한다.
③ 'Bring your own drone for the race.'의 내용과 일치한다.
④ '$500 and a medal will be awarded to the winner.'의 내용과 일치한다.

● drone ⓝ 드론, 무인 항공기
● take an opportunity 기회를 잡다
● requirement ⓝ 필수 요건
● souvenir ⓝ 기념품
● championship ⓝ 선수권
● prove ⓥ 증명하다
● bring ⓥ 가져오다, 지참하다

---

28 스쿠버 다이빙 일일 수업 광고   정답률 86% | 정답 ⑤

Summer Scuba Diving One–day Class에 관한 다음 안내문의 내용과 일치하는 것은?
① 오후 시간에 바다에서 다이빙 기술을 연습한다.
② 그룹 수업의 최대 정원은 4명이다.
③ 다이빙 장비를 유료로 대여할 수 있다.
④ 연령에 관계없이 참가할 수 있다.
✔ 적어도 수업 시작 5일 전까지 등록해야 한다.

Summer Scuba Diving One-day Class
여름 스쿠버 다이빙 일일 수업
Join our summer scuba diving lesson for beginners, / and become an underwater explorer!
초보자용 여름 스쿠버 다이빙 수업에 참여하여 / 수중 탐험가가 되세요!
Schedule
일정
10:00 – 12:00 Learning the basics
10시 – 12시 기초 배우기
「13:00 – 16:00 Practicing diving skills in a pool」 ①의근거 불일치
13시 – 16시 수영장에서 다이빙 기술 연습하기
Price
가격
Private lesson: $150
개인 수업: $150
「Group lesson (up to 3 people): $100 per person」 ②의근거 불일치
그룹 수업 (최대 3명): 1인당 $100
「Participants can rent our diving equipment for free.」 ③의근거 불일치
참가자는 다이빙 장비를 무료로 대여할 수 있습니다.
Notice
알림
「Participants must be 10 years old or over.」 ④의근거 불일치
참가자는 10세 이상이어야 합니다.
「Participants must register / at least 5 days before the class begins.」 ⑤의근거 일치
참가자는 등록해야 합니다. / 적어도 수업 시작 5일 전까지
For more information, / please go to www.ssdiver.com.
더 많은 정보를 원하시면, / www.ssdiver.com을 방문하세요.

Summer Scuba Diving One-day Class(여름 스쿠버 다이빙 일일 수업)

초보자용 여름 스쿠버 다이빙 수업에 참여하여 수중 탐험가가 되세요!

일정
• 10시 – 12시 기초 배우기
• 13시 – 16시 수영장에서 다이빙 기술 연습하기

가격
• 개인 수업: $150
• 그룹 수업 (최대 3명): 1인당 $100
• 참가자는 다이빙 장비를 무료로 대여할 수 있습니다.

알림
• 참가자는 10세 이상이어야 합니다.
• 참가자는 적어도 수업 시작 5일 전까지 등록해야 합니다.

더 많은 정보를 원하시면, www.ssdiver.com을 방문하세요.

Why? 왜 정답일까?

'Participants must register at least 5 days before the class begins.'에서 참가를 원하면 적어도 수업 시작 5일 전까지 등록하라고 하므로, 안내문의 내용과 일치하는 것은 ⑤ '적어도 수업 시작 5일 전까지 등록해야 한다.'이다.

Why? 왜 오답일까?

① '13:00–16:00 Practicing diving skills in a pool'에서 다이빙 기술을 연습하는 장소는 바다가 아니라 수영장이라고 하였다.
② 'Group lesson (up to 3 people): ~'에서 그룹 수업은 최대 3명까지라고 하였다.
③ 'Participants can rent our diving equipment for free.'에서 다이빙 장비는 무료로 대여할 수 있다고 하였다.
④ 'Participants must be 10 years old or over.'에서 참가 가능 연령은 10세 이상이라고 하였다.

● one-day class 일일 수업
● explorer ⓝ 탐험가
● private lesson 개인 레슨
● underwater ⓐ 물속의, 수중의
● basics ⓝ 기본, 필수적인 것들
● equipment ⓝ 장비

---

29 칭찬이 아이들의 자존감에 미치는 효과   정답률 55% | 정답 ④

다음 글의 밑줄 친 부분 중, 어법상 틀린 것은? [3점]

Although praise is one of the most powerful tools / available for improving young children's behavior, / it is equally powerful / for improving your child's self-esteem.
칭찬은 가장 강력한 도구 중 하나이지만, / 어린 아이들의 행동을 개선하는 데 사용할 수 있는 / 그것은 똑같이 강력하다. / 아이의 자존감을 향상시키는 데에도
Preschoolers believe / what their parents tell ① them / in a very profound way.
미취학 아동들은 여긴다. / 그들의 부모가 그들에게 하는 말을 / 매우 뜻 깊게
They do not yet have the cognitive sophistication / to reason ② analytically and reject false information.
그들은 인지적 정교함을 아직 가지고 있지 않다. / 분석적으로 추론하고 잘못된 정보를 거부할 수 있는
If a preschool boy consistently hears from his mother / ③ that he is smart and a good helper, / he is likely to incorporate that information into his self-image.
만약 미취학 소년이 그의 어머니로부터 계속 듣는다면, / 그가 똑똑하고 좋은 조력자라는 것을 / 그는 그 정보를 자기 자아상으로 통합시킬 가능성이 높다.
Thinking of himself as a boy / who is smart and knows how to do things / ✔ is likely to make him endure longer in problem-solving efforts / and increase his confidence in trying new and difficult tasks.
스스로를 소년으로 생각하는 것은 / 똑똑하고 일을 어떻게 하는지 아는 / 그가 문제 해결 노력에 있어 더 오래 지속하게 만들 가능성이 높다. / 그리고 새롭고 어려운 일을 시도할 때 그의 자신감을 높일
Similarly, / thinking of himself as the kind of boy / who is a good helper / will make him more likely / to volunteer ⑤ to help with tasks at home and at preschool.
마찬가지로, / 자신을 그런 부류의 소년으로 생각하는 것은 / 좋은 조력자인 / 그가 ~할 가능성이 더 커지게 할 것이다. / 집과 유치원에서 일을 자발적으로 도울

칭찬은 어린 아이들의 행동을 개선하는 데 사용할 수 있는 가장 강력한 도구 중 하나이지만, 그것은 아이의 자존감을 향상시키는 데에도 똑같이 강력하다. 미취학 아동들은 그들의 부모가 그들에게 하는 말을 매우 뜻 깊게 여긴다. 그들은 분석적으로 추론하고 잘못된 정보를 거부할 수 있는 인지적 정교함을 아직 가지고 있지 않다. 만약 미취학 소년이 그의 어머니로부터 그가 똑똑하고 좋은 조력자라는 것을 계속 듣는다면, 그는 그 정보를 자기 자아상으로 통합시킬 가능성이 높다. 스스로를 똑똑하고 일을 어떻게 하는지 아는 소년으로 생각하는 것은 그가 문제 해결 노력에 있어 더 오래 지속하게 하고, 새롭고 어려운 일을 시도할 때 그의 자신감을 높일 가능성이 높다. 마찬가지로, 자신을 좋은 조력자인 그런 부류의 소년으로 생각하는 것은 그가 집과 유치원에서 일을 자발적으로 도울 가능성이 더 커지게 할 것이다.

Why? 왜 정답일까?

주어인 동명사구(Thinking of himself as a boy ~) 뒤에 동사가 있어야 하므로, being을 is로 고쳐야 한다. 따라서 어법상 틀린 것은 ④이다.

Why? 왜 오답일까?

① tell의 주어는 their parents인데, 목적어는 문맥상 문장의 주어인 Preschoolers이다. 따라서 재귀대명사를 쓰지 않고, 인칭대명사 them을 썼다.
② to부정사구 to reason을 수식하는 부사 analytically이다.
③ hears의 목적절을 이끄는 접속사로 that이 알맞다. from his mother가 동사 앞으로 들어간 구조이다.
⑤ volunteer는 to부정사를 목적어로 취하므로 to help가 알맞다.

● self-esteem ⓝ 자존감
● profound ⓐ 뜻 깊은
● sophistication ⓝ 정교화(함)
● analytically ⓐⓓ 분석적으로
● incorporate A into B A를 B로 통합시키다
● preschooler ⓝ 미취학 아동
● cognitive ⓐ 인지적인
● reason ⓥ 추론하다
● consistently ⓐⓓ 지속적으로
● endure ⓥ 지속하다, 참다

구문 풀이

6행 If a preschool boy consistently hears from his mother {that he is smart
        동사   부사구   ( ): hears의 목적어
and a good helper}, he is likely to incorporate that information into his self-image.

---

30 광고주의 메시지 조절   정답률 55% | 정답 ②

다음 글의 밑줄 친 부분 중, 문맥상 낱말의 쓰임이 적절하지 않은 것은?

Advertisers often displayed considerable facility / in ① adapting their claims / to the market status of the goods they promoted.
광고주들은 상당한 능력을 자주 보여주었다. / 그들의 주장을 맞추는 데 있어 / 그들이 홍보하는 상품의 시장 지위에
Fleischmann's yeast, / for instance, / was used / as an ingredient for cooking homemade bread.
Fleischmann의 효모는 / 예를 들어, / 사용되었다. / 집에서 만든 빵을 요리하는 재료로
Yet / more and more people in the early 20th century / were buying their bread from stores or bakeries, / so consumer demand for yeast ✔ declined.
하지만 / 20세기 초의 점점 더 많은 사람들이 / 가게나 빵집에서 빵을 사고 있었고, / 그래서 효모에 대한 소비자 수요는 감소했다.
The producer of Fleischmann's yeast / hired the J. Walter Thompson advertising agency / to come up with a different marketing strategy / to ③ boost sales.
Fleischmann의 효모의 생산자는 / J. Walter Thompson 광고 대행사를 고용했다. / 다른 마케팅 전략을 고안하려고 / 판매를 촉진하기 위해서
No longer the "Soul of Bread," / the Thompson agency first turned yeast / into an important source of vitamins / with significant health ④ benefits.
더 이상 "Soul of Bread"를 쓰지 않고, / Thompson 광고 대행사는 먼저 효모를 바꾸었다. / 중요한 비타민 공급원으로 / 상당한 건강상의 이점이 있는
Shortly thereafter, / the advertising agency transformed yeast into a natural laxative.
그 이후 얼마 안 되어, / 광고 대행사는 효모를 천연 완하제로 바꾸었다.
⑤ Repositioning yeast / helped increase sales.
효모의 이미지 전환은 / 매출을 증가시키는 것을 도왔다.

광고주들은 그들이 홍보하는 상품의 시장 지위에 주장을 ① 맞추는 상당한 능력을 자주 보여주었다. 예를 들어, Fleischmann의 효모는 집에서 만든 빵을 요리하는 재료로 사용되었다. 하지만 20세기 초에 점점 더 많은 사람들이 가게나 빵집에서 빵을 사고 있었고, 그래서 효모에 대한 소비자 수요는 ② 증가했다(→ 감소했다). Fleischmann의 효모의 생산자는 판매를

③ 촉진하기 위해서 다른 마케팅 전략을 고안하려고 J. Walter Thompson 광고 대행사를 고용했다. 더 이상 "Soul of Bread"를 쓰지 않고, Thompson 광고 대행사는 먼저 효모를 상당한 건강상의 ④ 이점이 있는 중요한 비타민 공급원으로 바꾸었다. 그 이후 얼마 안 되어, 광고 대행사는 효모를 천연 완하제로 바꾸었다. 효모의 ⑤ 이미지 전환은 매출을 증가시키는 것을 도왔다.

Why? 왜 정답일까?

과거 효모는 집에서 굽는 빵의 재료로 쓰였지만, 20세기에 접어들어 사람들이 점점 가게에서 구운 빵을 사면서 효모에 대한 수요가 '떨어졌다'는 설명이 되도록 increased를 declined로 고쳐야 한다. 따라서 문맥상 낱말의 쓰임이 적절하지 않은 것은 ②이다.

- **considerable** ⓐ 상당한
- **ingredient** ⓝ 재료
- **come up with** 떠올리다, 고안하다
- **significant** ⓐ 상당한, 중요한
- **laxative** ⓝ 완하제(배변을 쉽게 하는 약·음식·음료)
- **facility** ⓝ 능력, 재능
- **hire** ⓥ 고용하다
- **strategy** ⓝ 전략
- **transform** ⓥ 변모시키다
- **reposition** ⓥ (제품의) 이미지를 바꾸다

구문 풀이

1행 Advertisers often displayed considerable facility in adapting their claims 〜하는 데 있어, 〜할 때 to the market status of the goods [(that) they promoted].
선행사 ↖ 생략

★★★ 등급을 가르는 문제!

31 탁월함과 타인의 신뢰   정답률 50% | 정답 ④

다음 빈칸에 들어갈 말로 가장 적절한 것을 고르시오.

① Patience – 인내심   ② Sacrifice – 희생   ③ Honesty – 정직함
✔④ Excellence – 탁월함   ⑤ Creativity – 창의력

Individuals / who perform at a high level in their profession / often have instant credibility with others.
사람들은 / 자기 직업에서 높은 수준으로 수행하는 / 흔히 다른 사람들에게 즉각적인 신뢰를 얻는다.
People admire them, / they want to be like them, / and they feel connected to them.
사람들은 그들을 존경하고, / 그들처럼 되고 싶어 하고, / 그들과 연결되어 있다고 느낀다.
When they speak, / others listen — / even if the area of their skill / has nothing to do with the advice they give.
그들이 말할 때, / 다른 사람들은 경청한다. / 비록 그들의 기술 분야가 / 그들이 주는 조언과 전혀 관련이 없을지라도
Think about a world-famous basketball player.
세계적으로 유명한 농구 선수에 대해 생각해 보라.
He has made more money from endorsements / than he ever did playing basketball.
그는 광고로부터 더 많은 돈을 벌었다. / 그가 농구를 하면서 그간 벌었던 것보다
Is it because of / his knowledge of the products he endorses?
그것이 〜 때문일까? / 그가 광고하는 제품에 대한 그의 지식
No.
아니다.
It's because of / what he can do with a basketball.
그것은 〜 때문이다. / 그가 농구로 할 수 있는 것
The same can be said of an Olympic medalist swimmer.
올림픽 메달리스트 수영 선수도 마찬가지이다.
People listen to him / because of what he can do in the pool.
사람들은 그의 말을 경청한다. / 그가 수영장에서 할 수 있는 것 때문에
And when an actor tells us / we should drive a certain car, / we don't listen / because of his expertise on engines.
그리고 어떤 배우가 우리에게 말할 때, / 우리가 특정 자동차를 운전해야 한다고 / 우리는 경청하는 것은 아니다. / 엔진에 대한 그의 전문 지식 때문에
We listen / because we admire his talent.
우리는 경청한다. / 그의 재능을 존경하기 때문에
Excellence connects.
탁월함이 연결된다.
If you possess a high level of ability in an area, / others may desire to connect with you / because of it.
만약 당신이 어떤 분야에서 높은 수준의 능력을 갖고 있다면, / 다른 사람들은 당신과 연결되기를 원할 수도 있다. / 그것 때문에

자기 직업에서 높은 수준으로 수행하는 사람들은 흔히 다른 사람들에게 즉각적인 신뢰를 얻는다. 사람들은 그들을 존경하고, 그들처럼 되고 싶어 하고, 그들과 연결되어 있다고 느낀다. 그들이 말할 때, 다른 사람들은 비록 그들의 기술 분야가 그들이 주는 조언과 전혀 관련이 없을지라도 경청한다. 세계적으로 유명한 농구 선수에 대해 생각해 보라. 그는 그가 농구를 하면서 그간 벌었던 것보다 광고로부터 더 많은 돈을 벌었다. 그것이 그가 광고하는 제품에 대한 그의 지식 때문일까? 아니다. 그것은 그가 농구로 할 수 있는 것 때문이다. 올림픽 메달리스트 수영 선수도 마찬가지이다. 사람들은 그가 수영장에서 할 수 있는 것 때문에 그의 말을 경청한다. 그리고 어떤 배우가 우리에게 특정 자동차를 운전해야 한다고 말할 때, 우리는 엔진에 대한 그의 전문 지식 때문에 경청하는 것은 아니다. 우리는 그의 재능을 존경하기 때문에 경청한다. 탁월함이 연결된다. 만약 당신이 어떤 분야에서 높은 수준의 능력을 갖고 있다면, 다른 사람들은 그것 때문에 당신과 연결되기를 원할 수도 있다.

Why? 왜 정답일까?

처음(Individuals who perform at a high level in their profession often have instant credibility with others.)과 마지막(If you possess a high level of ability in an area, others may desire to connect with you because of it.)에서 자기 분야에서 '높은 수준의 능력'을 가진 사람들은 다른 이들의 신뢰를 사기 쉽다고 언급하는 것으로 보아, 빈칸에 들어갈 말로 가장 적절한 것은 ④ '탁월함'이다.

- **profession** ⓝ 직업
- **credibility** ⓝ 신뢰
- **have nothing to do with** 〜와 관련이 없다
- **endorsement** ⓝ (유명인의 텔레비전 등에서의) 상품 보증 선전
- **endorse** ⓥ (유명인이 광고에 나와 특정 상품을) 보증하다, 홍보하다
- **medalist** ⓝ 메달리스트
- **patience** ⓝ 인내심
- **instant** ⓐ 즉각적인
- **admire** ⓥ 존경하다
- **world-famous** ⓐ 세계적으로 유명한
- **expertise** ⓝ 전문 지식
- **sacrifice** ⓝ 희생

[문제편 p.089]

구문 풀이

6행 He has made more money from endorsements than he ever did playing basketball.
대동사(= made money)

★★ 문제 해결 꿀~팁 ★★

▶ 많이 틀린 이유는?
빈칸 바로 앞에서 '전문 지식' 때문이 아니라 '재능' 때문에 유명인들의 말을 듣게 된다고 하는데, 이것을 ② '희생'이나 ③ '정직함'의 사례로 볼 수는 없다.

▶ 문제 해결 방법은?
글 처음과 마지막에 요지가 반복 제시된다. 즉 주제문인 첫 문장을 보고 빈칸을 완성하면 간단하다.

★★★ 등급을 가르는 문제!

32 도시처럼 상호작용으로 작동하는 뇌   정답률 43% | 정답 ①

다음 빈칸에 들어갈 말로 가장 적절한 것을 고르시오. [3점]

✔① operates in isolation – 독립적으로 작동하지
② suffers from rapid changes – 급속한 변화로 고생하지
③ resembles economic elements – 경제적 요소를 닮지
④ works in a systematic way – 체계적으로 작동하지
⑤ interacts with another – 서로 상호 작용하지

Think of the brain as a city.
뇌를 도시라고 생각해보라.
If you were to look out over a city / and ask "where is the economy located?" / you'd see / there's no good answer to the question.
만약 당신이 도시를 내다보며 / "경제는 어디에 위치해 있나요?"라고 묻는다면 / 당신은 알게 될 것이다. / 그 질문에 좋은 답이 없다는 것을
Instead, / the economy emerges / from the interaction of all the elements / — from the stores and the banks / to the merchants and the customers.
대신, / 경제는 나타난다. / 모든 요소의 상호 작용으로부터 / 상점과 은행에서 / 상인과 고객에 이르기까지
And so it is with the brain's operation: / it doesn't happen in one spot.
뇌의 작용도 그렇다. / 즉 그것은 한 곳에서 일어나지 않는다.
Just as in a city, / no neighborhood of the brain / operates in isolation.
도시에서처럼, / 뇌의 어떤 지역도 〜않는다. / 독립적으로 작동하지
In brains and in cities, / everything emerges / from the interaction between residents, / at all scales, / locally and distantly.
뇌와 도시 안에서, / 모든 것은 나타난다. / 거주자들 간의 상호 작용으로부터 / 모든 규모로, / 근거리든 원거리든
Just as trains bring materials and textiles into a city, / which become processed into the economy, / so the raw electrochemical signals from sensory organs / are transported along superhighways of neurons.
기차가 자재와 직물을 도시로 들여오고, / 그것이 경제 속에 처리되는 것처럼, / 감각 기관으로부터의 가공되지 않은 전기화학적 신호는 / 뉴런의 초고속도로를 따라서 전해진다.
There / the signals undergo processing / and transformation into our conscious reality.
거기서 / 신호는 처리를 겪는다. / 그리고 우리의 의식적인 현실로의 변형을

뇌를 도시라고 생각해보라. 만약 당신이 도시를 내다보며 "경제는 어디에 위치해 있나요?"라고 묻는다면 그 질문에 좋은 답이 없다는 것을 알게 될 것이다. 대신, 경제는 상점과 은행에서 상인과 고객에 이르기까지 모든 요소의 상호 작용으로부터 나타난다. 뇌의 작용도 그렇다. 즉 그것은 한 곳에서 일어나지 않는다. 도시에서처럼, 뇌의 어떤 지역도 독립적으로 작동하지 않는다. 뇌와 도시 안에서, 모든 것은 모든 규모로, 근거리든 원거리든, 거주자들 간의 상호 작용으로부터 나타난다. 기차가 자재와 직물을 도시로 들여오고, 그것이 경제 속으로 처리되는 것처럼, 감각 기관으로부터의 가공되지 않은 전기화학적 신호는 뉴런의 초고속도로를 따라서 전해진다. 거기서 신호는 처리와 우리의 의식적인 현실로의 변형을 겪는다.

Why? 왜 정답일까?

경제가 모든 요소의 상호 작용으로 작동하는 것처럼 뇌 또한 그렇다(And so it is with the brain's operation: it doesn't happen in one spot. / ~ everything emerges from the interaction ~)는 내용이므로, 빈칸에 들어갈 말로 가장 적절한 것은 ① '독립적으로 작동하지'이다.

- **think of A as B** A를 B로 여기다
- **element** ⓝ 요소
- **operation** ⓝ 작동, 작용
- **distantly** ⓐⓓ 멀리, 원거리로
- **process** ⓥ 가공하다, 처리하다
- **electrochemical** ⓐ 전기화학의
- **transport** ⓥ 수송하다, 실어 나르다
- **transformation** ⓝ 변화, 변모
- **in isolation** 고립되어
- **emerge** ⓥ 나타나다, 생겨나다
- **merchant** ⓝ 상인
- **locally** ⓐⓓ 국지적으로
- **textile** ⓝ 직물
- **raw** ⓐ 원재료의, 날것의
- **sensory organ** 감각 기관
- **undergo** ⓥ 거치다, 겪다
- **conscious** ⓐ 의식적인

구문 풀이

2행 If you were to look out over a city and ask "where is the economy
「if + 주어 + were to + 동사원형1 + ~   동사원형2 ~
located?" you'd see there's no good answer to the question.
주어 + 조동사 과거형 + 동사원형 : 가정법 미래(거의 불가능한 상황에 대한 가정)

★★ 문제 해결 꿀~팁 ★★

▶ 많이 틀린 이유는?
도시가 많은 경제 주체의 상호 작용을 통해 돌아가듯이 뇌 또한 수많은 요소의 상호 작용으로 돌아간다는 내용이다. 주어가 「no + 명사」 형태이므로, 빈칸에는 주제와 반대되는 말을 넣어야 문장 전체가 주제를 나타내게 된다. 하지만 ③은 '경제 주체와 비슷하다'는 주제를 직접 제시하므로, 이를 빈칸에 넣어 읽으면 '뇌의 그 어느 구역도 경제 주체와 비슷하지 않다'는 의미가 되어버린다. 즉 ③은 주제와 정반대되는 의미를 완성한다.

▶ 문제 해결 방법은?
'뇌 = 도시'라는 비유를 확인하고, 둘의 공통점이 무엇인지 파악한 후, 선택지를 하나씩 대입하며 빈칸 문장의 의미를 주의 깊게 이해해 보자.

다음 빈칸에 들어갈 말로 가장 적절한 것을 고르시오. [3점]

① language guides our actions – 언어가 우리 행동을 이끈다
② emotions arise from our bodies – 감정이 우리 신체에서 발생한다
③ body language hides our feelings – 신체 언어는 우리 감정을 숨긴다
④ what others say affects our mood – 다른 사람들의 말이 우리 감정에 영향을 미친다
⑤ negative emotions easily disappear – 부정적 감정은 쉽게 사라진다

Someone else's body language affects our own body, / which then creates an emotional echo / that makes us feel accordingly.
다른 사람의 신체 언어는 우리 자신의 신체에 영향을 미치며, / 그것은 그 후 감정적인 메아리를 만들어낸다. / 우리가 그에 맞춰 느끼게 하는

As Louis Armstrong sang, / "When you're smiling, / the whole world smiles with you."
Louis Armstrong이 노래했듯이, / "당신이 미소 지을 때, / 전 세계가 당신과 함께 미소 짓는다."

If copying another's smile / makes us feel happy, / the emotion of the smiler / has been transmitted via our body.
만약 다른 사람의 미소를 따라 하는 것이 / 우리를 행복하게 한다면, / 그 미소 짓는 사람의 감정은 / 우리의 신체를 통해 전달된 것이다.

Strange as it may sound, / this theory states / that emotions arise from our bodies.
이상하게 들릴지 모르지만, / 이 이론은 말한다. / 감정이 우리 신체에서 발생한다고

For example, / our mood can be improved / by simply lifting up the corners of our mouth.
예를 들어, / 우리의 기분은 좋아질 수 있다. / 단순히 입꼬리를 올리는 것으로

If people are asked / to bite down on a pencil lengthwise, / taking care not to let the pencil touch their lips / (thus forcing the mouth into a smile-like shape), / they judge cartoons funnier / than if they have been asked to frown.
만약 사람들이 요구받으면, / 연필을 긴 방향으로 꽉 물라고 / 연필이 입술에 닿지 않도록 조심하면서 / (그래서 억지로 입을 미소 짓는 것과 같은 모양이 되도록), / 그들은 만화를 더 재미있다고 판단한다. / 그들이 인상을 찌푸리라고 요구받은 경우보다

The primacy of the body / is sometimes summarized in the phrase / "I must be afraid, / because I'm running."
신체가 우선한다는 것은 / 때때로 구절로 요약된다. / "나는 분명 두려운가보다, / 왜냐하면 나는 도망치고 있기 때문이다."라는

다른 사람의 신체 언어는 우리 자신의 신체에 영향을 미치며, 그것은 그 후 우리가 그에 맞춰 (감정을) 느끼게 하는 감정적인 메아리를 만들어낸다. Louis Armstrong이 노래했듯이, "당신이 미소 지을 때, 전 세계가 당신과 함께 미소 짓는다." 만약 다른 사람의 미소를 따라 하는 것이 우리를 행복하게 한다면, 그 미소 짓는 사람의 감정은 우리의 신체를 통해 전달된 것이다. 이상하게 들릴지 모르지만, 이 이론은 감정이 우리 신체에서 발생한다고 말한다. 예를 들어, 우리의 기분은 단순히 입꼬리를 올리는 것으로 좋아질 수 있다. 만약 사람들이 연필을 긴 방향으로 꽉 물라고 요구받으면, 연필이 입술에 닿지 않도록 조심하면서 (그래서 억지로 입을 미소 짓는 것과 같은 모양이 되도록), 그들은 인상을 찌푸리라고 요구받은 경우보다 만화를 더 재미있다고 판단한다. 신체가 (감정에) 우선한다는 것은 "나는 분명 두려운가보다, 왜냐하면 나는 도망치고 있기 때문이다."라는 구절로 때때로 요약된다.

Why? 왜 정답일까?

빈칸 뒤의 실험에서 우리가 입꼬리를 올리고 있다 보면 더 기분이 좋아질 수 있다(~ our mood can be improved by simply lifting up the corners of our mouth.)고 설명하고, 이를 마지막 문장에서는 '(감정에 대한) 신체의 우선(The primacy of the body)'이라고 요약했다. 따라서 빈칸에 들어갈 말로 가장 적절한 것은 ② '감정이 우리 신체에서 발생한다'이다.

- **emotional** ⓐ 정서적인
- **transmit** ⓥ 전달하다
- **theory** ⓝ 이론
- **lift up** ~을 들어올리다
- **bite down on** ~을 깨물다
- **frown** ⓥ 얼굴을 찌푸리다
- **summarize** ⓥ 요약하다
- **hide** ⓥ 숨기다
- **accordingly** 〈ad〉 그에 따라
- **via** 〈prep〉 ~을 통해서
- **state** ⓥ 진술하다
- **be asked to** ~하도록 요청받다
- **lengthwise** 〈ad〉 길게
- **primacy** ⓝ 우선함
- **arise from** ~에서 생겨나다

구문 풀이

[5행] Strange as it may sound, this theory states that emotions arise from our bodies.
「보어+as+주어+동사 : 비록 ~일지라도(양보 구문)」

다음 빈칸에 들어갈 말로 가장 적절한 것을 고르시오. [3점]

① Promoting products through social media
소셜 미디어를 통해 제품을 홍보하는 것
② Reducing the risk of producing poor quality items
질이 좋지 않은 제품을 생산할 위험을 낮추는 것
③ Restricting the number of items customers can buy
고객이 구입할 수 있는 품목의 개수를 제한하는 것
④ Offering several options that customers find attractive
고객들이 매력적이라고 생각하는 몇 가지 선택 사항을 제시하는 것
⑤ Emphasizing the safety of products with research data
연구 데이터로 제품의 안전성을 강조하는 것

Restricting the number of items customers can buy / boosts sales.
고객이 구입할 수 있는 품목의 개수를 제한하는 것은 / 매출을 증가시킨다.

Brian Wansink, / Professor of Marketing at Cornell University, / investigated the effectiveness of this tactic in 1998.
Brian Wansink는 / Cornell University의 마케팅 교수인 / 1998년에 이 전략의 효과를 조사했다.

He persuaded three supermarkets in Sioux City, Iowa, / to offer Campbell's soup at a small discount: / 79 cents rather than 89 cents.
그는 Iowa 주 Sioux City에 있는 세 개의 슈퍼마켓을 설득했다. / Campbell의 수프를 약간 할인하여 제공하도록 / 즉 89센트가 아닌 79센트로

The discounted soup was sold in one of three conditions: / a control, / where there was no limit on the volume of purchases, / or two tests, / where customers were limited to either four or twelve cans.
할인된 수프는 세 가지 조건 중 하나의 조건으로 판매되었다. / 즉 하나의 통제 집단, / 구매량에 제한이 없는 / 또는 두 개의 실험 집단 / 고객이 4캔 아니면 12개의 캔으로 제한되는

In the unlimited condition / shoppers bought 3.3 cans on average, / whereas in the scarce condition, / when there was a limit, / they bought 5.3 on average.

무제한 조건에서 / 구매자들은 평균 3.3캔을 구입했고, / 반면 희소 조건에서는 / 제한이 있던 / 그들은 평균 5.3캔을 구입했다.

This suggests / scarcity encourages sales.
이것은 보여준다. / 희소성이 판매를 장려한다는 것을

The findings are particularly strong / because the test took place / in a supermarket with genuine shoppers.
그 결과는 특히 타당하다. / 이 실험이 진행되었기 때문에 / 진짜 구매자들이 있는 슈퍼마켓에서

It didn't rely on claimed data, / nor was it held in a laboratory / where consumers might behave differently.
그것은 주장된 데이터에 의존하지 않았고, / 그것은 실험실에서 이루어진 것도 아니었다. / 소비자들이 다르게 행동할지도 모르는

고객이 구입할 수 있는 품목의 개수를 제한하는 것은 매출을 증가시킨다. Cornell University의 마케팅 교수인 Brian Wansink는 1998년에 이 전략의 효과를 조사했다. 그는 Iowa 주 Sioux City에 있는 세 개의 슈퍼마켓이 Campbell의 수프를 약간 할인하여 89센트가 아닌 79센트로 제공하도록 설득했다. 할인된 수프는 세 가지 조건 중 하나의 조건으로 판매되었다. 구매량에 제한이 없는 하나의 통제 집단, 또는 고객이 4캔 아니면 12개의 캔으로 제한되는 두 개의 실험 집단이 그것이었다. 무제한 조건에서 구매자들은 평균 3.3캔을 구입했던 반면, 제한이 있던 희소 조건에서는 평균 5.3캔을 구입했다. 이것은 희소성이 판매를 장려한다는 것을 보여준다. 이 실험은 진짜 구매자들이 있는 슈퍼마켓에서 진행되었기 때문에 그 결과는 특히 타당하다. 그것은 주장된 데이터에 의존하지 않았고, 소비자들이 다르게 행동할지도 모르는 실험실에서 이루어진 것도 아니었다.

Why? 왜 정답일까?

빈칸 뒤로 소개된 연구에서, 구매 개수에 제한이 있었던 실험군이 제품을 가장 많이 구입했다고 설명하며, 희소성이 판매를 장려한다는 결론을 정리하고 있다(~ scarcity encourages sales.). 따라서 빈칸에 들어갈 말로 가장 적절한 것은 ③ '고객이 구입할 수 있는 품목의 개수를 제한하는 것'이다.

- **investigate** ⓥ 조사하다
- **tactic** ⓝ 전략
- **rather than** ~ 대신에
- **control** ⓝ 통제 집단(실험에서 처치를 가하지 않고 둔 집단)
- **unlimited** ⓐ 제한되지 않은, 무제한의
- **genuine** ⓐ 진짜의
- **laboratory** ⓝ 실험실
- **differently** 〈ad〉 다르게
- **emphasize** ⓥ 강조하다
- **effectiveness** ⓝ 유효성, 효과 있음
- **persuade** ⓥ 설득하다
- **condition** ⓝ 조건
- **scarcity** ⓝ 희소성
- **rely on** ~에 의존하다
- **behave** ⓥ 행동하다
- **attractive** ⓐ 매력적인

구문 풀이

[13행] It didn't rely on claimed data, nor was it held in a laboratory where consumers might behave differently.
부정문 「부정어+be+주어+p.p. : 도치 구문(~도 없다)」

다음 글에서 전체 흐름과 관계 없는 문장은?

Although technology has the potential / to increase productivity, / it can also have a negative impact on productivity.
기술은 잠재력을 가지고 있지만, / 생산성을 높일 수 있는 / 그것은 또한 생산성에 부정적인 영향을 미칠 수 있다.

For example, / in many office environments / workers sit at desks with computers / and have access to the internet.
예를 들어, / 많은 사무실 환경에서 / 직원들은 컴퓨터가 있는 책상에 앉아 / 인터넷에 접속한다.

① They are able to check their personal e-mails / and use social media / whenever they want to.
그들은 개인 이메일을 확인하고 / 소셜 미디어를 사용할 수 있다. / 그들이 원할 때마다

② This can stop them from doing their work / and make them less productive.
이것은 그들이 일을 하는 것을 방해하고 / 생산성이 떨어지게 할 수 있다.

③ Introducing new technology / can also have a negative impact on production / when it causes a change to the production process / or requires workers to learn a new system.
새로운 기술을 도입하는 것은 / 또한 생산에 부정적인 영향을 미칠 수 있다. / 그것이 생산 공정에 변화를 야기하거나 / 직원들에게 새로운 시스템을 배우도록 요구할 때

④ Using technology / can enable businesses / to produce more goods / and to get more out of the other factors of production.
기술을 사용하는 것은 / 기업이 ~할 수 있게 한다. / 더 많은 제품을 생산하고 / 다른 생산 요소들로부터 더 많은 것을 얻게

⑤ Learning to use new technology / can be time consuming and stressful for workers / and this can cause a decline in productivity.
새로운 기술 사용법을 배우는 것은 / 직원들에게 시간이 많이 드는 일이고 스트레스를 줄 수 있으며, / 이것은 생산성 저하를 야기할 수 있다.

기술은 생산성을 높일 수 있는 잠재력을 가지고 있지만, 또한 생산성에 부정적인 영향을 미칠 수 있다. 예를 들어, 많은 사무실 환경에서 직원들은 컴퓨터가 있는 책상에 앉아 인터넷에 접속한다. ① 그들은 원할 때마다 개인 이메일을 확인하고 소셜 미디어를 사용할 수 있다. ② 이것은 그들이 일을 하는 것을 방해하고 생산성이 떨어지게 할 수 있다. ③ 또한 새로운 기술을 도입하는 것은 생산 공정에 변화를 야기하거나 직원들에게 새로운 시스템을 배우도록 요구할 때 생산에 부정적인 영향을 미칠 수 있다. ④ 기술을 사용하는 것은 기업이 더 많은 제품을 생산하고 다른 생산 요소들로부터 더 많은 것을 얻게 할 수 있다. ⑤ 새로운 기술 사용법을 배우는 것은 직원들에게 시간이 많이 드는 일이고 스트레스를 줄 수 있으며, 이것은 생산성 저하를 야기할 수 있다.

Why? 왜 정답일까?

기술이 생산성을 떨어뜨릴 수 있다는 내용인데, ④는 기술 사용이 더 많은 제품 생산에 도움이 되고 생산 요소로부터 더 많은 것을 얻게 한다는 긍정적 내용이다. 따라서 전체 흐름과 관계 없는 문장은 ④이다.

- **impact** ⓝ 영향, 충격
- **production** ⓝ 생산, 제조
- **require** ⓥ 요구하다
- **time-consuming** ⓐ 시간이 많이 걸리는
- **have access to** ~에 접근하다, ~을 이용하다
- **cause** ⓥ 야기하다
- **factor** ⓝ 요인, 요소

구문 풀이

[5행] This can stop them from doing their work and make them less productive.
「stop+A+from+B : A가 B하지 못하게 하다」   5형식 동사 목적어   형용사 보어

36 시계의 발명 | 정답률 78% | 정답 ②

주어진 글 다음에 이어질 글의 순서로 가장 적절한 것을 고르시오. [3점]

① (A) – (C) – (B)
✓② (B) – (A) – (C)
③ (B) – (C) – (A)
④ (C) – (A) – (B)
⑤ (C) – (B) – (A)

Up until about 6,000 years ago, / most people were farmers.
약 6,000년 전까지 / 대부분의 사람들은 농부였다.

Many lived in different places throughout the year, / hunting for food / or moving their livestock to areas with enough food.
많은 사람들은 일 년 내내 여러 장소에서 살았고, / 식량을 찾아다니거나 / 가축을 충분한 먹이가 있는 지역으로 옮겼다.

(B) There was no need to tell the time / because life depended on natural cycles, / such as the changing seasons or sunrise and sunset.
시간을 알 필요가 없었다 / 삶이 자연적인 주기에 달려 있었기 때문에 / 변화하는 계절이나 일출과 일몰 같은

Gradually more people started to live in larger settlements, / and some needed to tell the time.
점점 더 많은 사람들이 더 큰 정착지에서 살기 시작했고, / 어떤 사람들은 시간을 알 필요가 있었다.

(A) For example, / priests wanted to know / when to carry out religious ceremonies.
예를 들어, / 성직자들은 알고 싶었다 / 언제 종교적인 의식을 수행해야 하는지

This is when people first invented clocks / — devices that show, measure, and keep track of passing time.
이때 사람들이 처음으로 발명했다 / 시간을 보여주고, 측정하고, 흐르는 시간을 추적하는 장치인 시계를

(C) Clocks have been important ever since.
시계는 그 이후로도 중요했다.

Today, / clocks are used for important things / such as setting busy airport timetables / — if the time is incorrect, / aeroplanes might crash into each other / when taking off or landing!
오늘날, / 시계는 중요한 일에 사용된다 / 바쁜 공항 시간표를 설정하는 것과 같은 / 만약 시간이 부정확하다면, / 비행기는 서로 충돌할지도 모른다! / 이륙하거나 착륙할 때

약 6,000년 전까지 대부분의 사람들은 농부였다. 많은 사람들은 일 년 내내 여러 장소에서 살았고, 식량을 찾아다니거나 가축을 충분한 먹이가 있는 지역으로 옮겼다.
(B) 변화하는 계절이나 일출과 일몰 같은 자연적인 주기에 삶이 달려 있었기 때문에 시간을 알 필요가 없었다. 점점 더 많은 사람들이 더 큰 정착지에서 살기 시작했고, 어떤 사람들은 시간을 알 필요가 있었다.
(A) 예를 들어, 성직자들은 언제 종교적인 의식을 수행해야 하는지 알고 싶었다. 이때 사람들이 시간을 보여주고, 측정하고, 흐르는 시간을 추적하는 장치인 시계를 처음으로 발명했다.
(C) 시계는 그 이후로도 중요했다. 오늘날, 시계는 바쁜 공항 시간표를 설정하는 것과 같은 중요한 일에 사용된다. 만약 시간이 부정확하다면, 비행기는 이륙하거나 착륙할 때 서로 충돌할지도 모른다!

Why? 왜 정답일까?

사람들이 대부분 농부였던 시절을 언급하는 주어진 글 뒤로, 이때는 시계가 필요 없었다는 내용으로 시작하는 (B)가 연결된다. 한편, (B)의 후반부는 그러다 일부 사람들이 시계를 필요로 하기 시작했다는 내용이고, (A)는 그런 사람들의 예로 성직자를 언급한다. (C)는 시계가 처음 발명된 이후로 시계의 중요성이 높아졌고, 오늘날에도 시계가 중요한 역할을 담당하고 있음을 설명한다. 따라서 글의 순서로 가장 적절한 것은 ② '(B) – (A) – (C)'이다.

- **hunt for** ~을 사냥하다
- **carry out** 수행하다
- **device** ⓝ 장치
- **keep track of** ~을 추적하다, 기록하다
- **gradually** [ad] 점차
- **tell the time** 시간을 알다
- **take off** 이륙하다
- **livestock** ⓝ 가축
- **religious** ⓐ 종교적인
- **measure** ⓥ 측정하다
- **natural cycle** 자연적 주기
- **settlement** ⓝ 정착(지)
- **crash into** ~에 충돌하다
- **land** ⓥ 착륙하다

구문 풀이

12행 Today, clocks are used for important things such as setting busy airport timetables — if the time is incorrect, aeroplanes might crash into each other when taking off or landing!
접속사를 포함한 분사구문(= when they take off or land)

37 생산성과 노동 분업 | 정답률 58% | 정답 ⑤

주어진 글 다음에 이어질 글의 순서로 가장 적절한 것을 고르시오.

① (A) – (C) – (B)
② (B) – (A) – (C)
③ (B) – (C) – (A)
④ (C) – (A) – (B)
✓⑤ (C) – (B) – (A)

Managers are always looking for ways / to increase productivity, / which is the ratio of costs to output in production.
관리자들은 항상 방법을 찾고 있는데, / 생산성을 높일 수 있는 / 이것은 생산에서 비용 대비 생산량의 비율이다.

Adam Smith, / writing when the manufacturing industry was new, / described a way / that production could be made more efficient, / known as the "division of labor."
Adam Smith는 / 제조 산업이 새로 등장했을 때 저술한 / 방식을 설명했고 / 생산이 더 효율적으로 될 수 있는 / 이것은 '노동 분업'으로 알려져 있다.

(C) Making most manufactured goods / involves several different processes / using different skills.
대부분의 공산품을 만드는 것은 / 여러 가지 다른 과정을 포함한다 / 다른 기술을 사용하는

Smith's example was the manufacture of pins: / the wire is straightened, / sharpened, / a head is put on, / and then it is polished.
Smith의 예는 핀의 제조였다 / 철사가 곧게 펴지고, / 뾰족해지고, / 머리가 끼워지고, / 그리고 나서 그것은 다듬어진다.

(B) One worker could do all these tasks, / and make 20 pins in a day.
한 명의 노동자가 이 모든 작업들을 할 수 있고, / 하루에 20개의 핀을 만들 수도 있다.

But this work can be divided into its separate processes, / with a number of workers each performing one task.
그러나 이 일은 별개의 과정으로 분리될 수 있다 / 많은 노동자가 각각 한 가지 작업을 수행하며

(A) Because each worker specializes in one job, / he or she can work much faster / without changing from one task to another.
각 노동자는 한 가지 작업을 전문으로 하기 때문에, / 이 사람은 훨씬 더 빠르게 일할 수 있다 / 한 작업에서 다른 작업으로 옮겨가지 않으면서

Now 10 workers can produce thousands of pins in a day / — a huge increase in productivity / from the 200 / they would have produced before.
이제 10명의 노동자가 하루에 수천 개의 핀을 생산할 수 있다. / 이는 큰 증가이다 / 이는 생산성의 큰 증가이다. / 200개로부터 / 이전에 그들이 생산했던

관리자들은 항상 생산성을 높일 수 있는 방법을 찾고 있는데, 생산성은 생산에서 비용 대비 생산량의 비율이다. 제조 산업이 새로 등장했을 때 저술한 Adam Smith는 생산이 더 효율적으로 될 수 있는 방식을 설명했고, 이것은 '노동 분업'으로 알려져 있다.
(C) 대부분의 공산품을 만드는 것은 다른 기술을 사용하는 여러 가지 다른 과정을 포함한다. Smith의 예는 핀의 제조였다. 철사를 곧게 펴고, 뾰족하게 만들고, 머리를 끼운 다음, 그것을 다듬는다.
(B) 한 명의 노동자가 이 모든 작업들을 할 수 있고, 하루에 20개의 핀을 만들 수도 있다. 그러나 이 일은 많은 노동자가 각각 한 가지 작업을 수행하며 별개의 과정으로 분리될 수 있다.
(A) 각 노동자는 한 가지 작업을 전문으로 하기 때문에, 이 사람은 한 작업에서 다른 작업으로 옮겨가지 않으면서 훨씬 더 빠르게 일할 수 있다. 이제 10명의 노동자가 하루에 수천 개의 핀을 생산할 수 있다. 이는 이전에 그들이 생산했던 200개로부터 생산성 측면에서 크게 증가한 것이다.

Why? 왜 정답일까?

'노동 분업'의 개념을 소개하는 주어진 글 뒤로, 핀 제조 과정을 예로 설명하는 (C), 이 제조 과정은 한 사람에 의해 수행될 수도 있지만, 분업으로 진행될 수도 있다고 설명하는 (B), 분업 상황의 장점을 소개하는 (A)가 차례로 이어져야 자연스럽다. 따라서 글의 순서로 가장 적절한 것은 ⑤ '(C) – (B) – (A)'이다.

- **ratio** ⓝ 비율
- **manufacturing industry** 제조업
- **efficient** ⓐ 효율적인
- **specialize in** ~에 특화되다
- **involve** ⓥ 포함하다, 수반하다
- **sharpen** ⓥ 뾰족하게 하다
- **output** ⓝ 산출
- **describe** ⓥ 설명하다
- **division of labor** 분업
- **a number of** 많은
- **straighten** ⓥ 곧게 펴다
- **polish** ⓥ 다듬다

구문 풀이

12행 But this work can be divided into its separate processes, with a number of workers each performing one task.
「with + 명사 + 분사 : ~이 …한 채로(부대상황 분사구문)」

★★★ 등급을 가르는 문제!

38 느리게라도 계속 진행되는 변화 | 정답률 39% | 정답 ②

글의 흐름으로 보아, 주어진 문장이 들어가기에 가장 적절한 곳을 고르시오.

Sometimes the pace of change is far slower.
때때로 변화의 속도는 훨씬 더 느리다.

① The face you saw / reflected in your mirror this morning / probably appeared no different / from the face you saw the day before / — or a week or a month ago.
당신이 본 얼굴은 / 오늘 아침 거울에 비춰진 / 아마도 다르지 않게 보였을 것이다 / 당신이 그 전날에 본 얼굴과 / 또는 일주일이나 한 달 전에

✓② Yet we know / that the face that stares back at us from the glass / is not the same, / cannot be the same, / as it was 10 minutes ago.
그러나 우리는 안다. / 거울에서 우리를 마주보는 얼굴이 / 같지 않고, / 같을 수 없다는 것을 / 10분 전과

The proof is in your photo album: / Look at a photograph / taken of yourself 5 or 10 years ago / and you see clear differences / between the face in the snapshot / and the face in your mirror.
증거는 당신의 사진 앨범에 있다. / 사진을 보라 / 5년 또는 10년 전에 당신을 찍은 / 그러면 당신은 명확한 차이를 보게 될 것이다. / 스냅사진 속의 얼굴과 / 거울 속 얼굴 사이의

③ If you lived in a world without mirrors for a year / and then saw your reflection, / you might be surprised by the change.
만약 당신이 일 년간 거울이 없는 세상에 살고 / 그 이후 (거울에) 비친 당신의 모습을 본다면, / 당신은 그 변화 때문에 깜짝 놀랄지도 모른다.

④ After an interval of 10 years / without seeing yourself, / you might not at first recognize the person / peering from the mirror.
10년의 기간이 지난 후, / 스스로를 보지 않고 / 당신은 그 사람을 처음에는 알아보지 못할지도 모른다. / 거울에서 쳐다보고 있는

⑤ Even something as basic as our own face / changes from moment to moment.
심지어 우리 자신의 얼굴같이 아주 기본적인 것조차도 / 순간순간 변한다.

때때로 변화의 속도는 훨씬 더 느리다. ① 오늘 아침 당신이 거울에 비춰진 것을 본 얼굴은 아마도 당신이 그 전날 또는 일주일이나 한 달 전에 본 얼굴과 다르지 않게 보였을 것이다. ② 그러나 우리는 거울에서 우리를 마주보는 얼굴이 10분 전과 같지 않고, 같을 수 없다는 것을 안다. 증거는 당신의 사진 앨범에 있다. 5년 또는 10년 전에 찍은 당신의 사진을 보면 당신은 스냅사진 속의 얼굴과 거울 속 얼굴 사이의 명확한 차이를 보게 될 것이다. ③ 만약 당신이 일 년간 거울이 없는 세상에 살고 그 이후 (거울에) 비친 당신의 모습을 본다면, 당신은 그 변화 때문에 깜짝 놀랄지도 모른다. ④ 스스로를 보지 않고 10년의 기간이 지난 후, 당신은 거울에서 쳐다보고 있는 사람을 처음에는 알아보지 못할지도 모른다. ⑤ 심지어 우리 자신의 얼굴같이 아주 기본적인 것조차도 순간순간 변한다.

Why? 왜 정답일까?

② 앞은 오늘 아침 거울로 본 얼굴이 전날, 일주일 전, 또는 한 달 전에 본 얼굴과 다르지 않았을 것이라는 내용인데, ② 뒤는 얼굴이 명확히 '달라졌다'는 것을 알 수 있는 증거에 관한 내용이다. 즉 ② 앞뒤로 상반된 내용이 제시되어 흐름이 어색하게 끊기므로, 주어진 문장이 들어가기에 가장 적절한 곳은 ②이다.

- **reflect** ⓥ 반사하다
- **snapshot** ⓝ 스냅사진, 짧은 묘사
- **surprised** ⓐ 놀란
- **peer** ⓥ 응시하다
- **clear** ⓐ 명확한
- **reflection** ⓝ (물이나 거울에 비친) 그림자
- **interval** ⓝ 간격
- **from moment to moment** 시시각각

구문 풀이

12행 Even something as basic as our own face changes from moment to moment.
「as + 원급 + as : ~만큼 …한」

09회

★★★ 등급을 가르는 문제!

39 나이가 들면서 호기심이 줄어드는 까닭　정답률 31% | 정답 ⑤

글의 흐름으로 보아, 주어진 문장이 들어가기에 가장 적절한 곳을 고르시오. [3점]

According to educational psychologist Susan Engel, / curiosity begins to decrease / as young as four years old.
교육 심리학자 Susan Engel에 따르면, / 호기심은 줄어들기 시작한다. / 네 살 정도라는 어린 나이에

By the time we are adults, / we have fewer questions and more default settings.
우리가 어른이 될 무렵, / 질문은 더 적어지고 기본값은 더 많아진다.

As Henry James put it, / "Disinterested curiosity is past, / the mental grooves and channels set."
Henry James가 말했듯이, / '무관심한 호기심은 없어지고, / 정신의 고랑과 경로가 자리잡는다.'

① The decline in curiosity / can be traced / in the development of the brain through childhood.
호기심의 감소는 / 원인을 찾을 수 있다. / 유년 시절 동안의 뇌의 발달에서

② Though smaller than the adult brain, / the infant brain contains millions more neural connections.
비록 성인의 뇌보다 작지만, / 유아의 뇌는 수백만 개 더 많은 신경 연결을 가지고 있다.

③ The wiring, however, is a mess; / the lines of communication between infant neurons / are far less efficient / than between those in the adult brain.
그러나 연결 상태는 엉망인데, / 유아의 뉴런 간의 전달은 / 훨씬 덜 효율적이다. / 성인 뇌 속 뉴런끼리의 전달보다

④ The baby's perception of the world / is consequently both intensely rich and wildly disordered.
세상에 대한 아기의 인식은 / 결과적으로 매우 풍부하면서도 상당히 무질서하다.

✔ As children absorb more evidence / from the world around them, / certain possibilities become much more likely and more useful / and harden into knowledge or beliefs.
아이들이 더 많은 증거를 흡수함에 따라, / 그들 주변의 세상으로부터 / 특정한 가능성들이 훨씬 더 커지게 되고 더 유용하게 되며 / 지식이나 믿음으로 굳어진다.

The neural pathways / that enable those beliefs / become faster and more automatic, / while the ones / that the child doesn't use regularly / are pruned away.
신경 경로는 / 그러한 믿음을 가능하게 하는 / 더 빠르고 자동적으로 이루어지게 되고, / 반면에 경로는 / 아이가 주기적으로 사용하지 않는 / 제거된다.

교육 심리학자 Susan Engel에 따르면, 호기심은 네 살 정도라는 어린 나이에 줄어들기 시작한다. 우리가 어른이 될 무렵, 질문은 더 적어지고 기본값은 더 많아진다. Henry James가 말했듯이, '무관심한 호기심은 없어지고, 정신의 고랑과 경로가 자리잡는다.' ① 호기심의 감소는 유년 시절 동안의 뇌의 발달에서 원인을 찾을 수 있다. ② 비록 성인의 뇌보다 작지만, 유아의 뇌는 수백만 개 더 많은 신경 연결을 가지고 있다. ③ 그러나 연결 상태는 엉망인데, 유아의 뉴런 간의 전달은 성인 뇌 속 뉴런끼리의 전달보다 훨씬 덜 효율적이다. ④ 결과적으로 세상에 대한 아기의 인식은 매우 풍부하면서도 상당히 무질서하다. ⑤ 아이들이 그들 주변의 세상으로부터 더 많은 증거를 흡수함에 따라, 특정한 가능성들이 훨씬 더 커지게 되고 더 유용하게 되며 지식이나 믿음으로 굳어진다. 그러한 믿음을 가능하게 하는 신경 경로는 더 빠르고 자동적으로 이루어지게 되고, 반면에 아이가 주기적으로 사용하지 않는 경로는 제거된다.

Why? 왜 정답일까?
⑤ 앞은 아기의 인식이 성인에 비해 무질서하다는 내용인데, ⑤ 뒤에서는 갑자기 '믿음'을 언급하며, 신경 경로의 자동화와 제거를 설명한다. 이때 주어진 문장을 보면, 아이들이 주변 세상에서 더 많은 근거를 얻고 더 유용한 가능성들을 취하면서 '믿음'이 굳어지기 시작한다고 한다. 이 '믿음'이 ⑤ 뒤와 연결되는 것이므로, 주어진 문장이 들어가기에 가장 적절한 곳은 ⑤이다.

- absorb ⓥ (정보를) 받아들이다
- educational ⓐ 교육의
- decrease ⓥ 감소하다
- disinterested ⓐ 무관심한
- channel ⓝ 경로
- neural ⓐ 신경의
- perception ⓝ 지각, 인식
- intensely ⓐⓓ 대단히, 강렬하게
- pathway ⓝ 경로
- prune ⓥ 가지치기하다

- harden ⓥ 굳어지다
- curiosity ⓝ 호기심
- default setting 기본값
- groove ⓝ 고랑
- infant ⓝ 유아
- mess ⓝ 엉망
- consequently ⓐⓓ 그 결과
- disordered ⓐ 무질서한
- automatic ⓐ 자동적인

구문 풀이

1행 As children absorb more evidence from the world around them, certain
　　　접속사(~함에 따라)　　　　　　　　　　　　　　　　　　　　=children
possibilities become much more likely and more useful and harden into
　　　　　　　동사1　　　주격 보어(비교급 형용사)　　　동사2
knowledge or beliefs.

▶ 문제 해결 방법은?
연결어 힌트가 없어서 난해하게 느껴질 수 있지만, 지시어 힌트를 활용하면 아주 쉽다. ⑤ 뒤에는 '그러한 믿음(those beliefs)'이라는 표현이 나오는데, 이는 앞에서 '믿음'을 언급했어야만 쓸 수 있는 표현이다. 하지만 ⑤ 앞까지는 beliefs가 전혀 등장하지 않고, 오로지 주어진 문장에만 knowledge or beliefs가 등장한다.

★★★ 등급을 가르는 문제!

40 식단의 좋고 나쁨　정답률 53% | 정답 ②

다음 글의 내용을 한 문장으로 요약하고자 한다. 빈칸 (A), (B)에 들어갈 말로 가장 적절한 것은?

	(A)	(B)		(A)	(B)
①	incorrect 부정확한	limited to ~에 한정된	✔③	appropriate 적절한	composed of ~로 구성되는
②	wrong 틀린	aimed at ~을 목표로 하는	④	appropriate 적절한	tested on ~에 시험된
⑤	incorrect 부정확한	adjusted to ~에 맞춰진			

Nearly eight of ten U.S. adults believe / there are "good foods" and "bad foods."
미국 성인 10명 중 거의 8명이 믿는다. / '좋은 음식'과 '나쁜 음식'이 있다고

Unless we're talking / about spoiled stew, poison mushrooms, or something similar, / however, / no foods can be labeled as either good or bad.
우리가 이야기하고 있지 않는 한, / 상한 스튜, 독버섯, 또는 이와 유사한 것에 관해 / 하지만 / 어떤 음식도 좋고 나쁨으로 분류될 수 없다.

There are, / however, / combinations of foods / that add up to a healthful or unhealthful diet.
~이 있다. / 하지만 / 음식들의 조합 / 결국 건강에 좋은 식단이나 건강에 좋지 않은 식단이 되는

Consider the case of an adult / who eats only foods thought of as "good" / — for example, / raw broccoli, apples, orange juice, boiled tofu, and carrots.
성인의 경우를 생각해보라. / '좋은' 음식이라고 생각되는 음식만 먹는 / 가령 / 생브로콜리, 사과, 오렌지 주스, 삶은 두부와 당근과 같이

Although all these foods are nutrient-dense, / they do not add up to a healthy diet / because they don't supply / a wide enough variety of the nutrients we need.
비록 이 모든 음식들이 영양이 풍부하지만, / 그것들은 결국 건강한 식단이 되지 않는다. / 그것들이 공급하진 않기에 / 우리가 필요로 하는 충분히 다양한 영양소를

Or take the case of the teenager / who occasionally eats fried chicken, / but otherwise stays away from fried foods.
또는 십 대의 경우를 예로 들어보자. / 튀긴 치킨을 가끔 먹지만, / 다른 경우에는 튀긴 음식을 멀리하는

The occasional fried chicken / isn't going to knock his or her diet off track.
가끔 먹는 튀긴 치킨은 / 이 십 대의 식단을 궤도에서 벗어나게 하지 않을 것이다.

But the person / who eats fried foods every day, / with few vegetables or fruits, / and loads up on supersized soft drinks, candy, and chips for snacks / has a bad diet.
하지만 사람은 / 매일 튀긴 음식을 먹고, / 채소나 과일을 거의 먹지 않으면서 / 간식으로 초대형 탄산음료, 사탕, 그리고 감자 칩으로 배를 가득 채우는 / 식단이 나쁜 것이다.

➡ Unlike the common belief, / defining foods as good or bad / is not (A) appropriate; / in fact, / a healthy diet is determined / largely by what the diet is (B) composed of.
일반적인 믿음과 달리, / 음식을 좋고 나쁨으로 정의하는 것은 / 적절하지 않고, / 사실 / 건강에 좋은 식단이란 결정된다. / 대체로 그 식단이 무엇으로 구성되는지에 의해

미국 성인 10명 중 거의 8명이 '좋은 음식'과 '나쁜 음식'이 있다고 믿는다. 하지만, 우리가 상한 스튜, 독버섯, 또는 이와 유사한 것에 관해 이야기하고 있지 않는 한, 어떤 음식도 좋고 나쁨으로 분류될 수 없다. 하지만, 결국 건강에 좋은 식단이나 건강에 좋지 않은 식단이 되는 음식들의 조합이 있다. 가령 생브로콜리, 사과, 오렌지 주스, 삶은 두부와 당근과 같이 '좋은' 음식이라고 생각되는 음식만 먹는 성인의 경우를 생각해보라. 비록 이 모든 음식들이 영양이 풍부하지만, 그것들은 우리가 필요로 하는 충분히 다양한 영양소를 공급하진 않기에 결국 건강한 식단이 되지 않는다. 또는 튀긴 치킨을 가끔 먹지만, 다른 경우에는 튀긴 음식을 멀리하는 십 대의 경우를 예로 들어보자. 가끔 먹는 튀긴 치킨은 이 십 대의 식단을 궤도에서 벗어나게 하지 않을 것이다. 하지만 채소나 과일을 거의 먹지 않으면서 매일 튀긴 음식을 먹고, 간식으로 초대형 탄산음료, 사탕, 그리고 감자 칩으로 배를 가득 채우는 사람은 식단이 나쁜 것이다.

➡ 일반적인 믿음과 달리, 음식을 좋고 나쁨으로 정의하는 것은 (A) 적절하지 않고, 사실 건강에 좋은 식단이란 대체로 그 식단이 무엇으로 (B) 구성되는지에 의해 결정된다.

Why? 왜 정답일까?
첫 세 문장에서 음식을 절대적으로 좋고 나쁘다고 분류할 수는 없고(~ no foods can be labeled as either good or bad.), 그 조합이 중요하다(There are, however, combinations of foods that add up to a healthful or unhealthful diet.)고 말한다. 따라서 요약문의 빈칸 (A), (B)에 들어갈 말로 가장 적절한 것은 ② '(A) appropriate(적절한), (B) composed of(~로 구성되는)'이다.

- nearly ⓐⓓ 거의
- spoiled ⓐ 상한
- label A as B A를 B라고 분류하다
- add up to 결국 ~이 되다
- broccoli ⓝ 브로콜리
- nutrient-dense ⓐ 영양이 풍부한
- nutrient ⓝ 영양분
- otherwise ⓐⓓ 그렇지 않으면, 다른 경우에는
- off track 제 길에서 벗어난
- composed of ~로 구성된

- unless ⓒⓞⓝⓙ ~하지 않는 한
- poison mushroom 독버섯
- combination ⓝ 조합
- healthful ⓐ 건강에 좋은
- tofu ⓝ 두부
- a wide variety of 매우 다양한
- occasionally ⓐⓓ 가끔
- stay away from ~을 멀리하다
- load up on ~로 배를 가득 채우다

구문 풀이

2행 Unless we're talking about spoiled stew, poison mushrooms, or something
　　　　접속사(~하지 않는 한)
similar, however, no foods can be labeled as either good or bad.
　　　　　　　　　　　　　　「A+be labeled as+B : A가 B라고 분류되다」

★★ 문제 해결 꿀~팁 ★★

▶ 많이 틀린 이유는?
두 번째 문장에서 음식을 절대적으로 좋고 나쁘다고 분류할 수 없다고 언급하는 것으로 보아, 음식의 분류가 '부정확하지' 않다. 즉 '정확하다'는 의미를 완성하는 ①과 ⑤의 incorrect를 (A)에 넣기는 부적절하다.

▶ 문제 해결 방법은?
글 초반에 however가 두 번 연속해 등장하여 주제를 강조한다. Consider 이하는 이 주제에 대한 사례이므로 결론만 가볍게 확인하며 읽어도 충분하다.

41-42 농업 발전과 생활 변화

Early hunter-gatherer societies had (a) minimal structure.
초기 수렵 채집인 사회는 최소한의 구조만 가지고 있었다.

A chief or group of elders / usually led the camp or village.
추장이나 장로 그룹이 / 주로 캠프나 마을을 이끌었다.

Most of these leaders / had to hunt and gather / along with the other members / because the surpluses of food and other vital resources / were seldom (b) sufficient / to support a full-time chief or village council.
대부분의 이러한 지도자들은 / 사냥과 채집을 해야 했다. / 다른 구성원들과 함께 / 왜냐하면 식량과 기타 필수 자원의 잉여분이 / 충분한 경우가 드물었기 때문에 / 전임 추장이나 마을 의회를 지원할 만큼

『The development of agriculture changed work patterns.』 ◀41번의 근거
농업의 발전은 작업 패턴을 변화시켰다.

Early farmers could reap 3-10 kg of grain / from each 1 kg of seed planted.
초기 농부들은 3–10kg의 곡물을 수확할 수 있었다. / 심은 씨앗 1kg마다

Part of this food/energy surplus / was returned to the community / and (c) provided support for nonfarmers / such as chieftains, village councils, men who practice medicine, priests, and warriors.
이 식량/에너지 잉여분의 일부는 / 지역 사회에 환원되었고 / 비농민에 대한 지원을 제공했다. / 족장, 마을 의회, 의술가, 사제, 전사와 같은

『In return, / the nonfarmers provided leadership and security / for the farming population, / enabling it / to continue to increase food/energy yields / and provide ever larger surpluses.』 ◀42번의 근거
그 대가로, / 비농민들은 리더십과 안보를 제공하여, / 농업 인구에게 / 그들이 ~할 수 있게 하였다. / 식량/에너지 생산량을 지속적으로 늘리고 / 항상 더 많은 잉여를 제공할 수 있게

With improved technology and favorable conditions, / agriculture produced consistent surpluses of the basic necessities, / and population groups grew in size.
개선된 기술과 유리한 조건으로, / 농업은 기본 생필품의 지속적인 흑자를 창출했고, / 인구 집단은 규모가 커졌다.

These groups concentrated in towns and cities, / and human tasks (d) specialized further.
이러한 집단은 마을과 도시에 집중되었고, / 인간의 업무는 더욱 전문화되었다.

Specialists / such as carpenters, blacksmiths, merchants, traders, and sailors / developed their skills / and became more efficient / in their use of time and energy.
전문가들은 / 목수, 대장장이, 상인, 무역업자, 선원과 같은 / 기술을 계발하고 / 더 효율적이 되었다. / 자신의 시간과 에너지 사용 면에서

『The goods and services they provided / brought about / an (e) improved quality of life, / a higher standard of living, / and, for most societies, / increased stability.』 ◀41번의 근거
그들이 제공한 재화와 서비스는 / 가져왔다. / 삶의 질 향상 / 생활 수준 개선 / 그리고 대부분의 사회에서 / 안정성의 향상을

초기 수렵 채집인 사회는 (a) 최소한의 구조만 가지고 있었다. 추장이나 장로 그룹이 주로 캠프나 마을을 이끌었다. 식량과 기타 필수 자원의 잉여분이 전임 추장이나 마을 의회를 지원할 만큼 (b) 충분한 경우가 드물었기 때문에 대부분의 이러한 지도자들은 다른 구성원들과 함께 사냥과 채집을 해야 했다. 농업의 발전은 작업 패턴을 변화시켰다. 초기 농부들은 심은 씨앗 1kg마다 3–10kg의 곡물을 수확할 수 있었다. 이 식량/에너지 잉여분의 일부는 지역 사회에 환원되었고 족장, 마을 의회, 의술가, 사제, 전사와 같은 비농민에 대한 지원을 (c) 제한했다(→ 제공했다). 그 대가로, 비농민들은 농업 인구에게 리더십과 안보를 제공하여, 그들이 식량/에너지 생산량을 지속적으로 늘리고 항상 더 많은 잉여를 제공할 수 있게 하였다.

개선된 기술과 유리한 조건으로, 농업은 기본 생필품의 지속적인 흑자를 창출했고, 인구 집단은 규모가 커졌다. 이러한 집단은 마을과 도시에 집중되었고, 인간의 업무는 더욱 (d) 전문화되었다. 목수, 대장장이, 상인, 무역업자, 선원과 같은 전문가들은 기술을 계발하고 자신의 시간과 에너지 사용을 더 효율적으로 하게 되었다. 그들이 제공한 재화와 서비스로 인해 삶의 질 (e) 향상, 생활 수준 개선, 그리고 대부분의 사회에서 안정성의 향상을 가져왔다.

- hunter-gatherer ⓝ 수렵 채집인
- vital ⓐ 필수적인, 매우 중요한
- reap ⓥ (농작물을) 베어들이다
- practice medicine 의사로 개업하다, 의술을 행하다
- warrior ⓝ 전사
- yield ⓝ 수확량
- concentrate ⓥ 집중되다
- blacksmith ⓝ 대장장이
- bring about ~을 야기하다, 초래하다, 가져오다
- surplus ⓝ 잉여, 흑자
- sufficient ⓐ 충분한
- chieftain ⓝ 수령, 두목
- security ⓝ 안보
- basic necessity 기본 필수품
- carpenter ⓝ 목수
- sailor ⓝ 선원
- stability ⓝ 안정성

구문 풀이

20행 The goods and services [they provided] brought about an improved quality
주어 ———— 동사 ———— 목적어1
of life, a higher standard of living, and, for most societies, increased stability.
목적어2 ———— 목적어3

41 제목 파악
정답률 61% | 정답 ①

윗글의 제목으로 가장 적절한 것은?

✔ ① How Agriculture Transformed Human Society
농업은 어떻게 인간 사회를 바꿨나
② The Dark Shadow of Agriculture: Repetition
농업의 어두운 그늘: 반복
③ How Can We Share Extra Food with the Poor?
우리는 가난한 사람들과 남은 음식을 어떻게 나눌 수 있을까?
④ Why Were Early Societies Destroyed by Agriculture?
왜 초기 사회는 농업으로 파괴되었나?
⑤ The Advantages of Large Groups Over Small Groups in Farming
농업에 있어 대규모 집단이 소규모 집단보다 유리한 점

Why? 왜 정답일까?

농업 이전 사회에서는 비교적 단순했던 사회 구조가 농업 이후에 어떻게 변화했는지 설명하는 내용이다. 우선 작업의 패턴이 변하고(The development of agriculture changed work patterns.), 잉여 생산물이 늘어남에 따라 사회 규모도 바뀌면서 삶의 질도 향상되었다(~ an improved quality of life, a higher standard of living, and, for most societies, increased stability.)는 설명이 주를 이룬다. 따라서 글의 제목으로 가장 적절한 것은 ① '농업은 어떻게 인간 사회를 바꿨나'이다.

42 어휘 추론
정답률 58% | 정답 ③

밑줄 친 (a) ~ (e) 중에서 문맥상 낱말의 쓰임이 적절하지 않은 것은? [3점]
① (a) ② (b) ✔ ③ (c) ④ (d) ⑤ (e)

Why? 왜 정답일까?

In return 앞뒤는 농민이 비농민에게 무언가를 해준 '보답으로' 비농민 또한 농민에게 안보를 제공하여 생산에 집중하게 했다는 내용이다. 즉 (c)는 농민의 잉여 생산물이 비농민에 대한 지원을 '제공하는 데' 쓰였다는 의미일 것이므로, limited 대신 provided를 써야 자연스럽다. 따라서 문맥상 낱말의 쓰임이 적절하지 않은 것은 ③ '(c)'이다.

43-45 모르는 노인의 임종을 지킨 군인

(A)

A nurse took a tired, anxious soldier to the bedside.
한 간호사가 피곤하고 불안해하는 군인을 침대 곁으로 데려갔다.

"Jack, your son is here," / the nurse said to an old man / lying on the bed.
"Jack, 당신 아들이 왔어요."라고 / 간호사가 노인에게 말했다. / 침대에 누워있는

She had to repeat the words several times / before the old man's eyes opened.
그녀는 그 말을 여러 번 반복해야 했다. / 그 노인이 눈을 뜨기 전에

『Suffering from the severe pain / because of heart disease, / he barely saw the young uniformed soldier / standing next to him.』 ◀45번 ①의 근거 일치
극심한 고통을 겪고 있던 / 심장병 때문에 / 그는 제복을 입은 젊은 군인을 간신히 보았다. / 자기 옆에 서 있는

(a) He reached out his hand to the soldier.
그는 손을 그 군인에게 뻗었다.

(D)

The soldier gently wrapped his fingers / around the weak hand of the old man.
그 군인은 부드럽게 자기 손가락을 감쌌다. / 노인의 병약한 손 주위로

『The nurse brought a chair / so that the soldier could sit beside the bed.』 ◀45번 ④의 근거 일치
간호사는 의자를 가져왔다. / 군인이 침대 옆에 앉을 수 있도록

All through the night / the young soldier sat there, / holding the old man's hand / and offering (e) him words of support and comfort.
밤새 / 젊은 군인은 거기에 앉아, / 노인의 손을 잡고 / 그에게 지지와 위로의 말을 건넸다.

『Occasionally, / she suggested / that the soldier take a rest for a while.
가끔, / 그녀는 제안했다. / 군인에게 잠시 쉬라고

He politely said no.』 ◀45번 ⑤의 근거 일치
그는 정중하게 거절했다.

(B)

Whenever the nurse came into the room, / she heard the soldier say a few gentle words.
간호사가 병실에 들어올 때마다, / 그녀는 그 군인이 상냥한 말을 하는 것을 들었다.

The old man said nothing, / only held tightly to (b) him all through the night.
노인은 아무 말도 하지 않았다. / 밤새도록 그에게 손만 꼭 잡힌 채로

Just before dawn, / the old man died.
동트기 직전에, / 그 노인은 죽었다.

『The soldier released the old man's hand / and left the room to find the nurse.』 ◀45번 ②의 근거 일치
그 군인은 노인의 손을 놓고 / 간호사를 찾기 위해 병실을 나갔다.

After she was told what happened, / she went back to the room with him.
그녀가 무슨 일이 있었는지 들은 후, / 그녀는 그와 함께 병실로 돌아갔다.

The soldier hesitated for a while and asked, / "Who was this man?"
군인은 잠시 머뭇거리고는 물었다. / "그분은 누구였나요?"라고

(C)

She was surprised and asked, / "Wasn't he your father?"
그녀는 깜짝 놀라서 물었다. / "그가 당신의 아버지가 아니었나요?"라고

『"No, he wasn't. / I've never met him before," / the soldier replied.』 ◀45번 ③의 근거 불일치
"아니요. 저는 그분을 이전에 만난 적이 없어요."라고 / 군인이 대답했다.

She asked, / "Then why didn't you say something / when I took you to (c) him?"
그녀는 물었다. / "그러면 당신은 왜 아무 말도 하지 않았나요? / 내가 당신을 그에게 안내했을 때"

He said, / "I knew there had been a mistake, / but when I realized / that he was too sick to tell / whether or not I was his son, / I could see how much (d) he needed me. / So, I stayed."
그가 말했다. / "저는 실수가 있었다는 것을 알았지만, / 제가 알게 되었을 때, / 그분이 너무도 위독해서 구별할 수 없다는 걸 / 제가 아들인지 아닌지 / 저는 그가 얼마나 저를 필요로 하는지 알 수 있었습니다. / 그래서 저는 머물렀습니다."

(A)

한 간호사가 피곤하고 불안해하는 군인을 침대 곁으로 데려갔다. "Jack, 당신 아들이 왔어요."라고 간호사가 침대에 누워있는 노인에게 말했다. 그 노인이 눈을 뜨기 전에 그녀는 그 말을 여러 번 반복해야 했다. 심장병 때문에 극심한 고통을 겪고 있던 그는 제복을 입은 젊은 군인이 자기 옆에 선 것을 간신히 보았다. (a) 그는 손을 그 군인에게 뻗었다.

(D)

그 군인은 노인의 병약한 손을 부드럽게 감쌌다. 간호사는 군인이 침대 옆에 앉을 수 있도록 의자를 가져왔다. 밤새 젊은 군인은 거기에 앉아, 노인의 손을 잡고 (e) 그에게 지지와 위로의 말을 건넸다. 가끔, 그녀는 군인에게 잠시 쉬라고 제안했다. 그는 정중하게 거절했다.

(B)

간호사가 병실에 들어올 때마다, 그녀는 그 군인이 상냥한 말을 하는 것을 들었다. 밤새도록 (b) 그에게 손만 꼭 잡힌 채로 노인은 아무 말도 하지 않았다. 동트기 직전에, 그 노인은 죽었다. 그 군인은 노인의 손을 놓고 간호사를 찾기 위해 병실을 나갔다. 그녀가 무슨 일이 있었는지 들은 후, 그녀는 그와 함께 병실로 돌아갔다. 군인은 잠시 머뭇거리고는 "그분은 누구였나요?"라고 물었다.

(C)

그녀는 깜짝 놀라서 물었다. "그가 당신의 아버지가 아니었나요?" "아니요. 저는 그분을 이전에 만난 적이 없어요."라고 군인이 대답했다. 그녀는 물었다. "그러면 내가 당신을 (c) 그에게 안내했을 때 왜 아무 말도 하지 않았나요?" 그가 말했다. "저는 실수가 있었다는 것을 알았지만, 그분이 너무도 위독해서 제가 아들인지 아닌지 구별할 수 없다는 걸 알게 되었을 때, 저는 (d) 그가 얼마나 저를 필요로 하는지 알 수 있었습니다. 그래서 저는 머물렀습니다."

- severe ⓐ 극심한
- reach out one's hand 손을 뻗다
- hesitate ⓥ 주저하다
- barely ⓐⓓ 간신히 ~하다, 거의 못 ~하다
- dawn ⓝ 새벽

(A) 4행 Suffering from the severe pain because of heart disease, he barely saw
분사구문　　　　전치사(~ 때문에)　　　　지각동사
the young uniformed soldier standing next to him.
목적어　　　　　현재분사

(D) 2행 The nurse brought a chair so that the soldier could sit beside the bed.
접속사(~하도록)

---

43 | 글의 순서 파악 | 정답률 77% | 정답 ④

주어진 글 (A)에 이어질 내용을 순서에 맞게 배열한 것으로 가장 적절한 것은?

① (B) – (D) – (C)
② (C) – (B) – (D)
③ (C) – (D) – (B)
✔④ (D) – (B) – (C)
⑤ (D) – (C) – (B)

Why? 왜 정답일까?

간호사가 한 군인을 임종이 임박한 노인에게 데려갔다는 내용의 (A) 뒤로, 군인이 노인 곁에 밤새 있었다는 내용의 (D), 마침내 노인이 임종한 뒤 군인이 그 노인이 누구였는지 물었다는 내용의 (B), 간호사가 놀라서 왜 노인 곁에 있었는지 묻고 군인이 답했다는 내용의 (C)가 순서대로 이어져야 자연스럽다. 따라서 글의 순서로 가장 적절한 것은 ④ '(D) – (B) – (C)'이다.

---

44 | 지칭 추론 | 정답률 64% | 정답 ②

밑줄 친 (a) ~ (e) 중에서 가리키는 대상이 나머지 넷과 다른 것은?

① (a)　✔② (b)　③ (c)　④ (d)　⑤ (e)

Why? 왜 정답일까?

(a), (c), (d), (e)는 the old man, (b)는 the soldier를 가리키므로, (a) ~ (e) 중에서 가리키는 대상이 다른 하나는 ② '(b)'이다.

---

45 | 세부 내용 파악 | 정답률 75% | 정답 ③

윗글에 관한 내용으로 적절하지 않은 것은?

① 노인은 심장병으로 극심한 고통을 겪고 있었다.
② 군인은 간호사를 찾기 위해 병실을 나갔다.
✔③ 군인은 노인과 이전에 만난 적이 있다고 말했다.
④ 간호사는 군인이 앉을 수 있도록 의자를 가져왔다.
⑤ 군인은 잠시 쉬라는 간호사의 제안을 정중히 거절하였다.

Why? 왜 정답일까?

(C) "No, he wasn't. I've never met him before."에서 군인은 노인을 만난 적이 없다고 말하므로, 내용과 일치하지 않는 것은 ③ '군인은 노인과 이전에 만난 적이 있다고 말했다.'이다.

Why? 왜 오답일까?

① (A) 'Suffering from the severe pain because of heart disease, ~'의 내용과 일치한다.
② (B) 'The soldier ~ left the room to find the nurse.'의 내용과 일치한다.
④ (D) 'The nurse brought a chair so that the soldier could sit beside the bed.'의 내용과 일치한다.
⑤ (D) 'Occasionally, she suggested that the soldier take a rest for a while. He politely said no.'의 내용과 일치한다.

어휘 Review Test 09

문제편 096쪽

A	B	C	D
01 명상	01 familiar	01 ⓗ	01 ⑨
02 불안한	02 possess	02 ⓞ	02 ①
03 가능성, 확률	03 productivity	03 ①	03 ⨍
04 ~보다 우월한	04 experienced	04 ⓢ	04 ⓡ
05 허구의	05 unpaid	05 ⓠ	05 ⓓ
06 지위	06 decline	06 ⓝ	06 ⓚ
07 지속적으로	07 award	07 ⓚ	07 ⓐ
08 도움을 요청하다	08 hire	08 ⓓ	08 ⓑ
09 능력, 재능	09 state	09 ⓔ	09 ⓟ
10 나타나다, 생겨나다	10 emphasize	10 ①	10 ⓜ
11 응시하다	11 curiosity	11 ⓟ	11 ⓢ
12 잉여, 흑자	12 barely	12 ①	12 ⓒ
13 주저하다	13 vital	13 ①	13 ⓓ
14 지속하다, 참다	14 stability	14 ⓜ	14 ⓞ
15 지역	15 contribution	15 ⓐ	15 ①
16 특유의, 독특한, 뚜렷한	16 embarrassed	16 ⓑ	16 ①
17 현상	17 considerable	17 ⓒ	17 ⓔ
18 바람직한	18 composed of	18 ⓖ	18 ①
19 추구하다	19 unless	19 ⓡ	19 ⓝ
20 주의 산만, 정신을 흩뜨리는 것	20 reflect	20 ①	20 ⓗ

10회 | 2022학년도 6월 학력평가 | 고1
| 정답과 해설 |

• 정답 •

01 ② 02 ① 03 ⑤ 04 ⑤ 05 ① 06 ③ 07 ① 08 ⑤ 09 ⑤ 10 ④ 11 ① 12 ③ 13 ③ 14 ④ 15 ④
16 ② 17 ③ 18 ② 19 ② 20 ⑤ 21 ③ 22 ① 23 ② 24 ① 25 ⑤ 26 ③ 27 ④ 28 ② 29 ④ 30 ②
31 ★ 32 ③ 33 ③ 34 ③ 35 ④ 36 ③ 37 ⑤ 38 ④ 39 ★ 40 ③ 41 ① 42 ④ 43 ④ 44 ② 45 ④

★ 표기된 문항은 [등급을 가르는 문제]에 해당하는 문항입니다.

---

01 | 건물 벽 페인트 작업 공지 | 정답률 97% | 정답 ②

다음을 듣고, 남자가 하는 말의 목적으로 가장 적절한 것을 고르시오.

① 사생활 보호의 중요성을 강조하려고
✔② 건물 벽 페인트 작업을 공지하려고
③ 회사 근무시간 변경을 안내하려고
④ 새로운 직원 채용을 공고하려고
⑤ 친환경 제품 출시를 홍보하려고

M : Good afternoon, this is the building manager, Richard Carson.
안녕하세요, 건물 관리인인 Richard Carson입니다.
We are planning to have the walls painted on our building next week.
다음 주에 우리 건물 벽에 페인트를 칠할 계획입니다.
The working hours will be from 9 a.m. to 6 p.m.
작업 시간은 오전 9시부터 오후 6시로 예정되어 있습니다.
Don't be surprised to see workers outside your windows.
창문 밖으로 작업자들을 보고 놀라지 마세요.
Please keep your windows closed while they are painting.
그들이 칠하는 동안, 창문을 닫고 계시기 바랍니다.
There might be some smell from the paint.
페인트 냄새가 조금 날 수도 있습니다.
But don't worry. It is totally safe and eco-friendly.
하지만 걱정 마세요. 완전히 안전하고 친환경입니다.
Sorry for any inconvenience and thank you for your cooperation.
불편을 끼쳐 사과드리고 협조에 감사합니다.

Why? 왜 정답일까?

건물 벽 페인트 작업이 예정되어 있다(We are planning to have the walls painted on our building next week.)는 내용으로 보아, 남자가 하는 말의 목적으로 가장 적절한 것은 ② '건물 벽 페인트 작업을 공지하려고'이다.

● eco-friendly ⓐ 친환경적인　　● cooperation ⓝ 협조

---

02 | 속도 제한 준수 | 정답률 96% | 정답 ①

대화를 듣고, 여자의 의견으로 가장 적절한 것을 고르시오.

✔① 운전자는 제한 속도를 지켜야 한다.
② 교통경찰을 더 많이 배치해야 한다.
③ 보행자의 부주의가 교통사고를 유발한다.
④ 교통사고를 목격하면 즉시 신고해야 한다.
⑤ 대중교통을 이용하면 이동시간을 줄일 수 있다.

M : Hello, Veronica.
안녕, Veronica.
W : Hi, Jason. I heard that you are trying to get a driver's license these days. How is it going?
안녕, Jason. 나 네가 요새 운전 면허를 따려고 한다고 들었어. 어떻게 돼 가?
M : You know what? I already got it. Look!
있잖아, 이미 땄어. 이거 봐!
W : Oh, good for you! How was the driving test?
오, 잘됐네! 운전 시험은 어땠어?
M : Well, while taking the driving test, I was very nervous because some people were driving so fast.
음, 운전 시험을 보는 동안, 몇몇 사람들이 너무 빨리 달려서 난 아주 긴장했어.
W : But there are speed limit signs everywhere.
그치만 모든 곳에 속도 제한 표시가 있잖아.
M : Right, there are. But so many drivers ignore speed limits these days.
맞아, 있지. 하지만 요새 속도 제한을 무시하는 사람들이 너무 많아.
W : That's terrible. Those drivers could cause serious car accidents.
끔찍해. 그런 운전자들은 심각한 교통사고를 낼 수도 있어.
M : That's true. Driving too fast can be dangerous for everybody.
맞아. 너무 빨리 운전하는 건 모두에게 위험할 수 있어.
W : Exactly. In my opinion, all drivers should follow the speed limits.
바로 그 말이야. 내 생각에, 모든 운전자들은 속도 제한을 지켜야 해.
M : I totally agree with you.
네 말에 전적으로 동의해.

Why? 왜 정답일까?

모든 운전자들은 제한 속도를 따라야 한다(In my opinion, all drivers should follow the speed limits.)는 여자의 말로 보아, 여자의 의견으로 가장 적절한 것은 ① '운전자는 제한 속도를 지켜야 한다.'이다.

● get a driver's license 운전 면허를 따다　　● speed limit 속도 제한
● follow ⓥ 지키다, 따르다

---

03 | 숙제를 위해 책 빌리기 | 정답률 96% | 정답 ⑤

대화를 듣고, 두 사람의 관계를 가장 잘 나타낸 것을 고르시오.

① 작가 – 출판사 직원 　　　　② 관람객 – 박물관 해설사
③ 손님 – 주방장 　　　　　　④ 탑승객 – 항공 승무원
✔ 학생 – 사서

W : Excuse me. Can you help me find some books for my homework?
실례합니다. 제가 숙제에 필요한 책을 좀 찾게 도와주실래요?
M : Sure. What is your homework about?
물론이죠. 어떤 숙제인가요?
W : It's for my history class. The topic is the relationship between France and Germany.
역사 수업 숙제고요. 주제는 프랑스와 독일의 관계예요.
M : What about this world history book?
이 세계사 책은 어때요?
W : It looks good. Do you have any other books?
괜찮아 보여요. 다른 책도 있나요?
M : I can also recommend this European history book.
이 유럽사 책도 추천해 드릴게요.
W : Great. How many books can I borrow at a time?
좋아요. 제가 한 번에 책을 몇 권 빌릴 수 있나요?
M : You can borrow up to four books for three weeks each.
한 권당 3주 동안 네 권까지 빌릴 수 있어요.
W : Okay. I'll take these two books, then.
알겠습니다. 그럼 이 두 권을 빌릴게요.
M : All right. [Beep sound] Don't forget to return them on time.
알겠습니다. [삐 소리] 제때 반납하는 것 잊지 마세요.

Why? 왜 정답일까?

'Can you help me find some books for my homework?', 'You can borrow up to four books for three weeks each.' 등에서 여자는 숙제에 참고할 책을 찾는 학생이고, 남자는 도서관 사서임을 알 수 있으므로, 두 사람의 관계로 가장 적절한 것은 ⑤ '학생 – 사서'이다.

● up to ~까지　　　　　　　● return ⓥ 반납하다
● on time 제때

04　아이 방 구경하기　　　정답률 85% | 정답 ⑤

대화를 듣고, 그림에서 대화의 내용과 일치하지 않는 것을 고르시오.

M : Honey, come to Lucy's room. Look at what I did for her.
여보, Lucy 방에 좀 와 봐요. 내가 아이를 위해 해놓은 것 좀 봐요.
W : It looks great. 「Is that a toy bear on the bed?」 ①의 근거 일치
근사해 보이네요. 침대 위에 있는 저건 곰 인형이에요?
M : Yes. That's right. She can sleep with the toy bear.
네, 맞아요. 아이는 곰 인형과 함께 잠들 수 있어요.
W : It's cute. 「Oh, and I like the round clock on the wall.」 ②의 근거 일치
귀여워요. 오, 그리고 벽에 걸린 동그란 시계가 마음에 드네요.
M : The round clock goes well with the room, doesn't it? 「How do you like the family picture next to the window?」 ③의 근거 일치
동그란 시계가 방에 잘 어울려요. 그렇죠? 창문 옆에 있는 가족사진은 어때요?
W : That's so sweet. 「I also love the striped curtains on the window.」 ④의 근거 일치
정말 보기 좋아요. 창문에 걸린 줄무늬 커튼도 마음에 들어요.
M : I'm happy you like them. 「What do you think of the star-shaped rug on the floor?」 ⑤의 근거 불일치
당신이 좋아해주니 기뻐요. 바닥에 깔린 별 모양 깔개는 어때요?
W : It is lovely. Lucy will feel safe and warm on the rug.
귀여워요. Lucy가 깔개 위에서 안전하고 따뜻한 기분을 느낄 거예요.
M : Looks like everything's prepared.
모든 게 준비된 것 같네요.
W : Thanks, honey. You've done a great job.
고마워요, 여보. 정말 잘했어요.

Why? 왜 정답일까?

대화에서는 바닥에 별 모양 깔개가 있다(What do you think of the star-shaped rug on the floor?)고 하는데, 그림의 깔개는 동그란 모양이다. 따라서 그림에서 대화의 내용과 일치하지 않는 것은 ⑤이다.

● toy bear 곰 인형　　　　　● round ⓐ 원형의
● go well with ~와 잘 어울리다　　● How do you like ~? ~이 어때요?
● What do you think of ~? ~을 어떻게 생각해요?

05　영화 약속 전에 보고서 내기　　　정답률 95% | 정답 ①

대화를 듣고, 남자가 할 일로 가장 적절한 것을 고르시오.

✔ 보고서 제출하기 　　　　② 티켓 예매하기
③ 자전거 수리하기 　　　　④ 축구 연습하기
⑤ 팝콘 구입하기

W : David, did you fix your bicycle yesterday?
David, 너 어제 네 자전거 고쳤어?

M : Yes. Luckily, I was able to fix it by myself. How was your soccer practice, Christine?
응. 다행히도 나 혼자 고칠 수 있었어. 너 축구 연습은 어땠어, Christine?
W : A new coach came to our soccer club and we practiced very hard.
우리 축구 동아리에 새로운 코치님이 와서 우린 아주 열심히 연습했어.
M : You must be so tired. Do you still want to see a movie this afternoon?
되게 피곤하겠네. 그래도 오늘 오후에 영화 보러 가는 건 괜찮겠어?
W : Of course, I booked the tickets two weeks ago.
물론이지, 난 표를 2주 전에 예매한걸.
M : All right. Let's get going.
알겠어. 같이 가자.
W : Wait, did you email your science report to Mr. Smith? It's due today.
잠깐만, 너 Smith 선생님께 이메일로 과학 보고서 냈어? 오늘이 마감이야.
M : [Pause] Oh, no! I finished it but forgot to send it. What should I do?
[잠시 멈춤] 오, 이런! 나 그거 끝냈는데 보내는 걸 깜빡했어. 어떻게 해야 하지?
W : Why don't you send it before meeting me at the movie theater?
나랑 영화관에서 만나기 전에 그걸 보내 놓는 게 어때?
M : Good idea. I'll go home quickly and send the report, but can you buy some popcorn for me before I get there?
좋은 생각이야, 빨리 집으로 가서 보고서 낼게. 근데 내가 도착하기 전에 네가 팝콘 좀 사 놓을 수 있어?
W : No problem. See you there.
문제 없지, 거기서 봐.

Why? 왜 정답일까?

남자는 과학 보고서를 다 작성했지만 제출하는 것을 깜빡 잊어서, 여자를 영화관에서 만나기 전에 보고서를 메일로 제출하고 오겠다(I'll go home quickly and send the report, ~)고 하므로, 남자가 할 일로 가장 적절한 것은 ① '보고서 제출하기'이다.

● fix ⓥ 고치다　　　　　● due ⓐ 기한인, ~하기로 되어 있는

06　놀이공원 표 사기　　　정답률 85% | 정답 ③

대화를 듣고, 여자가 지불할 금액을 고르시오. [3점]
① $40　② $60　✔ $80　④ $100　⑤ $120

M : Good morning. Welcome to Happy Land.
안녕하세요. Happy Land에 잘 오셨습니다.
W : Hello. I'd like to buy some tickets. How much are they?
안녕하세요. 전 표를 좀 사고 싶어요. 얼마인가요?
M : $20 for the amusement park and $10 for the water park. How many tickets do you need?
놀이공원 표는 20달러이고, 워터파크 표는 10달러입니다. 표가 몇 장 필요하신가요?
W : We're five people in total, and we only want to go to the amusement park.
저희는 총 다섯 명이고, 놀이공원만 가고 싶어요.
M : Okay. Do you have any discount coupons?
알겠습니다. 할인 쿠폰 가지고 계신가요?
W : I printed out a birthday coupon from your website. It's my birthday today.
웹 사이트에서 생일 쿠폰을 출력해 왔어요. 오늘 제 생일이거든요.
M : It's your birthday? Just let me check your ID, please.
생일이세요? 그럼 신분증만 확인할게요.
W : Here you are.
여기 있어요.
M : Oh, happy birthday! With your birthday coupon, your ticket is free.
오, 생일 축하드립니다! 생일 쿠폰이 있으면 본인 표는 무료예요.
W : That's great. Please give me five tickets including my ticket.
잘됐네요. 제 거 포함해서 표 다섯 장 주세요.
M : Let me see. That'll be four people at the original price, and one person with a birthday coupon.
확인하겠습니다. 네 분은 정가이고, 한 분은 생일 쿠폰이 있으시고요.
W : Right. Here is my credit card.
맞아요. 여기 제 신용 카드요.

Why? 왜 정답일까?

대화에 따르면 여자는 일행 넷과 함께 놀이공원에 입장하려 하는데, 여자 본인은 생일 쿠폰이 있어 표 값을 내지 않아도 된다. 놀이공원 표는 1인당 20달러이므로, 여자가 지불할 금액은 4인 표의 정가인 ③ '$80'이다.

● amusement park 놀이공원　　● print out ~을 출력하다
● original price 정가

07　음식 부스에 갈 수 없는 이유　　　정답률 97% | 정답 ①

대화를 듣고, 남자가 음식 부스에 갈 수 없는 이유로 가장 적절한 것을 고르시오.

✔ 밴드 오디션 연습을 해야 해서
② 보드게임 부스를 설치해야 해서
③ 영어 프로젝트를 끝내야 해서
④ 샌드위치를 준비해야 해서
⑤ 친구를 만나러 가야 해서

W : Hi, Alex. How is it going?
안녕, Alex. 잘 지내니?
M : I'm good. Thanks. I've just finished my English project. How about you, Tracy?
잘 지내. 고마워. 영어 프로젝트를 막 끝낸 참이야. 넌 어때, Tracy?
W : I'm a little busy preparing for my food booth.
난 음식 부스를 준비하느라 약간 바빠.
M : A food booth? What for?
음식 부스? 뭐 때문에?
W : My school festival is next Tuesday. I'm running a food booth that day.
우리 학교 축제가 다음 주 화요일이야. 난 그날 음식 부스를 운영해.
M : That is so cool. What is on the menu?
근사하네. 메뉴가 뭐야?
W : We're making sandwiches. You should come.
우린 샌드위치를 만들 거야. 너도 와.
M : I'd love to, but I can't.
나도 가고 싶은데 그럴 수가 없네.

W : You can't? I was really looking forward to seeing you at my school.
못 온다고? 난 우리 학교에서 널 만나길 고대했는데.

M : I'm terribly sorry. I have to practice for a band audition.
진짜 미안해. 난 밴드 오디션을 위해 연습해야 해.

W : Oh, I see. Well, good luck with your audition.
오, 그렇구나. 그럼, 오디션에 행운을 빌어줄게.

M : Thank you.
고마워.

Why? 왜 정답일까?

남자는 밴드 오디션 연습 때문에(I have to practice for a band audition.) 여자가 학교 축제 때 운영하는 음식 부스에 가볼 수 없다고 하므로, 남자가 음식 부스에 갈 수 없는 이유로 가장 적절한 것은 ① '밴드 오디션 연습을 해야 해서'이다.

- be busy ~ing ~하느라 바쁘다
- look forward to ~을 고대하다
- run ⓥ 운영하다
- terribly [ad] 너무, 대단히

---

08 스페인 문화 수업 정답률 97% | 정답 ⑤

대화를 듣고, Spanish culture class에 관해 언급되지 <u>않은</u> 것을 고르시오.

① 강사 ② 활동 종류 ③ 수업 요일
④ 준비물 ✓⑤ 수강료

[Telephone rings.]
[전화벨이 울린다.]

W : Hello, this is the World Culture Center. How can I help you?
안녕하세요, World Culture Center입니다. 무엇을 도와드릴까요?

M : Hi, I'm calling about a Spanish culture class for my teenage son.
안녕하세요, 전 제 십 대 아들을 위한 스페인 문화 수업 때문에 전화 드렸어요.

W : Okay. We have an interesting class for teenagers.
그러시군요. 저희는 십대 들을 위한 흥미로운 수업을 열고 있어요.

M : Great. 「Who teaches it?
좋아요. 강사가 누구인가요?

W : A Korean teacher and a native speaker teach it together.」 ①의근거 일치
한국인 선생님 한 분과 원어민 선생님 한 분이 함께 가르칩니다.

M : 「What kind of activities are there in the class?
수업에서 어떤 활동을 하나요?

W : Students can cook traditional foods, learn new words, and try on traditional clothing.」 ②의근거 일치
학생들은 전통 음식을 만들고, 새로운 단어를 배우고, 전통 복장도 체험해요.

M : 「On what day is the class?
수업이 무슨 요일에 있나요?

W : It's on Wednesday and Friday afternoons.」 ③의근거 일치
수요일과 금요일 오후입니다.

M : I see. 「Is there anything my son should prepare before the class?
그렇군요. 제 아들이 수업 전에 준비해야 할 게 있나요?

W : He just needs to bring a pen and a notebook.」 The center provides all the other class materials. ④의근거 일치
그냥 펜하고 공책만 지참하시면 돼요. 다른 수업 자료는 센터에서 다 제공합니다.

M : Perfect. Thanks for the information.
완벽해요. 정보 감사합니다.

Why? 왜 정답일까?

대화에서 남자와 여자는 Spanish culture class의 강사, 활동 종류, 수업 요일, 준비물을 언급하므로, 언급되지 않은 것은 ⑤ '수강료'이다.

Why? 왜 오답일까?

① 'A Korean teacher and a native speaker teach it together.'에서 '강사'가 언급되었다.
② 'Students can cook traditional foods, learn new words, and try on traditional clothing.'에서 '활동 종류'가 언급되었다.
③ 'It's on Wednesday and Friday afternoons.'에서 '수업 요일'이 언급되었다.
④ 'He just needs to bring a pen and a notebook.'에서 '준비물'이 언급되었다.

- native speaker 원어민
- try on ~을 입어보다
- traditional ⓐ 전통적인
- class material 수업 자료

---

09 벼룩시장 행사 안내 정답률 91% | 정답 ⑤

Summer Flea Market에 관한 다음 내용을 듣고, 일치하지 <u>않는</u> 것을 고르시오. [3점]

① 일주일 동안 진행된다.
② 학교 주차장에서 열린다.
③ 장난감, 양초와 같은 물품을 살 수 있다.
④ 상태가 좋은 중고 물품을 판매할 수 있다.
✓⑤ 첫날 방문하면 할인 쿠폰을 선물로 받는다.

W : Good afternoon, residents.
안녕하세요, 주민 여러분.

This is the head of the Pineville Community Center.
Pineville 주민센터장입니다.

「We're holding the Summer Flea Market for one week.」 ①의근거 일치
저희는 일주일 동안 Summer Flea Market을 개최할 예정입니다.

「It'll be held in the parking lot of Pineville Middle School.」 ②의근거 일치
이 행사는 Pineville 중학교 주차장에서 열립니다.

「You can get many different kinds of items such as toys and candles at reasonable prices.」 ③의근거 일치
장난감과 양초 같은 아주 다양한 종류의 물건을 합리적인 가격에 구매할 수 있습니다.

「You can also sell any of your own used items if they are in good condition.」
또한 여러분의 중고 물품이 상태가 좋다면 어떤 것이든 팔 수 있습니다.

「On the first day, every resident visiting the market will get a shopping bag as a gift.」 ⑤의근거 불일치
첫날에 장을 방문하는 모든 주민에게 쇼핑백을 선물로 드립니다.

For more information, please check out the community center's website.
더 많은 정보를 얻으시려면, 주민센터 웹 사이트를 확인해 주세요.

Why? 왜 정답일까?

'On the first day, every resident visiting the market will get a shopping bag as a gift.'에서 첫날 방문하는 주민 전원에게 선물로 쇼핑백을 준다고 하므로, 내용과 일치하지 않는 것은 ⑤ '첫날 방문하면 할인 쿠폰을 선물로 받는다.'이다.

Why? 왜 오답일까?

① 'We're holding the Summer Flea Market for one week.'의 내용과 일치한다.
② 'It'll be held in the parking lot of Pineville Middle School.'의 내용과 일치한다.
③ 'You can get many different kinds of items such as toys and candles at reasonable prices.'의 내용과 일치한다.
④ 'You can also sell any of your own used items if they are in good condition.'의 내용과 일치한다.

- flea market 벼룩시장
- reasonable ⓐ 합리적인, 적당한
- parking lot 주차장
- used item 중고품

---

10 운동화 사기 정답률 86% | 정답 ④

다음 표를 보면서 대화를 듣고, 여자가 구입할 운동화를 고르시오.

Sneakers

	Model	Price	Style	Waterproof	Color
①	A	$50	casual	×	black
②	B	$60	active	×	white
③	C	$65	casual	○	black
✓④	D	$70	casual	○	white
⑤	E	$85	active	○	white

W : Kyle, I'm looking for some sneakers. Can you help me find some good ones?
Kyle, 나 운동화를 찾고 있는데, 좋은 거 좀 찾게 도와줄래?

M : Of course. Let me see… *[Pause]* Look. These are the five best-selling ones.
물론이지. 어디 보자… [잠시 멈춤] 봐봐. 이게 제일 잘 나가는 제품 다섯 개네.

W : Wow, they all look so cool. It's hard to choose among them.
와, 다 근사해 보인다. 여기서 고르기 어려워.

M : 「Well, what's your budget?
음, 예산이 얼마야?

W : I don't want to spend more than 80 dollars.」 근거1 Price 조건
80달러 넘게 쓰고 싶지 않아.

M : All right. 「Which style do you want, active or casual?」 근거2 Style 조건
알겠어. 어떤 스타일이 좋아, 활동적인 거 아니면 캐주얼한 거?

W : I prefer casual ones.」 I think they match my clothes better.
캐주얼한 게 좋아. 그게 내 옷하고 잘 어울릴 거 같아.

M : Good. 「And I'd like to recommend waterproof shoes for rainy days.」 근거3 Waterproof 조건
그래. 그리고 난 비 오는 날을 대비해서 방수가 되는 신발을 추천하겠어.

W : Okay, I will take your advice.
그래, 네 충고를 따를게.

M : So you have two options left. 「Which color do you prefer?
그럼 선택권이 둘 남았어. 어떤 색을 선호해?

W : Most of my shoes are black, so I'll buy white ones this time.」 근거4 Color 조건
내 운동화가 대부분 검은색이라, 이번에는 흰색을 사겠어.

M : You made a good choice.
잘 골랐네.

Why? 왜 정답일까?

대화에 따르면 여자는 가격이 80달러를 넘지 않고, 캐주얼한 스타일에, 방수가 되고, 색이 흰색인 운동화를 골랐으므로, 여자가 구입할 운동화는 ④ 'D'이다.

- cool ⓐ 근사한, 멋진
- waterproof ⓐ 방수의
- make a choice 선택하다, 고르다
- match ⓥ 어울리다
- take an advice 충고를 따르다

---

11 서점 행사 광고 정답률 60% | 정답 ①

대화를 듣고, 여자의 마지막 말에 대한 남자의 응답으로 가장 적절한 것을 고르시오.

✓① All children's books are 20% off. – 모든 어린이 책이 20% 할인이래.
② It takes time to write a good article. – 좋은 기사를 쓰려면 시간이 걸리지.
③ I like to read action adventure books. – 난 액션 어드벤처 책을 읽는 걸 좋아해.
④ There are too many advertisements on TV. – TV에 광고가 너무 많이 나와.
⑤ The store has been closed since last month. – 그 매장은 지난 달부터 문을 닫았어.

W : Justin, what are you reading?
Justin, 뭐 읽고 있어?

M : An advertisement. There's a special event at Will's Bookstore downtown.
광고야. 시내에 있는 Will's Bookstore에서 특별 행사가 있대.

W : What kind of event is it?
무슨 행사야?

M : All children's books are 20% off.
모든 어린이 책이 20% 할인이래.

Why? 왜 정답일까?

서점 행사 광고를 읽고 있다는 남자에게 여자는 무슨 행사인지 물어보므로(What kind of event is it?), 남자의 응답으로 가장 적절한 것은 ① '모든 어린이 책이 20% 할인이래.'이다.

- advertisement ⓝ 광고
- article ⓝ 기사, 논문
- take time to ~하는 데 시간이 걸리다

---

12 걱정거리 묻기 정답률 85% | 정답 ③

대화를 듣고, 남자의 마지막 말에 대한 여자의 응답으로 가장 적절한 것을 고르시오.

① You're welcome. I'm happy to help you. – 천만에. 도와주게 돼 기뻐.
② That's not true. I made it with your help. – 그건 사실이 아냐. 네 도움이 있어 내가 해낸 거지.
✔ Okay. Good food always makes me feel better. – 그래. 맛있는 음식은 언제나 날 기분 좋게 해.
④ Really? You should definitely visit the theater later. – 정말? 그 영화관 나중에 꼭 가 봐.
⑤ Never mind. You'll do better on the next presentation. – 신경 쓰지 마. 다음 번 발표는 더 잘할 거야.

M : You look so worried. What's wrong, Liz?
  너 되게 걱정하는 거 같아 보이네. 무슨 일이야, Liz?
W : I didn't do well on my presentation yesterday.
  난 어제 발표를 잘하지 못했어.
M : Sorry about that. To help take your mind off of it, how about having a nice meal?
  안됐네. 생각을 떨쳐내기 위해서 맛있는 밥을 먹는 건 어때?
W : Okay. Good food always makes me feel better.
  그래. 맛있는 음식은 언제나 날 기분 좋게 해.

Why? 왜 정답일까?
발표를 잘하지 못해서 속상하다는 여자에게 남자는 기분 전환 겸 맛있는 것을 먹어보라고 제안하므로(To help take your mind off of it, how about having a nice meal?), 여자의 응답으로 가장 적절한 것은 ③ '그래. 맛있는 음식은 언제나 날 기분 좋게 해.'이다.

● do well on ~을 잘하다
● definitely [ad] 꼭, 반드시
● take one's mind off of ~의 생각을 떨쳐내다

13 방학 때 들을 수업 고르기 정답률 85% | 정답 ③

대화를 듣고, 여자의 마지막 말에 대한 남자의 응답으로 가장 적절한 것을 고르시오.
Man:
① I'm excited to buy a new guitar. – 난 새 기타를 살 생각에 신나.
② Summer vacation starts on Friday. – 여름방학은 금요일부터야.
✔ You can find it on the school website. – 학교 웹 사이트에서 볼 수 있어.
④ Let's go to the school festival together. – 학교 축제 같이 가자.
⑤ You can get some rest during the vacation. – 넌 방학 동안에 좀 쉴 수 있겠네.

M : Jenny, what class do you want to take this summer vacation?
  Jenny, 너 여름 방학 때 무슨 수업 듣고 싶어?
W : Well, [Pause] I'm thinking of the guitar class.
  음, [잠시 멈춤] 난 기타 수업을 생각 중이야.
M : Cool! I'm interested in playing the guitar, too.
  멋지다! 나도 기타 연주에 관심이 있어.
W : Really? It would be exciting if we took the class together.
  정말? 같이 수업 들으면 재밌겠다.
M : I know, but I am thinking of taking a math class instead. I didn't do well on the final exam.
  그러게. 그런데 난 대신 수학 수업을 들을까 해. 기말고사를 망쳤거든.
W : Oh, there is a math class? I didn't know that.
  오, 수학 수업이 있어? 몰랐네.
M : Yes. Mrs. Kim said she is offering a math class for first graders.
  응. Kim 선생님이 1학년을 대상으로 수학 수업을 열 거래.
W : That might be a good chance to improve my skills, too. Where can I check the schedule for the math class?
  내 수학 실력도 늘릴 수 있는 좋은 기회가 될지도 모르겠네. 수학 수업 시간표는 어디서 확인할 수 있어?
M : You can find it on the school website.
  학교 웹 사이트에서 볼 수 있어.

Why? 왜 정답일까?
방학 때 수학 수업이 열린다는 남자의 말에 여자는 수학 수업 시간표를 어디서 확인하면 되는지 물어보므로(Where can I check the schedule for the math class?), 남자의 응답으로 가장 적절한 것은 ③ '학교 웹 사이트에서 볼 수 있어.'이다.

● first grader 1학년생
● get rest 휴식을 취하다
● improve [v] 향상시키다

14 온라인 운동 수업 정답률 92% | 정답 ④

대화를 듣고, 남자의 마지막 말에 대한 여자의 응답으로 가장 적절한 것을 고르시오.
Woman:
① I agree. There are many benefits of exercising at the gym.
  동의해. 체육관에서 운동하면 이점이 많아.
② You're right. Not all exercise is helpful for your brain.
  네 말이 맞아. 모든 운동이 머리에 도움이 되는 건 아냐.
③ Don't worry. It's not too difficult for me to exercise.
  걱정하 마. 내가 운동하는 게 그렇게 어렵진 않아.
✔ That sounds great. Can I join the course, too?
  그거 괜찮다. 나도 거기 합류할 수 있나?
⑤ That's too bad. I hope you get well soon.
  안됐네. 빨리 낫길 바랄게.

M : Hi, Claire! How are you doing?
  안녕, Claire! 어떻게 지내?
W : I'm good. You're looking great!
  좋아. 너 멋져 보인다!
M : Thanks. I've been working out these days.
  고마워. 난 요새 운동하고 있어.
W : I need to start working out, too. What kind of exercise do you do?
  나도 운동을 시작해야 해. 무슨 운동 하고 있어?
M : I do yoga and some stretching at home.
  난 집에서 요가랑 스트레칭 좀 하고 있어.
W : At home? Do you exercise alone?
  집에서 한다고? 혼자 운동하는 거야?
M : Yes and no. I exercise online with other people.
  맞기도 하고 아니기도 해. 난 온라인에서 다른 사람들하고 운동해.
W : Exercising online with others? What do you mean by that?
  온라인에서 다른 사람들하고 운동을 한다고? 그게 무슨 의미야?

[문제편 p.098]

M : I'm taking an online fitness course. We work out together on the Internet every evening at 7.
  난 온라인 운동 수업을 듣고 있어. 우린 인터넷에서 매일 저녁 7시에 같이 운동해.
W : That sounds great. Can I join the course, too?
  그거 괜찮다. 나도 거기 합류할 수 있나?

Why? 왜 정답일까?
온라인 운동 수업을 통해 집에서 다른 사람들과 함께 운동하고 있다(I'm taking an online fitness course. We work out together on the Internet every evening at 7.)는 남자의 말에 대한 여자의 응답으로 가장 적절한 것은 ④ '그거 괜찮다. 나도 거기 합류할 수 있나?'이다.

● work out 운동하다
● get well (병 등이) 낫다
● benefit [n] 이점, 이득

15 선거 포스터 제작 부탁하기 정답률 83% | 정답 ④

다음 상황 설명을 듣고, Ted가 Monica에게 할 말로 가장 적절한 것을 고르시오. [3점]
Ted:
① Can I draw your club members on the poster? – 내가 포스터에 너희 동아리 회원들을 그려도 돼?
② Are you interested in joining my drawing club? – 너 우리 그림 동아리 드는 거 관심 있어?
③ Could you tell me how to vote in the election? – 선거 투표 방법을 알려줄 수 있니?
✔ Can you help me make posters for the election? – 내가 선거 포스터 만드는 거 도와줄래?
⑤ Would you run in the next school president election? – 너 다음 전교 회장 선거에 출마해줄래?

M : Ted is a high school student.
  Ted는 고등학생이다.
  He is planning to run for school president this year.
  그는 올해 전교 회장에 입후보할 계획이다.
  He really wants to win the election.
  그는 정말로 선거에서 이기고 싶다.
  He thinks using posters is an effective way to make a strong impression on his schoolmates.
  그는 포스터를 사용하는 것이 자기 학우들에게 강한 인상을 주는 데 효과적인 방법이라고 생각한다.
  But he is not good at drawing.
  하지만 그는 그림을 잘 그리지 못한다.
  His friend, Monica, is a member of a drawing club and she is good at drawing.
  그의 친구인 Monica는 그림 동아리 회원이고 그림을 잘 그린다.
  So, he wants to ask her to help him draw posters.
  그래서 그는 그녀에게 포스터 그리는 것을 도와달라고 청하고 싶다.
  In this situation, what would Ted most likely say to Monica?
  이 상황에서, Ted는 Monica에게 뭐라고 말할 것인가?
Ted : Can you help me make posters for the election?
  내가 선거 포스터 만드는 거 도와줄래?

Why? 왜 정답일까?
상황에 따르면 전교 회장 선거에 쓸 포스터를 만들려는 Ted는 본인이 그림을 잘 그리지 못해 친구 Monica에게 도와달라고 부탁하려 하므로(So, he wants to ask her to help him draw posters.), Ted가 Monica에게 할 말로 가장 적절한 것은 ④ '내가 선거 포스터 만드는 거 도와줄래?'이다.

● run for ~에 입후보하다
● election [n] 선거
● school president 전교 회장
● make an impression on ~에게 인상을 주다

16-17 건강한 아침 식사를 위한 식품 소개

W : Good morning, listeners.
  안녕하세요, 청취자 여러분.
  This is your host Rachel at the Morning Radio Show.
  Morning Radio Show의 진행자 Rachel입니다.
  What do you eat for breakfast?
  아침으로 뭘 드셨나요?
  「Today I will introduce a healthy breakfast food list.」 16번의 근거
  오늘 저는 건강한 아침 식사 음식 목록을 소개하려고 합니다.
  「Eggs are an excellent choice because they are high in protein.」 17번 ①의 근거 일치
  달걀은 단백질 함량이 높아서 탁월한 선택입니다.
  High-protein foods such as eggs provide energy for the brain.
  달걀 같은 고단백 음식은 뇌에 에너지를 공급해 주죠.
  「Cheese is another good option.」 17번 ②의 근거 일치
  치즈도 또 다른 좋은 선택입니다.
  It reduces hunger so it supports weight loss.
  이것은 배고픔을 줄여서 체중 감량을 도와주죠.
  「Yogurt is also great to eat in the morning.」 17번 ④의 근거 일치
  요거트도 아침에 먹기 아주 좋습니다.
  It contains probiotics that can improve digestion.
  여기에는 소화를 증진할 수 있는 프로바이오틱스가 들어 있습니다.
  「Eating berries such as blueberries or strawberries is another perfect way to start the morning.」 17번 ⑤의 근거 일치
  블루베리나 딸기 같은 베리를 먹는 것도 아침을 시작하는 데 완벽한 또 한 가지 방법입니다.
  They are lower in sugar than most other fruits, but higher in fiber.
  이것들은 대부분의 과일보다 당이 적지만, 섬유소는 더 많습니다.
  Add them to yogurt for a tasty breakfast.
  이것들을 요거트에 넣어 맛있는 아침을 만들어 보세요.
  Start every day with a healthy meal. Thank you.
  매일을 건강한 식사로 시작하세요. 고맙습니다.

● protein [n] 단백질
● digestion [n] 소화
● downside [n] 단점
● weight loss 체중 감량
● fiber [n] 섬유소

16 주제 파악 정답률 97% | 정답 ②

여자가 하는 말의 주제로 가장 적절한 것은?

① downsides of fatty food – 지방이 많은 식품의 단점
☑ healthy foods for breakfast – 아침 식사를 위한 건강 식품
③ ways to avoid eating snacks – 간식 섭취를 피하는 방법
④ easy foods to cook in 5 minutes – 5분만에 요리하기 쉬운 음식
⑤ the importance of a balanced diet – 균형 잡힌 식사의 중요성

Why? 왜 정답일까?

'Today I will introduce a healthy breakfast food list.'에서 여자는 아침에 먹기 좋은 건강 식품을 소개하겠다고 하므로, 여자가 하는 말의 주제로 가장 적절한 것은 ② '아침 식사를 위한 건강 식품'이다.

---

17 언급 유무 파악   정답률 94% | 정답 ③

언급된 음식이 아닌 것은?

① eggs – 달걀   ② cheese – 치즈   ☑ potatoes – 감자
④ yogurt – 요거트   ⑤ berries – 베리

Why? 왜 정답일까?

담화에서 여자는 아침에 먹기 좋은 건강식의 예로 달걀, 치즈, 요거트, 베리를 언급하므로, 언급되지 않은 것은 ③ '감자'이다.

Why? 왜 오답일까?

① 'Eggs are an excellent choice because they are high in protein.'에서 '달걀'이 언급되었다.
② 'Cheese is another good option.'에서 '치즈'가 언급되었다.
④ 'Yogurt is also great to eat in the morning.'에서 '요거트'가 언급되었다.
⑤ 'Eating berries is another perfect way to start the morning.'에서 '베리'가 언급되었다.

---

18 분실물 확인 요청   정답률 96% | 정답 ②

다음 글의 목적으로 가장 적절한 것은?

① 제품의 고장 원인을 문의하려고
☑ 분실물 발견 시 연락을 부탁하려고
③ 시설물의 철저한 관리를 당부하려고
④ 여행자 보험 가입 절차를 확인하려고
⑤ 분실물 센터 확장의 필요성을 건의하려고

Dear Boat Tour Manager,
보트투어 담당자께
On March 15, / my family was on one of your Glass Bottom Boat Tours.
3월 15일에 / 저희 가족은 귀사의 Glass Bottom Boat Tours 중 하나에 참여했습니다.
When we returned to our hotel, / I discovered that I left behind my cell phone case.
저희가 호텔에 돌아왔을 때, / 제가 휴대 전화 케이스를 놓고 왔다는 것을 발견했습니다.
The case must have fallen off my lap and onto the floor / when I took it off my phone to clean it.
제 무릎에서 케이스가 바닥으로 떨어졌던 것이 틀림없습니다. / 제가 케이스를 닦기 위해 휴대 전화에서 분리했을 때
I would like to ask you / to check if it is on your boat.
저는 당신에게 부탁드리고 싶습니다. / 그것이 보트에 있는지 확인해 주시길
Its color is black / and it has my name on the inside.
그것의 색깔은 검은색이며 / 안쪽에 제 이름이 있습니다.
If you find the case, / I would appreciate it if you would let me know.
만약 케이스가 발견된다면, / 저에게 알려주시면 감사하겠습니다.
Sincerely, // Sam Roberts
Sam Roberts 드림

보트 투어 담당자께

3월 15일에 저희 가족은 귀사의 Glass Bottom Boat Tours 중 하나에 참여했습니다. 호텔에 돌아왔을 때, 제가 휴대 전화 케이스를 놓고 왔다는 것을 발견했습니다. 케이스를 닦기 위해 휴대 전화에서 분리했을 때 케이스가 제 무릎에서 바닥으로 떨어졌던 것이 틀림없습니다. 그것이 보트에 있는지 확인해 주시길 부탁드립니다. 그것의 색깔은 검은색이며 안쪽에 제 이름이 있습니다. 만약 케이스가 발견된다면, 저에게 알려주시면 감사하겠습니다.

Sam Roberts 드림

Why? 왜 정답일까?

보트 투어 중 잃어버린 휴대 전화 케이스가 보트에 있는지 확인해줄 것을 부탁하는(I would like to ask you to check if it is on your boat.) 글이다. 따라서 글의 목적으로 가장 적절한 것은 ② '분실물 발견 시 연락을 부탁하려고'이다.

● leave behind ~을 남겨놓고 오다
● lap ⓝ 무릎
● fall ⓥ 떨어지다
● appreciate ⓥ 감사하다

구문 풀이

4행 The case must have fallen off my lap and onto the floor when I took it off
「must have+과거분사 : ~했음에 틀림없다」
my phone to clean it.
부사적 용법(~하기 위해)

---

19 공원에 놀러갔다가 얼마 못 놀고 돌아가게 된 Matthew   정답률 93% | 정답 ②

다음 글에 드러난 Matthew의 심경 변화로 가장 적절한 것은?

① embarrassed → indifferent   ☑ excited → disappointed
    당황한 → 무심한   신난 → 실망한
③ cheerful → ashamed   ④ nervous → touched
    즐거운 → 수치스러운   긴장한 → 감동한
⑤ scared → relaxed
    겁에 질린 → 느긋한

One Saturday morning, / Matthew's mother told Matthew / that she was going to take him to the park.
어느 토요일 아침, / Matthew의 어머니는 Matthew에게 말했다. / 자신이 그를 공원으로 데리고 가겠다고
A big smile came across his face.
그의 얼굴에 환한 미소가 드리워졌다.
As he loved to play outside, / he ate his breakfast and got dressed quickly / so they could go.
그가 밖에 나가서 노는 것을 좋아했기 때문에, / 그는 서둘러 아침을 먹고 옷을 입었다. / 그들이 나가기 위해
When they got to the park, / Matthew ran all the way over to the swing set.
그들이 공원에 도착했을 때, / Matthew는 그네를 향해 바로 뛰어갔다.
That was his favorite thing to do at the park.
그것은 그가 공원에서 가장 좋아하는 것이었다.
But the swings were all being used.
하지만 그네는 이미 모두 이용되고 있었다.
His mother explained / that he could use the slide / until a swing became available, / but it was broken.
그의 어머니는 말했지만, / 그가 미끄럼틀을 탈 수 있다고 / 그네를 이용할 수 있을 때까지 / 그것은 부서져 있었다.
Suddenly, his mother got a phone call / and she told Matthew they had to leave.
갑자기 그의 어머니가 전화를 받고 / 그녀는 Matthew에게 떠나야 한다고 말했다.
His heart sank.
그는 가슴이 내려앉았다.

어느 토요일 아침, Matthew의 어머니는 Matthew에게 공원으로 데리고 가겠다고 말했다. 그의 얼굴에 환한 미소가 드리워졌다. 그는 밖에 나가서 노는 것을 좋아했기 때문에, 나가기 위해 서둘러 아침을 먹고 옷을 입었다. 공원에 도착했을 때, Matthew는 그네를 향해 바로 뛰어갔다. 그것은 그가 공원에서 가장 좋아하는 것이었다. 하지만 그네는 이미 모두 이용되고 있었다. 그의 어머니는 그네를 이용할 수 있을 때까지 미끄럼틀을 탈 수 있다고 말했지만, 그것은 부서져 있었다. 갑자기 그의 어머니가 전화를 받고 Matthew에게 떠나야 한다고 말했다. 그는 가슴이 내려앉았다.

Why? 왜 정답일까?

아침에 어머니와 함께 공원으로 가게 되어 기뻐하던 Matthew가(A big smile came across his face.) 제대로 놀지도 못한 채 갑자기 떠나야 한다는 이야기를 듣고 실망했다(His heart sank.)는 내용의 글이다. 따라서 Matthew의 심경 변화로 가장 적절한 것은 ② '신난 → 실망한'이다.

● swing ⓝ 그네
● broken ⓐ 고장난, 부서진
● embarrassed ⓐ 당황한
● slide ⓝ 미끄럼틀
● sink ⓥ 가라앉다
● touched ⓐ 감동한

구문 풀이

3행 As he loved to play outside, he ate his breakfast and got dressed quickly
접속사(이유)   동사1   동사2
so (that) they could go.
접속사(목적 : ~하도록)

---

20 회의 안건을 사전에 작성해 공유하기   정답률 88% | 정답 ⑤

다음 글에서 필자가 주장하는 바로 가장 적절한 것은?

① 회의 결과는 빠짐없이 작성해서 공개해야 한다.
② 중요한 정보는 공식 회의를 통해 전달해야 한다.
③ 생산성 향상을 위해 정기적인 평가회가 필요하다.
④ 모든 참석자의 동의를 받아서 회의를 열어야 한다.
☑ 회의에서 다룰 사항은 미리 작성해서 공유해야 한다.

Meetings encourage creative thinking / and can give you ideas / that you may never have thought of on your own.
회의는 창의적 사고를 촉진하며 / 아이디어들을 당신에게 제공할 수 있다. / 당신이 혼자서는 절대 떠올리지 못할 만한
However, on average, / meeting participants consider / about one third of meeting time / to be unproductive.
그러나, 평균적으로, / 회의 참석자들은 여긴다. / 회의 시간의 대략 3분의 1 정도를 / 비생산적으로
But you can make your meetings / more productive and more useful / by preparing well in advance.
하지만 당신은 회의를 만들 수 있다. / 더 생산적이고 유용하게 / 사전에 잘 준비함으로써
You should create a list of items to be discussed / and share your list with other participants / before a meeting.
당신은 논의하게 될 사항들의 목록을 만들고 / 다른 회의 참석자들에게 공유해야 한다. / 회의 전에
It allows them / to know what to expect in your meeting / and prepare to participate.
그것은 참석자들이 ~하도록 만들어 준다. / 회의에서 무엇을 기대하는지를 알고 / 회의 참석을 준비할 수 있도록

회의는 창의적 사고를 촉진하며, 당신이 혼자서는 절대 떠올리지 못했을 만한 아이디어들을 당신에게 제공할 수 있다. 그러나, 평균적으로, 회의 참석자들은 회의 시간의 대략 3분의 1 정도를 비생산적으로 여긴다. 하지만 당신은 사전에 잘 준비함으로써 회의를 더 생산적이고 유용하게 만들 수 있다. 당신은 논의하게 될 사항들의 목록을 만들어 그 목록을 회의 전에 다른 회의 참석자들에게 공유해야 한다. 그것은 참석자들이 회의에서 무엇을 기대할지를 알고 회의 참석을 준비할 수 있도록 만들어 준다.

Why? 왜 정답일까?

'You should create a list of items to be discussed and share your list with other participants before a meeting.'에서 회의 전 논의 사항을 미리 작성해 공유하는 것이 좋다고 하므로, 필자가 주장하는 바로 가장 적절한 것은 ⑤ '회의에서 다룰 사항은 미리 작성해서 공유해야 한다.'이다.

● encourage ⓥ 촉진하다, 격려하다
● on average 평균적으로
● on one's own 혼자서, 스스로
● unproductive ⓐ 비생산적인

구문 풀이

7행 It allows them to know {what to expect in your meeting} and (to) prepare
동사   목적어   목적격 보어1   { } : 명사구(무엇을 ~할지)   목적격 보어2
to participate.

21 스트레스 관리의 원칙

정답률 80% | 정답 ③

밑줄 친 put the glass down이 다음 글에서 의미하는 바로 가장 적절한 것은? [3점]

① pour more water into the glass - 잔에 물을 더 부어야
② set a plan not to make mistakes - 실수하지 않기 위해 계획을 세워야
✓③ let go of the stress in your mind - 마음속에서 스트레스를 떨쳐내야
④ think about the cause of your stress - 스트레스의 원인을 생각해 보아야
⑤ learn to accept the opinions of others - 다른 사람들의 의견을 받아들이는 법을 배워야

A psychology professor raised a glass of water / while teaching stress management principles to her students, / and asked them, / "How heavy is this glass of water I'm holding?"
한 심리학 교수가 물이 든 유리잔을 들어 올리고 / 학생들에게 스트레스 관리 원칙을 가르치던 중 / 그들에게 물었다. / "제가 들고 있는 이 물 잔의 무게는 얼마나 될까요?"라고

Students shouted out various answers.
학생들은 다양한 대답을 외쳤다.

The professor replied, / "The absolute weight of this glass doesn't matter. / It depends on how long I hold it. / If I hold it for a minute, / it's quite light.
그 교수가 답했다. / "이 잔의 절대 무게는 중요하지 않습니다. / 이는 제가 이 잔을 얼마나 오래 들고 있느냐에 달려 있죠. / 만약 제가 이것을 1분 동안 들고 있다면, / 꽤 가볍죠.

But, if I hold it for a day straight, / it will cause severe pain in my arm, / forcing me to drop the glass to the floor.
하지만, 만약 제가 이것을 하루종일 들고 있다면 / 이것은 제 팔에 심각한 고통을 야기하고 / 잔을 바닥에 떨어뜨리게 할 것입니다.

In each case, / the weight of the glass is the same, / but the longer I hold it, / the heavier it feels to me."
각 사례에서, / 잔의 무게는 같지만, / 제가 오래 들고 있을수록 / 그것은 저에게 더 무겁게 느껴지죠."

As the class nodded their heads in agreement, / she continued, / "Your stresses in life are like this glass of water. / If you still feel the weight of yesterday's stress, / it's a strong sign / that it's time to put the glass down."
학생들은 동의하며 고개를 끄덕였고, / 교수는 이어 말했다. / "여러분이 인생에서 느끼는 스트레스들도 이 물 잔과 같습니다. / 만약 아직도 어제 받은 스트레스의 무게를 느낀다면, / 그것은 강한 신호입니다. / 잔을 내려놓아야 할 때라는"

한 심리학 교수가 학생들에게 스트레스 관리 원칙을 가르치던 중 물이 든 유리잔을 들어 올리고 "제가 들고 있는 이 물 잔의 무게는 얼마나 될까요?"라고 물었다. 학생들은 다양한 대답을 외쳤다. 그 교수가 답했다. "이 잔의 절대 무게는 중요하지 않습니다. 이는 제가 이 잔을 얼마나 오래 들고 있느냐에 달려 있죠. 만약 제가 이것을 1분 동안 들고 있다면, 꽤 가볍죠. 하지만, 만약 제가 이것을 하루종일 들고 있다면 이것은 제 팔에 심각한 고통을 야기하고 잔을 바닥에 떨어뜨릴 수밖에 없게 할 것입니다. 각 사례에서 잔의 무게는 같지만, 제가 오래 들고 있을수록 그것은 저에게 더 무겁게 느껴지죠." 학생들은 동의하며 고개를 끄덕였고, 교수는 이어 말했다. "여러분이 인생에서 느끼는 스트레스들도 이 물 잔과 같습니다. 만약 아직도 어제 받은 스트레스의 무게를 느낀다면, 그것은 잔을 내려놓아야 할 때라는 강한 신호입니다."

Why? 왜 정답일까?

물 잔의 무게를 느낄 때 중요한 것은 잔의 절대적 무게가 아니라 얼마나 오래 들고 있는지(It depends on how long I hold it.)이며, 같은 잔이라고 할지라도 더 오래 들고 있을수록 더 무겁게 느껴진다(the longer I hold it, the heavier it feels to me.)고 한다. 이를 스트레스 상황에 적용하면, 스트레스의 무게가 더 무겁게 느껴질수록 그 스트레스를 오래 안고 있었다는 뜻이므로 '스트레스를 떨쳐내기' 위해 노력해야 한다는 것을 알 수 있다. 따라서 밑줄 친 부분이 의미하는 바로 가장 적절한 것은 ③ '마음속에서 스트레스를 떨쳐내야'이다.

- **principle** ⓝ 원칙, 원리
- **nod** ⓥ 끄덕이다
- **put down** ~을 내려놓다
- **let go of** ~을 내려놓다, 버리다, 포기하다
- **severe** ⓐ 심각한
- **in agreement** 동의하며
- **pour** ⓥ 쏟다, 붓다

구문 풀이

6행 But, if I hold it for a day straight, it will cause severe pain in my arm,
접속사(조건) 동사(현재) 동사(미래)
forcing me to drop the glass to the floor.
분사구문(= and will force ~)

22 상황을 오해하게 하는 감정

정답률 82% | 정답 ①

다음 글의 요지로 가장 적절한 것은?

✓① 자신의 감정으로 인해 상황을 오해할 수 있다.
② 자신의 생각을 타인에게 강요해서는 안 된다.
③ 인간관계가 우리의 감정에 영향을 미친다.
④ 타인의 감정에 공감하는 자세가 필요하다.
⑤ 공동체를 위한 선택에는 보상이 따른다.

Your emotions deserve attention / and give you important pieces of information.
당신의 감정은 주목할 만하고 / 당신에게 중요한 정보를 준다.

However, / they can also sometimes be / an unreliable, inaccurate source of information.
그러나, / 감정은 또한 될 수도 있다. / 가끔 신뢰할 수 없고, 부정확한 정보의 원천이

You may feel a certain way, / but that does not mean / those feelings are reflections of the truth.
당신이 분명히 느낄지 모르지만, / 그것은 뜻하지는 않는다. / 그러한 감정들이 사실의 반영이라는 것을

You may feel sad / and conclude that your friend is angry with you / when her behavior simply reflects / that she's having a bad day.
당신은 슬플지도 모르고 / 그녀가 당신에게 화가 났다고 결론을 내릴지도 모른다. / 단지 친구의 행동이 나타낼 때에도, / 그 친구가 안 좋은 날을 보내고 있음을

You may feel depressed / and decide that you did poorly in an interview / when you did just fine.
당신은 기분이 우울할지도 모르고 / 자신이 면접에서 못했다고 판단할지도 모른다. / 자신이 잘했을 때도

Your feelings can mislead you into thinking things / that are not supported by facts.
당신의 감정은 당신을 속여 생각하게 할 수 있다. / 사실에 의해 뒷받침되지 않는 것들을

당신의 감정은 주목할 만하고 당신에게 중요한 정보를 준다. 그러나, 감정은 또한 가끔 신뢰

할 수 없고, 부정확한 정보의 원천이 될 수도 있다. 당신이 특정하게 느낄지 모르지만, 그것은 그러한 감정들이 사실의 반영이라는 뜻은 아니다. 친구의 행동이 단지 그 친구가 안 좋은 날을 보내고 있음을 나타낼 때에도, 당신이 슬퍼서 그녀가 당신에게 화가 났다고 결론을 내릴지도 모른다. 당신은 기분이 우울해서 면접에서 잘했을 때도 못했다고 판단할지도 모른다. 당신의 감정은 당신을 속여 사실에 의해 뒷받침되지 않는 것들을 생각하게 할 수 있다.

Why? 왜 정답일까?

'However, they can also sometimes be an unreliable, inaccurate source of information.'와 'Your feelings can mislead you into thinking things that are not supported by facts.'을 통해, 감정이 상황을 오해하게 하는 경우가 생길 수 있다는 중심 내용을 파악할 수 있으므로, 글의 요지로 가장 적절한 것은 ① '자신의 감정으로 인해 상황을 오해할 수 있다.'이다.

- **deserve** ⓥ ~을 받을 만하다
- **inaccurate** ⓐ 부정확한
- **reflection** ⓝ 반영
- **depressed** ⓐ 우울한
- **support** ⓥ 뒷받침하다, 지지하다
- **unreliable** ⓐ 믿을 만하지 않은
- **source of information** 정보 출처
- **conclude** ⓥ 결론 짓다
- **mislead A into B** A를 속여 B하게 하다

구문 풀이

8행 Your feelings can mislead you into thinking things [that are not supported by facts].
「mislead + A + into + B : A를 잘못 인도해 B하게 하다」 선행사 주격 관·대

23 아이들이 수학적 개념을 익혀 가는 방식

정답률 78% | 정답 ②

다음 글의 주제로 가장 적절한 것은?

① difficulties of children in learning how to count - 아이들이 수를 세는 법을 배우는 데 있어 어려움
✓② how children build mathematical understanding - 아이들은 수학적 이해를 어떻게 쌓아나가는가
③ why fingers are used in counting objects - 수를 셀 때 왜 손가락을 쓰는가
④ importance of early childhood education - 아동 조기 교육의 중요성
⑤ advantages of singing number songs - 숫자 노래 부르기의 이점

Every day, / children explore and construct relationships among objects.
매일, / 아이들은 사물 사이의 관계들을 탐구하고 구성한다.

Frequently, / these relationships focus on / how much or how many of something exists.
빈번히, / 이러한 관계들은 ~에 초점을 맞춘다. / 무언가가 얼마만큼 혹은 몇 개 존재하는지

Thus, / children count / — "One cookie, / two shoes, / three candles on the birthday cake, / four children in the sandbox."
따라서, / 아이들은 센다. / "쿠키 하나, / 신발 두 개, / 생일 케이크 위에 초 세 개, / 모래놀이 통에 아이 네 명."

Children compare / — "Which has more? Which has fewer? Will there be enough?"
아이들은 비교한다. / "무엇이 더 많지? 무엇이 더 적지? 충분할까?"

Children calculate / — "How many will fit? Now, I have five. I need one more."
아이들은 계산한다. / "몇 개가 알맞을까? 나는 지금 다섯 개가 있어. 하나 더 필요하네."

In all of these instances, / children are developing a notion of quantity.
이 모든 예시에서, / 아이들은 양의 개념을 발달시키는 중이다.

Children reveal and investigate mathematical concepts / through their own activities or experiences, / such as figuring out how many crackers to take at snack time / or sorting shells into piles.
아이들은 수학적 개념을 밝히고 연구한다. / 그들만의 활동이나 경험을 통해 / 간식 시간에 몇 개의 크래커를 가져갈지 알아내거나 / 조개껍질들을 더미로 분류하는 것과 같은

매일, 아이들은 사물 사이의 관계들을 탐구하고 구성한다. 빈번히, 이러한 관계들은 무언가가 얼마만큼 혹은 몇 개 존재하는지에 초점을 맞춘다. 따라서, 아이들은 센다. "쿠키 하나, 신발 두 개, 생일 케이크 위에 초 세 개, 모래놀이 통에 아이 네 명." 아이들은 비교한다. "무엇이 더 많지? 무엇이 더 적지? 충분할까?" 아이들은 계산한다. "몇 개가 알맞을까? 나는 지금 다섯 개가 있어, 하나 더 필요하네." 이 모든 예시에서, 아이들은 수량의 개념을 발달시키는 중이다. 아이들은 간식 시간에 몇 개의 크래커를 가져갈지 알아내거나 조개껍질들을 더미로 분류하는 것과 같은, 그들만의 활동이나 경험을 통해 수학적 개념을 밝히고 연구한다.

Why? 왜 정답일까?

아이들은 자기만의 활동이나 경험을 통해 수학적 개념을 익혀 간다(Children reveal and investigate mathematical concepts through their own activities or experiences ~)는 것이 핵심 내용이므로, 글의 주제로 가장 적절한 것은 ② '아이들은 수학적 이해를 어떻게 쌓아나가는가'이다.

- **explore** ⓥ 탐구하다
- **sandbox** ⓝ (어린이가 안에서 노는) 모래놀이 통
- **fit** ⓥ 맞다, 적합하다
- **notion** ⓝ 개념
- **investigate** ⓥ 연구하다, 조사하다
- **shell** ⓝ (조개 등의) 껍데기
- **construct** ⓥ 구성하다
- **calculate** ⓥ 계산하다
- **instance** ⓝ 예시, 사례
- **quantity** ⓝ (측정 가능한) 양, 수량
- **sort A into B** A를 B로 분류하다

구문 풀이

2행 Frequently, these relationships focus on {how much or how many of something exists}. [ ] : 「how + 형/부 + 주어 + 동사 : 얼마나 ~한지」

24 알고리듬의 시대

정답률 76% | 정답 ①

다음 글의 제목으로 가장 적절한 것은?

✓① We Live in an Age of Algorithms - 우리는 알고리듬의 시대에 산다
② Mysteries of Ancient Civilizations - 고대 문명의 미스터리
③ Dangers of Online Banking Algorithms - 온라인 뱅킹 알고리듬의 위험성
④ How Algorithms Decrease Human Creativity - 알고리듬은 어떻게 인간의 창의력을 떨어뜨리는가
⑤ Transportation: A Driving Force of Industry - 교통: 산업 발달의 원동력

Only a generation or two ago, / mentioning the word *algorithms* / would have drawn a blank from most people.

한두 세대 전만 해도, *알고리듬*이라는 단어를 언급하는 것은 / 대부분의 사람들로부터 아무 반응을 얻지 못했을 것이다.
Today, algorithms appear in every part of civilization.
오늘날, 알고리듬은 문명의 모든 부분에서 나타난다.
They are connected to everyday life.
그것들은 일상에 연결되어 있다.
They're not just in your cell phone or your laptop / but in your car, your house, your appliances, and your toys.
그것들은 당신의 휴대 전화나 노트북 속뿐 아니라 / 당신의 자동차, 집, 가전과 장난감 안에도 있다.
Your bank is a huge web of algorithms, / with humans turning the switches here and there.
당신의 은행은 알고리듬의 거대한 망이다. / 인간들이 여기저기서 스위치를 돌리고 있는
Algorithms schedule flights / and then fly the airplanes.
알고리듬은 비행 일정을 잡고 / 비행기를 운항한다.
Algorithms run factories, / trade goods, / and keep records.
알고리듬은 공장을 운영하며, / 상품을 거래하며, / 기록 문서를 보관한다.
If every algorithm suddenly stopped working, / it would be the end of the world / as we know it.
만일 모든 알고리듬이 갑자기 작동을 멈춘다면, / 이는 세상의 끝이 될 것이다. / 우리가 알고 있는

한두 세대 전만 해도, 알고리듬이라는 단어를 언급하는 것은 대부분의 사람들로부터 아무 반응을 얻지 못했을 것이다. 오늘날, 알고리듬은 문명의 모든 부분에서 나타난다. 그것들은 일상에 연결되어 있다. 그것들은 당신의 휴대 전화나 노트북 속뿐 아니라 당신의 자동차, 집, 가전과 장난감 안에도 있다. 당신의 은행은 인간들이 여기저기서 스위치를 돌리고 있는, 알고리듬의 거대한 망이다. 알고리듬은 비행 일정을 잡고 비행기를 운항한다. 알고리듬은 공장을 운영하고, 상품을 거래하며, 기록 문서를 보관한다. 만일 모든 알고리듬이 갑자기 작동을 멈춘다면, 이는 우리가 알고 있는 세상의 끝이 될 것이다.

Why? 왜 정답일까?

오늘날 문명의 모든 영역에서 알고리듬을 찾아볼 수 있다(Today, algorithms appear in every part of civilization.)는 것이 핵심 내용이므로, 글의 제목으로 가장 적절한 것은 ① '우리는 알고리듬의 시대에 산다'이다.

- generation ⑩ 세대
- civilization ⑩ 문명
- fly an airplane 비행기를 운항하다
- draw a blank 아무 반응을 얻지 못하다
- appliance ⑩ 가전 (제품)
- trade ⓥ 거래하다, 교역하다

구문 풀이

8행 If every algorithm suddenly stopped working, it would be the end of the world as we know it.
「if + 주어 + 과거시제 동사 ~, 주어 + 조동사 과거형 + 동사원형」: 가정법 과거(현재 사실 반대)

---

25 | 미국에서 반려동물을 키우는 가정의 비율   정답률 88% | 정답 ⑤

다음 도표의 내용과 일치하지 않는 것은?

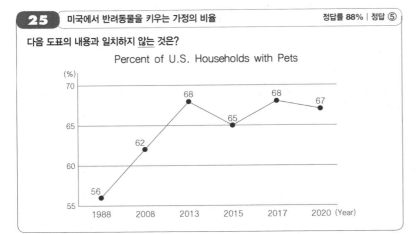

Percent of U.S. Households with Pets

The graph above shows the percent of households with pets / in the United States (U.S.) / from 1988 to 2020.
위 그래프는 반려동물을 기르는 가정의 비율을 보여준다. / 미국의 / 1988년부터 2020년까지
① In 1988, / more than half of U.S. households owned pets, / and more than 6 out of 10 U.S. households / owned pets from 2008 to 2020.
1988년에는 / 절반 이상의 미국 가정이 반려동물을 길렀고, / 10개 중 6개 이상의 미국 가정이 / 2008년에서 2020년까지 반려동물을 길렀다.
② In the period between 1988 and 2008, / pet ownership increased among U.S. households / by 6 percentage points.
1988년과 2008년 사이, / 반려동물 보유는 미국 가정들에서 증가했다. / 6퍼센트포인트만큼
③ From 2008 to 2013, / pet ownership rose an additional 6 percentage points.
2008년과 2013년 사이, / 반려동물 보유는 6퍼센트포인트가 추가적으로 올랐다.
④ The percent of U.S. households with pets in 2013 / was the same as that in 2017, / which was 68 percent.
2013년의 반려동물을 기르는 미국 가정의 비율은 / 2017년의 비율과 같고, / 68퍼센트였다.
✔ In 2015, / the rate of U.S. households with pets / was 3 percentage points lower than in 2020.
2015년에는, / 반려동물을 기르는 미국 가정의 비율이 / 2020년보다 3퍼센트포인트 더 낮았다.

위 그래프는 1988년부터 2020년까지 반려동물을 기르는 미국 가정의 비율을 보여준다. ① 1988년에는 절반 이상의 미국 가정이 반려동물을 길렀고, 2008년에서 2020년까지 10개 중 6개 이상의 미국 가정이 반려동물을 길렀다. ② 1988년과 2008년 사이, 반려동물 보유는 미국 가정들에서 6퍼센트포인트 증가했다. ③ 2008년과 2013년 사이, 반려동물 보유는 6퍼센트포인트가 추가적으로 올랐다. ④ 2013년의 반려동물을 기르는 미국 가정의 비율은 2017년의 비율과 같고, 68퍼센트였다. ⑤ 2015년에는, 반려동물을 기르는 미국 가정의 비율이 2020년보다 3퍼센트포인트 더 낮았다.

Why? 왜 정답일까?

도표에 따르면 미국에서 반려동물을 기르는 가정의 비율은 2015년 65%, 2020년 67%로, 두 해 간 비율은 2퍼센트포인트의 격차를 보인다. 따라서 도표와 일치하지 않는 것은 ⑤이다.

- household ⑩ 가정, 가구
- rise ⓥ 오르다
- ownership ⑩ 보유, 소유

---

26 | Claude Bolling의 생애   정답률 93% | 정답 ③

Claude Bolling에 관한 다음 글의 내용과 일치하지 않는 것은?

① 1930년에 프랑스에서 태어났다.
② 학교 친구를 통해 재즈를 소개받았다.
✔ 20대에 Best Piano Player 상을 받았다.
④ 성공적인 영화 음악 작곡가였다.
⑤ 1975년에 플루트 연주자와 협업했다.

「Pianist, composer, and big band leader, / Claude Bolling, was born on April 10, 1930, / in Cannes, France, / but spent most of his life in Paris.」 **①의 근거** 일치
피아니스트, 작곡가, 그리고 빅 밴드 리더인 / Claude Bolling은 1930년 4월 10일 태어났지만, / 프랑스 칸에서 / 삶의 대부분을 파리에서 보냈다.
He began studying classical music as a youth.
그는 젊었을 때 클래식 음악을 공부하기 시작했다.
「He was introduced to the world of jazz / by a schoolmate.」 **②의 근거** 일치
그는 재즈의 세계를 소개받았다. / 학교 친구를 통해
Later, / Bolling became interested in the music of Fats Waller, / one of the most excellent jazz musicians.
후에 / Bolling은 Fats Waller의 음악에 관심을 가졌다. / 최고의 재즈 음악가들 중 한 명인
「Bolling became famous as a teenager / by winning the Best Piano Player prize / at an amateur contest in France.」 **③의 근거** 불일치
그는 10대 때 유명해졌다. / Best Piano Player 상을 수상하며 / 프랑스의 아마추어 대회에서
「He was also a successful film music composer, / writing the music for more than one hundred films.」 **④의 근거** 일치
그는 또한 성공적인 영화 음악 작곡가였고, / 100편이 넘는 영화의 음악을 작곡했다.
「In 1975, he collaborated with flutist Rampal / and published *Suite for Flute and Jazz Piano Trio*, / which he became most well-known for.」 **⑤의 근거** 일치
1975년에, 그는 플루트 연주자 Rampal과 협업했고, / *Suite for Flute and Jazz Piano Trio*를 발매했으며, / 이것으로 가장 잘 알려지게 되었다.
He died in 2020, / leaving two sons, David and Alexandre.
그는 2020년 사망했다. / 두 아들 David와 Alexandre를 남기고

피아니스트, 작곡가, 그리고 빅 밴드 리더인 Claude Bolling은 1930년 4월 10일 프랑스 칸에서 태어났지만, 삶의 대부분을 파리에서 보냈다. 그는 젊었을 때 클래식 음악을 공부하기 시작했다. 그는 학교 친구를 통해 재즈의 세계를 소개받았다. 후에 Bolling은 최고의 재즈 음악가들 중 한 명인 Fats Waller의 음악에 관심을 가졌다. 그는 10대 때 프랑스의 아마추어 대회에서 Best Piano Player 상을 수상하며 유명해졌다. 그는 또한 성공적인 영화 음악 작곡가였고, 100편이 넘는 영화의 음악을 작곡했다. 1975년에, 그는 플루트 연주자 Rampal과 협업했고, *Suite for Flute and Jazz Piano Trio*를 발매했으며, 이것으로 가장 잘 알려지게 되었다. 그는 두 아들 David와 Alexandre를 남기고 2020년 사망했다.

Why? 왜 정답일까?

'Bolling became famous as a teenager by winning the Best Piano Player prize at an amateur contest in France.'에서 Claude Bolling이 아마추어 재즈 연주자 대회에서 Best Piano Player 상을 받은 것은 10대 시절이었다고 하므로, 내용과 일치하지 않는 것은 ③ '20대에 Best Piano Player 상을 받았다.'이다.

Why? 왜 오답일까?

① 'Claude Bolling, was born on April 10, 1930, in Cannes, France, ~'의 내용과 일치한다.
② 'He was introduced to the world of jazz by a schoolmate.'의 내용과 일치한다.
④ 'He was also a successful film music composer, ~'의 내용과 일치한다.
⑤ 'In 1975, he collaborated with flutist Rampal ~'의 내용과 일치한다.

- composer ⑩ 작곡가
- introduce ⓥ 소개하다
- flutist ⑩ 플루티스트
- well-known for ~로 유명한
- youth ⑩ 젊은 시절, 청춘
- collaborate with ~와 협업하다
- publish ⓥ 발매하다, 출간하다

구문 풀이

1행 Pianist, composer, and big band leader, Claude Bolling, was born on April 10, 1930, in Cannes, France, but spent most of his life in Paris.
주어 동격 / 주어 / 동사1 / 동사2

---

27 | 여름방학 태권도 프로그램   정답률 94% | 정답 ④

Kids Taekwondo Program에 관한 다음 안내문의 내용과 일치하지 않는 것은?

① 8월 8일부터 3일간 운영한다.
② 5세 이상의 어린이가 참가할 수 있다.
③ 자기 방어 훈련 활동을 한다.
✔ 참가비에 간식비는 포함되지 않는다.
⑤ 물병과 수건을 가져와야 한다.

Kids Taekwondo Program
Kids Taekwondo Program(어린이 태권도 프로그램)
Enjoy our taekwondo program this summer vacation.
이번 여름방학에 태권도 프로그램을 즐기세요.
Schedule
일정
「Dates: August 8th – August 10th」 **①의 근거** 일치
날짜: 8월 8일~8월 10일
Time: 9:00 a.m. – 11:00 a.m.
시간: 오전 9시~오전 11시
Participants
참가자
「Any child aged 5 and up」 **②의 근거** 일치
5세 이상 어린이 누구나
Activities
활동

『Self-defense training』 **③의 근거** 일치
자기 방어 훈련
Team building games to develop social skills
사교성 발달을 위한 팀 빌딩 게임
Participation Fee
참가비
『$50 per child (includes snacks)』 **④의 근거** 불일치
1인당 $50 (간식 포함)
Notice
알림
『What to bring: water bottle, towel』 **⑤의 근거** 일치
가져올 것: 물병, 수건
What not to bring: chewing gum, expensive items
가져오지 말아야 할 것: 껌, 비싼 물건

Kids Taekwondo Program(어린이 태권도 프로그램)

이번 여름방학에 태권도 프로그램을 즐기세요.

□ 일정
• 날짜: 8월 8일 ~ 8월 10일
• 시간: 오전 9시 ~ 오전 11시

□ 참가자
• 5세 이상 어린이 누구나

□ 활동
• 자기 방어 훈련
• 사교성 발달을 위한 팀 빌딩 게임

□ 참가비
• 1인당 $50 (간식 포함)

□ 알림
• 가져올 것: 물병, 수건
• 가져오지 말아야 할 것: 껌, 비싼 물건

Why? 왜 정답일까?

'$50 per child (includes snacks)'에서 참가비는 50달러인데, 간식이 포함된 금액이라고 한다. 따라서 안내문의 내용과 일치하지 않는 것은 ④ '참가비에 간식비는 포함되지 않는다.'이다.

Why? 왜 오답일까?

① 'Dates: August 8th – August 10th'의 내용과 일치한다.
② 'Participants / Any child aged 5 and up'의 내용과 일치한다.
③ 'Activities / Self-defense'의 내용과 일치한다.
⑤ 'What to bring: water bottle, towel'의 내용과 일치한다.

● self-defense ⑪ 자기 방어   ● social skill 사교성
● expensive ⓐ 비싼

---

28 초콜릿 공장 투어   정답률 93% | 정답 ②

Moonlight Chocolate Factory Tour에 관한 다음 안내문의 내용과 일치하는 것은?
① 주말 오후 시간에 운영한다.
✓ ② 초콜릿 제조 과정을 볼 수 있다.
③ 네 가지 종류의 초콜릿을 시식한다.
④ 마스크 착용은 참여자의 선택 사항이다.
⑤ 공장 내부에서 사진 촬영이 가능하다.

Moonlight Chocolate Factory Tour
Moonlight Chocolate Factory Tour(Moonlight 초콜릿 공장 투어)
Take this special tour / and have a chance to enjoy our most popular chocolate bars.
이 특별한 투어에 참여하여 / 우리의 가장 인기 있는 초콜릿 바를 즐길 기회를 가지세요.
Operating Hours
운영 시간
『Monday – Friday, 2:00 p.m. – 5:00 p.m.』 **①의 근거** 불일치
월요일 ~ 금요일, 오후 2시 ~ 오후 5시
Activities
활동
『Watching our chocolate-making process』 **②의 근거** 일치
초콜릿 제조 과정 견학
『Tasting 3 types of chocolate (dark, milk, and mint chocolate)』 **③의 근거** 불일치
초콜릿 3종 (다크, 밀크 및 민트 초콜릿) 시식
Notice
알림
Ticket price: $30
티켓 가격 : $30
『Wearing a face mask is required.』 **④의 근거** 불일치
마스크 착용은 필수입니다.
『Taking pictures is not allowed inside the factory.』 **⑤의 근거** 불일치
공장 내부에서 사진 촬영은 허용되지 않습니다.

Moonlight Chocolate Factory Tour (Moonlight 초콜릿 공장 투어)

이 특별한 투어에 참여하여 우리의 가장 인기 있는 초콜릿 바를 즐길 기회를 가지세요.

□ 운영 시간
• 월요일 ~ 금요일, 오후 2시 ~ 오후 5시
□ 활동
• 초콜릿 제조 과정 견학
• 초콜릿 3종 (다크, 밀크 및 민트 초콜릿) 시식
□ 알림

• 티켓 가격: $30
• 마스크 착용은 필수입니다.
• 공장 내부에서 사진 촬영은 허용되지 않습니다.

Why? 왜 정답일까?

'Activities / Watching our chocolate-making'에서 초콜릿 제조 과정을 견학할 수 있다고 하므로, 안내문의 내용과 일치하는 것은 ② '초콜릿 제조 과정을 볼 수 있다.'이다.

Why? 왜 오답일까?

① 'Monday – Friday, 2:00 p.m. – 5:00 p.m.'에서 운영 시간은 평일 오후라고 하였다.
③ 'Tasting 3 types of chocolate (dark, milk, and mint chocolate)'에서 시식할 수 있는 초콜릿은 세 종류라고 하였다.
④ 'Wearing a face mask is required.'에서 마스크 착용은 필수라고 하였다.
⑤ 'Taking pictures is not allowed inside the factory.'에서 공장 내부 사진 촬영은 불가하다고 하였다.

● have a chance to ~할 기회를 갖다   ● operating hour 운영 시간

---

29 더 많은 것을 소비하게 하는 첨단 생활방식   정답률 59% | 정답 ④

다음 글의 밑줄 친 부분 중, 어법상 틀린 것은?

Despite all the high-tech devices / that seem to deny the need for paper, / paper use in the United States / ① has nearly doubled recently.
모든 첨단 기기들에도 불구하고, / 종이의 필요성을 부정하는 것처럼 보이는 / 미국에서 종이 사용은 / 최근 거의 두 배로 증가했다.
We now consume more paper than ever: / 400 million tons globally and growing.
우리는 현재 그 어느 때보다도 더 많은 종이를 소비하고 있어서, / 전 세계에서 4억 톤을 쓰고 있으며 그 양은 증가하고 있다.
Paper is not the only resource / ② that we are using more of.
자원은 종이만이 아니다. / 우리가 더 많이 사용하고 있는
Technological advances often come / with the promise of ③ using fewer materials.
기술의 발전은 흔히 온다. / 더 적은 재료의 사용 가능성과 함께
However, / the reality is / that they have historically caused more materials use, / making us ✓ dependent on more natural resources.
그러나, / 현실은 ~이다. / 그것들이 역사적으로 더 많은 재료 사용을 야기해 / 우리가 더 많은 천연자원 사용에 의존하게 한다는 것
The world now consumes far more "stuff" / than it ever has.
세계는 이제 훨씬 더 많은 '것'을 소비한다. / 그것이 그 어느 때 그랬던 것보다
We use twenty-seven times more industrial minerals, / such as gold, copper, and rare metals, / than we ⑤ did just over a century ago.
우리는 산업 광물을 27배 더 많이 사용한다. / 금, 구리, 희귀 금속과 같은 / 우리가 고작 1세기 이전에 그랬던 것보다
We also each individually use more resources.
우리는 또한 각자 더 많은 자원을 사용한다.
Much of that is due to our high-tech lifestyle.
그중 많은 부분은 우리의 첨단 생활방식 때문이다.

종이의 필요성을 부정하는 것처럼 보이는 모든 첨단 기기들에도 불구하고, 미국에서 종이 사용은 최근 거의 두 배로 증가했다. 우리는 현재 그 어느 때보다도 더 많은 종이를 소비하고 있어서, 전 세계에서 4억 톤을 쓰고 있으며 그 양은 증가하고 있다. 우리가 더 많이 사용하고 있는 자원은 종이만이 아니다. 기술의 발전은 흔히 더 적은 재료의 사용 가능성을 수반한다. 그러나, 현실은 그것들이 역사적으로 더 많은 재료 사용을 야기해 우리가 더 많은 천연자원에 의존하게 한다는 것이다. 세계는 이제 그 어느 때보다도 훨씬 더 많은 '재료'를 소비한다. 우리는 금, 구리, 희귀 금속과 같은 산업 광물을 고작 1세기 이전보다 27배 더 많이 사용한다. 우리는 또한 각자 더 많은 자원을 사용한다. 그중 많은 부분은 우리의 첨단 생활방식 때문이다.

Why? 왜 정답일까?

make는 형용사를 목적격 보어로 취하는 5형식 동사이므로, 부사 dependently를 형용사 dependent로 고쳐 making의 보어 자리를 채워야 한다. 따라서 어법상 틀린 것은 ④이다.

Why? 왜 오답일까?

① 주어 paper use가 불가산명사이므로 단수 동사 has가 어법상 적절하다.
② 선행사 the only resource 뒤로 목적어가 없는 불완전한 절을 이끌고자 관계대명사 that이 알맞게 쓰였다. 참고로 선행사에 the only가 있으면 관계대명사 that이 주로 쓰인다.
③ 전치사 of 뒤에 목적어인 동명사 using이 알맞게 쓰였다.
⑤ 앞에 나온 일반동사 use를 대신하는데 시제가 과거이므로(over a century ago) 대동사 did가 알맞게 쓰였다.

● high-tech ⓐ 첨단 기술의   ● consume ⓥ 소비하다
● material ⑪ 물질, 자재, 재료   ● historically ⓐⓓ 역사적으로
● dependently ⓐⓓ 의존적으로, 남에게 의지하여   ● industrial ⓐ 산업의
● rare ⓐ 희귀한

구문 풀이

6행 However, the reality is {that they have historically caused more materials use, making us dependently on more natural resources}. { } : 명사절(주격 보어)
분사구문(= and they make ~)

---

30 삶을 사랑하는 법   정답률 61% | 정답 ②

다음 글의 밑줄 친 부분 중, 문맥상 낱말의 쓰임이 적절하지 않은 것은? [3점]

Do you sometimes feel like / you don't love your life?
당신은 가끔 느끼는가? / 당신이 삶을 사랑하지 않는다고
Like, deep inside, something is missing?
마치 마음 깊은 곳에서 뭔가가 빠진 것처럼?
That's because we are living someone else's life.
왜냐하면 우리가 타인의 삶을 살고 있기 때문이다.
We allow other people to ① influence our choices.
우리는 타인이 우리의 선택에 영향을 주도록 허용한다.
We are trying to meet their expectations.

우리는 그들의 기대감을 만족시키기 위해 노력하고 있다.
Social pressure is deceiving / — we are all impacted without noticing it.
사회적 압력은 현혹시킨다. / 우리 모두는 그것을 눈치채지도 못한 채 영향을 받는다.
Before we realize / we are losing ownership of our lives, / we end up ✔envying how other people live.
우리가 깨닫기도 전에, / 우리의 삶에 대한 소유권을 잃었다는 것을 / 우리는 결국 다른 사람들이 어떻게 사는지를 부러워하게 된다.
Then, we can only see the greener grass / — ours is never good enough.
그러면, 우리는 더 푸른 잔디만 볼 수 있게 된다. / 우리의 삶은 만족할 만큼 충분히 좋아질 수 없다.
To regain that passion for the life you want, / you must ③ recover control of your choices.
당신이 원하는 삶에 대한 열정을 되찾기 위해서는 / 당신은 당신의 선택에 대한 통제력을 회복해야 한다.
No one but yourself / can choose how you live.
당신 자신을 제외한 그 누구도 / 당신이 어떻게 살지를 선택할 수 없다.
But, how?
하지만 어떻게 해야 할까?
The first step to getting rid of expectations / is to treat yourself ④ kindly.
기대감을 버리는 첫 단계는 / 자신을 친절하게 대하는 것이다.
You can't truly love other people / if you don't love yourself first.
당신은 다른 사람을 진정으로 사랑할 수 없다. / 당신이 자신을 먼저 사랑하지 않으면
When we accept who we are, / there's no room for other's ⑤ expectations.
우리가 우리 있는 그대로를 받아들일 때, / 타인의 기대를 위한 여지는 남지 않는다.

당신은 가끔 삶을 사랑하지 않다고 느끼는가? 마치 마음 깊은 곳에서 뭔가가 빠진 것처럼? 왜냐하면 우리가 타인의 삶을 살고 있기 때문이다. 우리는 타인이 우리의 선택에 ① 영향을 주도록 허용한다. 우리는 그들의 기대감을 만족시키기 위해 노력하고 있다. 사회적 압력은 (우리를) 현혹시켜서, 우리 모두는 그것을 눈치채지도 못한 채 영향을 받는다. 우리의 삶에 대한 소유권을 잃어가고 있다는 것을 깨닫기도 전에, 우리는 결국 다른 사람들이 어떻게 사는지를 ② 무시하게(→ 부러워하게) 된다. 그러면, 우리는 더 푸른 잔디(타인의 삶이 더 좋아 보이는 것)만 볼 수 있게 되어, 우리의 삶은 (만족할 만큼) 충분히 좋아질 수 없다. 당신이 원하는 삶에 대한 열정을 되찾기 위해서는 당신의 선택에 대한 통제력을 ③ 회복해야 한다. 당신 자신을 제외한 그 누구도 당신이 어떻게 살지를 선택할 수 없다. 하지만 어떻게 해야 할까? 기대감을 버리는 첫 단계는 자기 자신에게 ④ 친절하게 대하는 것이다. 자신을 먼저 사랑하지 않으면 다른 사람을 진정으로 사랑할 수 없다. 우리가 우리 있는 그대로를 받아들일 때, 타인의 ⑤ 기대를 위한 여지는 남지 않는다.

Why? 왜 정답일까?

타인의 기대를 만족시키는 삶을 살아갈 때에는 삶을 사랑할 수 없기에 자신을 친절하게 대하며 삶에 대한 주도권을 회복해 나가야 한다는 내용의 글이다. 흐름상 ② 앞뒤는 타인의 삶을 살다 보면 자신의 삶에 대한 통제력을 잃었음을 알기도 전에 이미 타인의 삶을 더 좋게 보고 '부러워하게' 된다는 문맥이므로, ignoring을 envying으로 고쳐야 한다. 따라서 문맥상 낱말의 쓰임이 적절하지 않은 것은 ②이다.

- **missing** ⓐ 빠진, 실종된
- **meet the expectation** 기대를 충족하다
- **impact** ⓥ 영향을 미치다
- **recover** ⓥ 회복하다
- **influence** ⓥ 영향을 미치다 ⓝ 영향
- **deceiving** ⓐ 현혹시키는, 속이는
- **ownership** ⓝ 소유권
- **get rid of** ~을 없애다

구문 풀이

9행 No one but yourself can choose {how you live}. [ ] : 간접의문문(어떻게 ~할지)
~을 제외하고(= except)

★★★ 등급을 가르는 문제!

| 31 | 혁신 지속에 도움이 되는 가상 환경의 특징 | 정답률 49% | 정답 ① |

다음 빈칸에 들어갈 말로 가장 적절한 것을 고르시오.
✔① restrictions – 제한점
② responsibilities – 책임감
③ memories – 기억
④ coincidences – 우연의 일치
⑤ traditions – 전통

One of the big questions faced this past year / was how to keep innovation rolling / when people were working entirely virtually.
작년에 직면한 가장 큰 질문 중 하나는 / 어떻게 혁신을 지속할 것인가 하는 것이었다. / 사람들이 완전히 가상 공간에서 작업할 때
But experts say / that digital work didn't have a negative effect / on innovation and creativity.
그러나 전문가들은 말한다. / 디지털 작업이 부정적인 영향을 미치지 않았다고 / 혁신과 창의성에
Working within limits / pushes us to solve problems.
한계 내에서 일하는 것은 / 우리에게 문제를 해결하도록 독려한다.
Overall, / virtual meeting platforms put more constraints / on communication and collaboration / than face-to-face settings.
전반적으로, / 가상 미팅 플랫폼은 더 많은 제약을 가한다. / 의사소통과 협업에 / 대면 설정보다
For instance, / with the press of a button, / virtual meeting hosts can control the size of breakout groups / and enforce time constraints; / only one person can speak at a time; / nonverbal signals, / particularly those below the shoulders, / are diminished; / "seating arrangements" are assigned by the platform, / not by individuals; / and visual access to others may be limited / by the size of each participant's screen.
예를 들어, / 버튼을 누르면, / 가상 회의 진행자는 소모임 그룹의 크기를 제어하고 / 시간 제한을 시행할 수 있다. / 한 번에 한 사람만이 말할 수 있다. / 비언어적 신호, / 특히 어깨 아래의 신호는 / 줄어든다. / '좌석 배치'는 플랫폼에 의해 할당된다. / 개인이 아닌 / 그리고 다른 사람에 대한 시각적 접근은 제한될 수 있다. / 각 참가자의 화면 크기에 따라
Such restrictions are likely to stretch participants / beyond their usual ways of thinking, / boosting creativity.
이러한 제한점은 참가자들을 확장시킬 가능성이 높다. / 일반적인 사고방식 너머까지 / 그리고 창의력을 증진시킬

작년에 직면한 가장 큰 질문 중 하나는 사람들이 완전히 가상 공간에서 작업할 때 어떻게 혁신을 지속할 것인가 하는 것이었다. 그러나 전문가들은 디지털 작업이 혁신과 창의성에 부정적인 영향을 미치지 않았다고 말한다. 한계 내에서 일하는 것은 우리에게 문제를 해결하도록 독려한다. 전반적으로, 가상 미팅 플랫폼은 대면 환경보다 의사소통과 협업에 더 많은 제약들을 가한다. 예를 들어, 버튼을 누르면, 가상 회의 진행자는 소모임 그룹의 크기를 제어하고 시간 제한을 시행할 수 있다. 한 번에 한 사람만이 말할 수 있다. 비언어적 신호, 특히 어깨 아래의 신호는 줄어든다. '좌석 배치'는 개인이 아닌 플랫폼에 의해 할당된다. 그리고 다른 사람에 대한 시각적 접근은 각 참가자의 화면 크기에 따라 제한될 수 있다. 이러한 제한점은 참가자들을 일반적인 사고방식 너머까지 확장시켜 창의력을 증진시킬 가능성이 높다.

Why? 왜 정답일까?

'Working within limits pushes us to solve problems.'에서 한계 내에서 작업하는 것이 문제 해결을 독려한다고 언급하는 것으로 보아, 빈칸에 들어갈 말로 가장 적절한 것은 ① '제한점'이다.

- **virtually** ⓐⓓ (컴퓨터를 이용해) 가상으로
- **have a negative effect on** ~에 부정적 영향을 미치다
- **constraint** ⓝ 제한, 한계
- **breakout group** (전체에서 나누어진) 소집단
- **enforce** ⓥ 시행하다
- **diminish** ⓥ 줄이다
- **seating arrangement** 좌석 배치
- **assign** ⓥ 배정하다, 할당하다
- **stretch** ⓥ 늘이다, 확장하다
- **coincidence** ⓝ 우연의 일치, 동시 발생

구문 풀이

1행 One of the big questions faced this past year was {how to keep innovation
주어(one of the + 복수명사) 과거분사 동사(단수)
rolling when people were working entirely virtually}.
{ } : 주격 보어(how+to부정사 : ~하는 방법)

★★ 문제 해결 꿀~팁 ★★

▶ 많이 틀린 이유는?
Working within limits가 핵심 표현으로, 제약이나 제한이 혁신과 업무 수행에 도움이 된다는 것이 글의 주제이다. 최다 오답인 ②의 responsibilities는 '책임, (맡은) 책무'라는 뜻이므로 글 내용과 관련이 없다.

▶ 문제 해결 방법은?
핵심어인 limits, constraints와 동의어를 찾으면 된다. 빈칸 앞에 not 등 부정어도 없어, 복잡하게 사고할 필요가 없는 비교적 단순한 빈칸 문제이다.

★★★ 등급을 가르는 문제!

| 32 | 전통적 수요 법칙의 예외인 기펜재 | 정답률 56% | 정답 ② |

다음 빈칸에 들어갈 말로 가장 적절한 것을 고르시오. [3점]
① order more meat – 더 많은 고기를 주문한다
✔② consume more rice – 더 많은 쌀을 소비한다
③ try to get new jobs – 새로운 일자리를 구하려 한다
④ increase their savings – 저축액을 늘린다
⑤ start to invest overseas – 해외에 투자하기 시작한다

The law of demand is / that the demand for goods and services increases / as prices fall, / and the demand falls / as prices increase.
수요의 법칙은 ~이다. / 상품과 서비스에 대한 수요가 증가하고, / 가격이 하락할수록 / 수요가 감소하는 것 / 가격이 상승할수록
Giffen goods are special types of products / for which the traditional law of demand does not apply.
기펜재는 특별한 유형의 상품이다. / 전통적인 수요 법칙이 적용되지 않는
Instead of switching to cheaper replacements, / consumers demand more of giffen goods / when the price increases / and less of them when the price decreases.
저렴한 대체품으로 바꾸는 대신 / 소비자들은 기펜재를 더 많이 필요로 한다. / 가격이 상승할 때 / 그리고 가격이 하락할 때 덜
Taking an example, / rice in China is a giffen good / because people tend to purchase less of it / when the price falls.
예를 들어, / 중국의 쌀은 기펜재이다. / 사람들이 그것을 덜 구매하는 경향이 있기 때문에 / 가격이 하락할 때
The reason for this is, / when the price of rice falls, / people have more money / to spend on other types of products / such as meat and dairy / and, therefore, change their spending pattern.
그 이유는 ~이다. / 쌀값이 하락하면, / 사람들이 돈이 많아지고, / 다른 종류의 상품에 쓸 / 고기나 유제품 같은 / 그 결과 소비 패턴을 바꾸기 때문에
On the other hand, / as rice prices increase, / people consume more rice.
반면에, / 쌀값이 상승하면, / 사람들은 더 많은 쌀을 소비한다.

수요의 법칙은 가격이 하락할수록 상품과 서비스에 대한 수요가 증가하고, 가격이 상승할수록 수요가 감소하는 것이다. 기펜재는 전통적인 수요 법칙이 적용되지 않는 특별한 유형의 상품이다. 저렴한 대체품으로 바꾸는 대신 소비자들은 가격이 상승할 때 기펜재를 더 많이, 가격이 하락할 때 덜 필요로 한다. 예를 들어, 중국의 쌀은 가격이 하락할 때 사람들이 덜 구매하는 경향이 있기 때문에 기펜재이다. 그 이유는, 쌀값이 하락하면, 사람들이 고기나 유제품 같은 다른 종류의 상품에 쓸 돈이 많아지고, 그 결과 소비 패턴을 바꾸기 때문이다. 반면에, 쌀값이 상승하면, 사람들은 더 많은 쌀을 소비한다.

Why? 왜 정답일까?

전통적인 수요 법칙에 따르면 가격과 수요는 반비례하지만, 이 법칙의 예외에 있는 기펜재는 가격과 상승 및 하락 흐름을 같이한다(Instead of switching to cheaper replacements, consumers demand more of giffen goods when the price increases and less of them when the price decreases.)는 내용의 글이다. 중반부 이후로 중국의 쌀이 기펜재의 예시로 언급되므로, 쌀 가격이 오를 때 오히려 사람들은 '쌀을 더 산다'는 내용이 결론이어야 한다. 따라서 빈칸에 들어갈 말로 가장 적절한 것은 ② '더 많은 쌀을 소비한다'이다.

- **demand** ⓝ 수요 ⓥ 필요로 하다, 요구하다
- **switch to** ~로 바꾸다
- **dairy** ⓝ 유제품
- **apply for** ~에 적용되다
- **replacement** ⓝ 대체(품)
- **overseas** ⓐⓓ 해외에

구문 풀이

3행 Giffen goods are special types of products [for which the traditional law
선행사 「전치사+관계대명사」
of demand does not apply].

★★ 문제 해결 꿀~팁 ★★

▶ 많이 틀린 이유는?
기펜재의 개념을 잘 이해하고 사례에 적용해야 하는 빈칸 문제이다. 최다 오답 ④는 '저축액을 늘린다'는 의미인데, 글에서 기펜재와 저축액을 연결짓는 내용은 언급되지 않았다.

▶ 문제 해결 방법은?

글에 따르면 기펜재는 일반적 재화와 달리 가격이 오를 때 수요도 오르고, 가격이 떨어질 때 수요도 떨어지는 재화이다. 빈칸 문장에서는 '쌀 가격이 오르는' 상황을 상정하고 있으므로, '쌀에 대한 수요도 덩달아 오른다'는 결과를 예측할 수 있다.

★★★ 등급을 가르는 문제!

33 지적 능력 발달에 있어 천성보다 중요한 양육 정답률 44% | 정답 ③

다음 빈칸에 들어갈 말로 가장 적절한 것을 고르시오. [3점]

① by themselves for survival – 생존을 위해 스스로
② free from social interaction – 사회적 상호작용 없이
☑ based on what is around you – 여러분 주변에 있는 것에 따라
④ depending on genetic superiority – 유전적 우월성에 따라
⑤ so as to keep ourselves entertained – 우리 자신을 계속 즐겁게 하기 위해

In a study at Princeton University in 1992, / research scientists looked at two different groups of mice.
1992년 프린스턴 대학의 한 연구에서, / 연구 과학자들은 두 개의 다른 쥐 집단을 관찰했다.

One group was made intellectually superior / by modifying the gene for the glutamate receptor.
한 집단은 지적으로 우월하게 만들어졌다. / 글루타민산염 수용체에 대한 유전자를 변형함으로써

Glutamate is a brain chemical / that is necessary in learning.
글루타민산염은 뇌 화학 물질이다. / 학습에 필수적인

The other group was genetically manipulated / to be intellectually inferior, / also done by modifying the gene for the glutamate receptor.
다른 집단도 유전적으로 조작되었다. / 지적으로 열등하도록 / 역시 글루타민산염 수용체에 대한 유전자를 변형함으로써 이루어진

The smart mice were then raised in standard cages, / while the inferior mice were raised in large cages / with toys and exercise wheels / and with lots of social interaction.
그 후 똑똑한 쥐들은 표준 우리에서 길러진 반면, / 열등한 쥐들은 큰 우리에서 길러진 반면 / 장난감과 운동용 쳇바퀴가 있고 / 사회적 상호작용이 많은

At the end of the study, / although the intellectually inferior mice were genetically handicapped, / they were able to perform just as well / as their genetic superiors.
연구가 끝날 무렵, / 비록 지적 능력이 떨어지는 쥐들이 유전적으로 장애가 있었지만, / 그들은 딱 그만큼 잘 수행할 수 있었다. / 그들의 유전적인 우월군들만큼

This was a real triumph for nurture over nature.
이것은 천성에 대한 양육의 진정한 승리였다.

Genes are turned on or off / based on what is around you.
유전자는 작동하거나 멈춘다. / 여러분 주변에 있는 것에 따라

1992년 프린스턴 대학의 한 연구에서, 연구 과학자들은 두 개의 다른 쥐 집단을 관찰했다. 한 집단은 글루타민산염 수용체에 대한 유전자를 변형함으로써 지적으로 우월하게 만들어졌다. 글루타민산염은 학습에 필수적인 뇌 화학 물질이다. 다른 집단도 역시 글루타민산염 수용체에 대한 유전자를 변형함으로써, 지적으로 열등하도록 유전적으로 조작되었다. 그 후 똑똑한 쥐들은 표준 우리에서 길러진 반면 열등한 쥐들은 장난감과 운동용 쳇바퀴가 있고 사회적 상호작용이 많은 큰 우리에서 길러졌다. 연구가 끝날 무렵, 비록 지적 능력이 떨어지는 쥐들이 유전적으로 장애가 있었지만, 그들은 딱 유전적인 우월군들만큼 잘 수행할 수 있었다. 이것은 천성(선천적 성질)에 대한 양육(후천적 환경)의 진정한 승리였다. 유전자는 여러분 주변에 있는 것에 따라 작동하거나 멈춘다.

Why? 왜 정답일까?

빈칸이 있는 문장 바로 앞에서 양육, 즉 후천적 환경이 타고난 천성을 이겼다(a real triumph for nurture over nature)는 말로 연구 결과를 정리하고 있다. 따라서 빈칸에 들어갈 말로 가장 적절한 것은 '환경, 양육'과 같은 의미의 ③ '여러분 주변에 있는 것에 따라'이다.

● intellectually ad 지적으로
● receptor n 수용체
● inferior a 열등한
● triumph n 승리
● free from ~ 없이, ~을 면하여
● modify v 수정하다, 바꾸다
● genetically ad 유전적으로
● handicapped a 장애가 있는, 불리한 입장인
● nurture n 양육

구문 풀이

5행 The other group was genetically manipulated to be intellectually inferior, / 선행사 (which was) also done by modifying the gene for the glutamate receptor. / 생략(계속적 용법) 과거분사

★★ 문제 해결 꿀~팁 ★★

▶ 많이 틀린 이유는?

지적으로 우월하게(superior) 만들어진 쥐와 열등하게(inferior) 만들어진 쥐를 비교하는 실험 내용상 '유전적 우월함'을 언급하는 ④가 정답처럼 보인다. 하지만 실험의 결과를 보면, 결국 유전적으로 지능이 높게 만들어진 쥐와 열등하게 만들어진 쥐 사이에 차이가 없었다는 것이 핵심이다. 따라서 '유전적 우월함에 따라' 유전자가 작동하거나 작동하지 않을 수 있다는 의미를 완성하는 ④는 빈칸에 적절하지 않다.

▶ 문제 해결 방법은?

유전적으로 유도된 지능 차이보다도, 다른 어떤 요인이 쥐의 수행에 영향을 미칠 수 있는지 살펴봐야 한다. 글 중반부를 보면, 열등한 쥐들이 자란 환경은 우월한 쥐들이 자란 환경에 비해 사회적 상호작용이 활발한 공간이었다고 한다. 나아가 빈칸 앞에서는 이 실험 결과가 유전보다도 양육, 즉 후천적 환경(nurture)의 중요성을 말해준다고 한다. 따라서 빈칸에도 '환경'과 관련된 내용이 들어가야 한다.

★★★ 등급을 가르는 문제!

34 기후 변화에 대한 대처가 '현재' 이루어지지 않는 이유 정답률 45% | 정답 ②

다음 빈칸에 들어갈 말로 가장 적절한 것을 고르시오. [3점]

① it is not related to science – 그것이 과학과 관련이 없다
☑ it is far away in time and space – 그것이 시공간적으로 멀리 떨어져 있다

---

③ energy efficiency matters the most – 에너지 효율이 가장 중요하다
④ careful planning can fix the problem – 신중한 계획이 문제를 해결할 수 있다
⑤ it is too late to prevent it from happening – 그것이 일어나지 않도록 막기에는 너무 늦었다

Researchers are working on a project / that asks coastal towns / how they are preparing for rising sea levels.
연구원들은 프로젝트를 진행하고 있다 / 해안가 마을에게 묻는 / 해수면 상승에 어떻게 대비하고 있는지

Some towns have risk assessments; / some towns even have a plan.
어떤 마을들은 위험 평가를 하고 / 어떤 마을들은 심지어 계획을 가지고 있다.

But it's a rare town / that is actually carrying out a plan.
하지만 마을은 드물다 / 실제로 계획을 실행하고 있는

One reason we've failed to act on climate change / is the common belief / that it is far away in time and space.
우리가 기후 변화에 대처하는 데 실패한 한 가지 이유는 / 일반적인 믿음 때문이다 / 그것이 시공간적으로 멀리 떨어져 있다는

For decades, / climate change was a prediction about the future, / so scientists talked about it in the future tense.
수십 년 동안, / 기후 변화는 미래에 대한 예측이었기 때문에 / 과학자들은 미래 시제로 기후 변화에 대해 이야기했다.

This became a habit — / so that even today / many scientists still use the future tense, / even though we know / that a climate crisis is ongoing.
이것이 습관이 되어 / 그 결과 오늘날에도 / 많은 과학자들이 여전히 미래 시제를 사용하고 있다. / 우리가 알고 있음에도, / 기후 위기가 진행중이라는 것을

Scientists also often focus on regions / most affected by the crisis, / such as Bangladesh or the West Antarctic Ice Sheet, / which for most Americans are physically remote.
과학자들은 또한 지역에 초점을 맞추고 있으며, / 위기의 영향을 가장 많이 받는 / 방글라데시나 서남극 빙상처럼 / 그 지역은 대부분의 미국인들에게는 물리적으로 멀리 떨어져 있다.

연구원들은 해안가 마을들이 해수면 상승에 어떻게 대비하고 있는지 묻는 프로젝트를 진행하고 있다. 어떤 마을들은 위험 평가를 하고 어떤 마을들은 심지어 계획을 가지고 있다. 하지만 실제로 계획을 실행하고 있는 마을은 드물다. 우리가 기후 변화에 대처하는 데 실패한 한 가지 이유는 그것이 시공간적으로 멀리 떨어져 있다는 일반적인 믿음 때문이다. 수십 년 동안, 기후 변화는 미래에 대한 예측이었기 때문에 과학자들은 미래 시제로 기후 변화에 대해 이야기했다. 이것이 습관이 되어, 비록 우리가 기후 위기가 진행중이라는 것을 알고 있음에도, 많은 과학자들이 오늘날에도 여전히 미래 시제를 사용하고 있다. 과학자들은 또한 방글라데시나 서남극 빙상처럼 위기의 영향을 가장 많이 받는 지역에 초점을 맞추고 있으며, 그 지역은 대부분의 미국인들에게는 물리적으로 멀리 떨어져 있다.

Why? 왜 정답일까?

빈칸 뒤에 따르면, 기후 변화는 현재가 아닌 미래의 사건으로 여겨져 늘 미래 시제로 묘사되며(use the future tense), 기후 위기에 취약한 지역 또한 과학자들에게는 물리적으로 멀리 떨어진(physically remote) 곳이다. 다시 말해 기후 변화와 그로 인한 여파는 늘 '지금 여기와는 동떨어진' 사건으로 취급되고 있다는 것이 글의 핵심 내용이므로, 빈칸에 들어갈 말로 가장 적절한 것은 ② '그것이 시공간적으로 멀리 떨어져 있다'이다.

● sea level 해수면
● prediction n 예측
● crisis n 위기
● Antarctic a 남극의
● remote a 멀리 떨어진
● assessment n 평가
● tense n (문법) 시제
● ongoing a 진행 중인
● physically ad 물리적으로, 신체적으로

구문 풀이

4행 One reason [we've failed to act on climate change] is the common belief
주어 [관계부사절] 동사(단수) 주격 보어
{that it is far away in time and space}. { }: 동격절(= the common belief)

★★ 문제 해결 꿀~팁 ★★

▶ 많이 틀린 이유는?

⑤는 일반적으로 많이 언급되는 내용이지만 글에서 보면 기후 변화를 막기에 '시간적으로 너무 늦었다'는 내용은 글에서 다뤄지지 않았다.

▶ 문제 해결 방법은?

빈칸이 글 중간에 있으면 주로 뒤에 답에 대한 힌트가 있다. 여기서도 빈칸 뒤를 보면, 과학자들은 기후 변화에 관해 아직도 미래 시제로 말하며, 지리적으로도 멀리 떨어진 곳을 연구하는 데 집중한다는 점을 지적하고 있다. 이는 기후 변화를 '시간·공간적으로 동떨어진' 일로 여기는 경향을 비판하는 것이다.

---

35 패션의 의미 정답률 66% | 정답 ④

다음 글에서 전체 흐름과 관계 없는 문장은?

According to Marguerite La Caze, / fashion contributes to our lives / and provides a medium for us / to develop and exhibit important social virtues.
Marguerite La Caze에 따르면, / 패션은 우리의 삶에 기여하고 / 우리에게 수단을 제공한다. / 중요한 사회적 가치를 개발하고 나타낼

① Fashion may be beautiful, innovative, and useful; / we can display creativity and good taste in our fashion choices.
패션은 아름다울 수 있고, 혁신적일 수 있으며, 유용할 수 있다. / 우리는 패션을 선택하는 데 있어서 창의성과 좋은 취향을 드러낼 수 있다.

② And in dressing with taste and care, / we represent / both self-respect and a concern for the pleasure of others.
그리고 취향과 관심에 따라 옷을 입을 때, / 우리는 보여준다. / 자아존중과 타인의 즐거움에 대한 관심 모두를

③ There is no doubt / that fashion can be a source of interest and pleasure / which links us to each other.
의심의 여지가 없다. / 패션은 흥미와 즐거움의 원천이 될 수 있다는 것은 / 우리와 타인을 연결해 주는

☑ Although the fashion industry / developed first in Europe and America, / today it is an international and highly globalized industry.
비록 패션 산업은 / 유럽과 미국에서 처음 발달했지만, / 오늘날에는 국제적이고 매우 세계화된 산업이 되었다.

⑤ That is, / fashion provides a sociable aspect / along with opportunities to imagine oneself differently — / to try on different identities.
다시 말해, / 패션은 친교적인 측면을 제공한다. / 자신을 다르게 상상하는 기회와 더불어 / 즉, 다른 정체성을 시도하는

Marguerite La Caze에 따르면, 패션은 우리의 삶에 기여하고, 우리가 중요한 사회적 가치를 개발하고 나타낼 수단을 제공한다. ① 패션은 어쩌면 아름다울 수 있고, 혁신적일 수 있으며, 유용할 수 있다. 우리는 패션을 선택하는 데 있어서 창의성과 좋은 취향을 드러낼 수 있다. ② 그리고 취향과 관심에 따라 옷을 입을 때, 우리는 자아존중과 타인의 즐거움에 대한 관심 모두를 보여준다. ③ 의심의 여지없이, 패션은 우리를 서로 연결해 주는 흥미와 즐거움의 원천이 될 수 있다. ④ 패션 산업은 유럽과 미국에서 처음 발달했지만, 오늘날에는 국제적이고 매우 세계화된 산업이 되었다. ⑤ 다시 말해, 패션은 자신을 다르게 상상하는, 즉 다른 정체성을 시도하는 기회와 더불어 친교적인 측면을 제공한다.

Why? 왜 정답일까?

패션이 삶에서 갖는 의미를 설명한 글로, 개인의 삶과 타인과의 상호작용에서 어떤 의미를 갖는지가 주로 언급된다. 하지만 ④는 패션 사업의 발달에 관해 언급하며 글의 흐름에서 벗어나므로, 전체 흐름과 관계 없는 문장은 ④이다.

- contribute to ~에 기여하다, ~의 원인이 되다
- exhibit ⓥ 보여주다, 드러내다
- represent ⓥ 나타내다, 표현하다
- link A to B A와 B를 연결하다
- sociable ⓐ 사교적인, 사람들과 어울리기 좋아하는
- medium ⓝ 수단, 매체
- taste ⓝ 취향
- concern ⓝ 관심, 우려
- highly ⓐ 매우
- along with ~와 더불어

구문 풀이

6행 There is no doubt {that fashion can be a source of interest and pleasure
부정 주어   { } : doubt의 동격절   선행사
[which links us to each other]}.
주격 관·대

---

36 선생님에게 그림으로 감사를 표현한 Douglas   정답률 79% | 정답 ③

주어진 글 다음에 이어질 글의 순서로 가장 적절한 것을 고르시오.

① (A) − (C) − (B)　　　　② (B) − (A) − (C)
✔③ (B) − (C) − (A)　　　　④ (C) − (A) − (B)
⑤ (C) − (B) − (A)

Mrs. Klein told her first graders / to draw a picture of something to be thankful for.
Klein 선생님은 1학년 학생들에게 말했다. / 감사히 여기는 것을 그려보라고
She thought / that most of the class would draw turkeys or Thanksgiving tables.
그녀는 생각했다. / 반 아이들 대부분이 칠면조나 추수감사절 식탁을 그릴 것으로
But Douglas drew something different.
하지만 Douglas는 색다른 것을 그렸다.
(B) Douglas was a boy / who usually spent time alone and stayed around her / while his classmates went outside together during break time.
Douglas는 소년이었다. / 보통 혼자 시간을 보내고 그녀 주변에 머무르는 / 그의 반 친구들이 쉬는 시간에 함께 밖으로 나가 있는 동안
What the boy drew was a hand.
그 소년이 그린 것은 손이었다.
But whose hand?
그런데 누구의 손일까?
His image immediately attracted the other students' interest.
그의 그림은 즉시 다른 학생들의 관심을 끌었다.
(C) So, / everyone rushed to talk / about whose hand it was.
그래서, / 모두들 앞다투어 말하려 했다. / 그것이 누구의 손인지에 관해
"It must be the hand of God / that brings us food," / said one student.
"그것은 신의 손이 틀림없어. / 우리에게 음식을 가져다주는" / 한 학생이 말했다.
"A farmer's," / said a second student, / "because they raise the turkeys."
"농부의 손이야," / 두 번째 학생이 말했다. / "왜냐하면 그들은 칠면조를 기르거든."이라고
"It looks more like a police officer's," / added another, / "they protect us."
"경찰관의 손과 더 비슷해 보여," / 또 다른 학생이 덧붙였다. / "그들은 우리를 보호해 줘."라고
(A) The class was so responsive / that Mrs. Klein had almost forgotten about Douglas.
반 아이들이 몹시 호응해서 / Klein 선생님은 Douglas에 대해 하마터면 잊어버릴 뻔했다.
After she had the others at work on another project, / she asked Douglas whose hand it was.
그녀가 나머지 아이들에게 다른 과제를 하도록 지도한 후, / 그녀는 Douglas에게 그 손이 누구 손인지 물었다.
He answered softly, / "It's yours. Thank you, Mrs. Klein."
그는 조용히 대답했다. / "선생님 손이에요. 고마워요, Klein 선생님."이라고

Klein 선생님은 1학년 학생들에게 감사히 여기는 것을 그려보라고 말했다. 그녀는 반 아이들 대부분이 칠면조나 추수감사절 식탁을 그릴 것으로 생각했다. 하지만 Douglas는 색다른 것을 그렸다.

(B) Douglas는 그의 반 친구들이 쉬는 시간에 함께 밖으로 나가 있는 동안, 보통 혼자 시간을 보내고 그녀 주변에 머무르는 소년이었다. 그 소년이 그린 것은 손이었다. 그런데 누구의 손일까? 그의 그림은 즉시 다른 학생들의 관심을 끌었다.

(C) 그래서, 모두들 그것이 누구의 손인지에 관해 앞다투어 말하려 했다. "그것은 우리에게 음식을 가져다주는 신의 손이 틀림없어."라고 한 학생이 말했다. "농부의 손이야, 왜냐하면 그들은 칠면조를 기르거든."이라고 두 번째 학생이 말했다. "경찰관의 손과 더 비슷해 보여, 그들은 우리를 보호해 줘."라고 또 다른 학생이 덧붙였다.

(A) 반 아이들의 호응에 Klein 선생님은 Douglas에 대해 하마터면 잊어버릴 뻔했다. 그녀는 나머지 아이들에게 다른 과제를 하도록 지도한 후, Douglas에게 그 손이 누구 손인지 물었다. "선생님 손이에요. 고마워요, Klein 선생님."이라고 그는 조용히 대답했다.

Why? 왜 정답일까?

고마운 것을 그려보는 시간에 Douglas가 무언가 색다른 것을 그렸다는 내용의 주어진 글 뒤에는, Douglas가 그린 것이 손이었다는 내용의 (B), 아이들이 누구의 손인지 맞춰보려 했다는 내용의 (C), 나중에 Douglas가 그것이 선생님의 손임을 말했다는 내용의 (A)가 차례로 이어져야 자연스럽다. 따라서 글의 순서로 가장 적절한 것은 ③ '(B) − (C) − (A)'이다.

- turkey ⓝ 칠면조
- immediately ⓐ 즉시
- raise ⓥ 기르다, 키우다
- responsive ⓐ 즉각 반응하는, 관심을 보이는
- attract one's interest ~의 관심을 끌다

1행 Mrs. Klein told her first graders to draw a picture of something to be thankful for.
동사　목적어　　목적격 보어　　　　(대명사-thing)
형용사적 용법

---

37 흡혈귀가 존재했을 수 없는 이유   정답률 62% | 정답 ⑤

주어진 글 다음에 이어질 글의 순서로 가장 적절한 것을 고르시오. [3점]

① (A) − (C) − (B)　　　　② (B) − (A) − (C)
③ (B) − (C) − (A)　　　　④ (C) − (A) − (B)
✔⑤ (C) − (B) − (A)

According to legend, / once a vampire bites a person, / that person turns into a vampire / who seeks the blood of others.
전설에 따르면, / 흡혈귀가 사람을 물면 / 그 사람은 흡혈귀로 변한다. / 다른 사람의 피를 갈구하는
A researcher came up with some simple math, / which proves that these highly popular creatures can't exist.
한 연구자는 간단한 계산법을 생각해냈다. / 이 잘 알려진 존재가 실존할 수 없다는 것을 증명하는
(C) University of Central Florida physics professor / Costas Efthimiou's work breaks down the myth.
University of Central Florida의 물리학과 교수인 / Costas Efthimiou의 연구가 그 미신을 무너뜨렸다.
Suppose / that on January 1st, 1600, / the human population was just over five hundred million.
가정해 보자. / 1600년 1월 1일에 / 인구가 5억 명이 넘는다고
(B) If the first vampire came into existence / that day and bit one person a month, / there would have been two vampires by February 1st, 1600.
그날 최초의 흡혈귀가 생겨나서 / 한 달에 한 명을 물었다면, / 1600년 2월 1일까지 흡혈귀가 둘 있었을 것이다.
A month later there would have been four, / the next month eight, / then sixteen, / and so on.
한 달 뒤면 넷이 되었을 것이고 / 그다음 달은 여덟, / 그리고 열여섯 / 등등이 되었을 것이다.
(A) In just two-and-a-half years, / the original human population / would all have become vampires / with no humans left.
불과 2년 반 만에, / 원래의 인류는 / 모두 흡혈귀가 되었을 것이다. / 인간이 하나도 남지 않은 채로
But look around you.
하지만 주위를 둘러보라.
Have vampires taken over the world?
흡혈귀가 세상을 정복하였는가?
No, because there's no such thing.
아니다. 왜냐하면 흡혈귀는 존재하지 않으니까.

전설에 따르면, 흡혈귀가 사람을 물면 그 사람은 다른 사람의 피를 갈구하는 흡혈귀로 변한다. 한 연구자는 이 대단히 잘 알려진 존재가 실존할 수 없다는 것을 증명하는 간단한 계산법을 생각해냈다.

(C) University of Central Florida의 물리학과 교수 Costas Efthimiou의 연구가 그 미신을 무너뜨렸다. 1600년 1월 1일에 인구가 막 5억 명을 넘겼다고 가정해 보자.

(B) 그날 최초의 흡혈귀가 생겨나서 한 달에 한 명을 물었다면, 1600년 2월 1일까지 흡혈귀가 둘 있었을 것이다. 한 달 뒤면 넷, 그다음 달은 여덟, 그리고 열여섯 등등으로 계속 늘어났을 것이다.

(A) 불과 2년 반 만에, 원래의 인류는 모두 흡혈귀가 되어 더 이상 남아 있지 않았을 것이다. 하지만 주위를 둘러보라. 흡혈귀가 세상을 정복하였는가? 아니다. 왜냐하면 흡혈귀는 존재하지 않으니까.

Why? 왜 정답일까?

흡혈귀가 존재했음을 부정하는 계산식을 생각해낸 사람이 있다는 내용의 주어진 글 뒤에는, 먼저 1600년 1월 1일에 인구가 5억 명이 넘었다고 가정해 보자며 계산식에 관해 설명하기 시작하는 (C)가 연결된다. 이어서 (B)는 (C)에서 언급한 날짜를 that day로 가리키며, 흡혈귀가 달마다 두 배씩 늘어가는 상황을 가정해 보자고 설명한다. 마지막으로 (A)는 (C) − (B)의 상황이 성립한다면 5억 명의 사람들이 불과 2년 반 만에 모두 흡혈귀로 변했을 것인데, 인류는 현재까지 지속되고 있으므로 흡혈귀가 존재했을 수 없다는 결론을 제시하고 있다. 따라서 글의 순서로 가장 적절한 것은 ⑤ '(C) − (B) − (A)'이다.

- legend ⓝ 전설
- come into existence 생기다, 나타나다
- myth ⓝ 미신, (잘못된) 통념
- take over ~을 지배하다, 장악하다
- break down 무너뜨리다

구문 풀이

5행 In just two-and-a-half years, the original human population would all have become vampires with no humans left.
「would have + 과거분사 : ~했을 것이다(가정법 과거완료 주절)」
「with + 명사 + 과거분사 : ~이 …된 채로」

---

38 마찰력의 특징   정답률 73% | 정답 ④

글의 흐름으로 보아, 주어진 문장이 들어가기에 가장 적절한 곳을 고르시오.

Friction is a force / between two surfaces / that are sliding, or trying to slide, / across each other.
마찰력은 힘이다. / 두 표면 사이에 작용하는 / 미끄러지거나 미끄러지려고 하는 / 서로 엇갈리는
For example, / when you try to push a book along the floor, / friction makes this difficult.
예를 들어, / 당신이 바닥 위 책을 밀려고 할 때, / 마찰이 이를 어렵게 만든다.
Friction always works in the direction / opposite to the direction / in which the object is moving, or trying to move.
마찰은 항상 방향으로 작용한다. / 방향과 반대인 / 물체가 움직이거나 움직이려고 하는
So, friction always slows a moving object down.
그래서 마찰은 항상 움직이는 물체를 느리게 만든다.
① The amount of friction depends on the surface materials.
마찰의 양은 표면 물질에 따라 달라진다.
② The rougher the surface is, / the more friction is produced.
표면이 거칠수록 / 더 많은 마찰력이 발생한다.

---

③ Friction also produces heat.
마찰은 또한 열을 발생시킨다.

☑For example, / if you rub your hands together quickly, / they will get warmer.
예를 들어, / 만약 당신이 손을 빠르게 비비면, / 손이 더 따뜻해질 것이다.

Friction can be a useful force / because it prevents our shoes slipping on the floor / when we walk / and stops car tires skidding on the road.
마찰력은 유용한 힘으로 작용할 수 있는데, / 그것이 신발이 바닥에서 미끄러지는 것을 방지하고 / 우리가 걸을 때 / 자동차 타이어가 도로에서 미끄러지는 것을 막아주기 때문이다.

⑤ When you walk, / friction is caused / between the tread on your shoes and the ground, / acting to grip the ground and prevent sliding.
당신이 걸을 때, / 마찰은 발생하며, / 당신의 신발 접지면과 바닥 사이에 / 땅을 붙잡아 미끄러지는 것을 방지하는 역할을 한다.

마찰력은 서로 엇갈리게 미끄러지거나 미끄러지려고 하는 두 표면 사이에 작용하는 힘이다. 예를 들어, 당신이 바닥 위 책을 밀려고 할 때, 마찰이 이를 어렵게 만든다. 마찰은 항상 물체가 움직이거나 움직이려고 하는 방향과 반대 방향으로 작용한다. 그래서 마찰은 항상 움직이는 물체를 느려지게 만든다. ① 마찰의 양은 표면 물질에 따라 달라진다. ② 표면이 거칠수록 더 많은 마찰력이 발생한다. ③ 마찰은 또한 열을 발생시킨다. ④ 예를 들어, 만약 당신이 손을 빠르게 비비면, 손이 더 따뜻해질 것이다. 마찰력은 우리가 걸을 때 신발이 바닥에서 미끄러지는 것을 방지하고 자동차 타이어가 도로에서 미끄러지는 것을 막아주므로 유용한 힘이 될 수 있다. ⑤ 걸을 때, 마찰은 당신의 신발 접지면과 바닥 사이에 발생하여 땅을 붙잡아 미끄러지는 것을 방지하는 역할을 한다.

Why? 왜 정답일까?

주어진 문장은 마찰과 열을 관련지어 설명하고 있으므로, 앞에 열에 관한 내용이 언급된 후 예시(For example)로 이어질 수 있다. 글에서 열에 관해 언급하는 문장은 ④ 앞의 문장이므로, 주어진 문장이 들어가기에 가장 적절한 곳은 ④이다.

- rub ⓥ 문지르다
- surface ⓝ 표면
- slow down ~을 느려지게 하다
- slip ⓥ (넘어지거나 넘어질 뻔하게) 미끄러지다
- friction ⓝ 마찰
- opposite ⓐ 반대의
- rough ⓐ 거친
- grip ⓥ 붙잡다

구문 풀이

9행 The rougher **the surface is**, the more **friction is produced**.
「the+비교급 ~, the+비교급 … : ~할수록 더 …하다」

★★★ 등급을 가르는 문제!
39 선천적 시각장애인의 세상 이해 │ 정답률 46% │ 정답 ⑤

글의 흐름으로 보아, 주어진 문장이 들어가기에 가장 적절한 곳을 고르시오.

Humans born without sight / are not able to collect visual experiences, / so they understand the world / entirely through their other senses.
선천적으로 시각장애가 있는 사람은 / 시각적 경험을 수집할 수 없어서, / 그들은 세상을 이해한다. / 전적으로 다른 감각을 통해

① As a result, / people with blindness at birth / develop an amazing ability / to understand the world / through the collection of experiences and memories / that come from these non-visual senses.
그 결과, / 선천적으로 시각장애가 있는 사람들은 / 놀라운 능력을 발달시킨다. / 세상을 이해하는 / 경험과 기억의 수집을 통해 / 이러한 비시각적 감각에서 오는

② The dreams of a person / who has been without sight since birth / can be just as vivid and imaginative / as those of someone with normal vision.
사람이 꾸는 꿈은 / 선천적으로 시각장애가 있는 / 생생하고 상상력이 풍부할 수 있다. / 정상 시력을 가진 사람의 꿈처럼

③ They are unique, however, / because their dreams are constructed / from the non-visual experiences and memories / they have collected.
그러나 그들은 특별하다. / 그들의 꿈은 구성되기 때문에 / 비시각적 경험과 기억으로부터 / 그들이 수집한

④ A person with normal vision / will dream about a familiar friend / using visual memories of shape, lighting, and colour.
정상적인 시력을 가진 사람들은 / 친숙한 친구에 대해 꿈을 꿀 것이다. / 형태, 빛 그리고 색의 시각적 기억을 사용하여

☑But, / a blind person will associate the same friend / with a unique combination of experiences / from their non-visual senses / that act to represent that friend.
하지만, / 시각장애인은 그 친구를 연상할 것이다. / 독특한 조합의 경험으로 / 비시각적 감각에서 나온 / 그 친구를 구현하는 데 작용하는

In other words, / people blind at birth / have similar overall dreaming experiences / even though they do not dream in pictures.
다시 말해, / 선천적 시각장애인들은 / 전반적으로 비슷한 꿈을 경험한다. / 그들이 시각적인 꿈을 꾸지는 않지만

선천적으로 시각장애가 있는 사람은 시각적 경험을 수집할 수 없어서, 전적으로 다른 감각을 통해 세상을 이해한다. ① 그 결과, 선천적으로 시각장애가 있는 사람들은 이러한 비시각적 감각에서 오는 경험과 기억의 수집을 통해 세상을 이해하는 놀라운 능력을 발달시킨다. ② 선천적으로 시각장애가 있는 사람이 꾸는 꿈은 정상 시력을 가진 사람의 꿈처럼 생생하고 상상력이 풍부할 수 있다. ③ 그러나 그들의 꿈은 그들이 수집한 비시각적 경험과 기억으로부터 구성되기 때문에 특별하다. ④ 정상적인 시력을 가진 사람들은 형태, 빛 그리고 색의 시각적 기억을 사용하여 친숙한 친구에 대해 꿈을 꿀 것이다. ⑤ 하지만, 시각장애인은 그 친구를 구현하는 데 작용하는 자신의 비시각적 감각에서 나온 독특한 조합의 경험으로 바로 그 친구를 연상할 것이다. 다시 말해, 선천적 시각장애인들은 시각적인 꿈을 꾸지는 않지만, 전반적으로 비슷한 꿈을 경험한다.

Why? 왜 정답일까?

선천적 시각장애인은 시각적 경험이 없지만 비시각적 경험과 기억을 통해 세상을 이해하는 특별한 방법을 구성해 나간다는 내용의 글로, ② 이후로 시각장애인이 꿈꾸는 방식을 예로 들고 있다. ⑤ 앞의 문장에서 비시각장애인은 시각적 경험을 이용해 친구에 관한 꿈을 꾼다고 언급하는데, 주어진 문장은 But으로 흐름을 뒤집으며 선천적 시각장애인은 비시각적 감각 경험을 토대로 친구를 연상한다고 설명한다. In other words로 시작하는 ⑤ 뒤의 문장은 주어진 문장의 의미를 풀어볼 때 시각장애인도 결국 꿈을 비슷하게 경험한다는 것을 알 수 있다고 결론 짓는다. 따라서 주어진 문장이 들어가기에 가장 적절한 곳은 ⑤이다.

- associate A with B A와 B를 연결 짓다, 연상하다
- combination ⓝ 조합
- vivid ⓐ 생생한
- sight ⓝ 시력
- imaginative ⓐ 상상력이 풍부한

구문 풀이

9행 The dreams of a person [who has been without sight since birth] can be just as vivid and imaginative as those of someone with normal vision.
주어(복수) / 주격 관·대(a person 수식) / 전치사(~이후로) / 동사
「as + 원급 + as : ~만큼 …한」 / 대명사(= the dreams)

★★ 문제 해결 꿀~팁 ★★

▶ 많이 틀린 이유는?
가장 헷갈리는 ③ 앞을 보면, 선천적 시각 장애인의 꿈도 비장애인의 꿈과 마찬가지로 생생하고 상상력이 풍부하다는 내용이다. 이어서 ③ 뒤에서는 however와 함께, '그런데' 이들의 꿈은 비시각적 경험과 기억에 바탕을 두기 때문에 '특별하다'는 내용을 추가하고 있다. 즉, ③ 앞뒤는 역접어 however를 기점으로 '우리와 다르지 않다 → 특별하다'로 자연스럽게 전환되는 흐름인 것이다.

▶ 문제 해결 방법은?
⑤ 앞에서 언급된 a familiar friend가 주어진 문장의 the same friend, that friend로 이어진다. 또한, In other words로 시작하는 ⑤ 뒤의 문장은 주어진 문장을 일반화한 내용이다.

40 권위가 있는 부모 밑에서 자란 자녀들의 학업 성취 │ 정답률 65% │ 정답 ③

다음 글의 내용을 한 문장으로 요약하고자 한다. 빈칸 (A), (B)에 들어갈 말로 가장 적절한 것은? [3점]

	(A)		(B)		(A)		(B)
①	likely 가능성이 크며	·····	random 무작위적인	②	willing 자발적이며	·····	minimal 최소한의
☑	willing 자발적이며	·····	active 적극적인	④	hesitant 망설이며	·····	unwanted 원치 않는
⑤	hesitant 망설이며	·····	constant 지속적인				

According to a study of Swedish adolescents, / an important factor of adolescents' academic success / is how they respond to challenges.
스웨덴 청소년들에 대한 연구에 따르면, / 청소년들의 학업 성공의 중요한 요인은 / 그들이 어려움에 반응하는 방식이다.

The study reports / that when facing difficulties, / adolescents exposed to an authoritative parenting style / are less likely to be passive, helpless, and afraid to fail.
이 연구는 보고하고 있다. / 어려움에 직면했을 때 / 권위가 있는 양육 방식에 노출된 청소년들은 / 덜 수동적이고, 덜 무기력하며, 실패를 덜 두려워한다는

Another study of nine high schools / in Wisconsin and northern California / indicates / that children of authoritative parents do well in school, / because these parents put a lot of effort / into getting involved in their children's school activities.
9개 고교에서 진행된 또 다른 연구는 / Wisconsin과 northern California의 / 밝히고 있다. / 권위가 있는 부모들의 아이들이 학습을 잘하는데, / 그 이유는 이러한 부모들이 많은 노력을 기울이기 때문이라고 / 아이들의 학교 활동에 관여하고자

That is, / authoritative parents are significantly more likely / to help their children with homework, / to attend school programs, / to watch their children in sports, / and to help students select courses.
즉, / 권위가 있는 부모들은 ~할 가능성이 훨씬 더 크다. / 아이들의 숙제를 도와주고, / 학교 프로그램에 참여하며, / 스포츠에 참여하는 아이들을 지켜보고, / 아이들의 과목 선택을 도와줄

Moreover, / these parents are more aware / of what their children do and how they perform in school.
게다가, / 이러한 부모들은 더 잘 인지하고 있다. / 아이들이 학교에서 하고 있는 일과 수행하는 방식에 대해

Finally, / authoritative parents / praise academic excellence and the importance of working hard more / than other parents do.
마지막으로, / 권위가 있는 부모들은 / 학문적 탁월함과 근면함의 중요성을 더 많이 칭찬한다. / 다른 부모들에 비해

➡ The studies above show / that the children of authoritative parents / often succeed academically, / since they are more (A) willing to deal with their difficulties / and are affected by their parents' (B) active involvement.
위 연구는 보여준다. / 권위가 있는 부모의 아이들이 / 학업 성취가 좋다는 것을 / 그들이 어려움에 대처하는 데 더 자발적이며, / 그 부모들의 적극적인 관여에 영향을 받기 때문에

스웨덴 청소년들에 대한 연구에 따르면, 청소년들의 학업 성공의 중요한 요인은 그들이 어려움에 반응하는 방식이다. 이 연구는 어려움에 직면했을 때 권위가 있는 양육 방식에 노출된 청소년들은 덜 수동적이고, 덜 무기력하며, 실패를 덜 두려워한다고 보고하고 있다. Wisconsin과 northern California의 9개 고교에서 진행된 또 다른 연구는 권위가 있는 부모의 아이들이 학습을 잘하는데, 그 이유는 이러한 부모들이 아이들의 학교 활동에 관여하고자 많은 노력을 기울이기 때문이라고 밝히고 있다. 즉, 권위가 있는 부모들은 아이들의 숙제를 도와주고, 학교 프로그램에 참여하며, 스포츠에 참여하는 아이들을 지켜보고, 아이들의 과목 선택을 도와줄 가능성이 훨씬 더 크다. 게다가, 이러한 부모들은 아이들이 학교에서 무엇을 하는지, 어떤 성과를 내는지 더 잘 인지하고 있다. 마지막으로, 권위가 있는 부모들은 다른 부모들에 비해 학문적 탁월함과 근면함의 중요성을 더 많이 칭찬한다.

➡ 위 연구는 권위가 있는 부모의 아이들이 어려움에 대처하는 데 더 (A) 자발적이며, 그 부모들의 (B) 적극적인 관여에 영향을 받기 때문에 학업 성취가 좋다는 것을 보여준다.

Why? 왜 정답일까?

두 번째 문장인 '~ when facing difficulties, adolescents exposed to an authoritative parenting style are less likely to be passive ~'에서 권위적인 양육 방식에 노출된 자녀는 어려움 앞에서 덜 수동적이라고 한다. 이어서 '~ children of authoritative parents do well in school, because these parents put a lot of effort into getting involved in their children's school activities.'에서 권위가 있는 부모는 자녀의 학습에 더 적극 관여하기 때문에, 이들 자녀의 학업 성취가 실제로 더 좋다는 연구 결과를 언급하고 있다. 따라서 요약문의 빈칸 (A), (B)에 들어갈 말로 가장 적절한 것은 ③ '(A) willing(자발적이며), (B) active(적극적인)'이다.

- adolescent ⓝ 청소년
- authoritative ⓐ 권위적인
- put effort into ~에 노력을 쏟다
- hesitant ⓐ 망설이는
- factor ⓝ 요인
- helpless ⓐ 무기력한
- significantly ⓐⓓ 상당히

구문 풀이

3행 The study reports that when facing difficulties, adolescents exposed to an
분사구문(~할 때) / 주어 / 과거분사
authoritative parenting style are less likely to be passive, helpless, and afraid to fail.
동사구(~할 가능성이 적다) / 주격 보어1 / 주격 보어2 / 주격 보어3

「U.K. researchers say / a bedtime of between 10 p.m. and 11 p.m. is best.
영국 연구원들은 이야기한다. / 밤 10시와 밤 11시 사이의 취침 시간이 가장 좋다고

They say / people who go to sleep between these times / have a (a) lower risk of heart disease.」 41번의 근거
그들은 이야기한다. / 이 시간대 사이에 잠드는 사람들이 / 더 낮은 심장 질환의 위험성을 가지고 있다고

Six years ago, / the researchers collected data / on the sleep patterns of 80,000 volunteers.
6년 전, / 그 연구원들은 데이터를 수집했다. / 8만 명의 자원자들의 수면 패턴에 관해

The volunteers had to wear a special watch for seven days / so the researchers could collect data / on their sleeping and waking times.
그 자원자들은 7일간 특별한 시계를 착용해야만 했고, / 그래서 연구원들은 데이터를 수집할 수 있었다. / 그들의 수면과 기상 시간에 대한

The scientists then monitored the health of the volunteers.
그러고 나서 연구원들은 그 자원자들의 건강을 관찰했다.

Around 3,000 volunteers later showed heart problems.
약 3천 명의 자원자들이 이후에 심장 문제를 보였다.

「They went to bed earlier or later / than the (b) ideal 10 p.m. to 11 p.m. timeframe.」 42번의 근거
그들은 더 이르거나 더 늦게 잠자리에 들었다. / 밤 10시에서 밤 11시라는 이상적인 시간대보다

One of the authors of the study, Dr. David Plans, / commented on his research / and the (c) effects of bedtimes on the health of our heart.
그 연구 저자 중 한 명인 Dr. David Plans는 / 자신의 연구에 대해 언급했다. / 그리고 취침 시간이 우리의 심장 건강에 끼치는 영향에 대해

He said / the study could not give a certain cause for their results, / but it suggests / that early or late bedtimes may be more likely / to disrupt the body clock, / with (d) negative consequences for cardiovascular health.
그는 이야기했다. / 그 연구가 결과의 특정한 원인을 시사하지는 못하지만, / 그것을 제시한다고 / 이르거나 늦은 취침 시간이 ~할 가능성이 더 높을 수 있다는 것을 / 체내 시계를 혼란케 할 / 심혈관 건강에 부정적인 결과와 함께

He said / that it was important for our body / to wake up to the morning light, / and that the worst time to go to bed / was after midnight / because it may (e) reduce the likelihood of seeing morning light / which resets the body clock.
그는 말했다. / 우리의 몸에 중요하고, / 아침 빛에 맞추어 일어나는 것이 / 잠자리에 드는 가장 나쁜 시간이 / 자정 이후인데, / 그것이 아침 빛을 볼 가능성을 낮출 수도 있기 때문이라고 / 우리의 체내 시계를 재설정하는

He added / that we risk cardiovascular disease / if our body clock is not reset properly.
그는 덧붙였다. / 우리가 심혈관 질환의 위험을 안게 된다고 / 만약 우리의 체내 시계가 적절하게 재설정되지 않으면

영국 연구원들은 밤 10시와 밤 11시 사이의 취침 시간이 가장 좋다고 이야기한다. 그들은 이 시간대 사이에 잠드는 사람들이 (a) 더 낮은 심장 질환의 위험성을 가지고 있다고 이야기한다. 6년 전, 그 연구원들은 8만 명의 자원자들의 수면 패턴 데이터를 수집했다. 그 자원자들은 연구원들이 그들의 수면과 기상 시간에 대한 데이터를 수집할 수 있도록 7일간 특별한 시계를 착용해야만 했다. 그러고 나서 연구원들은 그 자원자들의 건강을 관찰했다. 약 3천 명의 자원자들이 이후에 심장 문제를 보였다. 그들은 밤 10시에서 밤 11시 사이라는 (b) 이상적인 시간대보다 더 이르거나 더 늦게 잠자리에 들었다. 그 연구 저자 중 한 명인 Dr. David Plans는 자신의 연구와 취침 시간이 우리의 심장 건강에 끼치는 (c) 영향에 대해 언급했다. 그는 그 연구가 결과의 특정한 원인을 시사하지는 못하지만, 이르거나 늦은 취침 시간이 심혈관 건강에 (d) 긍정적인(→ 부정적인) 결과와 함께 체내 시계를 혼란케 할 가능성이 더 높을 수 있다는 것을 제시한다고 이야기했다. 그는 우리의 몸이 아침 빛에 맞추어 일어나는 것이 중요하고, 잠자리에 드는 가장 나쁜 시간이 자정 이후인데, 우리의 체내 시계를 재설정하는 아침 빛을 볼 가능성을 (e) 낮출 수도 있기 때문이라고 말했다. 그는 만약 우리의 체내 시계가 적절하게 재설정되지 않으면 우리가 심혈관 질환의 위험을 안게 된다고 덧붙였다.

- **author** ⓝ 저자
- **consequence** ⓝ 결과, 영향
- **likelihood** ⓝ 가능성, 공산
- **sound** ⓐ 좋은, 건전한
- **body clock** 생체 시계
- **reduce** ⓥ 낮추다, 줄이다
- **properly** ⓐ 적절하게

구문 풀이

15행 He said {that it was important for our body to wake up to the morning light,} and {that the worst time to go to bed was after midnight because it may reduce the likelihood of seeing morning light [which resets the body clock]}.

41 제목 파악 정답률 67% | 정답 ①

윗글의 제목으로 가장 적절한 것은?
✔ ① The Best Bedtime for Your Heart – 당신의 심장을 위한 최적의 취침 시간
② Late Bedtimes Are a Matter of Age – 늦은 취침 시간은 나이 문제이다
③ For Sound Sleep: Turn Off the Light – 숙면을 위해: 불을 끄세요
④ Sleeping Patterns Reflect Personalities – 수면 패턴은 성격을 반영한다
⑤ Regular Exercise: A Miracle for Good Sleep – 규칙적인 운동: 숙면을 위한 기적

Why? 왜 정답일까?

취침 시간이 심혈관 건강에 미치는 영향에 관한 연구 내용을 들어 적절한 취침 시간의 중요성을 설명하는 글로, 첫 두 문장에 화제가 잘 제시된다(~ a bedtime of between 10 p.m. and 11 p.m. is best. ~ people who go to sleep between these times have a lower risk of heart disease.)이다. 따라서 글의 제목으로 가장 적절한 것은 ① '당신의 심장을 위한 최적의 취침 시간'이다.

42 어휘 추론 정답률 68% | 정답 ④

밑줄 친 (a)~(e) 중에서 문맥상 낱말의 쓰임이 적절하지 않은 것은?
① (a) ② (b) ③ (c) ✔ ④ (d) ⑤ (e)

Why? 왜 정답일까?

연구 결과를 언급하는 첫 문단의 마지막 두 문장에 따르면, 이상적인 취침 시간보다 이르거나 늦게 잠드는 사람들은 이후 심장 문제가 생길 가능성이 높았다(Around 3,000 volunteers later showed

---

heart problems. They went to bed earlier or later than the ideal 10 p.m. to 11 p.m. timeframe.)고 한다. 즉 이상적인 취침시간보다 빨리 자든 늦게 자든, 그로 인해 '부정적인' 영향을 입을 수 있다는 것이므로, (d)의 positive를 negative로 고쳐야 한다. 따라서 문맥상 낱말의 쓰임이 적절하지 않은 것은 ④ '(d)'이다.

(A)
Once, / a farmer lost his precious watch / while working in his barn.
어느 날, / 한 농부가 그의 귀중한 시계를 잃어버렸다. / 헛간에서 일하는 동안

It may have appeared to be an ordinary watch to others, / but 「it brought a lot of happy childhood memories to him.」 45번 ①의 근거 일치
그것은 다른 이들에게는 평범한 시계로 보일 수도 있었지만 / 그것은 그에게 어린 시절의 많은 행복한 기억을 불러왔다

It was one of the most important things to (a) him.
그것은 그에게 가장 중요한 것들 중 하나였다.

After searching for it for along time, / the old farmer became exhausted.
오랜 시간 동안 그것을 찾아본 뒤에 / 그 나이 든 농부는 지쳐버렸다.

(D)
However, / the tired farmer did not want to give up / on the search for his watch / and asked a group of children playing outside to help him.
그러나, / 그 지친 농부는 포기하고 싶지 않았기에 / 자기 시계를 찾는 것을 / 밖에서 놀던 한 무리의 아이들에게 도와 달라고 요청했다.

(e) He promised an attractive reward / for the person who could find it.
그는 매력적인 보상을 약속했다. / 자기 시계를 찾는 사람에게

「After hearing about the reward, / the children hurried inside the barn / and went through and round the entire pile of hay / looking for the watch.」 45번 ④의 근거 불일치
보상에 대해 듣고 난 뒤, / 그 아이들은 헛간 안으로 서둘러 들어갔고 / 전체 건초 더미 사이와 주변으로 걸어갔다. / 시계를 찾으려

「After a long time searching for it, / some of the children got tired and gave up.」 45번 ⑤의 근거 일치
시계를 찾느라 오랜 시간을 보낸 후, / 아이들 중 일부는 지쳐서 포기했다.

(B)
The number of children looking for the watch / slowly decreased / and only a few tired children were left.
시계를 찾는 아이들의 숫자가 / 천천히 줄어들었고 / 지친 아이들 몇 명만이 남았다.

The farmer gave up all hope of finding it / and called off the search.
그 농부는 시계를 찾을 거라는 모든 희망을 포기하고 / 찾는 것을 멈추었다.

「Just when the farmer was closing the barn door, / a little boy came up to him / and asked the farmer to give him another chance.」 45번 ②의 근거 일치
농부가 막 헛간 문을 닫고 있었을 때 / 한 어린 소년이 그에게 다가와서 / 자신에게 또 한 번의 기회를 달라고 요청했다.

The farmer did not want / to lose out on any chance of finding the watch / so let (b) him in the barn.
농부는 원하지 않아서 / 시계를 찾을 어떤 가능성도 놓치는 것을 / 그를 헛간 안으로 들어오게 해주었다.

(C)
「After a little while / the boy came out with the farmer's watch in his hand.」 45번 ③의 근거 일치
잠시 후 / 그 소년이 한 손에 농부의 시계를 들고 나왔다.

(c) He was happily surprised / and asked how he had succeeded to find the watch / while everyone else had failed.
그는 행복에 겨워 놀랐고 / 소년이 어떻게 시계를 찾는 데 성공했는지를 물었다. / 다른 모두가 실패했던 반면

He replied / "I just sat there and tried listening for the sound of the watch. / In silence, / it was much easier / to hear it and follow the direction of the sound."
그는 답했다. / "저는 거기에 앉아서 시계의 소리를 들으려고 했어요. / 침묵 속에서, / 훨씬 쉬웠어요. / 그것을 듣고 소리의 방향을 따라가는 것이"

(d) He was delighted to get his watch back / and rewarded the little boy as promised.
그는 시계를 되찾아 기뻤고 / 그 어린 소년에게 약속했던 대로 보상해 주었다.

(A)
어느 날, 한 농부가 헛간에서 일하는 동안 그의 귀중한 시계를 잃어버렸다. 그것은 다른 이들에게는 평범한 시계로 보일 수도 있었지만 그것은 그에게 어린 시절의 많은 행복한 기억을 불러일으켰다. 그것은 (a) 그에게 가장 중요한 것들 중 하나였다. 오랜 시간 동안 그것을 찾아본 뒤에 그 나이 든 농부는 지쳐버렸다.

(D)
그러나, 그 지친 농부는 자기 시계를 찾는 것을 포기하고 싶지 않았기에 밖에서 놀던 한 무리의 아이들에게 도와 달라고 요청했다. (e) 그는 자기 시계를 찾는 사람에게 매력적인 보상을 약속했다. 보상에 대해 듣고 난 뒤, 그 아이들은 헛간 안으로 서둘러 들어갔고 시계를 찾으려 전체 건초 더미 사이와 주변을 다녔다. 시계를 찾느라 오랜 시간을 보낸 후, 아이들 중 일부는 지쳐서 포기했다.

(B)
시계를 찾는 아이들의 숫자가 천천히 줄어들었고 지친 아이들 몇 명만이 남았다. 그 농부는 시계를 찾을 거라는 모든 희망을 포기하고 찾는 것을 멈추었다. 농부가 막 헛간 문을 닫고 있었을 때 한 어린 소년이 그에게 다가와서 자신에게 또 한 번의 기회를 달라고 요청했다. 농부는 시계를 찾을 어떤 가능성도 놓치고 싶지 않아서 (b) 그를 헛간 안으로 들어오게 해주었다.

(C)
잠시 후 그 소년이 한 손에 농부의 시계를 들고 나왔다. (c) 그는 행복에 겨워 놀랐고 다른 모두가 실패했던 반면 소년이 어떻게 시계를 찾는 데 성공했는지를 물었다. 그는 "저는 거기에 앉아서 시계의 소리를 들으려고 했어요. 침묵 속에서, 그것을 듣고 소리의 방향을 따라가는 것이 훨씬 쉬웠어요."라고 답했다. (d) 그는 시계를 되찾아 기뻤고 그 어린 소년에게 약속했던 대로 보상해 주었다.

- **precious** ⓐ 소중한, 귀중한
- **lose out on** ~을 놓치다, ~에게 지다
- **pile** ⓝ 더미
- **call off** ~을 중단하다, 멈추다
- **attractive** ⓐ 매력적인
- **hay** ⓝ 건초

구문 풀이

(B) 1행 The number of children looking for the watch slowly decreased and only a few tired children were left.

(C) 5행 In silence, it was much easier to hear it and follow the direction of the sound.

43 글의 순서 파악 정답률 77% | 정답 ④

주어진 글 (A)에 이어질 내용을 순서에 맞게 배열한 것으로 가장 적절한 것은?

① (B) – (D) – (C) ② (C) – (B) – (D)
③ (C) – (D) – (B) ✔④ (D) – (B) – (C)
⑤ (D) – (C) – (B)

Why? 왜 정답일까?

아끼던 시계를 잃어버린 농부를 소개하는 (A) 뒤로, 농부가 아이들에게 시계 찾기를 맡겼다는 내용의 (D), 모두가 실패한 가운데 한 소년이 다시 자원했다는 내용의 (B), 소년이 시계를 찾아냈다는 내용의 (C)가 차례로 이어져야 자연스럽다. 따라서 글의 순서로 가장 적절한 것은 ④ '(D) – (B) – (C)'이다.

44 지칭 추론 정답률 73% | 정답 ②

밑줄 친 (a) ~ (e) 중에서 가리키는 대상이 나머지 넷과 다른 것은?

① (a) ✔② (b) ③ (c) ④ (d) ⑤ (e)

Why? 왜 정답일까?

(a), (c), (d), (e)는 the farmer, (b)는 a little boy이므로, (a) ~ (e) 중에서 가리키는 대상이 다른 하나는 ② '(b)'이다.

45 세부 내용 파악 정답률 76% | 정답 ④

윗글에 관한 내용으로 적절하지 않은 것은?

① 농부의 시계는 어린 시절의 행복한 기억을 불러일으켰다.
② 한 어린 소년이 농부에게 또 한 번의 기회를 달라고 요청했다.
③ 소년이 한 손에 농부의 시계를 들고 나왔다.
✔④ 아이들은 시계를 찾기 위해 헛간을 뛰쳐나왔다.
⑤ 아이들 중 일부는 지쳐서 시계 찾기를 포기했다.

Why? 왜 정답일까?

(D) 'After hearing about the reward, the children hurried inside the barn ~'에서 아이들은 농부가 잃어버린 시계를 찾기 위해 헛간을 나온 것이 아니라 들어갔다고 하므로, 내용과 일치하지 않는 것은 ④ '아이들은 시계를 찾기 위해 헛간을 뛰쳐나왔다.'이다.

Why? 왜 오답일까?

① (A) '~ it brought a lot of happy childhood memories to him.'의 내용과 일치한다.
② (B) 'a little boy came up to him and asked the farmer to give him another chance.'의 내용과 일치한다.
③ (C) 'After a little while the boy came out with the farmer's watch in his hand.'의 내용과 일치한다.
⑤ (D) 'After a long time searching for it, some of the children got tired and gave up.'의 내용과 일치한다.

어휘 Review Test 10 문제편 108쪽

A	B	C	D
01 현혹시키는, 속이는	01 process	01 ①	01 ⓓ
02 매력적인	02 overseas	02 ⓝ	02 ①
03 원칙, 원리	03 consume	03 ①	03 ⓞ
04 자기 방어	04 participant	04 ⓐ	04 ①
05 논의하다	05 surface	05 ⓜ	05 ⓖ
06 탐구하다	06 modify	06 ⓟ	06 ⓖ
07 물리적으로, 신체적으로	07 raise	07 ⓡ	07 ⓢ
08 붙잡다	08 superior	08 ⓖ	08 ①
09 반영	09 household	09 ⓔ	09 ⓡ
10 믿을 만하지 않은	10 construct	10 ⓠ	10 ⓑ
11 우연의 일치, 동시 발생	11 recover	11 ①	11 ⓗ
12 예측	12 inaccurate	12 ⓑ	12 ⓗ
13 유전적으로	13 assessment	13 ⓢ	13 ①
14 독특한	14 sink	14 ⓓ	14 ⓚ
15 보유, 소유	15 historically	15 ⓗ	15 ⓔ
16 양, 수량	16 introduce	16 ⓚ	16 ⓐ
17 결과, 영향	17 precious	17 ⓕ	17 ①
18 양육	18 constraint	18 ⓞ	18 ⓜ
19 감동한	19 comment	19 ⓒ	19 ⓟ
20 발매하다, 출간하다	20 concern	20 ①	20 ⓒ

· 정답 ·

01 ② 02 ② 03 ② 04 ④ 05 ④ 06 ① 07 ③ 08 ③ 09 ④ 10 ③ 11 ② 12 ⑤ 13 ① 14 ⑤ 15 ③
16 ③ 17 ④ 18 ① 19 ③ 20 ① 21 ③ 22 ⑤ 23 ② 24 ① 25 ⑤ 26 ③ 27 ⑤ 28 ④ 29 ⑤ 30 ③
31 ① 32 ⑤ 33 ① 34 ④ 35 ④ 36 ⑤ 37 ② 38 ③ 39 ④ 40 ① 41 ⑤ 42 ④ 43 ② 44 ② 45 ⑤

★ 표기된 문항은 [등급을 가르는 문제]에 해당하는 문항입니다.

01 독감 예방 주사 접종 권유 정답률 90% | 정답 ②

다음을 듣고, 남자가 하는 말의 목적으로 가장 적절한 것을 고르시오.

① 건강 검진 일정을 공지하려고
✔② 독감 예방 접종을 권장하려고
③ 개인 위생 관리를 당부하려고
④ 보건소 운영 기간을 안내하려고
⑤ 독감 예방 접종 부작용을 경고하려고

M : Hello, students.
안녕하세요, 학생 여러분.
This is Allan, your school nurse.
저는 보건 교사인 Allan입니다.
Many students get sick with seasonal influenza.
많은 학생들이 계절성 독감에 걸립니다.
Some cases can lead to serious pain or even hospitalization.
몇몇 경우는 심각한 통증이나 심지어 입원으로 이어지기도 합니다.
I would recommend you to get a flu vaccine.
여러분이 독감 백신을 접종하기를 권장합니다.
A flu shot can keep you from getting sick.
독감 백신이 여러분을 아프지 않게 해줄 것입니다.
Also, since flu viruses keep changing, flu vaccines are updated to protect against such viruses.
또한, 독감 바이러스는 계속 바뀌므로, 그러한 바이러스로부터 보호되기 위해 독감 백신을 새로 맞아야 합니다.
Please get a flu shot offered in doctors' offices or health departments by the end of this month.
이번 달까지 병원 또는 보건부에서 제공하는 독감 주사를 맞기 바랍니다.
Thank you.
감사합니다.

Why? 왜 정답일까?

'I would recommend you to get a flu vaccine.'에서 남자는 학생들에게 독감 예방 주사를 맞기를 권장한다고 언급했고, 후반부에서 백신 접종을 이번 달까지 완료해 달라고 요청하였다. 따라서 남자가 하는 말의 목적으로 가장 적절한 것은 ② '독감 예방 접종을 권장하려고'이다.

- **school nurse** 보건 교사
- **seasonal** ⓐ 계절성의
- **hospitalization** ⓝ 입원
- **keep A from B** A를 B로부터 막다
- **health department** 보건부
- **get sick with** (병에) 걸리다
- **lead to** ~로 이어지다, ~을 낳다
- **recommend** ⓥ 권장하다
- **protect against** ~로부터 지키다

02 지역 서점 이용하기 정답률 87% | 정답 ②

대화를 듣고, 여자의 의견으로 가장 적절한 것을 고르시오.

① 독서 습관을 기르자.
✔② 지역 서점을 이용하자.
③ 지역 특산품을 애용하자.
④ 중고 서점을 활성화시키자.
⑤ 온라인을 통한 도서 구입을 늘리자.

M : Irene, where are you heading?
Irene, 어디 가고 있어?
W : Hello, Mason. I'm going to the bookstore to buy some books.
안녕, Mason. 난 책을 좀 사려고 서점에 가는 길이야.
M : The bookstore? Isn't it more convenient to order books online?
서점? 온라인에서 책을 주문하는 게 더 편하지 않아?
W : Yes, but I like to flip through the pages at bookstores.
응, 그런데 난 서점에서 책을 좀 훑어보는 게 좋아.
M : Yeah, but buying books online is cheaper.
응, 하지만 온라인에서 책을 사는 게 더 싸잖아.
W : Right. But we can help bookstore owners when we buy books from them.
맞아. 하지만 우리가 서점에서 책을 사면 서점 주인을 도울 수 있어.
M : I guess you're right. The bookstore near my house shut down last month.
네 말이 맞는 것 같네. 우리 집 근처 서점이 지난달에 문을 닫았어.
W : It's a pity to see local bookstores going out of business nowadays.
지역 서점이 요새 문을 닫는 것을 보게 되어 유감이야.
M : I agree. Next time I need a book, I'll try to go to a local bookstore.
동의해. 다음번에 내가 책이 필요할 때 지역 서점을 가 봐야겠어.

Why? 왜 정답일까?

'But we can help bookstore owners when we buy books from them.'에서 여자는 지역 서점에서 책을 사면 서점 주인들에게 도움이 된다고 언급하며 책을 살 때 서점을 이용한다고 말한다. 따라서 여자의 의견으로 가장 적절한 것은 ② '지역 서점을 이용하자.'이다.

- **convenient** ⓐ 편리한
- **go out of business** (가게가) 문을 닫다, 폐업하다
- **flip through** ~을 훑어보다

03 문이 잠겨서 열쇠 수리 요청하기 정답률 89% | 정답 ②

대화를 듣고, 두 사람의 관계를 가장 잘 나타낸 것을 고르시오.

① 호텔 직원 – 투숙객
✔② 열쇠 수리공 – 집주인

③ 경비원 – 입주민　　　　　④ 은행원 – 고객
⑤ 치과의사 – 환자

① 부엌 청소하기　　　　　② 점심 준비하기
③ 카메라 구매하기　　　　　✔ 딸 데리러 가기
⑤ 요리법 검색하기

[Telephone rings.]
[전화벨이 울린다.]

M : Hello. This is G-Solution. How may I help you?
여보세요. G-Solution입니다. 무엇을 도와드릴까요?

W : Hello. I'm locked out of my home. The keypad on my door isn't responding.
여보세요. 전 집 문이 잠겨서 못 들어가고 있어요. 제 문에 있는 키패드가 반응이 없어요.

M : It might be an electric problem. It's probably a simple fix and it won't cost much.
전기 문제일 수 있습니다. 아마 간단히 수리하면 될 거고 비용은 많이 안 들 거예요.

W : How much is it?
얼마죠?

M : It's 30 dollars including the service charge. But you'll have to pay extra if there're any additional problems.
출장비까지 포함해서 30달러입니다. 하지만 추가적인 문제가 혹시 있다면 추가 비용을 내셔야 할 겁니다.

W : I got it. Can you come over right away?
알겠습니다. 지금 바로 와주실 수 있나요?

M : I'm afraid not. I'm doing a job at the Capital Bank.
지금은 어렵습니다. Capital Bank에서 작업 중이거든요.

W : How long will it take you to finish?
끝내시는 데 얼마나 걸릴까요?

M : Just one hour. I'll call you as soon as I'm done. Address, please?
1시간이면 됩니다. 다 되는 대로 전화를 드리겠습니다. 주소 불러주시겠어요?

W : 705 Cozy Street near Lee's Dental Clinic.
Lee's Dental Clinic 근처의 Cozy Street 705번지예요.

M : Okay. See you soon.
네, 곧 뵙겠습니다.

Why? 왜 정답일까?

'I'm locked out of my home.', 'It might be an electric problem. It's probably a simple fix and it won't cost much.'를 통해 남자가 열쇠 수리공이고, 여자가 집주인임을 알 수 있다. 따라서 두 사람의 관계로 가장 적절한 것은 ② '열쇠 수리공 – 집주인'이다.

● **lock out of** 열쇠가 없어서 ~에 못 들어가다　● **electric** ⓐ 전기의
● **additional** ⓐ 추가적인

04 새로 꾸민 방 구경하기　　　정답률 65% | 정답 ④

대화를 듣고, 그림에서 대화의 내용과 일치하지 <u>않는</u> 것을 고르시오.

M : Grace, let me show you my newly designed room.
Grace, 내가 새로 꾸민 방을 보여줄게.

W : Wow, Jake! It's so cool.
와, Jake! 정말 멋지다.

M : 「Look at the monitor between the speakers.」 I changed my old monitor for this new one. ①의 근거 일치
스피커 사이에 있는 모니터를 봐. 내 오래된 모니터를 이걸로 바꿨어.

W : Looks nice. 「But isn't your desk too crowded to put your electric keyboard on it?」 ②의 근거 일치
근사해 보이네. 그런데 전자 키보드를 놓기에는 네 책상이 너무 꽉 차지 않니?

M : It's fine with me. I find it convenient there.
난 괜찮아. 그걸 거기 두는 게 편하더라고.

W : 「Is that a microphone in the corner?」 Do you sing? ③의 근거 일치
구석에 있는 건 마이크야? 너 노래해?

M : Yes. Singing is my all-time favorite hobby.
응. 노래는 언제나 내가 제일 좋아하는 취미야.

W : 「What's that star-shaped medal on the wall?」 Where did you get it? ④의 근거 불일치
벽에 있는 별 모양 메달은 뭐야? 어디서 났어?

M : I won that medal at a guitar contest with my dad.
난 우리 아빠랑 나간 기타 대회에서 저 메달을 얻었어.

W : Incredible! Do you often practice the guitar with your dad?
멋지다! 너는 아버지랑 종종 기타를 연습해?

M : Sure. 「That's why there're two guitars in the room.」 ⑤의 근거 일치
물론이지. 그래서 방에 기타가 두 대 있는 거야.

Why? 왜 정답일까?

대화에서는 벽에 별 모양 메달이 걸려 있다고 하는데(What's that star-shaped medal on the wall?), 그림의 벽에는 원 모양 메달이 걸려 있다. 따라서 그림에서 대화의 내용과 일치하지 않는 것은 ④이다.

● **crowded** ⓐ (~이) 가득한, 빽빽한　● **incredible** ⓐ 멋진, 믿을 수 없는
● **practice** ⓥ 연습하다

05 아이를 대신 데리러 가기로 하기　　　정답률 79% | 정답 ④

대화를 듣고, 남자가 여자를 위해 할 일로 가장 적절한 것을 고르시오. [3점]

---

① 부엌 청소하기　　　　　② 점심 준비하기
③ 카메라 구매하기　　　　　✔ 딸 데리러 가기
⑤ 요리법 검색하기

W : Smells nice, Daniel. What did you make for lunch?
냄새 좋네요, Daniel. 점심으로 뭘 만들었어요?

M : Creamy pasta. I found the recipe online.
크림 파스타예요. 온라인에서 레시피를 찾았어요.

W : Fantastic. But don't you think the kitchen is a little bit messy?
환상적이네요. 그런데 부엌이 좀 지저분하다고 생각하지 않아요?

M : Sorry. I'll clean it up later.
미안해요. 나중에 내가 치울게요.

W : You promise?
약속하는 거죠?

M : Yes. Let's have lunch. *[Pause]* By the way, do you remember you have to pick up our daughter from the library this afternoon?
네. 점심 먹죠. *[잠시 멈춤]* 그나저나, 오늘 오후 당신이 우리 딸을 도서관에서 데리고 오기로 했던 거 기억해요?

W : Oh, my! I totally forgot. What should I do? My friend Amy is coming in an hour.
오, 이런! 완전히 잊고 있었어요. 어떻게 하죠? 내 친구 Amy가 한 시간 뒤에 오기로 했어요.

M : Don't worry. I planned to go camera shopping, but I'll pick up Betty, instead.
걱정 마요. 난 카메라를 사러 갈 계획이었는데, 그 대신 내가 Betty를 데려올게요.

W : Thanks. How sweet of you! Then I'll clean the kitchen.
고마워요. 상냥하기도 하죠! 그럼 내가 부엌을 치울게요.

Why? 왜 정답일까?

대화에 따르면 남자는 딸을 도서관에 데리러 가기로 한 사실을 잊은 여자 대신 딸을 데리러 가기로 한다(~ I'll pick up Betty, instead.). 따라서 남자가 여자를 위해 할 일로 가장 적절한 것은 ④ '딸 데리러 가기'이다.

● **messy** ⓐ 지저분한, 엉망인　　　● **by the way** 그나저나
● **pick up** (~을 차로) 데려오다

06 노트북 가방 사기　　　정답률 85% | 정답 ①

대화를 듣고, 여자가 지불할 금액을 고르시오.

✔ $30　　② $50　　③ $63　　④ $65　　⑤ $70

M : Good afternoon. May I help you?
안녕하세요. 도와드릴까요?

W : Yes, please. I want to buy a bag for my laptop. Can you recommend one?
네. 전 노트북 가방을 사고 싶어요. 하나 추천해 주실래요?

M : How about this one? It's only 30 dollars on sale. The original price was 65 dollars.
이건 어떠신가요? 할인해서 30달러밖에 안 한답니다. 원래 가격은 65달러예요.

W : Wow, more than 50% off!
와, 50퍼센트나 더 할인하네요.

M : It's a very good deal.
아주 잘 사시는 거죠.

W : I like the design and color, but it's not big enough.
디자인하고 색은 마음에 드는데, 크기가 충분히 크지 않네요.

M : If you want something bigger, how about this one? It has a USB charging port, too.
좀 더 큰 것을 찾으신다면, 이건 어떠신가요? USB 충전 포트도 있어요.

W : I like it, but it looks expensive.
마음에 드는데, 비싸 보이네요.

M : It's 70 dollars. But I can give you a 10% discount.
70달러입니다. 하지만 10달러 할인을 해드릴 수 있어요.

W : Well... It's still beyond my budget. Let me look at the first one again.
음... 그래도 제 예산을 넘네요. 처음 봤던 것을 다시 볼게요.

M : Here it is. 30 dollars is a bargain.
여기 있습니다. 30달러면 거저죠.

W : Okay. I'll take it.
네, 이걸 살게요.

Why? 왜 정답일까?

대화에 따르면 여자는 처음 보았던 30달러짜리 노트북 가방이 크기가 작아 보여서 고민했지만 결국 이 가방을 사기로 한다. 따라서 여자가 지불할 금액은 ① '$30'이다.

● **laptop** ⓝ 노트북 컴퓨터　　　● **bargain** ⓝ 싼 물건, 특가

07 뮤지컬 공연에 갈 수 없는 이유　　　정답률 78% | 정답 ③

대화를 듣고, 남자가 공연장에 갈 수 <u>없는</u> 이유로 가장 적절한 것을 고르시오.

① 출장을 가야 해서　　　　② 숙제를 끝내야 해서
✔ 조카를 돌봐야 해서　　　④ 이사 준비를 해야 해서
⑤ 친구와 만날 약속을 해서

W : Hi, Chris. How was your business trip?
안녕, Chris. 출장 어땠니?

M : It went fine. By the way, I heard Emma is moving out this Saturday.
괜찮았어. 그나저나 난 Emma가 이번 토요일에 이사 간다고 들었어.

W : You're right. She's very busy preparing to move. So she gave me two tickets for a musical because she can't go.
맞아. 그녀는 지금 이사 준비에 몹시 바빠. 그래서 자기가 갈 수 없는 뮤지컬 티켓을 나한테 두 장 줬어.

M : Good for you. What's the name of the musical?
잘됐네. 뮤지컬 이름이 뭔데?

W : It's "Heroes."
'Heroes'야.

M : Really? I heard it's popular. Who are you going with?
정말? 그거 되게 유명한 거라고 들었어. 누구랑 같이 가?

W : No one, yet. My sister turned me down because she has to finish her homework.
아직 안 정했어. 우리 언니가 숙제를 끝내야 한다면서 거절했어.

M : Well, can I go with you instead?
음, 그럼 내가 대신 같이 가도 될까?

W : Sure. Why not? The show is at 8 p.m. this Friday.
물론이지. 왜 안 되겠어? 공연은 이번 주 금요일 저녁 8시야.

M : Friday? Oh, no! I promised to take care of my niece at that time.
금요일이라고? 이런! 그때엔 내 조카를 돌봐주기로 약속했어.

W : No problem. I'll ask Susan to go with me then.
괜찮아. 그럼 Susan한테 같이 가자고 할게.

Why? 왜 정답일까?

대화에 따르면 남자는 금요일에 조카를 돌봐주기로 약속했기에(I promised to take care of my niece at that time.) 공연에 갈 수 없다. 따라서 남자가 공연장에 갈 수 없는 이유로 가장 적절한 것은 ③ '조카를 돌봐야 해서'이다.

● business trip 출장
● be busy ~ing ~하느라 바쁘다
● turn down ~을 거절하다
● take care of ~을 돌보다

---

08 강아지 키우기 정답률 77% | 정답 ③

대화를 듣고, 강아지 키우기에 관해 언급되지 <u>않은</u> 것을 고르시오.
① 산책시키기
② 먹이 주기
✓③ 목욕시키기
④ 배변 훈련시키기
⑤ 소변 패드 치우기

W : Dad, I want to have a puppy just like my friend, Julie.
아빠, 전 제 친구 Julie처럼 강아지를 한 마리 갖고 싶어요.

M : Why not? But do you know how hard it is to raise a dog?
안 될 게 뭐 있니? 그런데 개를 키우는 게 얼마나 어려운지 알고 있어?

W : Yes, but I'm ready. I think I will name my puppy Toby.
네, 하지만 전 준비됐어요. 전 제 강아지를 Toby라고 이름 지으려고 생각 중이에요.

M : Okay. 「But will you walk Toby every day?」①의근거 일치
그래. 그런데 넌 Toby를 매일 산책시킬 거니?

W : That'll be easy.
그건 간단하죠.

M : 「Also, you'll have to feed Toby three times a day.」②의근거 일치
게다가, 넌 Toby에게 하루에 세 번 먹이를 줘야 해.

W : No big deal. Anything else?
별거 아니네요. 다른 건요?

M : 「You'll have to toilet train Toby, too.」④의근거 일치
넌 Toby에게 배변 훈련도 시켜야 하지.

W : Really?
정말요?

M : Of course. 「Plus, you'll need to clean up the dog's pee pads.」⑤의근거 일치
물론이지. 더구나, 개 소변 패드도 치워야 할 거야.

W : Hmm... Dad, you'll help me, right?
흠... 아빠, 저를 도와주실 거죠, 그렇죠?

M : Sometimes. But remember having a dog takes responsibility.
가끔은 도와주지. 하지만 개를 키우는 것에는 책임감이 필요하다는 점을 기억해 둬.

Why? 왜 정답일까?

대화에서 남자와 여자는 강아지 키우기와 관련하여 매일 산책시키기, 하루에 세 번 먹이 주기, 배변 훈련시키기, 소변 패드 치우기를 언급하였다. 따라서 언급되지 않은 것은 ③ '목욕시키기'이다.

Why? 왜 오답일까?

① 'But will you walk Toby every day?'에서 '산책시키기'가 언급되었다.
② 'Also, you'll have to feed Toby three times a day.'에서 '먹이 주기'가 언급되었다.
④ 'You'll have to toilet train Toby, too.'에서 '배변 훈련시키기'가 언급되었다.
⑤ 'Plus, you'll need to clean up the dog's pee pads.'에서 '소변 패드 치우기'가 언급되었다.

● raise ⓥ 기르다, 키우다
● toilet train 배변 훈련을 시키다

---

09 기부 운동 참여 권유 정답률 91% | 정답 ④

Sharing Friday Movement에 관한 다음 내용을 듣고, 일치하지 <u>않는</u> 것을 고르시오. [3점]
① 매주 금요일에 2달러씩 기부하는 운동이다.
② 2001년 핀란드에서 시작되었다.
③ 기부금은 가난한 지역에 깨끗한 물을 공급하는 데 쓰인다.
✓④ 올해 20명의 학생에게 장학금을 지급했다.
⑤ 추가 정보는 홈페이지를 통해 얻을 수 있다.

W : Good afternoon, listeners.
안녕하세요, 청취자 여러분.

「Why don't you join the Sharing Friday Movement and donate two dollars to our fund every Friday?」①의근거 일치
Sharing Friday Movement에 참여하셔서 매주 금요일마다 저희 펀드에 2달러씩 기부하시는 건 어떠세요?

「This movement started in 2001 in Finland as an idea to encourage people to do good.」②의근거 일치
이 운동은 사람들에게 좋은 일을 하도록 독려하고자 하는 아이디어로 2001년 핀란드에서 시작되었습니다.

Since then, this idea has grown into a global movement.
그 이후로 이 아이디어는 세계적인 운동으로 발전했죠.

「Most of the donations go to poor areas across the world and help people get clean water.」③의근거 일치
기부금의 대부분은 세계 가난한 지역으로 보내져 사람들이 깨끗한 물을 얻을 수 있게 도움을 주는 데 쓰입니다.

「This year, scholarships were given to 100 students in these areas to celebrate our 20th anniversary.」④의근거 불일치
올해는 저희 20주년을 기념하여 이러한 지역의 학생 100명에게 장학금이 지급되었습니다.

Please join us, and help make a difference.
저희와 함께 해주시고, 변화를 가져오는 데 도움을 주세요.

「If you want to get more information, visit our homepage.」⑤의근거 일치
더 많은 정보를 얻고 싶으시다면, 저희 홈페이지를 방문해주세요.

Why? 왜 정답일까?

'This year, scholarships were given to 100 students in these areas to celebrate our 20th anniversary.'에서 기부 운동 20주년을 맞이해 100명의 학생들에게 장학금이 수여되었다고 하므로, 내용과 일치하지 않는 것은 ④ '올해 20명의 학생에게 장학금을 지급했다.'이다.

Why? 왜 오답일까?

① 'Why don't you join the Sharing Friday Movement and donate two dollars to our fund every Friday?'의 내용과 일치한다.
② 'This movement started in 2001 in Finland ~'의 내용과 일치한다.
③ 'Most of the donations go to poor areas across the world and help people get clean water.'의 내용과 일치한다.
⑤ 'If you want to get more information, visit our homepage.'의 내용과 일치한다.

● donate ⓥ 기부하다
● do good 선행하다
● celebrate ⓥ 기념하다
● make a difference 변화를 가져오다, 차이를 낳다
● encourage ⓥ 독려하다
● scholarship ⓝ 장학금
● anniversary ⓝ 기념일

---

10 셀카봉 구입하기 정답률 91% | 정답 ③

다음 표를 보면서 대화를 듣고, 여자가 구입할 모델을 고르시오.

Selfie Sticks

	Model	Weight	Maximum Length	Bluetooth Remote Control	Price
①	A	150g	60cm	×	$10
②	B	150g	80cm	○	$30
✓③	C	180g	80cm	○	$20
④	D	180g	100cm	×	$15
⑤	E	230g	100cm	○	$25

W : Kevin, I'm looking for a selfie stick. Can you help me?
Kevin, 난 셀카봉을 찾고 있어. 나 좀 도와줄래?

M : Sure, mom. You can buy one on your smartphone. [Pause] What kind of selfie stick do you want?
네, 엄마. 스마트폰으로 하나 사시면 돼요. [잠시 멈춤] 어떤 종류의 셀카봉을 원하세요?

W : I'd prefer a light one.
난 가벼운 게 좋아.

M : 「Then I don't recommend a selfie stick over 200 grams.」 How about the length? 근거1 Weight 조건
그럼 200그램 이상인 셀카봉은 추천하지 않겠어요. 길이는요?

W : I have no idea. What's your opinion?
잘 모르겠어. 네 의견은 어때니?

M : Hmm... 「It should extend up to 80cm at least.」 근거2 Maximum Length 조건
흠.... 적어도 80센티미터까지는 늘어나야죠. 근거3 Bluetooth Remote Control 조건

W : Okay. 「I also want a bluetooth remote control.」 I heard they're convenient to use.
알겠어. 그리고 난 블루투스 리모컨을 원해. 그게 쓰기 편하다고 들었어.

M : Then you have two options left. Which one do you want?
그럼 선택권이 두 개 남았어요. 어느 걸 원하세요?

W : 「I'll buy this cheaper one.」 근거4 Price 조건
더 싼 이걸로 살래.

M : Great choice.
탁월한 선택이에요.

Why? 왜 정답일까?

대화에 따르면 여자는 무게가 200g 이하이고, 80cm 이상 늘어나고, 블루투스 리모컨이 포함되어 있으며, 가격은 더 싼 셀카봉을 구입하려고 한다. 따라서 여자가 구입할 모델은 ③ 'C'이다.

● selfie stick 셀카봉
● convenient ⓐ 편리한
● extend ⓥ 늘어나다

---

11 지리산 여행 준비하기 정답률 84% | 정답 ②

대화를 듣고, 남자의 마지막 말에 대한 여자의 응답으로 가장 적절한 것을 고르시오.
① Again? You've lost your bag twice. – 또? 넌 가방을 두 번이나 잃어버렸어.
✓② You're right. I'll take a warm jacket. – 네 말이 맞아. 따뜻한 재킷을 가져가겠어.
③ Why? I know you prefer cold weather. – 왜? 난 네가 추운 날씨를 더 좋아하는 걸 알아.
④ What? I finished packing a present for you. – 뭐? 난 네 선물을 다 쌌는데.
⑤ Sorry. But you can't join the trip at this point. – 미안해. 그런데 넌 지금 와서 여행에 참여할 수 없어.

M : Have you finished packing your bags for your trip to Mount Jiri?
너 지리산 여행을 위해 짐 다 쌌니?

W : I think so. Look! What else do I need?
그런 것 같아. 봐봐! 뭐가 더 필요할까?

M : You'd better prepare for the cold weather at night.
밤에 추워질 날씨를 대비하는 게 좋을 거야.

W : You're right. I'll take a warm jacket.
네 말이 맞아. 따뜻한 재킷을 가져가겠어.

Why? 왜 정답일까?

지리산 여행을 준비하고 있는 여자에게 남자는 밤에 추워질 날씨를 대비해야 한다고 말하므로(You'd better prepare for the cold weather at night.), 여자의 응답으로 가장 적절한 것은 ② '네 말이 맞아. 따뜻한 재킷을 가져가겠어.'이다.

● pack ⓥ (짐을) 싸다, 챙기다
● prepare for ~을 대비하다

---

12 외식 취소하기 정답률 69% | 정답 ⑤

대화를 듣고, 여자의 마지막 말에 대한 남자의 응답으로 가장 적절한 것을 고르시오.
① No thank you. I've had enough.
괜찮아요. 이제 됐습니다.
② Great. I'll book for five people at six.
좋아요. 내가 6시에 다섯 명 예약할게요.
③ That's a good choice. The food is wonderful.
좋은 선택이네요. 음식이 훌륭해요.

④ Okay. I'll set a place and time for the meeting.
알겠어요. 내가 회의 장소와 시간을 잡아볼게요.
☑ Sorry to hear that. I'll cancel the reservation now.
그 말을 들으니 유감이네요. 예약 지금 취소할게요.

W : Honey, we can't eat out tomorrow evening.
여보, 우리 내일 저녁에 외식 못할 것 같아.
M : Why not? I've already booked a table at the restaurant.
왜요? 난 이미 식당에 자리를 예약했어요.
W : I'm sorry. I have an important business meeting at that time.
미안해요. 그때 중요한 업무 회의가 있어요.
M : Sorry to hear that. I'll cancel the reservation now.
그 말을 들으니 유감이네요. 예약 지금 취소할게요.

Why? 왜 정답일까?

여자는 남자와 외식하기로 한 시간에 중요한 업무 회의가 잡혔다면서(I'm sorry. I have an important business meeting at that time.) 남자에게 외식을 못 할 것 같다고 이야기하고 있다. 따라서 남자의 응답으로 가장 적절한 것은 ⑤ '그 말을 들으니 유감이네요. 예약 지금 취소할게요.'이다.

● eat out 외식하다
● I've had enough. 이제 됐어요.
● book ⓥ 예약하다

---

13 팀 프로젝트 역할 분담 | 정답률 81% | 정답 ①

대화를 듣고, 남자의 마지막 말에 대한 여자의 응답으로 가장 적절한 것을 고르시오.

Woman :

☑ I'm in charge of giving the presentation.
난 발표 담당이야.
② I think you're the right person for that role.
난 네가 그 역할에 적격이라고 생각해.
③ It's important to choose your team carefully.
네 팀을 신중하게 고르는 것이 중요해.
④ The assignment is due the day after tomorrow.
과제는 내일 모레까지야.
⑤ I hope we don't stay up late to finish the project.
난 우리가 프로젝트를 끝내느라 늦게까지 깨어 있지 않으면 좋겠어.

M : Why do you look so busy?
왜 그렇게 바빠 보여?
W : I'm working on a team project.
난 팀 프로젝트 작업 중이야.
M : What's it about?
뭐에 관한 거야?
W : It's about 'Climate Change.'
'기후 변화'에 관한 거야.
M : Sounds interesting. Who's on your team?
재미있겠네! 누가 너네 팀에 있어?
W : You know Chris? He's the leader.
너 Chris 알아? 걔가 팀장이야.
M : I know him very well. He's responsible and smart.
나 걔 아주 잘 알아. 걔는 책임감이 있고 똑똑해.
W : Jenny is doing the research and Alex is making the slides.
Jenny가 자료 조사를 하고 Alex가 슬라이드를 만들고 있어.
M : What a nice team! Then what's your role?
근사한 팀이네! 그럼 네 역할은 뭐야?
W : I'm in charge of giving the presentation.
난 발표 담당이야.

Why? 왜 정답일까?

'기후 변화'에 관한 팀 프로젝트를 진행 중인 여자가 팀원들의 역할을 소개하자 남자는 여자의 역할이 무엇인지 묻고 있다(Then what's your role?). 따라서 여자의 응답으로 가장 적절한 것은 ① '난 발표 담당이야.'이다.

● work on ~을 작업하다, ~에 공을 들이다
● assignment ⓝ 과제
● stay up late 늦게까지 깨어 있다
● in charge of ~을 담당하는, 책임지는
● due ⓐ 예정인

---

14 시간 관리 앱 추천하기 | 정답률 81% | 정답 ⑤

대화를 듣고, 여자의 마지막 말에 대한 남자의 응답으로 가장 적절한 것을 고르시오.

Man :

① I'm good at public speaking.
난 공개 연설을 잘해.
② I'm sorry for forgetting my assignment.
내 과제를 잊어버려서 유감이야.
③ Unfortunately, my alarm doesn't wake me up.
안타깝게도 알람이 나를 깨워주지 않았어.
④ The speech contest is just around the corner.
말하기 대회가 코앞에 다가왔어.
☑ It helps me keep deadlines to complete specific tasks.
그것은 내가 특정 과제를 마쳐야 하는 기한을 지키게 해줘.

M : Hi, Diana. You look down. What's the problem?
안녕, Diana. 우울해 보이네. 무슨 문제 있어?
W : Hi, Peter. I missed the deadline for the speech contest. It was yesterday.
안녕, Peter. 난 말하기 대회 기한을 놓쳤어. 어제였거든.
M : No way. You'd been waiting for it for a long time.
세상에. 넌 그걸 아주 오랫동안 기다려 왔잖아.
W : Yeah. It totally slipped my mind. I'm so forgetful.
응. 완전히 잊어버리고 있었어. 난 너무 잘 까먹어.
M : Why don't you write notes to remember things?
일들을 기억하기 위해서 메모를 하면 어떠니?
W : I've tried, but it doesn't work. I even forget where I put the notes.
시도해 봤는데, 효과가 없어. 난 심지어 내가 메모를 어디다 뒀는지도 까먹어.
M : How about using a time management application like me?
나처럼 시간 관리 앱을 써 보는 게 어때?
W : Well... What's good about your app?
음... 그 앱의 장점이 뭐야?

M : It helps me keep deadlines to complete specific tasks.
그것은 내가 특정 과제를 마쳐야 하는 기한을 지키게 해줘.

Why? 왜 정답일까?

건망증이 심해 고민이라는 여자에게 남자가 시간 관리 앱을 사용해볼 것을 추천해주자, 여자는 앱을 쓰면 좋은 점이 무엇이냐고 묻는다(What's good about your app?). 따라서 남자의 응답으로 가장 적절한 것은 ⑤ '그것은 내가 특정 과제를 마쳐야 하는 기한을 지키게 해줘.'이다.

● slip one's mind 잊어버리다, 생각나지 않다
● around the corner 코앞에, 목전에
● specific ⓐ 특정한, 구체적인
● forgetful ⓐ 잘 잊어버리는
● complete ⓥ 마치다, 완수하다

---

15 시합 참가를 고집하는 선수를 달래기 | 정답률 66% | 정답 ③

다음 상황 설명을 듣고, Harold가 Kate에게 할 말로 가장 적절한 것을 고르시오. [3점]

Harold :

① Okay. You'd better put your best effort into the match. - 알겠어. 넌 시합에 최선을 다해야 해.
② I see. You should play the match instead of her. - 알겠어. 네가 그녀 대신 시합에 나가겠어.
☑ Take it easy. Take good care of yourself first. - 쉬엄쉬엄해. 우선 네 몸을 잘 챙겨.
④ You deserve it. Practice makes perfect. - 넌 자격이 있어. 연습하다 보면 완벽해지지.
⑤ Don't worry. You'll win this match. - 걱정하지 마. 넌 이 시합을 이길 거야.

M : Harold is a tennis coach.
Harold는 테니스 코치이다.
He's been teaching Kate, a talented and passionate player, for years.
그는 여러 해 동안 재능 있고 열정적인 선수인 Kate를 지도하고 있다.
While practicing for an upcoming match, Kate injured her elbow badly.
다가오는 시합을 위해 연습하다가, Kate는 팔꿈치를 심하게 다친다.
Her doctor strongly recommends she stop playing tennis for a month.
의사는 그녀가 한 달 동안 테니스를 그만 쳐야 한다고 강력하게 권한다.
However, Kate insists on playing the match.
하지만 Kate는 시합에 나가기를 고집한다.
Harold knows how heartbroken she would be to miss the match.
Harold는 그녀가 시합을 놓치면 얼마나 상심할지 알고 있다.
But he's concerned about her tennis career if her elbow doesn't recover.
하지만 그는 그녀의 팔꿈치가 낫지 않을 경우 테니스 경력(이 어떻게 될지)에 관해 걱정하고 있다.
So he wants to persuade her to calm down and focus on her recovery.
그래서 그는 그녀에게 진정하고 회복에 집중하라고 설득하고 싶어 한다.
In this situation, what would Harold most likely say to Kate?
이 상황에서, Harold는 Kate에게 뭐라고 말할 것인가?
Harold : Take it easy. Take good care of yourself first.
쉬엄쉬엄해. 우선 네 몸을 잘 챙겨.

Why? 왜 정답일까?

상황에 따르면 팔꿈치 부상을 입은 선수 Kate에게 코치인 Harold는 우선 회복에 집중하라고 권유하고 싶어 한다(So he wants to persuade her to calm down and focus on her recovery.). 따라서 Harold가 Kate에게 할 말로 가장 적절한 것은 ③ '쉬엄쉬엄해. 우선 네 몸을 잘 챙겨.'이다.

● talented ⓐ 재능 있는
● upcoming ⓐ 다가오는
● insist on ~을 고집하다
● concerned ⓐ 우려하는, 걱정하는
● Take it easy. 쉬엄쉬엄해. 진정해.
● Practice makes perfect. 자꾸 연습하다 보면 잘하게 된다. 연습이 완벽을 만든다.
● passionate ⓐ 열정적인
● injure ⓥ 다치다, 부상을 입다
● heartbroken ⓐ 상심한
● put effort into ~에 공을 들이다

16-17 빛 공해가 야생 동물의 생존에 미치는 영향

W : This is Linda from "Life and Science."
'Life and Science'의 Linda입니다.
『Did you know light pollution from bright lights at night can drive wildlife to death?』 **16번의 근거**
밤에 환한 불빛으로 인한 빛 공해가 야생 동물들을 죽음으로 몰아갈 수 있다는 걸 아셨나요?
『For example, sea turtles lay eggs on beaches and their babies find their way to the sea with the help of moonlight.』 **17번 ①의 근거** 일치
예컨대, 바다거북은 해변에 알을 낳고 그 새끼들은 달빛의 도움을 받아 바다로 향하는 길을 찾습니다.
But artificial lights can confuse them and cause them not to reach the sea and die.
하지만 인공조명이 이들을 헷갈리게 해서 바다에 닿지 못하고 죽게 만들 수 있죠.
『Fireflies have been disappearing across the globe.』 **17번 ②의 근거** 일치
반딧불이는 전 세계적으로 사라져가고 있습니다.
Male fireflies get disturbed by artificial lights when they try to attract mates.
수컷 반딧불이는 짝을 유혹하려 할 때 인공조명 때문에 방해를 받습니다.
This means less fireflies are born.
이것은 반딧불이가 더 적게 태어난다는 것을 뜻하죠.
『Also, salmon migrate randomly when exposed to artificial lights at night.』 **17번 ③의 근거** 일치
또한, 연어는 밤에 인공조명에 노출되면 아무 데나 이주해버립니다.
This threatens their chances of survival.
이것은 그들의 생존 가능성을 떨어뜨리죠.
『Lastly, light pollution interrupts the mating calls of tree frogs at night.』 **17번 ⑤의 근거** 일치
마지막으로, 빛 공해는 밤에 청개구리의 짝 찾는 울음을 방해합니다.
As male frogs reduce the number of their mating calls, the females don't reproduce.
수컷 개구리가 짝 찾는 울음의 횟수를 줄이면서, 암컷들은 번식하지 않게 됩니다.
So light pollution can be a matter of life and death for some animals.
그래서 빛 공해는 몇몇 동물들에게 생사의 문제가 될 수 있습니다.

● light pollution 빛 공해
● lay ⓥ (알 등을) 낳다
● artificial ⓐ 인공의
● disturb ⓥ 방해하다, 지장을 주다
● migrate ⓥ 이주하다
● interrupt ⓥ 방해하다, 끼어들다
● illegal ⓐ 불법의
● endangered ⓐ 멸종 위기에 처한
● wildlife ⓝ 야생 동물
● with the help of ~의 도움으로
● disappear ⓥ 사라지다
● attract ⓥ 유혹하다, 매혹시키다
● threaten ⓥ 위태롭게 하다
● reproduce ⓥ 번식하다
● characteristic ⓝ 특성, 특징
● habitat ⓝ 서식지

16 주제 파악
정답률 79% | 정답 ③

여자가 하는 말의 주제로 가장 적절한 것은?

① problems with illegal hunting – 불법 사냥의 문제점
② characteristics of migrating animals – 이주하는 동물의 특성
③ effects of light pollution on wild animals – 빛 공해가 야생 동물에 미치는 영향
④ various ways to save endangered animals – 멸종 위기에 처한 동물들을 구하는 다양한 방법
⑤ animal habitat change due to water pollution – 수질 오염으로 인한 동물 서식지 변화

Why? 왜 정답일까?

'Did you know light pollution from bright lights at night can drive wildlife to death?'에서 여자는 야간의 빛 공해가 야생 동물들을 죽음으로 몰아갈 수 있다는 핵심 내용을 제시한 뒤, 빛 공해로 인해 피해를 입고 있는 동물들의 예시를 들고 있다. 따라서 여자가 하는 말의 주제로 가장 적절한 것은 ③ '빛 공해가 야생 동물에 미치는 영향'이다.

17 언급 유무 파악
정답률 92% | 정답 ④

언급된 동물이 아닌 것은?

① sea turtles – 바다거북
② fireflies – 반딧불이
③ salmon – 연어
④ honey bees – 꿀벌
⑤ tree frogs – 청개구리

Why? 왜 정답일까?

담화에서 여자는 빛 공해로 피해를 입는 동물들의 예로 바다거북, 반딧불이, 연어, 청개구리를 언급하였다. 따라서 언급되지 않은 것은 ④ '꿀벌'이다.

Why? 왜 오답일까?

① 'For example, sea turtles lay eggs on beaches ~'에서 '바다거북'이 언급되었다.
② 'Fireflies have been disappearing across the globe.'에서 '반딧불이'가 언급되었다.
③ 'Also, salmon migrate randomly when exposed to artificial lights at night.'에서 '연어'가 언급되었다.
⑤ 'Lastly, light pollution interrupts the mating calls of tree frogs at night.'에서 '청개구리'가 언급되었다.

18 브랜드 로고 제작 요청
정답률 89% | 정답 ①

다음 글의 목적으로 가장 적절한 것은?

① 회사 로고 제작을 의뢰하려고
② 변경된 회사 로고를 홍보하려고
③ 회사 비전에 대한 컨설팅을 요청하려고
④ 회사 창립 10주년 기념품을 주문하려고
⑤ 회사 로고 제작 일정 변경을 공지하려고

Dear Mr. Jones,
Jones씨에게,
I am James Arkady, PR Director of KHJ Corporation.
저는 KHJ Corporation의 홍보부 이사 James Arkady입니다.
We are planning / to redesign our brand identity / and launch a new logo / to celebrate our 10th anniversary.
저희는 계획하고 있습니다. / 저희 회사 브랜드 정체성을 다시 설계하고 / 새로운 로고를 선보이려고 / 회사의 창립 10주년을 기념하기 위해서
We request you to create a logo / that best suits our company's core vision, / 'To inspire humanity.'
저희는 당신께 로고를 제작해 주시기를 요청합니다. / 저희 회사의 핵심 비전을 가장 잘 반영한 / '인류애를 고양하자'
I hope / the new logo will convey our brand message / and capture the values of KHJ.
저는 바랍니다. / 새로운 로고가 저희 회사 브랜드 메시지를 전달하고 / KHJ의 가치를 담아내기를
Please send us your logo design proposal / once you are done with it.
로고 디자인 제안서를 보내 주십시오. / 당신이 완성하는 대로
Thank you.
감사합니다.
Best regards, // James Arkady
James Arkady 드림

Jones씨에게,

저는 KHJ Corporation의 홍보부 이사 James Arkady입니다. 저희 회사의 창립 10주년을 기념하기 위해서 저희 회사 브랜드 정체성을 다시 설계하고 새로운 로고를 선보일 계획입니다. 저희 회사의 핵심 비전 '인류애를 고양하자'를 가장 잘 반영한 로고를 제작해 주시기를 요청합니다. 새로운 로고가 저희 회사 브랜드 메시지를 전달하고 KHJ의 가치를 담아내기를 바랍니다. 로고 디자인 제안서를 완성하는 대로 보내 주십시오. 감사합니다.

James Arkady 드림

Why? 왜 정답일까?

'We request you to create a logo that best suits our company's core vision, ~'에서 회사 핵심 비전을 잘 반영한 로고를 제작해줄 것을 요청한다고 하므로, 글의 목적으로 가장 적절한 것은 ① '회사 로고 제작을 의뢰하려고'이다.

- identity ⓝ 정체성
- launch ⓥ 시작하다, 런칭하다
- celebrate ⓥ 기념하다
- anniversary ⓝ 기념일
- suit ⓥ ~에 적합하다
- inspire ⓥ 고무시키다
- humanity ⓝ 인류애

구문 풀이

4행 We request you to create a logo [that best suits our company's core vision, 'To inspire humanity.']
5형식 동사 목적어 목적격 보어 / 선행사 / 주격 관계대명사

19 카페에서 우연히 유명한 화가를 마주친 Cindy
정답률 79% | 정답 ③

다음 글에 드러난 Cindy의 심경 변화로 가장 적절한 것은?

① relieved → worried
   안도한   걱정하는
② indifferent → embarrassed
   무관심한   당황한
③ excited → surprised
   들뜬   놀란
④ disappointed → satisfied
   실망한   만족한
⑤ jealous → confident
   질투하는   자신 있는

One day, / Cindy happened to sit next to a famous artist in a café, / and she was thrilled to see him in person.
어느 날, / Cindy는 카페에서 우연히 유명한 화가 옆에 앉게 되었고, / 그녀는 그를 직접 만나게 되어 몹시 기뻤다.
He was drawing on a used napkin over coffee.
그는 커피를 마시면서 사용하던 냅킨에 그림을 그리고 있었다.
She was looking on in awe.
그녀는 경외심을 가지고 지켜보고 있었다.
After a few moments, / the man finished his coffee / and was about to throw away the napkin / as he left.
잠시 후에, / 그 남자는 커피를 다 마시고 / 그 냅킨을 버리려고 했다. / 그가 자리를 뜨면서
Cindy stopped him.
Cindy는 그를 멈춰 세웠다.
"Can I have that napkin you drew on?", she asked.
"당신이 그림을 그렸던 냅킨을 가져도 될까요?"라고 그녀가 물었다.
"Sure," he replied.
"물론이죠."라고 그가 대답했다.
"Twenty thousand dollars."
"2만 달러입니다."
She said, with her eyes wide-open, / "What? It took you like two minutes to draw that."
그녀는 눈을 동그랗게 뜨고 말했다. / "뭐라구요? 그리는 데 2분밖에 안 걸렸잖아요."
"No," he said.
"아니요." 라고 그가 말했다.
"It took me over sixty years to draw this."
"나는 이것을 그리는 데 60년 넘게 걸렸어요."
Being at a loss, / she stood still rooted to the ground.
어쩔 줄 몰라 / 그녀는 여전히 꼼짝 못한 채 서 있었다.

어느 날, Cindy는 카페에서 우연히 유명한 화가 옆에 앉게 되었고, 그를 직접 만나게 되어 몹시 기뻤다. 그는 커피를 마시면서 사용하던 냅킨에 그림을 그리고 있었다. 그녀는 경외심을 가지고 지켜보고 있었다. 잠시 후에, 그 남자는 커피를 다 마시고 자리를 뜨면서 그 냅킨을 버리려고 했다. Cindy는 그를 멈춰 세웠다. "당신이 그림을 그렸던 냅킨을 가져도 될까요?"라고 그녀가 물었다. "물론이죠."라고 그가 대답했다. "2만 달러입니다." 그녀는 눈을 동그랗게 뜨고 말했다. "뭐라구요? 그리는 데 2분밖에 안 걸렸잖아요." "아니요."라고 그가 말했다. "나는 이것을 그리는 데 60년 넘게 걸렸어요." 그녀는 어쩔 줄 몰라 여전히 꼼짝 못한 채 서 있었다.

Why? 왜 정답일까?

첫 문장에서 우연히 유명한 화가를 카페에서 만난 Cindy가 몹시 기뻐했다(~ she was thrilled to see him in person.)는 것을 알 수 있고, 마지막 문장에서 그가 냅킨에 그린 그림을 가져다가 너무 비싼 값을 들은 Cindy가 말문이 막힐 정도로 놀랐다(Being at a loss, she stood still rooted to the ground.)는 것을 알 수 있다. 따라서 Cindy의 심경 변화로 가장 적절한 것은 ③ '들뜬 → 놀란'이다.

- thrilled ⓐ 몹시 기쁜, 황홀해하는
- in person 직접
- awe ⓝ 경외심
- at a loss (무슨 말을 해야 할지) 모르는
- rooted ⓐ (~에) 붙박인
- indifferent ⓐ 무관심한
- embarrassed ⓐ 당황한
- disappointed ⓐ 실망한
- jealous ⓐ 질투하는

구문 풀이

1행 One day, Cindy happened to sit next to a famous artist in a café, and she
우연히 / ~하다
was thrilled to see him in person.
감정 형용사 / 부사적 용법(~해서)

20 성공을 위해 변화를 시도하기
정답률 90% | 정답 ①

다음 글에서 필자가 주장하는 바로 가장 적절한 것은?

① 불편할지라도 성공하기 위해서는 새로운 것을 시도해야 한다.
② 일과 생활의 균형을 맞추는 성공적인 삶을 추구해야 한다.
③ 갈등 해소를 위해 불편함의 원인을 찾아 개선해야 한다.
④ 단계별 목표를 설정하여 익숙한 것부터 도전해야 한다.
⑤ 변화에 적응하기 위해 직관적으로 문제를 해결해야 한다.

Sometimes, / you feel the need to avoid something / that will lead to success / out of discomfort.
가끔씩, / 당신은 무언가를 피할 필요가 있다고 느낀다. / 성공으로 이끌어 줄 / 불편함을 벗어나
Maybe you are avoiding extra work / because you are tired.
아마도 당신은 추가적인 일을 피하고 있다. / 당신이 피곤하기 때문에
You are actively shutting out success / because you want to avoid being uncomfortable.
당신은 적극적으로 성공을 차단하고 있다. / 당신이 불편한 것을 피하고 싶어서
Therefore, / overcoming your instinct / to avoid uncomfortable things at first / is essential.
따라서 / 당신의 본능을 극복하는 것이 / 처음에는 불편한 것을 피하려는 / 필요하다.
Try doing new things outside of your comfort zone.
편안함을 주는 곳을 벗어나서 새로운 일을 시도하라.
Change is always uncomfortable, / but it is key to doing things differently / in order to find that magical formula for success.
변화는 항상 불편하지만, / 일을 색다르게 하는 데 있어서의 핵심이다. / 성공을 위한 마법의 공식을 찾기 위해

가끔씩은 당신은 불편함을 벗어나서 성공으로 이끌어 줄 무언가를 피할 필요가 있다고 느낀다. 아마도 당신은 피곤하기 때문에 추가적인 일을 피하고 있다. 당신은 불편한 것을 피하고 싶어서 적극적으로 성공을 차단하고 있다. 따라서 처음에는 불편한 것을 피하려는 당신의 본능을 극복하는 것이 필요하다. 편안함을 주는 곳을 벗어나서 새로운 일을 시도하라. 변화는

항상 불편하지만, 성공을 위한 마법의 공식을 찾기 위해 일을 색다르게 하는 데 있어서는 핵심이다.

마지막 두 문장에서 성공하기 위해서는 변화가 핵심이므로 불편하더라도 이를 감수하고 새로운 것을 시도할 필요가 있다(Try doing new things ~. Change is always uncomfortable, but it is key to doing things differently in order to find that magical formula for success.)고 조언하고 있다. 따라서 필자가 주장하는 바로 가장 적절한 것은 ① '불편할지라도 성공하기 위해서는 새로운 것을 시도해야 한다.'이다.

- discomfort ⓝ 불편함
- instinct ⓝ 본능
- comfort zone 안전지대, 일을 적당히 하거나 요령을 피우는 상태
- formula ⓝ 공식, 제조법
- overcome ⓥ 극복하다
- essential ⓐ 필수적인, 본질적인

구문 풀이

4행 Therefore, overcoming your instinct to avoid uncomfortable things at first
동명사구 주어 / 형용사적 용법
is essential.
동사(단수)

---

21 선택적 지각 정답률 50% | 정답 ③

밑줄 친 want to use a hammer가 다음 글에서 의미하는 바로 가장 적절한 것은? [3점]

① are unwilling to stand out
두드러지기를 꺼리면
② make our effort meaningless
우리의 노력을 무의미하게 만들면
③ intend to do something in a certain way
무언가를 특정한 방식으로 하려고 하면
④ hope others have a viewpoint similar to ours
다른 사람들이 우리와 비슷한 관점을 지니기를 바라면
⑤ have a way of thinking that is accepted by others
다른 사람들에게 받아들여지는 사고 방식을 갖고 있다면

We have a tendency / to interpret events selectively.
우리는 경향이 있다. / 사건을 선택적으로 해석하는

If we want things to be "this way" or "that way" / we can most certainly select, stack, or arrange evidence / in a way that supports such a viewpoint.
만약 우리가 일이 '이렇게' 혹은 '저렇게' 되기를 원한다면, / 우리는 틀림없이 증거를 선택하거나 쌓거나 배열할 수 있다. / 그러한 관점을 뒷받침하는 방식으로

Selective perception is based / on what seems to us to stand out.
선택적인 지각은 기반을 둔다. / 우리에게 두드러져 보이는 것에

However, / what seems to us to be standing out / may very well be related / to our goals, interests, expectations, past experiences, or current demands of the situation / — "with a hammer in hand, / everything looks like a nail."
그러나 / 우리에게 두드러져 보이는 것은 / 매우 관련 있을지도 모른다 / 우리의 목표, 관심사, 기대, 과거의 경험 또는 상황에 대한 현재의 요구와 / "망치를 손에 들고 있으면, / 모든 것은 못처럼 보인다."

This quote highlights the phenomenon of selective perception.
이 인용문은 선택적 지각의 현상을 강조한다.

If we want to use a hammer, / then the world around us / may begin to look / as though it is full of nails!
만약 우리가 망치를 사용하기를 원하면, / 우리 주변의 세상은 / 보이기 시작할지도 모른다! / 못으로 가득 찬 것처럼

우리는 사건을 선택적으로 해석하는 경향이 있다. 만약 우리가 일이 '이렇게' 혹은 '저렇게' 되기를 원한다면, 우리는 틀림없이 그러한 관점을 뒷받침하는 방식으로 증거를 선택하거나 쌓거나 배열할 수 있다. 선택적인 지각은 우리에게 두드러져 보이는 것에 기반을 둔다. 그러나 우리에게 두드러져 보이는 것은 우리의 목표, 관심사, 기대, 과거의 경험 또는 상황에 대한 현재의 요구와 매우 관련 있을지도 모른다 — "망치를 손에 들고 있으면, 모든 것은 못처럼 보인다." 이 인용문은 선택적 지각의 현상을 강조한다. 만약 우리가 망치를 사용하기를 원하면, 우리 주변의 세상은 못으로 가득 찬 것처럼 보이기 시작할지도 모른다!

우리의 지각은 우리 눈에 두드러져 보이는 것에 초점이 맞추어져 있다는 내용 뒤로, 사실 이 눈에 띄는 것들은 우리의 목표나 기대 등과 관련되어 있다는 내용이 제시된다(However, what seems to us to be standing out may very well be related to our goals, ~). 특히 망치를 손에 들고 있으면 모두 못처럼 보인다는 직접 인용구의 내용으로 미루어볼 때, 밑줄이 포함된 부분은 우리가 특정한 목표나 기대를 갖고 상황을 바라볼 때 그 목표나 기대를 적용하기 유리한 대로 상황을 해석할 가능성이 크다는 의미여야 한다. 따라서 밑줄 친 부분이 의미하는 바로 가장 적절한 것은 ③ '무언가를 특정한 방식으로 하려고 하면'이다.

- interpret ⓥ 해석하다
- stack ⓥ 쌓다, 포개다
- quote ⓝ 인용구
- phenomenon ⓝ 현상
- selectively ⓐⓓ 선택적으로
- stand out 두드러지다
- highlight ⓥ 강조하다
- unwilling ⓐ (~하기를) 꺼리는, 마지못해 하는

구문 풀이

9행 If we want to use a hammer, then the world around us may begin to look
접속사(만일 ~라면) / 주어 / 동사
as though it is full of nails!
접속사(마치 ~처럼)

---

22 형편없는 과제에 개선의 기회를 주기 정답률 71% | 정답 ⑤

다음 글의 요지로 가장 적절한 것은?

① 학생에게 평가 결과를 공개하는 것은 학습 동기를 떨어뜨린다.
② 학생에게 추가 과제를 부여하는 것은 학업 부담을 가중시킨다.
③ 지속적인 보상은 학업 성취도에 장기적으로 부정적인 영향을 준다.
④ 학생의 자기주도적 학습 능력은 정서적으로 안정된 학습 환경에서 향상된다.
⑤ 학생의 과제가 일정 수준에 도달하도록 개선 기회를 주면 동기 부여에 도움이 된다.

Rather than attempting to punish students / with a low grade or mark / in the hope / it will encourage them to give greater effort in the future, / teachers can better motivate students / by considering their work as incomplete / and then requiring additional effort.
학생에게 벌을 주는 대신, / 낮은 성적이나 점수로 / 희망하며 / 그것이 학생으로 하여금 미래에 더 노력을 기울이도록 독려할 것이라 / 교사는 학생들에게 동기 부여를 더 잘할 수 있다. / 그들의 과제를 미완성으로 보고 / 추가적인 노력을 요구함으로써

Teachers at Beachwood Middle School in Beachwood, Ohio, / record students' grades as A, B, C, or I (Incomplete).
오하이오 주 Beachwood의 Beachwood 중학교 교사는 / 학생의 성적을 A, B, C 또는 I(미완성)로 기록한다.

Students who receive an I grade / are required to do additional work / in order to bring their performance / up to an acceptable level.
I 성적을 받은 학생 / 추가적인 과제를 하도록 요구받는다. / 자신의 과제 수행을 끌어올리기 위해서 / 수용 가능한 수준까지

This policy is based on the belief / that students perform at a failure level / or submit failing work / in large part because teachers accept it.
이런 방침은 믿음에 근거한다. / 학생이 낙제 수준으로 수행하거나 / 낙제 과제를 제출하는 것이 / 대체로 교사가 그것을 받아들이기 때문이라는

The Beachwood teachers reason / that if they no longer accept substandard work, / students will not submit it.
Beachwood의 교사는 생각한다. / 만약 그들이 더 이상 기준 이하의 과제를 받아들이지 않는다면, / 학생이 그것을 제출하지 않을 것이라고

And with appropriate support, / they believe / students will continue to work / until their performance is satisfactory.
그리고 적절한 도움을 받아서 / 그들은 믿는다. / 학생들이 계속 노력할 것이라고 / 자신의 과제 수행이 만족스러울 때까지

낮은 성적이나 점수가 학생으로 하여금 미래에 더 노력을 기울이도록 독려할 것이라 희망하며 학생에게 그것으로 벌을 주는 대신, 교사는 그들의 과제를 미완성으로 보고 추가적인 노력을 요구함으로써 학생들에게 동기 부여를 더 잘할 수 있다. 오하이오 주 Beachwood의 Beachwood 중학교 교사는 학생의 성적을 A, B, C 또는 I(미완성)로 기록한다. I 성적을 받은 학생은 자신의 과제 수행을 수용 가능한 수준까지 끌어올리기 위해서 추가적인 과제를 하도록 요구받는다. 이런 방침은 학생이 낙제 수준으로 수행하거나 낙제 과제를 제출하는 것이 대체로 교사가 그것을 받아들이기 때문이라는 믿음에 근거한다. Beachwood의 교사는 만약 그들이 더 이상 기준 이하의 과제를 받아들이지 않는다면, 학생이 그것을 제출하지 않을 것이라고 생각한다. 그리고 그들은 학생들이 적절한 도움을 받아서 자신의 과제 수행이 만족스러울 때까지 계속 노력할 것이라고 믿는다.

첫 문장에서 학생들의 과제가 일정 수준 미만일 때 그저 점수를 낮게 주기보다는 '미완성된' 과제로 보고 더 노력을 들이도록 요구하는 것이 동기 부여에 좋다(~ teachers can better motivate students by considering their work as incomplete and then requiring additional effort.)고 하므로, 글의 요지로 가장 적절한 것은 ⑤ '학생의 과제가 일정 수준에 도달하도록 개선 기회를 주면 동기 부여에 도움이 된다.'이다.

- punish ⓥ 처벌하다
- additional ⓐ 추가적인
- substandard ⓐ 수준 이하의, 열악한
- satisfactory ⓐ 만족스러운
- incomplete ⓐ 미완성된
- acceptable ⓐ 수용 가능한
- appropriate ⓐ 적절한

구문 풀이

1행 Rather than attempting to punish students with a low grade or mark in the hope (that) it will encourage them to give greater effort in the future, teachers
~라는 희망으로 / 「encourage + 목적어 + to부정사」: ~이 …하도록 독려하다 / 주어
can better motivate students by considering their work as incomplete and then
동사구 / 전치사 / 동명사1
requiring additional effort.
동명사2

---

23 긍정적 재구성에 도움이 되는 호기심 정답률 60% | 정답 ②

다음 글의 주제로 가장 적절한 것은?

① importance of defensive reactions in a tough situation – 힘든 상황에서 방어적인 반응의 중요성
② curiosity as the hidden force of positive reframes – 긍정적 재구성의 숨은 동력인 호기심
③ difficulties of coping with stress at work – 직장에서의 스트레스에 대처하는 것의 어려움
④ potential threats caused by curiosity – 호기심으로 인한 잠재적 위험
⑤ factors that reduce human curiosity – 인간의 호기심을 떨어뜨리는 요인

Curiosity makes us / much more likely to view a tough problem / as an interesting challenge to take on.
호기심은 우리를 만든다. / 어려운 문제를 더 여기게 / 맡아야 할 흥미로운 도전으로

A stressful meeting with our boss / becomes an opportunity to learn.
상사와의 스트레스를 받는 회의는 / 배울 수 있는 기회가 된다.

A nervous first date / becomes an exciting night out with a new person.
긴장이 되는 첫 데이트는 / 새로운 사람과의 멋진 밤이 된다.

A colander becomes a hat.
주방용 체는 모자가 된다.

In general, / curiosity motivates us / to view stressful situations as challenges / rather than threats, / to talk about difficulties more openly, / and to try new approaches to solving problems.
일반적으로, / 호기심은 우리에게 동기를 부여해 준다. / 스트레스를 받는 상황을 도전으로 여기게 하고, / 위협보다는 / 어려움을 더 터놓고 말하게 하고, / 문제 해결에 있어 새로운 접근을 시도하도록

In fact, / curiosity is associated / with a less defensive reaction to stress / and, as a result, less aggression / when we respond to irritation.
실제로, / 호기심은 관련이 있다. / 스트레스에 대한 방어적인 반응이 줄어드는 것과 / 그리고 그 결과 공격성이 줄어드는 것과 / 우리가 짜증에 반응할 때

호기심은 우리가 어려운 문제를 맡아야 할 흥미로운 도전으로 더 여기게 한다. 상사와의 스트레스를 받는 회의는 배울 수 있는 기회가 된다. 긴장이 되는 첫 데이트는 새로운 사람과의 멋진 밤이 된다. 주방용 체는 모자가 된다. 일반적으로, 호기심은 우리가 스트레스를 받는 상황을 위협보다는 도전으로 여기게 하고, 어려움을 더 터놓고 말하게 하고, 문제 해결에 있어 새로운 접근을 시도하도록 동기를 부여해 준다. 실제로 호기심은 스트레스에 대한 방어적인 반응이 줄어들고, 그 결과 짜증에 반응할 때 공격성이 줄어드는 것과 관련이 있다.

Why? 왜 정답일까?

'Curiosity makes us much more likely to view a tough problem as an interesting challenge to take on.'에서 호기심은 우리가 어려운 문제를 흥미로운 도전처럼 여길 수 있게 해준다고 언급한 데 이어, 'In general, curiosity motivates us to view stressful situations as challenges ~'에서도 같은 내용을 제시한다. 따라서 글의 주제로 가장 적절한 것은 ② '긍정적인 재구성의 숨은 동력인 호기심'이다.

- curiosity ⓝ 호기심
- threat ⓝ 위협
- aggression ⓝ 공격
- cope with ~에 대처하다
- take on (책임이나 일을) 맡다, 지다
- defensive ⓐ 방어적인
- irritation ⓝ 짜증

구문 풀이

1행 Curiosity makes us much more likely to view a tough problem as an
　　　　 5형식 동사 ┃ 목적어 ┃ 목적격 보어 ┃ 「view + A + as + B : A를 B로 여기다」
interesting challenge to take on.

---

24 더 높은 고층 건물 건축에 이바지하는 엘리베이터　　정답률 73% | 정답 ①

다음 글의 제목으로 가장 적절한 것은?

☑① Elevators Bring Buildings Closer to the Sky
　 엘리베이터는 빌딩이 하늘에 더 가까워지게 만든다
② The Higher You Climb, the Better the View
　 더 높이 오를수록 경치가 더 좋다
③ How to Construct an Elevator Cheap and Fast
　 엘리베이터를 싸고 빠르게 짓는 방법
④ The Function of the Ancient and the Modern City
　 고대 및 현대 도시의 기능
⑤ The Evolution of Architecture: Solutions for Overpopulation
　 건축의 진화: 인구 과잉의 해결책

When people think about the development of cities, / rarely do they consider / the critical role of vertical transportation.
사람들이 도시 발전에 대해 생각할 때, / 그들은 거의 고려하지 않는다. / 수직 운송 수단의 중요한 역할을
In fact, each day, / more than 7 billion elevator journeys / are taken in tall buildings all over the world.
실제로 매일 / 70억 회 이상의 엘리베이터 이동이 / 전 세계 높은 빌딩에서 이루어진다.
Efficient vertical transportation / can expand our ability / to build taller and taller skyscrapers.
효율적인 수직 운송 수단은 / 우리의 능력을 확장시킬 수 있다. / 점점 더 높은 고층 건물을 만들 수 있는
Antony Wood, / a Professor of Architecture at the Illinois Institute of Technology, / explains / that advances in elevators over the past 20 years / are probably the greatest advances / we have seen in tall buildings.
Antony Wood는 / Illinois 공과대학의 건축학과 교수인 / 설명한다. / 지난 20년 간 엘리베이터의 발전은 / 아마도 가장 큰 발전이라고 / 우리가 높은 건물에서 봐 왔던
For example, / elevators in the Jeddah Tower in Jeddah, Saudi Arabia, / under construction, / will reach a height record of 660m.
예를 들어, / 사우디아라비아 Jeddah의 Jeddah Tower에 있는 엘리베이터는 / 건설 중인 / 660미터라는 기록적인 높이에 이를 것이다.

사람들은 도시 발전에 대해 생각할 때, 수직 운송 수단의 중요한 역할을 거의 고려하지 않는다. 실제로 매일 70억 회 이상의 엘리베이터 이동이 전 세계 높은 빌딩에서 이루어진다. 효율적인 수직 운송 수단은 점점 더 높은 고층 건물을 만들 수 있는 우리의 능력을 확장시킬 수 있다. Illinois 공과대학의 건축학과 교수인 Antony Wood는 지난 20년 간 엘리베이터의 발전은 아마도 우리가 높은 건물에서 봐 왔던 가장 큰 발전이라고 설명한다. 예를 들어, 건설 중인 사우디아라비아 Jeddah의 Jeddah Tower에 있는 엘리베이터는 660미터라는 기록적인 높이에 이를 것이다.

Why? 왜 정답일까?

'Efficient vertical transportation can expand our ability to build taller and taller skyscrapers.'에서 수직 운송 수단, 즉 엘리베이터가 더 높은 고층 건물을 짓도록 도와준다고 언급하는 것으로 보아, 글의 제목으로 가장 적절한 것은 ① '엘리베이터는 빌딩이 하늘에 더 가까워지게 만든다'이다.

- critical ⓐ 중요한
- transportation ⓝ 운송, 수송
- skyscraper ⓝ 고층 건물
- overpopulation ⓝ 인구 과잉
- vertical ⓐ 수직의
- expand ⓥ 확장하다
- under construction 건설 중인

구문 풀이

1행 When people think about the development of cities, rarely do they consider
　　　　　　　　　　　　　　　　　　　　　　　　　　　　　「부정어구 + 조동사 + 주어 + 동사원형 : 도치 구문」
the critical role of vertical transportation.

---

25 국가별 GDP 대비 의료 지출　　정답률 81% | 정답 ⑤

다음 도표의 내용과 일치하지 <u>않는</u> 것은?

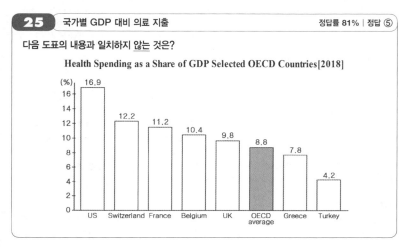

Health Spending as a Share of GDP Selected OECD Countries[2018]

(%) 막대 그래프: US 16.9, Switzerland 12.2, France 11.2, Belgium 10.4, UK 9.8, OECD average 8.8, Greece 7.8, Turkey 4.2

[문제편 p.111]

The above graph shows health spending / as a share of GDP / for selected OECD countries / in 2018.
위 그래프는 의료 지출을 보여준다. / GDP 점유율로 / 선택된 OECD 국가들의 / 2018년에
① On average, / OECD countries were estimated / to have spent 8.8 percent of their GDP on health care.
평균적으로, / OECD 국가들은 추정되었다. / GDP의 8.8%를 의료에 지출한 것으로
② Among the given countries above, / the US had the highest share, / with 16.9 percent, / followed by Switzerland at 12.2 percent.
위 국가들 중 / 미국은 가장 높은 점유율을 보였고, / 16.9%로 / 이어 스위스는 12.2%를 보였다.
③ France spent more than 11 percent of its GDP, / while Turkey spent less than 5 percent of its GDP on health care.
프랑스는 GDP의 11% 이상을 지출했던 반면, / 터키는 GDP의 5% 이하를 의료에 지출했다.
④ Belgium's health spending as a share of GDP / sat between that of France and the UK.
GDP 점유율로서 벨기에의 의료 지출은 / 프랑스와 영국 사이였다.
☑ There was a 3 percentage point difference / in the share of GDP / spent on health care / between the UK and Greece.
3%p의 차이가 있었다. / GDP의 점유율에 있어 / 의료에 지출된 / 영국과 그리스 사이에

위 그래프는 2018년 선택된 OECD 국가들의 의료 지출을 GDP 점유율로 보여준다. ① 평균적으로, OECD 국가들은 GDP의 8.8%를 의료에 지출한 것으로 추정되었다. ② 위 국가들 중 미국은 GDP의 16.9%로 가장 높은 점유율을 보였고, 이어 스위스는 12.2%를 보였다. ③ 프랑스는 GDP의 11% 이상을 지출했던 반면, 터키는 GDP의 5% 이하를 의료에 지출했다. ④ GDP 점유율로서 벨기에의 의료 지출은 프랑스와 영국 사이였다. ⑤ 영국과 그리스 사이에는 의료에 지출된 GDP의 점유율에 있어 3%p의 차이가 있었다.

Why? 왜 정답일까?

도표에 따르면 GDP를 기준으로 영국의 의료 지출은 9.8%, 그리스의 의료 지출은 7.8%였다. 즉 두 국가 간 비율의 차이는 2%p이므로, 도표와 일치하지 않는 것은 ⑤이다.

- on average 평균적으로
- estimate ⓥ 추정하다, 추산하다

---

26 Lithops의 특징　　정답률 63% | 정답 ③

Lithops에 관한 다음 글의 내용과 일치하지 <u>않는</u> 것은?

① 살아있는 돌로 불리는 식물이다.
② 원산지는 남아프리카 사막 지역이다.
☑③ 토양의 표면 위로 대개 1인치 이상 자란다.
④ 줄기가 없으며 땅속에 대부분 묻혀 있다.
⑤ 겉모양은 수분 보존 효과를 갖고 있다.

『Lithops are plants / that are often called 'living stones' / on account of their unique rock-like appearance.』 ①의 근거 일치
Lithops는 식물이다. / 종종 '살아있는 돌'로 불리는 / 독특한 바위 같은 겉모양 때문에
『They are native to the deserts of South Africa / but commonly sold in garden centers and nurseries.』 ②의 근거 일치
이것은 원산지가 남아프리카 사막이지만, / 식물원과 종묘원에서 흔히 팔린다.
Lithops grow well / in compacted, sandy soil with little water / and extreme hot temperatures.
Lithops는 잘 자란다. / 수분이 거의 없는 빡빡한 모래 토양과 / 극히 높은 온도에서
『Lithops are small plants, / rarely getting more than an inch above the soil surface / and usually with only two leaves.』 ③의 근거 불일치
Lithops는 작은 식물로, / 토양의 표면 위로 1인치 이상 거의 자라지 않고 / 보통 단 두 개의 잎을 가지고 있다.
The thick leaves resemble the cleft in an animal's foot / or just a pair of grayish brown stones gathered together.
두꺼운 잎은 동물 발의 갈라진 틈과 닮았다. / 혹은 함께 모여있는 한 쌍의 회갈색 빛을 띠는 돌과
『The plants have no true stem / and much of the plant is underground.』 ④의 근거 일치
이 식물은 실제 줄기는 없고 / 식물의 대부분이 땅속에 묻혀 있다.
『Their appearance has the effect of conserving moisture.』 ⑤의 근거 일치
겉모양은 수분을 보존하는 효과를 가지고 있다.

Lithops는 독특한 바위 같은 겉모양 때문에 종종 '살아있는 돌'로 불리는 식물이다. 이것은 원산지가 남아프리카 사막이지만, 식물원과 종묘원에서 흔히 팔린다. Lithops는 수분이 거의 없는 빡빡한 모래 토양과 극히 높은 온도에서 잘 자란다. Lithops는 작은 식물로, 토양의 표면 위로 1인치 이상 거의 자라지 않고 보통 단 두 개의 잎을 가지고 있다. 두꺼운 잎은 동물 발의 갈라진 틈이나 함께 모여있는 한 쌍의 회갈색 빛을 띠는 돌과 닮았다. 이 식물은 실제 줄기는 없고 식물의 대부분이 땅속에 묻혀 있다. 겉모양은 수분을 보존하는 효과를 가지고 있다.

Why? 왜 정답일까?

'Lithops are small plants, rarely getting more than an inch above the soil surface ~'에서 Lithops는 토양 표면 위로 1인치 이상 자라는 일이 거의 없다고 하므로, 내용과 일치하지 않는 것은 ③ '토양의 표면 위로 대개 1인치 이상 자란다.'이다.

Why? 왜 오답일까?

① 'Lithops are plants that are often called 'living stones' ~'의 내용과 일치한다.
② 'They are native to the deserts of South Africa ~'의 내용과 일치한다.
④ 'The plants have no true stem and much of the plant is underground.'의 내용과 일치한다.
⑤ 'Their appearance has the effect of conserving moisture.'의 내용과 일치한다.

- on account of ~ 때문에
- native to ~이 원산지인
- compacted ⓐ 빡빡한, 탄탄한
- gather ⓥ 모으다, 모이다
- conserve ⓥ 보존하다
- appearance ⓝ 겉모습
- desert ⓝ 사막
- extreme ⓐ 극도의
- stem ⓝ 줄기

구문 풀이

1행 Lithops are plants [that are often called 'living stones' on account of their
　　　　　　　　　　 선행사　　　　　　5형식 수동태　　　　　　　보어
unique rock-like appearance].

"Go Green" Writing Contest에 관한 다음 안내문의 내용과 일치하지 <u>않는</u> 것은?

① 대회 주제는 환경 보호이다.
② 참가자는 한 부문에만 참가해야 한다.
③ 마감 기한은 7월 5일이다.
④ 작품은 이메일로 제출해야 한다.
☑ 수상자는 개별적으로 연락받는다.

"Go Green" Writing Contest
"Go Green" Writing Contest
Share your talents & conserve the environment
여러분의 재능을 나누세요 & 환경을 보존하세요
Main Topic: 『Save the Environment』 ①의근거 일치
주제: 환경을 보호하자
Writing Categories
글쓰기 부문
Slogan // Poem // Essay
표어 // 시 // 에세이
Requirements:
요구 사항:
Participants: High school students
참가자: 고등학생
『Participate in one of the above categories』 ②의근거 일치
위 글쓰기 부문 중 하나에 참가하세요.
(only one entry per participant)
(참가자 1인당 한 작품만)
『Deadline: July 5th, 2021』 ③의근거 일치
마감 기한: 2021년 7월 5일
『Email your work to apply@gogreen.com.』 ④의근거 일치
apply@gogreen.com으로 작품을 이메일로 보내세요.
Prize for Each Category
부문별 상금
1st place: $80
1등: 80달러
2nd place: $60
2등: 60달러
3rd place: $40
3등: 40달러
『The winners will be announced / only on the website on July 15th, 2021.』 ⑤의근거 불일치
수상자는 공지될 예정입니다. / 2021년 7월 15일에 웹 사이트에서만
No personal contact will be made.
개별 연락은 없을 것입니다.
For more information, visit www.gogreen.com.
추가 정보를 원한다면, www.gogreen.com을 방문하시오.

"Go Green" Writing Contest

여러분의 재능을 나누세요 & 환경을 보존하세요

□ 주제 : 환경을 보호하자
□ 글쓰기 부문
 • 표어 • 시 • 에세이
□ 요구 사항:
 • 참가자 : 고등학생
 • 위 글쓰기 부문 중 하나에 참가하세요.
 (참가자 1인당 한 작품만)
□ 마감 기한 : 2021년 7월 5일
 • apply@gogreen.com으로 작품을 이메일로 보내세요.
□ 부문별 상금
 • 1등 : 80달러 • 2등 : 60달러 • 3등 : 40달러
□ 수상자는 2021년 7월 15일에 웹 사이트에서만 공지될 예정입니다. 개별 연락은 없습니다.
□ 추가 정보를 원한다면, www.gogreen.com을 방문하시오.

Why? 왜 정답일까?
'The winners will be announced only on the website on July 15th, 2021. No personal contact will be made.'에서 수상자는 웹 사이트에만 공지되며, 개별 연락은 없을 예정이라고 하였다. 따라서 안내문의 내용과 일치하지 않는 것은 ⑤ '수상자는 개별적으로 연락받는다.'이다.

Why? 왜 오답일까?
① 'Main Topic : Save the Environment'의 내용과 일치한다.
② 'Participate in one of the above categories'의 내용과 일치한다.
③ 'Deadline : July 5th, 2021'의 내용과 일치한다.
④ 'Email your work to apply@gogreen.com.'의 내용과 일치한다.

● go green 친환경적이 되다 ● conserve ⓥ 보존하다
● entry ⓝ 출품작

Virtual Idea Exchange에 관한 다음 안내문의 내용과 일치하는 것은?

① 동아리 회원이라면 누구나 참여 가능하다.
② 티켓 판매는 논의 대상에서 제외된다.
③ 회의는 3시간 동안 열린다.
☑ 접속 링크를 문자로 받는다.
⑤ 채팅방 입장 시 동아리명으로 참여해야 한다.

Virtual Idea Exchange
Virtual Idea Exchange
Connect in real time / and have discussions about the upcoming school festival.
실시간으로 접속하여 / 다가오는 학교 축제에 관해 토론하세요.
Goal
목표
Plan the school festival and share ideas for it.
학교 축제를 계획하고 아이디어를 공유하세요.
『Participants: Club leaders only』 ①의근거 불일치
참가자: 동아리장만
What to Discuss
토론 내용
Themes // 『Ticket sales』 // Budget
주제 // 티켓 판매 // 예산 ②의근거 불일치
『Date & Time: 5 to 7 p.m. on Friday, June 25th, 2021』 ③의근거 불일치
날짜 & 시간: 2021년 6월 25일 금요일 오후 5시 ~ 7시
Notes
참고사항
『Get the access link by text message / 10 minutes before the meeting / and click it.』
문자 메시지로 전송되는 접속 링크를 받아서 / 회의 10분 전에 / 클릭하세요. ④의근거 일치
『Type your real name / when you enter the chatroom.』 ⑤의근거 불일치
실명을 입력하세요. / 당신이 대화방에 들어올 때

Virtual Idea Exchange

실시간으로 접속하여 다가오는 학교 축제에 관해 토론하세요.

□ 목표
 • 학교 축제를 계획하고 아이디어를 공유하세요.
□ 참가자 : 동아리장만
□ 토론 내용
 • 주제 • 티켓 판매 • 예산
□ 날짜 & 시간 : 2021년 6월 25일 금요일 오후 5시 ~ 7시
□ 참고사항
 • 회의 10분 전에 문자 메시지로 전송되는 접속 링크를 받아서 클릭하세요.
 • 대화방에 들어올 때 실명을 입력하세요.

Why? 왜 정답일까?
'Get the access link by text message 10 minutes before the meeting and click it.'에서 회의 10분 전에 회의 접속 링크가 문자 메시지로 전송된다고 하므로, 안내문의 내용과 일치하는 것은 ④ '접속 링크를 문자로 받는다.'이다.

Why? 왜 오답일까?
① 'Participants: Club leaders only'에서 동아리장들만 참여 가능하다고 하였다.
② 'What to Discuss / Ticket sales'에서 티켓 판매가 논의 대상에 포함된다고 하였다.
③ 'Date & Time: 5 to 7 p.m. on Friday, June 25th, 2021'에서 회의는 오후 5시부터 7시까지 2시간 동안 열린다고 하였다.
⑤ 'Type your real name when you enter the chatroom.'에서 채팅방에 들어올 때 실명을 입력해야 한다고 하였다.

● virtual ⓐ (컴퓨터를 이용한) 가상의 ● real time 실시간
● upcoming ⓐ 다가오는 ● budget ⓝ 예산

다음 글의 밑줄 친 부분 중, 어법상 틀린 것은? [3점]

There have been occasions / ① in which you have observed a smile / and you could sense it was not genuine.
경우가 있었다. / 당신이 미소를 관찰했는데 / 당신이 그것이 진짜가 아니라고 느낄 수 있는
The most obvious way / of identifying a genuine smile from an insincere ② one / is / that a fake smile / primarily only affects the lower half of the face, / mainly with the mouth alone.
가장 명확한 방법은 / 진짜 미소와 진실하지 못한 미소를 알아보는 / ~이다. / 가짜 미소는 / 주로 얼굴의 아랫부분에만 영향을 미친다는 것 / 주로 입에만
The eyes don't really get involved.
눈은 별로 관련이 없다.
Take the opportunity to look in the mirror / and manufacture a smile / ③ using the lower half your face only.
거울을 볼 기회를 잡아서 / 미소를 지어보라. / 당신의 얼굴 아랫부분만을 사용하여
When you do this, / judge ④ how happy your face really looks / — is it genuine?
당신이 이렇게 할 때, / 당신의 얼굴이 실제로 얼마나 행복해 보이는지를 판단해 보라. / 그것은 진짜인가?
A genuine smile will impact / on the muscles and wrinkles around the eyes / and less noticeably, / the skin between the eyebrow and upper eyelid / ☑ is lowered slightly with true enjoyment.
진짜 미소는 영향을 주며, / 눈가 근육과 주름에 / 티가 좀 덜 나게 / 눈썹과 윗눈꺼풀 사이의 피부는 / 진정한 즐거움으로 살짝 내려온다.
The genuine smile can impact on the entire face.
진짜 미소는 얼굴 전체에 영향을 줄 수 있다.

당신이 미소를 관찰했는데 그것이 진짜가 아니라고 느낄 수 있는 경우가 있었다. 진짜 미소와 진실하지 못한 미소를 알아보는 가장 명확한 방법은 가짜 미소는 주로 얼굴의 아랫부분, 주로 입에만 영향을 미친다는 것이다. 눈은 별로 관련이 없다. 거울을 볼 기회를 잡아서 당신의 얼굴 아랫부분만을 사용하여 미소를 지어보라. 당신이 이렇게 할 때, 당신의 얼굴이 실제로 얼마나 행복해 보이는지를 판단해 보라. 그것은 진짜인가? 진짜 미소는 눈가 근육과 주름에 영향을 주며, 티가 좀 덜 나게 눈썹과 윗눈꺼풀 사이의 피부는 진정한 즐거움으로 살짝 내려온다. 진짜 미소는 얼굴 전체에 영향을 줄 수 있다.

Why? 왜 정답일까?
and 앞에 'A genuine smile will impact ~'라는 '주어＋동사' 한 쌍이 나온 뒤 and 뒤로 새로운 '주어＋동사'가 이어지고 있다. 이때 단수 명사 주어인 the skin에 맞추어 동사인 are를 is로 고쳐야 한

다. 따라서 어법상 틀린 것은 ⑤이다.

① 뒤에 and로 연결된 두 문장 'you have observed a smile and you could sense ~'가 모두 완전한 3형식 구조이다. 따라서 '전치사＋관계대명사' 형태인 in which가 바르게 쓰였다.
② 앞에 나온 **smile**을 지칭하기 위해 단수 부정대명사 **one**이 바르게 쓰였다.
③ 분사 뒤에 목적어 **the lower half your face only**가 나오는 것으로 보아 현재분사 **using**이 바르게 쓰였다.
④ 뒤에 '형용사＋주어＋동사'가 이어지는 것으로 보아 의문부사 how가 바르게 쓰였다. 의문부사 how가 '얼마나'라는 뜻이면 주로 'how＋형/부＋주어＋동사' 어순으로 쓰인다.

- **occasion** ⓝ 경우
- **obvious** ⓐ 명백한, 분명한
- **insincere** ⓐ 진실하지 않은
- **manufacture** ⓥ 만들다
- **noticeably** ⓐⓓ 눈에 띄게, 두드러지게
- **entire** ⓐ 전체의
- **genuine** ⓐ 진짜인
- **identify** ⓥ 알아보다, 식별하다
- **primarily** ⓐⓓ 주로
- **impact** ⓥ 영향을 미치다
- **slightly** ⓐⓓ 살짝, 약간

구문 풀이

2행 The most obvious way of identifying a genuine smile from an insincere [주어]
one is that a fake smile primarily only affects the lower half of the face, mainly
[동사(단수)] [주어] [동사] [목적어]
with the mouth alone.

30 자연계의 복잡한 형태 　　　　정답률 34% | 정답 ③

다음 글의 밑줄 친 부분 중, 문맥상 낱말의 쓰임이 적절하지 않은 것은? [3점]

Detailed study over the past two or three decades / is showing / that the complex forms of natural systems / are essential to their functioning.
지난 20년 혹은 30년 동안의 상세한 연구는 / 보여주고 있다. / 자연계의 복잡한 형태가 / 그 기능에 필수적이라는 것을
The attempt / to ① straighten rivers / and give them regular cross-sections / is perhaps the most disastrous example / of this form-and-function relationship.
시도는 / 강을 직선화하고 / 규칙적인 횡단면으로 만들고자 하는 / 아마도 가장 피해 막심한 사례가 될 수 있다. / 이러한 형태-기능 관계의
The natural river has a very ② irregular form: / it curves a lot, / spills across floodplains, / and leaks into wetlands, / giving it an ever-changing and incredibly complex shoreline.
자연 발생적인 강은 매우 불규칙한 형태를 가지고 있다. / 그것은 많이 굽이치고, / 범람원을 가로질러 넘쳐 흐르고, / 습지로 스며 들어가서 / 끊임없이 바뀌고 엄청나게 복잡한 강가를 만든다.
This allows the river / to ✓accommodate variations in water level and speed.
이것은 강이 ~하게 한다. / 강의 수위와 속도 변화를 조절할 수 있게
Pushing the river into tidy geometry / ④ destroys functional capacity / and results in disasters / like the Mississippi floods of 1927 and 1993 / and, more recently, the unnatural disaster of Hurricane Katrina.
강을 질서정연한 기하학적 형태에 맞춰 넣는 것은 / 기능적 수용 능력을 파괴하고 / 재난을 초래한다. / 1927년과 1993년의 미시시피 강의 홍수와 같은 / 그리고 또 최근인 허리케인 Katrina라는 비정상적인 재난을
A $50 billion plan to "let the river loose" in Louisiana / recognizes / that the ⑤ controlled Mississippi / is washing away / twenty-four square miles of that state annually.
루이지애나에서 "강이 자유롭게 흐르도록 두라(let the river loose)"라는 500억 달러 계획은 / 인정한 것이다. / 통제된 미시시피 강이 / 유실시키고 있다는 것을 / 매년 그 주의 24제곱마일을

지난 20년 혹은 30년 동안의 상세한 연구는 자연계의 복잡한 형태가 그 기능에 필수적이라는 것을 보여주고 있다. 강을 ① 직선화하고 규칙적인 횡단면으로 만들고자 하는 시도는 아마도 이러한 형태 — 기능 관계의 가장 피해 막심한 사례가 될 수 있다. 자연 발생적인 강은 매우 ② 불규칙한 형태를 가지고 있다. 그것은 많이 굽이치고, 범람원을 가로질러 넘쳐 흐르고, 습지로 스며 들어가서 끊임없이 바뀌고 엄청나게 복잡한 강가를 만든다. 이것은 강의 수위와 속도 변화를 ③ 막을(→ 조절할) 수 있게 한다. 강을 질서정연한 기하학적 형태에 맞춰 넣는 것은 기능적 수용 능력을 ④ 파괴하고 1927년과 1993년의 미시시피 강의 홍수와 더 최근인 허리케인 Katrina와 같은 비정상적인 재난을 초래한다. 루이지애나에서 "강이 자유롭게 흐르도록 두라(let the river loose)"라는 500억 달러 계획은 ⑤ 통제된 미시시피 강이 매년 그 주의 24제곱마일을 유실시키고 있다는 것을 인정한 것이다.

첫 문장에서 자연계의 복잡한 형태는 자연계가 기능하는 데 필수적이라는 주제를 제시하고 있다. 'The natural river ~'에서 자연 발생적인 강이 예시로 나오는데, 이러한 강이 매우 복잡한 형태를 띠고 있지만 바로 그 형태로 인해 물의 수위 변화와 속도를 조절할 수 있다는 내용이 이어져야 하므로 ③의 **prevent**를 accommodate로 고쳐야 한다. 따라서 문맥상 낱말의 쓰임이 적절하지 않은 것은 ③이다.

- **essential** ⓐ 필수적인
- **straighten** ⓥ 바로 펴다, 똑바로 하게 하다
- **irregular** ⓐ 불규칙한
- **spill** ⓥ 흐르다, 쏟아지다
- **incredibly** ⓐⓓ 엄청나게, 믿을 수 없게
- **attempt** ⓝ 노력, 시도
- **disastrous** ⓐ 처참한, 피해가 막심한
- **curve** ⓥ 굽이치다
- **leak into** ~에 새어 들어가다
- **annually** ⓐⓓ 매년, 연마다

구문 풀이

3행 The attempt to straighten rivers and give them regular cross-sections is
[주어] [형용사적 용법1] [형용사적 용법2] [동사(단수)]
perhaps the most disastrous example of this form-and-function relationship.
[주격 보어]

▶ 많이 틀린 이유는?
자연의 복잡한 형태가 자연의 기능 수행에 도움이 된다는 다소 생소한 내용의 지문이다. 특히 글의 마지막 부분에서 강의 모양을 인위적으로 변형시키려 한 이례적인 재난이 야기될 수 있어서 루이지애나 주 등에서 강의 모양을 '통제하려는' 시도를 그만두고 있다는 내용이 제시된다. 이러한 맥락으로 보아 최다 오답인 ⑤ 'controlled'는 적절하게 쓰였다.

▶ 문제 해결 방법은?
③이 포함된 문장에서 주어인 **This**는 앞 문장 내용, 즉 자연 발생적인 강이 복잡한 형태를 띤다는 내용을 받는다. 이러한 복잡한 형태가 자연의 기능 수행에 도움이 되는 요소임을 고려하면, 복잡한 형태가 강의 수위나 속도 변화를 '막아버린다'는 설명은 흐름상 어색하다.

31 원하는 것과 해야 할 것 　　　　정답률 41% | 정답 ①

다음 빈칸에 들어갈 말로 가장 적절한 것을 고르시오.
✓**desires** - 욕망　　② **merits** - 장점　　③ **abilities** - 능력
④ **limitations** - 한계　　⑤ **worries** - 걱정

In a culture / where there is a belief / that you can have anything you truly want, / there is no problem in choosing.
문화에서는 / 믿음이 있는 / 당신이 진정으로 원하는 것은 무엇이든지 가질 수 있다는 / 선택이 문제가 안 된다.
Many cultures, however, / do not maintain this belief.
그러나 많은 문화들은 / 이러한 믿음을 유지하지 못한다.
In fact, / many people do not believe / that life is about getting what you want.
사실, / 많은 사람들은 믿지 않는다. / 삶이란 당신이 원하는 것을 얻는 것이라고
Life is about doing what you are *supposed* to do.
인생은 당신이 *해야 할* 것을 하는 것이다.
The reason they have trouble making choices / is / they believe / that what they may want is not related / to what they are supposed to do.
그들이 선택을 하는 데 있어 어려움을 겪는 이유는 / ~이다. / 그들이 믿기 때문에 / 그들이 원하는 것이 관련이 없다고 / 그들이 해야 할 일과
The weight of outside considerations / is greater than their desires.
외적으로 고려할 문제의 비중이 / 그들의 욕망보다 더 크다.
When this is an issue in a group, / we discuss what makes for good decisions.
이것이 어떤 집단에서 논의 대상이 될 때, / 우리는 어떤 것이 좋은 결정인지 의논을 한다.
If a person can be unburdened from their cares and duties / and, just for a moment, / consider what appeals to them, / they get the chance / to sort out what is important to them.
만약 어떤 사람이 걱정과 의무로부터 벗어나 / 잠시 동안 / 자신에게 호소하는 것이 무엇인지를 생각해 볼 수 있다면, / 그들은 기회를 얻게 된다. / 자신에게 무엇이 중요한지를 가려낼
Then they can consider and negotiate / with their external pressures.
그리고 나서 그들은 고려하고 협상할 수 있다. / 외적인 부담에 대해

당신이 진정으로 원하는 것은 무엇이든지 가질 수 있다고 믿는 문화에서는 선택이 문제가 안 된다. 그러나 많은 문화들은 이러한 믿음을 유지하지 못한다. 사실, 많은 사람들은 삶이란 당신이 원하는 것을 얻는 것이라고 믿지 않는다. 인생은 당신이 *해야 할* 것을 하는 것이다. 그들이 선택을 하는 데 있어 어려움을 겪는 이유는 그들이 원하는 것이 그들이 해야 할 일과 관련이 없다고 믿기 때문이다. 외적으로 고려할 문제의 비중이 그들의 욕망보다 더 크다. 이것이 어떤 집단에서 논의 대상이 될 때, 우리는 어떤 것이 좋은 결정인지 의논을 한다. 만약 어떤 사람이 걱정과 의무로부터 벗어나 자신에게 호소하는 것이 무엇인지를 잠시 동안 생각해 볼 수 있다면, 그들은 자신에게 무엇이 중요한지를 가려낼 기회를 얻게 된다. 그리고 나서 그들은 외적인 부담에 대해 고려하고 협상할 수 있다.

첫 두 문장에 따르면 많은 문화권에서 원하는 것을 다 가질 수 있다는 믿음이 유지되지 못한다고 한다. 이를 근거로 할 때, 빈칸이 포함된 문장은 '원하는 것' 이외에 고려할 문제가 더 많다는 의미여야 한다. 따라서 빈칸에 들어갈 말로 가장 적절한 것은 ① '욕망'이다.

- **maintain** ⓥ 유지하다
- **weight** ⓝ 비중, 무게
- **negotiate** ⓥ 협상하다
- **desire** ⓝ 욕망
- **limitation** ⓝ 한계
- **have trouble ~ing** ~하는 데 어려움을 겪다
- **consideration** ⓝ 고려 사항
- **external** ⓐ 외부적인
- **merit** ⓝ 장점

구문 풀이

1행 In a culture [where there is a belief {that you can have anything you truly
[선행사] [관계부사] { }: 동격(= a belief)
want}], there is no problem in choosing.
[동사] [주어]

▶ 많이 틀린 이유는?
이 글은 우리가 원하는 바를 모두 성취하지 못하고 해야 하는 일 등 외부적 요소를 고려하여 선택을 하는 경우가 대부분이라는 내용을 다루고 있다. '능력'에 관해서는 중요하게 언급되지 않으므로 ③은 빈칸에 부적절하다.

▶ 문제 해결 방법은?
'what you want'와 'what you are *supposed* to do'가 두 가지 핵심 소재인데, 빈칸 문장의 outside consideration은 이중 'what you are *supposed* to do'와 같은 말이다. 따라서 빈칸에는 'what you want'를 달리 표현하는 말이 들어가야 한다.

32 선수의 인성 및 도덕성 함양에 양면적으로 작용하는 승리 　　　　정답률 43% | 정답 ⑤

다음 빈칸에 들어갈 말로 가장 적절한 것을 고르시오.
① a piece of cake - 식은 죽 먹기
② a one-way street - 일방통행로
③ a bird in the hand - 수중에 든 새
④ a fish out of water - 물 밖에 나온 고기
✓a double-edged sword - 양날의 검

Research has confirmed / that athletes are less likely to participate in unacceptable behavior / than are non-athletes.

연구는 확인해준다. / 운동선수는 받아들여지지 않는 행동을 덜 할 것이라고 / 선수가 아닌 사람들보다
However, / moral reasoning and good sporting behavior / seem to decline / as athletes progress to higher competitive levels, / in part because of the increased emphasis on winning.
그러나 / 도덕적 분별력과 바람직한 스포츠 행위가 / 감소하는 것 같다. / 운동선수가 더 높은 경쟁적 수준까지 올라감에 따라 / 부분적으로 승리에 대한 강조가 커지기 때문에
Thus winning can be a double-edged sword / in teaching character development.
그래서 승리라는 것은 양날의 검이 될 수 있다. / 인성 함양을 가르치는 데 있어서
Some athletes may want to win so much / that they lie, cheat, and break team rules.
어떤 선수는 너무나 이기려고 하다 보니 / 그 결과 거짓말하고 속이고 팀 규칙을 위반한다.
They may develop undesirable character traits / that can enhance their ability to win in the short term.
그들은 바람직하지 못한 인격 특성을 계발할지 모른다. / 단시간에 이길 수 있는 자신의 능력을 강화할 수 있는
However, / when athletes resist the temptation / to win in a dishonest way, / they can develop positive character traits / that last a lifetime.
그러나 / 선수가 유혹에 저항할 때 / 부정직한 방법으로 이기고자 하는 / 그들은 긍정적인 인격 특성을 계발할 수 있다. / 일생동안 지속되는
Character is a learned behavior, / and a sense of fair play develops / only if coaches plan to teach those lessons systematically.
인성이라는 것은 학습되는 행동이며 / 페어플레이 정신이 발달한다. / 코치가 그러한 교훈을 체계적으로 가르치고자 계획할 때 비로소

연구에 따르면 운동선수는 선수가 아닌 사람들보다 (사회적으로) 받아들여지지 않는 행동을 덜 할 것이라고 한다. 그러나 운동선수가 더 높은 경쟁적 수준까지 올라감에 따라 부분적으로 승리에 대한 강조가 커지기 때문에 도덕적 분별력과 바람직한 스포츠 행위가 감소하는 것 같다. 그래서 승리라는 것은 인성 함양을 가르치는 데 있어서 양날의 검이 될 수 있다. 어떤 선수는 너무나 이기려고 하다 보니 그 결과 거짓말하고 속이고 팀 규칙을 위반한다. 그들은 단시간에 이길 수 있는 자신의 능력을 강화할 수 있는 바람직하지 못한 인격 특성을 계발할지 모른다. 그러나 선수가 부정직한 방법으로 이기고자 하는 유혹에 저항할 때 그들은 일생동안 지속되는 긍정적인 인격 특성을 계발할 수 있다. 인성이라는 것은 학습되는 행동이며 코치가 그러한 교훈을 체계적으로 가르치고자 계획할 때 비로소 페어플레이 정신이 발달한다.

Why? 왜 정답일까?

첫 두 문장에 따르면 운동선수는 선수가 아닌 사람들에 비할 때 사회적으로 용인되지 않는 행동을 덜 하는 경향이 있지만, 승리가 강조되는 환경에 살기 때문에 경쟁이 심해질수록 도덕적 분별력이 떨어질 수 있다고 한다(~ athletes are less likely to participate in unacceptable behavior ~. However, moral reasoning and good sporting behavior seem to decline ~.). 따라서 빈칸에 들어갈 말로 가장 적절한 것은 승리라는 것이 선수의 인격 또는 도덕성 함양에 양면적으로 작용할 수 있다는 의미의 ⑤ '양날의 검'이다.

- **confirm** ⓥ (맞다고) 확인하다
- **reasoning** ⓝ 추론 (능력)
- **competitive** ⓐ 경쟁하는, 경쟁력 있는
- **undesirable** ⓐ 바람직하지 않은
- **resist** ⓥ 저항하다
- **dishonest** ⓐ 부정직한
- **systematically** ⓐⓓ 체계적으로
- **a bird in the hand** 수중에 든 새, 확실한 일
- **a fish out of water** 물 밖에 나온 고기, 낯선 환경에서 불편해하는 사람
- **a double-edged sword** 양날의 검, 양면성을 가진 상황

- **unacceptable** ⓐ 받아들여지지 않는, 용인되지 않는
- **decline** ⓥ 감소하다
- **emphasis** ⓝ 강조
- **enhance** ⓥ 강화하다
- **temptation** ⓝ 유혹
- **learned** ⓐ 학습된, 후천적인
- **a piece of cake** 식은 죽 먹기, 아주 쉬운 일

구문 풀이

1행 Research has confirmed that athletes are less likely to participate in
접속사(~것) / be less likely + to부정사: 덜 ~하는 경향이 있다
unacceptable behavior than are non-athletes.
than + 동사 + 주어: 도치 구문

★★ 문제 해결 꿀~팁 ★★

▶ 많이 틀린 이유는?
빈칸 뒤에 따르면 선수들은 승리를 위해 부도덕한 행동을 저지르면서 바람직하지 못한 인격 특성을 키우게 될 수 있지만, 한편으로 부정직한 승리의 유혹에 저항하는 과정에서 좋은 인격 특성을 함양하게 될 수도 있다고 한다. 이는 결국 승리가 선수에게 좋은 쪽과 나쁜 쪽 둘 다로 작용할 수 있다는 의미이므로, ② 'a one-way street(일방통행로)'은 빈칸에 적합하지 않다. 또한 ① 'a piece of cake(식은 죽 먹기)'는 글의 내용과 전혀 관련이 없다.

▶ 문제 해결 방법은?
빈칸 뒤의 세부 진술을 읽고 일반적인 결론을 도출한 뒤, 이를 다시 비유적으로 잘 나타낸 선택지를 찾아야 하는 문제이다. 핵심은 승리의 '양면성'에 있음을 염두에 둔다.

★★★ 등급을 가르는 문제!

33 개인에게 넘어간 음악 선택권   정답률 38% | 정답 ①

다음 빈칸에 들어갈 말로 가장 적절한 것을 고르시오. [3점]

☑ choose and determine his or her musical preferences
자신이 선호하는 음악을 선택하고 결정해야
② understand the technical aspects of recording sessions
녹음 세션의 기술적 측면을 이해해야
③ share unique and inspiring playlists on social media
독특하고 영감을 주는 재생 목록을 소셜 미디어에 공유해야
④ interpret lyrics with background knowledge of the songs
노래에 대한 배경지식으로 가사를 해석해야
⑤ seek the advice of a voice specialist for better performances
더 나은 공연을 위해 음성 전문가의 조언을 구해야

Due to technological innovations, / music can now be experienced by more people, / for more of the time than ever before.
기술 혁신으로 인해, / 음악은 이제 더 많은 사람에 의해 경험될 수 있다. / 이전보다 더 많은 시간 동안
Mass availability has given individuals unheard-of control / over their own sound-environment.
대중 이용 가능성은 개인들에게 전례 없는 통제권을 주었다. / 각자의 음향 환경에 대한
However, / it has also confronted them / with the simultaneous availability of countless genres of music, / in which they have to orient themselves.
하지만 / 그것은 그들을 맞닥뜨리게 했고 / 무수한 장르의 음악을 동시에 이용할 수 있는 상황에 / 그들은 그 상황에 적응해야만 한다.

People start filtering out and organizing their digital libraries / like they used to do with their physical music collections.
사람들은 자신들의 디지털 라이브러리를 걸러 내고 정리하기 시작한다. / 이전에 그들이 물리적 형태를 지닌 음악을 수집했던 것처럼
However, / there is the difference / that the choice lies in their own hands.
하지만 / 차이가 있다. / 선택권은 자신이 가진다는
Without being restricted to the limited collection of music-distributors, / nor being guided by the local radio program / as a 'preselector' of the latest hits, / the individual actively has to choose and determine his or her musical preferences.
음악 배급자의 제한된 컬렉션에 국한되지 않고, / 또한 지역 라디오 프로그램의 안내를 받지 않고, / 최신 히트곡의 '사전 선택자'인 / 개인은 적극적으로 자신이 선호하는 음악을 선택하고 결정해야 한다.
The search for the right song / is thus associated with considerable effort.
적절한 노래를 찾는 것은 / 따라서 상당한 노력과 관련이 있다.

기술 혁신으로 인해, 음악은 이제 이전보다 더 많은 시간 동안 더 많은 사람에 의해 경험될 수 있다. 대중 이용 가능성은 개인들에게 각자의 음향 환경에 대한 전례 없는 통제권을 주었다. 하지만 그들은 무수한 장르의 음악을 동시에 이용할 수 있는 상황에 맞닥뜨리게 되었고 그 상황에 적응해야만 한다. 사람들은 이전에 물리적 형태를 지닌 음악을 수집했던 것처럼 자신들의 디지털 라이브러리를 걸러 내고 정리하기 시작한다. 하지만 선택권은 자신이 가진다는 차이가 있다. 음악 배급자의 제한된 컬렉션에 국한되지 않고, 또한 최신 히트곡의 '사전 선택자'인 지역 라디오 프로그램의 안내를 받지 않고, 개인은 적극적으로 자신이 선호하는 음악을 선택하고 결정해야 한다. 따라서 적절한 노래를 찾는 것은 상당한 노력과 관련이 있다.

Why? 왜 정답일까?

첫 두 문장에서 기술 혁신으로 인해 개인이 자신의 음향 환경을 통제할 수 있는 권한을 갖게 되었다고 한다. 특히 'However, there is the difference that the choice lies in their own hands.'에서는 무수한 장르의 음악 속에서 자신의 디지털 라이브러리를 어떻게 구성할 것인지에 대한 선택권이 개인 자신에게 있다고 언급한다. 따라서 빈칸에 들어갈 말로 가장 적절한 것은 ① '자신이 선호하는 음악을 선택하고 결정해야'이다.

- **availability** ⓝ 이용 가능성
- **confront A with B** A를 B와 대면시키다
- **orient** ⓥ (새로운 상황에) 적응하다, 익숙해지다, 자기 위치를 알다
- **restrict** ⓥ 국한시키다, 제한하다
- **considerable** ⓐ 상당한
- **unheard-of** ⓐ 전례 없는
- **distributor** ⓝ 배급 업자
- **interpret** ⓥ 해석하다

구문 풀이

4행 However, it has also confronted them with the simultaneous availability
confront + A + with + B : A를 B와 대면시키다
of countless genres of music, in which they have to orient themselves.
계속적 용법(= where)

★★ 문제 해결 꿀~팁 ★★

▶ 많이 틀린 이유는?
기술 혁신으로 개인이 음악 선택권을 갖게 되었다는 내용의 글이다. 최다 오답인 ③은 개인이 소셜 미디어에 플레이리스트를 공유해야 한다는 의미인데, 개인이 직접 만든 플레이리스트를 공유해야 하는지는 글에서 언급되지 않았다. 특히 '소셜 미디어'라는 소재 자체가 글에서 아예 언급되지 않았다.

▶ 문제 해결 방법은?
주제가 드러나는 'However ~.' 문장을 잘 읽으면 쉽다. 'the choice lies in their own hands'가 문제 해결에 핵심적인 표현이다.

34 관객과의 상호 작용을 요하는 창작 행위   정답률 49% | 정답 ④

다음 빈칸에 들어갈 말로 가장 적절한 것을 고르시오. [3점]

① exploring the absolute truth in existence
현존하는 절대적 진리를 탐구하는 것
② following a series of precise and logical steps
정확하고 논리적인 일련의 단계를 따르는 것
③ looking outside and drawing inspiration from nature
밖을 보고 자연으로부터 영감을 얻는 것
☑ internalizing the perspective of others on one's work
다른 사람의 관점을 자신의 작품 속에 내면화하는 것
⑤ pushing the audience to the limits of its endurance
관객을 인내심의 한계까지 밀어붙이는 것

It is common to assume / that creativity concerns primarily the relation / between actor(creator) and artifact(creation).
가정하는 것이 일반적이다. / 창조성은 주로 관계와 연관되어 있다고 / 행위자(창작자)와 창작물(창작) 간의
However, from a sociocultural standpoint, / the creative act is never "complete" / in the absence of a second position / — that of an audience.
그러나 사회 문화적 관점에서 볼 때, / 창작 행위는 결코 '완전'하지 않다. / 제2의 입장이 부재한 상황에서는 / 다시 말해 관객의 부재
While the actor or creator him/herself / is the first audience of the artifact being produced, / this kind of distantiation can only be achieved / by internalizing the perspective of others on one's work.
행위자나 창작자 자신은 / 만들어지고 있는 창작물의 첫 번째 관객이지만, / 이런 거리두기는 오로지 이루어진다. / 다른 사람의 관점을 자신의 작품 속에 내면화하는 것으로서만
This means / that, in order to be an audience to your own creation, / a history of interaction with others is needed.
이것은 의미한다. / 자신의 창작 활동에 관객이 되기 위해서는 / 다른 사람들과 상호 작용하는 역사가 필요하다는 것
We exist in a social world / that constantly confronts us with the "view of the other."
우리는 사회적인 세상에 살고 있다. / 끊임없이 '상대방의 관점'에 마주하는
It is the view / we include and blend into our own activity, / including creative activity.
그것은 관점이다. / 우리가 우리 자신의 활동에 통합시키고 뒤섞게 되는 / 창조적인 행위를 포함하여
This outside perspective is essential for creativity / because it gives new meaning and value / to the creative act and its product.
이러한 외부 관점은 창조성에는 필수적이다. / 그것이 새로운 의미와 가치를 부여하기 때문에 / 창작 행위와 그 결과물에

창조성은 주로 행위자(창작자)와 창작물(창작) 간의 관계와 연관되어 있다고 가정하는 것이 일반적이다. 그러나 사회 문화적 관점에서 볼 때, 창작 행위는 관객의 부재, 다시 말해 제2의 입장이 부재한 상황에서는 결코 '완전'하지 않다. 행위자나 창작자 자신은 만들어지고 있는 창작물의 첫 번째 관객이지만, 이런 거리두기는 다른 사람의 관점을 자신의 작품 속에 내면화하는 것으로서만 이루어진다. 이것은 자신의 창작 활동에 관객이 되기 위해서는 다른 사람

들과 상호 작용하는 역사가 필요하다는 것을 의미한다. 우리는 끊임없이 '상대방의 관점'에 마주하는 사회적인 세상에 살고 있다. 그것은 창조적인 행위를 포함해서 우리가 우리 자신의 활동에 통합시키고 뒤섞게 되는 관점이다. 이러한 외부 관점은 창작 행위와 그 결과물에 새로운 의미와 가치를 부여하기 때문에 창조성에는 필수적이다.

Why? 왜 정답일까?

두 번째 문장에서 사회 문화적 관점에 따르면 창작 행위는 제2의 관점, 즉 관객의 시각이 빠진 상태에서는 결코 완전할 수 없다고 한다. 이어서 'This means that, ~' 이하로 창작 활동에는 다른 사람과 상호 작용하는, 즉 '상대방의 관점'이 창조적 활동에 통합되는 과정이 꼭 필요하다는 내용이 이어진다. 따라서 빈칸에 들어갈 말로 가장 적절한 것은 ④ '다른 사람의 관점을 자신의 작품 속에 내면화하는 것'이다.

- primarily ⓐ 주로
- in the absence of ~이 없을 때에
- distantiation ⓝ 거리두기
- blend into ~에 뒤섞다
- absolute ⓐ 절대적인
- precise ⓐ 정확한
- endurance ⓝ 인내심, 참을성
- standpoint ⓝ 관점
- audience ⓝ 관객, 청중
- constantly ⓐ 지속적으로
- essential ⓐ 필수적인, 본질적인
- in existence 현존하는
- internalize ⓥ 내면화하다

구문 풀이

8행 This means that, in order to be an audience to your own creation, a history
접속사(~것)   부사적 용법(~하기 위해)   주어
of interaction with others is needed.
                                동사(단수)

---

35 전염병의 확산과 이에 대한 도시 환경의 대응력   정답률 58% | 정답 ④

다음 글에서 전체 흐름과 관계 <u>없는</u> 문장은? [3점]

Health and the spread of disease / are very closely linked / to how we live and how our cities operate.
건강과 질병의 확산은 / 매우 밀접하게 연관되어 있다 / 우리가 어떻게 살고 우리의 도시가 어떻게 작동하느냐와

The good news is / that cities are incredibly resilient.
좋은 소식은 ~이다 / 도시가 믿을 수 없을 정도로 회복력이 있는 것

Many cities have experienced epidemics in the past / and have not only survived, but advanced.
많은 도시는 과거에 전염병을 경험했고 / 살아있었을 뿐만 아니라 발전했다

① The nineteenth and early-twentieth centuries / saw destructive outbreaks of cholera, typhoid, and influenza / in European cities.
19세기와 20세기 초 / 콜레라, 장티푸스, 독감의 파괴적인 창궐을 목격했다 / 유럽의 도시에서

② Doctors such as Jon Snow, from England, / and Rudolf Virchow, of Germany, / saw the connection / between poor living conditions, overcrowding, sanitation, and disease.
영국 출신의 Jon Snow와 같은 의사들은 / 그리고 독일의 Rudolf Virchow와 같은 / 연관성을 알게 되었다 / 열악한 주거 환경, 인구 과밀, 위생과 질병의

③ A recognition of this connection / led to the replanning and rebuilding of cities / to stop the spread of epidemics.
이 연관성에 대한 인식은 / 도시 재계획과 재건축으로 이어졌다 / 전염병의 확산을 막기 위한

④ In spite of reconstruction efforts, / cities declined in many areas / and many people started to leave.
재건 노력에도 불구하고 / 많은 지역에서 도시는 쇠퇴하였고 / 많은 사람이 떠나기 시작했다.

⑤ In the mid-nineteenth century, / London's pioneering sewer system, / which still serves it today, / was built / as a result of understanding the importance of clean water / in stopping the spread of cholera.
19세기 중반에, / 런던의 선구적인 하수 처리 시스템은 / 오늘날까지도 사용되고 있는 / 만들어졌다. / 깨끗한 물의 중요성에 대한 이해의 결과로 / 콜레라의 확산을 막는 데 있어

건강과 질병의 확산은 우리가 어떻게 살고 우리의 도시가 어떻게 작동하느냐와 매우 밀접하게 연관되어 있다. 좋은 소식은 도시가 믿을 수 없을 정도로 회복력이 있다는 것이다. 많은 도시는 과거에 전염병을 경험했고 살아있었을 뿐만 아니라 발전했다. ① 19세기와 20세기 초 유럽의 도시들은 콜레라, 장티푸스, 독감의 파괴적인 창궐을 목격했다. ② 영국 출신의 Jon Snow와 독일의 Rudolf Virchow와 같은 의사들은 열악한 주거 환경, 인구 과밀, 위생과 질병의 연관성을 알게 되었다. ③ 이 연관성에 대한 인식은 전염병의 확산을 막기 위한 도시 재계획과 재건축으로 이어졌다. ④ 재건 노력에도 불구하고 많은 지역에서 도시는 쇠퇴하였고 많은 사람이 떠나기 시작했다. ⑤ 19세기 중반에 지어진, 오늘날까지도 사용되고 있는 런던의 선구적인 하수 처리 시스템은 깨끗한 물이 콜레라의 확산을 막는 데 중요하다는 이해의 결과로 만들어졌다.

Why? 왜 정답일까?

첫 문장에서 전염병의 확산은 우리의 생활방식 및 도시 환경과 밀접하게 연관되어 있다는 주제를 제시한 뒤, ①, ②, ③, ⑤는 19~20세기 각종 전염병의 창궐을 경험한 유럽 도시들이 도시 환경의 개선을 통해 전염병을 극복했다는 예시를 든다. 하지만 ④는 도시가 재건 노력에도 불구하고 쇠퇴했다는 무관한 내용을 제시한다. 따라서 전체 흐름과 관계 없는 문장은 ④이다.

- spread ⓝ 확산 ⓥ 퍼지다
- epidemic ⓝ 전염병
- outbreak ⓝ 발발, 창궐
- sanitation ⓝ 위생 (관리)
- incredibly ⓐ 놀라울 정도로
- destructive ⓐ 파괴적인
- overcrowding ⓝ 과밀 거주, 초만원
- reconstruction ⓝ 재건

구문 풀이

1행 Health and the spread of disease are very closely linked to how we live
          주어   동사구(복수)   간접의문문1
and how our cities operate.
      간접의문문2

---

36 아기가 사람 얼굴을 선호하는 이유   정답률 69% | 정답 ⑤

주어진 글 다음에 이어질 글의 순서로 가장 적절한 것을 고르시오.

① (A) - (C) - (B)
② (B) - (A) - (C)

---

③ (B) - (C) - (A)
④ (C) - (A) - (B)
✓ (C) - (B) - (A)

Starting from birth, / babies are immediately attracted to faces.
태어나면서부터, / 아기는 즉각적으로 사람 얼굴에 끌린다.

Scientists were able to show this / by having babies look at two simple images, / one that looks more like a face than the other.
과학자들은 이것을 보여줄 수 있었다. / 아기에게 간단한 두 개의 이미지를 보여줌으로써 / 하나가 다른 것에 비해 더 사람 얼굴처럼 보이는 이미지

(C) By measuring where the babies looked, / scientists found / that the babies looked at the face-like image more / than they looked at the non-face image.
아기가 바라보는 곳을 유심히 살펴보면서, / 과학자들은 발견하게 되었다. / 아기가 얼굴처럼 보이는 이미지를 더 바라본다는 것을 / 그들이 얼굴처럼 보이지 않는 이미지를 보는 것보다

Even though babies have poor eyesight, / they prefer to look at faces.
아기는 시력이 좋지 않음에도 불구하고 / 그들은 얼굴을 보는 것을 더 좋아한다.

But why?
그런데 왜 그럴까?

(B) One reason babies might like faces / is because of something called evolution.
아기가 얼굴을 좋아하는 것 같은 하나의 이유는 / 진화라고 불리는 것 때문이다.

Evolution involves changes / to the structures of an organism(such as the brain) / that occur over many generations.
진화는 변화를 수반한다 / 유기체 구조(뇌와 같은 것)에 있어서의 / 여러 세대를 거쳐 발생하는

(A) These changes help the organisms to survive, / making them alert to enemies.
이런 변화들은 유기체가 생존하도록 도와준다. / 적들을 경계하게 해서

By being able to recognize faces / from afar or in the dark, / humans were able to know / someone was coming / and protect themselves from possible danger.
얼굴을 알아볼 수 있음으로써, / 멀리서 또는 어둠 속에서 / 인간은 알 수 있었고 / 누군가가 다가오는지 / 있을 법한 위험으로부터 자신을 보호할 수 있었다.

태어나면서부터, 아기는 즉각적으로 사람 얼굴에 끌린다. 과학자들은 아기에게 간단한 두 개의 이미지, 하나가 다른 것에 비해 더 사람 얼굴처럼 보이는 이미지를 보여줌으로써 이것을 보여줄 수 있었다.

(C) 과학자들은 아기가 바라보는 곳을 유심히 살펴보면서, 아기가 얼굴처럼 보이지 않는 이미지보다는 얼굴처럼 보이는 이미지를 더 바라본다는 것을 발견하게 되었다. 아기는 시력이 좋지 않음에도 불구하고 얼굴을 보는 것을 더 좋아한다. 그런데 왜 그럴까?

(B) 아기가 얼굴을 좋아하는 것 같은 하나의 이유는 진화라고 불리는 것 때문이다. 진화는 여러 세대를 거쳐 발생하는 유기체 구조(뇌와 같은 것)의 변화를 수반한다.

(A) 이런 변화들은 적들을 경계하게 해서 유기체가 생존하도록 도와준다. 멀리서 또는 어둠 속에서 얼굴을 알아볼 수 있음으로써, 인간은 누군가가 다가오는지 알 수 있었고 있을 법한 위험으로부터 자신을 보호할 수 있었다.

Why? 왜 정답일까?

주어진 글에서 아기들은 태어나면서부터 사람 얼굴에 끌리고, 이를 뒷받침하는 실험이 있다고 언급한다. (C)는 주어진 글의 실험에 따르면 아기들이 시력이 좋지 않은데도 불구하고 얼굴 이미지를 선호하는데 '왜 그런 것인지' 의문을 던진다. (B)는 (C)에서 제시된 질문에 '진화' 때문이라는 답을 제시한다. (A)는 (B)에서 언급된 '진화'를 보충 설명하는 내용이다. 따라서 글의 순서로 가장 적절한 것은 ⑤ '(C) - (B) - (A)'이다.

- alert ⓐ 경계하는
- structure ⓝ 구조
- evolution ⓝ 진화
- eyesight ⓝ 시력

구문 풀이

8행 One reason [babies might like faces] is because of something called
       주어   동사(단수)   전치사   명사   과거분사
evolution.

---

37 미디어상의 잘못된 정보 공유 문제   정답률 65% | 정답 ②

주어진 글 다음에 이어질 글의 순서로 가장 적절한 것을 고르시오.

① (A) - (C) - (B)
✓ (B) - (A) - (C)
③ (B) - (C) - (A)
④ (C) - (A) - (B)
⑤ (C) - (B) - (A)

People spend much of their time / interacting with media, / but that does not mean / that people have the critical skills / to analyze and understand it.
사람들은 많은 시간을 소비하지만, / 미디어를 이용해 상호작용하는 데 / 그렇다고 해서 뜻하지는 않는다. / 사람들이 중요한 기술을 가지고 있다는 것 / 미디어를 분석하고 이해하는 데

(B) One well-known study from Stanford University in 2016 / demonstrated / that youth are easily fooled by misinformation, / especially when it comes through social media channels.
2016년 Stanford 대학의 잘 알려진 한 연구는 / 보여주었다. / 젊은이들이 잘못된 정보에 쉽게 속는다는 것을 / 특히 그것이 소셜 미디어 채널을 통해 올 때

This weakness is not found only in youth, however.
그러나 이러한 약점은 젊은이에게서만 발견되는 것은 아니다.

(A) Research from New York University found / that people over 65 / shared seven times as much misinformation / as their younger counterparts.
New York 대학의 조사에서 밝혔다. / 65세 이상의 사람들이 / 7배나 더 많은 잘못된 정보를 공유한다고 / 젊은이들보다

All of this raises a question:
이 모든 것이 의문을 제기한다.

What's the solution to the misinformation problem?
잘못된 정보 문제에 대한 해결책은 무엇인가?

(C) Governments and tech platforms / certainly have a role / to play in blocking misinformation.
정부와 기술 플랫폼은 / 분명 해야 할 역할을 가지고 있다. / 잘못된 정보를 막아내는 데 있어

However, / every individual needs to take responsibility / for combating this threat / by becoming more information literate.
그러나 / 모든 개인은 책임을 지닐 필요가 있다. / 이러한 위험에 맞서 싸울 / 정보를 더 잘 분별함으로써

사람들은 미디어를 이용해 상호작용하는 데 많은 시간을 소비하지만, 그렇다고 해서 사람들이 미디어를 분석하고 이해하는 데 중요한 기술을 가지고 있는 것은 아니다.

(B) 2016년 Stanford 대학의 잘 알려진 한 연구는 특히 정보가 소셜 미디어 채널을 통해 올 때 젊은이들이 잘못된 정보에 쉽게 속는다는 것을 보여주었다. 그러나 이러한 약점은 젊은이에게서만 발견되는 것은 아니다.

(A) New York 대학의 조사에서 65세 이상의 사람들이 젊은이들보다 7배나 더 많은 잘못된 정보를 공유한다고 밝혔다. 이 모든 것이 (다음의) 의문을 제기한다. 잘못된 정보 문제에 대한 해결책은 무엇인가?

(C) 정부와 기술 플랫폼은 분명 잘못된 정보를 막아내는 데 있어 해야 할 역할을 가지고 있다. 그러나 모든 개인은 정보를 더 잘 분별함으로써 이러한 위협에 맞서 싸울 책임을 지닐 필요가 있다.

Why? 왜 정답일까?

주어진 글에서 오늘날 사람들은 미디어를 많이 쓰고 있음에도 미디어를 분석하고 이해하는 데 필요한 능력을 갖추고 있지는 못하다고 지적한다. 이어서 (B)는 한 연구를 사례로 들며, 특히 젊은이들이 잘못된 정보에 쉽게 속는다는 점을 언급한다. (A)에서는 (B)의 말미에 언급된 대로 '젊은 사람들뿐 아니라' 65세 이상의 연령대에서도 잘못된 정보 공유 문제가 발생한다고 언급한다. 이어서 (C)는 (A)의 마지막에 제시된, 정보 공유 문제에 대한 해결책을 묻는 질문에 대해 정부와 개인의 역할을 나누어 답하고 있다. 따라서 글의 순서로 가장 적절한 것은 ② '(B) – (A) – (C)'이다.

- critical ⓐ 중요한
- misinformation ⓝ 오보, 잘못된 정보
- demonstrate ⓥ 입증하다
- combat ⓥ 싸우다
- literate ⓐ ~을 다룰 줄 아는, 정통한, 글을 읽고 쓸 줄 아는
- analyze ⓥ 분석하다
- raise a question 의문을 제기하다
- take responsibility for ~을 책임지다

구문 풀이

1행 People spend much of their time interacting with media, but that does
「spend + 시간 + 동명사」: ~하는 데 …을 소비하다 지시대명사(but 앞 문장)
not mean that people have the critical skills to analyze and understand it.
접속사(~것) 형용사적 용법1 형용사적 용법2

---

38 소리가 들리는 원리   정답률 59% | 정답 ③

글의 흐름으로 보아, 주어진 문장이 들어가기에 가장 적절한 곳을 고르시오.

Sound and light travel in waves.
소리와 빛은 파장으로 이동한다.
An analogy often given for sound / is that of throwing a small stone / onto the surface of a still pond.
소리 현상에 대해 자주 언급되는 비유는 작은 돌멩이를 던지는 것이다. / 고요한 연못 표면에
Waves radiate outwards from the point of impact, / just as sound waves radiate from the sound source.
파장은 충격 지점으로부터 바깥으로 퍼져나간다. / 음파가 음원으로부터 사방으로 퍼지는 것처럼
① This is due to a disturbance / in the air around us.
이것은 교란 작용 때문이다. / 우리 주변 공기 중의
② If you bang two sticks together, / you will get a sound.
만약에 당신이 막대기 두 개를 함께 꽝 친다면 / 당신은 소리를 듣게 될 것이다.
✔ As the sticks approach each other, / the air immediately in front of them / is compressed / and energy builds up.
막대기들이 서로 가까워질 때, / 막대 바로 앞에 있는 공기가 / 압축되고 / 에너지는 축적된다.
When the point of impact occurs, / this energy is released as sound waves.
충돌점이 발생하면 / 이 에너지는 음파로 퍼져나간다.
④ If you try the same experiment with two heavy stones, / exactly the same thing occurs, / but you get a different sound / due to the density and surface of the stones, / and as they have likely displaced more air, / a louder sound.
당신이 두 개의 무거운 돌을 가지고 같은 실험을 해보면 / 똑같은 일이 일어나지만, / 당신은 다른 소리를 듣게 된다. / 돌의 밀도와 표면 때문에 / 그리고 그 돌이 아마 더 많은 공기를 바꿔 놓았기 때문에 / 더 큰 소리
⑤ And so, / a physical disturbance in the atmosphere around us / will produce a sound.
따라서 / 우리 주변의 대기 중에서 일어나는 물리적 교란 작용이 / 소리를 만든다.

소리와 빛은 파장으로 이동한다. 소리 현상에 대해 자주 언급되는 비유는 작은 돌멩이를 고요한 연못 표면에 던지는 것이다. 음파가 음원으로부터 사방으로 퍼지는 것처럼 파장은 충격 지점으로부터 바깥으로 퍼져나간다. ① 이것은 우리 주변 공기 중의 교란 작용 때문이다. ③ 만약에 당신이 막대기 두 개를 함께 꽝 친다면 소리를 듣게 될 것이다. ③ 막대기들이 서로 가까워질 때, 막대 바로 앞에 있는 공기가 압축되고 에너지는 축적된다. 충돌점이 발생하면 이 에너지는 음파로 퍼져나간다. ④ 두 개의 무거운 돌을 가지고 같은 실험을 해보면 똑같은 일이 일어나지만, 돌의 밀도와 표면 때문에 당신은 다른 소리를 듣게 되고, 그 돌이 아마 더 많은 공기를 바꿔 놓았기 때문에 당신은 더 큰 소리를 듣게 된다. ⑤ 따라서 우리 주변의 대기 중에서 일어나는 물리적 교란 작용이 소리를 만든다.

Why? 왜 정답일까?

소리를 듣게 되는 원리를 설명한 글로, ③ 앞의 문장에서 막대기 두 개를 함께 쳐서 소리를 듣는 상황을 예로 들고 있다. 주어진 문장은 두 막대기(the sticks)가 서로 가까워질 때 막대 바로 앞의 공기가 압축되고 에너지가 모인다고 설명한다. ③ 뒤의 문장은 그러다 충돌점이 발생하면 모였던 에너지(this energy)가 음파 형태로 퍼져나간다고 언급한다. 따라서 주어진 문장이 들어가기에 가장 적절한 곳은 ③이다.

- compress ⓥ 압축하다
- surface ⓝ 표면
- disturbance ⓝ 교란, 방해
- density ⓝ 밀도
- build up 축적되다
- impact ⓝ 충격, 여파
- release ⓥ 방출하다
- displace ⓥ 대체하다, (평소의 위치에서) 옮겨 놓다

구문 풀이

3행 An analogy often given for sound is that of throwing a small stone onto
주어 과거분사 동사 └ 지시대명사(= analogy)
the surface of a still pond.

---

39 먹이 사슬의 특징   정답률 58% | 정답 ④

글의 흐름으로 보아, 주어진 문장이 들어가기에 가장 적절한 곳을 고르시오. [3점]

Food chain means the transfer of food energy / from the source in plants / through a series of organisms / with the repeated process of eating and being eaten.
먹이 사슬은 식품 에너지가 이동하는 것을 의미한다. / 식물 안에 있는 에너지원으로부터 / 일련의 유기체를 통해 / 먹고 먹히는 반복되는 과정 속에서
① In a grassland, / grass is eaten by rabbits / while rabbits in turn are eaten by foxes.
초원에서 / 풀은 토끼에게 먹히지만 / 토끼는 이윽고 여우에게 먹힌다.
② This is an example of a simple food chain.
이것은 단순한 먹이 사슬의 예이다.
③ This food chain implies the sequence / in which food energy is transferred / from producer to consumer or higher trophic level.
이 먹이 사슬은 연쇄를 의미한다. / 식품 에너지가 전달되는 / 생산자로부터 소비자 또는 더 높은 영양 수준으로
✔ It has been observed / that at each level of transfer, / a large proportion, 80 − 90 percent, of the potential energy / is lost as heat.
관찰되어 왔다. / 각 이동 단계에서 / 잠재적 에너지의 상당한 부분인 80 ~ 90%가 / 열로 손실되는 것으로
Hence / the number of steps or links in a sequence / is restricted, / usually to four or five.
그래서 / 하나의 사슬 안에 있는 단계나 연결의 수는 / 제한된다. / 보통 4 ~ 5개로
⑤ The shorter the food chain / or the nearer the organism is to the beginning of the chain, / the greater the available energy intake is.
먹이 사슬이 짧을수록 / 또는 유기체가 사슬의 시작 단계에 가까울수록 / 이용 가능한 에너지 섭취량이 더 커진다.

먹이 사슬은 식물 안에 있는 에너지원으로부터 먹고 먹히는 반복되는 과정 속에서 일련의 유기체를 통해 식품 에너지가 이동하는 것을 의미한다. ① 초원에서 풀은 토끼에게 먹히지만 토끼는 이윽고 여우에게 먹힌다. ② 이것은 단순한 먹이 사슬의 예이다. ③ 이 먹이 사슬은 식품 에너지가 생산자로부터 소비자 또는 더 높은 영양 수준으로 전달되는 연쇄를 의미한다. ④ 각 이동 단계에서 잠재적 에너지의 상당한 부분인 80 ~ 90%가 열로 손실되는 것으로 관찰되어 왔다. 그래서 하나의 사슬 안에 있는 단계나 연결의 수는 보통 4 ~ 5개로 제한된다. ⑤ 먹이 사슬이 짧을수록 또는 유기체가 사슬의 시작 단계(하위 영양 단계)에 가까울수록 이용 가능한 에너지 섭취량이 더 커진다.

Why? 왜 정답일까?

④ 앞의 문장에서 먹이 사슬은 식품 에너지가 생산자에서 소비자로, 즉 더 높은 영양 수준으로 이동하는 연쇄적 과정을 의미하는 것이라고 한다. 이어서 주어진 문장은 먹이 사슬의 각 이동 단계(each level of transfer)에서 에너지의 80 ~ 90%가 열로 손실되어 버린다는 사실을 언급한다. ④ 뒤의 문장은 주어진 문장에서 언급된 이유로(Hence) 한 먹이 사슬 안의 단계 수가 4 ~ 5개로 제한된다고 설명한다. 따라서 주어진 문장이 들어가기에 가장 적절한 곳은 ④이다.

- transfer ⓝ 이동
- in turn 이윽고, 차례로
- restrict ⓥ 제한하다
- proportion ⓝ 비율
- imply ⓥ 암시하다
- intake ⓝ 섭취량

구문 풀이

11행 The shorter the food chain or the nearer the organism is to the beginning
「the + 비교급1 ~ the + 비교급2 ~」
of the chain, the greater the available energy intake is.
the + 비교급 …: ~하거나 ~할수록 더 …하다

---

40 공공재의 비극을 막을 방법   정답률 63% | 정답 ①

다음 글의 내용을 한 문장으로 요약하고자 한다. 빈칸 (A), (B)에 들어갈 말로 가장 적절한 것은?

	(A)		(B)
✔①	reminder 상기물	……	shared 공유
②	reminder 상기물	……	recycled 재활용된
③	mistake 실수	……	stored 저장된
④	mistake 실수	……	borrowed 빌려온
⑤	fortune 행운	……	limited 제한된

A woman named Rhonda / who attended the University of California at Berkeley / had a problem.
Rhonda라는 여자에게는 / Berkeley에 있는 California 대학에 다니는 / 한 가지 문제 상황이 있었다.
She was living near campus with several other people / — none of whom knew one another.
그녀는 여러 사람들과 함께 캠퍼스 근처에 살고 있었는데 / 그들 중 누구도 서로를 알지 못했다.
When the cleaning people came each weekend, / they left several rolls of toilet paper / in each of the two bathrooms.
청소부가 주말마다 왔을 때 / 그들은 몇 개의 두루마리 화장지를 두고 갔다. / 화장실 두 칸 각각에
However, / by Monday all the toilet paper would be gone.
그러나 / 월요일 즈음 모든 화장지가 없어지곤 했다.
It was a classic tragedy-of-the-commons situation: / because some people took more toilet paper / than their fair share, / the public resource was destroyed for everyone else.
그것은 전형적인 공유지의 비극 상황이었다. / 일부 사람들이 더 많은 휴지를 가져갔기 때문에 / 자신들이 사용할 수 있는 몫보다 / 그 외 모두를 위한 공공재가 파괴됐다.
After reading a research paper about behavior change, / Rhonda put a note in one of the bathrooms / asking people not to remove the toilet paper, / as it was a shared item.
행동 변화에 대한 연구논문을 읽고 나서, / Rhonda는 쪽지를 화장실 한 곳에 두었다. / 사람들에게 화장실 화장지를 가져가지 말라고 요청하는 / 그것이 공유지이므로
To her great satisfaction, / one roll reappeared in a few hours, / and another the next day.
아주 만족스럽게도, / 몇 시간 후에 화장지 한 개가 다시 나타나고 / 그다음 날에는 또 하나가 다시 나타났다.
In the other note-free bathroom, however, / there was no toilet paper until the following weekend, / when the cleaning people returned.
하지만 쪽지가 없는 화장실에서는 / 청소부가 돌아오는 / 다음 주말까지 화장지가 없었다.
➡ A small (A) reminder brought about a change / in the behavior of the people / who had taken more of the (B) shared goods / than they needed.
자그마한 상기물은 변화를 일으켰다. / 사람들의 행동에 / 더 많은 공유 재화를 가져갔던 / 그들이 필요한 것보다

Berkeley에 있는 California 대학에 다니는 Rhonda라는 여자에게는 한 가지 문제 상황이 있었다. 그녀는 여러 사람들과 함께 캠퍼스 근처에 살고 있었는데 그들 중 누구도 서로를 알지 못했다. 청소부가 주말마다 왔을 때 화장실 두 칸 각각에 몇 개의 두루마리 화장지를 두고 갔다. 그러나 화요일 즈음 모든 화장지가 없어지곤 했다. 그것은 전형적인 공유지의 비극 상황이었다. 일부 사람들이 자신들이 사용할 수 있는 몫보다 더 많은 휴지를 가져갔기 때문에 그 외 모두를 위한 공공재가 파괴됐다. 행동 변화에 대한 한 연구논문을 읽고 나서, Rhonda는 화장실 화장지는 공유재이므로 사람들에게 가져가지 말라고 요청하는 쪽지를 화장실 한 곳에 두었다. 아주 만족스럽게도, 몇 시간 후에 화장지 한 개가 다시 나타났고 그다음 날에는 또 하나가 다시 나타났다. 하지만 쪽지가 없는 화장실에서는 청소부가 돌아오는 그다음 주말까지 화장지가 없었다.

➡ 자그마한 (A) 상기물은 필요한 것보다 더 많은 (B) 공유 재화를 가져갔던 사람의 행동에 변화를 일으켰다.

Why? 왜 정답일까?

실험을 소개한 글이므로 결과 부분에 주목한다. 마지막 세 문장에 따르면, 화장실 휴지가 공유재임을 상기시키는 쪽지를 붙인 화장실에는 없어졌던 휴지가 다시 돌아온 반면, 쪽지를 붙이지 않은 화장실에는 휴지가 돌아오지 않았다고 한다. 이를 토대로, 어떤 것이 공유재임을 '환기시켜 주는' 장치가 있을 때 '공유 재'를 가져갔던 이들의 행동에 변화가 일어날 수 있다는 결론을 도출할 수 있다. 따라서 요약문의 빈칸 (A), (B)에 들어갈 말로 가장 적절한 것은 ① 'A) (상기물), (B) shared(공유)'이다.

- **classic** ⓐ 고전적인
- **destroy** ⓥ 파괴하다
- **bring about** ~을 야기하다
- **tragedy of the commons** 공유지의 비극
- **reappear** ⓥ 다시 나타나다
- **reminder** ⓝ (잊고 있었던 것을) 상기시켜주는 것

구문 풀이

2행 She was living near campus with several other people — none of whom
선행사(사람)　　　　　계속적 용법
knew one another.

41-42　사회적 두려움을 극복하는 방법

If you were afraid of standing on balconies, / you would start on some lower floors / and slowly work your way up to higher ones.
당신이 발코니에 서 있는 것을 두려워한다면, / 당신은 더 낮은 층에서 시작해서 / 천천히 더 높은 층으로 올라갈 것이다.

It would be easy / to face a fear of standing on high balconies / in a way that's totally controlled.
쉬울 것이다. / 높은 발코니에 서 있는 두려움을 직면하기는 / 완전히 통제된 방식으로

Socializing is (a) trickier.
사람을 사귄다는 것은 더 까다롭다.

People aren't like inanimate features of a building / that you just have to be around to get used to.
사람은 건물과 같은 무생물이 아니다. / 그저 주변에 있어서 여러분이 익숙해지는

You have to interact with them, / and their responses can be unpredictable.
당신은 그들과 상호 작용을 해야 하며 / 그들의 반응을 예측하기가 힘들 수 있다.

Your feelings toward them / are more complex too.
그들에 대한 당신의 느낌도 / 역시 더 복잡하다.

Most people's self-esteem / isn't going to be affected that much / if they don't like balconies, / but your confidence can (b) suffer / if you can't socialize effectively.
대부분의 사람들의 자존감은 / 그렇게 많이 영향을 받지 않을 것이지만, / 그들이 발코니를 좋아하지 않는다고 해도 / 당신의 자신감은 상처받을 수 있다. / 당신이 효과적으로 사람들을 사귈 수 없다면

It's also harder / to design a tidy way / to gradually face many social fears.
또한 더 어렵다. / 깔끔한 방법을 설계하는 것 / 점차적으로 마주할 여러 사교적 두려움을

『The social situations / you need to expose yourself to / may not be (c) available / when you want them, / or they may not go well enough / for you to sense / that things are under control.』 ◀ 42번의 근거
사교적 상황이 / 당신을 드러낼 필요가 있는 / 형성되지 않을 수 있고, / 당신이 원할 때 / 또는 그것들은 충분히 잘 진행되지 않을지도 모른다. / 당신이 감지할 만큼 / 상황이 통제 가능하다고

The progression from one step to the next / may not be clear, / creating unavoidable large (d) increases in difficulty / from one to the next.
한 단계에서 다음 단계로의 진행은 / 분명하지 않을 수 있으며, / 피할 수 없이 어려움이 크게 늘어나게 된다. / 한 단계에서 다음 단계로 진행할 때

People around you aren't robots / that you can endlessly experiment with / for your own purposes.
당신 주변의 사람들은 로봇이 아니다. / 당신이 끝임없이 실험해 볼 수 있는 / 당신 자신의 목적을 위해서

This is not to say / that facing your fears is pointless / when socializing.
이것은 말하는 것이 아니다. / 당신의 두려움을 직면하는 것이 의미가 없고 / 사람을 사귈 때

『The principles of gradual exposure / are still very (e) useful.』
점진적인 노출의 원칙은 / 여전히 매우 유용하다.

The process of applying them / is just messier, / and knowing that before you start / is helpful.』 ◀ 41번의 근거
그것들을 적용하는 과정은 / 더 복잡하지만, / 시작하기 전에 그것을 아는 것은 / 도움이 된다.

발코니에 서 있는 것을 두려워한다면, 당신은 더 낮은 층에서 시작해서 천천히 더 높은 층으로 올라갈 것이다. 완전히 통제된 방식으로 높은 발코니에 서 있는 두려움을 직면하기는 쉬울 것이다. 사람을 사귄다는 것은 (a) 더 까다롭다. 사람은 그저 주변에 있어서 익숙해지는 건물과 같은 무생물이 아니다. 당신은 그들과 상호 작용을 해야 하며 그들의 반응을 예측하기가 힘들 수 있다. 그들에 대한 당신의 느낌도 역시 더 복잡하다. 대부분의 사람들의 자존감은 그들이 발코니를 좋아하지 않는다고 해도 그렇게 많이 영향을 받지 않을 것이지만, 당신이 효과적으로 사람들을 사귈 수 없다면 당신의 자신감은 (b) 상처받을 수 있다. 점차적으로 마주할 여러 사교적 두려움을 깔끔한 방법을 설계하는 것 또한 더 어렵다. 당신을 드러낼 필요가 있는 사교적 상황이 당신이 원할 때 (c) 형성되지 않을 수 있고, 또는 그것들은 상황이 통제 가능하다고 감지할 만큼 충분히 잘 진행되지 않을지도 모른다. 한 단계에서 다음 단계로의 진행은 분명하지 않을 수 있으며, 한 단계에서 다음 단계로 진행할 때 피할 수 없이 어려움이 크게 (d) 줄어들게(→ 늘어나게) 된다. 당신 주변의 사람들은 당신 자신의 목적을 위해서 끝임없이 실험해 볼 수 있는 로봇이 아니다. 이것은 사람을 사귈 때 당신의 두려움을 직면하는 것이 의미가 없다는 말이 아니다. 점진적인 노출의 원칙은 여전히 매우 (e) 유용하다. 그것들을 적용하는 과정은 더 복잡하지만, 시작하기 전에 그것을 아는 것은 도움이 된다.

- **socialize** ⓥ (사람과) 사귀다, 사회화하다
- **inanimate** ⓐ 무생물의
- **unpredictable** ⓐ 예측 불가한
- **confidence** ⓝ 자신감
- **under control** 통제되는
- **unavoidable** ⓐ 피할 수 없는
- **pointless** ⓐ 의미 없는
- **tricky** ⓐ 까다로운, 다루기 힘든
- **get used to** ~에 익숙해지다
- **self-esteem** ⓝ 자존감
- **gradually** ⓐⓓ 점차적으로
- **progression** ⓝ 진전
- **endlessly** ⓐⓓ 끝임없이
- **principle** ⓝ 원칙, 원리

구문 풀이

1행 If you were afraid of standing on balconies, you would start on some
「if＋주어＋과거 동사 ~,　　　　　　주어＋조동사 과거형＋동사원형1＋
lower floors and slowly work your way up to higher ones.
동사원형2 : 가정법 과거」

★★★ 등급을 가르는 문제! ★★★

41　제목 파악　　　정답률 39% | 정답 ⑤

윗글의 제목으로 가장 적절한 것은?
① How to Improve Your Self-Esteem
　자존감을 높이는 방법
② Socializing with Someone You Fear: Good or Bad?
　당신이 두려워하는 사람과 어울리는 것: 좋을까, 나쁠까?
③ Relaxation May Lead to Getting Over Social Fears
　휴식은 사회적 두려움을 극복하게 해줄 수 있다
④ Are Social Exposures Related with Fear of Heights?
　사회적 노출은 고소공포증과 연관이 있을까?
☑⑤ Overcoming Social Anxiety Is Difficult; Try Gradually!
　사회적 불안을 극복하기는 어렵지만, 점진적으로 시도하라!

Why? 왜 정답일까?

마지막 두 문장에 따르면 사교적으로 불안을 느끼는 상황에 점진적 노출 기법을 적용하기는 어렵지만 그래도 여전히 이 기법은 유용하다고 한다. 따라서 글의 제목으로 가장 적절한 것은 ⑤ '사회적 불안을 극복하기는 어렵지만, 점진적으로 시도하라'이다.

★★ 문제 해결 꿀~팁 ★★

▶ 많이 틀린 이유는?
사교에 대한 두려움을 고소공포증 극복처럼 점진적 노출 기법, 즉 두려운 상황의 강도를 조금씩 높여가며 노출되는 방식으로 극복해나갈 수 있는지 논한 글이다. 무서워하는 사람과 상호작용을 하는 것이 좋은지 나쁜지 판단하는 내용은 없으므로 ②는 답으로 부적절하다.

▶ 문제 해결 방법은?
명확한 주제문 없이 '사교적 두려움 극복'이라는 소재에 관해 설명하고 마지막 부분에서 결론을 내리는 구조의 글이므로, 전체적으로 글을 다 읽되 필자의 의견이 가장 잘 드러난 부분을 찾아 답으로 연결시켜야 한다.

42　어휘 추론　　　정답률 57% | 정답 ④

밑줄 친 (a)~(e) 중에서 문맥상 낱말의 쓰임이 적절하지 않은 것은?
① (a)　② (b)　③ (c)　☑④ (d)　⑤ (e)

Why? 왜 정답일까?

두 번째 단락의 첫 두 문장에서 사회적 불안을 점진적으로 직면할 수 있는 상황을 형성하거나 통제하는 것은 어렵다고 설명하고 있다. 이를 근거로 볼 때, (d)가 포함된 문장은 상황의 단계가 진행할수록 어려움이 '커진다'는 내용이어야 하므로, (d)의 decreases를 increases로 고쳐야 한다. 따라서 문맥상 낱말의 쓰임이 적절하지 않은 것은 ④ '(d)'이다.

43-45　아버지의 연설문을 보고 감동한 필자

(A)

When I was 17, / I discovered a wonderful thing.
내가 17살 때 / 나는 놀라운 물건을 발견했다.

My father and I were sitting on the floor of his study.
아버지와 나는 서재 바닥에 앉아 있었다.

『We were organizing his old papers.』 ◀ 45번 ①의 근거 일치
우리는 아버지의 오래된 서류를 정리하고 있었다.

Across the carpet I saw a fat paper clip.
나는 카펫 너머에 있는 두꺼운 종이 클립을 보았다.

Its rust dusted the cover sheet of a report of some kind.
그것의 녹이 어떤 보고서의 표지를 더럽혔다.

I picked it up.
나는 그것을 집어 들었다.

『I started to read.
나는 읽기 시작했다.

Then I started to cry.』 ◀ 45번 ②의 근거 일치
그러고 나서 나는 울기 시작했다.

(C)

『It was a speech / he had written in 1920, in Tennessee.
그것은 연설이었다. / 1920년 Tennessee 주에서 아버지가 썼던

Then only 17 himself and graduating from high school, / he had called for equality for African Americans.』 ◀ 45번 ④의 근거 일치
당시 단지 17살에 고등학교를 졸업했을 뿐인데 / 아버지는 아프리카계 미국인들을 위한 평등을 요구했다.

(b) I marvelled, / proud of him, / and wondered / how, in 1920, / so young, so white, / and in the deep South, / where the law still separated black from white, / (c) he had had the courage to deliver it.
나는 놀라웠고, / 아버지를 자랑스럽게 여기면서 / 궁금했다. / 어떻게 1920년에 / 그렇게 어리고 백인이었던 / 그리고 최남부 지역에서 / 법으로 백인과 흑인을 여전히 분리시키고 있었던 / 그가 그 연설을 할 용기를 가지고 있었는지

I asked him about it.
나는 그에게 그것에 관해 물었다.

(B)

"Daddy," I said, / handing him the pages, / "this speech — how did you ever get permission to give it?
"아빠," 나는 말했다. / 아빠에게 서류를 건네 드리며 / "이 연설, 어떻게 이렇게 하도록 허락을 받으셨나요?

And weren't you scared?"
두렵지 않으셨나요?"

"Well, honey," he said, / "'I didn't ask for permission.」 45번 ③의 근거 일치
"아들아," 그가 말했다. / "'난 허락을 구하지 않았단다.

I just asked myself, / 'What is the most important challenge / facing my generation?'
단지 나 자신에게 물었지. / '가장 중요한 도전 과제는 무엇인가? / 우리 세대가 직면하고 있는'

I knew immediately.
난 즉시 알았어.

Then (a) I asked myself, / 'And if I weren't afraid, / what would I say about it in this speech?'"
그 뒤 나는 스스로에게 물었어. / '내가 두려워하지 않는다면, / 이 연설에서 이것에 대해 무엇을 말할까?'라고

(D)

"I wrote it.
"난 글을 썼어.

And I delivered it.
그리고 연설을 했지.

『About half way through / I looked out to see / the entire audience of teachers, students, and parents / stand up — and walk out.」 45번 ⑤의 근거 불일치
대략 반쯤 연설을 했을 때 / 나는 바라보았어. / 교사, 학생, 학부모로 이루어진 전체 청중이 / 일어나더니 나가 버리는 것을

Left alone on the stage, / (d) I thought to myself, / 'Well, I guess I need to be sure / to do only two things with my life: / keep thinking for myself, and not get killed.'"
무대에 홀로 남겨진 채 / 나는 마음속으로 생각했어. / '그래, 나는 확실히 하면 되겠구나. / 내 인생에서 두 가지만 해내는 것을 / 계속 스스로 생각하는 것과 죽임을 당하지 않는 것'이라고

He handed the speech back to me, and smiled.
아버지는 연설문을 나에게 돌려주며 미소 지으셨다.

"(e) You seem to have done both," I said.
"아빠는 그 두 가지 모두를 해내신 것 같네요."라고 나는 말했다.

(A)

17살 때 나는 놀라운 물건을 발견했다. 아버지와 나는 서재 바닥에 앉아 있었다. 우리는 아버지의 오래된 서류들을 정리하고 있었다. 나는 카펫 너머에 있는 두꺼운 종이 클립을 보았다. 그것의 녹이 어떤 보고서의 표지를 더럽혔다. 나는 그것을 집어 들었다. 나는 읽기 시작했다. 그러고 나서 나는 울기 시작했다.

(C)

그것은 1920년 Tennessee 주에서 아버지가 썼던 연설문이었다. 아버지는 당시 단지 17살에 고등학교를 졸업했을 뿐인데 아프리카계 미국인들을 위한 평등을 요구했다. 아버지를 자랑스럽게 여기면서 (b) 나는 놀라워했고, 1920년에 법으로 백인과 흑인을 여전히 분리시키고 있었던 최남부 지역에서 그렇게 어리고 백인이었던 (c) 그가 어떻게 그 연설을 할 용기를 가지고 있었는지 궁금했다. 나는 그에게 그것에 관해 물었다.

(B)

아빠에게 서류를 건네 드리며 "아빠, 이 연설, 어떻게 이렇게 하도록 허락을 받으셨나요? 두렵지 않으셨나요?"라고 말했다. "아들아," 그가 말했다. "난 허락을 구하지 않았단다. 단지 '우리 세대가 직면하고 있는 가장 중요한 도전 과제는 무엇인가?'라고 나 자신에게 물었지. 난 즉시 알았어. 그 뒤 '내가 두려워하지 않는다면, 이 연설에서 이것에 대해 무엇을 말할까?' 라고 (a) 나는 스스로에게 물었어."

(D)

"난 글을 썼어. 그리고 연설을 했지. 대략 반쯤 연설을 했을 때 교사, 학생, 학부모로 이루어진 전체 청중이 일어나더니 나가 버리는 것을 바라보았어. 무대에 홀로 남겨진 채 '그래, 내 인생에서 두 가지만 확실히 해내면 되겠구나. 계속 스스로 생각하는 것과 죽임을 당하지 않는 것.'이라고 (d) 나는 마음속으로 생각했어." 아버지는 연설문을 나에게 돌려주며 미소 지으셨다. "(e) 아빠는 그 두 가지 모두를 해내신 것 같네요."라고 나는 말했다.

- **study** ⓝ 서재
- **permission** ⓝ 허락
- **call for** ~을 요구하다, 필요로 하다
- **marvel** ⓥ 놀라다
- **courage** ⓝ 용기
- **entire** ⓐ 전체의
- **rust** ⓝ 녹
- **generation** ⓝ 세대
- **equality** ⓝ 평등
- **separate** ⓥ 분리시키다
- **deliver** ⓥ (연설이나 강연을) 하다

구문 풀이

(B) 5행 And if I weren't afraid, what would I say about it in this speech?
「if + 주어 + 과거 동사 ~, 조동사 과거형 + 주어 + 동사원형 ~」: 가정법 과거 의문문

(C) 3행 I marvelled, (being) proud of him, and wondered {how, in 1920, (being) so
동사1 생략(분사구문) 동사2 의문사
young, so white, and in the deep South, where the law still separated black from
선행사 관계부사 생략(분사구문: he 보충 설명)
white, he had had the courage to deliver it}. ( ): 목적어(간접의문문)
주어 동사

(D) 3행 Left alone on the stage, I thought to myself, 'Well, I guess (that) I need to
분사구문 생략(접속사)
be sure to do only two things with my life: keep thinking for myself, and not get
동격(= two things)
killed.'

---

43 글의 순서 파악
정답률 68% | 정답 ②

주어진 글 (A)에 이어질 내용을 순서에 맞게 배열한 것으로 가장 적절한 것은?
① (B) – (D) – (C) ✓② (C) – (B) – (D)
③ (C) – (D) – (B) ④ (D) – (B) – (C)
⑤ (D) – (C) – (B)

Why? 왜 정답일까?
필자가 아버지와 서재를 정리하다가 아버지가 17살 때 썼던 연설문을 발견했다는 내용의 **(A)** 뒤에, 연설문을 읽은 필자가 아버지에게 어떻게 그런 연설을 할 용기를 냈는지 물었다는 내용의 **(C)**가 연결된다.

이어서 **(B)**에서 아버지는 아들인 필자의 물음에 답하기 시작하고, **(D)**에서는 답을 마무리한다. 따라서 글의 순서로 가장 적절한 것은 ② '(C) – (B) – (D)'이다.

44 지칭 추론
정답률 44% | 정답 ②

밑줄 친 (a) ~ (e) 중에서 가리키는 대상이 나머지 넷과 다른 것은?
① (a) ✓② (b) ③ (c) ④ (d) ⑤ (e)

Why? 왜 정답일까?
(a), (c), (d), (e)는 My father, (b)는 필자인 'I'를 가리키므로, (a) ~ (e) 중에서 가리키는 대상이 다른 하나는 ② '(b)'이다.

45 세부 내용 파악
정답률 68% | 정답 ⑤

윗글에 관한 내용으로 적절하지 않은 것은?
① 아버지와 나는 서류를 정리하고 있었다.
② 나는 서재에서 발견한 것을 읽고 나서 울기 시작했다.
③ 아버지는 연설을 하기 위한 허락을 구하지 않았다.
④ 아버지가 연설문을 썼을 당시 17세였다.
✓⑤ 교사, 학생, 학부모 모두 아버지의 연설을 끝까지 들었다.

Why? 왜 정답일까?
(D) 'About half way through I looked out to see the entire audience of teachers, students, and parents stand up — and walk out.'에 따르면 필자의 아버지가 절반쯤 연설을 진행했을 때 교사, 학생, 학부모 등 전체 관중이 모두 일어나 나갔다고 하므로, 내용과 일치하지 않는 것은 ⑤ '교사, 학생, 학부모 모두 아버지의 연설을 끝까지 들었다.'이다.

Why? 왜 오답일까?
① (A) 'We were organizing his old papers.'의 내용과 일치한다.
② (A) 'I started to read. Then I started to cry.'의 내용과 일치한다.
③ (B) 'I didn't ask for permission.'의 내용과 일치한다.
④ (C) 'It was a speech he had written in 1920, in Tennessee. Then only 17 himself and graduating from high school, ~'의 내용과 일치한다.

어휘 Review Test 11			문제편 120쪽

A	B	C	D
01 모으다, 모이다	01 appearance	01 ⓚ	01 ⓛ
02 축적되다	02 temptation	02 ⓟ	02 ⓝ
03 섭취량	03 progression	03 ⓠ	03 ⓒ
04 확산, 퍼지다	04 spill	04 ⓕ	04 ⓠ
05 적절한	05 instinct	05 ⓘ	05 ⓐ
06 한계	06 permission	06 ⓙ	06 ⓙ
07 감소하다	07 demonstrate	07 ⓐ	07 ⓚ
08 인용구	08 curiosity	08 ⓒ	08 ⓢ
09 공격	09 standpoint	09 ⓜ	09 ⓜ
10 분석하다	10 humanity	10 ⓗ	10 ⓔ
11 의미 없는	11 enhance	11 ⓝ	11 ⓛ
12 평등	12 impact	12 ⓛ	12 ⓗ
13 ~에 뒤섞다	13 sanitation	13 ⓘ	13 ⓘ
14 경우	14 additional	14 ⓓ	14 ⓟ
15 경외심	15 messy	15 ⓞ	15 ⓡ
16 정체성	16 approach	16 ⓘ	16 ⓖ
17 상당한	17 skyscraper	17 ⓔ	17 ⓓ
18 비율	18 self-esteem	18 ⓢ	18 ⓘ
19 다시 나타나다	19 negotiate	19 ⓑ	19 ⓑ
20 수직의	20 maintain	20 ⓖ	20 ⓑ